APPLYING
IFRS®
Standards

FIFTH EDITION

IFRS®
Standards

FIFTH EDITION

RUTH *PICKER*

LEO *VAN DER TAS*

DAVID *KOLITZ*

GILAD *LIVNE*

JANICE *LOFTUS*

MIRIAM *KONING*

CATHRYNNE *SERVICE*

WILEY

Library of Congress Cataloging-in-Publication Data is Available:

ISBN 9781394235933 (Paperback)
ISBN 9781394235926 (ePDF)
ISBN 9781394235919 (ePub)

Cover Design: Wiley
Cover Image: © Dmitry Kovalchuk/Adobe Stock

Set in 9.5/11pt ITC Giovanni Std by Straive, Chennai, India.
Printed and bound by CPI Group (UK) Ltd, Croydon, CR0 4YY

C9781394235933_150325

The manufacturer's authorized representative according to the EU General Product Safety Regulation is Wiley-VCH GmbH, Boschstr. 12, 69469 Weinheim, Germany, e-mail: Product_Safety@wiley.com.

FROM THE PROFESSION

EY is delighted to support *Applying IFRS Standards*, fifth edition. With International Financial Reporting Standards (IFRS®) now being mandated, or permitted, for the financial reporting of listed entities in most parts of the world, it has become the global language of accounting. This means that comparing financial statements from companies across the globe has become much easier, increasing transparency and improving decision-making by stakeholders of companies. It also has led to reductions in training costs and greater mobility of accounting staff and professionals across countries. You, as accountancy students and professionals, will benefit greatly from being able to carry your knowledge and experience from country to country without always having to study local accounting standards each time you cross a border.

The business environment and capital markets are developing continuously. Financial reporting needs to adapt with these changes. The International Accounting Standards Board (IASB®) not only introduced new and amended existing standards, but also recognised the growing importance of the impact of climate and other sustainability topics on the financial performance and position of companies. In doing so, it works closely with its sister Board in the IFRS Foundation, the International Sustainability Standards Board (ISSB®) that sets IFRS Sustainability Disclosure Standards®, which we hope will get a similar acceptance as the IFRS Accounting Standards. In this new edition of *Applying IFRS Standards* these developments have been incorporated and illustrated with extracts from recent financial statements.

Applying IFRS Standards aims to help you master the complex world of IFRS Standards; as such, it is truly global in the wealth of insights and examples it provides, as well as extracts from financial statements of companies across the globe. I am sure this book will be instructive not only to those learning about financial reporting standards for the first time, but also to accountancy professionals keeping abreast of developments in IFRS Standards and trying to find their way in applying IFRS Standards to transactions and events.

Now that IFRS Standards have been adopted in most parts of the world, it is important to interpret and apply the standards consistently to make it a truly single global set of accounting standards. I hope and trust this book will help in achieving a common and consistent understanding and application of IFRS Standards.

Michiel van der Lof
Global Leader — Corporate Reporting Services, Global Professional Practice
EY
London

March 2025

BRIEF CONTENTS

Part 1   CONCEPTUAL FRAMEWORK   1

1   The IASB and its *Conceptual Framework*   3

Part 2   ELEMENTS   23

2   Financial statement presentation   25
3   Revenue from contracts with customers   55
4   Inventories   83
5   Property, plant and equipment   109
6   Intangible assets   151
7   Impairment of assets   173
8   Fair value measurement   199
9   Leases   223
10   Provisions, contingent liabilities and contingent assets   259
11   Employee benefits   279
12   Owners' equity: share capital and reserves   307
13   Financial instruments   331
14   Share-based payment   379
15   Income taxes   403

Part 3   PRESENTATION AND DISCLOSURES   433

16   Statement of cash flows   435
17   Key notes disclosures   457
18   Operating segments   479
19   Business combinations   497

Part 4   ECONOMIC ENTITIES   523

20   Consolidation: controlled entities   525
21   Consolidation: wholly owned subsidiaries   539
22   Consolidation: intragroup transactions   561
23   Consolidation: non-controlling interest   585
24   Translation of foreign currency transactions and the financial statements of foreign entities   625

CONTENTS

Preface xiii
About the Authors xv
Acronyms xvii

Part 1

CONCEPTUAL FRAMEWORK 1

1 The IASB and its *Conceptual Framework* 3

Introduction 4
1.1 The IFRS Foundation and the International Accounting Standards Board (IASB) 4
1.2 The purpose of a conceptual framework 7
1.3 Qualitative characteristics of useful financial information 8
1.4 Going concern assumption 10
1.5 Definition of elements in financial statements 11
1.6 Recognition of elements of financial statements 14
1.7 Derecognition 16
1.8 Measurement of the elements 16
1.9 Unit of account 18
1.10 Presentation and disclosure 18
1.11 Concepts of capital 19
Summary 19
Discussion questions 20
References 20
Academic perspective 21
References 22

Part 2

ELEMENTS 23

2 Financial statement presentation 25

Introduction 26
2.1 Components of financial statements 26
2.2 General principles of financial statements 27
2.3 Statement of financial position 29
2.4 Statement of profit or loss and other comprehensive income 33
2.5 Statement of changes in equity 39
2.6 Notes 41
2.7 Accounting policies, changes in accounting estimates and errors 45
2.8 Events after the reporting period 49
2.9 Future developments 50
Summary 51
Discussion questions 51
References 51
Academic perspective 52
References 53

3 Revenue from contracts with customers 55

3.1 Introduction 56
3.2 Scope 56
3.3 Identify the contract with the customer 57
3.4 Identify the performance obligations 58
3.5 Determine the transaction price 61
3.6 Allocate the transaction price 65
3.7 Satisfaction of performance obligations 67
3.8 Contract costs 70
3.9 Other application issues 72
3.10 Presentation and disclosures 76
Summary 79
Discussion questions 80
Reference 80
Academic perspective 81
References 81

4 Inventories 83

4.1 Introduction 84
4.2 The nature of inventories 84
4.3 Measurement of inventory 87
4.4 Determination of cost 88
4.5 Recording inventory transactions 92
4.6 End-of-period accounting 95
4.7 Assigning costs to inventory on sale 98
4.8 Net realisable value 103
4.9 Recognition as an expense 106
4.10 Disclosure 106
Summary 107
Academic perspective 108
References 108

5 Property, plant and equipment 109

5.1 The nature of property, plant and equipment 110
5.2 Initial recognition of property, plant and equipment 112
5.3 Initial measurement of property, plant and equipment 113
5.4 Measurement subsequent to initial recognition 117
5.5 The cost model 118
5.6 The revaluation model 123
5.7 Choosing between the cost model and the revaluation model 133
5.8 Derecognition 133
5.9 Disclosure 135
5.10 Investment properties 136
Summary 139
Discussion questions 146
References 147
Academic perspective 148
References 149

6 Intangible assets   151

Introduction   152
6.1 The nature of intangible assets   153
6.2 Recognition and initial measurement   155
6.3 Measurement subsequent to initial recognition   161
6.4 Retirements and disposals   164
6.5 Disclosure   164
Summary   167
Discussion questions   169
References   170
Academic perspective   171
References   172

7 Impairment of assets   173

7.1 Introduction to IAS 36   174
7.2 When to undertake an impairment test   175
7.3 Impairment test for an individual asset   176
7.4 Cash-generating units — excluding goodwill   182
7.5 Cash-generating units and goodwill   186
7.6 Reversal of an impairment loss   188
7.7 Disclosure   190
Summary   191
Discussion questions   195
References   195
Academic perspective   196
References   197

8 Fair value measurement   199

8.1 Introduction   200
8.2 The definition of fair value   201
8.3 The fair value framework   202
8.4 Application to non-financial assets   209
8.5 Application to liabilities   212
8.6 Application to measurement of an entity's own equity   215
8.7 Disclosure   215
Summary   219
Discussion questions   219
References   219
Academic perspective   220
References   221

9 Leases   223

9.1 Introduction   224
9.2 Background of current lease accounting   224
9.3 Scope and lessee exemptions   225
9.4 What is a lease?   225
9.5 Lessee accounting   234
9.6 Lessee presentation and disclosure   241
9.7 Lease classification by lessors   243
9.8 Accounting for finance leases by lessors   246
9.9 Accounting for finance leases by manufacturer or dealer lessors   250
9.10 Accounting for operating leases by lessors   251
9.11 Accounting for sale and leaseback transactions   253
Summary   255
Academic perspective   257
References   257

10 Provisions, contingent liabilities and contingent assets   259

10.1 Introduction to IAS 37   260
10.2 Scope   260
10.3 What is a provision?   260
10.4 What is a contingent liability?   262
10.5 Distinguishing a contingent liability from a provision   263
10.6 Measurement of provisions   263
10.7 Application of the definitions, recognition and measurement rules   268
10.8 Contingent assets   273
10.9 Disclosure   273
Summary   275
Discussion questions   275
References   275
Academic perspective   276
References   276

11 Employee benefits   279

11.1 Introduction to accounting for employee benefits   280
11.2 Scope and purpose of IAS 19   280
11.3 Defining employee benefits   280
11.4 Short-term employee benefits   280
11.5 Post-employment benefits   287
11.6 Accounting for defined contribution post-employment plans   288
11.7 Accounting for defined benefit post-employment plans   289
11.8 Other Long-term employee benefits   297
11.9 Termination benefits   301
Summary   302
Discussion questions   302
References   303
Academic perspective   304
References   304

12 Owners' equity: share capital and reserves   307

12.1 Equity   308
12.2 For-profit companies   309
12.3 Key features of corporate structure   309
12.4 Different forms of share capital   310
12.5 Contributed equity: issue of share capital   312

12.6 Contributed equity: subsequent movements in share capital 314

12.7 Share capital: subsequent decreases in share capital 318

12.8 Reserves 320

12.9 Disclosure 324

Summary 324

Discussion questions 327

References 327

Academic perspective 328

References 329

13 Financial instruments 331

13.1 Introduction 332

13.2 What is a financial instrument? 334

13.3 Financial assets and financial liabilities 335

13.4 Distinguishing financial liabilities from equity instruments 336

13.5 Compound financial instruments 339

13.6 Interest, dividends, gains and losses 340

13.7 Financial assets and financial liabilities: scope 341

13.8 Derivatives and embedded derivatives 342

13.9 Financial assets and financial liabilities: categories of financial instruments 344

13.10 Financial assets and financial liabilities: recognition criteria 348

13.11 Financial assets and financial liabilities: measurement 348

13.12 Financial assets and financial liabilities: offsetting 359

13.13 Hedge accounting 360

13.14 Disclosures 368

Summary 374

Discussion questions 374

Reference 375

Academic perspective 376

References 377

14 Share-based payment 379

Introduction 380

14.1 Application and scope 382

14.2 Cash-settled and equity-settled share-based payment transactions 382

14.3 Recognition 383

14.4 Equity-settled share-based payment transactions 383

14.5 Vesting 386

14.6 Other considerations 390

14.7 Modifications to terms and conditions on which equity instruments were granted 391

14.8 Cash-settled share-based payment transactions 392

14.9 Disclosure 397

Summary 399

Discussion questions 399

References 400

Academic perspective 401

References 401

15 Income taxes 403

15.1 The nature of income tax 404

15.2 Differences between accounting profit and taxable profit 404

15.3 Accounting for income taxes 407

15.4 Calculation of current tax 407

15.5 Recognition of current tax 412

15.6 Payment of tax 412

15.7 Tax losses 413

15.8 Calculation of deferred tax 414

15.9 Recognition of deferred tax liabilities and deferred tax assets 421

15.10 Change of tax rates 424

15.11 Other Issues 424

15.12 Presentation in the financial statements 425

15.13 Disclosures 426

Summary 429

Discussion questions 430

References 430

Academic perspective 431

References 432

Part 3

PRESENTATION AND DISCLOSURES 433

16 Statement of cash flows 435

Introduction and scope 436

16.1 Purpose of a statement of cash flows 436

16.2 Defining cash and cash equivalents 436

16.3 Classifying cash flow activities 437

16.4 Format of the statement of cash flows 439

16.5 Preparing a statement of cash flows 441

16.6 Other disclosures 450

16.7 Future developments 453

Summary 454

Discussion questions 454

References 454

Academic perspective 455

References 456

17 Key notes disclosures 457

Introduction 458

17.1 Related party disclosures 458

17.2 Earnings per share 464

Summary 475

Discussion questions 476

Academic perspective 477

References 478

18 Operating segments 479

18.1 Objectives of financial reporting by segments 480
18.2 Scope 480
18.3 Management approach vs risks and rewards approach 481
18.4 Identifying operating segments 481
18.5 Identifying reportable segments 484
18.6 Applying the definition of reportable segments 486
18.7 Disclosure 487
18.8 Applying the disclosures in practice 490
Summary 494
Discussion questions 494
References 494
Academic perspective 495
References 496

19 Business combinations 497

19.1 The nature of a business combination 498
19.2 Accounting for a business combination — basic principles 499
19.3 Subsequent accounting for a business combination 510
19.4 Disclosure — business combinations 513
Summary 515
Discussion questions 520
References 520
Academic perspective 521
References 522

Part 4

ECONOMIC ENTITIES 523

20 Consolidation: controlled entities 525

20.1 Introduction 526
20.2 Consolidated financial statements 526
20.3 Control as the criterion for consolidation 528
20.4 Preparation of consolidated financial statements 534
20.5 Business combinations and consolidation 535
20.6 Disclosure 536
Discussion questions 537

21 Consolidation: wholly owned subsidiaries 539

21.1 The consolidation process 540
21.2 Consolidation worksheets 541
21.3 The acquisition analysis: determining goodwill or bargain purchase 542
21.4 Worksheet entries at the acquisition date 545
21.5 Worksheet entries subsequent to the acquisition date 550
21.6 Consolidation worksheet when the parent company accounts for investment in subsidiary using the equity method 555
21.7 Disclosure 557
Summary 560
Discussion questions 560

22 Consolidation: intragroup transactions 561

Introduction 562
22.1 Rationale for adjusting for intragroup transactions 562
22.2 Transfers of inventory 564
22.3 Intragroup services 570
22.4 Intragroup dividends 571
22.5 Intragroup borrowings 573
Summary 574
Discussion questions 583

23 Consolidation: non-controlling interest 585

23.1 Non-controlling interest explained 586
23.2 Effects of NCI on the consolidation process 588
23.3 Calculating the NCI share of equity 594
23.4 Adjusting for the effects of intragroup transactions 608
23.5 Gain on bargain purchase 612
Summary 613
Discussion questions 624

24 Translation of foreign currency transactions and the financial statements of foreign entities 625

24.1 Translation of foreign currency transactions and foreign subsidiary's statements 626
24.2 Key concepts in foreign currency translation 626
24.3 Functional and presentation currencies 627
24.4 Identifying the functional currency 630
24.5 Translation of transactions into the functional currency 632
24.6 Translation of financial statements into the functional currency 632
24.7 Translation into the presentation currency 638
24.8 Consolidating acquired foreign subsidiaries — where the functional currency is not the presentation currency 640
24.9 Consolidating acquired foreign subsidiaries — where functional currency is the parent's reporting currency 648
24.10 Net Investment in a foreign operation 649
24.11 Disclosure 650
Summary 651
Discussion questions 651
References 651

Online chapter A **Exploration for and evaluation of mineral resources**
Online chapter B **Agriculture**
Online chapter C **Associates and joint ventures**
Online chapter D **Joint arrangements**

Glossary 653

Index 663

PREFACE

IFRS Accounting Standards have firmly established their role as the global standard for financial reporting, mandated in more than 140 countries, with many other countries adopting the Standards. Over the years, IFRS Accounting Standards have also been the example for national accounting standards. As economic conditions and global markets continue to change in a world of shifting political landscapes, the importance of a stable and widely accepted set of financial reporting standards remains essential, providing a foundation for transparency and consistency in the complexities of today's world.

An understanding of the IFRS Accounting Standards is therefore paramount for all those involved in financial reporting or preparing to attain such a role. It provides not just technical knowledge and in-depth understanding of the financial reporting process, but does so in a global business environment. *Applying IFRS Standards*, fifth edition, has been written to meet the needs of accountancy students and practitioners in understanding the complexities of IFRS Accounting Standards.

This publication is the fifth edition of the book. It has now established itself as a text that is used by academics and practitioners throughout the world. We have welcomed the comments and suggestions received from various people and have tried to ensure that these are reflected in this edition.

What's new in this edition?

The fifth edition incorporates the release of new IFRS Accounting Standards and amendments of existing accounting standards. Some of the more prominent changes made include:
- an update of the chapter on the IASB's Conceptual Framework for Financial Reporting due to its amendment
- a complete rewrite of the chapter on leases following the adoption of IFRS 16 Leases
- a significant update of the chapters on revenue recognition and financial instruments with more illustrative examples and extracts from IFRS financial statements now that IFRS 9 and IFRS 15 have been applied for some years
- expanded scope of the chapter on translation of financial statements to include foreign currency transactions
- a re-ordering of the chapters in section 2 to better align with the structure of the statement of financial position and statement of profit or loss and other comprehensive income
- an update of all other chapters including recent extracts and incorporating IFRIC agenda decisions and smaller changes to the standards.

Also the academic perspectives, to be found at the end of all chapters in the first three parts of the book (i.e. chapters 1 to 19), have been updated. These academic perspectives summarise and highlight certain findings from published research in accounting and other fields that pertain to a chapter's topic. Referring to these perspectives should give the reader a basic understanding of questions that accounting researchers have attempted to address. Note, however, that the academic perspectives do not furnish a comprehensive review of related literature. Rather, they provide a starting point for further reading and exploration of relevant academic research.

Applying IFRS Standards, fifth edition, also comes equipped with discussion questions at the end of each chapter, specifically designed to test the reader's understanding of the content. A wealth of additional learning materials can also be found at www.wiley.com/go/picker5e/student; www.wiley.com/go/picker5e/instructor, including:
- Four additional chapters entitled: Exploration for and evaluation of mineral resources; Agriculture; Associates and joint ventures; Joint arrangements
- Instructor slides
- Testbank
- Exercises
- Solutions manual
- Access to the IFRS Learning Resources

In writing this book, we have endeavoured to ensure that the following common themes flow throughout the text:
- *Accounting standards are underpinned by a conceptual framework*. Accounting standards are not simply a rulebook to be learnt by heart. An understanding of the conceptual basis of accounting, and the rationale behind the principles espoused in particular standards, is crucial to their consistent application in a variety of practical applications.

- *The International Accounting Standards Board (IASB®) IFRS Accounting Standards are principles-based.* Although a specific standard is a stand-alone document, the principles in any standard relate to and are interpreted in conjunction with other standards. To appreciate the application of a specific standard, an understanding of the reasoning within other standards is required. We have endeavoured where applicable to refer to other IFRS Accounting Standards that are connected in principle and application. In particular, extensive references are made to the Basis for Conclusions documents accompanying each standard issued by the IASB. This material, although not integral to the standards, explains the reasoning process used by the IASB and provides indicators of changes in direction being proposed by the IASB.
- *Accounting standards have a practical application.* The end product of the standard-setting process must be applied by accounting practitioners in a variety of organisational structures and practical settings. While a theoretical understanding of a standard is important, practitioners should be able to apply the relevant standard. The author of each chapter has demonstrated the practical application of the accounting standards by providing case studies, examples and journal entries (where relevant). The references to practical situations require the reader to pay close attention to the detailed information discussed, given that such a detailed examination is essential to an understanding of the standards. Having only a broad overview of the basic principles is insufficient.

Writing a book like this is impossible without the help and input from many people. Much of the knowledge and insights reflected in this book have been gained through discussions and debates with many colleagues and with staff associated with the standard-setting bodies, particularly at the IASB. We thank them for sharing their perspectives and experience. We would like to thank the following people in particular. A team of people from EY's Global Corporate Reporting Services team in London, consisting of Angela Covic, Pieter Dekker and Victor Chan, wrote or reviewed individual chapters of the book. Richard Barker from Saïd Business School, Oxford University reviewed the chapters in Part 4. Erik Roelofsen from Rotterdam School of Management, Erasmus University Rotterdam and PwC reviewed the Academic Perspectives. Elisabetta Barone from Brunel Business School updated the testbank. We would also like to thank Natalie Forde from Cardiff Business School and other anonymous reviewers who have provided valuable feedback and recommendations during the development of the fifth edition. In addition, we extend our thanks to the people at Wiley and professional freelancers for their help realising this edition, including Juliet Booker, Steve Hardman, Georgia King, Joyce Poh and Joshua Poole as well as Jennifer Mair and Paul Stringer. Last but not least, writing a book takes huge commitment, and this has left less time for family and friends. We thank them also for their support and understanding.

Finally, in a time when the world, with its increasing sophistication, seems to produce situations and pronouncements that have added complexity, we hope that this book assists in the lifelong learning process that we and the readers of this book are continuously engaged in.

Ruth Picker
Leo van der Tas
David Kolitz
Miriam Koning
Gilad Livne
Janice Loftus
Cathrynne Service

March 2025

Ruth Picker

Ruth Picker AM, B.A., F.C.A., FSIA, FCPA, is an experienced finance, accounting, audit, and risk management specialist with many years of international senior executive leadership experience as a Lead Partner in the corporate finance sector. Born and educated in Cape Town, South Africa, where she graduated with a Bachelor of Arts, Ruth then studied to qualify as a Chartered Accountant.

Prior to retiring in June 2021 Ruth had a long corporate relationship with the firm Ernst & Young (EY), where she was most recently the Asia-Pacific Risk Management Leader, a member of the Asia-Pacific Executive and a member of EY's Asia-Pacific Diversity and Inclusion Committee. She also chaired the EY Asia-Pacific Ethics Oversight Group and was one of the leaders of the Asia-Pacific COVID Response Team. She was also a member of EY's Global Risk Management Committee. Prior to that she was EY's Global Leader – International Financial Reporting Standards – based in London. Prior to that she held various senior partner roles within Australia including as an IFRS specialist, Managing Partner of the Melbourne Office and Oceania Leader – Climate Change & Sustainability Services. She has held many voluntary committee positions, both in Australia and internationally. Ruth is a strong advocate for women's leadership, and diversity and inclusion more broadly. In 2020 Ruth was inducted into the Australian Accounting Hall of Fame for services to the accounting profession internationally and in Australia. Ruth is also a published author (including lead author of 'Applying International Financial Reporting Standards' published by Wiley), published songwriter & composer and speaker on topics including accounting, auditing, risk management, ethics, mentoring and leadership. She features as a case study on quiet leadership styles in Megumi Miki's award-winning book 'Quietly Powerful'.

Ruth was appointed a Member of the Order of Australia (AM) in the King's Birthday Honours on 12 June 2023.

Leo van der Tas

Leo van der Tas (PhD, RA) is full professor of financial reporting at Tilburg University, the Netherlands, since 2010 and before that at Erasmus University Rotterdam, the Netherlands.

Leo was the Global Corporate Reporting Services Leader at EY in London until 2022, before which he was the Global IFRS Technical Director at EY in London. In these roles he was responsible for the IFRS policy of EY in the area of IFRS Accounting Standards and IFRS Sustainability Disclosure Standards and the consistency of their application within the EY network. He was senior technical partner at EY in the Netherlands until 2022.

He is a member of the Connectivity Advisory Panel of the European Financial Reporting Advisory Group, tasked with advising on the connectivity between financial reporting and sustainability reporting.

Leo was a member of the International Financial Reporting Interpretations Committee (IFRIC and predecessor Standing Interpretations Committee) of the IASB between 1997 and 2006 and a member of the IFRS Foundation Advisory Council between 2009 and 2013.

Leo has been a member of the Consultative Working Group of the Standing Corporate Reporting Committee of the European Securities and Market Authority (ESMA) in Paris, France, and of the Advisory Committee on Financial Reporting of the Netherlands Authority for the Financial Markets (AFM) in Amsterdam, the Netherlands.

He has published many books and articles in the area of international accounting and is a frequent speaker and teacher on the subject.

He was seconded to the European Commission in Brussels, Belgium, for a period of 2 years to assist in the development of the Commission's policy in the area of European accounting harmonisation.

David Kolitz

David Kolitz, BComm (Natal), BCom (Hons) (SA), MCom (Wits), SFHEA is Senior Lecturer in the Business School at the University of Exeter. He was previously Associate Professor and Assistant Dean in the Faculty of Commerce, Law and Management at the University of the Witwatersrand, Johannesburg. He is an experienced accounting academic and the lead author/co-author of three other books in the area of Financial Accounting.

Gilad Livne

Gilad Livne, PhD, CPA, is a professor of accounting at the School of Business and Management at Queen Mary University of London. Previously Gilad served on the accounting faculty of the London Business

School, Bayes Business School, University of Exeter and University of Bristol. Gilad received his MSc and PhD in accounting at the University of California at Berkeley, and BA (Accounting and Economics) at Tel Aviv University.

Gilad's teaching involves financial statement analysis, international accounting and advanced financial accounting courses. Gilad has taught in Undergraduate, MBA, Executive MBA, and MSc programmes. He has also been invited to teach at other schools and universities, such as EDHEC, HEC Lausanne, HEC Paris, London School of Economics, New Economic School (Moscow) and on various company-specific programmes.

Gilad's research looks into auditor independence, international accounting, fair value accounting and compensation. Gilad currently serves on a number of editorial boards of accounting journals. His research has been published in several journals including *Accounting and Business Research, Auditing: A Journal of Practice & Theory, European Accounting Review, Journal of Banking and Finance, Journal of Business Finance and Accounting, Journal of Corporate Finance, Review of Accounting Studies* and *The Accounting Review.*

Janice Loftus

Janice Loftus, BBus, MCom (Hons), FCPA, is an associate professor in accounting at the University of Adelaide. Her teaching interests are in the areas of financial accounting and accounting theory, and she has written several study guides for professional and tertiary programs. Janice's research interests are primarily in the area of financial reporting, including recent work on the understandability of accounting standards in collaboration with the Australian Accounting Standards Board. Janice has numerous publications on international financial reporting standards, risk reporting, solvency, earnings management, corporate governance, social and environmental reporting and developments in standard setting in Australian and international journals. Janice is the lead author of *Financial Reporting*, published by Wiley. She is an executive member of the Financial Reporting Interest Group of the Accounting and Finance Association of Australia and New Zealand and a member of the Australian Accounting Standards Board's Academic Advisory Panel. Prior to embarking on an academic career, Janice held several senior accounting positions in Australian and multinational corporations.

Miriam Koning

Miriam Koning, PhD, is associate professor at Rotterdam School of Management, Erasmus University (RSM). Her research addresses international accounting issues, in particular the impact of standards, institutions and intermediaries (financial regulators, standard setters, the business press, auditors and analysts) on corporate disclosure decisions and financial market participants. Her work is published in leading academic journals, including the *Journal of International Business Studies, Abacus* and the *International Review of Financial Analysis*. She is an associate member of the Erasmus Research Institute of Management (ERIM).

Miriam is the academic director of the MScBA in Accounting and Financial Management at RSM. She teaches various courses in accounting and financial reporting, at the bachelor and master's level, including the core course in international financial reporting in the master's program. In addition to pre- and post-experience courses at RSM, Miriam designs and teaches courses targeted toward senior level executives and professional audiences. Her educational style can be characterized as a blended approach, combining elements of lecture-based instruction, problem-based learning (PBL), technology-enhanced learning (including flipped classroom models) and in-class, interactive discussions.

Miriam holds an MSc in Economics from the Erasmus School of Economics and a PhD from Rotterdam School of Management. Prior to joining RSM, she worked in international assurance services at Ernst & Young.

Cathrynne Service

Cathrynne Service is a chartered accountant, passionate academic, educationist, independent IFRS consultant and a professional authoress. She has lectured at a variety of prestigious universities, including the University of Queensland, Griffith University and University of KwaZulu-Natal. During this time, she ran a variety of undergraduate and postgraduate programs (some leading to the highly sought-after qualification of "chartered accountant") and served in various positions, such as Head of Financial Accounting and Chairman of Cost and Management Accounting. She was also elected to several posts within the Southern African Accounting Association, which promotes excellence in accounting education and research, including serving as the National Chairman of Financial Accounting.

Cathrynne has authored (as sole, lead and co-author) numerous publications on the application of International Financial Reporting Standards. These are published through international publishers such as Wiley, LexisNexis and Juta and also through professional institutes, such as the Institute of Chartered Accountants of Pakistan, and are used by academics and professionals internationally.

ACRONYMS

AFS	Available-for-sale
AGM	Annual general meeting
ASC	Accounting Standards Codification
BCVR	Business combinations value reserve
CEO	Chief Executive Officer
CGU	Cash-generating unit
CODM	Chief Operating Decision Maker
COO	Chief Operating Officer
DBL(A)	Defined benefit liability (asset)
DBO	Defined benefit obligation
ED	Exposure draft
EFRAG	European Financial Reporting Advisory Group
EPS	Earnings per share
FAS	Financial Accounting Standards
FASB	US Financial Accounting Standards Board
FIFO	First-in, first-out
FV	Fair value
FVOCI	Fair value through other comprehensive income
FVPL	Fair value through profit or loss
GAAP	US Generally Accepted Accounting Principles
IAS®	International Accounting Standards
IASB®	International Accounting Standards Board
IASC	International Accounting Standards Committee, predecessor of the IASB
IDC	Initial direct costs
IFRIC®	International Financial Reporting Interpretations Committee, now the IFRS® Interpretations Committee
IFRS®	International Financial Reporting Standards
IPO	Initial public offering
LIBOR	London Interbank Offered Rate
MLP	Minimum lease payments
NCI	Non-controlling interest
OCI	Other comprehensive income
PV	Present value
R&D	Research and development
ROA	Return on assets
SAC	Standards Advisory Council
SARs	Share appreciation rights
SFAS	US Statement of Financial Accounting Standards
SPPI	Solely payments of principal and interest
TSR	Total shareholder return
US GAAP	see GAAP

APPLYING

IFRS®
Standards

FIFTH EDITION

Part 1

Conceptual Framework

1 The IASB and its *Conceptual Framework*   3

1 The IASB and its *Conceptual Framework*

After studying this chapter, you should be able to:

 1 describe the organisational structure of the key players in setting International Financial Reporting Standards (IFRS® Standards)

 2 describe the purpose of a conceptual framework — who uses it and why

 3 explain the qualitative characteristics that make information in financial statements useful and the constraint thereon

 4 explain the going concern assumption

 5 define the basic elements in financial statements — assets, liabilities, equity, income and expenses

 6 explain the principles for recognising the elements of financial statements

 7 distinguish between alternative bases for measuring the elements of financial statements

 8 explain the principles for measuring the elements of financial statements

 9 explain the difference between presentation and disclosure and the principles for presenting and disclosing information in the financial statements

 10 explain what is meant by a unit of account and in what context it is used

 11 outline two concepts of capital and explain the relevance of the term capital maintenance

INTRODUCTION

The purpose of this book is to identify and explain the major concepts and principles of International Financial Reporting Standards (generally referred to as IFRS Standards, or simply IFRSs) and to help you develop skills in applying them in business contexts. You may be familiar with the accounting treatment for various transactions, such as the purchase of inventory. The text will build on that knowledge and consider the principles and techniques required or permitted by IFRS Standards in accounting for a range of transactions, events and circumstances.

This first chapter provides an outline of the International Accounting Standards Board (IASB®) and its role in setting international accounting standards (IFRS Standards). It also explains that the IASB develops those IFRS Standards using certain fundamental concepts and principles, which are set out in the *Conceptual Framework for Financial Reporting* (the *Conceptual Framework*). The *Conceptual Framework's* key concepts and principles will also be outlined in this chapter. Interestingly, although the IFRSs are supposed to be built on the concepts and principles contained in the *Conceptual Framework*, it is possible for an IFRS to not reflect these concepts and principles. This situation may arise when an IFRS was developed prior to the current revision of the *Conceptual Framework* (the latest major revision occurred in 2018), and in situations such as these, the requirements of that IFRS take precedence over the *Conceptual Framework*. IFRS Standards are principles-based standards, rather than rules-based standards, even though the volume of guidance under IFRS Standards might suggest otherwise. Since the IFRS Standards are principles-based, we need *professional judgement* when applying them. An example of needing to apply principles rather than rules is the requirement that investment property be measured either using the cost model or fair value model, where this decision is based on the principle that the model chosen should be the one that provides the most useful information to the user. Identifying the most useful information is frequently a subjective task. To assist in this process, the *Conceptual Framework* establishes the qualitative characteristics financial information must have for it to be considered useful. The *Conceptual Framework* also provides definitions and recognition criteria that must be met before including elements in the financial statements and explains a variety of principles, including, for example, the concepts of recognition and derecognition, measurement, presentation and disclosure as well as concepts of capital. These principles are an important source of guidance to standard setters in the development of new IFRS standards referred to as IFRS Standards or simply IFRSs and to preparers of financial statements in the absence of an applicable IFRS standard. Accordingly, study of the *Conceptual Framework* provides a useful foundation to understanding and applying IFRS Standards.

1.1 THE IFRS FOUNDATION AND THE INTERNATIONAL ACCOUNTING STANDARDS BOARD (IASB)

The purpose of this section is to provide an understanding of the structure of the IFRS Foundation and how the IASB fits into this structure, and in particular, the IASB's role in the determination of IFRS Standards. Much of this information has been obtained from the website of the IASB, www.ifrs.org. To keep up to date with what the IASB is doing, this website should be regularly visited.

1.1.1 Formation of the IASB

In 1972, at the 10th World Congress of Accountants in Sydney, Australia, a proposal was put forward for the establishment of an International Accounting Standards Committee (IASC). In 1973, the IASC was formed by 16 national professional accountancy bodies from nine countries — Canada, the United Kingdom, the United States, Australia, France, Germany, Japan, the Netherlands and Mexico. By December 1998, the membership of the IASC had expanded and the committee had completed its core set of accounting standards.

However, the IASC was seen as having a number of shortcomings:
- It had weak relationships with national standard setters; this was due in part to the fact that the representatives on the IASC were not representative of the national standard setters but rather of national professional accounting bodies.
- There was a lack of convergence between the IASC standards and those adopted in major countries, even after 25 years of trying.
- The board only functioned on a part-time basis.
- The board lacked resources and technical support.

In 1998, the committee responsible for overseeing the operations of the IASC began a review of the IASC's operations. The results of the review were recommendations that the IASC be replaced with a smaller, full-time International Accounting Standards Board. At the same time, the IASC's Standing Interpretations Committee of the IASC was replaced by the IFRS Interpretations Committee of the IASB (commonly referred to as IFRIC). In 1999, the IASC board approved the constitutional changes necessary for the restructuring of the IASC. A new International Financial Reporting Standards Foundation was established and its trustees appointed. By early 2001, the members of the IASB and the Standards Advisory Council (SAC) were appointed, as were technical staff to assist the IASB.

The IASB initially adopted the International Accounting Standards (IAS® Standards), with some modifications, as issued by the IASC (e.g. IAS 2 *Inventories*). As standards were revised or newly issued by the IASB, they were then called International Financial Reporting Standards (e.g. IFRS 8 *Operating Segments*). This means that the term International Financial Reporting Standards (IFRSs) includes both IFRS Standards and IAS Standards. For the sake of brevity, this chapter will refer to all standards as IFRSs, whether prefixed with 'IFRS' or IAS'.

1.1.2 The IFRS Foundation: purpose and governance

The *IFRS Foundation* has a three-tiered governance structure:
- The International Accounting Standards Board (IASB), together with its IFRS Interpretations Committee (IFRIC), and the International Sustainability Standards Board (ISSB)
- The IFRS Foundation Trustees
- IFRS Foundation Monitoring Board

What these levels do and how they interact is explained below.
- The ***International Accounting Standards Board* (IASB)** is an independent standard-setting board. It is this body that publishes the International Financial Reporting Standards (IFRSs).
- The IASB has a committee called the ***IFRS Interpretations Committee* (IFRIC)**. This committee reviews newly identified financial reporting issues that are not specifically dealt with in the IFRSs, and issues for which unsatisfactory or conflicting interpretations have emerged or may emerge. The committee endeavours to reach a consensus on appropriate accounting treatment and provides authoritative guidance on the issue concerned. This may take the form of (i) a proposal to the Board to amend a standard; (ii) the issuance of an interpretation of a standard; or (iii) the issuance of an agenda decision explaining why neither is necessary. The latter often implicitly contains guidance on how to apply an IFRS.

  Once approved, or not objected to, by the IASB, the interpretations have equivalent status to standards (IFRSs); that is, although they are technically not standards (IFRSs), they are regarded as forming part of the standards (IFRSs) such that stating that there is compliance with the standards (IFRSs) means that there has been compliance with both the standards issued by the IASB (IFRSs) and any guidance issued by IFRIC. More recently the *IFRS Interpretations Committee* has been asked by the IASB to help with the drafting of minor amendments to standards and with the Annual Improvement Projects. The latter are annual packages of changes to standards that are minor or narrow in scope.

- The ***International Sustainability Standards Board* (ISSB)** was created in 2022, and is the body that will focus on the standard setting for 'sustainability reporting', called IFRS Sustainability Disclosure Standards. Sustainability disclosure standards are not covered in this book. However, the two Boards will work together closely in areas of mutual interest, where uncertainties regarding sustainability may have an impact on financial statements.

  The members of the ISSB, the IASB and IFRIC are appointed and overseen by a geographically and professionally diverse group of trustees, referred to as the *IFRS Foundation Trustees*. The trustees are publicly accountable to the *IFRS Foundation Monitoring Board*.

- The trustees appoint an ***IFRS Advisory Council* (IFRS AC)**, which provides strategic advice to the IASB, the ISSB, and informs the *IFRS Foundation Trustees*.

  In addition to the IFRSAC, ***other formal advisory bodies*** that provide a means for the IASB to consult and engage with interested parties from a range of backgrounds and geographical areas include:
  - Capital Markets Advisory Committee
  - Emerging Economies Group
  - Global Preparers Forum
  - SME Interpretations Group.

  Furthermore, ***working groups*** may be established for major projects to provide the IASB with access to additional expertise as required; for example, the Insurance Working Group was set up when the IASB was developing a standard on accounting for insurance contracts.

  Further information about advisory bodies and working groups, including reports and summaries of discussions, can be obtained from the IASB's website.

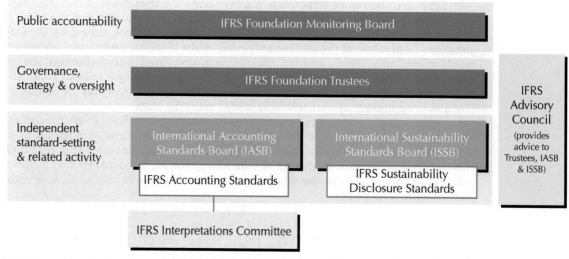

FIGURE 1.1 Institutional structure of international standard setting
Source: IASB (accessed 2024): http://www.ifrs.org/about-us/our-structure.

A pictorial view of the structure of the IFRS Foundation is given in figure 1.1.

1.1.3 The IFRS Foundation: due process

The *IFRS Foundation Trustees* approved the publication of the booklet *IASB and IFRS Interpretations Committee Due Process Handbook* (DP Handbook) in 2020 (available on the IASB's website). This handbook sets out the due process to be followed when, for example, publishing a new or revised IFRS Standard, or an IFRS Interpretation. The requirements laid out in the DP Handbook have been carefully crafted to ensure the development process is 'thorough, inclusive and transparent', which, in turn, ensures that the *IFRS Foundation* is successful in its stated aim of developing high-quality standards that will be accepted and adopted globally.

By way of a brief overview, the DP Handbook sets out:

- 'how the Board determines whether to add a project to its work plan;
- the stages of standard-setting and the types of consultation documents and other materials published by the Board and the Interpretations Committee;
- the minimum consultation requirements, including the duration of consultations;
- the advisory bodies and consultative groups established to provide input to the standard-setting process, and when and how they should be consulted;
- the minimum voting requirements for the Board and the Interpretations Committee to advance proposals or finalise documents at different stages in standard-setting; and
- the procedures followed if a stakeholder complains about the due process'.

    Source: 'What is Due Process and Why Does it Matter?' by Alan Beller; on the IFRS website: https://www.ifrs.org/news-and-events/news/2020/08/what-is-the-due-process-and-why-does-it-matter/#:~:text=The%20due%20process%20is%20essential,global%20acceptance%20of%20the%20 Standards.

1.1.4 Due process: publishing an IFRS

By way of an example, the summarised process involved in publishing an IFRS Standard (IFRS) is presented below.

1. *Research programme.* This stage of the process involves analysing 'perceived shortcomings' and assessing possible improvements and remedies to these alleged problems. A wide variety of bodies and interested parties are involved in this step (e.g. national and regional accounting standard-setting bodies, other bodies associated therewith, academics and any other interested persons). The involvement of a wide array of bodies is made possible through the use of the Accounting Standards Advisory Forum (ASAF). Evidence of possible problems and their solutions is put forward through documents such as discussion papers, requests for information or research papers. After a process of deliberation and debate, some of these matters will be considered important enough to progress to stage 2, whereas others may be dismissed as not sufficiently important to require modifications or revisions to existing standards or pronouncements.

2. *Developing a proposal for publication.* After mandatory consultation with the IFRS Trustees, IFRS Advisory Council (IFRSAC) and the Accounting Standards Advisory Forum (ASAF), the project must then be formally added to the IASB's agenda (this is done by a simple majority vote at a public IASB meeting). If the project is considered major, the IASB must then consider whether a consultative group (e.g. involving a group of expert advisors) needs to be established. Proposals must then be developed and debated in public meetings (this involves reviewing papers prepared by the IASB's technical staff and also the possible feedback from any discussion papers). Then, an exposure draft is prepared and published (sometimes with additional supporting materials). This must be done with a press release, requesting public comment.

3. *Redeliberations and finalisation.* After the exposure draft is published (see prior stage 2), there is a mandatory period during which the public is given time to comment (the period depends on what the exposure draft relates to). When this period ends, the IASB must then consider the feedback. Based on feedback received, the IASB must consider whether a revised exposure draft is necessary and whether additional consultation is necessary (or, if significant negative feedback is received, the IASB may need to consider cancelling the entire project). Unless the project is cancelled, the final draft IFRS will need to be prepared for balloting, whereupon the Due Process Oversight Committee (DPOC) needs to be informed that the balloting milestone has been reached (and, if relevant, the DPOC will need to be told why a revised exposure draft was not necessary). The IFRS is published (normally together with an accompanying document called the 'Basis of Conclusions') if the ballot results yield a supermajority of IASB members (this is 8 votes if there are only 13 members, or 9 votes if there are 14 members). If the IFRS was a new standard or had been subject to major amendments, then the publication of the IFRS will be accompanied by other supporting materials, such as a project summary, feedback statements and possibly even podcasts and Q&As.

4. *Post-implementation reviews.* If the IFRS (published in stage 3) was a new standard or arose due to major amendments to a pre-existing standard, then a post-implementation review must be conducted roughly 2.5–3 years after the IFRS became effective (the review may be deferred in certain circumstances). This review may also be performed for other reasons (e.g. changes to the concerns voiced by stakeholders).
Source: Summarised from ifrs.org website — IASB Due Process
https://www.iasplus.com/en/resources/ifrsf/due-process/iasb-due-process

The above is a summary of the Due Process followed by the IASB before publishing IFRS Standards or amendments thereto. A slightly different due process would be followed when publishing an Interpretation or Agenda decision by IFRIC. The detailed Due Process can be found in the Due Process Handbook, which is available on the IFRS Foundation's website (IFRS.Org: https://www.ifrs.org/content/dam/ifrs/about-us/legal-and-governance/constitution-docs/due-process-handbook-2020.pdf)

1.2 THE PURPOSE OF A CONCEPTUAL FRAMEWORK

1.2.1 Overview

The first international 'framework' was adopted in 1989, then superseded by a replacement in 2010, and then largely rewritten in 2018. This latest version is called the *Conceptual Framework for Financial Reporting* (CF). Some fairly significant changes were made in this latest revision, including formalising concepts not previously referred to (e.g. derecognition), clarifying concepts that had previously been interpreted in a variety of ways (e.g. prudence) and completely revising the definitions of the elements and their recognition criteria. Before getting into the details, however, it is important to understand a few important points about this CF.

Firstly, the CF is not an IFRS. Instead, the purpose of the CF is:

- to assist the IASB to develop IFRSs;
- to assist preparers of financial statements to develop their own accounting policies in the event there is no suitable IFRS or the existing IFRS allows for an alternative policy to be developed;
- to assist everyone (e.g. the IASB, the preparers of financial statements and users of financial statements) to understand and interpret the application of IFRSs.

The revised CF consists of eight chapters:

- Chapter 1: The objective of general-purpose financial reporting
- Chapter 2: Qualitative characteristics of useful financial information
- Chapter 3: Financial statements and the reporting entity
- Chapter 4: The elements of financial statements
- Chapter 5: Recognition and derecognition

- Chapter 6: Measurement
- Chapter 7: Presentation and disclosure
- Chapter 8: Concepts of capital and capital maintenance.

Aspects of these eight chapters will be explained in the rest of this chapter.

1.2.2 The objective of general purpose financial reporting

The IASB's *Conceptual Framework* deals only with the objective of general purpose financial reporting; that is, financial reporting intended to meet the information needs common to a range of users who are unable to command the preparation of reports tailored to satisfy their own particular needs. For example, IFRSs are not designed to be used in the preparation of special purpose reports for stakeholders such as tax authorities and banking supervisors, both of which are able to demand this information directly.

Paragraph 1.2 of the *Conceptual Framework* states the objective of general purpose financial reporting:

> The objective of general purpose financial reporting is to provide financial information about the reporting entity that is useful to existing and potential investors, lenders and other creditors in making decisions relating to providing resources to the entity. Those decisions involve decisions about (a) buying, selling or holding equity and debt instruments, (b) providing or settling loans and other forms of credit, or (c) exercising rights to vote on, or otherwise influence, management's actions that affect the use of the entity's economic resources.

In order to achieve the objective of general purpose financial reporting (i.e. to provide useful information), the CF specifies certain qualitative characteristics of financial reporting information, defines the elements (assets, liabilities, income, expenses and equity), clarifies the concepts to be used when deciding whether to recognise (and derecognise) them, how to measure them and how to present and disclose them.

1.3 QUALITATIVE CHARACTERISTICS OF USEFUL FINANCIAL INFORMATION

What characteristics should financial information have in order to be included in general purpose financial reporting? The following section discusses both the qualitative characteristics of useful information and the constraint on providing useful information. The qualitative characteristics are divided into fundamental qualitative characteristics and enhancing qualitative characteristics.

1.3.1 Fundamental qualitative characteristics

For financial information to be decision-useful, it must possess two fundamental qualitative characteristics:
- relevance
- faithful representation.

Relevance

Paragraphs 2.6–2.11 of the IASB's *Conceptual Framework* elaborate on the qualitative characteristic of *relevance*.

Information is relevant if:
- it is capable of making a difference in the decisions made by users of financial information.

Information is considered to have the ability to make a difference in a user's decision-making if the information provides predictive value, confirmatory value or both.
- *Predictive value* occurs where the information is useful as an input into the users' decision models and affects their expectations about the future.
- *Confirmatory value* arises where the information provides feedback that confirms or changes past or present expectations based on previous evaluations

Notice that the information needs merely to be *capable* of making a difference. It is not necessary that the information has actually made a difference in the past or will make a difference in the future.

Information about the financial position and past performance is often used as the basis for predicting future financial position and performance and other matters in which users are directly interested, such as future dividends and wage payments, future share prices, and the ability of the reporting entity to pay its debts when they fall due. The predictive ability of information may be improved if unusual or infrequent transactions and events are reported separately in the statement of profit or loss and other comprehensive income.

Materiality is not a qualitative characteristic, but is a concept used when assessing the relevance of information. Simply put, if something is *immaterial*, it would be *irrelevant* to the users. Information is *material* if it is reasonable to expect that a primary user's decisions relating to the specific reporting entity might change if the information were to be omitted, misstated or obscured (paragraph 2.11).

Small expenditures for non-current assets (e.g. tools) are often expensed immediately rather than depreciated over their useful lives to save the clerical costs of recording depreciation and because the effects on performance and financial position over their useful lives are not large enough to affect decisions. Another example of the application of materiality is the common practice by large companies of rounding amounts to the nearest thousand units of currency (e.g. euros or dollars) in their financial statements.

An important aspect of materiality is that it is *entity-specific*. In other words, materiality is a relative matter — what is material for one entity may be immaterial for another. A $10,000 error may not be important in the financial statements of a multimillion-dollar company, but it may be critical to a small business. The materiality of an item may depend not only on its relative size but also on its nature. For example, the discovery of a $10,000 bribe may be a material event even for a large company. Professional judgements as to the materiality of an item or event are often difficult.

Faithful representation

Paragraphs 2.12–2.19 of the IASB's *Conceptual Framework* elaborate on the concept of faithful representation. Faithful representation is attained when the depiction of an economic phenomenon is complete, neutral, and free from material error. This results in the depiction of the economic substance of the underlying transaction. Note the following in relation to these characteristics:

- A depiction is *complete* if it includes 'all information necessary for a user to understand the phenomenon being depicted'. (Paragraph 2.14).
- *Neutrality* is the absence of bias. Bias refers to the manipulation of information to achieve a response, whether it be favourable or unfavourable. In order to achieve neutrality, we must exercise prudence. Prudence requires preparers to be cautious whenever dealing with information that has a level of uncertainty so that they do not prepare financial information with a favourable bias (e.g. overstating assets or understating liabilities), or unfavourable bias (e.g. understating assets or overstating liabilities). (Paragraphs 2.15–2.17).
- Information that is *free from error* does not mean accurate in all respects. Instead, it means that there is no error or omission either in the description thereof or in the selection and application of processes used to produce it. By way of an example, including an estimated amount in a set of financial statements does not render the information erroneous and thus no longer a faithful representation. Although measurement uncertainty has now been introduced into the financial statements, the amount is still a faithful representation of the phenomena 'if the amount is described clearly and accurately as being an estimate, the nature and limitations of the estimating process are explained and no errors have been made in selecting and applying an appropriate process for developing the estimate'. (Paragraphs 2.18–2.19).

It should be noted that the term 'faithful representation' has replaced the previous term 'reliability'. As explained in the *Basis for Conclusions*, the boards noted that there were various notions as to what is meant by reliability. The boards believed that the term 'faithful representation' provided a better understanding of the quality of information required. (Paragraphs BC 2.22–2.30).

The two fundamental qualitative characteristics of financial information (relevance and faithful representation) may give rise to conflicting guidance on how to account for phenomena. For example, the measurement base that provides the most relevant information about an asset will not always provide the most faithful representation. The *Conceptual Framework* (paragraphs 2.21–2.22) explains how to balance the fundamental qualitative characteristics. First, the criterion of relevance is applied to information to determine which economic information should be contained in the financial statements. Thereafter, the criterion of faithful representation is applied to determine how to depict those phenomena in the financial statements. The two characteristics work together. Either irrelevance (the economic phenomenon is not going to make a difference to the users' decision-making) or unfaithful representation (the depiction of the phenomenon is incomplete, biased or contains error) will result in information that is not useful to users in their decision-making.

1.3.2 Enhancing qualitative characteristics

The *Conceptual Framework* (paragraphs 2.23–2.36) identifies four enhancing qualitative characteristics. These four enhancing characteristics, expanded upon below, are *complementary* to the two fundamental characteristics. These enhancing characteristics distinguish *more useful* information from *less useful* information.

Comparability

Comparability is the quality that enables users to identify similarities in and differences between two or more sets of economic phenomena. Effective decision-making about an entity is enhanced when it is possible to compare current year financial information with that of the prior year/s (enabling the identification of trends within the entity). Similarly, decision-making is enhanced when it is possible to compare an entity's information with that of other similar entities.

It is important to note the difference between the terms comparability and consistency. For effective comparisons to be possible, there needs to be an appropriate level of consistency e.g. there needs to be a consistent method of calculating earnings per share across the various entities being compared, or from one year to the next, if we are simply comparing the earnings per share of a single entity across a period of years. *Consistency* enables or enhances *comparability*.

Note that the need for consistency does not require a given accounting method to be applied throughout an entity. For example, an entity may well use different methods to account for different types of inventory. *(These inventory costing methods are discussed in chapter 4.)* Similarly, a variety of different measurement techniques may be appropriate; for example, land may need to be measured at cost, plant may be best measured at depreciated cost and investment property may be best measured at fair value.

Consistency from year to year, or entity to entity, enhances comparability in the presentation of financial information but the need for such consistency should not be allowed to hinder the change to better accounting methods. The need for comparability should not demand blind uniformity or consistency. For example, it would not be appropriate for an entity to continue to apply an accounting policy if the policy ceases to meet the fundamental qualitative characteristics of relevance and faithful representation.

Verifiability

Verifiability is the quality that helps assure users that information faithfully represents the economic phenomena that it purports to represent. Verifiability is achieved if different knowledgeable and independent observers would reach the same general conclusions that a particular description or amount is a faithful representation. That said, and as explained in the Basis of Conclusions, information that is not verifiable is not useless. In fact, many forward-looking estimates cannot be verified, and yet the financial statements would be far less useful without them, which is why verifiability is 'very desirable but not necessarily required'. (BC2.62)

Timeliness

Timeliness means having information available to users before it loses its capacity to influence their decisions. If such capacity is lost, then the information loses its relevance. Information may continue to be timely after it has been initially provided, for example, in trend analysis.

Understandability

Understandability is the quality that enables users to comprehend the meaning of the information. Information may be more understandable if it is 'classified, characterised and presented clearly and concisely'. In this regard, preparers of financial information may assume that the users thereof 'have a reasonable knowledge of business and economic activities', that they will 'review and analyse the information diligently' and will obtain the 'aid of an advisor' to understand complex issues.

1.3.3 Cost constraint on useful financial reporting

Paragraphs 2.39 to 2.43 of the *Conceptual Framework* note that cost is the constraint that limits the information provided by financial reporting. The provision of information incurs *costs*. The benefits of supplying information should always be greater than the costs. Costs include costs of collecting and processing information, costs of verifying information, and costs of disseminating information. The non-provision of information also imposes costs on the users of financial information as they seek alternative sources of information.

1.4 GOING CONCERN ASSUMPTION

Financial statements are prepared under the assumption that the entity will continue to operate for the foreseeable future. Thus, it is assumed that an entity will continue to operate at least long enough to carry out its existing commitments. This assumption is called the *going concern assumption* or sometimes the *continuity assumption*.

Adoption of the going concern assumption has important implications in accounting. For example, it is an assumption used by some to justify the use of historical costs in accounting for non-current assets and for the systematic allocation of their costs to depreciation expense over their useful lives. Because it is assumed that the assets will not be sold in the near future but will continue to be used in operating activities, current market values of the assets are sometimes assumed to be of little importance. If the entity continues to use the assets, fluctuations in their market values cause no gain or loss; nor do they increase or decrease the usefulness of the assets. The going concern assumption also supports the inclusion of some assets, such as prepaid expenses and acquired goodwill, in the statement of financial position (balance sheet) even though they may have little, if any, sales value.

If management intends to liquidate the entity or to cease trading, or has no realistic alternative than to do so, the going concern assumption is set aside. In that case the financial statements are prepared on a different basis, but the *Conceptual Framework* provides no guidance on what that basis would be. However, paragraph 25 of IAS 1 *Presentation of Financial Statements* prescribes disclosures when an entity does not prepare financial statements on a going concern basis, including the basis on which it prepared the financial statements *(see chapter 16)*.

1.5 DEFINITION OF ELEMENTS IN FINANCIAL STATEMENTS

The *Conceptual Framework* (CF) identifies and defines the elements of financial statements; namely assets, liabilities, equity, income and expenses. The 2018 CF introduced some fairly significant changes to these definitions.

1.5.1 Assets

An *asset* is defined in paragraph 4.3 of the *Conceptual Framework* as:

A present economic resource controlled by the entity resulting from past events.

This definition refers to an *economic resource*, which is defined in paragraph 4.4 as:

A right that has the potential to produce economic benefits.

Applying these two definitions means that, for an item to represent an asset to an entity, an assessment needs to be made as to:
1. whether it is an economic resource, being a *right* that has the *potential* to produce economic benefits;
2. whether this right is *controlled* by the entity; and
3. whether the right exists at reporting date as a result of a *past event*.
Each of these characteristics will now be explained in a little more depth.

Rights with potential

One of the most significant changes to the asset definition brought about by the publication of the latest Conceptual Framework in 2018 was the notion that assets represent *rights*. This means that, for example, when considering an entity's manufacturing plant, we 'look past' the physical object and, instead, we 'look into' it in order to identify whether that physical object contains any rights; for example, the plant gives the entity both the right to use it to manufacture certain items and the right to benefit from it by selling the plant's output. This example (of a physical plant) raises another important point in that some resources (e.g. a plant) contain multiple rights (e.g. the right to use and the right to benefit). In such situations, the multiple rights are often accounted for as a single asset, being a *set* of rights. In other words, we do not record the 'right to use the plant' and 'right to benefit from the plant' as two separate assets on our statement of financial position. Another important point is that, where an asset is conceptually a 'set of rights' (consider the example of the plant, which represented two rights: a right to use and a right to benefit), the set of rights will often be described as the physical object to which they relate. This is because describing it as the physical object would be a faithful representation and often the most concise and understandable method of describing the rights.

The next aspect related to the right is that, for a *right* to meet the definition of an *economic resource*, it must also have the *potential* to produce economic benefits for the entity. These economic benefits could come in many forms; for example, they could be cash inflows (e.g. a plant that represents the right to manufacture items would lead to a potential cash inflow from the sale of these items) or the avoidance of cash outflows (e.g. electricity prepaid represents a right that avoids future cash outflows for electricity). Other examples of ways in which a right could economically benefit an entity (whether the right is used singly or in combination with other rights) include the ability to:
• exchange it for another right under favourable conditions,
• extinguish a liability, and
• use it to create goods or services.
Finally, although the right must have the potential to create economic benefits for the entity, this potential does not need to be probable or even likely. Instead, the level of probability that the potential economic benefits would occur is built into the next stage, being the assessment of the recognition criteria (in other words, the conclusion may be made that an asset exists but because it does not meet the recognition criteria, it is not recognised) and/or into the measurement of the asset.

Control

The entity must have *control* over the right if it is to meet the definition of an asset. This does not mean legal ownership is necessary. Instead, control arises through either:

- the ability to enforce legal rights (e.g. through a legal contract); or
- the ability to both 'direct the use' of the resource (meaning that the entity can decide how it is to be used) and 'obtain the benefits' from it.

Past event

For a right to meet the definition of an asset, it must have arisen by way of a past event on or before reporting date, such that it exists at reporting date.

1.5.2 Liabilities

A *liability* is defined in paragraph 4.26 of the *Conceptual Framework* as:

> a present obligation of the entity to transfer an economic resource as a result of past events.

This definition refers to a *present obligation*, which is defined in paragraph 4.29 as:

> a duty or responsibility that an entity has no practical ability to avoid.

Applying these two definitions means that, for an item to represent a liability to an entity, an assessment needs to be made as to:

1. whether there is a *present obligation*, being a duty or responsibility that the entity has no practical ability to avoid;
2. whether a transfer of *economic benefits* is possible; and
3. whether the present obligation at reporting date results from a *past event*.

Each of these characteristics will now be explained in a little more depth:

Present obligation

A duty or responsibility the entity has no practical ability to avoid

One of the most significant changes to the liability definition brought about by the publication of the latest Conceptual Framework in 2018, is that the term *'present obligation'* has now been clarified to mean there must be a 'duty or responsibility that an entity has *no practical ability to avoid'*. Thus, if an entity could avoid the duty or responsibility only through, for example, the cessation of trading, it would meet the definition of a present obligation because, unless the entity is not applying the going concern assumption, the cessation of trade is not a practical option.

The obligation is a duty or responsibility that always involves a third party

Another important point is that obligations always involve a *duty or responsibility owed to a third party* but that it is not necessary to know who the third party is. (Paragraph 4.29)

The obligation can be legal, constructive or conditional

Legal obligations are duties or responsibilities that cannot practically be avoided because the third party can legally force the entity to fulfil its obligations (e.g. through a legally enforceable contract).

Constructive obligations are duties or responsibilities that cannot practically be avoided due to the entity's own 'customary practices, published policies or specific statements' that will have caused third parties to have certain expectations of the entity (e.g. an entity may have a policy of rectifying faults in its products even after the warranty period has expired, in which case, amounts expected to be spent on repairs in respect of goods already sold are liabilities).

Conditional obligations are duties or responsibilities that will arise due to an entity's own future actions, but where these future actions cannot practically be avoided (e.g. a duty to rehabilitate a specific area if it gets damaged due to mining would be a conditional obligation of a mining company that has been granted a licence to mine in that area, since a mining company has no practical ability to avoid mining).

Present obligations are not the same as future commitments

A future commitment, or intention to sacrifice economic resources in the future, would not meet the definition of a present obligation because the entity has the ability to avoid the future outflow. For example, a decision by management to buy an asset in the future does not give rise to a present obligation. Instead, an obligation would arise when, for example, the entity has entered into an irrevocable agreement to buy the asset, with a substantial penalty if the agreement is revoked.

Transfer of economic resources

The *economic resource* that the entity may need to transfer can be anything, for example, paying in cash, providing the right to cash, providing goods or services or other assets or even converting the obligation to equity.

Past event

The liability definition requires that the obligation be *present* at reporting date, having arisen from a *past event*. Although the asset definition used the term 'past event', it did not explain it. From the perspective of the liability definition, however, two criteria must be met for a *past event* to have occurred (the cause and effect criteria):

- the entity must have either obtained a benefit or taken an action (the cause); and
- as a result, the entity may have to transfer an economic benefit (the effect).

For example, work done by staff gives rise to wages payable. By contrast, wages to be paid to staff for work they will do in the *future* is not a liability as there is no past transaction or event and thus no present obligation.

1.5.3 Income

The *Conceptual Framework* defines *income* in paragraph 4.68 as:

> Increases in assets, or decreases in liabilities, other than those relating to contributions from holders of equity claims.

The definition of income is directly linked to the definitions of assets and liabilities: if assets increase, we have income. . . if liabilities decrease, we have income. The only exception is if the assets or liabilities changed due to a contribution made to the entity by 'a holder of an equity claim', in which case the movement in the asset or liability is *not* income, but an *equity movement* instead. For example, if an investor buys shares in the entity in exchange for cash, the entity's bank account, an asset, will increase. However, by definition, this is not income because the cash contribution came from a person in his role as a 'holder of an equity claim' (i.e. a shareholder). Thus, the only option is to record the contra entry to the increase in assets (i.e. cash in bank) as a direct increase in equity (i.e. share capital). In other words, the entity's assets increased with no change to its liabilities, with the result that equity, as defined, has increased and since it is not income, the equity must be increased directly.

Income arises once there is an increase in an asset, provided there is no equivalent increase in liabilities. For example, in the case of magazine subscriptions received in advance, although the bank account has increased (i.e. an asset has increased) no income exists on receipt of the cash because an equivalent obligation has also arisen for services to be performed through the obligation to supply magazines to subscribers in the future (i.e. a liability has increased). Thus, there is no *net* increase in assets and thus no income.

Income can also exist through a reduction in liabilities. An example of a liability reduction is the forgiveness of an entity's loan liability. Income arises from that forgiveness, unless it is a contribution by a holder of an equity claim (e.g. if the party who forgives the entity's debt is given shares in the entity in return, in which case the decrease in the liability is not income but a direct increase in equity, instead).

Under the *Conceptual Framework*, income encompasses both revenue and gains. A definition of *revenue* is contained in paragraph 7 of IAS 18 *Revenue* as follows:

> [T]he gross inflow of economic benefits during the period arising in the course of the ordinary activities of an entity when those inflows result in increases in equity, other than increases relating to contributions from equity participants.

Thus, *revenue* represents income that has arisen from 'the ordinary activities of an entity'. Income that does not arise from the entity's ordinary activities (i.e. it does not meet the definition of revenue) is referred to as a *gain* (e.g. income made from the sale of a non-current asset). Gains are usually disclosed in the statement of profit or loss and other comprehensive income *net* of any related expenses, (e.g. when selling an item of plant, we would deduct its carrying amount from the proceeds on sale thereof and show as income the net 'gain on sale of plant'). Revenue, on the other hand, is reported at a gross amount. Revenues and gains are both income, meaning that they are not separate elements under the *Conceptual Framework*.

1.5.4 Expenses

The *Conceptual Framework* defines *expenses* in paragraph 4.69 as:

> Decreases in assets, or increases in liabilities, other than those relating to distributions to holders of equity claims.

The definition of expenses is directly linked to the definitions of assets and liabilities: if assets decrease, we have an expense . . . if liabilities increase, we have an expense. The only exception is if the assets or liabilities changed due to a distribution made by the entity to 'a holder of an equity claim'. For example, if the entity paid a cash dividend to its shareholders, the entity's bank account, an asset, would decrease. However, by definition, this would not be regarded as an expense because a shareholder is a 'holder of an equity claim'. Therefore, in this case, the only option would be to regard this decrease in assets as a direct decrease in equity (the entity's assets decreased with no change to its liabilities, with the result that equity, as defined, has decreased and since it was a payment to a holder of an equity claim (e.g. a shareholder), the decrease is a direct reduction in equity).

A transaction that involves the payment for electricity credits (e.g. electricity prepaid) will not create an expense. This is because the net effect on assets and liabilities is nil since one asset decreases and another asset increases: the payment decreases the 'cash in bank' asset but it increases the 'electricity prepaid' asset ('electricity prepaid' is an asset to the entity because it represents an economic resource, being a right to use electricity in the future and where this right has the potential to lead to economic benefits). Conversely, a transaction that involves the payment for electricity that has already been used would result in an expense. This is because there is a net decrease in the entity's assets (the payment decreases the 'cash in bank' asset but since it is a payment for electricity that has already been used, it has not created an economic resource that can be used by the entity — in other words, the payment has not created an asset).

1.5.5 Equity

Paragraph 4.63 of the *Conceptual Framework* defines *equity* as:

the residual interest in the assets of the entity after deducting all its liabilities.

Defining equity in this manner shows clearly that it cannot be defined independently of the other elements in the statement of financial position. The characteristics of equity are as follows:

- Equity is a residual, that is, something left over. In other words:

$$\text{Equity} = \text{Assets} - \text{Liabilities}$$

- Equity is increased by profitable operations, that is, the excess of income over expenses, and by contributions by owners (e.g. investing in the entity through the purchase of equity shares). Similarly, equity is diminished by unprofitable operations and by distributions to owners (drawings and dividends). The proof of the connection between 'equity' and 'income and expenses' is contained within the definitions. In this regard, like equity, the definitions of income and expenses (see the sections below) are linked directly to assets and liabilities, although income and expenses are defined by the *movement* in assets and liabilities. Thus, since the income definition states that income arises from, for example, an increase in assets, and since the equity definition states that total equity increases through increased assets, it can be seen that increased income leads to increased equity.
- Since equity is the residual of assets and liabilities, equity will clearly also be affected by how those assets and liabilities are measured and by the concepts of capital and capital maintenance adopted in the preparation of general purpose financial statements. (Concepts of capital and capital maintenance are discussed later in the chapter.)
- Equity may be subclassified in the statement of financial position, for example, into contributed funds from owners, retained earnings, other reserves representing appropriations of retained earnings, and reserves representing capital maintenance adjustments.

1.6 RECOGNITION OF ELEMENTS OF FINANCIAL STATEMENTS

1.6.1 Overview

Recognising an item as an element refers to the process of incorporating it into the accounting records such that it will eventually be included in either the statement of financial position or statement of profit or loss and other comprehensive income, where it will either be presented separately, or aggregated with other items.

Before an item may be recognised as one of the five elements (e.g. an asset, liability, income, expense or equity), it must:

- Meet the definition of that element; and
- Meet the recognition criteria.

1.6.2 Recognition criteria

Regarding recognition criteria, the 2018 *Conceptual Framework* states, in paragraph 5.7, that elements should only be recognised in the financial statements if it means providing information that is both:

- relevant; and
- a faithful representation.

Interestingly, these are the two *fundamental qualitative characteristics* of *useful* financial information and thus the essence of the two recognition criteria is simply that, by recognising an element, we must be providing useful information.

These recognition criteria are used for all five elements. This represents a significant departure from the previous *Conceptual Framework* of 2010, in which there were different recognition criteria relevant to each of the five elements.

1.6.3 The three uncertainties: Impact on recognition criteria and the balancing act

When deciding whether a definition is met, and thus that an element exists, there are uncertainties that were ignored. These uncertainties, however, are considered when deciding whether to recognise the element. For example, when deciding if an asset exists (i.e. whether it meets the asset definition), we consider only whether it has the potential to produce economic benefits and ignore the fact that the potential for economic benefits may be only a remotely possible outcome. This is referred to as *outcome* uncertainty. Other uncertainties include *measurement* uncertainty and *existence* uncertainty.

Existence uncertainty affects *relevance*. For example, the existence of an obligation may be dependent on future actions that may or may not be avoidable, such as an entity's obligation to rehabilitate land that will only arise if a certain level of activity on the land is exceeded. If, on balance, the obligation (the liability element) probably won't eventuate because the entity does not plan to exceed the level of activity beyond which rehabilitation would become necessary, information about this element may be considered irrelevant and would thus not be recognised.

Outcome uncertainty also affects *relevance*. Outcome uncertainty refers to the uncertainty regarding the amount and timing of the potential flow of economic benefits. For example, if an entity is aware that there is a present obligation due to the fact that it is being sued for something that has already happened, but is unsure of the amount of the obligation or when the amount will become payable, there is outcome uncertainty regarding the obligation. If, for example, it is virtually certain that the amount measured will be insignificant, information about this obligation would probably be regarded as irrelevant and not recognised.

Measurement uncertainty affects *faithful representation*. Measurement uncertainty arises when the amount attributed to an element cannot be directly observed and thus has to be estimated. Financial information contains many estimates and thus the mere fact that an amount is estimated does not mean the financial information is not useful. The level of measurement uncertainty must simply be considered acceptable.

Measurement uncertainty may also impact *relevance*. For example, the most relevant information regarding an asset may be its fair value rather than its cost. However, the fair value may involve such a high degree of estimation that the measurement uncertainty reaches an unacceptable level. In such a case, it may be necessary to measure the asset at cost (being information that is a faithful representation although possibly less relevant to the users) instead of at fair value (being information that would be more relevant but information that is not a faithful representation). In other words, in order to achieve useful information, there is a necessary and natural balancing act between the two requirements of relevance and faithful representation. In this example, the most relevant information (fair value) was not able to be faithfully represented and thus the next most relevant information (cost) was substituted instead.

1.6.4 Items that may not be recognised

If an item does not meet the definition or recognition criteria, the item must not be recognised in the statement of financial position or statement of profit or loss and other comprehensive income. Information about the item may, however, be useful to the users of the financial statements and thus it may be necessary to include this information in the notes to the financial statements. If an item is not recognised in the current period because the recognition criteria are not currently met, this item may be recognised in a future period when the recognition criteria are met.

1.7 DERECOGNITION

Although derecognition has always existed (involving the removal of an asset or liability from the accounting records), the 2018 *Conceptual Framework* introduced a new section to clarify the meaning of derecognition, which it describes as the:

- 'removal of all or part of
- a recognised asset or liability
- from the statement of financial position'.

Derecognition normally occurs when an asset or liability, which was previously recognised, subsequently fails to meet the relevant definition. For example, an entity may 'lose control' over the asset (or part of the asset), in which case all of (or part of) an asset would be derecognised. Similarly, a liability will be derecognised if the entity 'no longer has a present obligation for all or part of the recognised liability'.

When part of an asset or liability is derecognised, care must be exercised to ensure that the financial statements faithfully represent both:

- the portion of the asset or liability that remains; and
- the change in the asset or liability arising from the transaction or event that led to the derecognition.

1.8 MEASUREMENT OF THE ELEMENTS

1.8.1 Overview

Chapter 6 of the 2018 *Conceptual Framework* deals with measurement. This chapter explains and describes various measurement bases and the factors to consider when deciding which would be the most appropriate. Interestingly, however, this chapter is one that is designed largely for use by the IASB in preparing IFRSs. Preparers of financial statements, on the other hand, generally do not need to refer to chapter 6 because they simply need to comply with the relevant IFRSs, which are normally quite prescriptive in terms of which measurement bases may be used. That said, however, where an IFRS provides a preparer with measurement options (e.g. IAS 40 *Investment property* allows the choice between the cost model and fair value model), preparers who are battling to decide which option to use would find it helpful to refer to the explanations behind the various measurement bases and factors to consider when choosing which to use.

1.8.2 Measurement and the measurement bases

According to paragraph 6.1 of the *Conceptual Framework*, measurement refers to the quantification, using monetary terms, of the elements recognised in the financial statements. This requires the 'selection of a measurement basis'.

Since equity, income and expenses are elements that, by definition, flow from assets and liabilities, the *Conceptual Framework* tends to focus on how the measurement basis is applied to assets and liabilities. In other words, the measurement of the asset or liability will tend to automatically affect the measurement of the related income and expenses and ultimately equity.

Since the objective is to produce useful information, which requires balancing the qualitative characteristics against the cost constraint, it is generally necessary to use different measurement bases for different assets, liabilities, income and expenses.

1.8.3 Various measurement bases

The *Conceptual Framework* provides various examples of measurement bases, which are categorised under the following headings:

- historical cost; or
- current value.

The *Conceptual Framework* emphasises that both are useful measurements, but that, in particular situations, one method may provide more useful information than the other.

Historic cost

Historic cost refers to measurement bases that are based upon 'the price of the transaction or other event that gave rise to the asset or liability'. (Paragraph 6.24)

A measurement at historic cost will normally include transaction costs, and may involve reductions in cost to reflect usage (e.g. depreciation or amortisation) and impairments. Historic cost is an example of an *entry price* (in other words, it is a measurement that reflects the cost of acquisition).

Examples of IFRSs that utilise the historic cost measurement include:

- IAS 16 *Property, plant and equipment*: Land, which generally does not diminish in value through usage, is often measured at historic cost, whereas plant, which does diminish in value through usage, is often measured at depreciated historic cost.
- IAS 2 *Inventory*: Inventory is measured at lower of cost and net realisable value, where 'cost' is an example of a measurement at historic cost.
- IFRS 9 *Financial instruments*: Certain financial liabilities are measured at amortised cost.

Current value

A current value measurement is one that presents the 'current conditions' at measurement date. There are three examples of the current value method referred to in the *Conceptual Framework*:

- Fair value
- Current cost
- Value in use of an asset or fulfilment value of a liability.

The **fair value** is an exit price that reflects the price that would be received to sell an asset, or paid to transfer a liability, in an orderly transaction between market participants at the measurement date. The measurement of fair value is sufficiently complex that there is an IFRS dedicated to this (IFRS 13 *Fair value measurement*). An example of an IFRS that allows measurement at fair value is IAS 40 *Investment property*.

The **current cost** is an entry price, but it reflects the consideration that would be paid to acquire an *equivalent* asset, (i.e. in its current second-hand condition), at measurement date, or, if it is a liability, the consideration that would be received for an *equivalent* liability. It includes transaction costs: in the case of an asset, transaction costs are added; whereas, in the case of a liability, transaction costs are deducted. An example would be a machine that was purchased new for $1,000, but which, at measurement date, is now 3 years old. On this date, purchasing a new replacement machine would cost $1,500, whereas a second-hand 3-year old machine would cost $900. The current cost is $900 (note that the historic cost is $1,000).

Value in use is an exit price that reflects the present value of an asset's economic benefits that an entity expects to obtain from the combination of its use and eventual disposal. This measurement is often used to test certain assets for impairment. For example, it is one of the measures referred to in IAS 36 *Impairment of assets* used to test assets accounted for in terms of IAS 16 *Property plant and equipment* and IAS 38 *Intangible assets*.

Fulfilment value of a liability is an exit price that reflects the present value of the outflow of economic benefits that an entity expects to be obliged to transfer in fulfilment (settlement) of its liability.

The measurement basis most commonly adopted by entities is the historic cost basis, although over time, IFRSs have increasingly allowed or mandated the use of the current value basis, for example, through the use of fair values to measure property and value in use, used to test assets for impairment. There is little use of current cost (replacement cost) in financial statements, being a measurement basis appropriate for entities using the physical concept of capital (this is explained in a later section of this chapter).

1.8.4 Choosing a measurement basis

Significant professional judgement is needed when choosing which measurement basis to use. Consideration must be given to 'the nature of the information that the choice of measurement basis will produce in both the statement of financial position and the statement of financial performance' (paragraph 6.43). Ultimately, the objective is to present *useful* information. In other words, the measurement basis chosen must reflect information that is relevant and a faithful representation (these are fundamental qualitative characteristics). The information should ideally also be comparable, timely, verifiable and understandable.

As mentioned above, selecting a measurement basis that produces a faithful representation is not the only objective. In this regard, a measurement basis that reflects a directly observable price would be a faithful representation (it is 100% accurate), but it may not necessarily be relevant information. For example, measuring a plant at fair value, where this plant has an active market and a fair value that is directly observable, may be considered a faithful representation but, if it is to be used internally and not sold, its fair value would not be relevant information. Thus, it is advisable to first decide what information is relevant to users and then select a measurement basis that is a faithful representation thereof.

It should be noted that a measurement that is a faithful representation is not necessarily 'free from error'. Information that is relevant may require a measurement involving estimates. The use of estimates introduces 'measurement uncertainty', but even a high degree of measurement uncertainty does not necessarily mean the information is not a faithful representation. Conversely, some estimates may involve such a high level of uncertainty that the information ceases to be a faithful representation, in which case, a different measurement basis must be sought that will still produce relevant information. (Paragraphs 59–60)

Not only does *measurement* uncertainty sometimes arise, but *outcome* uncertainty and *existence* uncertainty may also exist.

- *outcome* uncertainty refers to the uncertainty regarding the timing and amount of the cash flows; and
- *existence* uncertainty refers to the uncertainty as to whether an asset or liability exists. (Paragraph 61)

Existence uncertainty normally affects the decision as to whether to recognise the asset or liability but, like *outcome* uncertainty, it can also affect measurement uncertainty. (Paragraph 62)

When selecting a measurement basis, its usefulness in terms of both the initial measurement *and* subsequent measurement must be considered. This is because, if different measurement bases were to be used for each of the initial measurement and subsequent measurement, it could happen that income or expenses arise when the initial measurement basis is switched to the subsequent measurement basis when, in fact, no transaction or event had occurred. (Paragraph 6.48)

Although different measurement bases may be used for different assets, liabilities, income and expenses, the *Conceptual Framework* cautions that 'measurement inconsistencies' (also called 'accounting mismatches') might arise if different measurement bases are used for assets and liabilities that are 'related in some way' (e.g. when the cash flows from an asset are linked to the cash flows from a liability). Such accounting mismatches may lead to financial information that is not a faithful representation. (Paragraph 6.58)

1.9 UNIT OF ACCOUNT

A unit of account is a term used when deciding how to recognise and measure assets and liabilities. The 'unit of account' is defined as:

- the right or group of rights, the obligation or group of obligations, or the group of rights and obligations, to which recognition criteria and measurement concepts are applied. (Paragraph 4.48)

When deciding what the 'unit of account' is, we must be guided by the objective of general-purpose financial reporting, which is to provide *useful* financial information. This means that the decision regarding the 'unit of account' must result in relevant information that is faithfully represented and, as with all financial reporting decisions, the cost constraint (cost versus benefit) must be considered. Achieving the objective of useful information may necessitate using different 'units of account' for recognition and for measurement.

By way of example, an entity may decide that when *recognising* its contracts, the unit of account is the 'individual contract' whereas, when *measuring* the contract, for reasons of cost-effectiveness, the unit of account is a larger 'portfolio of contracts'. In other words, this entity looks at each contract to decide whether that specific individual contract should be recognised, but, once recognised, that contract, instead of being individually measured, is measured as part of a larger *portfolio* of contracts (i.e. in this example, the unit of account for recognition purposes is the 'individual contract' but the unit of account for measurement purposes is the 'portfolio of contracts').

Since information should always faithfully represent the substance of transactions and events, care must be taken when identifying the unit of account. For example, it may be necessary to account for rights and obligations as separate units of account even if they arose from a single source transaction. Conversely, however, it may be necessary to account for rights and obligations arising from multiple source transactions as a single unit of account.

1.10 PRESENTATION AND DISCLOSURE

Elements that meet the definition and recognition criteria are recognised and included in the statement of financial position or statement of profit or loss and other comprehensive income. These are financial statements that are presented on the accrual basis. These elements will need to also be presented using the cash basis and included in the statement of cash flows. Further detailed information may be needed regarding these recognised elements and also regarding those elements that were not recognised because they failed to meet the definitions and/or recognition criteria. This detailed information is provided in the notes to the financial statements.

Guidance regarding the level of presentation and disclosure is generally stipulated in the specific IFRSs. However, the 2018 *Conceptual Framework* introduces a chapter (chapter 7) dedicated to understanding the concepts of presentation and disclosure. This chapter reiterates that, as with recognition and measurement, presentation and disclosure decisions must be guided by the overall objective of providing users with financial information that is relevant and a faithful representation of the transactions and events (i.e. useful information). Similarly, these decisions may need to be constrained when assessing the cost versus benefit.

The essence of this chapter on presentation and disclosure is that effective communication in the financial information requires:
- focusing on presentation and disclosure objectives and principles rather than focusing on rules;
- classifying information in a manner that groups similar items and separates dissimilar items; and
- aggregating information in such a way that it is not obscured either by unnecessary detail or by excessive aggregation. (Paragraph 7.2)

1.11 CONCEPTS OF CAPITAL

The concept of capital has a direct impact on profits, with the concept of capital maintenance referring to the specific point at which profit may be recognised. In this regard, profit is recognised only to the extent that the capital existing at the end of a period exceeds the capital that existed at the beginning of that period. In other words, profit is only recognised if the closing capital exceeds that required for capital maintenance. It is thus imperative that entities identify the capital that they seek to maintain. In this regard, two main concepts of capital are discussed in the *Conceptual Framework*, namely financial capital and physical capital.

Under the *financial capital concept*, capital is synonymous with the *net assets* (i.e. *equity*) of the entity. Profit exists only after the entity has maintained its capital, measured as the financial amount of *equity*, using either nominal monetary units (currency) or units of constant purchasing power. In other words, profit is only recognised if the *equity* at the end of the period exceeds the *equity* at the beginning of the period, adjusted for distributions to and contributions from owners. (Paragraph 8.3 (a))

Under the *physical capital concept*, capital represents the *operating capability* of the entity. Profit exists only after the entity has maintained its capital, measured as its *operating capability*. In other words, profit is recognised if the *operating capability* at the end of the period exceeds the *operating capability* (or the resources or funds needed to achieve that capacity) that existed at the beginning of the period, after adjusting for distributions to and contributions from owners. (Paragraph 8.3 (b))

The decision as to which capital concept to adopt is driven by the needs of users. Most entities use the financial capital concept. If an entity adopted the physical capital concept, it would need to use the current cost basis of measurement. (Paragraphs 8.2–8.5)

1.12 SUMMARY

This chapter has provided an overview of the structure of the IASB and the process of setting IFRSs, including IFRIC Interpretations. The adoption of IFRSs in many parts of the world has increased the importance of developments in international standards setting. This chapter also provides an overview of some of the most important aspects of the *Conceptual Framework*.

The *Conceptual Framework* describes the basic concepts that underlie financial statements prepared in conformity with IFRSs. It mainly serves as a guide to the standard setters in developing accounting standards but is also a guide for preparers in resolving accounting issues that are not addressed directly in an accounting standard and for users to assist in better understanding financial reports.

The *Conceptual Framework* identifies the principal classes of users of an entity's general purpose financial statements and states that the objective of financial statements is to provide information — about the financial position, performance and changes in financial position of an entity — that is useful to certain users of the financial statements. It specifies the fundamental qualities that make financial information useful, namely relevance and faithful representation, and the qualities that enhance usefulness, being comparability, verifiability, timeliness and understandability, and admits that achieving all these qualities may be constrained by cost.

The *Conceptual Framework* also defines the basic elements in financial statements (assets, liabilities, equity, income and expenses) and discusses the criteria for both recognising and derecognising them. It also provides an overview of various measurement bases and principles to consider when measuring these elements. The concept of 'unit of account', used when making decisions regarding recognition, derecognition and measurement, is also introduced. The concepts of presentation and disclosure are also explained. The *Conceptual Framework* also describes two alternative concepts of capital maintenance, which directly influence when profit may be recognised.

Discussion questions

1. Describe the standard-setting process of the IASB.
2. Identify the potential benefits of a globally accepted set of accounting standards.
3. Outline the fundamental qualitative characteristics of financial reporting information to be considered when preparing general purpose financial statements.
4. Discuss the importance of the going concern assumption to the practice of accounting.
5. Discuss the essential characteristics of an asset as described in the *Conceptual Framework*.
6. Discuss the essential characteristics of a liability as described in the *Conceptual Framework*.
7. Discuss the difference, if any, between income, revenue and gains.
8. Distinguish between the financial and physical concepts of capital and their implications for the measurement of profit.

References

IFRS Foundation 2020, *IASB and IFRS Interpretations Committee Due Process Handbook,* www.ifrs.org.

IFRS Foundation and the International Accounting Standards Board 2018, *IASB and the IASC Foundation: Who We Are and What We Do,* www.ifrs.org.

The *Conceptual Framework* highlights the decision useful-ness property of accounting numbers and identifies certain underlying qualities that enhance it. It is therefore an impor-tant question, in light of the large resources society expends on accounting regulation and profession, whether pub-lished financial statements do in fact provide useful infor-mation. In attempting to address this question, accounting research largely has focused on the 'value relevance' prop-erty of accounting numbers as a way to operationalise cri-teria such as relevance and faithful representation (or, as previously known, reliability). There may be several ways to assess the value relevance and reliability of specific num-bers or disclosures, but a common approach in the archival empirical academic literature has been to examine the asso-ciation between specific disclosures and stock prices or stock returns. Extensive reviews that go well beyond the scope of this section are offered by, for example, Barth et al. (2001) and Kothari (2001).

Modern empirical accounting research traces its origin to the seminal paper of Ball and Brown (1968) which shows that stock returns and earnings surprises tend to move in the same direction. From this evidence one can infer that earnings and share prices impound similar information, although causality (i.e., whether accounting numbers shape stock prices and trading decisions) is more difficult to show. Beaver's (1968) seminal paper on trading volume around earnings announcements provides more persuasive evidence that earnings announcements furnish useful *news* to market participants. Specifically, he documents a spike in trading activity around earnings announcements, suggesting infor-mation conveyed in these announcements leads investors to revise their prior beliefs and hence trade. Notwithstanding the centrality of the value relevance strand in accounting research, it is not without shortcomings. Criticisms of the value relevance literature can be found in Holthausen and Watts (2001) and the interested reader should bear these in mind. In particular, many academics stress the role of accounting in contracting, such as in debt and compensa-tion. However, contracting is not a consideration in the *Con-ceptual Framework*.

Of the extensive research that links earnings to stock prices and returns, we mention here only a few important papers. Kormendi and Lipe (1987) link returns to earnings surprises (or, earnings innovations) by regressing stock returns on earnings surprises. The coefficient on the earnings surprise is called the earnings response coefficient (ERC). If the surprise is permanent *and* value relevant, then $1 of a surprise should translate into more than $1 of return. Kormendi and Lipe (1987) show that greater earnings persistence translates to a larger ERC.

Using changes in earnings as a proxy for new information can shed light on how informative earnings are when they are announced. Because earnings may not be timely, in the sense that news from other sources is already impounded in prices before the earnings are announced (Beaver et al. 1980), changes in annual or quarterly earnings may be only weakly related to returns. Therefore, a smaller earnings response coefficient may indicate a lack of timeliness (rather than weaker persistence), which is an enhancing qualitative characteristic of accounting information. The relatively small magnitude observed for earnings response coefficients from the extant research (Kothari, 2001) may be then attributed to the fact that earnings lag behind share prices. Another, not mutually exclusive, explanation for the low magnitude of the earnings response coefficient is that the quality of accounting standards is poor (Lev and Zarowin, 1999).

Research that followed includes Easton and Harris (1991) who refine the specification used in Kormendi and Lipe (1987) to show that prices and returns are also related to earnings levels as well as earnings changes. Kothari and Sloan (1992) argue that the earnings response coefficient is a function of news about future growth in earnings that is con-tained in current earnings. As is suggested by Kormendi and Lipe (1987), the earnings response coefficient may also be smaller when earnings changes are transitory. In particular, losses are transitory because they cannot continue for a long time; in such a case the reporting entity will go out of busi-ness or be purchased by another company. Hayn (1995) pro-vides evidence on the earnings response coefficient in loss firms that is consistent with this idea.

Surprisingly, only in recent years have accounting researchers started to look at the value relevance of earnings in the much larger debt markets. Easton et al. (2009) find that bond returns and earnings are positively associated, and more so for negative earnings surprises. This is explained by the sensitivity of investors in bonds to bad news, as this may affect the return on their investments (whereas increases in firm value normally benefit equity investors). They also find that trading activity in bonds increases around earnings announcements, evidence that extends the findings of Beaver (1968) to debt markets. Overall, therefore, the accounting literature has provided evidence that accounting numbers are capable of, and likely are, providing information that is useful to investors.

The qualitative characteristic that received most scrutiny in more recent accounting research is probably faithful rep-resentation. Faithful representation requires the accounting treatment to be unbiased and neutral. In particular, it negates the concept of conservatism that requires estimates to be cautious in that, if a range of estimates is available for an item of assets or income, a lower estimate should be selected. The opposite holds for liabilities and expenses. It should be noted that historically conservatism has been one of the fundamental principles in accounting (Watts, 2003) and the requirement for neutral and unbiased treatment is relatively new. That many standards, old and new, are never-theless conservative may be surprising given standard setters' insistence on neutrality as per the *Conceptual Framework* of 2010 and 2018. However, as Watts (2003) argues, conserva-tism reduces political cost for standard setters and so when they promulgate specific standards they still require conserv-atism in measurement procedures. Consistent with this argu-ment, Barker and McGeachin (2015) find many examples in accounting standards promulgated by the IASB that show that IAS and IFRS are, in practice, conservative. Basu (1997) operationalised the concept of conservatism to predict that bad news is incorporated into earnings at a faster rate than good news. Employing negative share returns as a proxy for bad news he finds that in a regression of earnings on returns and negative returns the coefficient on negative returns is positively associated with earnings. This implies that negative returns (bad news) reduce earnings more than positive returns (good news) increase earnings, thus confirming his conjecture. Basu (1997) has been a highly influential paper. It has spawned a very large number of studies that investigate the relation between conservatism and an array of economic phenomena. As of writing this section, Basu (1997) has been cited more than 7100 times (source: Google Scholar on 7 January 2025).

Other qualitative characteristics may be less amenable to empirical research. For example, several accounting researchers attempted to look at the economic consequences of comparability. De Franco et al. (2011) propose a novel approach to the operationalisation of comparability. The underlying concept in their paper is that two accounting systems are comparable if the same economic event maps into earnings in a similar way. They employ time series of earnings and stock returns for each firm in their sample to regress the former on the latter. The regression coefficients are then used to calculate expected earnings given an economic event, which is proxied by returns. Comparability is defined with respect to the difference between expected earnings between any two firms within the same industry and financial year assuming both firms experience the same return. The smaller the absolute difference, the greater the comparability. Employing this measure De Franco et al. (2011) show that analyst following increases in comparability of one firm's earnings to other firms. This suggests that comparability reduces barriers for analysts. Chen et al. (2018) use the same measure of comparability as De Franco et al. (2011) to further show that greater comparability assists in making more profitable acquisition decisions and Zhang (2018) shows that greater comparability within the same industry assists auditors in reducing erroneous audit opinions.

In concluding this perspective, it is important to note that although the *Conceptual Framework* provides the 'accounting constitution' for standard-setting, whether the IASB has adhered to its own constitution in setting standards is unclear. This is because, as several researchers have argued, standard-setting is a political process rather than purely technical (e.g., André et al. 2009) resulting in, for example, the conceptual departure from neutrality discussed above, and more recently in developing IFRS 16 for leases (Kabir and Rahman, 2018).

References

André, P., Cazavan-Jeny, A., Dick, W., Richard, C., and Walton, P. 2009. Fair value accounting and the banking crisis in 2008: shooting the messenger. *Accounting in Europe*, 6(1), 3–24.

Ball, R., and P. Brown, 1968. An empirical evaluation of accounting income numbers. *Journal of Accounting Research*, 159–178.

Barker, R., and McGeachin, A., 2015. An analysis of concepts and evidence on the question of whether IFRS should be conservative. *Abacus*, 51(2), 169–207.

Barth, M.E., Beaver, W.H., and Landsman, W.R., 2001. The relevance of the value relevance literature for financial accounting standard setting: another view. *Journal of Accounting and Economics*, 31(1), 77–104.

Basu, S., 1997. The conservatism principle and the asymmetric timeliness of earnings. *Journal of Accounting and Economics*, 24(1), 3–37.

Beaver, W., 1968. The information content of annual earnings announcements. *Journal of Accounting Research*, 6, 67–92.

Beaver, W., Lambert, R., and Morse, D., 1980. The information content of security prices. *Journal of Accounting and Economics*, 2(1), 3–28.

Chen, C. W., Collins, D. W., Kravet, T. D., and Mergenthaler, R. D., 2018. Financial statement comparability and the efficiency of acquisition decisions. *Contemporary Accounting Research*, 35(1), 164–202.

De Franco, G., Kothari S.P., and Verdi, R.S., 2011. The benefits of financial statement comparability. *Journal of Accounting Research*, 49(4), 895–931.

Easton, P., and Harris, T., 1991. Earnings as an explanatory variable for returns. *Journal of Accounting Research*, 19–36.

Easton, P., Monahan, S., and Vasvari, F., 2009. Initial evidence on the role of accounting earnings in the bond market. *Journal of Accounting Research*, 47(3), 721–766.

Hayn, C., 1995. The information content of losses. *Journal of Accounting and Economics*, 20(2), 125–153.

Holthausen, R.W., and Watts, R.L., 2001. The relevance of the value relevance literature for financial accounting standard setting. *Journal of Accounting and Economics*, 31(1), 3–75.

Kabir, H., and Rahman, A., 2018. How does the IASB use the conceptual framework in developing IFRSs? An examination of the development of IFRS 16 leases. *Journal of Financial Reporting*, 3(1), 93–116.

Kormendi, R., and Lipe, R., 1987. Earnings innovations, earnings persistence and stock returns. *Journal of Business*, 60(3), 23–345.

Kothari, S.P., 2001. Capital markets research in accounting. *Journal of Accounting and Economics*, 31(1), 105–231.

Kothari, S.P., and Sloan, R., 1992. Information in prices about future earnings: implications for earnings response coefficients. *Journal of Accounting and Economics*, 15(2), 143–171.

Lev, B., and Zarowin, P., 1999. The boundaries of financial reporting and how to extend them. *Journal of Accounting Research*, 37(2), 353–385.

Watts, R., 2003. Conservatism in accounting part I: explanations and implications. *Accounting Horizons*, 17(3), 207–221.

Zhang, J.H., 2018. Accounting comparability, audit effort, and audit outcomes. *Contemporary Accounting Research*, 35(1), 245–276.

Part 2

Elements

2 Financial statement presentation 25
3 Revenue from contracts with customers 55
4 Inventories 83
5 Property, plant and equipment 109
6 Intangible assets 151
7 Impairment of assets 173
8 Fair value measurement 199
9 Leases 223

10 Provisions, contingent liabilities and contingent assets 259
11 Employee benefits 279
12 Owners' equity: share capital and reserves 307
13 Financial instruments 331
14 Share-based payment 379
15 Income taxes 403

2 Financial statement presentation

ACCOUNTING STANDARDS IN FOCUS

IAS 1 *Presentation of Financial Statements*

IAS 8 *Accounting Policies, Changes in Accounting Estimates and Errors*

IAS 10 *Events after the Reporting Period*

LEARNING OBJECTIVES

After studying this chapter, you should be able to:

 1   describe the main components of financial statements

 2   explain the general principles underlying the preparation and presentation of financial statements

 3   apply the requirements for the classification of items reported in the statement of financial position, and apply the requirements for the presentation of information in the statement of financial position and/or in the notes

 4   apply the requirements for the presentation of information in the statement of profit or loss and other comprehensive income and/or in the notes

 5   apply the requirements for the presentation of information in the statement of changes in equity and/or in the notes

 6   discuss other disclosures required by IAS 1 in the notes to the financial statements

 7   apply the requirements of IAS 8 regarding the selection and application of accounting policies, and in respect of accounting for changes in accounting policies, changes in accounting estimates and errors

 8   distinguish between adjusting and non-adjusting events after the reporting period in accordance with IAS 10

 9   be aware of future developments and changes in relation to IAS 1.

INTRODUCTION

IAS 1 *Presentation of Financial Statements* sets out the overall requirements for financial statements, including how they should be structured, the minimum requirements for their content and overriding concepts such as going concern and the accrual basis of accounting.

You are probably already familiar with financial statements. In this chapter we will build on your existing knowledge as we take a closer look at the requirements of IFRS Standards for dealing with some complex and technical issues in the presentation of financial statements. You have probably noticed that current and non-current assets and liabilities are usually separately identified in the statement of financial position. Do they have to be classified this way? How do preparers decide whether an asset should be classified as current or non-current? Why is there so much variation in the way that companies report on profit and comprehensive income?

What should preparers do if they realise there has been an error in the financial statements of previous periods? How should entities account for changes of accounting policies and accounting estimates? If events occur after the end of the reporting period, can they be reflected in the financial statements? IFRS Standards are principles-based accounting standards.

In this chapter we will consider the principles that underlie the preparation of general purpose financial statements in order to provide information that is useful for creditors, investors and other users in making decisions about providing resources to the entity.

2.1 COMPONENTS OF FINANCIAL STATEMENTS

The principles and other considerations relating to the presentation of financial statements are contained in IAS 1 *Presentation of Financial Statements*. A complete set of financial statements is defined in paragraph 10 and comprises:

- a statement of financial position
- a statement of profit or loss and other comprehensive income
- a statement of changes in equity
- a statement of cash flows
- notes, comprising significant accounting policies and other explanatory information
- comparative information, such as financial statements and notes for the preceding period, are also a component of a complete set of financial statements: when an entity retrospectively applies an accounting policy or makes retrospective adjustments to the amount or classification of items in financial statements, the complete set of financial statements includes a statement of financial position as at the beginning of the preceding period *(we will return to this requirement in section 2.7)*.

Each component of the financial statements must be clearly identified in the financial statements and distinguished from other information reported in the same document (IAS 1 paragraphs 49–51). While IAS 1 refers to the statements as a 'statement of financial position', a 'statement of profit or loss and other comprehensive income', a 'statement of changes in equity' and a 'statement of cash flows', reporting entities may use other labels when presenting these financial statements in accordance with IAS 1. For example, some companies label their statement of financial position a 'balance sheet'.

Paragraph 51 requires identification of the following:

- name of the reporting entity and any change in that name since the preceding reporting period
- whether the financial statement covers an individual entity or a group of entities
- the date of the end of the reporting period (e.g. for a statement of financial position) or the reporting period covered by the financial statement (for reports on flows, such as the statement of profit or loss and other comprehensive income)
- the presentation currency, as defined in IAS 21 *The Effects of Changes in Foreign Exchange Rates*
- the level of rounding used in presenting amounts in the financial statements, usually thousands or millions.

Entities often present other information, such as certain financial ratios or a narrative review of operations by management or the directors. These reports are sometimes referred to as 'management discussion and analysis'. In addition, some entities voluntarily prepare sustainability reports or corporate social responsibility reports. This other information is reported outside the financial statements and is not within the scope of pronouncements issued by the International Accounting Standards Board (IASB®).

Issued in December 2010, IFRS Practice Statement 1, *Management Commentary*, provides a broad, non-binding framework for the presentation of management commentary that relates to financial statements that have been prepared in accordance with IFRS Standards.

Management commentary should provide users of financial statements with integrated information providing a context for the related financial statements, including the entity's resources and the claims against the entity and its resources, and the transactions and other events that change them. It also provides management with an opportunity to explain its objectives and its strategies for achieving those objectives.

IAS 1 applies to all general purpose financial statements, except that its requirements relating to the structure and content of financial statements do not apply to condensed interim financial statements prepared in accordance with IAS 34 *Interim Financial Reporting*. This chapter deals with the requirements of IAS 1 for the presentation of the statement of financial position, the statement of profit or loss and other comprehensive income, the statement of changes in equity and notes. *(The statement of cash flows is considered in chapter 16.)* The requirements of IAS 8 *Accounting Policies, Changes in Accounting Estimates and Errors* and IAS 10 *Events after the Reporting Period* are also considered *(see sections 2.7 and 2.8, respectively)*.

In addition to the disclosure requirements covered in this chapter, IFRS Standards prescribe disclosures relating to specific financial statement elements and transactions and events. Specific disclosures relevant to the topics of the various chapters of this book are outlined in those chapters.

2.2 GENERAL PRINCIPLES OF FINANCIAL STATEMENTS

IAS 1 describes eight general principles that need to be applied in the presentation of financial statements, each of which is addressed in the *sections 2.2.1–2.2.8*. These requirements are intended to ensure that the financial statements of an entity are a faithful presentation of its financial position, financial performance and cash flows in accordance with the *Conceptual Framework (see chapter 1)*.

2.2.1 Fair presentation and compliance with IFRS standards

Paragraph 15 of IAS 1 states that 'financial statements shall present fairly the financial position, financial performance and cash flows of an entity'. This means that the *Conceptual Framework*'s definitions and recognition criteria for assets, liabilities, equity, income and expenses should be applied in faithfully representing the effects of transactions, other events and conditions.

Does compliance with IFRS Standards result in financial statements that 'present fairly'? Paragraph 10 makes the explicit assumption that it does, subject to additional disclosures, when necessary. This is reiterated in paragraph 17, which states that compliance with IFRS Standards achieves fair presentation in virtually all circumstances. Fair presentation requires (paragraph 17):
- selecting and applying accounting policies in accordance with IAS 8 *(see section 2.7.1)*;
- presenting information in a way that provides relevant, reliable, comparable and understandable information; and
- providing additional disclosures, where necessary.

However, paragraph 19 of IAS 1 notes that, in extremely rare circumstances, management may conclude that compliance with the requirements of an IFRS Standard would be so misleading that it would conflict with the objective of financial statements specified in the *Conceptual Framework*. The reporting requirements that arise in this situation are considered later *(see section 2.6.1)*.

2.2.2 Going concern

Paragraph 25 of IAS 1 states that financial statements shall be prepared on a going concern basis unless management intends to either liquidate the entity or cease trading, or has no realistic alternative but to do so. The *Conceptual Framework* makes a similar underlying assumption. When management is aware of any material uncertainties that cast doubt upon the entity's ability to continue as a going concern, those uncertainties must be disclosed (IAS 1 paragraph 25). When financial statements are not prepared on a going concern basis, that fact must be disclosed, together with the basis on which the financial statements are prepared and the reason why the entity is not regarded as a going concern.

If, for example, an entity has been placed in receivership and it is anticipated that liquidation will follow, the going concern assumption would be inappropriate. IFRS does not provide any guidance in such circumstances. If the going concern assumption is no longer valid, this could mean that the financial statements are prepared on a 'liquidation' basis, which means that assets and liabilities are measured at the amounts expected to be received or settled on liquidation.

2.2.3 Accrual basis of accounting

Financial statements, except for the statement of cash flows, must be prepared using the accrual basis of accounting. This is discussed further in the *Conceptual Framework (see chapter 1)*.

2.2.4 Materiality and aggregation

Paragraph 7 of IAS 1 states:

> Information is material if omitting, misstating or obscuring it could reasonably be expected to influence decisions that the primary users of general purpose financial statements make on the basis of those financial statements, which provide financial information about a specific reporting entity.

The standard clarifies that materiality depends on the nature or magnitude of information, or both. An entity needs to assess whether the information, either individually or in combination with other information, is material in the context of the financial statements.

Information is obscured if it is presented in a way that would have a similar effect as omitting or misstating the information. Paragraph 7 provides examples of circumstances where material information may be obscured:

- information regarding a material item, transaction or other event is disclosed in the financial statements but the language used is vague or unclear *or* the information is scattered throughout the financial statements;
- Dissimilar items, transactions or events are inappropriately aggregated *or conversely*, if similar items are inappropriately disaggregated.

Note that the definition of material in paragraph 7 refers to information that 'could reasonably be expected to influence' primary users. This wording is intended to ensure that the financial statements do not include excess information that is not capable of influencing the decisions of the primary users.

Financial statements result from processing large volumes of transactions that are then aggregated into classes according to their nature or function. These classes form the line items on the statement of financial position, statement of profit or loss and other comprehensive income, statement of changes in equity, and statement of cash flows. Paragraph 29 requires separate presentation of each material class of similar items in the financial statements.

The minimum line items specified by IAS 1 are discussed later in the chapter (*see sections 2.3, 2.4 and 2.5*). Paragraph 31 confirms that these minimum requirements and requirements for disclosures in the notes prescribed by IAS 1 and other IFRS Standards are subject to materiality.

2.2.5 Offsetting

- If certain assets and liabilities are offset in the statement of financial position, it means they are represented on a net basis. For example, if a receivable of $10,000 were offset against a payable of $25,000, a net liability of $15,000 would be reported. Paragraph 32 of IAS 1 states that an entity shall not offset assets and liabilities, or income and expenses, unless required or permitted by an IFRS Standard. For example, IAS 32 *Financial Instruments: Presentation* permits financial assets and liabilities to be offset if there is a legal right of set-off and the entities intend to settle amounts owed to/by each other on a net basis.
- Offsetting detracts from the understandability of financial statements unless it reflects the substance of transactions or events (paragraph 33). For example, in reporting on the disposal of a non-current asset, it is usually appropriate to offset the carrying amount of the asset against the proceeds to report a net gain or loss. However, measuring assets net of valuation allowances, for example, obsolescence allowances on inventories and doubtful debt allowances on receivables, is not regarded as offsetting. The application of offsetting is an area of considerable judgement and subjectivity.

2.2.6 Frequency of reporting

Financial statements must be prepared at least annually. If an entity's reporting period changes, the length of the reporting period will be greater or less than a year in the period of the change. For example, if an entity with a reporting period ending on 31 March changed its reporting period to end on 31 December the first financial statements it prepares for the period ending 31 December would either cover a 9-month period or a 21-month period. When this occurs, paragraph 36 of IAS 1 requires the entity to disclose why the reporting period is longer or shorter and the fact that the amounts presented in the financial statements are not entirely comparable.

2.2.7 Comparative information

IAS 1 has requirements for *minimum* comparative information (paragraphs 38 to 38B). For all statements in a set of financial statements, a minimum of the preceding year's comparative information is required. In other words, there would be two columns of figures in, for example, a statement of financial position: one for the current year and one for the prior year. The need to present comparative information applies equally to both numerical information (i.e. the amounts) and narrative information. However, in the case of narrative information, comparative narrative information is only needed if it is relevant to understanding the current period financial statements.

IAS 1 also allows an entity to provide voluntary additional comparative information covering, say, two or more preceding years (paragraphs 38C to 38D). This may be done on condition that this extra comparative information is also prepared according to IFRSs. Note that the comparative information need not be provided for all the components of the financial statements. For example, an entity may give extra comparative information for its statement of comprehensive income but not for its statement of financial position.

Finally, IAS 1 has requirements for compulsory additional comparative information (paragraphs 40A to 44). This comes about in the event of changes in accounting policies or corrections of errors. The accounting treatment of changes in accounting policies and correction of errors, including additional disclosure requirements for retrospective adjustments, are dealt with in IAS 8 (and addressed later in this chapter).

2.2.8 Consistency of presentation

Paragraph 45 of IAS 1 requires the presentation and classification of items in the financial statements to be consistent from one period to the next. However, this requirement does not apply where an IFRS Standard requires a change in presentation. A change in presentation is also permitted if there has been a significant change in the nature of the entity's operations and a change in presentation is considered appropriate using the criteria specified in IAS 8 for the selection of accounting policies.

When such a change is made, the comparative information must also be reclassified. For example, if, after a major change in operations, an entity elects to change the way it classifies expenses, the comparative financial information must also be reclassified.

2.3 STATEMENT OF FINANCIAL POSITION

The statement of financial position summarises the elements directly related to the measurement of financial position: an entity's assets, liabilities and equity. It thus provides the basic information for evaluating an entity's capital structure and analysing its liquidity, solvency and financial flexibility. It also provides a basis for computing summary indicators, such as return on total assets and the ratio of liabilities to equity.

2.3.1 Statement of financial position classifications

The statement of financial position presents a structured summary of the assets, liabilities and equity of an entity. To help users of financial statements to evaluate an entity's financial structure and its liquidity, solvency and financial flexibility, assets and liabilities are classified according to their function in the operations of the entity, and their liquidity and financial flexibility characteristics.

Paragraph 60 of IAS 1 requires an entity to classify assets and liabilities as current or non-current in its statement of financial position, unless a presentation based on liquidity is considered to provide more relevant and reliable information. When that exception arises, all assets and liabilities are required to be presented broadly in order of liquidity.

IAS 1 specifies criteria for classification of assets and liabilities as current. When an entity applies the current/non-current classification, assets and liabilities that do not meet the criteria for classification as current are classified as non-current.

Current assets are described in paragraph 66 of IAS 1 as those that:
(a) are expected to be realised, sold or consumed within the entity's normal operating cycle;
(b) are held for trading;
(c) are expected to be realised within 12 months after the reporting period; or
(d) are cash or cash equivalents.
For example, inventory is classified as current because it is expected to be sold within the entity's normal operating cycle. This applies even to inventory which is expected to be sold more than 12 months after the reporting period, such as maturing wine or cheese.

Current liabilities are described in paragraph 69 of IAS 1 as those that:
(a) are expected to be settled within the entity's normal operating cycle;
(b) are held for trading;
(c) are due to be settled within 12 months after the reporting period; or
(d) the entity does not have the right at the end of the reporting period to defer settlement of the liability for at least 12 months after the reporting period.

Paragraph 69 (d) is of particular importance as the classification of liabilities with conditions as current or non-current could significantly affect a company's presentation of its financial position and, hence, the company's financial ratios. For a liability to be classified as non-current, a company must have the right to defer settlement of the liability for at least 12 months after the reporting period and the right must have substance and exist at the end of the reporting period (paragraph 72A).

An entity's right to defer settlement of a liability for at least 12 months after the reporting period may be subject to the entity complying with conditions in that arrangement (the standard refers to conditions as covenants).

If a company is required to comply with covenants on or before the end of the reporting period, these covenants will affect whether such a right exists at the end of the reporting period. This is the case even if compliance with the covenant is assessed only after the reporting period. For example, a covenant based on the company's financial position at the end of the reporting period, but where the assessment for compliance is performed only after the reporting period (paragraph 72B (a)).

A covenant does not affect whether the right to defer settlement exists at the end of the reporting period if a company is required to comply with the covenant only after the end of the reporting period. For example, where a covenant is based on the company's financial position, say, six months after the end of the reporting period (paragraph 72B (b)).

Finally, paragraph 76ZA sets out the disclosure requirements for situations where an entity classifies liabilities arising from loan arrangements as non-current and the entity's right to defer settlement of those liabilities for at least 12 months is subject to the entity complying with one or more covenants within 12 months after the reporting period. In such situations, the standard requires the entity to disclose information in the notes that enables users of financial statements to understand the risk that the liabilities could become repayable within 12 months after the reporting period, including:

(i) information about the covenants (including the nature of the covenants and when the entity is required to comply with them) and the carrying amount of related liabilities; (ii) facts and circumstances, if any, that indicate the entity may have difficulty complying with the covenants.

Paragraph 73 of IAS 1 deals with rollovers. Instead of repaying the loan at maturity, an entity rolls it over into a new loan. When an entity has the right to roll over an obligation under an existing loan facility for at least 12 months after the reporting period, the liability is classified as non-current.

Figure 2.1 shows the classification of assets in the consolidated statement of financial position of GSK at 31 December 2023, while figure 2.2 shows the classification of liabilities at that date. Note that some of GSK's borrowings are classified as current liabilities and some as non-current liabilities.

FIGURE 2.1 Consolidated current and non-current assets of GSK at 31 December 2023

	Notes	2023 £m	2022 £m
Non-current assets			
Property, plant and equipment	17	9,020	8,933
Right of use assets	18	937	687
Goodwill	19	6,811	7,046
Other intangible assets	20	14,768	14,318
Investments in associates and joint ventures	21	55	74
Other investments	23	1,137	1,467
Deferred tax assets	14	6,049	5,658
Other non-current assets	24	1,584	1,194
Total non-current assets		40,361	39,377
Current assets			
Inventories	25	5,498	5,146
Current tax recoverable	14	373	405
Trade and other receivables	26	7,385	7,053
Derivative financial instruments	44	130	190
Current equity investments	22	2,204	4,087
Liquid investments	30	42	67
Cash and cash equivalents	27	2,936	3,723
Assets held for sale	28	76	98
Total current assets		18,644	20,769
Total assets		59,005	60,146

Source: GSK (2023, p. 454).

FIGURE 2.2 Consolidated current and non-current liabilities of GSK at 31 December 2023

	Notes	2023 £m	2022 £m
Current liabilities			
Short-term borrowings	30	(2,813)	(3,952)
Contingent consideration liabilities	33	(1,053)	(1,289)
Trade and other payables	29	(15,844)	(16,263)
Derivative financial instruments	44	(114)	(183)
Current tax payable	14	(500)	(471)
Short-term provisions	32	(744)	(652)
Total current liabilities		(21,068)	(22,810)
Non-current liabilities			
Long-term borrowings	30	(15,205)	(17,035)
Corporation tax payable	14	(75)	(127)
Deferred tax liabilities	14	(311)	(289)
Pensions and other post-employment benefits	31	(2,340)	(2,579)
Other provisions	32	(495)	(532)
Contingent consideration liabilities	33	(5,609)	(5,779)
Other non-current liabilities	34	(1,107)	(899)
Total non-current liabilities		(25,142)	(27,240)
Total liabilities		(46,210)	(50,050)

Source: GSK (2023, p. 454).

The current/non-current classification is ordinarily considered to be more relevant when an entity has a clearly identifiable operating cycle. This is because it distinguishes between those assets and liabilities that are expected to circulate within the entity's operating cycle and those used in the entity's operations over the long term. The typical cycle operates from cash, purchase of inventory (in the case of a manufacturer, production) and then receivables through sales of inventory and finally back to cash through collection of the receivables. The average time of the operating cycle varies with the nature of the operations and may extend beyond 12 months. Long operating cycles are common in real estate development, construction and forestry.

Current assets may include inventories and receivables that are expected to be sold, consumed or realised as part of the normal operating cycle beyond 12 months after the reporting period. Similarly, current liabilities may include payables that are expected to be settled more than 12 months after the reporting period if the operating cycle exceeds 12 months. Because of these possibilities paragraph 61 of IAS 1 requires disclosure that distinguishes between the amount that is expected to be recovered or settled within 12 months after the reporting period and more than 12 months after the reporting period for each line item of assets and liabilities. This requirement is irrespective of whether assets and liabilities are classified on the current/non-current basis or in order of liquidity.

A presentation based broadly on order of liquidity is usually considered to be more relevant than a current/non-current presentation for the assets and liabilities of financial institutions. This is because financial institutions do not supply goods or services within a clearly identifiable operating cycle.

The classification of assets and liabilities as current or non-current is a particularly important issue for calculating summary indicators for assessing an entity's liquidity and solvency. For example, an entity's current ratio (current assets to current liabilities) is often used as an indicator of liquidity and solvency. Lenders may also include terms in debt contracts requiring the borrower to maintain a minimum ratio of current assets to current liabilities. If the entity falls below that ratio then the financier has the right to demand repayment of the borrowing, which may, in turn, affect the assessment of whether the entity is a going concern.

2.3.2 Information required to be presented in the statement of financial position

IAS 1 does not prescribe a standard format that must be adopted for the statement of financial position. Rather, it prescribes a list of items that are considered to be sufficiently different in nature or function to warrant presentation in the statement of financial position as separate line items. These items are listed in paragraph 54:

(a) property, plant and equipment;
(b) investment property;
(c) intangible assets;
(d) financial assets (excluding amounts under (e), (h) and (i));
(da) portfolios of contracts within the scope of IFRS 17, Insurance Contracts that are assets;
(e) investments accounted for using the equity method;
(f) biological assets;
(g) inventories;
(h) trade and other receivables;
(i) cash and cash equivalents;
(j) the total of assets classified as held for sale and assets included in disposal groups classified as held for sale in accordance with IFRS 5 *Non-current Assets Held for Sale and Discontinued Operations*;
(k) trade and other payables;
(l) provisions;
(m) financial liabilities (excluding amounts shown under (k) and (l));
(ma) portfolios of contracts within the scope of IFRS 17, Insurance Contracts that are liabilities;
(n) liabilities and assets for current tax, as defined in IAS 12 *Income Taxes*;
(o) deferred tax liabilities and deferred tax assets, as defined in IAS 12;
(p) liabilities included in disposal groups classified as held for sale in accordance with IFRS 5;
(q) non-controlling interests, presented within equity; and
(r) issued capital and reserves attributable to owners of the parent.

Most entities would not present all of the items shown above because they may not have any amounts to report for particular items, or the item may be considered to be immaterial. As an example, compare the list from paragraph 54 with the line items reported by GSK in its statement of financial position, *as shown in* figures 2.1 and 2.2.

Paragraph 55 of IAS 1 requires additional line items, headings and subtotals to be included in the statement of financial position when they are relevant to an understanding of the entity's financial position. In accordance with paragraph 58 of IAS 1, judgement about the presentation of additional items should be based on an assessment of the nature and liquidity of assets, the function of assets, and the amounts, nature and timing of liabilities.

Figure 2.3 presents the equity section of GSK's consolidated balance sheet (statement of financial position) at 31 December 2023. Does GSK present any additional line items of equity beyond the minimum listed in paragraph 54 of IAS 1?

FIGURE 2.3 Consolidated equity of GSK at 31 December 2023

	Notes	2023 £m	2022 £m
Equity			
Share capital	37	1,348	1,347
Share premium account	37	3,451	3,440
Retained earnings	38	7,239	4,363
Other reserves	38	1,309	1,448
Shareholders' equity		13,347	10,598
Non-controlling interests		(552)	(502)
Total equity		12,795	10,096

Source: GSK (2023, p. 454).

2.3.3 Information required to be presented in the statement of financial position or in the notes

To provide greater transparency and enhance the understandability of the statement of financial position, paragraph 77 of IAS 1 requires the subclassification of line items to be reported either in the statement or in the notes. For example, an entity might provide subclassification of intangible assets as brand names, licences and patents. Paragraph 78 of IAS 1 explains that subclassifications of line items in the statement of financial position are also dependent on the size, nature and function of the amounts involved. Judgement about the need for subclassifications should be made with regard to the same factors previously outlined when judging whether additional line items should be presented in the statement of financial position *(see section 2.2.4)*. Some subclassifications are governed by specific IFRS Standards. For example, IAS 16 requires items of property, plant and equipment to be disaggregated into classes *(see chapter 5)*. Entities typically report land and buildings as a separate class from machinery and equipment.

Figure 2.4 shows the subclassifications of inventories reported in note 25 to the 2023 consolidated financial statements of GSK. The Group subclassifies its inventory as raw materials, work in progress and finished goods. Amounts measured at cost and net realisable value are separately identified.

FIGURE 2.4 Inventories of GSK at 31 December 2023

	2023 £m	2022 £m
Raw materials and consumables	1,594	1,576
Work in progress	2,449	2,286
Finished goods	1,455	1,284
	5,498	5,146

Source: GSK (2023, p. 220).

Paragraph 79(a) of IAS 1 requires additional disclosures about the entity's shares in the statement of financial position, the statement of changes in equity, or in the notes. The most commonly applicable of these disclosures include, for each class of capital:
- the number of authorised shares, issued and fully paid shares, and issued but not fully paid shares
- par value, or that there is no par value
- a reconciliation of the number of outstanding (issued) shares at the beginning and end of the period.

Other required disclosures about equity pertain to: rights, preferences and restrictions on dividends and repayment of capital; shares held by the entity, its subsidiaries or its associates; and shares subject to options and contracts. Paragraph 79(b) requires disclosure of the nature and purpose of each reserve within equity.

Entities that have no share capital must disclose equivalent information to that required by paragraph 79(a) for each category of equity interests. For example, a unit trust would report on the number of units authorised by the trust deed, details about units issued, par value, a reconciliation of the number of units at the beginning and end of the period, rights to and restrictions on distributions, equity held in subsidiaries and units reserved under options and contracts.

2.4 STATEMENT OF PROFIT OR LOSS AND OTHER COMPREHENSIVE INCOME

The statement of profit or loss and other comprehensive income is the prime source of information about an entity's financial performance. It can also be used to assist users to predict an entity's future performance and future cash flows.

2.4.1 Items of comprehensive income

The statement of profit or loss and other comprehensive income reports on all non-owner transactions and valuation adjustments affecting net assets during the period. Profit or loss is the most common measure of an entity's performance. It is used in the determination of other summary indicators, such as earnings per share and the return on equity. Profitability ratios may be used in contracts, such as executive remuneration plans.

While the statement of profit or loss and other comprehensive income incorporates all income and expenses, a distinction is made between profit or loss for the period and other comprehensive income. However, the distinction between items recognised in profit or loss and those recognised in other comprehensive income is dependent upon prescriptions of accounting standards and accounting policy choices, rather than being driven by conceptual differences. The other comprehensive section is sometimes referred to as a 'political wasteland' for standard setters. In other words, if an item of income or expense is too contentious to recognise in profit or loss, it is moved to other comprehensive income to get the standard approved.

For example, IAS 16 requires asset revaluation losses to be recognised in profit or loss, unless reversing a previous revaluation gain. However, IAS 16 also requires asset revaluation gains to be recognised in other comprehensive income, unless reversing a previous revaluation loss (*see chapter 5*). Accordingly, a revaluation loss would be reported in profit or loss while a revaluation gain would be reported below the profit line in other comprehensive income.

2.4.2 Information required to be presented in the statement of profit or loss and other comprehensive income

IAS 1 does not prescribe a standard format for the statement of profit or loss and other comprehensive income. It does, however, require that the statement of profit or loss and other comprehensive income be presented either as:

- a single statement with a profit or loss section and another section for comprehensive income; or
- a statement of profit or loss and a separate statement presenting comprehensive income.

The single statement format is illustrated in figure 2.5. Paragraph 81A requires disclosure of:

- profit or loss
- total other comprehensive income
- total comprehensive income.

Can you find each of these items in figure 2.5?

FIGURE 2.5 Statement of profit or loss and other comprehensive income in one statement with expenses classified according to function

XYZ GROUP Statement of Profit or Loss and Other Comprehensive Income for the year ended		
	2024 $'000	2023 $'000
Revenue	390,000	355,000
Cost of sales	(245,000)	(230,000)
Gross profit	145,000	125,000
Other income	20,667	11,300
Distribution costs	(9,000)	(8,700)
Administrative expenses	(20,000)	(21,000)
Other expenses	(2,100)	(1,200)
Finance costs	(8,000)	(7,500)
Share of profit of associates	35,100	30,100
Profit before tax	161,667	128,000
Income tax expense	(40,417)	(32,000)
Profit for the year from continuing operations	121,250	96,000
Loss for the year from discontinued operations	—	(30,500)
PROFIT FOR THE YEAR	121,250	65,500
Other comprehensive income:		
Items that will not be reclassified to profit or loss:		
Gains on property revaluations	933	3,367
Remeasurements of defined benefit pension plans	(667)	1,333
Share of gain (loss) on property revaluation of associates	400	(700)
Income tax relating to items that will not be reclassified	(166)	(1,000)
	500	3,000

FIGURE 2.5 *(continued)*

Items that may be reclassified subsequently to profit or loss:		
Exchange differences on translating foreign operations	5,334	10,667
Available-for-sale financial assets	(24,000)	26,667
Cash flow hedges	(667)	(4,000)
Income tax relating to items that may be reclassified	4,833	(8,334)
	(14,500)	25,000
Other comprehensive income for the year, net of tax	(14,000)	28,000
TOTAL COMPREHENSIVE INCOME FOR THE YEAR	107,250	93,500
Profit attributable to:		
Owners of the parent	97,000	52,400
Non-controlling interests	24,250	13,100
	121,250	65,500
Total comprehensive income attributable to:		
Owners of the parent	85,800	74,800
Non-controlling interests	21,450	18,700
	107,250	93,500
Earnings per share:	$	$
Basic and diluted	0.46	0.30

Source: Adapted from IAS 1, Implementation Guidance, IG6.

(Check: profit for 2024 = $121,250,000; other comprehensive income for 2024 = a loss of $14,000,000; and total comprehensive income for 2024 = $107,250,000.)

Paragraph 81B of IAS 1 requires the following items to be presented in the statement of profit or loss and other comprehensive income:

(a) profit or loss for the period attributable to:
  (i) non-controlling interests; and
  (ii) owners of the parent; and
(b) comprehensive income for the period attributable to:
  (i) non-controlling interests; and
  (ii) owners of the parent.

These items may arise when preparing consolidated financial statements for groups *(see chapter 23)*. Can you find each of these items in figure 2.5?

(Check: profit attributable to non-controlling interests for 2024 = $24,250,000; and total comprehensive income attributable to non-controlling interests for 2024 = $21,450,000.)

IAS 1 identifies certain items that are considered to be of sufficient importance to the reporting of the performance of an entity to warrant their presentation in the statement of profit or loss and other comprehensive income. The profit or loss section and the other comprehensive income section are considered separately.

Profit or loss section

Profit or loss is the total of income less expenses, excluding the items of other comprehensive income (IAS 1 paragraph 7). Paragraph 82 of IAS 1 identifies the items that must be presented in the profit or loss section:

  (a) revenue;
 (aa) gains and losses from the derecognition of financial assets measured at amortised cost;
 (ab and ac) certain income or expenses from insurance and reinsurance contracts within the scope of IFRS 17;
  (b) finance costs;
 (ba) impairment losses (including reversals) determined in accordance with IFRS 9;
 (bb and bc) certain income or expenses from insurance or reinsurance contracts issued within the scope of IFRS 17;
  (c) share of profit or loss of associates and joint ventures accounted for using the equity method
     (see online chapter C);
 (ca and cb) certain gains or losses associated with the reclassification of financial assets

(d) tax expense;

(e) [deleted]

(ea) a single amount for the total of discontinued operations (see IFRS 5).

Other comprehensive income section

Income and expenses are recognised in other comprehensive income if that treatment is required or permitted by another IFRS Standard. Paragraph 82A of IAS 1 requires the presentation of items of other comprehensive income classified by nature and grouped on the basis of whether, in accordance with another IFRS Standard:

(a) they will not be reclassified subsequently to profit or loss; and

(b) they will be reclassified subsequently to profit or loss when specific conditions are met.

Reclassification of items to profit or loss is discussed further in section 2.4.3. If an entity recognises the share of other comprehensive income of associates and joint ventures accounted for using the equity method, these amounts must be presented as separate items. *(See online chapter C.)* Similar to other items presented in this section, items that may be reclassified subsequent to profit or loss are distinguished from those that will not be reclassified to profit or loss.

Examples of the items of other comprehensive income include:

- asset revaluation gains *(see chapter 5)*
- foreign currency gains and losses on translation of the financial statements of net investments in foreign operations *(see chapter 24)*
- remeasurement of the net defined benefit liability (asset) *(see chapter 11)*.

Items classified as other comprehensive income may be reported net of tax in the statement of profit or loss and other comprehensive income. Alternatively, each item of other comprehensive income may be shown on a before-tax basis, along with aggregate amounts of income tax relating to other comprehensive income, distinguishing between income tax applicable to the group of items that might be subsequently reclassified to profit or loss, and the group of items that will not be subsequently reclassified to profit or loss. Further, an entity must disclose the amount of income tax relating to each item of other comprehensive income, in accordance with paragraph 90 of IAS 1. This may be presented either in the statement of profit or loss and other comprehensive income or in the notes.

Additional line items and labelling

Paragraph 85 of IAS 1 requires additional line items, headings and subtotals to be presented in the statement of profit or loss and other comprehensive income when they are relevant to understanding the entity's financial performance. Disclosure of additional line items may help users to understand the entity's performance and to make predictions about future earnings and cash flow because items may vary in frequency and the extent to which they recur. When an entity presents subtotals, Paragraph 85A requires those subtotals to be comprised of line items made up of amounts recognised and measured in accordance with IFRS; be presented and labelled in a clear and understandable manner; be consistent from period to period; not be displayed with more prominence than the required subtotals and totals; and reconciled with the subtotals or totals required in IFRS.

Paragraph 86 further explains that the nature, function and materiality of the items of income and expense should be considered in making judgements concerning the inclusion of additional line items.

An entity may also amend the descriptions used and the ordering of items when this is necessary to explain the elements of financial performance. However, paragraph 87 of IAS 1 specifically prohibits the presentation of any items of income and expense as 'extraordinary items' either in the statement of profit or loss and other comprehensive income or in the notes.

2.4.3 Information required to be presented in the statement of profit or loss and other comprehensive income or in the notes

To enhance the understandability of the statement of profit or loss and other comprehensive income, paragraph 97 of IAS 1 requires the separate disclosure of the nature and amount of material items of income and expense. Paragraph 98 identifies circumstances that would give rise to the separate disclosure of items of income and expense as including:

(a) write-downs of inventories to net realisable value or of property, plant and equipment to recoverable amount, as well as reversals of such write-downs;

(b) restructurings of the activities of an entity and reversals of any provisions for the costs of restructuring;

(c) disposals of items of property, plant and equipment;

(d) disposals of investments;

(e) discontinued operations;
(f) litigation settlements; and
(g) other reversals of provisions.

Disclosure of material items is important to users of financial statements wishing to predict the likely future profit and cash flows. For example, a gain or loss on disposal of operations is typically non-recurring and the disposal may have implications for the generation of future cash flows.

Paragraph 99 of IAS 1 requires an entity to present an analysis of expenses classified either by their function or nature. Classification by function (e.g. cost of sales, distribution expenses) is illustrated in figure 2.5. Classification by nature (e.g. raw materials and consumables used, employee benefits expense, depreciation expense) is illustrated in figure 2.6. An entity should adopt the presentation that provides more relevant and reliable information. Disclosure of the subclassification of expenses helps users of financial statements to identify relationships between expenses and various measures of the volume of activity, such as the ratio of cost of sales to sales revenue. If the classification of expenses is by function, the entity must disclose additional information about the nature of expenses, including depreciation and amortisation expense and employee benefits expense, because it is useful for predicting future cash flows (IAS 1 paragraph 105).

FIGURE 2.6 Profit or loss section with expenses classified according to nature

ALPHA LTD Statement of Profit or Loss and Other Comprehensive Income (EXTRACT) for the year ended		
	2024 $'000	2023 $'000
Revenue	330,000	300,000
Other income	16,700	13,500
Changes in inventories of finished goods and work in progress	(85,000)	(78,000)
Raw materials and consumables used	(80,500)	(73,000)
Employee benefits expense	(92,000)	(90,000)
Depreciation and amortisation expense	(18,000)	(18,000)
Impairment of property, plant and equipment	(2,200)	—
Other expenses	(5,000)	(4,500)
Finance costs	(9,000)	(10,000)
Profit before tax	55,000	40,000
Income tax expense	(16,500)	(12,000)
Profit for the year from continuing operations	38,500	28,000
Loss for the year from discontinued operations	(3,500)	—
PROFIT FOR THE YEAR	35,000	28,000
Profit attributable to:		
Owners of the parent	30,000	25,000
Non-controlling interests	5,000	3,000
	35,000	28,000
Earning per share:	$	$
Basic and diluted	0.60	0.50

Some income and expense items are required to be initially recognised in other comprehensive income and subsequently reclassified to profit or loss. For example, *as discussed in chapter 8*, gains and losses on a financial instrument held that is a debt instrument measured at fair value through other comprehensive income are recognised in other comprehensive income and accumulated in equity, and when the financial asset is derecognised, the accumulated gain or loss is reclassified from equity to profit or loss. The subsequent recognition in profit or loss of an item previously recognised in other comprehensive income is referred to as a reclassification adjustment in IAS 1. While the standard uses the term 'reclassification', in practice, it is also commonly referred to as recycling of gains and losses through profit or loss.

Not all items recognised in other comprehensive income are subject to potential reclassification. For example, revaluation gains recognised in accordance with IAS 16 *Property, Plant and Equipment* are not reclassified to profit or loss.

Paragraph 92 of IAS 1 requires the disclosure of reclassification adjustments relating to items of other comprehensive income. A reclassification adjustment is included with the related item of other comprehensive income in the period that the adjustment is reclassified to profit or loss. These amounts may have been recognised in other comprehensive income in a previous period. They could also have been recognised in other comprehensive income in the same period. For example, some of the gains and losses accumulated in equity pertaining to a financial instrument may have been recognised in other comprehensive income in both the current reporting period and previous periods.

In accounting for a reclassification adjustment, gains previously recognised in other comprehensive income are deducted from other comprehensive income in the period in which they are recognised in profit or loss. This is to avoid double counting of the gain. Conversely, losses previously recognised in other comprehensive income are added back to other comprehensive income in the period in which they are recognised in profit or loss. Illustrative example 2.1 demonstrates how to present a reclassification adjustment in the statement of profit or loss and other comprehensive income.

ILLUSTRATIVE EXAMPLE 2.1 Reclassification adjustment

During March 2022 Investor Ltd purchased listed bonds issued by another company for $120,000, which was their fair value at that time. The bonds were measured at fair value and Investor Ltd elected to present in other comprehensive income any gains and losses arising from changes in fair value of the bonds, as permitted by IFRS 9 *Financial Instruments*, taking into consideration the characteristics of the bonds and the business model under which the bonds are held *(see chapter 13)*. To illustrate reclassification here, we ignored the required loan loss provision on the bonds.

On 31 December 2022 Investor Ltd revalued the bonds to their fair value of $146,000. The gain was $20,000, net of income tax of $6,000.

On 31 December 2023 Investor Ltd revalued the bonds to their fair value of $170,000. The gain was $18,000, net of income tax of $6,000.

The gains and losses on revaluation of the bonds are recognised in other comprehensive income and accumulated in the 'Investment in debt instruments reserve' in equity.

On 31 December 2023, Investor Ltd sold the bonds for $170,000. At that time the accumulated credit in the 'Investment in debt instruments' in relation to the bonds was $38,000 (net of tax of $12,000). There were no other items of other comprehensive income for the year ended 31 December 2022 or 31 December 2023.

INVESTOR LTD Statements of Profit or Loss and Other Comprehensive Income for the year ended 31 December			
	Notes	2023 $'000	2022 $'000
Revenue	2	980	740
Cost of sales	3	(400)	(300)
Selling and administrative expenses	4	(240)	(200)
Finance costs	4	(100)	(100)
Reclassification of gain on financial instruments	5	50	—
Profit before taxation		290	140
Income tax expense	6	(100)	(40)
PROFIT FOR THE YEAR		190	100
Other comprehensive income:			
Items that may be reclassified subsequently to profit or loss:			
Gain on revaluation of financial instruments	7	18	20
Reclassification adjustment for gains on revaluation of financial instruments	7	(38)	—
Other comprehensive income for the year, net of tax		(20)	20
TOTAL COMPREHENSIVE INCOME FOR THE YEAR		170	120

Profit attributable to:		
Owners of Investor Ltd	180	95
Non-controlling interests	10	5
	190	100
Total comprehensive income attributable to:		
Owners of Investor Ltd	(20)	20
Non-controlling interests	0	0
	(20)	120

Prior to the disposal of the bonds, Investor Ltd had recognised gains in other comprehensive income over two periods, comprising $20,000 in 2022 and $18,000 in 2023. On the disposal and derecognition of the bonds the accumulated gain of $38,000 must be reclassified to profit. The gain is presented as $50,000, being the amount before tax. The related tax effect of $12,000 is included in the income tax expense line item. To avoid double counting, the gain is deducted from other comprehensive income and added to profit. Thus, the reclassification adjustment of $38,000 has no net effect on total comprehensive income in 2023 because it increases profit by $38,000 and decreases other comprehensive income by the same amount.

2.5 STATEMENT OF CHANGES IN EQUITY

The statement of changes in equity provides a reconciliation of the opening and closing amounts of each component of equity for the period. The purpose of the statement of changes in equity is to report transactions with owners, such as the issue of new shares and the payment of dividends, and the effects of any retrospective adjustments to beginning-of-period components of equity (see section 2.7).

2.5.1 Presentation of the statement of changes in equity

The statement of changes in equity presents information about movements in the components of equity, which include share capital, retained earnings and amounts accumulated in equity for each class of items recognised in other comprehensive income, such as the asset revaluation surplus and the foreign currency translation reserve. The statement is often presented as a table with the components of equity listed in separate columns. The opening balance, current period movements and closing balance are shown in different rows. As for the other financial statements, comparative amounts are required to be reported in the statement of changes in equity. The comparative figures are often presented in a separate table from the current period figures.

2.5.2 Information required to be reported in the statement of changes in equity

Paragraph 106 of IAS 1 requires the following information to be presented in the statement of changes in equity:
- total comprehensive income for the period, distinguishing between amounts attributable to owners of the parent entity and to non-controlling interests;
- the effects of retrospective application or retrospective restatement recognised in accordance with IAS 8 for each component of equity; and
- a reconciliation between the carrying amount at the beginning and the end of the period for each item of equity.

The reconciliation of the carrying amount must include, as a minimum, the changes resulting from profit or loss, other comprehensive income; and transactions with owners in their capacity as owners, showing separately contributions by and distributions to owners and changes in ownership interests in subsidiaries.

Profit (loss) for the period increases (decreases) retained earnings. Other items of comprehensive income affect other components of equity. For example, a gain on revaluing assets, net of its tax effect, increases the asset revaluation surplus.

Figure 2.7 shows the consolidated statement of changes in equity of GSK for the year ended 31 December 2023 (comparative figures for the year ended 31 December 2021 have been excluded). The complete statement also presents comparative information, following the same tabular format.

FIGURE 2.7 Consolidated statement of changes in equity of GSK for the year ended 31 December 2023

	Share capital £m	Share premium £m	Retained earnings £m	Other reserves* £m	Total £m	Non-controlling interests £m	Total equity £m
					Shareholders' equity		
At 31 December 2021	1,347	3,301	7,944	2,463	15,055	6,287	21,342
Profit for the year	—	—	14,956	—	14,956	665	15,621
Other comprehensive income/(expense) for the year	—	—	(89)	(714)	(803)	(28)	(831)
Total comprehensive income/(expense) for the year	—	—	14,867	(714)	14,153	637	14,790
Distributions to non-controlling interests	—	—	—	—	—	(1,409)	(1,409)
Non-cash distribution to non-controlling interests	—	—	—	—	—	(2,960)	(2,960)
Contributions from non-controlling interests	—	—	—	—	—	8	8
Changes to non-controlling interests	—	—	—	—	—	(20)	(20)
Deconsolidation of former subsidiaries	—	—	—	—	—	(3,045)	(3,045)
Dividends to shareholders	—	—	(3,467)	—	(3,467)	—	(3,467)
Non-cash dividend to shareholders	—	—	(15,526)	—	(15,526)	—	(15,526)
Realised after tax losses on disposal or liquidation of equity investments	—	—	14	(14)	—	—	—
Share of associates and joint ventures realised profits on disposal of equity investments	—	—	7	(7)	—	—	—
Shares issued	—	25	—	—	25	—	25
Write-down of shares held by ESOP Trusts	—	—	(911)	911	—	—	—
Shares acquired by ESOP Trusts	—	114	1,086	(1,200)	—	—	—
Share-based incentive plans	—	—	357	—	357	—	357
Tax on share-based incentive plans	—	—	(8)	—	(8)	—	(8)
Hedging gain after taxation transferred to non-financial asset	—	—	—	9	9	—	9
At 31 December 2022	1,347	3,440	4,363	1,448	10,598	(502)	10,096
Profit for the year	—	—	4,928	—	4,928	380	5,308
Other comprehensive income/(expense) for the year	—	—	(45)	(247)	(292)	(25)	(317)
Total comprehensive income/(expense) for the year	—	—	4,883	(247)	4,636	355	4,991
Distributions to non-controlling interests	—	—	—	—	—	(412)	(412)
Contributions from non-controlling interests	—	—	—	—	—	7	7
Dividends to shareholders	—	—	(2,247)	—	(2,247)	—	(2,247)
Realised after tax losses on disposal or liquidation of equity investments	—	—	(26)	26	—	—	—
Share of associates and joint ventures realised profits on disposal of equity investments	—	—	(7)	7	—	—	—
Shares issued	1	9	—	—	10	—	10
Write-down of shares held by ESOP Trusts	—	—	(324)	324	—	—	—
Shares acquired by ESOP Trusts	—	2	283	(285)	—	—	—
Share-based incentive plans	—	—	307	—	307	—	307
Hedging gain/(loss) after taxation transferred to non-financial asset	—	—	—	36	36	—	36
Tax on share-based incentive plans	—	—	7	—	7	—	7
At 31 December 2023	1,348	3,451	7,239	1,309	13,347	(552)	12,795

Source: GSK (2023, p. 182).

2.5.3 Information to be presented in the statement of changes in equity or in the notes

An analysis of other comprehensive income by item must be included in the statement of changes in equity or in the notes. Similarly, the amount of dividends recognised as distributions to owners during the period and the amount of dividends per share for the period must be disclosed either in the statement of changes in equity or in the notes.

2.6 NOTES

Notes are an integral part of the financial statements. Their purpose is to enhance the understandability of the statement of financial position, statement of profit or loss and other comprehensive income, statement of cash flows and statement of changes in equity. An entity should present the notes in a systematic order and cross-reference each item in the financial statements to any related information in the notes, in accordance with paragraph 113 of IAS 1.

The following information must be disclosed in the notes in accordance with paragraph 112 of IAS 1:
- information about the basis of preparation of the financial statements and the specific accounting policies used, in accordance with paragraphs 117–24
- information required by IFRS Standards unless presented elsewhere in the financial statements
- other information that is relevant to understanding the financial statements, unless presented elsewhere.

We will first consider the statements about compliance with IFRS Standards followed by the summary of significant accounting policies used and sources of estimation uncertainty, information about capital, and other disclosures.

2.6.1 Compliance with IFRS standards

An explicit and unreserved statement of compliance with IFRS Standards should be made if, and only if, the financial statements comply with the requirements of IFRS Standards (IAS 1 paragraph 16). If applicable, the statement is often included in the note about the basis of preparation of the financial statements.

In extremely rare circumstances, management may conclude that compliance with a requirement in an IFRS Standard would be so misleading that it would conflict with the objective of financial statements. Does this mean that management should depart from compliance with IFRS Standards in order to present financial statements that serve the decision-making needs of present and potential investors, lenders and other creditors? The answer to this question depends on domestic reporting requirements. In some countries the law may require compliance with IFRS Standards. In some jurisdictions departure from the requirements of an IFRS Standard may be permitted in the extremely rare circumstances referred to in IAS 1, where management believe it would be misleading.

When assessing whether compliance would be misleading, management must consider why the objectives of financial statements would not be achieved in the current circumstances and how the entity's circumstances differ from other entities that do comply with the requirement.

What should managers do if they conclude that compliance with IFRS Standards would be so misleading as to defeat the objectives of financial reporting? The answer to this depends on whether departure from IFRS Standards is permitted in the domestic reporting regime, as shown in figure 2.8.

FIGURE 2.8 Reporting requirements when management concludes compliance with an IFRS Standard would be misleading

Disclosures required by IAS 1 when management concludes compliance with an IFRS Standard would be misleading		
Domestic reporting regime	Domestic reporting regime permits departure from an IFRS Standard	Domestic reporting regime prohibits departure from an IFRS Standards
Action	Depart from the IFRS Standard	Do not depart from the IFRS Standards
Disclosure	• that management has concluded that the financial statements present fairly the entity's financial position, financial performance and cash flows	• the title of the relevant IFRS Standard • the nature of the requirement • the reason for management's conclusion that compliance is misleading and

FIGURE 2.8 *(continued)*

• that the financial statements are in compliance with IFRS Standards except for the specific departure to achieve a fair presentation
• the title of the IFRS Standard from which the entity has departed
  – the treatment required by the IFRS Standard
  – the nature of the departure
  – why the treatment would be so misleading in the circumstances that it would be in conflict with the objectives of financial statements specified in the *Conceptual Framework*
  – the financial effect of the departure on each item in the financial statements for each period presented.
	• the adjustments necessary to each item for each period presented that are required to achieve a fair presentation.

Relevant paragraphs	IAS 1, paragraphs 19–22	IAS 1, paragraphs 23–24

2.6.2 Disclosure of accounting policy information

Paragraph 117 of IAS 1 requires an entity to disclose *material* accounting policy information. Previous versions of the standard used the word 'significant', but in the absence of a definition of the term 'significant' in IFRS, the IASB decided to replace it with 'material' in the context of disclosing accounting policy information.

Material accounting policy information is defined as follows in paragraph 117 of IAS 1:

'Accounting policy information is material if, when considered together with other information included in an entity's financial statements, it can reasonably be expected to influence decisions that the primary users of general purpose financial statements make on the basis of those financial statements.'

Application of the materiality definition

Paragraph 117A of IAS 1 clarifies that accounting policy information that is immaterial need not be disclosed. In assessing the materiality of accounting policy information, entities need to consider both the *size* of the transactions, other events or conditions and the *nature* of them. In other words, accounting policy information may be material because of the nature of the related transaction, even if the amounts are immaterial.

Further, although a transaction to which the accounting policy information relates may be material, it does not necessarily mean that all accounting policy information in respect of that transaction, other event or circumstances, is material to the entity's financial statements.

According to paragraph 117B of IAS 1, accounting policy information is expected to be material if it helps users to understand other material information in the financial statements. This will be the case, if, for example:

– The entity changed its accounting policy, causing a material change to the information in the financial statements
– The accounting policy relates to an IFRS that permits a choice such as IAS 38 where certain intangible assets can be measured either under the cost model or revaluation model
– An entity develops an accounting policy in accordance with IAS 8 Accounting Policies, Changes in Accounting Estimates and Errors in the absence of an IFRS that specifically applies
– Application of accounting policy requires significant judgements or assumptions
– The method of accounting for a material transaction, events or condition is so complex that users need the accounting policy information to understand it, such as when more than one IFRS is applied.

Paragraph 117D of IAS 1 acknowledges that disclosure of immaterial accounting policy information is permitted, although it is not required. However, if an entity decides to disclose immaterial accounting policy information, it needs to ensure that such information does not obscure material information, for example, by giving the immaterial accounting policy information more importance.

The application of the materiality judgements of IAS 1 can be summarised as shown in figure 2.9.

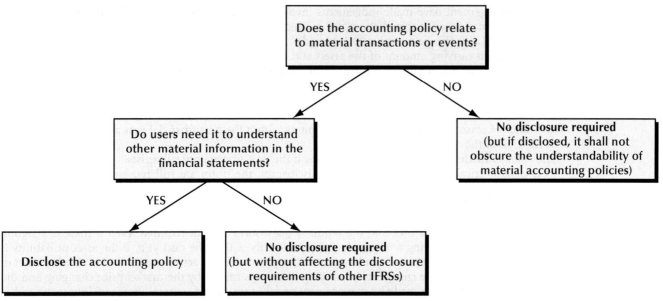

FIGURE 2.9 Applying the IAS 1 materiality judgements
Source: Deloitte. dReport, How to disclose accounting policies from 1 January 2023.

Disclosure of standardised information

Paragraph 117C of IAS 1 highlights that accounting policy information that focuses on how an entity has applied IFRS requirements to its own circumstances provides entity-specific information that is more useful to users of the financial statements than standardised information, or information that only duplicates or summarises the IFRS requirements. This idea is discussed in more detail in IFRS Practice Statement 2: Making Materiality Judgements, which states that entity-specific accounting policy information is mostly useful when that information relates to a scenario where an entity has exercised judgement; for example, when an entity applies an IFRS differently from similar entities in the same industry.

According to IFRS Practice Statement 2, material accounting policy information could sometimes include information that is standardised, or that duplicates or summarises the IFRS requirements. Such information may be material if, for example:

– Users of the entity's financial statements need that information to understand other material information provided in the financial statements;
– The accounting required by IFRS is complex, and users need to understand the required accounting, for example, when more than one IFRS is applied.

2.6.3 Judgements made in applying accounting policies

The application of IFRS Standards often requires the exercise of judgement. For example, an entity may need to apply judgement to determine whether an item of plant has met the requirements to be accounted for in terms of IFRS 5 *Non-current assets held for sale* rather than being accounted for in terms of IAS 16, *Property, plant and equipment.*

Paragraph 122 of IAS 1 requires disclosure, along with material accounting policy information, of the judgements that have the most significant effect on the amounts recognised in financial statements. Note that this excludes judgements involving estimates, referred to as estimation uncertainty and discussed in paragraph 2.6.4.

2.6.4 Sources of information uncertainty

The preparation of financial statements involves many estimates that require professional judgement, such as estimating depreciation rates and estimating the amount of a provision.

Disclosure is required about the assumptions and estimates where there is a significant risk that a material adjustment to the carrying amount of an asset or liability may need to be made within the next financial year (IAS 1, paragraph 125).

Where management have made judgements involving 'assumptions about the future and other major sources of estimation uncertainty' the notes are required to include disclosure of the following (IAS 1, paragraph 125 (a) & (b); paragraph 129 (a) to (d):

- the nature and carrying amount of the assets and liabilities affected;
- the nature of the assumption or estimation uncertainty;
- the sensitivity of the carrying amounts to the methods, assumptions and estimates used in their calculation;
- the reasons for the sensitivity;
- the range of reasonably possible carrying amounts within the next financial year and the expected resolution of the uncertainty;
- the changes made (if any) to past assumptions if the past uncertainty still exists.

If it is impracticable to provide the above disclosures, the notes are still required to disclose (IAS 1, paragraph 131):

- the source/s of uncertainty;
- the nature and carrying amount of the assets and liabilities affected.

IAS 1, paragraph 128 clarifies that the required disclosures are not required, even if there is a significant risk of an item's carrying amount changing materially within the next year, if the asset or liability is measured at a fair value that has been based on a quoted price in an active market for an identical asset or liability. This is because the change in its carrying amount is caused by the market price changing and did not arise from assumptions made by management or other sources of estimation uncertainty at the end of the reporting period.

2.6.5 Information about capital

Paragraph 134 of IAS 1 requires disclosure of information that enables users of financial statements to evaluate the entity's management of capital. This requirement encompasses qualitative information about objectives, policies and processes, including a description of what is managed as capital, the nature of any externally imposed capital requirements, whether the entity has complied with externally imposed requirements, and, if the entity has not complied with external requirements, the implications of non-compliance.

Quantitative disclosures are also required, including summary data of what is managed as capital. This may differ from reported equity because an entity may exclude some components of equity, such as foreign currency translation reserves, from what is managed as capital, while including some items that are classified as liabilities, such as subordinated debt.

The standard adopts a management perspective by focusing on how capital is viewed by management, rather than prescribing specific definitions of capital for the purposes of the disclosures. The entity is required to base its capital disclosures on the information provided internally to key management personnel (paragraph 135).

2.6.6 Other disclosures

It is not uncommon for dividends to be proposed or declared (i.e. approved by the appropriate authorising body, such as the board of directors) after the reporting date but before the financial statements are issued. Unless the dividends are declared before the end of the reporting period they cannot be recognised in the financial statements. IAS 10 *Events after the Reporting Period* requires disclosure in the notes of any dividends that have been proposed or declared before the release of the financial statements but not recognised in the financial statements. Paragraph 137(a) of IAS 1 requires the disclosure to include the amount of the dividends that have been proposed or declared but not recognised, and the related amount per share. The amount of any cumulative preference dividends that have not been recognised as liabilities must also be disclosed (paragraph 137(b)).

Paragraph 138 of IAS 1 requires disclosure of certain non-financial information including:

- the legal form of the entity, such as whether it is a company or a trust
- the country of incorporation
- the address of the registered office or the principal place of business (if different from the registered office)
- a description of the nature of the entity's operations and its principal activities
- the name of the parent and the ultimate parent of the group
- if a limited-life company, the length of its life.

2.7 ACCOUNTING POLICIES, CHANGES IN ACCOUNTING ESTIMATES AND ERRORS

We will now consider how to:
- select and account for changes in accounting policies
- account for changes in accounting estimates
- correct prior period errors.

The requirements are specified in IAS 8 *Accounting Policies, Changes in Accounting Estimates and Errors*.

The term *accounting policy* refers to principles or conventions applied in preparing the financial statements, such as historical cost or revaluation method for property, plant and equipment. An *accounting estimate* is a judgement applied in determining the carrying amount of an item in the financial statements such as an estimate of the useful life of a depreciable asset. The use of reasonable estimates is an essential part of the process of preparing financial statements because many items reported in the financial statements — such as provisions for warranties — cannot be calculated with precision. For example, the measurement of a provision for warranty claims may be based on historical data, such as the volume of sales and the length of outstanding warranty periods. The *calculation* of the amount of the warranty provision is an accounting *estimate* that applies this accounting policy.

A *prior period error* is an omission or misstatement in the financial statements of a prior period resulting from the misuse or failure to use reliable information. Errors may arise from mathematical miscalculations, mistakes in applying accounting policies, oversights or misinterpretations of facts, and fraud (IAS 8 paragraph 5). For example, assume Company C owns a building from which it derives rental income. In testing for impairment, Company C measures the value in use of the building by discounting future rental income. The amount of rental income should be reduced by any waivers of rent allowed to tenants, such as rent-free periods offered to new tenants. Assume that in measuring the value in use in a prior period, the cash inflows forgone from rent-free periods were added to annual rentals, instead of being deducted, and that this resulted in an overstated carrying amount of the building. The misstatement would be classified as an error in the prior-period financial statements because it results from a mistake in the application of information that was available at the time. In contrast, if, in hindsight, the building was found to have been overstated because the estimated rental growth rates used in a prior period were too high, the subsequent restatement of the carrying amount of the building would be treated as a change of accounting estimate.

2.7.1 Selecting and changing accounting policies

Accounting standards prescribe accounting policies for certain topics, transactions or events. Paragraph 10 of IAS 8 specifies that where there is no IFRS Standard dealing with a particular transaction, preparers should use judgement in developing and applying accounting policies so that the resulting information is relevant and reliable. The concept of reliability encompasses:
- faithful representation
- reflecting economic substance over legal form
- neutrality, freedom from bias
- prudence and
- completeness in all material respects.

IAS 8 provides what is commonly termed the 'hierarchy' of relevant sources of information to be used by management in selecting and applying accounting policies. Paragraph 11 states that management must firstly consider the requirements and guidance of any IFRS Standard dealing with similar or related issues. Secondly, management must consider the *Framework*'s definitions, recognition criteria and measurement concepts of assets, liabilities, income and expenses. Provided they do not conflict with the sources in paragraph 11, management may also consider the most recent pronouncements of other standard setters that use a similar conceptual framework, other accounting literature and accepted industry practices.

Paragraph 13 of IAS 8 requires an entity to apply accounting policies consistently for similar transactions, events or conditions unless otherwise required by an accounting standard. Accordingly, IAS 8 paragraph 14 specifies only two circumstances in which an entity is permitted to change an accounting policy. These are:
- if the change is *required* by an IFRS Standard; or
- if the change, *made voluntarily*, results in the financial statements providing reliable and more relevant information about the effects of transactions, other events or conditions on the entity's financial position, financial performance or cash flows.

However, the initial application of a policy to revalue assets in accordance with IAS 16 *Property, Plant and Equipment* or IAS 38 *Intangible Assets* must be accounted for as a revaluation in accordance with those standards and not as a change in accounting policy under IAS 8. Note that this applies to the *initial* application of a revaluation policy only. IAS 8 would apply if an entity initially chooses the revaluation method under IAS 16 or IAS 38, and then changes to the cost method at a later date.

Where an entity changes an accounting policy because it is required to do so, it must account for that change in accordance with the transitional provisions of the accounting standard requiring the change. If the accounting standard does not specify how to account for the change, then the change must be applied *retrospectively*. Retrospective application is also required for all voluntary changes in accounting policy (IAS 8 paragraph 19). Retrospective application means applying a new accounting policy to transactions, other events and conditions as if that policy had always been applied (paragraph 5). When an entity retrospectively applies a change of accounting policy, the *opening* balance of each affected component of equity for the earliest prior period presented must be adjusted, and the other comparative amounts must be disclosed for each prior period presented as if the new accounting policy had always been applied (IAS 8 paragraph 22). Further, when an entity applies an accounting policy retrospectively (or other retrospective restatement or reclassification), paragraph 40A of IAS 1 requires presentation of a statement of financial position as at the beginning of the preceding period if it has a material effect on the information presented. As clarified in paragraph 40B, the entity would be required to present three statements of financial position as at:

- the end of the current period;
- the end of the preceding period; and
- the beginning of the preceding period.

IAS 8 requires extensive disclosures when an entity changes its accounting policy. These include:

- the nature of the change in accounting policy
- for the current period and each prior period presented, to the extent practicable, the amount of the adjustment for:
  - each financial statement line item affected and
  - basic and diluted earnings per share, if IAS 33 *Earnings per Share* applies to the entity
- the amount of the adjustment relating to periods before those presented, to the extent practicable
- if retrospective application is impracticable, the reason for that condition and a description of how and from when the change in accounting policy has been applied.

Additional disclosures are required for changes required by an IFRS Standard and for voluntary changes, as follows:

- Change of accounting policy required by an IFRS Standard
  - the title of the IFRS Standard
  - that the change in accounting policy is made in accordance with its transitional provisions, if applicable
  - a description of the transitional provisions, if applicable
  - the transitional provisions that might have an effect on future periods, if applicable.
- Voluntary change of accounting policy
  - the reasons why the new accounting policy provides reliable and more relevant information.

As noted in section 2.5.2, paragraph 106(b) of IAS 1 requires disclosure of the effects of retrospective adjustments for each component of equity in the statement of changes in equity.

Illustrative example 2.2 shows how to apply retrospectively a change in accounting policy.

ILLUSTRATIVE EXAMPLE 2.2 Applying a voluntary change in accounting policy

Spade Ltd is a large manufacturer. The company has a 28 February year-end. With effect from 1 March 2024, the company adopted a new accounting policy in relation to revenue recognition.

If the new policy had been adopted in previous years, the effect on revenue and accounts receivable for the years ended 28 February 2023 and 28 February 2024 are as follows:

	Year ended 28/02/2023 £	Year ended 28/02/2024 £
Increase in revenue	350,000	600,000
Increase in accounts receivable	350,000	950,000

There is no effect in any earlier year.

An extract from the company's draft statement of profit or loss for the year to 28 February 2025 (with comparatives for 2024 as originally stated) is as follows:

SPADE LIMITED DRAFT STATEMENT OF PROFIT OR LOSS FOR THE YEAR ENDED 28 FEBRUARY 2025		
	2025 £000	2024 £000
Revenue	5,200	4,800
Operating expense	(4,100)	(3,900)
Profit before taxation	1,100	900
Taxation	(220)	(180)
Profit after taxation	880	720

The draft financial statements for the year to 28 February 2025 show only the effect of the new policy on the 2025 figures. The 2024 figures are as originally reported.

The company's taxation expense is equal to 20% of its profit before taxation. The retained earnings at 28 February 2023 and 28 February 2024 were originally reported at £885,000 and £1,605,000 respectively.

No dividends were paid during the two years to 28 February 2025.

The effect of the change in accounting policy is accounted for retrospectively. The comparative figures on the statement of profit or loss for the year ended 28 February 2024 need to be restated to take into account the effect of the increased revenue. The taxation is adjusted accordingly.

SPADE LIMITED STATEMENT OF PROFIT OR LOSS FOR THE YEAR ENDED 28 FEBRUARY 2025		
	2025	2024 (Restated)
	£000	£000
Revenue	5,200	5,400
Operating expenses	(4,100)	(3,900)
Profit before taxation	1,100	1,500
Taxation	(220)	(300)
Profit after taxation	880	1,200

The cumulative effect of the change in policy on the opening balance in retained earnings for the earliest year presented is disclosed as well as the effect on the opening balance in retained earnings for the current year.

SPADE LIMITED EXTRACT FROM STATEMENT OF CHANGES IN EQUITY FOR THE YEAR ENDED 28 FEBRUARY 2025	
	Retained earnings £000
Balance at 28/02/23	1,165
As previously reported	885
Change in accounting policy (350 × 80%)	280
Profit after tax for year ended 28/02/24 (as restated)	1,200
Balance at 28/02/24	2,365
As previously reported	1,605
Change in accounting policy (950 × 80%)	760
Profit after tax for year ended 28/02/25	880
Balance at 28/02/25	3,245

Paragraphs 23–25 of IAS 8 deal with circumstances where retrospective application of a change in accounting policy is impracticable and thus cannot be applied. In the context of IAS 8 'impracticable' means 'the entity cannot apply it after making every reasonable effort to do so' (paragraph 5). For example, the retrospective application of an accounting policy would be impracticable if it required assumptions about what management's intent might have been at a prior point in time. Hindsight is not used when applying a new accounting policy retrospectively. For example, an asset measured on the fair value basis retrospectively should be measured at the fair value as at the date of the retrospective adjustment and should not take into account subsequent events. When it is impracticable for an entity to apply a new accounting policy retrospectively because it cannot determine the cumulative effect of applying the policy to all prior periods, the entity should apply the new policy prospectively from the start of the earliest period practicable. This may be the current period.

2.7.2 Changes in accounting estimates

Accounting estimates are monetary amounts in financial statements that are subject to measurement uncertainty (IAS 8, paragraph 5). Entities develop accounting estimates if accounting policies require items in financial statements to be measured in a way that involves measurement uncertainty. Remember that making estimates is an integral part of preparing financial statements and, if they are based on reasonable judgements and assumptions, they will not undermine the reliability of the financial statements.

An estimate may need to be revised if changes occur in the circumstances on which it was based, or as a result of new information or more experience. Paragraph 36 of IAS 8 requires changes in accounting estimates to be accounted for *prospectively*. Prospective application is defined in paragraph 5. When a new accounting estimate is applied prospectively the effect of the change is recognised in the current period and any future periods affected by the change but no adjustment is made to prior periods.

Paragraph 34A of IAS 8 clarifies that a change in accounting estimate that results from new information or new developments is not the correction of an error.

Paragraph 37 of IAS 8 states that if the change in estimate affects assets, liabilities or equity, then the carrying amounts of those items shall be adjusted in the period of the change. Paragraphs 39 and 40 prescribe disclosures for changes in accounting estimates that have an effect in the current or future periods. The entity must disclose the nature and amount of the change. However, if it is impracticable to estimate the effect on future periods the entity must disclose that fact.

Illustrative example 2.3 demonstrates accounting for a change in an accounting estimate, including the required disclosures.

ILLUSTRATIVE EXAMPLE 2.3 Accounting for a change in an accounting estimate

Company Z installed factory plant in January 2022. The company had been depreciating its factory plant on a straight-line basis, with an estimated useful life of 15 years and nil residual value. Four years later, in January 2026, the directors of Company Z determined that, due to technological developments, the factory plant's useful life was 10 years in total – that is, it had a remaining useful life of 6 years. Company Z's reporting period ends on 31 December. As at 1 January 2026, the balance of factory plant was as follows:

Cost	$150,000
Accumulated depreciation	(40,000)
Carrying amount	110,000

For the year ended 31 December 2026, Company Z's depreciation expense will be $18,333. This is calculated as $110,000/6 (being the carrying amount of the asset at 1 July 2026 divided by the remaining useful life).

Extract from Company Z's financial statements for the year ended 31 December 2026:

Company Z has historically depreciated its factory plant over 15 years. The company's directors determined that, effective from 1 January 2026, the factory plant should be depreciated over 10 years. The effect of the change in the estimated useful life of the factory plant in the current period is to increase the depreciation expense from $10,000 to $18,333 and to increase accumulated depreciation by $8,333. In future periods, annual depreciation expense for the factory plant will be $18,333 over the remaining useful life of the plant.

2.7.3 Correction of prior period errors

IAS 8 refers to three categories of errors:
- Current period errors
- Prior period errors that are immaterial
- Prior period errors that are material.

Current period errors are errors that are *made* in the current year, are *discovered* in the current year and thus *corrected* in the current year. No disclosure is made of the error or its correction because it does not affect users' decision making.

A 'prior period error' is an omission from, or misstatement in, the financial statements of one or more prior periods. Prior period errors are errors that occurred *before* the current year but which are only discovered in the current year. They can include the effects of mathematical mistakes, mistakes in applying accounting policies, oversights or misinterpretations of facts and fraud.

Immaterial prior period errors are corrected, but are not subject to the disclosure requirements of IAS 8.

If a *material prior period error* is discovered in a subsequent period, paragraph 42 of IAS 8 requires retrospective correction by restating comparative amounts for each prior period presented in which the error occurred. Where the error occurred before the first prior period presented, the entity must restate opening balances of assets, liabilities and equity of the earliest period presented.

Retrospective restatement is required unless it is impracticable to do so (IAS 8 paragraphs 43–45). Similar disclosures are required for correction of errors as for changes in accounting policy (paragraph 49). However, as the correction of errors requires the retrospective restatement of items in the financial statements, a statement of financial position as at the beginning of the earliest comparative period must also be presented if that statement of financial position is affected by the error (IAS 1 paragraph 40A).

2.8 EVENTS AFTER THE REPORTING PERIOD

The objective of IAS 10 is to prescribe when an entity should adjust its financial statements for events after the reporting period, and what disclosures the entity should make about events after the reporting period. IAS 10 paragraph 3 defines an *event after the reporting period* as occurring after the end of the reporting period but before the financial statements are authorised for issue. Events after the reporting period are classified as being:

- adjusting events, which provide further evidence of conditions that existed at the end of the reporting period, and can include an event that indicates that the going concern assumption may be inappropriate; and
- non-adjusting events, which indicate conditions that arose after the end of the reporting period, such as the unintended destruction of property that existed at the end of the reporting period.

Usually the date at which financial statements are authorised for issue is when the directors or other governing body formally approve the financial statements for issue to shareholders and/or other users. Although subsequent ratification by the shareholders at an annual meeting may be required, that is not usually the date of authorisation for issue.

2.8.1 Adjusting events after the reporting period

Paragraph 8 of IAS 10 requires an entity to adjust the amounts recognised in its financial statements to reflect adjusting events after the reporting period. Examples of adjusting events after the reporting period include the following:

- the receipt of information after the reporting period that indicates an asset was impaired as at the end of the reporting period – this may occur, for example, if a trade receivable recorded at the end of the reporting period is shown to be irrecoverable because of the insolvency of the customer that occurs after the reporting period
- the sale of inventories after the reporting period that provides evidence of their net realisable value at the end of the reporting period
- the judge's decision on a court case, after the reporting period, confirming that the entity had a present obligation at the end of the reporting period.

Illustrative example 2.4 demonstrates accounting for an adjusting event after the reporting period.

Blue Ltd's financial statements for the year ended 31 December 2023 included a receivable of $35,000 in respect of a major customer, Red Ltd On 31 January 2024 the liquidator of Red Ltd advised that the company was insolvent and would be unable to repay the full amount owed. The liquidator advised Blue Ltd in writing that Red Ltd's creditors would receive 10 cents in the dollar (i.e. 10 cents for every dollar owed). The liquidator estimated that the amount would be paid in November 2024. Blue Ltd's financial statements were authorised for issue by the directors on 25 February 2024.

In accordance with IAS 10, the insolvency of Red Ltd is an adjusting event after the reporting period because it provides further evidence of the collectability of the receivable at 31 December 2023. Blue Ltd will adjust the receivable from $35,000 to $3,500 as follows:

Impairment loss	Dr	31,500	
Receivables	Cr		31,500
(Impairment of receivable)			

2.8.2 Non-adjusting events after the reporting period

Paragraph 10 of IAS 10 states that an entity shall not adjust the amounts recognised in its financial statements to reflect non-adjusting events after the reporting period. Examples of non-adjusting events include:
- a major business combination after the reporting period
- the destruction of property by fire after the reporting period
- the issuance of new share capital after the reporting period
- commencing major litigation arising solely out of events that occurred after the reporting period.

Although these events are not adjusted for, paragraph 21 of IAS 10 requires the following disclosure for each material category of non-adjusting event after the reporting period:
- the nature of the event; and
- an estimate of its financial effect, or a statement that such an estimate cannot be made.

Paragraph 11 of IAS 10 refers to a controversial area of accounting for events after the reporting period. It states that a decline in the market value of investments between the end of the reporting period and the date when the financial statements are authorised for issue is a non-adjusting event, because the decline in market value does not normally relate to the condition of the investments at the end of the reporting period but instead reflects circumstances that have arisen subsequently. This appears to be inconsistent with the treatment of the receivables referred to in paragraph 9(b)(i) of IAS 10, regarding the insolvency of a debtor after the reporting period. IAS 10 paragraph 9(b)(i) states that this would constitute an adjusting event because the insolvency confirms that a loss existed at the end of the reporting period. The critical issue here is the amount and uncertainty of the future cash flows arising from the receivable, not whether the debtor was insolvent at the end of the reporting period. There may have been some concerns about collectability at the end of the reporting period.

A view that reconciles the differing treatment is that the additional information about the debtor's insolvency provides further evidence that the receivable was impaired and enables a better assessment of the extent of impairment. However, for assets, such as investments in securities that are traded in an active market, the market value at the reporting date would have been observable. Thus, the position taken in paragraph 11 is that the change in market value of the securities observed after the reporting period is indicative of conditions that arose after the reporting period, and, as such, is a non-adjusting event after the reporting period.

2.9 FUTURE DEVELOPMENTS

IAS 1 will be superseded by IFRS 18 *Presentation and Disclosure in Financial Statements*, effective for periods beginning on or after 1 January 2027. In brief, IFRS 18 introduces new requirements on presentation within the statement of profit or loss, including specified totals and subtotals. Items of income and expense will be classified into operating, financing, investing, income tax or discontinued operations categories. This classification will depend on a combination of an assessment of the entity's main business activities and certain accounting policy choices. A subtotal for operating profit (a defined term in IFRS 18) will be required to be presented in financial statements.

It also requires disclosure of management-defined performance measures, with reconciliations to the nearest IFRS-compliant subtotal. It also includes new requirements for aggregation and disaggregation of financial information based on the identified roles of the primary financial statements and the notes.

2.10 SUMMARY

IAS 1 *Presentation of Financial Statements*, IAS 8 *Accounting Policies, Changes in Accounting Estimates and Errors* and IAS 10 *Events after the Reporting Period* deal with fundamental disclosures and considerations that underpin financial statement presentation.

IAS 1 prescribes overall considerations to be applied in the preparation of financial statements, and the structure and content of financial statements, which comprise a statement of financial position, statement of profit or loss and other comprehensive income, statement of cash flows, statement of changes in equity and notes. The prescribed disclosures are designed to enhance the understandability of the financial statements for the users of general purpose financial statements in their economic decision making.

IAS 8 prescribes the accounting treatment for changes in accounting policies, changes in accounting estimates and correction of prior period errors. Changes in accounting policies and corrections of errors are applied retrospectively, while changes in accounting estimates are recognised prospectively.

IAS 10 distinguishes between two types of events after the reporting period — adjusting and non-adjusting. Adjusting events must be recognised in the financial statements, whereas non-adjusting events must be disclosed only.

Discussion questions

1. Describe the eight general principles to be applied in the presentation of financial statements. Which principles are more subjective? Explain your answer.
2. Why is it important for entities to disclose the measurement bases used in preparing the financial statements?
3. How do the presentation and disclosure requirements of IFRS Standards reflect the objectives of financial statements? Illustrate your argument with examples from IAS 1, IAS 8 and IAS 10.
4. What is the purpose of a statement of financial position? What comprises a complete set of financial statements in accordance with IAS 1?
5. What are the major limitations of a statement of financial position as a source of information for users of general purpose financial statements?
6. Under what circumstances are assets and liabilities ordinarily classified broadly in order of liquidity rather than on a current/non-current classification?
7. Can an asset that is not realisable within 12 months be classified as a current asset? If so, under what circumstances?
8. Explain the difference between classification of expenses by nature and by function.
9. Does the separate identification of profit and items of other comprehensive income provide a meaningful distinction between the effects of different types of non-owner transactions and events?
10. What is the objective of a statement of changes in equity?
11. Why is a summary of accounting policies important to ensuring the understandability of financial statements to users of general purpose financial statements?
12. Provide an example of a judgement made in preparing the financial statements that can lead to estimation uncertainty at the end of the reporting period. Describe the disclosures that would be required in the notes.
13. What disclosures are required in the notes in regard to accounting policy judgements?
14. What is the difference between an accounting policy and an accounting estimate? Provide an example of each.
15. Explain the difference between retrospective application of a change in accounting policy and prospective application of a change in accounting estimate. Why do you think the standard setters require prospective application of a change in accounting estimate?
16. Explain the difference between adjusting and non-adjusting events after the reporting period. Provide examples to illustrate your answer.

References

Deloitte 2023, Deloitte dReport, How to disclose accounting policies from 1 January 2023c, https://www.dreport.cz/en/blog/how-to-disclose-accounting-policies-from-1-january-2023
GSK 2023, Annual Report 2023, 2023 Annual Report (gsk.com)

Under IAS 1 certain changes in net assets are reported as other comprehensive income (OCI) rather than in the income statement (IS). One concern that academics have raised is whether items reported in OCI are interpreted differently than items reported in the IS. Dhaliwal et al. (1999) examine a sample of over 11,000 firm-year observations between 1994 and 1995 and find that most companies report non-zero OCI. They then examine the association between stock returns and the sum of net income and OCI – or, adjusted income – and establish that it is positive. The explanatory power of adjusted income for stock return is larger than that of net income alone. This is consistent with decision useful-ness of OCI. However, further investigation reveals that the additional usefulness primarily stems from fair-value adjust-ments of available-for-sale securities that are reported in OCI and not from other sources of OCI. The authors also explore the association between net income and adjusted income with stock prices. They find that the association is stronger for net income. Moreover, net income is more closely related to future cash flows and future net income than adjusted income. The conclusion the authors draw from this evidence is that OCI is a noisy measure of performance and hence is not as useful as net income. However, this finding may be due to the fact that Dhaliwal et al. (1999) do not separate between net income and OCI to see how each component individually and incrementally is used by investors. This task is performed by Barton et al. (2010) employing a very large international sample (46 countries) between 1996 and 2005. They examine an alternative specification whereby net income and total comprehensive income are tested sepa-rately and incrementally to each other. This alternative speci-fication, however, does not change the insight that OCI is measured with considerable noise and is not value relevant. However, conflicting evidence is provided by Chambers et al. (2007). Specifically, they find from a US sample of 2705 firm-year observations in the 1998–2003 period that OCI is positively related to stock returns. The contrast with Dhaliwal et al. (1999) is explained by the fact that Dhaliwal et al. (1999) do not actually use OCI numbers as prescribed by SFAS 130 (now ASC 220) (FASB, 1997), but proxy for these numbers. Similarly, Barton et al. (2010) largely employ reports prepared under older versions of IAS 1.

While IFRS® Standards now require the reporting of OCI either immediately following the income statement or in the statement of comprehensive income, this has not always been the case. In the US, for example, certain items of OCI could be reported in the statement of changes in equity. Adopting this approach therefore shifts the location of OCI from a performance-focused statement – the statement of comprehensive income – to the balance sheet. But, does the location of OCI reporting matter? One may argue that the most important issue is that the relevant figures are clearly reported, regardless of their location. However, if investors have limited attention, as is argued by Hirshleifer and Teoh (2003), they may focus on performance measures at the expense of information disclosed elsewhere in the financials (e.g., the statement of changes in equity). Experimental evi-dence indeed suggests that location may matter. Maines and

McDaniel (2000) provide evidence that non-professional investors ignore the volatility of OCI if it is reported in the statement of changes in equity. Hirst and Hopkins (1998) run an experiment based on professional subjects who examine a case where a fictitious firm sells available-for-sale (AFS) instruments to realise a holding gain. The sale of the AFS instruments is not expected to affect the firms' value because they were already carried at fair value. However, Hirst and Hopkins (1998) find that the location of infor-mation about this gain matters for valuation. Specifically, reporting the resulting changes in comprehensive income attracts lower valuations than reporting in the statement of changes in equity. The implication is that professional inves-tors focus on performance measures such as comprehensive income and analyse related disclosures more diligently.

Bamber et al. (2010) build on the above-mentioned research to argue that managers believe that reporting OCI in a performance statement will increase investors' percep-tion of performance volatility. This acts as an incentive to report OCI in the statement of changes in equity. Consistent with this, Bamber et al. (2010) find that when managers had discretion where to report OCI 81% of their sample firms report OCI in the statement of changes in equity. Cao and Dong (2020) find evidence supporting managers' concern that including OCI in a performance statement, rather than in statement of changes in equity, increases perceived vola-tility, with resultant lower valuations.

Older versions of IAS 1 required that financial statements give a 'true and fair view' (TFV) of the financial affairs of the reporting entity. Older versions of IAS 1 further required that a reporting entity departs from promulgated stand-ards if by following them the reporting will be misleading, and hence inconsistent with TFV. Such a departure is called TFV override. In preparation for the 2005 adoption of IFRS® Standards in Europe, IAS 1 was revised to require fair pres-entation, and, furthermore, to discourage TFV overrides (the language of the standard now speaks about *rare* circum-stances in which an override can be invoked). An important question in this context is whether companies use TFV over-rides to improve the quality of financial reports, or do so only when it is convenient for them. There is unfortunately scarce empirical research on this topic, in part because fol-lowing the adoption of IFRS® Standards most firms have been discouraged from overrides. An exception is the study by Livne and McNichols (2009) who examine TFV overrides in the UK prior to the 2005 adoption of IFRS® Standards. The authors first develop a classification system to assess the severity of an override. A more costly override is expected to be invoked to the extent that it delivers better outcomes to managers. Livne and McNichols (2009) find that more costly overrides (overrides of UK GAAP) are associated with poor performance. This evidence therefore suggests that over-rides were invoked opportunistically in an effort to improve reported performance and financial position. Further, firms that invoked TFV overrides are associated with poorer quality of financial statements. This evidence suggests that allowing more flexibility to invoke an override may lead to unin-tended consequences.

Relatively little is known about changes in accounting estimates, which are required when forward-looking information changes during the reporting period. Chung et al. (2021) analyse 4771 reported changes in accounting estimates. They find that the three most frequently-affected accounts are revenues, liabilities and depreciation. However, there is considerable variation in affected accounts across industries. They also find that these changes in estimates tend to positively affect net income.

References

Bamber, L.S., Jiang, J., Petroni, K.R., and Wang, I.Y., 2010. Comprehensive income: who's afraid of performance reporting? *The Accounting Review*, 85(1), 97–126.

Barton, J., Hansen, T.B., and Pownall, G., 2010. Which performance measures do investors around the world value the most—and why? *The Accounting Review*, 85(3), 753–789.

Cao, Y., and Dong, Q., 2020. Does reporting position affect the pricing of the volatility of comprehensive income? *Journal of Business Finance & Accounting*, 47(9–10), 1113–1150.

Chambers, D., Linsmeier, T.J., Shakespeare, C., and Sougiannis, T., 2007. An evaluation of SFAS no. 130 comprehensive income disclosures. *Review of Accounting Studies*, 12(4), 557–593.

Chung, P.K., Geiger, M.A., Paik, G.H., and Rabe, C., 2021. Materiality thresholds: empirical evidence from change in accounting estimate disclosures. *Accounting Horizons*, 35(3), pp.113–141.

Dhaliwal, D., Subramanyam, K.R., and Trezevant, R., 1999. Is comprehensive income superior to net income as a measure of firm performance? *Journal of Accounting and Economics*, 26(1), 43–67.

Financial Accounting Standards Board (FASB), 1997. Reporting comprehensive income. SFAS No. 130. Stamford, CT: FASB

Hirshleifer, D., and Teoh, S.H., 2003. Limited attention, information disclosure, and financial reporting. *Journal of Accounting and Economics*, 36(1), 337–386.

Hirst, D.E., and Hopkins, P.E., 1998. Comprehensive income reporting and analysts' valuation judgments. *Journal of Accounting Research*, 36, 47–75.

Livne, G., and McNichols, M., 2009. An empirical investigation of the true and fair override in the United Kingdom. *Journal of Business Finance & Accounting*, 36(1–2), 1–30.

Maines, L.A., and McDaniel, L.S., 2000. Effects of comprehensive-income characteristics on nonprofessional investors' judgments: the role of financial-statement presentation format. *The Accounting Review*, 75(2), 179–207.

3 Revenue from contracts with customers

ACCOUNTING STANDARDS IN FOCUS

IFRS 15 *Revenue from Contracts with Customers*

LEARNING OBJECTIVES

After studying this chapter, you should be able to:

1. discuss the background behind the issuance of IFRS 15
2. identify the types of contracts that are within the scope of IFRS 15
3. apply the five-step model for measuring and recognising revenue under IFRS 15
4. understand how to account for contract related costs
5. identify other significant application issues associated with IFRS 15
6. explain the presentation and disclosure requirements of IFRS 15.

3.1 INTRODUCTION

The International Accounting Standards Board (IASB®) issued IFRS 15 *Revenue from Contracts with Customers* ('IFRS 15' or 'the standard') in May 2014. The standard was developed jointly with the US FASB (collectively, 'the Boards'). The US FASB issued its new revenue standard at the same time that the IASB issued IFRS 15. The new revenue standards issued by the Boards are largely converged. IFRS 15 became effective for periods starting on or after 1 January 2018.

The IASB has performed a Post-Implementation Review (PIR) of IFRS 15. During this process, the effect of the standard on investors, preparers and auditors is assessed. In addition, issues that were important or contentious during the development of the standard as well as issues that have come to the attention of the IASB subsequently are considered and feedback is sought from stakeholders. The IASB concluded that there were no fundamental flaws in the requirements of the standard but will consider some low priority matters in their next agenda consultation.

IFRS 15 outlines the accounting treatment for all revenue arising from contracts with customers and provides a model for the measurement and recognition of gains and losses on the sale of certain non-financial assets, such as intangible assets, property, plant or equipment or investment properties.

The core principle of IFRS 15 is that an entity will recognise revenue at an amount that reflects the consideration to which the entity expects to be entitled in exchange for transferring goods or services to a customer. This requires entities to apply a five-step model as follows:

1. Identify the contract(s) with a customer *(discussed in section 3.3)*.
2. Identify the performance obligations in the contract *(discussed in section 3.4)*.
3. Determine the transaction price *(discussed in section 3.5)*.
4. Allocate the transaction price to the performance obligations in the contract *(discussed in section 3.6)*.
5. Recognise revenue when (or as) the entity satisfies a performance obligation *(discussed in section 3.7)*.

Figure 3.1 depicts these five steps.

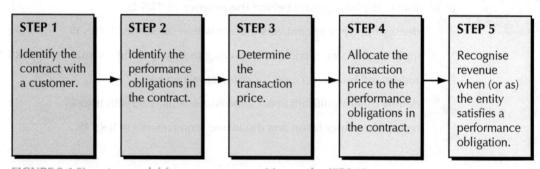

FIGURE 3.1 Five-step model for revenue recognition under IFRS 15

3.2 SCOPE

All contracts with customers to provide goods or services in the ordinary course of business are included within the scope of IFRS 15, except for the following contracts and arrangements:

- lease contracts accounted for under IFRS 16 *Leases* (see Chapter 9);
- insurance contracts accounted for under IFRS 17 *Insurance Contracts*;
- financial instruments and other contractual rights or obligations accounted for under IFRS 9 *Financial Instruments* (see Chapter 13), IFRS 10 *Consolidated Financial Statements* (see Chapter 20), IFRS 11 *Joint Arrangements*, IAS 27 *Separate Financial Statements* and IAS 28 *Investments in Associates and Joint Ventures* (see online chapters Joint arrangements and Associates and joint ventures); and
- non-monetary exchanges between entities in the same line of business to facilitate sales to customers or potential customers.

Entities have to evaluate their relationship with the counterparty to the contract in order to determine whether a vendor–customer relationship exists, which may be particularly judgemental for certain arrangements. For example, some collaboration arrangements are more akin to a partnership, while others represent a vendor–customer relationship. Only transactions that are with a customer are within the scope of IFRS 15.

Entities may enter into transactions with customers that are partially within the scope of IFRS 15 and partially within the scope of other standards. In these situations, the standard requires that an entity apply requirements (if any) in the other standard(s) first, to separate and/or measure the different parts in the contract, before applying the requirements in IFRS 15.

3.3 IDENTIFY THE CONTRACT WITH THE CUSTOMER

An entity must identify the contract, or contracts, to provide goods and services to customers as the first step in the model in IFRS 15. Any contracts that create enforceable rights and obligations fall within the scope of the standard. Such contracts may be written, oral or implied through an entity's customary business practice and this may impact an entity's determination of when an arrangement meets the definition of a contract with a customer. Since enforceability is driven by the laws within the jurisdiction, the assessment of whether there are legally enforceable rights and obligations will depend on the facts and circumstances.

Take, for example, an entity that has an established business practice of starting performance based on oral agreements with its customers. The entity may assess that such oral agreements result in a contract as defined in IFRS 15 and, therefore, account for a contract as soon as performance begins, instead of delaying until there is a signed agreement. Certain arrangements may require a written agreement to comply with jurisdictional law or trade regulation. In those cases, the assessment may differ and a contract may exist only when there is a written document.

3.3.1 Arrangements that meet the definition of a contract

To help entities determine whether (and when) their arrangements with customers are contracts within the scope of the standard, the Boards provided five criteria that must be met at the commencement of the arrangement. Once the criteria are met, an entity would apply the five-step model in IFRS 15 to account for the contract and it is not required to reassess these criteria unless there is a significant change in facts and circumstances.

Paragraph 9 of IFRS 15 provides five criteria, as summarised below:

(a) the contract is approved by all parties, whether in writing, orally or in accordance with other customary business practices, and the parties are committed to carrying out their respective obligations;

(b) the entity can identify the rights of each party with regard to the goods or services that are to be transferred under the contract;

(c) the entity can identify the payment terms for the goods or services to be transferred;

(d) the contract has commercial substance; and

(e) collectability of the amount of consideration that an entity will be entitled to in exchange for the goods and services that will be transferred to the customer is probable.

The purpose of these criteria is to help an entity assess whether a contract with its customer is genuine and entered into for a valid business purpose. If the criteria are not met, then the arrangement is not considered a revenue contract under IFRS 15. *Instead, the requirements discussed in section 3.3.2 must be applied.* In addition, entities are required to continue assessing the criteria throughout the term of the arrangement to determine if they are subsequently met, at which point the five-step model applies. Illustrative example 3.1 describes a scenario where an agreement is signed but still no contract exists that meets all of the above criteria.

ILLUSTRATIVE EXAMPLE 3.1 Determining whether a contract exists

Entities S and C sign a Master Purchase and Sale Agreement (MPSA) whereby the conditions under which S will deliver staple consumables to C are laid down such as prices of the various goods, rebates, payment conditions and shipping terms. The MPSA has a term of 18 months. Under the agreement C will place orders over the next 18 months specifying the exact goods and quantities to be delivered.

In this scenario S concludes that the criteria of IFRS 15 have not been fulfilled at the date of signing the MPSA since criterion (b) is not met as the exact type and quantity of goods to be delivered have not been agreed yet. The criteria of IFRS 15 are likely to be met when C places an order as in that case the MPSA in combination with the order will meet all criteria.

3.3.2 Arrangements that do not meet the definition of a contract

Paragraph 15 of IFRS 15 indicates that when a contract with a customer does not meet the criteria for a revenue contract *(i.e. the criteria discussed in section 3.3.1)* and an entity receives consideration from the customer, the entity can only recognise the consideration received as revenue when such amounts are non-refundable and either of the following events has occurred:

(a) the entity has completed performing all of its obligations under the contract and has received all, or substantially all, of the consideration promised by the customer; or

(b) the contract has been terminated.

The standard goes on to specify that an entity must recognise any consideration received from a customer as a liability until one of the events described above occurs or until the contract meets the contract criteria *(see section 3.3.1)* to be accounted for within the revenue model.

3.3.3 Contracts that are combined

Entities have to combine individual contracts entered into at, or near, the same time with the same customer (or related parties of the customer) if they meet one or more of the following criteria in paragraph 17 of IFRS 15:

(a) the contracts are negotiated as a package with the intent of meeting a single business purpose (e.g. where a contract would be loss-making without taking into account the consideration received under another contract);

(b) the amount of consideration that a customer has to pay in one contract is impacted by the price or performance of the other contract (e.g. where failure to perform under one contract affects the amount paid under another contract); or

(c) some or all of the goods or services promised in the individual contracts form a single performance obligation (e.g. a contract for the sale of specialised equipment and a second contract entered into at the same time with the same customer for significant customisation and modification of that specialised equipment may give rise to a single performance obligation).

Note that only contracts entered into at or near the same time are assessed under the contract combination requirements. Arrangements entered into at a much later date that were not anticipated at the start of the contract or implied based on the entity's customary business practices may need to be accounted for as contract modifications, *which are discussed in section 3.9.1.*

3.4 IDENTIFY THE PERFORMANCE OBLIGATIONS

Once an entity has identified the contract with the customer, the second step in the model requires an entity to identify the promised goods and services in the contract. This assessment is performed at the commencement of the contract.

The entity has to determine which of the promised goods or services (individually or as a bundle of promised goods or services) will be treated as separate performance obligations. Under IFRS 15, a promised good or service that is not distinct on its own must be combined with other goods or services until a distinct bundle of goods or services is formed. Each separate performance obligation is an individual unit of account for purposes of applying the standard. These concepts are discussed further below.

3.4.1 Separate performance obligations

Paragraph 26 of IFRS 15 provides a non-exhaustive list of examples of promised goods or services that may be identified in a contract. Such promised goods or services are accounted for as separate performance obligations if they are distinct (either by themselves or as part of a bundle of goods and services) or they are part of a series of distinct goods and services that are substantially the same and have the same pattern of transfer to the customer *(see section 3.4.2).*

In assessing whether a promised good or service (or a bundle of goods and services) is distinct, an entity has to meet both of the criteria below:

• the goods or services are capable of being distinct; and
• the promise to transfer the good or service is distinct when considered in the context of the entire contract.

Capable of being distinct

A good or service is capable of being distinct if the customer can benefit from it (i.e. it could be used, consumed, sold for an amount greater than scrap value or otherwise held in a way that generates economic benefits). In assessing this, an entity considers the individual characteristics of the good or service, rather than how a customer may use the good or service.

A customer may be able to benefit from some goods or services on their own or in conjunction with other readily available resources. Readily available resources are goods and services that may be sold separately by the entity (or another entity) or that the customer has already obtained from the entity (including goods or services that have already been transferred to the customer under the contract) or from other transactions or events. Separately selling a good or service on a regular basis indicates that a customer can benefit from that good or service on its own or with readily available resources.

Distinct within the context of the contract

The second criterion requires that the entity considers whether the promise to transfer goods or services is separately identifiable. The entity determines whether the nature of the promise, within the context of the contract, is to transfer each of those goods or services individually, or, instead to transfer a combined item or items to which the promised goods or services are inputs. The standard provides a non-exhaustive list of indicators that an entity's promise to transfer a good or service to a customer is <u>not</u> separately identifiable. The indicators are summarised as follows:

(a) The entity is using the goods or services as inputs into a single process or project that is the output of the contract. That is, the entity is not providing a significant integration service.

(b) One or more of the goods or services significantly modify or customise other promised goods and services promised in the contract.

(c) The goods or services are highly interdependent, or highly interrelated with, other promised goods or services in the contract. For example, two or more goods or services are significantly affected by each other when the entity would not be able to fulfil its promise by transferring each of the goods or services independently.

If a promised good or service is not distinct, an entity is required to combine that good or service with other promised goods or services until it identifies a bundle of goods or services that is distinct. As a consequence, an entity may end up accounting for all the goods or services promised in a contract as a single performance obligation if the bundle of promised goods and services is the only distinct item identified.

Illustrative example 3.2 demonstrates how an entity might apply the two-step process for determining whether promised goods or services in a contract are distinct and how an entity might bundle inseparable goods and services.

ILLUSTRATIVE EXAMPLE 3.2 Determining whether goods or services are distinct

Entity Z is a software development company that provides hosting services to a variety of retailers. Entity Z offers a hosted inventory management software product that requires the retailers to purchase hardware from Entity Z. In addition, retailers may purchase professional services from Entity Z to migrate historical data and create interfaces with existing back-office accounting systems. Entity Z always delivers the hardware first, followed by professional services and finally, the ongoing hosting services.

Scenario A — All goods and services are also sold separately

Entity Z determines that all of the individual goods and services in the contract are capable of being distinct because the entity regularly sells each element of the contract separately. Entity Z also determines that the goods and services are separable from other promises in the contract (i.e. distinct within the context of the contract), because it is not providing a significant service of integrating the goods and services and the level of customisation is not significant. Furthermore, because the customer could purchase (or not purchase) each good and service without significantly affecting the other goods and services purchased, the goods and services are not highly dependent on, or highly interrelated with, each other. Accordingly, the hardware, professional services and hosting services are each accounted for as separate performance obligations.

Scenario B — Hardware is not sold separately

In this scenario Entity Z determines that the professional services are distinct because it frequently sells those services on a stand-alone basis (e.g. Entity Z also performs professional services related to hardware and software it does not sell). Furthermore, the entity determines that the hosting services are distinct because it also sells those services on a stand-alone basis. For example, customers that have completed their initial contractual term and elect each month to continue purchasing the hosting services are purchasing those services on a stand-alone basis. The hardware, however, is always sold in a package with the professional and hosting services and the customer cannot use the hardware on its own or with resources that are readily available to it. Therefore, Entity Z determines the hardware is not distinct.

Entity Z must determine which promised goods and services in the contract to bundle with the hardware. Entity Z likely would conclude that because the hardware is integral to the delivery of the hosted software, the hardware and hosting services should be accounted for as one performance obligation, and the professional services, which are distinct, would be a separate performance obligation.

Please note that even if an entity (implicitly) promises to perform certain activities, this does not necessarily mean that the performance of those activities transfers a good or service, and therefore, would not be included in a performance obligation. The IFRS Interpretations Committee, in January 2019 clarified this when answering a question about revenue recognition for listing services by stock exchanges. Illustrative example 3.3 is based upon the agenda decision that the IFRS Interpretations Committee issued on this question.

ILLUSTRATIVE EXAMPLE 3.3 Determining goods or services transferred — listing services

Stock Exchange F provides listing services to companies seeking listing on its stock exchange. F charges companies a non-refundable upfront fee at the time of initial listing and an ongoing listing fee. F undertakes various activities at or near contract inception to enable admission to the exchange such as due diligence, reviewing the company's listing application, issuing reference numbers and tickers for the new security, processing the listing and admission to the markets. The question is whether these activities are admission services that are distinct from the listing service.

In this scenario, the activities performed by F at or near inception of the contract (i.e. during the initial listing phase) are required to transfer the service for which the listed company has contracted, i.e. the service of being listed on the stock exchange. However, F's performance of those activities does not transfer a service to the listed company. The listing service transferred to the listed company is the same on initial listing and on all subsequent days for which the listed company remains listed. So, F does not promise to transfer any good or service to the listed company other than the service of being listed on the exchange.

We will see in section 3.6 that the implication is that the non-refundable upfront fee is not recognised as revenue upfront when the admission activities are performed, but allocated to the period over which the listing services are promised.

3.4.2 Series of distinct goods and services that are substantially the same and have the same pattern of transfer

Even if a good or service is determined to be distinct, if it is part of a series of goods or services that are substantially the same and have the same pattern of transfer, that series of goods or services must be treated as a single performance obligation when both of the following criteria are met:
- each distinct good or service in the series is a performance obligation that would be satisfied over time *(see section 3.7.1)* if it were accounted for separately; and
- the measure used to assess the entity's progress towards satisfaction of the performance obligation is the same for each distinct good or service in the series *(see section 3.7.2)*.

An example would be a contract with a one-year life where the service provider promises the customer to clean the windows of a specific office every month for a fixed amount. In this case, there are not twelve separate performance obligations, but only one performance obligation, consisting of a series of monthly services.

3.4.3 Customer options for additional goods or services

Some entities frequently give customers the option to purchase additional goods or services ('customer options'). These additional goods or services may be priced at a discount or may even be free of charge. Customer options also come in many forms, including sales incentives, customer award credits (e.g. frequent flyer programmes offered by airlines), contract renewal options (e.g. waiver of certain fees, reduced future rates) or other discounts on future goods or services.

IFRS 15 indicates that a customer option is a separate performance obligation only if it provides the customer with a material right that the customer would not have received without entering into the contract (e.g. a discount that exceeds the range of discounts typically given for those goods or services to that class of customer in that geographical area or market). The purpose of this requirement is for entities to identify and account for options that customers are essentially paying for as part of the current transaction.

If the discounted price of the customer option reflects the stand-alone selling price *(see section 3.6.1)*, separate from any existing relationship or contract, the entity is deemed to have made a marketing offer rather than having granted a material right. This is the case even if the customer option can only be exercised because the customer entered into the earlier transaction.

Illustrative example 3.4 provides two scenarios highlighting the circumstances under which a separate performance obligation may or may not arise.

ILLUSTRATIVE EXAMPLE 3.4 Determining whether customer options constitute a separate performance obligation

Scenario A
Retailer H grants coupons to its customers. For every €100 of purchases the customer gets a €5 coupon that can only be used to pay for further purchases during a specific period. The coupon is not exchangeable for cash and can only be spent in shops of retailer H. H determines that the coupons have substance and concludes that upon the first sales transaction there are two performance obligations, i.e. (i) the transfer of the goods purchased by the customer, and (ii) the promise to the same customer to get a rebate of €5 on the next purchase. The two are distinct goods.

Scenario B
Retailer J provides every customer that buys two boxes of toothpaste a coupon with a 50% discount on the next purchase of toothpaste. The same coupon, however, can be found on the website of retailer J available to anybody. J concludes that the coupon is merely a marketing offer, available to anybody and therefore not conditional upon an original purchase by a customer. Upon the sale of the two boxes of toothpaste, J determines there is only one performance obligation, i.e. the transfer to the customer of the two boxes of toothpaste.

3.5 DETERMINE THE TRANSACTION PRICE

The third step in the model requires an entity to determine the transaction price. This is the amount of consideration to which an entity expects to be entitled in exchange for transferring promised goods or services to a customer. This excludes amounts collected on behalf of third parties (e.g. some sales taxes). In determining the transaction price, the entity has to consider the contractual terms and its customary business practices.

In many cases, the transaction price can be readily determined because the entity receives a fixed payment when it transfers promised goods or services to the customer (e.g. the sale of goods in a retail store). Determining the transaction price can be more challenging in other situations, such as:
- when the transaction price is variable
- when a customer pays for the goods or services before or after the entity's performance
- when a customer pays in a form other than cash
- when the entity pays consideration to the customer, or
- when the customer has a right of return.
The effects of these items on the determination of the transaction price are discussed in sections 3.5.1–3.5.5.

Determining the transaction price is an important step in the model because this amount is subsequently allocated to the identified performance obligations in the fourth step of the model. It is also the amount that will be recognised as revenue when (or as) those performance obligations are satisfied.

3.5.1 Variable consideration

Paragraph 50 of IFRS 15 requires that if the consideration promised in a contract includes a variable amount, the entity must estimate the amount of consideration to which it will be entitled and include that amount in the transaction price, subject to a constraint (which is discussed further below).

Variable consideration may include discounts, rebates, refunds, credits, price concessions, incentives, performance bonuses, penalties or other similar items. If an entity's entitlement to the consideration is contingent on the occurrence or non-occurrence of a future event, the transaction price is considered to be variable. An example of this is when a portion of the transaction price depends on an entity meeting specified performance conditions and there is uncertainty about the outcome and, therefore, whether the entity will receive that amount of consideration.

Estimating variable consideration
An entity is required to estimate the variable consideration using either an 'expected value' or a 'most likely amount' approach. An entity has to decide which approach better predicts the amount of consideration

to which it expects it will be entitled and apply that approach. That is, an entity will need to select the method not based on a 'free choice' but rather on what is most suitable given the specific facts and circumstances. In some cases, an entity may have to use different approaches (i.e. expected value or most likely amount) for estimating different types of variable consideration within a single contract.

The selected method(s) must be applied consistently throughout the contract and an entity will have to update the estimated transaction price at the end of each reporting period. Furthermore, an entity is required to apply the selected approach consistently to similar types of contracts.

The expected value approach is based on probability-weighting the possible outcomes of a contract. As a result, it may better predict the expected consideration when an entity has a large number of contracts with similar characteristics. Using the most likely amount approach, an entity will select the amount that is most likely to be received considering the range of possible amounts. The most likely amount approach may be the better method to use when there are a limited number of possible amounts expected (e.g. a contract in which an entity is entitled to receive all or none of a specified commission payment, but not a portion of that commission).

When applying either of these approaches, all information (historical, current and forecast) that is reasonably available to the entity must be considered.

Constraining the cumulative amount of revenue recognised

As mentioned earlier, after estimating the amount of variable consideration, an entity must apply the 'constraint' to the estimated amount. The constraint is aimed at preventing revenue from being overstated. To include variable consideration in the estimated transaction price, the entity has to conclude that it is 'highly probable' that a significant revenue reversal will not occur in future periods when the uncertainties related to the variability are subsequently resolved. This conclusion involves considering both the likelihood and magnitude of a potential revenue reversal. In assessing the magnitude, an entity needs to consider if the potential revenue reversal is 'significant' relative to cumulative revenue recognised for the entire contract, rather than just the variable consideration. The estimate of the variable consideration (which is subject to the effect of the constraint) included in the transaction price is updated throughout the contractual period to reflect the conditions that exist at the end of each reporting period.

Illustrative example 3.5 provides an example of estimating the variable consideration using the 'expected value' and the 'most likely amount' approaches, and the effect of the constraint on both approaches.

ILLUSTRATIVE EXAMPLE 3.5 Estimating variable consideration

Scenario A

Entity A provides transportation to theme park customers to and from accommodation in the area under a 1-year agreement. It is required to provide scheduled transportation throughout the year for a fixed fee of $400,000 annually. Entity A also is entitled to performance bonuses for on-time performance and average customer wait times. Its performance may yield a bonus from $0 to $600,000 under the contract. Based on its history with the theme park, customer travel patterns and its current expectations, Entity A estimates the probabilities for different amounts of bonus within the range as follows:

Bonus amount	Probability of outcome
$0	30%
$200,000	30%
$400,000	35%
$600,000	5%

Analysis

Expected value

Because Entity A believes that there is no one amount within the range that is most likely to be received, Entity A determines that the expected value approach is most appropriate to use. As a result, Entity A estimates variable consideration to be $230,000 (($200,000 × 30%) + ($400,000 × 35%) + ($600,000 × 5%)) before considering the effect of the constraint.

Assume that Entity A is a calendar year-end entity and it entered into the contract with the theme park during its second quarter. Customer wait times were slightly above average during the second quarter. Based on this experience, Entity A determines that it is highly probable that a significant revenue reversal for $200,000 of variable consideration will not occur. Therefore, after applying the constraint, Entity A only includes $200,000 in its estimated transaction price. At the end of its third quarter, Entity A updates its analysis and expected value calculation. The updated analysis again results in estimated variable consideration of $230,000, with a probability outcome of 75%. Based on analysis of the factors in paragraph 57 of IFRS 15 and in light of slightly better-than-expected average customer wait times during the third quarter, Entity A determines that it is highly probable that a significant revenue reversal for the entire $230,000 estimated transaction price will not occur. Entity A updates its estimate to include the entire $230,000 in the transaction price. Entity A will continue to update its estimate of the transaction price at each subsequent reporting period.

Scenario B

Assume the same facts as in Scenario A, except that the potential bonus will not be an amount along a range between $0 and $600,000, but one of four stated amounts: $0, $200,000, $400,000 or $600,000. Based on its history with the theme park and customer travel patterns, Entity A estimates the probabilities for each bonus amount as follows:

Bonus amount	Probability of outcome
$0	30%
$200,000	30%
$400,000	35%
$600,000	5%

Analysis

Expected value

Entity A determined that the expected value approach was the most appropriate to use when estimating its variable consideration. Under that approach, it estimates the variable consideration is $230,000. Entity A must then consider the effect of the constraint on the amount of variable consideration included in the transaction price. Entity A notes that, because there are only four potential outcomes under the contract, the constraint essentially limits the amount of revenue Entity A can recognise to one of the stated bonus amounts. In this example, Entity A would be limited to including $200,000 in the estimated transaction price until it became highly probable that the next bonus level (i.e. $400,000) would be achieved. This is because any amount over $200,000 would be subject to subsequent reversal, unless $400,000 was received.

Most likely amount

As there are only a limited number of outcomes for the amount of bonus that can be received, Entity A is concerned that a probability-weighted estimate may result in an amount that is not a potential outcome. Therefore, Entity A determines that estimating the transaction price by identifying the most likely outcome would be the best predictor.

The standard is not clear about how an entity would determine the most likely amount when there are more than two potential outcomes and none of the potential outcomes is significantly more likely than the others. A literal reading of the standard might suggest that, in this example, Entity A would select $400,000 because that is the amount with the highest estimated probability. However, Entity A must then apply a constraint on the amount of variable consideration included in the transaction price.

To include $400,000 in the estimated transaction price, Entity A has to believe it is highly probable that the bonus amount will be at least $400,000. Based on the listed probabilities above, however, Entity A believes it is only 40% likely to receive a bonus of at least $400,000 (i.e. 35% + 5%) and 70% likely it will receive a bonus of at least $200,000 (i.e. 30% + 35% + 5%). As a result, Entity A would include only $200,000 in its estimate of the transaction price.

3.5.2 Significant financing component

For some transactions, customers may pay in advance or in arrears of the goods or services being transferred to them. When the customer pays before (or after) the goods or services are provided, the entity is effectively receiving financing from (or providing financing to) the customer. Paragraph 60 of IFRS 15 requires that the entity adjusts the transaction price for the effects of the time value of money if either the customer or the entity is provided with a significant financing benefit due to the timing of payments.

As a practical expedient, an entity is only required to assess whether the arrangement contains a significant financing component when the period between the customer's payment and the entity's transfer of the goods or services is greater than 1 year. This assessment, performed at the commencement of the contract, will likely require entities to exercise significant judgement. Furthermore, a financing component only affects the transaction price when it is considered significant to the contract.

For contracts with a significant financing component, the transaction price is calculated by discounting the amount of promised consideration, using the same discount rate that an entity would use if it were to enter into a separate financing transaction with the customer. Using a risk-free rate or a rate that is explicitly specified in the contract that does not reflect the borrower's credit characteristics would not be acceptable. An entity does not need to update the discount rate for changes in circumstances or interest rates after the commencement of the contract.

3.5.3 Non-cash consideration

A customer might pay in cash or in forms other than cash (e.g. goods, services, equity shares). Paragraph 66 of IFRS 15 requires an entity to include the fair value of any non-cash consideration it receives (or expects to receive) in the transaction price. An entity applies the requirements of IFRS 13 *Fair Value Measurement* when measuring the fair value of any non-cash consideration. If an entity cannot reasonably estimate the fair value of non-cash consideration, it measures the non-cash consideration indirectly by reference to the estimated stand-alone selling price of the promised goods or services.

The fair value of non-cash consideration may change either: (i) because of the performance considerations that affect the amount of consideration; or (ii) because of the fair value of the non-cash consideration (e.g. changes in the price of shares that the seller is entitled to). The transaction price is updated for these changes. It should be noted, though, that the changes in non-cash consideration caused by a change in performance consideration are subject to the requirements for constraining variable consideration *(as discussed in section 3.5.1)*. This would, for example, be the case if the seller were entitled to a variable number of shares, depending on whether or not certain milestones are met.

3.5.4 Consideration paid or payable to a customer

It is not uncommon for entities to make payments to their customers or, in some cases, to other parties that purchase the entity's goods or services from the customer (e.g. indirect customers, such as customers of a reseller or distributor). Such payments might be explicitly stated in the contract or implied by the entity's customary business practice.

In addition, the term 'payments' does not only refer to cash payments. Paragraph 70 of IFRS 15 provides that consideration paid or payable can also be in the form of other items (e.g. discounts, coupons, vouchers) that a customer can apply against amounts owed to the entity.

To determine the appropriate accounting treatment, an entity would need to assess the purpose of the payments. That is, an entity must first determine whether the consideration paid or payable to a customer is:
- a payment for a distinct good or service *(see discussion in section 3.4.1)*; or
- to reduce the transaction price; or
- a combination of both.

If the consideration paid or payable to a customer is a payment for a distinct good or service from the customer, an entity accounts for the purchase of the good or service like any other purchase from a supplier. Otherwise, such payments are accounted for as a reduction to the transaction price and recognised at the later of when the entity:
- transfers the promised goods or services to the customer; or
- pays or promises to pay the consideration.

In some cases, the payments could be for both a distinct good or service and to reduce the transaction price. If the payments to the customer exceed the fair value of the distinct good or service received from the customer, the excess is accounted for as a reduction of the transaction price. If the fair value of the good or service received from the customer cannot be reasonably estimated, the entire payment to the customer is accounted for as a reduction of the transaction price.

Furthermore, the consideration paid or payable to a customer may be fixed or variable in amount (e.g. in the form of a discount or refund for goods or services provided). If the discount or refund is subject to variability, an entity would estimate it using either of the two approaches *discussed in section 3.5.1* and apply the constraint to the estimate to determine the effect of the discount or refund on the transaction price or related revenues.

3.5.5 Sale with a right of return

Often sales of goods occur with a right of return by the customer within a certain period (for example because the customer is dissatisfied with the good). The question arises whether a sale has occurred and, if so, for what amount? IFRS 15 provides guidance on how to account for these transactions. The seller estimates the extent to which transferred goods will be returned (using the requirements for estimating and constraining variable consideration). Revenue is only recognised for those goods that are not expected to be returned. For transferred goods that are expected to be returned, no revenue is recognised. Instead, a refund liability is recognised, together with an asset for the right to recover these goods from customers on settling the refund liability. Illustrative example 3.6 describes a scenario with a right of return. In figure 3.2 the accounting policy of Adidas AG for rights of return is depicted.

ILLUSTRATIVE EXAMPLE 3.6 Right of return

Online sales platform P sells fashion clothes. Customers have a right to return the goods bought within 2 weeks to get their money back. In the 2 weeks before its 31 December 20X1 balance sheet date P has sold 100 sweaters of a particular type at $80 each. The costs of these sweaters amount to $60. P has many years of return statistics and, using the requirements for estimating variable consideration (including the constraint), it estimates that five sweaters will be returned by customers.

In 20X1 it will recognise revenue only for those sweaters sold that are not expected to be returned, so 95. However, cash is received for all 100 sweaters sold. So the journal entry would be:

Cash: 100 * $80	Dr	8,000
Revenue (100 − 5) * $80	Cr	7,600
Refund liability: 5 * $80	Cr	400
Cost of goods sold: (100 − 5) * $60	Dr	5,700
Right to returned assets: 5 * $60	Dr	300
Inventory: 100 * $60	Cr	6,000

FIGURE 3.2 Right of return

Under certain conditions and in accordance with contractual agreements, the company's customers have the right to return products and to either exchange them for similar or other products or to return the products against the issuance of a credit note. Amounts for estimated returns related to revenues are accrued based on past experience of average return rates and average actual return periods by means of a refund liability. The return assets are measured at the carrying amount of the inventories/products, less any handling costs and any potential impairment.

Source: Adidas Annual report 2023, note 2, p. 212.

3.6 ALLOCATE THE TRANSACTION PRICE

In the fourth step of the model, IFRS 15 requires an entity to allocate the transaction price to each performance obligation that has been identified. In this step, an entity allocates the transaction price to each identified performance obligation based on the proportion of the stand-alone selling price of that performance obligation to the sum of the total stand-alone selling prices of all performance obligations. This is known as the relative stand-alone selling price method. Under this method, any discount within the contract will be allocated proportionally to all of the separate performance obligations in the contract.

There are two exceptions to using the relative stand-alone selling price method:
- An entity must allocate variable consideration to one or more (but not all) performance obligations, or one or more (but not all) distinct goods or services promised in a series of distinct goods or services that forms part of a single performance obligation *(as discussed in section 3.4.1)*, in a contract if the terms of the variable consideration specifically refer to that performance obligation and such allocation is consistent with the overall objective of allocation to performance obligations.
- An entity must allocate a discount in an arrangement proportionally to all performance obligations, unless there is observable evidence that the discount relates to one or more (but not all) performance obligations in a contract. The latter will only be the case if the entity regularly sells each distinct performance obligation separately and regularly sells the performance obligation (or bundle of performance obligations) separately at a discount and that discount is consistent with the overall discount in the contract.

3.6.1 Stand-alone selling prices

In applying the relative stand-alone selling price method, an entity must first determine the stand-alone selling price for each identified performance obligation. The stand-alone selling price is the price at which a good or service is, or would be, sold separately by the entity. This price is determined by the entity at the commencement of the contract and is not typically updated subsequently. However, if the contract is modified and that modification is not treated as a separate contract, the entity would update its estimate of the stand-alone selling price at the time of the modification (*see section 3.9.1*).

Under IFRS 15, an entity should use the observable price of a good or service sold separately, when it is readily available. In situations in which there is no observable stand-alone selling price, the entity must estimate the stand-alone selling price. Paragraph 79 of IFRS 15 highlights the following methods, which may be, but are not required to be, used:

- **Adjusted market assessment approach** — this approach considers the amount that the market is willing to pay for a good or service and focuses primarily on external factors rather than entity-specific factors.
- **Expected cost plus margin approach** — this approach is based primarily on internal factors (e.g. incurred costs). However, it factors in a margin that the entity believes the market would be willing to pay, not the margin that an entity would like to get.
- **Residual approach** — this approach allows an entity to estimate the stand-alone selling price of a promised good or service as the difference between the total transaction price and the observable (i.e. not estimated) stand-alone selling prices of other promised goods or services in the contract, provided certain criteria are met. However, the use of this approach may be limited because it requires that the selling price of the goods or services be either highly variable or uncertain because the goods or services have not yet been sold. The latter is meant to avoid revenue being recognised too early.

An entity is required to consider all reasonably available information (including market conditions, entity-specific factors and information about the customer or class of customer) when determining the estimated stand-alone selling price. The standard requires an entity to make as much use of observable inputs as reasonably possible and to apply estimation methods consistently to similar circumstances. This will require an entity to consider a variety of data sources.

3.6.2 Application of the relative stand-alone selling price method

Under the relative stand-alone selling price method, once the stand-alone selling price of each performance obligation is determined, the entity will then allocate the transaction price to each performance obligation based on the proportion of the stand-alone selling price of each performance obligation to the sum of the stand-alone selling prices of all the performance obligations in the contract. Illustrative example 3.7 shows a relative stand-alone selling price allocation.

ILLUSTRATIVE EXAMPLE 3.7 Relative stand-alone selling price allocation

Manufacturing Co. entered into a contract with a customer to sell a machine for £100,000. The total contract price included installation of the machine and a 2 year extended warranty. Assume that Manufacturing Co. determined there were three performance obligations and the stand-alone selling prices of those performance obligations were as follows: machine — £75,000, installation services — £14,000 and extended warranty — £20,000.

The aggregate of the stand-alone selling prices (£109,000) exceeds the total transaction price of £100,000, indicating there is a discount inherent in the contract. There is no observable evidence that the discount relates to one specific performance obligation. That means the discount must be allocated to each of the individual performance obligations based on the relative stand-alone selling price of each performance obligation. Therefore, the amount of the £100,000 transaction price is allocated to each performance obligation as follows:

Machine	—	£68,807 (£75,000 × (£100,000/£109,000))
Installation	—	£12,844 (£14,000 × (£100,000/£109,000))
Warranty	—	£18,349 (£20,000 × (£100,000/£109,000))

The entity would recognise as revenue the amount allocated to each performance obligation when (or as) each performance obligation is satisfied.

Source: Ernst & Young (International GAAP 2024, chapter 27, section 6.2 illustration 6-5).

3.7 SATISFACTION OF PERFORMANCE OBLIGATIONS

Under IFRS 15, revenue can only be recognised when (or as) an entity satisfies an identified performance obligation by transferring a promised good or service to a customer. A good or service is considered transferred when the customer obtains control over the promised good or service (i.e. the customer can direct the use of, and receive benefits from, the good or service, or prevent others from doing the same).

For each performance obligation identified in the contract, an entity must determine at the commencement of the contract, whether the performance obligation will be satisfied over time or at a point in time. If a performance obligation does not meet the criteria to be satisfied over time, it is presumed to be satisfied at a point in time.

3.7.1 Performance obligations satisfied over time

Paragraph 35 of IFRS 15 provides the criteria to help an entity determine if a performance obligation is satisfied over time. An entity has to meet one of the following criteria in order to recognise revenue over time:
(a) the benefits provided by the entity's performance are simultaneously received and consumed by the customer;
(b) the customer controls an asset that is being created or enhanced by the entity's performance; or
(c) the asset created has no alternative use to the entity and there is an enforceable right to payment for the performance completed to date.

Illustrative example 3.8 demonstrates the application of each of the above criteria:

ILLUSTRATIVE EXAMPLE 3.8 Application of the criteria for recognition over time

Scenario A — Customer simultaneously receives and consumes the benefits

Sparkle and Co. enters into a contract to provide weekly cleaning services to a customer for 2 years.

The promised cleaning services are accounted for as a single performance obligation *as discussed in section 3.4.2*. The performance obligation is satisfied over time because the customer simultaneously receives and consumes the benefits of Sparkle and Co.'s cleaning services as and when Sparkle and Co. performs. The fact that another entity would not need to re-perform the cleaning services that Sparkle and Co. has provided to date also demonstrates that the customer simultaneously receives and consumes the benefits of Sparkle and Co.'s performance as Sparkle and Co. performs. As such, Sparkle and Co. recognises revenue over time by measuring its progress towards satisfaction of that performance obligation *as discussed in section 3.7.2*.

Scenario B — Customer controls asset as it is created or enhanced

Sakalian enters into an agreement to build an integrated IT system that interfaces sales, procurement and accounting functions. Sakalian is expected to take 1 year to complete the work.

During the development of the integrated system, Sakalian works extensively with the customer to design and configure the system as well as to run tests to check its operability. All work is being performed at the customer's site so that throughout the different stages of development, the customer takes ownership and physical possession of the integrated system as it is being built.

Because the customer controls the integrated IT system as it is built, Sakalian determines that the performance obligation is satisfied over time (i.e. the control over the asset is transferred over time), rather than at a point in time.

Scenario C — Asset with no alternative use and right to payment

Novak Ltd enters into a contract to construct a highly customised piece of equipment subject to specifications provided by the customer. If the customer were to terminate the contract for reasons other than Novak Ltd's failure to perform as promised, the contract requires the customer to compensate Novak Ltd for its costs incurred plus a 10% margin. The 10% margin approximates the profit margin that Novak Ltd earns from similar contracts.

Novak Ltd therefore concludes that at any point in time during the construction it has an enforceable right to payment for its performance completed to date for its costs plus a reasonable margin, which approximates the profit margin in other contracts.

In the event of contract cancellation, the contract also contains an enforceable restriction on Novak Ltd's ability to direct the equipment (regardless of the extent of completion) for another use, such as selling the equipment to another customer. As a result, the equipment does not have an alternative use to Novak Ltd.

As a result, Novak Ltd meets the conditions for recognising revenue over time.

Determining whether the criteria for over time revenue recognition are met may require a careful analysis of all facts and circumstances. Several questions have been posed to the IASB about the interpretation of these criteria, particularly in the area of construction contracts. Illustrative example 3.9 is based upon one of those questions.

ILLUSTRATIVE EXAMPLE 3.9 Recognition at a point in time or over time?

Scenario A — Asset with right to payment and no alternative use

Hammersmith Ltd develops and constructs residential multi-unit complexes. When entering into a sale of a real estate unit the customer is required to prepay 15% of the purchase price and pay the rest upon delivery of the finished unit. However, if the customer cancels the contract, Hammersmith Ltd is entitled to payment that covers costs incurred plus a reasonable profit margin. The contract is irrevocable and Hammersmith Ltd is not allowed to sell the unit to another party, nor to substitute units or make changes to the design without the consent of the customer. The customer will receive legal title to the specific real estate unit as well as an undivided interest in the land underneath the multi-unit complex and the joint facilities, when construction is complete.

Hammersmith Ltd concludes that the criteria for over time recognition are met because the asset has no alternative use and Hammersmith Ltd has an enforceable right to payments for performance completed to date.

Scenario B — Asset with no right to payment and no alternative use

Assume the same scenario, but courts have accepted requests from customers to cancel contracts in particular circumstances, for example when it has been proven that the customer is financially unable to fulfil the terms of the contract (such as unemployment, illness or other significant deterioration of ability to pay). In those cases any amounts already paid by the customer are returned (except for an amount withheld as a cancellation fee). These court decisions provide evidence of legal precedent, making it relevant to similar contracts.

Hammersmith Ltd concludes that although the asset has no alternative use, there is no enforceable right to payments for performance completed to date as the contract can be cancelled at any time outside the control of Hammersmith Ltd. So, the criteria for over time recognition are not met and revenue on these real estate units can only be recognised upon delivery of the unit.

Figure 3.3 shows how Airbus determines which contracts to deliver aircraft meet the criteria for 'over time' recognition and which do not.

If a performance obligation is satisfied over time, an entity would recognise revenue over time by using a method that best reflects its progress in satisfying that performance obligation *(see section 3.7.2)*.

3.7.2 Measure of progress

When an entity has determined that a performance obligation is satisfied over time, paragraph 40 of IFRS 15 requires an entity to select a single revenue recognition method to measure the entity's progress in transferring the promised goods or services over time. In selecting the method that best reflects the transfer of the promised goods or services, the entity considers both the nature of the goods or services and the work to be performed by the entity. The selected method must be applied consistently to similar performance obligations and in similar circumstances, and the standard does not allow a change in methods. That is, a performance obligation is accounted for under the method the entity selects until it has been fully satisfied. However, the standard does require an entity to update its estimates related to the measure of progress selected at each reporting date. The effect of changes in the measure of progress is accounted for as a change in estimate under IAS 8 *Accounting Policies, Changes in Accounting Estimates and Errors*.

There are two methods for recognising revenue on arrangements involving the transfer of goods and services over time:

- **Output methods** — measure the value of goods or services transferred to date relative to the remaining goods or services promised under the agreement (e.g. surveys of performance completed to date, appraisals of results achieved, milestones reached, time elapsed and units produced or units delivered).

FIGURE 3.3 Point in time and over time recognition

Revenue recognition — Revenue is recognised when the Company transfers control of the promised goods or services to the customer. The Company measures revenue, for the consideration to which the Company is expected to be entitled in exchange for transferring promised goods or services. Variable considerations are included in the transaction price when it is highly probable that there will be no significant reversal of the revenue in the future. The Company identifies the various performance obligations of the contract and allocates the transaction price to these performance obligations. Advances and pre-delivery payments (contract liabilities) are received in the normal course of business and are not considered to be a significant financing component as they are intended to protect the Company from the customer failing to complete its contractual obligations.

Revenue from the sale of commercial aircraft is recognised at a point in time (*i.e.* at delivery of the aircraft). The Company estimates the amount of price concession granted by the Company's engine suppliers to their customers as a reduction of both revenue and cost of sales.

An aircraft can remain in storage under a bill-and-hold arrangement. In such cases, revenue is recognised when the requirements for the transfer of control under a bill-and-hold arrangement are fulfilled.

Revenue from the sale of military aircraft, space systems and services — When control of produced goods or rendered services is transferred over time to the customer, revenue is recognised over time, *i.e.* under the percentage of completion method ("PoC" method).

The Company transfers control over time when:

- it produces a good with no alternative use and the Company has an irrevocable right to payment (including a reasonable margin) for the work completed to date, in the event of contract termination at the convenience of customers (*e.g.* Tiger contract); or

- it creates a good which is controlled by the customer as the good is created or enhanced (*e.g.* Eurofighter contracts, some border security contracts, A400M development); or

- the customer simultaneously receives and consumes the benefits provided by the Company (*e.g.* maintenance contracts).

For the application of the over time method (PoC method), the measurement of progress towards complete satisfaction of a performance obligation is based on inputs (*i.e.* cost incurred).

When none of the criteria stated above have been met, revenue is recognised at a point in time. For instance, revenue is recognised at the delivery of aircraft under IFRS 15 from the sale of military transport aircraft, from the A400M launch contract and most of NH90 serial helicopters' contracts.

Source: Airbus SE 2023 financial statements, note 4, p. 13.

- **Input methods** — measure the inputs/efforts put in by the entity relative to the total expected inputs needed to transfer the promised goods or services to the customer (e.g. resources consumed, labour hours expended, costs incurred, time elapsed or machine hours used). Using a straight-line basis to recognise revenue is appropriate only if the entity's efforts or inputs are expended evenly throughout the period that an entity performs. This is illustrated in illustrative example 3.10.

ILLUSTRATIVE EXAMPLE 3.10 Revenue recognition over time

Hammersmith Ltd enters into a contract to build a house for £480,000 on 23 April 2024. Construction will start in September 2024 and is expected to be finished in the course of 2025. The contract meets the criteria for over time revenue recognition and Hammersmith Ltd uses an input method to measure progress, based on costs incurred.

At the balance sheet date 31 December 2024 costs incurred amount to £180,000 and Hammersmith Ltd expects to need another £240,000 to complete construction. Hammersmith also analyses the £180,000 costs incurred and concludes it does not contain inefficiencies, i.e. costs incurred can serve as a basis for estimating progress. The amount of revenue Hammersmith Ltd will recognise on this construction contract in 2024 is the transaction price multiplied by the percentage of costs incurred to the total expected costs.

$$£480,000 \times \left(£180,000 / \left(£180,000 + £240,000 \right) \right) = £205,714$$

If an entity does not have a reasonable basis to measure its progress, revenue is not recognised until the entity is able to measure its progress. However, in cases in which the entity is not able to reasonably estimate the amount of profit but is able to determine that a loss will not be incurred, the entity will recognise revenue but only up to the amount of the costs incurred, until the outcome/profit can be reasonably estimated.

3.7.3 Performance obligation satisfied at a point in time

For performance obligations in which control is not transferred over time, control is transferred at a point in time. In many situations, the determination of the point at which control is transferred is relatively straightforward. However, there are instances when this determination could be more complicated. To help entities determine the point in time when a customer obtains control of a particular good or service, the standard provides a non-exhaustive list of indicators of the transfer of control, as follows:

(a) The entity has a present right to payment for the asset.
(b) The asset's legal title is held by the customer.
(c) Physical possession of the asset has been transferred by the entity.
(d) The significant risks and rewards of ownership of the asset reside with the customer.
(e) The customer has accepted the asset.

These indicators are not individually determinative and no one indicator is more important than the others. Rather, an entity must consider all relevant facts and circumstances to determine when control has been transferred. Furthermore, this list of indicators is not intended to be a 'checklist'. That is, an entity does not need to meet all of these indicators to determine that the customer has gained control. Rather, they are just some common factors that are often present when a customer has obtained control of an asset.

3.8 CONTRACT COSTS

IFRS 15 requires an entity to capitalise, as an asset, two types of costs relating to a contract with a customer:
- any incremental costs to obtain the contract that would otherwise not have been incurred, if the entity expects to recover them;
- costs incurred to fulfil a contract with the customer, if certain criteria are met.
We will discuss these two types of costs further in section 3.8.1.

Any capitalised contract costs are then amortised on a systematic basis that reflects the pattern of transfer of the related promised goods or services to the customer. Entities will also have to assess any capitalised contract costs for impairment at the end of each reporting period. *See further discussion in section 3.8.2.*

3.8.1 Contract costs to be capitalised

Incremental costs to obtain a contract

Under IFRS 15, the costs that an entity incurs in order to obtain a contract are capitalised only if they are incremental and expected to be recoverable (IFRS 15 paragraph 91). Incremental refers to costs that would not have been incurred if the contract would not have been obtained. Recoverable means that the costs need to be either explicitly reimbursable under the contract or implicitly recoverable through the margin inherent in the contract. Costs that would have been incurred regardless of whether the contract is obtained or those costs that are not directly related to obtaining a contract would not be capitalisable.

To illustrate this distinction, consider the following examples:
- Sales commissions paid to an employee if a contract with a customer is successfully won would likely meet the requirements for capitalisation.
- Bonuses paid to an employee based on quantitative or qualitative metrics that are unrelated to winning a contract (e.g. profitability, earnings per share, performance evaluations) would likely not meet the criteria for capitalisation.

If the amortisation period of the incremental costs would be 1 year or less, an entity can choose to expense these costs immediately, as a practical expedient, instead of capitalising such costs.

Costs to fulfil a contract

IFRS 15 addresses the question of when and how much revenue to recognise from contracts with customers. It does not provide comprehensive guidance on when and how to recognise all related costs and refers the reader to other standards. This means that for all costs to fulfil a contract an entity will first have to determine if such contract fulfilment costs are within the scope of other standards (e.g. IAS 2 *Inventories*,

IAS 16 *Property, Plant and Equipment*, IAS 38 *Intangible Assets*). The requirements of IFRS 15 will apply only if such costs do not fall within the scope of other standards.

So, if an entity incurs costs to produce goods before it has entered into a contract with a customer, it applies IAS 2 or any other relevant standard to determine which of those costs can be capitalised and which are expensed. When subsequently a contract is entered into and the goods are sold, any costs incurred to satisfy that performance obligation are expensed (including the carrying amount of the inventory produced and delivered to the customer).

For the same reason, if an entity enters into a contract to construct an asset, but the criteria for over time revenue recognition are not met, any costs incurred to produce the asset are accounted for in accordance with the relevant standard such as IAS 2. At the point in time of revenue recognition any capitalised costs in relation to that performance obligation are expensed.

There may also be costs incurred necessary to fulfil a contract, but that do not transfer goods or services to the customer. For example, the entity may have to set up a software platform or train its personnel before it can deliver certain services to the customer it contracted with. Those costs may or may not benefit the entity beyond this specific contract with this customer. Again, IFRS 15 would require the entity to first look whether these expenditures are scoped within another standard. If they are not, IFRS 15 applies, which states (paragraph 95) that the costs incurred to fulfil a contract are capitalised only if all the following criteria are met:

(a) they are directly related to a specific contract or to a specific anticipated contract (e.g. direct labour, direct materials);

(b) they generate or enhance resources of the entity that will be used in satisfying (or in continuing to satisfy) performance obligations in the future; and

(c) they are expected to be recovered (*see discussion above on incremental costs to obtain a contract*).

If the above criteria are not met, an entity will expense the contract fulfilment costs as they are incurred. In assessing the above criteria, an entity must consider its specific facts and circumstances.

Criterion (a) above indicates that such costs may be incurred even before the related contract is finalised. However, such costs need to be associated with a specifically identifiable anticipated contract in order to be capitalisable. In illustrative example 3.11 a scenario is described in which certain costs to fulfil a contract are capitalised and others are expensed.

ILLUSTRATIVE EXAMPLE 3.11 Costs to fulfil a contract

IT Consultancy firm Bits & Bytes SE enters into a contract with a customer to deliver IT services. Before it can start providing these specific IT services, hardware of CU100,000 needs to be acquired together with related software (CU50,000). Bits & Bytes personnel working on this contract will get special training at a cost of CU20,000. Finally, design, data migration and other activities necessary to be able to provide the services under the contract amount to CU35,000.

Bits & Bytes SE considers that the accounting for the hardware is scoped within IAS 16, requiring it to capitalise the CU100,000. The acquired software is scoped within IAS 38, so it capitalises the CU50,000 as an intangible asset. The training costs of CU20,000 also are scoped within IAS 38, which requires these to be expensed as incurred as they do not meet the criteria for recognition of an intangible asset. Finally, the costs of designing, migrating and other activities are not scoped within any standard, so they fall within IFRS 15 and need to be assessed under the criteria mentioned in paragraph 95.

3.8.2 Amortisation and impairment of contract costs

An entity has to amortise any capitalised contract costs and recognise the expense in the statement of profit or loss. *As discussed earlier in the introduction to section 3.8*, an entity amortises the capitalised contract costs on a systematic basis that reflects the pattern of transfer of the related promised goods or services to the customer.

In some cases, the capitalised costs may relate to multiple goods and services that are transferred under multiple contracts. Entities will need to consider this aspect when determining the amortisation period to apply. Entities are also required to update the amortisation period to reflect a significant change in the expected timing of transfer to the customer of the goods or services to which the asset relates. Such a change would need to be treated as a change in accounting estimate under IAS 8.

Capitalised contract costs must continue to be recoverable throughout the arrangement. As such, any contract costs asset recognised under IFRS 15 is subject to an impairment assessment at the end of each reporting period. An impairment loss is recognised in the statement of profit or loss for the difference between:

- the carrying amount of the capitalised contract costs; and
- the remaining amount of consideration that an entity expects to receive in exchange for providing the associated goods and services, less the remaining costs that relate directly to providing those good and services.

3.9 OTHER APPLICATION ISSUES

3.9.1 Contract modifications

Paragraph 18 of IFRS 15 states that:

> A contract modification is a change in the scope or price (or both) of a contract that is approved by the parties to the contract. In some industries and jurisdictions, a contract modification may be described as a change order, a variation or an amendment. A contract modification exists when the parties to a contract approve a modification that either creates new or changes existing enforceable rights and obligations of the parties to the contract. A contract modification could be approved in writing, by oral agreement or implied by customary business practices. If the parties to the contract have not approved a contract modification, an entity shall continue to apply this Standard to the existing contract until the contract modification is approved.

As evident in the definition, an approved contract modification can be explicit or implicit; however, as long as it results in enforceable changes to the rights and obligations of the parties involved in the contract, it would need to be accounted for.

Once an entity has determined that a contract has been modified, the entity has to determine the appropriate accounting treatment under IFRS 15. Certain modifications are treated as separate, stand-alone contracts, while others are combined with the existing contract and accounted for together.

Two criteria must be met for a modification to be treated as a separate contract:

(a) The scope of the contract increases because of the promise of additional goods or services that are distinct from those already promised in the original contract.

This assessment is done in accordance with IFRS 15's requirements for determining whether promised goods and services are distinct *as discussed in section 3.4.1*. Although a contract modification may add a new good or service that would be distinct in a stand-alone transaction, the new good or service may not be distinct when it is considered within the context of a contract modification. Furthermore, only modifications that add distinct goods or services to the arrangement can be treated as separate contracts. Arrangements that reduce the amount of promised goods or services or change the scope of the original promised goods or services cannot, by their very nature, be considered separate contracts. Instead, they would be considered modifications of the original contract.

(b) The expected amount of consideration for the additional promised goods or services reflects the entity's stand-alone selling price(s) of those goods or services.

However, when determining the stand-alone selling price, entities have some flexibility to adjust that price, depending on the facts and circumstances. For example, a discount may be given to a customer who decides to purchase additional goods and the discount relates to selling-related costs that are only incurred for new customers. In this example, the entity may determine that the adjusted selling price meets the stand-alone selling price requirement, even though the discounted price is less than the stand-alone selling price of that good or service for a new customer.

If the two criteria are not met, the contract modification would be accounted for as a change to the original contract (i.e. not accounted for as a separate contract). Such types of contract modifications (which may include changes that modify or remove previously agreed-upon goods and services) may be accounted for in any of the following three ways depending on the specific facts and circumstances:

1. **Termination of the old contract and the creation of a new contract.**

This accounting treatment applies if the remaining goods or services after the contract modification are distinct from the goods or services transferred on or before the contract modification. Under this approach, an entity does not adjust the revenue previously recognised. Instead, the remaining portion of the original contract and the modification are accounted for, together, on a prospective basis by allocating the total remaining consideration to the remaining performance obligations.

2. **Continuation of the original contract.**

This accounting treatment applies if the remaining goods and services to be provided after the contract modification are not distinct from those already provided. That is, the remaining goods or services constitute part of a single performance obligation that is partially satisfied at the date of modification. Under this approach, the entity adjusts the revenue previously recognised, either up or down, for any changes to the transaction price and the measure of progress as a result of the contract modification, on a cumulative catch-up basis.

3. Modification of the existing contract and the creation of a new contract.

This accounting treatment is a combination of the two above treatments. In this case, an entity does not adjust the revenue previously recognised for the goods or services already transferred that are distinct from the modified goods or services.

However, for the transferred goods or services that are not distinct from the modified goods or services, the entity would have to adjust the revenue previously recognised, either up or down, for any changes to the estimated transaction price and the measure of progress as a result of the contract modification, on a cumulative catch-up basis.

Figure 3.4 provides a decision tree covering the four scenarios described above.

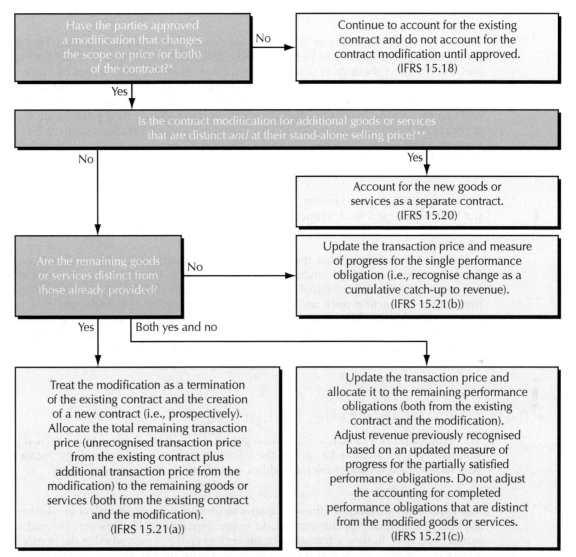

* Under IFRS 15, a contract modification can be approved in writing, by oral agreement or implied by customary business practices. IFRS 15.19 states that an entity may have to account for a contract modification prior to the parties reaching final agreement on changes in scope or pricing (or both), provided the rights and obligations that are created or changed by a modification are enforceable.

** In accordance with IFRS 15.20, an entity may make appropriate adjustments to the stand-alone selling price to reflect the circumstances of the contract and still meet the criteria to account for the modification as a separate contract.

FIGURE 3.4 Decision tree on accounting for contract modifications
Source: EY, International GAAP® 2024, chapter 27, section 3.4.

The various scenarios are illustrated in illustrative example 3.12.

ILLUSTRATIVE EXAMPLE 3.12 Contract modification

In July 20X1, construction company Hammer BV enters into a contract to construct a house for customer F for an amount of €1,200,000. Construction starts in October 20X1. Hammer BV concludes that the criteria for over time revenue recognition are met and uses an input method based on costs incurred to measure progress. On 31 December 20X1 Hammer has spent €500,000 on this construction and there are no inefficiencies. A further €500,000 is expected to be needed to complete construction. The amount of revenue recognised on this contract in 20X1 therefore is €500,000/€ 1,000,000 * €1,200,000 = €600,000.

Scenario A

In January 20X2, F asks Hammer BV to also build a shed on the same piece of land. The total consideration for the construction is increased by €50,000 to €1,250,000. Because the shed is not connected to the house and will not affect the costs of constructing the house itself, the price agreed by Hammer BV represents the stand-alone price of the shed. Hammer BV therefore concludes that the performance obligation under the modification, i.e. building the shed, is distinct from the performance obligation to build the house and that the increase in consideration represents its stand-alone selling price, so the modification of the contract is a separate contract under IFRS 15. Hammer BV also concludes the criteria for over time revenue recognition are met for the separate contract. Hammer BV recognises revenue separately for the house and the shed based upon the costs incurred for each of the house and shed respectively.

Scenario B

In January 20X2, F asks Hammer BV to make changes to the design of the part of the house that has not been constructed yet. Hammer BV and F agree on an increase in the transaction price of €350,000 resulting in a total price of €1,550,000. Hammer expects the total costs to increase from €1,000,000 to €1,250,000.

Hammer BV concludes that the services to be provided under the modification are not distinct from the services promised under the original contract. Therefore, this is not a separate contract, nor a termination of the original contract, but a continuation of the existing contract. Hammer BV updates the transaction price and the measure of progress on the single performance obligation (to construct the house). The total transaction price is now €1,550,000 and the measure of progress is €500,000/€1,250,000 = 40%, so the cumulative amount of revenue to be recognised is €620,000, resulting in a cumulative catch-up of revenue of €20,000 upon modification of the contract.

3.9.2 Licences of intellectual property

The standard provides separate application guidance specific to licences of intellectual property ('licences') that will apply to licences for any of the following: software and technology, media and entertainment (e.g. motion pictures and music), franchises, patents, trademarks and copyrights.

Determining whether a licence is distinct

The application guidance on licences applies to distinct licences regardless of whether they are promised explicitly or implicitly in the contract. In many transactions, licences may be sold together with other goods or services. In these circumstances, the entity needs to assess whether the licence is a separate performance obligation (i.e. whether the benefit derived from the licence can only be obtained when it is used together with another good or service or whether it can be of use to the customer on its own) *as discussed in section 3.4.1.*

If the licence is distinct, the entity then has to determine the nature of its promise to the customer (discussed further below) to determine if the licence revenue is recognised over time or at a point in time.

If the licence is not distinct, then an entity would look to the other requirements in IFRS 15 to account for the combined performance obligation that includes the licence. However, in some cases, it could be necessary for an entity to consider the nature of the entity's promise in granting a licence (discussed further below) even when the licence is not distinct (e.g. when the licence is the primary or dominant component of a combined performance obligation) in order to appropriately determine whether the performance obligation is satisfied over time or at a point in time and/or to determine the appropriate measure of progress.

Determining the nature of the entity's promise

For distinct licences (and in some cases, combined performance obligations for which the licence is the primary or dominant component), an entity must determine whether the licence is a 'right to access' or a 'right to use'.

If the entity has promised a customer a right to access the intellectual property (including any updates) throughout the licence period, revenue is recognised over time. In making this assessment as to whether the nature of the promise is a right to access, all of the following criteria must be met:

(a) the entity is required to (or the customer reasonably expects that the entity will) perform activities that significantly affect the intellectual property to which the licence relates, such as changes in form or functionality of the intellectual property of the ongoing activities of the entity to support or maintain the value of a brand name;

(b) the customer is directly exposed to any affects (both positive and negative) of those activities in (a) as a result of the rights granted under the licence; and

(c) the activities in (a) do not transfer any goods or services to the customer.

If the licenced intellectual property does not have the above characteristics, the nature of the entity's promise will be a right to use (i.e. the customer is granted the use of the intellectual property as it exists at the point in time in which the licence is granted). Therefore, the revenue for a right to use licence is recognised at a point in time.

It is critical for an entity to assess the above criteria and judgement will be required to assess whether a customer has a reasonable expectation that the entity will perform the relevant activities. For example, the existence of a shared economic interest between the parties (e.g. sales or usage-based royalties which are discussed further below) may be an indicator that the customer has a reasonable expectation for the entity to perform such activities. These activities need not be specifically linked to the contract but they can be part of an entity's ongoing business activities and customary business practices. Examples of right to use versus right to access can be found in illustrative example 3.13.

ILLUSTRATIVE EXAMPLE 3.13 Nature of licences

Scenario A

Archie SpA runs a digital archive of historical maps. Customers can buy a licence granting them the right to receive a digital copy of a specific map and use the intellectual property for a period of time to provide services to their own customers, for example by incorporating the information in their own software. Archie SpA is not required to update the digital copy for any technological developments, nor to provide any further services. Archie SpA concludes that after sending the digital copy of a map, it has no further obligations, so the criteria for 'right to access' are not met. Therefore, the licence is a right to use the intellectual property of Archie SpA and the licence fee is recognised as revenue at a point in time, the transfer of the right to use.

Scenario B

Beta NV develops anti-virus software. Customers enter into a licence to the software, which is continuously updated. Beta NV concludes that it is required throughout the licence period to undertake activities that significantly affect the intellectual property to which the customer has rights and that those activities benefit the customer and do not result in the transfer of goods or services. So, the criteria for right to access are met and revenue from the licence fee is recognised over time, during the period of the licence.

Sales or usage-based royalties on licences of intellectual property

IFRS 15 includes an exception to the accounting for variable consideration *(see section 3.5.1)* in which sales-based or usage-based royalties on licences of intellectual property are excluded from the estimate of variable consideration. Under the standard, these amounts are recognised only at the later of:

- when the subsequent sale or usage occurs; or
- the performance obligation to which some or all of the sales-based or usage-based royalty has been allocated is wholly or partially satisfied.

This exception is applicable to all licences of intellectual property, regardless of whether they have been determined to be distinct. However, the exception is not applicable to all arrangements involving sales or usage-based royalties. It only applies to sales- or usage-based royalties related to licences of intellectual property.

3.9.3 Principal versus agent considerations

In arrangements that have three or more parties, an entity will have to determine whether it is acting as a principal or an agent in order to determine the amount of revenue to which it is entitled. An entity is a principal (and, therefore, records revenue on a gross basis) if it controls a promised good or service before transferring that good or service to the customer (IFRS 15 paragraph B35). An entity is an agent (and, therefore, records as revenue the net amount that it retains for its agency services) if its role is to arrange for another entity to provide the goods or services (IFRS 15 paragraph B36).

Given that the identification of the principal and agent in a contract is not always straightforward, IFRS 15 provides the following indicators to help entities assess if they control the specified good or service before it is transferred to the customer:

(a) the entity has primary responsibility for fulfilling the contract
(b) the entity has inventory risk over the specified good transferred (or to be transferred)
(c) the entity has discretion in establishing the prices for the specified goods or services.

After an entity identifies its promise and determines whether it is the principal or the agent, the entity recognises the revenue to which it is entitled when it satisfies that performance obligation *(see section 3.7)*.

3.10 PRESENTATION AND DISCLOSURES

3.10.1 Presentation of contract assets, contract liabilities and revenue

Under the standard, when either party to a contract performs, a contract asset or contract liability must be recognised in the statement of financial position.

A contract liability arises if the customer performs first (e.g. by prepaying the promised consideration before the promised goods or services are transferred). Conversely, a contract asset represents an entity's conditional right to consideration from the customer when (or as) it satisfies a performance obligation under the contract. This right may be conditional because the entity must first satisfy another performance obligation in the contract before it is entitled to invoice the customer. When the entity's right to collect the consideration becomes unconditional (i.e. there is nothing other than the passage of time before the customer pays the entity), a receivable is recognised in place of the contract asset.

The standard does not require entities to specifically use the terms 'contract assets' or 'contract liabilities'. However, the standard does require that the unconditional rights to consideration (i.e. receivables) be clearly distinguished from the conditional rights to receive consideration (i.e. contract assets). After initial recognition, receivables and contract assets are subject to an impairment assessment in accordance with IFRS 9.

Other assets, such as capitalised contract costs *(see section 3.8)*, are required to be presented separately from contract assets and contract liabilities in the statement of financial position, if they are material. In addition, revenue from contracts with customers is required to be separately presented or disclosed from other sources of revenue.

3.10.2 Disclosure objective and general requirements

The overall disclosure objective is set out in paragraph 110 of IFRS 15:

> The objective of the disclosure requirements is for an entity to disclose sufficient information to enable users of financial statements to understand the nature, amount, timing and uncertainty of revenue and cash flows arising from contracts with customers.

As a result, qualitative and quantitative information about the following must be disclosed:

(a) contracts with customers *(see section 3.10.3)*;
(b) the significant judgements, and changes in the judgements, made in applying the standard *(see section 3.10.4)*; and
(c) any assets recognised from the costs to obtain or fulfil a contract with a customer *(see section 3.10.5)*.

Entities are required to ensure that useful information is not obscured by either the inclusion of a large amount of insignificant detail or the aggregation of items that have substantially different characteristics.

The disclosures are required for (and as at) each annual period for which a statement of comprehensive income and a statement of financial position are presented. The standard also requires information on disaggregated revenue in both an entity's annual and interim financial statements *(see section 3.10.3)*.

3.10.3 Disclosures on contracts with customers

These disclosures comprise information on disaggregation of revenue, contract asset and liability balances and an entity's performance obligations.

The main purpose of the disaggregated revenue disclosures is to illustrate how the nature, amount, timing and uncertainty about revenue and cash flows are affected by economic factors. Please note that these go beyond the revenue per segment disclosures already required by IFRS 8 *Operating Segments (see chapter 18)*. Entities would have to determine how they should present the disaggregated revenue information according to their facts and circumstances because the standard does not specify how revenue should be disaggregated. However, the application guidance suggests categories, including: by major product line, by country or region, by type of customer, by type of contract or by contract duration. This is illustrated in figure 3.5 which contains disaggregated revenue numbers for Sanofi. Sanofi has two operating segments, Biopharma and Consumer Healthcare, and reports revenue per product line and per region, next to the segment disclosures.

Furthermore, an entity is required to disclose:

- the opening and closing balances of receivables, contract assets and contract liabilities from contracts with customers, if not otherwise separately presented or disclosed;
- revenue recognised in the reporting period that was included in the contract liability balance at the beginning of the period; and
- revenue recognised in the reporting period from performance obligations satisfied (or partially satisfied) in previous periods (e.g. changes in transaction price).

In addition, an entity is required to explain the interaction between the revenue recognised and significant movements in the contract asset and the contract liability balances during the reporting period. This requires both qualitative and quantitative information to be disclosed, such as how the timing of satisfaction of the entity's performance obligations relates to the typical timing of payment and the effect that those factors have on the contract asset and the contract liability balances. This is illustrated in figure 3.6, which is an extract from the ASML Holding NV annual report 2023.

Separate disclosure of an entity's remaining performance obligations is also required, as well as the amount of the transaction price allocated to the remaining performance obligations and an explanation of the expected timing of recognition for those amount(s). This disclosure can be provided on either a quantitative basis (e.g. amounts to be recognised in given time bands, such as between 1 and 2 years or between 2 and 3 years) or by disclosing a mix of quantitative and qualitative information. This disclosure is important to provide insight into the order book of the entity and the impact on future revenue.

Note that there is a practical expedient exempting an entity from making these particular disclosures if the remaining performance obligation is for contracts with an original expected duration of less than 1 year or the entity is recognising revenue based on invoiced amounts.

3.10.4 Significant judgements

IFRS 15 requires an entity to disclose the significant accounting estimates and judgements made in applying Steps 3–5 of the model in IFRS 15 *(see section 3.1)*. These requirements are in addition to the requirements in IAS 1 *Presentation of Financial Statements*.

Entities will need to exercise significant judgement when applying the model in IFRS 15, such as when estimating the variable consideration included in the transaction price and application of the constraint (Step 3), when estimating the stand-alone selling prices used to allocate the transaction price (Step 4) and when measuring obligations for returns, refunds and other similar obligations. Paragraph 126 of IFRS 15 requires entities to disclose qualitative information about the methods, inputs and assumptions used in all of the above judgements in their annual financial statements.

IFRS 15 also requires entities to provide disclosures about the significant judgements made in determining when performance obligations are satisfied. For performance obligations that are satisfied over time, entities must disclose the output or input method used to recognise revenue and how the selected method reflects the pattern of goods or services that are transferred.

For performance obligations satisfied at a point in time, entities must disclose the significant judgements made in determining the point at which the entity transfers control of the promised goods or services to the customer.

3.10.5 Assets recognised from the costs to obtain or fulfil a contract

IFRS 15 requires entities to disclose information on contract costs that are capitalised to help users understand the amounts and types of costs that have been capitalised, the amortisation methods applied or any impairment losses that have been recognised. The information includes an explanation of any judgements made in applying the requirements under IFRS 15.

FIGURE 3.5 Disaggregation of revenue

D.35.1.1. Analysis of net sales

The table below sets forth Sanofi's net sales for the years ended December 31, 2023, 2022 and 2021:

(€ million)	Europe	United States	Other countries	2023	Europe	United States	Other countries	2022[a]	Europe	United States	Other countries	2021[b]
Biopharma	8,835	17,265	11,790	37,890	8,498	16,985	12,329	37,812	8,426	13,246	11,621	33,293
Specialty Care	3,206	11,917	2,917	18,040	3,016	10,848	2,593	16,457	2,764	7,847	2,141	12,752
of which DUPIXENT	1,224	8,145	1,346	10,715	940	6,346	1,007	8,293	649	3,971	629	5,249
AUBAGIO	437	460	53	955	511	1,420	100	2,031	512	1,312	131	1,955
CEREZYME	229	189	269	687	239	194	274	707	244	173	266	683
FABRAZYME	241	503	247	991	228	471	239	938	223	395	226	844
MYOZYME/LUMIZYME	341	254	188	783	408	318	232	958	410	373	220	1,003
JEVTANA	12	230	78	320	33	275	83	391	112	253	90	455
ALPROLIX	—	440	100	540	—	406	98	504	—	332	82	414
ELOCTATE	—	341	130	471	—	450	130	580	—	429	134	563
General Medicines	3,932	2,084	6,360	12,376	4,141	2,846	7,140	14,127	4,437	2,637	7,144	14,218
Core Assets	1,988	1,485	2,797	6,270	1,917	1,653	2,819	6,389	1,868	1,315	2,585	5,768
of which LOVENOX	622	7	496	1,125	658	17	635	1,310	703	29	754	1,486
TOUJEO	441	213	469	1,123	421	283	413	1,117	394	259	316	969
PLAVIX	96	8	844	948	101	9	873	983	115	9	805	929
Non-Core Assets	1,396	592	3,536	5,524	1,637	1,176	4,305	7,118	1,846	1,281	4,515	7,642
of which LANTUS	357	281	782	1,420	426	757	1,076	2,259	474	861	1,159	2,494
Other non-core assets	961	302	2,424	3,687	1,129	412	2,840	4,381	1,285	410	3,034	4,729
Industrial sales	548	7	27	582	587	17	16	620	723	41	44	808
Vaccines	1,697	3,264	2,513	7,474	1,341	3,291	2,596	7,228	1,225	2,762	2,336	6,323
of which Polio/Pertussis/Hib Vaccines	297	398	1,470	2,165	325	456	1,504	2,285	306	470	1,383	2,159
Influenza Vaccines	694	1,406	569	2,669	681	1,737	559	2,977	729	1,366	533	2,628
Consumer Healthcare	1,557	1,247	2,376	5,180	1,501	1,290	2,394	5,185	1,333	1,139	1,996	4,468
of which Allergy	70	412	287	769	55	439	276	770	49	371	192	612
Pain Care	502	180	424	1,106	555	212	424	1,140	515	196	382	1,093
Digestive Wellness	520	138	844	1,502	432	144	822	1,449	389	124	618	1,131
Total net sales	10,392	18,512	14,166	43,070	9,999	18,275	14,723	42,997	9,759	14,385	13,617	37,761

(a) 2022 figures have been adjusted to take account of the two new operating segments, Biopharma and Consumer Healthcare, effective January 1, 2023.

(b) Due to a lack of available data and the complex adjustments that would be required (particularly for our reporting tools), the 2021 figures have not been restated to reflect changes arising from our new organizational structure.

Source: Sanofi, Form 20-F 2023, note D.35.1.1, p. F-93.

FIGURE 3.6 Interaction between contract assets and liabilities, revenue and cash flows

CONTRACT assets and liabilities

The contract assets relate to our right to a consideration in exchange for goods or services delivered, when that right is conditional on something other than the passage of time. The contract assets are transferred to the receivables when the receivables become unconditional. The contract liabilities primarily relate to remaining performance obligations for which consideration has been received for systems not yet recognized in revenue, as well as deferred revenue from system shipments, based on the allocation of the consideration to the related performance obligations in the contract.

The majority of our customer contracts result in both asset and liability positions. At the end of each reporting period, these positions are netted on a contract basis and presented as either an asset or a liability in the Consolidated Statement of Financial Position. Consequently, a contract balance can change between periods from a net contract asset balance to a net contract liability balance in the balance sheet. Significant changes in the contract assets and the contract liabilities balances during the periods are as follows.

Year ended December 31 (€, in millions)	2022		2023	
	Contract Assets	Contract Liabilities	Contract Assets	Contract Liabilities
Balance at beginning of the year	164.6	11,160.9	131.9	17,750.9
Transferred from contract assets to accounts receivables	(393.4)	—	(402.0)	—
Revenue recognized during the year ending in contract assets	116.5	—	135.1	—
Revenue recognized that was included in contract liabilities	—	(6,326.6)	—	(11,106.1)
Changes as a result of cumulative catch-up adjustments arising from changes in estimates	—	(118.0)	—	(24.9)
Remaining performance obligations for which considerations have been received, or for which we have an unconditional right to consideration	—	12,790.4	—	9,416.3
Transfer between contract assets and liabilities	244.2	244.2	375.1	375.1
Other	—	—	—	(144.8)
Total	131.9	17,750.9	240.1	16,266.5

The decrease in the net contract liabilities to €16.0 billion as of December 31, 2023 compared to €17.6 billion as of December 31, 2022 is mainly driven by a lower volume of fast shipment systems shipped for which revenue has not yet been recognized. This is partially offset by an increase of down payments for systems which will be shipped in the future. Cumulative catch-up adjustments recognized in our current year revenue are due to updated estimates for system volume, discounts and credits included in our volume purchase agreements.

Source: ASML Holding NV. Annual report 2023, note 2, pp. 256–257.

3.10.6 Practical expedients

In addition, IFRS 15 has several practical expedients that entities can elect to use. If either or both of the practical expedients relating to a significant financing component *(see section 3.5.2)* or incremental costs of obtaining a contract *(see section 3.8.1)* are applied, the entity must disclose this fact.

3.11 SUMMARY

IFRS 15 specifies the accounting treatment for all revenue arising from contracts with customers. It applies to all entities that enter into contracts to provide goods or services to their customers, unless the contracts are within the scope of other IFRS Standards. The standard outlines the principles an entity must apply to measure and recognise revenue and the related cash flows. Under the standard, an entity applies the five-step model outlined in *sections 3.3–3.7* to recognise revenue at an amount that reflects the consideration to which the entity expects to be entitled in exchange for transferring goods or services to a customer. In addition, entities are required to disclose significant judgements made in applying the five-step model as well as disaggregating revenue to provide users insight into the various types of revenue and their nature, amount, timing and uncertainties.

Discussion questions

1. What are the main accounting issues associated with the recognition of revenue and how does IFRS 15 address those?
2. What is the five-step model in connection with revenue recognition?
3. What is the distinction between revenue and income?
4. Why might it be necessary to combine individual contracts?
5. Describe some common forms of variable consideration.
6. Explain the disclosure objectives and general requirements of IFRS 15.

Reference

EY, 2024, International GAAP® 2024, Chapter 32: Revenue from contracts with customers (IFRS 15).

Perhaps no other line-item in the income statement invites as much scrutiny as the top line of sales (or, revenues). Wagenhofer (2014)[1] states that 'Revenue is one of the most important measures of companies' financial performance'. He bases this assertion, in part, on reference to analysts' view of revenues as hard to manipulate, persistent and more responsive to underlying changes in the business environment than expenses. There is only scant research on the effects of IFRS 15 on the value-relevance of earnings. Onie et al. (2023) find in Australia that the adoption of IFRS 15 has not improved the value-relevance of earnings.

If revenues are so important to users of financial statements, we would expect them to be highly value-relevant and perhaps more so than other numbers in the financial statements. Ertimur et al. (2003) analyse market reaction to earnings surprises. They claim that expenses reported in the income statement aggregate variety of expense types, which makes this information harder to analyse than revenues. Consistent with this argument they find that surprises in revenues are incorporated into prices with a larger magnitude than surprises in expenses. Jegadeesh and Livnat (2006) extend this line of research. They examine the relation between both earnings surprises and revenue surprises on one hand and current and future stock return on the other hand. They are motivated by the question of whether any reaction to earnings surprises is driven by news about revenue growth or contraction of costs (or vice versa). They show that both earnings surprises and revenue surprises are associated with current and future stock returns. However, the association with current returns is considerably weaker for revenue surprises. At the same time, future stock returns are more closely associated with current revenue surprises than current earnings surprises. This suggests that market participants may under-react to the information content in the revenue surprises.

Revenues cannot be recognised without the recognition of costs of expenses associated with the revenue-generation process. This is broadly known as the matching process. The Conceptual Framework (IASB 2018, section 5.5) describes the process of matching as the: 'simultaneous recognition of income and related expenses', and which must comply with the definitions of assets, liabilities and equity. Dichev and Tang (2008) argue that more recent standards deviate from the previous tradition of matching expenses to revenues on some other basis than changes in the balance sheet. Dichev and Tang (2008) posit that poor matching is manifested in lower correlation between revenues and expenses, higher variability of earnings and lower persistence. Examining a long period (1967–2003), they find lower association between current expenses and current revenues for the sub-period of 1986–2003 than the earlier period of 1967–1985. Moreover, consistent with Givoly and Hayn (2000), they find evidence of early recognition of expenses in the latter sub-period, which is indicative of increasing conservatism. In addition, Dichev and Tang (2008) find that earnings persistence declined in the latter period relative to the earlier period.

While Dichev and Tang's (2008) paper is consistent with the notion of poorer matching in recent years, a limitation of their study is the way they define expenses. Specifically, expenses are captured as the difference between revenues and profits. Hence, their study is silent on which expense line-item contributes the most to the documented decline in matching. Donelson et al. (2011) take up this task by looking at cost of goods sold; selling, general, and administrative expense; depreciation; taxes; other income/expenses and special items. Their evidence suggests that the decline in the association between revenues and expenses is mostly attributable to special items. Special items include a variety of 'one-off' events, such as impairments and restructuring charges. Once these one-off items are excluded, Donelson et al. (2011) find no evidence of poorer matching in recent years.

The US Securities and Exchange Commission (SEC) raised the concern that firms advance recognition of revenues. As a result, the SEC issued in 1999 Staff Accounting Bulletin (SAB) No. 101. The essence of this pronouncement is the tightening of revenue recognition criteria to reduce the incidence of premature revenue recognition. To the extent that the new regulation was effective, it is expected that firms that had to adopt SAB 101 would exhibit evidence of greater earnings management before adoption than after it. Altamuro et al. (2005) investigate this hypothesis. They find evidence suggesting that firms that adopted SAB 101 managed earnings more prior to adoption and less subsequently. This is supportive for the motivation behind the SEC's decision to pass SAB 101. This also speaks to the success of this promulgation. To provide further support for this result and remove suspicion it only captures time effect, Altamuro et al. (2005) compare earnings management in firms that were unaffected by SAB 101 around adoption time. Unlike firms subject to SAB 101, unaffected firms do not exhibit a decline in earnings management following the enactment of SAB 101.

References

Altamuro, J., Beatty, A.L., and Weber, J., 2005. The effects of accelerated revenue recognition on earnings management and earnings informativeness: Evidence from SEC Staff Accounting Bulletin No. 101. *The Accounting Review*, 80, 373–401.

Dichev, I.D., and Tang, V.W., 2008. Matching and the changing properties of accounting earnings over the last 40 years. *The Accounting Review*, 83, 1425–1460.

Donelson, D.C., Jennings, R., and McInnis, J., 2011. Changes over time in the revenue–expense relation: Accounting or economics? *The Accounting Review*, 86, 945–974.

Ertimur, Y., Livnat, J., and Martikainen, M., 2003. Differential market reactions to revenue and expense surprises. *Review of Accounting Studies*, 8, 185–211.

---

[1]This paper provides a more extensive review of the literature and is recommended for the interested reader.

Givoly, D., and Hayn, C., 2000. The changing time-series properties of earnings, cash flows and accruals: Has financial reporting become more conservative? *Journal of Accounting and Economics*, 29, 287–320.

IASB, 2018. The Conceptual Framework for Financial Reporting. London: IASB.

Jegadeesh, N., and Livnat, J., 2006. Revenue surprises and stock returns. *Journal of Accounting and Economics*, 41, 147–171.

Onie, S., Ma, L., Spiropoulos, H., and Wells, P., 2023. An evaluation of the impacts of the adoption of IFRS 15 Revenue from Contracts with Customers. *Accounting & Finance*, 63, 953–973.

Securities and Exchange Commission (SEC), 1999. Revenue recognition. Staff Accounting Bulletin No. 101. Washington DC: Government Printing Office.

Wagenhofer A., 2014. The role of revenue recognition in performance reporting. *Accounting and Business Research*, 44, 349–379.

4 Inventories

ACCOUNTING STANDARDS IN FOCUS

IAS 2 *Inventories*

LEARNING OBJECTIVES

After studying this chapter, you should be able to:

 1   discuss the nature of inventories

 2   explain how to measure inventories

 3   explain what is included in the cost of inventory

 4   account for inventory transactions using both the periodic and the perpetual methods

 5   explain and apply end-of-period procedures for inventory under both periodic and perpetual methods

 6   explain why cost flow assumptions are required and apply both FIFO and weighted average cost formulas

 7   explain the net realisable value basis of measurement and account for adjustments to net realisable value

 8   identify the amounts to be recognised as inventory expenses

 9   implement the disclosure requirements of IAS 2.

4.1 INTRODUCTION

For many companies, especially in retail and manufacturing, inventory is one of the most important assets. In the statement of financial position, it makes up a significant proportion of current assets of such entities. In addition, cost of sales (which is directly related to the measurement of inventory) is normally the largest expense on the income statement.

For companies that use IFRS, the main accounting standard when reporting inventories is IAS 2 *Inventories*. This is the standard that is central to this chapter. The standard was originally issued in December 1993 when it replaced IAS 2 *Valuation and Presentation of Inventories in the Context of the Historical Cost System* (issued in October 1975) and has been amended several times.

This chapter discusses accounting for inventory as follows:
- nature of inventories — the definition of inventory and the scope of the standard IAS 2 (section 4.2)
- initial recognition of inventory — the measurement principles for inventory (section 4.3) and determining the cost of inventory acquired or made (section 4.4)
- recording of inventory transactions using either the periodic or perpetual inventory methods (section 4.5), including end-of-period procedures and adjustments (section 4.6)
- assignment of costs to inventory using the first-in, first-out (FIFO), weighted average cost formulas or other measurement techniques (section 4.7)
- measurement subsequent to initial recognition — determining the amount at which the asset is reported subsequent to acquisition, including any write-down to net realisable value (section 4.8)

4.2 THE NATURE OF INVENTORIES

Before we discuss how inventory is recognised, measured and reported in financial statements, it is important to understand the nature of inventories under IFRS. In this section, we take a closer look at the definition, classification and scope of the inventory accounting standard IAS 2.

4.2.1 Definition

Assets used by the entity are classified based on their nature, which may place them under IAS 2 or other standards. For example, IAS 16 *Property, Plant and Equipment* covers tangible assets like production equipment, and IAS 38 *Intangible Assets* covers intangible assets such as patents. IAS 2 specifically addresses items that are intended for sale or are in the process of being produced for sale or consumed in that process. Assets must be appropriately classified based on their intended use and role in the production process, and the definitions in the standards provide guidance for the classification.

Paragraph 6 of IAS 2 defines inventories as follows:

> Inventories are assets:
> (a) held for sale in the ordinary course of business;
> (b) in the process of production for such sale; or
> (c) in the form of materials or supplies to be consumed in the production process or in the rendering of services.

This definition clarifies that there are different types of inventories. For example, inventories include goods or other assets purchased for resale, but also raw materials and components purchased for consumption during production of those products or the rendering of services. It includes finished goods, but also products and services in intermediate stages of completion. Usually, three types of inventory are distinguished: finished goods, raw materials and work in progress.

Holding an asset for sale does not automatically mean it is classified as inventory. The term 'inventories' applies only when the asset that is held for sale is intended for sale in the ordinary course of business. Finished goods inventory, for example, are assets intended for sale in the ordinary course of business. In contrast, if an entity decides to sell equipment that it previously used for production, this equipment would typically not be classified as inventories because it is not held for sale in the ordinary course of business.

IAS 2, paragraph 6(c), includes in its definition of inventories the 'materials or supplies to be consumed in the production process or in the rendering of services'. This connects to IAS 16, paragraph 8, which states that spare parts, standby equipment and servicing equipment are classified as inventory unless they meet the definition of property, plant and equipment. This illustrates that the distinction between inventory and other classes of assets can be complex, as it depends on the intended use and role of the items within the production process. For example, items regularly consumed during production, such as fasteners (bolts, nuts and screws) for a car manufacturer are treated as inventory. Conversely, items like stationery are not considered inventories unless they are held for sale or used in the production of saleable goods.

4.2.2 Classification

Inventories are classified as current assets if they meet the conditions in IAS 1 *Presentation of Financial Statements*, which they typically do. Based on paragraph 66 of IAS 1, assets are current assets if they satisfy the following criteria:

- the asset is expected to be realised in, or is intended for sale or consumption in the entity's normal operating cycle
- it is held primarily for the purpose of being traded
- it is expected to realise the asset within 12 months after the reporting period, or
- it is cash or a cash equivalent as defined in IAS 7 *Statement of Cash Flows* unless the asset is restricted from being exchanged or used to settle a liability for at least 12 months after the reporting period

The operating cycle of an entity, defined in IAS 1, paragraph 68, is the time between acquiring assets for processing and their realisation in cash or cash equivalents. While the operating cycle may be short in industries like retailing, it can span several years in industries such as winemaking. If the operating cycle is not clearly identifiable, it is assumed to be 12 months.

To illustrate, LVMH, a French multinational company specialising in luxury goods, prepares its financial statements in accordance with IFRS. In its 2023 statement of financial position, LVMH reports a total amount of €22,952 million in Inventories (53% of its current assets). The extract from LVMH's notes to the consolidated financial statements at 31 December 2023, as shown in figure 4.1, illustrates what is contained in inventories.

FIGURE 4.1 Extract from Note 11 Inventories and work in progress to the consolidated financial statements 2023 of LVMH

(EUR millions)	2023	2022
	Net	Net
Wines and *eaux-de-vie* in the process of aging	6,582	5,932
Other raw materials and work in progress	4,559	4,187
	11,141	**10,120**
Goods purchased for resale	2,650	2,410
Finished products	9,161	7,790
	11,811	**10,200**
Total	**22,952**	**20,319**

Source: LVMH, Consolidated Financial Statements, 31 December 2023, p. 30.

4.2.3 Scope

According to paragraph 2 of IAS 2, the standard applies to all inventories except financial instruments and biological assets related to agricultural activity and agricultural produce at the point of harvest (IAS 41 *Agriculture*). Work in progress is scoped in IFRS 15 *Revenue from Contracts with Customers* unless it gives rise to inventories (or assets within the scope of another standard).

Developments in business practices and technology may pose challenges to the application of the scope and recognition requirements of IAS 2. The discussion considering broadcast rights, emission rights and crypto assets demonstrates how the logic of IAS 2 is interpreted and applied in such situations.

Broadcast rights

Media companies, such as Netflix, the BBC or the RTL Group, acquire programmes through various arrangements, often committing to purchase them at an early development stage, sometimes even as mere concepts. They may obtain exclusive broadcasting rights or limited rights to broadcast for a specific period or number of times. However, IFRS accounting standards do not provide clear guidance on how to classify and recognise these rights.

In many cases broadcast rights would be considered intangible assets, as defined by IAS 38, which explicitly includes licencing rights for items like motion picture films and video recordings within its scope. However, rights to programmes intended for sale in the ordinary course of business to other parties qualify as inventory under IAS 2. Similarly, acquired rights for a broadcaster's programming schedule can be seen as 'materials or supplies to be consumed in the production process or in the rendering of services', also falling under the scope of IAS 2 (paragraph 6). The appropriate classification depends on the particular facts and circumstances. As an illustration, consider the disclosures on programme rights by the RTL Group, a media conglomerate based in Luxembourg. In its consolidated financial statements for 2023, the RTL Group reports an amount of €1,562 million of current program rights (38% of its current assets) which are essentially classified as inventory. Figure 4.2 shows a fragment of the accounting policy for current program rights, as described in Note 1.11 to the consolidated financial statements of the RTL Group.

FIGURE 4.2 Extract from Note 1.11 Current programme rights to the consolidated financial statements 2023 of the RTL Group

RTL Group, Consolidated Financial Statements

1.11 Current programme rights

Current programme rights are initially recognised at acquisition cost or Group production cost when the Group controls, in substance, the respective assets and the risks and rewards attached to them. Current programme rights include programmes in progress, (co-)productions and rights acquired with the primary intention to broadcast or sell them in the normal course of the Group's operating cycle. Current programme rights include an appropriate portion of overheads and are stated at the lower of cost and net realisable value. The net realisable value assessment is based on the advertising revenue expected to be generated when broadcast, and on estimated net sales. Weak audience shares or changes from a prime-time to a late-night slot constitute indicators that a valuation allowance may be applicable. They are consumed based on either the expected number of transmissions or expected revenue in order to match the costs of consumption with the benefits received. The rates of consumption applied for broadcasting rights are as follows:
- Free television thematic channels: programme rights are consumed on a straight-line basis over a maximum of six runs
- Free television other channels:
  - Blockbusters (films with high cinema ticket sales), mini-series (primarily own productions with a large budget), other films, series, TV movies and (co-)productions are consumed, run by run, over a maximum of four transmissions following a degressive approach for amortisation depending on the agreed total number of transmissions
  - Soaps, in-house productions, quiz and game shows, sports and other events, documentaries and music shows are fully consumed upon the first transmission
  - Children's programmes and cartoons are consumed over the licence period on a linear basis as there is a very slow saturation and a very high number of repetitions for the target group kids (three to 13-year-olds)
- Pay television channels: programme rights are consumed on a straight-line basis over the licence period.

Source: RTL Group, Consolidated Financial Statements, 31 December 2023, pp. 114–115.

Emission rights

To encourage the reduction of pollutants, governments worldwide have introduced schemes involving tradeable emissions allowances or permits. For example, the European Union launched an Emissions Trading System (EU ETS) in 2005 to facilitate compliance with its greenhouse gas emissions reduction targets. Companies can receive emission allowances from the government or purchase these rights from a third party. The accounting for emission rights is not clear-cut and remains a topic of discussion. However, companies must choose and consistently apply an accounting policy for emission rights, whether granted by the government or purchased.

At the time of writing, there is no specific IFRS standard for these rights, or 'pollutant pricing mechanisms' more generally. This leads to diversity in how such mechanisms are accounted for. Under IFRS, emissions rights held by an emitter are often classified as intangible assets, as defined under IAS 38. Alternatively, in some cases, emission rights are classified as inventory within the scope of IAS 2. Emissions allowances can arguably be considered an input in the production process and, as such, recognised as inventory in accordance with IAS 2. When granted or purchased emission rights are recognised as inventories, the measurement requirements of IAS 2 are subsequently applied.

If an entity acquires emissions rights with the intention of selling them to another market participant in the ordinary course of business, then the company would be acting as a broker or trader. In such circumstances, emissions allowances would still be classified as inventory, but they would be considered commodities, thus meeting the broker-trader exemption (paragraph 3.b of IAS 2). Broker-traders account for emission rights as inventory and may measure them at either the lower of cost and net realisable value or at fair value less costs to sell, as permitted by IAS 2.

It is important for companies to consider the nature of the arrangement and the business purpose for which they purchased or received the emission rights. In the absence of a specific IFRS standard, the facts and circumstances determine whether the emission allowances should be classified as intangible assets or inventory.

Crypto assets

Crypto assets, or more specifically cryptocurrencies, have very distinct characteristics due to their unique digital nature. In recent years, numerous cryptocurrencies have been launched, of which Bitcoin is the most widely known. Although there is currently no specific IFRS standard to address the classification and measurement of these assets, the IFRS Interpretation Committee (IFRS IC) has discussed how the IFRS accounting standards apply to holdings of crypto assets. In their agenda decision in June 2019, the IFRS IC listed the following characteristics of cryptocurrencies:

(a) a digital or virtual currency recorded on a distributed ledger that uses cryptography for security
(b) not issued by a jurisdictional authority or other party
(c) does not give rise to a contract between the holder and another party.

The IFRS IC concluded that cryptocurrencies meet the definition of an intangible asset. However, this does not automatically imply that cryptocurrencies are in scope of IAS 38 *Intangible Assets*. Intangible assets that are held for sale in the ordinary course of business, are in scope of IAS 2. This could be the case when a commodity broker-trader holds cryptocurrencies. In that circumstance, a broker-trader would classify its holding of cryptocurrency as inventory and IAS 2 would apply. The IFRS IC noted that in practice, crypto assets are generally not used in the production of inventory, and therefore they would normally not be considered 'materials and supplies to be consumed in the production process'. The IFRS IC concluded that if IAS 2 is not applicable, an entity applies IAS 38 to holdings of cryptocurrencies.

The examples of broadcasting rights, emission allowances and cryptocurrencies illustrate how developments in business and practice lead to debate on the scope and application of existing standards. For IAS 2, the discussion on these issues further clarified the nature of inventories, for example by reemphasizing that IAS 2 does not require inventory to be tangible.

4.3 MEASUREMENT OF INVENTORY

According to paragraph 9 of IAS 2, 'Inventories shall be measured at the lower of cost and net realisable value'. As the purpose of acquiring or manufacturing inventory items is to sell them at a profit, inventory will initially be recognised at cost. Net realisable value is defined as 'the estimated selling price in the ordinary course of business less the estimated costs of completion and the estimated costs necessary to make the sale'. This differs from fair value, which IAS 2 (paragraph 6) defines according to IFRS 13 *Fair Value Measurement* as 'the price that would be received to sell an asset or paid to transfer a liability in an orderly transaction between market participants at the measurement date'.

The main difference between net realisable value and fair value is that net realisable value is entity-specific, representing the amount the entity actually expects to realise from selling the inventory in the ordinary course of business. In contrast, fair value is not entity-specific; it reflects the price at which an orderly transaction to sell the same inventory would occur between market participants in the principal (or most advantageous) market at the measurement date. Consequently, net realisable value may differ from fair value less costs to sell.

Two specific industry groups have been exempted from applying the lower of cost and net realisable value rule (IAS 2 paragraph 3), namely:

(a) producers of agricultural and forest products, agricultural produce after harvest and minerals and mineral products, to the extent that they are measured at net realisable value in accordance with well-established practices in those industries. (. . .)
(b) commodity broker-traders who measure their inventories at fair value less costs to sell

In these cases, movements in net realisable value or fair value less costs to sell incurred during the period are recognised in profit or loss. Where inventories in these industries are measured by reference to historical cost, the lower of cost and net realisable value rule mandated by paragraph 9 would still apply.

In both cases, the standard stresses that these inventories are only scoped out from the measurement requirements of IAS 2; the standard's other requirements, such as disclosure, continue to apply.

The measurement rule in IAS 2 highlights two concepts: 'cost' and 'net realisable value'. The cost principle is a fundamental concept in inventory, and we discuss the complexities of its application in the next sections. In section 4.8 we shift the attention to the concept of net realisable value.

4.4 DETERMINATION OF COST

The first step in accounting for inventory is its initial recognition at cost. Identifying the cost is an important step, as it determines both the costs of goods sold and the value of inventory on the statement of financial position (the closing inventory). IAS 2, paragraph 10, specifies three components of cost:

- costs of purchase
- costs of conversion
- other costs incurred in bringing the inventories to their present location and condition.

We discuss each of the three components separately in this section.

4.4.1 Costs of purchase

Under IAS 2, the cost of purchase includes more than just the price paid for acquiring the inventory. Paragraph 11 of IAS 2 states that 'the costs of purchase of inventories comprise the purchase price, import duties and other taxes (other than those subsequently recoverable by the entity from the taxing authorities), and transport, handling and other costs directly attributable to the acquisition of finished goods, materials and services. Trade discounts, rebates and other similar items are deducted in determining the costs of purchase'.

Below, each of the elements of the cost of purchase are briefly discussed:

1. *Purchase price*

Usually, where an item of inventory is acquired for cash or short-term credit, determination of the purchase price is relatively straightforward. In the case that some or all of the cash payment is deferred, as noted in paragraph 18 of IAS 2, the purchase cost contains a financing element — the difference between the amount paid and a purchase on normal credit terms — which must be recognised as interest expense over the period of deferral.

2. *Import duties and other taxes (other than those subsequently recoverable by the entity from the taxing authorities)*

Taxes are included in the cost of purchase, unless they are recoverable. Effectively this means that most transaction taxes are explicitly excluded from the cost of purchase. Many countries levy taxes on transactions involving the exchange of goods and services, requiring buyers to pay these taxes at the point of purchase. If such a 'goods and services tax' or 'value added tax' exists, care must be taken to exclude these amounts from the costs of purchase if they are recoverable by the entity from the taxing authorities.

3. *Transport, handling and other costs directly attributable to the acquisition of finished goods, materials and services*

This means any expenses incurred to bring these items to their current location and condition for use or sale, such as shipping fees, import duties and delivery charges, should be added to the purchase cost. This approach aligns with other IFRS standards and the IASB's conceptual framework, which emphasise the need to recognise all costs necessary to bring an asset to its present location and condition.

4. *Trade discounts, rebates and other similar items*

Trade discounts are reductions in the selling price that a seller offers to its customers. These discounts can serve various purposes: they can incentivise purchases, help clear out ageing inventory, or reward customers for placing large orders. IAS 2 explicitly requires that trade discounts, rebates and other similar items be treated as deductions from the cost of purchase.

Settlement discounts, also known as cash discounts, are incentives offered by the supplier to encourage early payment of credit sales. Unlike trade discounts, these discounts are directly linked to the credit terms of the purchase. For example, a supplier might offer a 2% discount if payment is made within 10 days instead of the usual 30 days. IAS 2 does not provide specific guidance on the accounting treatment of settlement discounts by the buyer. However, in November 2004, the IFRS IC issued an agenda decision stating that 'settlement discounts should be deducted from the cost of inventories'. This means that if inventory costs €1,000 and a 2% settlement discount is available, the inventory should be recorded at €980 if the discount is taken. The committee also clarified that 'rebates that specifically and genuinely refund selling expenses should not be deducted from the cost of inventories'. But what is the appropriate accounting if the discount is available, but the buyer does not take advantage of it? In the previous example: what happens if the company pays after 10 days and therefore pays the full amount? In the absence of authoritative guidance on this issue, there are essentially two approaches to account for discounts that are not taken. The first approach is to still record the inventory at the net amount as if the discount had been taken. The difference between the amount actually paid and the discounted price is treated as a finance charge. This finance charge reflects the cost of not taking advantage of the discount, which is essentially an additional financing cost. The alternative approach is to record the inventory at the full amount paid if the discount is not taken, as long as the payment terms are within normal credit terms.

4.4.2 Costs of conversion

Costs of conversion appear only in manufacturing entities where raw materials and other supplies are purchased and then converted to other products. IAS 2, paragraph 12, identifies costs of conversion as 'the costs directly related to the units of production, such as direct labour, plus a systematic allocation of fixed and variable production overheads that are incurred in converting materials into finished goods'. Variable production overheads are indirect costs of production that vary directly with the volume of production and are allocated to each unit of production on the basis of actual use of production facilities. Fixed overheads, such as depreciation of production machinery, remain relatively constant regardless of the volume of production. With the requirement to include variable and fixed production costs in the cost of inventory, IAS 2 essentially requires the adoption of absorption costing. Direct costing, which would treat fixed production costs as period costs by recognising them as expenses in the period in which they incurred, is not allowed. Where a production process simultaneously produces one or more products, the costs of conversion must be allocated between products on a systematic and rational basis (IAS 2 paragraphs 12–14).

Under IAS 2, fixed production overheads must be allocated to inventory based on normal capacity, which is the average production expected under normal circumstances, considering maintenance and other regular downtimes. For example, if a factory normally produces 10,000 units per month, this figure is used to allocate fixed costs. If actual production closely matches this normal capacity, it can be used instead. However, during periods of low output or idle capacity, not all overheads are allocated to inventory, and the excess overheads are expensed. Conversely, during periods of unusually high production, the fixed overhead rate must be reduced to avoid overstating inventory costs.

When disruptions such as natural disasters, epidemics or wars lead to decreased production volumes, the allocation of fixed overhead costs to each unit cannot be increased. Instead, any unallocated overheads are expensed. For example, during the COVID-19 pandemic, many companies had to re-evaluate their fixed overhead cost absorption practices due to abnormally low production volumes resulting from plant closures or reduced product demand. In such scenarios, the amount of overheads that could be included in the inventory cost was impacted. Conversely, if production unexpectedly increases due to events like panic buying, the overhead rate per unit must be reduced to prevent inventories from being valued above their cost. Furthermore, any abnormal waste of materials, labour or other production costs, including costs incurred for repackaging goods for a different market, should be expensed as they are incurred.

Costing methodologies to allocate fixed costs to inventories (such as activity-based-costing) are a managerial accounting issue and outside the scope of this book.

4.4.3 Other costs

The third component of the cost of inventories, specified in IAS 2, is 'other costs incurred in bringing the inventories to their present location and condition'. Other costs can be included only if they are 'incurred in bringing the inventories to their present location and condition' (IAS 2 paragraph 15). Such costs could include specific design expenses incurred in producing goods for individual customers. IAS 23 *Borrowing Costs* allows borrowing costs such as interest to be included in the cost of inventories, but only where such inventories are a qualifying asset; that is, one which 'takes a substantial period of time to get ready for its intended use or sale' (IAS 23 paragraph 5). Inventory items would rarely meet this criterion. For example, a winery could include the directly attributable interest from borrowed money in the cost of wine inventory, as the wine requires several years of ageing before it is ready for sale.

In paragraph 16, IAS 2 explicitly lists examples of costs that cannot be included in the cost of inventories and must be recognised as expenses when incurred:
- abnormal amounts of wasted materials, labour or other production costs
- storage costs, unless necessary in the production process before a further production stage
- administrative overheads that do not contribute to bringing inventories to their present location and condition
- selling costs.

Illustrative example 4.1 demonstrates how to calculate the initial cost of inventory for purchased goods, using the information provided in the invoice.

Magenta Fashion SA, a Paris-based fashion company, received the following invoice from Coral Garments Ltd, an Italian garment manufacturer.

Coral Garments
Since 1860

Invoice #5465
22-5-2025

TO	CUSTOMER ID	ADDRESS	PHONE
Magenta Fashion	ABK967	118 Boulevard Saint-Germain 75006 Paris La France	640-555-0146

SALESPERSON	JOB	PAYMENT TERMS	Terms of sale
Mario	Account Manager Retail	on credit 2/15 net 60 days	FCA

QTY	DESCRIPTION	UNIT PRICE		LINE TOTAL	
60	Basic T-shirt size 16	€	8.25	€	495.00
1200	Glamour Tee size 14	€	11.22	€	13,464.00
560	Superseded T-shirt size 10*	€	5.90	€	3,304.00
	* 15% discount on list price applies				

SUBTOTAL	€	17,263.00
Freight costs	€	695.00

VAT %: 15%

VAT INCL 00.00

TOTAL	€	17,958.00

CoralGarments@gmail.com
Largo Brugnatelli - Angolo Via Volta
20090 BUCCINASCO MI

THANK YOU

The goods arrived at the airport in Paris on 29 May 2025 and were held in a customs bonded warehouse pending payment of import duties and taxes. After the payment of storage costs of €145, import duty at 1.5% of the total value of goods in euros, goods and services tax (GST) of 10% and local freight charges of €316, the goods were finally delivered to Magenta Fashion SA's warehouse on 6 June 2025. The invoice was received on 8 June and a liability of €17,958 recorded at that date. The invoice was paid in full on 8 July which was within the credit terms of 60 days. Upon receipt of the goods, Magenta Fashion SA attaches its own logo to the T-shirts and repackages them for sale. The cost of this further processing is €2.54 per T-shirt.

Problem

What is the cost of this inventory?

Solution

The cost of inventory would include the following amounts:

Purchase price	€17,263.00
Shipping costs	695.00
	€17,958.00
Available credit discount 2%	353.90
Net of discount	17,604.10
Storage costs — customs bonding warehouse	145.00
Import duty (€17,263 × 1.5%)	258.95
Freight costs	316.00
Logo and repackaging (1820 items × €2.54)	4,622.80
Total cost	€22,946.85

Notes:
- Credit terms specify an early payment incentive. Discount of 2% when paid within 15 days. This is indicated on the invoice under 'payment terms' as '2/15 net 60 days', meaning Magenta receives a discount of 2% when paid within 15 days and that the regular payment term is 60 days. The available credit discount is deducted from the cost of inventories. If Magenta pays after 15 days, the discount will not be applied. The additional amount that Magenta pays for not taking the discount is recorded as a finance charge. (If the discount is not taken, an acceptable alternative accounting treatment would be to record the inventory at the full, undiscounted amount.)
- The GST of 10% payable is not included as it is a transaction tax recoverable by Magenta Fashion SA against GST collected on sale of inventory.
- The invoice also states FCA, which is an international commercial term used in foreign trade contracts to clarify the obligations of buyers and sellers. It specifies at which point the obligations, costs and risk involved in the delivery of goods shift from the seller to the buyer. Under FCA (Free Carrier), the seller's responsibility ends once the goods are delivered to the carrier at the agreed location, and the buyer takes over responsibility from that point onward. Where a cost per unit for each type of T-shirt is required, some method of allocating the 'generic' costs of shipping, storage, freight and the credit discount would need to be employed. In this case, such costs could be allocated on a per garment basis. For example, the cost per unit for the Basic T-shirts would be:

	€
Purchase price	8.25
Import duty 1.5%	0.12
Shipping and other costs[a]	0.44
Logo and repackaging	2.54
Cost per unit	€11.351

[a] €145 + 316 + 167 + €695 − 353.80 = €802.10/1820 garments = €0.44 per garment.

4.5 RECORDING INVENTORY TRANSACTIONS

The method chosen to record inventory movements plays an important role in determining the cost of sales and the value of closing inventories. Two primary methods exist in inventory accounting: the periodic inventory system and the perpetual inventory system. IAS 2 does not specifically address which inventory system entities should use, as long as they comply with the measurement and recognition principles outlined in the standard. The choice between these systems — perpetual or periodic — significantly influences how a company calculates the cost of goods sold (which appears on the statement of comprehensive income) and the cost of closing inventory (reported on the statement of financial position). In the following sections, we will discuss both the periodic and perpetual inventory systems and their respective procedures.

4.5.1 Periodic method

Under the periodic method, the amount of inventory is determined periodically (normally annually) by conducting a physical count and multiplying the number of units by a cost per unit to value the inventory on hand. This amount is then recognised as a current asset. This balance remains unchanged until the next count is taken. Purchases and returns of inventory during the reporting period are recorded on a separate expense account (the 'Purchases' account). Cost of sales (or, cost of goods sold) during the year is determined as a balancing figure at the end of the accounting period, by adding total purchases to the beginning inventory and subtracting ending inventory, as follows:

$$\text{Cost of sales} = \text{opening inventory} + \text{purchases} - \text{closing inventory}$$

Under the periodic method, inventory must be counted at the end of each accounting period to determine the carrying value of closing inventory. The way in which the physical count is conducted will depend on the type of inventory and the accounting system of the entity. Stockpiled inventory such as mineral sands may require the use of surveyors to measure quantities on hand and assay tests to determine mineral content.

Accounting for inventory using the periodic method is cost effective and easy to apply, but its major disadvantage is that the exact quantity and cost of inventory cannot be determined on a day-to-day basis, and this might result in lost sales or unhappy customers. Additionally, it is not possible to identify stock losses or posting errors, resulting in accounting figures that might be inaccurate or misleading.

4.5.2 Perpetual method

Under the perpetual method, inventory records are updated with every transaction involving inventory. This keeps the quantity and cost of inventory on hand continuously current, allowing the entity to provide better customer service and maintain tighter control over its inventory. Although once more complex and costly than the periodic method, advancements in technology have made the perpetual system more accessible. Modern, user-friendly accounting software and integrated point-of-sale systems have become widely available and affordable, making the perpetual method a viable option for many businesses today.

The perpetual method requires a subsidiary ledger to be maintained with a separate record for each inventory item detailing all movements in both quantity and cost. This subsidiary record is linked to the general ledger account for inventory, and regular reconciliations are carried out to ensure the accuracy and completeness of the accounting records. *This reconciliation process is discussed in section 4.6.*

Also under the perpetual system, periodic counts are made. Under the perpetual method, the objective of the inventory count is to verify the accuracy of recorded quantities for each inventory item, although not necessarily at the end of the reporting period, if inventory differences are historically found to be immaterial.

Illustrative example 4.2 shows the journal entries necessary to record the normal inventory transactions that would occur during an accounting period, and the reporting of gross profit from the sale of inventory under both inventory systems.

Emerald Ltd sells garden furniture settings. The inventory account in the general ledger of Emerald Ltd at the beginning of the year under both methods (periodic and perpetual) is shown below.

Inventory

1/1/24	Balance b/d	6,700
	(10 units @ $670)	

The following transactions took place during the year:
(a) Purchased 354 settings at $670 each on credit terms of 2/10, *n*/30 from Greenery Ltd
(b) Sold, on credit, 352 settings for $975 each.
(c) Returned four settings to the supplier.
(d) Seven settings were returned by customers.
The journal entries necessary to record these transactions under both inventory accounting methods are shown below.

EMERALD LTD
Journal entries

Perpetual inventory method   *Periodic inventory method*

(a) Purchased 354 settings at $670 each on credit terms of 2/10, *n*/30 from Greenery Ltd

	Dr	Cr		Dr	Cr
Inventory	237,180		Purchases	237,180	
Accounts payable		237,180	Accounts payable		237,180

(b) Sold, on credit, 352 settings for $975 each.

	Dr	Cr		Dr	Cr
Accounts receivable	343,200		Accounts receivable	343,200	
Sales revenue		343,200	Sales revenue		343,200
Cost of sales	235,840				
Inventory		235,840			

(c) Returned four settings to the supplier.

	Dr	Cr		Dr	Cr
Accounts payable	2,680		Accounts payable	2,680	
Inventory		2,680	Purchase returns		2,680

(d) Seven settings were returned by customers.

	Dr	Cr		Dr	Cr
Sales returns	6,825		Sales returns	6,825	
Accounts receivable		6,825	Accounts receivable		6,825
Inventory	4,690				
Cost of sales		4,690			

After posting the journal entries, the general ledger account would appear as shown below.

	Perpetual inventory method		Periodic inventory method

Perpetual inventory method

Inventory

1/1/24	Balance b/d	6,700	Cost of sales	235,840
	Accounts payable	237,180	Accounts payable	2,680
	Cost of sales	4,690	Balance c/d	10,050
		248,570		248,570
	Balance c/d	10,050		

Periodic inventory method

Inventory

1/1/24	Balance b/d	6,700

Assuming that the physical count at the end of the reporting period found 15 settings on hand at a cost of $670 each, in total (15 × $670 =) $10,050. This equals the amount of the closing balance under the perpetual system, which means that there are no corrections required. Under the periodic method, the outcome of the physical count is recorded as the closing inventory with the following entries:

Perpetual inventory method			Periodic inventory method		
	Dr	Cr		Dr	Cr
			Inventory	234,500	
			Purchase returns	2,680	
			Purchases		237,180
			(To transfer purchases to inventory)		
(No entries required)			Cost of sales	231,150	
			Inventory		231,150
			(Record closing inventory based on physical count)		

After these journal entries, closing inventory is recorded under the periodic method as follows:

Closing inventory = opening inventory + purchases − cost of sales
= $ 6,700 + 237,180 − 2,680 − 231,150
= $10,050

The gross profit earned for the perpetual and periodic method would be determined as follows:

EMERALD LTD Determination of Gross Profit		
Perpetual inventory method		
Sales revenue		343,200
Less: Sales returns and allowances		(6,825)
Net sales revenue		336,375
Cost of sales		(231,150)
Gross profit		$ 105,225
Periodic inventory method		
Sales revenue		343,200
Less: Sales returns		(6,825)
Net sales revenue		336,375
Cost of sales		
Opening inventory	6,700	
Add: Purchases	237,180	
	243,880	
Less: Purchase returns	(2,680)	
Goods available for sale	241,200	
Less: Closing inventory	(10,050)	
Cost of sales		(231,150)
Gross profit		$ 105,225

Note that, in this example, the same gross profit is reported irrespective of the inventory recording method adopted. However, where adjustments are made for damaged or lost inventory, the gross profit will be different under the perpetual method. If as a result of a physical count discrepancies are discovered, this may reveal losses of goods caused by damage or fraud. Under the perpetual system, the value of goods that have been lost would be written off using the following entry:

Inventory losses	Dr	xxx
Inventory	Cr	xxx
(Recognition of inventory losses during the period)		

Under the periodic method, inventory losses and fraud cannot be identified and recorded as a separate expense. The movement in inventory balances plus the cost of purchases is presumed to represent the cost of sales during the reporting period.

4.6 END-OF-PERIOD ACCOUNTING

To ensure that reported figures for inventory, cost of sales and other expenses are accurate and complete, certain procedures must be carried out at the end of each accounting period. It is essential that good internal controls are in place to ensure that inventory is protected from fraud or loss and that inventory figures are complete and accurate. The physical count that we discussed in the previous section is part of the end-of-period procedure. This section examines end-of-year cut-off procedures and essential reconciliation procedures.

4.6.1 Cut-off procedures

Under both periodic and perpetual methods there is a need to ensure that, when a physical count is conducted, there is a proper cut-off of the record keeping so that the accounting records reflect the results of the physical count and include all transactions relevant to the accounting period, while excluding those that belong to other periods. For all inventory transactions (sales, purchases and returns), it is possible for inventory records to be updated before transaction details are posted to the general ledger accounts. For example, goods are normally entered into inventory records when the goods are received, but accounts payable records will not record the liability until the invoice arrives because shipping documents may not record price details. Under the periodic method, there is a need to ensure a proper cut-off between the general ledger recording of goods received, shipped and returned, and the inventory counted. Under the perpetual method, there is a need to ensure that all inventory movements are properly recorded in the perpetual records, so a valid comparison is made between inventory counted and the perpetual record quantities. Further, if the perpetual method is not integrated with the general ledger, there is also a need to ensure a proper cut-off between the general ledger and the perpetual records. Thus, at the end of the reporting period it is essential that proper cut-off procedures be implemented.

The following cut-off errors could arise:
- Goods have been received into inventory, but the purchase invoice has not been processed.
- Goods have been returned to a supplier, and deleted from inventory, but the credit note has not been processed.
- Goods have been sold and dispatched to a customer, but the invoice has not been raised.
- Goods have been returned by a customer, but the credit note has not been issued. If inventory movements have been processed before invoices and credit notes, adjusting entries are needed to bring both sides of the transaction into the same accounting period.

4.6.2 Goods in transit

At the end of a reporting period, goods that have been shipped by a seller but not yet received by the buyer must be accounted for based on the terms of trade. These terms specify when ownership of the goods transfers from the supplier to the customer and who is liable for damages during shipping. In international trade, it is common to use the standardised terminology published by the International Chamber of Commerce (ICC), such as FOB (Free On Board) and FCA (Free Carrier), although there are some variations in the definitions. These terms determine when goods should be accounted for as inventory by the buyer or the seller.

For example, if the purchase agreement indicates that the goods belong to the purchaser from the time they are loaded onto the carrier at the port of shipment (we will call this FOB Shipping Point), the purchaser should include the goods in inventory and accounts payable from the shipping date. At the end of the reporting period, all such purchases in transit need to be identified, and the following adjusting journal entry should be posted:

Goods in transit (Inventory)	Dr	xxx	
Accounts payable	Cr		xxx
(Recognition of inventory in transit at the end of the reporting period)			

Alternatively, the trade terms may specify that the goods remain the property of the supplier until they reach the buyer's location (we will call this FOB Destination). From the perspective of the buyer, if goods are purchased under these terms, no adjustment is required for goods in transit at the end of the reporting period because they still belong to the supplier.

However, if an entity sells goods under these terms, it must make end-of-period adjustments to account for the sold goods in transit. Since these goods belong to the selling entity until they arrive at the customer's premises, and the sale has been recorded in the current financial period, the following adjusting entries will be necessary to remove the sale and reinstate the inventory:

Inventory	Dr	xxx	
Cost of sales	Cr		xxx
(Reversal of sale for goods in transit at the end of the reporting period)			

Sales revenue	Dr	xxx	
Accounts receivable	Cr		xxx
(Reversal of sale for goods in transit at the end of the reporting period)			

4.6.3 Consignment inventory

Care must be taken in the treatment of consignment inventory. Under a consignment arrangement, an agent (the consignee) agrees to sell goods on behalf of the consignor on a commission basis. The transfer of goods to the consignee is not a legal sale/purchase transaction. Legal ownership remains with the consignor until the agent sells the goods to a third party. For example, car dealerships often operate on consignment, displaying vehicles from manufacturers or private sellers without owning them until sold. Steps must be taken to ensure that goods held on consignment are not included in the physical count. Equally, goods owned by the entity that are held by consignees must be added to the physical count. The accounting for such consignment arrangements is outlined in IFRS 15 *Revenue from Contracts with Customers*.

4.6.4 Control account/subsidiary ledger reconciliation

Under the perpetual inventory system, the reconciliation of the control account and/or the subsidiary ledger is an essential end-of-period procedure. The general ledger account balance must be reconciled with the total of the subsidiary ledger. Recording errors and omissions will cause the reconciliation process to fail. Any material discrepancies should be investigated and corrected. This process will identify only amounts that have not been posted to both records; it cannot identify errors within the subsidiary records, such as posting a purchase to the wrong inventory item code. However, the physical count/recorded figure reconciliation will isolate these errors.

Illustrative example 4.3 shows the process for making an end-of-period inventory adjustment under the perpetual system, in the case of a difference between the inventory ledger account and the physical count.

Bob Rose, trading as Indigo Ltd, completed his first year of trading as a paint wholesaler on 31 December 2024. He is worried about his end-of-year physical and cut-off procedures.

The inventory ledger account balance at 31 December 2024, under the perpetual inventory method, was £78,700. His physical count, however, revealed the cost of inventory on hand at 31 December 2024 to be only £73,400. While Bob expected a small inventory shortfall due to breakage and petty theft, he considered this shortfall to be excessive.

Upon investigating reasons for the inventory 'shortfall', Bob discovered the following:

- Goods costing £800 were sold on credit to Lavender Company for £1,300 on 27 December 2024 on FOB destination terms. The goods were still in transit at 31 December 2024. Indigo Ltd recorded the sale on 27 December 2024 and did not include these goods in the physical count.
- Included in the physical count were £2,200 of goods held on consignment.
- Goods costing £910 were purchased on credit from Violet Ltd on 23 December 2024 and received on 28 December 2024. The purchase was unrecorded at 31 December 2024, but the goods were included in the physical count.
- Goods costing £400 were purchased on credit from Lime Supplies on 22 December 2024 on FOB shipping terms. The goods were delivered to the transport company on 27 December 2024. The purchase was recorded on 27 December 2024, but, as the goods had not yet arrived, Indigo Ltd did not include these goods in the physical count.
- At 31 December 2024 Indigo Ltd had unsold goods costing £3,700 out on consignment. These goods were not included in the physical count.
- Goods costing £2,100 were sold on credit to Maroon Ltd for £3,200 on 24 December 2024 on FOB shipping terms. The goods were shipped on 28 December 2024. The sale was unrecorded at 31 December 2024 and Indigo Ltd did not include these goods in the physical count.
- Goods costing £1,500 had been returned to Azure Coatings on 31 December 2024. A credit note was received from the supplier on 5 January 2025. No payment had been made for the goods prior to their return.

These transactions and events must be analysed to determine if adjustments are required to the ledger accounts (general and subsidiary) and/or the physical count records as follows:

Workings

	Recorded balance £	Physical count £
Balance prior to adjustment	78,700	73,400
Add: Goods sold, FOB destination and in transit at 31 December	800	800
Less: Goods held on consignment	—	(2,200)
Add: Unrecorded purchase	910	—
Add: Goods purchased, FOB shipping and in transit at 31 December	—	400
Add: Goods out on consignment	—	3,700
Less: Unrecorded sale	(2,100)	—
Less: Unrecorded purchase returns	(1,500)	—
	£76,810	£76,100

If, after all adjustments are made, the recorded balance cannot be reconciled to the physical count, the remaining discrepancy is presumed to represent inventory losses and a final adjustment is made as follows:

Adjusted balances	76,810	76,100
Inventory shortfall	(710)	—
	£76,100	£76,100

The following journal entries are necessary on 31 December 2024 to correct errors and adjust the inventory ledger accounts:

INDIGO LTD General Journal			
2024			
31 December			
Sales revenue	Dr	1,300	
Accounts receivable (Lavender)	Cr		1,300
(Correction of sale recorded incorrectly)			
Inventory	Dr	800	
Cost of Sales	Cr		800
(Correction of sale recorded incorrectly)			
Inventory	Dr	910	
Accounts payable (Violet Ltd)	Cr		910
(Correction of unrecorded purchase)			
Accounts receivable (Maroon Ltd)	Dr	3,200	
Sales Revenue	Cr		3,200
(Correction of unrecorded sale)			
Cost of Sales	Dr	2,100	
Inventory	Cr	2,100	
(Correction of unrecorded sale)			
Accounts payable (Azure Coatings)	Dr	1,500	
Inventory	Cr		1,500
(Correction of unrecorded purchase return)			
Inventory losses and write-downs	Dr	710	
Inventory	Cr		710
(Unexplained variance [physical/records] written off)			

4.7 ASSIGNING COSTS TO INVENTORY ON SALE

When inventory is first recorded by an entity, it is typically recognised at its cost, regardless of its nature. But when it is sold, the type or characteristics of the inventory becomes significant and determines how costs are assigned. As shown in illustrative example 4.2, under the perpetual system the cost of inventory items is transferred to a 'Cost of Sales' expense account on sale, and under the periodic system a 'Cost of Sales' figure is calculated at the end of the reporting period. This is an easy task if the nature of inventory is such that it is possible to clearly identify the exact inventory item that has been sold and its cost, but what if it is not possible to identify exactly the cost of the item sold? How can you measure the cost of a tonne of wheat when it is extracted from a stockpile consisting of millions of tonnes acquired at different prices over the accounting period?

IAS 2 addresses this problem by mandating two different rules for the assigning of cost to inventory items sold. The rules differ depending on the nature of inventory held. The first rule, in paragraph 23 of IAS 2, states that:

> The cost of inventories of items that are not ordinarily interchangeable and goods or services produced and segregated for specific projects shall be assigned by using specific identification of their individual costs.

Thus, if the inventory held consists of items that can be individually identified because of their unique nature or by some other means, or cannot be individually identified, but have been acquired for a specific project, then the exact cost of the item sold must be recorded as cost of sales expense. This method, known as the specific identification method, is particularly useful for high-value items with significant cost variations. For example, a car dealership might use this method, as each car, identifiable by a unique vehicle identification number, has a specific cost.

The second rule for the assignment of costs, in paragraph 25 of IAS 2, states that:

The cost of inventories, other than those dealt with in paragraph 23, shall be assigned by using the first-in, first-out (FIFO) or weighted average cost formula.

This means that, where a specific cost cannot be identified because of the nature of the item sold, then some method has to be adopted to estimate that cost. This process is known as 'assigning' cost. Most inventory items fall into this category, for example, identical items of food and clothing and bulk items like oil and minerals. There are many methods of assigning a cost to inventory items sold, but IAS 2 restricts entities to a choice between two methods — FIFO and weighted average.

4.7.1 First-In, First-Out (FIFO) cost formula

The FIFO formula assumes that items of inventory that were purchased or produced first are sold first, and the items remaining in inventory at the end of the period are those most recently purchased or produced (IAS 2 paragraph 27). Thus, more recent purchase costs are assigned to the inventory asset account, and older costs are assigned to the cost of sales expense account.

Consider this example: assume an online shop has 515 drones on hand at 31 December 2025, and recent purchase invoices showed the following costs:

28 December	180 drones at €49.00
15 December	325 drones at €48.50
30 November	200 drones at €47.00

The value of ending inventory is found by starting with the most recent purchase and working backward until all items on hand have been priced (on the assumption that it is not known when any particular drone was sold). The value of ending inventory would be €25,052.50 (being 180 drones at €49 + 325 drones at €48.50 + 10 drones at €47).

Many proponents of the FIFO method argue that this method best reflects the physical movement of inventory, particularly perishable goods or those subject to changes in fashion or rapid obsolescence. If the oldest goods are normally sold first, then the oldest costs should be assigned to expense.

4.7.2 Weighted average cost formula

Under the weighted average cost formula, the cost of each item sold is determined from the cost of similar items purchased or produced during the period. The average may be calculated on a periodic basis (weighted average), or as each additional shipment is received (moving average).

Using a *periodic basis*, the cost of inventory on hand at the beginning of the period plus all inventory purchased during the year is divided by the total number of items available for sale during the period (opening quantity plus purchased quantity). This produces the cost per unit. For example: assume an online shop in gaming supplies has inventory on hand at 1 January 2026 that was valued at £3,439.78, consisting of 134 game consoles at an average of £25.67 each. During the year the following purchases were made:

$$200 \text{ units at } £27.50 = £5,500.00$$
$$175 \text{ units at } £28.35 = £4,961.25$$
$$300 \text{ units at } £29.10 = £8,730.00$$
$$120 \text{ units at } £29.00 = £3,480.00$$

At the end of the year, the weighted average cost of inventory would be calculated as:

$$£3,439.78 + £5,500.00 + £4,961.25 + £8,730.00 + £3,480.00 = £26,111.03 \div 929 \text{ units} = £28.11 \text{ per unit}$$

When entities keep *perpetual* inventory records, the average unit cost is recalculated each time there is an inventory purchase or purchase return. This is called the *moving weighted average method*. Companies often apply average-cost methods, even for goods that can be traced by their serial numbers. Figures 4.3 and 4.4 show fragments of the notes to the financial statements of Sony and Nintendo, respectively. These leading electronic companies, that both produce game consoles, apply the (moving) weighted average cost method to their inventories.

FIGURE 4.3 Fragment from the inventory accounting policies as applied by Sony

FIGURE 4.3 Fragment from the inventory accounting policies as applied by Sony

3. Summary of material accounting policies
I. Material accounting policies
(. . .)
(6) Inventories – Inventories are measured at the lower of cost or net realizable value. The cost of inventories is determined on the "weighted average cost" basis.

Source: Sony Group Corporation and Consolidated Subsidiaries, Form F-20 for year ended 31 March 2024, Page 145 Note 3 Summary of material accounting policies.

FIGURE 4.4 Fragment from the inventory accounting policies as applied by Nintendo

4. Accounting procedures
(1) Valuation basis and method for important assets
(. . .)

(iii) Inventories – They are mainly stated at cost using the moving-average method (the figures shown in the balance sheets have been calculated by writing them down based on decline in profitability).

Source: Nintendo Co., Ltd, Annual Report 2024 for the fiscal year ended 31 March 2024. Page 59, Note 4 Accounting procedures.

The application of the FIFO cost formula and the moving weighted average method is demonstrated in illustrative example 4.4.

ILLUSTRATIVE EXAMPLE 4.4 Application of cost formulas

The following information has been extracted from the records of Sunglow Parts about one of its products. Sunglow Parts uses the perpetual inventory method and its reporting period ends on 31 December.

		No. of units	Unit cost $	Total cost $
2025				
01/01	Beginning balance	800	7.00	5,600
06/01	Purchased	300	7.05	2,115
05/02	Sold @ $12.00 per unit	1,000		
19/03	Purchased	1,100	7.35	8,085
24/03	Purchase returns	80	7.35	588
10/04	Sold @ $12.10 per unit	700		
22/06	Purchased	8,400	7.50	63,000
31/07	Sold @ $13.25 per unit	1,800		
04/08	Sales returns @ $13.25 per unit	20		
04/09	Sold @ $13.50 per unit	3,500		
06/10	Purchased	500	8.00	4,000
27/11	Sold @ $15.00 per unit	3,100		

1. Calculate the cost of inventory on hand at 31 December 2025 and the cost of sales for the year ended 31 December 2025, assuming:
    (a) the FIFO cost flow assumption
    (b) the moving average cost flow assumption (round the average unit costs to the nearest cent, and round the total cost amounts to the nearest dollar).
2. Prepare the trading section of the statement of profit or loss for the year ended 31 December 2025, assuming:
    (a) the FIFO cost flow assumption
    (b) the moving average cost flow assumption.

Part 1. (a) First-in, first-out cost formula

		Purchases			Cost of sales			Balance[a]		
Date	Details	No. units	Unit cost	Total cost	No. units	Unit cost	Total cost	No. units	Unit cost	Total cost
01/01	Inventory balance							800	7.00	5,600
06/01	Purchases	300	7.05	2,115				800	7.00	5,600
								300	7.05	2,115
05/02	Sales				800	7.00	5,600			
					200	7.05	1,410	100	7.05	705
19/03	Purchases	1,100	7.35	8,085				100	7.05	705
								1,100	7.35	8,085
24/03	Purchase returns	(80)	7.35	(588)				100	7.05	705
								1,020	7.35	7,497
10/04	Sales				100	7.05	705			
					600	7.35	4,410	420	7.35	3,087
22/06	Purchases	8,400	7.50	63,000				420	7.35	3,087
								8,400	7.50	63,000
31/07	Sales				420	7.35	3,087			
					1.380	7.50	10,350	7,020	7.50	52,650
04/08	Sales returns[b]				(20)	7.50	(150)	7,040	7.50	52,800
04/09	Sales				3,500	7.50	26,250	3,540	7.50	26,550
06/10	Purchases	500	8.00	4,000				3,540	7.50	26,550
								500	8.00	4,000
22/11	Sales				3,100	7.50	23,250	440	7.50	3,300
								500	8.00	4,000
				76,612			74,912			

a As it is assumed the earliest purchases are sold first, a separate balance of each purchase at a different price must be maintained.
b The principle of 'last-out, first-in' is applied to sales returns.

Part 1. (b) Moving average cost formula

Date	Details	Purchases			Cost of sales[a]			Balance		
		No. units	Unit cost	Total cost	No. units	Unit cost	Total cost	No. units	Unit cost[b]	Total cost
01/01	Inventory balance							800	7.00	5,600
06/01	Purchases	300	7.05	2,115				1,100	7.01	7,715
05/02	Sales				1,000	7.01	7,010	100	7.01	705
19/03	Purchases	1,100	7.35	8,085				1,200	7.33	8,790
24/03	Purchase returns	(80)	7.35	(588)				1,120	7.32	8,202
10/04	Sales				700	7.32	5,124	420	7.32	3,078
01/01	Inventory balance	8,400	7.50	63,000				8,820	7.49	66,078
06/01	Purchases				1,800	7.49	13,482	7,020	7.49	52,596
05/02	Sales				(20)	7.49	(150)	7,040	7.49	52,746
19/03	Purchases				3,500	7.49	26,215	3,540	7.49	26,531
24/03	Purchase returns	500	8.00	4,000				4,040	7.56	30,531
10/04	Sales				3,100	7.56	23,436	940	7.56	7,095
				76,612			75,117			

a The 'average' cost on the date of sale is applied to calculate the 'cost of sales'.
b The average cost per unit is recalculated each time there is a purchase or a purchase return at a different cost.

Part 2

	SUNGLOW PARTS Statement of Profit or Loss (extract) for the year ended 31 December 2025		
		FIFO $	Moving average $
Sales revenue		138,070	138,070
Less: Sales returns		(265)	(265)
Net sales		137,805	137,805
Less: Cost of sales		(74,912)	(75,117)
Gross profit		$ 62,893	$ 62,688

Because the purchase price has been rising throughout the year, using the FIFO formula produces a lower cost of sales (higher gross profit) and a higher inventory balance than the moving average formula.

4.7.3 Which cost formula to use?

The choice of method is a matter for management judgement and depends upon the nature of the inventory, the information needs of management and financial statement users and the cost of applying the formulas. For example, the weighted average method is easy to apply and is particularly suited to inventory where homogeneous products are mixed together, like iron ore or spring water. On the other hand, FIFO may be a better reflection of the actual physical movement of goods, such as those with use-by dates where the first produced must be sold first to avoid loss due to obsolescence, spoilage or legislative restrictions. Entities with diversified operations may use both methods because they carry different types of inventory.

Using diverse methods is acceptable under IAS 2, but paragraph 26 cautions that 'a difference in geographical location of inventories (or in the respective tax rules), by itself, is not sufficient to justify the use of different cost formulas'. The nature of the inventory itself should determine the choice of formula.

4.7.4 Consistent application of costing methods

Once a cost formula has been selected, management cannot randomly switch from one formula to another. Because the choice of method can have a significant impact on an entity's reported profit and asset figures, particularly in times of volatile prices, indiscriminate changes in formulas could result in the reporting of financial information that is neither comparable nor reliable. Accordingly, paragraph 13 of IAS 8 *Accounting Policies, Changes in Accounting Estimates and Errors* requires that 'accounting policies be consistently applied to ensure comparability of financial information. Changes in accounting policies are allowed (IAS 8 paragraph 14) only when required by an accounting standard or where the change results in reporting more relevant and reliable financial information'. Therefore, unless the nature of inventory changes, it is unlikely that the cost formulas will change. The requirements when a company voluntarily changes its accounting policies are described in IAS 8 (*see section 2.7.1 in this book for a more detailed discussion*).

4.7.5 Other cost measurement techniques

In some situations, applying FIFO or weighted average can be very complex. This is particularly true for manufacturers producing a wide range of products with repetitive processes, or for retailers with large volumes of similar inventory items. Under IAS 2, alternative techniques such as the standard cost method or the retail method may be used, provided the resulting values approximate actual cost (paragraph 21). The standard cost method involves assigning pre-determined costs to inventory items based on expected costs of materials, labour and overhead for each product. These costs are based on normal levels of efficiency and capacity utilisation. Adjustments are made at the end of the reporting period to account for variances between standard and actual costs. The retail method is used to measure inventories of large numbers of rapidly changing items with similar margins, for which it is impractical to use other costing methods. This method is commonly used by supermarkets and department stores. Cost is determined by reducing the sales value of the inventory by an appropriate percentage gross margin or an average percentage margin. Care must be taken to ensure that gross margins are adjusted for goods that have been discounted below their original selling price.

Figure 4.5 shows a fragment from the inventory accounting policies applied by Ahold Delhaize, a large food retailer, that explains the use of the retail method in conjunction with other costing principles as set out in IAS 2.

FIGURE 4.5 Fragment from the inventory accounting policies as applied by Koninklijke Ahold Delhaize NV

INVENTORIES

Inventories are stated at the lower of cost or net realizable value. Cost consists of all costs of purchase, cost of conversion and other costs incurred in bringing the inventories to their location and condition ready for sale, net of vendor allowances attributable to inventories. For certain inventories, cost is approximated using the retail method, in which the sales value of the inventories is reduced by the appropriate percentage of gross margin. The cost of inventories is determined using either the first-in, first-out (FIFO) method or the weighted average cost method, depending on their nature or use. Net realizable value is the estimated selling price in the ordinary course of business, less the estimated marketing, distribution and selling expenses.

Source: Ahold Delhaize Annual Report 2023, Note 17 Inventories, p. 231.

4.8 NET REALISABLE VALUE

As the measurement rule mandated by IAS 2 for inventories is the 'lower of cost and net realisable value' (paragraph 9), an estimate of net realisable value must be made to determine if inventory must be written down. Normally, this estimate is done at the end of the reporting period, but, where management become aware during the reporting period that goods or services can no longer be sold at a price above cost, inventory values should be written down to net realisable value. The rationale for this measurement rule, according to paragraph 28 of IAS 2, is that 'assets should not be carried in excess of amounts expected to be realised from their sale or use'.

Net realisable value is the net amount that an entity expects to realise from the sale of inventory in the ordinary course of business. It is defined in paragraph 6 of IAS 2 as 'the estimated selling price in the ordinary course of business less the estimated costs of completion and the estimated costs necessary to make the sale'. Net realisable value is specific to an individual entity and is not necessarily equal to fair value less selling costs. Fair value is defined as 'the price that would be received to sell an asset or paid to transfer a liability in an orderly transaction between market participants at the measurement date. (See IFRS 13 *Fair Value Measurement*.)' (IAS 2 paragraph 6).

Net realisable value may fall below cost for a number of reasons including:

- a fall in selling price (e.g. fashion garments)
- physical deterioration of inventories (e.g. fruit and vegetables)
- product obsolescence (e.g. computers and electrical equipment)
- a decision, as part of an entity's marketing strategy, to manufacture and sell products for the time being at a loss (e.g. new products)
- miscalculations or other errors in purchasing or production (e.g. over-stocking)
- an increase in the estimated costs of completion or the estimated costs of making the sale (e.g. air-conditioning plants).

4.8.1 Estimating net realisable value

Estimates of net realisable value must be based on the most reliable evidence available at the time the estimate is made (normally the end of the reporting period) of the amount that the inventories are expected to realise. Thus, estimates must be made of:

- expected selling price
- estimated costs of completion (if any)
- estimated selling costs.

These estimates take into consideration fluctuations of price or cost occurring after the end of the reporting period to the extent that such events confirm conditions existing at the end of the reporting period. The purpose for which inventory is held should be taken into account when reviewing net realisable values. For example, the net realisable value of inventory held for a specific contract should be based on the contract price. In addition, for inventory such as unused office supplies that are held for internal use, the replacement cost is the best available measure of their net realisable value.

Estimated selling costs include all costs likely to be incurred in securing and filling customer orders such as advertising costs, sales personnel salaries and operating costs and the costs of storing and shipping finished goods.

It is possible to use formulas based on predetermined criteria to initially estimate net realisable value. These formulas normally take into account, as appropriate, the age, past movements, expected future movements and estimated scrap values of the inventories. However, the results must be reviewed in the light of any special circumstances not anticipated in the formulas, such as changes in the current demand for inventories or unexpected obsolescence.

In addition, natural disasters, epidemics and wars may affect consumer behaviour and, as a result, lead to increased estimation uncertainty when estimating net realisable value. In such situations, the calculation of net realisable value will likely require more detailed methods or assumptions. As an illustration, figure 4.6 shows a fragment taken from the financial statements of Burberry plc, a luxury clothing company, for the financial year 2019–20 where it explains how the net realisable value of its inventories was affected by the lockdowns during the COVID-19 pandemic.

FIGURE 4.6 An example disclosure of inventory impairment, related to the impact of COVID-19

Burbery Annual Report 2019–20
Impairment of inventory
Management assesses the recoverability of the carrying value of inventories at every reporting period and, where the expected recoverable amount is lower than the carrying value, a provision is recorded. Typically, inventory provisions are recorded against aged inventory or specific products which have been identified as having a low expectation of future sale. Due to the impact of COVID-19, the closure of many of the Group's retail stores worldwide and the associated build-up of inventory, management have reassessed their plans for the usage of inventory over the next 12 months, taking into account the expected length of the shutdown, products ordered for future seasons and the Group's projected future sales. As a result of this reassessment, management have identified additional inventory which is no longer expected to realise its carrying value. Provisions of £68.3 million have been recorded against this additional inventory, which relates to current and recent seasons that under more normal circumstances would be expected to sell through with limited loss. This additional charge for inventory provisions has been presented as an adjusting item arising as a result of COVID-19, in accordance with the Group's accounting policy, as it is considered material and one-off in nature. A related taxcredit of £12.5 million has also been recognised in the year. Refer to note 17 for details of inventory provisions.

Source: Burberry plc Annual Report 2019–20, 6. ADJUSTING ITEMS Impact of COVID-19, p. 225.

4.8.2 Materials and other supplies

IAS 2, paragraph 32, states that 'materials and other supplies held for use in the production of inventories are not written down below cost if the finished goods in which they will be incorporated are expected to be sold at or above cost'. When the sale of finished goods is not expected to recover the costs, then materials are to be written down to net realisable value. IAS 2 suggests that the replacement cost of the materials or other supplies is probably the best measure of their net realisable value.

4.8.3 Write-down to net realisable value

Inventories are usually written down to net realisable value on an item-by-item basis. Paragraph 29 of IAS 2 states that 'it is not appropriate to write inventories down on the basis of a classification of inventory, for example, finished goods, or all the inventories in a particular operating segment'. Where it is not practical to separately evaluate the net realisable value of each item within a product line, the write-down may be applied on a group basis provided that the products have similar purposes or end uses, and are produced and marketed in the same geographical area. IAS 2 generally requires that service providers apply the measurement rule only on an item-by-item basis, as each service ordinarily has a separate selling price.

The journal entry to process the write-down would be:

Inventory write-down expense	Dr	xxx	
Inventory	Cr		xxx
(Write-down to net realisable value)			

4.8.4 Reversal of prior write-down to net realisable value

If the circumstances that previously caused inventories to be written down below cost change, or if a new assessment confirms that net realisable value has increased, the amount of a previous write-down may have to be reversed (subject to an upper limit of the original write-down). This could occur if an item of inventory written down to net realisable value because of falling sales prices is still on hand at the end of a subsequent period and its selling price has recovered.

The journal entry to process the reversal would be:

Inventory	Dr	xxx	
Inventory write-down expense	Cr		xxx
(Write-up to revised net realisable value)			

Illustrative example 4.5 demonstrates how the lower of cost or net realisable value (NRV) rule, applied on an item-by-item basis, affects the valuation of inventory.

ILLUSTRATIVE EXAMPLE 4.5 Application of lower of cost or NRV measurement rule

Dandelion Ltd retails gardening equipment and has four main product lines: mowers, vacuum blowers, edgers and garden tools. At 31 December 2025, cost and net realisable value (NRV) for each line were as shown below.

Application of lower of cost and net realisable value measurement rule				
Inventory item	Quantity	Cost per unit €	NRV per unit €	Lower of cost and NRV €
Mowers	16	215.80	256.00	3,452.80
Vacuum blowers	113	62.35	60.00	6,780.00
Edgers	78	27.40	36.00	2,137.20
Garden tools	129	12.89	11.00	1,419.00
Inventory at the lower of cost and net realisable value				€13,789.00

The standard states that inventories are usually written down to net realisable value on an item-by-item basis (paragraph 29 of IAS 2), which leads to a more conservative and accurate valuation of inventory, preventing overstatement. If the NRV rule were applied to the inventory items as a group — a method allowed in certain circumstances — items with significant declines in NRV could be offset by others with higher NRV, resulting in an overall inflated inventory value.

In this example, applying the lower of cost or NRV to the group of inventory items would result in no write-down, as the total cost (€14,298.36) is less than the total NRV (€15,103.00). However, when assessed on an item-by-item basis, two items — vacuum blowers and garden tools — must be written down to their individual NRVs.

The following journal entry would be required to adjust inventory values to net realisable value:

31 December 2025 Inventory write-down expense Inventory (Write-down to net realisable value — vacuum blowers €265.55 (113 × €2.35) and garden tools €243.81 (129 × €1.89))	Dr Cr	509.36	 509.36

4.9 RECOGNITION AS AN EXPENSE

Paragraph 34 of IAS 2 requires the following items to be recognised as expenses:
- carrying amount of inventories in the period in which the related revenue is recognised, in other words, cost of sales
- write-down of inventories to net realisable value and all losses
- reversals of write-downs to net realisable value (reduction of the expense).

The only exception to this rule relates to inventory items allocated to other asset accounts, e.g. used by an entity as components in self-constructed property, plant or equipment. The cost of these items would be capitalised and recognised as an expense via depreciation.

4.10 DISCLOSURE

Paragraph 36 of IAS 2 contains the required disclosures relating to inventories. Before preparing the disclosure note, inventories on hand will need to be classified into categories because paragraph 36(b) requires 'the carrying amount in classifications appropriate to the entity' to be disclosed. Common classifications suggested in paragraph 37 are 'merchandise, production supplies, materials, work in progress and finished goods'. In addition, paragraph 36 (d) requires companies to disclose the amount of inventory recognised as an expense. This amount is usually included in cost of sales. Figure 4.7 provides an illustration of the disclosures required by IAS 2, showing how the BMW Group reports the relevant information in its consolidated financial statements.

29 Inventories
Inventories comprise the following:

in € million	31.12.2023	31.12.2022
Finished goods and goods for resale	16,103	12,563
Work in progress, unbilled contracts	3,190	3,235
Raw materials and supplies	3,722	3,424
Vehicles held for sale in the financial services business	693	524
Advance payments to suppliers	11	259
Inventories	**23,719**	**20,005**

FIGURE 4.7 An example of illustrative disclosures required by IAS 2

Out of the total amount recognised for inventories at 31 December 2023, inventories measured at net realisable value amounted to €1,346 million (2022: €1,940 million). Write-downs to net realisable value in the financial year 2023 amounted to €189 million (2022: €112 million), while reversals of write-downs amounted to €13 million (2022: €11 million).

The expense recorded in conjunction with inventories during the financial year 2023 amounted to €81,497 million (2022: €76,014 million).

At 31 December 2023, the carrying amounts of inventories expected to be realised after more than 12 months amount to €86 million (2022: €98 million).

Source: BMW Group Report 2023, Notes to the Group Financial Statements, Note 29 Inventories, p.189.

4.11 SUMMARY

This chapter provides a comprehensive overview of inventory accounting, analysing the principles and guidelines set by IAS 2 *Inventories*. The principal issue in accounting for inventories is the determination of cost and its subsequent recognition as an expense, including any write-down to net realisable value (IAS 2 paragraph 1). One key decision in recognising inventory is the selection of an appropriate method for allocating costs between individual items of inventory to determine the cost of sales and the cost of inventory on hand. Following the initial recognition of the inventory, cost must be compared to net realisable value, and the value of inventory written down where net realisable value falls below cost. IAS 2 requires disclosures to be made in relation to the inventories held by an entity and the accounting policies adopted with respect to these assets.

There is only scant literature on inventories and IAS 2, perhaps because the accounting treatment is not controversial. The main research interest therefore rests with the information content of inventory and inventory changes. There is also some research into earnings management through production costs.

Starting with the information role of inventory, Lev and Thiagarajan (1993) postulate that increases in inventory above the level of increases in sales serve as a fundamental signal to investors. Specifically, they argue that when inventory increases more than sales do, this is likely associated with unwarranted inventory buildup. One consequence of this is that future sales will decline as managers will have to offer discounts to customers. Alternatively, such an increase is likely to be followed by inventory write-offs. At the same time, over-production of inventory may entail a positive effect on current earnings in manufacturing firms. This is because overhead costs are allocated to a larger number of units, and hence reduces the per-unit cost of sales. Lev and Thiagarajan (1993) show that inventory buildup is negatively associated with stock returns. This is consistent with market participants regarding inventory buildup as a negative signal. Abarbanell and Bushee (1997) formally show that Lev and Thiagarajan's (1993) conjecture about the negative association between inventory buildup and future earnings is borne out in the data. However, they do not find that financial analysts revise their predictions in line with the empirical evidence. This raises a concern that financial analysts do not fully appreciate the consequences of inventory buildup. Abarbanell and Bushee's (1998) subsequent analysis employs the same fundamental signal as Lev and Thiagarajan (1993), but this time to show it can help form a profitable buy-and-hold strategy. Specifically, a portfolio that takes a long (short) position in firms with increases in inventory below (above) the levels of increase in sales generates positive returns.

Thomas and Zhang (2002) link inventory changes to another important empirical finding that was previously established by Sloan (1996). Sloan (1996) finds that accruals are inversely related to future stock returns. This suggests that market participants do not fully understand the reversal property of accruals. Thomas and Zhang (2002) investigate if this is primarily caused by inventory changes. They find that both inventory and other components of accruals explain this phenomenon. However, the contribution of changes in inventory is the largest.

Roychowdhury (2006) examines real earnings management, which he defines as 'manipulating real activities to avoid reporting annual losses'. This contrasts with manipulating accruals, which is the convention in accounting research for earnings management. One of the real activities subject to such manipulations is overproduction of inventory. As Lev and Thiagarajan (1993) note, this can help reduce cost of sales, and hence improve reported profitability. Roychowdhury (2006) estimates production costs as cost of goods sold plus the change in inventory. He focuses on firms that report the smallest profit among available observations during the 1987–2001 period. Based on past research these are firms suspected of using earnings management to avoid losses (e.g. Burgstahler and Dichev 1997). Consistent with his conjecture that real earnings management takes place in inventory production cost, he finds that suspect firms are characterised by high production costs, low operating cash flows and lower level of accruals than non-suspect firms.

Gunny (2010) extends this line of research to examine future operating performance of firms that engage in real earnings management to meet earnings benchmarks. She argues that engaging in real earnings management (in part through inventory production) may serve as a signal about future performance. She finds that firms that overproduce to avoid reporting losses show higher return on equity (ROE) and operating cash flows in the subsequent year than firms that report small losses while not engaging in real earnings management. However, the higher ROE may be also indicative of higher equity risk. Kim and Sohn (2013) find that real earnings management is also associated with higher implied cost of capital, supporting this interpretation of Gunny (2010).

References

Abarbanell, J., and Bushee. B. 1997. Fundamental analysis, future earnings, and stock prices. *Journal of Accounting Research*, 35, 1–24.

Abarbanell, J., and Bushee. B. 1998. Abnormal returns to a fundamental analysis strategy. *The Accounting Review*, 73, 19–45.

Burgstahler, D., and Dichev, I., 1997. Earnings management to avoid earnings decreases and losses. *Journal of Accounting and Economics*, 24, 99–126.

Gunny, K. A. 2010. The relation between earnings management using real activities manipulation and future performance: evidence from meeting earnings benchmarks. *Contemporary Accounting Research*, 27(3), 855–888.

Kim, J.B. and Sohn, B.C., 2013. Real earnings management and cost of capital. *Journal of Accounting and Public Policy*, 32(6), 518–543.

Lev, B., and Thiagarajan, R. 1993. Fundamental information analysis. *Journal of Accounting Research*, 31, 190–215.

Roychowdhury, S. 2006. Earnings management through real activities manipulation. *Journal of Accounting and Economics*, 42(3), 335–70.

Sloan, R. G. 1996. Do stock prices fully reflect information in accruals and cash flows about future earnings? *The Accounting Review*, 71, 289–315.

Thomas, J. K., and Zhang, H., 2002. Inventory changes and future returns. *Review of Accounting Studies*, 7(2–3), 163–187.

5 Property, plant and equipment

ACCOUNTING STANDARDS IN FOCUS

IAS 16 *Property, Plant and Equipment*

IAS 40 *Investment Property*

LEARNING OBJECTIVES

After studying this chapter, you should be able to:

 1   describe the nature of property, plant and equipment

 2   recall the recognition criteria for initial recognition of property, plant and equipment

 3   demonstrate how to measure property, plant and equipment on initial recognition

 4   explain the alternative ways in which property, plant and equipment can be measured subsequent to initial recognition

 5   explain the cost model and account for the calculation of depreciation

 6   explain the revaluation model

 7   discuss the factors to consider when choosing which measurement model to apply

 8   account for derecognition

 9   implement the disclosure requirements of IAS 16

 10   explain the accounting issues relating to investment properties.

5.1 THE NATURE OF PROPERTY, PLANT AND EQUIPMENT

The accounting standard described in this chapter is IAS 16 *Property, Plant and Equipment*. IAS 16 was reissued in December 2003 and applies to annual periods beginning on or after 1 January 2005.

According to paragraph 2 of IAS 16, the standard applies in accounting for property, plant and equipment except where another standard requires or permits a different accounting treatment. IAS 16 does not apply to property, plant and equipment classified as held for sale in accordance with IFRS 5 *Non-current Assets Held for Sale and Discontinued Operations*; biological assets related to agricultural activity as these are accounted for under IAS 41 *Agriculture*; or mineral rights and mineral reserves such as oil, gas and similar non-regenerative resources. However, IAS 16 does apply to property, plant and equipment used to develop or maintain biological assets and mineral rights and reserves.

Paragraph 6 of IAS 16 defines property, plant and equipment as follows:

Property, plant and equipment are tangible items that:

(a) are held for use in the production or supply of goods or services, for rental to others, or for administrative purposes; and

(b) are expected to be used during more than one period.

Note the following:

- The assets are 'tangible' assets. *The distinction between tangible and intangible assets is discussed in depth in chapter 6.* However, a key feature of tangible assets is that they are physical assets, such as land, rather than non-physical, such as patents and trademarks.
- The assets have specific uses within an entity; namely, for use in production/supply, rental or administration. Assets that are held for sale, including land, or held for investment are not included under property, plant and equipment. Instead, assets held for sale are accounted for in accordance with IFRS 5 and investment properties are accounted for in accordance with IAS 40 *(see section 5.10)*.
- The assets are non-current assets, the expectation being that they will be used for more than one accounting period.

Property, plant and equipment may be divided into classes for disclosure purposes, a class of assets being a grouping of assets of a similar nature and use in an entity's operations. Examples of classes of property, plant and equipment are land, machinery, motor vehicles and office equipment. The property, plant and equipment note to the statement of financial position of Marks & Spencer plc, at 1 April 2023, as shown in figure 5.1, provides an indication of the classes of property, plant and equipment disclosed by Marks & Spencer plc (land and buildings; fixtures, fittings and equipment; assets in the course of construction) as well as details of the movements in those classes. It is interesting to see in the preamble to this note that Marks and Spencer state that their property, plant and equipment incorporates both 'owned assets' as well as 'right-of-use assets', which are a separate category of non-current assets comprising leased assets *(see chapter 9)*.

In this chapter, accounting for property, plant and equipment is considered as follows:

- recognition of the asset — the point at which the asset is brought into the accounting records
- initial measurement of the asset — determining the initial amount at which the asset is recorded in the accounts
- measurement subsequent to initial recognition — determining the amount at which the asset is reported subsequent to acquisition, including the recording of any depreciation of the asset
- derecognition of the asset.

FIGURE 5.1 Property, plant and equipment

15 PROPERTY, PLANT AND EQUIPMENT

The Group's property, plant and equipment of £5,203.7m (last year: £4,902.3m) consists of owned assets of £3,747.7m (last year: £3,486.5m) and right-of-use assets of £1,456.0m (last year: £1,415.8m).

Property, plant and equipment – owned

	Land and buildings £m	Fixtures, fittings and equipment £m	Assets in the course of construction £m	Total £m
At 3 April 2021				
Cost	2,809.9	5,450.2	67.5	8,327.6
Accumulated depreciation, impairments and write-offs	(787.5)	(3,959.3)	(18.2)	(4,765.0)
Net book value	2,022.4	1,490.9	49.3	3,562.6

FIGURE 5.1 *(continued)*

	Land and buildings £m	Fixtures, fittings and equipment £m	Assets in the course of construction £m	Total £m
Year ended 2 April 2022				
Opening net book value	2,022.4	1,490.9	49.3	3,562.6
Additions	0.9	17.7	238.0	256.6
Transfers and reclassifications	3.0	175.8	(164.3)	14.5
Disposals	(15.9)	(1.9)	–	(17.8)
Impairment reversals	34.5	27.6	–	62.1
Impairment charge	(57.6)	(31.4)	–	(89.0)
Asset write-offs	0.9	(11.4)	–	(10.5)
Depreciation charge	(34.2)	(256.1)	–	(290.3)
Exchange difference	(1.7)	–	–	(1.7)
Closing net book value	1,952.3	1,411.2	123.0	3,486.5
At 2 April 2022				
Cost	2,764.8	5,275.7	141.2	8,181.7
Accumulated depreciation, impairments and write-offs	(812.5)	(3,864.5)	(18.2)	(4,695.2)
Net book value	1,952.3	1,411.2	123.0	3,486.5
Year ended 1 April 2023				
Opening net book value	**1,952.3**	**1,411.2**	**123.0**	**3,486.5**
Additions	**0.8**	**40.0**	**296.2**	**337.0**
Acquired through business combinations	**150.5**	**38.7**	**3.8**	**193.0**
Transfers and reclassifications	**15.0**	**292.3**	**(280.7)**	**26.6**
Disposals	**(2.2)**	**(2.2)**	**–**	**(4.4)**
Impairment reversals	**25.8**	**14.4**		**40.2**
Impairment charge	**(22.5)**	**(9.3)**	**–**	**(31.8)**
Asset write-offs	**2.2**	**1.5**		**3.7**
Depreciation charge	**(59.9)**	**(250.4)**	**–**	**(310.3)**
Exchange difference	**5.5**	**1.6**	**0.1**	**7.2**
Closing net book value	**2,067.5**	**1,537.8**	**142.4**	**3,747.7**
At 1 April 2023				
Cost	**2,911.4**	**5,532.3**	**160.6**	**8,604.3**
Accumulated depreciation, impairments and write-offs	**(843.8)**	**(3,994.6)**	**(18.2)**	**(4,856.6)**
Net book value	**2,067.6**	**1,537.7**	**142.4**	**3,747.7**

Asset write-offs in the year include assets with gross book value of £240.9m (last year: £383.3m) and £nil (last year: £nil) net book value that are no longer in use and have therefore been retired.

Source: Marks & Spencer plc (*Annual Report* 2023, p. 178).

5.2 INITIAL RECOGNITION OF PROPERTY, PLANT AND EQUIPMENT

Paragraph 7 of IAS 16 contains the principles for recognition of property, plant and equipment:

The cost of an item of property, plant and equipment shall be recognised as an asset if, and only if:
(a) it is probable that future economic benefits associated with the item will flow to the entity; and
(b) the cost of the item can be measured reliably.

This is a *general* recognition principle for property, plant and equipment. This recognition principle shall be applied to all costs at the time they are incurred, both incurred initially to acquire or construct an item of property, plant and equipment and incurred subsequently after recognition to add to, replace part of or service it.

5.2.1 Asset versus expense

For most items of property, plant and equipment, the entity will incur some initial expenditure. After incurring the initial costs of acquiring or constructing an asset, further related costs may continue to be incurred, referred to as 'subsequent costs'. The issue is whether these subsequent costs should be recognised as an asset or whether they should be expensed. The same recognition criteria that apply to initial costs apply equally to subsequent costs. Thus, a subsequent cost may only be capitalised if it can be measured reliably and leads to probable future economic benefits.

Examples of subsequent costs include day-to-day servicing of the asset, adding to the asset, replacing parts and performing major inspections. Assets need maintenance and although these costs may be very large and will lead to probable future economic benefits, they are always expensed. Typically, day-to-day servicing costs include labour, consumables and small parts.

Further, some parts of an item of property, plant and equipment may require replacement at regular intervals; for example, aircraft interiors. In such a case, the carrying amount of the older part is derecognised and the cost of the new part is recognised into the carrying amount of the item. The same applies to major inspections for faults, overhauling and similar items (*see section 5.2.2*).

5.2.2 Separate assets – significant parts

If an item of property, plant and equipment has significant parts, each significant part must be recognised in a separate asset account. A part of an asset is 'significant' if the cost of that part is significant in relation to the total cost of the asset. The rationale behind recognising each part separately is that it enables management to make more accurate estimates of depreciation because each part is depreciated separately. This is important because significant parts often have different useful lives and residual values to the remaining parts of the item of property, plant and equipment, both of which will affect the amount of depreciation.

A condition of continuing to operate an item of property, plant and equipment may be the performing of regular major inspections. When the general recognition criteria of paragraph 7 of IAS 16 are met, the cost of the major inspection is recognised as an asset; simultaneously the cost and accumulated depreciation of the previous major inspection is derecognised. It may be necessary to estimate the cost of a previous major inspection if not identified in the initial cost (IAS 16, paragraph 14).

An entity allocates the amount initially recognised in respect of an asset to its significant parts and accounts for each part separately. Paragraph 9 of IAS 16 notes that the identification of what constitutes a separate item of plant and equipment requires the exercise of judgement, because the standard does not prescribe the unit of measure for recognition.

For example, consider an aircraft as an item of property, plant and equipment. Is it sufficient to recognise the aircraft as a single asset? An analysis of the aircraft may reveal that there are various parts of the aircraft that have different useful lives. Parts of the aircraft include the engines, the frame of the aircraft and the fittings (seats, floor coverings and so on). It may be necessary to refit the aircraft every five years, whereas the engines may last twice as long. Similarly, an entity that deals with the refining of metals may have a blast furnace, the lining of which needs to be changed periodically. The lining of the blast furnace therefore needs to be separated from the external structure in terms of asset recognition and subsequent accounting for the asset. Further, as noted in paragraph 9 of IAS 16, it may be appropriate to aggregate individually insignificant items (such as moulds, tools and dies) and apply the criteria to the aggregate value.

5.2.3 Generation of future benefits

Paragraph 11 of IAS 16 notes that certain assets may not of themselves generate future benefits, but instead it may be necessary for the entity itself to generate future benefits. For example, some items of property, plant and equipment may be acquired for safety or environmental reasons, such as equipment associated with the safe storage of dangerous chemicals. The entity's generation of the benefits from use of the chemicals can occur only if the safety equipment exists. Hence, even if the safety equipment does not of itself generate cash flows, its existence is necessary for the entity to be able to use chemicals within the business.

5.3 INITIAL MEASUREMENT OF PROPERTY, PLANT AND EQUIPMENT

Having established that an asset can be recognised, the entity must then assign to it a monetary amount. Paragraph 15 of IAS 16 contains the principles for initial measurement of property, plant and equipment: 'An item of property, plant and equipment that qualifies for recognition as an asset shall be measured at its cost.' Paragraph 16 specifies three elements of cost, namely:

- purchase price
- directly attributable costs
- initial estimate of the costs of dismantling and removing the item or restoring the site on which it is located.

These elements are considered separately in the following sections.

5.3.1 Purchase price

'Purchase price' is not defined in IAS 16, but paragraph 16(a) states that the purchase price includes import duties and non-refundable purchase taxes, and is calculated after deducting any trade discounts and rebates. The essence of what constitutes purchase price is found in the definition of cost in paragraph 6 of the standard, which states: 'Cost is the amount of cash or cash equivalents paid or the fair value of the other consideration given to acquire an asset at the time of its acquisition or construction.'

Where an item of property, plant and equipment is acquired for cash, determination of the purchase price is relatively straightforward. One variation that may arise is that some or all of the cash payment is deferred. In this case, as noted in paragraph 23 of IAS 16, the cost is the cash price equivalent at the recognition date, determined by measuring the cash payments on a present value basis (done by discounting the cash flows). Interest is then recognised as the payments are made.

More difficulties arise where the exchange involves assets other than cash. In a non-cash exchange, the acquiring entity receives a non-cash asset and in return provides a non-cash asset to the seller. In measuring the cost of the asset acquired, the question is whether the measurement should be based on the value of the asset given up by the acquirer, or by reference to the value of the asset acquired from the seller. In relation to the application of the cost principle of measurement, note the following:

1. Cost is determined by reference to the fair value of what is given up by the acquirer rather than by the fair value of the item acquired. The cost represents the sacrifice made by the acquirer. This principle is inherent in the definition of cost in paragraph 6 of IAS 16. Further, paragraph 26 states that where both the fair value of what is given up by the acquirer and the asset received are reliably measurable, then the fair value of the asset given up is used to measure the cost of the asset received, unless the fair value of the asset received is more clearly evident. 'More clearly evident' presumably relates to the cost and difficulty of determining the fair value as, in the paragraph 26 example, the fair values of both the asset received and the asset given up can be measured reliably.

2. Cost is measured by reference to fair value (paragraph 24). The term fair value is defined in paragraph 6 of IAS 16 as 'the price that would be received to sell an asset or paid to transfer a liability in an orderly transaction between market participants at the measurement date'.

   Fair value is an exit price. The process of determining fair value necessarily involves judgement and estimation. The acquiring company is not actually trading the items given up in the marketplace for cash, but is trying to estimate what it would get for those items if it did so. Hence, the determination of fair value is only an estimation. A further practical problem in determining fair value is that the nature of the market in which the goods given up are normally traded may make estimation difficult. The market may be highly volatile with prices changing daily, or the market may be relatively inactive. *Chapter 8 contains detailed information on the measurement of fair value.*

   If the acquirer gives up an asset at fair value, and the carrying amount of the asset is different from the fair value, then the entity will recognise a gain or a loss. According to paragraph 34 of IAS 1 *Presentation of Financial Statements*, gains and losses on the disposal of non-current assets are reported by deducting from the proceeds on disposal the carrying amount of the asset and related selling expenses.

   Assume that an entity acquires a piece of machinery and gives in exchange a block of land. The land is carried by the entity at original cost of £100,000 and has a fair value of £150,000. The journal entry to record the acquisition of the machinery is:

Machinery	Dr	150,000	
Gain on Sale of Land	Cr		50,000
Land	Cr		100,000
(Acquisition of machinery in exchange for land)			

The entity then reports a gain on sale of land of £50,000.

If, instead of giving land in exchange, the entity issued shares having a fair value of £150,000 this is accounted for as a share-based payment in accordance with paragraph IFRS 2 *(see chapter 14)*, the journal entry is:

Machinery	Dr	150,000	
Share Capital	Cr		150,000
(Acquisition of machinery by issue of shares)			

Further discussion on the measurement of the fair value of equity instruments issued by the acquirer in exchange for assets is found in chapter 19.

3. Paragraph 24 of IAS 16 requires the use of fair value to measure the cost of an asset received unless the exchange transaction lacks commercial substance. Commercial substance is concerned with whether the transaction has a discernible effect on the economics of an entity. Paragraph 25 states that an exchange transaction has commercial substance if:

(a) *the configuration (risk, timing and amount) of the cash flows of the asset received differs from the configuration of the cash flows of the asset transferred.* This would not occur if similar assets (e.g. an exchange of commodities such as oil or milk) were exchanged as would occur where, for example, suppliers exchanged inventories in various locations to fulfil demand on a timely basis in a particular location; or

(b) *the entity-specific value of the portion of the entity's operations affected by the transaction changes as a result of the exchange.* Paragraph 6 defines entity-specific value as 'the present value of the cash flows an entity expects to arise from the continuing use of an asset and from its disposal at the end of its useful life or expects to incur when settling a liability'. If there is no change in the expected cash flows to the entity as a result of the exchange, as in the case of the exchange of similar items, then the transaction lacks commercial substance; and

(c) *the difference in (a) or (b) is significant relative to the fair value of the assets exchanged.* In both (a) and (b), the change in cash flows or configuration must be material, with materiality being measured in relation to the fair value of the assets exchanged.

Where the transaction lacks commercial substance, the asset acquired is measured at the carrying amount of the asset given up.

4. Paragraph 24 of IAS 16 also covers the situation where, in an exchange of assets, neither the fair value of the assets given up nor the fair value of the assets acquired can be measured reliably. Such situations could occur where the assets exchanged are both traded in weak markets where market transactions are infrequent. In this situation, the acquirer measures the cost of the asset acquired at the carrying amount of the asset given up.

Acquisition date

One of the problems in recording the acquisition of an item of property, plant and equipment relates to the determination of the fair values of the assets involved in the exchange. As noted above, accounting for the asset exchange requires that potentially both the fair values of the assets acquired and assets given up must be determined. However, where the markets for these assets are volatile, choosing the appropriate fair value may be difficult. This can be seen where an entity issues shares in exchange for an asset. The fair value of the shares issued may change on a daily basis. At what point in time should the fair values be measured?

Some likely dates that may be considered are:
• the date the contract to exchange the assets is signed
• the date the consideration is paid
• the date on which the assets acquired are received by the acquirer
• the date on which an offer becomes unconditional.

The advantage of these dates is that they relate to a point of time that can be determined objectively, such as the date the item of property, plant and equipment arrives at the acquirer's premises. A problem is that there may be a number of dates involved if, for example, an item of equipment arrives in stages or payment for the equipment is to be made in instalments over time.

The date on which the fair values should be measured is the date on which the acquirer *obtains control of the asset or assets acquired* — hereafter referred to as the 'acquisition date'. The definition of cost in paragraph 6 of IAS 16 refers to the 'time of its [the asset's] acquisition'. There is no specific date defined in the standard. In IFRS 3 *Business Combinations*, acquisition date is defined as 'the date on which the acquirer obtains control of the acquiree'. If the consideration is paid in own shares, IFRS 2 paragraph 7 applies which clarifies that the fair value must be measured at the date the good is obtained.

The measurement of the fair value relates to the date the assets acquired are recognised in the records of the acquirer. At this date, the acquirer must be able to reliably measure the cost of the asset. Recognition of an asset requires the acquirer to have control of expected future benefits. Hence, when the item acquired becomes the asset of the acquirer (i.e. when the expected benefits come under the control of the acquirer), this is the point in time when the measurements of the fair values of assets acquired and given up are made. Paragraph 23 of IAS 16 states that the cost of an item of property, plant and equipment is the cash price equivalent at the 'recognition date'. Recognition date is normally the same as acquisition date.

Acquisition of multiple assets

The above principles as stated in IAS 16 apply to the acquisition of individual items of property, plant and equipment. However, an acquisition may consist of more than one asset, such as a block of land and a number of items of machinery. The acquirer may acquire the assets as a group, paying one total amount for the bundle of assets. The cost of acquiring the bundle of assets is determined as per IAS 16, namely by measuring the fair value of what is given up by the acquirer to determine the purchase price, and adding to this any directly attributable costs. However, even if the total cost of the bundle of assets can be determined, for accounting purposes it is necessary to determine the cost of each of the separate assets as they may be in different classes, or some may be depreciable and others not. No guidance is given in this standard for determining the costs of each of the assets. However, IFRS 3 *Business Combinations* paragraph 2(b) states:

> The cost of the group shall be allocated to the individual identifiable assets and liabilities on the basis of their relative *fair values* at the date of purchase. Such a transaction or event does not give rise to goodwill.

In this situation, the cost of each asset to be recorded separately is calculated by allocating the cost of the bundle of assets over the assets acquired in proportion to the fair values of the assets acquired. To illustrate this allocation procedure, assume an entity acquired land, buildings and furniture at a total cost of £300,000 cash. In order to separately record each asset acquired at cost, the entity determines the fair value of each asset, for example:

Land	£ 40,000
Buildings	200,000
Furniture	80,000
	£320,000

The total cost of £300,000 is then allocated to each asset on the basis of these fair values as follows:

Land	£40,000/£320,000 × £300,000	=	£ 37,500
Buildings	£200,000/£320,000 × £300,000	=	187,500
Furniture	£80,000/£320,000 × £300,000	=	75,000
			£300,000

The acquisition of the three assets is recorded by the entity as follows:

Land	Dr	37,500	
Buildings	Dr	187,500	
Furniture	Dr	75,000	
Cash	Cr		300,000
(Acquisition of assets for cash)			

Under IAS 16, the basic principle of recording assets acquired is to record at cost. Where a bundle of assets is acquired, the cost of the separate assets must be estimated, and the fair values of the assets acquired can be used in this process. Where the cost of the assets in total is less than the sum of the fair values of the assets acquired, a bargain purchase has been made. However, as the assets are to be recognised initially at cost, no gain is recognised on acquisition.

5.3.2 Directly attributable costs

Directly attributable costs are the costs necessary to get the asset into a location and condition enabling it to be capable of operating in the manner intended by management. These costs must be capitalised (i.e. included in the cost of the asset). (IAS 16 paragraph 16(b)). Conversely, costs that are not considered 'directly attributable' are expensed.

Costs to be included

Paragraph 17 of IAS 16 provides examples of directly attributable costs:

- costs of site preparation
- initial delivery and handling costs
- installation and assembly costs — where buildings are acquired, associated costs could be the costs of renovation
- professional fees
- costs of employee benefits arising directly from the construction or acquisition of the item of property, plant and equipment
- costs of testing whether the asset is functioning properly (but if any products made during the testing phase are sold, the costs incurred relating to these products are recognised as inventory and the proceeds are recognised in profit and loss together with the cost of the related inventory).

It can be seen that all these costs are incurred before the asset is used, and are necessary in order for the asset to be usable by the entity. Note, however, the use of the word 'necessary'. There may be costs incurred that were not necessary; for example, the entity may have incurred fines, or a concrete platform may have been placed in the wrong position and had to be destroyed and a new one put in the right place. These costs should be written off to an expense rather than being capitalised as part of the cost of the acquired asset.

A further cost that may be capitalised into the cost of an item of property, plant and equipment is that of borrowing costs. Borrowing costs (i.e. interest and other costs associated with the borrowing of funds) are accounted for under IAS 23 *Borrowing Costs*. Paragraph 8 of IAS 23 states that borrowing costs that are directly attributable to the acquisition, construction or production of a qualifying asset must be capitalised as part of the cost of the asset. (A qualifying asset is one that necessarily takes a substantial period of time to get ready for its intended use or sale, such as a building.)

Costs not to be included

Paragraphs 19 and 20 of IAS 16 contain examples of costs that should not be included in directly attributable costs:

- *costs of opening a new facility.* These costs are incurred after the item of property, plant and equipment is capable of being used; the opening ceremony, for example, does not enhance the operating ability of the asset.
- *costs of introducing a new product or service, including costs of advertising and promotional activities.* These costs do not change the location or working condition of the asset.
- *costs of conducting business in a new location or with a new class of customer (including costs of staff training).* Unless the asset is relocated, there is no change in the asset's ability to operate.
- *administration and other general overhead costs.* These costs are not directly attributable to the asset, but are associated generally with the operations of the entity.
- *costs incurred while an item capable of operating in the manner intended by management has yet to be brought into use or is operated at less than full capacity.* These costs are incurred because of management's decisions regarding the timing of operations rather than being attributable to getting the asset in a position for operation.
- *initial operating losses, such as those incurred while demand for the item's output builds up.* These are not incurred before the asset is ready for use.
- *costs of relocating or reorganising part or all of the entity's operations.* If a number of currently operating assets are relocated to another site, then the costs of relocation are general, and not directly attributable to the item of property, plant and equipment.

5.3.3 Costs of dismantling, removal or restoration

At the date an asset is initially recognised, an entity is required to estimate any costs necessary to eventually dismantle and remove the asset and restore its site. For example, when an asset such as an offshore oil platform is constructed, an entity knows that in the future it is required by law to dismantle and remove the platform in such a manner that the environment is cared for. The construction of the platform gives rise to a liability for restoration under IAS 37 *Provisions, Contingent Liabilities and Contingent Assets*. The expected costs, measured on a present value basis, are capitalised into the cost of the platform as the construction of the platform brings with it the responsibility of disposing of it. Acceptance of the liability for dismantling and removal is an essential part of bringing the asset to a position of intended use. As with directly attributable costs, the dismantling and removal costs are depreciated over the life of the asset. There may be restoration costs associated with the use of land, such as where the land is used for mining or farming. These costs are capitalised into the cost of the land at the acquisition date and, although the land is not depreciated, the restoration costs are depreciated over the period in which the benefits from use of the land are received.

The provision for future costs may require adjustment over time, resulting from a change in the expected outflow of economic benefits or a change in the estimated current market discount rate. Further, if the provision is measured at its present value, its measurement will change through the unwinding of the discount (it increases as one gets closer to the date on which an asset has to be decommissioned). Issues relating to accounting for the effect of changes in the measurement of existing decommissioning, restoration and similar liabilities are addressed in IFRIC 1 *Changes in existing decommissioning, restoration and similar liabilities.*

The unwinding of the discount is expensed in profit or loss as a finance cost. Capitalisation of these finance costs under IAS 23 Borrowing costs is not permitted. However, both a change in the expected future outflows (for example, a change in the amount of the future decommissioning cost) and a change in the estimated current market discount rate will lead to adjustments to the asset's carrying amount. An increase in expected future cash outflows results in the asset's cost increasing. Note also that in terms of IFRIC 1, paragraph 5, a decrease in the liability that would lead to a negative asset is recognised in profit or loss.

5.4 MEASUREMENT SUBSEQUENT TO INITIAL RECOGNITION

As previously mentioned, at the point of initial recognition of an item of property, plant and equipment, the asset is measured at *cost*. After this initial recognition, an entity has a choice on the measurement basis to be adopted. IAS 16 paragraph 29 recognises two possible measurement models:
- the cost model
- the revaluation model.

The choice of model is an accounting policy decision. That policy is not applied to individual assets but to an entire *class* of property, plant and equipment. Hence, for each class of assets, an entity must decide the measurement model to be used. Having chosen a particular measurement model for a specific class of assets, the entity may not change to the alternative basis unless the principles of IAS 8 *Accounting Policies, Changes in Accounting Estimates and Errors* allow such a change. Paragraph 14 of IAS 8 states:

> An entity shall change an accounting policy only if the change:
>
> (a) is required by an IFRS; or
>
> (b) results in the financial statements providing reliable and more relevant information about the effects of transactions, other events or conditions on the entity's financial position, financial performance or cash flows.

It is part (b) that establishes the principle for change. The key is whether the change in measurement basis will make the financial statements more useful to users; in particular, will the information be more relevant and/or more reliable? In general, a change from the cost model to the revaluation model would be expected to increase the relevance of information provided because more current information is being made available. However, the change may make the information less reliable, as the determination of fair value requires estimation to occur. The entity would need to assess the overall benefit of the change in order to justify the change. In contrast, changing from the revaluation model would generally lead to a decrease in the relevance of the information. However, it may be that the determination of fair value has become so unreliable that the fair values determined have little meaning. Again, a judgement of the relative trade-offs between relevance and reliability needs to be made.

Paragraph 17 of IAS 8 notes that the accounting for a change from the cost model to the revaluation model constitutes a change in accounting policy, but the accounting for such a change is done in accordance with the principles in IAS 16 rather than those in IAS 8, namely by applying the principles of the revaluation model. No such statement is made about a change from fair value back to cost. It would appear that the accounting for this is based on IAS 8, paragraph 22 in particular. This paragraph requires the change to be applied retrospectively, and the information disclosed as if the new accounting policy had always been applied. Hence, a change from the revaluation model to the cost model would require adjustments to the accounting records to show the information as if the cost model had always been applied. Adjustments can be taken through the opening balance of retained earnings. Comparative information would also need to be restated.

5.5 THE COST MODEL

Paragraph 30 of IAS 16 states:

> After recognition as an asset, an item of property, plant and equipment shall be carried at its cost less any accumulated depreciation and any accumulated impairment losses.

The cost is as described in *section 5.3*, and includes outlays incurred up to the point where the asset is at the location and in the working condition to be capable of operating in the manner intended by management. Note that this entails management determining a level of operations, a capacity of production or a use for the item of property, plant and equipment. In getting a machine to an appropriate working condition, management may need to undertake certain outlays to keep the machine running efficiently at that level. In relation to a vehicle that is needed to take a driver from point A to point B, the car needs to run efficiently and at a required safety level, without breaking down. In order for this to occur, the car needs to be regularly serviced, have tune-ups and incur any other routine checks. Costs associated with keeping the item of property, plant and equipment at the required working condition are expensed, and not added to the depreciable cost of the asset. These costs are generally referred to as repairs and maintenance.

Similar examples can be seen with other assets, such as escalators that need to be regularly maintained to ensure they achieve the basic task of moving passengers from one level to another. Most items of plant with moving parts require some form of regular maintenance. Paragraph 12 of IAS 16 notes the existence of these 'repairs and maintenance' costs, stating that these costs should not be capitalised into the cost of the asset. These costs relate to the day-to-day servicing of the asset and consist mainly of labour and consumables, but may also include the cost of small parts. Costs of repairs and maintenance are expensed as incurred.

After acquisition, management may also outlay funds refining the ability of the asset to operate. These are not outlays associated with repairs, maintenance or replacement. Examples of such expenditures relate to outlays designed to increase the remaining useful life of the asset, increase its capacity, improve the quality of the output, and adjust the asset to reduce operating costs.

A decision to capitalise these outlays requires the application of the recognition principle in paragraph 7 of IAS 16. Capitalisation requires there to be an increase in probable future economic benefits associated with the asset; that is, it should be probable that the expenditure increases the future economic benefits embodied in the asset in excess of its standard of performance assessed at the time the expenditure is made. Note the timing of the assessment process: at the time the expenditure is *incurred*. The comparison is not with the original capacity to operate or the expected future benefits at acquisition, but with the capacity existing at the time the subsequent expenditure is incurred. Hence, if the capacity of the asset had reduced over time, expenditure to revive the asset to its original capacity would be capitalised. The assessment of capacity requires judgement, and needs to take into account matters such as the level of maintenance performed before the incurrence of the subsequent expenditure. The latter could not include the costs of any as yet unperformed maintenance work.

5.5.1 Depreciation

Under the cost model, after initial recognition, an asset continues to be recorded at its original cost. The subsequent carrying amount is determined after adjustments are made only for depreciation and impairment losses. *(Impairment losses are discussed in chapter 7.)* The main point of the following discussion is to determine the depreciation in relation to an item of property, plant and equipment.

In order to understand the accounting principles for depreciation, it is necessary to consider the definitions of depreciation, depreciable amount, useful life and residual value contained in paragraph 6 of IAS 16:

> *Depreciation* is the systematic allocation of the depreciable amount of an asset over its useful life.

> *Depreciable amount* is the cost of an asset, or other amount substituted for cost, less its residual value.

> The *residual value* of an asset is the estimated amount that an entity would currently obtain from disposal of the asset, after deducting the estimated costs of disposal, if the asset were already of the age and in the condition expected at the end of its useful life.

> *Useful life* is:
> (a) the period over which an asset is expected to be available for use by an entity; or
> (b) the number of production or similar units expected to be obtained from the asset by an entity.

Process of allocation

Depreciation is a process of allocation. *As noted in section 5.2*, the initial recognition of an item of property, plant and equipment requires that it is probable that the future benefits will flow to the entity. On acquiring these benefits, an entity will have expectations as to the period over which these benefits are to be received and the pattern of these benefits (e.g. they could be received evenly over the life of the asset). The purpose of determining the depreciation charge for the period is to measure the consumption of benefits allocable to the current period, ensuring that, over the useful life of the asset, each period will be allocated its fair share of the cost of the asset acquired. This principle is found in paragraphs 50 and 60 of IAS 16:

> 50 The depreciable amount of an asset shall be allocated on a systematic basis over its useful life.

> 60 The depreciation method used shall reflect the pattern in which the asset's future economic benefits are expected to be consumed by the entity.

By describing depreciation as a process of allocation, the IASB is effectively arguing that an increase in value is not sufficient justification for not depreciating an asset. The IASB considers separately the consumption of benefits and the changes in value over a period. As paragraph 52 of the standard states, depreciation is recognised even if the fair value of an asset is greater than its carrying amount (which is the amount at which an asset is recognised after deducting any accumulated depreciation and accumulated impairment losses). However, depreciation is not recognised if the asset's residual value exceeds the carrying amount.

Methods of depreciation

The accounting policy that an entity must adopt for depreciation is specified in paragraphs 50 and 60 of IAS 16, namely the systematic allocation of the cost or other revalued amount of an asset over its useful life in a manner that reflects the pattern in which the asset's future economic benefits are expected to be consumed. There are many methods of allocation, depending on the pattern of benefits. Paragraph 62 of the standard notes three methods:

- *Straight-line method.* This is used where the benefits are expected to be consumed evenly over the useful life of the asset. The depreciation charge for the period is calculated as:

$$\text{Depreciation expense} = \frac{\text{Cost less residual value}}{\text{Useful life}}$$

If an item of plant had an original cost of £100,000, a residual value of £10,000, and a useful life of four years, the depreciation expense each year is:

$$\text{Depreciation expense} = \frac{(£100,000 - £10,000)}{4}$$

The journal entry is:

Depreciation Expense — Plant	Dr	22,500	
Accumulated Depreciation — Plant	Cr		22,500
(Depreciation on plant per annum)			

Note that both the residual value and the useful life may change during the life of the asset as expectations change.

- *Diminishing-balance method.* This method is used where the pattern of benefits is such that more benefits are consumed in the earlier years in the life of the asset. As the asset increases in age, the benefits consumed each year are expected to reduce.

It is possible to calculate a rate of depreciation that would result in the depreciable amount being written off over the useful life, with the depreciation charge each year being calculated by multiplying the rate by the carrying amount at the beginning of the year. The formula is:

$$\text{Depreciation rate} = 1 - \sqrt[n]{\frac{r}{c}}$$

where n = useful life
r = residual value
c = cost or other revalued amount

Using the same information as in the example for the straight-line method, the depreciation rate under the diminishing-balance method is:

$$\text{Depreciation rate} = 1 - \sqrt[4]{\frac{10,000}{100,000}}$$

$$= 44\% \text{ approximately}$$

The depreciation expense for each year of the asset's useful life is:

Year 1 depreciation expense = 44% × £100,000   = £ 44,000
Year 2 depreciation expense = 44% × £56,000   = £ 24,640
Year 3 depreciation expense = 44% × £31,360   = £ 13,798
Year 4 depreciation expense = £13,798 − £10,000 = £ 3,798

Note that the depreciation rate is applied to the *carrying amount* at the beginning of each year (the carrying amount at the beginning of year 1 is the cost of £100,000; the carrying amount at the beginning of year 2 is £56,000). The depreciation charge then reflects a decreasing pattern of benefits over the asset's useful life.

- *Units-of-production method.* This method is based on the expected use or output of the asset. Variables used could be production hours or production output.

    Using the above example again, assume that over the 4-year life of the asset the expected output of the asset is as follows:

Year 1	17,000 units
Year 2	15,000 units
Year 3	12,000 units
Year 4	6,000 units
	50,000 units

The depreciation expense in each of the four years is:

Year 1 depreciation expense = 17/50 × £90,000 = £ 30,600
Year 2 depreciation expense = 15/50 × £90,000 = £ 27,000
Year 3 depreciation expense = 12/50 × £90,000 = £ 21,600
Year 4 depreciation expense = 6/50 × £90,000 = £ 10,800
£ 90,000

Note that the apportionment of the units of production each year is applied to the *depreciable amount*, and not the carrying amount as with the diminishing balance method.

IAS 16 does not specify the use of any specific method of depreciation. The method chosen by an entity should be based on which method most closely reflects the expected pattern of consumption of the future economic benefits embodied in the asset.

Paragraph 61 of IAS 16 requires an entity to review the depreciation method chosen to ensure that it is providing the appropriate systematic allocation of benefits. The review process should occur at least at the end of each financial year. If there has been a change in the pattern of benefits such that the current method is inappropriate, the method should be changed to one that reflects the changed pattern of benefits. This change is not a change in an accounting policy, simply rather a change in depreciation method. As such it is accounted for as a change in an accounting estimate, with the application of IAS 8. Under paragraph 36 of IAS 8, the change is recognised prospectively with adjustments being made to the amounts recognised in the current period and future periods as appropriate.

The depreciation method is applied from the date the asset is available for use; that is, when it is in the location and condition necessary for it to perform as intended by management. As noted in paragraph 55 of IAS 16, depreciation continues even if the asset is temporarily idle, dependent on movements in residual value and expected useful life. However, under methods such as the units-of-production method, no depreciation is recognised where production ceases.

Useful life

Determination of useful life requires estimation on the part of management, because the way in which an item of property, plant and equipment is used and the potential for changes in the market for that item affect estimates of useful life. Paragraph 56 of IAS 16 provides the following list of factors to consider in determining useful life:

(a) the *expected usage* of the asset by the entity; this is assessed by reference to the asset's expected capacity or physical output

(b) the expected *physical wear and tear*, which depends on operational factors such as the number of work shifts for which the asset will be used and the repair and maintenance programme of the entity, and the care and the maintenance of the asset while it is idle

(c) *technical or commercial obsolescence* arising from changes or improvements in production, or from a change in the market demand for the product or service output of the asset. For example, computers may be regarded as having a relatively short useful life. The actual period over which they may be expected to work is probably considerably longer than the period over which they may be considered to be technologically efficient. The useful life for depreciation purposes is related to the period over which the entity intends to use them, which is probably closer to their technological life than the period over which they would be capable of being used.

(d) *legal or similar limits* on the use of the asset, such as expiry dates of related leases.

There is no necessary relationship between useful life to the entity and the economic life of the asset. Management may want to hold only relatively new assets, and a policy of replacement after specified periods of time may mean that assets are held for only a proportion of their economic lives. In other words, useful life for the purpose of calculating depreciation is defined in terms of the asset's expected usefulness to the entity. As noted earlier, the useful life of an asset covers the entire time the asset is available for use, including the time the asset is idle but available for use.

As noted in paragraph 58 of IAS 16, land is a special type of asset. Unless the land is being used for a purpose where there is a limited life imposed on the land, such as a quarry (where the land is depreciated), it is assumed to have an unlimited life (and not depreciated). Hence, when accounting for land and buildings, these assets are dealt with separately so that buildings are subject to depreciation. If, however, the cost of land includes the expected costs of dismantling, removal or restoration, then these costs are depreciated over the period in which the benefits from use of the land are received.

Just as the depreciation method requires a periodic review, so the useful life of an asset is subject to review. According to paragraph 51 of IAS 16, the review should occur at least at each financial year-end. A change in the assessment of the useful life will result in a change in the depreciation rate used. As this is a change in accounting estimate, changes are made prospectively in accordance with IAS 8 paragraph 36.

ILLUSTRATIVE EXAMPLE 5.1 Assessment of useful life

Future View is in the business of making camera lenses. The machine used in this process is very well made, and could be expected to provide a service in making the lenses currently demanded for another 20 years. As the machine is computer-driven, the efficiency of making lenses is affected by the sophistication of the computer program to define what is required in a lens. Technological advances are being made all the time, and it is thought that a new machine with advanced technology will be available within the next five years. The type of lens required is also a function of what cameras are considered to be in demand by consumers. Even if there is a change in technology, it is thought that cameras with the old style lens could still be marketable for another seven years.

Required

What useful life should management use in calculating depreciation on the machine?

Solution

Three specific time periods are mentioned:
- physical life: 20 years
- technical life: 5 years
- commercial life: 7 years.

A key element in determining the appropriate life is assessing the strategy used by management in marketing its products. If management believes that to retain market share and reputation it needs to be at the cutting edge of technology, five years will be appropriate. If, however, the marketing strategy is aimed at the general consumer, seven years will be appropriate. In essence, management needs to consider at what point it expects to replace the machine.

Residual value

Note again the definition of residual value in paragraph 6 of IAS 16:

> The *residual value* of an asset is the estimated amount that the entity would currently obtain from disposal of the asset, after deducting the estimated costs of disposal, if the asset were already of the age and in the condition expected at the end of its useful life.

Residual value is an estimate based on what the entity would *currently* obtain from the asset's disposal; that is, what could be obtained at the time of the estimate — not at the expected date of disposal at the end of the useful life. The estimate is based on what could be obtained from disposal of *similar* assets that are currently, at the date of the estimate, at the end of their useful lives, and which have been used in a similar fashion to the asset being investigated. Where assets are unique, this estimation process is much more difficult than for assets that are constantly being replaced. For an asset such as a vehicle, which may have a useful life of 10 years, the residual value of a new vehicle is the net amount that could be obtained now for a 10-year-old vehicle of the same type as the one being depreciated. In many cases, the residual value will be negligible or scrap value.

This form of assessment means that the residual value will not be adjusted for expected changes in prices. Basing the residual value calculation on current prices relates to the adoption in IAS 16 of depreciation as a process of allocating economic benefits. If the residual value were adjusted for future prices, then there may be no measure of benefits consumed during the period as the residual value may exceed the carrying amount at the beginning of the period. Management is not required to be a predictor of future inventions. Expectations of technological change are already built into current second-hand asset prices. Management should then take into account reasonable changes in technological development and the effect on prices. Where assets are expected to be used for the whole or the majority of their useful lives, the residual values are zero or immaterial in amount.

Where residual values are material, an entity must, under paragraph 51 of IAS 16, review the residual value at each financial year-end. If a change is required, again the change is a change in estimate and is accounted for prospectively as an adjustment to future depreciation.

Significant parts depreciation

It has been mentioned previously in this chapter that a significant parts approach requires an entity to allocate the cost of an asset to its significant parts and account for each part separately; for example, the cost of an aeroplane is allocated to such parts as the frame, the engines and the fittings. According to paragraph 43 of IAS 16, *each part* of an item of property, plant and equipment with a *cost that is significant* in relation to the total cost of the item must be depreciated *separately*. In other words, an entity is required to separate each item of property, plant and equipment into its significant parts, with each part being separately depreciated. Any remainder is also depreciated separately.

Paragraph 13 of the standard discusses the replacement or renewal of the parts of an asset:

> Under the recognition principle in paragraph 7, an entity recognises in the carrying amount of an item of property, plant and equipment the cost of replacing part of such an item when that cost is incurred if the recognition criteria are met. The carrying amount of those parts that are replaced is derecognised in accordance with the derecognition provisions of this Standard (see paragraphs 67–72).

As is consistent with accounting for all separate items of property, plant and equipment, once an acquired asset is separated into the relevant significant parts, if one of those parts needs regular replacing or renewing, the part is generally accounted for as a separate asset. The replaced asset is depreciated over its useful life, and derecognised on replacement.

To illustrate the accounting for parts, consider the case of a building with a roof that periodically needs replacing. If the roof is accounted for as a separate part, then the roof is accounted for as a separate asset and is depreciated separately. On replacement, paragraph 13 of IAS 16 is applied, and the carrying amount (if any) of the old roof is written off. In order for this derecognition to occur, it is necessary to know the original cost of the roof and the depreciation charged to date. The new roof is accounted for as the acquisition of a new asset, assessed under paragraph 7 and, if capitalised as an asset, subsequently depreciated. If, however, the roof is not treated as a separate part from the acquisition date of the building, then on replacement of the roof, calculation of the amount to be derecognised is more difficult. An estimation may need to be made of the cost of the roof at acquisition date in order to derecognise the roof.

Another example of dealing with a part of an asset arises where assets are subject to regular major inspections to ensure that they reach the requisite safety and quality requirements. Under paragraph 14 of IAS 16, such major inspections may be capitalised as a replacement part. In order for the cost of the inspection to be capitalised, the recognition criteria in paragraph 7 of the standard must be met. In particular, it must be probable that future economic benefits associated with the outlay will flow to the entity. For example, if there is a 5-year inspection of aircraft by a specific party, and this is required every 5 years in order for the aircraft not to be grounded, then the cost of the inspection provides benefits to the owner of the aircraft for that period of time by effectively providing a licence to continue flying. The capitalised amount is then depreciated over the relevant useful life, most probably the time until the next inspection.

5.6 THE REVALUATION MODEL

Use of the revaluation model of measurement is the alternative treatment to the cost model. Paragraph 31 of IAS 16 states:

> After recognition as an asset, an item of property, plant and equipment whose fair value can be measured reliably shall be carried at a revalued amount, being its fair value at the date of the revaluation less any subsequent accumulated depreciation and subsequent accumulated impairment losses. Revaluations shall be made with sufficient regularity to ensure that the carrying amount does not differ materially from that which would be determined using fair value at the end of the reporting period.

In relation to this paragraph, note the following points:

1. The measurement basis is fair value, defined in Appendix A of IFRS 13 *Fair Value Measurement* as 'the price that would be received to sell an asset or paid to transfer a liability in an orderly transaction between market participants at the measurement date'. Fair value is an exit price and is measured in accordance with IFRS 13. Under this standard, there are a number of methods that may be used to measure fair value such as the market approach, the cost approach and the income approach. There are also a variety of inputs to these valuation techniques which are prioritised into three levels — Level 1, Level 2 and Level 3. This fair value hierarchy gives highest priority to observable inputs rather than unobservable inputs. *See chapter 8 for more information on fair value measurement.*

2. IAS 16 does not specify how often revaluations must take place. The principle established is that the revaluations must be of sufficient regularity such that the carrying amount of the asset does not materially differ from fair value. The frequency of revaluations depends on the nature of the assets themselves. For some assets, frequent revaluations are necessary because of continual change in the fair values owing to a volatile market. For other assets, revaluation every 3 or 5 years may be appropriate (paragraph 34). Paragraph 38 notes that assets may be revalued on a rolling basis provided that the total revaluation is completed within a short period of time, and that at no time is the total carrying amount of the class of assets materially different from fair value.

3. To understand the type of information that might be observed in determining whether there is a need to revalue an asset, it is useful to note the inputs into the valuation techniques. For example, in paragraph B35(g) of IFRS 13, in relation to buildings held and used, it is noted that a Level 2 input would be the price per square metre for the building derived from observable market data; for example, multiples derived from process in observed transactions involving comparable or similar buildings in similar locations.

Paragraph 36 of IAS 16 notes that the revaluation model is not applied to individual items of property, plant and equipment; instead, the accounting policy is applied to a class of assets. Hence, for each class of assets, management must choose whether to apply the cost model or the revaluation model.

A class of property, plant and equipment 'is a grouping of assets of a similar nature and use in an entity's operations' (IAS 16 paragraph 37). Examples of separate classes are:

- land
- land and buildings
- machinery
- ships
- aircraft
- motor vehicles
- furniture and fixtures
- office equipment.

There are two purposes for requiring revaluation to be done on a class rather than on an individual asset basis. First, this limits the ability of management to selectively choose which assets to revalue. Thus in order to be able to adopt the revaluation model, the fair values need to be capable of being reliably measured for all assets within the class. Second, the requirement to have all assets within the class measured on a fair value basis means that there is consistent measurement for the same type of assets in the entity.

According to paragraph 31 of IAS 16, where an asset is carried at a revalued amount, recognition of the asset should occur only when the fair value can be measured reliably. This is unlikely to be an issue as IFRS 13 allows the use of unobservable inputs in measuring fair value.

5.6.1 Applying the revaluation model: revaluation increases

Paragraphs 39 and 40 of IAS 16 contain the principles for applying the fair value method to revaluation increases. These paragraphs apply to individual items of property, plant and equipment. In other words, even though revaluations are done on a class-by-class basis, the accounting is done on an asset-by-asset basis.

The first part of paragraph 39 states:

> If an asset's carrying amount is increased as a result of a revaluation, the increase shall be recognised in other comprehensive income and accumulated in equity under the heading of revaluation surplus.

Note two points here:

1. *The increase is recognised in other comprehensive income.* In the statement of profit or loss and other comprehensive income, the comprehensive income for a period is divided into profit or loss (P/L) for the period and other comprehensive income (OCI). Revaluation increases are recognised in other comprehensive income, not profit or loss. An example of a statement of profit or loss and other comprehensive income showing the disclosure of profit for the year separately from the other comprehensive income items is given in figure 5.2.

FIGURE 5.2 Statement of profit or loss and other comprehensive income

XYZ GROUP Statement of Profit or Loss and Other Comprehensive Income for the year ended 31 December 20X7		
(illustrating the presentation of profit or loss and other comprehensive income in one statement and the classification of expenses within profit by function) *(in thousands of currency units)*		
	20X7	20X6
Revenue	390,000	355,000
Cost of sales	(245,000)	(230,000)
Gross profit	145,000	125,000
Other income	20,667	11,300
Distribution costs	(9,000)	(8,700)
Administrative expenses	(20,000)	(21,000)
Other expenses	(2,100)	(1,200)
Finance costs	(8,000)	(7,500)
Share of profit of associates	35,100	30,100
Profit before tax	161,667	128,000
Income tax expense	(40,417)	(32,000)
Profit for the year from continuing operations	121,250	96,000
Loss for the year from discontinued operations		(30,500)
Profit for the year	121,250	65,500
Other comprehensive income		
Items that will not be reclassified to profit or loss		
Gains on property revaluation	933	3,367
Actuarial gains (losses) on defined benefit pension plans	(667)	1,333
Share of gain (loss) on properly revaluation of associates	400	(700)
Income tax relating to items that will not be reclassified	(166)	(1,000)
	500	3,000
	20X7	20X6
Items that may be reclassified subsequently to profit or loss		
Exchange differences on translating foreign operations	5,334	10,667
Debt instruments at fair value through other comprehensive income	(24,000)	26,667
Cash flow hedges	(667)	(4,000)
Income tax relating to items that may be reclassified	4,833	(8,334)
	(14,500)	25,000
Other comprehensive income for the year, net of tax	(14,000)	28,000
TOTAL COMPREHENSIVE INCOME FOR THE YEAR	107,250	93,500

Source: Based upon the illustration in IAS 1 paragraph IG 6.

Hence the initial journal entry for a revaluation increase is:

Asset	Dr	xxx
Gain on Revaluation of Non-Current Asset (OCI)	Cr	xxx
(Revaluation of asset)		

In accordance with paragraph 42 of IAS 16, the effects of any taxes resulting from the revaluation of property, plant and equipment need to be accounted for in accordance with IAS 12 *Income Taxes*. A revaluation of an asset may give rise to a difference between the tax base and the carrying amount of the asset, leading to a taxable temporary difference, in which case a deferred tax liability needs to be raised (see paragraph 20 of IAS 12). Paragraph 90 of IAS 1 *Presentation of Financial Statements* requires the disclosure of 'the amount of income tax relating to each item of other comprehensive income'. To reflect the tax effect of the gain, the required entry is:

Gain on Revaluation of Asset (OCI)	Dr	xxx
Deferred Tax Liability	Cr	xxx
(Recognition of tax effect of revaluation increase)		

The reason for the immediate recognition of the deferred tax effect is because, as explained below, the gain on revaluation of non-current assets is accumulated in equity.

2. Having recognised the gain in other comprehensive income, the gain, net of tax, is transferred to equity under the heading of revaluation surplus. The required entry is:

Gain on Revaluation of Non-Current Asset (OCI)	Dr	xxx
Asset Revaluation Surplus	Cr	xxx
(Accumulation of net revaluation gain in equity)		

The asset revaluation surplus is disclosed in the reserve section of the statement of financial position.

ILLUSTRATIVE EXAMPLE 5.2 Revaluation increases and tax effect

On 1 January 2024, XYZ Group carries an item of land at a cost of £100,000, this amount also being the tax base of the asset. The land is revalued to £120,000. The tax rate is 30%.

The new carrying amount is £120,000 and the tax base of the asset is £100,000, giving rise to a taxable temporary difference of £20,000. A deferred tax liability of £6,000 must be raised to account for the expected tax to be paid in relation to the increase in expected benefits from the asset. The asset revaluation surplus raised will be the net after-tax increase in the asset (£20,000 − £6,000 = £14,000). The appropriate accounting entries on revaluation of the asset are shown in figure 5.3.

FIGURE 5.3 Journal entries for revaluation with associated tax effect

Land	Dr	20,000	
Gain on Revaluation of Land (OCI)	Cr		20,000
(Recognition of revaluation increase: £120,000 – £100,000)			
Gain on Revaluation of Land (OCI)	Dr	6,000	
Deferred Tax Liability	Cr		6,000
Gain on Revaluation of Land (OCI)	Dr	14,000	
Asset Revaluation Surplus	Cr		14,000
(Accumulation of net revaluation gain in equity)			

Where the item of property, plant and equipment is depreciable, there are two possible accounting treatments under paragraph 35 of IAS 16:

1. restate proportionately with the change in the gross carrying amount of the asset so that the carrying amount of the asset after revaluation equals its revalued amount; or
2. eliminate the accumulated depreciation balance against the gross carrying amount of the asset and then restate the net amount to the fair value of the asset. This method is applied in this chapter.

ILLUSTRATIVE EXAMPLE 5.3 Revaluation increases and depreciable assets

On 30 June 2024, an item of plant has a carrying amount of £42,000, being the original cost of £70,000 less accumulated depreciation of £28,000. The fair value of the asset is £50,000. The tax rate is 30%. The entries are shown in figure 5.4.

FIGURE 5.4 Revaluation increase and depreciable assets

The revaluation is done in two steps:

The first step is to write off the accumulated depreciation of the plant, reducing the asset to its carrying amount of £42,000.

Accumulated Depreciation Plant	Dr	28,000
Plant	Cr	28,000
(Write down asset to its carrying amount)		

The second step is to adjust the carrying amount of £42,000 to the fair value of the asset, £50,000, being an increase of £8,000. This increase is tax-effected, and the net gain accumulated to equity.

Plant	Dr	8,000
Gain on Revaluation of Plant (OCI)	Cr	8,000
(Revaluation of asset to fair value)		
Gain on Revaluation of Plant (OCI)	Dr	2,400
Deferred Tax Liability	Cr	2,400
(Tax effect of revaluation increase)		
Gain on Revaluation of Plant (OCI)	Dr	5,600
Asset Revaluation Surplus	Cr	5,600
(Accumulation of net revaluation gain in equity)		

Revaluation increase reversing previous revaluation decrease

The full text of paragraph 39 of IAS 16 is as follows:

> If an asset's carrying amount is increased as a result of a revaluation, the increase shall be recognised in other comprehensive income and accumulated in equity under the heading of revaluation surplus. However, the increase shall be recognised in profit or loss to the extent that it reverses a revaluation decrease of the same asset previously recognised in profit or loss.

Hence, a revaluation increase is credited to an asset revaluation surplus unless the increase reverses a revaluation decrease previously recognised as an expense in which case it is recognised as income (within profit or loss). The accounting treatment for revaluation decreases is discussed in the next section.

5.6.2 Applying the revaluation model: revaluation decreases

Paragraph 40 of IAS 16 states:

> If an asset's carrying amount is decreased as a result of a revaluation, the decrease shall be recognised in profit or loss. However, the decrease shall be recognised in other comprehensive income to the extent of any credit balance existing in the revaluation surplus in respect of that asset.

As with revaluation increases, this paragraph covers two situations: a revaluation decrease, and a revaluation decrease following a previous revaluation increase.

The accounting for a revaluation decrease involves an immediate recognition of a loss in the period of the downward revaluation. As the change in the carrying amount of the asset directly affects income, the tax effect is dealt with in the normal workings of tax-effect accounting. Hence, no extra tax-effect entries outside those generated via the tax-effect worksheet are necessary in accounting for revaluation decrease.

ILLUSTRATIVE EXAMPLE 5.4 Revaluation decrease

An item of plant has a carrying amount of £50,000, comprising the original cost of £60,000 less accumulated depreciation of £10,000. If the asset is revalued downwards to £24,000, the appropriate journal entries are:

Accumulated Depreciation	Dr	10,000	
Plant	Cr		10,000
(Eliminating accumulated depreciation on revaluation)			
Loss – Downward Revaluation of Plant (P/L)	Dr	26,000	
Plant	Cr		26,000
(Revaluation of asset from carrying amount of £50,000 to fair value of £24,000)			

In relation to the tax-effect worksheet, if the carrying amount and the tax base in this example were the same immediately before the revaluation and the revaluation would only be tax deductible in future years, then there would be a deductible temporary difference of £26,000. A deferred tax asset of £7,800 would be raised via the tax-effect worksheet analysis at the end of the reporting period. If, however, the decrease in value would be tax deductible, no deferred tax asset is recognised, instead the current tax liability would be lower.

Decrease reversing previous revaluation increase

Where an asset revaluation surplus has been raised via a previous revaluation increase, in accounting for a subsequent revaluation decrease for the same asset, the surplus must be eliminated before any expense is recognised. In adjusting for the previous revaluation increase, both the asset revaluation surplus and the related deferred tax liability must be reversed.

ILLUSTRATIVE EXAMPLE 5.5 Decrease reversing previous increase

XYZ Group has a block of land with a cost of £100,000. When the land was revalued upwards to £200,000, the following entries were passed:

Land	Dr	100,000	
Gain on Revaluation of Land (OCI)	Cr		100,000
(Revaluation of asset to fair value)			
Gain on revaluation of land (OCI)	Dr	30,000	
Deferred Tax Liability	Cr		30,000
(Tax effect of revaluation increase)			
Gain on Revaluation of Land (OCI)	Dr	70,000	
Asset Revaluation Surplus	Cr		70,000
(Accumulation of net revaluation gain in equity)			

If the land is subsequently *revalued downwards* to £160,000, the £40,000 write-down is a partial reversal of the previous upward revaluation. The accounting entries then reflect:
- a recognition of the decrease in other comprehensive income, and
- a decrease in accumulated equity, namely, asset revaluation surplus.

Loss on Revaluation of Land (OCI)	Dr	40,000	
Land	Cr		40,000
(Revaluation downwards of land)			
Deferred Tax Liability	Dr	12,000	
Loss on Revaluation of Land (OCI)	Cr		12,000
(Tax effect of revaluation decrease)			
Asset Revaluation Surplus	Dr	28,000	
Loss on Revaluation of Land (OCI)	Cr		28,000
(Reduction in accumulated equity due to revaluation decrease on land)			

However, if the land is subsequently *revalued downwards* to £80,000, which is a reduction of £120,000, the land is written down to an amount £20,000 less than the original cost of the land.

In accordance with paragraph 40, the downward revaluation requires a loss to be recognised in profit or loss, as well as a decrease to be recognised in other comprehensive income. Effectively this will result in the elimination of the deferred tax liability and the asset revaluation surplus previously raised. The appropriate entries are:

Loss on Revaluation of Land (P/L)	Dr	20,000	
Loss on Revaluation of Land (OCI)	Dr	100,000	
Land	Cr		120,000
(Revaluation downwards of land)			
Deferred Tax Liability	Dr	30,000	
Loss on Revaluation of Land (OCI)	Cr		30,000
(Tax effect of loss on revaluation of land)			
Asset Revaluation Surplus	Dr	70,000	
Loss on Revaluation of Land (OCI)	Cr		70,000
(Reduction in accumulated equity due to revaluation decrease on land)			

The tax-effect worksheet, assuming the original revaluation increase occurred in a previous period, is shown in figure 5.5.

FIGURE 5.5 Tax-effect worksheet on revaluation of assets

	Carrying amount	Tax base	Taxable temporary differences	Deductible temporary differences
Land	£80,000	£100,000		£20,000
Temporary difference				20,000
Deferred tax liability — closing balance			—	
Deferred tax asset — closing balance				6,000 Dr
Beginning balance			£30,000 Cr	
Movement during the year			30,000 Dr	
Adjustment				6,000 Dr

The tax-effect worksheet shows that XYZ Group would recognise a deferred tax asset of £6,000, reflecting the fact that the carrying amount of the asset is £20,000 less than the tax base.

Net revaluation increase reversing previous revaluation decrease

Where an asset is revalued upwards, an asset revaluation surplus is credited except where the increase reverses a revaluation decrease previously recognised as a loss. In this case, the revaluation increase must be recognised as a gain.

ILLUSTRATIVE EXAMPLE 5.6 Revaluation increase reversing previous decrease

XYZ Group has an item of plant that cost £300,000. Depreciation is on the diminishing balance basis at 10% per annum. At the end of the first year, the plant was revalued downwards to £220,000, with the following accounting entries being passed:

Accumulated Depreciation	Dr	30,000	
Plant	Cr		30,000
(Eliminating accumulated depreciation [£300,000 × 10%] on downward revaluation)			

Loss – Downward Revaluation of Plant (P/L)	Dr	50,000	
Plant	Cr		50,000
(Revaluation of asset from carrying amount of £270,000 [£300,000 – £30,000] to fair value of £220,000)			

If at the end of the second year, the plant is assessed as having a fair value of £230,000, there is a revaluation increase of £32,000 [£230,000 – (£220,000 – £22,000). However as there was a previous decrease of £50,000, the appropriate revaluation entry must reverse part of this previously recognised revaluation loss. The entries are:

Accumulated Depreciation	Dr	22,000	
Plant	Cr		22,000
(Eliminating accumulated depreciation [£220,000 × 10%] on revaluation)			
Plant	Dr	32,000	
Gain on Revaluation of Plant (P/L)	Cr		32,000
(Revaluation of plant from carrying amount of £198,000 (£220,000 – £22,000) to fair value of £230,000, subsequent to prior write-down of the plant)			

However, if at the end of the second year, the plant is assessed as having a fair value of £280,000, the accounting entries recognise the increase of £82,000 as consisting of two parts:
1. the reversal of the previously recognised write-down loss of £50,000; this reversal is recognised as a gain, and disclosed in profit or loss
2. the £32,000 increase recognised in other comprehensive income and accumulated in asset revaluation surplus.

The entries are:

Accumulated Depreciation	Dr	22,000	
Plant	Cr		22,000
(Eliminating accumulated depreciation [£220,000 × 10%] on revaluation)			
Plant	Dr	80,000	
Gain on Revaluation of Plant (P/L)	Cr		50,000
Gain on Revaluation of Plant (OCI)	Cr		32,000
(Revaluation of plant from carrying amount of £198,000 (£220,000 – £22,000) to fair value of £280,000)			
Gain on Revaluation of Plant (OCI)	Dr	9,600	
Deferred Tax Liability	Cr		9,600
(Tax effect of revaluation gain)			
Gain on Revaluation of Plant (OCI)	Dr	22,400	
Asset Revaluation Surplus	Cr		22,400
(Accumulation of revaluation gain in equity)			

5.6.3 Effects of accounting on an asset-by-asset basis

If the fair value basis of measurement is chosen, IAS 16 requires it to be applied to items of property, plant and equipment on a class-by-class basis. However, in accounting for revaluation increases and decreases, the accounting is done on an individual asset basis within the class. Practising accountants and standard setters have often argued that a better accounting treatment would be to account for revaluation increases and decreases on a class-by-class basis. The rationale for this is that under IAS 16 revaluation increases (gains) and revaluation decreases (losses) above amortised cost are recognised in other comprehensive income and accumulated in equity while revaluation increases (gains) and revaluation decreases (losses) below amortised cost are recognised in profit or loss in the period the revaluation occurs. If revaluation was done on a class-by-class basis, then it would be the net increase that would be accounted for, providing a netting of the gains and losses. Figure 5.6 illustrates this.

FIGURE 5.6 Revaluation by asset or class of asset?

Assets	Carrying amount £	Fair value £	Increase/(decrease) £
Plant A	1,500,000	2,000,000	500,000
Plant B	1,500,000	1,200,000	(300,000)
Total	3,000,000	3,200,000	200,000

Applying IAS 16, both Plant A and Plant B, being in the one class of assets, have to be revalued to fair value if the revaluation model is applied to plant. However, in accounting for the movements in fair value, each asset is dealt with separately. With Plant A, as there is a revaluation increase of £500,000, the increase results in a £500,000 gain being recognised in other comprehensive income and £350,000 (assuming a tax rate of 30%) being accumulated in equity affecting an asset revaluation surplus. With Plant B, the revaluation decrease of £300,000 is recognised as an expense affecting current period profit or loss. For those who argue that revaluations should be accounted for on a class-by-class basis, the net revaluation increase on plant is £200,000. Accounting on a class basis would result in recognising a £200,000 gain in other comprehensive income and then accumulating £140,000 in an asset revaluation surplus with no effect on current period profit or loss. The argument for the class method of accounting is that it reduces the biased effect that the IAS 16 method has on current period profit or loss. However the two methods produce the same total comprehensive income for the period.

5.6.4 Applying the revaluation model: transfers from asset revaluation surplus

Paragraph 41 of IAS 16 covers the accounting for the asset revaluation surplus subsequent to its creation. There are two circumstances where the asset revaluation surplus may be transferred to retained earnings. Note that there is no requirement that the asset revaluation surplus must be transferred, only a specification of situations where it may be transferred. The *first* situation is where the asset is derecognised (i.e. removed from the statement of financial position, for example, by sale of the asset). In this case, the whole or part of the surplus may be transferred. The *second* situation is where an asset is being used up over its useful life, a proportion of the revaluation surplus may be transferred to retained earnings, the proportion being in relation to the depreciation on the asset. In this case, the amount of the surplus transferred would be equal to the difference between depreciation based on the original cost, and depreciation based on the revalued amount, adjusted for the tax effect relating to the surplus. This second situation is shown in illustrative example 5.7.

ILLUSTRATIVE EXAMPLE 5.7 Transferring revaluation surplus to retained earnings

An item of plant is acquired at a cost of £100,000. The plant is depreciated using the straight-line method over a useful life of 10 years. The tax rate is 30%.

At the end of the first year, the plant is revalued to a fair value of £126,000. The useful life of the plant remained unchanged.

The revaluation entries at the end of the first year are:

Accumulated Depreciation	Dr	10,000	
Plant	Cr		10,000
(Eliminating accumulated depreciation [£100,000 × 10%] on revaluation)			

Plant	Dr	36,000	
Gain on Revaluation of Plant (OCI)	Cr		36,000
(Revaluation of plant from £90,000 to £126,000)			
Gain on Revaluation of Plant (OCI)	Dr	10,800	
Deferred Tax Liability	Cr		10,800
(Tax effect of revaluation of plant)			
Gain on Revaluation of Plant (OCI)	Dr	25,200	
Asset Revaluation Surplus	Cr		25,200
(Accumulation of revaluation gain in equity)			
(£36,000 − £10,800)			

The remaining useful life of the asset at revaluation date (end of the first year) is nine years. Therefore, at the end of the second year, depreciation expense of £14,000 (£126,000 / 9 yrs) is recorded. In addition, XYZ Group may transfer £2,800 (£25,200 / 9 yrs) of the asset revaluation surplus to retained earnings. Note that there is no transfer of the asset revaluation surplus to retained earnings at the end of the first year as the revaluation only took place on that date. The entries at the end of the second year are:

Depreciation	Dr	14,000	
Accumulated Depreciation	Cr		14,000
(Depreciation expense for the second year)			
Asset Revaluation Surplus	Dr	2,800	
Retained earnings	Cr		2,800
(Transfer from asset revaluation surplus to retained earnings)			

5.6.5 Applying the revaluation model: depreciation of revalued assets

Section 5.5.1 discusses the accounting treatment for depreciation under IAS 16. As noted, the term 'depreciable amount' includes 'other amount substituted for cost'. This includes fair value. Paragraph 50 of IAS 16 notes that depreciation is a process of allocation. Hence, even though an asset is measured at fair value, depreciation is not determined simply as the change in fair value of the asset over a period. As with the cost method, depreciation for a period is calculated after considering the pattern of economic benefits relating to the asset and the residual value of the asset.

ILLUSTRATIVE EXAMPLE 5.8 Depreciation of revalued assets

XYZ Group has an item of plant that was revalued to £1,000 at 30 June 2024. The asset is expected to have a remaining useful life of five years, with benefits being received evenly over that period. The residual value is assessed to be £100. The tax rate is 30%. Consider two situations.

Situation 1

One year later, at 30 June 2025, no formal revaluation occurs and the management of XYZ Group assess that the carrying amount of the plant is not materially different from fair value.

The appropriate journal entry for the 2024–2025 period is:

2025			
June 30	Depreciation Expense	Dr	180	
	Accumulated Depreciation	Cr		180
	(Depreciation on plant 1/5[£1,000 − £100])			

The asset is reported in the statement of financial position at a carrying amount of £820, equal to a gross amount of £1,000 less accumulated depreciation of £180, the carrying amount being equal to fair value.

Situation 2

One year later, at 30 June 2025, a formal revaluation occurs and the external valuers assess the fair value of the plant to be £890.

The appropriate journal entries for the 2024–2025 period are:

2025				
June 30	Depreciation Expense	Dr	180	
	Accumulated Depreciation	Cr		180
	(Depreciation on plant 1/5[£1,000 − £100])			
	Accumulated Depreciation	Dr	180	
	Plant	Cr		180
	(Elimination of accumulated depreciation on revaluation)			
	Plant	Dr	70	
	Gain on Revaluation of Plant (OCI)	Cr		70
	(Revaluation of plant from £820 to £890)			
	Gain on Revaluation of Plant (OCI)	Dr	21	
	Deferred Tax Liability	Cr		21
	(Tax effect of revaluation of plant)			
	Gain on Revaluation of Plant (OCI)	Dr	49	
	Asset Revaluation Surplus	Cr		49
	(Accumulation of net revaluation gain in equity)			

In other words, there is a two-step process. Depreciation is allocated in accordance with normal depreciation principles. Then, as a formal revaluation occurs, the accumulated depreciation is written off and the asset revalued to fair value. The asset is reported in the statement of financial position at fair value of £890 with no associated accumulated depreciation.

It may be argued that the accounting in situation 2 is inappropriate. Whereas the depreciation charge affects profit or loss, the gain on the revaluation of the asset affects other comprehensive income. The economic benefits in relation to the asset for the period are not only those achieved by consumption of the asset, but also those obtained by changes in the market value of the asset. However, these are accounted for differently under IAS 16. It could then be argued that the appropriate depreciation in situation 2 should be the change in fair value over the period, namely £110 (£1,000 − £890), with the journal entry being:

	Depreciation Expense	Dr	110	
	Accumulated Depreciation	Cr		110
	(Depreciation on plant)			

No revaluation entry is then necessary. Note, however, that this entry is not allowed under IAS 16.

Subsequent to revaluation, XYZ Group should reassess the useful life and residual value of the revalued asset because these may change as a result of economic changes affecting XYZ Group and its use of assets. Using the example in scenario 2, following the revaluation at 30 June 2025, assume XYZ Group determines that the residual value is £110 and the remaining useful life is four years. In the 2025–2026 period, the depreciation entry is:

	Depreciation Expense	Dr	195	
	Accumulated Depreciation	Cr		195
	(Depreciation on plant 1/4[£890 − £110])			

5.7 CHOOSING BETWEEN THE COST MODEL AND THE REVALUATION MODEL

Given that IAS 16 allows entities a choice between the cost model and the revaluation model, it is of interest to consider what motivates entities to choose between the two measurement models.

Arguments relating to the choice of models generally claim that a current price (a fair value) will provide more relevant information than a past price (the original cost). However, the requirement under IAS 16 to continuously adjust the carrying amounts of assets measured at fair value so that they are not materially different from current fair values provides a cost disincentive to management to adopt the revaluation model. Costs associated with adopting the revaluation model include the cost of employing valuers, annual costs associated with reviewing the carrying amounts to assess whether a revaluation is necessary, extra record-keeping costs associated with the revaluations, including accounting for the associated revaluation increases and decreases, and increased audit costs relating to the review of changing revalued amounts.

A further factor that influences some entities' measurement choice in favour of the cost model is harmonisation with US GAAP, which does not allow the revaluation of non-current assets. Another factor that entities have to consider when choosing their measurement bases for classes of property, plant and equipment is the effect of the model on the statement of profit or loss and other comprehensive income. Where assets are measured on a fair value basis, the depreciation per annum is expected to be higher as the depreciable amount is higher.

Besides the effect of higher depreciation, there will be the effect on the disposal of the asset. Where an asset is measured at fair value, there is expected to be an immaterial amount of profit or loss on sale as, at the time of sale, the recorded amount of the asset should be close to that of the market price. For an asset measured at cost, the full difference between sales proceeds and carrying amount based upon historical cost will be reported in profit or loss.

What, apart from increased relevance and reliability arguments, are the incentives for management to use the revaluation model? The effect of adopting the revaluation model is to increase the entity's assets and equities (via the revaluation surplus). Hence, entities that want to report higher amounts in these areas would consider adoption of the revaluation model. The incentives for entities to adopt fair value measures then tend to be entity-specific because the entities face pressures relating to external circumstances. Examples of such pressures are:

- Entities with debt covenants generally have constraints relating to their debt–asset ratios, such as the requirement that the debt–asset ratio must not exceed 50%. Hence, for an entity with increasing debt, adoption of the revaluation model for a class of assets that is increasing in value will ease pressures on the debt–asset ratio by increasing the asset base of the entity. This assumes that the debt covenant allows revaluations to be taken into account in measuring assets.
- An entity's reported profit figure may be under scrutiny from a specific source, such as a trade union seeking reasons to support claims for higher pay, or regulators looking at monopoly control within an industry.

Where there are pressures to report lower profits, adoption of the revaluation model provides scope for higher depreciation charges. These are reflected in the profit or loss for the period. The increases in the values of the non-current assets do not affect profit or loss but are reported in other comprehensive income. If ratios such as rates of return on assets or equity are based on profit rather than comprehensive income, lower reported profits and higher asset/equity bases will result in an entity being seen in a less favourable light.

However, as noted above, the incentives relating to playing with profit and asset numbers tend to rely on users of the information having no knowledge of accounting rules or movements in prices within industries or sectors, or being unable to make comparisons across entities within an industry segment. One of the key elements of analysing entities within an industry is comparability of information. If all entities in the sector are applying the cost model, analysts can make their judgements by comparing the information between the entities and applying information from sources other than accounting reports, such as movements in price indexes. The entity then has less reason to incur the costs of adopting the revaluation model of measurement.

5.8 DERECOGNITION

As noted in paragraph 3 of IAS 16, the standard does not apply to non-current assets classified as held for sale and accounted for under IFRS 5. IAS 16 then deals with the disposal of non-current assets that have not previously been classified as held for sale.

Paragraph 67 of IAS 16 identifies two occasions where derecognition of an item of property, plant and equipment should occur:

- on disposal, such as the sale of the asset
- when no future economic benefits are expected, either from future use or from disposal.

When items of property, plant and equipment are sold, regardless of whether there are many or few remaining economic benefits, the selling entity will recognise a gain or loss on the asset, this being determined as the difference between the net proceeds from sale and the carrying amount of the asset at the time of sale (IAS 16 paragraph 71). In calculating the net proceeds from sale, any deferred consideration must be discounted, and the proceeds calculated at the cash price equivalent (IAS 16 paragraph 72). As the carrying amount is net of depreciation and impairment losses, it is necessary to calculate the depreciation from the beginning of the reporting period to the point of sale. Failing to do this, whether under the cost model or the revaluation model, would be out of step with the key principle established in IAS 16 that depreciation is a process of allocation and each period must bear its fair share of the cost or revalued amount of the asset.

The gain or loss on sale is included in the profit or loss for the period. Note paragraph 34 of IAS 1 *Presentation of Financial Statements*:

(a) an entity presents gains and losses on the disposal of non-current assets, including investments and operating assets, by deducting from the proceeds on disposal the carrying amount of the asset and related selling expenses; . . .

Paragraph 34 (a) requires only the disclosure of the gain or loss on sale, as opposed to separate disclosure of the income and the carrying amount of the asset (see also paragraph 98(c) of IAS 1). The argument for the netting of the income and expense is that gains/losses on the disposal of property, plant and equipment result from activities that are not considered to be the main revenue-generating activities of an entity.

In paragraph BC35 of the Basis of Conclusions on IAS 16, the IASB argued:

users of financial statements would consider these gains and the proceeds from an entity's sale of goods in the course of its ordinary activities differently in their evaluation of an entity's past results and their projections of future cash flows. This is because revenue from the sale of goods is typically more likely to recur in comparable amounts than are gains from sales of items of property, plant and equipment. Accordingly, the Board concluded that an entity should not classify as revenue gains on disposals of items of property, plant and equipment.

However, in preparing a cash flow statement, proceeds from the sale of property, plant and equipment are normally shown as a cash flow from investing activities.

ILLUSTRATIVE EXAMPLE 5.9 Disposals of assets

XYZ Group acquired an item of plant on 1 July 2023 for £100,000. The asset had an expected useful life of 10 years and a residual value of £20,000. On 1 January 2026, XYZ Group sold the asset for £81,000.

Required

Prepare the journal entries relating to this asset in the year of sale.

Solution

At the point of sale, the depreciation on the asset must be calculated for that part of the year for which the asset was held before the sale. Hence, for the half-year before the sale, under the straight-line method, depreciation of £4,000 (i.e. $0.5 \times 1/10[£100,000 - £20,000]$) must be charged as an expense. The entry is:

Depreciation Expense	Dr	4,000	
Accumulated Depreciation	Cr		4,000
(Depreciation charge up to point of sale)			

The gain or loss on sale is the difference between the proceeds on sale of £81,000 and the carrying amount at time of sale of £80,000 (i.e. $£100,000 - 2.5[1/10 \times £80,000]$), which is £1,000. The required journal entry is:

Cash	Dr	81,000	
Accumulated Depreciation	Dr	20,000	
Plant	Cr		100,000
Gain on Sale of Plant	Cr		1,000
(Gain on sale of asset)			

In this example, the asset was sold for £81,000. Assume that the asset, now referred to as Plant A, was traded in for another asset, Plant B. Plant B had a fair value of £280,000, with XYZ Group making a cash payment of £202,000 as well as giving up Plant A. The trade-in amount is then £78,000. The journal entries to record this transaction are:

Plant B	Dr	280,000	
Loss on Sale of Plant A (P/L)	Dr	2,000	
Accumulated Depreciation – Plant A	Dr	20,000	
Plant A	Cr		100,000
Cash	Cr		202,000
(Acquisition of Plant B and trade-in of Plant A)			

5.9 DISCLOSURE

Paragraphs 73–79 of IAS 16 contain the required disclosures relating to property, plant and equipment. Information in paragraph 73 is required on a class-by-class basis, and paragraph 77 relates only to assets stated at revalued amounts. Paragraph 79 contains information that entities are encouraged to disclose, but are not required to do so. Figure 5.7 provides an illustration of the disclosures required by IAS 16.

FIGURE 5.7 Illustrative disclosures required by IAS 16

	IAS 16 paragraph
Note 1: Summary of accounting policies (extract)	
Property, plant and equipment	
Freehold land and buildings on freehold land are measured on a fair value basis. At the end of each reporting period, the value of each asset in these classes is reviewed to ensure that it does not differ materially from the asset's fair value at that date. Where necessary, the asset is revalued to reflect its fair value. In June 2024, revaluations were carried out by an independent valuer; since then valuations have been made internally. The basis for the assessment of fair value has been by reference to observable transactions in the property market, including an analysis of prices paid in recent market transactions for similar properties. No other valuation techniques were used.	73(a) 77(a) 77(b) 77(a)
All other classes of property, plant and equipment are measured at cost.	73(a)
Depreciation	
Depreciation is provided on a straight-line basis for all property, plant and equipment, other than freehold land.	73(b)
The useful lives of the assets are:	73(c)

	2026	2025
Freehold buildings	40 years	40 years
Plant and equipment	5 to 15 years	5 to 15 years

Note 10: Property, plant and equipment

	Land and buildings		Plant and equipment		
	2026	2025	2026	2025	
	£'000	£'000	£'000	£'000	
Balance at beginning of year	1,861	1,765	2,840	2,640	73(d)
Accumulated depreciation	(400)	(364)	(732)	(520)	
Carrying amount	1,461	1,401	2,108	2,120	
Additions	—	123	755	372	73(e)(i)
Disposals	(466)	(18)	(181)	(158)	73(e)(ii)
Acquisitions via business combinations	739	—	412	—	73(e)(iii)

(continued)

FIGURE 5.7 *(continued)*

Impairment losses	—	—	(100)	—	73(e)(v)
Depreciation	(20)	(36)	(161)	(212)	73(e)(vii)
Transfer to assets held for sale	(438)	—	(890)	—	73(e)(ix)
Net exchange differences	11	(9)	8	(14)	73(e)(viii)
Carrying amount at end of year	1,287	1,461	1,951	2,108	73(d)
Property, plant and equipment:					
At cost	1,707	1,861	2,944	2,840	
Accumulated depreciation and impairment losses	(420)	(400)	(993)	(732)	
Carrying amount at end of year	1,287	1,461	1,951	2,108	73(d)

For the freehold land and buildings measured at fair value, the carrying amount that would have been recognised if they had been carried at cost is:			77(e)
	2026 £'000	2025 £'000	
Carrying amount at end of year	942	824	

Plant and equipment of £420,000 have been pledged as security for loans to the company.	74(a)
The company has entered into a contract to acquire £640,000 of plant equipment over the next 2 years.	74(c)

Activity in the revaluation surplus for land and buildings is as follows:			77(f)
	2026 £'000	2025 £'000	
Balance at beginning of year	309	303	
Revaluation of gains on land and buildings	42	9	
Deferred tax liability	(13)	(3)	
Balance at end of year	338	309	

5.10 INVESTMENT PROPERTIES

IAS 40 *Investment Properties* requires that an entity differentiate between investment properties and other properties, such as owner-occupied property.

For an item to be classified as investment property, it must meet the definition of investment property. Investment property is essentially property from which the entity intends to earn capital appreciation or rental income or both.

5.10.1 Definition and classification

Investment property is defined in paragraph 5 of IAS 40 as land or buildings (or both, or part of a building), held by an owner or leased by a lessee under a finance lease:

- to earn rentals or for capital appreciation or both;
- rather than for use in the production or supply of goods or services or for administrative purposes or sale in the ordinary course of business.

In addition, a property held under an operating lease may be classified as an investment property (see below). The following are examples of properties that *are* classified as investment property:

- property held for long-term capital appreciation (i.e. not held for a short-term sale);
- a building (owned by the entity or held as a right-of-use asset) that is leased out to a third party under an operating lease; or a vacant building that is held with the intention to lease it out under an operating lease;
- a property being constructed or developed for future use as an investment property; and
- land whose use is undecided (the standard assumes that the land is held for capital appreciation).

The following are examples of properties that *are not* classified as investment property:

- property that is owner-occupied (it is classified as property, plant and equipment in terms of IAS 16 *Property, Plant and Equipment*);

- property that is leased out to a third party under a finance lease (it is treated in terms of IFRS 16, *Leases*); and
- property held for sale in the ordinary course of business (it is classified as inventory in terms of IAS 2 *Inventory*).

5.10.2 Transfers in and out of investment property

Transfers in and out of investment property take place when and only when there is a change in use. Examples of such a change in use where a property that was classified as investment property would cease to be classified as an investment property include:
- when the investment property becomes owner-occupied — in which case it must be transferred to property, plant and equipment;
- when there is commencement of development of the investment property with the view to resale — in which case it must be transferred to inventory.

Conversely, examples of such a change in use where a property that *was not* classified as investment property would become classified as an investment property would include:
- when a property that was owner-occupied ceases to be occupied by the owners — in which case it is immediately transferred from property, plant and equipment to investment property; and
- when a property that was held for sale in the ordinary course of business is rented out under an operating lease — in which case it is immediately transferred from inventories to investment property.

Note that if the rental agreement is structured as a finance lease instead of an operating lease, the property would not become classified as investment property but would instead be accounted for under IFRS 16, *Leases (see chapter 9)*.

5.10.3 Joint use properties

It is common for land and buildings to be used for a variety of purposes, for example, a portion of the property is used to earn rental income and a portion of the property is used in the production or supply of goods or services.

The result is that a portion of the property meets the definition of investment property (the part used to earn rental income) and a portion of the property meets the definition of property, plant and equipment (the part used in the production or supply of goods or services). These properties are referred to as joint use properties.

Paragraph 10 of IAS 40 provides guidance on how to classify joint use properties. If each portion can be sold or leased out separately (under a finance lease), then each portion is classified separately (one as an investment property and the other as an owner-occupied property). On the other hand, if each portion cannot be sold or leased out separately, then the entire property is classified as property, plant and equipment if the owner-occupied portion is not insignificant; if the owner-occupied portion is an insignificant portion the entire property is classified as investment property.

Professional judgement is required to determine whether the owner-occupied portion is insignificant and the resultant classification of the property.

5.10.4 Ancillary services

An entity may provide ancillary services to the occupants of its property, for example, maintenance of the building or security. In such circumstances, the property may only be classified as an investment property if these services are insignificant or incidental.

If the ancillary services provided are considered to be significant, then the entity can no longer be considered to be an inactive investor and classification as investment property may not be appropriate.

5.10.5 Measurement of investment properties

On acquisition, an owned investment property is initially measured at cost as defined in IAS 40. Investment property held as a right of use (leased as lessee) is recognised initially at cost as defined in IFRS 16. Subsequent measurement permits a choice between the cost model and the fair value model, which must then be applied to all investment property, including investment property held as a right of use under a lease. The fair value model is encouraged by the standard.

Note, however, that the cost model is compulsory if the fair value is not reliably measurable on a continuing basis. This scenario then forces the property to be measured under the cost model and it may not be measured under the fair value model at a later stage, but this does not prevent the entity from using the fair value model for its other investment properties.

It is important to note that if the fair value model is chosen, it is almost impossible to subsequently change to the cost model. Paragraph 55 of IAS 40 does not permit a change from the fair value model to the cost model if the fair value becomes difficult to measure. Rather, the property is then measured at the last known fair value until such time that a revised fair value becomes available.

Further, IAS 8 *Accounting Policies, Changes in Accounting Estimates and Errors*, only allows a change in policy if the new accounting policy results in reliable and more relevant information, which is unlikely to be the case when considering a change in policy from the fair value model to the cost model.

Use of the cost model

The cost model used for investment properties is the same as the cost model used for property, plant and equipment.

An investment property held under the cost model is measured at cost and depreciated annually (in terms of IAS 16 *Property, Plant and Equipment*); it is also tested for impairments (in terms of IAS 36 *Impairment of Assets*).

Use of the fair value model

The fair value model requires that the investment property be initially measured at cost and at the end of the reporting period it is remeasured to its fair value. For investment property held as a right of use under a lease, fair value is determined by reference to the fair value of the right of use, not the underlying property. Any subsequent gains or losses resulting from a change in the fair value of the investment property are recognised in profit or loss for the period in which they arise in terms of paragraph 35 of IAS 40.

It is important to note that the fair value model used to measure investment properties differs from the revaluation model used for property, plant and equipment. Revalued property, plant and equipment is depreciated and tested for impairment; revaluations are recognised in other comprehensive income. However, investment property measured at fair value is not depreciated or tested for impairment; and fair value changes are recognised in profit or loss.

Fair value is a market-based value measured in terms of IFRS 13, which must reflect, inter alia, rental incomes from current leases, and other assumptions that market participants would use when pricing investment property under current market conditions.

5.10.6 Disclosure

Paragraph 75(a) and (c) of IAS 40 requires that the accounting policy note should disclose:
- whether the fair value model or cost model is used;
- where it was difficult to decide, the criteria that the entity used to determine whether a property is classified as investment property, owner-occupied property or inventory.

Paragraphs 75 (e) and (g) of IAS 40 requires that the investment property note should disclose:
- whether the fair value was measured by an independent, suitably qualified valuer with relevant experience in the location and type of property;
- any restrictions on the property;

Paragraph 75(f) of IAS 40 requires the disclosure of:
- rental income earned from investment property;
- direct operating expenses related to all investment property, split into:
  - those that earned rental income, and
  - those that did not earn rental income (IAS 40 paragraph 75(f)).

    There are additional disclosure requirements specific to the fair value model or cost model. Paragraphs 76–78 of IAS 40 require the following disclosure if the fair value model was used:
- a reconciliation between the opening balance and closing balance of investment property;
- if a specific property is measured using the cost model because the fair value could not be reliably measured then the following must be disclosed in relation to that property:
  - a description of the property;
  - a separate reconciliation from opening balance to closing balance;
  - an explanation as to why the fair value could not be measured reliably;
  - the range of estimates within which the fair value is highly likely to lie;
  - if such a property is disposed of, a statement to this effect including the carrying amount at the time of sale and the resulting gain or loss on disposal.

Paragraph 79(c)–(d) of IAS 40 requires the following disclosure if the cost model had been used:
- a reconciliation between the opening balance and closing balance of investment property must show all:
  - the gross carrying amount and accumulated depreciation (at the beginning and end of the year);
  - depreciation for the current year (and in the profit before tax note);
  - impairments (and reversals) for the current year (and in the profit before tax note);
  - additions (either through acquisition or a business combination);
  - subsequent expenditure that was capitalised;
  - transfers to and from inventories and property, plant and equipment;
  - exchange differences;
  - other changes.

5.11 SUMMARY

'Property, plant and equipment' covers a wide range of assets such as vehicles, aircraft, all types of buildings, and specific structures such as oil and gas offshore platforms. These assets have a variety of useful lives, expected benefits, risk of receipt of benefits, movements in value over time, and expected value at point of derecognition. In some cases at derecognition, assets such as oil platforms require entities to incur costs rather than receive a residual value on sale. IAS 16, although recognising this variety, provides common principles to be applied to all items of property, plant and equipment.

Initial recognition occurs when the recognition criteria are met and assets are then recorded at cost. Subsequent to initial recognition, entities have a choice of measurement model, namely the cost model and the revaluation model. Under both measurement models, assets are subject to depreciation, this being a process of allocation and not a process of change in value. The measurement of depreciation requires judgements to be made by the accountant, including useful lives, residual values and pattern of receipt of benefits. Use of the revaluation model has additional accounting complications with revaluation increases and decreases potentially affecting asset revaluation surplus accounts, and having tax-effect consequences. Because of the judgements having to be made, IAS 16 requires extensive disclosures to be made.

DEMONSTRATION PROBLEM 5.1 Movements in assets, depreciation

Munich Manufacturing Ltd's post-closing trial balance at 30 June 2025 included the following balances:

Machinery Control (at cost)	£244,480
Accumulated Depreciation – Machinery Control	113,800
Fixtures (at cost; purchased 2 December 2022)	308,600
Accumulated Depreciation – Fixtures	134,138

The Machinery Control and Accumulated Depreciation — Machinery Control accounts are supported by subsidiary ledgers. Details of machines owned at 30 June 2025 are as follows:

Machine	Acquisition date	Cost	Estimated useful life	Estimated residual value
1	28 April 2021	£74,600	5 years	£3,800
2	4 February 2023	82,400	5 years	4,400
3	26 March 2024	87,480	6 years	5,400

Additional information
(a) Munich Manufacturing Ltd uses the general journal for all journal entries, records depreciation to the nearest month, balances its books every six months, and records amounts to the nearest pound.
(b) The company uses straight-line depreciation for machinery and diminishing-balance depreciation at 20% per annum for fixtures.

The following transactions and events occurred from 1 July 2025 onwards:

2025		
July 3	Exchanged items of fixtures (having a cost of £100,600; a carrying amount at exchange date of £56,872; and a fair value at exchange date of £57,140) for a used machine (Machine 4). Machine 4's fair value at exchange date was £58,000. Machine 4 originally cost £92,660 and had been depreciated by £31,790 to exchange date in the previous owner's accounts. Munich Manufacturing Ltd estimated Machine 4's useful life and residual value to be three years and £4,580 respectively.	
Oct. 10	Traded in Machine 2 for a new machine (Machine 5) that cost £90,740. A trade-in allowance of £40,200 was received and the balance was paid in cash. Freight charges of £280 and installation costs of £1,600 were also paid in cash. Munich Manufacturing Ltd estimated Machine 5's useful life and residual value to be six years and £5,500 respectively.	

2026		
April 24	Overhauled Machine 3 at a cash cost of £16,910, after which Munich Manufacturing Ltd revised its residual value to £5,600 and extended its useful life by two years.	
May 16	Paid for scheduled repairs and maintenance on the machines of £2,370.	
June 30	Recorded depreciation and scrapped Machine 1.	

Required

1. Prepare journal entries to record the above transactions and events.
2. Prepare the Accumulated Depreciation — Machinery Control and Accumulated Depreciation — Fixtures ledger accounts for the period 30 June 2025 to 30 June 2026.

Solution

1. *Journal entries*

Calculate the depreciation on each of the depreciable assets so that when events such as a sale occur, depreciation up to the date of the transaction can be calculated. Depreciation is calculated as:

$$\text{(Cost – residual value)/expected useful life}$$

For the three items of machinery, the depreciation per month is calculated as follows:

> Machine 1 depreciation = (£74,600 – £3,800)/60 months = £1,180 per month
> Machine 2 depreciation = (£82,400 – £4,400)/60 months = £1,300 per month
> Machine 3 depreciation = (£87,480 – £5,400)/72 months = £1,140 per month

On 3 July the company exchanges items of fixtures for a machine. After assessing that the transaction has commercial substance, the fixtures are derecognised by eliminating both the asset account and the accumulated depreciation. The acquired machine (Machine 4) is recognised at cost. Cost is measured using the fair value of the consideration given by the acquirer. As cost is the measurement used, the fair value of the machine is not relevant. Similarly, the carrying amount of the asset in the seller's records is also not relevant. The entry also records the profit on sale.

2025				
July 3	Machinery (M4)	Dr	57,140	
	Accumulated Depreciation – Fixtures*	Dr	43,728	
	Fixtures	Cr		100,600
	Profit on sale of fixtures (P/L)	Cr		268
	*£100,600 – £56,872			

The depreciation per month for Machine 4 is then calculated:

> Machine 4 depreciation = (£57,140 – £4,580)/36 months = £1,460 per month

On 10 October, Machine 2 is traded in for Machine 5. Depreciation up to point of sale on Machine 2 is determined, being £1,300 per month for the three months from July to September.

Oct. 10	Depreciation – Machinery (M2)*	Dr	3,900	
	Accumulated Depreciation – Machinery (M2)	Cr		3,900
	*£1,300 × 3 months			

Machine 2 is derecognised with the machine and related accumulated depreciation being written out of the records. Machine 5 is recorded at cost. Cost is determined as the sum of the purchase price and directly attributable costs. Purchase price is the fair value of consideration given up by the acquirer. In the absence of a fair value for Machine 2, the consideration is based on the fair value of Machine 5, namely £90,740. The directly attributable costs are the freight charges of £280 and installation costs of £1,600, both being necessarily incurred to get the asset into the condition for management's intended use. The cash outlay is then the sum of the balance paid to the seller of Machine 5 and the directly attributable costs.

	Machinery (M5)*	Dr	92,620	
	Accumulated Depreciation – Machinery (M2)**	Dr	41,600	
	Loss on sale of Machinery (P/L)	Dr	600	
Machinery (M2)		Cr		82,400
	Cash	Cr		52,420
	*£90,740 + £280 + £1,600			
	**£1,300 × 32 months			

The depreciation per month for Machine 5 is then calculated:

$$\text{Machine 5 depreciation} = (£92{,}620 - £5{,}500)/72 \text{ months} = £1{,}210 \text{ per month}$$

On 24 April 2026, Machine 3 received an overhaul. This resulted in a change in the capacity of the machine, which increased the residual value and extended its useful life. Because this results in a change in the depreciation per month, depreciation based on the rate before the overhaul for the period up to the date of the overhaul is recorded.

2026				
April 24	Depreciation – Machinery (M3)*	Dr	11,400	
	Accumulated Depreciation – Machinery (M3).	Cr		11,400
	*£1,140 × 10 months			

Because the overhaul increases the expected benefits from the asset — that is, the outlay for the overhaul results in probable future benefits, the cost of the overhaul is capitalised, increasing the overall cost of the asset.

| Machinery (M3) | | Dr | 16,910 | |
| Cash | | Cr | | 16,910 |

The overhaul results in a change in expectations, so it is necessary to calculate a revised depreciation per month:

M3:	New depreciable amount	= £87,480 + £16,910 – £5,600	= £98,790
	Accumulated depreciation balance	= £1,140 × 25 months	= £28,500
	Carrying amount to be depreciated	= £98,790 – £28,500	= £70,290
	New useful life	= 72 months – 25 months +24 months	= 71 months
	Revised depreciation	= £70,290/71 months	= £990 per month

Because outlays on repairs and maintenance do not lead to increased future benefits, these outlays are expensed.

May 16	Repairs and Maintenance Expense	Dr	2,370	
	Cash	Cr		2,370

At the end of the reporting period, depreciation is recognized on all depreciable assets:

Machinery:	M1	1,180 × 10 months	£ 11,800
	M3	£990 × 2 months	1,980
	M4	£1,460 × 12 months	17,520
	M5	£1,210 × 9 months	10,890
			£ 42,190*
Fixtures:		£308,600 − £100,600	£208,000
		Less: £134,138 − £43,728	(90,410)
			£117,590
		20% × £117,590	£23,518**

June 30	Depreciation – Machinery*	Dr	42,190	
	Depreciation – Fixtures**	Dr	23,518	
	Accumulated Depreciation – Machinery	Cr		42,190
	Accumulated Depreciation – Fixtures	Cr		23,518

Machine 1 is scrapped, so the asset is derecognised by writing off the asset and related accumulated depreciation. The undepreciated amount is recognised as an expense. A residual value of £3,800 was expected but not received, so the company incurs a loss of £3,800.

Accumulated Depreciation – Machinery (M1)*	Dr	70,800	
Loss on scrapping (P/L) (M1)**	Dr	3,800	
Machinery (M1)	Cr		74,600
*£1,180 × 60 months			
**£74,600 − $70,800			

2. *Ledger accounts*

Accumulated Depreciation – Machinery

10/10/25	Machinery	41,600	30/6/25	Balance b/d	113,800
31/12/25	Balance c/d	76,100	10/10/25	Depreciation	3,900
		117,700			117,700
30/6/26	Machinery	70,800	31/12/25	Balance b/d	76,100
	Balance c/d	58,890	24/4/26	Depreciation	11,400
			30/6/26	Depreciation	42,190
		129,690			129,690
			30/6/26	Balance b/d	58,890

Accumulated Depreciation – Fixtures

3/7/25	Fixtures	43,728	30/6/25	Balance b/d	134,138
31/12/25	Balance c/d	90,410			
		134,138			134,138
			31/12/25	Balance b/d	90,410
30/6/26	Balance c/d	113,928	30/6/26	Depreciation	23,518
		113,928			113,928
			30/6/26	Balance b/d	113,928

On 1 July 2024, Weinheim Ltd acquired a number of assets from Berlin Ltd. The assets had the following fair values at that date:

Plant A	£300,000
Plant B	180,000
Furniture A	60,000
Furniture B	50,000

In exchange for these assets, Weinheim Ltd issued 200,000 shares with a fair value of £2.95 per share. The directors of Weinheim Ltd decided to measure plant at fair value under the revaluation model and furniture at cost. The plant was considered to have a further 10-year life with benefits being received evenly over that period, whereas furniture is depreciated evenly over a 5-year period.

At 31 December 2024, Weinheim Ltd assessed the carrying amounts of its assets as follows:
- Plant A was valued at £296,000, with an expected remaining useful life of eight years.
- Plant B was valued at £168,000, with an expected remaining useful life of eight years.
- Furniture A's carrying amount was considered to be less than its recoverable amount.
- Furniture B's recoverable amount was assessed to be £40,000, with an expected remaining useful life of four years.

Appropriate entries were made at 31 December 2024 for the half-yearly accounts.

At 30 June 2025, Weinheim Ltd assessed the carrying amounts of its assets as follows:
- Plant A was valued at £274,000.
- Plant B was valued at £161,500.
- The carrying amounts of furniture were less than their recoverable amounts. The tax rate is 30%.

Required

Prepare the journal entries passed during the 2024–25 period in relation to the non-current assets in accordance with IAS 16 *Property, Plant and Equipment*.

Solution

The assets acquired are recorded at cost. The total cost of the assets is the fair value of the shares issued, namely £590,000 (i.e. 200,000 shares at £2.95 per share). This exactly equals the sum of the fair values of the assets acquired, hence the cost of each of the assets acquired is assumed to be equal to its fair value. If the amount were different from £590,000, say £550,000, then the cost of each asset would be determined based on the proportion of fair value to total fair value.

2024				
1 July	Plant A	Dr	300,000	
	Plant B	Dr	180,000	
	Furniture A	Dr	60,000	
	Furniture B	Dr	50,000	
	Share Capital	Cr		590,000
	(Acquisition of assets)			

At the end of each reporting period, depreciation is calculated and recorded. The next two entries record the depreciation on Plant A and Plant B after six months, at 31 December 2024.

31 Dec.	Depreciation Expense – Plant A	Dr	15,000	
	Accumulated Depreciation	Cr		15,000
	(Depreciation, 10% × ½ × £300,000)			
	Depreciation Expense – Plant B	Dr	9,000	
	Accumulated Depreciation	Cr		9,000
	(Depreciation, 10% × ½ × £180,000)			

Plant is measured using the revaluation model. At 31 December the fair values of plant are assessed. In relation to Plant A, the carrying amount of the asset is £285,000 (i.e. £300,000 − £15,000). The fair value is assessed to be £296,000. There is then a revaluation increase of £11,000. The first journal entry is to write off any accumulated depreciation at the point of revaluation:

Accumulated Depreciation – Plant A	Dr	15,000	
Plant A	Cr		15,000
(Write down Plant A to its carrying amount)			

The second journal entry recognises the increase in other comprehensive income:

Plant A	Dr	11,000	
Gain on Revaluation of Plant (OCI)	Cr		11,000
(Revaluation of Plant A from carrying amount of £285,000 to fair value of £296,000)			

The third entry recognises the tax effect of the gain:

Gain on Revaluation of Plant (OCI)	Dr	3,300	
Deferred Tax Liability	Cr		3,300
(Tax effect of gain on revaluation of plant)			

The fourth entry accumulates the after-tax gain in equity, in the asset revaluation surplus account:

Gain on Revaluation of Plant (OCI)	Dr	7,700	
Asset Revaluation Surplus – Plant A	Cr		7,700
(Accumulation of net revaluation gain in equity)			

Assets are revalued by class. However, accounting for revaluations is on an asset-by-asset basis. It is therefore important to associate any revaluation surplus with the asset that created that surplus. Accordingly, in the above entry the surplus is associated with Plant A.

With Plant B, the carrying amount at 31 December is £171,000 (i.e. £180,000 − £9,000). The fair value is assessed to be £168,000. The revaluation decrease is £3,000. This amount is recognised as a loss in current period profit or loss.

Accumulated Depreciation – Plant B	Dr	9,000	
Plant B	Cr		9,000
(Write down Plant B to its carrying amount)			
Loss on Revaluation of Plant (P/L)	Dr	3,000	
Plant B	Cr		3,000
(Revaluation of Plant B from carrying amount of £171,000 to fair value of £168,000)			

Furniture is measured under the cost model. Depreciation for the 6-month period is calculated based on an allocation of the cost over a 5-year period:

Depreciation Expense – Furniture A	Dr	6,000	
Accumulated Depreciation	Cr		6,000
(Depreciation, $\frac{1}{5} \times \frac{1}{2} \times £60,000$)			
Depreciation Expense – Furniture B	Dr	5,000	
Accumulated Depreciation	Cr		5,000
(Depreciation, $\frac{1}{5} \times \frac{1}{2} \times £50,000$)			

The carrying amount of Furniture B at 31 December is £45,000 (i.e. £50,000 − £5,000). The recoverable amount is £40,000. The asset is written down to recoverable amount, with the write-down being added to the accumulated depreciation account, and reported as an impairment loss.

Impairment Loss – Furniture B		Dr	5,000	
Accumulated Depreciation and Impairment Losses – Furniture B		Cr		5,000
(Write-down of asset to recoverable amount)				

At 30 June depreciation is recorded for plant assets based on an allocation of the fair values at 31 December 2024.

30 June	Depreciation Expense – Plant A	Dr	18,500	
	Accumulated Depreciation	Cr		18,500
	(Depreciation, $\frac{1}{8} \times \frac{1}{2} \times £296,000$)			
	Depreciation Expense – Plant B	Dr	10,500	
	Accumulated Depreciation	Cr		10,500
	(Depreciation, $\frac{1}{8} \times \frac{1}{2} \times £168,000$)			

The fair value of Plant A is assessed to be £274,000. Since the carrying amount is £277,500 (i.e. £296,000 − £18,500), there is a revaluation decrease of £3,500. Before recognising any expense on the revaluation decrease, there needs to be a reversal of the effects of any previous revaluation increase. For Plant A, at 31 December 2014, there was a revaluation increase of £11,000 which resulted in the recording of a £3,300 deferred tax liability and a £7,700 asset revaluation surplus. Hence, with the revaluation decrease of £3,500, the normal adjustment would be to debit the deferred tax liability with £1,050 (being 30% × £3,500) and debit the asset revaluation surplus with £2,450 (being 70% × £3,500). However, because of the bonus dividend, the balance in the asset revaluation surplus for Plant A is only £2,100 (i.e. £7,700 − £5,600). There is a deficiency of £350 in relation to the surplus.

The required journal entries at 30 June 2015 for Plant A are:
- *the elimination of the accumulated depreciation account:*

Accumulated Depreciation – Plant A		Dr	18,500	
Plant A		Cr		18,500
(Write down Plant A to its carrying amount)				

- *the recognition of the revaluation decrease in other comprehensive income:*

Loss on Revaluation of Plant (OCI)		Dr	3,500	
Plant A		Cr		3,500
(Revaluation of Plant A from carrying £277,500 to fair value of £274,000)				

- *the tax effect of the revaluation write-down:*

Deferred Tax Liability		Dr	1,050	
Loss on Revaluation of Plant (OCI)		Cr		1,050
(Tax effect of loss on revaluation of plant)				

- *the accumulation of the loss on revaluation to equity:*

Asset Revaluation Surplus – Plant A		Dr	2,450	
Loss on Revaluation of Plant (OCI)		Cr		2,450
(Accumulation of revaluation loss to equity)				

For Plant B, the carrying amount is £157,500 (i.e. £168,000 − £10,500). The fair value is £161,500. There is a revaluation increase of £4,000. The accounting for this increase requires a reversal of any prior decrease. With Plant B at 31 December 2024, an expense of £3,000 was recognised as a result of a revaluation decrease. The reversal of the previous decrease requires the recognition of income of £3,000. The £1,000 balance of the current increase (i.e. £4,000 − £3,000) is accounted for as other comprehensive income with a deferred tax liability and asset revaluation surplus being recognised.

The required journal entries for Plant B are:

- *the elimination of the accumulated depreciation account:*

Accumulated Depreciation – Plant B		Dr	10,500	
Plant B		Cr		10,500
(Write down Plant B to its carrying amount)				

- *the recognition of both a gain in profit or loss (for the reversal of the prior decrease) and a gain in other comprehensive income on the revaluation of Plant B:*

Plant B		Dr	4,000	
Gain on Revaluation of Plant (OCI)		Cr		1,000
Gain on Revaluation of Plant (P/L)		Cr		3,000
(Recognition of revaluation increase in profit or loss and other comprehensive income)				

- *Tax effect of revaluation gain:*

Gain on Revaluation of Plant (OCI)		Dr	300	
Deferred Tax Liability		Cr		300
(Tax effect of gain on revaluation of plant)				

- *accumulation of the revaluation gain in equity:*

Gain on Revaluation of Plant (OCI)		Dr	700	
Asset Revaluation Surplus – Plant B		Cr		700
(Accumulation of net revaluation gain in equity)				

Furniture at cost is depreciated for the final six months of the year.

Depreciation Expense – Furniture A		Dr	6,000	
Accumulated Depreciation		Cr		6,000
(Depreciation, $1/_5 \times 1/_2 \times$ £60,000)				
Depreciation Expense – Furniture B		Dr	5,000	
Accumulated Depreciation		Cr		5,000
(Depreciation, $1/_5 \times 1/_2 \times$ £40,000)				

Discussion questions

1. How should items of property, plant and equipment be measured at point of initial recognition, and would gifts be treated differently from acquisitions?
2. How is cost determined?
3. What choices of measurement model exist subsequent to assets being initially recognised?
4. What factors should entities consider in choosing alternative measurement models?
5. What is meant by 'depreciation expense'?
6. How is useful life determined?
7. What is meant by 'residual value' of an asset?
8. Should accounting for revaluation increases and decreases be done on an asset-by-asset basis or on a class-of-assets basis?
9. What differences occur between asset-by-asset or class-of-asset bases in accounting for revaluation increases and decreases?
10. When should property, plant and equipment be derecognised?

References

International Accounting Standards Board 2014, IAS 1 *Presentation of financial statements*, https://www.ifrs. org/issued-standards/list-of-standards

International Accounting Standards Board 2014, IAS 16 *Property, plant & equipment*, https://www.ifrs.org/ issued-standards/list-of-standards

International Accounting Standards Board 2014, IAS 40 *Investment property*, https://www.ifrs.org/ issued-standards/list-of-standards

Marks & Spencer plc 2023, *Annual Report*, https://corporate.marksandspencer.com/sites/marksandspencer/ files/2023-06/M-and-S-2023-Annual-Report.pdf.

Depreciation is an inter-period allocation method that is subject to considerable managerial discretion. It is therefore interesting to learn whether it could be relevant to users of financial statements. Barth et al. (2001) argue that if investments in depreciable assets generate total cash flows in excess of cost, the annual depreciation should be positively associated with future operating cash flows. Their findings are broadly consistent with this prediction, although this does not hold in several industries analysed in this paper. In a more direct test of how investors perceive depreciation, Kang and Zhao (2010) find that annual changes in depreciation expense are not associated with stock returns. They also fail to find that accumulated depreciation is associated with stock prices. Therefore, taken together from these two papers, the evidence on the usefulness to investors of depreciation and accumulated depreciation is mixed.

IAS 16 permits companies to adopt the revaluation model for property, plant and equipment (PPE). Casual observation nevertheless suggests that fewer companies have revalued their PPE in recent years and that the method was more common prior to the adoption of IFRS® Standards. The research on revaluations therefore goes several years back. Easton et al. (1993) examine a sample of Australian companies that revalued their PPE in the 1980s. Based on interviews with the chief financial officers, the authors conjecture that revaluations are reported with the view to lower the debt-to-equity ratio in order to be seen as less leveraged. This opportunistic behaviour possibly contrasts with a motivation to give a 'true and fair view' of the financial statements, which was also highlighted as another reason for revaluations given by company officers. Consistent with information usefulness perspective, this paper documents a positive association between revaluation reserve (and changes in the reserve) and the market-to-book ratio. The documented association, however, is stronger for higher debt-to-equity firms. A potential explanation of this is that revaluing firms avoid violation of debt covenants and that the market perceives this as a beneficial outcome. However, stock returns are unrelated to the change in the revaluation reserve in almost all years examined. The latter may be explained by poor timeliness of revaluation disclosure.

Aboody et al. (1999) examine 347 UK firms that revalued their PPE upward during 1983–1995. They find that these have predictive ability with respect to 1–3-year ahead changes in operating income and changes in operating cash flows. Similar to Easton et al. (1993) they examine the association of revaluation information with stock prices and stock returns and find it is positive and significant. In additional analysis the authors find that their results are weaker for high debt-to-equity firms. This is suggestive of opportunistic revaluations. Notwithstanding the statistical significance of these results, they are somewhat hard to interpret. First, the authors do not outline the theoretical link between revaluations and future performance. Second, the exclusion of negative revaluations does not permit a more comprehensive view of the information role of revaluations. More recent analysis of revaluations of fixed assets is presented by Lopes and Walker (2012). They analyse 177 Brazilian firms that revalued their

fixed assets during 1998–2004. Employing research design similar to Aboody et al. (1999) they find that future performance is *negatively* related to revaluations. Furthermore they find that the revaluation balance is negatively related to share price and that the revaluation increment is negatively related to stock returns. An interpretation of these results is that Brazilian firms that anticipate deterioration in performance take a pre-emptive action to fortify their balance sheets.

The above-mentioned conflicting results may be explained, at least in part, by whether the revaluations are based on managers' estimates or external assessors' valuations. The latter may be perceived as more reliable estimates by investors. Barth and Clinch (1998) find in an Australian sample that revaluations of PPE by both internal directors and external appraisers are positively associated with stock prices. However, their evidence seems to suggest that this association is stronger for internal valuations. This is inconsistent with the notion that internal valuations are more prone to manipulations and is indicative of superior information held by insiders. Cotter and Richardson (2002) extend this analysis to model the choice of the appraiser, again using an Australian sample. Their analysis suggests that the likelihood of selecting an independent appraiser is negatively related to measures of a CEO's control of the board of directors. Cotter and Richardson (2002) then further examine if upward revaluations are followed by reversals, and whether this is dependent on appraiser type. They argue that reversals can be used as a measure of the reliability of the initial upward revaluation. For plant and equipment they find that independent revaluations are more reliable than internal revaluations. However, this result is not robust to an alternative measure of reliability.

Prior to the adoption of IFRS® Standards it was required in the UK that fair values are recognised for investment property companies. Dietrich et al. (2001) argue that the reliability of fair values reported can be examined by reference to gains or losses booked when the properties are sold. If revaluations are good estimates of sale prices, one should not observe large losses or gains upon disposal of the properties. They examine a sample of 76 firms for the period 1988–1996 and find that, on average, disposals of investment properties entail a gain that is equivalent to 6% of the selling price. This is consistent with conservative fair value estimates used for revaluations. An alternative explanation is that managers select to sell assets that increased in value after the last revaluation. Dietrich et al. (2001) further find that annual revaluations are positively related to future debt issues, which is broadly consistent with the debt-related motivation identified by Easton et al. (1993). Muller and Riedl (2002) also employ a sample of UK investment property companies to investigate if the choice of internal vs. external appraiser is capable of reducing information asymmetry. They provide evidence from an analysis of bid–ask spreads that suggests valuations carried out by external appraisers reduce information asymmetry more than internal appraisers. This is indicative of higher accuracy of externally generated estimates.

There are only a few studies that directly examine reporting requirements set in IAS 16 and IAS 40. Muller et al. (2011)

provide direct evidence as to the effect of mandating IAS 40 following the adoption of IFRS® Standards on information asymmetry. In a sample of European investment property companies they find that companies that disclosed fair values of their investment properties prior to IFRS® Standards did not benefit from a decline in information asymmetry. However, such a decline was observed for firms that disclosed the required information only following the adoption. This evidence suggests that investors benefit from the disclosure of fair value estimates of certain long-lived assets.

What factors affect the selection of the fair value option? Quagli and Avallone (2010) examine a sample of public real-estate firms from seven European countries. They find that larger firms tend to select fair values less than smaller firms. Surprisingly, they do not find that leverage explains this choice. Christensen and Nikolaev (2013) postulate that market forces are a factor in firms' choice whether to revalue their PPE when IFRS® Standards offer this option. Specifically, they argue that the demand for revaluations is stronger in the UK than in Germany. They also conjecture that revaluations are more common for investment properties than PPE. They find that UK (German) firms are more likely to use fair value model (historical cost basis), but that in both countries investment property companies tend to use the fair value model more than companies from other industries.

References

Aboody, D., Barth, M.E., and Kasznik, R., 1999. Revaluations of fixed assets and future firm performance, evidence from the UK. *Journal of Accounting and Economics*, 26(1–3), 149–178.

Barth, M., and Clinch, G., 1998. Revalued financial, tangible, and intangible assets: associations with share prices and non-market based value estimates. *Journal of Accounting Research*, 36 (Supplement), 199–233.

Barth, M., Cram, D.P., and Nelson K. K., 2001. Accruals and the prediction of future cash flows. *The Accounting Review*, 76(1), 27–58.

Christensen, H. B., and Nikolaev, V. V. 2013. Does fair value accounting for non-financial assets pass the market test? *Review of Accounting Studies*, 18(3), 734–775.

Cotter, J., and Richardson, S., 2002. Reliability of asset revaluations: the impact of appraiser independence. *Review of Accounting Studies*, 7(4), 435–457.

Dietrich, D., Harris, M., and Muller, K., 2001. The reliability of investment property fair value estimates. *Journal of Accounting and Economics*, 30(2), 125–158.

Easton, P., Eddey, P., and Harris, T., 1993. An investigation of revaluations of tangible long-lived assets. *Journal of Accounting Research*, 31 (Supplement), 1–38.

Kang, S. H., and Zhao, Y., 2010. Information content and value relevance of depreciation: a cross-industry analysis. *The Accounting Review*, 85(1), 227–260.

Lopes, A.B., and Walker, M., 2012. Asset revaluations, future firm performance and firm-level corporate governance arrangements: new evidence from Brazil. *The British Accounting Review*, 44(2), 53–67.

Muller, K., and Riedl. E., 2002. External monitoring of property appraisal estimates and information asymmetry. *Journal of Accounting Research*, 40(3), 865–881.

Muller, K., Riedl, E., and Sellhorn, T., 2011. Mandatory fair value accounting and information asymmetry: evidence from the European real estate industry. *Management Science*, 57(6), 1138–1153.

Quagli, A. and Avallone, F., 2010. Fair value or cost model? Drivers of choice for IAS 40 in the real estate industry. *European Accounting Review*, 19(3), 461–493.

6 Intangible assets

ACCOUNTING STANDARDS IN FOCUS

IAS 38 *Intangible Assets*

LEARNING OBJECTIVES

After studying this chapter, you should be able to:

 1   understand the key characteristics of an intangible asset

 2   explain the criteria relating to the initial recognition of intangible assets and their measurement at point of initial recognition, distinguishing between acquired and internally generated intangibles

 3   explain how to measure intangibles subsequent to initial recognition, including the principles relating to the amortisation of intangibles

 4   explain the accounting for retirement and disposal of intangible assets

 5   apply the disclosure requirements of IAS 38.

INTRODUCTION

Chapter 5 discusses the accounting standards for the tangible assets of property, plant and equipment. This chapter examines the standards for intangible assets. The International Accounting Standards Board (IASB®) believes it is necessary to distinguish between tangible assets (such as property, plant and equipment) and intangible assets (such as patents and brand names). In analysing the accounting for intangible assets, the question that must always be kept in mind is whether there should be any difference in the accounting treatment for tangible and intangible assets. What is it that is different about intangible assets that makes a separate accounting standard, and presumably different accounting rules, for intangible and tangible assets necessary?

Historically, it is common for entities to report all their tangible assets on the statement of financial position but be less consistent in the reporting of intangible assets. As a result, there are sometimes large differences between the market value of an entity and its recorded net assets.

The accounting for intangibles are contained in IAS 38 *Intangible Assets*. The standard covers the accounting for all intangible assets except, as detailed in paragraphs 2 and 3, those specifically covered by another accounting standard; financial assets; and mineral rights and expenditure on exploration for, or development and extraction of, minerals, oil, natural gas and similar non-regenerative resources. Other intangible assets specifically covered by standards other than IAS 38 are:

- intangible assets held by an entity for sale in the ordinary course of business (IAS 2 *Inventories*)
- deferred tax assets (IAS 12 *Income Taxes*)
- leases of intangible assets within the scope of IFRS 16 *Leases*
- assets arising from employee benefits (IAS 19 *Employee Benefits*)
- goodwill acquired in a business combination (IFRS 3 *Business Combinations*)
- contracts within the scope of IFRS 17 *Insurance Contracts*
- non-current intangible assets held for sale (IFRS 5 *Non-current Assets Held for Sale and Discontinued Operations*).

An example of the assets that are being considered in this chapter is shown in figure 6.1, which contains the intangible assets disclosed by Diageo in its 2023 annual report. Note that brands comprise the majority of the intangible assets but other intangibles include goodwill and computer software.

FIGURE 6.1 Examples of intangible assets

	Brands £ million	Goodwill £ million	Other intangibles £ million	Computer software £ million	Total £ million
Cost					
At 30 June 2021	8,458	2,627	1,421	673	13,179
Hyperinflation adjustment in respect of Turkey	315	208	–	1	524
Exchange differences	639	145	194	28	1,006
Additions	109	70	55	67	301
Disposals	(23)	(42)	–	(23)	(88)
Reclassification to asset held for sale	(560)	–	–	(8)	(568)
At 30 June 2022	8,938	3,008	1,670	738	14,354
Hyperinflation adjustment in respect of Turkey	81	60	–	–	141
Exchange differences	(531)	(257)	(64)	(16)	(868)
Additions	338	92	13	155	598
Disposals	–	–	–	(26)	(26)
Reclassification from/(to) asset held for sale	453	(29)	–	–	424
At 30 June 2023	9,279	2,874	1,619	851	14,623
Amortisation and impairment					
At 30 June 2021	1,097	670	80	568	2,415
Exchange differences	51	60	(1)	25	135
Amortisation for the year	–	–	7	38	45
Impairment	317	19	–	–	336
Disposals	(23)	(28)	–	(20)	(71)
Reclassification to asset held for sale	(400)	–	–	(8)	(408)

FIGURE 6.1 *(continued)*

At 30 June 2022	1,042	721	86	603	2,452
Exchange differences	(96)	(61)	(1)	(15)	(173)
Amortisation for the year	–	–	16	40	56
Impairment	498				498
Disposals	–	–	–	(24)	(24)
Reclassification from/(to) asset held for sale	315	(13)	–	–	302
At 30 June 2023	1,759	647	101	604	3,111
Carrying amount					
At 30 June 2023	7,520	2,227	1,518	247	11,512
At 30 June 2022	7,896	2,287	1,584	135	11,902
At 30 June 2021	7,361	1,957	1,341	105	10,764

(a) Brands

The principal acquired brands, all of which are regarded as having indefinite useful economic lives, are as follows:

	Principal markets	2023 £ million
Crown Royal whisky	United States	1,162
Captain Morgan rum	Global	954
Smirnoff vodka	Global	654
Johnnie Walker whisky	Global	625
Casamigos tequila	United States	479
McDowell's No.1 whisky, rum and brandy	India	308
Don Papa rum	Europe	282
Yenì raki	Turkey	249
Shui Jing Fang Chinese white spirit	Greater China	246
Don Julio tequila	United States	235
Aviation American gin	United States	209
Seagram's 7 Crown whiskey	United States	177
Signature whisky	India	176
Zacapa rum	Global	152
Black Dog whisky	India	149
Antiquity whisky	India	145
Windsor Premier whisky	Korea	137
Gordon's gin	Europe	119
Bell's whisky	Europe	102
Other brands		960
		7,520

Source: Diageo (2023, pp. 190, 191).

6.1 THE NATURE OF INTANGIBLE ASSETS

Paragraph 8 of IAS 38 defines an intangible asset as follows:

an identifiable non-monetary asset without physical substance.

The intangible asset definition refers to an 'asset', which IAS 38 also defines in paragraph 8 as:

a resource controlled by the entity as a result of past events and from which an inflow of future economic benefits are expected to flow to the entity.

Note that IAS 38 uses the asset definition from the old 2010 *Conceptual Framework* and not the asset definition in the new 2018 *Conceptual Framework*; however, the essence of the two definitions is the same.

The asset definition refers to an expectation of future economic benefits. These benefits could take any form; for example, revenue, other income or even cost savings such as lower costs from a new formula.

An important part of the asset definition is control. This means that for an item to be an intangible asset, it will need to be controlled by the entity.

Control over an intangible asset is difficult to prove, but it may be achieved if the entity has the ability to restrict accessibility by others to the asset's future economic benefits; and the power to obtain the asset's future economic benefits (IAS 38, paragraph 13).

An asset's future economic benefits can be controlled through legally enforceable rights, such as copyright, but legal rights are not necessary to prove control; it is just more difficult to prove that control exists if legal rights do not exist.

For example, an entity may be able to identify a portfolio of customers, market share or technical knowledge that will give rise to future economic benefits. However, the lack of control over the flow of future economic benefits means that these items seldom meet the definition of an intangible asset. Conversely, control over technical knowledge and market knowledge may be protected by legal rights such as copyrights and restraint of trade agreements, in which case these would meet the requirement of control.

The difficulties in determining whether certain intangibles meet the definition of an asset caused the standard setters to introduce the further test of identifiability. By requiring identifiability for recognition of intangibles, they diffused the debate as to whether an item such as good staff relations is an asset. Regardless of whether it is an asset, it is not an intangible asset because it does not meet the identifiability criterion, and so can only be recognised, if at all, as part of goodwill. However, reducing the number of assets recognised in the financial statements because of measurement problems may also reduce the relevance of the information provided in those financial statements.

Turning back to the IAS 38 definition of an intangible asset, the standard identifies three key characteristics of an intangible asset: identifiable, non-monetary in nature and without physical substance. Each characteristic is there for a reason, generally to exclude certain assets from being classified as intangible assets or recognised at all.

6.1.1 Non-monetary in nature

Monetary assets are defined in IAS 38 as 'money held and assets to be received in fixed or determinable amounts of money'. The reason for including 'non-monetary' in the definition of intangible assets is to exclude financial assets such as loans and receivables from being classified as intangible assets. The accounting for financial assets is covered in IFRS 9 *Financial Instruments* and IAS 39 *Financial Instruments: Recognition and Measurement (see chapter 13)*.

6.1.2 Identifiable

IAS 38 does not contain a definition of 'identifiable'. However, paragraph 12 of the standard sets down two criteria, either of which must be met for an asset to be identifiable and thus be classified as an intangible asset. Paragraph 12 states:

An asset is identifiable if it either:
(a) is separable, i.e. is capable of being separated or divided from the entity and sold, transferred, licensed, rented or exchanged, either individually or together with a related contract, identifiable asset or liability, regardless of whether the entity intends to do so; or
(b) arises from contractual or other legal rights, regardless of whether those rights are transferable or separable from the entity or from other rights and obligations.

There are thus two parts to the concept of identifiability.

First, consider the criterion of separability. Separability tests whether an entity can divide an asset from other assets and transfer it to another party.

Consider the cost of the advertising campaign. It is not separable as it cannot be separated from the entity and sold, transferred, rented or exchanged. Furthermore, the advertising campaign does not arise from contractual or legal rights. Thus the cost of the advertising campaign is not identifiable.

Although many intangible assets are both separable and arise from contractual or legal rights, under the laws of some jurisdictions, for example, some licences granted to an entity are not transferable except by sale of the entity as a whole.

IAS 38's requirement that an intangible asset must be 'identifiable' was introduced to try to distinguish it from internally generated goodwill (which, outside a business combination, should not be recognised as an asset), but also to emphasise that, especially in the context of a business combination, there will be previously unrecorded items that should be recognised in the financial statements as intangible assets separately from goodwill. Examples include trademarks, newspaper mastheads and customer lists.

The criterion of separability is included in the definition of an intangible asset to ensure reliability of measurement. If an asset can be transferred to another entity, then probably a market exists for that asset. If no transfer can occur, then there will be no market and therefore no market price. It would seem that the standard setters are afraid that preparers of financial statements will include assets such as customer relationships on their balance sheet at some form of non-market valuation, and they are concerned about the reliability of such measurements. By including separability in the definition of intangible assets, there is a limit placed on the assets that could potentially appear on a balance sheet.

The second criterion to the concept of identifiability is if it 'arises from contractual or other legal rights'. As noted earlier, this criterion is an alternative to separability. Hence there are some intangible assets that are not separable but meet the definition of an intangible asset because of part (b) in paragraph 12 of IAS 38. In paragraph BC10 of the Basis for Conclusions on IAS 38, the IASB stated:

> Some contractual-legal rights establish property interests that are not readily separable from the entity as a whole. For example, under the laws of some jurisdictions some licences granted to an entity are not transferable except by sale of the entity as a whole.

Examples of assets fitting into this category generally relate to situations where a government gives or sells a right to an entity, such as:
- an entity has a right to use two million litres of water per annum in its production process
- an entity has a right to emit a specified quantity of greenhouse gases into the atmosphere per annum.

A condition of receiving this right may be that the right cannot be transferred between entities; hence, if an entity used only one million litres of water, it could not sell/transfer the remaining right to one million litres of water to another entity. The right is then not separable. However the IASB believed that these assets could be distinguished from other assets held by an entity and should be disclosed as intangible assets. Separability was then not seen as the only criterion for identifiability.

6.1.3 Lack of physical substance

Lack of physical substance is the third characteristic in the definition of an intangible asset. It is the characteristic that separates assets such as property, plant and equipment from intangible assets, in that property, plant and equipment would generally meet both the other criteria of an intangible asset; that is, IAS 16 *Property, Plant and Equipment* provides accounting policies for identifiable, non-monetary assets.

Note that some intangible assets may be associated with a physical item, such as software contained on a computer disk. However, the asset is really the software and not the disk itself. As noted in paragraph 4 of IAS 38, judgement in some cases is required to determine which element, tangible or intangible, is most important to the classification of the asset.

6.2 RECOGNITION AND INITIAL MEASUREMENT

IAS 38 sets out the principles in relation to the recognition and initial measurement of intangible assets.

6.2.1 Criteria for recognition and initial measurement

After determining that an asset exists and that it meets the definition of an intangible asset, the asset must meet the two criteria in paragraph 21 of IAS 38 before it can be recognised. The criteria are:
- it is *probable* that the future economic benefits attributable to the asset will flow to the entity
- the *cost* of the asset can be measured *reliably*.

These criteria are the same as those for the recognition of property, plant and equipment in IAS 16 *Property, Plant and Equipment*. If the cost of the asset cannot be reliably measured, but the fair value is determinable, an asset cannot be recognised under either IAS 16 or IAS 38 because both standards require initial measurement at cost. As noted later, this has consequences for the recognition of intangible assets that are internally generated rather than acquired, as well as causing differences in the statements of financial position of entities that internally generate assets and those that acquire assets.

In relation to the initial measurement of an intangible asset, paragraph 24 of IAS 38 states:

> An intangible asset shall be measured initially at cost.

With the reliable measurement of cost as one of the recognition criteria, this cost forms the basis for initial measurement.

These recognition criteria and the requirement for initial measurement should be viewed as general principles only. Having established these criteria, IAS 38 then proceeds to examine the accounting for intangibles based upon how these assets were generated. The standard analyses intangibles in terms of four ways in which an entity could have obtained the assets:

- separate acquisition
- acquisition as part of a business acquisition
- acquisition by way of a government grant
- internally generated assets.

For each of these situations, IAS 38 provides specific recognition criteria and measurement rules. It is these that are applied in accounting for intangibles rather than the general criteria noted in paragraphs 21 and 24. Presumably the standard setters considered that there were particular measurement issues that arose under each of these situations requiring different principles to be established for each situation.

6.2.2 Separate acquisition

In recognising assets acquired separately, paragraph 25 of IAS 38 notes that:

> the probability recognition criterion in paragraph 21(a) is always considered to be satisfied for separately acquired intangible assets.

The standard setters argue that the price paid for the asset automatically takes into account the probability of the expected benefits being received; hence, it is unnecessary to apply a further probability test. For example, if an asset had expected cash inflows of £1,000, and the probability of these inflows being received was 40%, then an acquirer would pay £400 for the asset. The standard setters argue that these benefits are now automatically probable. Further, paragraph 26 of IAS 38 states:

> In addition, the cost of a separately acquired intangible asset can usually be measured reliably. This is particularly so when the purchase consideration is in the form of cash or other monetary assets.

The measurement of cost may, however, be more difficult if the exchange involves the acquirer giving up non-monetary assets rather than cash.

An intangible asset acquired separately is initially measured at cost. As with property, plant and equipment, the cost of an asset is the sum of the purchase price and the directly attributable costs (IAS 38 paragraph 27). The purchase price is measured as the fair value of what is given up by the acquirer in order to acquire the asset, and the directly attributable costs are those necessarily incurred to get the asset into the condition where it is capable of operating in the manner intended by management. *(These concepts are discussed further in sections 5.3.1 and 5.3.2 in relation to property, plant and equipment.)* The principles of accounting for separately acquired intangibles and property, plant and equipment are the same.

If an intangible asset is acquired together with other assets in a transaction that is not a business combination, IFRS 3 paragraph 2(b) clarifies that the cost of the group of assets (and liabilities if any) must be allocated to the individual identifiable assets and liabilities on the basis of their relative fair values at the date of the purchase.

In summary, where an entity acquires an intangible asset as a separate asset, there is only one recognition criterion to be applied, namely reliable measurement of the cost of the asset.

6.2.3 Acquisition as part of a business combination

Where assets are acquired as part of a business combination, IFRS 3 *Business Combinations* is applied. Appendix A of this standard contains a definition of a 'business combination' and a 'business'. *This standard is discussed in detail in chapter 19.* In this section, a reference to a business combination indicates that the acquiring entity has acquired a group of assets rather than a single asset and one of the assets in that group is an intangible asset. The group of assets could be an operating division or a segment of another entity. The key issue is then how to account for the acquisition of an intangible asset when it is acquired as part of a group of assets rather than as a single asset. Note, however, that IFRS 3 prescribes different accounting for the acquisition of a group of assets that constitutes a business and for a group that does not constitute a business. In applying the principles in IAS 38 relating to acquisition of assets as part of a business combination, it is first necessary to ensure that the group of assets being acquired is a business.

With respect to recognition criteria to apply when intangible assets are acquired in a business combination, IAS 38 states that *no* recognition criteria need be applied. Provided the assets meet the definition of an intangible asset, they must be recognised as separate assets. As with separately acquired intangible assets, paragraph 33 of IAS 38 provides that, where intangible assets are acquired as part of a business combination, the effect of probability is reflected in the measurement of the asset. Hence, the probability recognition criterion is automatically met. Further, it is argued in paragraph 33 of IAS 38 that the requirement for reliability of measurement is always met as sufficient information always exists to measure reliably the fair value of the asset. This non-application of recognition criteria in accounting for intangibles acquired in a business combination is also seen in IFRS 3 where paragraphs 11 and 12 note that the recognition conditions for the identifiable assets must meet the definition of an asset in the *Conceptual Framework*, as well as be a part of what the acquirer and the acquiree exchanged in the business combination transaction.

The application of these recognition requirements means that an acquirer must, in recognising separately the acquiree's intangible assets, recognise intangible assets that the acquiree has not recognised in its records, such as in-process research and development that cannot be recognised under IAS 38 as internally generated assets (discussed later in this section). As noted in paragraph 34, recognition by an acquirer of an acquiree's in-process research and development project only depends on whether the project meets the definition of an intangible asset. It can be seen that entities that acquire intangible assets in a business combination will be able, and in fact are required, to recognise intangible assets that are not separately recognisable when acquired by other means.

The measurement of intangible assets acquired in a business combination is established in paragraph 33 of IAS 38:

> In accordance with IFRS 3 *Business Combinations*, if an intangible asset is acquired in a business combination, the cost of that intangible asset is its fair value at the acquisition date.

Note firstly that it is IFRS 3 that determines the measurement of assets acquired in a business combination. Under IFRS 3 acquired assets are measured at fair value. Hence, intangible assets acquired in a business combination must be measured at initial recognition at fair value. This is then a departure from the general measurement rule in paragraph 24 of IAS 38. Paragraph 33 of IAS 38 does say that 'the cost . . . is its fair value'; however, the acquiring entity does not attempt to measure the cost, rather it measures the fair value.

The measurement of fair value is determined in accordance with IFRS 13 *Fair Value Measurement*. IFRS 13 defines fair value in Appendix A as:

> The price that would be received to sell an asset or paid to transfer a liability in an orderly transaction between market participants at the measurement date.

Chapter 8 provides information on the measurement of fair value under IFRS 13.

6.2.4 Acquisition by way of a government grant

According to paragraph 44 of IAS 38, some intangible assets, such as licences to operate radio or television stations, are allocated to entities via government grants. These intangibles are accounted for in accordance with IAS 20 *Accounting for Government Grants and Disclosure of Government Assistance*, whereby an entity may choose to initially recognise both the intangible asset and the grant at fair value. If an entity does not choose to use the fair value measurement option, it will recognise the asset initially at a nominal amount plus directly attributable costs.

6.2.5 Internally generated intangible assets

The recognition criteria and measurement rules are different for intangible assets acquired as a separate asset or acquired in a business combination. The approach taken in accounting for internally generated assets is different again. The recognition criteria in paragraph 21 are not applied at all. The measurement approach used is one of capitalisation of outlays incurred by the entity.

This continuous change in accounting for intangible assets leaves the standard setters open to criticism for lack of consistency in the accounting for acquired intangibles versus internally generated intangibles. The problem from an accounting point of view with internally generated intangibles is determining at what point in time an asset should be recognised. An entity may outlay funds in an exploratory project, such as developing software to overcome a specific problem, or designing a tool for a special purpose. There is no guarantee of success at the start of the project. The program may not work or the tool may be unsatisfactory for the purpose. Should the entity capitalise the costs from the beginning of the project, or wait until there is some indication of success? A further problem with some intangible assets such as brand names is whether the costs outlaid relate solely to increasing the worth of the brand name or simply to enhancing the overall reputation of the entity.

The standard setters' solution to the problem of when to begin capitalising costs is to classify the generation of the asset into two phases: the research phase and the development phase. These terms are defined in paragraph 8 of IAS 38 as follows:

> *Research* is original and planned investigation undertaken with the prospect of gaining new scientific or technical knowledge and understanding.

Development is the application of research findings or other knowledge to a plan or design for the production of new or substantially improved materials, devices, products, processes, systems or services before the start of commercial production or use.

It can be seen from these definitions that the earlier stages of a project are defined as research and, at some point in time, the project moves from a research phase to a development phase. Examples of research activities are given in paragraph 56 of IAS 38, such as the search for new knowledge or for alternatives for materials, devices, products, processes, systems or services. Examples of development activities are found in paragraph 59, such as the design, construction and operation of a non-commercial pilot plant, and the design of pre-production prototypes and models. From an accounting perspective, expenditure on research is expensed when incurred (paragraph 54), and expenditure on development is capitalised as an intangible asset. It is obviously important to be able to distinguish one phase from the other.

Paragraph 57 of IAS 38 is the key paragraph in this regard. It contains a list of criteria, all of which must be met in order for a development outlay to be capitalised. In order to capitalise development outlays, an entity must be able to demonstrate all of the following:

(a) the technical feasibility of completing the intangible asset so that it will be available for use or sale;
(b) its intention to complete the intangible asset and use or sell it;
(c) its ability to use or sell the intangible asset;
(d) how the intangible asset will generate probable future economic benefits. Among other things, the entity can demonstrate the existence of a market for the output of the intangible asset or the intangible asset itself or, if it is to be used internally, the usefulness of the intangible asset;
(e) the availability of adequate technical, financial and other resources to complete the development and to use or sell the intangible asset; and
(f) its ability to measure reliably the expenditure attributable to the intangible asset during its development.

The criteria in paragraph 57 are designed to help determine whether, in relation to a project, it is probable that there will be future benefits flowing to the entity. If there are markets for the output, the project is feasible, and the resources are available to complete the project, then it becomes probable that there will be future cash inflows. This approach in IAS 38 provides more certainty in obtaining comparable accounting across entities than simply relying on an accounting principle that states that, if there are probable expected future benefits, an entity should capitalise the outlay.

If the criteria in paragraph 57 are all met, IAS 38 requires the intangible asset to be measured at cost. This cost is not, however, the total cost relating to the project. The amount to be capitalised is the 'sum of expenditure incurred from the date when the intangible asset first meets the recognition criteria in paragraphs 21, 22 and 57' (paragraph 65). Paragraph 71 explicitly prohibits the reinstatement of amounts previously expensed. Recognition of an asset that is not yet available for use requires an entity to subject that asset to an annual impairment test as per IAS 36 *Impairment of Assets*. Paragraphs 66–67 of IAS 38 note that the cost comprises all directly attributable costs necessary to create, produce and prepare the asset to be capable of operating in a manner intended by management, and provide examples of such costs as well as items that are not components of the cost.

It may seem that the use of the terms 'research' and 'development', which may be associated with such assets as patents and software development, are not applicable to all internally generated intangibles, such as brand names. However, it needs to be remembered that all intangible assets must meet the identifiability criterion, one part of which is separability, which is the capability of being separated and sold or transferred. In relation to certain assets, paragraph 63 of IAS 38 provides a major exclusion in an entity's ability to capitalise internally generated intangibles:

Internally generated brands, mastheads, publishing titles, customer lists and items similar in substance shall not be recognised as intangible assets.

The standard setters concluded that, even though the criteria in paragraph 57(a)–(f) are met, the listed items in paragraph 63 cannot be recognised. As paragraph 64 states, the standard setters do not believe that the costs associated with developing the listed assets can be distinguished from the cost of developing the business as a whole. For example, it may be argued that funds spent on developing a brand name also enhance the overall image of the entity, and therefore the outlays cannot be solely attributable to the brand name.

6.2.6 Explaining the non-recognition of internally generated assets

There are a number of problems associated with the treatment of internally generated assets versus that required for acquired intangibles. In particular, there are inconsistencies in the accounting for internally generated intangibles and intangibles acquired in a business combination. Note, in this regard:

(a) *The initial recognition of intangible assets.* IAS 38 requires intangible assets to be initially recognised at cost. However, for assets acquired in a business combination, an intangible asset can be recognised at fair value. Internally generated intangibles cannot be recognised, even if the fair value can be reliably measured. For example, outlays on research cannot be recognised as an asset. However, if an entity acquires another entity that has in-process research, an intangible asset can be recognised if the fair value can be measured reliably.

(b) *The measurement of fair value.* One of the reasons given in paragraph BCZ38(c) of the Basis for Conclusions on IAS 38 for disallowing the recognition of internally generated intangible assets is the impossibility of determining the fair value of an intangible asset reliably if no active market exists for the asset, and active markets are unlikely to exist for internally generated intangible assets. However, for intangible assets recognised in a business combination, it is assumed that fair value can be measured (reliably, it is hoped) without the existence of active markets. IAS 38 allows the use of other measurement techniques or even what an entity would have paid based on the best information available. Hence, in a business combination, the fair values of intangibles can be measured reliably using measures determined outside an active market, but these same measures cannot be used to measure the fair values of internally generated assets for asset recognition purposes. As a protection, the requirements of IAS 36 *Impairment of Assets* can be applied to both acquired and internally generated intangible assets.

(c) *Brands, mastheads, publishing titles and customer lists.* Paragraph 63 of IAS 38 prohibits the recognition of internally generated brands and items similar in substance. However, such assets can be recognised when acquired in a business combination (as well as if acquired as a separate asset). As far as the measurement of the fair value of these assets goes, the argument presented in point (b) applies — if the fair value of a brand can be determined in a business combination then it can be determined if internally generated. Further, it has been noted previously that the reason given in paragraph 64 of IAS 38 for non-recognition of internally generated brands is that the cost of these items 'cannot be distinguished from the cost of developing the business as a whole'. If this argument is true for internally generated brands, the same argument could be applied to acquired brands.

An interesting application of the concepts discussed in this section is in relation to football players playing for professional football clubs. For most clubs, there are two broad groups of players. The first group consists of those players whose contracts have been bought by the club on the transfer market. The second group consists of those players who have come up through the youth development schemes at the club.

Figure 6.2 is an extract from the balance sheet of Arsenal Holdings Limited, a British premier league club. The intangible assets of £417,044 million comprise over half of the total fixed (non-current) assets.

FIGURE 6.2 Extract from balance sheet of Arsenal Holdings Limited

ARSENAL HOLDINGS LIMITED
BALANCE SHEET
As at 31 May 2023

		Group	
		2023	2022
	Note	£'000	£'000
Fixed assets			
Tangible assets	9	388,644	389,041
Intangible assets	10	417,044	333,490
Investments	11	750	2,140
		806,438	724,671
Current assets			
Stock - development properties	12	10,068	9,106
Stock - retail merchandise		11,498	4,235
Debtors - due within one year	13	72,207	53,758
- due after one year	13	11,916	11,360
Cash at bank and in hand	14	42,769	29,956
		148,458	108,415

Source: Arsenal Holdings Limited (2023, p18).

The note to intangible assets (see figure 6.3) reveals that the entire intangible assets balance comprises the net book value of 'player registrations'. The 'cost of player registrations' represents the amounts paid by Arsenal for player contracts bought on the transfer market. Note that the financial statements refer to 'player registrations' and not 'players' as it is the contract that is the intangible asset and not the players themselves. The cost of player registrations meets the definition of an intangible asset and is measurable.

However, what about the players that have come up through the youth development schemes? These players play alongside the players bought on the transfer market but as all of the costs associated with their development are not separable and thus not measurable, there is no recognition of their contracts as an intangible asset on the financial statements.

FIGURE 6.3 Extract from intangible assets note of Arsenal Holdings Limited

Intangible assets	£'000
Cost of player registrations	
At 1 June 2022	648,717
Additions	251,126
Disposals	(126,170)
At 31 May 2023	773,673
Amortisation of player registrations	
At 1 June 2022	315,227
Charge for the year	139,060
Impairment	18,091
Disposals	(115,749)
At 31 May 2023	356,629
Net book value	
At 31 May 2023	417,044
At 31 May 2022	333,490

The figures for cost of player registrations are historic figures for the costs associated with acquiring players' registrations or extending their contracts. Accordingly, the net book amount of player registrations will not reflect, nor is it intended to, the current market value of these players nor does it take any account of players developed through the Group's youth system.

The directors consider the net realisable value of intangible assets to be significantly greater than their book value.

Source: Arsenal Holdings Limited (2023, pp. 31, 32).

6.2.7 Recognition of an expense

Paragraphs 68–71 of IAS 38 cover the issue of when expenditure on an intangible asset should be expensed. However, if the previous rules in IAS 38 are followed, then the appropriate outlays are expensed when the criteria are not met. These paragraphs add nothing particularly new to the accounting for intangible assets. However, paragraph 69 provides a list of other examples of outlays that should always be recognised as an expense when incurred, these being expenditures on:

- start-up activities
- training activities
- advertising and promotional activities
- relocating or reorganising part or all of an entity.

Provision of this list ensures no asset will be recognised in relation to these activities, taking the judgement away from preparers of the financial statements.

Note that there is an important distinction between expenditure incurred on future advertising and promotional activities and prepayments for advertising and promotional activities.

Where an entity has received goods or services that it would use to develop or communicate an advertisement or promotion (for example, brochures), the entity should not recognise as an asset goods or services in respect of its future advertising or promotional activities. This expenditure should be expensed on receipt of the goods or services and not when they are used (for example, when the brochures are distributed). However, if an entity pays for advertising goods or services in advance and the other party has not yet provided those goods or services, the entity has a different asset. That asset is the right to receive those goods and services. This is set out in paragraph 69A and elaborated in paragraph BC46 of the Basis for Conclusions.

Paragraph 71 is important. This paragraph prohibits the recognition at a later date of past expenditure as assets. In other words, if amounts relating to research have been expensed, these amounts cannot then be capitalised, nor can appropriate adjustments to equity be made, when an intangible asset is created at the development stage.

6.2.8 Internally generated goodwill

Paragraph 49 of IAS 38 states categorically that internally generated goodwill is not recognised as an asset. Hence, goodwill can be recognised only when it is acquired as part of a business combination and measured in accordance with IFRS 3 *Business Combinations*.

The reason given in paragraph 49 of IAS 38 for non-recognition is that goodwill is not identifiable; that is, it is not separable, nor does it arise from contractual or other legal rights. A second reason given for non-recognition, as stated in paragraph 49, is that the cost of internally generated goodwill cannot be reliably determined. The fair value of goodwill could be determined by comparing the fair value of the entity as a whole and subtracting the sum of the fair values of the identifiable assets and liabilities of the entity. However, under IAS 38, the principle for recognition is that identifiable intangible assets as well as goodwill must initially be measured at cost, not at fair value. As is discussed in more detail in the next section, this principle makes the recognition of internally generated intangibles harder than the recognition of acquired intangibles.

6.3 MEASUREMENT SUBSEQUENT TO INITIAL RECOGNITION

6.3.1 Measurement basis

Consistent with IAS 16, after the initial recognition of an intangible asset at cost, an entity must choose for each class of intangible asset whether to measure the assets using the *cost model* or the *revaluation model* – see paragraph 72. *(These models are discussed in greater detail in chapter 5.)*

Cost model

Under the cost model, the asset is recorded at the initial cost of acquisition and is then subject to amortisation *(see section 6.3.3)* and impairment testing *(see chapter 7)*.

Revaluation model

Under the revaluation model, the asset is carried at fair value, and is subject to amortisation and impairment charges. As with property, plant and equipment, if this model is chosen, revaluations are made with sufficient regularity so that the carrying amount of the asset does not materially differ from the current fair value at the end of the reporting period.

One specification that applies to intangible assets but is not required for property, plant and equipment is how the fair value is to be measured. Under paragraph 75 of IAS 38, the fair value must be measured by reference to an active market. An active market is defined in IFRS 13 as a market in which transactions for the asset or liability take place with sufficient frequency and volume to provide pricing information on an ongoing basis. This means that an intangible asset acquired in a business combination and measured at fair value using some measurement technique cannot subsequently use that same measurement technique if it adopts the revaluation model. In the absence of an active market, the intangible asset would be kept at the fair value determined at the date of the business combination and accounted for on the cost basis. As paragraph 76 notes, the choice of revaluation model does not allow the recognition of intangible assets that cannot be recognised initially at cost. However, paragraph 77 allows an asset for which only part of the cost was recognised to be fully revalued to fair value.

Paragraph 78 of IAS 38 states that intangibles such as brands, newspaper mastheads, patents and trademarks cannot be measured at fair value, as there is no active market for these assets because they are unique. As with the recognition of these types of intangible assets, the standard setters have stated specifically that they can be measured only at cost.

Selection of the revaluation model requires all assets in the one class to be measured at fair value. Because of the insistence on using active markets for the measurement of fair value, the standard recognises that there will be cases where fair values cannot be determined for all assets within one class. Hence, under paragraph 81 of IAS 38, where there is no active market for an asset, the asset can be measured at cost even if the class is measured using the revaluation model. Further, if the ability to measure the asset at fair value disappears because the market for the asset no longer meets the criteria to be classified as active, the asset is carried at the latest revalued amount and effectively accounted for under the cost model. If the market again becomes active, the revaluation model can be resumed.

Accounting for intangible assets measured using the revaluation model is exactly the same as for property, plant and equipment *(see chapter 5)*. Where there is a revaluation increase, the asset is increased and the increase is credited directly to a revaluation surplus. However, if the revaluation increase reverses a previous revaluation decrease relating to the same asset, the revaluation increase is recognised as income (IAS 38 paragraph 85). Any accumulated amortisation is eliminated at the time of revaluation.

Where there is a revaluation decrease, the decrease is recognised as an expense unless there has been a previous revaluation increase. In the latter case, the adjustment must first be made against any existing revaluation surplus before recognising an expense (IAS 38 paragraph 86). Any accumulated amortisation is eliminated at the time of the revaluation.

As with a revaluation surplus on property, plant and equipment, paragraph 87 of IAS 38 states that the revaluation surplus may be transferred to retained earnings when the surplus is realised on the retirement or disposal of the asset. Alternatively, the revaluation surplus may progressively be taken to retained earnings in proportion to the amortisation of the asset.

6.3.2 Subsequent expenditure

Paragraph 20 of IAS 38 discusses subsequent expenditure in general. Subsequent expenditure refers to the costs incurred after the intangible asset is acquired or after its internal generation is complete. It is argued in this paragraph that the unique nature of intangibles means that subsequent expenditure should be expensed rather than capitalised. Subsequent expenditure maintains expected benefits rather than increases them.

In addition, and consistent with paragraph 63, subsequent expenditure on brands, mastheads, publishing titles, customer lists and items similar in substance (whether externally acquired or internally generated) is always recognised in profit or loss as incurred. This is because such expenditure cannot be distinguished from expenditure to develop the business as a whole.

Paragraph 42 provides specific guidance on subsequent expenditures relating to acquired in-process research and development projects. Effectively, the same criteria for initially recognising an asset and expensing are applied to account for subsequent expenditures. The results of this application are:
- to expense research outlays
- to expense development outlays not meeting the criteria in paragraph 57
- to add to the acquired in-process research or development project if the development expenditure satisfies the paragraph 57 criteria.

6.3.3 Amortisation of intangible assets

Useful life

A key determinant in the amortisation process for intangible assets is whether the useful life is finite or indefinite. If finite, then the asset has to be amortised over that life. If the asset has an indefinite life, then there is no annual amortisation charge. Paragraph 88 of IAS 38 states:

> An entity shall assess whether the useful life of an intangible asset is finite or indefinite and, if finite, the length of, or number of production or similar units constituting, that useful life. An intangible asset shall be regarded by the entity as having an indefinite useful life when, based on an analysis of all the relevant factors, there is no foreseeable limit to the period over which the asset is expected to generate net cash inflows for the entity.

The term 'indefinite' does not mean that the asset has an infinite life; that is, that it is going to last forever. As paragraph 91 notes, an indefinite life means that, with the proper maintenance, there is no foreseeable end to the life of the asset. Paragraph 90 provides a list of factors that should be considered in determining the useful life of the asset:
- the expected use of the asset by the entity and whether the asset could be managed efficiently by another management team
- typical product life cycles for the asset, and public information on estimates of useful lives of similar assets that are used in a similar way
- technical, technological, commercial or other types of obsolescence
- the stability of the industry, and changes in market demand
- expected actions by competitors
- the level of maintenance expenditure required and the entity's ability and intent to reach such a level

- the period of control over the asset and legal or similar limits on the use of the asset
- whether the useful life of the asset depends on the useful lives of other assets of the entity.

Paragraph 94 of IAS 38 notes that, as a general rule, assets whose lives depend on contractual or legal lives will be amortised over those lives or shorter periods in some cases. If renewal is possible, then the useful life applied can include the renewal period providing there is evidence to support renewal by the entity without significant cost.

Figure 6.4 contains two examples from those in the illustrative examples accompanying IAS 38 in relation to the assessment of useful lives.

FIGURE 6.4 Examples of indefinite lives for intangible assets.

Example: An acquired broadcasting licence that expires in 5 years
The broadcasting licence is renewable every 10 years if the entity provides at least an average level of service to its customers and complies with the relevant legislative requirements. The licence may be renewed indefinitely at little cost and has been renewed twice before the most recent acquisition. The acquiring entity intends to renew the licence indefinitely and evidence supports its ability to do so. Historically, there has been no compelling challenge to the licence renewal. The technology used in broadcasting is not expected to be replaced by another technology at any time in the foreseeable future. Therefore, the licence is expected to contribute to the entity's net cash inflows indefinitely.

The broadcasting licence would be treated as having an indefinite useful tile because it is expected to contribute to the entity's net cash inflows indefinitely. Therefore, the licence would not be amortised until its useful life is determined to be finite. The licence would be tested for impairment under IAS 36 annually and whenever there is an indication that it may be impaired.

Example: An acquired trademark used to identify and distinguish a leading consumer product that has been a market-share leader for the past 8 years
The trademark has a remaining legal life of 5 years but is renewable every 10 years at little cost. The acquiring entity intends to renew the trademark continuously and evidence supports its ability to do so. An analysis of (1) product life cycles, (2) market, competitive and environmental trends, and (3) brand extension opportunities provides evidence that the trademarked product will generate net cash inflows for the acquiring entity for an indefinite period.

The trademark would be treated as having an indefinite useful life because it is expected to contribute to net cash inflows indefinitely. Therefore, the trademark would not be amortised until its useful life is determined to be finite. It would be tested for impairment under IAS 36 annually and whenever there is an indication that it may be impaired.

Rather than considering the existence of an indefinite life for intangible assets, the standard setters could have set a maximum useful life such as 40 years. However, as noted in paragraph BC63 of the Basis for Conclusions on IAS 38, the IASB considers that writing standards in such a fashion would not accord with the principle that the accounting numbers should be representationally faithful. The principles in IAS 38 provide management with more discretion but allow for the provision of more relevant information. In order for an intangible asset (such as a trademark) to have an indefinite life, an entity is required to outlay funds on an annual basis to maintain the trademark. Consider in this regard the annual expenditure by soft-drink companies to maintain the value of their trademarks. The annual profit figure is then affected by these outlays. To require amortisation charges to be levied as well, when the asset is being maintained, would be to affect the statement of profit or loss and other comprehensive income twice.

Intangible assets with finite useful lives

Paragraph 97 of IAS 38 sets out the principles relating to the amortisation period and choice of amortisation method. In general, the principles of amortisation are the same as those for depreciating property, plant and equipment under IAS 16. In both cases, the process involves the allocation of the depreciable amount on a systematic basis over the useful life, with the method chosen reflecting the pattern in which the expected benefits are expected to be consumed by the entity. Paragraph 98 notes that an amortisation method will rarely result in an amortisation charge that is lower than if a straight-line method had been used. Further, in accordance with paragraph 104, the amortisation period and amortisation method should be reviewed at least at the end of each annual reporting period, which is the same for property, plant and equipment.

However, IAS 38 contains a number of rules that are specific to intangible assets, presumably because of the relative uncertainty associated with intangible assets:

- Where the pattern of benefits cannot be determined reliably, the straight-line method is to be used (paragraph 97). This is, presumably, to bring some consistency and comparability into the calculations.

- The residual value is assumed to be zero unless there is a commitment by a third party to purchase the asset at the end of its useful life, *or* there is an active market for the asset, and:
  - residual value can be determined by reference to that market and
  - it is probable that such a market will exist at the end of the asset's useful life (paragraph 100).

Any changes in residual value, amortisation method or useful life are changes in accounting estimates, and accounted for prospectively with an effect on the current and future amortisation charges.

Intangible assets with indefinite useful lives

As noted earlier, where an intangible asset has an indefinite useful life, there is no amortisation charge (IAS 38 paragraph 107). As with finite useful lives, the useful life of an intangible that is not being amortised must be reviewed each period (paragraph 109). Any change from indefinite to finite useful life for an asset is treated as a change in estimate and affects the amortisation charge in current and future periods. Intangible assets with indefinite useful lives are subject to annual impairment tests *(see chapter 7)*.

6.4 RETIREMENTS AND DISPOSALS

Accounting for the retirements and disposals of intangible assets is identical to that for property, plant and equipment under IAS 16. In particular, under IAS 38:
- intangible assets are to be derecognised on disposal or when there are no expected future benefits from the asset (paragraph 112)
- gains or losses on disposal are calculated as the difference between the proceeds on disposal and the carrying amount at point of sale, with amortisation calculated up to the point of sale (paragraph 113)
- amortisation of an intangible with a finite useful life does not cease when the asset becomes temporarily idle or is retired from active use (paragraph 117).

6.5 DISCLOSURE

Paragraph 118 of IAS 38 requires disclosures for each class of intangibles, and for internally generated intangibles to be distinguished from other intangibles. Examples of separate classes are given in paragraph 119:
- brand names
- mastheads and publishing titles
- computer software
- licences and franchises
- copyrights, patents and other industrial property rights, service and operating rights
- recipes, formulas, models, designs and prototypes
- intangible assets under development.

Disclosures required by paragraph 118(a) and (b) would be contained in the summary of significant accounting policies, as illustrated in figure 6.5. Disclosures required by paragraphs 118 (c) to (e) and 122 of IAS 38 are illustrated in figure 6.6.

FIGURE 6.5 Illustrative disclosures required by paragraph 118(a) and (b) of IAS 38

Note 1: Summary of significant accounting policies (extract)	IAS 38 paragraph 118
Intangible assets Intangible assets are initially recognised at cost. Intangible assets that have indefinite useful lives are tested for impairment on an annual basis. Intangible assets that have finite useful lives are amortised over those lives on a straight-line basis.	*(b)*

Patents and copyrights
These have all been acquired by the company. Costs relating to these assets are capitalised and amortised on a straight-line basis over the following periods:
    Patent — packaging 5 years
    Patent — tools 10 years
    Copyright 10 years
	(b)

Licence The licence relating to television broadcasting rights is determined to be indefinite.	*(a)*

FIGURE 6.5 *(continued)*

Research and development Research costs are expensed as incurred. Development costs are expensed except those that it is probable will generate future economic benefits, this being determined by an analysis of factors such as technical feasibility and the existence of markets. Such costs are currently being amortised on a straight-line basis over the following periods:	*(a)*
Tool design project 5 years Water cooling project 10 years	*(b)*

Other disclosures required, where relevant, by paragraph 118 of IAS 38 are:
- the line item in the statement of profit or loss and other comprehensive income in which any amortisation of intangible assets is included (paragraph 118(d))
- increases or decreases during the period resulting from revaluations under paragraphs 75, 85 and 86 and from impairment losses recognised or reversed directly in equity (paragraph 118(e)(iii))
- impairment losses reversed in profit or loss during the period (paragraph 118(e)(v)).

FIGURE 6.6 Illustrative disclosures required by paragraphs 118 and 122 of IAS 38

Note 11: Intangible assets	IAS 38 paragraph 122
Details about the Company's intangible assets are provided below. All intangibles are considered to have finite useful lives except for a patent held for a tool used in the manufacture of steel windmills. As this tool is able to substantially lessen the cost of manufacturing windmills, and all entities manufacturing windmills acquire the special tool from the company for use in their production process, the continued use of the tool in the manufacturing process is considered to be infinite. Hence, the patent is considered to have an indefinite life. The tool has a carrying amount of £155,000 [2013: £155,000].	*(a)*

Note 11: Intangible assets

IAS 38 paragraph 122

	Patents and copyrights		Deferred development expenditure		paragraph 188
Beginning of year	2024 £'000	2023 £'000	2024 £'000	2023 £'000	
At cost	576	545	592	361	*(c)*
Accumulated amortisation	276	234	166	110	
Carrying amount	300	311	426	251	
Additions:					*(e)(i)*
Acquisition of subsidiary	—	22	—	54	
Internal development	—	—	72	182	
Acquired separately	10	15	—	—	
Disposals	(15)	—	—	—	*(e)(ii)*
Amortisation	(38)	(32)	(52)	(44)	*(e)(vi)*
Impairment	—	(10)	—	(12)	*(e)(iv)*
Exchange differences	5	(6)	5	(5)	*(e)(vii)*
Carrying amount at end of year	262	300	451	426	
At cost	557	576	669	592	*(c)*
Accumulated amortisation	295	276	218	166	
Carrying amount at end of year	262	300	451	426	

Paragraph 122 of IAS 38 also requires the following disclosures, if relevant:
- for intangible assets acquired by way of a *government grant* and initially recognised at fair value (paragraph 122(c)):
  - the fair value initially recognised for these assets
  - their carrying amount
  - whether they are measured after recognition under the cost model or the revaluation model.

- the existence and carrying amounts of intangible assets whose *title is restricted* and the carrying amounts of intangible assets *pledged as security* for liabilities (paragraph 122(d)).
- the amount of *contractual commitments* for the acquisition of intangible assets (paragraph 122(e)).

Paragraph 124 details further disclosures where intangible assets are carried at revalued amounts. An example of this disclosure is contained in figure 6.7.

FIGURE 6.7 Disclosures required by paragraph 124 of IAS 38

FIGURE 6.7 Disclosures required by paragraph 124 of IAS 38

		IAS 38 paragraph 124
Intangibles carried at revalued amounts		
The company has recognised its Internet domain name as an intangible asset. The asset was recognised initially at cost in 2020. The revaluation model was used to measure this asset from 1 January 2023. At the end of the reporting period, 31 December 2024, the carrying amount of this asset is £52,500. If the cost method had continued to be applied, the carrying amount would have been £33,600.		(a)(i) (a)(ii) (a)(iii)
The revaluation surplus in relation to this asset is as follows:	2024 / 2023	(b)
Balance at beginning of year	£48,000 / £45,000	
Increase	4,500 / 3,000	
Balance al end of year	£52,500 / £48,000	
There are no restrictions on the distribution of this balance to shareholders.		

Paragraph 126 requires disclosure of the aggregate amount of research and development expenditure recognised as an expense during the period. Disclosures in paragraph 128 that are encouraged but not required include a description of any fully amortised intangible asset that is still in use, and a brief description of significant intangible assets controlled by the entity but not recognised as assets because they did not meet the recognition criteria in IAS 38.

An example of disclosure of intangible assets is in figure 6.8, which shows the intangible assets disclosed by GSK in its 2023 annual report.

FIGURE 6.8 Example of disclosure of intangible assets

20. Other intangible assets

	Computer software £m	Licences, parents, amortised brands £m	Indefinite life brands £m	Total £m
Cost at 1 January 2022	2,424	21,439	18,626	42,489
Exchange adjustments	63	934	1,112	2,109
Capitalised development costs	–	317	–	317
Additions through business combinations	–	2,964	–	2,964
Other additions	149	626	–	775
Disposals and asset write-offs	(203)	(33)	–	(236)
Transfer to assets held for sale/distribution	(513)	(496)	(19,772)	(20,781)
Reclassifications	39	(34)	34	39
Cost at 31 December 2022	1,959	25,717	–	27,676
Exchange adjustments	(30)	(664)	–	(694)
Capitalised development costs	–	363	–	363
Additions through business combinations	–	1,438	–	1,438
Other additions	144	525	–	669
Disposals and asset write-offs	(125)	(13)	–	(138)

FIGURE 6.8 *(continued)*

Transfer to assets held for sale/distribution	2	–	–	2
Reclassifications	34	(3)	–	31
Cost at 31 December 2023	1,984	27,363	–	29,347
Amortisation at 1 January 2022	(1,369)	(8,262)	–	(9,631)
Exchange adjustments	(33)	(307)	–	(340)
Charge for the year	(204)	(931)	–	(1,135)
Disposals and asset write-offs	129	19	–	148
Transfer to assets held for sale	254	300	–	554
Amortisation at 31 December 2022	(1,223)	(9,181)	–	(10,404)
Exchange adjustments	18	174	–	192
Charge for the year	(203)	(1,009)	–	(1,212)
Disposals and asset write-offs	100	8	–	108
Transfer to assets held for sale/distribution	(3)	–	–	(3)
Reclassifications	4	1	–	5
Amortisation at 31 December 2023	(1,307)	(10,007)	–	(11,314)
Impairment at 1 January 2022	(91)	(2,480)	(208)	(2,779)
Exchange adjustments	(2)	(138)	(1)	(141)
Impairment losses	(72)	(313)	(17)	(402)
Transfer to assets held for sale/distribution	10	34	226	270
Reversal of impairments	1	17	–	18
Disposals and asset write-offs	73	7	–	80
Impairment at 31 December 2022	(81)	(2,873)	–	(2,954)
Exchange adjustments	1	70	–	71
Impairment losses	(23)	(398)	–	(421)
Transfer to assets held for sale/distribution	–	–	–	–
Reversal of impairments	3	–	–	3
Disposals and asset write-offs	25	11	–	36
Impairment at 31 December 2023	(75)	(3,190)	–	(3,265)
Total amortisation and impairment at 31 December 2022	(1,304)	(12,054)	–	(13,358)
Total amortisation and impairment at 31 December 2023	(1,382)	(13,197)	–	(14,579)
Net book value at 1 January 2022	964	10,697	18,418	30,079
Net book value at 31 December 2022	655	13,663	–	14,318
Net book value at 31 December 2023	602	14,166	–	14,768

Source: GSK (2023, p. 210).

6.6 SUMMARY

Intangible assets are considered to be sufficiently different from other assets such as property, plant and equipment for the standard setters to provide a separate standard. The reason for having such a standard is that the nature of intangibles is such that there are particular measurement problems associated with these assets that require specific accounting principles to be established. IAS 38 *Intangible Assets* is concerned with the definition, recognition, measurement and disclosure of intangibles.

The characteristic of 'identifiability' is critical to the identification of intangibles, and is the same concept that arises in IFRS 3 *Business Combinations* in relation to identifiable assets, liabilities and contingent liabilities recognised by the acquirer. In considering the accounting for intangibles, it is important to consider the differences in accounting depending on the source of the intangibles. The conditions for recognising intangibles acquired (separately or within a business combination) are less onerous than those for internally generated intangibles.

Amortisation of intangibles raises particular issues in terms of the useful lives of assets. The potential to assess some intangible assets as having indefinite useful lives and hence not subject to amortisation makes the decision on what is the useful life of an asset very significant. It is important to understand how to make such a decision. Aspects of that decision process are required to be specifically disclosed.

DEMONSTRATION PROBLEM 6.1 Development outlays

This demonstration problem illustrates the application of the criteria in paragraph 57 of IAS 38, determining when development outlays are capitalised or expensed.

Pretoria Ltd is a highly successful engineering company that manufactures filters for air conditioning systems. Due to its dissatisfaction with the quality of the filters currently available, on 1 January 2024 it commenced a project to design a more efficient filter. The following notes record the events relating to that project:

2024	
January	Paid £145,000 in salaries of company engineers and consultants who conducted basic tests on available filters with varying modifications.
February	Spent £165,000 on developing a new filter system, including the production of a basic model. It became obvious that the model in its current form was not successful because the material in the filter was not as effective as required.
March	Acquired the fibres division of Durban Ltd for £330,000. The fair values of the tangible assets of this division were: property, plant and equipment, £180,000; inventories, £60,000.
	This business was acquired because one of the products it produced was a fibrous compound, sold under the brand name Springbok, that Pretoria Ltd considered would be excellent for including in the filtration process.
	By buying the fibres division, Pretoria Ltd acquired the patent for this fibrous compound.
	Pretoria Ltd valued the patent at £50,000 and the brand name at £40,000, using a number of valuation techniques. The patent had a further 10-year life but was renewable on application.
	Further costs of £54,000 were incurred on the new filter system during March.
April	Spent a further £135,000 on revising the filtration process to incorporate the fibrous compound. By the end of April, Pretoria Ltd was convinced that it now had a viable product because preliminary tests showed that the filtration process was significantly better than any other available on the market.
May	Developed a prototype of the filtration component and proceeded to test it within a variety of models of air conditioners. The company preferred to sell the filtration process to current manufacturers of air conditioners if the process worked with currently available models. If this proved not possible, the company would then consider developing its own brand of air conditioners using the new filtration system. By the end of May, the filtration system had proved successful on all but one of the currently available commercial models. Costs incurred were £65,000.
June	Various air conditioner manufacturers were invited to demonstrations of the filtration system. Costs incurred were £25,000, including £12,000 for food and beverages for the prospective clients. The feedback from a number of the companies was that they were prepared to enter negotiations for acquiring the filters from Pretoria Ltd. The company now believed it had a successful model and commenced planning the production of the filters. Ongoing costs of £45,000 to refine the filtration system, particularly in the light of comments by the manufacturers, were incurred in the latter part of June.

Explain the accounting for the various outlays incurred by Pretoria Ltd.

Solution

The main problem in accounting for the costs is determining at what point of time costs can be capitalised. This is resolved by applying the criteria in paragraph 57 of IAS 38:

- *Technical feasibility*. At the end of April, the company believed that the filtration process was technically feasible.
- *Intention to complete and sell*. At the end of April, the company was not yet sure that the system was adaptable to currently available models of air conditioners. If it wasn't adaptable, the company would have to test whether development of its own brand of air conditioners would be a commercial proposition. Hence, it was not until the end of May that the company was convinced it could complete the project and had a product that it could sell.
- *Ability to use or sell*. By the end of May, the company had a product that it believed it had the ability to sell. Being a filter manufacturer, it knew the current costs of competing products and so could make an informed decision about the potential for the commercial sale of its own filter.
- *Existence of a market*. The market comprised the air conditioning manufacturers. By selling to the manufacturers, the company had the potential to generate probable future cash flows. This criterion was met by the end of May.*Availability of resources*. From the beginning of the project, the company was not short of resources, being a highly successful company in its own right.
- *Ability to measure costs reliably*. Costs are readily attributable to the project throughout its development.

On the basis of the above analysis, the criteria in paragraph 57 of IAS 38 were all met at the end of May. Therefore, costs incurred before this point are expensed, and those incurred after this point are capitalised. Hence, the following costs would be written off as incurred:

January	£145,000
February	165,000
March	54,000
April	135,000
May	65,000

In acquiring the fibres division from Durban Ltd, Pretoria Ltd would pass the following entry:

Property, plant and equipment	Dr	180,000	
Inventories	Dr	60,000	
Brand	Dr	40,000	
Patent	Dr	50,000	
Cash	Cr		330,000
(Acquisition of assets)			

The patent would initially be depreciated over a 10-year useful life. However, this would need to be reassessed upon application of the fibrous compound to the air conditioning filtration system. This alternative use may extend the expected useful life of the product, and hence of the patent. The brand name would be depreciated over the same useful life of the patent, because it is expected that the brand has no real value unless backed by the patent.

The company would then capitalise development costs of £45,000 in June. The marketing costs incurred in June of £25,000 would be expensed because they are not part of the development process.

Discussion questions

1. What are the key characteristics of an intangible asset?
2. Explain what is meant by 'identifiability'.
3. How do the principles for amortisation of intangible assets differ from those for depreciation of property, plant and equipment?
4. Explain what is meant by an 'active market'.
5. How is the useful life of an intangible asset determined?
6. What intangibles can never be recognised if internally generated? Why?
7. Explain the difference between 'research' and 'development'.
8. Explain when development outlays can be capitalised.

References

Arsenal Holdings Limited 2023, Annual Report, https://www.arsenal.com/the-club/corporate-info/arsenal-holdings-financial-results

Diageo plc 2023, *Annual Report*, https://media.diageo.com/diageo-corporate-media/media/p1bljst1/diageo-annual-report-2023.pdf.

GSK plc 2023, *Annual Report*, https://www.gsk.com/media/11007/annual-report-2023.pdf.

Service, CL (2024), Gripping GAAP, LexisNexis.

There is an extant accounting literature on intangibles, only a small fraction of which can be reviewed here. Wyatt (2008) offers a comprehensive review of the literature for the interested reader. Broadly, the literature can be split into two strands. The first is with respect to intangible assets that are recognised on the balance sheet (other than goodwill — *see chapter 19*). The second strand assesses the adequacy of the expensing requirements that apply to most internally generated intangibles.

Starting with recognised intangibles, Aboody and Lev (1998) examine the value relevance of capitalised software development costs in a sample of 163 software companies between 1987 and 1995. They argue that software firms reporting under US GAAP (SFAS 86 [FASB, 1985] and now ASC 985–20) face considerable flexibility with the capitalisation decision. As a result, about one fifth of sample firms expensed the development cost in full in every year examined. They find that the annual amount capitalised is smaller in bigger and more profitable firms, and is larger when the development costs (before capitalisation) are larger. They further find that stock returns are positively related to changes in annual amounts of capitalisation, but unrelated to the change in development expense recognised in the income statement. Because capitalising firms amortise the intangible asset, the amortisation figures may be informative, for example with respect to managers' estimate of the useful life. Consistent with that, the authors find that changes in amortisation expense are negatively related to stock returns. Further analysis also confirms that stock prices are positively related to the amount of software development cost recognised on the balance sheet. Collectively, this evidence suggests that investors regard capitalised amounts as assets. Mohd (2005) extends this analysis by looking at differences in information asymmetry between capitalising and expensing firms. He employs bid–ask spreads and trading volume as measures of information asymmetry. Consistent with the view that investors better understand the financials of capitalising firms, he finds evidence of lower information asymmetry for capitalising firms. Hence, both Aboody and Lev (1998) and Mohd (2005) are supportive of capitalisation of software development cost because it provides more useful information to investors.

Markarian et al. (2008) provide evidence from Italy about capitalisation of R&D expenses prior to the adoption of IFRS® Standards in 2005. Domestic Italian rules were quite similar to the capitalisation rules set in IAS 38 for development cost. Therefore this study is helpful in understanding how managers can use accounting discretion under IAS 38. This paper employs 130 firm-year observations during 2001–2003. The degree of capitalisation is on average 10% of total R&D costs. The paper fails to find consistent evidence as to the determinants of the amount capitalised, although some evidence suggests that more profitable firms capitalise less. Cazavan-Jeny and Jeanjean (2006) focus on a French sample, also pre IFRS® Standards. During 1993–2002 domestic French rules allowed considerable flexibility to managers with respect to the capitalisation decision. Their sample consists of 197 firms and 770 firm-year observations, with 250 observations under capitalisation. Unlike Aboody and Lev (1998) they find that (1) capitalised amounts are negatively related to stock prices, and (2) changes in capitalised amounts are negatively related to stock returns. This evidence is consistent with usefulness of reported numbers under capitalisation. Nevertheless, the negative relation could be indicative of investor perception that the decision to capitalise is opportunistic in nature and is adopted by weaker firms.

Wyatt (2005) employs an Australian sample during 1993–1997. During this period Australian GAAP allowed considerable flexibility for companies as to whether to capitalise internally generated intangibles. Wyatt (2005) examines several hypotheses as to what drives the capitalisation decision. In particular she predicts that the degree to which a firm can capture future benefits positively influences the capitalisation decision. Wyatt (2005) provides evidence that is consistent with this prediction using several proxies. This suggests that Australian firms used the discretion to capitalise in line with underlying economic fundamentals rather than in an opportunistic fashion.

IAS 38 axiomatically assumes that acquired intangibles always satisfy asset-recognition criteria. Nevertheless, to the extent that uncertainty about future benefits is an inherent feature of intangibles, it is questionable if acquired intangibles should be initially capitalised. Amir and Livne (2005) raise this point when they examine human-capital intangibles. Specifically, they take advantage of a unique industry arrangement – the football industry – whereby clubs that sign up new players often pay a transfer fee to the player's former club. This fee normally corresponds to the talent and stature of the player. Nevertheless, as the form of the player and his fit with the new team and coach are far from being certain, it is not clear that they should be capitalised. Amir and Livne (2005) examine the relation between measures of future benefits and transfer fees paid, employing financials of 58 UK football clubs between 1990 and 2003. While they find a positive association between current sales, operating profit and operating cash flows on one hand and past transfer fees on the other hand, it seems that the investments are not fully recoverable. In addition, the useful life of transfer fees is found to be shorter than the amortisation period used by the clubs. Amir and Livne (2005) also examine the relation between transfer fees paid and stock prices and establish it is positive. They therefore conclude that market participants do regard fees paid as an asset. While the setting examined in Amir and Livne (2005) is industry-specific, it nevertheless raises some doubt about the requirement to show purchased intangibles as assets.

Turning to unrecognised intangibles, a number of studies have criticised the immediate expensing rule that applies to internally generated intangibles, mostly advertising and R&D. Hirschey and Weygandt (1985) is one of the earlier studies to suggest advertising and R&D should be capitalised. Specifically, they examine the association between the ratio of market value of equity to replacement cost of equity (a measure of the premium of market price over book value of equity) and advertising and R&D expenses. Inconsistent with standard-setters' view, the results indicate a positive relation, which is expected if investors regard these expenditures as assets.

Lev and Sougiannis (1996) advance a method for estimating the amortised cost of intangible R&D assets. They employ more than 11,600 observations to estimate economic amortisation rates that subsequently were used to estimate the hypothetical amount to be recognised as an R&D asset in the balance sheet. They also calculate the difference between reported earnings (and equity) and capitalisation-with-amortisation adjusted earnings (and equity). Lev and Sougiannis (1996) find that these differences are positively associated with stock prices, especially for high R&D-intensity firms. A stock returns analysis modestly supports the levels analysis. Barth et al. (2023) find a positive relation between prices and R&D expense using a large sample from 1962 to 2018. This evidence collectively suggests that investors pay attention to these differences, which in turn indicates that for R&D-intensive firms investors adjust reported numbers as if R&D expense is capitalised.

Lev and Zarowin (1999) take the charge against expensing of R&D a step further. They look at the ability of earnings and changes in earnings to explain stock returns over a period of 20 years. In addition to the changes analysis they look at the ability of earnings and book value of equity to explain stock prices (levels analysis) over the same period. They provide evidence that suggests that (1) the usefulness of accounting numbers has declined over the period examined and (2) at the same time there has been an increase in the rate of change businesses have faced. The central claim of the Lev and Zarowin's (1999) paper is that the changes in business environment are attributable to the role of R&D and technology. To support this assertion they show that firms that increase (decrease) their R&D intensity over time exhibit lower (higher) usefulness of their financial reports. They then argue that the expensing rule may have contributed to the decline in usefulness, although in this paper they do not furnish direct evidence pertaining to this claim.

Not all studies agree that R&D should be capitalised. Kothari et al. (2002) show that the variability of future profits is increasing with R&D expense, and more so than capital expenditure (CAPEX). This is consistent with standard setters' view that the uncertainty surrounding future benefits is high in the case of R&D. Amir et al. (2007) nevertheless argue, and provide evidence to that effect, that the risk in CAPEX can exceed that of R&D in several industries. The evidence provided in Amir et al. (2007) is intriguing because it challenges the view that CAPEX should always be capitalised.

Further research has been conducted also with respect to other intangibles that existing accounting rules disallow their capitalisation. For example, Barth et al. (1998) employ brand estimates reported by Financial World that, in turn, are based on valuation methodology developed by Interbrand Ltd. The authors find evidence supporting the view that unrecognised brands are regarded as assets by market participants. Livne et al. (2011) examine the valuation role of customer acquisition cost, a major expense in several service-based firms. They provide evidence from the wireless industry that these expenses are positively related to customer retention and future operating profit. This suggests that such expenses meet asset recognition criteria. Bonacchi et al. (2014) extend this research by looking at subscription-based enterprises. They develop a valuation model for customer equity using 576 firm-year observations and find that it is positively related to stock prices. Since internally generated customer relationships cannot be capitalised, the evidence in Livne et al. (2011) and Bonacchi et al. (2014) calls for a change in existing rules regarding customer relationships.

References

Aboody, D., and Lev, B., 1998. The value relevance of intangibles: the case of software capitalization. *Journal of Accounting Research*, 36, 161–191.

Amir, E., Guan, Y., and Livne, G., 2007. The association of R&D and capital expenditures with subsequent earnings variability. *Journal of Business Finance & Accounting*, 34 (1 and 2), 222–246.

Amir, E., and Livne, G., 2005. Accounting, valuation and duration of football player contracts. *Journal of Business Finance & Accounting*, 32(3–4), 549–586.

Barth, M.E., Clement, M.B., Foster, G., and Kasznik, R., 1998. Brand values and capital market valuation. *Review of Accounting Studies*, 3(1), 41–68.

Barth, M.E., Li, K., and McClure, C.G., 2023. Evolution in value relevance of accounting information. *The Accounting Review*, 98(1), 1–28.

Bonacchi, M., Kolev, K., and Lev, B. 2014. Customer franchise—a hidden, yet crucial asset. *Contemporary Accounting Research*, 32(3), 1024–1049.

Cazavan-Jeny, A., and Jeanjean, T. 2006. The negative impact of R&D capitalization: a value relevance approach. *European Accounting Review*, 15(1), 37–61.

Financial Accounting Standards Board. 1985. Accounting for the Costs of Computer Software to Be Sold, Leased, or Otherwise Marketed. SFAS 86. Stamford, CT.

Hirschey, M., and Weygandt, J.J., 1985. Amortization policy for advertising and research and development expenditures. *Journal of Accounting Research*, 23 (1), 326–335.

Kothari, S.P., Laguerre, T.E., and Leone, A.J., 2002. Capitalization versus expensing: evidence on the uncertainty of future earnings from capital expenditures versus R&D outlays. *Review of Accounting Studies*, 7(4), 355–382.

Lev, B., and Sougiannis, T., 1996. The capitalization, amortization, and value-relevance of R&D. *Journal of Accounting and Economics*, 21(1), 107–138.

Lev, B., and Zarowin, P., 1999. The boundaries of financial reporting and how to extend them. *Journal of Accounting Research*, 37(2), 353–385.

Livne, G., Simpson, A., and Talmor, E., 2011. Do customer acquisition cost, retention and usage matter to firm performance and valuation? *Journal of Business Finance & Accounting*, 38(3), 334–363.

Markarian, G., Pozza, L., and Prencipe, A., 2008. Capitalization of R&D costs and earnings management: evidence from Italian listed companies. *The International Journal of Accounting*, 43(3), 246–267.

Mohd, E., 2005. Accounting for software development costs and information asymmetry. *The Accounting Review*, 80(4), 1211–1231.

Wyatt, A., 2005. Accounting recognition of intangible assets: theory and evidence on economic determinants. *The Accounting Review*, 80(3), 967–1003.

Wyatt, A., 2008. What financial and non-financial information on intangibles is value-relevant? A review of the evidence. *Accounting and Business Research*, 38(3), 217–256.

7 Impairment of assets

ACCOUNTING STANDARDS IN FOCUS

IAS 36 *Impairment of Assets*

LEARNING OBJECTIVES

After studying this chapter, you should be able to:

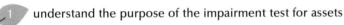 understand the purpose of the impairment test for assets

 understand when to undertake an impairment test

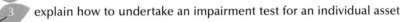 explain how to undertake an impairment test for an individual asset

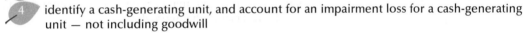 identify a cash-generating unit, and account for an impairment loss for a cash-generating unit — not including goodwill

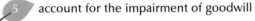 account for the impairment of goodwill

 account for reversals of impairment losses

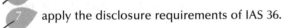 apply the disclosure requirements of IAS 36.

7.1 INTRODUCTION TO IAS 36

Chapters 5 and 6 discuss the measurement and recognition criteria for property, plant and equipment, and intangible assets. These assets are measured at cost or revalued amount and, for each asset, the cost or revalued amount is allocated over its useful life. The exception is where intangible assets have indefinite useful lives, in which case no amortisation is charged. In the statement of financial position at the end of a reporting period, the assets are reported at cost or revalued amount less the accumulated depreciation/amortisation. Because there are many judgements involved in the depreciation/amortisation process — estimates of useful life, residual values and the pattern of benefits — it is important to investigate if at the end of the reporting period the carrying amounts of the assets in the statement of financial position overstate the worth of the assets. In other words, can an entity expect to recover in future periods the carrying amounts of its assets? Recovery can be from continuing use of the asset and/or from the disposal of the asset. The entity has an impairment loss in relation to an asset if the expected recovery is less than the carrying amount of that asset. Paragraph 6 of IAS 36 *Impairment of Assets* defines an impairment loss as follows:

> An impairment loss is the amount by which the carrying amount of an asset or a cash-generating unit exceeds its recoverable amount.

This chapter examines the impairment test for assets. The accounting standard covering impairment is IAS 36 *Impairment of Assets*. The standard was issued initially by the International Accounting Standards Board (IASB®) in July 1998 and amended on numerous occasions, including an amendment in 2013.

Under IAS 36, an entity is required to conduct impairment tests for its assets to see whether it has incurred any impairment losses. The purpose of the impairment test is to ensure that assets are not carried at amounts that exceed their recoverable amounts or, more simply, that assets are not overstated.

Key questions in relation to the impairment test are:

- How does the test work?
- Is the test the same for all assets?
- Should the test apply to individual assets or to groups of assets? If to groups, which groups?
- Is the accounting treatment the same for assets measured at cost and for those measured at revalued amount?
- When should the test be carried out? Should it be done annually, every 3 years or some other time?
- Can the results of the impairment test be reversed; that is, if an asset is written down because it is impaired, can later events lead to the reversal of that write-down?

7.1.1 Scope of IAS 36

Paragraph 2 of IAS 36 notes that the standard does not apply to all assets; that is, not all assets are subject to impairment testing. Assets to which IAS 36 does not apply are:

(a) inventories (IAS 2 *Inventories*); *see chapter 4*
(b) contract assets and assets arising from costs to obtain or fulfil a contract that are recognised in accordance with IFRS 15 *Revenue from Contracts with Customers*; *see chapter 3*
(c) deferred tax assets (IAS 12 <u>Income Taxes</u>); *see chapter 15*
(d) assets arising from employee benefits (IAS 19 *Employee Benefits*); *see chapter 11*
(e) financial assets that are within the scope of IFRS 9 *Financial Instruments*; *see chapter 13*
(f) investment property that is measured at fair value (IAS 40 *Investment Property*); *see chapter 5*
(g) biological assets related to agricultural activity within the scope of IAS 41 *Agriculture* that are measured at fair value less costs to sell; *see online chapter Agriculture*
(h) contracts within the scope of IFRS 17 *Insurance Contracts* that are assets and any assets for insurance acquisition cash flows as defined in IFRS 17; and
(i) non-current assets (or disposal groups) classified as held for sale in accordance with IFRS 5 *Non-current Assets Held for Sale and Discontinued Operations*.

The accounting standards listed contain the principles for recognition and measurement of the particular assets covered by those standards. Note that in some of these standards the assets are required to be recorded at fair value, or fair value less costs of disposal. *Fair value is discussed in detail in chapter 8.* Where assets are recorded at fair value, through profit and loss there is no need to test for recoverability of the carrying amount of the asset. Examples of this would include investment property or financial assets measured at fair value through profit and loss as well as certain biological assets. Under IAS 2, inventory is recorded at the lower of cost and net realisable value. As net realisable value is defined in terms of estimated selling price, IAS 2 has an inbuilt impairment test requiring inventory to be written down when the cost is effectively greater than the recoverable amount.

7.2 WHEN TO UNDERTAKE AN IMPAIRMENT TEST

As noted earlier, the purpose of the impairment test is to ensure that disclosed assets do not have carrying amounts in excess of their recoverable amounts. However, under IAS 36 it is not necessary at the end of each reporting period to test each asset in order to determine whether it is impaired. The only assets that need to be tested at the end of the reporting period are those where there is any *indication* that an asset may be impaired (see paragraph 9 of IAS 36). An entity therefore must determine by looking at various sources of information whether there is sufficient evidence to suspect that an asset may be impaired. If there is no such evidence, then an entity can assume that impairment has not occurred.

For most assets, the need for an impairment test can be assessed by analysing sources of evidence. However, there are some assets for which an impairment test *must* be undertaken *every year*. Paragraph 10 identifies these assets:

- intangible assets with indefinite useful lives
- intangible assets not yet available for use
- goodwill acquired in a business combination.

The reason for singling out these assets for automatic impairment testing is that the carrying amounts of these assets are considered to be more uncertain than those of other assets. None of these assets are subject to an annual amortisation charge, and so there is no ongoing reduction in the carrying amounts of the assets. As the assets are not being reduced via amortisation, it is considered essential that the carrying amounts be tested against the recoverable amounts.

Another important reason for remeasuring assets and testing for impairment relates to the concept of depreciation adopted by the IASB. *As noted in chapter 5*, depreciation is viewed as a process of allocation rather than as a valuation process, even when an asset is measured at a revalued amount. Therefore, the carrying amount of an asset reflects the unallocated measure of the asset rather than the benefits to be derived from the asset in the future. The impairment test relates to the assessment of recoverability of the asset, which is not a feature of the depreciation allocation process.

7.2.1 Collecting evidence of impairment

The purpose of the impairment test is to determine whether the carrying amount of an asset exceeds its recoverable amount. The recoverable amount will be discussed in more detail below, but it is essentially the higher of the asset's fair value and the net present value of the cash flows that will be generated by that asset. Time and effort can be saved by establishing whichever of the two figures is the easier to determine. If that figure exceeds the carrying value, then the asset cannot be impaired and the other figure is unnecessary. For example, an entity owns property with a carrying value of $10 million. Management believes that the fair value is 'at least' $12 million. The value of the cash flows associated with the property is irrelevant and so there is no need to establish it.

IAS 36 requires management to consider sources of evidence that might indicate the possibility of impairment. Evidence can come from external and internal sources.

External sources of information

Paragraph 12 of IAS 36 lists four sources of information relating to the external environment in which the entity operates:

1. *Asset's value.* Might the asset's value have declined more than would normally be expected during the period? For example, are revenues from the products made using the asset declining? Are observable market prices for similar assets declining on the open market?
2. *Entity's environment/market.* Have significant adverse changes occurred or will they occur in the technological, market, economic or legal environment in which the entity operates, or in the market to which the asset is dedicated? For example, a competitor may have developed a product or technology that is likely to cause or has caused a significant and permanent reduction in the entity's market share.
3. *Interest rates.* Have market interest rates or market rates of return increased during the period? If so, then discounting future cash flows at this higher rate will reduce their net present value.
4. *Market capitalisation.* Is the carrying amount of the net assets of the entity greater than the market capitalisation of the entity?

Internal sources of information

Paragraph 12 of IAS 36 lists three sources of information based on events within the entity itself:

1. *Obsolescence or physical damage.* Does an analysis of the asset reveal physical damage or obsolescence?
2. *Changed use within the entity.* Is the asset expected to be used differently within the entity? For example, the asset may become idle; there may be a restructure in the entity that changes the use of the asset; there may be plans to sell the asset; or the useful life of an intangible may be changed from indefinite to finite.

3. *Economic performance of the asset.* Do internal reports indicate that the economic performance of the asset is worse than expected? Evidence of this consists of:
– actual cash flows for maintenance or operating the asset may be significantly higher than expected
– actual cash inflows or profits may be lower than expected
– expected cash flows for maintenance of operations may have increased, or expected profits may be lower.

In analysing the information from the above sources, paragraph 15 of IAS 36 notes that materiality must be taken into account. For example, an increase in short-term interest rates that is not expected to persist would have very little impact on net present values.

In its notes to the 2023 consolidated financial statements, Nokia provided details of the factors that trigger an impairment review for the entity (see figure 7.1).

FIGURE 7.1 Indicators of impairment for Nokia Corporation

Nokia tests the carrying value of goodwill for impairment annually. In addition, Nokia assesses the recoverability of the carrying value of goodwill and intangible assets if events or changes in circumstances indicate that the carrying value may be impaired. Factors that Nokia considers when it reviews indications of impairment include, but are not limited to, underperformance of the asset relative to its historical or projected future results, significant changes in the manner of using the asset or the strategy for the overall business, and significant negative industry or economic trends.

Source: Nokia Corporation (2023, p. 160).

7.3 IMPAIRMENT TEST FOR AN INDIVIDUAL ASSET

The impairment test involves comparing the carrying amount of an asset with its recoverable amount. To understand the nature of this test, it is necessary to understand a number of definitions given in paragraph 6 of IAS 36:

The recoverable amount of an asset or a cash-generating unit is the higher of its fair value less costs of disposal and its value in use.

Fair value is the price that would be received to sell an asset or paid to transfer a liability in an orderly transaction between market participants at the measurement date. *(See IFRS 13 Fair Value Measurement.)*

Costs of disposal are incremental costs directly attributable to the disposal of an asset or cash-generating unit, excluding finance costs and income tax expense.

Value in use is the present value of the future cash flows expected to be derived from an asset or cash-generating unit.

Note the phrase 'an asset or cash-generating unit' in the above definitions. The discussion in this section focuses on an individual asset, and it is assumed that, for the asset being tested for impairment, there are specific cash flows that can be associated with the asset. *Cash-generating units are discussed in section 7.4.*

From the definition of recoverable amount, there are two possible amounts against which the carrying amount can be tested for impairment: (i) fair value less costs of disposal and (ii) value in use. Although the definition of recoverable amount refers to the 'higher' of these two amounts, an impairment occurs if the carrying amount exceeds recoverable amount (paragraph 8). However, it is not always necessary to measure both amounts when testing for impairment. If either one of these amounts is greater than carrying amount, the asset is not impaired (paragraph 19). Where there are active markets, determining fair value less costs of disposal is probably easier than calculating value in use. However, where the carrying amount exceeds the fair value less costs of disposal, it is necessary to calculate the value in use. Figure 7.2 is a diagrammatic representation of the impairment test.

In calculating either fair value less costs of disposal or value in use, paragraph 23 of IAS 36 notes that in 'some cases, estimates, averages and computational shortcuts may provide reasonable approximations', rather than an entity having to perform in-depth calculations annually. It is also possible to use the most recent detailed calculation of recoverable amount made in a preceding year (paragraph 24) in the case of an intangible asset with an indefinite useful life. The latter is possible if *all* the following criteria are met:

• for the intangible asset, if tested as part of a cash-generating unit *(see section 7.4)*, the other assets and liabilities in the unit have not changed significantly
• in the preceding year's calculation, the difference between the carrying amount and recoverable amount was substantial
• an analysis of all evidence relating to events affecting the asset suggests that the likelihood of the recoverable amount being less than carrying amount is remote.

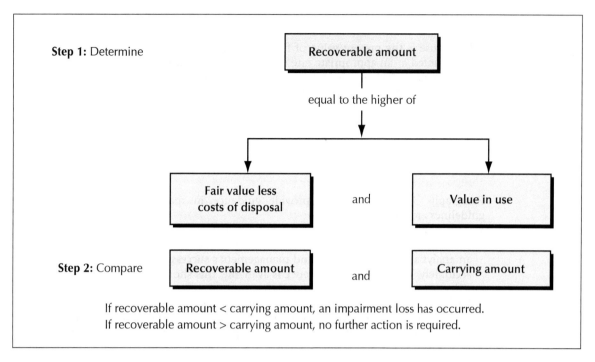

Step 1: Determine — Recoverable amount

equal to the higher of

Fair value less costs of disposal — and — Value in use

Step 2: Compare — Recoverable amount — and — Carrying amount

If recoverable amount < carrying amount, an impairment loss has occurred.
If recoverable amount > carrying amount, no further action is required.

FIGURE 7.2 The impairment test

7.3.1 Calculating fair value less costs of disposal

There are two parts to the determination of fair value less costs of disposal, namely *fair value* and *costs of disposal*. Fair value is measured in accordance with IFRS 13 *Fair Value Measurement* and is discussed in detail in *chapter 8*. Amongst other things, this means that fair value is defined as an exit price and can be measured using a number of valuation techniques using various observable or unobservable inputs.

Paragraph 28 of IAS 36 provides the following examples of costs of disposal: legal costs, stamp duty and similar transaction taxes, costs of removing the asset, and direct incremental costs to bring the asset into condition for sale. The costs must be directly associated with either the sale of the asset or getting the asset ready for sale. Any costs arising after the sale of the asset, even if arising as a result of the sale, are not regarded as costs of disposal.

Paragraph 5 of IAS 36 provides guidance where an asset is measured at a revalued amount (i.e. fair value). Fair value as a measure does not include a consideration of disposal costs. Hence, if an asset's fair value is equal to its market value, the difference between fair value and fair value less costs of disposal is the disposal costs of the asset. If the disposal costs are immaterial, then there is no significant difference between fair value and fair value less costs of disposal and no impairment needs to be reported. If the fair value is up to date, then the asset may be impaired if the disposal costs were material. However, disposal costs become relevant only if the fair value less the cost of disposal exceeds value in use, because then the recoverable amount is set equal to fair value less cost of disposal. In contrast, if the asset's value in use is the recoverable amount, the cost of disposal does not affect the impairment decision and amount.

Companies normally describe this process when discussing their accounting policies. Figure 7.3 is an example of such disclosure and is taken from Nokia's 2023 financial statements.

FIGURE 7.3 Nokia's accounting policies regarding impairment of assets

Nokia conducts its impairment testing by determining the recoverable amount for an asset, a cash-generating unit or groups of cash-generating units. The recoverable amount of an asset, a cash-generating unit or groups of cash-generating units is the higher of its fair value less costs of disposal and its value-in-use. The recoverable amount is compared to the asset's, cash-generating unit's or groups of cash-generating units' carrying value. If the recoverable amount for the asset, cash-generating unit or groups of cash-generating units is less than its carrying value, the asset is considered impaired and is written down to its recoverable amount. Impairment losses are presented in cost of sales, research and development expenses or selling, general and administrative expenses, except for impairment losses on goodwill, which are presented in other operating expenses.

Source: Nokia Corporation (2023, p. 160).

7.3.2 Calculating value in use

Value in use is the present value of future cash flows relating to the asset being measured. These should be discounted at an appropriate rate that takes account of the risks inherent in future cash flows from the asset. Paragraph 53A of IAS 36 *Impairment of Assets* notes that fair value differs from value in use because of factors that are likely to be specific to the entity:

(a) additional value derived from the grouping of assets (such as the creation of a portfolio of investment properties in different locations);
(b) synergies between the asset being measured and other assets;
(c) legal rights or legal restrictions that are specific only to the current owner of the asset; and
(d) tax benefits or tax burdens that are specific to the current owner of the asset.

Determining future cash flows

Paragraphs 33–54 of IAS 36 provide guidance in measuring future cash flows. Some important guidelines are:

- Cash flow projections should be based on *management's best estimate* of the range of economic conditions that will exist over the remaining useful life of the asset. These should be modified by an analysis of past cash flows and management's success in the past in predicting future cash flows accurately. Where external evidence is available, this should be given greater weight than simple reliance on management's expectations.
- Cash flow projections should be based on the most recent *financial budgets and forecasts*. These projections should cover a maximum period of 5 years unless a longer period can be justified. For most entities, a detailed analysis of future operations rarely extends beyond 5 years.
- Expectations concerning *growth rate* should be realistic and in line with observable rates. The cash inflows should include those from *continuing use* of the asset over its expected useful life as well as those expected to be received on *disposal* of the asset. Further, any cash *outflows* necessary to achieve the projected inflows must be taken into account.
- Projected cash flows must be estimated for the asset in its *current* condition (paragraph 44). Where there is an expected restructuring of the entity in future periods, or where there are possibilities for improving or enhancing the performance of the asset by subsequent expenditure, projections of cash flows will not take these possible events into consideration. Such enhancements can only be taken into consideration once the entity is committed to the restructure. Day-to-day servicing costs are included in the outflows used to measure value in use, as are the costs of major inspections.
- Cash flows relating to *financing activities* or *income tax* are not included in the calculations of future cash flows. As the discount rate is based on a pre-tax basis, the future cash flows must also be on a pre-tax basis.
- In assessing cash flows from *disposal*, the expected disposal price will take into account specific future price increases/decreases, and be based on an analysis of prices prevailing at the date of the estimate for similar assets in conditions similar to those expected for the asset under consideration at the end of its useful life.
- Appendix A to IAS 36, described as an 'integral part of the standard', contains guidance on the use of present value techniques in measuring value in use. Essentially, expected values may be used when probabilities can be estimated.

Although the current version of IAS 36 does not refer to climate change, recent developments in the sphere of climate-related disclosures compel firms to consider the effects of climate change on future cash flows and possible impairments. In particular, many companies adhere to the disclosure recommendations of the Task Force on Climate-Related Financial Disclosures (TCFD). In the UK, a 2022 revision to the Companies Act places legal requirements to incorporate climate disclosures in the annual report. In addition, the IASB (2023) has reproduced some educational materials about climate risks including how to apply IAS 36. As companies assess climate-change risk, they need to consider the implications for impairment. For example, in its 2023 annual report Diageo states that it considers 'the impact of climate change on forecasts of future cash flows used (including forecast depreciation in line with capital expenditure plans for Diageo's net zero carbon emission commitment) in impairment assessments of value-in-use of non-current assets, including goodwill' (Diageo 2023, p. 174).

Determining the discount rate

Paragraph 55 of IAS 36 notes that the discount rate should be pre-tax and:
- reflect the time value of money
- reflect the risks specific to the asset for which the future cash flow estimates have not been adjusted.

The rate may be determined by viewing rates used for similar assets in the market, or from the weighted average cost of capital of a listed entity that has a single asset, or portfolio of assets, similar to the asset under review (paragraph 56). It should be noted that valuators typically assess fair values on a post-tax basis, using post-tax cash flows and post-tax discount rates. This has probably led to a practice where companies started to apply the same methodology and subsequently consider whether this leads to a materially different outcome compared to using pre-tax cash flows and pre-tax discount rates. To help companies and simplify the impairment process, the IASB has issued a proposed amendment to IAS 36 in 2024, explicitly allowing companies to use post-tax discount rates (and post-tax cash flows).

Figure 7.4 contains information provided in Note 9 to the financial statements in the 2023 annual report of Rolls-Royce. As can be seen, Rolls-Royce uses different discount rates for the two main cash generating units. In the case of its Power System AG it uses a post-tax rate of 9.2% whereas for its Rolls-Royce Deutchland Ltd & Co KG it uses a pre-tax rate of 14.4%. Also note, in the case of Power System AG Rolls-Royce uses fair value less cost of disposal as the recoverable amount whereas in the case of Rolls-Royce Deutchland Ltd & Co KG it uses VIU as the recoverable amount.

FIGURE 7.4 Testing of goodwill impairment at Rolls-Royce 2023 using different discount rates

Goodwill

In accordance with the requirements of IAS 36, goodwill is allocated to the Group's CGUs, or groups of CGUs, that are expected to benefit from the synergies of the business combination that gave rise to the goodwill as follows:

Cash-generating unit (CGU) or group of CGUs

	Primary operating segment	2023 £m	2022 £m
Rolls-Royce Power Systems AG	Power Systems	798	818
Rolls-Royce Deutschland Ltd & Co KG	Civil Aerospace	237	241
Other	Various	31	40
		1,066	1,099

Goodwill has been tested for impairment during 2023 on the following basis:
- The carrying values of goodwill have been assessed by reference to the recoverable amount, being the higher of value in use or fair value less costs of disposal (FVLCOD).
- The recoverable amount has been estimated using cash flows from the most recent forecasts prepared by the Directors, which are consistent with past experience and external sources of information on market conditions. These forecasts generally cover the next five years. Growth rates for the period not covered by the forecasts are based on growth rates of 2% which reflects the products, industries and countries in which the relevant CGU or group of CGUs operate. Inflation has been included based on contractual commitments where relevant. Where general inflation assumptions have been required, these have been estimated based on externally sourced data. General inflation assumptions of 2% to 4% have been included in the forecasts, depending on the nature and geography of the flows.
- The key forecast assumptions for the impairment tests are the discount rate and the cash flow projections, in particular the programme assumptions (such as sales volumes and product costs), the impact of foreign exchange rates on the relationship between selling prices and costs, and growth rates. Impairment tests are performed using prevailing exchange rates.
- The Group believes there are significant business growth opportunities to come from Rolls-Royce playing a leading role in the transition to net zero, whilst at the same time climate change poses potentially significant risks. The assumptions used by the Directors are based on past experience and external sources of information. Based on the climate scenarios prepared, the forecasts do not assume a significant deterioration of demand for Civil Aerospace (including Rolls-Royce Deutschland) programmes given that all commercial aero-engines were compatible with sustainable fuels by the end of 2023. Similarly, 80% of the engines in Power Systems are compatible with sustainable fuels. The investment required to ensure our new products will be compatible with net zero operation, and to achieve net zero scope 1 + 2 GHG emissions is reflected in the forecasts used.

A 1.5°C scenario has been prepared using key data points from external sources, including Oxford Economics, Global Climate Service and Databank and the International Energy Agency. This scenario has been used as the basis of a sensitivity. It is assumed that governments adopt stricter product and behavioural standards and measures that result in higher carbon pricing. Under these conditions, it is assumed that markets are willing to pay for low carbon solutions and that there is an economic return

(continued)

FIGURE 7.4 *(continued)*

from strategic investments in low carbon alternatives. The sensitivity has considered the likelihood of demand changes for our products based on their relative fuel efficiency in the marketplace and the probability of alternatives being introduced earlier than currently expected. The sensitivity also reflects the impact of a broad range of potential casts imposed by policy or regulatory interventions (through carbon pricing). This sensitivity does not indicate the need far an impairment charge.

The principal assumptions for goodwill balances considered to be individually significant are:

Rolls-Royce Power Systems AG

- Recoverable amount represents FVLCOD to reflect the future strategy of the business. The Directors consider that disclosing information prepared on a FVLCOD basis here is a more useful representation of the recoverable amount when considering the future strategy of the business, including the impact of climate-related risks and opportunities. Due to the unavailability of observable market inputs or inputs based on market evidence, the fair value is estimated by discounting future cash flows (Level 3 as defined by IFRS 13 *Fair Value Measurement*) modified for market participants views;
- Trading assumptions (e.g. volume of equipment deliveries, pricing achieved and cost escalation) that are based on current and known future programmes, estimates of market share and long-term economic forecasts;
- Plausible downside scenario in relation to macro-economic factors included with a 25% weighting;
- Cash flows beyond the five-year forecasts are assumed to grow at 2.0% (2022: 1.0%); and
- Nominal post-tax discount rate 9.2% (2022: 10.0%.)

The Directors do not consider that any reasonably possible changes in the key assumptions (including taking consideration of the climate-related risks above) would cause the FVLCOD of the business to fall below its carrying value of goodwill.

Rolls-Royce Deutschland Ltd & Co KG

- Recoverable amount represents the value in use of the assets in their current condition;
- Trading assumptions (e.g. volume of engine deliveries, flying hours of installed fleet, including assumptions on the recovery of the aerospace industry, and cost escalation) that are based on current and known future programmes, estimates of market share and long-term economic forecasts;
- Plausible downside scenario in relation to macro-economic factors included with a 25% weighting;
- Cash flows beyond the five-year forecasts are assumed to grow at 2.0% (2022: 2.0%); and
- Nominal pre-tax discount rate 14.4% (2022: 13.2%).

The Directors do not consider that any reasonably possible changes in the key assumptions (including taking consideration of the climate-related risks above) would cause the value in use of the goodwill to fall below its carrying value.

Other CGUs

Goodwill balances across the Group that are not considered to be individually significant were also tested for impairment, resulting in no impairment charge (2022: £nil) being recognised at 31 December 2023.

Source: Rolls-Royce (2023, pp. 152–53).

7.3.3 Recognition and measurement of an impairment loss for an individual asset

Paragraphs 58–64 of IAS 36 provide the principles for recognition and measurement of an impairment loss for an individual asset. If the recoverable amount of an asset is less than its carrying amount, an impairment loss occurs, and the asset must be written down from its carrying amount to the recoverable amount.

Where an asset is measured using the *cost model*, according to paragraph 60 of IAS 36 an impairment loss is recognised immediately in profit or loss. In relation to the other side of the accounting entry to the loss, reference should be made to paragraph 73(d) of IAS 16 *Property, Plant and Equipment*. According to this paragraph, for items of property, plant and equipment 'the gross carrying amount and the accumulated depreciation (aggregated with accumulated impairment losses) at the beginning and end of the period' should be disclosed. When impairment occurs, there is no need to write off any existing accumulated depreciation or create a separate accumulated impairment account. The impairment write-down can be included in accumulated depreciation, preferably referred to as 'Accumulated Depreciation and Impairment Losses'.

Hence, if an asset having a carrying amount of $100 (original cost $160) has a recoverable amount of $90, the appropriate journal entry to account for the impairment loss is:

Impairment loss	Dr	10
Accumulated depreciation and impairment losses	Cr	10
(Impairment loss on asset)		

Where an asset is measured using the *revaluation model* (i.e. at fair value), according to paragraph 60 of IAS 36 any impairment loss is treated as a revaluation decrease and accounted for as set out in IAS 16. *See chapter 5* for further discussion of the treatment revaluations for property plant and equipment.

Revaluation of Asset (P/L)	Dr	10
Accumulated Depreciation	Cr	10
(Downward Revaluation of Asset)		

Regardless of whether the cost model or the revaluation model is used, once the impairment loss is recognised, any subsequent depreciation/amortisation is based on the new recoverable amount. In accordance with paragraph 63 of IAS 36, the depreciation charge is that necessary to allocate the asset's revised carrying amount (the recoverable amount) less its residual value (if any) on a systematic basis over its remaining useful life, which may have to be reviewed in light of the circumstances leading to the impairment.

In cases where the recoverable amount is negative owing to large expected future cash outflows (rather than cash inflows) relating to the asset, the impairment loss could be greater than the carrying amount of the asset. According to paragraph 62 of IAS 16, a liability for the excess should be raised only if another standard requires it.

Figure 7.5 contains information disclosed in Note 9 to the 2022/23 financial statements of Diageo relating to its impairment of specific intangible assets.

FIGURE 7.5 Impairment of intangible assets at Diageo 2022/23

	Brands £ million	Goodwill £ million	Other intangibles £ million	Computer software £ million	Total £ million
Cost					
At 30 June 2021	8,458	2,627	1,421	673	13,179
Hyperinflation adjustment in respect of Turkey	315	208	–	1	524
Exchange differences	639	145	194	28	1,006
Additions	109	70	55	67	301
Disposals	(23)	(42)	–	(23)	(88)
Reclassification to asset held for sale	(560)	–	–	(8)	(568)
At 30 June 2022	**8,938**	**3,008**	**1,670**	**738**	**14,354**
Hyperinflation adjustment in respect of Turkey	**81**	**60**	–	–	**141**
Exchange differences	**(531)**	**(257)**	**(64)**	**(16)**	**(868)**
Additions	**338**	**92**	**13**	**155**	**598**
Disposals	–	–	–	**(26)**	**(26)**
Reclassification from/(to) asset held for sale	**453**	**(29)**	–	–	**424**
At 30 June 2023	**9,279**	**2,874**	**1,619**	**851**	**14,623**
Amortisation and impairment					
At 30 June 2021	1,097	670	80	568	2,415
Exchange differences	51	60	(1)	25	135
Amortisation for the year	–	–	7	38	45
Impairment	317	19	–	–	336

(continued)

FIGURE 7.5 *(continued)*

Disposals	(23)	(28)	–	(20)	(71)
Reclassification to asset held for sale	(400)	–	–	(8)	(408)
At 30 June 2022	**1,042**	**721**	**86**	**603**	**2,452**
Exchange differences	**(96)**	**(61)**	**(1)**	**(15)**	**(173)**
Amortisation for the year	–	–	16	40	56
Impairment	498	–	–	–	498
Disposals	–	–	–	(24)	(24)
Reclassification from/(to) asset held for sale	315	(13)	–	–	302
At 30 June 2023	**1,759**	**647**	**101**	**604**	**3,111**
Carrying amount					
At 30 June 2023	**7,520**	**2,227**	**1,518**	**247**	**11,512**
At 30 June 2022	7,896	2,287	1,584	135	11,902
At 30 June 2021	7,361	1,957	1,341	105	10,764

Source: Diageo (2023, p. 190).

As can be seen the impairment charges are substantial in both years. For example, in the year ending 30 June 2023 there is an impairment charge to brands of £498 million. This is more than 10% of Diageo's operating profit for the same period of £4,632.

7.4 CASH-GENERATING UNITS — EXCLUDING GOODWILL

The discussion above *(section 7.3)* focuses on individual assets and whether they have been impaired. The impairment test in such cases involves the determination of recoverable amount, and this requires the measurement of fair value less costs of disposal and value in use of the asset being tested for impairment. However, for some assets, fair value less costs of disposal may be determinable, because the asset is separable and a market for that asset exists, but it may be impossible to determine the value in use. Value in use requires determining the expected cash flows to be received from an asset.

Most assets do not individually generate cash flows because the cash flows generated are the result of a combination of several assets. For example, a machine in a factory works in conjunction with the rest of the assets in the factory to produce sellable goods. For such assets, if the carrying amount exceeds the fair value less costs of disposal, some other measure relating to value in use must be used.

Paragraph 66 of IAS 36 requires that, where there is any indication an asset may be impaired, if possible the recoverable amount should be estimated for the individual asset.

However, if this is not possible, the entity should 'determine the recoverable amount of the cash-generating unit to which the asset belongs'. In other words, the impairment test is applied to a cash-generating unit rather than to an individual asset. Paragraph 6 contains the following definition of a cash-generating unit:

> A cash-generating unit is the smallest identifiable group of assets that generates cash inflows that are largely independent of the cash inflows from other assets or groups of assets.

7.4.1 Identifying a cash-generating unit

The identification of a cash-generating unit requires considerable judgement. As is stated in the definition, the key is to determine the 'smallest identifiable group of assets', and this group must create 'independent' cash flows from continuing use. Guidelines given in paragraphs 67–73 of IAS 36 include the following:
- Consider how management monitors the entity's operations, such as by product lines, businesses, individual locations, districts or regional areas.
- Consider how management makes decisions about continuing or disposing of the entity's assets and operations.
- If an active market exists for the output of a group of assets, this group constitutes a cash-generating unit.
- Cash-generating units should be identified consistently from period to period for the same group of assets.

For example, an entity owns eight shops, spread across the same city. Head office sets selling prices and designs shop layout. All inventory is purchased centrally. Factors that would indicate that each store is a cash generating unit include the following:

- Does management monitor the profitability of each store separately?
- Does the location of the store suggest that each will have its own unique customer base?

Or consider a steel mill that manufactures a particular grade of steel that is transferred to another factory owned by the entity. If the steel could be sold on the open market (even if all output is transferred internally) then the mill is likely to be a separate cash-generating unit. If there is no external market, then the mill and the factory may have to be combined into a single cash-generating unit.

The abovementioned guidelines leave much discretion to managers in identifying the cash-generating units. For example, managers might combine assets that are likely to decrease in value with others that are likely to increase, so that impairment losses are unlikely to be recognised.

7.4.2 Impairment loss for a cash-generating unit — excluding goodwill

An impairment loss occurs when the carrying amount of the assets of a cash-generating unit exceeds their recoverable amount.

Determining the impairment loss

In determining the carrying amount of the assets, all those assets that are directly attributable to the cash-generating unit and that contribute to generating the cash flows used in measuring recoverable amount must be included. There must be consistency between what is being measured for recoverable amount — namely cash flows relating to a group of assets — and the measurement of the carrying amount of those assets.

The principles for determining the recoverable amount of a cash-generating unit are the same as those previously described for an individual asset (section 7.3). However, note that paragraph 76(b) of IAS 36 requires that the carrying amount of a cash-generating unit does not include the carrying amount of any recognised liability, unless the recoverable amount of the cash-generating unit cannot be determined without consideration of this liability. Consistent with this, and to avoid double counting, the calculation of the future cash flows of the cash-generating unit does not include cash outflows that relate to obligations that have been recognised as liabilities, such as payables and provisions (see paragraph 43(b)).

Accounting for an impairment loss in a cash-generating unit

If an impairment loss is recognised in a cash-generating unit that has not recorded any goodwill, paragraph 104 of IAS 36 states that the impairment loss should be allocated to reduce the carrying amount of the assets of the unit by allocating the impairment loss pro rata based on the carrying amount of each asset in the unit. The reduction in each carrying amount relates to each specific asset and should be treated as an impairment of each asset, even though the impairment loss was based on an analysis of a cash-generating unit. The loss is accounted for in the same way as that for an individual asset *as described in section 7.3*, with losses relating to an asset measured at cost being recognised immediately in profit or loss.

Paragraph 105 of IAS 36 places some restrictions on an entity's ability to write down assets as a result of the allocation of the impairment loss across the carrying amounts of the assets of the cash-generating unit. For each asset, the carrying amount should not be reduced below the highest of:

(a) its fair value less costs of disposal (if measurable);
(b) its value in use (if determinable); and
(c) zero.

Assuming the sum of the fair values of the individual assets is not higher than the recoverable amount and the recoverable amount of the CGU is positive, these guidelines effectively set the impaired amount, if any, to the recoverable amount. If the sum of the fair values of the individual assets within the CGU is higher than the recoverable amount, or if the recoverable amount is negative, then it is possible that only a portion of the loss is recognised, because recognising the loss in full will result in negative carrying values or carrying values of individual assets below their fair value. Of course, in such a case, one would question the reasonability of keeping the impaired asset, rather than selling it.

If there is an amount of impairment loss allocated to an asset, but a part of it would reduce the asset below, say, its fair value less costs of disposal, then that part is allocated across the other assets in the cash-generating unit on a pro rata basis (see illustrative example 7.1). However, as paragraph 106 notes, if the recoverable amount of each of the assets cannot be estimated without undue costs or effort, then an arbitrary allocation of the impairment loss between the assets of the unit will suffice because all the assets of a cash-generating unit work together.

A cash-generating unit has been assessed for impairment and it has been determined that the unit has incurred an impairment loss of $12,000. The carrying amounts of the assets and the allocation of the impairment loss on a proportional basis are as shown below.

	Carrying amount (before impairment)	Proportion	Allocation of impairment loss	Net carrying amount (after impairment)
Buildings	$ 500,000	5/12	$ 5,000	$ 495,000
Equipment	300,000	3/12	3,000	297,000
Land	250,000	2.5/12	2,500	247,500
Fittings	150,000	1.5/12	1,500	148,500
	$1,200,000		$12,000	$1,188,000

However, if the recoverable amount of the buildings was $497,000, then this is the maximum to which these assets could be reduced. Hence, the balance of the allocated impairment loss to buildings of $2,000 (i.e. $5,000 − [$500,000 − $497,000]) has to be allocated across the other assets:

	Carrying amount	Proportion	Allocation of impairment loss	Net carrying amount
Buildings				$497,000
Equipment	$297,000	297/693	$ 857	296,143
Land	247,500	247.5/693	714	246,786
Fittings	148,500	148.5/693	429	148,071
	$693,000		$2,000	

The journal entry to reflect the recognition of the impairment loss is:

Impairment loss	Dr	12,000	
Accumulated depreciation and impairment Losses — buildings	Cr		3,000
Accumulated depreciation and impairment Losses — equipment	Cr		3,857
Land	Cr		3,214
Accumulated depreciation and impairment Losses — fittings	Cr		1,929

Corporate assets

One problem that arises when dividing an entity into separate cash-generating units is dealing with corporate assets. Corporate assets, such as the headquarters building or the information technology support centre, are integral to all cash-generating units generating cash flows but do not by themselves independently generate cash flows. Paragraph 102 of IAS 36 sets out how corporate assets should be dealt with in determining impairment losses for an entity:

Step 1: If any corporate assets can be allocated on a reasonable and consistent basis to cash-generating units, then this should be done. Each unit is then, where appropriate, tested for an impairment loss. Where a loss occurs in a cash-generating unit, the loss is allocated pro rata across the assets including the portion of the corporate asset allocated to the unit.

Step 2: If some corporate assets cannot be allocated across the cash-generating units, the entity:
• compares the carrying amount of each unit being tested (excluding the unallocated corporate asset) with its recoverable amount and recognises any impairment loss by allocating the loss across the assets of the unit;
• identifies the smallest cash-generating unit that includes the unit under review and to which a portion of the unallocated corporate asset can be allocated on a reasonable and consistent basis;
• compares the carrying amount of the larger cash-generating unit, including the portion of the corporate asset, with its allocated amount. Any impairment loss is then allocated across the assets of the larger cash-generating unit.

Illustrative example 7.2 provides the accounting for corporate assets.

Singapore Engineering has two cash generating units, A and B. The assets of the two units are as follows:

	Unit A	Unit B
Plant	$500	$400
Land	300	220

Singapore Engineering has two corporate assets: the headquarters building and a research centre. The headquarters is assumed to be used equally by both units. The carrying amount of the research centre cannot be allocated on a reasonable basis to the two units. The headquarters building has a carrying amount of $160. The research centre's assets consist of furniture of $40 and equipment of $30. Neither of the corporate assets directly generates cash flows for Singapore Engineering.

The recoverable amounts of the two cash-generating units are:

Unit A	$900
Unit B	$665

Note that the overall recoverable amount is $1,565, while the total carrying value of Singapore Engineering's assets is $1,650. Hence, there is an overall impairment of $85.

The *first* step is to calculate the impairment losses for each of the cash generating units, which could differ from the overall impairment loss that needs to be recognised. To do this, the carrying amount of the headquarters building is allocated equally between the two units as it is used equally by those units. Impairment losses are then as follows:

	Unit A	Unit B
Plant	$ 500	$ 400
Land	300	220
Headquarters building	80	80
	880	700
Recoverable amount	900	665
Impairment loss	$ 0	$ 35

The impairment loss of $35 for Unit B is then allocated across all assets in that unit and the headquarters building, but leaving out the research centre's assets:

	Carrying amount	Proportion of loss	Loss	Adjusted carrying amount
Plant	$400	400/700	$20 = 35 × 400/700	$380
Land	220	220/700	11 = 35 × 220/700	209
Headquarters building	80	80/700	4 = 35 × 80/700	76
			$35	$665

The second step is to deal with the research centre (which was left out from step 1). This requires the determination of any impairment loss for the smallest cash-generating unit that includes the research centre. In this case, the smallest cash generating unit is the entity as a whole. The impairment loss is calculated as follows:

Unit A	
Plant	$ 500
Land	300
Headquarters building [$80]	80
	880

Unit B		
	Plant	380
	Land	209
Headquarters building [$76]		76
		665
Research Centre		
Furniture		40
Equipment		30
		70
		1,615
Recoverable amount [$900 + $665]		1,565
Impairment loss		$ 50

This additional impairment loss of $50 is then allocated across all of the entity's assets on a pro rata basis, using in the case of Unit B the previously calculated carrying values after impairment, so the total recoverable amount is $1,565:

	Carrying amount	Proportion of loss	Further impairment loss (rounded)	Adjusted carrying amount
Unit A				
Plant	$ 500	500/1,615	$ 15 = 50 × 500/1,615	$ 485
Land	300	300/1,615	9 = 50 × 300/1,615	291
Headquarters building]	80	80/1,615	2 = 50 × 80/1,615	78
Unit B				
Plant	380	380/1,615	12 = 50 × 380/1,615	368
Land	209	209/1,615	6 = 50 × 209/1,615	203
Headquarters building	76	76/ 1,615	4 = 50 × 76/1,615	72
Research Centre				
Furniture	40	40/1,615	1 = 50 × 40/1,615	39
Equipment	30	30/1,615	1 = 50 × 30/1,615	29
	$1,615		$ 50	$1,565

7.5 CASH-GENERATING UNITS AND GOODWILL

In accounting for impairment losses for cash-generating units, one of the assets that may be recorded by an entity is goodwill. IAS 36 contains specific requirements for accounting for goodwill and how its existence affects the allocation of impairment losses across the assets of a cash-generating unit.

Goodwill is recognised only when it is acquired in a business combination. It is not possible to determine a fair value less costs of disposal for goodwill, or to identify a set of cash flows that relates specifically to goodwill.

Accounting for goodwill acquired in a business combination is specified in paragraph 32 of IFRS 3 *Business Combinations*. The acquirer measures goodwill acquired in a business combination at cost less any accumulated impairment losses. Goodwill is not subject to amortisation. Instead, the acquirer tests the carrying amount of goodwill annually in accordance with IAS 36.

When a business combination occurs, and goodwill is calculated as part of accounting for that combination, the goodwill acquired is allocated to one or more cash-generating units (IAS 36 paragraph 80). Even though goodwill was acquired in relation to the entity as a whole, the cash flow earning capacity of goodwill must be allocated across the cash-generating units. The aim is to allocate all assets, whether corporate assets or goodwill, to the cash-generating units so they can be associated with the cash flows received by those units.

When deciding which units should have goodwill allocated to them, consideration should be given to how internal management monitors the goodwill. According to paragraph 80, the goodwill should be allocated to the *lowest level* at which management monitors the goodwill. When the business combination occurred, the acquirer would have analysed the earning capacity of the entity it proposed to acquire, and would have equated aspects of goodwill to various cash-generating units. It is possible that the allocation of goodwill would be made to each of the operating segments identified by management under the application of IFRS 8 *Operating Segments*. Paragraph 80 of IAS 36 states that the units to which goodwill is allocated should not be larger than an operating segment based on either the entity's primary or secondary reporting format. This is due to the fact that IFRS 8 requires the determination of business and geographical segments based on areas that are subject to different risks and return, and the internal financial reporting system within the entity is used as a basis for identifying these segments.

Under IFRS 3, there is an allowance for a provisional initial accounting for the business combination. Paragraph 84 of IAS 36 therefore provides, consistent with IFRS 3, that where the allocation of goodwill cannot be completed before the end of the annual period in which the business combination occurred, the initial allocation is to be completed before the end of the first annual period beginning after the acquisition date.

7.5.1 Impairment testing of goodwill

A cash-generating unit that has goodwill allocated to it must be tested for impairment *annually* or more frequently if there is an indication the unit may be impaired (IAS 36 paragraph 90). As with other impairment tests, this involves comparing the carrying amount of the unit's assets, including goodwill, with the recoverable amount of the unit's assets.

Recoverable amount exceeds carrying amount

If the recoverable amount exceeds the carrying amount, there is no impairment loss. In particular, there is no impairment of goodwill. The goodwill balance remains unadjusted; that is, it is not reduced due to impairment loss.

In practice, it is impossible to distinguish purchased goodwill from other assets that might increase the recoverable amount:

- *internally generated goodwill* — possibly created since the business combination.
- *unrecognised identifiable net assets* — intangibles may exist which do not meet the recognition criteria under IAS 38 *Intangible Assets*.
- *excess value over carrying amount of recognised assets* — the impairment test uses the carrying amount of the unit's recognised assets. If the fair values of these assets are greater than their carrying amounts, the extra benefits relating to these assets increase the recoverable amount of the unit.

The IASB acknowledges that these factors create a 'shielding effect' that could reduce the likelihood of recognising impairment losses for goodwill. The shielding effect may even arise from the date of the business combination when goodwill is allocated to a wider CGU or group of CGUs than the business acquired. In that case unrecognised internally generated goodwill and recognised purchased goodwill are tested together. The impairment test for goodwill is, at best, ensuring that the carrying amount of goodwill is recoverable from cash flows generated by both acquired and internally generated goodwill. While this may be inconsistent with the requirement that purchased goodwill should be reviewed annually for impairment, it simplifies that annual review. As part of its project 'Business Combinations — Disclosures, Goodwill and Impairment' the IASB has published a Discussion Paper in March 2020 and an Exposure Draft in March 2024 discussing potential ways to address this shielding effect (see: https://www.ifrs.org/content/dam/ifrs/project/goodwill-and-impairment/exposure-draft-2024/iasb-ed-2024-1-bcdgi.pdf).

Users of the financial statements can take appropriate care when interpreting financial statements that show a significant goodwill balance.

Carrying amount exceeds recoverable amount

If the carrying amount exceeds the recoverable amount, there is an impairment loss, and this loss is recognised in accordance with paragraph 104 of IAS 36. This paragraph states that the impairment loss must be allocated to reduce the carrying amount of the assets of the unit, or group of units, in the following order:

- firstly, to reduce the carrying amount of any goodwill allocated to the cash-generating unit
- then, to the other assets of the unit pro rata on the basis of the carrying amount of each asset in the unit.

These reductions in carrying amounts are treated as impairment losses on the individual assets of the unit and recognised as any other impairment losses on assets.

However, paragraph 105 of IAS 36 provides some restrictions on the write-downs to individual assets:

> In allocating an impairment loss in accordance with paragraph 104, an entity shall not reduce the carrying amount of an asset below the highest of:
> (a) its fair value less costs of disposal (if measurable);
> (b) its value in use (if determinable); and
> (c) zero.
> The amount of the impairment loss that would otherwise have been allocated to the asset shall be allocated pro rata to the other assets of the unit (group of units).

Timing of impairment tests

As noted earlier, goodwill has to be tested for impairment annually. However, the test does not have to occur at the end of the reporting period. As paragraph 96 of IAS 36 notes, the test may be performed at any time during the year, provided it is performed at the same time every year. According to paragraph BC171 of the Basis for Conclusions on IAS 36, this measure was allowed as a means of reducing the costs of applying the test. However, if a business combination has occurred in the current period, and an allocation has been made to one or more cash-generating units, all units to which goodwill has been allocated must be tested for impairment before the end of that year — *see paragraph 96 of IAS 36*.

It is not necessary for all cash-generating units to be tested for impairment at the same time. If there are two units being tested for impairment, one being a smaller cash-generating unit within a larger unit and the larger unit contains an allocation of goodwill, it is necessary to test the smaller unit for impairment first. This ensures that, if necessary, the assets of the smaller unit are adjusted before the testing of the larger unit. Similarly, if the assets of a cash-generating unit containing goodwill are being tested at the same time as the unit, then the assets must be tested first.

Other impairment issues relating to goodwill

IAS 36 raises a number of other issues that need to be considered in accounting for the impairment of goodwill within a cash-generating unit:

- *Disposal of an operation within a cash-generating unit.* Where the cash-generating unit has a number of distinct operations and goodwill has been allocated to the unit, if one of the operations is disposed of, it is necessary to consider whether any of the goodwill relates to the operation disposed of. If it does, the amount of goodwill is measured on the basis of the relative values of the operation disposed of and the portion of the cash-generating unit retained, unless the entity can demonstrate that some other method better reflects the goodwill associated with the operation disposed of. In calculating the gain or loss on disposal of the operation, the allocated portion of the goodwill is included in the carrying amount of the assets sold (paragraph 86).

  For example, if part of a cash-generating unit was sold for $200 and the recoverable amount of the remaining part of the unit is $600, then it is assumed that 25% (200/[200 + 600]) of the goodwill has been sold and is included in the carrying amount of the operation disposed of.

- *Reorganisation of the entity.* Where an entity containing a number of cash-generating units restructures, changing the composition of the cash-generating units, and where goodwill has been allocated to the original units, paragraph 87 requires the reallocation of the goodwill to the new units. The allocation is done on a relative value basis similar to that used where a cash-generating unit is disposed of, again unless the entity can demonstrate that some other method better reflects the goodwill associated with the operation disposed of.

7.6 REVERSAL OF AN IMPAIRMENT LOSS

An impairment loss is recognised after an entity analyses the future prospects of an individual asset or a cash-generating unit. Subsequent to an impairment loss occurring because of doubts about the performance of assets, it is possible for circumstances to change such that, when the recoverable amount of the assets increases, consideration can be given to a reversal of a past impairment loss. Paragraph 110 of IAS 36 requires an entity to assess *at the end of each reporting period* whether there are indications that an impairment loss recognised in previous periods may not exist or may have decreased. If such indications exist, the entity should estimate the recoverable amount of the asset or unit.

If there is evidence of a favourable change in the estimates in relation to an asset (and only if there has been a change in the estimates), a reversal of impairment loss can be recognised. The reversal process requires the recognition of an increase in the carrying amount of the asset to its recoverable amount.

The ability to recognise a reversal of an impairment loss and the accounting for that reversal depend on whether the reversal relates to an individual asset, a cash-generating unit or goodwill.

7.6.1 Reversal of an impairment loss — individual assets

Where the recoverable amount is greater than the carrying amount of an individual asset (other than goodwill), the reversal of a previous impairment loss requires adjusting the carrying amount of the asset to recoverable amount. In determining the amount by which the carrying amount is to be adjusted, one limitation, as outlined in paragraph 117 of IAS 36, is that the carrying amount cannot be increased to an amount in excess of the carrying amount that would have been determined had no impairment loss been recognised.

7.6.2 Reversal of an impairment loss — cash-generating unit

If the reversal of the impairment loss relates to a cash-generating unit, in accordance with paragraph 122 of IAS 36 the reversal of the impairment loss is allocated pro rata to the assets of the unit, except for goodwill, with the carrying amounts of those assets. These reversals will then relate to the specific assets of the cash-generating unit and will be accounted for as detailed above for individual assets. In relation to those individual assets, the carrying amount of an asset cannot, as per paragraph 123 of IAS 36, be increased above the lower of its recoverable amount (if determinable) and the carrying amount that would have been determined had no impairment loss been recognised for the asset in previous periods.

If the situation envisaged in paragraph 123 occurs, then the amount of impairment loss reversal that cannot be allocated to an individual asset is then allocated on a pro rata basis to the other assets of the cash-generating unit, except for goodwill.

7.6.3 Reversal of an impairment loss — goodwill

Paragraph 124 of IAS 36 states that an impairment loss recognised for goodwill shall *not* be reversed in a later period.

Illustrative example 7.3 demonstrates the treatment of a reversal of impairment loss related to individual assets when goodwill is also impaired.

ILLUSTRATIVE EXAMPLE 7.3 Reversal of impairment loss

At 30 June 2022, Jimena Ltd incurred an impairment loss of $5,000, of which $3,000 was used to write off the goodwill and $2,000 to write down the assets. The allocation of the impairment loss to the assets was as follows:

	Carrying amount	Proportion of loss	Loss	Adjusted carrying amount
Land	$10,000	1/5	$ 400	$ 9,600
Plant	40,000	4/5	1,600	38,400
	$50,000		$2,000	

The plant had previously cost $100,000 and was being depreciated at 5% per annum, requiring a depreciation charge of $5,000 per annum. Subsequent to the impairment, the plant was depreciated on a straight-line basis over 8 years, at $4,800 per annum.

Jimena Ltd's financial year end is 30 June. At 30 June 2025, the business situation had improved and Jimena Ltd believed that it should reverse past impairment losses. A comparison of the carrying amounts of the assets at 30 June 2025 that were previously impaired and their recoverable amounts revealed:

Land	$ 9,600
Plant [$38,400 − 3 × $4,800]	24,000
	33,600
Recoverable amount	36,800
Excess of recoverable amount over carrying amount	$ 3,200

The excess cannot be allocated to the goodwill as impairment losses on goodwill can never be reversed. If the excess were allocated to the assets, it can only be allocated to the assets existing at the previous impairment write-down as assets cannot be written up above their original cost. The excess of recoverable amount is then allocated to the relevant assets on a pro rata basis:

	Carrying amount	Share of impairment reversal (rounded)	Adjusted carrying amount
Land	$ 9,600	$ 914 = 3,200 × 9,600/33,600	$ 10,514
Plant	24,000	2,286 = 3,200 × 24,000/33,600	26,286
	$ 33,600	$ 3,200	$ 36,800

These assets cannot be written up above the amounts that they would have been recorded at if there had been no previous impairment. These amounts would be:

Land	$10,000
Plant	$25,000 [$40,000 − 3 × $5,000 annual depreciation for 3 years]

As the land cannot be written up above $10,000, $514 of the $914 reversal that was allocated may be reallocated to the plant. However, the adjusted carrying value of the plant ($26,286) exceeds $25,000, the carrying amount that would have been reported absent impairment. The entry below therefore restores the original amounts:

Land	Dr	400	
Accumulated depreciation and impairment loss – plant	Dr	1,000	
Income – reversal of impairment loss	Cr		1,400
(Reversal of impairment loss)			

7.7 DISCLOSURE

Paragraph 126 of IAS 36 requires the following disclosures for each class of assets:
- (a) the amount of impairment losses recognised in profit or loss during the period and the line item(s) of the statement of comprehensive income in which those impairment losses are included;
- (b) the amount of reversals of impairment losses recognised in profit or loss during the period and the line item(s) of the statement of comprehensive income in which those impairment losses are reversed;
- (c) the amount of impairment losses on revalued assets recognised in other comprehensive income during the period; and
- (d) the amount of reversals of impairment losses on revalued assets recognised in other comprehensive income during the period.

As noted in chapter 5, paragraph 73(e) of IAS 16 *Property, Plant and Equipment* requires, in relation to the reconciliation of the carrying amount at the beginning and end of the period for each class of property, plant and equipment, disclosure of:
- increases or decreases during the period resulting from impairment losses recognised or reversed in other comprehensive income
- impairment losses recognised in profit or loss during the period
- impairment losses reversed in profit or loss during the period.

Similar disclosures are required for intangibles under paragraph 118 of IAS 38 *Intangible Assets* for each class of intangible asset.

As paragraph 128 of IAS 36 states, the disclosures required by paragraph 126 may be presented or included in a reconciliation of the carrying amount of assets at the beginning and end of the period. (*Such disclosures were illustrated in chapter 11.*) For parts (a) and (b) of paragraph 126, disclosure is required of the relevant line item(s) used. If these were included in other expenses or other income then information relating to impairment losses or reversals would be required in the note to the statement of profit or loss and other comprehensive income relating to these line items in the statement of profit or loss and other comprehensive income.

Paragraph 129 of IAS 36 details information to be disclosed for each reportable segment where an entity applies IFRS 8 *Operating Segments*.

Paragraph 133 of IAS 36 requires disclosures in relation to any goodwill that has not been allocated to a cash-generating unit at the end of the reporting period. In particular, an entity must disclose the amount of the unallocated goodwill and the reasons that amount has not been allocated to the cash-generating units in the entity.

Because the calculation of recoverable amount requires assumptions and estimates relating to future cash flows, IAS 36 requires disclosures relating to the calculation of recoverable amount. Paragraph 132 encourages, but does not require, disclosure of *key assumptions* used to determine the recoverable amounts of assets or cash-generating units.

Paragraph 134 of IAS 36 requires disclosures about the *estimates* used to measure the recoverable amount of a cash-generating unit when goodwill or an intangible asset with an indefinite life is included in the carrying amount of the unit, and the carrying amount of goodwill or intangible assets with indefinite useful lives allocated to that unit is *significant* in comparison with the entity's total carrying amount of goodwill or intangible assets with indefinite useful lives. Where the carrying amount of goodwill or intangible assets is not significant for a unit, paragraph 135 requires that fact to be disclosed. If, for a number of such units, the recoverable amounts are based on the same key assumptions and the aggregate carrying amount of goodwill or intangible assets with indefinite lives is significant in comparison to the total for the entity, paragraph 135 requires similar, but not as extensive, disclosures to those in paragraph 134.

7.8 SUMMARY

It is important that users of financial statements can rely on the information provided. In particular, they need to be assured that the assets in the statement of financial position are not stated at amounts greater than an entity could expect to recover from those assets. An entity can obtain cash flows from two sources in relation to any asset: (i) by using the asset, or (ii) by selling the asset. One of these involves an ongoing use of the asset whereas the other relates to an immediate sale of the asset. Any test of the carrying amounts of assets against their recoverable amounts must take both alternative sources of cash flows into account.

For an entity to conduct an impairment test, there must be indications of impairment. Entities then need to continuously obtain information about factors that may indicate that assets are impaired. These sources of information may consist of an analysis of economic factors external to the organisation, such as actions of competitors, or economic factors within the entity itself, such as the performance of the entity's property, plant and equipment over time. When there are indications of impairment, an entity conducts an impairment test, comparing the carrying amounts of relevant assets and their recoverable amounts. The latter involves measurement of value in use and fair value less costs of disposal.

In many cases, single assets do not produce cash flows for the entity. Instead, the assets of the entity are allocated to units, called cash-generating units, as each unit produces independent cash flows for an entity. In such cases, impairment tests are conducted on the cash-generating units, rather than on individual assets. Where an impairment loss occurs, the loss must be allocated across the assets of the unit, with goodwill being the first asset affected. Where corporate assets such as research facilities, data centres, management offices, etc., exist, it may be necessary to combine a number of cash-generating units together in order to test for impairment of the corporate asset.

Having written down assets following impairment tests, entities may see potential improvement in the recoverable amounts of assets by observing the same indicators used for detecting impairment losses. In such cases, where the recoverable amounts of assets have increased, impairment losses may be reversed, subject to certain constraints. Impairment losses relating to goodwill, however, can never be reversed.

DEMONSTRATION PROBLEM 7.1 Impairment losses, corporate assets can be allocated

Eastern Ltd has two divisions, Kamal and Katherine, each of which is a separate cash-generating unit (CGU). Eastern Ltd adopts a decentralised management approach whereby unit managers are expected to operate their units. However, there is one corporate asset, the information technology network, which is centrally controlled and provides a computer network to the company as a whole. The information technology network is not a depreciable asset.

At 31 December 2024 the net assets of each division, including its allocated share of the information technology network, were as follows:

	Kamal	Katherine
Information technology (IT) network	$ 284,000	$ 116,000
Land	450,000	290,000
Plant (20% p.a. straight-line depreciation)	1,310,000	960,000
Accumulated depreciation (plant)	(917,000)	(384,000)
Goodwill	46,000	32,000
Patent (10% straight-line amortisation)	210,000	255,000
Accumulated amortisation (patent)	(21,000)	(102,000)
Cash	20,000	12,000
Inventory	120,000	80,000
Receivables	34,000	40,000
	1,536,000	1,299,000
Liabilities	(276,000)	(189,000)
Net assets	$1,260,000	$1,110,000

Additional information as at 31 December 2024:
- Kamal's land had a fair value less costs of disposal of $437,000.
- Katherine's patent had a carrying amount below its recoverable amount.
- Katherine's plant had a recoverable amount of $540,000.
- Receivables were considered to be collectable.
- The IT network is not depreciated, as it is assumed to have an indefinite life.

Eastern Ltd's management undertook impairment testing at 31 December 2024 and determined the recoverable amount of each cash-generating unit to be: $1,430,000 for Kamal and $1,215,000 for Katherine

Required

Prepare any journal entries necessary to record the results of the impairment testing for each of the CGUs.

Solution

The first step is to determine whether either CGU has an impairment loss. This is done by comparing the carrying amount of the assets of each CGU with the recoverable amount of these assets. Note that it is the carrying amount of the assets not the net assets that is used — the test is for the impairment of assets, not net assets.

	Kamal	Katherine
Carrying amount of assets	$1,536,000	$1,299,000
Recoverable amount	1,430,000	1,215,000
Impairment loss	$ (106,000)	$ (840,00)

As a result of the comparison, both CGUs have suffered impairment losses.

For each CGU, the impairment loss is used to write off any goodwill and then to allocate any balance across the other assets in proportion to their carrying amounts.

Kamal CGU

Kamal has goodwill of $46,000. Therefore, the first step is to write off goodwill of $46,000.

The second step is to allocate the remaining impairment loss of $60,000 (i.e. $106,000 − $46,000).

Note that although all the assets are included in the calculation to determine whether the CGU has incurred an impairment loss, the allocation of that loss is only to those assets that can be written down as a result of the allocation process. Cash and receivables are not written down as they are recorded at amounts equal to fair value. The inventory is recorded under IAS 2 at the lower of cost and net realisable value, and as such is excluded from the impairment test write-down under IAS 36. The allocation of the balance of the impairment loss is done on a pro rata basis, in proportion to the assets' carrying amounts.

	Carrying amount	Proportion	Allocation of loss	Adjusted carrying amount
IT network	$ 284,000	284/1316	$12,948	$271,052
Land	450,000	450/1316	20,517	429,483
Plant	393,000	393/1316	17,918	375,082
Patent	189,000	189/1316	8,617	180,383
	$1,316,000		$60,000	

After the initial allocation across the assets, a check has to be made on the amount of each write-down as IAS 36 places limitations on the amount to which assets can be written down. Paragraph 105 of IAS 36 states that for each asset the carrying amount should not be reduced below the highest of the following:
- its fair value less costs of disposal
- its value in use
- zero.

In this example, because the land has a recoverable amount of $437,000, it cannot be written down to $429,483 as per the above allocation table. Only $13,000 (to write the asset down from $450,000 to $437,000) of the impairment loss can be allocated to it. Therefore, the remaining $7,517 allocated loss (i.e. $20,517 − $13,000) must be allocated to the other assets. This allocation is based on the adjusted carrying amounts, the right-hand column of the table above.

	Carrying amount	Proportion	Allocation of loss	Adjusted carrying amount
IT Network	$271,052	271,052/826,517	$2,465	$ 268,587
Plant	375,082	375,082/826,517	3,411	371,671
Patent	180,383	180,383/826,517	1,641	178,742
	$826,517		$7 517	

The impairment loss for each asset is then based, where relevant, on the accumulation of both allocations. With non-depreciable assets such as land, the asset is simply written down, whereas with depreciable assets such as plant, the account increased is the Accumulated Depreciation and Impairment losses account.

The journal entry for Kamal is:

Impairment loss	Dr	106,000	
Goodwill	Cr		46,000
Land	Cr		13,000
IT network [$12,948 + $2,465]	Cr		15,413
Accumulated depreciation and Impairment			
Losses – plant [$17,918 + $3,411]	Cr		21,329
Accumulated depreciation and impairment			
Losses – patent [$8,617 + $1,641]	Cr		10,258

Katherine CGU

As with the Kamal CGU, the impairment loss is used to first write off the goodwill balance, $32,000, and then the balance of the impairment loss, $52,000 (i.e. $84,000 − $32,000), is allocated across the remaining assets, except for cash, receivables and inventory. Further, as the patent's carrying amount is below its recoverable amount, no impairment loss can be allocated to it.

	Carrying amount	Proportion	Allocation of loss	Adjusted carrying amount
IT network	$116,000	116/982	$ 6,143	$109,857
Land	290,000	290/982	15,356	274,644
Plant	576,000	576/982	30,501	545,499
	$982,000		$52,000	

Because the plant has a fair value less costs of disposal of $540,000 and this is below the adjusted carrying amount of $545,499, the full impairment loss of $30,501 can be allocated to it.

The journal entry for Katherine is:

Impairment Loss	Dr	84,000	
Goodwill	Cr		32,000
IT Network	Cr		6,143
Land	Cr		15,356
Accumulated depreciation and impairment			
Losses — Plant	Cr		30,501

DEMONSTRATION PROBLEM 7.2 Impairment losses, some corporate assets cannot be allocated, no goodwill

Parkes Ltd has three CGUs, a head office and a data centre. The carrying amounts of the assets and their recoverable amounts are as follows:

	Unit A	Unit B	Unit C	Head office	Data centre	Parkes Ltd
Carrying amount	$100	$150	$200	$150	$50	$650
Recoverable amount	129	164	271			584

The assets of the head office are allocable to the three units as follows:
- Unit A: $19
- Unit B: $56
- Unit C: $75

The assets of the data centre facility cannot be reasonably allocated to the CGUs.

Required

Assuming all assets can be adjusted for impairment, prepare the journal entry relating to any impairment of the assets of Parkes Ltd.

Solution

For each unit there needs to be a comparison between the carrying amounts of the assets of the units and their recoverable amounts to determine which, if any, of the CGUs is impaired. As the asset of the head office can be allocated to each of the units, the carrying amounts of each of the units must then include the allocated part of the head office.

Calculation of impairment losses for units

	Unit A	Unit B	Unit C
Carrying amount	$100	$150	$200
Add head office allocation	19	56	75
	119	206	275
Recoverable amount	129	164	271
Impairment loss	$ 0	$ 42	$ 4

Because the assets of Unit A are not impaired, no write-down is necessary. For Units B and C, the impairment losses must be allocated to the assets of the units. The allocation is in proportion to the carrying amounts of the assets.

Allocation of impairment loss

	Unit A (unaffected)	Unit B		Unit C	
To head office		$11	[42 × 56/206]	$1	[4 × 75/275]
To carrying amount of assets		31	[42 × 150/206]	3	[4 × 200/275]
		$42		$4	

In relation to the data centre, the assets of the centre cannot be allocated to the units, so the impairment test is based on the smallest CGU that contains the research centre, which in this case is the entity as a whole, Parkes Ltd. For this calculation, the carrying amounts of the assets of the units as well as the head office are reduced by the impairment losses already allocated. The total assets of Parkes Ltd consist of all the assets of the entity.

Impairment testing for CGU as a whole

	Unit A	Unit B	Unit C	Head office	Data centre	Parkes Ltd
Carrying amount	100	150	200	150	50	650
Impairment loss	—	31	3	12	—	46
Net	100	119	197	138	50	604
Recoverable amount						584
Impairment loss						20

Because the carrying amount of the assets of Parkes Ltd is greater than the recoverable amount of the entity, the entity as a whole has incurred an impairment loss. This loss is allocated across all the assets of the entity in proportion to their carrying amounts (taking into account impairments recorded in the previous step).

Allocation of impairment loss

	Carrying amount	Proportion	Allocation of loss	Adjusted carrying amount
Unit A	$ 100	100/604 × 20	$ 3	$ 97
Unit B	119	119/604 × 20	4	116
Unit C	197	197/604 × 20	6	191
Head office	138	138/604 × 20	5	132
Data centre	50	50/604 × 20	2	48
	$ 604		$ 20	$ 584

Journal entry for impairment loss

The journal entry for the impairment loss recognises the reduction in each of the assets. As the composition of the assets is not detailed in this question, the credit adjustments are made against the asset accounts. They could also have been made against an Accumulated Depreciation and Impairment losses account. Obviously if the composition of each of the assets of each unit had been given, the impairment loss would have been allocated to specific assets rather than assets as a total category as in the solution here.

Impairment Loss	Dr	66 = 660 − 584	
Assets — Unit A	Cr		3
Assets — Unit B	Cr		35 = 31 + 4
Assets — Unit C	Cr		9 = 3 + 6
Assets — Head Office	Cr		17 = 15 + 2
Assets — Data centre	Cr		2

Discussion questions

1. What is an impairment test?
2. Why is an impairment test considered necessary?
3. When should an entity conduct an impairment test?
4. What are some external indicators of impairment?
5. What are some internal indicators of impairment?
6. What is meant by recoverable amount?
7. How is an impairment loss calculated in relation to a single asset accounted for?
8. What are the limits to which an asset can be written down in relation to impairment losses?
9. What is a cash-generating unit?
10. How are impairment losses accounted for in relation to cash-generating units?
11. Are there limits in adjusting assets within a cash-generating unit when impairment losses occur?
12. How is goodwill tested for impairment?
13. What is a corporate asset?
14. How are corporate assets tested for impairment?
15. When can an entity reverse past impairment losses?
16. What are the steps involved in reversing an impairment loss?

References

Diageo, 2023, *Annual Report 2023*, https://media.diageo.com/diageo-corporate-media/media/p1bljst1/diageo-annual-report-2023.pdf

International Accounting Standard Board (IASB), 2023. Educational material: Effects of climate-related matters on financial statements. https://www.ifrs.org/content/dam/ifrs/supporting-implementation/documents/effects-of-climate-related-matters-on-financial-statements.pdf

Nokia, 2023, *Annual Report 2023* https://www.nokia.com/system/files/2024-03/nokia-annual-report-2023.pdf

Rolls-Royce Holdings PLC, 2023, *Annual Report 2023*, https://www.rolls-royce.com/investors/results-reports-and-presentations/annual-report-2023.aspx

The two main types of impairment examined in accounting research are of long-term tangible assets and goodwill. We start with long-term tangible assets. Bartov et al. (1998) examine the market reaction to announcements of these impairments. They observe that the stock market reaction seems to be small relative to the magnitude of recorded impairments. One possible explanation for this is that the recording of the impairment is delayed relative to the underlying economic loss event. If this is the case, then the market might have reacted beforehand and so the accounting impairment conveys no new information. Another explanation may be that markets do not initially fully comprehend the significance of the impairment. To explore these explanations Bartov et al. (1998) examine 373 impairments during the 1981–1985 period. For impairments recorded in the context of business changes (e.g. restructuring) they do not find significant market reactions, but for other impairments they document negative stock return during a 4-day window around the impairment announcement. Nevertheless, all impairment-announcing firms experience a decline in stock prices in the 2 years leading up to the announcement. This evidence therefore suggests that markets reacted to the underlying economic events before the recording of the loss in the books. Interestingly, the trend in falling prices continues for an additional year following the impairment announcement. Hence, the evidence suggests both that the loss recognition is delayed relative to the underlying economic event and that it is not fully assessed by market participants.

Alciatore et al. (2000) examine write-downs in a specific industry — the oil and gas industry — and provide interesting evidence that pertains to the delay in loss recognition. Companies in this industry who trade on a US exchange are required to compare the cost of wells recorded on the balance sheet to the present value of future cash flows, which in this industry are closely tied to oil prices. Thus, the economic loss event is clearly identifiable. Focusing on the period of 1984 to mid-1988 when oil and gas prices declined, the authors provide evidence that the recording of the write-downs takes place after the decline in oil and gas prices. This is broadly consistent with managerial incentive to delay recognition of bad news (Kothari et al. 2009).

Riedl (2004) further explores the link between impairments and underlying economic factors. He postulates that the quality of recorded impairments should be judged with respect to whether they capture the effect of underlying economic factors. He employs several proxies for economic factors, including changes in gross domestic product (GDP), change in industry return on assets (ROA), and change in sales. His sample is based on over 2750 firm-year observations including 455 firm-year observations with impairment charges (including impairments of goodwill). Some of these impairments were recorded following the implementation of SFAS 121 (FASB 1995) in the US, which is similar to IAS 36 in many respects. In his sample, impairment firms generally perform worse than non-impairment firms. His most intriguing result, however, is that whereas impairments are related to economic factors pre-SFAS 121, they are not in the post-standard period. As Riedl (2004) points out, the aim of the standard was to reduce the level of discretion that was available to managers before SFAS 121. His evidence therefore suggests that the standard did not succeed in curtailing managerial discretion.

While managers may wish to under-record impairments, auditors are expected to monitor and curtail opportunistic behaviour. Stein (2019) examines the role of auditors in impairment recognition. She finds that impairments are larger when auditors are industry specialists, and that impairments are recorded in a timelier manner.

Turning to studies of goodwill, Henning et al. (2000) provide evidence consistent with the view that goodwill is an asset (see also the Academic Perspective to chapter 19). Specifically, they find that goodwill is positively related to the firm's market value. This positive association indicates that capital markets perceive goodwill as an asset. Hayn and Hughes (2006) turn attention to impairments by attempting to quantify the delay in such impairments. They identify 58 companies who had impaired goodwill 6 or more years after the acquisition. Hayn and Hughes (2006) then provide evidence of unusual poor performance by the acquirers of up to 5 years before the impairment is recognised. This evidence therefore suggests that impairments of goodwill are recorded with considerable delay.

One possible underlying reason for goodwill impairments is that the acquiring firms overpay for target firms in the first place. This is more likely in cases where the acquisition is financed by the acquirer's own shares. Gu and Lev (2011) argue that the overpayment problem is more pronounced when the acquirer's stock is overpriced itself. They develop an index that captures the overpricing of the acquirer's stock. The index is based on three underlying measures, including industry-adjusted price-to-earnings ratio, discretionary accruals, and net equity issues. They then employ a large sample for 1990–2006 including 7055 acquisitions and show that stock-funded acquisitions are associated with larger increases in recorded goodwill than cash-funded acquisitions. The difference in recorded goodwill between stock- and cash-bidders becomes larger with the measure of overpricing of the acquirers' own stock. Gu and Lev (2011) then examine goodwill impairments recorded in 2001–2006 for firms that were involved in acquisition activity in 1990–2000. They find that the magnitude of the impairment is positively related to the overpricing of the acquirers' own stock.

Impairment of goodwill is based on managers' estimates of the underlying cash flows that the cash-generating unit is expected to produce in the future. This estimate is largely subject to managerial discretion. Ramanna and Watts (2012) examine a sample of firms for which the book-to-market (BM) ratio is greater than 1 for 2 consecutive years. The authors argue that goodwill impairment is more likely in such firms as the market-based value of goodwill is negative. Hence, firms that exhibit BM > 1 for 2 consecutive years may be avoiding recognising impairments. One reason for this could be because managers of these firms expect improvement in future performance that would negate the need to impair goodwill. That is, these managers possess good news not known to investors.

Ramanna and Watts (2012) proxy for insider good news is insider purchase of own stock. However, they do not find that insider purchase of own stock is at a different level than of insiders of firms that do recognise goodwill impairments. The authors therefore conclude that delayed impairments of goodwill are not owed to impending good news.

Filip et el. (2021) conduct a cross-country analysis of firms impairing goodwill. They find that the strength of a country's accounting enforcement is associated with impairment events. Specially, they find that recognition of goodwill impairment is more likely in countries with stricter enforcement.

Taken together, the literature reviewed here suggests that impairments are prone to significant managerial discretion, albeit with auditors' and regulators' constraining effects. This is manifested in delayed recording of impairments, impairments that are divorced from underlying economic events, and in the case of goodwill, these impairments are predictable insofar as they are more likely to take place in stock-for-stock acquisitions where the acquirer's stock is overpriced.

References

Alciatore, M., Easton, P., and Spear, N., 2000. Accounting for the impairment of long-lived assets: Evidence from the petroleum industry. *Journal of Accounting and Economics*, 29(2), 151–172.

Bartov, E., Lindahl, F. W., and Ricks, W. E., 1998. Stock price behavior around announcements of write-offs. *Review of Accounting Studies*, 3(4), 327–346.

Filip, A., Lobo, G.J., and Paugam, L., 2021. Managerial discretion to delay the recognition of goodwill impairment: The role of enforcement. *Journal of Business Finance & Accounting*, 48(1–2), 36–69.

Financial Accounting Standards Board (FASB), 1995. Accounting for the impairment of long-lived assets and for long-lived assets to be disposed of. SFAS No. 121. Norwalk, CT: FASB.

Gu, F., and Lev, B. 2011. Overpriced shares, ill-advised acquisitions, and goodwill impairment. *The Accounting Review*, 86(6), 1995–2022.

Hayn, C., and Hughes, P. J. 2006. Leading indicators of goodwill impairment. *Journal of Accounting, Auditing & Finance*, 21(3), 223–265.

Henning, S. L., Lewis, B. L., and Shaw, W. H. 2000. Valuation of the components of purchased goodwill. *Journal of Accounting Research*, 38(2), 375–386.

Kothari, S., Shu, S., and Wysocki, P. 2009. Do managers withhold bad news? *Journal of Accounting Research* 47(1), 241–276.

Ramanna, K., and Watts, R. L. 2012. Evidence on the use of unverifiable estimates in required goodwill impairment. *Review of Accounting Studies*, 17(4), 749–780.

Riedl, E. J. 2004. An examination of long-lived asset impairments. *The Accounting Review*, 79(3), 823–852.

Stein, S.E., 2019. Auditor industry specialization and accounting estimates: Evidence from asset impairments. *Auditing: A Journal of Practice & Theory*, 38(2), 207–234.

8 Fair value measurement

ACCOUNTING STANDARDS IN FOCUS

IFRS 13 *Fair Value Measurement*

LEARNING OBJECTIVES

After studying this chapter, you should be able to:

1. explain the need for an accounting standard on fair value measurement
2. understand the key characteristics of the term 'fair value'
3. understand the key concepts used in the fair value framework
4. explain the steps in determining the fair value of non-financial assets
5. understand how to measure the fair value of liabilities
6. explain how to measure the fair value of an entity's own equity instruments
7. discuss issues relating to the measurement of the fair value of financial instruments
8. understand the impact of climate-related matters on fair value
9. prepare the disclosures required by IFRS 13 *Fair Value Measurement*.

8.1 INTRODUCTION

8.1.1 The need for a standard on fair value measurement

Under accounting standards issued by the International Accounting Standards Board (IASB®), there are various ways in which assets are required to be measured. Many standards specify how assets are to be initially recognised, and most standards specify or give choices on measurement subsequent to initial recognition. The two main measures used are cost and fair value, for example:

- IAS 16 *Property, Plant and Equipment* requires an item of property, plant and equipment that qualifies for recognition as an asset to be measured initially at its cost (paragraph 15) and allows entities the choice, subsequent to initial recognition, of measuring assets using the cost model or the revaluation model (paragraph 29). The revaluation model means that assets are measured at their fair value at the date of the revaluation less any subsequent accumulated depreciation and subsequent accumulated impairment losses (paragraph 31). *See chapter 5.*
- IAS 38 *Intangible Assets* contains similar requirements for intangible assets (paragraphs 24, 72 and 75, respectively). *See chapter 6.*
- IFRS 9 *Financial Instruments* requires financial assets to be measured initially at fair value plus or minus transaction costs (paragraph 5.1.1). Subsequent measurement depends on the classification of the financial asset and could be at amortised cost or at fair value (paragraph 5.2.1). In addition, IFRS 7 *Financial Instruments: Disclosures* requires the disclosure of the fair value of all financial assets (paragraph 25). For more details *see chapter 13.*

Other measurement methods used in accounting standards include net realisable value, fair value less costs of disposal, recoverable amount and value in use.

In relation to the measurement of liabilities, IFRS 9 requires financial liabilities to be measured initially at fair value plus or minus transaction costs and IFRS 7 requires the disclosure of the fair value of all financial liabilities, while non-financial liabilities are measured, in accordance with paragraph 36 of IAS 37 *Provisions, Contingent Liabilities and Contingent Assets*, at the best estimate of the expenditure required to settle the present obligation.

It follows from the above that recognising or disclosing the fair value of assets and liabilities is a common phenomenon in IFRS financial reporting. For each category of asset and liability the various chapters in this book address the question *when* to recognise these assets and liabilities at fair value or disclose their fair values. In contrast, this chapter addresses the question *how* to measure fair value.

It is important that fair values are determined consistently. This resulted in the need for a separate standard on how to determine fair values in IFRS financial statements. This guidance came with the issuance of IFRS 13 *Fair Value Measurement* in May 2011. The standard was developed in cooperation with the United States Financial Accounting Standards Board and created a generally uniform framework for applying fair value measurement in both IFRS and US GAAP.

8.1.2 The objectives of IFRS 13

A primary goal of IFRS 13 is to increase the consistency and comparability of fair value measurements used in financial reporting. The objectives of IFRS 13 are succinctly stated in paragraph 1:

- to define fair value
- to set out in a single standard a framework for measuring fair value
- to require disclosures about fair value measurement.

8.1.3 When does IFRS 13 apply?

IFRS 13 applies whenever another accounting standard requires or permits the measurement or disclosure (i.e. those items that are not measured at fair value, but whose fair value is required to be disclosed) of fair value or measures based on fair value (e.g. fair value less costs of disposal). It also specifies when and what information about fair value measurement is to be disclosed.

IFRS 13 does not apply to share-based payment transactions within IFRS 2 *Share-based Payment*; leasing transactions accounted for in accordance with IFRS 16 *Leases*; and measurements that have similarities to, but are not, fair value, such as net realisable value in IAS 2 *Inventories* or value in use in IAS 36 *Impairment of Assets*.

8.2 THE DEFINITION OF FAIR VALUE

Fair value is defined in Appendix A of IFRS 13 as:

> The price that would be received to sell an asset or paid to transfer a liability in an orderly transaction between market participants at the measurement date.

Please note that the measurement of fair value is not based on an actual transaction, but a hypothetical one. In addition, the definition specifies that fair value is a market-based measurement, not an entity-specific measurement, and, as such, is determined based on the assumptions that market participants would use in pricing the asset or liability. It is also clear that it is the price of such a transaction at the measurement date, not some other date. The definition also clarifies that fair value is an exit (selling) price, rather than an entry (buying) price. In addition, it assumes an orderly transaction, not a forced transaction or a distress sale. Below we will discuss this in more detail.

8.2.1 Current exit price

Exit price is defined in Appendix A of IFRS 13 as follows:

> The price that would be received to sell an asset or paid to transfer a liability.

Paragraph 57 of IFRS 13 notes that, when an entity acquires an asset or assumes a liability in an exchange transaction, the transaction price is the amount paid by the entity. This is an *entry* price. In contrast, the fair value of the asset or liability is the price that would be received to sell the asset or paid to transfer the liability. This is an *exit* price.

Importantly, the definition of fair value is that it is an exit price based on the perspective of the entity that holds the asset or owes the liability.

An exit price is based on expectations about the future cash flows that will be generated by the asset subsequent to the sale of the asset or transfer of the liability. These cash flows may be generated from use of the asset or from sale of the asset by the acquiring entity. Even if the entity holding the asset intends to use it rather than sell it, fair value is measured as an exit price by reference to the sale of the asset to a market participant who will use the asset or sell it.

Similarly, with a liability, an entity may continue to hold a liability until settlement or transfer the liability to another entity. The fair value in both cases is based on market participants' expectations about cash outflows by the entity.

According to paragraph BC44 of the Basis for Conclusions to IFRS 13, the IASB concluded that a current entry price and a current exit price will be equal when they relate to the same asset or liability on the same date in the same form in the same market. However, valuation experts informed the IASB that, in a business combination, an exit price for an asset or liability acquired or assumed might differ from an exchange price — entry or exit — if:

- an entity's intended use for an acquired asset is different from its highest and best use
- a liability is measured on the basis of settling it with the creditor rather than transferring it to a third party.

This distinction between an entry price and exit price is significant and can have important implications for the initial recognition of assets and liabilities at fair value. Therefore, an entity must determine whether the transaction price represents the fair value of an asset or liability at initial recognition. For example, if the transaction takes place between related parties or if the transaction takes place under duress or the seller is forced to sell, the transaction price and fair value may not be the same (IFRS 13 paragraph B4).

8.2.2 Orderly transactions

The definition of fair value requires that an asset be sold or a liability transferred in an orderly transaction. An orderly transaction is not a forced or distressed sale, such as occurs in liquidations. It assumes that, before the measurement date, there is sufficient time and exposure to a market to allow the usual marketing activities to take place for that transaction.

Fair value is measured by considering a hypothetical transaction in a market. To determine that fair value, the entity will make observations in current markets. The markets to be observed must be those containing orderly transactions. Prices of goods sold in a liquidation or 'fire sale' are not appropriate to include in the measurement. Similarly, prices between entities that are not at arm's length are not prices from orderly transactions.

While fair value assumes an orderly transaction, in practice entities may need to consider prices from such transactions or from markets where there has been a decline in trading. An example relates to

2011 trading activity for Greek sovereign bonds. During that calendar year, the economic situation in Greece had deteriorated and some had questioned whether the Greek sovereign bonds were still being actively traded.

IFRS 13 is clear that fair value remains a market-based exit price that considers the current market conditions as at the measurement date, even if there has been a significant decrease in the volume and level of activity for the asset or liability (paragraph 15). Therefore, the standard provides guidance to assist entities in measuring fair value when the volume or level of activity for an asset or a liability has significantly decreased (paragraphs B37–B47 of Appendix B and Illustrative Example 14 paragraphs IE49–IE58).

8.2.3 Transaction and transportation costs

Both transaction and transport costs affect the determination of the fair value of an asset or liability. However, the price used to measure fair value is not adjusted for transaction costs, but would consider transportation costs.

Transaction costs are the incremental direct costs, that are essential to the transaction, to sell an asset or transfer a liability and are defined as the costs that would be incurred in the principal (or most advantageous) market and are directly attributable to the sale or transfer. Similar to other requirements, incremental costs are those that would not otherwise have been incurred had the entity not decided to enter into the transaction to sell or transfer.

Transportation costs are those that would be incurred to move the asset to the principal (or most advantageous) market.

As discussed in section 8.3.2, when determining the most advantageous market (in the absence of a principal market), an entity takes into consideration the transaction costs and transportation costs it would incur to sell the asset or transfer the liability. However, the price in that market that is used to measure the fair value of an asset or liability is not adjusted for transaction costs. The reason for this is that transaction costs are not considered to be a characteristic of the asset or liability. Instead, they are specific to a transaction and will change from transaction to transaction.

An asset may have to be transported from its present location to the principal (or most advantageous) market. As the location of an asset or a liability is a characteristic of the asset or liability, it will have a different fair value because of associated transport costs. For example, if an entity located in a capital city is considering buying a vehicle, then a vehicle located in a country town has a different fair value compared to one located in the capital city because of the transport costs associated with moving the vehicle from the country town. A price in the principal (or most advantageous) market is then adjusted for the transport costs. In contrast, transaction costs, such as registration costs, are not a characteristic of the asset. Illustrative example 8.1 shows how transport costs and transaction costs are considered in the measurement of fair value.

ILLUSTRATIVE EXAMPLE 8.1 Transaction costs and transport costs

Entity A holds a physical commodity measured at fair value in its warehouse in Europe. For this commodity, the London exchange is determined to be the principal market as it represents the market with the greatest volume and level of activity for the asset that the entity can reasonably access.

The exchange price for the asset is £25. However, the contracts traded on the exchange for this commodity require physical delivery to London. Entity A determines that it would cost £5 to transport the physical commodity to London and the broker's commission would be £3 to transact on the London exchange.

Since location is a characteristic of the asset and transportation to the principal market is required, the fair value of the physical commodity would be £20 — the price in the principal market for the asset £25, less transportation costs of £5. The £3 broker commission represents a transaction cost; therefore, no adjustment is made to the price in the principal market used to measure fair value.

Source: Adapted from EY, *International GAAP® 2024*, Chapter 14 *Fair value measurement*, Section 8.2, Illustration 8.1.

8.3 THE FAIR VALUE FRAMEWORK

In addition to providing a single definition of fair value, IFRS 13 includes a framework for applying this definition to financial reporting. Many of the key concepts used in the fair value framework are interrelated and their interaction needs to be considered in the context of the entire approach.

When measuring fair value, paragraph B2 of IFRS 13 requires an entity to determine all of the following:
- the particular asset or liability that is the subject of the measurement (consistent with its unit of account) — *see section 8.3.1*.
- the principal (or most advantageous) market for the asset or liability — *see section 8.3.2*.
- the valuation technique(s) appropriate for the measurement, considering the available inputs that represent market participants assumptions and their categorisation within the fair value hierarchy — *see sections 8.3.3–8.3.5*.
- for a non-financial asset, the valuation premise that is appropriate for the measurement (consistent with its highest and best use) — *see section 8.4*.

IFRS 13 provides specific requirements to assist entities in applying its fair value framework to:

(a) non-financial assets;
(b) liabilities and an entity's own equity instruments.

This application guidance is discussed in sections 8.4–8.6.

8.3.1 What is the particular asset or liability that is the subject of the measurement?

Paragraph 11 of IFRS 13 clarifies that in order to measure fair value for a particular asset or liability, an entity must take into account those characteristics that exist at the measurement date that a market participant would consider when pricing the asset or liability. Some of the key questions that need to be asked when determining the asset or liability to be measured are:

- *What is the unit of account? Is the asset a stand-alone asset or is it a group of assets?* The unit of account defines what is to be measured. Other standards specify this — that is, the level at which an asset or liability is aggregated or disaggregated for financial reporting purposes (Appendix A of IFRS 13). For example, where a fair value is being calculated for impairment purposes, the assets being valued may be a single asset or a cash generating unit, as defined in IAS 36. Similarly, if the fair value relates to a business, the definition of a business in IFRS 3 *Business Combinations* would need to be considered.
- *Are there any restrictions on sale or use of the asset or transfer of the liability?* There may be legal limits on the use of the asset (e.g. patents, licences or expiry dates of related lease contracts). A restriction that would transfer with the asset in an assumed sale would generally be a characteristic of the asset that market participants would consider. However, a restriction that is specific to the entity that holds the asset would not transfer with the asset and, therefore, would not be considered. A liability or an entity's own equity instrument may be subject to restrictions that prevent its transfer. IFRS 13 does not allow an entity to include a separate input (or an adjustment to other inputs) for such restrictions because the effect will either implicitly or explicitly be included in other inputs.
- *What is the condition of the asset?* Many of the factors that are considered in depreciating an asset will be of relevance, such as remaining useful life, physical condition, expected usage, and technical or commercial obsolescence.
- *What is the location of the asset?* If the location of a non-financial asset is different from the market in which it would hypothetically be sold, the asset would need to be transported in order to sell it. In such cases, location is considered a characteristic of the asset and the costs to transport the asset to market would be deducted from the price received in order to measure fair value.

A further consideration relates to whether or not the size of an entity's holding can be considered. Assume, for example, that an entity holds 100 shares that it needs to measure at fair value. The unit of account is the individual financial instrument. So, in order to measure fair value, does the entity use the price to sell a single share or the block of 100 shares? In general, the price per unit would be expected to fall if a large volume of the units were being sold as a package. This is referred to as a 'block discount' arising because the volume is a 'blockage factor'. Paragraph 69 prohibits the use of a blockage factor, arguing that a blockage factor is not relevant. As noted in paragraph BC42 of the Basis for Conclusions on IFRS 13, the transaction being considered between the market participants is a hypothetical transaction, and as such, the determination of fair value does not consider any entity-specific factors that might influence the transaction. The size of an entity's holding is entity-specific. Therefore, fair value must be measured based on the unit of account of the asset or liability being measured.

In addition to the above, for non-financial assets, an entity must consider the highest and best use of the asset and the valuation premise. *This is discussed further in section 8.4.*

8.3.2 What are the principal and most advantageous markets for the asset?

When measuring fair value, an entity is required to assume that the hypothetical transaction to sell the asset or transfer the liability takes place either (paragraph 16):

(a) in the *principal market* for the asset or liability; or
(b) in the absence of a principal market, in the *most advantageous market* for the asset or liability.

Appropriately determining the relevant exit market is important because an entity needs to determine the market participants to whom it would sell the asset or transfer the liability, *as is discussed in section 8.3.3*.

IFRS 13 is clear that, if there is a principal market for the asset or liability, the fair value measurement represents the price in that market at the measurement date (regardless of whether that price is directly observable or estimated using another valuation technique). The price in the principal market must be used even if the price in a different market is potentially more advantageous (paragraph 18).

Appendix A contains a definition of principal market, as follows:

The market with the greatest volume and level of activity for the asset or liability.

The principal market is, therefore, the deepest and most liquid market for the non-financial asset. However, an entity need not make an exhaustive search of all markets in order to determine which market is the principal market. IFRS 13 presumes that the market in which the entity usually enters to sell this type of asset or liability is the principal market, unless evidence to the contrary exists (paragraph 17).

Where there is no principal market, the entity needs to determine the most advantageous market.

The determination of the most advantageous market is based on a comparison of the amounts that would be received from transacting for the asset or liability in a number of markets. The most advantageous market is the one that offers the highest return when selling an asset or requires the lowest payment when transferring a liability, after taking into consideration transportation and transaction costs. Illustrative example 8.2 provides an example of determining the principal market and the most advantageous market.

ILLUSTRATIVE EXAMPLE 8.2 Principal market and most advantageous market

The following three markets exist for Entity X's fleet of vehicles. Entity X has the ability to transact in all three markets. The entity has 100 vehicles (same make, model and mileage) that it needs to measure at fair value. Volumes and prices in the respective markets are as follows:

Market	Price	The entity's volume for the asset in the market (based on history and/or intent)	Total market-based volume for the asset	Transportation costs	Transaction costs
A	£27,000	60%	15%	£3,500	£1,100
B	£25,000	25%	75%	£2,300	£900
C	£23,000	15%	10%	£900	£800

Based on this information, Market B would be the principal market as this is the market in which the majority of transactions for the asset occur. As such, the fair value of the 100 vehicles as at the measurement date would be £2,270,000 (£22,700 = £25,000 per car — transportation costs of £2,300). Actual sales of the assets in either Market A or C would result in a gain or loss to the entity, i.e. when compared to the fair value of £25,000 per car.

If none of the markets is the principal market for the asset, the fair value of the asset would be measured using the price in the most advantageous market.

The most advantageous market is the one that maximises the amount that would be received to sell the asset, after considering transaction costs and transportation costs (i.e. the net amount that would be received in the respective markets).

Assume in the fact pattern above that each of markets A, B and C would be equally used such that there is no principal market, entity X would need to consider the most advantageous market.

In Market A, the net amount received by the entity is £22,400 (= £27,000 − £3,500 − £1,100) per car.
In Market B, the net amount received by the entity is £21,800 (= £25,000 − £2,300 − £900) per car.

In Market C, the net amount received by the entity is £21,300 (= £23,000 − £900 − £800) per car.

Since the net amount that would be received is higher in Market A, that is the most advantageous market for entity X. Therefore, the fair value of each vehicle is £23,500, being the amount received net of transportation costs. Please note that although transaction costs are used to determine the most advantageous market, they are not used in the measurement of fair value.

Source: Adapted from EY, *International GAAP 2024*, Chapter 14 *Fair value measurement*, Sections 5.1 and 5.2, Illustrations 5–2 and 5–4.

The principal (or most advantageous) market is considered from the perspective of the reporting entity, which means that it could be different for different entities. An entity may also be able to access different markets at different points of time — that is, not all markets are always accessible to the entity. The principal (or most advantageous) market must be one that the entity can access at the measurement date (paragraph 19).

The IASB reasoned that the principal market was the most liquid market and provided the most representative input for a fair value measurement (paragraph BC52 of the Basis for Conclusions to IFRS 13). The IASB also believed that most entities made operational decisions based upon an objective of maximisation of profits; therefore entities would choose the most advantageous market in which to conduct operations. The most advantageous market would then often be the market that the entity usually enters, or expects to enter.

In some cases, there may be no observable market in which transactions take place for an asset or liability — for example, a patent or a trademark. Where this occurs, an entity must assume that a transaction takes place at the measurement date. The assumed transaction establishes a basis for estimating the price to sell the asset or transfer the liability.

8.3.3 Who are the market participants?

Market participants are 'buyers and sellers in the principal (or most advantageous) market for the asset or liability' (IFRS 13 Appendix A). IFRS 13 assumes they have all of the following characteristics:

- *They are independent of each other, that is, they are not related parties.* As a result, the hypothetical transaction is assumed to take place between market participants at the measurement date, not between the reporting entity and another market participant. While market participants are not related parties, the standard does allow the price in a related party transaction to be used as an input in a fair value measurement provided the entity has evidence the transaction was entered into at market terms.
- *They are knowledgeable, having a reasonable understanding about the asset or liability using all available information.* Market participants should have sufficient knowledge before transacting. However, this knowledge does not necessarily need to come from publicly available information. It could be obtained in the course of a normal due diligence process.
- *They are able and willing to enter into a transaction for the asset or liability.* When determining potential market participants, certain characteristics should be considered, including the legal capability and the operating or financial capacity of an entity to purchase the asset or assume the liability. As well as being able to transact, market participants must be willing to do so. That is, they are motivated but not forced or otherwise compelled to transact.

When measuring fair value, an entity is required to use the assumptions that market participants would use when pricing the asset or liability. Fair value is not the value specific to the reporting entity and it is not the specific value to any one market participant that may have a greater incentive to transact than other market participants. The reporting entity should consider those factors that market participants, in general, would consider.

There is no need to identify specific market participants. The focus should be on the characteristics of the participants (paragraph 22). For example, it is not necessary to identify, say, ArcelorMittal S.A. or Nippon Steel Corporation as potential market participants; rather, the entity would identify market participants as large steel producers and consider the characteristics of such producers.

Determining these characteristics takes into consideration factors that are specific to the asset or liability *(see section 8.3.1)*; the principal (or most advantageous) market *(see section 8.3.2)*; and the market participants in that market (paragraph 23).

The IASB staff clarified in the educational material *Effects of climate-related matters on financial statements* that climate-related matters may affect the fair value measurement of assets and liabilities; for example, market participants' views of potential climate-related legislation could affect the fair value of an asset or liability. This means an entity cannot just consider its own expectations about climate-related risks and opportunities, but must assess fair value taking a market participant perspective.

8.3.4 What are the appropriate valuation techniques for the measurement?

Having determined the nature of the asset being valued (including additional considerations for non-financial assets, *discussed in section 8.4 below*) and the principal (or most advantageous) market (the exit market) in which the asset would be sold or liability transferred, the next step is to determine the appropriate valuation technique(s) and inputs *(see section 8.3.5)* to use to estimate the exit price.

The appropriateness of a valuation technique and inputs may vary depending on the level of activity in the exit market. However, the objective of a fair value measurement does not change depending on the level of activity or the valuation technique(s) used (paragraph 62).

The following three possible valuation approaches are noted in paragraph 62. Within the application of each of these approaches, there may be a number of possible valuation techniques.
- The *market approach*: based on market transactions involving identical or similar assets or liabilities.
- The *income approach*: based on future amounts (e.g. cash flows or income and expenses) that are converted (discounted) to a single present amount. The fair value is based upon market expectations about future cash flows, or income and expenses associated with that asset. Present value techniques are an example of techniques used in applying the income approach. The fair value of an asset is then not based on an observed market price but rather is generated by discounting the expected earnings from the use of the asset by a market participant. Paragraphs B13–B30 of Appendix B provide details about present value techniques.
- The *cost approach*: based on the amount required to replace the service capacity of an asset (often referred to as current replacement cost). This may involve consideration of the amount to be paid for a new asset, with this amount then adjusted for both physical deterioration and technological obsolescence.

IFRS 13 does not propose a hierarchy of valuation techniques (with the exception of the requirement to measure identical financial instruments that trade in active markets at price multiplied by quantity [P × Q]). Instead, it prioritises the inputs used in the application of these techniques *(see section 8.3.5)*. Some valuation techniques are better in some circumstances than in others. Significant judgement is required in selecting the appropriate valuation technique for the situation. Sufficient knowledge of the asset or liability and an adequate level of expertise regarding the valuation techniques is also needed. However, some guidance in the choice of technique is provided in IFRS 13:
- The technique must be appropriate to the circumstances (paragraph 61).
- There must be sufficient data available to apply the technique (paragraph 61).
- The technique must maximise the use of observable inputs and minimise the use of unobservable inputs (paragraph 61).
- In some cases, multiple techniques may be appropriate. This is likely to result in a range of possible values. Therefore, an entity must evaluate the reasonableness of the range and select the point within the range that is most representative of fair value in the circumstances (paragraph 63). This could include weighting the results. However, evaluating the range does not necessarily require calibration of the approaches (i.e. the results from different approaches do not have to be equal). Paragraph 40 indicates that a wide range of fair value measurements may indicate that further analysis is needed.
- Valuation techniques used to measure fair value must be consistently applied. Paragraph 65 provides examples of situations where a change in technique may be appropriate, such as when new markets develop or new information becomes available.

Use of different valuation techniques is shown in illustrative example 8.3.

ILLUSTRATIVE EXAMPLE 8.3 Valuation techniques

MediaCo is a newspaper and magazine publishing company. It previously acquired another publishing company that had two weekly newspapers and five monthly magazines. As a result of a sustained decline in circulation for the two newspapers, MediaCo tests the related cash-generating units (including the newspaper mastheads) for impairment in accordance with IAS 36 and measures the fair value less costs of disposal.

MediaCo concludes the market and income approaches could be applied as follows:
- The market approach is applied by using prices for comparable business combinations, adjusted for differences between those business combinations and each cash-generating unit (including location, circulation) and changes in market conditions since those business combinations took place.
- The income approach is applied using a present value technique. The expected cash flows reflect market participants' expectations were a buyer to operate each cash-generating unit, in light of anticipated market conditions, including expectations about future circulation.

8.3.5 Which inputs should be used when measuring fair value?

Selecting inputs

According to Appendix A of IFRS 13, inputs are:

> The assumptions that market participants would use when pricing the asset or liability, including assumptions about risk, such as the following:
>
> (a) the risk inherent in a particular valuation technique used to measure fair value (such as a pricing model); and
> (b) the risk inherent in the inputs to the valuation technique.
>
> Inputs may be observable or unobservable.

Observable inputs are defined in Appendix A as:

> Inputs that are developed using market data, such as publicly available information about actual events or transactions, and reflect the assumptions that market participants would use when pricing the asset or liability.

Unobservable inputs are defined in Appendix A as:

> Inputs for which market data are not available and that are developed using the best information available about the assumptions that market participants would use when pricing the asset or liability.

Regardless of the selected valuation technique, the inputs an entity uses must be consistent with the characteristics of the asset or liability that market participants would take into account. In addition, inputs exclude premiums or discounts that reflect size as a characteristic of the entity's holding, as these are not a characteristic of the item being measured (for example, blockage factors, *see section 8.3.1*), and any other premiums or discounts that are inconsistent with the unit of account (paragraph 69).

Regardless of the technique used, an entity must maximise the use of observable inputs and minimise the use of unobservable inputs. Therefore, for example, an income approach valuation technique that maximises the use of observable inputs and minimises the use of unobservable inputs may provide a better measure of fair value than a market valuation technique that requires significant adjustment using unobservable inputs.

Inputs based on bid and ask prices

Some input measures are based on market prices where there are both bid prices — the price a dealer is willing to pay — and ask prices — the price a dealer is willing to sell. An example is a foreign exchange dealer who is willing to exchange one currency for another, such as exchanging Euros for Japanese Yen. In such cases paragraph 70 of IFRS 13 states that the price within a bid–ask spread that is most representative of fair value should be used to measure fair value. Paragraph 71 notes that mid-market pricing (that is, using the mid-point in the bid–ask spread), or another pricing convention that is used by market participants, may be used as a practical expedient.

Fair value hierarchy — prioritising inputs

To achieve consistency and comparability in the measurement of fair values, IFRS 13 provides a hierarchy of inputs showing which inputs are given higher priority in determining a fair value measurement.

Four important points critical to understanding the uses of these inputs are:

1. The inputs are prioritised into three levels — Level 1, Level 2 and Level 3.
2. The fair value hierarchy gives the highest priority to quoted market prices in active markets for identical assets and liabilities and the lowest priority to unobservable inputs (paragraph 72).
3. Where observable inputs are used, they must be *relevant* observable inputs (paragraph 67). As noted in paragraph BC151 of the Basis for Conclusions, some respondents to the IASB expressed concerns about being required to use observable inputs during the global financial crisis that started in 2007 when the available observable inputs were not representative of the asset or liability being measured at fair value. Observability is, therefore, not the only criterion applied when selecting inputs; the inputs must be relevant as well as observable. Market conditions may require adjustments to be made to current observable inputs in measuring fair value.
4. The availability of inputs and their relative subjectivity potentially affects the selection of the valuation technique; however, the fair value hierarchy prioritises the *inputs* to the valuation techniques, not the techniques themselves.

IFRS 13 also distinguishes between where an individual input may fall within the fair value hierarchy and where the entire measurement is categorised for disclosure purposes. *The latter is discussed in section 8.7.1.*

Level 1 inputs

Level 1 inputs are defined in Appendix A as:

> Quoted prices (unadjusted) in active markets for identical assets or liabilities that the entity can access at the measurement date.

An active market is defined in Appendix A as follows:

A market in which transactions for the asset or liability take place with sufficient frequency and volume to provide pricing information on an ongoing basis.

Observable markets in which debt instruments, equity instruments or commodities are regularly traded on a securities exchange would likely be active markets. However, the above definitions make it clear that pricing needs to be for *identical* items. Assets such as vehicles, intangibles and buildings, and many liabilities may be similar, but will not be identical. Therefore, it is unlikely that Level 1 inputs would be available for such items.

As noted in paragraph 77, a quoted price in an active market for the identical asset or liability provides the most reliable evidence of fair value. As a result, IFRS 13 requires this price (without adjustment) to be used whenever available (also known as price multiplied by quantity, or P × Q). Adjustments to this price are only permitted in the limited circumstances specified in paragraph 79 of IFRS 13.

A market may no longer be considered active if:

- there has been a significant decrease in the volume and level of activity for the asset or liability when compared with normal market activity
- there are few recent transactions
- price quotations are not based on current information
- price quotations vary substantially over time or among market-makers.

Level 2 inputs

Level 2 inputs are any inputs, other than Level 1 inputs, that are directly or indirectly observable.

These inputs, like Level 1 inputs, are observable. According to paragraph 82, level 2 inputs include:

- quoted prices for similar assets or liabilities in active markets
- quoted prices for identical or similar assets or liabilities in markets that are not active
- inputs, other than quoted prices, that are observable for the asset or liability, such as interest rates and yield curves
- inputs that are derived from, or corroborated, by observable market data by correlation or other means.

It may be necessary to make adjustments to Level 2 inputs. For example, in relation to quoted prices for similar assets, these may have to be adjusted for the condition of the assets or the location of the assets.

Paragraph B35 in Appendix B contains examples of Level 2 inputs:

- *Finished goods inventory at a retail outlet:* Level 2 inputs include either a price to customers in a retail market or a wholesale price to retailers in a wholesale market, adjusted for differences between the condition and location of the inventory item and the comparable (i.e. similar) inventory items.
- *Building held and used:* A Level 2 input would be the price per square metre for the building derived from observable market data, or derived from prices in observed transactions involving comparable buildings in similar locations.
- *Cash-generating unit:* A Level 2 input may involve obtaining a multiple of earnings or revenue from observable market data by observing transactions of similar businesses.

In all cases, the examples refer to market data or to prices being observable either directly (that is, the price itself is available) or indirectly (that is, price is derived from observable information).

Level 3 inputs

Level 3 inputs are those that are unobservable.

While Level 1 and Level 2 inputs are based on observable market data, Level 3 inputs are unobservable. The data used may be that of the entity itself, which may be adjusted for factors that market participants would build into the valuation, or to eliminate the effect of variables that are specific to this entity, but not relevant to other market participants.

Examples of Level 3 inputs include:

- *Cash-generating unit:* A Level 3 input would include a financial forecast of cash flow or earnings based on the entity's own data.
- *Trademark:* A Level 3 input would be the royalty rate expected by the entity that could be obtained by allowing other entities to use the trademark to produce the products covered by the trademark.
- *Accounts receivable:* A Level 3 input would be the amount expected to be recovered based upon the entity's historical record of recoverability of accounts receivable.

In illustrative example 8.4, an example is given where different valuation techniques could be used to measure the fair value of an asset, with a consideration of the level of inputs that might be used.

Van Hoff revalues its buildings, which are held and used, in accordance with IAS 16. All three valuation approaches could be applied to measure fair value. Van Hoff would evaluate the results of using these valuation techniques. It would consider the relevance, reliability and subjectivity of the information used in the valuations and the range of values given by the three techniques in order to select the point within the range that is most representative of fair value in the circumstances.

Market approach

Van Hoff applies the market approach using observable prices for comparable buildings in similar locations adjusted for differences between the buildings, including its location and condition. The prices for comparable buildings are Level 2 inputs. Both observable information (e.g. square-metres, age of the building) and unobservable information was used to determine the adjustments to the prices for comparable buildings. As such, the adjustments were generally Level 3 inputs.

Income approach

Van Hoff uses a present value technique using expected cash flows that reflect what market participants would expect to receive from renting the building to tenants. Van Hoff derives the price per square metre for the building and expected incentives to entice new tenants from observable market data, which are Level 2 inputs. Adjustments are made for differences in location and condition of the building. The expected cash flows also include market participants' expectations about costs to maintain the building, which Van Hoff estimates based on its own data, which are Level 3 inputs. The discount rate used is based on the risk-free rate, which is observable, but is adjusted for the premium a market participant would require to accept the uncertainty related to purchasing and renting the building. As such, the discount rate is a Level 3 input.

Cost approach

Van Hoff estimates the amount that would currently be required to construct a substitute building. Adjustments would be necessary for the effects of location and condition of the building. The inputs used are a mix of Level 2 and Level 3 inputs. Some inputs are based on observable market data; for example, costs related to materials and labour. Inputs related to estimated physical obsolescence to reflect the current condition of the building are derived from Van Hoff's own data, which is unobservable.

8.4 APPLICATION TO NON-FINANCIAL ASSETS

In addition to the general fair value framework *(discussed in section 8.3)*, the fair value of a non-financial asset must take into consideration the highest and best use of the asset from a market participant perspective. The highest and best use determines the valuation premise. *These concepts are discussed in sections 8.4.1 and 8.4.2.*

Paragraph BC63 of the Basis for Conclusions to IFRS 13 clarifies that the concepts of highest and best use and valuation premise in IFRS 13 are only relevant for non-financial assets (and not liabilities or financial assets). This is because:

- Financial assets have specific contractual terms; they do not have alternative uses. Changing the characteristics (i.e. contractual terms) of the financial asset causes the item to become a different asset and the objective of a fair value measurement is to measure the asset as it exists as at the measurement date.
- The different ways by which an entity may relieve itself of a liability (e.g. repayment) are not alternative uses. In addition, entity-specific advantages (or disadvantages) that enable an entity to fulfil a liability more or less efficiently than other market participants are not considered in a fair value measurement.

8.4.1 What is the highest and best use of a non-financial asset?

Unlike liabilities and financial assets, a non-financial asset may have several uses. The way in which the reporting entity uses a non-financial asset may not be the way market participants would use the asset. As such, the standard requires that the fair value of a non-financial asset be measured by considering the highest and best use from a market participant perspective. Highest and best use is defined in Appendix A of IFRS 13 as:

> The use of a non-financial asset by market participants that would maximise the value of the asset or the group of assets and liabilities (e.g. a business) within which the asset would be used.

Highest and best use is a valuation concept that considers how market participants would use a non-financial asset in order to maximise its benefit or value. This may come from its use: (i) in combination with other assets (or with other assets and liabilities); or (ii) on a stand-alone basis. This establishes the valuation premise to be used to measure the fair value of that asset (paragraph 31).

According to paragraph 28 of IFRS 13, the highest and best use must be:

- *Physically possible*, taking into account the physical characteristics of the asset.
- *Legally permissible*, considering any legal restrictions (e.g. zoning regulations on the use of property). A use of a non-financial asset need not be legal (or have legal approval) at the measurement date, but it must not be legally prohibited in the jurisdiction (paragraph BC69).
- *Financially feasible*, in that the use of the asset must result in the market participant obtaining an appropriate return from the asset.

IFRS 13 presumes that an entity's current use of an asset is its highest and best use, unless market or other factors suggest that a different use by market participants would maximise the value of that asset (paragraph 29). However, the highest and best use is determined from a market participant perspective. Therefore, despite the presumption, the highest and best use may not be the entity's current use. For example, an entity may have acquired a trademark that competes with its own trademark and chooses not to use it. If market participants would use the trademark, the current use may not be the highest and best use. Care is needed when the highest and best use is in combination with other non-financial assets to ensure that consistent assumptions are made about the highest and best use *(see illustrative example 8.6 in section 8.4.2)*.

If the highest and best use of the asset is something other than its current use:

- Any costs to transform the non-financial asset (e.g. obtaining a new zoning permit or converting the asset to the alternative use) and profit expectations from a market participant's perspective are also considered in the fair value measurement.
- An entity must disclose that fact and its basis.

8.4.2 What is the valuation premise?

Depending on its highest and best use, the fair value of the non-financial asset will either be measured assuming market participants would purchase the asset to benefit from the use or sale of the asset on a stand-alone basis or in combination with other assets (or other assets and liabilities) — that is, the asset's valuation premise.

Decisions concerning the highest and best use of an asset and the relevant valuation premise are considered in illustrative examples 8.5 and 8.6.

Stand-alone valuation premise

As noted in paragraph 31(b) of IFRS 13, under this premise, the fair value of the asset is the price that would be received in a current transaction to sell the asset to market participants *who would use the asset on a stand-alone basis*.

In-combination valuation premise

When a fair value is measured under this premise, the highest and best use of the asset is where the market participants obtain maximum value through using the asset *in combination with other assets and liabilities*.

Paragraph 31(a) states that, under this premise, the fair value is measured on the basis of the price that would be received in a current transaction to sell the asset such that the purchaser could use it with other assets and liabilities as a group and that those assets and liabilities (complementary assets and liabilities) would be available to market participants. The transaction is for the individual asset, consistent with its unit of account. The fair value measurement assumes that the complementary assets and liabilities would be available to market participants. For example, as noted in paragraph B3(c) of Appendix B *Application guidance* of IFRS 13, if the asset is work-in-progress that would be converted into finished goods, in determining the fair value of the work-in-progress, it is assumed that the market participants already have, or would be able to acquire, any necessary machinery for that conversion process.

The fair value is what the market participants would pay for the asset being measured knowing that they can use it with those complementary assets. For some specialised assets, the market price may not capture the value the asset contributes to the group of complementary assets and liabilities because the market price would be for an unmodified, stand-alone asset. As noted in paragraph BC79 of the Basis for Conclusions on IFRS 13, the IASB recognised that in some cases an entity will need to measure fair value using another valuation technique, such as an income approach, or the cost to replace or recreate the asset.

A further question considered by the IASB was whether the exit price for specialised equipment is equal to its scrap value (paragraph BC78 of the Basis for Conclusions on IFRS 13). An item of specialised equipment would generally be used in conjunction with other assets; hence the valuation premise would be in-use rather than in-exchange. The exit price is then based on the sale of the specialised equipment to market participants who will use the specialised equipment in conjunction with other assets to obtain a return. The in-use valuation premise assumes there are market participants who will use the asset in combination with other assets and that those assets are available to them (paragraph 31 of IFRS 13). This means the answer to the question raised would generally be no.

Under IAS 36 *Impairment of Assets*, recoverable amount is determined as the higher of value in use and fair value less costs of disposal. It should be noted that there is a difference between value in use and a fair value measure determined under the in-use valuation premise as the objective of each of those measures is different. Value in use measures the expected cash flows an entity expects to receive from using those assets. This is an entity-specific value. In contrast, fair value measured under the in-use premise is based on the cash flows that market participants would expect to receive from using the asset. However, the two measures may often be the same if determined as a market-based value. For further details about value in use *see chapter 7*.

ILLUSTRATIVE EXAMPLE 8.5 Determining highest and best use and valuation premise

Addison owns 100 restaurants in a large city. Each restaurant's land and buildings are accounted for using the revaluation model in IAS 16. Addison has no intention to sell. However, in the past it has sold the land and buildings and the buyers have either also used them as restaurants or converted them into grocery stores.

To measure the fair value, it is necessary to determine the highest and best use of the restaurants, from a market participant perspective, and the valuation premise. The highest and best use of each parcel of land and the building thereon may be to:
(a) continue using them (in combination with each other and other assets) as a restaurant. The fair value would be determined on the basis of the price that Addison would receive to sell the land and building to market participants, assuming that these market participants would use them in conjunction with their other assets as a group and that these assets are available to the market participants.
(b) convert the building into a grocery store. The fair value would be determined on the basis of the price that would be received to sell the land and building to market participants who would convert the building. This price would take into consideration the conversion costs that market participants would incur before being able to use the building as a grocery store.

ILLUSTRATIVE EXAMPLE 8.6 Consistent assumptions about highest and best use and valuation premise in an asset group

A wine producer owns and manages a vineyard and produces its own wine on site. The vines are measured at fair value less costs to sell in accordance with IAS 41 at the end of each reporting period. The grapes are measured at the point of harvest at fair value less costs to sell in accordance with IAS 41 (being its 'cost' when transferred to IAS 2, for further details see online chapter Agriculture). Before harvest, the grapes are considered part of the vines. The wine producer elects to measure its land using IAS 16's revaluation model (fair value less any subsequent accumulated depreciation and accumulated impairment). All other non-financial assets are measured at cost.

At the end of the reporting period, the entity assesses the highest and best use of the vines and the land from the perspective of market participants. The vines and land could continue to be used, in combination with the entity's other assets and liabilities, to produce and sell its wine (i.e. their current use). Alternatively, the land could be converted into residential property. Conversion would include removing the vines and plant and equipment from the land.

Scenario A

The entity determines that the highest and best use of these assets is in combination as a vineyard (that is, their current use). The entity must make consistent assumptions for assets in the group (for which highest and best use is relevant, i.e. non-financial assets). Therefore, the highest and best use of all non-financial assets in the group is to produce and sell wine, even if conversion into residential property might yield a higher value for the land on its own.

Scenario B

The entity determines that the highest and best use of these assets is to convert the land into residential property, even if the current use might yield a higher value for the vines on their own. The entity would need to consider what a market participant would do to convert the land, which could include the cost of rezoning, selling cuttings from the vines or simply removing the vines, and the sale of the buildings and equipment either individually or as an asset group.

Since the highest and best use of these assets is not their current use in this scenario, the entity would disclose that fact, as well as the reason why those assets are being used in a manner that differs from their highest and best use.

Source: EY, International GAAP 2024, Chapter 14 Fair value measurement, Section 9.2.2, Illustration 9–2.

8.5 APPLICATION TO LIABILITIES

The objective of a fair value measurement of a liability is to estimate the price that would be paid to transfer the liability between market participants at the measurement date under current market conditions. In all cases, an entity must maximise the use of relevant observable inputs and minimise the use of unobservable inputs.

This section applies to both financial and non-financial liabilities.

8.5.1 Settlement versus transfer

Prior to the issuance of IFRS 13, the measurement of a liability was commonly based on the amount required to *settle* the present obligation. However, as per its definition in IFRS 13, fair value is the amount paid to *transfer* a liability. The fair value measurement thus assumes that the liability is transferred to another market participant at the measurement date. According to paragraph 34(a) of IFRS 13, the transfer of a liability assumes:

> A liability would remain outstanding and the market participant transferee would be required to fulfil the obligation. The liability would not be settled with the counterparty or otherwise extinguished on the measurement date.

The liability is assumed to continue (i.e. it is not settled or extinguished), and the market participant to whom the liability is transferred would be required to fulfil the obligation. The IASB considered the settlement versus transfer in developing IFRS 13. In paragraph BC82 of the Basis for Conclusions on IFRS 13, the IASB explains that the thought-process to determine a settlement amount is similar to determining an amount at which to transfer a liability. This is because both settlement and transfer of a liability reflect all costs incurred, whether direct or indirect, and the entity faces the same risks as a market participant transferee. Despite this, the IASB concluded that the transfer notion was necessary in a fair value measurement.

Importantly, it captures market participants' expectations (e.g. about the liquidity and uncertainty), which may not be captured by a settlement notion because it may incorporate entity-specific factors. The clarification in IFRS 13 that fair value is not based on the price to settle a liability with the existing counterparty, but rather to transfer it to a market participant of equal credit standing, also affects the assumptions about the principal (or most advantageous) market and the market participants in the exit market for the liability.

8.5.2 Non-performance risk

In addition to the fair value framework *discussed in section 8.3*, when an entity measures the fair value of a liability it also considers the effect of non-performance risk. Non-performance risk is defined in Appendix A as:

> The risk that an entity will not fulfil an obligation. Non-performance risk includes, but may not be limited to, the entity's own credit risk.

Non-performance is discussed in paragraphs 42–44 of IFRS 13. When measuring the fair value of a liability, it is necessary to consider the effect of an entity's own credit risk and any other risk factors that may influence the likelihood that the obligation will not be fulfilled (paragraph 43). The requirement that non-performance risk remains unchanged before and after the transfer implies that the liability is hypothetically transferred to a market participant of equal credit standing. Illustrative example 8.7 demonstrates the valuation of liabilities with a consideration of non-performance risk.

Shore Ltd issues a zero-coupon loan of €5,000 to Cove Bank with a 5-year term. At the time, it has an AA credit rating and can borrow at 5% p.a. Shore Ltd measures the liability at fair value at initial recognition. The fair value of this loan is €3,918, being the present value of the payment in 5 years' time discounted at 5% p.a.

One year later, Shore Ltd issues another zero coupon loan of €5,000 to Cove Bank with a 5-year term. Due to a change in credit standing, it must now borrow at 7% p.a. Shore Ltd determines that the fair value of the second loan is €3,565, being the present value of the payment on the second loan in 5 years' time discounted at 7% p.a. As a result, the fair value of each liability reflects the credit standing of the entity at initial recognition.

Some respondents to the IASB questioned the decision to take non-performance risk into consideration when valuing a liability (paragraph BC95 of the Basis for Conclusions on IFRS 13). The problem they saw was that a change in an entity's credit standing — whether deterioration or improvement — would affect the fair value of the liability. This would lead to gains and losses being recognised in profit or loss for the period, potentially affecting the usefulness of the reported numbers. Furthermore, counterintuitively, a deterioration in the credit standing of the entity could lead to gains being recognised in profit or loss (this is considered in illustrative example 8.8 in section 8.5.3). However, the IASB noted that this issue was beyond the scope of the fair value measurement project and addressed these concerns when developing IFRS 9 Financial Instruments (see chapter 13).

8.5.3 Approaches to measuring the fair value of a liability

Where there is a quoted price for an identical or similar liability, an entity uses that price to measure fair value. However, in many cases, there will be no quoted prices available for the transfer of an instrument that is identical or similar to an entity's liability, particularly as liabilities are generally not transferred. For example, this might be the case for debt obligations that are legally restricted from being transferred or for decommissioning liabilities that the entity does not intend to transfer. In such situations, an entity must determine whether the identical item is held by another party as an asset:

- If the identical item is held by another party as an asset — measure fair value from the perspective of a market participant that holds the asset
- If the identical item is not held by another party as an asset — measure the fair value using a valuation technique from the perspective of a market participant that owes the liability.

In most circumstances, a liability will be held as an asset by another entity — for example, a loan is recognised as a payable by one entity, the recipient of the loan, and a receivable by another entity, the lender. The IASB considers that the fair value of a liability generally equals the fair value of a properly defined corresponding asset.

Paragraph 38 of IFRS 13 states that measurement of the corresponding asset should be in the following descending order of preference:

- the quoted price of the asset in an active market
- the quoted price for the asset in a market that is not active
- a valuation under a technique such as:
  - an income approach: present value techniques could be used based on the expected future cash flows a market participant would expect to receive from holding the liability as an asset
  - a market approach: the measure would be based on quoted prices for similar liabilities held by other parties as assets.

Illustrative example 8.8 demonstrates a situation where an entity uses a valuation technique under a market approach to measure the fair value of a liability. Refer to Example 13 of IFRS 13 for an illustration of an entity using an income approach to measure the fair value of a liability.

On 1 January 20X1, Urban Ltd issued at par $5 million exchange-traded 4-year fixed rate corporate bonds with annual coupon payments of 7.5%.

On 30 June 20X1, the instrument is trading as an asset in an active market at $1,015 per $1,000 of par value after payment of accrued interest. On 31 December 20X1, the quoted price is $830 per $1,000 of par value after payment of accrued interest. The decrease in the quoted price is partly caused by concerns about the entity's ability to pay. Urban Ltd determines there are no factors (e.g. third-party credit enhancements) that are included in the quoted price for the asset that would not be included in the price of the liability. Therefore, no adjustments are needed to the quoted price for the asset.

Urban Ltd uses the quoted price for the asset as its initial input into the fair value measurement of the bond. This results in a fair value of $5,075,000 (= $1,015/$1,000 × $5,000,000) at 30 June 20X1 and $4,150,000 (= $830/$1,000 × $5,000,000) at 31 December 20X1. *As noted in section 8.5.2,* counterintuitively a worsening of Urban Ltd's credit standing leads to a decrease in the fair value of the liability. If the financial liability would be measured at fair value through profit and loss (*see chapter 13*), a gain would be recognised in the income statement.

For some liabilities, the corresponding *asset is not held* by another entity, such as in the case of an entity that must decommission an oil platform when drilling ceases. The entity measuring the fair value of a liability must, therefore, use a valuation technique from the perspective of a market participant that owes the liability (paragraph 40). In such cases a present value technique could be applied, as is shown in illustrative example 8.9. This illustrative example also highlights the elements that are captured by using a present value technique (paragraph B13 of IFRS 13), being:
- an estimate of future cash flows
- expectations about variations in the amount and timing of the cash flows representing the uncertainty inherent in the cash flows
- the time value of money, represented by a risk-free interest rate
- a risk premium, being the price for bearing the uncertainty inherent in the cash flows
- other factors that market participants would take into account
- for a liability, non-performance risk.

ILLUSTRATIVE EXAMPLE 8.9 Present value technique: decommissioning liability

On 1 January 20X1, BigOil Ltd assumed a decommissioning liability in a business combination. The entity is legally required to dismantle and remove an offshore oil platform at the end of its useful life, which is estimated to be 10 years.

If BigOil Ltd were contractually allowed to transfer its decommissioning liability to a market participant, that market participant would need to take into account the following inputs:
- labour costs — these would be developed on the basis of current market wages, adjusted for expected wage increases with the final amount to be determined on a probability-weighted basis allocation of overhead costs
- compensation for undertaking the activity, including a reasonable profit margin and a premium for undertaking the risks involved effects of inflation time value of money, represented by the risk-free rate
- non-performance risk relating to the risk that BigOil Ltd will not fulfil the obligation, including BigOil Ltd's own credit risk.

The risk-free rate of interest for a 10-year maturity at 1 January 20X1 is 5%. BigOil Ltd adjusts that rate by 3.5% to reflect its risk of non-performance including its credit risk. Hence, the interest rate used in the present value calculation is 8.5%.

The fair value of the decommissioning liability at 1 January 20X1 determined using the present value technique is $194,879, calculated as follows:

Expected labour costs	$131,250
Allocated overhead and equipment costs	$105,000
Contractor's profit margin (20% of total costs of $236,250)	$47,250
Expected cash flows before inflation adjustment	$283,500
Inflation factor (4% for 10 years)	1.4802
Expected cash flows adjusted for inflation	$419,637
Market risk premium (0.05 × $419,637)	$20,982
Expected cash flows adjusted for market risk	$440,619
Expected present value using a discount rate of 8.5% for 10 years	$194,879

Source: Adapted from IASB 2011, IFRS 13 *Fair Value Measurement*, Illustrative Examples, Example 11 — Decommissioning liability.

8.6 APPLICATION TO MEASUREMENT OF AN ENTITY'S OWN EQUITY

The fair value of an entity's own equity instruments may need to be measured, for example, when an entity undertakes a business combination and issues its own equity instruments as part of the consideration for the exchange. Depending on the facts and circumstances, an instrument may be classified as either a liability or equity instrument (in accordance with other standards) for accounting purposes. Therefore, in developing the requirements in IFRS 13 for measuring the fair value of liabilities and an entity's own equity, paragraph BC106 in the Basis for Conclusions notes that the Boards concluded the requirements should generally be consistent with those for liabilities. Therefore, in general, the principles set out in *section 8.5* (in relation to liabilities) also apply to an entity's own equity instruments, except for the requirement to consider non-performance risk, which does not apply directly to an entity's own equity.

A fair value measurement assumes that an entity's own equity instruments are transferred to a market participant at the measurement date. Paragraph 34(b) of IFRS 13 notes that the transfer assumes the following:

> An entity's own equity instrument would remain outstanding and the market participant transferee would take on the rights and responsibilities associated with the instrument. The instrument would not be cancelled or otherwise extinguished on the measurement date.

In order to exit from its own equity, an entity would need to either cancel the share or repurchase the share. Since it cannot consider cancelling its own equity, an entity will likely need to measure the fair value of its own equity instruments from the perspective of a market participant that holds the corresponding instrument as an asset — for example, shareholders. *See section 8.5 for a discussion on measuring the fair value of a liability by reference to the corresponding asset.*

8.7 DISCLOSURE

8.7.1 Categorisation within the fair value hierarchy for disclosure purposes

IFRS 13 requires a fair value measurement *in its entirety to be categorised within the hierarchy* for disclosure purposes. Inputs used in a valuation technique may be within different levels in the fair value hierarchy *(as discussed in section 8.3.5)*. Therefore, the observability of a fair value measurement needs to reflect the observability of the various inputs used. Categorisation within the hierarchy is, therefore, based on the *lowest* level input that is significant to the entire measurement (paragraph 73). A valuation technique that relies solely on a Level 1 input ($P \times Q$) produces a fair value measurement categorised within Level 1. However, if a measurement uses even a single Level 3 input that is significant to the measurement in its entirety, the fair value measurement would be categorised within Level 3.

8.7.2 The disclosure requirements

The disclosure requirements in IFRS 13 apply to fair value measurements recognised in the statement of financial position after initial recognition and disclosures of fair value, with limited exceptions. The standard establishes a set of broad disclosure objectives and provides the minimum disclosures an entity must make. The disclosures are designed to provide users of financial statements with additional transparency regarding:

- the extent to which fair value is used to measure assets and liabilities;
- the valuation techniques, inputs and assumptions used in measuring fair value; and
- the effect of Level 3 fair value measurements on profit or loss (or other comprehensive income).

The minimum requirements vary depending on whether the fair value measurements are recurring or non-recurring and their categorisation within the fair value hierarchy (i.e. Level 1, 2 or 3). More disclosure is required for fair value measurements categorised in Level 3 of the fair value hierarchy than for those categorised in Levels 1 or 2.

To illustrate, in 2023 the IASB staff clarified in their educational material *Effects of climate-related matters on financial statements* that climate-related matters may affect the disclosures about fair value measurements. IFRS 13 requires that unobservable inputs reflect the assumptions that market participants would use when pricing, including assumptions about climate-related risks. This is particularly relevant for fair values categorised within Level 3, triggering the disclosure of inputs used, and for recurring fair value measurements, a narrative description of the sensitivity of the fair value measurement to changes in those inputs.

'Recurring' fair value measurements are those that other IFRSs require or permit in the statement of financial position at the end of the period. 'Non-recurring' fair value measurements are those that other IFRSs require or permit in particular circumstances — for example, under the application of IFRS 5 *Non-current Assets Held for Sale and Discontinued Operations* in relation to non-current assets held for sale. Disclosures must be presented by class of asset or liability. The appropriate classes may depend on the entity's specific facts and circumstances and the needs of users of its financial statements.

In order for users of the financial statements to be able to assess the relevance of the fair value information provided, IFRS 13 requires the disclosure of information that assists users in understanding:

- *An entity's policies and processes with regard to measuring fair value* — for example, its accounting policy choice with respect to the valuation processes used for fair value measurements categorised within *Level 3 of the fair value hierarchy, which is illustrated in figure 8.1.*
- *The specific assets and liabilities for which fair value is being measured* — for example, the reason for the measurement (if non-recurring); and the reason why the *current use* of a non-financial asset differs from its *highest and best use* (if applicable).
- *How fair value was measured* — for example, the fair value of the asset or liability; valuation technique(s) used; and the inputs used. For fair value measurements categorised within Level 3, an entity must disclose quantitative information about the significant unobservable inputs used in the fair value measurement.
- *The likelihood that fair value could change (i.e. the sensitivity)* — for example, quantitative and qualitative information about the sensitivity of the measurement to changes in inputs for any fair value measurement categorised within Level 3 of the fair value hierarchy.
- *The reasons for changes in fair value between periods* — examples of such disclosures include a reconciliation from the opening balances to the closing balances for fair value measurements categorised within *Level 3* of the fair value hierarchy, including what caused any change. In addition, disclosure is required of changes in valuation techniques used, as well as transfers between levels within the fair value hierarchy for recurring fair value measurements, along with the reasons for those transfers.

Many of these disclosure requirements apply regardless of whether the fair value measurement is recognised in the financial statements or only disclosed. Figures 8.1 and 8.2 provide illustrations of the type of information required for fair value measurements categorised within Level 3.

All fair value methods are considered to be able to provide reliable measures of fair value; however, users need disclosures about the methods, inputs used and the fair value in order to assess the extent of subjectivity of the techniques used. Irrespective of the frequency at which the measurements are made, the disclosures under IFRS 13 are intended to provide financial statement users with additional insight into the relative subjectivity of various fair value measurements and enhance their ability to broadly assess an entity's quality of earnings.

FIGURE 8.1 Disclosure requirements — valuation processes used for fair value measurements categorised within Level 3

b) Valuation governance

UBS's fair value measurement and model governance framework includes numerous controls and other procedural safeguards that are intended to maximize the quality of fair value measurements reported in the financial statements. New products and valuation techniques must be reviewed and approved by key stakeholders from the risk and finance control functions. Responsibility for the ongoing measurement of financial and non-financial instruments at fair value is with the business divisions.

Fair value estimates are validated by the risk and finance control functions, which are independent of the business divisions. Independent price verification is performed by Finance through benchmarking the business divisions' fair value estimates with observable market prices and other independent sources. A governance framework and associated controls are in place in order to monitor the quality of third-party pricing sources where used. For instruments where valuation models are used to determine fair value, independent valuation and model control groups within Finance and Risk Control evaluate UBS's models on a regular basis, including valuation and model input parameters, as well as pricing. As a result of the valuation controls employed, valuation adjustments may be made to the business divisions' estimates of fair value to align with independent market data and the relevant accounting standard.

›**Refer to Note 21d for more information**

Source: UBS Group AG Annual Report 2023, note 21 sub b, p 366.

e) Level 3 instruments: valuation techniques and inputs

The table below presents material Level 3 assets and liabilities, together with the valuation techniques used to measure fair value, the inputs used in a given valuation technique that are considered significant as of 31 December 2023 and unobservable, and a range of values for those unobservable inputs

The range of values represents the highest- and lowest-level inputs used in the valuation techniques. Therefore, the range does not reflect the level of uncertainty regarding a particular input or an assessment of the reasonableness of the Group's estimates and assumptions, but rather the different underlying characteristics of the relevant assets and liabilities held by the Group. The ranges will therefore vary from period to period and parameter to parameter based on characteristics of the instruments held at each balance sheet date. Furthermore, the ranges of unobservable inputs may differ across other financial institutions, reflecting the diversity of the products in each firm's inventory.

Valuation techniques and inputs used in the fair value measurement of Level 3 assets and liabilities

USD bn	Fair value — Asen 31.12.23	Asen 31.12.22	Liabilities 31.12.23	Liabilities 31.12.22	Valuation technique(s)	Significant unobservable Input(s)	Range of Inputs 31.12.23 low	31.12.23 high	31.12.23 weighted average[2]	31.12.22 low	31.12.22 high	31.12.22 weighted average[2]	unit[1]
Financial assets and liabilities at fair value held for trading and Financial assets at fair value not held far trading													
Corporate and municipal bonds	1.5	0.8	0.1	0.0	Relative value to market comparable	Bond price equivalent	5	126	99	14	112	85	points
					Discounted expected cash flaws	Discount margin	135	491	463	412	412	200	basis points
Traded loans, loans measured at fair value, loan commitments and guarantees	22.0	1.7	0.0	0.0	Relative value to market comparable	Loan price equivalent	1	120	88	30	100	97	points
					Discounted expected cash flows	Credit spread	19	2,681	614	200	200	200	basis points
					Market comparable and securitization model	Credit spread	162	1,849	318	145	1,350	322	basis points
					Option model	Gap risk	0	2	0				%
Auction rate securities	1.2	1.3			Discounted expected cash flows	Credit spread	135	205	150	115	196	144	basis points
Investment fund units[3]	0.8	0.3	0.0	0.0	Relative value to market comparable	Net asset value							
Equity instruments[3]	3.4	0.9	0.1	0.1	Relative value to market comparable	Price							
Debt issued designated at fair value[4]			15.3	10.5									

The following table reproduces the ranges of significant unobservable inputs, valuation techniques and related fair-value amounts. Numeric columns (left-to-right) represent the fair-value amounts (in italics), the range of significant unobservable inputs for the two reporting dates, and the unit of measure.

Instrument	Fair-value amounts	Valuation technique	Significant unobservable inputs	Low	High	Low	High	Unit
Other financial liabilities designated at fair value	*2.6* *0.7* / *0.4* *0.5*	Discounted expected cash flows	Funding spread	**51**	**201**	23	175	basis points
Derivative financial instruments								
Interest rate	*0.2* *0.1* / *0.5* *0.3*	Option model	Volatility of interest rates	**45**	**154**	75	143	basis points
			Volatility of inflation	**1**	**6**			%
			IR-to-IR correlation	**4**	**100**			%
Credit	*0.6* *0.3* / *0.5* *0.3*	Discounted expected cash flows	Credit spreads	**1**	**2,421**	9	565	basis points
			Credit correlation	**50**	**66**			%
			Credit volatility	**60**	**60**			%
			Bond price equivalent	**2**	**242**	3	277	points
			Recovery rates	**14**	**100**			%
		Option model	Credit spreads	**26**	**2,159**			basis points
Equity/index	*3.3* *1.2* / *1.3* *0.7*	Option motel	Equity dividend yields	**0**	**17**	0	20	%
			Volatility of equity stocks, equity and other indices	**4**	**142**	4	120	%
			Equity-to-FX correlation	**(40)**	**77**	(29)	84	%
			Equity-to-equity correlation	**(50)**	**100**	(25)	100	%
Loan commitments measured at FVTPL	*1.0*	Relative value to market comparable	Loan price equivalent	**35**	**102**			points

1 The ranges of significant unobservable inputs are represented in points, percentages and basis points. Points are a percentage of par (e.g., 100 points would be 100% of par). 2 Weighted averages are provided for most non-derivative financial instruments and were calculated by weighting inputs based on the fair values of the respective instruments. Weighted averages are not provided for inputs related to Other financial liabilities designated at fair value and Derivative financial instruments, as this would not be meaningful. 3 The range of inputs is not disclosed, as there is a dispersion of values given the diverse nature of the investments. 4 Debt issued designated at fair value primarily consists of UBS structured notes, which include variable maturity notes with various equity and foreign exchange underlying risks, as well as rates-linked and credit-linked notes, all of which have embedded derivative parameters that are considered to be unobservable The equivalent derivative instrument parameters far debt issued or embedded derivatives la over-the-counter debt instruments are presented in the respective derivative financial instruments lines in this table.

Source: UBS Group AG Annual Report 2023, note 21 sub e). pp 273–374.

8.8 SUMMARY

The debate over the best measurement method for assets and liabilities is not a new one. Discussions of the decision usefulness of various models of current value accounting have occupied many pages in accounting journals and were the focus of the research of many academics. Historically, accounting standards have relied primarily on the use of historical cost, but the use of fair values has become increasingly common, particularly with the focus on financial instruments. The standard setters therefore decided that it was time to produce an accounting standard on fair value measurement, with the focus on how to measure fair value rather than on when to use those fair values. This has resulted in the issue of IFRS 13 by the IASB.

A key feature of the definition is that fair value is a current exit price, rather than an entry price.

The fair value framework in IFRS 13 is based on a number of key concepts including unit of account, exit price, valuation premise, highest and best use, principal market, market participant assumptions and the fair value hierarchy. The requirements incorporate financial theory and valuation techniques, but are focused solely on how these concepts are to be applied when determining fair value for financial reporting purposes. Critical to the measurement process are the assumptions that market participants make when using a valuation technique. The assumptions or inputs are classified into three levels, the classification being based on the use of observable and unobservable inputs. In choosing a valuation technique an entity should seek to maximise the number of observable inputs used.

A key element of IFRS 13 is the requirement to disclose sufficient information about the fair value measures used. Users of financial statements should be able to assess the methods and inputs used to develop the fair value measurements and the effects on (comprehensive) income.

Discussion questions

1. Name three current accounting standards that permit or require the use of fair values.
2. What are the main objectives of IFRS 13?
3. What are the key elements of the definition of 'fair value'?
4. How does entry price differ from exit price?
5. Is the reporting entity a market participant?
6. Does the measurement of fair value take into account transport costs and transaction costs? Explain.
7. What are the key steps in measuring fair value?
8. Explain the difference between the current use of an asset and the highest and best use of that asset.
9. Explain the difference between the in-combination valuation premise and the stand-alone valuation premise.
10. What is the difference between the principal market for an asset or liability and its most advantageous market?
11. What valuation techniques are available to measure fair value?
12. Explain the fair value hierarchy.
13. Explain the different levels of fair value inputs.
14. How does the measurement of the fair value of a liability differ from that of an asset?
15. How do climate-related risks affect fair value measurement?

References

EY, International GAAP 2024® edition

IASB Staff 2023, Educational material *Effects of climate-related matters on financial statements*, effects-of-climate-related-matters-on-financial-statements.pdf (ifrs.org) London, July 2023.

Fair value measurement has increasingly replaced the historical cost measurement basis. One major concern for academic research has been whether fair value accounting is value relevant and sufficiently reliable. Historical cost accounting (HCA) is typically verifiable as it is based on past evidence (e.g. an invoice confirming the purchase cost of an asset). In contrast, by construction, fair value accounting is based on unrealised gains or losses. Moreover, fair value measurement may be based on unobservable and subjective inputs, as is the case, for example, with Level 3 inputs. Landsman (2007) provides a good discussion on the value relevance and reliability of fair value accounting, although his review of related empirical research precedes more recent rules and studies. Beatty and Liao's (2014) review of accounting in banks is also a very useful source of detailed discussion of issues related to fair value accounting.

Since the use of fair value accounting is more pronounced in financial firms, such as banks, early research has examined the value relevance of fair value accounting mostly in banks. Barth (1994) finds that fair value gains and losses on investment securities provide incremental explanatory power for stock returns over that of historical cost gains and losses. Nelson (1996) examines fair value disclosures in banks' financial statements but fails to find evidence that these disclosures are value relevant over historical cost measures. In contrast Eccher et al. (1996) and Barth et al. (1996) find that fair value disclosures are incorporated into share prices. Livne et al. (2011) examine assets that are recognised and measured at fair value. Their evidence suggests that the unrealised component of fair values of investment securities is positively associated with stock returns, but the historical cost component is not. This result is intriguing because the unrealised component is precisely the part in the fair value measure that may be susceptible to managerial discretion and manipulation. Yet, boards seem to doubt the reliability of fair values. DeFond et al. (2020) find that changes in fair values do not affect executive compensation to the same extent as performance measures that are based on HCA.

Evans et al. (2014) provide evidence that the unrealised component in fair value measurement has predictive ability with respect to future income and cash flows. This may explain the association of unrealised gains and losses with returns in that investors use this information to value shares. Consistent with the evidence in Livne et al. (2011), Evans et al. (2014) also show that unrealised gains and losses are associated with market value of equity. Beaver and Venkatachalam (2003) find that whether the discretionary component in fair value measurement (i.e. the unrealised gain or loss) is value relevant is dependent on managers' reporting incentives. They provide some evidence suggesting that when the discretionary component is measured in opportunistic fashion, investors find it less relevant than when opportunism does not play a role.

Does this evidence then suggest that historical cost accounting is not useful? An answer can be found by taking advantage of the accounting rules for available-for-sale (AFS) securities. These require that gains and losses arising upon the disposal of AFS assets are recorded on historical cost basis.

But, at the same time AFS securities are measured on the balance sheet at fair value. If historical cost accounting is superfluous when fair value accounting is used, it is not expected that historical cost measures of realised gains and losses would be value relevant incrementally over fair value measures of the underlying assets. Dong et al. (2014), however, show that these historical cost measures are incrementally value relevant. They conclude that historical cost measures can still be value relevant when fair value accounting is used. More recently, McInnis et al. (2018) analyse the relative usefulness of fair value accounting against HCA in banks. They find that HCA better explains share prices and returns than financial statement using fair value accounting.

IFRS 13, and SFAS 157 in the US (also known as ASC Topic 820), set fair value hierarchy as described in this chapter. Several researchers have conjectured that the value relevance and reliability of fair value decreases from Level 1 to Level 3. However, the evidence on this is quite mixed. Song et al. (2010) examine quarterly reports of banks in 2008 and find evidence consistent with this conjecture. In contrast, Altamuro and Zhang (2013) examine mortgage services rights that are fair-valued and find that Level 3 is more value relevant.

The relevance and reliability of Level 2 and Level 3 may be a function of both noisy inputs, as well as managerial discretion. Altamuro and Zhang (2013) argue that managers can convey useful information using their discretion in Level 3 reporting and that this effect may be more pronounced when the underlying asset is not traded in an active market. Song et al. (2010) find that the value relevance of Level 3 fair values increases with the strength of corporate governance. Taken together, this suggests that opportunism plays a role but can be constrained by board monitoring.

Relying on markets to supply objective inputs into fair value measurement can introduce noise even absent discretion and corporate governance effects. Banks often rely on market-based indices when valuing mortgage portfolios. Stanton and Wallace (2011) show that the pricing of a leading default risk index used by many banks in marking-to-market loan portfolios was inconsistent with reasonable assumptions about future default rates. They argue that, consequently, certain banks that relied on this index wrote off billions of dollars' worth of assets during the financial crisis of 2008, potentially unnecessarily.

The above-mentioned research is mostly focused on fair value accounting for financial assets and liabilities. However, fair value accounting is also employed in non-financial assets (see also the Academic Perspective to chapter 5). Aboody et al. (1999) examine revaluations of property plant and equipment under UK GAAP (prior to IFRS adoption in 2005). They provide evidence that the revalued balances of these assets are positively associated with share prices and that changes in revaluation amounts are positively associated with stock returns. They also provide evidence suggesting that revaluations predict future performance. Liang and Riedl (2014) examine the value relevance of unrealised gains and losses recorded when investment properties are measured at fair value. They find that analyst forecasts of EPS are less accurate when investment properties are measured at fair value than when they are measured at historical cost. However, analysts are better able to forecast the balance sheet for firms employing the fair value model.

References

Aboody, D., Barth, M., and Kasznik, R., 1999. Revaluations of fixed assets and future firm performance: evidence from the UK. Journal of Accounting and Economics, 26, 149–178.

Altamuro, A., and Zhang, H., 2013. The financial reporting of fair value based on managerial inputs versus market inputs: evidence from mortgage servicing rights. Review of Accounting Studies, 18, 833–858.

Barth, M., 1994. Fair value accounting: evidence from investment securities and the market valuation of banks. The Accounting Review, 69, 1–25.

Barth, M., Beaver, W., and Landsman, W., 1996. Value-relevance of banks' fair value disclosures under SFAS No. 107. The Accounting Review, 71, 513–537.

Beatty, A., and Liao, S., 2014. Financial accounting in the banking industry: a review of the empirical literature. Journal of Accounting and Economics, 58, 339–383.

Beaver, W., and Venkatachalam, M., 2003. Differential pricing of components of bank loan fair values. Journal of Accounting, Auditing and Finance, 18, 41–67.

DeFond, M., Hu, J., Hung, M., and Li, S., 2020. The effect of fair value accounting on the performance evaluation role of earnings. Journal of Accounting and Economics, 70(2–3), 101341.

Dong, M., Ryan, S., and Zhang, X.-J., 2014. Preserving amortized costs within a fair-value-accounting framework: reclassification of gains and losses on available-for-sale securities upon realization. Review of Accounting Studies, 19, 242–280.

Eccher, E., Ramesh, K., and Thiagarajan, S., 1996. Fair value disclosures by bank holding companies. Journal of Accounting and Economics, 22, 79–117.

Evans, M.E., Hodder, L., and Hopkins, P.E., 2014. The predictive ability of fair values for future financial performance of commercial banks and the relation of predictive ability to banks' share prices. Contemporary Accounting Research, 31, 13–44.

Landsman, W., 2007. Is fair value accounting information relevant and reliable? Evidence from capital market research. Accounting and Business Research, 37, 19–30.

Liang, L., and Riedl, E., 2014. The effect of fair value versus historical cost reporting model on analyst forecast accuracy. The Accounting Review, 89, 1151–1177.

Livne, G., Markarian, G., and Milne, A., 2011. Bankers' compensation and fair value accounting. Journal of Corporate Finance, 17, 1096–1115.

McInnis, J. M., Yu, Y., and Yust, C. G., 2018. Does fair value accounting provide more useful financial statements than current GAAP for banks?. The Accounting Review, 93(6), 257–279.

Nelson, K.K., 1996. Fair value accounting for commercial banks: an empirical analysis of SFAS 107. The Accounting Review, 161–182.

Song, C., Thomas, W., and Yi, H., 2010. Value relevance of FAS 157 fair value hierarchy information and the impact of corporate governance mechanisms. The Accounting Review, 85, 1375–1410.

Stanton, R., and Wallace, N., 2011. The Bear's lair: index credit defaults swaps and the subprime mortgage crisis. Review of Financial Studies, 24, 3250–3280.

9 Leases

ACCOUNTING STANDARDS IN FOCUS	IFRS 16 *Leases*

LEARNING OBJECTIVES

After studying this chapter, you should be able to:

1. explain the main accounting challenge for leases
2. discuss the background of the current lease accounting standard
3. explain the scope of the standard and the lessee exemptions
4. discuss the definition of a lease and apply the definition to identify a lease
5. account for leases from the perspective of a lessee
6. describe the presentation and disclosure requirements for a lessee
7. understand and apply the guidance necessary to classify leases from the perspective of a lessor
8. account for finance leases from the perspective of a lessor
9. account for finance leases by manufacturer or dealer lessors
10. account for operating leases from the perspective of a lessor
11. explain and account for sale and leaseback transactions.

9.1 INTRODUCTION

A lease is a contract where the owner of an asset — the lessor — grants another party — the lessee — the right to use that asset. In exchange for this right (known as a right-of-use asset), the lessee makes periodic payments to the lessor. While the lessor typically maintains legal ownership of the asset, it is the lessee who benefits from its use during the lease term. Leasing is a popular financing instrument in business, because of the flexibility and other advantages over ownership that it offers.

The accounting challenge for leases revolves around capturing the economic substance of lease contracts to maintain comparability. Essentially, a lease can resemble either a legal purchase or a rental agreement. Previously, accounting standards attempted to separate leases into two categories: finance leases and operating leases. Finance leases were treated similarly to asset purchases, while operating leases were expensed similarly to rentals, without recognising the leased asset and liability. However, this approach raised concerns about transparency and comparability, particularly in the accounting by lessees. The current lease accounting standard, IFRS 16, was introduced to address these concerns. This standard abolishes the distinction between finance and operating leases for lessees, but retains it for lessors.

The next section discusses the background of lease accounting and the continuing debate surrounding this topic. After that, the chapter discusses the requirements for lessees under IFRS 16. Lessor accounting is discussed in the final sections.

9.2 BACKGROUND OF CURRENT LEASE ACCOUNTING

Leasing gained popularity in the 1970s as a way to access the economic benefits of assets. However, concerns arose among standard setters and stakeholders worldwide regarding the usefulness of financial reports due to extensive use of off-balance-sheet arrangements. In response, leasing standards were issued by both international and national standard-setting bodies in the 1980s.

The first lease accounting standard issued by the International Accounting Standards Board (IASB), IAS 17, was introduced in 1982 and was used for several decades without any substantial changes. The standard required companies to classify leases as either finance leases or operating leases. A lease was treated as a finance lease if it transferred substantially all risks and rewards incidental to ownership to the lessee. This meant treating the lease as equivalent to the purchase of an asset on credit by the lessee, and as a sale or financing by the lessor. The justification for recognising the asset and liability relating to a finance lease was twofold. Firstly, although legally the lessee may not acquire legal title to the leased asset, in substance and financial reality, the lessee gains the economic benefits of the asset for most of its economic life, in return for an obligation to pay an amount approximating the fair value of the asset and related finance charge. Secondly, failure to reflect such lease transactions in the lessee's statement of financial position would understate the entity's economic resources and level of obligations, distorting financial ratios. Only those leases that did not meet the criteria for a finance lease would be classified as operating leases and were treated as an executory arrangement, with lessees recognising no asset or liability on their statement of financial position.

Under IAS 17, many lease obligations were kept off the balance sheet, raising concerns regarding transparency and comparability. Moreover, the distinction between finance and operating leases was criticised as arbitrary, permitting manipulation. Critics contended that IAS 17 understated lessees' assets and liabilities, thereby failing to offer a faithful representation of their financial position. Despite these criticisms, the standard remained essentially unchanged. It was not until 2006, the IASB and the Financial Accounting Standards Board (FASB) in the United States jointly added a leasing project to their respective agendas, recognising the need to address concerns about off-balance-sheet financing and improve transparency in financial reporting. However, the proposed changes faced considerable pushback from industry and practice, particularly regarding the idea of capitalising all leases for lessees.

The comments led to extensive deliberations and revisions over the years. In 2009, a discussion paper titled 'Leases — Preliminary Views' was issued, laying out initial proposals and seeking feedback from stakeholders. The discussion paper proposed a 'right of use' model to leasing, which was fundamentally different from the 'substance over form' approach of IAS 17. Due to the focus on rights of use, the new standard developed in a direction that would have a much bigger impact on lessees than on lessors. The discussion paper was followed by nearly identical exposure drafts (EDs) of a proposed, converged new standard on leases in 2010. However, significant differences in opinion and concerns about the potential impact on various industries led to prolonged discussions and revisions.

Recognising virtually all leases on balance sheets, as proposed in the discussion paper, was highly controversial because it would significantly impact financial reporting. Companies heavily reliant on leasing, such as retailers, airlines and transportation firms, were particularly concerned. Capitalising leases would increase reported assets and liabilities, potentially affecting debt covenants, credit ratings and investor perceptions. Moreover, it would require significant changes in accounting systems and processes.

After years of deliberation and redeliberation, the IASB issued its new standard, IFRS 16 *Leases*, in 2016. This standard represented a significant departure from previous lease accounting standards, particularly for lessees. Effective from 1 January 2019, IFRS 16 requires lessees to recognise right-of-use assets and lease liabilities for most leases. Lessees applying IFRS have a single accounting model for all leases, with exemptions for leases of 'low-value assets' and short-term leases. Lessor accounting for IFRS reporters is substantially unchanged from the previous accounting standard, IAS 17.

Although the lease accounting project started as a joint project with the intention to converge, the differences in opinion and approaches between the IASB and the FASB led to the development of separate lease accounting standards. The FASB issued a new standard, ASC 842 *Leases* in 2016, which introduced changes to lease accounting under US GAAP. While both IFRS 16 and ASC 842 require lessees to recognise right-of-use assets and lease liabilities on the balance sheet, there are important differences in expense recognition for lessees. Under IFRS 16, lessees recognise depreciation of the right-of-use asset and interest expense on the lease liability separately. In contrast, under US GAAP (ASC 842), there remains a distinction between finance leases and operating leases for lessees, albeit with changes to classification criteria. For finance leases, lessees recognise interest expense on the lease liability and amortise the right-of-use asset. For operating leases, however, lease expense is recognised on a straight-line basis over the lease term and is reported as a single lease expense in the income statement, rather than separately recognising interest and amortisation expenses. This means that, although both standards require leases to be recognised on the balance sheet, the treatment of lease-related expenses, and thereby the reporting of financial performance, is different.

The extensive debate and remaining differences in standards underscore the complexity and impact of lease accounting.

9.3 SCOPE AND LESSEE EXEMPTIONS

IFRS 16 should be applied to account for all leases, with a few exceptions. These exceptions include leases related to the exploration for and use of non-regenerative natural resources (such as oil, gas and minerals) and certain licencing agreements (such as motion pictures, patents, and other intellectual property within the scope of IAS 38 *Intangible Assets*, or licences granted by the lessor within the scope of IFRS 15 *Revenue from Contracts with Customers*). Additionally, certain service concession arrangements and leases of biological assets accounted for under IAS 41 *Agriculture* are also exempt.

For some leases that fall within the scope of IFRS 16, a lessee may be able to simplify its accounting for that lease. The standard provides exemptions for leases of short-term and low-value assets (paragraph 5 of IFRS 16). Short-term leases, with a lease term of 12 months or less, are allowed not to be recognised as lease assets and liabilities on their balance sheets. Instead, lease payments can be recognised as expenses on a straight-line basis over the lease term (or on another systematic basis if more appropriate). For low-value assets, typically valued at $5,000 or less when new, lessees can also opt not to recognise lease assets and liabilities, instead recognising lease payments as expenses. These exemptions aim to simplify accounting for leases of lower significance, reducing administrative burden for lessees.

9.4 WHAT IS A LEASE?

Under IFRS 16, a lease is defined as 'a contract, or part of a contract, that conveys the right to use an asset (the underlying asset) for a period of time in exchange for consideration' (IFRS 16 *Leases*, Appendix A). This definition applies to all rights of use, regardless of the legal nature of the contract, including leases, rentals, hires, hire-purchases and service agreements. At the inception of the contract, customers (lessees) and suppliers (lessors) should verify whether the contract is or contains a lease. Determining if a contract is or contains a lease dictates whether it is recorded on or off the statement of financial position for a customer (lessee) at the commencement date of the lease.

Note that in the context of IFRS 16, the inception date and the commencement date are two important concepts that should not be confused. The inception date refers to the date when a lease is agreed upon by the parties involved, typically when the lease contract is signed or when the lessee commits to lease the asset under the terms of the contract. The commencement date is the date when the lessee actually gains the right to use the leased asset. In other words, the inception date marks the beginning of the lease contract itself, while the commencement date marks the beginning of the lease term, when the lessee starts using the asset. It may be the same date as the inception of the lease or a later date.

Entities should evaluate whether a contract contains separate components to determine how to account for them under IFRS 16. A contract can contain multiple lease components and non-lease components that should be identified and separated. For example, if a contract grants the rights to use multiple assets, such as a building and equipment, each asset is considered a separate lease component if certain criteria are met. Firstly, the lessee must be able to benefit from the use of the asset either independently or with other readily available resources, such as goods or services that can be leased or purchased separately. Secondly, the underlying asset should not be highly dependent on or interrelated with other assets in the contract. Once identified as a lease component, it should be accounted for separately from other components of the contract. If the criteria are not met, the multiple assets are treated as a single lease component. Non-lease components are typically identified by considering whether they represent goods or services that are distinct from the right to use the underlying asset.

However, IFRS 16 paragraph 15 allows a lessee to simplify accounting by choosing, for each class of underlying asset, not to separate non-lease components from lease components. Instead, as a practical expedient, the lessee can treat both the lease and associated non-lease components as a single lease component.

Illustrative example 9.1 applies the criteria for identifying separate lease components.

ILLUSTRATIVE EXAMPLE 9.1 Identifying separate lease components

Scenario 1: The lessee operates a woodworking shop and leases a specialised CNC (computer numerical control) router for carving original designs into wooden furniture. This type of router is used in advanced woodworking machinery, but the equipment is sensitive and needs special maintenance. Along with the CNC router, the lessee leases a high-pressure cleaner specifically designed for cleaning woodworking equipment, that is offered in combination with the CNC router only. The CNC router requires specialised cleaning due to the fine sawdust generated during operation, and therefore a specific cleaning machine tailored for woodworking equipment is needed. The cleaning machine does not have an alternative use within the context of the lessee's operations.

Assessment: The cleaning machine is tailored for cleaning woodworking equipment such as the CNC router. Therefore, the cleaning machine is only useful for the lessee in combination with the other asset in the contract: the CNC router. Thus, from the perspective of the lessee, the contract contains one lease component.

Scenario 2: In another scenario, the lessee operates a construction company and leases a heavy-duty excavator for digging foundations on construction sites. Along with the excavator, the lessee leases a specialised cleaning machine specifically designed for heavy equipment. Similar cleaners are sold elsewhere. The high-pressure cleaner has an alternative use, as it can be used for cleaning a wide range of surfaces, including outdoor surfaces and other equipment and vehicles that the lessee owns.

Assessment: The cleaning machine has alternative use and can be used independently from the excavator. The lessee can benefit from the cleaner by cleaning other equipment and surfaces. Therefore, from the perspective of the lessee, the contract contains two lease components: the lease of the excavator and the cleaning machine. The use of the excavator and the specialised cleaning machine should be accounted for as separate lease components.

Verifying whether a contract is or contains a lease is usually straightforward. However, judgement may be necessary in applying the definition, especially in more complex arrangements. The key elements of the definition of a lease can be summarised in three questions that together constitute a test to determine whether a contract is or contains a lease:
1. Is there an identified asset?
2. Does the customer have the right to obtain substantially all of the economic benefits from use of the identified asset?
3. Does the customer have the right to direct the use of the identified asset?

The first question establishes whether a specific asset is the subject of the contract and ensures that the asset can be distinctly identified. This is the foundational step because, without an identified asset, there can be no lease. The second and third question determine whether the contract grants the lessee control over the use of the asset. In general, this is the case when the lessee has the right to obtain the economic benefits from using the assets and has the authority to control how and for what purpose the asset is used throughout the lease period. If each of the three questions is answered with 'yes', the contract is or contains a lease and the lessee would apply the lease accounting model set out in the standard. Once it is determined that a contract is or contains a lease, the accounting is determined by other important elements of the definition, i.e. (4) the period of time, usually called the lease term, and (5) the consideration (lease payments and other payments in a lease contract). Each of these 5 elements is discussed in more detail in the remainder of this section.

9.4.1 Identified asset

The first step in determining if a contract between a customer and a supplier constitutes a lease is to establish whether there is an identified asset. If the leased asset is explicitly specified in the contract, this step may be straightforward. However, there may be more complicated situations, for example when the asset is implicitly specified, when an asset is partially leased or when the leased asset may be substituted by another asset. In this section, we briefly discuss each of these situations.

The underlying asset is often *explicitly* specified in a contract. For example, in the case of the lease of a car, the contract would specify details such as the registration or chassis number, manufacturer and model. An asset can also be *implicitly* specified when it becomes available for use. For example, if the leased car has yet to be manufactured at the inception of the agreement, the contract may outline key characteristics like the model, colour, and optional features. Based on these characteristics, the car becomes identifiable when it is made available to the customer. In other words, the car is identified by being implicitly specified at the time it is made available for use by the customer (paragraph B13 of IFRS 16).

In some cases, a customer leases only a portion of an asset, such as a floor in a building or a portion of the capacity of a pipeline. According to IFRS 16 a portion of an asset can be considered an identified asset if it is physically distinct (like the office space in the larger building) or represents substantially all of the capacity of the asset (for example when assessing whether the portion of the capacity of the pipeline represents substantially all of the capacity).

Another situation in which it is more complicated to establish whether there is an identified asset, is when the supplier retains the right to substitute the leased asset. For example if a customer leases a large number of cars or printers, it is not uncommon that the supplier has the right to replace these assets. For this type of agreement, it is important to assess whether the supplier's right to replace the leased asset effectively means that the customer does not control the use of the asset. If both of the following conditions are met, the supplier's substitution rights are considered substantive, meaning that the customer does not control the use of the asset (paragraph B14 of IFRS16):

- the supplier has the practical ability to substitute alternative assets throughout the period of use; and
- the supplier would benefit economically from the exercise of its right to substitute the asset.

Illustrative example 9.2 demonstrates how to determine whether a contract contains an identified asset and to clarify the role of the supplier's substitution rights under IFRS 16. Specifically, it highlights the difference between a contract that grants the customer control over specific assets (thus qualifying as a lease) and a contract where the supplier retains control and the ability to substitute assets (which does not qualify as a lease).

ILLUSTRATIVE EXAMPLE 9.2 Determining whether a contract contains an identified asset

Scenario A: Icarus Airfreight Ltd (the Customer) is a global logistics company specialising in air cargo transportation. They have a contract with Daedalus Corp (the Supplier) to use 10 specific cargo planes (Model X200, each identified by a unique registration number) for 5 years. These specific aircraft belong to Daedalus, but Icarus Airfreight controls when and where the planes fly and what goods they transport. When not in use, the planes are stationed at Icarus Airfreight's preferred airport facilities. The aircraft can also be used for storage, but they are restricted from transporting hazardous chemicals, such as flammable substances.

If one of the specific planes needs maintenance or repairs, Daedalus is required to provide a replacement plane of the same model (Model X200). However, the contract specifically states that substitution can only occur in these situations (repairs or maintenance). Apart from that, Daedalus cannot take back or swap the planes for different ones during the five-year contract period.

Assessment: The contract includes a lease for the 10 identified Model X200 planes because:

1. The planes are specifically identified in the contract by their registration numbers, and Daedalus cannot freely substitute them except when repairs or maintenance are needed. This makes them identified assets.
2. Icarus Airfreight has exclusive control over the specific planes during the five-year period and decides how and when they are used.
3. Although Daedalus provides pilots and crew, this does not affect Icarus Airfreight's control over the planes themselves.

Scenario B: In another contract, Icarus Airfreight agrees with Daedalus Corp for the transportation of a specific amount of cargo using Model X200 cargo planes for 5 years. The contract specifies the type of plane (Model X200), but it does not assign individual planes by registration numbers. Daedalus operates a large fleet of Model X200 planes and can substitute any of those planes to fulfil the contract.

Daedalus also benefits economically from this arrangement, as it can optimise the use of its fleet. For example, if a Model X200 plane is already positioned close to a scheduled flight's departure location, Daedalus can allocate that plane, reducing costs. Additionally, by rotating planes, Daedalus can make more efficient use of the fleet, minimising downtime and coordinating return flights, thus maximising plane utilisation.

Because Daedalus has a large pool of similar planes that are readily available, they can freely substitute planes as needed throughout the contract, without needing approval from Icarus Airfreight.

Assessment: This contract does not contain a lease because:

1. The planes are not identified assets (i.e., they are not assigned specific registration numbers); Daedalus can substitute any plane of the same model.
2. Daedalus has the practical ability to substitute the planes, as they are readily available from their fleet.
3. Daedalus benefits economically from this substitution right, as it allows them to optimise fleet usage, reduce costs by positioning planes strategically and improve efficiency through coordinated return flights.

Therefore, Daedalus retains control over which planes are used, and Icarus Airfreight is purchasing air cargo services, not leasing specific, identified planes.

9.4.2 Rights to economic benefits

The second question to determine whether a contract contains a lease, is 'Does the customer have the right to obtain substantially all of the economic benefits from use of the identified asset?' This question determines whether the customer is entitled to most of the economic benefits derived from using the asset.

The right to substantially all economic benefits is a necessary condition to control the use of the identified asset. This helps to confirm that the customer is effectively using the asset as if it were their own.

These benefits can come from using the asset or holding it for rental income. This means considering the primary output of the asset, any by-products, and other economic benefits from its use that could be gained through transactions with third parties, like sub-leasing. Benefits associated with asset ownership, such as income tax credits, are excluded from this evaluation. The lessee also considers only the economic benefits that fall within the defined scope of the right to use the asset. For example, if a contract restricts the use of a vehicle to a specific territory, only the economic benefits from using the vehicle within that territory are taken into account.

Illustrative example 9.3 provides a practical application of this criterion.

ILLUSTRATIVE EXAMPLE 9.3 Assessing the right to obtain substantially all of the economic benefits from use of the identified asset

Scenario: Cervantes, a utility company, enters into a 15-year agreement with Don Quixote, a power company, to buy all the electricity generated by a new wind farm. Don Quixote owns the wind farm and will receive tax credits related to its construction and ownership, while Cervantes will get renewable energy credits from using the wind farm.

Assessment: Cervantes benefits substantially from the wind farm over the 15-year period. The benefits it receives represent substantially all the economic benefits from the use of the wind farm:

- all the electricity generated by the farm during the lease term, which is the primary product;
- and renewable energy credits, which are a by-product of using the farm.

Although Don Quixote gets economic benefits in the form of tax credits from owning the wind farm, these are unrelated to the use of the wind farm. Therefore, the tax credits are not considered in this assessment.

9.4.3 Right to direct the use

The third and final step is to assess whether the customer has the right to direct the use of the identified asset. This is determined by considering who has the right to direct how and for what purpose the asset is used. A company considers the 'relevant' decision-making rights, which means that the decisions should affect the economic benefits derived from the use of the asset. Relevant decisions that determine the use of the asset include questions about *what* to produce, *when* to produce it, *where* production or delivery would take place and *how much* the asset should produce.

The assessment should determine who makes these relevant decisions: the customer or the supplier. Alternatively, the use of the asset might be specified and predetermined, for example in the contract. In short:

- If the <u>customer</u> has the right to direct how and for what purpose the asset is used, then the contract is (or contains) a lease;
- If the <u>supplier</u> has the right to direct how and for what purpose the asset is used, then the contract does not contain a lease;
- If the relevant decisions about how and for what purpose the asset is used are predetermined, further analysis is needed.

Decisions about how and for what purpose an asset is used can be predetermined in various ways. For example, these decisions might be set during contract negotiations between the customer and supplier, with no changes allowed after the lease starts. Alternatively, the design of the asset itself might dictate its use. However, it is rare for all decisions to be completely predetermined. When the relevant decisions are predetermined, the customer is considered to control the use of an identified asset if either of the following conditions is met (IFRS 16 paragraph B24.b):

1. Right to operate: The customer has the authority to operate the asset (or to instruct others on how to operate it) throughout the lease period, and the supplier does not have the right to alter those operating instructions.
2. Asset design: The customer was involved in designing the asset (or specific features of it) in a way that determines how and for what purpose it will be used for the duration of the lease.

To summarise the three key steps, figure 9.1 visualises the decision process to determine whether a contract is or constitutes a lease, or to identify a lease. It is based on the decision tree that is part of the application guidance in IFRS 16 (paragraph B31).

Illustrative example 9.4 provides a comprehensive example of the application of the lease definition to determine whether a contract is or contains a lease.

ILLUSTRATIVE EXAMPLE 9.4 Identification of a lease in a contract

Scenario: Thales Holding enters into an agreement with Miletus Company granting the use of a specific retail unit in a large shopping mall for 6 years. As the owner of the property, Miletus has retained the right to relocate the customer to another retail unit. If Miletus would require Thales to move to another retail unit, Miletus would have to cover the cost of the relocation. However, under these conditions, the likelihood of this relocation benefiting Miletus economically is low. Under the agreement, Thales is required to comply with the opening hours of the shopping mall and to exploit its shop and sell its goods during those hours. Thales can decide which goods it sells, as well as pricing and inventory quantities. Additionally, Thales can manage physical access to the unit throughout the six-year term. The agreement specifies that Thales pays a monthly rent that includes a fixed amount plus a percentage of sales from the unit.

Assessment: To determine whether the contract is, or contains, a lease, the three key questions should be answered.

1. Is there an identified asset?
   The retail unit is explicitly specified, and although the property owner Miletus (the supplier) can substitute it, this right is not substantive due to unlikely beneficial circumstances. Therefore, the retail unit is an identified asset.
2. Does the customer have the right to obtain substantially all of the economic benefits from use of the identified asset?
   Thales (the customer) has exclusive use of the unit, despite paying the property owner a portion of sales. Thus, Thales enjoys substantially all economic benefits from its use.
3. Does the customer have the right to direct the use of the identified asset?
   Thales (the customer) makes all decisions about how to use the unit during the lease. While the contract specifies selling hours, it doesn't restrict the customer's control over the unit's use.

Conclusion: The contract contains a lease of the retail space.

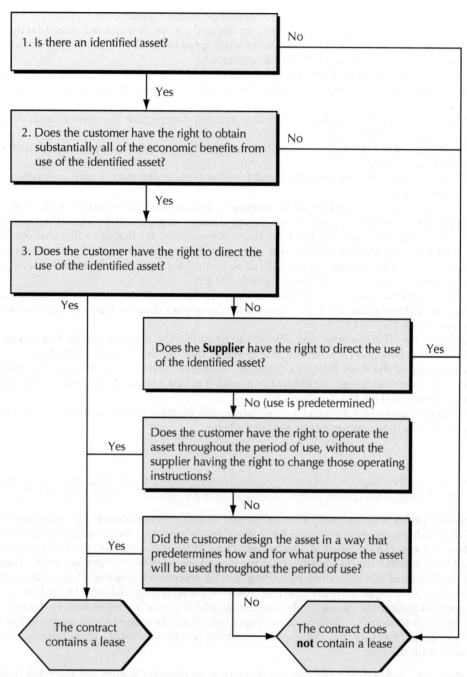

FIGURE 9.1 Decision tree to determine whether a contract is or contains a lease (based on IFRS 16 application guidance)

9.4.4 Lease term

Determining the length of the lease can be complex in contracts that contain options to cancel or renew the arrangements. Under IFRS 16, estimating the lease term is an essential element of the lease definition. For lessees, it determines the amount of the lease liability and the corresponding right-of-use asset. In addition, it determines whether the lease qualifies for the 'short-term'-lease exemption for lessees. For lessors, the lease term is a critical estimate for the classification of the lease. Determining the lease term is complex and requires a significant amount of judgement. The lease term is defined in IFRS 16 (Appendix A) as:

The non-cancellable period for which a lessee has the right to use an underlying asset, together with both:
(a) periods covered by an option to extend the lease if the lessee is reasonably certain to exercise that option; and
(b) periods covered by an option to terminate the lease if the lessee is reasonably certain not to exercise that option.

In other words, the lease term is the non-cancellable period of a lease, plus any optional periods that the lessee is reasonably certain to use. The lease term should reflect the company's reasonable expectation of the period during which the underlying asset will be used (paragraph BC 156 of IFRS 16). To determine the lease term, a company takes the following steps:

1. Determine the length of the non-cancellable period. This is the minimum length of the lease, because during this period the lessee has no option to terminate the lease.
2. Determine the maximum potential length of the lease. This is the enforceable period, which includes all optional periods in the lease that are enforceable. A lease arrangement is no longer enforceable when both the lessee and the lessor have the option to terminate it without permission of the other party and without a significant penalty.
3. Determine where — within the range between the minimum and maximum length of the lease — the lease term falls based upon the 'reasonably certain' tests described above.

When determining the length of the non-cancellable period and the enforceable period of a lease, an entity must consider both the definition of a contract and the period for which the contract is enforceable. According to IFRS 16, a contract is an agreement between two or more parties that creates enforceable rights and obligations. However, the interpretation of a contract can vary based on the contract law of the country where the lease is executed. For example, in some jurisdictions, there might be statutory provisions or legal precedents that allow for early termination of a lease under certain circumstances, even if the lease agreement specifies it as non-cancellable. Therefore, to determine the enforceability of a lease contract, both the written agreement and the legal framework provided by local laws and regulations that dictate the rights and responsibilities of the parties involved must be taken into account. Whether a contract is legally binding depends on the laws of the jurisdiction in question, and each contract must be assessed based on its specific terms and conditions. This example in lease accounting illustrates how international regulations work in conjunction with national laws and that the application of IFRS standards may interact with and depend on the legal context.

Deciding whether an extension or termination option is 'reasonably certain' involves substantial judgement. Both lessees and lessors must consider all relevant factors that create an economic incentive for the lessee to exercise such options. One critical consideration is the significance of the leased asset to the lessee's operations.

For example, a company leasing a specialised facility, such as a manufacturing plant or corporate headquarters, may heavily rely on that asset for its core activities. Opting not to renew the lease or purchase the facility could result in severe challenges, such as difficulty finding a suitable replacement, operational disruptions, increased costs, and lost revenue during the transition to a new location. These potential consequences, which amount to a significant economic penalty, make it more likely that the company will exercise the renewal or purchase option to avoid such risks.

This example also highlights how IFRS 16 requires taking a broad view of the term 'penalty' when assessing the lease term. Penalties from early termination are not limited to contractual termination payments but also include broader economic impacts. The standard emphasises considering the 'broader economics of the contract,' which means factoring in costs such as relocating, operational disruptions, damage to customer relationships, and lost revenue.

Simple lease contracts usually don't have any optional periods. In that case, the non-cancellable term, enforceable term and the lease term are all the same. For contracts with multiple optional periods, the relationship between the different terms is summarised in the diagram in figure 9.2 (based on a staff paper by the IFRS IC).

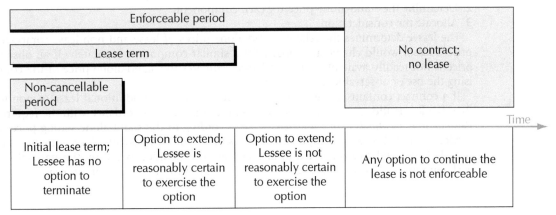

FIGURE 9.2 Determining Lease Term: Relationship Between Non-Cancellable and Enforceable Periods
Source: IFRS IC (2019, November). Agenda paper 4. Lease term and useful life of leasehold improvements (IFRS 16 and IAS 16). IFRS Foundation.

Illustrative example 9.5 demonstrates how to determine the lease term under IFRS 16 in case of termination rights in the lease agreement. The example focuses on the concept of the enforceable period and what constitutes a significant penalty that would make termination impractical for one of the parties.

ILLUSTRATIVE EXAMPLE 9.5 Determining the enforceable period

Apollo Diagnostics, a medical equipment supplier, leases a state-of-the-art MRI scanner to Artemis Health, a private hospital. The contract specifies an initial non-cancellable lease period of one year. After the first year, the lease automatically renews annually unless either party gives notice to terminate at least six weeks before the renewal date. Both Apollo and Artemis can terminate the lease at these intervals.

The contract specifies additional conditions that should be considered. If Artemis decides to terminate, it must cover the costs of returning the MRI scanner to Apollo's headquarters. These costs are substantial due to the machine's size, specialised packaging requirements, and the need for secure transportation. Additionally, installing a replacement MRI scanner involves significant expenses, including structural adjustments to the diagnostic room and hiring technicians to oversee the installation.

Artemis relies heavily on the scanner for its radiology department. Without it, the hospital would need to halt critical diagnostic services, leading to patient rescheduling, potential reputational damage, and a significant loss of revenue. While equivalent MRI scanners are available from other suppliers, transitioning would still involve considerable downtime and costs.

Apollo, on the other hand, faces no penalties or additional costs if the lease is terminated. It has a strong customer base and can easily lease the scanner to another healthcare provider.

Assessment of the lease term: Although both Apollo and Artemis have termination rights, Artemis is effectively bound by economic penalties that make termination impractical. These penalties include the high costs of returning the scanner, the expense and complexity of installing a replacement, and the financial impact of disrupted operations. Consequently, the lease is enforceable beyond the initial one-year period. The enforceable lease period is determined by when Artemis could terminate without incurring more-than-insignificant costs. Additional facts are needed to determine when this would occur.

9.4.5 Consideration

The consideration includes all payments in the lease agreement. Under IFRS 16, both the lessee and the lessor must allocate the total consideration in the lease contract to the lease and non-lease components, proportionately to the stand-alone price of each component. The following steps are taken to allocate the consideration:

1. Determine the consideration. Total consideration includes the costs related to the lease components (lease payments), costs related to non-lease components and other payments which are not separate components (e.g. payments relating to items such as taxes).
2. Determine the stand-alone price for each component.
3. Allocate the consideration.

The lessee determines the relative stand-alone prices of lease and non-lease components based on the price a lessor would charge a company for a similar component separately. If an observable stand-alone price is not readily available, then the lessee estimates the stand-alone price of the components, maximising the use of observable information.

If a contract contains a lease component and one or more additional lease or non-lease components, then the lessor allocates the consideration in the contract in accordance with the requirements of IFRS 15 *Revenue from Contracts with Customers* — i.e. according to the stand-alone selling prices of the goods and services included in each component. If the sum of the components does not equal the total consideration, IFRS 15 guidance is applied to allocate the consideration based on the stand-alone selling prices of each component. *The requirements of IFRS 15 are discussed in chapter 3 of this book.*

Illustrative example 9.6, taken from the examples provided in IFRS 16, shows how lessees identify and separate lease and non-lease components of a contract, and allocate consideration in the contract to the components (illustrative example 12 from IFRS 16).

Diogenes leases a bulldozer, a truck and a long-reach excavator to Zeno for use in Zeno's mining operations for 4 years. Diogenes also agrees to maintain each item of equipment throughout the lease term. The total consideration in the contract is €600,000, payable in annual instalments of €150,000, and a variable amount that depends on the hours of work performed in maintaining the long-reach excavator. The variable payment is capped at 2% of the replacement cost of the long-reach excavator. The consideration includes the cost of maintenance services for each item of equipment.

Zeno accounts for the non-lease components (maintenance services) separately from each lease of equipment applying paragraph 12 of IFRS 16. Zeno does not elect the practical expedient in paragraph 15 of IFRS 16. Zeno considers the requirements in paragraph B32 of IFRS 16 and concludes that the lease of the bulldozer, the lease of the truck and the lease of the long-reach excavator are each separate lease components. This is because:

(a) Zeno can benefit from the use of each of the three items of equipment on its own or together with other readily available resources (for example, Zeno could readily lease or purchase an alternative truck or excavator to use in its operations); and

(b) although Zeno is leasing all three items of equipment for one purpose (i.e., to engage in mining operations), the machines are neither highly dependent on, nor highly interrelated with, each other.

Zeno's ability to derive benefit from the lease of each item of equipment is not significantly affected by its decision to lease, or not lease, the other equipment from Diogenes. Consequently, Zeno concludes that there are three lease components and three non-lease components (maintenance services) in the contract. Zeno applies the guidance in paragraphs 13–14 of IFRS 16 to allocate the consideration in the contract to the three lease components and the non-lease components.

Several suppliers provide maintenance services for a similar bulldozer and a similar truck. Accordingly, there are observable stand-alone prices for the maintenance services for those two items of leased equipment. Zeno is able to establish observable stand-alone prices for the maintenance of the bulldozer and the truck of €32,000 and €16,000, respectively, assuming similar payment terms to those in the contract with Diogenes. The long-reach excavator is highly specialised and, accordingly, other suppliers do not lease or provide maintenance services for similar excavators. Nonetheless, Diogenes provides four-year maintenance service contracts to customers that purchase similar long-reach excavators from Diogenes. The observable consideration for those four-year maintenance service contracts is a fixed amount of €56,000, payable over 4 years, and a variable amount that depends on the hours of work performed in maintaining the long-reach excavator. That variable payment is capped at 2% of the replacement cost of the long-reach excavator. Consequently, Zeno estimates the stand-alone price of the maintenance services for the long-reach excavator to be €56,000 plus any variable amounts. Zeno is able to establish observable stand-alone prices for the leases of the bulldozer, the truck and the long-reach excavator of €170,000, €102,000, and €224,000, respectively.

Zeno allocates the fixed consideration in the contract (€600,000) to the lease and non-lease components as follows:

(in €)	Bulldozer	Truck	Long-reach excavator	Total
Lease	170,000	102,000	224,000	496,000
Non-lease				104,000
Total fixed consideration				600,000

Zeno allocates all of the variable consideration to the maintenance of the long-reach excavator, and, thus, to the non-lease components of the contract. Zeno then applies the guidance in IFRS 16 to account for each lease component, treating the allocated consideration as the lease payments for each lease component.

9.5 LESSEE ACCOUNTING

This section focuses on the requirements for the lessee, which is the entity that obtains the right to use an underlying asset. Related to this right, the lessee makes payments to the lessor (see figure 9.3).

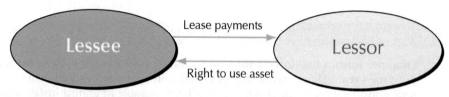

FIGURE 9.3 Lessee perspective

9.5.1 Initial measurement

When a contract is (or contains) a lease, the lessee must recognise a right-of-use asset representing its right to use the underlying asset and a lease liability representing its obligation to make payments at the commencement date of the lease. This requirement applies to all leases, except for short-term leases and leases of low value if the lessee chooses to apply the exemptions for these categories.

Right-of-use assets

Initially, a lessee measures the right-of-use asset at a cost that includes the following (IFRS 16, paragraph 24):
(a) The amount of the initial measurement of the lease liability.
(b) Any lease payments made to the lessor at or before the commencement date, less any lease incentives received from the lessor.
(c) Any initial direct costs incurred by the lessee.
(d) An estimate of the costs to be incurred by the lessee in dismantling and removing the underlying asset, restoring the site on which the underlying asset is located or restoring the underlying asset to the condition required by the terms and conditions of the lease, unless those costs are incurred to produce inventories.

The structure of this list is consistent with the cost of property, plant and equipment, as described in IAS 16 *Property, Plant and Equipment*. Similar to property, plant and equipment, cost at initial recognition consists of three elements: the cost of the asset, other direct costs and cost of dismantling the asset. However, for property, plant and equipment, the cost notion used to determine which costs can be attributed to the initial cost of the asset is broader than the 'incremental' direct cost in IFRS 16.

Initial direct costs are the incremental costs of obtaining the leased asset that would otherwise not have been incurred. The emphasis is on costs that are contingent on successfully obtaining the lease. An example of an initial direct cost is the so-called 'key money' in certain retail property leases, where a payment is made to the existing lessee in return for vacating the property. Costs incurred in the process of seeking a lease but are paid regardless of whether the lease is actually acquired are not considered initial direct costs (such as legal advice, professional fees, internal costs). This narrow definition of initial direct cost is similar to the incremental cost notion in IFRS 15 *Revenue from Contracts with Customers*. Both the lessee and the lessor apply the same definition of initial direct costs.

When a lessee first recognises a lease, costs related to dismantling, removing, or restoring the leased asset must be included as part of the right-of-use asset. This is because these costs are often an unavoidable part of using the asset. For example, if a company leases a building and needs to restore it to its original condition at the end of the lease, the estimated restoration costs are included in the asset's value. The corresponding liability for these costs is recognised separately and measured following IAS 37 *Provisions, Contingent Liabilities and Contingent Assets*.

The most significant part of the initial measurement of the right-of-use asset will normally be the amount of the lease liability (a). The measurement of the liability is central to the next section.

Lease liabilities

At the start of the lease (commencement date), the lessee calculates the lease liability as the present value of all future lease payments that have not yet been made. This means the lessee needs to discount the future lease payments to their value in today's terms. To do this, the lessee should use the interest rate implicit in the lease contract — if this rate can be readily determined. If the implicit rate cannot be determined, the lessee must use their own incremental borrowing rate instead (IFRS 16, paragraph 26). The standard provides a list of the amounts that must be included in the lease payments, to determine the lease liability (IFRS 16, paragraph 27):
(a) fixed payments, less any lease incentives receivable
(b) variable lease payments that depend on an index or a rate (e.g. payments linked to the consumer price index, a benchmark interest rate, change in market rentals), initially measured using the index or rate as at the commencement date

(c) amounts expected to be payable by the lessee under residual value guarantees

(d) the exercise price of a purchase option if the lessee is reasonably certain to exercise that option

(e) payments or penalties for terminating the lease if the lease term reflects the lessee exercising an option to terminate the lease.

Lease incentives received by the lessee reduce the net lease payments. A lease agreement with a lessor might offer incentives to the lessee to sign the lease, like providing an initial cash payment, covering expenses (like relocation costs), or taking over the lessee's existing lease with a third party. IFRS 16 defines lease incentives as payments made by a lessor to a lessee associated with a lease, or the reimbursement or assumption by a lessor of costs of a lessee.

A lessee may provide the lessor a guarantee that the value of the underlying asset, when returned at the end of the lease, will be at least a certain amount. These guarantees are enforceable obligations the lessee has assumed as part of the lease agreement. If it is expected that the lessee will have to pay the guaranteed amount, it will be included as a lease payment. However, an unguaranteed residual value is always excluded from the lessee's determination of lease payments.

In addition, lease arrangements may contain an option for the lessee to purchase the underlying asset at the end of the lease term. A purchase option is included as a lease payment if the lessee is reasonably certain to exercise it. When assessing whether a lessee is reasonably certain to exercise an option to purchase the underlying asset, the lessee considers all relevant facts and circumstances (both monetary and non-monetary) that create an economic incentive for the lessee to exercise or not exercise that option. This is similar to the assessment whether the lessee will extend the lease (or not exercise an option to terminate) when determining the lease term.

The lessee initially measures the lease liability at the present value of the lease payments to be made over the lease term. The discount rate used to determine the present value of the lease payments is the interest rate implicit in the lease, which is the rate that causes the equation in figure 9.4 to hold:

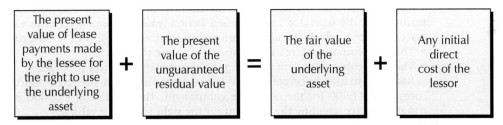

FIGURE 9.4 Interest rate implicit in the lease as defined by IFRS 16 (Appendix A)

Determining the interest rate implicit in a lease can be challenging for lessees due to several factors. Firstly, in most cases the implicit rate differs from the rate stated in the lease contract. Additionally, lessees often lack access to crucial information from the lessor, such as the lessor's initial direct costs, the initial fair value of the underlying asset and residual value estimates. Estimating the implicit rate is not allowed for lessees under the standard; it must be 'readily available'. As a result, it may be impossible for lessees to determine the implicit interest rate. The standard specifies that if that rate cannot be readily determined, the lessee should use the incremental borrowing rate as the discount rate. The incremental borrowing rate represents the interest that the lessee would pay to borrow funds over a similar term and with similar security to purchase the asset. Essentially, it serves as a substitute discount rate when the implicit rate is unavailable or challenging to ascertain.

Once the initial amount of the right-of-use asset and the lease liability have been established, the lessee recognises an asset and a liability at the commencement of the lease. In its simplest form, the entry is:

| Right-of-use asset | Dr | PV of lease payments | |
| Lease Liability | Cr | | PV of lease payments |

If the lessee incurs initial direct costs associated with negotiating and securing the lease arrangement, these costs are added to the amount recognised as an asset. The journal entry is:

Right-of-use asset	Dr	PV of lease payments plus initial direct cost	
Cash	Cr		Initial direct cost
Lease Liability	Cr		PV of lease payments

Illustrative example 9.7 demonstrates the initial recognition of a lease by the lessee.

On 31 December 2026, Poseidon Group leased a vehicle to Athena Company. Poseidon had purchased the vehicle on that day at an amount equal to its fair value of €89,721. At inception of the lease, Athena determines that the arrangement contains a lease. The vehicle is the identified (underlying) asset. The lease agreement, which cost Poseidon €1,457 to have drawn up, contained the following terms: This cost was disclosed during lease negotiations and included in the lease documentation provided by the lessor. In addition, Athena collected the following information in relation to the lease agreement:

Lease term	4 years
Annual payment, payable in advance on 31 December each year	€23,900
Economic life of vehicle	6 years
Residual value at end of lease term expected by lessor	€15,000
Residual value guaranteed by lessee	€7,500

If Athena terminates the lease before the end of the 4-year lease term, it will incur a monetary penalty equivalent to 2 years, rental payments. Included in the annual payments is an amount of €1,900 to cover reimbursement for the cost of maintenance paid by Poseidon.

At lease commencement, based on Athenas expected heavy use of the vehicle, Athena expects the vehicle to have a residual value of €0 at the end of the lease. Therefore, as a result of the guaranteed residual value, Athena determines it is reasonably certain that it will owe Poseidon €7,500 at the end of the lease.

Assessment:

1. *Identify and separating non-lease components*

The lease agreement includes an annual payment that reimburses maintenance costs, representing a service rather than the right to use an asset. IFRS 16 requires that payments for services, such as maintenance, be separated and classified as non-lease components. In this example, where the lease agreement for a vehicle includes maintenance services, the contract is divided into two components:
- The lease component, relating to the right to use the vehicle.
- The non-lease component, covering the maintenance services provided.

Based on market information, the lessee determined that the fixed annual payment of €23,900 consists of €1,900 for the non-lease component. The remaining €22,000 is allocated to the lease component, representing the payment for the right to use the vehicle.

2. *Determine the lease term*

Because Athena is required to pay a termination payment equivalent to the present value of the remaining lease payments, the lease is essentially non-cancellable as it is reasonably certain that Athena will not exercise the option to terminate the lease before the 4-year term specified in the contract. At lease commencement, Athena therefore concludes that the lease term is 4 years, as specified in the lease agreement.

3. *Determine lease payments*

The lease payments consist of:

Fixed lease payments, excluding non-lease component (maintenance)	an immediate payment €22,000 (being €23,900 – €1,900); and three subsequent payments of €22,000, payable annually on 31 December
Guaranteed residual value	an amount of €7,500 is part of the lease payments, because the expected residual value is lower than the guaranteed residual value. Therefore, €7,500 is the expected amount owed to Poseidon at the end of the fourth year

Lease payments do not include payments allocated to non-lease components of a contract, unless the lessee elects to combine non-lease components with a lease component and to account for them as a single component (paragraph 15 of IFRS 16). The penalties for terminating the lease are not included in the lease payments, because Athena determined that it is unlikely to terminate the lease before the 4-year term. The lessee expects that the residual value guarantee of €7,500 made to the lessor will result in an amount owed to the lessor of €7,500 at the end of the lease term. This amount is included as a lease payment in the calculation of the lease liability.

4. *Measure initial lease liability*

Athena determines the lease liability at the commencement of the lease as the present value of the lease payments to be made over the lease term. As discount rate, the lessee should use the rate implicit in the lease, if this can be readily determined. The implicit rate should be calculated from the perspective of the lessor, using the lessor specific information such as initial direct cost and estimated residual value. Based on the facts provided, Athena obtained the relevant information from the lessor during the lease negotiation process to calculate the implicit rate. The interest rate implicit in the lease is the rate that discounts the lease payments and the unguaranteed residual value to €91,178, which is the sum of the vehicle's fair value at 31 December 2026 of €89,721 and the initial direct costs (IDC) of €1,457 incurred by Poseidon Ltd. This rate is found by trial and error using present value tables or a financial calculator.

It can be determined that the implicit interest rate in this example is 7%, in which the following equation holds:

PV of lease payments made by the lessee	+	PV of the unguaranteed residual value	=	FV of the underlying asset	+	Initial direct cost of the lessor
€85,456.50	+	€5,721.50	=	€89,721	+	€1,457

Thus, the lease liability, calculated as PV of the lease payments discounted at 7%, is €85,456.50, of which €22,000 is paid immediately at commencement of the lease.

Note the following:
The present value of the lease payments is calculated as follows:

$$\text{PV of lease payments} = €22,000 + €22,000 \times \frac{1}{(1.07)} + €22,000 \times \frac{1}{(1.07)^2} + €22,000 \times \frac{1}{(1.07)^3}$$

$$+ €7,500 \times \frac{1}{(1.07)^4} = €85,456.50$$

Or, using the formula for an annuity (in advance):

$$\text{PV of lease payments} = €22,000 + €22,000 \times \frac{1-(1.07)^{-3}}{0.07} + €7,500 \times \frac{1}{(1.07)^4} = €85,456.50$$

The present value of the fixed lease payments is calculated as an annuity (in advance) based on three equal payments of €22,000 for the next 3 years at 7%. As the first payment is made at the inception of the lease, it is not discounted.

The present value of the unguaranteed residual value is based on a single amount of €7,500 at the end of the lease term (€15,000 residual value estimated by the lessor minus €7,500 residual value guarantee) in 4 years at a rate of 7%.

The present value of the lease payments plus unguaranteed residual value is €91,178 (€85,456.50 + €5,721.50), which is equal to the fair value (FV) plus IDC (€89,721 + €1,457), so the interest rate implicit in the lease is 7%.

5. *Measure initial right-of-use (ROU) asset*

Based on the previous steps, the right-of-use asset as at 31 December 2026 before the first lease payment can be determined as follows:

Initial measurement of lease liability	€85,456.50
Prepaid lease payments	—
Lease incentives (minus)	—
Lessee's initial direct costs	—
Estimated dismantling costs	(not applicable)
Total	**€85,456.50**

6. *Initial recognition of right-of-use asset and lease liability*

At the commencement of the lease, Athena would recognise the lease-related asset and liability as follows (rounded at euros)

Right-of-use asset — Vehicle	Dr	€85,457	
Lease liability	Cr		€85,457

9.5.2 Subsequent measurement

After initial recognition, IFRS 16 prescribes differing accounting treatments for the right-of-use asset and the lease liability.

Right-of-use assets

After initial recognition, the right-of-use asset is measured at cost, less accumulated depreciation and accumulated impairment losses and adjusted for any remeasurement of the lease liability (paragraph 29 of IFRS 16).

To depreciate the right-of-use asset, the lessee applies the requirements in IAS 16 *Property, Plant and Equipment*. The asset is depreciated over its useful life or the shorter lease term. The length of a right-of-use asset's depreciation period depends on whether or not ownership of the asset will transfer at the end of the lease term. If the asset is to be returned to the lessor, then depreciation will be allocated over the lease term. If ownership is reasonably certain to transfer to the lessee, then the right-of-use asset is depreciated over its useful life. Additionally, if the right-of-use asset consists of components with costs that are significant relative to the total asset, component depreciation applies, as required by IAS 16. This means the cost attributed to each significant part must be depreciated separately. Additionally, to determine whether a right-of-use asset has become impaired, the lessee must apply IAS 36 *Impairment of Assets*.

Generally, a lessee applies the cost model to right-of-use assets. There are two exceptions in the standard, in which case lessee applies other measurement models:

1. If the right-of-use asset meets the definition of investment property in IAS 40 *Investment Property*, then the lessee measures it in accordance with its accounting policy for all investment property, which may be the fair value model.
2. If a lessee applies the revaluation model in IAS 16 to a class of property, plant, and equipment, then it may choose to apply the revaluation model to all right-of-use assets that belong to the same class.

Lease liability

After initial recognition, the measurement of the lease liability is affected by the following factors (paragraph 36 of IFRS 16):

- interest accrued on the lease liability, increasing the carrying amount;
- lease payments made, reducing the carrying amount; and
- remeasurements due to any reassessment or lease modifications.

The interest expense is calculated by applying the same rate to the outstanding lease liability at the beginning of the payment period. This rate is equal to the discount rate determined at commencement of the lease (and used to calculate the present value of the lease payments). As a result, interest on the lease liability in each period during the lease term is the amount that produces a constant periodic rate of interest on the remaining balance of the lease liability. A payments schedule can be used to determine the interest expense and the reduction in the liability over the lease period. Lessees cannot choose to measure lease liabilities subsequently at fair value.

If the lease payments change during the lease term, the lessee may have to remeasure the lease liability. Reassessment of the lease liability may be required under the following circumstances (paragraph 40 and 42 of IFRS 16):

- a change in the lease term;
- a reassessment of a purchase option;
- a revision to the amounts expected to be payable under a residual value guarantee;
- an adjustment to future lease payments resulting from a change in an index or rate used to determine those payments.

Reassessment of the terms of the initial lease agreement do not constitute a lease modification. A lease modification refers to a change in the scope of the lease or the consideration for the lease that was not part of the original terms and conditions. Depending on the circumstances, lease modifications must be accounted for as either a new lease or an adjustment to the original lease agreement. Specific recognition and measurement elements for lease contract modifications are outlined in the standard (paragraphs 44–46 of IFRS 16).

Remeasurements of the lease liability are considered adjustments to the right-of-use asset. If the carrying amount of the asset decreases to zero, any additional reduction is immediately recognised in profit or loss (paragraph 39 of IFRS 16).

9.5.3 Expense recognition

After the lease starts, the lessee records two main expenses in profit or loss:
1. Depreciation of the right-of-use asset,
2. Interest on the lease liability.

Additionally, any variable lease payments not included in the lease liability are recognised in the period when the event or condition triggering them occurs (as required by paragraph 38 of IFRS 16).

The expense pattern for leases under IFRS 16 often shows higher costs in the earlier stages of the lease. This happens when the lessee depreciates the right-of-use asset evenly over time (straight-line depreciation), while interest expense is based on the effective interest method, leading to higher interest costs at the start of the lease and lower costs as payments reduce the liability. The result is an expense pattern, with higher total costs at the start of the lease and lower costs toward the end. This pattern is similar to financing an asset purchase with a loan. In both cases, more interest is charged at the beginning, and this gradually decreases as the loan (or lease liability) is paid off. The subsequent measurement for leases in the financial statements of lessees under IFRS 16 is demonstrated in illustrative example 9.8.

ILLUSTRATIVE EXAMPLE 9.8 Subsequent measurement for leases by lessees

Using the facts from illustrative example 9.7, the lease payments schedule prepared by Athena, based on annual lease payments of €22,000 for the vehicle and an interest rate of 7%, would be:

ATHENA Lease Payments schedule				
	Lease payments[a]	Interest expense[b]	Reduction in liability[c]	Balance of liability[d]
31 December 2026[e]				€85,457[f]
31 December 2026	€22,000	€ —	€22,000	63,457
31 December 2027	22,000	4,442	17,558	45,899
31 December 2028	22,000	3,213	18,787	27,112
31 December 2029	22,000	1,898	20,102	7,010
31 December 2030	7,500	490	7,010	—
	€95,500	€10,043	€85,457	

a Four annual payments of €22,000 payable in advance on 31 December of each year, plus an expected payment for guaranteed residual value of €7,500 on the last day of the lease.
b Interest expense = balance of liability each prior year-end multiplied by 7%. No interest expense is incurred in the year ended 31 December 2026 because payment is made at 31 December 2026, the commencement of the lease.
c Reduction in liability = lease payments less interest expense. The total of this column must equal the initial liability, which may require rounding the final interest expense figure.
d The balance is reduced each year by the amount in previous column.
e At lease commencement.
f Initial liability = present value of lease payments.

The payment schedule is used to prepare lease journal entries and financial statement disclosures each year. The journal entries recorded by Athena for the 4 years of the lease in accordance with IFRS 16 are:

ATHENA General Journal			
Year ended 31 December 2026 31 December 2026:			
Right-of-use asset −Vehicle	Dr	85,457	
Lease Liability	Cr		85,457
(Initial recording of right-of-use asset and lease liability)			
Lease Liability	Dr	22,000	
Prepaid Maintenance Costs[a]	Dr	1,900	
Cash	Cr		23,900
(First lease payment)			

a Maintenance costs have been recognised as an asset because the insurance and maintenance benefits will not be received until the next reporting period.

Year ended 31 December 2027
1 January 2027:

Maintenance Costs	Dr	1,900	
Prepaid Maintenance Costs	Cr		1,900

(Reversal of prepayment)[b]

31 December 2027

Lease Liability	Dr	17,558	
Interest Expense	Dr	4,442	
Prepaid Maintenance Costs	Dr	1,900	
Cash	Cr		23,900

(Second lease payment)

Depreciation Expense	Dr	19,489	
Accumulated Depreciation	Cr		19,489

(Depreciation charge for the period [€85,457 − €7,500]/4)[c]

Year ended 31 December 2028
1 January 2028:

Maintenance Costs	Dr	1,900	
Prepaid Maintenance Costs	Cr		1,900

(Reversal of prepayment)[b]

31 December 2028:

Lease Liability	Dr	18,787	
Interest Expense	Dr	3,213	
Prepaid Maintenance Costs	Dr	1,900	
Cash	Cr		23,900

(Third lease payment)

Depreciation Expense	Dr	19,489	
Accumulated Depreciation	Cr		19,489

(Depreciation charge for the period [€85,457 − €7,500]/4)

Year ended 31 December 2029
1 January 2029

Maintenance Costs	Dr	1,900	
Prepaid Maintenance Costs	Cr		1,900

(Reversal of prepayment)[b]

31 December 2029:

Lease Liability	Dr	20,102	
Interest Expense	Dr	1,898	
Prepaid Maintenance Costs	Dr	1,900	
Cash	Cr		23,900

(Fourth lease payment)

Depreciation Expense	Dr	19,489	
Accumulated Depreciation	Cr		19,489

(Depreciation charge for the period [€85,457 − €7,500]/4)

Year ended 31 December 2030
1 January 2030:

Maintenance Costs	Dr	1,900	
Prepaid Maintenance Costs	Cr		1,900

(Reversal of prepayment)[b]

b For simplicity, reversal of maintenance costs is shown on 1 January. However, maintenance costs are recognised as incurred, which in this example would be over the entire year.

c Because the asset will be returned at the end of the lease term, the useful life is the lease term of 4 years and the depreciable amount is the net present value of the lease payments less the guaranteed residual value.

31 December 2030:

Lease Liability	Dr	7,010	
Interest Expense	Dr	490	
Leased Vehicle	Cr		7,500

(Return of leased vehicle)[d]

Depreciation Expense	Dr	19,490	
Accumulated Depreciation	Cr		19,490

(Depreciation charge for the period [€85,457 − €7,500]/4)

Accumulated Depreciation	Dr	77,957	
Leased Vehicle	Cr		77,957

(Fully depreciated asset written off)

d The final 'payment' is the return of the asset at its guaranteed residual value. If the asset is being purchased, this entry will record a cash payment. Another entry will then be required to reclassify the undepreciated balance of the asset from a 'leased' asset to an 'owned' asset.

9.6 LESSEE PRESENTATION AND DISCLOSURE

LO6

Under IFRS 16, lessees must either separately present right-of-use assets on the statement of financial position or disclose the line items where they are included. Similarly, lease liabilities should be presented separately or their inclusion in specific line items should be disclosed. Interest on lease liabilities should be classified as finance costs in the statement of comprehensive income.

Figure 9.5 summarises how lease-related amounts and activities are presented in the lessee's financial statements.

FIGURE 9.5 Overview of presentation of lease-related items in financial statements

Statement of financial position	
Right-of-use asset	**Lease liability**
Separately from other assets (e.g. owned assets) in the statement of financial position or disclosure in the notes to the financial statements Right-of-use assets that meet the definition of investment property are presented within investment property	Separate from other liabilities in the statement of financial position or disclosure in the notes

Statement of profit or loss	Statement of cash flows
Depreciation expense **Interest expense** Lease-related depreciation and lease-related interest expense are presented separately (i.e., lease-related depreciation and lease-related interest expense cannot be combined). Interest expense on the lease liability is a component of finance costs.	**Operating activities** Variable lease payments not included in the lease liability Payments for short-term and low-value leases (subject to use of recognition exemption) **Financing activities** Cash payments for principal portion of lease liability **Depending on 'general' allocation** Cash payments for the interest portion are classified in accordance with other interest paid

The lessee provides detailed information to allow users of financial statements to understand the impact of leases on its financial position, performance and cash flows. The lessee includes lease-related disclosures in a single note or a separate section of the financial statements. However, duplicating information from other parts of the financial statements is unnecessary if cross-referenced (paragraph 52 of IFRS 16).

IFRS 16 imposes extensive disclosure requirements on lessees, as elaborated in paragraph 40-52 of IFRS 16. These include:

- depreciation charge for right-of-use assets, split by the class of underlying asset;
- interest expenses on lease liabilities;
- expenses related to leases of short-term assets and low-value items, where the lessee has chosen not to recognise a right-of-use asset and lease liability; and
- carrying amount of right-of-use assets at the end of the reporting period, split by class of underlying asset.

Additionally, lessees must apply and disclose a maturity analysis of the lease liability, similar to the disclosure requirements to other financial liabilities in accordance with IFRS 7 *Financial Instruments: Disclosures*.

To illustrate the information that lessees disclose in accordance with IFRS 16, consider the example of PostNL, a mail, parcel and e-commerce corporation located in the Netherlands. Figure 9.6 depicts the information disclosed in their financial statements of 2023 with respect to their right-of-use assets. First, they describe the accounting policies applied and thereafter they present a breakdown of the recognised amounts for the right-of-use assets. In the same note the lease liabilities related to their leasing activities as lessee are explained in detail.

FIGURE 9.6 Extract from Note 3.4 Leases to the consolidated financial statements 2023 of PostNL

3.4 Leases

Accounting policies

PostNL leases sorting centres, sorting machines, distribution centres, offices, warehouses, trucks, vans, cars, transport equipment and other equipment. Leases are recognised as a right-of-use asset and a corresponding liability at the date at which the leased asset is available for use by the group. At the commencement date of the lease, the lease liabilities are measured at the present value of lease payments to be made over the lease term. Right-of-use assets are measured at cost, less any accumulated depreciation and impairment losses, and adjusted for any remeasurement of lease liabilities. The cost of right-of-use assets includes the amount of lease liabilities recognised, initial direct costs incurred, and lease payments made at or before the commencement date less any lease incentives received.

The lease payments are discounted using the interest rate implicit in the lease. If that rate cannot be readily determined, the incremental borrowing rate is used, being the rate that would have to be paid to borrow the funds necessary to obtain an asset of similar value to the right-of-use asset in a similar economic environment with similar terms, security and conditions.

The lease payments include the exercise price of a purchase option reasonably certain to be exercised by PostNL and payments of penalties for terminating the lease, if the lease term reflects PostNL exercising the option to terminate. Lease payments to be made under reasonably certain extension options are also included in the measurement of the liability.

PostNL elected to apply the practical expedient not to separate non-lease components from lease components, and instead account for each lease component and any associated non-lease components as a single lease component. PostNL also elected the practical expedient not to apply the requirements for short-term leases (with a lease term of 12 months or less and which do not contain a purchase option) and leases for which the underlying asset is of low value (<€5,000). The lease payments associated with these leases are recognised as an expense on a straight line basis over the lease term.

FIGURE 9.6 (continued)

PostNL Right-of-use assets in € million
2023

	Land and buildings	Transport	Other	Total
Depreciation percentage	0%-10%	10%-33%	10%-33%	
Historical cost	298	153	24	474
Accumulated depreciation and impairments	(89)	(79)	(12)	(180)
Balance at 1 January 2023	**209**	**75**	**11**	**295**
New leases	15	44	2	61
Lease modifications/reassessments	8	2		10
Disposals	(2)			(2)
Depreciation	(37)	(32)	(2)	(72)
Total changes	**(16)**	**15**		**(2)**
Historical cost	311	183	25	519
Accumulated depreciation and impairments	(119)	(93)	(14)	(226)
Balance at 31 December 2023	**192**	**89**	**11**	**293**

PostNL Lease liabilities in € million
2022, 2023

At 31 December	2022	2023
Long-term lease liabilities	255	240
Short-term lease liabilities	75	80
Total	**331**	**320**

The total cash outflow from leases amounted to €94 million (2022: €86 million) and related for €81 million to repayments of lease liabilities (2022: €74 million), and for €13 million to rent and lease expenses (2022: €12 million). Refer to note 4.1 for further information on the lease liabilities.

In 2023, rent and lease expenses of €13 million (2022: €12 million) relate for €11 million (2022: €10 million) to short-term leases and for €2 million (2022: €2 million) to leases for which the underlying asset is of low value. The interest expenses on lease liabilities amounted to €9 million (2022: €9 million).

Source: PostNL, Annual report 2023, p. 186–187.

9.7 LEASE CLASSIFICATION BY LESSORS

In the following sections, we focus on the other party in lease arrangements: the lessor. The lessor is essentially the supplier of the asset that is leased under a lease agreement to the lessee. Typically, the lessor is the legal owner of the asset and gives the lessee the right to use the asset for a specific period. During the agreement, the lessor retains the right of ownership of the property and is entitled to receive periodic payments from the lessee based on their initial agreement. The perspective of the lessor is depicted in figure 9.7.

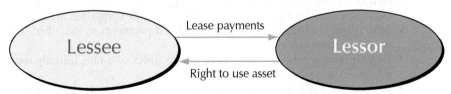

FIGURE 9.7 Lessor perspective

According to IFRS 16, lessors must follow the same guidelines as lessees to determine if a contract is considered a lease. Once it is confirmed that a contract is (or contains) a lease, lessors need to categorise each lease as either an operating lease or a finance lease. This classification is crucial in lessor accounting, as there are significant accounting differences between these two types of leases. The criteria for classification are discussed in detail below.

A finance lease is defined as a lease that 'transfers substantially all the risks and rewards incidental to ownership of an asset'. An operating lease is simply defined as the opposite, namely as a lease that 'does not transfer substantially all the risks and rewards incidental to ownership of an asset' (paragraph 62 of IFRS 16).

The key criterion of a finance lease is the transfer of substantially all the risks and rewards without a transfer of ownership. The classification process, therefore, consists of two steps. First, the potential rewards and potential risks associated with the asset must be identified. Second, the lease agreement must be analysed to determine the nature and extent of the rewards and risks transferred from the lessor to the lessee.

Risks could include possible losses due to unused capacity or technological advancements making the asset obsolete, as well as fluctuations in returns caused by changes in economic conditions. Conversely, rewards may arise from the anticipation of profitable operation over the asset's economic life and the potential to gain value or realise a residual value (IFRS 16.B53).

IFRS 16 (paragraph 63) provides examples (a)–(e) of situations that individually or in combination would normally lead to a lease transaction being classified as a finance lease. Each of the examples are discussed below.

(a) *the lease transfers ownership of the underlying asset to the lessee by the end of the lease term;*

When ownership of the underlying asset transfers to the lessee at the end of the lease term, the arrangement is, in effect, a purchase and sale of the asset. As such, the lessor has transferred the risks and rewards of ownership to the lessee.

(b) *the lessee has the option to purchase the underlying asset at a price that is expected to be sufficiently lower than the fair value at the date the option becomes exercisable for it to be reasonably certain, at the inception date, that the option will be exercised;*

Lease arrangements often contain an option for the lessee to purchase the underlying asset at the end of the lease term. IFRS 16 does not define 'reasonably certain'. In practice, a purchase option is considered reasonably certain of exercise when the option price is significantly below market (i.e. a bargain purchase option).

(c) *the lease term is for the major part of the economic life of the underlying asset even if title is not transferred;*

When a lease is for the major part of the economic life of an asset, it is unlikely that the lessor expects to earn its return on the asset from another party. However, this guideline is not necessarily conclusive as there may be other factors that suggest the lessor retains the risks and rewards associated with the asset, such as obsolescence risks. Therefore, judgement is required when evaluating this guideline.

(d) *at the inception date, the present value of the lease payments amounts to at least substantially all of the fair value of the underlying asset;*

The lease payments represent payments for benefits transferred to the lessee. At lease inception date, the relationship of the present value of the lease payments to the fair value of the asset indicates the proportion of benefits being paid for by the lessee.

To apply this guideline, the following information must be gathered or determined at the inception of the lease:

- fair value of the leased asset;
- lease payments for each period;
- discount rate.

For the purpose of lessor accounting, fair value is defined as 'the amount for which an asset could be exchanged, or a liability settled, between knowledgeable, willing parties in an arm's length transaction'. (Appendix A to IFRS 16).

This definition of fair value is different from the definition in IFRS 13 *Fair Value Measurement (see chapter 3 for extensive discussion of fair value measurement)*. Under IFRS 16 fair value is normally a market price. However, if the lease relates to specialised equipment constructed or obtained for the lease contract, a fair value may be difficult to obtain. The fair value is regarded as representing the future rewards available to the user of the asset, discounted by the market to allow for the risk that the rewards will not eventuate and for changes in the purchasing power of money over time.

Lease payments from the perspective of the lessor are comprised of the following (IFRS 16, paragraph 70):

- fixed payments (including in-substance fixed payments as described in paragraph B42), less any lease incentives payable;
- variable lease payments that depend on an index or a rate, initially measured using the index or rate as at the commencement date;
- any residual value guarantees provided to the lessor by the lessee, a party related to the lessee or a third party unrelated to the lessor that is financially capable of discharging the obligations under the guarantee;
- the exercise price of a purchase option if the lessee is reasonably certain to exercise that option; and
- payments of penalties for terminating the lease, if the lease term reflects the lessee exercising an option to terminate the lease.

To discount the lease payments, the lessor will need to determine the interest rate implicit in the lease.

(e) *the underlying asset is of such a specialised nature that only the lessee can use it without major modifications.*

In some arrangements, the lessor manufactures an asset for the specific needs of the lessee and the asset is not able to be used by another lessee without the lessor incurring significant costs to modify it. In this situation, it is likely that other guidelines above also have been met as the arrangement would be designed for the lessor to generate all of its returns from the one lessee.

IFRS 16 (paragraph 64) also provides indicators of situations that individually or in combination also could lead to a lease being classified as a finance lease, that we discuss below under (f)–(h).

(f) *if the lessee can cancel the lease, the lessor's losses associated with the cancellation are borne by the lessee;*

This guideline suggests that the residual value risk is essentially borne by the lessee. Suppose a lessee leases a car for 5 years and is required to compensate the lessor for any decreases in the residual value if the lessee decides to cancel the lease after 3 years. If the residual value is lower than anticipated, the lessee bears more of the risks and rewards associated with the asset, which may indicate a finance lease.

(g) *gains or losses from the fluctuation in the fair value of the residual accrue to the lessee (for example, in the form of a rent rebate equalling most of the sales proceeds at the end of the lease);*

If, for example, a lessee is required to reimburse the lessor for declines in the fair value of the asset at the end of the lease, the lessee would be exposed to the risks of the residual value in the asset. This would indicate that the lessor was compensated for the asset from the payments received from the lessee and suggests a finance lease.

(h) *the lessee has the ability to continue the lease for a secondary period at a rent that is substantially lower than market rent.*

An option to renew a lease at substantially less than market rent, i.e. a 'bargain renewal option', is considered reasonably certain of exercise. Therefore, the periods covered by such an option are included in the lease term when assessing whether the lease term is for a major part of the economic life of the leased asset, as discussed above. Depending on the number of renewal terms and the renewal period in relation to the economic life of the asset, such options could result in a finance lease.

Note that these examples and indicators are guidelines in assessing whether substantially all the risks and rewards are transferred. Each example or indicator then relates to some measure of risk or reward. Applying the examples and indicators to classify a lease requires substantial judgement. The standard specifically uses the terms 'examples' and 'indicators' and emphasises that they are not always conclusive (IFRS 16 paragraph 65). The examples and indicators should be evaluated either individually or in combination, which implies that they should not be applied as stand-alone tests. Unlike the application of similar tests in US GAAP, the existence of only one of the examples or indicators would not necessarily result in a lease being classified as a finance lease. The overriding consideration is whether the lease transfers substantially all the risks and rewards incidental to ownership of an underlying asset from the lessor to the lessee.

IFRS 16 does not define the terms 'major part' (example [c] above) or 'substantially all' (example [d] above) or prescribe classification criteria. This is left as a judgement call. By omitting quantitative examples, the IASB has placed the classification decision in the hands of account preparers, who must decide what is 'major' and 'substantially all' for their entity and particular circumstances. The disadvantage of this approach is that similar or even identical lease agreements may be classified differently because of varying interpretations of what the terms 'major part' and 'substantially all' mean. Some national GAAPs (e.g. US GAAP) include indicators of 90% for 'substantially all' and 75% for 'major part'. In practice IFRS reporters often use this as a guideline.

An application of the principles of lease classification for lessors is provided in illustrative example 9.9.

ILLUSTRATIVE EXAMPLE 9.9 Lessor classification of a lease agreement

On 31 December 2026, Poseidon Group leased a vehicle to Athena Company. Poseidon had purchased the vehicle on that day at an amount equal to its fair value of €89,721. At inception of the lease, Poseidon determines that the arrangement contains a lease. The vehicle is the identified (underlying) asset. The lease agreement, which cost Poseidon €1,457 to have drawn up, contained the following terms:

Lease term	4 years
Annual payment, payable in advance on 31 December each year	€23,900
Economic life of vehicle	6 years
Residual value at the end of lease term expected by lessor	€15,000
Residual value guaranteed by lessee	€7,500

If Athena terminates the lease before the end of the 4-year lease term, it will incur a monetary penalty equivalent to 2 years rental payments. Included in the annual payments is an amount of €1,900 to cover reimbursement for the cost of maintenance paid by Poseidon.

Assessment:
At inception, lessor Poseidon Group classifies the lease. IFRS 16 requires the lease to be classified as either a finance lease or an operating lease, based on the extent to which the risks and rewards associated with the vehicle have been transferred from Poseidon Group to Athena Company (lessee).

Does the lease transfer ownership of the vehicle by the end of the lease term?
The lease terms do not transfer ownership of the vehicle to Athena.

Is Athena reasonably certain to exercise an option to purchase the vehicle?
The lease terms do not contain an option to purchase the underlying asset.

Is the lease term for a major part of the economic life of the vehicle?
The lease term is 4 years, which is 66% of the vehicle's economic life of 6 years. If expected benefits were receivable evenly over the vehicle's useful life, it would be doubtful that the lease arrangement is for the major part of its life.

Is the present value of the lease payments substantially all of the fair value of the vehicle?
Absent any residual value guarantees by parties other than the lessee, we can assume that the lease payments following from the agreement will be the same amounts for the lessor as for the lessee. Therefore, at inception date the present value of the lease payments is equal to the amount established for the lessee (in illustrative example 9.7) which is €85,456.50. The fair value of the vehicle, including the initial direct cost for the lessor, is €91,178. Based on this, the lessor can determine that the present value of the lease payments amounts to 93.7% of the fair value, as follows:

$$(€85,456.50 / €91,178) \times 100\% = 93.7\%$$

At a 93.7% level, Poseidon considers the present value of the lease payments to be substantially all of the fair value of the vehicle.

Other considerations required by IFRS 16
- Is the leased asset of such a specialised nature that it is expected to have no alternative use to Poseidon Ltd at the end of the lease term? No.
- Is Athena responsible for any losses incurred by Poseidon Ltd if Athena decides to cancel the lease before the end of the lease term? No.
- Is Athena entitled to the gains or losses from the fluctuation in the fair value of the residual asset? No.
- Can Athena continue to use the leased asset for further periods at rent substantially less than market rent? No. The terms of the lease agreement do not contain any renewal options. If Athena decides to continue to lease the vehicle, this would be subject to new negotiations with Poseidon Ltd and a new agreement, which would require a new analysis of classification under IFRS 16.

Classification of the lease
Application of the lease classification guidelines provides mixed signals. The key criterion in classifying leases is whether substantially all the risks and rewards incidental to ownership have been transferred. This requires an overall analysis of the arrangement. The different signals coming from the lease term guideline and the present value guideline may be due to the fact that the majority of the rewards will be transferred in the early stages of the life of the asset, which is the case with motor vehicles. This is reflected in the relatively low residual value at the end of the lease term. These mixed signals demonstrate that the classification guidelines must be used for guidance only and not treated as specific criteria that must be met.

Based on the nature of the asset and the assessment that the lessee will pay substantially all of the fair value of the asset over the lease term, Poseidon concludes that the lease agreement should be classified as a finance lease because substantially all the risks and rewards incident to ownership have been passed to the lessee.

9.8 ACCOUNTING FOR FINANCE LEASES BY LESSORS

Under a finance lease agreement, substantially all the risks and rewards incidental to ownership are transferred to the lessee. Therefore, at commencement of the lease, the lessor essentially derecognises the underlying asset and replaces it with a lease receivable.

9.8.1 Initial recognition

At lease commencement, the lessor recognises an asset held under a finance lease in its statement of financial position and presents it as a receivable at an amount equal to the net investment in the lease (paragraph 67 of IFRS 16). In other words, a lessor initially accounts for a finance lease as follows:
- derecognises the carrying amount of the underlying asset;
- recognises the net investment in the lease; and
- recognises, in profit or loss, any selling profit or selling loss.

In Appendix A to IFRS 16 the net investment in the lease is defined as 'the gross investment in the lease discounted at the interest rate implicit in the lease' and the gross investment as the sum of:

(a) the lease payments receivable by the lessor under a finance lease; and

(b) any unguaranteed residual value accruing to the lessor.

This value would normally equal the fair value of the asset at the inception of the lease. Initial direct costs (except those incurred by manufacturer or dealer lessors) are included in the initial measurement of the finance lease receivable and in the calculation of the implicit interest rate, thereby reducing the amount of interest revenue recognised over the lease term.

The recognition of the fair value of the leased asset as a receivable raises a conceptual issue in that the 'receivable', for leases with no purchase option, has both a monetary component (the rent payments) and non-monetary component (the return of the asset).

9.8.2 Subsequent measurement

Because the lease payments are received from the lessee over the lease term, the lease receivable is increased by interest revenue earned and decreased by the lease payments received (i.e. lease payments excluding payments for services and contingent rent). The lease receivable recognised at the commencement of the lease term represents the present value of future lease payments relating to the use of the asset. This present value is determined by applying the interest rate implicit in the lease. The interest revenue can be obtained by applying the same rate to the outstanding lease receivable at the beginning of the payment period. A receipts schedule can be used to determine the interest revenue and the reduction in the receivable over the lease period.

Illustrative example 9.10 demonstrates the accounting for finance leases for the lessor.

ILLUSTRATIVE EXAMPLE 9.10 Accounting for finance leases by lessors

Using the facts from illustrative example 9.9 regarding the lease of a vehicle, Poseidon Group prepares the following calculations to record the lease arrangement with Athena Company.

Poseidon applies the IFRS guidelines and classifies the lease as a finance lease. See illustrative example 9.9 for workings.

Initial recognition

Under IFRS 16, the lessor recognises the receivable at an amount equal to the net investment in the lease, which equals the discounted gross investment.

	Gross investment in the lease	Net investment in the lease (Present value at 7%[(a)])
Lease payments 4 × €22,000 + €7,500 =	€ 95,500	€85,456.50
Unguaranteed residual value	€ 7,500	€ 5,721.50
	€103,000	€ 91,178

a 7% is the rate implicit in the lease. The present value is calculated for the periodic lease payments of €22,000 and the final payment for the guaranteed residual value of €7,500. See also the calculations in illustrative example 9.7.

At commencement of the lease, Poseidon derecognises the carrying amount of the underlying asset (the vehicle) and recognises the net investment in the lease. Initial direct cost (IDC) is included in the initial measurement, as follows:

POSEIDON General Journal			
Year ended 31 December 2026			
31 December 2026:			
Vehicle	Dr	89,721	
Cash	Cr		89,721
(Purchase of motor vehicle)			
Lease Receivable	Dr	91,178	
Vehicle	Cr		89,721
Cash	Cr		1,457

(Initial recognition of lease of vehicle to Athena Company and payment of IDC.)

Subsequent measurement

A lease receipts schedule is used to prepare lease journal entries and financial statement disclosures each year. The lease receipts schedule based on annual payments of €22,000 for the vehicle and an interest rate implicit in the lease of 7% shows:

POSEIDON Lease Receipts Schedule				
	Lease receipts[a]	Interest revenue[b]	Reduction in receivable[c]	Balance of receivable[d]
31 December 2026[e]				€91,178[f]
31 December 2026	€ 22,000	€ –	€22,000	69,178
31 December 2027	22,000	4,842	17,158	52,020
31 December 2028	22,000	3,641	18,359	33,661
31 December 2029	22,000	2,356	19,644	14,017
31 December 2030	15,000	983	14,017	–
	€103,000[g]	€11,822	€91,178	

a Four annual receipts of €22,000 payable in advance on 31 December of each year, plus a residual value of €15,000 (of which €7,500 is guaranteed by the lessee) on the last day of the lease.

b Interest revenue = balance of receivable each prior year-end multiplied by 7%. No interest revenue is earned in the year ended 31 December 2026 because the payment is received at 31 December 2026, the commencement of the lease.

c Reduction in receivable = lease payments received less interest revenue. The total of this column must equal the initial receivable, which may require rounding the final interest revenue figure.

d The balance is reduced each year by the amount in the previous column. The receivable equals the net investment.

e At lease inception.

f Initial receivable = vehicles fair value of €89,721 plus IDC of €1,457. This figure equals the present value of lease payments receivable and the present value of the unguaranteed residual value. See calculation details in illustrative example 9.7.

g The rentals receivable over the lease period and the residual value, in total €103,000, comprise the gross investment in the lease.

The journal entries recorded by Poseidon, after initial recognition, for the 4 years of the lease in accordance with IFRS 16 are:

POSEIDON General Journal			
Year ended 31 December 2026			
31 December 2026:			
Cash	Dr	23,900	
Lease Receivable	Cr		22,000
Reimbursement in Advance[a]	Cr		1,900
(Receipt of first lease payment)			

a The reimbursement of maintenance cost has been carried forward to 2026, when Poseidon will pay the costs.

Year ended 31 December 2027			
1 January 2027:			
Reimbursement in Advance	Dr	1,900	
Reimbursement Revenue	Cr		1,900
(Reversal of accrual)[b]			
31 December 2027:			
Maintenance[b]	Dr	1,900	
Cash	Cr		1,900
(Payment of costs on behalf of lessee)			

b For simplicity, recognition of maintenance costs and associated revenue are recognised on 1 January and 31 December each year, respectively. However, the costs would be incurred and associated revenue generally would be earned over the entire year.

Cash	Dr	23,900	
Lease Receivable	Cr		17,158
Interest Revenue	Cr		4,842
Reimbursement in Advance	Cr		1,900
(Receipt of second lease payment)			

Year ended 31 December 2028
1 January 2028:

Reimbursement in Advance	Dr	1,900	
Reimbursement Revenue	Cr		1,900
(Reversal of accrual)[(b)]			

31 December 2028:

Maintenance[(b)]	Dr	1,900	
Cash	Cr		1,900
(Payment of costs on behalf of lessee)			

Cash	Dr	23,900	
Lease Receivable	Cr		18,359
Interest Revenue	Cr		3,641
Reimbursement in Advance	Cr		1,900
(Receipt of third lease payment)			

Year ended 31 December 2029
1 January 2029:

Reimbursement in Advance	Dr	1,900	
Reimbursement Revenue	Cr		1,900
(Reversal of accrual)[(b)]			

31 December 2029:

Maintenance[(b)]	Dr	1,900	
Cash	Cr		1,900
(Payment of costs on behalf of lessee)			

Cash	Dr	23,900	
Lease Receivable	Cr		19,644
Interest Revenue	Cr		2,356
Reimbursement in Advance	Cr		1,900
(Receipt of fourth lease payment)			

Year ended 31 December 2030
1 January 2030

Reimbursement in Advance	Dr	1,900	
Reimbursement Revenue	Cr		1,900
(Reversal of accrual)[(b)]			

31 December 2030:

Maintenance[(b)]	Dr	1,900	
Cash	Cr		1,900
(Payment of costs on behalf of lessee)			

At the end of the lease Athena returns the vehicle to Poseidon. Due to the heavy use of the vehicle by the lessee Athena, it is clear that the vehicle has no residual value. Poseidon therefore determines that the residual value is €0, instead of the anticipated €15,000. Athena pays the guaranteed amount of €7,500. Poseidon records the following journal entry:

Cash	Dr	7,500	
Loss on finance lease	Dr	7,500	
Interest Revenue	Cr		983
Lease Receivable	Cr		14,017
(Return of vehicle at end of lease).			

9.9 ACCOUNTING FOR FINANCE LEASES BY MANUFACTURER OR DEALER LESSORS

For manufacturers and dealers, leases can function as an effective marketing tool, as leasing options attract potential customers who may not have the means or desire to purchase assets outright with cash. Car manufacturers, for example, frequently provide lease options to help customers finance their purchases, thereby stimulating overall sales. When manufacturers or dealers offer customers the choice of either buying or leasing an asset, a lease arrangement classified as a finance lease gives rise to two types of income:
- profit or loss equivalent to the outright sale of the asset being leased
- finance income over the lease term.

Accounting for the lease is identical to that required by non-manufacturer/dealer lessors except for an initial entry to recognise profit or loss and the treatment of costs incurred in connection with obtaining the lease, which is described below.

Manufacturer and dealer lessors must recognise selling profit or loss at the lease commencement in line with their sales policy (and to which IFRS 15 *Revenue from Contracts with Customers* applies). If artificially low interest rates are used to attract customers to the lease, the recorded selling profit should be restricted to the profit that would be earned if a market interest rate were applied.

According to IFRS 16 (paragraph 71), the recognised sales revenue should equal the assets fair value or, if lower, the present value of the lease payments calculated using a market interest rate. The cost of sales is determined by the asset's cost or carrying amount minus the present value of any unguaranteed residual value. Selling profit or loss is calculated as the difference between sales revenue and the cost of sales. Furthermore, any cost that the manufacturer or dealer lessor incurs to obtain the lease should be expensed immediately at the commencement of the lease. These costs are explicitly excluded from the definition of initial direct costs because they are considered part of the sales profit rather than leasing costs.

The following example of a sales-type lease (illustrative example 9.11) demonstrates the accounting from the perspective of a manufacturer or dealer lessor.

ILLUSTRATIVE EXAMPLE 9.11 Initial recognition of finance lease by manufacturer lessor

Argos S.A. manufactures specialised moulding machinery. The company offers its customers the choice to either buy or lease the machinery. On 1 January 2024, Argos S.A. leased a machine to Perseus S.A., incurring €1,500 in costs to negotiate, prepare and execute the lease document. The machine cost Argos S.A. €195,000 to manufacture, and its fair value at the inception of the lease was €212,515. The interest rate implicit in the lease is 10%, which is in line with current market rates. Under the terms of the lease, Perseus S.A. is required to make five annual lease payments of €50,000, payable in arrears. In addition, Perseus has guaranteed €25,000 of the asset's expected residual value of €37,000 at the end of the 5-year lease term.

After determining that the lease is a finance lease, Argos S.A. records the following entries on 1 January 2024:

Lease Receivable[a]	Dr	212,515	
Cost of Sales[b]	Dr	187,549	
Inventory[c]	Cr		195,000
Sales Revenue[d]	Cr		205,064
(Initial recognition of lease receivable and recording sale of machinery)			
Lease Costs[e]	Dr	1,500	
Cash	Cr		1,500
Payment of cost incurred to obtain the lease			

a The lease receivable represents the net investment in the lease and is equal to the fair value of the leased machine.
b Cost of sales represents the cost of the leased machine (€195,000) less the present value of the unguaranteed residual value

$$(€12,000 \times \frac{1}{(1,10)^5} = €7,451).$$

---

c Inventory is reduced by the cost of the leased machine.

d Sales revenue represents the present value of the lease payments, which in this situation is less than the fair value of the asset due to the existence of an unguaranteed residual value. The lease payments consist of the annual payment of €50,000 and the guaranteed residual value of €25,000. The present value is calculated as follows:

$$\text{PV of lease payments} = €50,000 \times \frac{1}{(1,10)} + €50,000 \times \frac{1}{(1,10)^2} + €50,000 \times \frac{1}{(1,10)^3} + €50,000 \times \frac{1}{(1,10)^4} +$$

$$€50,000 \times \frac{1}{(1,10)^5} + €25,000 \times \frac{1}{(1,10)^5} = €205,064$$

Or, using the formula for an ordinary annuity:

$$= €50,000 \times \frac{1-(1.10)^{-5}}{0.10} = \frac{1}{(1,10)^5} \text{PV of lease payments} = €50,000 \times \frac{1-(1.10)^{-5}}{0.10} + €25,000 \times \frac{1}{(1.10)^5} = €205,064$$

$$\frac{1}{(1,10)} = €3,900 \times \frac{1-(1.06)(1.06)^{-3}}{0.06}$$

e The costs to negotiate, prepare and execute the lease documents (of €1,500) are clear examples of 'incremental costs of obtaining the lease'. For manufacturer or dealer lessors, these are excluded from the definition of initial direct costs. Instead, they should be expensed at commencement of the lease, when the selling profit or loss is recognised.

9.10 ACCOUNTING FOR OPERATING LEASES BY LESSORS

Lessors classify lease arrangements as either finance leases (as discussed in the previous sections on lessors) or as operating leases. Operating leases are leases that do not transfer substantially all the risks and rewards incidental to ownership to an underlying asset (Appendix A to IFRS 16). A lessor recognises lease payments from operating leases as income on either a straight-line basis or another systematic basis, if that is more representative of the 'pattern in which benefit from the use of the underlying asset is diminished' (paragraph 81 of IFRS 16). For operating leases, there is no distinction in the treatment of manufacturer or dealer lessors.

Any initial direct costs incurred by lessors in negotiating operating leases are added to the carrying amount of the leased asset and recognised as an expense over the lease term on the same basis as the lease income (paragraph 83). The treatment of initial direct cost in the carrying amount of the asset is illustrated as follows:

Initial cost of the asset	€ xxx
Less: Accumulated depreciation	(xxx)
	xxx
Plus: remaining balance in initial direct costs	xxx
Carrying amount	xxx

Under IFRS 16, lessors continue to recognise the underlying asset on the statement of financial position. The leased assets are required to be presented according to the nature of the asset. In other words, if the leased asset is a piece of land, it is included in the category 'Land' on the statement of financial position. For depreciable assets, depreciation under operating leases must be consistent with the lessor's normal depreciation policy for similar assets, and calculated in accordance with IAS 16 and IAS 38. In addition, a lessor applies IAS 36 to determine whether an underlying asset subject to an operating lease is impaired.

In illustrative example 9.12, the mechanics of accounting for operating leases by lessors are demonstrated.

On 1 January 2025, Medusa Corporation leased a bobcat from Pegasus Inc. The bobcat cost Pegasus Inc. €35,966 on that same day. The lease agreement, which cost Pegasus Inc. €381 to have drawn up, contained the following terms:

Lease term	3 years
Estimated economic life of the bobcat	10 years
Annual rental payment, in arrears (commencing 31 December 2025)	€3,900
Residual value at end of the lease term	€31,000
Residual value guaranteed by Medusa Corporation	€0
Interest rate implicit in lease	6%

IFRS 16 requires the lessor (Pegasus Inc.) to classify the lease as either a finance lease or an operating lease based on the extent to which the risks and rewards associated with the vehicle have been effectively transferred between Medusa Corporation and Pegasus Inc.

Does the lease transfer ownership of the bobcat by the end of the lease term?
The lease terms do not transfer ownership of the bobcat to Medusa Corporation.

Is Medusa Corporation reasonably certain to exercise an option to purchase the bobcat?
The lease agreement does not contain an option for Medusa Corporation to purchase the bobcat.

Is the lease term for the major part of the economic life of the bobcat?
The lease term is 3 years, which is only 30% of the bobcat's economic life of 10 years. Therefore, it would appear that the lease arrangement is not for the major part of the asset's life.

Is the present value of the lease payments substantially all of the fair value of the bobcat?
The lease payments consist of three payments, in arrears, of €3,900. There are no residual value guarantees by any party.

$$\text{PV of lease payments} = €3,900 \times \frac{1}{(1.06)} + €3,900 \times \frac{1}{(1.06)^2} + €3,900 \times \frac{1}{(1.06)^3} = €10,425$$

$$\text{Or : PV of lease payments} = €3,900 \times \frac{1-(1.06)^{-3}}{0.06} = €10,425$$

Fair value of underlying asset : €35,966

PV / FV = €10,425 / €35,966 = 29%

At 29%, the present value of the lease payments is not substantially all of the fair value of the bobcat.

Other considerations required by IFRS 16
Is the bobcat of such a specialised nature that it is expected to have no alternative use to Pegasus Inc. at the end of the lease term? No.
- Is Medusa Corporation responsible for any losses incurred by Pegasus Inc. if Medusa Corporation decides to cancel the lease before the end of the lease term? No.
- Is Medusa Corporation entitled to the gains or losses from the fluctuation in the fair value of the residual asset? No.
- Can Medusa Corporation continue to use the bobcat for further periods at rent substantially less than market rent? No. The terms of the lease agreement do not contain any renewal options. If Medusa Corporation decides to continue to lease the bobcat, this would be subject to new negotiations with Pegasus Inc. and a new agreement, which would require a new analysis of classification under IFRS 16.

Classification of the lease
On the basis of the facts presented, there has not been a transfer of substantially all the risks and rewards associated with the bobcat to Medusa Corporation. Hence, the lease would be classified and accounted for by the lessor, Pegasus Inc. as an operating lease.

Journal entries
The following journal entries would be recorded in the books of Pegasus Inc.

PEGASUS INC. GENERAL JOURNAL			
1 January 2025:			
Plant and Equipment	Dr	35,966	
Cash	Cr		35,966
(Purchase of bobcat)			
Deferred IDC— Plant and Equipment	Dr	381	
Cash	Cr		381
(IDC incurred for lease)			
31 December 2025:			
Cash	Dr	3,900	
Lease Income	Cr		3,900
(Receipt of first year's rental in arrears)			
Depreciation Expense	Dr	127	
Deferred IDC— Plant and Equipment	Cr		127
(Recognition of initial direct cost: €381/3 years)			
Depreciation Expense	Dr	3,597	
Accumulated Depreciation	Cr		3,597
(Depreciation charge for the period: €35,966/10).			

LO11 9.11 ACCOUNTING FOR SALE AND LEASEBACK TRANSACTIONS

A 'sale and leaseback' is a type of arrangement that involves the sale of an asset that is then leased back from the purchaser for all or part of its remaining economic life. Hence, the original owner becomes the lessee. In substance, the lessee gives up legal ownership or control of the asset, but still retains the right to control the use of the underlying asset for the period of the lease.

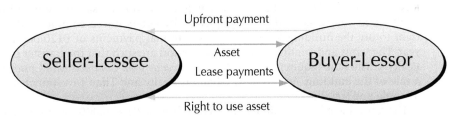

FIGURE 9.8 Sale and leaseback transaction

Figure 9.8 visualises the exchange of payments and rights between the seller-lessee and the buyer-lessor.

Entities normally enter into sale and leaseback arrangements to generate immediate cash flows while still retaining the use of the asset. Such arrangements are particularly attractive when the fair value of an asset is considerably higher than its carrying amount, or when a large amount of capital is tied up in property and plant. Traditionally, sale and leaseback transactions were a popular method for lessees to achieve off-balance-sheet financing. However, under IFRS 16, leaseback arrangements must be recognised on the balance sheet as a lease liability and a corresponding right-of-use asset. As a result, lessees can no longer use these transactions to avoid reporting lease obligations on the balance sheet.

The accounting for sale and leaseback transactions depends on whether the transfer of the asset qualifies as a sale. Therefore, the first step is to determine whether the initial transfer of the underlying asset from the seller-lessee to the buyer-lessor qualifies as a sale. This assessment is crucial. Both the seller-lessee and the buyer-lessor apply IFRS 15 *Revenue from Contracts with Customers* to determine whether control of the underlying asset has indeed passed to the buyer-lessor (*see chapter 3*). IFRS 15 provides several indicators to determine whether control of the asset has been transferred, but all relevant facts and circumstances must be considered.

9.11.1 Transactions that qualify as a sale

If the transaction qualifies as a sale, the seller-lessee accounts for it as follows:

- Derecognition: The seller-lessee derecognises the underlying asset from its balance sheet.
- Leaseback: The seller-lessee recognises a right-of-use asset and a corresponding lease liability for the leaseback arrangement.
- Gain or loss on sale: The seller-lessee recognises any gain or loss relating to the rights transferred to the buyer-lessor and adjusted for off-market terms.

Calculating the gain or loss on the sale can be complex, especially in case of any off-market terms in sale and leaseback transactions. Sales transactions and the resulting leases are often negotiated together, as a package, which can lead to situations where the agreed-upon sales price and lease payments are not at fair market value. Such off-market terms can affect the reported gain or loss on the sale and the subsequent lease expenses and income. To correct for potential distortions, IFRS 16 requires adjustments for these off-market terms based on the differences between the fair value and contractual values. These adjustments are based on the more readily determinable differences between the fair value of the sale consideration and the asset's fair value, and between the present value of the contractual lease payments and the present value of lease payments at market rates (paragraph 102 of IFRS 16).

When the terms of a sale and leaseback transaction deviate from market value, IFRS 16 requires adjustments to reflect the true economic substance. If the sales price is below the asset's fair value, or lease payments are below market rates, the seller-lessee treats the shortfall as a lease prepayment. This adjustment increases the recorded sales price and the initial right-of-use asset value, aligning the transaction with market terms. Conversely, if the sales price exceeds the fair value, or lease payments are above market rates, the seller-lessee treats the excess as additional financing received from the buyer-lessor. This reduces the recorded sales price and accounts for the financing effect.

The buyer-lessor mirrors these adjustments: any difference between the purchase price and fair value is recorded as either a lease prepayment or additional financing provided to the seller-lessee. Illustrative example 9.13 (based on IE 11 Example 24 from IFRS 16) clarifies the accounting for sale and leaseback transactions in case of above-market terms, with fixed payments. The standard and following interpretations also discuss the treatment of sale and leaseback transactions with variable payments extensively. This complex issue is considered out-of-scope for this chapter.

ILLUSTRATIVE EXAMPLE 9.13 Sale and leaseback transaction with fixed payments and above-market terms

An entity, Olympus Realty (seller-lessee), sells a building to another entity, Titan Investments (buyer-lessor), for cash of €2,000,000. Immediately before the transaction, the building is carried at a cost of €1,000,000. At the same time, Olympus Realty enters into a contract with Titan Investments for the right to use the building for 18 years, with annual payments of €120,000 payable at the end of each year. The terms and conditions of the transaction are such that the transfer of the building by Olympus Realty satisfies the requirements of IFRS 15 *Revenue from Contracts with Customers* to be accounted for as a sale of the building. Accordingly, Olympus Realty and Titan Investments account for the transaction as a sale and leaseback.

The fair value of the building at the date of sale is €1,800,000. Because the consideration for the sale of the building is not at fair value, Olympus Realty and Titan Investments make adjustments to measure the sales proceeds at fair value. Applying paragraph 101(b) of IFRS 16, the amount of the excess sales price of €200,000 (€2,000,000 – €1,800,000) is recognised as additional financing provided by Titan Investments to Olympus Realty.

The interest rate implicit in the lease is 4.5% per annum, which is readily determinable by Olympus Realty. The present value of the annual payments (18 payments of €120,000, discounted at 4.5% per annum) is €1,459,200, of which €200,000 relates to the additional financing and €1,259,200 relates to the lease, corresponding to 18 annual payments of €16,447 and €103,553, respectively. For the purpose of this example, we assume that Titan Investments classifies the lease of the building as an operating lease.

Olympus Realty (seller-lessee)

Applying paragraph 100(a) of IFRS 16, at the commencement date, Olympus Realty measures the right-of-use asset arising from the leaseback of the building at the proportion of the previous carrying amount of the building that relates to the right-of-use retained by Olympus Realty, which is €699,555. Olympus Realty calculates this amount as: €1,000,000 (the carrying amount of the building) × €1,259,200 (the discounted lease payments for the 18-year right-of-use asset) ÷ €1,800,000 (the fair value of the building).

Olympus Realty recognises only the amount of the gain that relates to the rights transferred to Titan Investments of €240,355 calculated as follows. The gain on sale of the building amounts to €800,000 (€1,800,000 – €1,000,000), of which:

(a) €559,645 relates to the right to use the building retained by Olympus Realty (calculated as: €800,000 × [€1,259,200 ÷ €1,800,000]); and

(b) €240,355 relates to the rights transferred to Titan Investments (calculated as: €800,000 × ([€1,800,000 – €1,259,200] ÷ €1,800,000)).

At the commencement date, Olympus Realty accounts for the transaction as follows:

Cash	Dr	2,000,000	
Right-of-use asset	Dr	699,555	
Building	Cr		1,000,000
Lease liability	Cr		1,259,200
Financial liability	Cr		200,000
Gain on rights transferred	Cr		240,355
(Sale and leaseback of building)			

Titan Investments (buyer-lessor)

At the commencement date, Titan Investments accounts for the transaction as follows:

Building[a]	Dr	800,000	
Financial asset[b]	Dr	200,000	
Cash	Cr		1,000,000
(Purchase of building under a sale-and-leaseback agreement)			

a Fair value of the building at the date of the sale.
b Financial asset is initially measured at the present value of the financing payments (18 payments of €16,447, discounted at 4.5% per annum).

After the commencement date, Titan Investments accounts for the lease by treating €103,553 of the annual payments of €120,000 as lease payments. The remaining €16,447 of annual payments received from Olympus Realty are accounted for as (a) payments received to settle the financial asset of €200,000 and (b) interest revenue.

9.11.2 Transactions that do not qualify as a sale

When the transfer of an asset is not considered a sale (based on the requirements of IFRS 15 *Revenue from Contracts with Customers*), the seller-lessee treats the transaction as a financing arrangement. IFRS 16 explains in paragraph 103 that, in this case, the seller-lessee keeps the transferred asset on its balance sheet and records the received amount as a financial liability, following IFRS 9 guidelines. The seller-lessee then reduces this financial liability with the payments made, minus the interest expense portion.

Similarly, if the transfer is not a sale, the buyer-lessor does not record the transferred asset. Instead, the buyer-lessor treats the amount paid as a receivable, also in accordance with IFRS 9.

9.12 SUMMARY

The main accounting challenge for lessees under IFRS 16 is recognising and measuring lease liabilities and right-of-use assets on the balance sheet to reflect the true economic impact of lease transactions. IFRS 16 was introduced to replace IAS 17, addressing off-balance-sheet financing and improving transparency and comparability by requiring most leases to be recognised on the balance sheet. The standard applies to nearly all leases, with exemptions available for short-term leases and leases of low-value assets.

Under IFRS 16, a lease is defined as a contract that conveys the right to use an asset for a period of time in exchange for consideration, and identifying a lease involves determining whether the contract grants control over an identified asset. Lessees must recognise a right-of-use asset and a lease liability, with the liability measured at the present value of lease payments and the asset at cost. Lessees must present right-of-use assets and lease liabilities separately and disclose detailed information about the nature, amounts, and maturity of leases. Lessors classify leases as finance or operating based on the transfer of risks and rewards of ownership. For finance leases, lessors recognise a receivable equal to the net investment in the lease, while income is recognised over the lease term. Manufacturer or dealer lessors recognise selling profit or loss on finance leases at lease commencement, with sales revenue being the lower of fair value or the present value of lease payments minus the cost of sales. Operating leases require lessors to recognise lease income on a straight-line or systematic basis, keeping the leased asset on the balance sheet and depreciated over its useful life. Sale and leaseback transactions are accounted for as a sale under IFRS 15 or as a financing transaction if they do not qualify as a sale.

Reporting and analysing lease transactions under IFRS 16 helped financial statements to reflect the economic realities of leasing activities. The ongoing debate among accounting standard setters continues to focus on balancing transparency, complexity and the practical implementation of these comprehensive lease accounting requirements.

Under rules before IFRS 16, research into the accounting for leases was concerned with measuring the magnitude of the off-balance-sheet financing that operating leases represent. In particular, the concern has been that leaving assets and debt off the balance sheet distorts commonly used ratios. Imhoff et al. (1991) posit that it is quite plausible that managers 'game' the accounting rules to avoid classifying lease contracts as finance leases. They propose a method for capitalisation of operating leases and assess its impact for a small sample of firms chosen from several industries. Their calculations suggest that the effect of capitalising operating leases on ratios such as return on assets (ROA) and debt-to-equity can be very large. For example, they calculate that ROA can decrease by 55% while debt-to-equity can increase by more than 300%. Beattie et al. (1998) employ the method suggested by Imhoff et al. (1991) to a large UK sample comprising 300 firms that reported operating leases during 1981 to 1994. They examine a wide range of ratios for this sample and demonstrate that the effect of capitalisation on many of the ratios can be very large. Cornaggia et al. (2013) provide recent analysis that also looks at the trend over time in the use of operating leases. They document an increasing tendency by US firms to use off-balance-sheet financing through operating leases in the past three decades. Over the same time, on-balance-sheet financing through finance leases has fallen. This suggests that for analytical purposes it is increasingly important to capitalise operating leases.

Researchers have also been interested in the degree to which leases are used as a substitute, or perhaps as a complement, to ordinary debt financing. Ang and Peterson (1984) expect to find a substitutive effect whereby more (less) debt is associated with less (more) lease financing. However, in a study spanning the 1976 to 1981 period that includes only finance leases they fail to find consistent relation. Adedeji and Stapleton (1996) rectify several methodological problems in the approach taken by Ang and Peterson (1984) using a UK sample and find that there is a substitution effect whereby a reduction of £1 in debt is associated with an increase in leases of roughly £2. Further evidence supporting a substitutive effect is provided by Schallheim et al. (2013) who examine a sample of sale-and-leaseback transactions. The advantage of this sample vis-à-vis other studies is that the underlying asset base is kept the same because the leased-back asset is retained by the lessee. Beattie et al. (2000) take this research further by incorporating measures of capitalised operating leases. They examine a sample of more than 560 UK firms during 1990 to 1994 and find that, once operating leases are capitalised, debt and leases are substitutes. Moreover, since most of lease-borrowing stems from operating leases, this result suggests that the substitutive effect is largely due to operating lease financing.

All the above-mentioned studies, however, do not address the question of whether users of financial statements regard operating leases as debt financing. Altamuro et al. (2014) provide helpful and rare input into this question. They examine whether banks regard operating leases as debt (that is, as finance leases) or periodic expense. They argue that if operating leases are in-substance debt, then banks should adjust the interest charge accordingly. In other words, the interest banks charge on their loans is expected to be a function of leverage and other ratios that are adjusted for the capitalisation of operating leases. They first report that the interest charge is higher the larger the amount of outstanding payments on operating leases. They then show that models that feature adjusted ratios explain the variations in interest charges. However, this is not the case for operating leases in the retail business. They conclude that leases of store space are regarded as periodic expense by lending banks.

Ely (1995) adopts a shareholders' perspective rather than creditors' perspective as in Altamuro et al. (2014). She argues that the distinguishing factor between operating and finance leases is the degree to which the lessee is exposed to risk from employing the leased assets. She therefore relates equity risk to two key ratios: ROA (capturing asset risk) and debt-to-equity (capturing financial risk). Her sample is based on 212 US firms that provide disclosures about minimum lease payments (MLPs) that are classified as operating leases in 1987 and 102 firms that disclosed no information about operating leases. As with other studies, Ely (1995) capitalises these MLPs to examine, in her case, the association with a measure of equity risk. She finds that debt-to-equity ratios adjusted for the capitalised amounts are positively related to equity risk. This result suggests that investors perceive operating lease obligations as similar to debt. Nevertheless, the results regarding ROA are mixed and it is not clear if investors perceive operating leases as increased asset risk.

In the US, the FASB adopted similar rules to IFRS 16. Ma and Thomas (2023) investigate the effects of the new standard on several key financial measures, and find that firms reported similar profitability and credit rating under the new rules and old rules. However, they also find that firms reduced the use of long-term leases, and increased the use of lease contracts under 1 year (i.e., short-term leases that are not capitalised). They also find that after the adoption of the new rules, firms spend more on capital expenditure (CAPEX). CAPEX is a cheaper investment option than lease contracts (Ma and Thomas 2023). Thus, use of long-term operating leases under previous rules was self-serving for managers. Once the incentives to use these leases has been removed by the new rules, managers shift to CAPEX.

References

Adedeji, A., and Stapleton, R. C. 1996. Leases debt and taxable capacity. *Applied Financial Economics*, 6, 71–83.

Altamuro, J., Johnston, R., Pandit, S. S., and Zhang, H. H. 2014. Operating leases and credit assessments. *Contemporary Accounting Research*, 31(2), 551–580.

Ang, J., and Peterson, P. P. 1984. The leasing puzzle. *Journal of Finance*, 39, 1055–1065.

Beattie, V. A., Edwards, K., and Goodacre, A. 1998. The impact of constructive operating lease capitalisation on key accounting ratios. *Accounting and Business Research*, 28, 233–254.

Beattie, V., Goodacre, A., and Thomson, S. 2000. Operating leases and the assessment of lease–debt substitutability. *Journal of Banking & Finance*, 24(3), 427–470.

Cornaggia, K. J., Franzen, L. A., and Simin, T. T. 2013. Bringing leased assets onto the balance sheet. *Journal of Corporate Finance*, 22, 345–360.

Ely, K. M. 1995. Operating lease accounting and the market's assessment of equity risk. *Journal of Accounting Research*, 33(2), 397–415.

Imhoff, E. A., Lipe, R. C., and Wright, D. A. 1991. Operating leases: impact of constructive capitalization. *Accounting Horizons*, 5, 51–63.

Ma, M.S. and Thomas, W.B., 2023. Economic consequences of operating lease recognition. *Journal of Accounting and Economics*, 75(2-3), p.101566.

Schallheim, J., Wells, K., and Whitby, R. J. 2013. Do leases expand debt capacity? *Journal of Corporate Finance*, 23, 368–381.

10

Provisions, contingent liabilities and contingent assets

ACCOUNTING STANDARDS IN FOCUS

IAS 37 *Provisions, Contingent Liabilities and Contingent Assets*

IFRIC 1 *Changes in Existing Decommissioning, Restoration and Similar Liabilities*

IFRIC 21 *Levies*

LEARNING OBJECTIVES

After studying this chapter, you should be able to:

 1 describe the background to IAS 37

 2 identify which items are included within the scope of the standard

 3 outline the concept of a provision

 4 outline the concept of a contingent liability

 5 describe how to distinguish a provision from a contingent liability

 6 explain how a provision should be measured

 7 apply the definitions, recognition and measurement criteria for provisions and contingent liabilities to practical situations

 8 outline the concept of a contingent asset

 9 describe the disclosure requirements for provisions, contingent liabilities and contingent assets.

10.1 INTRODUCTION TO IAS 37

As its name suggests, IAS 37 *Provisions, Contingent Liabilities and Contingent Assets* deals with the accounting for
- a provision, which is a liability that involves uncertainty in either the timing and/or amount of its settlement
- a contingent liability, which is either a *possible* obligation or a *present* obligation that does not meet the recognition criteria for a provision
- a contingent asset, which is a possible asset, the existence of which is still to be confirmed.
  The standard remains largely unchanged since its original issue date of 1998 by the IASC.

10.2 SCOPE

IAS 37 prescribes the accounting and disclosure for all provisions, contingent liabilities and contingent assets except:

(a) those resulting from financial instruments *(see chapter 13)* and those arising in insurance entities from contracts with policy holders

(b) those resulting from executory contracts, except where the contract is onerous (Executory contracts or a portion of a contract, that is equally unperformed—neither party has fulfilled any of its obligations, or both parties have partially fulfilled their obligations to an equal extent.)

(c) those specifically covered by another IAS®/IFRS® Standard. For example, certain types of provisions are also addressed in standards on:
- income taxes *(see IAS 12 Income Taxes, covered in chapter 15)*
- leases *(see IFRS 16 Leases, covered in chapter 9)*. However, IAS 37 applies to any lease that becomes onerous before the commencement date of the lease as defined in IFRS 16. IAS 37 also applies to short-term leases and leases for which the underlying asset is of low value accounted for in accordance with paragraph 6 of IFRS 16 and that have become onerous
- employee benefits *(see IAS 19 Employee Benefits, covered in chapter 11)*
- insurance contracts *(see IFRS 17 Insurance Contracts)*.
- revenue from contracts with customers. However, as IFRS 15 contains no specific requirements to address contracts with customers that are, or have become, onerous, IAS 37 applies to such cases *(see IFRS 15 Revenue from Contracts with Customers, covered in chapter 3)*.

Sometimes the term 'provision' is also used in the context of items such as depreciation, impairment of assets and doubtful debts. These are adjustments to the carrying amounts of assets and are not related to the concept of a provision in IAS 37. *Refer to IAS 36 Impairment of Assets, which is covered in chapter 7.*

IAS 37 applies to provisions for restructuring (including discontinued operations). Where a restructuring meets the definition of a discontinued operation, additional disclosures may be required by IFRS 5 *Non-current Assets Held for Sale and Discontinued Operations*. IFRS 3 *Business Combinations* deals with accounting for restructuring provisions arising in business combinations.

10.3 WHAT IS A PROVISION?

10.3.1 Definition of a provision

As a starting point, IAS 37, paragraph 10 defines a provision as

> A liability of uncertain timing or amount.

The key principle is that a provision is a type of liability; in other words, all provisions are liabilities but not all liabilities are provisions. A provision involves uncertainty in relation to the timings of the outflows and/or the amount of the outflows.

The standard clarifies in paragraph 11 that provisions can be distinguished from other liabilities such as trade payables and accruals because of the uncertainty related to a provision. By contrast, trade payables are liabilities to pay for goods or services typically based on an invoiced amount (certainty of amount); accruals are liabilities to pay for goods or services that typically have not been invoiced and although it is sometimes necessary to estimate the amount or timing of accruals, the uncertainty is generally much less than for provisions. Accruals are often reported as part of trade payables but provisions are always reported separately.

Even though a provision is a type of liability, there are important differences between an actual liability, a provision and what is referred to as a contingent liability. These differences hinge upon their alignment with the definition of a liability and the recognition criteria in IAS 37.

IAS 37 defines a liability in paragraph 10 as follows:

A liability is a present obligation of the entity arising from past events, the settlement of which is expected to result in an outflow from the entity of resources embodying economic benefits.

This definition of a liability is taken from the previous (2010) *Conceptual Framework*. Paragraph 4.26 of the current (2018) *Conceptual Framework* defines a liability as:

A present obligation of the entity to transfer an economic resource as a result of past events

However, the *Conceptual Framework* states clearly in paragraph SP1.2 that it is not a Standard and that nothing in the *Conceptual Framework* overrides any Standard or any requirement in a Standard.

A crucial part of both definitions is that there must be a ***present obligation*** arising from a ***past event***. Deciding if there actually is an obligation at the reporting date can be difficult and require professional judgement.

For a present obligation to exist, there must be a past event that is also an obligating event. Where it is difficult to determine if there is a present obligation or a past event, guidance is given in paragraph 16 of IAS 37:

- if it is more likely than not that a present obligation exists at the end of the reporting period (interpreted as greater than 50% chance), in which case a provision is recognised; or
- if it is more likely that no present obligation exists at the end of the reporting period (interpreted as less than 50% chance), in which case a contingent liability is disclosed (unless the possible outflow of future economic benefits is remote, in which case it is ignored).

In assessing the likelihood of a present obligation, the entity uses its professional judgement, other expert opinions (such as legal opinions) and events after the reporting period.

An example of where an entity may be uncertain of whether or not there is a present obligation due to a past event, is a court case in progress at year-end where there is uncertainty as to whether certain events have actually occurred (i.e. whether there is a past event) and further, whether or not the events will lead to a fine or other settlement (i.e. whether there is a resulting present obligation).

For a past event to exist, it must have occurred on or before the reporting date. IAS 37, paragraph 17 refers to a past event that leads to a present obligation as an *obligating event*. An obligating event is an event where the entity has no realistic alternative but to settle the obligation created by the event. The standard goes on to identify two types of obligating events:

- a legal obligation, where the settlement of the obligation can be enforced by law; or
- a constructive obligation, where the event creates a valid expectation in other parties that the entity will discharge the obligation.

The obligating event must both exist independently of the entity's future actions (IAS 37, paragraph 19) *and* always involve another party (IAS 37, paragraph 20).

Examples of obligations that exist independently of their future actions are penalties or clean-up costs for unlawful environmental damage, both of which would lead to an outflow of resources embodying economic benefits in settlement regardless of the future actions of the entity. Similarly, an entity recognises a provision for the decommissioning costs of an oil installation or a nuclear power station to the extent that the entity is obliged to rectify damage already caused.

In contrast, because of commercial pressures or legal requirements, an entity may intend or need to carry out expenditure to operate in a particular way in the future (for example, by fitting smoke filters in a certain type of factory). Because the entity can avoid the future expenditure by its future actions, for example by changing its method of operation, it has no present obligation for that future expenditure and no provision is recognised.

Because an obligation always involves a commitment to another party, it follows that a management decision does not give rise to a constructive obligation at the end of the reporting period unless the decision has been communicated before the end of the reporting period to those affected by it in a sufficiently specific manner to raise a valid expectation in them that the entity will discharge its responsibilities.

An interesting application of the principles discussed in this section is set out in an IFRS Interpretations Committee document (Climate-related commitments – Agenda Paper 2, November 2023). The scenario involves a manufacturer, that in 20X0, publicly states its commitment to gradually reduce its annual greenhouse gas emissions, reducing them by at least 60% of their current level by 20X9; and, to offset its remaining annual emissions in 20X9 and in subsequent years by buying carbon credits and retiring them from the carbon market.

The issue is whether the entity has a constructive obligation in 20X0 and does it satisfy the criteria for recognising a provision? The Committee concluded that:

- the obligation is not a present obligation as a result of a past event when the entity publicly states the commitments in 20X0. The costs that the entity will incur to reduce its annual greenhouse gas emissions and to offset the greenhouse gases it emits in 20X9 do not exist independently of the entity's future actions.
- only when the entity has emitted the greenhouse gases that it has committed to offset will it have a present obligation to offset those greenhouse gases. The entity will have that present obligation only if and when it emits greenhouse gases in 20X9 and in subsequent years.

10.3.2 Recognition criteria for a provision

IAS 37, paragraph 14 states that a provision is recognised when:

(a) an entity has a present obligation (legal or constructive) as a result of a past event;
(b) it is probable that an outflow of resources embodying economic benefits will be required to settle the obligation; and
(c) a reliable estimate can be made of the amount of the obligation.

If these conditions are not met, no provision shall be recognised. Note also that part of the definition of a liability is repeated within part (a) of the recognition criteria. This has been addressed in the previous section. Effectively, therefore, part (a) of paragraph 14 related to the definition of a provision and parts (b) and (c) relate to the recognition criteria.

Turning to the future outflow of resources, IAS 37 paragraph 23 states that an outflow of resources is probable if the event is more likely than not to occur, in which case a provision should be recognised. If it is *not* more likely than not that the event will occur, then a contingent liability should be disclosed (unless the possible outflow is remote).

Paragraphs 25 and 26 of IAS 37 deal with the reliable estimate of the obligation. The use of estimates is an essential part of the preparation of financial statements and does not undermine their reliability. This means that, although a provision is a liability of uncertain timing or amount, it does not mean that this liability cannot be reliably measured. In almost all cases, an entity will be able to determine a range of possible outcomes and can therefore make an estimate of the obligation that is sufficiently reliable to use in recognising a provision. In the extremely rare case where no reliable estimate can be made, the recognition criteria are not met and a contingent liability is disclosed.

10.4 WHAT IS A CONTINGENT LIABILITY?

IAS 37, paragraph 10 defines a contingent liability as:

(a) a possible obligation that arises from past events and whose existence will be confirmed only by the occurrence or non-occurrence of one or more uncertain future events not wholly within the control of the entity; or
(b) a present obligation that arises from past events but is not recognised because:
 (i) it is not probable that an outflow of resources embodying economic benefits will be required to settle the obligation; or
 (ii) the amount of the obligation cannot be measured with sufficient reliability.

The definition of a contingent liability encompasses two distinctly different concepts. The first, part (a) of the definition, is the concept of a *possible* obligation. This fails one of the essential characteristics of a liability — the requirement for the existence of a present obligation. If there is no present obligation, but only a possible one, there is no liability. Hence, part (a) of the definition does not meet the definition of a liability which may lead one to argue that the term 'contingent *liability*' is misleading, because items falling into category (a) are not liabilities by definition.

Part (b) of the definition, on the other hand, deals with liabilities that fail the recognition criteria. They are present obligations, so they meet the essential requirements of the definition of liabilities, but they do not meet the recognition criteria (probability of outflow of economic benefits and reliability of measurement).

However, the definition and recognition criteria need to be considered together. An obligation whose existence is yet to be confirmed does not meet the definition of a liability; and a present obligation in respect of which an outflow of resources is not probable, or which cannot be measured reliably, does not qualify for recognition. On that basis a contingent liability under IAS 37 means one of the following:

• an obligation that is estimated to have less than a 50% likelihood of existing (i.e. it does not meet the definition of a liability). Where it is more likely than not that a present obligation exists at the end of the reporting period, a provision is recognised (see IAS 37 paragraph 16(a)). Where it is *not* more likely than not that a present obligation exists, a contingent liability is disclosed (unless the possibility is remote); or
• a present obligation that has a likelihood of 50% or less of requiring an outflow of economic benefits (i.e. it meets the definition of a liability but does not meet the recognition criteria). Where it is not probable that there will be an outflow of resources, an entity discloses a contingent liability (unless the possibility is remote); or
• a present obligation for which a sufficiently reliable estimate cannot be made (i.e. it meets the definition of a liability but does not meet the recognition criteria). In these rare circumstances, a liability cannot be recognised and it is disclosed as a contingent liability (see IAS 37 paragraph 26).

10.5 DISTINGUISHING A CONTINGENT LIABILITY FROM A PROVISION

A provision is recognised as a liability if it meets the definition and recognition criteria as set out in IAS 37. A contingent liability, on the other hand, is never recognised as it fails to meet either the definition or recognition criteria. In summary, therefore, a contingent liability exists where

- The liability definition is not met, i.e. there is only a possible obligation rather than a present obligation, whose existence will be confirmed only by the occurrence or non-occurrence of one or more uncertain future events, not wholly within the control of the entity, or
- The liability definition is met but it cannot be recognised because one or more of the recognition criteria are not met, i.e. there is a present obligation, from past events, that is not recognised because
  - it is not probable that an outflow of economic benefits will be needed to settle the obligation; or
  - the amount of the obligation cannot be measured sufficiently reliably.

However, and as mentioned previously, contingent liabilities, although not recognised in the financial statements, must be disclosed in the financial statements unless the possibility of an outflow in settlement is remote.

Illustrative example 10.1 illustrates the difference between a contingent liability and a provision.

ILLUSTRATIVE EXAMPLE 10.1 Example of the difference between a provision and a contingent liability

Legal proceedings against Lemon Pharma Co. started after several people became ill, possibly as a result of taking the health supplements manufactured and sold by Lemon. Lemon disputes any liability and, up to the authorised date of issue of its financial statements for 31 December 2023, its lawyers have advised that it is probable that Lemon will not be found liable. However, when Lemon prepares its financial statements for 31 December 2024, its lawyers advise that, owing to the developments in the case, it is probable that Lemon will be found liable and a reliable estimate of the amount of damages can be made.

For 31 December 2023, no provision is recognised and the matter is disclosed as a contingent liability unless the probability of any outflow is regarded as remote. On the basis of the evidence available when the financial statements were approved, there is no obligation as a result of a past event.

For 31 December 2024, a provision is recognised for the best estimate of the amount required to settle the obligation. The fact that an outflow of economic benefits is now believed to be probable and a reliable estimate can be made means that this is no longer a contingent liability, but a provision.

In sections 10.3–10.5 we discussed the definitions of provisions and contingent liabilities, the recognition criteria for provisions and when a contingent liability must be disclosed. The decision tree (figure 10.1) summarises this discussion. The decision tree is based on IAS 37, Implementation Guidance sub B.

10.6 MEASUREMENT OF PROVISIONS

10.6.1 Best estimate

When measuring a provision, the amount recognised should be the *best estimate* of the consideration required to settle the present obligation at the end of the reporting period (IAS 37 paragraph 36). This amount is often expressed as the amount which represents, as closely as possible, what the entity would rationally pay to settle the present obligation at the end of the reporting period or to provide consideration to a third party to assume it. The fact that it is difficult to measure the provision and that estimates have to be used does not mean that the provision is not reliably measurable.

The standard provides guidance on estimation of a provision which involves a large population of items. In such circumstances, the obligation is estimated using the expected value method, i.e. weighting all possible outcomes by their associated probabilities. For example, in January 20X1 Haifa Industries sells 10,000 units of good Y with a 1-year warranty which covers manufacturing defects that become apparent within the first 12 months after purchase. If minor defects are detected, repair costs of $200 per unit of good Y would result. If major defects are detected, repair costs of $1000 per unit of good Y would result. Based upon past experience and future expectations Haifa Industries expects at the end of January 20X1 that, for the goods sold in January, 85% will have no defects, 10% will have minor defects and 5% will have major defects within 12 months after sale. Therefore, Haifa Industries assesses the probability of an outflow for the warranty obligations as a whole. The expected value as at the end of January 20X1 of the cost of repairs will be (85% of nil) + (10% of [$200 × 10,000]) + (5% of [$1,000 × 10,000]) = $700,000.

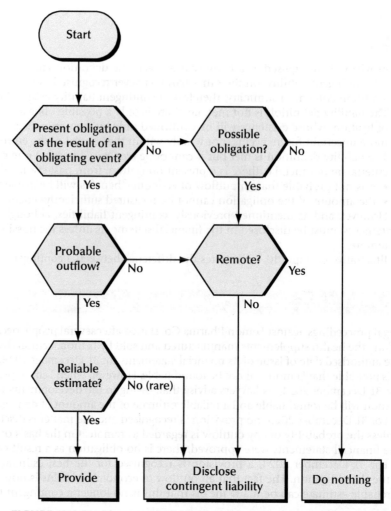

FIGURE 10.1 Decision tree (IAS 37, Implementation Guidance, Section B)

In situations where there is only one single obligation to measure, the individual most likely outcome may be the best estimate of the liability. However, the entity has to consider other possible outcomes as well. Where other possible outcomes are either mostly higher or mostly lower than the most likely outcome, the best estimate will be a higher or lower amount. For example, if an entity has to rectify a serious fault in a major plant that it has constructed for a customer, the individual most likely outcome may be for the repair to succeed at the first attempt at a cost of €100,000, but a provision for a larger amount is made if there is a significant chance that further attempts might be necessary.

The provision is measured before tax. Any tax consequences are accounted for in accordance with IAS 12 *Income Taxes*.

10.6.2 Risks and uncertainties

IAS 37 paragraph 42 requires that the risks and uncertainties surrounding the events and circumstances should be taken into account in reaching the best estimate of a provision. The standard also requires a risk adjustment to be made when measuring liabilities. However, uncertainty is not a justifiable reason for making excessive provisions or deliberately overstating liabilities.

Furthermore, disclosure of the uncertainties surrounding the amount or timing of expected outflows is required by paragraph 85(b) of the standard.

10.6.3 Present value

Provisions are required to be *discounted to present value* where the effect of discounting is material (IAS 37 paragraph 45). IAS 37 (paragraph 47) requires that the discount rate used must be a pre-tax rate that reflects current market assessments of the time value of money and the *risks specific to the liability*. Where future cash flow estimates have been adjusted for risk, the discount rate should not reflect this risk—otherwise the effect of risk would be double-counted.

In practical terms it is often difficult to determine reliably a liability-specific discount rate. Usually entities use a rate available for a liability with similar terms and conditions or, if a similar liability is not available, a risk-free rate for a liability with the same term (e.g. a government bond[1] with a five-year term may be used as the basis for a company's specific liability with a five-year term) and this rate is then adjusted for the risks pertaining to the liability in question.

The mechanism for risk-adjusting a discount rate may seem counterintuitive at first as a risk-adjusted rate for a liability would be a *lower* rate than the risk-free rate. This is demonstrated and further explained in illustrative example 10.2.

ILLUSTRATIVE EXAMPLE 10.2 Calculation of a risk-adjusted rate

A company has a provision for which the expected value of the cash outflow in three years' time is £150 and the risk-free rate is 5%. However, the possible outcomes from which the expected value has been determined lie within a range between £100 and £200. The company is risk-averse and would settle instead for a certain payment of, say, £160 in three years' time rather than be exposed to the risk of the actual outcome being as high as £200. The effect of risk in calculating present value can be expressed as either:
(a) discounting the risk-adjusted cash flow of £160 at the risk-free (unadjusted) rate of 5%, giving a present value of £138; or
(b) discounting the expected cash flow (which is unadjusted for risk) of £150 at a risk-adjusted rate that will give the present value of £138, i.e. a rate of 2.8%.

As can be seen from this example, the risk-adjusted discount rate is a lower rate than the unadjusted (risk-free) discount rate. This may seem counterintuitive initially, because the experience of most borrowers is that lenders will charge a higher rate of interest on loans that are assessed to be higher risk to the lender. However, in the case of a provision a risk premium is being suffered to eliminate the possibility of the actual cost being higher (thereby capping a liability), whereas in the case of a loan receivable a premium is required to compensate the lender for taking on the risk of not recovering its full value (setting a floor for the value of the lender's financial asset). In both cases the actual cash flows incurred by the paying entity are higher to reflect a premium for risk. In other words, the discount rate for an asset is increased to reflect the risk of recovering less and the discount rate for a liability is reduced to reflect the risk of paying more.

Source: Based upon EY International GAAP (2024, chapter 26 section 4.2).

Illustrative example 10.3 shows the way a provision should be measured, taking into account risks and the time value of money.

ILLUSTRATIVE EXAMPLE 10.3 Measuring a provision

Iconic plc estimates that the expected cash outflows to settle its warranty obligations at the end of the reporting period are as follows. (Note that the probability of cash outflows has already been adjusted for risk and, accordingly, no further adjustment for risk is made to the discount rate.) Iconic plc has used a discount rate based on government bonds with the same term and currency as the expected cash outflows as a proxy for the risk-free rate.

Expected cash outflow	Timing	Discount rate	Present value of cash outflow
£400,000	In one year	6.0%	£377,358
100,000	In two years	6.5%	88,166
20,000	In three years	6.9%	16,371
Present value			481,895

---

[1] Assumed to be risk-free although this may not always be the case.

10.6.4 Future events

Anticipated future events expected to affect the amount required to settle the entity's present obligation must be reflected in the amount provided, when there is reliable evidence that they will occur. For example, an entity may believe that the cost of cleaning up a site at the end of its life will be reduced by future changes in technology. The amount recognised reflects a reasonable expectation of technically qualified, objective observers, taking account of all available evidence as to the technology that will be available at the time of the clean-up. Therefore, it is appropriate to include, for example, expected cost reductions associated with increased experience in applying existing technology or the expected cost of applying existing technology to a larger or more complex clean-up operation than has previously been carried out.

10.6.5 Expected disposal of assets

Gains from the expected disposal of assets must not be taken into account when measuring the amount of a provision (IAS 37 paragraph 51), even if the expected disposal is closely linked to the event giving rise to the provision. Rather, when the gain on disposal is made, it should be recognised at that time, in accordance with the relevant IFRS.

10.6.6 Reimbursements

When some of the amount required to settle a provision is expected to be recovered from a third party (e.g. through an insurance contract held that covers the specific loss), IAS 37 requires that the recovery be recognised as an asset, but only when it is *virtually certain* that the reimbursement will be received if the entity settles the obligation (paragraph 53). This differs from the normal asset recognition criteria, which require that the inflow of future economic benefits be *probable*. Presumably, the standard setters were concerned with recognition of an uncertain asset related to a liability of uncertain timing and amount, and therefore decided to make the recognition criteria stricter for these types of assets to avoid variability in the balance sheet. When such an asset is recognised, the amount should not exceed the amount of the provision. No 'netting off' is allowed in the statement of financial position, with any asset classified separately from any provision in accordance with paragraph 53 of IAS 37. However, IAS 37 allows the income from the asset to be set off against the expense relating to the provision in the income statement.

10.6.7 Changes in provisions and use of provisions

IAS 37 requires provisions to be reviewed at the end of each reporting period and adjusted to reflect the current best estimate. If it is no longer probable that an outflow of resources embodying economic benefits will be required to settle the obligation, the provision should be reversed (IAS 37 paragraph 59).

Where discounting is used, the carrying amount of a provision increases in each period to reflect the passage of time. This increase is recognised as borrowing cost.

A provision is recognised for future costs. When these costs are eventually paid, the provision is reduced. However, a provision should be used only for expenditures for which the provision was originally recognised; if a payment is set off against a provision that was recognised for a different purpose, it would conceal the impact of two different events (IAS 37, paragraphs 61 & 62). For example, a provision recognised for legal costs for breach of contract may not be used to set off a provision for legal costs for alleged environmental damage.

Illustrative example 10.4 shows how a provision is accounted for where discounting is applied and where the provision is adjusted to reflect the current best estimate.

ILLUSTRATIVE EXAMPLE 10.4 Accounting for a provision

Weber AG estimates that it will be required to pay €100,000 in three years' time to settle a warranty obligation. The risk-free discount rate applied is 5.5%. The probability of cash outflows has been assessed (i.e. adjusted for risk) in determining the €100,000.

The following table shows how the provision is accreted over the three years:

A. Year	B. Present value at the beginning of the year	C. Interest expense at 5.5% (B × 5.5%)	D. Cash flows	E. Present value at the end of the year (B + C − D)
1	85,161	4,683	—	89,844
2	89,844	4,942	—	94,786
3	94,786	5,214	(100,000)	—

Journal entries are as follows:

On initial recognition in year 1:			
Warranty Expense	Dr	85,161	
Warranty Provision	Cr		85,161

On recognition of interest in year 1:			
Interest Expense	Dr	4,683	
Warranty Provision	Cr		4,683

On recognition of interest in year 2:			
Interest Expense	Dr	4,942	
Warranty Provision	Cr		4,942

On recognition of interest in year 3:			
Interest Expense	Dr	5,214	
Warranty Provision	Cr		5,214

On settlement of provision, end of year 3:			
Warranty Provision	Dr	100,000	
Cash	Cr		100,000

Now assume the same facts as above except that, at the end of year 2, Weber AG re-estimates the amount to be paid to settle the obligation at the end of year 3 to be €90,000. The appropriate discount rate remains at 5.5%.

The present value of €90,000 at the end of year 2 is €85,306. Company A thus adjusts the provision by €9,480 (€94,786 − €85,306) to reflect the revised estimated cash flows.

Journal entries are as follows:

Revision of estimate at end of year 2:			
Warranty Provision	Dr	9,480	
Warranty Expense (statement of comprehensive income)	Cr		9,480

On recognition of interest in year 3:			
Interest Expense (€85,306 × 5.5% rounded)	Dr	4,694	
Warranty Provision	Cr		4,694

On settlement of provision, end of year 3:			
Warranty Provision	Dr	90,000	
Cash	Cr		90,000

The re-estimated cash flows are adjusted against the warranty expense recorded in the statement of comprehensive income, while the unwinding of the discount continues to be recorded as interest expense (IAS 37 paragraph 60).

10.7 APPLICATION OF THE DEFINITIONS, RECOGNITION AND MEASUREMENT RULES

10.7.1 Future operating losses

IAS 37 disallows recognition of provisions for future operating losses (paragraph 63). Even if a sacrifice of future economic benefits is expected, a provision for future operating losses is not recognised because a past event creating a present obligation has not occurred. This is because the entity's management will generally have the ability to avoid incurring future operating losses by either disposing of or restructuring the operation in question. An expectation of future operating losses may, however, be an indicator that an asset is impaired and the requirements of IAS 36 *Impairment of Assets* should be applied.

10.7.2 Onerous contracts

IAS 37 defines an onerous contract as a contract in which the unavoidable costs of meeting the obligations under the contract exceed the economic benefits expected to be received under it.

If an entity is a party to an onerous contract, a provision for the present obligation under the contract must be recognised (IAS 37 paragraph 66). The reason these losses should be provided for is that the entity is contracted to fulfil the contract. Therefore an onerous contract gives rise to a present obligation. Examples of onerous contracts include:

- where an electricity supplier has entered into a contract to supply electricity at a price lower than the price at which it is contracted to receive
- where a manufacturer has entered into a supply contract to provide goods to a customer at a price below its costs of production.

In May 2020, the IASB issued amendments to IAS 37 (paragraph 68A) to specify which costs an entity needs to include when assessing whether a contract is onerous or loss-making. The amendments apply a 'directly related cost approach'. The costs that relate directly to a contract to provide goods or services include both incremental costs (e.g. the costs of direct labour and materials) and an allocation of costs directly related to contract activities (e.g. depreciation of equipment used to fulfil the contract as well as costs of contract management and supervision). General and administrative costs do not relate directly to a contract and are excluded unless they are explicitly chargeable to the counterparty under the contract.

For the purpose of raising a provision in respect of an onerous contract, the amount to be recognised is the least net cost of exiting the contract; that is, the lesser of:

- the cost of fulfilling the contract, and
- any compensation or penalties arising from failure to fulfil the contract.

IAS 37 also requires that before a separate provision is made for an onerous contract, an entity must first recognise any impairment loss that has occurred on assets dedicated to that contract. This is shown in illustrative example 10.5.

ILLUSTRATIVE EXAMPLE 10.5 Accounting for an onerous contract

Alpha Ltd enters into a supply agreement with Beta Ltd on 1 January 2024. The agreement states that Alpha Ltd must supply Beta Ltd with 100 chairs at a price of $150 per chair. The agreement also states that if Alpha Ltd cannot deliver the chairs on time and under the terms of the contract it must pay Beta Ltd a penalty of $12,000. The delivery date is 31 March 2024. Alpha Ltd concludes that the sales contract does not meet the criteria for over-time revenue recognition *(see chapter 3)*. Alpha Ltd commences manufacturing the chairs on 1 March and experiences a series of production problems that result in the cost to produce each chair totalling $200 at 31 March 2024. As at 31 March Alpha Ltd identifies an onerous contract in accordance with IAS 37 because the costs of fulfilling the contract (100 × $200 = $20,000) exceed the agreed amount to be received (100 × $150 = $15,000). The cost of the chairs is recognised as inventory as at 31 March 2024. Assuming the end of Alpha Ltd's reporting period is 31 March it must first recognise an impairment loss on the inventory. This would be calculated and recorded as $5,000 (lower of cost and net realisable value [ignoring costs to sell] under IAS 2 *Inventories* — see chapter 4). Once this impairment loss has been recognised, there is no amount to be recorded as a provision under the onerous contract. However, if Alpha Ltd had not yet recorded any costs as inventory it would need to determine what amount to recognise as a provision for the onerous contract. This would be the lesser of the penalty required to be paid to Beta Ltd ($12,000) and the cost of fulfilling the contract ($5,000, which is only to the extent that costs are not covered by related revenues). Thus, Alpha Ltd would record a provision of $5,000.

10.7.3 Restructuring provisions

A restructuring is a programme that is planned and controlled by management, and materially changes either the scope of the business or the manner in which the business is conducted (IAS 37, paragraph 10).

Examples of restructurings are given in paragraph 70 and include:
(a) sale or termination of a line of business;
(b) the closure of business locations in a country or region or the relocation of business activities from one country or region to another;
(c) changes in management structure, for example, eliminating a layer of management; and
(d) fundamental reorganisations that have a material effect on the nature and focus of the entity's operations.

An entity that is planning a restructuring will expect to incur a variety of costs such as retrenchment packages or costs incurred in the sale of plant and machinery. For an entity to recognise a provision for the expected costs of restructuring, the same definition and recognition criteria for a provision must be met. In addition, IAS 37 provides further criteria to assist in determining whether the basic definition and recognition criteria have been met.

In broad terms, there are three additional criteria that need to be met. First, the entity must have a *present obligation (either legal or constructive)* to restructure such that it cannot realistically avoid going ahead with the restructuring and thus incurring the costs involved. Second, only costs that are *directly and necessarily* caused by the restructuring and *not associated with the ongoing activities* of the entity may be included in a restructuring provision. Third, if the restructuring involves the sale of an operation, no obligation is deemed to arise for the sale of an operation until the entity is committed to the sale by a *binding sale agreement*. Each of these requirements is considered in more detail below.

Present obligation

Usually management initiates a restructuring and thus it is uncommon that a legal obligation will exist for a restructuring. IAS 37 therefore focuses on the conditions that need to be met for a constructive obligation to exist.

In respect of restructuring provisions, a constructive obligation to restructure arises only when an entity:
(a) has a detailed formal plan for the restructuring identifying at least:
    (i) the business or part of a business concerned;
    (ii) the principal locations affected;
    (iii) the location, function, and approximate number of employees who will be compensated for terminating their services;
    (iv) the expenditures that will be undertaken; and
    (v) when the plan will be implemented; and
(b) has raised a valid expectation in those affected that it will carry out the restructuring by starting to implement that plan or announcing its main features to those affected by it *(see IAS 37 paragraph 72)*.

Therefore, we see that the entity needs to have a *detailed formal plan* and must have raised a *valid expectation* in those affected.

Qualifying restructuring costs

The second requirement for recognition of a restructuring provision is that the provision can include only costs that are directly and necessarily caused by the restructuring and not associated with the ongoing activities of the entity (IAS 37 paragraph 80).

Examples of the types of costs that would be included in a restructuring provision include the costs of terminating leases and other contracts as a direct result of the restructuring and costs of making employees redundant.

Paragraph 81 of IAS 37 specifically indicates that the types of costs excluded from provisions for restructuring would be the costs of retraining or relocating the continuing staff, marketing costs and costs related to investment in new systems and distribution networks. These types of costs relate to the future conduct of the entity and do not relate to present obligations.

These requirements relating to the types of costs that qualify as restructuring costs apply equally to internal restructurings as well as to restructurings occurring as part of an acquisition.

It is important to note that, although certain costs have occurred only because of restructuring (i.e. they would not have had to be incurred had the restructuring not taken place), this fact alone does not qualify them for recognition as restructuring costs. They also have to be costs that are not associated with the ongoing activities of the entity.

The final requirement for recognition of a restructuring provision is that if the restructuring involves the sale of an operation, no obligation is deemed to arise for the sale until the entity is committed to the sale by a binding sale agreement (IAS 37 paragraph 78). It is because, before there is a binding sale agreement, an entity could change its mind or take another course of action if a purchaser cannot be found on acceptable terms. For the treatment of non-current assets held for sale and discontinued operations, refer to IFRS 5 *Non-current Assets Held for Sale and Discontinued Operations* for further guidance.

10.7.4 Decommissioning provisions

When an entity is required to remove an asset at the end of its useful life and to restore the site where it was located, such decommissioning costs are required to be provided for (see IAS 37 IE Example 3). A provision is required to be recognised at the time the asset is being constructed as the environmental damage requiring restoration in the future presumably starts at that point in time.

For changes in estimates of the decommissioning provision, IAS 37 lacks relevant guidance, therefore IFRIC 1 *Changes in Existing Decommissioning, Restoration and Similar Liabilities* was issued in May 2004 to rectify this.

IFRIC 1 provides guidance on accounting for changes in decommissioning, restoration and similar liabilities that have previously been recognised both as part of the cost of an item of property, plant and equipment under IAS 16 and as a provision under IAS 37. This would apply, for example, to a liability that was recognised by an entity operating an oil rig for costs that it expects to incur in the future when the rig is decommissioned.

IAS 37 requires the amount recognised as a provision to be the best estimate of the expenditure required to settle the obligation at the reporting date. This is measured at its present value, which according to IFRIC 1, should be a current market-based discount rate.

The three kinds of change dealt with in the Interpretation are those that arise from:

(a) the revision of estimated outflows of resources embodying economic benefits (for example, the estimated costs of decommissioning an oil rig may vary significantly both in timing and amount)

(b) revisions to the current market-based discount rate

(c) an increase in the liability that reflects the passage of time — also referred to as the unwinding of the discount.

Most entities account for their property, plant and equipment using the cost model of IAS 16. For changes caused by (a) or (b), these changes are required to be capitalised as part of the cost of the item and depreciated over the remaining life of the item to which they relate. This is consistent with the treatment in terms of IAS 16 of other changes in estimate relating to property, plant and equipment.

A change caused by (c), the periodic unwinding of the discount, is recognised in profit or loss as a finance cost as it occurs.

10.7.5 Levies

IFRIC 21 provides guidance on when to recognise a liability for a levy imposed by a government. This includes levies that are accounted for in accordance with IAS 37 and levies where the timing and amount is certain.

Excluded from the ambit of IFRIC 21 are income taxes, fines and other penalties, liabilities arising from emissions trading schemes and outflows within the scope of other Standards.

IFRIC 21 identifies the obligating event for the recognition of a liability as the activity that triggers the payment of the levy in accordance with the relevant legislation. It also provides the following guidance on recognition of a liability to pay levies:

- The liability is recognised progressively if the obligating event occurs over a period of time;
- If an obligation is triggered on reaching a minimum threshold, the liability is recognised when that minimum threshold is reached.

IFRIC 21 does not deal with how to account for costs arising from the recognition of a liability to pay a levy, and instead other standards are applied in determining whether the recognition of a liability gives rise to an asset or expense.

Table 10.1 summarises the illustrative examples that accompany IFRIC 21.

Table 10.1 IFRIC 21 examples

Illustrative examples	Obligating event	Recognition of liability
Levy triggered progressively as revenue is generated in a specified period.	Generation of revenue in the specified period.	Recognise progressively. A liability must be recognised progressively because, at any point in time during the specified period, the entity has a present obligation to pay a levy on revenues generated to date.
Levy triggered in full as soon as revenue is generated in one period, based on revenues from a previous period.	First generation of revenue in subsequent period.	Full recognition at that point in time. Where an entity generates revenue in one period, which serves as the basis for measuring the amount of the levy in a subsequent year, the entity does not become liable for the levy, and therefore cannot recognise a liability, until it first starts generating revenue in the subsequent period.
Levy triggered in full if the entity operates as a bank at the end of the annual reporting period.	Operating as a bank at the end of the reporting period.	Full recognition at the end of the annual reporting period. Before the end of the annual reporting period, the entity has no present obligation to pay a levy, even if it is economically compelled to continue operating as a bank in the future. The liability is recognised only at the end of the annual reporting period.
Levy triggered if revenues are above a minimum specified threshold (e.g. when a certain level of revenue has been achieved).	Reaching the specified minimum threshold.	Recognise an amount consistent with the obligation at that point of time. A liability is recognised only at the point that the specified minimum threshold is reached. For example, a levy is triggered when an entity generates revenues above specified thresholds: 0% for the first $50 million and 2% above $50 million. In this example, no liability is accrued until the entity's revenues reach the revenue threshold of $50 million.

10.7.6 Other applications

Illustrative examples 10.6–10.13, sourced from IAS 37 and modified to aid understanding, illustrate the applications of the recognition requirements of IAS 37.

ILLUSTRATIVE EXAMPLE 10.6 Warranties

Eastern Systems gives warranties at the time of sale to purchasers of its product. Under the terms of the contract for sale Eastern Systems undertakes to make good, by repair or replacement, manufacturing defects that become apparent within three years from the date of sale. On past experience, it is probable (that is, more likely than not) that there will be some claims under the warranties.

In these circumstances the obligating event is the sale of the product with a warranty, which gives rise to a legal obligation. Because it is more likely than not that there will be an outflow of resources for some claims under the warranties as a whole, a provision is recognised for the best estimate of the costs of making good under the warranty for those products sold before the end of the reporting period.

Hadafa Petrochemical in the oil industry causes contamination but cleans up only when required to do so under the laws of the particular country in which it operates. One country in which it operates has had no legislation requiring cleaning up, and the entity has been contaminating land in that country for several years. At 31 December 2024, it is virtually certain that a draft law requiring a clean-up of land already contaminated will be enacted shortly after the year end.

In these circumstances, the virtual certainty of new legislation being enacted means that Hadafa has a present legal obligation as a result of the past event (contamination of the land), requiring a provision to be recognised.

Conch in the oil industry causes contamination and operates in a country where there is no environmental legislation. However, Conch has a widely published environmental policy in which it undertakes to clean up all contamination that it causes. Conch has a record of honouring this published policy.

In these circumstances a provision is still required because Conch has created a valid expectation that it will clean up the land, meaning that Conch has a present constructive obligation as a result of past contamination. It is therefore clear that where an entity causes environmental damage and has a present legal or constructive obligation to make it good, it is probable that an outflow of resources will be required to settle the obligation, and a reliable estimate can be made of the amount, a provision will be required.

Pearl operates an offshore oilfield where its licencing agreement requires it to remove the oil rig at the end of production and restore the seabed. Of the eventual costs, 90% relate to the removal of the oil rig and restoration of damage caused by building it, and 10% arise through the extraction of oil. At the end of the reporting period, the rig has been constructed but no oil has been extracted.

A provision is recognised at the time of constructing the oil rig (obligating event) in relation to the eventual costs that relate to its removal and the restoration of damage caused by building it. Additional provisions are recognised over the life of the oil field to reflect the need to reverse damage caused during the extraction of oil. A provision is recognised for the best estimate of 90% of the eventual costs that relate to the removal of the oil rig and restoration of damage caused by building it. These costs are included as part of the cost of the oil rig. The 10% of costs that arise through the extraction of oil are recognised as a liability when the oil is extracted.

Under new legislation, Karachi Ltd is required to fit smoke filters to its factories by 30 June 2023. Karachi Ltd has not fitted the smoke filters.

(a) At the end of the reporting period, 31 December 2022:

No event has taken place to create an obligation. Only once the smoke filters are fitted or the legislation takes effect will there be a present obligation as a result of a past event, either for the cost of fitting smoke filters or for fines under the legislation.

(b) At the end of the reporting period, 31 December 2023:

There is still no obligating event to justify provision for the cost of fitting the smoke filters required under the legislation because the filters have not been fitted. However, an obligation may exist as at the reporting date to pay fines or penalties under the legislation because Karachi Ltd is operating its factory in a non-compliant way. However, a provision would only be recognised for the best estimate of any fines and penalties if, as at 31 December 2023, it is determined to be more likely than not that such fines and penalties will be imposed.

Some assets require, in addition to routine maintenance, substantial expenditure every few years for major refits or refurbishment and the replacement of major components. IAS 16 *Property, Plant and Equipment* gives guidance on allocating expenditure on an asset to its component parts where these components have different useful lives or provide benefits in a different pattern.

An aircraft has an air-conditioning and pressurisation system that needs to be replaced every five years for technical reasons. At the end of the reporting period, the system has been in use for three years.

In these circumstances, a provision for the cost of replacing the system is not recognised because, at the end of the reporting period, no obligation to replace the system exists independently of the entity's future actions. Even the intention to incur the expenditure depends upon the entity deciding to continue operating the system or to replace the system. Instead of a provision being recognised, the initial cost of the system is treated as a significant part of the aircraft and depreciated over a period of five years. The replacement costs are then capitalised when incurred and depreciated over the next five years *(also see chapter 5).*

Sunshine Air is required by law to overhaul its aircraft once every three years.

Even with the legal requirement to perform the overhaul, there is no obligating event until the 3-year period has elapsed. As with the previous example, no obligation exists independently of Sunshine Air's future actions. Sunshine Air could avoid the cost of the overhaul by selling the aircraft before the 3-year period has elapsed. Instead of a provision being recognised, the overhaul cost is identified as a separate part of the aircraft asset under IAS 16 and is depreciated over three years *(also see chapter 5).*

10.8 CONTINGENT ASSETS

A contingent asset is a possible asset that arises from past events and whose existence will be confirmed only by the occurrence or non-occurrence of one or more uncertain future events not wholly within the control of the entity (IAS 37 paragraph 10). IAS 37 does not allow the recognition of a contingent asset and disclosures are required when an inflow of benefits is probable.

An example of a contingent asset would be the possible receipt of damages arising from a court case, which has been decided in favour of the entity as at the end of the reporting period. The hearing to determine damages, however, will be held after the end of the reporting period. The outcome of the hearing is outside the control of the entity, but the receipt of damages is probable because the case has been decided in the entity's favour. The asset meets the definition of a contingent asset because it is possible that the entity will receive the damages and the hearing is outside its control. In addition, the contingent asset is disclosed because it is probable that the damages (the inflow of economic benefits) will flow to the entity.

10.9 DISCLOSURE

The disclosure requirements of IAS 37 are self-explanatory and are described in paragraphs 84–92 of the standard.

Note that the disclosures required for contingent liabilities and assets involve judgement and estimation. Many analysts consider the contingent liabilities note to be one of the most important notes provided by a company because it helps the analyst in making decisions about the likely consequences for the company and is useful in providing an overall view of the company's exposures. Therefore, the use of the exemption for non-disclosure of information, which would prejudice an entity's position in a dispute with other parties as permitted in paragraph 92, should be treated with caution because it could be interpreted as a deliberate concealing of the company's exposures.

An example of disclosures of provisions and related assumptions is included in the annual report of Bidvest, a global enterprise based in South Africa, reporting under IFRS Standards. Figure 10.2 is an extract from the provisions note (note 8.1)

FIGURE 10.2 Example of disclosures of provisions

8.11. Provisions

					2023 R'000	2022 R'000
Long-term portion					**567,657**	671,955
Short-term portion					**639,343**	398,812
					1,207,000	1,070,767

	Onerous contracts R'000	Business Integration R'000	Insurance liabilities R'000	Legal claims R'000	Other R'000	Total R'000
Balance at 1 July 2021	44,818	322,533	226,505	459,271	42,863	1,095,990
Created	1,653	59,444	190,360	85,494	26,242	363,193
Utilised	(15,291)	(112,420)	(212,375)	(81,001)	(18,365)	(439,452)
Net acquisition of businesses	-	10,971	-	617	-	11,588
Exchange rate adjustments	259	1,031	-	38,158	-	39,448
Balance at 30 June 2022	31,439	281,559	204,490	502,539	50,740	1,070,767
Created	**1,438**	**54,930**	**120,949**	**59,469**	**28,999**	**265,785**
Utilised	**(21,751)**	**(63,111)**	**(77,431)**	**(46,738)**	**(19,723)**	**(228,754)**
Net disposal of businesses and disposal group	-	-	-	**(8,378)**	**4,369**	**(4,009)**
Exchange rate adjustments	**2,695**	**35,095**	-	**65,421**	-	**103,211**
Balance at 30 June 2023	**13,821**	**308,473**	**248,008**	**572,313**	**64,385**	**1,207,000**

Onerous contracts

Onerous contracts are identified through regular renews of the terms and conditions of contracts as well as on the acquisition of businesses. A provision for onerous contracts is calculated as the present value of the portion which management deem to be onerous in light of the current market conditions, discounted using market-related rates

Business integration

Provisions raised to restructure and re-align the Group's operations to reduced demand. Included are provisions for retrenchment arising from s 189 (of the Labour Relations Act) notice and consultation processes and other provisions necessary to right-size the business.

Insurance liabilities

Insurance liabilities include amounts provided for under IFRS 4 and include: unearned premiums, which represent the proportion of premiums written in the current year which relate to risks that have not expired by the end of the financial year and are calculated on a time proportionate basis; deferred acquisition costs, which are recognised on a basis consistent with the related provisions for unearned premiums; claims, which are calculated on the settlement amount outstanding at year end; and, claims incurred but not reported, for claims arising from events that occurred before the close of the accounting period but which had not been reported to the Group by that date, and are calculated based on the preceding six years' insurance premium revenue multiplied by percentages specified in the Short Term Insurance Act.

Legal claims

Legal claims include provisions raised under IAS37 for the estimated cost of claims not covered by the Group's insurance policies and in certain instances for the cost of claims below the Group's inner deductibles. Legal claims have long lead times and the provision is determined using actuarial assumptions.

Other

Included in other is a provision raised for the estimated cost of honouring warranties on certain products sold where the manufacturers' warranty is inadequate or not available, R63 million (2022: R40 million).

Source: Bidvest (*Annual Report 2023*, p. 56).

10.10 SUMMARY

IAS 37 deals with the recognition, measurement and presentation of provisions and contingent assets and contingent liabilities. The standard contains specific requirements regarding the recognition of restructuring provisions and onerous contracts.

The standard:
- defines provisions and specifies recognition criteria and measurement requirements for the recognition of provisions in financial statements
- defines contingent liabilities and contingent assets and prohibits their recognition in the financial statements but requires their disclosure when certain conditions are met
- requires that where provisions are measured using estimated cash flows, that the cash flows be discounted to their present value at the reporting date and specifies the discount rate to be used for this purpose
- prohibits providing for future operating losses
- defines onerous contracts and requires the estimated net loss under onerous contracts to be provided for
- specifies recognition criteria for restructuring provisions and identifies the types of costs that may be included in restructuring provisions
- requires extensive disclosures relating to provisions, recoveries, contingent liabilities and contingent assets.

The standard differs from IFRS 3 *Business Combinations* in respect of the recognition of contingent liabilities and contingent consideration. However, it is consistent with IFRS 3 in respect of restructuring provisions.

Discussion questions

1. How is present value related to the concept of a liability?
2. Define (a) a contingency and (b) a contingent liability.
3. What are the characteristics of a provision?
4. Define a constructive obligation.
5. What is the key characteristic of a present obligation?
6. What are the recognition criteria for provisions?
7. At what point would a contingent liability become a provision?
8. Compare and contrast the requirements of IFRS 3 and IAS 37 in respect of restructuring provisions and contingent liabilities.

References

Bidvest 2023, *Annual Report 2014*, Bidvest, group-afs.pdf (bidvest-reports.co.za).
IFRS Interpretations Committee (2023), Climate-related Commitments (IAS 37 Provisions, Contingent Liabilities and Contingent Assets)—Agenda Paper 2, https://www.ifrs.org/content/dam/ifrs/supporting-implementation/agenda-decisions/2024/climate-related-commitments-apr-24.pdf

As pointed out in the chapter, one of the main types of provision is the provision for restructuring costs. The requirements of IAS 37 with respect to restructuring likely had been influenced by some high-profile abuses of previous rules (e.g., the case of W.R. Grace & Co. and Lucent Technologies in the late 1990s). But what is the evidence supporting the notion that the restructuring provision is prone to earnings management? Nelson et al. (2002) surveyed over 250 auditors working in large audit firms about their experience with earnings management. One interesting insight that emerged from this survey is that provisions are most susceptible to earnings management. By initially inflating the provision, managers create a 'cookie jar' that can be used later to support future earnings. Consistent with this, Gu and Chen's (2004) analysis of non-recurring items indicates that restructuring charges are the leading type among such items.

Moehrle (2002) examines the financials of 121 firms that reversed their restructuring charges (reversing firms) to understand the motivation for the reversal. Reversed charges work to increase reported profit and hence may be opportunistically used by managers to meet market expectations. Consistent with this conjecture, he finds that reversing firms experience pre-reversal negative earnings, and pre-reversal earnings that fall short of analyst expectations. This evidence is consistent with 'cookie jar' earnings management that enables managers to reverse the charge when managers need to boost reported income to meet certain profit targets.

Environmental liabilities and environmental-related disclosures received considerable attention in the accounting literature. Firms that contaminate sites they use for their plants and operations need to estimate the 'clean-up' costs that will be needed after cessation of activity and accrue a provision. Barth and McNichols (1994) is one of the earliest studies of this provision. They provide evidence that suggests that clean-up provisions are understated. In a follow-up paper Barth et al. (1997) examine the determinants of the disclosures of clean-up provisions. They provide evidence that indicates that several factors influence these disclosures, including the regulatory environment, manager's information and threat of litigation. Lawrence and Khurana (1997) investigate the accrual of clean-up provisions in US municipalities. They find that two thirds of sample municipalities fail to accrue clean-up provisions and provide adequate disclosures.

Provisions need to be accrued and recognised, provided the resource outflow is probable, whereas (unrecognised) contingent liabilities arise when the outflow is only possible. For both accrued provisions and contingent liabilities there are additional disclosure requirements regarding expected amounts and timing. A powerful disincentive to provide detailed disclosures is present in the case of legal provisions. This is because disclosed information can be used by the opposing litigating party. Desir et al. (2010) examine 51 cases in which companies disclose details regarding the resolution of litigation cases. While 47 of these companies mention the exposure in the statements immediately preceding the loss resolution, only 24 quantify the magnitude of the expected loss. Nevertheless, only 31 firms accrue the loss before-hand. This evidence in Desir et al. (2010) is consistent with resistance of managers to disclose potentially harmful information. This conclusion is reinforced by Hennes's (2014) study of 212 resolved employee discrimination lawsuits.

There is little evidence on other types of provisions. Cohen et al. (2011) look at the provision for warranty cost. They posit that this provision can convey to the market managers' information about the underlying product quality. Specifically, employing signalling theory they argue greater warranty expense and larger provisions indicate better product quality and hence better future sales and return on assets. They provide evidence that is consistent with this view. In addition, they find that the market regards this provision similar to other liabilities. Finally, they provide evidence suggesting that the warranty provision is used opportunistically by managers of underperforming firms.

The accrual of a provision is dependent on how managers and auditors interpret the concept of 'probable' outflow. This can be quite subjective and prior accounting and psychology research reviewed in Amer et al. (1995) suggests probability measures vary quite significantly across individuals. Specifically, Amer et al. (1995) examine whether the meaning of 'probable' varies across loss contexts, an outcome that was not intended by standard setters. In particular, in experimental setting auditor-subjects were asked to assess risk of default of a customer of a hypothetical audit client. The subjects were also given background information about the health of the industry in which the hypothetical client operates in addition to information about the client's customer. The main finding was that the threshold for 'probable' was higher when industry conditions were good than when they were poorer (0.75 versus 0.68). Hence Amer et al. (1995) conclude that auditors' interpretation of what is probable may be sensitive to the context in which the assessment is applied.

Aharony and Dotan (2004) explore whether analysts and managers similarly interpret 'remote' and 'probable'. They analyse about 300 questionnaires sent to managers, analysts and auditors in the US. They report that analysts regard an outflow event as 'remote' when the probability is up to 0.17, on average. Mangers' probability assessment of a remote event is higher, at 0.20, on average. Analysts quantify 'probable' as an event whose chance is 0.67, on average, while managers assign it 0.75, on average. Auditors provide estimates that are identical to those of managers, on average. These findings suggest that managers' and auditors' threshold for accruing a provision are higher than market perceptions and that they tend to under-report loss events by arguing they are remote.

References

Aharony, J., and Dotan, A., 2004. A comparative analysis of auditor, manager and financial analyst interpretations of SFAS 5 disclosure guidelines. *Journal of Business Finance & Accounting*, 31, 475–504.

Amer, T., Hackenbrack, K., and Nelson, M.W., 1995. Context-dependence of auditors' interpretations of the SFAS no. 5 probability expressions. *Contemporary Accounting Research*, 12(1), 25–39.

Barth, M.E., and McNichols, M.C., 1994. Estimation and market valuation of environmental liabilities relating to superfund sites. *Journal of Accounting Research*, 32 (Supplement), 177–209.

Barth, M.E., McNichols, M.C., Wilson, G.P., 1997. Factors influencing firms' disclosures about environmental liabilities. *Review of Accounting Studies*, 2(1), 35–64.

Cohen, D., Darrough, M.N., Huang, R., and Zach, T., 2011. Warranty reserve: contingent liability, information signal, or earnings management tool? *The Accounting Review*, 86(2), 569–604.

Desir, R., Fanning, K., and Pfeiffer, R.J., 2010. Are revisions to SFAS No. 5 needed? *Accounting Horizons*, 24(4), 525–545.

Gu, Z., and Chen, T., 2004. Analysts' treatment of nonrecurring items in street earnings. *Journal of Accounting and Economics*, 38 (Conference Issue), 129–170.

Hennes, K.M., 2014. Disclosure of contingent legal liabilities. *Journal of Accounting and Public Policy*, 33(1), 32–50.

Lawrence, C.M., and Khurana, I.K., 1997. Superfund liabilities and governmental reporting entities: an empirical analysis. *Journal of Accounting and Public Policy*, 16(2), 155–186.

Moehrle, S.R., 2002. Do firms use restructuring charge reversals to meet earnings targets? *The Accounting Review*, 77(2), 397–413.

Nelson, M.W., Elliott, J.A., and Tarpley, R.L., 2002. Evidence from auditors about managers' and auditors' earnings management decisions. *The Accounting Review*, 77(s-1), 175–202.

11

Employee benefits

ACCOUNTING STANDARDS IN FOCUS

IAS 19 *Employee Benefits*

LEARNING OBJECTIVES

After studying this chapter, you should be able to:

1. outline the principles applied in accounting for employee benefits

2. discuss the scope and purpose of IAS 19

3. discuss the definition of employee benefits

4. prepare journal entries to account for short-term liabilities for employee benefits, such as wages and salaries, sick leave and annual leave

5. compare defined benefit and defined contribution post-employment benefit plans

6. prepare entries to account for expenses, assets and liabilities arising from defined contribution post-employment plans

7. prepare entries to record expenses, assets and liabilities arising from defined benefit post-employment plans

8. explain how to measure and record other long-term liabilities for employment benefits, such as long service leave

9. explain when a liability should be recognised for termination benefits and how it should be measured.

11.1 INTRODUCTION TO ACCOUNTING FOR EMPLOYEE BENEFITS

Employee benefits typically constitute a significant component of an entity's expenses, particularly in the services sector. For example, HSBC Holdings plc (a bank) reports in its 2023 financial statements that 'total operating expenses' of US$32,070 million include 'employee compensation and benefits' of US$18,220 million. Employees are remunerated for the services they provide. Employee remuneration is not limited to wages, which may be paid weekly, fortnightly, or monthly, but often includes entitlements to be paid, such as sick leave, annual leave, long service leave and post-employment benefits, such as pension plans. The measurement of short-term liabilities for employee benefits, such as sick leave and annual leave, is relatively straightforward. However, the measurement of other types of employee benefits, including post-employment benefits, other long-term benefits, such as long service leave, and termination benefits, is more complex because it requires estimation and present value calculations.

11.2 SCOPE AND PURPOSE OF IAS 19

IAS 19 *Employee Benefits* applies to all employee benefits except those to which IFRS 2 *Share-based Payment* applies. Employee benefits arise from formal employment contracts between an entity and its individual employees. Employee benefits also include requirements specified by legislation or industry arrangements for employers to contribute to an industry, state or national plan. Informal practices that generate a constructive obligation, such as payment of annual bonuses, also fall within the scope of employee benefits under IAS 19. Share-based employee benefits are beyond the scope of IAS 19. *Chapter 14 considers share-based payments, including share-based employee remuneration.*

The purpose of IAS 19 is to prescribe the recognition, measurement and disclosure requirements for expenses, assets and liabilities arising from services provided by employees. Liabilities arise when employees provide services in exchange for benefits to be provided later by the employer. Accounting for employee benefits is complicated because some benefits may be provided many years after employees have provided services. The measurement of liabilities for employee benefits is made more difficult because the payment of some employee benefits for past services may be conditional upon the continuation of employment.

11.3 DEFINING EMPLOYEE BENEFITS

Paragraph 8 of IAS 19 defines employee benefits as including all types of consideration that the employer may give in exchange for services provided by employees or for the termination of employment. Employee benefits are usually paid to employees but the term also includes amounts paid to their dependants or to other parties.

Wages, salaries and other employee benefits are usually recognised as expenses. However, the costs of employee benefits may be allocated to assets in accordance with other accounting standards. For example, the cost of labour used in the manufacture of inventory is included in the cost of inventory in accordance with IAS 2 *Inventories*. The cost of an internally generated intangible asset recognised in accordance with IAS 38 *Intangible Assets*, such as the development of a new production process, includes the cost of employee benefits for staff, such as engineers, employed in generating the new production process.

11.4 SHORT-TERM EMPLOYEE BENEFITS

Short-term employee benefits are expected to be settled wholly within 1 year after the end of the annual reporting period in which the employee renders the service. Examples of short-term employee benefits include wages, salaries, bonuses and profit-sharing arrangements. They also include various forms of paid leave entitlements for which employees may be eligible. Sick leave and annual leave are common forms of paid leave entitlements. IAS 19 refers to various forms of leave entitlements as paid absences.

Short-term employee benefits also include non-monetary benefits, which are often referred to as 'fringe benefits'. Non-monetary benefits include the provision of health insurance, housing and motor vehicles. An entity may offer non-monetary benefits to attract staff. For example, a mining company may provide housing to employees where there are no major towns located near its mining sites. Non-monetary benefits may also arise from salary sacrifice arrangements, otherwise referred to as salary packaging. A salary sacrifice arrangement involves the employee electing to forgo some of his or her salary or wages in return for other benefits, such as a motor vehicle, provided by the employer.

11.4.1 Payroll

The subsystem for regular recording and payment of employee benefits is referred to as the payroll. The payroll involves:

- recording the amount of wages or salaries for the pay period
- updating personnel records for the appointment of new employees
- updating personnel records for the termination of employment contracts
- calculating the amount to be paid to each employee, net of deductions
- remitting payment of net wages or salaries to employees
- remitting payment of deductions and employer taxes and charges to various external parties
- complying with regulatory requirements, such as reporting to taxation authorities.

Entities may process several payrolls. For example, an entity may process a payroll each fortnight for employees who are paid on a fortnightly basis and process a separate monthly payroll for employees paid on a monthly basis.

In return for providing services to the employer, employees regularly receive benefits, or remuneration, in the form of wages or salaries. Employers are typically required to deduct income tax from employees' wages and salaries. Thus the employee receives a payment that is net of tax, and the employer subsequently pays the amount of income tax to the taxation authority.

Employers may offer a service of deducting other amounts from employees' wages and salaries and paying other parties on their behalf. For example, the employer may deduct union membership fees from employees' wages and make payments to the various unions on behalf of the employees.

Payments made on behalf of an employee from amounts deducted from the employee's wages or salaries form part of the entity's wages and salaries expense. As these amounts are typically remitted in the month following the payment of wages and salaries, they represent a short-term liability for employee benefits at the end of each month.

Paragraph 11(a) of IAS 19 requires short-term employee benefits for services rendered during the period to be recognised as a liability after deducting any amounts already paid. Short-term liabilities for employee benefits must be measured at the nominal (undiscounted) amount that the entity expects to pay.

11.4.2 Accounting for the payroll

Illustrative example 11.1 demonstrates accounting for the payroll, including deductions from employees' remuneration, the remittance of payroll deductions and the measurement of resulting liabilities at the end of the period.

ILLUSTRATIVE EXAMPLE 11.1 Accounting for the payroll

Pacific Inc. pays its managers on a monthly basis. All managerial salaries are recognised as expenses. Pacific Inc.'s employees can elect to have their monthly private health insurance premiums deducted from their salaries and paid to their health insurance company on their behalf. Employees are also enrolled into a pension scheme which involves 5% deduction from gross pay. Pacific Inc. is required by law to withhold income tax and social security tax at the source, and transfer to the tax authorities within 30 days of payment to employees, but Pacific Inc. makes all payments to all external bodies by the 5th of the following month. Figure 11.1 summarises the managerial payrolls for May and June 2025.

FIGURE 11.1 Summary of Pacific Inc.'s payroll.

	$	May 2025 $	$	June 2025 $
Gross monthly payroll		2,400,000		2,500,000
Deductions:				
Income Tax payable to tax authority	530,000		540,000	
Social Security payable to tax authority	40,000		41,000	
Pension scheme	120,000		125,000	
Private health insurance	32,000		33,000	
		722,000		739,000
Net salaries paid		1,678,000		1,761,000

Each time the monthly payroll is processed, the cost of the salaries is charged to expense accounts and a liability is accrued for the gross wages payable. Payments of net wages and salaries and remittance of payroll deductions to taxation authorities and other parties reduce the payroll liability account.

The managerial payroll is processed and paid on the 25th of the month. During May, managers earned salaries of $2.4 million. After deducting amounts for income tax, social security tax, pension and private health insurance, Pacific Inc. paid its managers a net amount of $1,678,000 during May.

The balance of Pacific Inc.'s accrued managerial payroll account at 1 June 2025 is $722,000, being the deductions from managers' salaries for income tax, social security, pension, and insurance premiums for May 2025. These amounts are paid on 5 June 2025. A similar process is followed for the June salaries.

The journal entries to record Pacific Inc.'s payroll and remittances for the June 2025 payroll are as follows:

June 25	Salaries expense	Dr	2,500,000	
	Bank	Cr		1,761,000
	Income tax payable (including social security)	Cr		581,000
	Pension fund payable	Cr		125,000
	Private health insurance payable	Cr		33,000
	(Managerial payroll for June)			
July 5	Income tax payable	Dr	581,000	
	Pension fund payable	Dr	125,000	
	Private health insurance payable	Dr	33,000	
	Bank	Cr		739,000
	(Payment of income and social security taxes withheld, transfers to private health insurance company and transfer to pension fund for June payroll)			

Depending on the jurisdiction, companies may face employer taxes. These are charges that do not affect net pay to employees, but should also be recognised. For example, in addition to social security tax paid by employees, employers may also need to pay to social security. Such expenses should also be classified as part of employment expenses. Figure 11.2 shows employment costs reported by Rolls-Royce in 2023:

FIGURE 11.2 Employee expenses at Rolls-Royce 2023.

| | **2023** | 2022 | | |
	Total £m	Continuing operations £m	Discontinued operations £m	Total £m
Wages, salaries and benefits	**2,940**	2629	117	2,746
Social security costs	**416**	378	27	405
Share-based payments (note 24)	**66**	47	-	47
Pensions and other post-retirement scheme benefits (note 22)	**346**	268	2	270
Group employment costs	**3,768**	3,322	146	3,468

Source: Rolls-Royce 2023 annual report (p. 150).

11.4.3 Accrual of wages and salaries

The end of the payroll period often differs from the end of the reporting period because payrolls are usually determined on a weekly or fortnightly basis. Accordingly, it is usually necessary to recognise an expense and a liability for employee benefits for the business days between the last payroll period and the end of the reporting period. This is demonstrated in illustrative example 11.2.

Consider again illustrative example 11.1 and assume that Pacific Inc. has a financial year-end of June 30. Also now assume Pacific Inc. pays employees their salaries the following month (in this case June and July for the May and June payrolls, respectively). The last payroll in the financial year is therefore with respect to the month of June. Hence the entry on 25 June will now be:

June 25	Salaries expense	Dr	2,500,000	
	Accrued wages and salaries	Cr		1,761,000
	Income tax payable (including social security)	Cr		581,000
	Pension fund payable	Cr		125,000
	Private health insurance payable	Cr		33,000
	(Managerial payroll for June)			

The accrued wages and salaries is a liability for short-term employee benefits. Paragraph 16 of IAS 19 requires accrued short-term employee benefits to be measured at nominal value; that is, the amount expected to be paid to settle the obligation.

11.4.4 Short-term paid absences

Employees may be entitled to be paid during certain absences, such as annual leave (e.g. holiday) or short periods of illness. Some entities also offer other forms of paid leave, including, parental leave, carers' leave and bereavement leave. Entitlements to short-term paid absences are those entitlements that are expected to be settled within 12 months after the end of the reporting period.

Short-term paid absences may be either accumulating or non-accumulating. Non-accumulating paid absences are leave entitlements that the employee may not carry forward to a future period. For example, an employment contract may provide for 5 days of paid, non-cumulative sick leave. If the employee does not take sick leave during the year, the unused leave lapses; that is, it does not carry forward to an increased entitlement in the following year.

Accumulating paid absences are leave entitlements that the employee may carry forward to a future period, if unused in the current period. For example, an employment contract may provide for 20 days of paid annual leave. If the employee takes only 15 days of annual leave during the year, the remaining 5 days may be carried forward and taken in the following year.

Accumulating paid absences may be vesting or non-vesting. If accumulating paid absences are vesting, the employee is entitled, upon termination of employment, to cash settlement of unused leave. If accumulating paid absences are non-vesting, the employee has no entitlement to cash settlement of unused leave. For example, an employment contract may provide for cumulative annual leave of 20 days, vesting to a maximum of 30 days, and non-vesting cumulative sick leave of 10 days per annum. After 2 years of service, the employee would have been entitled to take 40 days of annual leave and 20 days of sick leave, but if the employee resigned after 2 years of employment, during which no annual leave or sick leave had been taken, the termination settlement would include payment for 30 days' unused annual leave (the maximum allowed by the employment contract). There would be no cash settlement of the unused sick leave because it was non-vesting.

Paragraph 13(a) of IAS 19 requires expected short-term accumulating paid absences to be recognised when the employee renders services that increase the entitlement. For example, if its employees are entitled to 2 weeks of cumulative sick leave for every year of service, the entity is required to accrue the sick leave throughout the year. The employee benefit — that is, the accumulated leave — is measured as the amount that the entity expects to pay to settle the obligation that has accumulated at the end of the reporting period. If the leave is cumulative but non-vesting, it is possible that there will not be a future settlement for some employees. The sick leave might remain unused when the employment contract is terminated. However, the sick leave must still be accrued throughout the period of employment because an obligation arises when the employee provides services that give rise to the leave entitlement. If the leave is non-vesting, it is necessary to estimate the amount of accumulated paid absence that the entity expects to pay.

For non-accumulating short-term paid absences, paragraph 13(b) requires the entity to recognise the employee benefit when the paid absence occurs. A liability is not recognised for unused non-accumulating leave entitlements because the employee is not entitled to carry them forward to a future period. Hence there is no obligation.

The alternative forms of short-term paid absences and the corresponding recognition and measurement requirements are depicted in figure 11.3.

FIGURE 11.3 Short-term paid absences.

Accumulation	Vesting/non-vesting	Recognition	Liability measurement
Accumulating — employee may carry forward unused entitlement	Vesting — employee is entitled to cash settlement of unused leave	Recognised as employee provides services giving rise to entitlement	Nominal, amount expected to be paid, i.e. total vested accumulated leave
	Non-vesting — no cash settlement of unused leave	Recognised as employee provides services giving rise to entitlement	Nominal, amount expected to be paid, requires estimation of amount that will be used
Non-accumulating — unused entitlement lapses each period		Recognised when paid absences occur	No liability is recognised

The following illustrative examples demonstrate accounting for short-term paid absences. First, illustrative example 11.3 demonstrates accounting for annual leave.

ILLUSTRATIVE EXAMPLE 11.3 Accounting for annual leave

Schnee AG has four employees in its Alpine branch. Each employee is entitled to 20 days of paid recreational leave per annum, referred to as annual leave (AL). At 1 January 2025, the balance of the liability for annual leave was €4,360. During the year employees took a total of 70 days of annual leave, which cost Schnee AG €9,160. After annual leave taken during the year had been recorded, the liability for annual leave account had a debit balance of €4,800 in the trial balance at 31 December 2025 before end-of-period adjustments. All annual leave accumulated at 31 December 2025 is expected to be paid by 31 December 2026. However, employees cannot roll onto the following year more than 12 days. The following information is obtained from the payroll records for the year ended 31 December 2025:

Employee	Wage per day	AL 1 January 2025 in days	Increase in entitlement in days	AL taken in days
Bauer	€120	9	20	16
Fiedler	€160	7	20	16
Goetz	€180	8	20	14
Wagner	€ 90	8	20	24

A liability must be recognised for accumulated annual leave at 31 December 2025. This is measured as the amount that is expected to be paid. As annual leave is vesting, all accumulated leave is expected to be paid. The first step in measuring the liability is to calculate the number of days of accumulated annual leave for each employee at 31 December 2025. Although this calculation would normally be performed by payroll software, we will manually calculate the number of days to enhance your understanding of the process. The next step is to multiply the number of days of accumulated annual leave by each employee's daily wage.

Employee	AL 1 January in days	Increase in entitlement in days	AL taken in days	Accumulated AL 31 December 2025 in days	Liability for AL 31 December 2025 €
Bauer	9	20	16	12 = 13–1	1,440
Fiedler	7	20	16	11	1,760
Goetz	8	20	14	12 = 14–2	2,160
Wagner	8	20	24	4	360
Total					**€5,720**

Note in the case of Bauer and Goetz the cap of 12 days. The calculation of accumulated annual leave in days and the resultant liability are as follows:

Thus, Schnee AG should recognise a liability of €5,720 for annual leave at 31 December 2025. After recording annual leave taken during the year, the unadjusted trial balance shows a debit balance of €4,800 for the liability for annual leave. Thus, a journal entry is required to record an increase of €11,000 (= 4,800 + 5,720).

Wages and Salaries Expense	Dr	10,520	
Liability for Annual Leave	Cr		10,520
(Accrual of Liability for Annual Leave)			

In illustrative example 11.3, an annual adjustment was made to the liability for annual leave. Some entities make accruals for annual leave more frequently to facilitate more comprehensive internal reporting to management. This is easily achieved with electronic accounting systems or payroll software.

Accounting for accumulating sick leave is demonstrated in illustrative example 11.4. In this illustration, the accumulating sick leave is non-vesting.

ILLUSTRATIVE EXAMPLE 11.4 Accounting for accumulating sick leave

Atlantic Inc. has 10 employees who are each paid $500 per week for a 5-day working week (i.e. $100 per day). Employees are entitled to 5 days of accumulating non-vesting sick leave each year. At 1 January 2025 the accumulated sick leave brought forward from the previous year was 10 days in total. During the year ended 31 December 2025 employees took 35 days of paid sick leave and 10 days of unpaid sick leave. One employee resigned at the beginning of the year. At the time of her resignation she had accumulated 5 days of sick leave. It is estimated that 60% of the unused sick leave will be taken during the following year and that the remaining 40% will not be taken at all.

After recording sick leave taken during the year, the unadjusted trial balance shows that the liability for sick leave had a debit balance of $3,000 at 31 December 2025.

The following table presents information used to calculate the amount of the provision for sick leave that Atlantic Inc. should recognise at 31 December 2025:

			Sick leave			Leave expected to be taken	
Number of employees	Base pay/day $	Balance 1 January 2025 Days	Accumulated in 2025 Days	Taken or lapsed Days		Within 12 months %	After 1 year %
10	100	10	50 = 10 employees × 5 days each	40 = 35 + 5		60	0

The 10 employees who were employed for all of the year ended 31 December 2025 each became entitled to 5 days of sick leave during the year. Thus, the total increase in entitlement during the year is 50 days. During the year, 35 days of paid sick leave were taken and 5 days of sick leave entitlement lapsed because an employee with 5 days' accumulated sick leave resigned without having used her entitlement. Thus, the aggregate sick leave entitlement reduced by 40 days during the year.

The first step in measuring the amount of the liability is to calculate the number of days of accumulated sick leave entitlement at 31 December 2025.

	Days
Brought forward 1 January 2025	10
Increase in entitlement for services provided in the current year	50
Sick leave entitlement taken or lapsed during the year	(40)
Sick leave carried forward 31 December 2025	20

The number of days of accumulated sick leave at the end of the reporting period is multiplied by the proportion of days expected to be taken, in this case, 60%. This amount, 12 days (20 days × 60%), is then multiplied by the current rate of pay per day, giving an ending balance of the liability of $1,200. The unadjusted balance of the liability for sick leave is (a debit of) $3,000 Dr. Accordingly, the liability must be increased by $4,200 as follows:

Wages and Salaries Expense	Dr	4,200	
Liability for Sick Leave	Cr		4,200
(Accrual of Liability for Sick Leave)			

For simplicity, the accrual adjustment to recognise sick leave is made at the end of the year in this example. Many companies make such adjustments throughout the year to provide more complete internal reporting to management. This is facilitated by payroll software that automates the calculation of accumulated entitlements.

11.4.5 Profit-sharing and bonus plans

Employers may offer profit-sharing arrangements and bonuses to their employees. Bonuses may be determined as a lump-sum amount or based on accounting or market-based measures of performance. Many large companies use bonuses in management incentive schemes. For example, the remuneration received by the senior executives of BHP Billiton includes base salary, both cash-based and share-based bonuses linked to short-term and long-term performance targets (incentive-based remuneration — *see chapter 14* for the accounting of share-based payments) and pension benefits. The components of remuneration for the chief executive officer (CEO) of BHP Billiton for 2023 are shown in figure 11.4. As is typical for CEOs, the majority of BHP Billiton's CEO's remuneration is in forms other than base salary.

FIGURE 11.4 BHP Billiton CEO remuneration.

US$('000)		Base salary	Benefits[1]	Pension[2]	CDP[3]	LTIP[4]	Total
Mike Henry	**FY2023**	**1,742**	**7**	**174**	**3,762**	**8,032**	**13,717**
	FY2022	1,700	168	170	3,917	9,353	15,308

1 Benefits are non-pensionable and include net movements in leave balances, private family health insurance, car parking, fringe benefits tax and personal tax return preparation in required countries.
2 FY2023 and FY2022 pension contributions were provided based on 10 per cent of base salary.
3 The values shown are the full CDP value (cash and deferred equity) earned based on performance during FY2023 and FY2022. The FY2023 CDP award will be provided one-third in cash in September 2023 and two-thirds in deferred equity, with one-third due to vest at the end of FY2025 and one-third due to vest at the end of FY2028 (on the terms of the CDP). The FY2022 CDP award was provided one-third in cash in September 2022 and two-thirds in deferred equity, with one-third due to vest at the end of FY2024 and one-third due to vest at the end of FY2027 (on the terms of the CDP).
4 The LTIP award values for FY2023 and FY2022 are based on the full awards Mike Henry received in 2018 and 2017, respectively, when he was President Operations, Minerals Australia (prior to becoming and with no proration applied for time as CEO), and 100 per cent of the awards vesting. The 2018 LTIP award value in FY2023 is an estimate calculated on the average share price for the month of July 2023 (which will be updated for the actual share price on the vesting date in the 2024 Remuneration Report); whereas the 2017 LTIP award value in FY2022 was calculated on the actual share price on the vesting date (and updated from the 2022 Remuneration Report in which the value was an estimate calculated on the average share price for the month of July 2022).

Source: BHP Billiton (2023, p. 121).

Paragraph 19 of IAS 19 requires an entity to recognise a liability for profit-sharing and bonus payments if it has a present obligation to make such payments and the amount can be estimated reliably. A present obligation exists if the entity has no realistic opportunity to avoid making the payments. The employee's performance under an employment contract may give rise to a legal obligation to pay a bonus. Alternatively, a constructive obligation may arise if the entity has a well-established practice of paying the bonus and has no realistic alternative but to pay the bonus because non-payment may be harmful to the entity's relations with its employees.

Liabilities for short-term profit-sharing arrangements and bonuses are measured at the nominal (i.e. undiscounted) amount that the entity expects to pay. Thus, if payment under a profit-sharing arrangement is subject to the employee still being employed when the payment is due (known as a service condition), the amount recognised as a liability is reduced by the amount that is expected to go unpaid due to staff turnover. For example, assume an entity has a profit-sharing arrangement in which it is obligated to pay 1% of profit for the period to employees and the amount becomes payable 3 months after the end of the reporting period. Based on staff turnover in prior years, the entity estimates that only 95% of employees will be eligible to receive a share of profit 3 months after the end of the reporting period. Accordingly, the amount of the liability that should be recognised for the profit-sharing scheme is equal to 0.95% of the entity's profit for the period. In this simple example it is assumed the bonus is distributed equally among employees.

11.5 POST-EMPLOYMENT BENEFITS

Post-employment benefits are benefits, other than termination benefits *(which are considered in section 11.9)*, that are payable after completion of employment, typically after the employee retires. Where post-employment benefits involve significant obligations, it is common (and in some countries compulsory) for employers to contribute to a post-employment benefit plan for employees.

Post-employment benefit plans are defined in paragraph 8 of IAS 19 as arrangements through which an entity provides post-employment benefits. They are also referred to as pension plans or employee retirement plans. The plan can be run by the entity itself or, more common, by a separate fund. In the latter case, the employer makes payments to the fund. The fund, which is a separate entity, typically a trust, invests the contributions and provides post-employment benefits to the employees, who are the members of the fund. Figure 11.5 shows the relations between the employer, the pension fund (plan) and the employees (members of the fund).

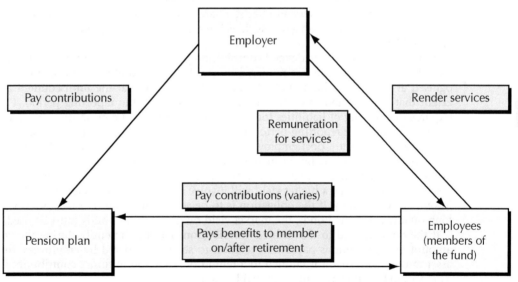

FIGURE 11.5 Relationships between the employer, pension plan and employees.

The two types of post-employment benefit plans are:
- defined benefit plans, and
- defined contribution plans, including, under certain conditions, multi-employer plans.

In practice the distinction between the two pension types may be more complex than what is depicted above, and the standard has not changed to keep up with innovations in provision of pension. This notwithstanding, paragraph 8 of IAS 19 refers to defined contribution plans as post-employment plans for which an entity pays fixed contributions into a separate entity. The contributions are normally based on the wages and salaries paid to employees. The contributing entity has no legal or constructive obligation to pay further contributions if the fund does not hold sufficient assets to pay all employee benefits relating to employees' services in the current and prior periods. Typically, the amount received by employees on retirement is dependent upon the level of contributions and the return earned by the fund on its investments.

In paragraph 8 of IAS 19, defined benefit plans are defined as post-employment plans other than defined contribution plans. If a post-employment plan is not classified as a defined contribution plan, by default, it is a defined benefit plan. Critical to the definition of a defined contribution post-employment benefit plan is the absence of an obligation for the employer to make further payments if the plan is unable to pay all the benefits accruing to members for their past service. Thus, defined benefit post-employment plans are those in which the employer has some obligation to pay further contributions to enable the plan to pay members' benefits. In a defined benefit post-employment plan, the benefit received by members on retirement is typically determined by a formula reflecting their years of service and level of remuneration. It is not solely dependent upon the performance of the plan. If the plan has insufficient funds to pay members' post-employment benefits, the trustee of the plan will require the employer, who is the sponsor of the plan, to make additional payments. Similarly, if the plan achieves higher returns than are required to pay members' post-employment benefits, the employer may be able to take a 'contribution holiday' or even a refund. Employers often prefer defined contribution plans because there is no risk of liability for further contributions if the plan fails to earn an adequate return.

IAS 19 prescribes the accounting treatment for contributions to post-employment benefit plans and assets and liabilities arising from post-employment benefit plans from the perspective of the employer. It does not prescribe accounting requirements for the post-employment benefit plan. Financial reporting by post-employment plans is dealt with in IAS 26 *Accounting and Reporting by Retirement Benefit Plans*, which is not further addressed in this book.

11.6 ACCOUNTING FOR DEFINED CONTRIBUTION POST-EMPLOYMENT PLANS

As described above, entities that participate in defined contribution post-employment plans make payments to a post-employment benefit plan. The amount is determined as a percentage of remuneration paid to employees who are members of the plan. Contributions payable to defined contribution funds are recognised in the period the employee renders services. The contributions payable during the period are recognised as expenses unless another standard permits the cost of employment benefits to be allocated to the carrying amount of an asset, such as internally constructed plant in accordance with IAS 16 *Property, Plant and Equipment*.

If the amount paid to the defined contribution plan by the entity during the year is less than the amount payable in relation to services rendered by employees, a liability for unpaid contributions must be recognised at the end of the period. The liability is measured at the undiscounted amount payable to the extent that contributions are due within 12 months after the reporting period. Paragraph 52 of IAS 19 requires discounting of liabilities for contributions to defined contribution plans that are due more than 12 months after the reporting period in which the employee provides the related services. The discount rate used to discount a post-employment benefit obligation is determined by reference to market yields on high-quality corporate bonds in accordance with IAS 19 paragraph 83. Since there are several corporate bonds that are regarded as high-quality, the yield for which likely varies, managers have discretion over the discount rate. Selecting a higher yield will involve a higher discount rate and hence, all else being equal, a lower pension liability. If the obligation is to be settled in a country that does not have a deep market in high-quality corporate bonds, the market yield on government bonds must be used.

If the amount paid to the defined contribution plan by the entity during the year is greater than the amount of contributions payable in relation to services rendered by employees, the entity recognises an asset to the extent that it is entitled to a refund or reduction in future contributions. In this situation, the asset would be a prepayment, or prepaid expenses.

ILLUSTRATIVE EXAMPLE 11.5 Accounting for defined contribution post-employment plans

Arctic Ltd provides a defined contribution pension plan for its employees. Arctic Ltd is required to contribute 9% of gross wages, salaries and commissions payable for services rendered by employees. It makes quarterly payments of $80,000 to the pension plan. If the amount paid to the pension plan during the financial year is less than 9% of gross wages, salaries and commissions for that year, Arctic Ltd must pay the outstanding contributions by 31 March of the following financial year. If the amount paid during the financial year is more than 9% of the gross wages, salaries and bonuses for the year, the excess contributions are deducted from amounts payable in the following year.

Arctic Ltd's annual reporting period ends on 31 December Arctic Ltd's employee benefits for the year ended 31 December 2026 comprise:

	$
Gross wages and salaries	3,900,000
Gross commissions	100,000
	4,000,000

The deficit in Arctic Ltd's pension plan contributions for 2026 is determined as follows:

	$
Contributions payable:	
9% × gross wages, salaries and commissions	360,000
Contributions paid during 2026: $80,000 × 4	320,000
Pension contribution payable	40,000

Arctic Ltd must recognise a liability for the unpaid pension plan contributions. The liability is not discounted because it is a short-term employee benefits liability. Arctic Ltd would record the following entry for 31 December 2026:

Wages and Salaries Expense	Dr	40,000	
Pension contributions payable	Cr		40,000
(Accrual of liability for unpaid pension plan contributions)			

11.7 ACCOUNTING FOR DEFINED BENEFIT POST-EMPLOYMENT PLANS

As described in section 11.5, typically the employer pays contributions to a plan, which is a separate entity from the employer. The plan accumulates assets through contributions and returns on investments. The accumulated assets are used to pay post-employment benefits to members (retired employees). The return on investments held by the pension plan comprises dividend and interest income and changes in the fair value of investments. The benefits paid to members are a function of their remuneration levels while employed and the number of years of service. The trustee of the plan may require the employer to make additional contributions if there is a shortfall. Thus, the employer effectively underwrites the actuarial and investment risks of the plan. In other words, the entity bears the risk of the plan being unable to pay benefits.

The assets of the pension plan, which are mostly investments, do not always equal its obligation to pay post-employment benefits to members. The pension plan has a deficit to the extent that the present value of the defined benefit obligation (i.e. post-employment benefits that are expected to be paid to employees for their services up to the end of the reporting period) exceeds the fair value of the plan assets. Conversely, a surplus arises when the fair value of the plan assets exceeds the present value of the defined benefit obligation.

Whether the deficit (surplus) of the defined benefit pension plan is a liability (asset) of the sponsoring employer is debatable. In the past, before the standard was amended to demonstrate the pension asset is recoverable, some argued that the surplus in the pension plan does not satisfy all of the characteristics of an asset. Arguably, the assets of the plan are not controlled by the employer because they cannot be used for its benefit. For example, the employer may not use the surplus of the defined benefit pension plan to pay its debts; the assets of the plan are only used to generate cash flows to pay post-employment benefits to the members of the plan. Although the surplus is expected to result in future cash savings, such as lower contributions in future, it could be argued that the employer has not obtained control over those benefits through a past event where the reduction in contributions is at the discretion of the trustee of the pension plan.

Similarly, it has been argued that a deficit in the defined benefit pension plan is not a liability of the sponsoring employer because it does not have a present obligation to make good the shortfall. For instance, the employer may modify the post-employment benefits payable so as to avoid some of the obligation. However, other than in exceptional cases, an employer cannot unilaterally reduce or negate the rights granted to plan participants without some form of compensation, which explains why the standard assumes there is a liability with the employer.

The perspective adopted in IAS 19 is that the surplus or deficit of the defined benefit pension plan is an asset, or liability, respectively, of the sponsoring employer. In some cases, the entity might not have a legal obligation to make good any shortfall in the pension plan. For example, the terms of the trust deed may allow the employer to change or terminate its obligation under the plan. Although the employer might not have a legal obligation to make up any shortfall, it typically has a constructive obligation because terminating its obligations under the plan may make it difficult to retain and recruit staff. Accordingly, the accounting treatment prescribed by IAS 19 for an entity's obligations arising from sponsorship of a defined benefit plan assumes that the entity will continue to promise the post-employment benefits over the remaining working lives of its employees.

If adopting the view that a deficit or surplus of the defined benefit pension plan is a liability or asset of the sponsoring employer, the next conceptual issue is whether it should be recognised and, if so, how it should be measured. Before looking at how the standard setters resolved these issues, we will consider the possibilities, which are shown in figure 11.6. At one extreme, the deficit or surplus is not recognised in the financial statements of the entity that sponsors the defined benefit pension plan. In other words, the deficit or surplus is 'off balance sheet'. At the other extreme, referred to as 'net capitalisation', the deficit (surplus) of the fund is recognised as a liability (asset) on the statement of financial position of the entity that sponsors the defined benefit pension plan. Under net capitalisation, the net pension liability or asset is usually measured as the difference between the present value of post-employment benefits earned by employees for services in the current and prior periods and the fair value of plan assets. Between these two extremes are various partial capitalisation methods in which some amount of the surplus or deficit of the fund remains off balance sheet. For example, an earlier version of IAS 19 permitted increments in the defined benefit obligation resulting from prior periods (referred to as past service costs) to be recognised progressively over the average remaining period until they became vested.

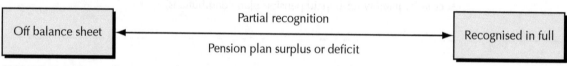

FIGURE 11.6 Alternative approaches to accounting for defined benefit pension plans.

In the absence of accounting regulation, preparers were able to select different approaches to accounting for defined benefit post-employment benefits, ranging from off balance sheet to net capitalisation.

Obviously, the use of different methods of accounting for post-employment benefits reduces the comparability of financial statements. Concerns were also raised about delays in recognition of liabilities perpetuated by partial capitalisation methods. Untimely recognition of assets or liabilities arising under post-employment benefit plans results in misleading information in the statement of financial position which is not adequately resolved by additional disclosures in the notes. The International Accounting Standards Board (IASB®) and the US Financial Accounting Standards Board (FASB) jointly undertook a project to enhance the comparability and transparency of accounting for post-employment benefits (IASB 2008), resulting in a revised version of IAS 19 *Employee Benefits*. We will now turn to the requirements of IAS 19 for accounting for defined benefit post-employment benefits.

The net capitalisation approach is adopted by IAS 19. Thus, the sponsoring employer recognises a net defined benefit liability or asset, representing its exposure to the defined benefit pension plan at the end of the reporting period. Contributions paid into the plan by the employer increase the assets of the plan, and thus increase a surplus or reduce any deficit of the plan. The employer accounts for its contributions to the plan as a decrease in the net defined benefit liability, or an increase in the net defined benefit asset. The employer recognises expenses in relation to its sponsorship of the defined benefit pension plan when service costs and interest costs are incurred, rather than when contributions are paid. This will become clear as we work through the revised requirements of IAS 19 for accounting for defined benefit pension plans.

The key steps involved in accounting by the employer for a defined benefit post-employment plan in accordance with IAS 19 (paragraph 57) are:
1. determining the deficit or surplus of the plan which involves (i) estimating the ultimate cost to the entity of the benefit that employees have earned in return for their service in the current and prior periods; (ii) discounting that benefit in order to determine the present value of the defined benefit obligation and the current service cost; and (iii) deducting the fair value of any plan assets from the present value of the defined benefit obligation
2. determining the amount of the net defined benefit liability (asset), which is the amount of the deficit or the surplus, adjusted for any effect of limiting a net-defined benefit asset to the asset ceiling, which is explained below

3. determining the amounts to be recognised in profit or loss for current service cost, any past service cost and net interest expense (income) on the net defined benefit liability (asset)
4. determining the remeasurement of the net defined benefit liability (asset) to be recognised in other comprehensive income, which comprises actuarial gains and losses, return on plan assets (other than amounts included in net interest), and any change in the effect of the asset ceiling (other than amounts included in net interest).

We will now take a closer look at each step.

11.7.1 Step 1: Determining the deficit or surplus of the plan

There are two elements to determining the deficit or surplus of the plan — the obligation to pay benefits and any plan assets. Paragraph 67 of IAS 19 requires an entity to use the projected unit credit method to determine the present value of post-employment benefits earned by employees for services in the current and prior periods. Other names for the projected unit credit method include the *accrued benefit method pro-rated on service* and the *benefits/years of service method*. The projected unit credit method, which attributes a proportionate amount of additional benefit to each period of service, is shown in illustrative example 11.6. In reading illustrative example 11.6 it is important to note that there is a need to project what the final salary may be, which is a function of pay policy (e.g. whether pay is adjusted for inflation), and so it is the final salary that affects current expense, rather than current salary.

ILLUSTRATIVE EXAMPLE 11.6 Determining the present value of the defined benefit obligation using the projected unit credit method

Dickens plc provides a defined benefit pension plan in which employees receive post-employment benefits determined as 15.0% of their final year salary, for every year of service. (This form of pension is now less common with many employers switching to either defined contribution plans, or average career salary. This example will flow through if final salary is replaced with career average.) Salaries are expected to increase by 5% (compound) each year, taking into account the effects of inflation. The managers reviewed the yield on high-quality-corporate bonds and determined that the appropriate discount rate is 4% p.a. Jane commenced working for Dickens plc on 1 January 2024 with an annual salary of £50,000 and is expected to retire on 31 December 2028. For simplicity, this example ignores the additional adjustment that would be necessary to reflect the probability that Jane will resign, die or retire at an earlier date. Dicken's financial year end is 31 December.

Consider Jane's accrued benefit on 31 December 2024. This is 4 years from retirement (31 December 2028), and so Jane's projected salary is £50,000 × 1.05^4, or £60,775. Having worked 1 year, she is entitled to 15% of £60,775, or £9,116 (rounded). Now consider Jane's accrued benefit on 31 December 2025. Having worked 2 years, she is now entitled to 2 × 15% × £60,775, or £18,233. The table below summarises Jane's accrued benefit over the 2024–2028 period following this process:

Year (£)	2024	2025	2026	2027	2028
Salary	50,000	52,500	55,125	57,881	60,775
Annual benefit = 15% of **final salary**	9,116	9,116	9116	9,116	9,116
Accrued benefit based on number of years served × final salary	9,116	18,233	27,349	36,465	45,581

The accrued benefit obligation should be measured as the present value of the final salary at the end of each period using the discount rate selected by the managers (4%). The present value of the accrued benefits increases as the expected settlement time approaches because the expected settlement is discounted over a shorter period of time. For example, at the end of 2024 the discount factor is 1.169859 = 1.04^4, but at the end of 2026 it is 1.0816 = 1.04^2.

The table below shows these present values, using 4% annual discount rate (compounding):

Year	2024	2025	2026	2027	2028
Accrued benefit based on final salary £	9,116	18,223	27,349	36,465	45,581
Discount factor at 4%	1.169859	1.124864	1.0816	1.04	1
Accrued defined benefit obligation at present value £	7,793	16,209	25,286	35,063	45,581

The annual increase in the present value of the accrued benefit is attributable to the current service cost — the increase in accrued benefit owing to one additional year of service — and interest accrued on the pension liability (i.e. the interest expense). The annual undiscounted service cost is £9,116, but this needs to be discounted to present time. For example, the 2026 annual service cost is £8,429 = £9,116/1.0816. The interest component is calculated for each period by multiplying the opening balance of the accrued benefit obligation by the interest rate. For example, for 2026 the interest expense is £648 = 4% × £16,209. The table below analyses the annual increases in accrued defined benefit between the current service cost and interest expense:

Year	2024	2025	2026	2027	2028
Opening balance £	0	7,793	16,209	25,286	35,063
Interest at 4%	0	312	648	1,011	1,403
Service cost	7,793	8,104	8,429	8,766	9,116
Accrued defined benefit obligation at present value £	7,793	16,209	25,286	35,063	45,581

To complete the first step, it is necessary to determine the difference between the fair value of plan assets and the present value of the defined benefit obligation. The excess of the defined benefit obligation over the fair value of the plan assets is the deficit of the plan. Conversely, any excess of the fair value of plan assets over the present value of the defined benefit obligation is a surplus of the plan. The previous example is based on an individual to simplify the calculations of accrued benefits. However, the plan would typically provide multiple members and the plan assets would generate cash inflows to be used to settle obligations to all members.

ILLUSTRATIVE EXAMPLE 11.7 Determining the deficit or surplus of the defined benefit pension plan

To illustrate the calculation of the deficit or surplus of the defined benefit pension plan, assume the following information about the assets and obligations for post-employment benefits of Dickens Employee Pension Plan in 2024–2026:

	31/12/24 £	31/12/25 £	31/12/26 £
Accrued defined benefit obligation value	7,793	16,209	25,286
Fair value of plan assets	4,500	11,100	26,800
Deficit (surplus) of the plan	3,293	5,109	(1,514)

The closing obligation is the present value of the defined benefit obligation at the end of each reporting period. The plan has a deficit of £3,293 at 31 December 2024. This amount is calculated as £7,793–£4,500, which is the amount by which the present value of the defined benefit obligation exceeds the fair value of plan assets. At 31 December 2025, the plan has a deficit of £5,109, being the excess of the obligation of £16,209 over the fair value of plan assets, £11,100. At 31 December 2026, the fair value of plan assets exceeds the defined benefit obligation. Accordingly, the defined benefit pension plan has a surplus of £1,514, being the fair value of plan assets, £26,800, less the defined benefit obligation, £25,286.

Obligations to pay pensions during employees' lives or that of their eligible dependants can further complicate the measurement of accrued benefits because the total payment is dependent upon the mortality rate of the employees and their eligible beneficiaries. Companies often rely on actuarial assessments to estimate the defined benefit obligation and the level of investment required to enable the plan to pay accumulated benefits as and when they fall due. Actuaries apply mathematical, statistical, economic and financial analysis to assess risks associated with contracts, such as insurance policies and pension plans. Actuarial estimates rely on assumptions, such as the employee retention rates and the rate at which salaries are expected to increase. Actuaries also provide financial planning advice, on matters such as the level of investment needed to generate sufficient future cash flows to meet the expected obligations as and when they fall due.

11.7.2 Step 2: Determining the amount of the net defined benefit liability (asset) adjusted for any effect of limiting a net-defined benefit asset to the asset ceiling

A net defined benefit liability arises when the defined benefit pension plan has a deficit. The net defined benefit liability is measured as the amount of the deficit of the defined benefit pension plan, which is calculated following the procedure described in step 1.

A net defined benefit asset arises when the defined benefit pension plan has a surplus. The net defined benefit asset is measured as the amount of the surplus, adjusted for any effect of limiting a net defined benefit asset to the asset ceiling. The asset ceiling is defined in paragraph 8 of IAS 19 as 'the present value of any economic benefits available in the form of refunds from the plan or reductions in future contributions to the plan'. The net defined benefit asset is the lower of the surplus of the defined benefit pension plan and the asset ceiling. For example, if we assume that the present value of reductions in Dickens plc's future contributions to the plan at 31 December 2026 were £2,800, the net defined benefit asset of Dickens plc would be measured as £1,514, being the lower of the surplus of the defined benefit plan and the asset ceiling. However, if the present value of reductions in Dickens plc's future contributions to the plan at 31 December 2026 were only £1,000, its net defined benefit asset would be measured as £1,000 rather than £1,514.

11.7.3 Step 3: Determining the amounts to be recognised in profit or loss

The amount of the net defined benefit liability (asset) is affected by the present value of the defined benefit obligation and the fair value of plan assets. The present value of the defined benefit obligation is affected by the service cost, which comprises current service cost, past service cost and any gain or loss on settlement of the defined benefit plan.

As explained above, the current service cost is 'the increase in the present value of defined benefit obligation resulting from employee service in the current period' (IAS 19 paragraph 8). The service cost for each year in illustrative example 11.6 is a current service cost to Dickens plc because it is the increase in the present value of the defined benefit obligation attributed to employment services rendered by Jane during each year.

Past service cost is defined in paragraph 8 of IAS 19 as the change in the present value of the defined benefit obligation for employee service in prior periods. This occurs if the plan is amended or curtailed. Illustrative example 11.8 draws on the same information as used in illustrative example 11.6, with the addition of an amendment to the terms of the pension plan.

Paragraph 8 of IAS 19 defines the *net interest on the net defined benefit liability (asset)* as the change in the net defined benefit liability (asset) that arises from the passage of time. The net interest on net defined benefit liability (asset) is measured by multiplying the discount rate that is used to measure the defined benefit obligation at the beginning of the period by the net defined benefit liability (asset) (IAS 19 paragraph 123). Paragraph 83 requires the discount rate to be determined with reference to market yields on high-quality corporate bonds. In the absence of a deep market in such bonds, the market yield on government bonds should be used. The standard requires contributions received and benefits paid by the plan to be taken into account when calculating interest. This involves recalculating interest for part of the year each time the plan assets are increased by a contribution or where payment of benefits resulted in settlement gains or losses, giving rise to change in the net defined benefit liability or asset. Throughout this text, this process is simplified by applying the discount rate to the opening balance of the net defined benefit liability (asset), effectively assuming contributions and benefits are paid at the end of each year.

When the pension plan pays benefits to a member, both the plan assets and the defined benefit obligation are reduced. If, at the time of settlement, the carrying amount of the obligation to the member is equal to the amount actually payable, the settlement will have no effect on the surplus or deficit of the plan. However, the carrying amount of the defined benefit obligation results from numerous actuarial estimates which may differ from amounts actually due at settlement. Differences between the part of the carrying amount of the defined benefit obligation of the plan that relates to a specific benefit and the amount actually paid to that participant represent an actuarial gain or loss which is recognised in other comprehensive income (*see section 11.7.4.*)

As per 1 January 2026 Dickens plc modified the terms of the defined benefit pension plan from 15.0% of final year salary per year of service to 12.5% of final year salary per year of service. The modification applied retrospectively to services rendered before 2026. Accordingly, after the modification the defined benefit payable at 31 December 2026 is expected to be 37.5% of final year salary instead of 45% of final salary, reflecting 3 years of service.

This modification requires to first remeasure the pension obligation as per the date of the modification, i.e. 1 January 2026, using the revised benefit rate. This is calculated as 25% of Jane's final year salary (25% × £60,775/1.124864 = £13,507). Comparing this to the amount reported at the end of 2025 (£16,209) indicates that the effect of this modification is a reduction of £2,702. Second, the revised annual service cost for 2026 needs to be calculated. It is £7,024 = 12.5% × 60,775/1.0816. Third, the revised interest expense needs to be calculated. The interest expense is now £540 = 4% × £13,507.

The following schedule shows the current service cost, interest cost and present value of the defined benefit obligation on the basis of the revised terms of the plan from 2026 to 2028. The calculations follow the same process as illustrated under the original terms.

Schedule of current service cost, interest and present value of the defined benefit obligation			
	Year ended 31/12/26 £	Year ended 31/12/27 £	Year ended 31/12/28 £
Opening obligation (revised in 2026)	13,507	21,071	29,219
Interest at 4%	540	843	1,169
Current service cost	7,024	7,305	7,597
Closing obligation	21,071	29,219	37,985

The following table shows how this modification is reported in 2026.

	Year ended 31/12/25 £	Year ended 31/12/26 £
Opening obligation	7,793	16,209
Past service costs arising from modifications to the plan	—	(2,702)
Adjusted obligation		13,507
Interest at 4%	312	540
Current service cost	8,104	7,024
Closing obligation	16,209	21,071

Current and past service cost, interest income or expense are recognised in profit or loss.

Notably, in illustrative example 11.8 there is no consideration of fair value of plan assets and the return these assets generate. As explained below, the return on plan assets may affect both income and other comprehensive income. But briefly, in determining net interest expense, it is required to use the discount rate used in calculating the accrued benefit obligation x beginning balance of plan assets (paragraph 123). To illustrate, assume the balance of plan assets on 1/1/26 is £5,000 (assumed to be fully recoverable), and so the net pension liability (after modification) is £8,507 (= £13,507 − £5,000). The net interest income is then £340 = 4% × £8,507.

11.7.4 Step 4: Determining the remeasurements of the net defined benefit liability (asset) to be recognised in other comprehensive income

Changes in the net defined benefit liability (asset) that result from remeasurements comprise actuarial gains and losses, return on plan assets (other than amounts included in net interest), and any change in the effect of the asset ceiling (excluding amounts included in net interest).

Actuarial gains and losses occur when changes in actuarial assumptions or experience adjustments affect the present value of the defined benefit obligation. The measurement of the defined benefit obligation is sensitive to assumptions such as employee turnover and the rate of increase in salaries. For example, an increase in the rate of salary increase used in measuring the defined benefit obligation would increase the expected future settlement and, hence, the present value of the defined benefit obligation. An increase in the rate of salary increase results in an actuarial loss because it increases the present value of the defined benefit obligation. Another example of a change in an actuarial assumption is a change in the discount rate used to determine the present value of the obligation. An increase in the discount rate results in an actuarial gain because it reduces the present value of the defined benefit obligation.

Experience adjustments refer to differences between the actual results and previous actuarial estimates used to measure the defined benefit obligation. An example is the difference between the estimated employee turnover for the year and the actual employee turnover during the year. Experience adjustments may also relate to early retirement, mortality rates and the rate of increase in salaries.

The return on plan assets is determined after deducting the costs of managing the plan assets and tax payable by the pension plan on its income derived from plan assets. Other administration costs are not deducted from the return on plan assets (IAS 19 paragraph 130).

The effects of remeasurements of the net defined benefit liability (asset) are recognised in other comprehensive income. Amounts recognised in other comprehensive income as a result of remeasurement of the net defined benefit liability are not able to be reclassified to profit or loss. *(The reclassification of items of other comprehensive income to profit or loss is considered in chapter 2.)* The recognition of actuarial gains and losses as items of other comprehensive income shields reported profit from the volatility that these items can cause.

ILLUSTRATIVE EXAMPLE 11.9 Accounting for a defined benefit pension plan

Gesundheit GmbH has a defined benefit pension plan for its senior managers. Members of the plan had been entitled to 10% of their average salary for every year of service.

The following information is available about the Gesundheit Pension Plan:

		€'000
31 December 2026		
Present value of defined benefit obligation (DBO) at 31 December 2026		26,000
Fair value of plan assets at 31 December 2026		30,000
Asset ceiling at 31 December 2026		4,200
Interest rate used to measure the defined benefit obligation (DBO) 31 December 2026	7%	
1 January 2027		
Past service costs		5,000
Year ended 31 December 2027		
Current service cost		4,000
Contributions received by the plan		4,500
Benefits paid by the plan		Nil
Actuarial gain on plan assets (return on plan assets in excess of interest accrual on opening plan assets)		800
Actuarial gain resulting from change in the discount rate, 31 December 2027		1,470
Present value of defined benefit obligation at 31 December 2027		35,700
Fair value of plan assets at 31 December 2027		37,400
Asset ceiling at 31 December 2027		2,500
Interest rate used to measure the defined benefit obligation (DBO) 31 December 2027	8%	

Additional information
(a) The current service cost is given as €4 million. This estimation is based on actuarial advice provided by the manager of the pension plan.
(b) Actuarial advice has been obtained for the present value of the defined benefit obligation at 31 December 2026 and 2027.
(c) On 1 January 2027 Gesundheit GmbH revised its defined benefits and increased the entitlement to 11% of average salary. The revision to the defined benefit plan resulted in an increase in the defined benefit obligation of €5 million on 1 January 2027.

(d) On 31 December 2027, Gesundheit GmbH contributed €4,500,000 to the plan. All of the contributions to the Gesundheit Pension Plan are paid by Gesundheit GmbH. The senior managers of Gesundheit GmbH, who are the members of the plan, do not pay any contributions.

(e) The discount rate used to measure the defined benefit obligation was increased from 7% to 8% on 31 December 2027, resulting in a decrease of €1,470,000 in the present value of the defined benefit obligation.

(f) The fair value of plan assets is derived from valuations performed by Helf and Gott Valuers each year.

The information shown above is used to prepare the journal entries to account for Gesundheit GmbH's pension liability (asset) for 2027 in accordance with IAS 19. But first we will determine the amount of the net defined benefit liability (asset) at 31 December 2026.

Gesundheit Pension Plan had a surplus of €4,000,000, being the excess of the fair value of plan assets over the present value of the defined benefit obligation, at 31 December 2026. Gesundheit GmbH recognised a net defined benefit asset of €4,000,000, being the lesser of the surplus and the asset ceiling of €4,200,000.

Next, we will consider the four steps involved in accounting by the employer for a defined benefit post-employment plan identified by IAS 19 (paragraph 57). The defined benefit worksheet, which is shown below for the Gesundheit Pension Plan, incorporates the four steps and provides workings for the summary journal entries to account for the defined benefit post-employment plan in the books of the employer and provides a basis for the disclosure requirements required by IAS 19.

Gesundheit Defined Benefit Pension Plan Worksheet for the year ended 31 December 2027						
	Gesundheit GmbH				Gesundheit Pension Plan	
	Profit/loss €'000	OCI €'000	Bank €'000	Net DBL(A) €'000	DBO €'000	Plan Assets €'000
Balance 31/12/26				4,000 Dr	26,000 Cr	30,000 Dr
Past service cost	5,000 Dr				5,000 Cr	
Revised balance 1/1/27				1,000 Cr	31,000 Cr	30,000 Dr
Interest at 7%	70 Dr				2,170 Cr	2,100 Dr
Current service cost	4,000 Dr				4,000 Cr	
Contributions to the plan			4,500 Cr			4,500 Dr
Benefits paid by the plan					0	0
Actuarial gain on plan assets (Return on plan assets in excess of interest income of £2100)		800 Cr				800 Cr
Actuarial gain: DBO		1,470 Cr			1,470 Dr	
Journal entry	9,070 Dr	2,270 Cr	4,500 Cr	2,300 Cr		
Balance 31/12/27				1,700 Dr	35,700 Cr	37,400 Dr
Adjustment for asset ceiling if < deficit				Not applicable		
Balance 31/12/27				1,700 Dr	35,700 Cr	37,400 Dr

Step 1: Determining the deficit or surplus of the fund

The pension plan has a surplus of €1,700,000 at 31 December 2027. This is shown in the last row of the defined benefit worksheet, and can be calculated as the excess of the fair value of plan assets (€37,400,000) over the present value of the defined benefit obligation (DBO) (€35,700,000).

Step 2: Determining the amount of the net defined benefit liability (asset) — DBL(A)

The net defined benefit asset (DBA) is €1,700,000, being the lesser of the surplus of €1,700,000 and the asset ceiling of €2,500,000 at 31 December 2027.

Step 3: Determining the amounts to be recognised in profit or loss

The sum of past service cost of €5,000,000, net interest income of €70,000 (calculated as 7% of the revised net opening balance of plan assets and DBO after accounting for past service cost), and the current service cost of €4,000,000 is recognised in profit or loss.

Step 4: Determining the amount of remeasurements to be recognised in other comprehensive income

The actuarial gains and losses on plan assets and the DBO are recognised in other comprehensive income. The actuarial gain on plan assets is the amount of return on plan assets less the interest income on the opening balance of the plan assets leading to an actuarial gain of 800,000. The actuarial gain on the DBO amounts to €1,470,000, as shown in the defined benefit worksheet. The effects of the remeasurements are recognised in other comprehensive income (OCI) as shown in the defined benefit worksheet.

The payment of contributions during 2027 increases the net defined benefit asset and increases the plan assets.

Any benefits paid to members during the period would reduce both the plan assets and the DBO. It appears in the pension plan columns only because it is a transaction of the plan, and not a transaction of the sponsoring employer.

The worksheet provides working papers for the journal entries to account for the defined benefit pension plan in the books of Gesundheit GmbH. The summary journal entries are shown below.

Summary entry	Pension Expense (P/L)	Dr	9,070,000	
	Pension Plan Gain (OCI)	Cr		2,270,000
	Bank	Cr		4,500,000
	Net Defined Benefit Pension Asset	Cr		2,300,000
	(Payment of pension contributions and recognition of changes in net pension asset)			

The defined benefit worksheet also provides a basis for preparation of notes to the financial statements for some of the disclosures required by IAS 19 in respect of defined benefit post-employment plans. Paragraph 140 includes a requirement for a reconciliation of the opening balance to the closing balance of the net defined benefit liability (asset), showing separate reconciliations for plan assets, the present value of the defined benefit obligation and the effect of the asset ceiling. Each reconciliation is required to show the effect, if applicable, of past service cost and gains and losses arising on settlement, current service cost, interest income or expense, and remeasurement of the net defined liability (asset), showing separately return on plan assets excluding amounts included in interest, actuarial gains arising from changes in demographic assumptions, actuarial gains and losses arising from changes in financial assumptions and changes in the effect, if any, of the asset ceiling (IAS 19 paragraph 141). Paragraph 141 also requires disclosure of contributions, distinguishing between those paid by the employer and those paid by the members of the plan, and benefits paid. Other reconciliation items include the effects of changes in foreign exchange rates and the effects of business combinations and disposals.

The net capitalisation method can result in large gains and losses being recognised in other comprehensive income, due to changes in the surplus or deficit of the fair value of plan assets over the present value of the defined benefit obligation. For instance, the present value of the defined benefit obligation increases if employee retention is greater than the amount assumed in the previous actuarial estimate. Similarly, an unexpected decline in the return on investment of plan assets may cause the plan assets to grow at a slower rate than the present value of the defined benefit obligation, giving rise to an increase in the net pension liability recognised by the employer. Although this volatility affects other comprehensive income and equity, it does not affect net profit or loss, which is what preparers and investors are probably more focused on.

11.8 OTHER LONG-TERM EMPLOYEE BENEFITS

Long-term employee benefits are benefits for services provided in the current or prior periods that will not be paid until more than 12 months after the end of the period. *Post-employment benefits were considered in section 11.5.* This section considers long-term employee benefits that are provided to employees during the period of their employment. A common form of long-term employee benefit is long service leave, which is a paid absence after the employee has provided a long period of service, such as 3 months of paid leave after 10 years of continuous employment.

Long service leave accrues to employees as they provide service to the entity. The principle adopted by IAS 19 is that an obligation arises for long service leave when the employees provide services to the employer, even though the employees may have no legal entitlement to the leave. Thus, a liability is recognised for long service leave as it accrues. Long service leave payments reduce the long service leave liability.

Accounting for other long-term employee benefits is similar to accounting for defined benefit post-employment plans except that the effects of remeasurements are not recognised in other comprehensive income (IAS 19 paragraphs 154–55). Thus, the net liability (asset) for long-term employee benefits is measured as the net of the present value of the defined benefit obligation at the reporting date minus the fair value at the reporting date of plan assets (if any) out of which the obligations are to be settled directly, subject to adjustment of a net asset for the effects of an asset ceiling, if applicable.

In some countries it is extremely unusual to establish plan assets to provide for the payment of long service leave benefits to employees. Thus, the accounting treatment for long service leave benefits is usually confined to the recognition of the present value of the obligation measured in accordance with the projected unit credit method.

The projected unit credit method measures the obligation for long-term employee benefits by calculating the present value of the expected future payments that will result from employee services provided to date. The measurement of the present value of the obligation for long service leave payments is complicated by the need to make several estimates. These include estimation of when the leave will be taken, projected salary levels, and the proportion of employees who will continue in the entity's employment long enough to become entitled to long service leave. Actuarial advice is often used in the measurement of long service leave obligations.

The steps involved in the measurement of a liability for long service leave are as follows:

1. *Estimate the number of employees who are expected to become eligible for long service leave.* The probability that employees will become eligible for long service leave generally increases with the period of employment. For example, if an entity provides long service leave after 10 years of employment, the probability that employees who have already been working for the entity for 7 years will continue in employment for another 3 years is very high, as the closer proximity to long service leave entitlement provides an incentive to employees to stay with their current employer.

2. *Estimate the projected wages and salaries at the time that long service leave is expected to be paid.* This step involves the application of expected inflation rates or other cost adjustment rates over the remaining period before long service leave is paid. Applying an estimated inflation rate:

$$\text{Projected salaries} = \text{current salaries} \times (1 + \text{inflation rate})^n$$

where n = number of years until long service leave is expected to be paid.

For example, for employees who have 3 years remaining before long service leave is expected to be paid, current salaries are projected over a period of 3 years.

3. *Determine the accumulated benefit.* The projected unit credit is determined as the proportion of projected long service leave attributable to services that have already been provided by the employee.

The accumulated benefit is calculated as:

$$\frac{\text{Years of employment}}{\text{Years required for LSL}} \times \frac{\text{weeks of paid leave}}{52} \times \text{projected salaries}$$

4. *Measure the present value of the accumulated benefit.* The accumulated benefit is discounted at a rate determined by reference to market yields on high-quality corporate bonds, in accordance with paragraph 83. If the country in which the long service leave entitlement will be paid does not have a deep market in high-quality corporate bonds, the government bond rate is used.

$$\text{Present value} = \frac{\text{accumulated benefit}}{(1+i)^n}$$

where i is the interest rate on high-quality corporate bonds maturing n years later.

The liability for long service leave is a provision. After determining the amount of the obligation for long service leave at the end of the period, following steps 1 to 4 above, the provision is increased or decreased as required.

Illustrative example 11.10 demonstrates the measurement of the obligation for long service leave, applying the projected unit credit method in accordance with IAS 19, and the entries to account for changes in the provision for long service leave.

Green Ltd commenced operations on 2 January 2026 and had 150 employees. Average salaries were $60,000 per annum for the year. Green Ltd accounts for all recognised employee costs as expenses. Employees are entitled to 13 weeks of long service leave after 10 years of employment. The following information is based on advice received from actuarial consultants at 31 December 2026:

Number of years unit credit	1 year
Number of years until long service leave is expected to be paid	9 years
Probability that long service leave will be taken (proportion of employees expected to stay long enough to become entitled to long service leave)	50%
Expected increase in salaries (based on inflation)	2% p.a.
Yield on 9-year high-quality corporate bonds at 31/12/26	10%

The discount rate is determined using 9-year bonds because the long service leave is expected to be paid 9 years after the end of the reporting period.

Step 1: Estimate the number of employees who are expected to become eligible for long service leave.

$$50\% \times 150 \text{ employees} = 75 \text{ employees}$$

Step 2: Estimate the projected salaries.

$$= \text{Salary} \times (1 + \text{inflation rate})^n$$
$$= \$60,000 \times 75 \text{ employees} \times (1 + 0.02)^9 = \$5,377,917$$

The current salary is inflated over 9 years because employees are expected to take long service leave 9 years after the end of the reporting period.

Step 3: Determine the accumulated benefit.

$$= \frac{\text{Years of employment}}{\text{Years required for LSL}} \times \frac{\text{weeks of paid leave}}{52} \times \text{projected salaries}$$
$$= \frac{1}{10} \times \frac{13}{52} \times \$6,573,009 = \$134,448$$

Step 4: Measure the present value of the accumulated benefit.

$$= \frac{\text{Accumulated benefit}}{(1 + i)^n}$$
$$= \$134,448 / (1 + 0.1)^9 \left[\text{or } \$134,448 \times 0.4241 \text{ from present value tables}\right]$$
$$= \$57,019$$

The change in the provision for long service leave is recorded by the following journal entry:

2026				
31 December	Long Service Leave Expense	Dr	57,019	
	Provision for Long Service Leave	Cr		57,019
	(Increase in provision for long service leave)			

Note there was no beginning of period provision for long service leave as this is the first year.

During the following year, Green Ltd's 150 employees continued to work for the company. Average salaries increased to $68,000 per annum for the year. The following information is based on advice received from actuarial consultants at 31 December 2027:

Number of years unit credit	2 years
Number of years until long service leave is expected to be paid	8 years
Probability that LSL will be taken (proportion of employees expected to stay long enough to be entitled)	55%
Expected increase in salaries (based on inflation)	2% p.a.
Yield on 8-year high-quality corporate bonds 31/12/27	9%

The discount rate is determined using 8-year bonds because the long service leave is expected to be paid 8 years after the end of the reporting period.

Step 1: Estimate the number of employees who are expected to become eligible for long service leave.

$$55\% \times 150 \text{ employees} = 82.5 \text{ employees}$$

Step 2: Estimate the projected salaries.

$$= \text{Salary} \times (1 + \text{inflation rate})^n$$
$$= \$68,000 \times 82.5 \text{ employees} \times (1 + 0.02)^8 = \$6,573,009$$

The current salary is inflated over 8 years because employees are expected to take long service leave 8 years after the end of the reporting period.

Step 3: Determine the accumulated benefit.

$$= \frac{\text{Years of employment}}{\text{Years required for LSL}} \times \frac{\text{weeks of paid leave}}{52} \times \text{projected salaries}$$
$$= \frac{2}{10} \times \frac{13}{52} \times \$6,573,009 = \$328,650$$

Step 4: Measure the present value of the accumulated benefit.

$$= \frac{\text{Accumulated benefit}}{(1+i)^n}$$
$$= \$328,650 / (1 + 0.09)^8 \text{ [or } \$328,650 \times 0.50187 \text{ from present value tables]}$$
$$= \$164,939$$

The increase in the long service leave is $107,920 (calculated as $164,939 less $57,019) because there have been no long service leave payments during the year to reduce the provision from the amount recognised at the end of the previous year. The change in the provision for long service leave is recorded by the following journal entry:

2027				
31 December	Long Service Leave Expense	Dr	107,920	
	Provision for Long Service Leave	Cr		107,920
	(Increase in provision for long service leave)			

The increase in the provision for long service leave during 2027 can be attributed to several factors:
- an increase in unit credit accumulated by employees. In the first year, the employees' accumulation was 10% of the leave, but, by the end of the second year, 20% had been accumulated because the employees had completed a second year of service.
- the interest cost, being the increase in the present value arising from discounting the future cash flows over a shorter period.
- an increase in projected salaries resulting from an increase in remuneration. That is, salaries increased beyond the projected 2% during 2027.
- a reduction in the interest rate used from 10% at 31 December 2026 to 9% at 31 December 2027.

11.9 TERMINATION BENEFITS

When an employee is retrenched or made redundant, the employer may be obliged to pay termination benefits. For example, a downturn in the economy may cause a manufacturer to reduce the scale of its operations, resulting in some portion of the entity's workforce being made redundant. Termination benefits are typically lump sum payments. Paragraph 8 of IAS 19 refers to termination benefits as employee benefits that are payable as a result of either the employer deciding to terminate an employment contract, other than through normal retirement, or an employee accepting an offer of benefits in return for termination of employment.

Thus, the obligation to pay termination benefits arises from the termination of an employment contract, rather than from past services provided by the employee. Although the obligation arises from a decision to terminate employment, the extent of past services provided by each employee is usually a factor in determining the amount of the payment.

The decision to undertake a redundancy programme is not sufficient for the recognition of a liability for termination benefits. Merely deciding to undertake a redundancy programme does not create an obligation to a third party and thus does not meet the definition of a liability in accordance with the *Conceptual Framework*.

As stated above, an obligation to pay termination benefits can result from a decision of the employee to accept an offer, such as a redundancy arrangement, or a decision by the employer to terminate the employment contract. These alternative decisions are reflected in the requirement to recognise a liability and expense for termination benefits at the earlier of the following dates in accordance with paragraph 165 of IAS 19:
(a) when the entity can no longer withdraw the offer of the benefits; and
(b) when the entity recognises costs for a restructuring that is within the scope of IAS 37 and that involves the payment of termination benefits.

Paragraph 166 elaborates on when the entity can no longer withdraw an offer for termination benefits that become payable as a result of the employee's acceptance of an offer. The entity is unable to withdraw an offer after the employee accepts it. Further, the entity may be prevented from withdrawing an offer by existing regulations, contracts or laws. The entity can no longer withdraw an offer once such restrictions take effect.

Paragraph 167 is concerned with termination benefits that become payable as a result of the entity's decision to terminate employment. In this case, the offer can no longer be withdrawn when the entity has communicated to affected employees a plan of termination that meets all the following criteria (IAS 19 paragraph 167):
(a) steps taken to complete the plan indicate that it is unlikely to change significantly;
(b) the plan identifies the location, function or job classification, the number of employees whose services are to be terminated, and the expected completion date; and
(c) the plan is sufficiently detailed to enable employees to determine the type and amount of benefits they will receive.

If at the time of initial recognition, termination benefits are expected to be settled wholly within 12 months after the end of the annual reporting period, they are measured at the nominal (undiscounted) amount that the entity expects to pay. However, if the termination benefits are not expected to be settled wholly within 12 months after the end of the reporting period, they must be measured at present value. The expected payments required to settle the obligation are discounted at a rate determined by reference to market yields on high-quality corporate bonds, in accordance with paragraph 83. This is consistent with the measurement of other long-term employee benefits.

ILLUSTRATIVE EXAMPLE 11.11 Termination benefits

During December 2026, the board of directors of Universal plc approved a plan to outsource its data processing operations. The closure of the data processing operations is expected to result in laying off 180 employees in England and Wales. The chief financial officer provided an estimate of redundancy costs of £1.2 million. The board expected that it would take at least 6 months to select a contractor for outsourcing the data processing and a further 3 months for training before internal data processing operations could be discontinued.

During November 2027, redundancy packages were negotiated with trade union representatives and communicated to employees. Data processing operations were to be transferred to an external service provider in India on 1 March 2028.

When should Universal plc recognise an expense and liability for the redundancy payments?

2026

Universal plc must recognise a liability for termination benefits when it can no longer withdraw from a plan of termination communicated to affected employees, and that plan meets the criteria specified in paragraph 167 of IAS 19. It does not require an offer being accepted by employees.

At 31 December 2026, the termination plan meets some of the criteria. Management had specified the location (England and Wales) and function (data processing) of the employees becoming redundant, and estimated their number at 180. The termination benefit payable for each job specification is likely to have formed the basis of the estimated redundancy costs of £1.2 million. However, until Universal plc has identified an alternative source of data processing, it will not be able to decide on a time at which the redundancy plan should be implemented. Further, although the decision to discontinue the internal data processing operation had been made by Universal plc's board of directors, it has not been communicated to the employees. Therefore, Universal plc should not recognise an expense and liability for termination benefits in association with the planned closure of its data processing operations at 31 December 2026 in accordance with IAS 19.

2027

By November 2027, the company had completed the formal detailed termination plan by specifying when it is to be implemented. The negotiations with unions over the amount of redundancy payments and entering into a contract with an external provider demonstrate that it is unlikely that significant changes will be made to the amount or timing of the redundancy plan. The termination plan has been communicated to affected employees. Accordingly, Universal plc should recognise an expense and a liability for termination benefits in association with the planned closure of its data processing operations in its financial statements for the period ended 31 December 2027 in accordance with IAS 19.

11.10 SUMMARY

Employee benefits are a significant expense for most reporting entities. Accounting for employee benefits is complicated by the diversity of arrangements for remuneration for services provided by employees. This area of accounting is further complicated by the different methods prescribed by IAS 19 to account for various forms and categories of employee benefits. Liabilities for short-term employee benefits, such as salaries, wages, sick leave, annual leave and bonuses payable within 12 months after the reporting period, are measured at the undiscounted amount that the entity expects to pay. Long-term liabilities for defined benefits, such as long service leave, are measured at the present value of the defined benefit obligations less the fair value of plan assets, if any, out of which the obligation is to be settled. The obligation for long service leave is measured using the projected unit credit method. IAS 19 also prescribes accounting treatment for post-employment benefit plans. Accounting for defined contribution post-employment plans is relatively straightforward: a liability is recognised by the entity for contributions payable for the period in excess of contributions paid. Conversely, an asset is recognised if contributions paid exceed the contributions payable to the extent that the entity expects the excess contributions to be refunded or deducted from future contributions. An entity's net exposure to a defined benefit post-employment plan is measured at the present value of the defined benefit obligations less the fair value of plan assets. If the defined benefit plan has a surplus, the net defined benefit asset recognised by the entity is subject to an asset ceiling. In this chapter, we have also considered termination benefits. The measurement of a liability for termination benefits depends on whether they are expected to be settled wholly within 12 months of the annual reporting period in which they were first recognised. The principles for the measurement of the termination benefits liability are consistent with those for short-term employee benefits and other long-term employee benefits.

Discussion questions

1. What is a paid absence? Provide an example.
2. What is the difference between accumulating and non-accumulating sick leave? How does the recognition of accumulating sick leave differ from the recognition of non-accumulating sick leave?
3. What is the difference between vesting and non-vesting sick leave? How does the recognition and measurement of vesting sick leave differ from the recognition and measurement of non-vesting sick leave?
4. Explain how a defined contribution pension plan differs from a defined benefit pension plan.
5. During October 2008, there was a sudden global decline in the price of equity securities and credit securities. Many pension funds made negative returns on investments during this period. How would

this event affect the wealth of employees and employers? Consider both defined benefit and defined contribution pension funds in your answer to this question.

6. Explain how an entity should account for its contribution to a defined contribution pension plan in accordance with IAS 19.

7. Compare the off-balance-sheet approach to accounting for a defined benefit post-employment plan with the net capitalisation approach adopted by IAS 19. Can these approaches be explained by different underlying views as to whether a deficit or surplus in the plan meets the definition of a liability or asset of the sponsoring employer?

8. In relation to defined benefit post-employment plans, paragraph 56 of IAS 19 states, 'the entity is, in substance, underwriting the actuarial and investment risks associated with the plan'. Evaluate whether the requirements for the recognition and measurement of the net defined benefit liability reflect the underlying assumptions about the entity's risks.

9. Identify and discuss the assumptions involved in the measurement of a provision for long service leave. Assess the consistency of these requirements with the fundamental qualitative characteristics of financial information prescribed by the *Conceptual Framework*.

10. Explain the projected unit credit method of measuring and recognising an obligation for long-term employee benefits. Illustrate your answer with an example.

11. The board of directors of City Scooters GmbH met in December 2026 and decided to close down a branch of the company's operations when the lease expired in the following August. The chief financial officer advised that termination benefits of €2.0 million are likely to be paid. Should the company recognise a liability for termination benefits in its financial statements for the year ended 31 December 2026? Justify your judgement with reference to the requirements of IAS 19.

References

BHP Billiton 2023, *Annual Report*, BHP Billiton, https://www.bhp.com/-/media/documents/investors/annual-reports/2023/230822_bhpannualreport2023.pdf

HSBC Holdings plc 2023, *Annual Report 2023*, https://www.hsbc.com/investors/results-and-announcements/annual-report

IASB 2008, *Discussion paper: Preliminary views on amendments to IAS 19 Employee Benefits*, www.ifrs.org.

Rolls-Royce Holdings PLC 2023, Annual Report 2023, https://www.rolls-royce.com/investors/results-reports-and-presentations/annual-report-2023.aspx

As discussed in the chapter, a fundamental question arises whether the pension asset or liability should be included in the sponsoring firm's balance sheet. While recognising a liability is consistent with future funding needs, it is not clear that plan assets that are owned by the employees (through a trust) should appear on the sponsoring firm's balance sheet. Landsman's (1986) analysis speaks to this question. He finds that the stock market regards pension assets similar to other assets and pension liabilities as similar to other liabilities. His results therefore support the notion that the net pension asset or liability should be included in the balance sheet.

IAS 19 changed disclosure and recognition rules relative to what was domestically required in many countries that adopted IFRS® Standards. One issue that has been of interest to accounting researchers is whether the new rules have influenced the trend observed in many countries to curtail defined benefit (DB) plans and replace them with defined contribution (DC) plans. A possible explanation for this trend is that many employers find it hard to manage the various uncertainties embedded in DB plans (e.g. increasing life expectancy, inflation, interest rates). It is also possible that employers have found DC to be cheaper to run in that contribution rates are lower than funding pension plan assets under DB programmes. Kiosse and Peasnell (2009) review comment letters sent to the UK's Accounting Standard Board (ASB) when it deliberated FRS 17 (which is very similar to IAS 19). They observe that many commentators were concerned that rules to fully recognise the pension liability may lead sponsors to shut down DB plans. The prime concern was the added volatility that new rules will introduce to the income statement and balance sheet.

Short of termination of the DB plans, the effect of IAS 19 adoption may be seen in the effect on the strategy of investment in plan assets. Amir et al. (2010) provide evidence that pertains to this effect. They find that UK companies shifted to investment in bonds in and after 2005 — when IFRS® Standards and IAS 19 were adopted. Moreover, they find that this shift was more pronounced in firms with larger pension plans. They argue that such firms were more exposed to higher volatility in the financial statements post-adoption and consequently had a greater incentive to reduce this volatility through the less-risky strategy of investment in bonds as opposed to investment in equities.

Prior to SFAS 158 (FASB 2006) in the US and the 2011 revision to IAS 19, sponsoring firms calculated pension expense on a different basis. In particular, the income from plan assets was based on the notional expected rate of return (ERR) on plan assets. Importantly the selection of ERR was to a large extent subject to managerial discretion. Researchers have therefore been interested in understanding the degree to which this discretion was employed. Amir and Benartzi (1998) examine a sample of US firms that reported under these previous rules. They take advantage of a proprietary dataset that provides details of the composition of plan assets and examine how ERR varies with this composition. Amir and Benartzi (1998) argue that firms that invest a greater proportion of pension plan assets in equity investments

should employ a higher ERR to reflect the higher level of risk associated with equity investments. Thus, a high correlation between the percentage of equities in plan assets and ERR should be observed. However, Amir and Benartzi (1998) find that this correlation is weak in that ERR changed only slightly as the percentage of equities increased. This suggests that managers were quite conservative in selecting ERR. This is further supported by the additional finding that ERR is a poorer predictor of future return on plan assets than the percentage of investment in equities.

More broadly, assumptions underlying the calculation of pension expense and liability could be used opportunistically by managers. Amir and Gordon (1996) find evidence consistent with this hypothesis. Specifically, they find that the assumptions employed by managers worked to reduce reported pension liability. Their evidence further suggests that this is more pronounced in highly leveraged firms. Bergstresser et al. (2006) show that firms whose plan assets are large relative to operating income tend to select higher ERR than other firms. Higher ERR is also observed in firms that meet certain earnings thresholds. Interestingly, in some circumstances, managers may prefer to increase reported pension expense and liability. Comprix and Muller (2011) examine cases where companies froze the pension plans (i.e. stopped accruing pension obligations for existing and new members) to be able to make future savings. Since this decision could lead to labour disputes, managers may be motivated to exaggerate the pension problem to reduce disagreement with employees. They find that the number of employees affected and presence of labour union is negatively related to the likelihood of the freezing decision. This is consistent with concerns about employee reaction influencing managers against freezing. Furthermore, Comprix and Muller (2011) find that the ERR and discount rate selected by freezing sponsor firms are lower than non-freezing firms in the years preceding the freezing year. Because such lower estimates work to increase pension expense and pension liability, the evidence in Comprix and Muller (2011) is consistent with managerial discretion to reduce the likelihood of labour disputes by worsening reported performance and financial position.

IAS 19 is silent on where interest on net pension asset (i.e. expected return on net pension assets) or on net pension liability (i.e. interest expense) should be reported. Thus, reporting entities have a choice to classify this item either as operating (i.e. included in earnings before interest and tax — EBIT) or financial in nature. Glaum et al. (2018) observe that this choice is not always clearly disclosed. However, using a sample of French, German, and UK firms they find that managers use discretion to boost EBIT.

References

Amir, E., and Benartzi, S., 1998. The expected rate of return on pension funds and asset allocation as predictors of portfolio performance. The Accounting Review, 73, 335–352.

Amir, E., and Gordon, E. A., 1996. Firms' choice of estimation parameters: empirical evidence from SFAS no. 106. Journal of Accounting, Auditing and Finance, 11, 427–448.

Amir, E., Guan, Y., and Oswald, D., 2010. The effect of pension accounting on corporate pension asset allocation. Review of Accounting Studies, 15, 345–366.

Bergstresser, D., Desai, M., and Rauh, J., 2006. Earnings manipulations, pension assumptions and managerial investment decisions. The Quarterly Journal of Economics, 121, 157–194.

Comprix, J., and Muller, K. A., 2011. Pension plan accounting estimates and the freezing of defined benefit pension plans. Journal of Accounting and Economics, 51(1), 115–133.

Financial Accounting Standards Board (FASB), 2006. Statement of financial accounting standards (SFAS) No. 158, employers' accounting for defined benefit pension and other postretirement plans — an amendment of FASB statements No. 87, 88, 106 and 132(R). Norwalk, CT: FASB

Glaum, M., Keller, T. and Street, D.L., 2018. Discretionary accounting choices: the case of IAS 19 pension accounting. Accounting and Business Research, 48(2), 139–170.

Kiosse, P.V., and Peasnell, K., 2009. Have changes in pension accounting changed pension provision? A review of the evidence. Accounting and Business Research, 39(3), 255–267.

Landsman, W., 1986. An empirical investigation of pension fund property rights. Accounting Review, 662–691.

12

Owners' equity: share capital and reserves

ACCOUNTING STANDARDS IN FOCUS

IAS 1 *Presentation of Financial Statements*

IAS 32 *Financial Instruments: Presentation*

LEARNING OBJECTIVES

After studying this chapter, you should be able to:

1. describe the essence of the equity section in the statement of financial position
2. describe in general terms what a for-profit company is
3. outline the key features of corporate structure
4. discuss the different forms of share capital
5. account for the issue of both no-par and par value shares
6. account for share placements, rights issues, options, and bonus issues
7. discuss the rationale behind and accounting treatment of share buy-backs
8. outline the nature of reserves and account for movements in retained earnings, including dividends
9. prepare note disclosures in relation to equity, as well as a statement of changes in equity.

12.1 EQUITY

LO1

The purpose of this chapter is to introduce the element of equity in financial statements, describe its various components and the accounting for transactions that give rise to these components.

Equity is part of the statement of financial position, or balance sheet. From an algebraic standpoint it is the difference between total assets and liabilities. The IASB's *Conceptual Framework* (IASB 2018 paragraph 4.63) defines it as a residual, implying shareholders' financial interest in a company is confined to the excess, if any, of its assets over its liabilities.[1] This definition largely stems from the notion that shareholders' claims on a firm's assets are typically inferior to other stakeholders' rights (e.g. creditors). It is important to note that the figure for equity reported in the balance sheet is based on accounting conventions (as explained throughout this book) and is typically quite different from the real worth of the company to its owners.[2]

The main components of the equity section of the statement of financial position are contributed capital (e.g. share capital), reserves and retained earnings. The specific element of capital will differ depending on the nature of the organisation, whether a sole proprietorship, partnership or company. Reserves comprise equity attributable to the owners of the entity other than amounts directly contributed by the owners. An example of the equity section of the statement of financial position of a for-profit entity is shown in figure 12.1. It contains an extract from the group (consolidated) balance sheet of Tesco as at 25 February 2023. Note that the sum of share capital and share premium — the first two components — represents the amount of cash the company raised upon issuing its shares, less any subsequent decreases *(see section 12.7)*. For example, total share capital and premium for Tesco as at 25 February 2023 is £5,628m. An alternative term to 'share premium' that is used, in particular by US firms, is 'additional paid-in capital'. The third component, other reserves, is all the other equity accounts, which may be set to satisfy certain legal requirements, or as a result of specific accounting treatments discussed elsewhere in this book. Other reserves, however, exclude retained earnings and non-controlling interest. In the case of Tesco 2023 other reserves amount to £3,123m. Retained earnings, the total amount of undistributed profits at the balance sheet date, is £3,490, and can be used to pay dividends in the future or to buy-back shares. Non-controlling interests represents the ownership interests of non-Tesco shareholders in other companies that Tesco controls but does not hold 100% of the voting rights. *(This is discussed in detail in chapter 23.)* In the case of Tesco 2023 this is a relatively very small amount.

FIGURE 12.1 Owners' equity of Tesco

Group balance sheet	25 February 2023 £m	26 February 2022 £m
Equity		
Share capital	463	484
Share premium	5,165	5,165
Other reserves	3,123	3,079
Retained earnings	3,490	6,932
Equity attributable to the owners of the parent	**12,241**	**15,660**
Non-controlling interests	(11)	(16)
Total equity	**12,230**	**15,644**

In contrast to a multi-shareholders company like Tesco, with a *sole proprietor*, having a single owner means there is little reason for distinguishing between capital (potentially the initial investment in the business) and profits retained in the business for investment purposes. Nevertheless, many single-owned companies could still adopt a similar presentation.

Traditionally with *partnerships*, the rights and responsibilities of the partners are specified in a partnership agreement. This document details how the profits or losses of the partnership are to be divided between

---

[1] See also chapter 1.
[2] IAS 1 employs the term 'owners' to mean 'shareholders'. In this chapter, the two terms are used interchangeably.

the partners, including rules relating to distributions on dissolution of the partnership. In accounting for partnerships, a distinction is generally made for each partner between a capital account, to which amounts invested by a partner are credited, and a current account or retained earnings account, to which a partner's share of profits are credited and from which any drawings are debited. As with a sole proprietorship, there generally is no real distinction between capital contributed and profits retained (unless there is some other specification in the partnership agreement, which is unlikely). Both amounts represent the ongoing investment by the partners. On dissolution of the partnership, the distribution to partners is unaffected by whether an equity balance is capital or retained earnings.

With *companies*, the focus of this chapter, the situation is different because their formation is generally governed by legislation, and there is normally a clear distinction made between contributed capital and profits retained in the entity. For example, the amount of dividend a company can pay may be restricted to what is reported in retained earnings.

12.2 FOR-PROFIT COMPANIES

Generally, companies can be distinguished by the nature of the ownership, and the rights and responsibilities of the shareholders. In particular, some companies are not-for-profit and some are for-profit. The focus of this chapter, however, is on for-profit companies.

For-profit companies may be:
- Listed (or, quoted) — their shares are traded on a stock exchange
- unlisted — the shares are traded through brokers and financial institutions
- limited by guarantee — the members undertake to contribute a guaranteed amount in the event of the company going into liquidation
- unlimited — members are liable for all the debts of the company
- no-liability — members are not required to pay any calls on their shares if they do not wish to continue being shareholders in the company.

The exact rights and responsibilities of shareholders in relation to the different forms of companies will differ according to the relevant companies' legislation and other laws specific to the country or countries in which the company operates. However, shareholders are generally regarded as the residual claimants on the company's assets.

Many global companies list on a number of stock exchanges. Nokia, for example, is now quoted on the NASDAQ Helsinki (Symbol: NOKIA), the New York Stock Exchange (Symbol: NOK), and Euronext Paris (Symbol: NOKIA).

12.3 KEY FEATURES OF CORPORATE STRUCTURE

The choice of the company as the preferred form of organisational structure brings with it certain advantages, such as limited liability to shareholders *(see section 12.3.2)*. It also comes with certain disadvantages, such as making the entity subject to increasing regulation, especially in cases where the company is regarded as a Public Interest Entity (PIE). Some features of the company structure that affect the subsequent accounting for a company are described below.

12.3.1 The use of share capital

The ownership rights in a company are generally represented by shares; that is, the share capital of a company comprises several units, or shares. Typically, each share represents a proportional right to the net assets of the company and, within a class of shares, all shares have the same equal rights. These shares are generally transferable between parties. As a result, markets have been established to provide investors with an ability to trade in shares. A further advantage of transferability is that a change in ownership by one shareholder selling shares to a new investor does not have an effect on the continued existence and operation of the company.

In addition, each share typically has other rights, including:
- *the right to vote for directors of the company.* This establishes the right of shareholders to have a say as owners in the strategic direction of the company. Where there are a large number of owners in a company, there is generally a separation between ownership and management. The shareholders thus employ professional managers (the directors) to manage the organisation; these managers then provide periodic reports to the shareholders on the financial performance and position of the

company. Some directors are executive directors, being employed as executives in the company, while others have non-executive roles. The directors are elected at the annual general meeting of the company, and shareholders exercise their voting rights to elect the directors. The shareholders may vote in person, or by proxy. In relation to the latter, a shareholder may authorise another party to vote on their behalf at the meeting; the other party could be the chairperson of the company's board.

- *the right to share in assets on the winding-up or liquidation of the company.* The rights and responsibilities of shareholders in the event of liquidation are generally covered in legislation specific to each country, as are the rights of creditors to receive payment in preference to shareholders. However, if upon liquidation the assets are insufficient to pay the outstanding liabilities, shareholders of limited liability companies will receive no consideration for their shares *(also see section 12.3.2)*.

- *the right to share proportionately in any new issues of shares of the same class.* This right is sometimes referred to as the pre-emptive right. It ensures that a shareholder is able to retain the same proportionate ownership in a company, and that this ownership percentage cannot be diluted by the company issuing new shares to other investors, possibly at prices lower than the current fair value. However, the directors may be allowed to make limited placements of shares under certain conditions.

12.3.2 Limited liability

When shares are issued, the maximum amount payable by each shareholder is set. Even if a company incurs losses or goes into liquidation, the company cannot require a shareholder to provide additional capital. In some countries, shares are issued with a specific amount stated on the share certificate, this amount being called the par value of the share. For example, a company may issue 1 million shares each with a par value of $1. The company then receives share capital of $1 million.

Shares may also be issued at a premium; that is, for an amount exceeding the par value. For example, where a company requires share capital of $2 million, 1 million $1 shares may be issued at a premium of $1 per share; in this case, each shareholder is required to pay $2 per share. Similarly, shares may be issued at a discount. For example, where a company issues $1 shares at a discount of 20c, the company requires each shareholder to initially pay 80c per share. The only real purpose of the par value is to establish the maximum liability of the shareholder in relation to the company, and so owners may be required to contribute a further 20c per share upon liquidation, or at a later stage, as agreed with the company. Legislation in some countries restricts the issue of shares at a discount, and also establishes the subsequent uses of any share premium received on a share.

Note that the par value does not represent a fair or market value of the share. At the issue date, it would be expected that the par value, plus the premium or minus the discount, would represent the market value of the share. In some countries the use of par value shares has been replaced by the issue of shares at a specified price with no par value. For example, a company may issue 1,000 shares in 2024 at $3 per share, and in 2025 it may issue another 1,000 shares at $5 per share. At the end of 2025, the company then has 2,000 shares and a share capital of $8,000. The issue price becomes irrelevant subsequent to the issue. The variables are the number of shares issued and the amount of share capital in total. The amount of potential loss each shareholder is exposed to is therefore limited to the issue price of the shares at the time of issue.

The feature of limited liability protects shareholders by limiting the contribution required of them, which in turn places limitations on the ability of creditors to access funds for the repayment of company debts. To protect creditors, many countries have enacted legislation that prohibits companies from distributing capital to shareholders in the form of dividends or share buy-back. Dividends are then payable only from retained profits, not out of capital *(see section 12.8.1)*. Other forms of legislation require that assets exceed liabilities immediately before a dividend is 'declared'.

12.4 DIFFERENT FORMS OF SHARE CAPITAL

Shares are issued with specific rights attached and these can vary considerably across companies. Nevertheless, the two most common labels are ordinary shares and preference shares.

12.4.1 Ordinary shares

The most common form of share capital is the ordinary share or common stock. These shares have no specific rights to any distributions of profit by the company, and ordinary shareholders are often referred to as 'residual' equity holders in that these shareholders obtain what is left after all other parties' claims have been met. An example of a company that has only one class of share is Nokia and each share entitles its holder to one vote (Nokia Corporation 2022, p. 109). Further information on its shares was provided in its 2022 annual report. Part of this information is shown in figure 12.2. Note the reference to about 45 million shares owned by Group companies. Such shares are called treasury shares and the accounting for treasury shares *is discussed in section 12.7.* Treasury shares result from share-buy-back implying the number of shares held by shareholders excludes treasury shares.

FIGURE 12.2 Share capital, Nokia Corporation

Shares and share capital

Nokia has one class of shares. Each Nokia share entitles the holder to one vote at general meetings of Nokia.

At 31 December 2022, the share capital of Nokia Corporation equaled EUR 245,896,461.96 and the total number of shares issued was 5,632,297,576. At 31 December 2022, the total number of shares included 45,281,539 shares owned by Group companies representing approximately 0.8% of the total number of shares and the total voting rights.

Source: Nokia Corporation (2022, p. 109).

Returns to shareholders

The shareholders of ordinary shares have no specific rights to dividends, and the managers of a company have the decision power whether to pay dividends. For example, Meta Platforms has not paid its shareholders a dividend until 2024. Regulations in some countries may specify from which equity accounts the dividends can be paid, or whether the company has to meet solvency tests before paying dividends. In some cases, the directors may be allowed to propose a dividend at year-end, but this proposal may have to be approved by the shareholders in the annual general meeting.

12.4.2 Preference shares

Another form of share capital is the preference share. Holders of preference shares generally have a preferential right to dividends over the ordinary shareholders. Note firstly that preference shares, notwithstanding the name, are not necessarily included in equity. *As is discussed in chapter 13,* some preference shares are in substance not equity but liabilities, or they may be compound instruments being partially debt and partially equity, sometimes referred to as hybrid, or compound, securities. Secondly, the rights of preference shareholders may be very diverse. Some preference shares have a fixed dividend; for example, a company may issue preference shares at $10 each with a 4% dividend per annum, thus entitling the shareholder to a 40c dividend per annum. Other common features of preference shares are:

- *cumulative* versus *non-cumulative shares*. Where a preference share is cumulative, if a dividend is not declared in a particular year, the right to the dividend is not lost but carries over to a subsequent year. The dividends are said to be in arrears. With non-cumulative shares, if a dividend is not paid in a particular year, the right to that dividend is lost.
- *participating* versus *non-participating shares*. A participating share gives the holder the right to share in extra dividends. For example, if a company has issued 8% participating preference shares and it pays a 10% dividend to the ordinary shareholders, the preference shareholders may be entitled to a further 2% dividend.
- *convertible* versus *non-convertible shares*. Convertible preference shares may give the holder the right to convert the preference shares into ordinary shares. The right to convert may be at the option of the holder of the shares or at the option of the company itself. *As explained in chapter 13,* convertible preference shares may need to be classified into debt and equity components.
- *redeemable preference shares*. Redeemable preference shares are shares that may be converted into cash under certain pre-specified conditions. *As explained in chapter 13,* if the terms of the issue are such that the shares are redeemed at the discretion of the shareholder, the issue of the preference shares is treated as a liability. However, if the terms are such that the decision to redeem is at the issuer's discretion, it will be reported as equity.

12.5 CONTRIBUTED EQUITY: ISSUE OF SHARE CAPITAL

Once a business has decided to form a public company, it will commence the procedures necessary to issue shares to the public. The initial offering of shares to the public to invest in the new company is called an initial public offering (IPO). To arrange the sale of the shares, the business that wishes to float the company usually employs a promoter, such as a stockbroker or a financial institution, with expert knowledge of the legal requirements and experience in this area. Once the promoter and the managers of the business agree on the structure of the new company, a prospectus is drawn up and lodged with the regulating authority. The prospectus contains information about the current status of the business and its future prospects.

To ensure that the statements in the prospectus are accurate, a process of due diligence is undertaken by an accounting firm. To ensure that the sale of shares is successful, an underwriter may be employed. The role of the underwriter is to advise on such matters as the pricing of the issue, the timing of the issue and how the issue will be marketed. One of the principal reasons for using an underwriter is to ensure that all the shares are sold, as the underwriter agrees to acquire all shares that are not taken up by the public.

12.5.1 Issue costs

The costs of issuing the shares, particularly in an IPO, can be quite substantial. The costs include those associated with preparing and distributing the relevant documentation, as well as the fees charged by the various experts consulted which could include bankers, accountants, lawyers and taxation specialists. Accounting for these costs is covered in paragraphs 35, 37 and 38 of IAS 32 *Financial Instruments: Presentation*. It distinguishes between costs that are incremental to issuance of new equity instruments and the costs of other activities that may occur at the same time (such as becoming a public company or acquiring an exchange listing). The former are offset against equity, whereas the latter are expensed as incurred. This may require judgement in determining what is incremental and how to allocate costs to the various activities that may take place at the same time. If the issue is aborted, costs are expensed in profit and loss (see IFRIC 2008).

The costs are then treated as a reduction in share capital such that the amount shown in share capital immediately after the share issue is the net amount available to the company for operations. *The accounting for share issue costs is demonstrated in the next section.*

Any costs associated with the formation of the company that cannot be directly related to the issue of the shares, such as registration of the company name, are expensed as the cost is incurred. These outlays do not meet the definition of an asset as there are no expected future economic benefits associated with these outlays that can be controlled by the company.

As discussed in 12.3.2, shares may be issued with a stated par value, or as no-par shares. Shares with stated par value may be issued at a premium, or a discount. *These possibilities are illustrated next.*

12.5.2 Issue of no-par shares

Illustrative example 12.1 shows the recording of issuing no-par shares.

ILLUSTRATIVE EXAMPLE 12.1 Issue of no-par shares

Quebec Ltd issues 500 no-par shares for cash at $10 each, incurring share issue costs of $450. Quebec Ltd records on its share register the number of shares issued, and makes the following journal entry:

Cash	Dr	5,000	
Share Capital	Cr		5,000
(Issue of 500 $10 shares)			
Share Capital	Dr	450	
Cash	Cr		450
(Share issue costs)			

12.5.3 Issue of par value shares

When shares certificates specify the par value, the share issue proceeds are compared to the par value. If proceeds exceed par value, shares are said to be issued at a premium. If proceeds fall below par value, then they are issued at a discount.

Shares issued at a premium

Where shares are issued at a premium, the excess over the par value is credited to an equity account which may be called share premium, additional paid-in capital, or share capital in excess of par. The share premium is then a component of contributed equity. Example of entries required when shares are issued at a premium is provided in illustrative example 12.2.

ILLUSTRATIVE EXAMPLE 12.2 Issue of par value shares at a premium

Bhutan Ltd issues 5,000 shares of $1 par value at $3 a share. Issuance costs (lawyers, accountants, registration, etc.) amount to $500. The net cash received therefore is $14,500 (5,000 × $3 − $500). The journal entry is:

Cash	Dr	14,500	
Share Capital	Cr		5,000
Share Premium	Cr		9,500
(Issue of shares at a premium after deducting issuance costs)			

Shares issued at a discount

Shares may be issued at a discount, subject to certain conditions and restrictions that are typically set by law; therefore, issuing shares at a discount is a relatively rare event. The account used in relation to the discount can be the same as that used for a premium, or it can be a separate discount account. The accounting treatment will vary depending on the regulations governing discounts in particular jurisdictions. Example of entries required when shares are issued at a discount is provided in illustrative example 12.3.

ILLUSTRATIVE EXAMPLE 12.3 Issue of par value shares at a discount

Aidan Ltd issues 5,000 shares of $2 par value at a 50c discount (or, alternatively, at $1.50 a share). Issuance costs are $500. The net cash received therefore is $7,000 (5000 × $1.5 − $500). The journal entry is:

Cash	Dr	7,000	
Discount on Shares	Dr	3,000	
Share Capital	Cr		10,000
(Issue of shares at a discount)			

12.5.4 Oversubscriptions

An issue of shares by a company may be so popular that it is oversubscribed (see illustrative example 12.4); that is, there are more applications for shares than shares to be issued. Some investors may then receive an allotment of fewer shares than they applied for, or may not be allotted any shares at all. In most cases, therefore, excess application monies are simply refunded to the applicants.

China Ltd was incorporated on 1 July 2024. The directors offered to the general public 100,000 ordinary shares for subscription at an issue price of $2. The company received applications for 200,000 shares and collected $400,000. The directors then decided to issue 150,000 shares, returning the balance of application money to the unsuccessful applicants.

The appropriate journal entries are:

Cash	Dr	400,000	
Application Reserve (Equity)	Cr		400,000
(Money received on application)			
Application Reserve	Dr	300,000	
Share Capital	Cr		300,000
(Issue of shares)			
Application Reserve	Dr	100,000	
Cash	Cr		100,000
(Refund of excess application money)			

12.6 CONTRIBUTED EQUITY: SUBSEQUENT MOVEMENTS IN SHARE CAPITAL

Having floated the company, the directors may at a later stage decide to make changes to the share capital. For example, the shareholders of Santander, a large Spanish bank, authorised its Board of Directors to issue new shares. This authorisation is shown in figure 12.3.

Share capital may be either increased or decreased. This section of the chapter discusses the methods a company may use to increase its share capital. *Section 12.7 examines how a company may decrease its share capital.*

FIGURE 12.3 An authorisation to increase share capital, Santander

Under Spanish law, shareholders at the general meeting have the authority to increase the share capital and may delegate power to the board of directors to increase the share capital by no more than 50%. Our Bylaws are consistent with Spanish law and do not set out special conditions for share capital increases. By 31 December 2023, our board of directors had received authorization from shareholders to approve or carry out the following capital increases:

- Authorised capital to 2025: Shareholders at the 2022 AGM granted authorization to the board to increase share capital on one or more occasions by up to EUR 4,335,160,325.50 (50% of the capital at the time of that AGM). The board was granted this authorization for a period of 3 years (until 1 April 2025).

Source: Santander (annual report 2023, p. 186).

12.6.1 Placements of shares

Rather than issue new shares to the public or current shareholders, the company may decide to place the shares with specific investors such as life insurance companies and pension funds. The advantages to the company of a placement of shares are:
- *speed* — a placement can be effected in a short period of time
- *price* — because a placement is made to other than existing shareholders, and to a market that is potentially more informed and better funded, the issue price of the new shares may be closer to the market price at the date of issue

- *direction* — the shares may be placed with investors who approve of the direction of the company, or who will not interfere in the formation of company policies
- *prospectus* — in some cases, a placement can occur without the need for a detailed prospectus to be prepared.

There are potential disadvantages to the existing shareholders from private placements in that the current shareholders will have their interest in the company diluted as a result of the placement. In some countries, the securities regulations place limits on the amounts of placements of shares without the approval of existing shareholders. Further disadvantages to current shareholders can occur if the company places the shares at a large discount. Again, securities laws are generally enacted to ensure that management cannot abuse the placement process and that current shareholders are protected. Example of entries required for placement of shares is provided in illustrative example 12.5.

ILLUSTRATIVE EXAMPLE 12.5 Placement of shares

Thailand Ltd placed 5,000 no-par ordinary shares at $5 each with Turkey Ltd
The entry in the journals of Thailand Ltd is:

Cash	Dr	25,000	
Share Capital	Cr		25,000
(Placement of shares)			

Note the entry in Thailand's books would be the same if the shares were issued to existing shareholders, or the public at large, although the explanation will naturally change.

12.6.2 Rights issues

A rights issue is an issue of new shares with the terms of issue giving existing shareholders the right to an additional number of shares in proportion to their current shareholding; that is, the shares are offered pro rata. For example, an offer could be made to each shareholder to buy two new shares on the basis of every 10 shares currently held. If all the existing shareholders exercise their rights and take up the shares, there is no change in each shareholder's percentage ownership interest in the company. Example of entries required for rights issue is provided in illustrative example 12.6. Rights issues are typical in the context of protecting shareholders from involuntary dilution of their interest, and may also be offered below market price to encourage shareholders' participation. This was the case for Santander, as well as other banks, which in the height of the financial crisis in 2008–2009 was forced to support its equity by a large share issue through a deeply discounted rights issue (*Santander's Rushed Rights Issue is Raising Hackles*, FT.com, 20 November 2008).

Rights issues may be tradeable or non-tradeable. If tradeable, existing shareholders may sell their rights to the new shares to another party during the offer period. If the rights are non-tradeable, a shareholder is not allowed to sell their rights to the new shares and must either accept or reject the offer to acquire new shares in the company.

ILLUSTRATIVE EXAMPLE 12.6 Rights issue

Pakistan Ltd planned to raise $3.6 million from shareholders through a one-for-six rights issue. The terms of the issue were 6 million no-par shares to be issued at 60c each, applications to be received by 15 April 2024. The rights issue was fully taken up. The shares were issued on 20 April 2024.
The journal entries in the company's records are passed only when the rights are exercised:

April 20	Cash	Dr	3,600,000	
	Share Capital	Cr		3,600,000
	(Issue of shares)			

12.6.3 Options

Companies often provide their employees with share-based compensation. In particular, under some of these arrangements employees are issued shares, or options to shares, that replace cash payment. This may involve entries to owners' equity that may increase share premium account or a specific reserve. *Chapter 14 discusses the specific requirements for such arrangements.*

More generally, a company-issued share option is an instrument that gives the holder the right but not the obligation to buy a certain number of shares in the company by a specified date at a stated price. For example, a company could issue options in 2023 that give an investor the right to acquire shares in the company at $20 each, with the options having to be exercised before 31 December 2027. The option holder is taking a risk in that the share price may not reach $20 (the option is 'out of the money') or the share price may exceed $20 (the option is 'in the money').

When the options are issued, the issuing entity will receive an initial amount of cash that corresponds to the fair value of the option at that time. Where the option holder exercises the option, the company increases its share capital as it issues the shares to the option holder.

To illustrate: assume Beckham Inc. company issues 100 options on 30 June 2026 with a fair value of $0.50 each to two investors in equal amounts (i.e. 50 options each). Each option entitles the investors to acquire a share in the company at a price of $3. The current market price of the company shares is $2.80. Assume that on 30 November 2026 the share price reaches $4 and one investor exercises the option. The journal entries required are shown below. The par value of each share is $1.[3]

June 30	Cash	Dr	50	
	Options reserve*	Cr		50
	(100 options issued at 50c each)			
November 30	Cash	Dr	150	
	Options reserve	Dr	25	
	Share Capital	Cr		100
	Share Premium	Cr		75
	(Exercise of 50 options issued in June)			

*This account is part of equity and can also be called 'Other Equity'.

Note that the issue price of those options exercised is treated as part of share capital; in essence, the investor who exercises the option is paying $3.50 ($0.50 + $3.0) in total for each share (and a total of 50 × $3.50 = $175) and gains $25 (50 × $4.00 − $175). Also note the specific use of accounts in this example. However, these accounts may not always be the appropriate ones across all legal jurisdictions and the choice of which accounts are used may also be affected by taxation implications.

Options generally have to be exercised by a specific date. Assume that in the case of Beckham Inc. the options had to be exercised by 31 December 2026, and only one investor exercised their right to acquire shares. Then there is no need to pass any additional journal entries. For the options that were not exercised, the entity could transfer the equity balance of $25 to share premium or a reserve account including retained earnings. Again, legal and taxation implications should be considered in choosing the appropriate accounts to be used. For the example above where the holder of 50 options did not exercise those options, the journal entry below may be required when the options lapse would be:

Options reserve	Dr	25	
Share Premium	Cr		25
(Transfer of lapsed options)			

---

[3]This is an example of 'gross-settled' share options (i.e. when the option is exercised the full amount of shares is issued). Option contracts that are 'cash-settled' are treated as a derivative liability, and hence are not recognised in equity. If the contract is net 'equity-settled' the initial amount raised is treated as a liability, which is subsequently adjusted to changes in the fair value of the option. Upon exercise, the entity issues shares so as to settle the balance. For example, if the share price on exercise day is $4 and the exercise price is $3, then the total value of outstanding options is $100 (($4 − $3) × 100), and hence the liability on that day stands at $100. When 25 ($100/$4) new shares are issued to settle the balance, the issuer debits the liability $100, and credits share capital $25 and share premium $75.

12.6.4 Share warrants and compound securities

Other forms of option are company-issued warrants and embedded options to convert debt to equity in a compound debt-equity instrument. While an option is a freestanding equity instrument, a warrant or an embedded option in a convertible bond is generally attached to another form of financing. For example, embedded options may be attached to an issue of debt, and warrants may be given as an incentive to acquire a large parcel of shares in a future capital raising activity. Warrants may be detachable or non-detachable, but typically upon exercise require the holder to contribute further funds. If warrants are non-detachable, then they cannot be traded separately from the shares or debt package to which they were attached. In either case the warrant or conversion option has a value that needs to be recorded in equity, although where in equity is not generally prescribed. *The measurement and accounting for convertible bonds is described in chapter 13.*

12.6.5 Bonus issues (or stock dividend)

A bonus issue is an issue of shares to existing shareholders in proportion to their current shareholdings at no cost to the shareholders. The company uses its reserves balances or retained earnings to make the issue. The bonus issue is a transfer from one equity account to another, so it does not increase or decrease the equity of the company. Instead, it increases the share capital and decreases another equity account of the company.

The standards do not provide guidance as to how a bonus issue should be measured. Reference to fair value of the bonus issue may be unwarranted, as firm valuation remains intact. Furthermore, when *all* shareholders receive *equal* bonus (on a pro rata basis), each shareholder's wealth is unaffected although the value of each share is smaller following the bonus. This suggests that the charge to the other equity account should be recorded at the par value. To illustrate: assume a company has a share capital consisting of 500,000 shares, $1 par value each. If it makes a 1-for-20 bonus issue from its retained earnings, it will issue 25,000 shares pro rata to its current shareholders. The journal entry required is:

Retained Earnings	Dr	25,000	
Share Capital	Cr		25,000
(Bonus issue of 25,000 shares from retained earnings)			

Nevertheless, in the case where a company assigns a value to the stock dividend that exceeds the par value, perhaps by reference to the prevailing share price, the charge to retained earnings, or any other permissible reserve, will be higher, with a balancing entry to the share premium account. Considering the previous example, assume the share bonus is valued at $100,000. Then the journal entry for issuing 25,000 bonus shares is:

Retained Earnings	Dr	100,000	
Share Capital	Cr		25,000
Share Premium	Cr		75,000
(Bonus issue of 25,000 shares at $100,000 from retained earnings)			

Depending on prevailing law, companies may use other equity accounts instead of retained earnings. In the example above, issuing the stock dividend at par value could be charged against the share premium account:

Share Premium	Dr	25,000	
Share Capital	Cr		25,000
(Bonus issue of 25,000 shares from retained earnings)			

On occasions where the debit to the share premium account exceeds its opening balance, the difference between the 25,000 and the opening balance may be debited to retained earnings, or any other reserve account permitted by the relevant country's regulations. *(See section 12.8 for the discussion of reserves.)*

12.6.6 Share split

Issuing shareholders bonus shares has the effect of reducing the value of each share, which consequently increases the liquidity and ease with which these shares can be exchanged or traded since there are more shares in circulation at a lower price. However, total equity is unaffected by share bonus and there also should not be any effect on total firm value. A similar effect on share value is reached via share splits. A share split involves increasing the number of shares outstanding while proportionally reducing the par value of each share. For example, if a company has 10,000 shares outstanding at 90c each, and carries out a 3-for-1 split, it will report after the split 30,000 shares at 30c each. Total share capital is therefore unchanged and, unlike a share bonus, no charge is required to any other equity account.

12.6.7 Share-based transactions

A company may acquire assets, including other entities, with the consideration for the acquisition being shares in the company itself. *Accounting for this form of transaction is covered in chapter 19. Accounting for share-based payments is covered in chapter 14.*

12.7 SHARE CAPITAL: SUBSEQUENT DECREASES IN SHARE CAPITAL

A company may decrease the number of shares issued by buying back some of its own shares. The extent to which a company may buy back its own shares and the frequency with which it may do so are generally governed by specific laws within a jurisdiction as well as the company's own charter. Shareholders typically need to authorise management to buy-back shares, although such authorisation may be valid for a number of years. For example, in its 2023 annual report Bayer refers to such authorisation which expires next financial year (see figure 12.4):

FIGURE 12.4 An authorisation to decrease share capital, Bayer 2023

> The Annual Stockholders' Meeting held on April 26, 2019, resolved that the Board of Management be authorised to purchase and dispose of own shares representing up to 10% of the capital stock existing at the time the resolution was adopted. This authorization expires on April 25, 2024.

Source: Bayer (2023, p. 125).

A key feature of such regulations is the protection of creditors, as the company is reducing equity by using cash that otherwise would have been available to repay creditors. Companies may undertake a share buy-back to:
- increase earnings-per-share (EPS) (which is often used in executive compensation contracts)
- manage the capital structure by reducing equity
- more efficiently return surplus funds held by the company to shareholders, rather than pay a dividend or reinvest in other ventures (specific tax rules may favour buy-backs to dividends).

Repurchased shares are called treasury shares. IAS 32 (paragraph 33) requires that the amount spent on buying back treasury shares is deducted from equity, reported in a contra-equity account. The standard, however, does not prescribe which element of equity should be reduced.

Consider Harlem Inc. which has issued 500,000 shares at $1 par value each over a period of years. Further assume the total equity of Harlem Inc. consists of:

Share Capital	$ 500,000
Share Premium	270,000
Retained Earnings	230,000
	$1,000,000

If Harlem Inc. now buys back 50,000 shares for $2.20 per share, the amount of treasury shares is $110,000. This is recorded as follows:

Treasury Shares	Dr	110,000
Cash	Cr	110,000
(Share buy-back 50,000 shares at $2.20 per share)		

The equity section will now report:

Share Capital	$ 500,000
Share Premium	270,000
Retained Earnings	230,000
Treasury Shares	(110,000)
	$ 890,000

Note that the treasury shares account is a contra-equity account, as it appears in equity, but with a negative sign.

Following the repurchase, treasury shares may be (i) kept by the company; (ii) reissued and (iii) cancelled. The accounting treatment for these different possibilities is described below.

12.7.1 Treasury shares kept in the company

As long as the treasury shares are kept in the company, the equity reports a deduction of $110,000, as illustrated above. Treasury shares are not regarded as issued for the purpose of voting, dividends and other rights that come along with ordinary shares.

12.7.2 Treasury shares are reissued

Companies may reuse treasury shares to satisfy demand for options that have been exercised (e.g. in employee share option schemes), or resell them in the open market or to other investors. Since the proceeds on such resell may differ from the original cost of the treasury shares, a gain or a loss may arise. However, IAS 32 (paragraph 33) disallows the recognition of such gain or loss in the income statement. Instead, it should be recognised directly in reserves.

Assume Harlem Inc. resells on the open market 10,000 treasury shares at $3 each. This generates a gain of $0.80 per share ($3.00 − $2.20), or a total gain of $8,000. A typical entry to record this would be:

Cash	Dr	30,000
Treasury Shares	Cr	22,000
Share Premium	Cr	8,000
(Resell of 10,000 treasury shares at $3.00 per share)		

If, on the other hand, Harlem Inc. resells 10,000 treasury shares at $1.40 a share, a loss of $8,000 is generated. This will be recorded as follows:

Cash	Dr	14,000
Share Premium	Dr	8,000
Treasury Shares	Cr	22,000
(Re-sell of 10,000 treasury shares at $1.40 per share)		

Again, on occasions where the debit to the share premium account exceeds its opening balance, the difference may be debited to retained earnings, or any other reserve account permitted by the relevant country's regulations. (*See section 12.8 for the discussion of reserves.*)

12.7.3 Treasury shares are cancelled

A repurchase of shares that is followed by a cancellation is equivalent from an economic perspective to a redistribution of wealth to owners. According to this view, when treasury shares are cancelled, a suitable reduction to retained earnings should be made. However, depending on the legal jurisdiction, other distributable reserves can be used (see section 12.8 for the discussion of reserves in equity). In addition, the original share capital should be cancelled. Assume that prior to the purchase of the 100,000 treasury shares at $2.20 each Harlem Inc. also had an asset revaluation surplus reserve of $20,000 that can be used for this purpose. The cancellation of 50,000 shares is therefore recorded as:

Share Capital	Dr	50,000	
Share Premium	Dr	27,000	
Revaluation Surplus	Dr	20,000	
Retained Earnings	Dr	13,000	
Treasury Shares	Cr		110,000
(Cancellation of 50,000 treasury shares with $1 par value each that were purchased at $2.20 each)			

Corporate law in some countries requires the maintenance of capital, as a means of protecting creditors (this is the case, for example, in the UK). This implies that a new non-distributable reserve in equity is also established at the amount of cancelled share capital. Employing the previous example, this can be recorded as follows:

Share Capital	Dr	50,000	
Share Premium	Dr	27,000	
Revaluation Reserve	Dr	20,000	
Retained Earnings	Dr	63,000	
Capital Redemption Reserve	Cr		50,000
Treasury Shares	Cr		110,000
(Cancellation of 50,000 treasury shares with $1 par value each that were purchased at $2.20 each)			

Creditors' protection is obtained through the larger debit to retained earnings, implying Harlem Inc.'s ability to further pay cash dividends in the future is reduced (by an additional $50,000).

In Nokia's 2023 balance sheet (see figure 12.2), the treasury shares are deducted from total equity because the share capital of the entity has effectively been reduced by the repurchase of the shares.

12.8 RESERVES

'Reserves' is the generic term for all equity accounts other than contributed equity. A major component is the retained earnings account. This account accumulates the sum of the periodic income earned by an entity, and certain other comprehensive income (OCI). IAS 1 requires entities to prepare a Statement of Comprehensive Income that lists both periodic income and items of OCI (see chapter 2). OCI includes all income items that certain accounting standards require (or allow) to flow directly through equity, net of related tax effects. Some notable examples of OCI are:

- remeasurements of financial assets measured at fair value through other comprehensive income and cash flow hedges (IFRS 9 — see chapter 13)
- remeasurement of defined benefit pension plans (IAS 19 [Revised] — see chapter 11)
- revaluation of property, plant and equipment (IAS 16 — see chapter 5)
- particular foreign exchange differences (IAS 21 — see chapter 24).

However, not all income items recognised in OCI need to be incorporated into retained earnings. They may be incorporated into a separate reserve, as discussed in section 12.8.2.

Retained earnings is the primary account from which distributions to owners are made in the form of dividends. Hence, in general, the retained earnings account will accumulate comprehensive income (that is not recognised in other reserves) earned over the life of the entity.

12.8.1 Retained earnings

'Retained earnings' has the same meaning as 'retained profits' and 'accumulated profit or loss'. The key change in this account is the addition of the comprehensive income or loss for the current period. The main other movements in the retained earnings account are:

- dividends declared
- cancellation of shares (*see section 12.7.3*)
- transfers to and from reserves
- changes in accounting policy and errors (see IAS 8 *Accounting Policies, Changes in Accounting Estimates and Errors, discussed in detail in chapter 2*).

Cash dividends. Cash dividends are a distribution from the company to its owners in the form of cash. It is generally the case, under companies legislation, that dividends can be paid only from profits, and not from capital. In some jurisdictions, companies must comply with a solvency test before paying dividends. The purpose in both situations is to protect the creditors, as any money paid to shareholders is money unavailable for paying creditors.

Scrip dividends. Companies often give shareholders a choice between cash dividend and receiving more shares in an equivalent value to the cash dividend. As an example, Sean plc declares a 10c per share dividend during 2025. The market value of its 1m shares is $10m at the time of the declaration. The par value of each share is $1. As the total cash dividend amounts to $100,000, the dividend is equal to 1% of the market value of its equity ($0.1 × 1m/$10m). Hence, Sean plc offers a 1-for-100 scrip alternative. Assuming 50% of shareholders opt for the scrip alternative, Sean plc would record these entries:

2025	Retained Earnings	Dr	100,000	
	Dividends Payable	Cr		100,000
	(Declaration of dividend of $100,000)			
	Dividends Payable	Dr	100,000	
	Cash	Cr		50,000
	Share Capital	Cr		5,000
	Retained Earnings	Cr		45,000
	(Payment of $50,000 cash dividend and issue of 5,000 new shares)			

The scrip alternative can be thought of as equivalent to a share bonus. Hence, if the share premium account can be used for the share bonus, it is possible to record the following entries when the dividend is paid and new shares are issued:

2025	Dividends Payable	Dr	100,000	
	Share Premium	Dr	5,000	
	Cash	Cr		50,000
	Share Capital	Cr		5,000
	Retained Earnings	Cr		50,000
	(Payment of $50,000 cash dividend and issue of 5,000 bonus shares)			

Note that in this case retained earnings are reduced only by the amount of cash dividend.

Interim and final dividends. Dividends are sometimes divided into interim and final dividends. Interim dividends are paid during the financial year, while final dividends are declared by the directors at financial year-end for payment sometime after the end of the reporting period. In some companies, the eventual payment of the final dividends is subject to approval of the dividend by the annual general meeting. With the final dividend, there is some debate as to when the company should raise a liability for the dividend, particularly where payment of the dividend is subject to shareholder approval. Some would argue that until approval is received there is only a contingent liability, the entity not having a present obligation to pay the dividend until approval is received. Others argue that there is a constructive obligation existing at year-end and, given customary business practice, the entity has a liability at the end of the reporting period.

In this regard, paragraphs 12 and 13 of IAS 10 *Events after the Reporting Period* state that if dividends are not declared *and* approved by the annual general meeting (AGM) by the end of the reporting period, no liability is recognised at the end of the reporting period. That is, a declaration without approval does not affect the balance sheet. Often, a declaration is made after the reporting date, but this does not give rise to the recognition of a dividend payable liability, even if the AGM subsequently approves it. When the declared dividend cannot be recognised as a liability, it should be reported only as a contingent liability. *(See chapter 10 for further discussion on provisions and contingencies.)* It is also important to note that the payment takes place some time after the declaration, as the declaring entity needs to identify all shareholders that are entitled to the dividend and this procedure takes time. Dividends paid after this date (the ex-dividend date) will be paid to the registered shareholders on declaration date, even if they subsequently sold their shares. This process is depicted in illustrative example 12.7.

ILLUSTRATIVE EXAMPLE 12.7 Interim and final dividends

During the period ending 30 June 2025, the following events occurred in relation to Oman Ltd:

2024

Sept. 25	Annual general meeting approves the final dividend of $10,000 relating to the results of the financial year that ended on 30 June 2024. It further authorises the Board to pay an interim dividend in February 2025 up to $8,000 in relation to 2025 profit.
Sept. 30	Oman Ltd pays the final dividend to shareholders.

2025

Jan. 5	Oman Ltd declares an interim dividend of $8,000
Feb. 10	Oman Ltd pays an interim dividend of $8,000.
June 30	Oman Ltd declares a final dividend of $12,000, this dividend requiring shareholder approval at the next AGM.

Required
Prepare the journal entries to record the dividend transactions of Oman Ltd

Solution

2024

Sept. 25	Retained Earnings	Dr	10,000	
	Dividends Payable	Cr		10,000
	(Dividend of $10,000 authorised by annual meeting)			
Sept. 30	Dividends Payable	Dr	10,000	
	Cash	Cr		10,000
	(Payment of dividend)			

2025

Jan. 5	Retained Earnings	Dr	8,000	
	Interim dividend payable	Cr		8,000
	(Declaration of interim dividend)			
Feb. 10	Interim dividend payable	Dr	8,000	
	Cash	Cr		8,000
	(Payment of interim dividend)			

No entry is required in relation to the final dividend of $12,000. A contingent liability would be recorded in the notes to the 2025 financial statements.

12.8.2 Other components of equity

In section 12.7 we encountered two special reserves: treasury shares (a contra-equity account) and capital redemption reserve. Some additional examples of reserves other than retained earnings are shown below.

Asset revaluation reserve

IAS 16 *Property, Plant and Equipment* allows entities a choice in the measurement of these assets. In particular, entities may choose between measuring the assets at cost (the cost model) or at fair value (the revaluation model). If the fair value basis is chosen, revaluation increases are recognised in other comprehensive income and accumulated in equity via an asset revaluation surplus. *(Details of the accounting under a fair value basis for property, plant and equipment are covered in chapter 5.)*

An asset revaluation surplus, may be used for payment of dividends or be transferred to other reserve accounts including retained earnings, depending on a jurisdiction's specific laws. Amounts recognised directly in the asset revaluation surplus cannot subsequently be recognised in profit or loss for the period even when the revalued asset is disposed of.

Foreign currency translation differences

Foreign currency translation differences arise when foreign operations are translated from one currency into another currency for presentation purposes. *(Details of the establishment of this account can be found in chapter 24.)* The changes in wealth as a result of the translation process are thereby not taken through profit or loss for the period, and are recognised in profit or loss only if and when the investor disposes of its interest in the foreign operation.

Fair value differences

Under IFRS 9 *Financial Instruments*, at initial recognition, financial assets and liabilities are measured at fair value. Paragraph 5.7.5 of IFRS 9 permits an entity to make an irrevocable election to present in other comprehensive income changes in the fair value of an investment in an equity instrument that is not held for trading. Because IFRS 9 (paragraph B5.7.1) does not allow such gains and losses to be transferred into profit and loss, they should be recorded in other reserves, or directly in retained earnings. Illustrative example 12.8 is taken from Diageo annual report for 2023 showing how Diageo reports its various reserves (see figure 12.5).

ILLUSTRATIVE EXAMPLE 12.8 Reserves

As an example of the disclosure of reserves, the note disclosure provided by Diageo in its 2023 annual report is shown in figure 12.5.

As illustrated earlier in the chapter, entities may make transfers between various reserves. For example, share premium may be used to issue bonus shares. Asset revaluation surplus can be transferred gradually to retained earnings, when the depreciation on the underlying asset exceeds the historical-cost depreciation. It may also be transferred into retained earnings when the underlying asset is sold. Example of entries required from transfers between reserves is provided in illustrative example 12.9.

ILLUSTRATIVE EXAMPLE 12.9 Reserve transfers

During the period ending 31 December 2023, the following events occurred in relation to the company Malaysia Ltd:

Jan. 1	$10,000 transferred from retained earnings to general reserve
July 18	$4,000 transferred from asset revaluation surplus to retained earnings
Oct. 15	Issuing bonus shares of $50,000, half against general reserve and half against retained earnings

Required
Prepare the journal entries to record these transactions.

Solution

2023				
Jan. 1	Retained Earnings	Dr	10,000	
	General Reserve	Cr		10,000
	(Transfer from retained earnings to general reserves)			
Jul. 18	Asset Revaluation Surplus	Dr	4,000	
	Retained Earnings	Cr		4,000
	(Transfer from asset revaluation surplus)			
Oct. 15	General Reserve	Dr	25,000	
	Retained Earnings	Dr	25,000	
	Share Capital	Cr		50,000
	(Issue of bonus shares)			

12.9 DISCLOSURE

Disclosures in relation to equity are detailed in IAS 1 *Presentation of Financial Statements*. The disclosures relate to specific items of equity as well as the preparation of a statement of changes in equity.

12.9.1 Specific disclosures

IAS 1 provides several disclosure requirements regarding the equity section in the balance sheet. The main ones appear in paragraphs 54, 79, 106, 136, 137 and 138 and require disclosures regarding:

1. The amount of non-controlling interest within the equity section (paragraph 54(q)).
2. The amount of issued capital and reserves attributed to parent company (paragraph 54(r)).
3. An entity shall disclose the following, either in the statement of financial position or the statement of changes in equity, or in the notes: (a) for each class of share capital: (i) the number of shares authorised; (ii) the number of shares issued and fully paid, and issued but not fully paid; (iii) par value per share, or that the shares have no par value; (iv) a reconciliation of the number of shares outstanding at the beginning and at the end of the period; (v) the rights, preferences and restrictions attaching to that class including restrictions on the distribution of dividends and the repayment of capital; (vi) shares in the entity held by the entity or by its subsidiaries or associates; and (vii) shares reserved for issue under options and contracts for the sale of shares, including terms and amounts; and (b) a description of the nature and purpose of each reserve within equity. (paragraph 79).
4. Statement of changes in equity, *as discussed in section 12.9.2* below (paragraph 106).
5. Puttable instruments classified as equity, including amounts and explanations as to the entity's objectives in respect to these instruments and expected cash flows (paragraph 136A).
6. The amounts of dividends proposed or declared, inclusive of preference dividend, which have not been recognised as a liability (paragraph 137).

12.9.2 Statement of changes in equity

Paragraph 106 of IAS 1 requires the preparation of a statement of changes in equity. This paragraph requires the statement to show the following:

(a) total comprehensive income for the period, showing separately the total amounts attributable to owners of the parent and to non-controlling interests;
(b) for each component of equity, the effects of retrospective application or retrospective restatement recognised in accordance with IAS 8; and
(c) [deleted]
(d) for each component of equity, a reconciliation between the carrying amount at the beginning and the end of the period, separately disclosing changes resulting from:
  (i) profit or loss;
  (ii) other comprehensive income; and
  (iii) transactions with owners in their capacity as owners, showing separately contributions by and distributions to owners and changes in ownership interests in subsidiaries that do not result in a loss of control.

These requirements can be met in several ways, including using a columnar format. The statement of changes in equity must contain the information in paragraph 106 of IAS 1. The information required by paragraph 107 in relation to dividends may be included in the statement of changes in equity or disclosed in the notes.

Figure 12.5, the statement of changes in equity disclosed in the 2023 annual report of Diageo plc, demonstrates a columnar format for this statement.

12.10 SUMMARY

The corporate form of organisational structure is a popular one in many countries, particularly because of the limited liability protection that it affords to shareholders. These companies' operations are financed by a mixture of equity and debt. In this chapter the focus is on the equity of a corporate entity. The components of equity recognised generally by companies are share capital, other reserves and retained earnings. Share capital in particular is affected by a variety of financial instruments developed in the financial markets, offering investors instruments with an array of risk–return alternatives. Each of these equity alternatives has its own accounting implications. The existence of reserves is driven by traditional accounting as well as the current restrictions in some accounting standards for some wealth increases to be recognised directly in equity rather than in current income. Even though definite distinctions are made between the

	Share capital £ million	Other reserves — Share premium £ million	Other reserves — Capital redemption reserve £ million	Other reserves — Hedging and exchange reserve £ million	Retained earnings/(deficit) — Own shares £ million	Retained earnings/(deficit) — Other retained earnings/(deficit) £ million	Retained earnings/(deficit) — Total £ million	Equity attributable to parent company shareholders £ million	Non-controlling interests £ million	Total equity £ million
At 30 June 2020	742	1,351	3,201	(929)	(1,936)	4,343	2,407	6,772	1,668	8,440
Profit for the year	—	—	—	—	—	2,660	2,660	2,660	139	2,799
Other comprehensive loss	—	—	—	(652)	—	(39)	(39)	(691)	(174)	(865)
Total comprehensive (loss)/income for the year	—	—	—	**(652)**	—	**2,621**	**2,621**	**1,969**	**(35)**	**1,934**
Employee share schemes	—	—	—	—	59	(10)	49	49	—	49
Share-based incentive plans	—	—	—	—	—	49	49	49	—	49
Share-based incentive plans in respect of associates	—	—	—	—	—	3	3	3	—	3
Tax on share-based incentive plans	—	—	—	—	—	9	9	9	—	9
Purchase of non-controlling interests	—	—	—	—	—	(15)	(15)	(15)	(27)	(42)
Associates' transactions with non-controlling interests	—	—	—	—	—	(91)	(91)	(91)	—	(91)
Change in fair value of put option	—	—	—	—	—	(2)	(2)	(2)	—	(2)
Share buyback programme	(1)	—	1	—	—	(200)	(200)	(200)	—	(200)
Dividend declared for the year	—	—	—	—	—	(1,646)	(1,646)	(1,646)	(72)	(1,718)
At 30 June 2021	741	1,351	3,202	(1,581)	(1,877)	5,061	3,184	6,897	1,534	8,431
Adjustment to 2021 closing equity in respect of hyperinflation in Turkey	—	—	—	—	—	251	251	251	—	251
Adjusted opening balance	741	1,351	3,202	(1,581)	(1,877)	5,312	3,435	7,148	1,534	8,682
Profit for the year	—	—	—	—	—	3,249	3,249	3,249	89	3,338
Other comprehensive income	—	—	—	535	—	777	777	1,312	170	1,482
Total comprehensive income for the year	—	—	—	**535**	—	**4,026**	**4,026**	**4,561**	**259**	**4,820**
Employee share schemes	—	—	—	—	39	50	89	89	—	89
Share-based incentive plans	—	—	—	—	—	59	59	59	—	59

Share-based incentive plans in respect of associates	—	—	—	—	—	4	4	4	—	4
Tax on share-based incentive plans	—	—	—	—	—	9	9	9	—	9
Share-based payments and purchase of own shares in respect of subsidiaries	—	—	—	—	—	(11)	(11)	(11)	(6)	(17)
Unclaimed dividend	—	—	—	—	—	3	3	3	1	4
Change in fair value of put option	—	—	—	—	—	(34)	(34)	(34)	—	(34)
Share buyback programme	(18)	—	18	—	—	(2,310)	(2,310)	(2,310)	—	(2,310)
Dividend declared for the year	—	—	—	—	—	(1,720)	(1,720)	(1,720)	(72)	(1,792)
At 30 June 2022	**723**	**1,351**	**3,220**	**(1,046)**	**(1,838)**	**5,388**	**3,550**	**7,798**	**1,716**	**9,514**
Profit for the year	—	—	—	—	—	3,734	3,734	3,734	32	3,766
Other comprehensive loss	—	—	—	(324)	—	(330)	(330)	(654)	(148)	(802)
Total comprehensive (loss)/income for the year	—	—	—	**(324)**	—	**3,404**	**3,404**	**3,080**	**(116)**	**2,964**
Employee share schemes	—	—	—	—	24	24	48	48	—	48
Share-based incentive plans	—	—	—	—	—	49	49	49	—	49
Share-based incentive plans in respect of associates	—	—	—	—	—	6	6	6	—	6
Tax on share-based incentive plans	—	—	—	—	—	6	6	6	—	6
Share-based payments and purchase of own shares in respect of subsidiaries	—	—	—	—	—	3	3	3	2	5
Purchase of non-controlling interests	—	—	—	—	—	(111)	(111)	(111)	(35)	(146)
Associates' transactions with non-controlling interests	—	—	—	—	—	(7)	(7)	(7)	—	(7)
Unclaimed dividend	—	—	—	—	—	1	1	1	—	1
Change in fair value of put option	—	—	—	—	—	(16)	(16)	(16)	—	(16)
Share buyback programme	(11)	—	11	—	—	(1,273)	(1,273)	(1,273)	—	(1,273)
Dividend declared for the year	—	—	—	—	—	(1,762)	(1,762)	(1,762)	(97)	(1,859)
At 30 June 2023	**712**	**1,351**	**3,231**	**(1,370)**	**(1,814)**	**5,712**	**3,898**	**7,822**	**1,470**	**9,292**

The accompanying notes are an integral part of these consolidated financial statements.

FIGURE 12.5 Statement of changes in equity for Diageo plc 2023

Source: Diageo plc (2023, pp. 171).

various components of equity, it needs to be recognised that they are all equity and differences relate to jurisdictional differences in terms of restrictions on dividend distribution, taxation effects and rights of owners. IAS 1 requires detailed disclosures in relation to each of the components of equity.

Discussion questions

1. Discuss the nature of a reserve. How do reserves differ from the other main components of equity?
2. A company announces a final dividend at the end of the financial year. Discuss whether a dividend payable should be recognised.
3. The telecommunications industry in a particular country has been a part of the public sector. As a part of its privatisation agenda, the government decided to establish a limited liability company called Telecom Plus, with the issue of 10 million $3 shares. These shares were to be offered to the citizens of the country. The terms of issue were such that investors had to pay $2 on application and the other $1 per share would be called at a later time. Discuss:
   (a) the nature of the limited liability company, and in particular the financial obligations of acquirers of shares in the company
   (b) the journal entries that would be required if applications were received for 11 million shares.
4. Why would a company wish to buy back its own shares? Discuss.
5. A company has a share capital consisting of 100,000 shares issued at $2 per share, and 50,000 shares issued at $3 per share. All shares have a par value of $1. Discuss the effects on the accounts if:
   (a) the company buys back 20,000 shares at $4 per share
   (b) the company buys back 20,000 shares at $2.50 per share.
6. Refer to the details provided in discussion question 5. Discuss the effects on the accounts if:
   (a) the company then sells 10,000 shares for $5 per share (assume these shares were bought back at $4 per share)
   (b) the company cancels 12,000 shares (assume these shares were bought back at $4 per share).
7. What is a rights issue? Distinguish between a tradeable and a non-tradeable issue.
8. What is a private placement of shares? Outline its advantages and disadvantages.
9. Discuss whether it is necessary to distinguish between the different components of equity rather than just having a single number for shareholders' equity.
10. For what reasons may a company make an appropriation of its retained earnings?

References

Bayer 2023, *Annual Report 2023*, https://www.bayer.com/sites/default/files/2024-03/bayer-annual-report-2023.pdf

Diageo plc 2023, *Annual Report 2023*, https://media.diageo.com/diageo-corporate-media/media/p1bljst1/diageo-annual-report-2023.pdfInternational Accounting Standards Board 2018, https://www.ifrs.org/content/dam/ifrs/publications/pdf-standards/english/2021/issued/part-a/conceptual-framework-for-financial-reporting.pdf,.

International Financial Reporting Interpretations Committee (IFRIC) 2008, September 2008 Newsletter, https://www.ifrs.org/content/dam/ifrs/news/updates/ifrs-ic/2008/september-2008-ifric-update.pdf

Nokia Corporation 2022, *Annual Report 2022*, https://www.nokia.com/system/files/2023-03/nokia-form-20-f-2022.pdf

Santander 2023, *Annual Report 2023*, https://www.santander.com/content/dam/santander-com/en/documentos/informe-financiero-anual/2023/ifa-2023-consolidated-annual-financial-report-en.pdf

Tesco plc 2023, *Annual Report 2023*, https://www.tescoplc.com/media/u1wlq2qf/tesco-plc-annual-report-2023.pdf

Equity transactions can be broadly classified into one of the following three categories: (i) issue of shares, inclusive of employee share options; (ii) share buy-back and (iii) cash dividends. Starting with new share issues, the academic literature has been largely concerned with attempts by managers to influence the prices of the new shares by the means of earnings management and abnormal accruals.[11] However, the academic literature has provided conflicting evidence as to the relation between abnormal accruals (a measure of earnings management) and pricing of new share issues. One strand of the literature argues that earnings in initial public offerings (IPOs) are inflated by managers because they attempt to increase IPO proceeds or IPO valuation. Teoh et al. (1998b) provide evidence suggesting that IPO managers inflate earnings and that the market is misled by this. They reach this conclusion from observing subsequent poor share price performance for earnings-inflating firms. Teoh and Wong (2002) report that analysts systematically fail to detect earnings management in IPOs and seasoned equity offerings (SEOs), and this may be a contributing factor to the post-issue share performance. Teoh et al. (1998a) examine SEOs and find evidence consistent with naive reaction of equity investors to earnings management pre-SEO. Shivakumar (2000), in contrast, shows that stock returns at the time when firms announce SEOs are negatively related to previously announced abnormal accruals. His evidence thus suggests that the SEO announcement prompts investors to revise their assessment of prior earnings, but also suggests that earnings management misleads market participants, at least for some time. A different view developed in the literature suggests that only strong IPOs inflate earnings as a costly signal of quality (Fan, 2007). According to this theory, earnings management is priced. However, this is not because investors are misled, rather because they understand that only good firms can inflate earnings and sustain the potential cost of litigation that earnings inflation may entail. More recently, Filatotchev et al. (2020) fail to find evidence supporting the notion that earnings management affects first-day share prices in foreign IPOs in the US.

When firms issue share options they typically do so in the context of employee compensation, in particular CEO compensation. This practice is commonly known as employee stock options, or ESOP. One typical feature of ESOP is that the exercise price is set equal to the share price on the grant day. The lower the exercise price, the greater the scope for managers to make a gain on their options when they are exercised. Yermack (1997) finds evidence of positive abnormal stock returns in the 2 days following the grant of ESOP. He argues that this is consistent with managers that time the terms of the ESOP to gain from lower share price, and hence exercise price. Aboody and Kasznik (2000) further show that managers delay voluntary disclosure of good news but advance disclosure of bad news before the grant day. Both studies therefore support the notion that managers manipulate the terms of the ESOP.

Returning money to shareholders can be done via either share buy-back or cash dividend. Skinner (2008) estimates that both methods were of similar magnitude in the mid-2000s, whereas share buy-back used to be smaller in magnitude in earlier years. Recently, the fraction of firms that only pay dividend has become very small. Skinner (2008) further reports that share buy-back programmes respond to variations in earnings more than cash dividends do. That is, dividends are quite 'sticky' and are largely unrelated to profitability.

Accounting researchers have been particularly interested in understanding what dividend and share buy-back programmes imply about past and future earnings and whether the information content in share buy-back or dividend announcements is incremental to the information content of earnings. With respect to share buy-back programmes, the literature has distinguished between two forms. The first is called a share repurchase tender offer. Here the firm asks shareholders to submit their offer as to how many shares they are willing to sell back to the firm and at what price. The firm then decides which offers to accept. The second method is an open-market buy-back programme. Under this method the company announces its plan to buy shares on the open market and, occasionally, how much cash is set aside for this purpose. Bartov (1991) claims that tender offers command a greater amount of cash that is distributed back to shareholders and hence the information content of these announcements may differ. For open-market offers he finds that earnings announced by repurchasing firms *before* tender offers outperform analyst expectations more than earnings announced by non-purchasing firms. Hertzel and Jain (1991) examine tender offers and find that analysts revise their forecasts of future (short-term) earnings upward for firms announcing repurchases. Taken together these studies suggest that share buy-back programmes are triggered by strong performance in the past but also indicate managers' expectations about future performance. These findings notwithstanding, it is not clear why managers engage in share buy-back programmes in practice. Survey evidence indicates that managers buy-back shares when they feel the share price is too low, or as a means to increase earnings per share, not necessarily to convey information about future earnings (Brav et al. 2005). Oswald and Young (2008) show that cash-rich firms are more likely to spend cash on buy-backs, casting some doubt on the signalling theory.

The Academic Perspective of chapter 1 discusses the information content, or value relevance, of earnings. A similar issue arises with dividends — are they informative? Furthermore, are they informative *incrementally* to earnings? One concern about the informativeness of dividends is that, unlike share repurchases, they are very 'sticky' and do not change much, suggesting they do not normally convey much news. Additionally, managers are reluctant to reduce dividends because they expect negative market reaction (Brav et al. 2005). To investigate the information content of dividends Aharony

---

[1]Earnings management refers to selection by managers of accounting policies, estimates and other assessments with the intention of meeting certain objectives.

and Swary (1980) investigate quarterly dividend and earnings announcements made on different dates (i.e. not concurrently). Most dividend announcements follow earnings announcements, but consistent with dividend 'stickiness', only 13% of sample firms change their dividends. The authors find that firms announcing dividend increases (decreases) experience positive (negative) abnormal stock returns (returns that are measured relative to the overall market return) on the announcement date. They also find that this was the case regardless of whether the dividend announcement preceded or followed the earnings announcement. Therefore, they conclude that changes in dividends do convey information incrementally to earnings. Healy and Palepu (1988) take this line of inquiry further by looking at specific types of changes: dividend initiations and omissions. They find that companies that start paying dividends experienced earnings growth prior and after the dividend initiation. The opposite holds for firms that omit dividend payments. They also find that initiations and omissions provide incremental predictive power for future earnings over and above changes in prior earnings. However, some of these results were contested in subsequent studies (see Lie 2005 for a summary of the follow-up literature as well as some more recent evidence).

Another form of dividend is stock dividend, or share bonus. However, unlike normal dividends (or share buyback), share bonus does not use cash and so the value of the company should remain unaffected, ignoring relatively minor administrative expenses. The same argument holds for stock splits. Nevertheless, this practice is not unusual and therefore begs the question: why do companies engage in it? Intrigued by evidence that such share issues are rewarded by capital markets, Lakonishok and Lev (1987) look at this question from the perspective of earnings growth. They find that firms that split their shares experienced a robust earnings growth in the 5-year period before the split. But this does not hold for firms using share dividends. Further examining stock returns they conclude that the aim of stock split is to bring high stock prices to a normal level. Asquith et al. (1989) provide additional evidence suggesting that share split announcements are perceived by the market to be associated with permanent earnings growth rather than a transitory one. This suggests that managers can communicate their positive outlook of firm performance via splits.

References

Aboody, D., and Kasznik, R., 2000. CEO stock option awards and the timing of corporate voluntary disclosures. Journal of Accounting and Economics 29, 73–100.

Aharony, J., and Swary, I., 1980. Quarterly dividend and earnings announcements and stockholders' returns: an empirical analysis. Journal of Finance, 35, 1–12.

Asquith, P., Healy, P., and Palepu, K., 1989. Earnings and stock splits. The Accounting Review, 64(3), 387–403.

Bartov, E., 1991. Open-market stock repurchases as signals for earnings and risk changes. Journal of Accounting and Economics, 14, 275–294.

Brav, A., Graham, J. R., Harvey, C. R., and Michaely, R., 2005. Payout policy in the 21st century. Journal of Financial Economics, 77, 483–527.

Fan, Q., 2007. Earnings management and ownership retention for initial public offering firms: theory and evidence. The Accounting Review, 82, 27–64.

Filatotchev, I., Jona, J., and Livne, G., 2020. Earnings management in domestic and foreign IPOs in the United States: do home country institutions matter?European Accounting Review, 29(2), 307–335.

Healy, P.M., and Palepu, K.G., 1988. Earnings information conveyed by dividend initiations and omissions. Journal of Financial Economics, 21, 149–175.

Hertzel, M., and Jain, P., 1991. Earnings and risk changes around stock repurchase tender offers. Journal of Accounting and Economics, 11, 253–274.

Lakonishok, J., and Lev, B., 1987. Stock splits and stock dividends: why, who, and when. The Journal of Finance, 42(4), 913–932.

Lie, E., 2005. Operating performance following dividend decreases and omissions. Journal of Corporate Finance, 12, 27–53.

Oswald, D., and Young, S., 2008. Share reacquisitions, surplus cash, and agency problems. Journal of Banking & Finance, 32(5), 795–806.

Shivakumar, L., 2000. Do firms mislead investors by overstating earnings before seasoned equity offerings? Journal of Accounting and Economics, 29(3), 339–371.

Skinner, D. J., 2008. The evolving relation between earnings, dividends, and stock repurchases. Journal of Financial Economics, 87, 582–609.

Teoh, S. H., and Wong, T. J., 2002. Why new issues and high-accrual firms underperform: the role of analysts' credulity. Review of Financial Studies, 15(3), 863–900.

Teoh, S. H., Welch I., and Wong, T. J., 1998a. Earnings management and the underperformance of seasoned equity offerings. Journal of Financial Economics, 50, 63–99.

Teoh, S. H., Welch I., and Wong, T. J., 1998b. Earnings management and the long-run market performance of initial public offerings. Journal of Finance, 53(6), 1935–1974.

Yermack, D., 1997. Good timing: CEO stock option awards and company news announcements. The Journal of Finance, 52, 449–476.

13

Financial instruments

ACCOUNTING STANDARDS IN FOCUS

IAS 32 Financial Instruments: Presentation

IFRS 7 Financial Instruments: Disclosures

IFRS 9 Financial Instruments

LEARNING OBJECTIVES

After studying this chapter, you should be able to:

1. describe the background to the development of accounting standards on financial instruments

2. define a financial instrument

3. outline and apply the definitions of financial assets and financial liabilities

4. distinguish between equity instruments and financial liabilities

5. explain the concept of a compound financial instrument

6. determine the classification of revenues and expenses arising from financial instruments

7. describe the scope of IFRS 9

8. explain the concept of an embedded derivative

9. distinguish between the categories of financial instruments specified in IFRS 9

10. apply the recognition criteria for financial instruments

11. understand and apply the measurement criteria for each category of financial instrument

12. determine when financial assets and financial liabilities may be offset

13. outline the rules of hedge accounting set out in IFRS 9 and be able to apply the rules to simple common cash flow and fair value hedges.

14. describe the main disclosure requirements of IFRS 7.

13.1 INTRODUCTION

Developing standards for financial instrument accounting has probably been the most controversial area in the history of the International Accounting Standards Board (IASB®). This already started right when the IASB was formed around the turn of the century and had to develop what later became IAS 39 *Financial Instruments — Recognition and Measurement* as part of the 'stable platform' of standards adopted in 2005. Many stakeholders including banks, other preparer groups, regulators and politicians lobbied during the process. The controversial aspects of the standards at that time were largely related to hedge accounting. The controversy continued during the financial crisis of 2008 when the IASB was put under enormous pressure to amend IAS 39 overnight in October 2008 and allow retrospective reclassification of financial assets to avoid fair value losses hitting banks' income statements.

Figure 13.1 provides an extract from the 2009 Report of the Financial Crisis Advisory Group[1], which illustrates the controversy and complexity surrounding the accounting for financial instruments at the time of the 2008 financial crisis.

In the wake of the credit crisis, in 2009, the IASB promised to replace IAS 39 with a new standard that would, amongst others, more closely align the measurement method of financial instruments with the business model of the holder and the characteristics of the financial instrument, and would improve the requirements for impairment of financial assets. It took the IASB more than 5 years to complete the development of that new standard IFRS 9 *Financial Instruments*. It became fully effective for financial statements starting on or after 1 January 2018. IFRS 9 introduced a new classification and measurement approach for financial assets, a forward-looking expected credit loss model, an improved hedge accounting model and a better approach to deal with the so-called 'own credit' issue *(see section 13.9.2)*. These changes were made to address the concerns that the Group of Twenty (G-20, an international forum for the governments and central bank governors from 20 major economies), the Financial Crisis Advisory Group and others had raised.

FIGURE 13.1 Effective financial reporting

Report of the Financial Crisis Advisory Group

While the post-mortems are still being written, it seems clear that accounting standards were not a root cause of the financial crisis. At the same time, it is clear that the crisis has exposed weaknesses in accounting standards and their application. These weaknesses reduced the credibility of financial reporting, which in part contributed to the general loss of confidence in the financial system. The weaknesses primarily involved (1) the difficulty of applying fair value ('mark-to-market') accounting in illiquid markets; (2) the delayed recognition of losses associated with loans, structured credit products, and other financial instruments by banks, insurance companies and other financial institutions; (3) issues surrounding the broad range of off-balance-sheet financing structures, especially in the US; and (4) the extraordinary complexity of accounting standards for financial instruments, including multiple approaches to recognizing asset impairment. Some of these weaknesses also highlighted areas in which International Financial Reporting Standards ('IFRS') and US generally accepted accounting principles ('US GAAP') diverged.

In the early part of the crisis, the principal criticism of financial reporting focused on fair value accounting. This criticism contended that fair value accounting contributed to the pro-cyclicality of the financial system. Prior to the crisis, it is argued, fair value accounting led to significant overstatement of profits; however, during the crisis, it was supposed to have led to a severe overstatement of losses and the consequent 'destruction of capital'. Thus, the argument went, a vicious cycle ensued: falling asset prices led to accounting write-downs; the write-downs led to forced asset sales by institutions needing to meet capital adequacy requirements; and the forced sales exacerbated the fall in asset prices. In the US, moreover, critics singled out the other-than-temporary impairment standards for available-for-sale and held-to-maturity securities as being particularly 'destructive' because institutions were forced to take charges against earnings as a consequence of what they believed to be temporary 'market irrationality'.

Proponents of fair value accounting do not deny that indeed mark-to-market accounting shows the fluctuations of the market, but they maintain that these cycles are a fact of life and that the use of fair value accounting does not exacerbate these cycles. Moreover, they argue that fair value accounting standards provided 'early warning' signals by revealing the market's discomfort with inflated asset

---

[1] Report of the Financial Crisis Advisory Group, 28 July 2009.

FIGURE 13.1 *(continued)*

values. In their view, this contributed to a more timely recognition of problems and mitigation of the crisis.

Whatever the final outcome of the debate over fair value accounting, it is unlikely that, on balance, accounting standards led to an understatement of the value of financial assets. While the crisis may have led to some understatement of the value of mark-to-market assets, it is important to recognize that, in most countries, a majority of bank assets are still valued at historic cost using the amortized cost basis. Those assets are not marked to market and are not adjusted for market liquidity. By now it seems clear that the overall value of these assets has not been understated — but overstated. The incurred loss model for loan loss provisioning and difficulties in applying the model — in particular, identifying appropriate trigger points for loss recognition — in many instances has delayed the recognition of losses on loan portfolios. (The results of the US stress tests seem to bear this out.) Moreover, the off-balance-sheet standards, and the way they were applied, may have obscured losses associated with securitizations and other complex structured products. Thus, the overall effect of the current mixed attribute model by which assets of financial institutions have been measured, coupled with the obscurity of off-balance sheet exposures, has probably been to understate the losses that were embedded in the system.

Even if the overall effect of accounting standards may not have been pro-cyclical, we consider it imperative that the weaknesses in the current standards be addressed as a matter of urgency. Improvements in accounting standards cannot 'cure' the financial crisis by resolving underlying economic and governance issues (for example, the massive overleveraging of the global economy, excessive risk taking, and the undercapitalization of the banking sector). However, as demonstrated by the positive market reaction to disclosure of the results of the US stress tests, improvements in standards that enhance transparency and reduce complexity can help restore the confidence of financial market participants and thereby serve as a catalyst for increased financial stability and sound economic growth. Conversely, any changes in financial reporting that reduce transparency and allow the impact of the crisis lo be obscured would likely have the opposite effect, by further reducing the confidence of market participants and thereby prolonging the crisis or by laying the foundation for future problems.

Source: Financial Crisis Advisory Group (2009).

Although the IASB worked closely with the US FASB in the initial stages of the development of IFRS 9, the efforts to develop a converged standard were ultimately unsuccessful when the IASB and the FASB decided to go their separate ways. As a result IFRS 9 differs in important respects from the accounting prescribed by the FASB.

IAS 32 sets out the definitions of financial instruments, financial assets and financial liabilities, the distinction between financial liabilities and equity instruments, and originally prescribed detailed disclosures. The standard was developed before IAS 39 because consensus on the recognition, derecognition, measurement and hedging rules for financial instruments was difficult to achieve. Therefore, the standard setters first established classification and disclosure rules, anticipating that increased disclosure by reporting entities would provide more information, not only for users, but also for the standard setters. Increased disclosure helps to provide standard setters with information that assists in developing further standards.

In 2006, IAS 32 was renamed *Financial Instruments: Presentation* and a new standard, IFRS 7 *Financial Instruments: Disclosures*, was introduced, applicable to annual periods beginning on or after 1 January 2007. IFRS 7 contains many of the disclosure requirements that were originally in IAS 32 and IAS 30 *Disclosures in the Financial Statements of Banks and Similar Financial Institutions*. It also introduced a number of new disclosure requirements.

Because IFRS 9, IAS 32 and IFRS 7 are complex standards, this chapter provides an overall explanation of the requirements. It emphasises those areas most commonly affecting the majority of reporting entities, and places less emphasis on specialised areas.

Each standard is addressed separately in this chapter.

IAS 32, IFRS 7 and IFRS 9 each contain Application Guidance, which is abbreviated in this chapter as AG. IFRS 7 and IFRS 9 also contain Implementation Guidance, commonly abbreviated to IG.

The main definitions and accounting requirements of IAS 32 are covered *in sections 13.2–13.6*, while its requirements on offsetting are dealt with *in section 13.12*. The IFRS 9 requirements on accounting for financial assets, financial liabilities and derivatives and its recognition, measurement and hedge accounting requirements are covered *in sections 13.7–13.13*. Finally, the disclosure requirements of IFRS 7 are covered *in section 13.14*.

13.2 WHAT IS A FINANCIAL INSTRUMENT?

13.2.1 Definition of a financial instrument

IAS 32, paragraph 11, defines a financial instrument as:

> any contract that gives rise to a financial asset of one entity and a financial liability or equity instrument of another entity.

Financial assets and financial liabilities are terms defined in IAS 32 *(see sections 13.3.1 and 13.3.2)*. Financial assets are defined from the perspective of the *holder* of the instrument, whereas financial liabilities and equity instruments are defined from the perspective of the *issuer* of the instrument.

An equity instrument is defined in paragraph 11 as:

> any contract that evidences a residual interest in the assets of an entity after deducting all of its liabilities.

The most common type of equity instrument is an ordinary share of a company. The holder of the shares is not entitled to any fixed return on or of its investment; instead, the holder receives the residual after all liabilities have been settled. This applies both to periodic returns (where dividends are paid after interest on liabilities has been paid) and capital returns (when a company is wound up, all liabilities are settled before shareholders are entitled to any return of their investment).

13.2.2 Two sides to the story

Note that the definition of a financial instrument is two-sided — the contract must always give rise to a financial asset of one party, with a corresponding financial liability or equity instrument of another party. For example, a contract that gives the seller of a product the right to receive cash from the purchaser creates a receivable for the seller (a financial asset) and a payable for the purchaser (a financial liability).

13.2.3 Common types of financial instruments

Financial instruments include primary instruments such as cash, receivables, investments and payables, as well as derivative financial instruments such as financial options and forward exchange contracts. Derivative financial instruments, or derivatives, are instruments that *derive* their value from another underlying item such as a share price or an interest rate. *(The definition of a derivative is discussed in section 7.8.)*

13.2.4 Contracts to buy or sell non-financial instruments

Financial instruments do *not* include non-financial assets such as property, plant and equipment, or non-financial liabilities such as provisions for restoration. Contracts to buy or sell non-financial items are also usually not financial instruments. Many commodity contracts fall into this category (contracts to buy or sell oil, cotton, wheat and so on). These commodity contracts are thus outside the scope of IAS 32. Certain commodity contracts are, however, included within the scope of IAS 32. These include contracts to buy or sell non-financial items that can be settled net (in cash) or by exchanging financial instruments, or in which the non-financial item is readily convertible into cash. Contracts to buy or sell gold might fall into the latter category and so might be caught by IAS 32 and IFRS 9 and trigger disclosure following the requirements of IFRS 7. An exception is made for 'own-use contracts *(refer section 13.7.1)*.

13.2.5 Other items that are *not* financial instruments

Note also that the definition of a financial instrument requires there to be a contractual right or obligation. Therefore, liabilities or assets that are not contractual — such as income taxes that are created as a result of statutory requirements imposed by governments, or constructive obligations as defined in IAS 37 *Provisions, Contingent Liabilities and Contingent Assets (see chapter 10)* — are not financial instruments.

In addition, certain financial assets and liabilities are outside the scope of IAS 32. These include employee benefits accounted for under IAS 19, and investments in subsidiaries, associates and joint ventures that are accounted for under IFRS 10 *Consolidated Financial Statements*, IAS 27 *Separate Financial Statements*, IAS 28 *Investments in Associates and Joint Ventures* and IFRS 11 *Joint Arrangements*.

13.3 FINANCIAL ASSETS AND FINANCIAL LIABILITIES

13.3.1 Financial assets

A financial asset is defined in paragraph 11 of IAS 32 as follows:

any asset that is:

(a) cash;
(b) an equity instrument of another entity;
(c) a contractual right:
    (i) to receive cash or another financial asset from another entity; or
    (ii) to exchange financial assets or financial liabilities with another entity under conditions that are potentially favourable to the entity; or
(c) a contract that will or may be settled in the entity's own equity instruments and meets certain additional conditions.

Examples of common financial assets in each of the categories of the definition include:

(a) cash — either cash on hand or the right of the depositor to obtain cash from the financial institution with which it has deposited the cash
(b) an equity instrument of another entity — ordinary shares held in another entity
(c) a contractual right
    (i) to receive cash or another financial asset — trade accounts receivable, notes receivable, loans receivable
    (ii) to exchange under potentially favourable conditions — an option held by the holder to purchase shares in a specified company at less than the market price.

Part (d) of the definition was added in response to issues arising from the classification of certain complex financial instruments as liabilities or equity. The IASB considered that to treat any transaction settled in the entity's own shares as an equity instrument would not deal adequately with transactions in which an entity is using its own shares as 'currency' (e.g. where it has an obligation to pay a fixed or determinable amount that is settled in a variable number of its own shares). In such transactions the counterparty bears no share price risk, and is therefore not in the same position as a 'true' equity provider. (This is further discussed *in section 13.4*.)

13.3.2 Financial liabilities

A financial liability is defined in paragraph 11 of IAS 32 as follows:

any liability that is:

(a) a contractual obligation:
    (i) to deliver cash or another financial asset to another entity; or
    (ii) to exchange financial assets or financial liabilities with another entity under conditions that are potentially unfavourable to the entity; or
(b) a contract that will or may be settled in the entity's own equity instruments and meets certain additional conditions.

Examples of common financial liabilities in each of the categories of the definition include:

(a) a contractual obligation
    (i) to deliver cash or another financial asset — trade accounts payable, notes payable, loans payable
    (ii) to exchange under potentially unfavourable conditions — an option written (i.e. issued) by the issuer to sell shares in a specified company at less than the market price.

Part (b) of the definition was added in response to issues arising from the classification of certain complex financial instruments as liabilities or equity (*See section 13.4.*)

Table 13.1 contains a summary of common financial instruments

Table 13.1 Summary of common financial instruments

Financial assets	Financial liabilities	Equity instruments
Cash	Bank overdraft	Ordinary shares
Accounts receivable	Accounts payable	Certain preference shares
Notes receivable	Notes payable	
Loans receivable	Loans payable	
Derivatives with potentially favourable exchange conditions	Derivatives with potentially unfavourable exchange conditions	
	Certain preference shares	

13.4 DISTINGUISHING FINANCIAL LIABILITIES FROM EQUITY INSTRUMENTS

IAS 32 is very prescriptive in the way it distinguishes between financial liabilities and equity instruments. This area, commonly known as the debt versus equity distinction, is of great concern to many reporting entities because instruments classified as liabilities rather than equity affect:

- a company's gearing and solvency ratios
- debt covenants with financial institutions (usually a requirement that specified financial ratios of the borrower are met; if they do not meet the prescribed thresholds, the financial institution has a right to require immediate repayment of the loan)
- whether periodic payments on these instruments are treated as interest (affecting profit or loss) or dividends (not affecting profit or loss)
- regulatory requirements for capital adequacy (banks and other financial institutions are required by their regulators to maintain a certain level of capital, which is calculated by reference to assets and equity).

Accordingly, reporting entities are often motivated, when raising funds, to issue instruments that are classified as equity for accounting purposes. In the years since IAS 32 was first issued, many complex instruments were devised by market participants specifically to achieve equity classification under IAS 32. Some of these instruments were liabilities in substance but were able to be classified technically as equity, notwithstanding a 'substance over form' test in IAS 32. As a result, the IASB amended IAS 32 to create specific rules designed to address these complex instruments. Unfortunately, the rules are now quite complicated, so this section will address the key principles of liability versus equity classification only.

13.4.1 The rules

IAS 32, paragraph 15, states:

> The issuer of a financial instrument shall classify the instrument, or its component parts, on initial recognition as a financial liability, a financial asset or an equity instrument in accordance with the substance of the contractual arrangement and the definitions of a financial liability, a financial asset and an equity instrument.

To avoid any doubt, paragraph 16 goes on to repeat and clarify the definition of a financial liability. It states that an instrument shall be classified as an equity instrument if, and only if, *both* conditions (a) and (b) below are met:

(a) The instrument includes no contractual obligation:
   (i) to deliver cash or another financial asset to another entity; or
   (ii) to exchange financial assets or financial liabilities with another entity under conditions that are potentially unfavourable to the issuer.
(b) If the instrument will or may be settled in the issuer's own equity instruments, it is:
   (i) a non-derivative that includes no contractual obligation for the issuer to deliver a variable number of its own equity instruments; or
   (ii) a derivative that will be settled only by the issuer exchanging a fixed amount of cash or another financial asset for a fixed number of its own equity instruments.

Part (a) is clearly referring to the definition of a financial liability. The rules in part (b) are trying to establish who bears 'equity risk' in complex transactions where an entity issues a financial instrument that will or may be settled in its own shares.

The concept of equity risk is useful for both part (b) of the test and generally in determining whether an instrument is equity or a liability. Note, however, that part (a) of the test turns only on whether or not the issuer has a contractual obligation.

Part (a) of the equity/liability test: contractual obligation

The examples in figure 13.2 apply part (a) of the equity/liability test, together with the equity risk concept.

FIGURE 13.2 Applying part (a) of the equity/liability test

> **Example 1: Ordinary shares**
>
> Company A wants to raise funds of $1 million. It does so by issuing ordinary shares to the public. The holders of those shares are exposed to equity risk (they are not entitled to any fixed or determinable return on or of their investment, and receive the residual left over after all liabilities have been settled) in respect of both periodic payments and capital returns. If there is no profit after interest on liabilities and other contractual obligations have been paid, then there are no dividends. If, on winding up, there are no assets after all liabilities have been settled, there is nothing returned to the shareholders.

FIGURE 13.2 *(continued)*

This is the fundamental nature of equity risk. The ordinary shares issued by Company A are equity instruments of Company A. Under part (a) of the test, Company A has no contractual obligation to its ordinary shareholders.

Company A would record the following journal entry on initial recognition:

Cash (financial asset)	Dr	1,000,000	
Ordinary Share Capital (equity)	Cr		1,000,000

Example 2: Non-cumulative, non-redeemable preference shares

Company A decides to issue preference shares instead of ordinary shares. It issues 1 million preference shares for $1 each. Each preference shareholder is entitled to a non-cumulative dividend of 5% annually. (A non-cumulative dividend means that, if in any year a dividend is not paid, the shareholder forfeits it.) In any year, the decision to pay a dividend to preference shareholders is at the discretion of management of company A. The preference shareholders rank ahead of ordinary shareholders on the winding up of the company. The preference shares are non-redeemable (the holders of the shares cannot get their money back).

Under part (a) of the test, Company A has no contractual obligation to the preference shareholders, either to pay dividends or to return the cash. Therefore, the preference shares are equity instruments of Company A. In addition, applying the concept of equity risk reveals that the preference shareholders are exposed to equity risk, although it is lower than for the ordinary shareholders.

Company A would record the following journal entry on initial recognition:

Cash (financial asset)	Dr	1,000,000	
Preference Share Capital (equity)	Cr		1,000,000

Example 3: Cumulative preference shares redeemable by the holder

Company A issues 1 million preference shares for $1 each, and each preference shareholder is entitled to a cumulative dividend of 5% annually. The preference share-holders rank ahead of ordinary shareholders on the winding-up of the company. The preference shares are redeemable for cash at the option of the holder.

Under part (a) of the test, Company A now has a contractual obligation to the preference shareholders — both in respect of dividends and to return the cash. Company A must pay the dividends and, if in any period it cannot pay, it must make up the payment with the next dividend. Furthermore, Company A must repay the money whenever the holder demands repayment. Therefore, the preference shares are financial liabilities of Company A. In addition, applying the concept of equity risk reveals that the preference shareholders are not exposed to equity risk — they are guaranteed a periodic return of 5% and they can require that their cash be returned. They bear a similar risk as would a lender to Company A, although a lender may rank ahead of cumulative preference shareholders in the winding-up of the company. A lender's risk is generally credit risk (the risk that Company A will fail to discharge its obligations) and liquidity risk (the risk that Company A will fail to raise funds to enable it to redeem the liability on demand).

Company A would record the following journal entry on initial recognition:

Cash (financial asset)	Dr	1,000,000	
Preference Share Liability (financial liability)	Cr		1,000,000

Paragraph 17 of IAS 32 reiterates that a critical feature in differentiating a financial liability from an equity instrument is the existence of a contractual obligation of the issuer. Paragraph 18 then goes on to state that the substance of a financial instrument, rather than its legal form, governs its classification on the entity's statement of financial position. Some financial instruments, such as the preference shares in example 3 of figure 13.2, may take the legal form of equity but are liabilities in substance. Sometimes the combined features result in the financial instrument being split into its component parts (*see section 13.5*).

Another example of a financial instrument whose legal form may be equity but whose accounting classification is a financial liability is a puttable instrument. A puttable instrument gives the holder the right to put the instrument back to the issuer for cash or another financial asset. This is so even when the amount of cash/other financial asset is determined based on an index or another amount that may increase or decrease. For example, certain mutual funds, unit trusts and partnerships provide their unit holders or members with a right to redeem their interests in the issuer at any time for cash equal to their proportionate share of the net asset value of the issuer. The puttable instruments may be the only instruments issued by the entity, in which case this may lead to the entity having no equity at all. The IASB allows those entities, under certain conditions, to classify these instruments as equity, as an exception to the definition of a liability (IAS 32 par. 16A–16F).

Paragraphs 19 and 20 of IAS 32 explain that an entity has a contractual obligation to deliver cash/other financial assets notwithstanding:

- any restrictions on the entity's ability to meet its obligation (such as access to foreign currency)
- that the obligation may be conditional on the counterparty exercising its redemption right (as in example 3 of figure 13.2 — redemption is at the option of the holder and therefore could be considered to be conditional on the holder exercising its right to redeem. However, this does not negate the fact that the issuer has a contractual obligation to redeem the shares, because it cannot avoid its obligation should it be required to redeem by the holder)
- that the financial instrument does not explicitly establish a contractual obligation to deliver cash/ other financial assets. A contractual obligation may be implied in the terms and conditions of the instrument. However, the guidance in paragraph 20 should be read in a narrow way given the guidance on preference shares. Paragraph AG26 states that non-redeemable preference shares are equity instruments, notwithstanding a term that prevents ordinary share dividends from being paid if the preference share dividend is not paid, or from being paid on the issuer's expectation of profit or loss for a period. A fairly common term in certain non-redeemable preference shares is that the dividend is 'discretionary' but, if the preference dividend is not paid, then ordinary dividends cannot be paid. If these terms exist in the preference shares of highly profitable companies, one could argue under paragraph 20 that the implicit terms and conditions of the preference shares require the dividend to be paid. However, paragraph AG26 states that such conditions do not create a financial liability of the issuer.

Part (b) of the equity/liability test: settlement in the entity's own equity instruments

Paragraph 21 of IAS 32 states that a contract is not an equity instrument solely because it may result in the receipt or delivery of the entity's own equity instruments. As noted earlier in this section, such an instrument can be classified as an equity instrument under paragraph 16(b) of IAS 32 only if it is:

(i) a non-derivative that includes no contractual obligation for the issuer to deliver a variable number of its own equity instruments; or

(ii) a derivative that will be settled only by the issuer exchanging a fixed amount of cash or another financial asset for a fixed number of its own equity instruments.

Part (i) will be examined first. Assume listed Company A has an obligation to deliver to Party B as many of Company A's own ordinary shares as will equal $100,000. The number of shares that Company A will have to issue will vary depending on the market price of its own shares. If Company A's shares are each worth $1 at the date of settlement of the contract, it will have to deliver 100,000 shares. If Company A's shares are each worth $0.50 at the date of settlement of the contract, it will have to deliver 200,000 shares. Company A has a contractual obligation at all times to deliver $100,000 to Party B; that is, the value is fixed, and so the number of shares to be delivered will vary. Therefore, Company A's financial instrument fails the test in part (i) and the instrument is a financial liability. Applying the concept of equity risk, the holder of the financial instrument (Party B) is not exposed to equity risk because it will always receive $100,000 regardless of the market price of Company A's shares. A true equity risk-taker will be exposed to share price fluctuations — this reflects the residual nature of an equity risk-taker's investment.

Now examine part (ii). Assume listed Company A issues a share option to Party B that entitles Party B to buy 100,000 shares in Company A at $1 each in 3 months' time. This financial instrument meets the conditions for equity classification under part (ii) because it is a derivative that will be settled by issuing a fixed number of shares for a fixed amount. Assume that, at the date of the grant of the option, Company A's share price is $1. If in 3 months' time Company A's share price exceeds $1, Party B will exercise its option and Company A must issue its shares to Party B for $100,000. If, however, in 3 months' time Company A's share price falls below $1, Party B will not exercise its option and Company A will not issue any shares. Applying the concept of equity risk reveals that the holder of the financial instrument (Party B) is exposed to equity risk because it is not guaranteed to receive $100,000 in value. Whether or not it receives $100,000 is entirely dependent on the market price of Company A's shares. As a true equity risk-taker, it is exposed to share price fluctuations; this reflects the residual nature of an equity risk-taker's investment. Party B will have paid a premium to Company A for the option. Paragraph 22 of IAS 32 states that this premium is added directly to Company A's equity, consistent with the classification of the instrument as an equity instrument.

13.4.2 Contingent settlement provisions and settlement options

Sometimes, when a financial instrument requires an entity to deliver cash/other financial assets, the terms of settlement are dependent on the occurrence or non-occurrence of uncertain future events that are beyond the control of both the issuer and the holder. Examples of such events include changes in a share market index, the consumer price index or the issuer's future revenues. The issuer of such an instrument does not have the unconditional right to avoid delivering the cash/other financial assets, so paragraph 25 of IAS 32 requires such instruments to be classified as financial liabilities. For example, assume that Company A issues preference shares to Party B, the terms of which entitle Party B to redeem the preference shares for cash if Company A's revenues fall below a specified level. Because neither Company A nor Party B can control the level of Company A's revenues, the settlement provision is considered to be contingent. However, because Company A cannot avoid repaying Party B should Company A's revenues fall below the specified level, Company A does not have an unconditional right to avoid repayment. Thus the preference shares are a financial liability of Company A.

Some financial instruments contain a choice of settlement. For example, preference shares may be redeemed for cash or for the issuer's ordinary shares. Sometimes the choice is the issuer's; sometimes it is the holder's. Paragraph 26 of IAS 32 requires that, when a *derivative* financial instrument gives one party a choice over how it is settled, it is a financial asset or a financial liability unless all of the settlement alternatives would result in it being an equity instrument. An example is a share option that the issuer can decide to settle net in cash or by exchanging its own shares for cash. Because not all of the settlement options would result in an equity instrument being issued, the option must be classified as a financial asset or liability. Note that the likelihood of each outcome is not relevant; the fact that cash settlement may be required is sufficient to create a financial asset or liability.

Paragraph 26 does not address *non-derivative* financial instruments. Therefore, where a non-derivative financial instrument such as a preference share may be redeemed for cash or for the issuer's own ordinary shares, paragraph 26 does not apply. Instead, paragraph 16 would be applied to determine whether or not there is (a) a contractual obligation to deliver cash/other financial assets, or (b) a contractual obligation to deliver a variable number of the issuer's ordinary shares. Note that both (a) and (b) must be answered with a 'no' for equity classification to apply. So, for example, if the *issuer* of the preference share has the option to redeem for cash or for a variable number of its ordinary shares, the first question to ask is: Does the issuer have a contractual obligation to deliver cash? If redemption is at the issuer's option, the issuer has *no* contractual obligation to redeem *at all* and therefore arguably the second question about the number of ordinary shares is irrelevant. Indeed, paragraph 16(b) asks whether or not the issuer has a contractual obligation to deliver a variable number of its own shares and, since redemption is at the issuer's option, it has no such contractual obligation, even though the number of shares that potentially will be issued is variable. Therefore, all other things being equal, the preference shares will be classified as equity. On the other hand, if redemption is at the *holder's* option, the instrument would be classified as a liability, because the issuer has a contractual obligation to deliver cash/other financial assets or ordinary shares because the holder has the right to call for redemption. This is so even if the number of ordinary shares is fixed, because the holder's right to redeem for cash means that paragraph 16(a) is met.

13.5 COMPOUND FINANCIAL INSTRUMENTS

Paragraph 28 of IAS 32 requires an issuer of a non-derivative financial instrument to determine whether it contains both a liability and an equity component. Such components must be classified separately as financial liabilities, financial assets or equity instruments.

Paragraph 29 goes on to explain that this means that an entity recognises separately the components of a financial instrument that (a) creates a financial liability of the entity, and (b) grants an option to the holder of the instrument to convert it into an equity instrument of the entity. A common example of such a financial instrument is a convertible bond or note that entitles the holder to convert the note into a fixed number of ordinary shares of the issuer. From the perspective of the *issuer*, such an instrument comprises two components: (a) a financial liability, being a contractual obligation to deliver cash/other financial assets in the form of interest payments and redemption of the note; and (b) an equity instrument, being an option issued to the holder entitling it to the right, for a specified period of time, to convert the note into a fixed number of ordinary shares of the issuer. Note that the number of shares to be issued must be fixed, otherwise the option would not meet the definition of an equity instrument under paragraph 16(b) *as discussed in section 13.4.1.*

Classification of the liability and equity components is made on initial recognition of the financial instrument and is not revised as a result of a change in the likelihood that the conversion option may be exercised. This is because, until such time as the conversion option is either exercised or lapses, the issuer has a contractual obligation to make future payments.

How does the issuer measure the separate liability and equity components? Paragraphs 31 and 32 of IAS 32 prescribe that the financial liability must be calculated first, with the equity component by definition being the residual. The example in figure 13.3 illustrates how this is done.

FIGURE 13.3 A convertible note, allocating the components between liability and equity

Compound financial instrument — a convertible note

Company A issues 2000 convertible notes on 1 July 2013. The notes have a 3-year term and are issued at par with a face value of €1000 per note, giving total proceeds at the date of issue of €2 million. The notes pay interest at 6% annually in arrears. The holder of each note is entitled to convert the note into 250 ordinary shares of Company A at any time up to maturity.

When the notes are issued, the prevailing market interest rate for similar debt (similar term, similar credit status of issuer and similar cash flows) without conversion options is 9%. This rate is higher than the convertible note's rate because the holder of the convertible note is prepared to accept a lower interest rate given the implicit value of its conversion option.

The issuer calculates the contractual cash flows using the market interest rate (9%) to work out the value of the holder's option, as follows:

Present value of the principal: €2 million payable in 3 years' time:	€ 1,544,367
Present value of the interest: €120,000 (€2 million × 6%) payable annually in arrears for 3 years	€ 303,755
Total liability component	€ 1,848,122
Equity component (by deduction)	€ 151,878
Proceeds of the note issue	€ 2,000,000

The journal entries at the date of issue are as follows:

Cash	Dr	2,000,000	
Financial Liability	Cr		1,848,122
Equity	Cr		151,878

The equity component is not remeasured and thus remains at €151,878 until the note is either converted or redeemed. The liability component accrues interest of 9% until it is redeemed or converted. If the note is converted, the remaining liability component is transferred to equity. If the note is not converted at the end of the 3-year term, the carrying amount has accreted up to €2,000,000 and the notes will be redeemed at €2,000,000. The equity component remains in equity.

Source: Adapted from IAS 32, Illustrative Example 9, paragraphs IE35–IE36.

13.6 INTEREST, DIVIDENDS, GAINS AND LOSSES

IAS 32 requires the statement of profit or loss and other comprehensive income (OCI) classification of items relating to financial instruments to match their statement of financial position classification. Thus, statement of profit or loss and OCI items relating to financial liabilities and financial assets are classified as income or expenses, or gains or losses. These are usually interest expense, interest income and dividend income. Distributions to holders of equity instruments are debited directly to equity. Usually these are dividends. These principles also apply to the component parts of a compound financial instrument.

Table 13.2 summarises these principles.

Table 13.2 Classification of revenues, expenses and equity distributions

Statement of financial position classification	Statement of profit or loss and other comprehensive income classification	Statement of changes in equity
Equity instrument		Dividends distributed
Financial liability	Interest expense	
Financial asset	Interest income, dividend income	

The transaction costs of an equity transaction are deducted from equity, but only to the extent to which they are incremental costs directly attributable to the equity transaction that otherwise would have been avoided. Examples of such costs include registration and other regulatory fees, legal and accounting fees and stamp duties. These costs are required to be shown separately under IAS 1 *Presentation of Financial Statements*.

13.7 FINANCIAL ASSETS AND FINANCIAL LIABILITIES: SCOPE

The objective of IFRS 9 is to set principles for financial reporting of financial assets and financial liabilities that is relevant and useful to users in assessing the amounts, timing and uncertainty of an entity's future cash flows. As the standard is very complex, particularly in its application to financial institutions, this chapter addresses only the more common applications of IFRS 9 and provides a general understanding of its requirements.

IFRS 9 applies to all entities and to all types of financial instruments, subject to a list of exceptions that in themselves are complicated. Therefore, the following is only an overview of the exceptions:

1. Investments in subsidiaries, associates and joint ventures that are accounted for under IFRS 10, IAS 27 or IAS 28. However, certain investments in such entities may be accounted for under IFRS 9 if so permitted by IFRS 10, IAS 27 or IAS 28. For example, IAS 27 permits investments in subsidiaries, associates and joint ventures to be carried at fair value under IFRS 9 in the investor's separate financial statements.
2. Rights and obligations under leases to which IFRS 16 *Leases* applies. However, finance lease receivables and operating lease receivables recognised by lessors are subject to the derecognition and impairment provisions of IFRS 9. Lease liabilities recognised by lessees are also subject to the derecognition requirements of IFRS 9. Finally, embedded derivatives in leases are subject to IFRS 9.
3. Employers' rights and obligations under employee benefit plans to which IAS 19 *Employee Benefits* applies.
4. Financial instruments issued by the entity that meet the definition of an equity instrument in IAS 32. This applies only to the issuer of the equity instrument. The holder of such an instrument will have a financial asset that is covered by IFRS 9.
5. Rights and obligations arising under an insurance contract as defined in IFRS 17 *Insurance contracts*, as well as investment contracts with discretionary participation features within the scope of IFRS 17, with certain exceptions. Scoped within IFRS 9 are embedded derivatives in contracts scoped within IFRS 17, unless they are insurance contracts themselves. The rights and obligations of an issuer of an insurance contract that also meets the definition of a financial guarantee contract are scoped within IFRS 9, unless the issuer has previously asserted explicitly and has used accounting that is applicable to insurance contracts, in which case the issuer may elect to apply either IFRS 9 or IFRS 17. Such choice can be made contract by contract and is irrevocable. If a credit card arrangement meets the definition of an insurance contract (for example because the cardholder is compensated for loss of goods purchased with the credit card), IFRS 9 and IFRS 17 contain specific requirements to determine whether these contracts are scoped in either standard, or need to be separated in components scoped within each standard.
6. Contracts between an acquirer and a vendor in a business combination to buy or sell an acquiree at a future date. However, this only applies if the term of the forward contract does not exceed a reasonable period normally necessary to obtain any required approvals and to complete the transaction.
7. Loan commitments that cannot be settled net in cash or another financial instrument, unless the loan commitment is measured at fair value through profit or loss (FVPL) *(see section 13.9)* under IFRS 9, in which case it is covered by IFRS 9. Loan commitments outside the scope of IFRS 9 are still subject to the impairment requirements *(see section 13.11.5)* of the standard.
8. Financial instruments to which IFRS 2 *Share-based Payment* applies.
9. Rights to payments to reimburse the entity for expenditure it is required to make to settle a liability that it recognises as a liability under IAS 37.
10. Financial instruments within the scope of IFRS 15 *Revenue from Contracts with Customers*, except those for which that standard specifies they should be accounted for under IFRS 9.

As discussed in section 13.2.4, contracts to buy or sell non-financial items are generally not financial instruments. Certain commodity contracts are, however, included within the scope of IAS 32. These include contracts to buy or sell non-financial items that can be settled net (in cash) or by exchanging financial instruments, or in which the non-financial item is readily convertible into cash.

13.7.1 'Own use' contracts

Contracts to buy or sell non-financial items do not generally meet the definition of a financial instrument. However, many such contracts are standardised in form and traded on organised markets in much the same way as some derivative financial instruments. The ability to buy or sell such a contract for cash, the ease with which it may be bought or sold, and the possibility of negotiating a cash settlement of the obligation to receive or deliver the commodity, do not alter the fundamental character of the contract in a way that creates a financial instrument. However, the IASB believes that there are many circumstances where these contracts should be accounted for as if they were financial instruments.

Accordingly, the provisions of IFRS 9 are normally applied to those contracts — effectively as if the contracts were financial instruments — to buy or sell non-financial items (1) that can be settled net in cash or another financial instrument or (2) that can be settled by exchanging financial instruments. However, there is an exception for what are commonly termed 'normal' purchases and sales or 'own use' contracts.

The provisions of IFRS 9 are not to be applied to those contracts to buy or sell non-financial items that can be settled net if they were entered into and continue to be held for the purpose of the receipt or delivery of the non-financial item in accordance with the entity's expected purchase, sale or usage requirements (a 'normal' purchase or sale). For example, an entity that enters into a contract to purchase 1,000 kg of copper in accordance with its expected usage requirements would not account for such a contract as a derivative under IFRS 9, even if it could be settled net in cash.

IFRS 9 includes a fair value option for those so-called 'own use' contracts. At inception of a contract, an entity may make an irrevocable designation to measure an own use contract at FVPL even if it was entered into for the purpose of the receipt or delivery of the non-financial item in accordance with the entity's expected purchase, sale or usage requirement. However, such designation is only allowed if it eliminates or significantly reduces an accounting mismatch.

13.8 DERIVATIVES AND EMBEDDED DERIVATIVES

The concept of a derivative may appear daunting because there are numerous derivative financial instruments in the market that seem complex and difficult to understand. However, as already noted, fundamentally all derivatives simply derive their value from another underlying item such as a share price or an interest rate. Derivative financial instruments create rights and obligations that have the effect of transferring between the parties to the instrument one or more of the financial risks inherent in an underlying primary financial instrument. On inception, derivative financial instruments give one party a contractual right to exchange financial assets or financial liabilities with another party under conditions that are potentially favourable, while the other party has a contractual obligation to exchange under potentially unfavourable conditions.

Figure 13.4 illustrates an option contract as an example of a derivative.

FIGURE 13.4 How an option contract works

> **An option contract**
>
> Party A buys an option that entitles it to purchase 1000 shares in Company Z at £3 a share, at any time in the next 6 months. The shares in Company Z are the underlying financial instruments from which the option derives its value. The option is thus the derivative financial instrument. The amount of £3 a share is called the exercise price of the option.
>
> Party B sells the option to Party A. Party A is called the holder of the option, and Party B is called the writer of the option. Party A will usually pay an amount called a premium to purchase the option. The amount of the premium is less than what Party A would have to pay for the shares in Company Z.
>
> Assume that at the date of the option contract the market price of shares in Company Z is £2.60.
>
> The financial instrument created by this transaction is a contractual right of Party A to purchase the 1000 shares in Company Z at £3 a share (a financial asset of Party A), and a contractual obligation of Party B to sell the shares in Company Z to Party A at £3 a share (a financial liability of Party B). Party A's right is a financial asset because it has the right to exchange under potentially favourable conditions to itself. Thus, if the share price of Company Z rises above £3, Party A will exercise its option and require Party B to deliver the shares at £3 a share. Party A will have benefited from this transaction by acquiring the shares in Company Z at less than the market price. Conversely, Parry B's obligation is a financial liability because it has the obligation to exchange under potentially unfavourable conditions to itself. Thus, if the shares in Company Z rise to £3.20, Party A

FIGURE 13.4 *(continued)*

will purchase the shares from Party B for £3,000. If Party A had had to purchase the shares on the market, it would have paid £3,200.

Party B may have made a loss from this transaction, depending on whether it already held the shares in Company Z, or had to go out and buy them for £3,200 and then sell them to Party A for £3,000, or had entered into other derivative contracts with other parties enabling it to purchase the shares at less than £3,000.

What it the share price in Company Z never exceeds £3 over the 6-month term of the option? In this case, Party A will not exercise the option and the option will lapse. The option is termed 'out of the money' from Party A's perspective — it has no value to Party A because the exercise price is higher than the market price. Once the share price rises above £3, the option is termed 'in the money'. Party A is not compelled to exercise its option, even if it is in the money. From Party A's perspective, it has a right to exercise the option should it so choose. However, if Party A exercises its option, Party B is then compelled to deliver the shares under its contractual obligation.

IAS 32 notes that the nature of the holder's right and of the writer's obligation is not affected by the likelihood that the option will be exercised.

In simple terms, parties to derivative financial instruments are taking bets on what will happen to the underlying financial instrument in the future. In the example in figure 13.4, Party A was taking a bet that the share price in Company Z would rise above £3 within 6 months, and Party B was taking a bet that it would not. Party B would most likely hedge its bet by doing something to protect itself should the market price rise above £3. It could do this by entering into another derivative with another party, enabling Party B to purchase shares from that other party at £3. Often a chain of derivative financial instruments will be created in this way. Party A will probably not know anything about the chain created. *(Hedging is discussed in section 13.13.)*

IAS 32 does not prescribe recognition and measurement rules for derivatives; these are addressed in IFRS 9. Instead, IAS 32 includes derivatives in the definition of financial instruments. Other types of derivatives include interest rate swaps, forward exchange contracts and futures contracts.

13.8.1 Three required characteristics

Appendix A of IFRS 9 defines a derivative. Derivatives derive their value from another underlying item such as a share price or an interest rate. The definition requires all of the following three characteristics to be met:
- its value must change in response to a change in an underlying variable such as a specified interest rate, price, credit rating, or foreign exchange rate
- it must require no initial net investment or an initial net investment that is smaller than would be required for other types of contracts with similar responses to changes in market factors
- it is settled at a future date.

13.8.2 Examples of derivatives

Typical examples of derivatives are futures and forwards, swap and option contracts. A derivative usually has a notional amount, which is an amount of currency, a number of shares or other units specified in a contract. However, a derivative does not require the holder or writer to invest or receive the notional amount at the inception of the contract. In the example in figure 13.4, where Party A buys an option that entitles it to purchase 1000 shares in Company Z at £3 a share at any time in the next 6 months, the 1000 shares is the notional amount. However, a notional amount is not an essential feature of a derivative. For example, a contract may require a fixed payment of £2,000 if a specified interest rate increases by a specified percentage. Such a contract is a derivative even though there is no notional amount.

Many option contracts require a premium to be paid to the writer of the option. The premium is less than what would be required to purchase the underlying shares or other underlying financial instruments and thus option contracts meet the definition of a derivative.

13.8.3 Embedded derivatives

Derivatives may exist on a stand-alone basis, or they may be embedded in other financial instruments. An embedded derivative is a component of a hybrid contract that also includes a non-derivative host contract, with the effect that some of the cash flows of the combined instrument vary in a way similar to a stand-alone instrument (IFRS 9 paragraph 4.3.1). An embedded derivative cannot be contractually detached from the host contract, nor can it have a different counterparty from that of the host instrument, as it would otherwise be considered a separate financial instrument.

Separation of embedded derivatives

The requirements for embedded derivatives differ between (i) those where the host is an *asset* that is scoped within IFRS 9 and (ii) those where the host is an asset not scoped within IFRS 9 or is a liability (regardless of whether it is scoped within IFRS 9 or not).

A derivative should not be separated from the host contract if it is embedded in an *asset* host that is within the scope of IFRS 9. Instead, an entity should apply the IFRS 9 requirements to such hybrid financial assets in their entirety (IFRS 9 paragraph 4.3.2).

For all embedded derivatives other than those where the host is an asset scoped within IFRS 9, paragraph 4.3.3 of IFRS 9 requires them to be separated from the host contract if, and only if, the following three conditions are met:

- the economic characteristics and risks of the embedded derivative are not closely related to the economic characteristics and risks of the host contract
- a separate instrument with the same terms as the embedded derivative would meet the definition of a derivative
- the hybrid contract is not measured at FVPL. This means that a derivative embedded in a hybrid contract measured at FVPL is not separated, even if it could be separated, as the separated embedded derivative would be required to be measured at FVPL anyway.

The following are examples of instruments scoped within IFRS 9 where the economic characteristics and risks of the embedded derivative are not closely related to the economic characteristics and risks of the host contract (and therefore the embedded derivative must be separated):

- a put option embedded in a host debt instrument that allows the holder to require the issuer to reacquire the instrument for an amount of cash that varies on the basis of the change in an equity or commodity price or index. This is because the host is a debt instrument and the variables are not related to the debt instrument
- an option to extend the remaining term to maturity of a debt instrument without a concurrent adjustment to the market rate of interest at the time of the extension
- equity-indexed interest or principal payments embedded in a host debt instrument or insurance contract by which the amount of interest or principal is indexed to a share price because the risks inherent in the host and the embedded derivative are dissimilar
- commodity-indexed interest or principal payments embedded in a host debt instrument or insurance contract by which the amount of interest or principal is indexed to the price of the commodity (such as gold).

A common example of an underlying contract not scoped within IFRS 9 where entities need to determine whether an embedded derivative needs to be separated is one where an entity enters into a purchase or sale contract in a currency other than its functional currency. IFRS 9 stipulates that the embedded foreign currency derivative in the host contract is only closely related to the host contract if (i) the host contract is not leveraged, and (ii) does not contain option features, and (iii) is denominated in either (a) the currency of one of the counterparties to the contract, or (b) the currency in which the price of the related good or service is routinely denominated such as the USD for oil, or (c) a currency that is commonly used in the specific economic environment.

IFRS 9 contains further examples of such instruments. In addition, it also gives examples of instruments where the economic characteristics and risks of the embedded derivative are closely related to the economic characteristics and risks of the host contract. These examples are very prescriptive and not clearly principle-based.

If an embedded derivative is separated, it is accounted for as a stand-alone derivative. If fair value of the separated derivative cannot be reliably measured, then the entire hybrid contract must be measured at FVPL (IFRS 9 paragraph 4.3.6).

LO9 13.9 FINANCIAL ASSETS AND FINANCIAL LIABILITIES: CATEGORIES OF FINANCIAL INSTRUMENTS

13.9.1 Financial assets

During the credit crisis commentators argued that IAS 39 contained too many categories of financial assets, that were not geared to the various business models, in particular of banks, and was not flexible enough to allow preparers to reclassify, for example when their business model changes. Some also argued that IAS 39 was biased towards the fair value model rather than the cost model.

In response to this feedback the IASB issued an initial proposal with only three categories of financial assets, no options and rigid criteria to classify financial assets which included the business model test. In the course of the consideration of these proposals though, at the request of groups of stakeholders, several options and additional categories were introduced and the criteria for classification were changed, including an additional business model to accommodate the insurance sector. The categories and the criteria for classification in the final standard are described below.

IFRS 9 has the following measurement categories for financial assets:
- Debt instruments at amortised cost.
- Debt instruments at fair value through other comprehensive income (FVOCI) with cumulative gains and losses reclassified to profit or loss upon derecognition.
- Equity instruments designated as measured at FVOCI with gains and losses remaining in OCI without subsequent reclassification to profit or loss.
- Debt instruments, derivatives and equity instruments at FVPL.

The classification is based on both the entity's business model for managing the financial assets and the contractual cash flow characteristics of the financial asset, as set out in figure 13.5.

Table 13.3 sets out the requirements of IFRS 9 in further detail.

Business models

An entity's business model for managing financial assets is a matter of fact typically observable through particular activities that the entity undertakes to achieve its stated objectives. An entity will need to use judgement to assess its business model for managing financial assets and that assessment is not determined by a single factor or activity. Rather, the entity must consider all relevant evidence that is available at the date of the assessment.

The business model assessment is not an instrument-by-instrument assessment, but it takes place at a higher level of aggregation, which is the level at which the key decision makers manage groups or portfolios of financial assets to achieve the business objective. IFRS 9 distinguishes between three types of business model:

1. In a 'hold to collect' business model, management's objective is to collect the instrument's contractual cash flows. Although IFRS 9 is slightly vague about the role of sales, expected future sales are the key determining factor and past sales are of relevance only as a source of evidence. Portfolios in which the expected sales are more than infrequent and significant in value do not meet the criteria of a 'hold to collect' business model. A typical example of such a business model is a liquidity buffer portfolio where an entity only sells assets in rare 'stress case' scenarios.

2. In the 'hold to collect and sell' business model, the entity's key management personnel have made a decision that both collecting contractual cash flows and selling are fundamental to achieving the objective of the business model. For example, the objective of the business model may be to manage everyday

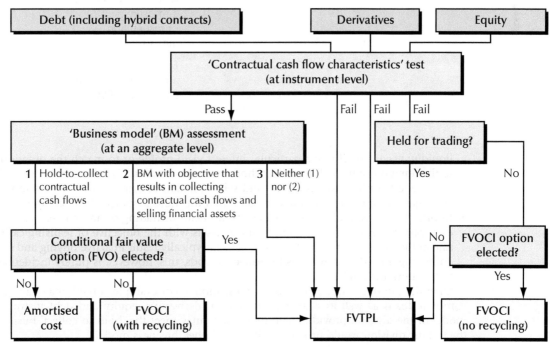

FIGURE 13.5 The categories of financial assets

Table 13.3 The categories of financial assets

Category	Characteristics of the instrument	Business model and other requirements	Examples
Debt instruments measured at amortised cost	The asset's contractual cash flows represent 'solely payments of principle and interest' (SPPI)	The asset is held within a 'hold to collect' business model whose objective is to collect contractual cash flows	Commercial bill investments; government bonds; corporate bonds; accounts receivable; mortgage loans
Debt instruments at fair value through other comprehensive income (FVOCI)	The asset's contractual cash flows represent 'solely payments of principal and interest'	Held within a 'hold to collect and sell' business model whose objective is achieved by both collecting contractual cash flows and selling financial assets	Commercial bill investments; government bonds; corporate bonds; mortgage loans
Equity instruments designated as measured at FVOCI	Equity instrument	Designation of the equity instrument not held for trading as measured at FVOCI with gains and losses remaining in other comprehensive income	Shares
Derivatives and debt and equity instruments at fair value through profit or loss (FVPL)	Any financial asset	Derivatives Debt instruments that fail the SPPI test or the business model tests above Debt instruments that are designated at fair value through profit or loss because it reduces or eliminates a measurement or recognition inconsistency Equity instruments that are not designated as measured at FVOCI	Forward exchange contracts; interest rate swaps; call options Commercial bill investments; government bonds; corporate bonds Share portfolio held for short-term gains

liquidity needs, to achieve a particular interest yield profile or to match the duration of financial assets to the duration of the liabilities that those assets are funding. To achieve these objectives, the entity will both collect contractual cash flows and sell the financial assets. This business model will typically involve greater frequency and value of sales than the 'hold to collect' business model.

3. In other business models, financial assets are held for trading or are managed on a fair value basis. In each case, the entity manages the financial assets with the objective of realising cash flows through the sale of the assets and the entity's objective will typically result in active buying and selling. Although the entity might hold certain assets for longer periods, this, however, is purely incidental and not essential to this business model.

An entity can have more than one business model. For example, a bank may have a division providing corporate loans as well as a division trading in derivatives, equity and debt instruments. The business model of the division providing corporate loans may meet the 'hold to collect' business model, whereas the trading division would probably fall in the 'other' business model.

Cash flow characteristics

The assessment of the characteristics of the contractual cash flows is done at the individual financial asset level and aims to identify whether the contractual cash flows are solely payments of principal and interest (SPPI) on the principal amount outstanding. For the purposes of the SPPI test, interest is typically the compensation for the time value of money and credit risk, but may also include consideration for other basic lending risks (e.g. liquidity risk) and costs (e.g. servicing or administrative costs) associated with holding the financial asset for a period of time, as well as a profit margin that is consistent with a basic lending agreement.

The SPPI test is designed to screen out financial assets for which the application of the effective interest method either is not viable from a purely mechanical standpoint (e.g. a share where the cash flows simply cannot be reflected by the effective interest method) or does not provide useful information about the uncertainty, timing and amount of the financial asset's contractual cash flows (e.g. a debt instrument that is linked to a commodity price where variability of cash flows is largely caused by the change in the commodity price). Accordingly, the SPPI test is based on the premise that the application of the effective interest method only provides useful information when the variability in the contractual cash flows arises to maintain the holder's return in line with a basic lending arrangement.

Sometimes, contractual provisions may modify the cash flows of an instrument so that it does not give rise only to a straightforward repayment of principal and interest. However, financial assets may still meet the SPPI test if:

- the contractual cash flow characteristic has only a *de minimis* (i.e. very minor) effect on the contractual cash flows of the financial asset (IFRS 9 paragraph B4.1.18)
- the contractual cash flow characteristic is *not genuine*, i.e. it affects the instrument's contractual cash flows only on the occurrence of an event that is extremely rare, highly abnormal and very unlikely to occur (IFRS 9 paragraph B4.1.18)
- the entity can determine, quantitatively or qualitatively, that the contractual cash flows that have a modified time value of money element of interest (e.g. a 6-month loan that pays 12-month LIBOR has such an element) do not differ significantly from the cash flows on a benchmark instrument that represent solely payments of principal and interest on the principal outstanding) (IFRS 9 paragraph B4.1.9B and C), or
- the interest rate is set by government or a regulatory authority. In such a case, the interest rate may be considered a proxy for the time value of money element for applying the contractual cash flow characteristics test if that regulated interest rate meets certain conditions. (IFRS 9, paragraph B4.1.9E)

Many financial assets have characteristics that could cause them to fail the SPPI test, even though they arise in the course of regular lending operations in the economy. Therefore, the IASB included detailed guidance in IFRS 9 — that deals with contingent events affecting cash flows, prepayment and extension options, contractually linked instruments and non-recourse lending — in order to limit the circumstances in which these instruments would have to be measured at fair value.

13.9.2 Financial liabilities

IFRS 9 has the following measurement categories for financial liabilities:
- Financial liabilities at amortised cost.
- Financial liabilities at FVPL.

The classification of financial liabilities under IFRS 9 does not follow the approach for the classification of financial assets, but follows the approach set out in table 13.4.

Table 13.4 The categories of financial liabilities

Category	Characteristics of the instrument	Other requirements	Examples
Financial liabilities at fair value through profit or loss (FVPL)	Financial liabilities	Financial liabilities that meet the definition of held for trading	Short positions in trading; derivatives
		Financial liabilities that are designated at fair value through profit or loss because it reduces or eliminates a measurement or recognition inconsistency	Bond issues
Financial liabilities at amortised cost	Financial liabilities	Financial liabilities that do not fall into the above category	Bond issues; trade creditors

Note that derivative financial liabilities are deemed to meet the definition of held for trading and are measured at FVPL.

For financial liabilities that do not meet the definition of held for trading, but are designated as at FVPL, the element of gains or losses attributable to changes in the entity's own credit risk is normally recognised in OCI. This avoids the counterintuitive effect of a deterioration of an entity's credit standing resulting in a gain recognised in profit and loss *(see section 8.5 on fair value measurement)*. However, if this creates or enlarges an accounting mismatch in profit or loss, gains and losses must be entirely presented in profit or loss.

13.9.3 Reclassifications

IFRS 9 contains various prescriptive rules on the reclassification of financial instruments. The rules are aimed at preventing inconsistent gain or loss recognition and the use of arbitrage between the categories. In summary:

- In certain rare circumstances when an entity changes its business model for managing financial assets, non-derivative debt assets are required to be reclassified between the amortised cost, FVPL, and FVOCI categories. Changes in the business model for managing financial assets are expected to be very rare and occur for example when an entity acquires a new business or disposes of an existing business. A business model may develop over time in a way that it no longer meets the requirements of the initial measurement category. Those cases are not reclassifications and existing assets remain in the old category while new assets are classified taking into consideration the new business model.
- Equity instruments measured at FVOCI and financial liabilities should not be reclassified.
- The following changes in circumstances are not reclassifications:
  - when an item is designated as (or ceases to be) an effective hedging instrument in a cash flow hedge or net investment hedge *(see section 13.13 on hedge accounting)*
  - changes in measurement in accordance with the guidance on designation of credit exposure as measured at FVPL to avoid an accounting mismatch *(see section 13.13.5)*.

13.10 FINANCIAL ASSETS AND FINANCIAL LIABILITIES: RECOGNITION CRITERIA

IFRS 9 states that an entity shall recognise a financial asset or a financial liability in its statement of financial position when, and only when, the entity becomes a party to the contractual provisions of the instrument. The standard provides examples of applying the recognition criteria, as follows:

- Unconditional receivables and payables are recognised as assets or liabilities when the entity becomes a party to the contract and, consequently, has a legal right to receive or a legal obligation to pay cash. Normal trade debtors and trade creditors would fall into this category.
- Assets to be acquired and liabilities to be incurred under a firm commitment to purchase or sell goods or services are generally not recognised until at least one of the parties has performed under the agreement. However, this is subject to the rules set out in the scope paragraph of IFRS 9 *(discussed in section 13.7)*. Thus, if a firm commitment to buy or sell non-financial items is within the scope of IFRS 9, its net fair value is recognised as an asset or liability on the commitment date.
- A forward contract within the scope of the standard is also recognised as an asset or liability at the commitment date. When an entity becomes party to a forward contract, the rights and obligations at the commitment date are often equal, so that the net fair value of the forward is zero. Note the following:
- Option contracts within the scope of the standard are recognised as assets or liabilities when the holder or writer becomes a party to the contract.
- Planned future transactions, no matter how likely, are not assets and liabilities because the entity has not become a party to a contract.

13.11 FINANCIAL ASSETS AND FINANCIAL LIABILITIES: MEASUREMENT

The measurement rules in IFRS 9 address:
1. initial measurement
2. subsequent measurement

3. reclassifications
4. gains and losses
5. impairment and collectability of financial assets.

The rules are applied distinctly to each of the categories of financial instruments *discussed in section 13.9.*

13.11.1 Initial measurement

Paragraph 5.1.1 of IFRS 9 requires that, on initial recognition, financial assets and financial liabilities must be measured at fair value. Fair value is defined by IFRS 13 as:

> the price that would be received to sell an asset or paid to transfer a liability in an orderly transaction between market participants at the measurement date.

The concept of fair value is discussed in chapter 8.

In addition, paragraph 5.1.1 requires that transaction costs directly attributable to the acquisition or issue of the financial asset or liability must be added to or deducted from the fair value, except for financial assets and liabilities measured at FVPL. Transaction costs are defined in IFRS 9 as:

> incremental costs that are directly attributable to the acquisition, issue or disposal of a financial asset or financial liability (see IFRS 9 paragraph B5.4.8). An incremental cost is one that would not have been incurred if the entity had not acquired, issued or disposed of the financial instrument.

Paragraph B5.4.8 of IFRS 9 provides further guidance. Examples of transaction costs include fees and commissions paid to agents, advisers, brokers and dealers; levies by regulatory agencies and securities exchanges; and transfer taxes and duties (such as stamp duties). Transaction costs do not include debt premiums or discounts, financing costs or internal administrative or holding costs.

The fair value of a financial instrument on initial recognition is normally the transaction price (the fair value of the consideration given or received). However, if part of the consideration given or received is for something other than the financial instrument, then the fair value must be estimated using valuation techniques. For example, if a company provides an interest-free loan to its employees, part of the consideration is given in the form of recognition of employee services or loyalty rather than for the loan itself. The fair value of the loan must be calculated by discounting the future cash flows using a market rate of interest for a similar loan (similar as to currency, term and credit rating). Any additional amount lent is accounted for as an expense unless it qualifies for recognition as some other type of asset. Figure 13.6 provides an example.

FIGURE 13.6 Initial measurement of an interest-free loan

Initial measurement of an interest-free loan

Company Z provides interest-free loans to 10 employees for a 5-year term, payable at the end of 5 years. The total loan amount is $200,000. A market rate of interest for a similar 5-year loan is 5%.

The present value of this receivable, being the future cash flows discounted at 5%, is approximately $157,000. Therefore, $43,000 is an employee expense to Company Z. Depending on the terms of the loan, this employee expense is either recognised immediately (e.g. if the employee can continue to benefit from the interest free loan even if he/she stops providing employee services), or deferred over the period that the employee is required to provide employee services to continue to benefit from the interest-free loan (e.g. if the loan needs to be repaid immediately on termination of employment).

Company Z would record the following journal entries:

Loans Receivable	Dr	157,000	
(Deferred) Expenses	Dr	43,000	
Cash	Cr		200,000

13.11.2 Subsequent measurement

Subsequent measurement depends on whether or not the item is a financial asset or financial liability, and on which of the categories applies.

Financial assets are measured as follows:

1. At amortised cost — debt instruments measured at amortised cost.
2. At fair value —
   (i) Debt instruments at FVOCI
   (ii) Equity instruments designated as measured at FVOCI
   (iii) Debt instruments, derivatives and equity instruments at FVPL.

If any of these financial assets are hedged items, they are subject to the hedge accounting measurement rules (*see section 13.13*).

Amortised cost is defined in IFRS 9 as follows:

> The amount at which the financial asset or financial liability is measured at initial recognition minus the principal repayments, plus or minus the cumulative amortisation using the effective interest method of any difference between that initial amount and the maturity amount and, for financial assets, adjusted for any loss allowance.

The effective interest method calculates the amortised cost of a financial asset or a financial liability and allocates interest revenue or interest expense in profit or loss over the relevant period. The effective interest rate is defined by IFRS 9 as:

> The rate that exactly discounts estimated future cash payments or receipts through the expected life of the financial asset or financial liability to the gross carrying amount of a financial asset [which is the asset's amortised cost before deducting any loss allowance] or to the amortised cost of a financial liability.

The effective interest rate must be calculated considering all contractual terms of the instrument. It includes all fees, transaction costs, premiums and discounts.

Illustrative example 13.1 provides an example of how amortised cost is calculated.

ILLUSTRATIVE EXAMPLE 13.1 Calculation of amortised cost (based on IFRS 9, Implementation Guidance B.26)

Cape Ventures purchases a debt instrument at 1 January 2026 with a 5-year term for its fair value of $1,000 (including transaction costs). The instrument has a principal amount of $1,250 (the amount payable on redemption) and carries fixed interest of 4.7% annually. The annual cash interest income is thus $59 ($1,250 × 0.047). Using a financial calculator, the effective interest rate is calculated as 10%. The debt instrument is classified as at amortised cost.

The following table sets out the cash flows and interest income for each period, using the effective interest rate of 10%:

A. Year	B. Amortised cost at beginning of year	C. Interest income (B × 10%)	D. Cash flows	E. Amortised cost at end of year (B + C − D)
2026	1,000	100	59	1,041
2027	1,041	104	59	1,086
2028	1,086	109	59	1,136
2029	1,136	113	59	1,190
2030	1,190	119	59 + 1,250	—

The journal entries to record this transaction on initial recognition and throughout the life of the instrument are as follows:

On initial recognition at 1 January 2026:

Debt instrument measured at amortised cost	Dr	1,000
Cash	Cr	1,000

On recognition of interest in 2026:

Debt instrument measured at amortised cost	Dr	41
Cash	Dr	59
Interest Income	Cr	100

On recognition of interest in 2027:

Debt instrument measured at amortised cost	Dr	45	
Cash	Dr	59	
Interest Income	Cr		104

On recognition of interest in 2028:

Debt instrument measured at amortised cost	Dr	50	
Cash	Dr	59	
Interest Income	Cr		109

On recognition of interest in 2029:

Debt instrument measured at amortised cost	Dr	54	
Cash	Dr	59	
Interest Income	Cr		113

On recognition of interest in 2030:

Debt instrument measured at amortised cost	Dr	60	
Cash	Dr	59	
Interest Income	Cr		119

On redemption of investment at 31 December 2030:

Cash	Dr	1,250	
Debt instrument measured at amortised cost	Cr		1,250

Financial liabilities are measured subsequent to initial recognition at amortised cost except for those designated as 'at fair value through profit or loss', which must be measured at fair value (IFRS 9 paragraph 4.2.2). There are four exceptions to this rule (IFRS 9 paragraph 4.2.1):

1. Financial liabilities arising in certain circumstances when a financial asset is transferred under the derecognition rules. These are outside the scope of this chapter.
2. Financial guarantee contracts scoped within IFRS 9 *(see section 13.7)*. These are initially measured at fair value and subsequently at the *higher* of:
   (i) the amount determined in accordance with the IFRS 9 requirements on impairment *(see section 13.11.5)* and
   (ii) the amount initially recognised less, where appropriate, cumulative amortisation recognised in accordance with IFRS 15 *Revenue from Contracts with Customers*.
   A common example of a financial guarantee contract is when a parent company guarantees the debts of its subsidiary to an external financier. The parent undertakes to pay the financier in the event that the subsidiary is unable to pay.
3. Commitments to provide a loan at a below-market interest rate. The measurement rules are the same as for (2) above.
4. Contingent consideration recognised in a business combination should be measured at fair value with changes recognised in profit or loss.

If any of these financial liabilities are hedged items, they are subject to the hedge accounting measurement rules *(see section 13.13)*. If any of the financial liabilities are measured at fair value, an entity would need to apply the specific requirements for effect of its own credit risk *(see section 13.9.2)*.

Illustrative example 13.2 provides an example of a financial liability measured at amortised cost.

Lenglen enters into an agreement with Bartoli to lend it $1 million on 1 January 2026. Bartoli incurs transaction costs of $25,000. The interest to be paid is 5% for each of the first 2 years and 7% for each of the next 2 years, annually in arrears. The loan must be repaid after 4 years. The annual cash interest expense is thus $50,000 ($1 million × 0.05) for each of the first 2 years and $70,000 ($1 million × 0.07) for each of the next 2 years. Using a financial calculator, the effective interest rate is calculated as 6.67%. Bartoli measures the financial liability at fair value less transaction costs on initial recognition and subsequently at amortised cost in accordance with IFRS 9.

The following table sets out the cash flows and interest expense for each period, using the effective interest rate of 6.67%.

A. Year	B. Amortised cost at beginning of year	C. Interest income (B × 6.67%)	D. Cash flows	E. Amortised cost at end of year (B + C − D)
2026	975,000	65,014	50,000	990,014
2027	990,014	66,015	50,000	1,006,029
2028	1,066,029	67,083	70,000	1,003,112
2029	1,003,112	66,888	70,000 + 1,000,000	—

The journal entries to record this transaction on initial recognition and throughout the life of the instrument in the books of Bartoli are as follows:

On initial recognition in 2026:

Cash	Dr	975,000
Bond—Liability	Dr	25,000
Bond—Liability	Cr	1,000,000

On recognition of interest in 2026:

Interest Expense	Dr	65,014
Bond—Liability	Cr	15,014
Cash	Cr	50,000

On recognition of interest in 2027:

Interest Expense	Dr	65,015
Bond—Liability	Cr	16,015
Cash	Cr	50,000

On recognition of interest in 2028:

Interest Expense	Dr	67,083
Bond—Liability	Dr	2,917
Cash	Cr	70,000

On recognition of interest in 2029:

Interest Expense	Dr	66,888
Bond—Liability	Dr	3,112
Cash	Cr	70,000

On repayment of liability in 2029:

Interest Expense	Dr	0	
Bond—Liability	Dr	1,000,000	
Cash	Cr		1,000,000

13.11.4 Gains and losses

A gain or loss on a financial asset or financial liability that is measured at fair value is recognised in profit or loss unless:

1. it is part of a hedge relationship. In that case the requirements on hedge accounting (*see section 13.13*) apply
2. it is an investment in an equity instrument for which the gains and losses are recognised in OCI
3. it is a financial liability for which the entity is required to present the effects of changes in own credit risk in OCI, or
4. it is a debt instrument at FVOCI — a gain or loss is recognised in profit or loss when the financial asset is derecognised, reclassified to measurement at FVPL, through the amortisation process or in order to recognise impairment gains or losses.

A gain or loss on a financial instrument that is measured at amortised cost and is not part of a hedging relationship should be recognised in profit or loss when:

1. financial assets are derecognised, reclassified to measurement at FVPL, through the amortisation process or in order to recognise impairment gains or losses
2. financial liabilities are derecognised through the amortisation process.

One could be forgiven for thinking that for debt and equity instruments at FVOCI, the cumulative amount in OCI in respect of that instrument is identical to its cumulative fair value changes. Although this may be true in simple scenarios, it often is not. For example, equity instruments at FVOCI are initially measured at fair value less transaction costs. This will lead to the cumulative amount in OCI on this equity instrument to be the cumulative fair values changes less transaction costs. For debt instruments the same applies and in addition there may be differences due to impairment losses (*see section 13.11.5*).

13.11.5 Impairment and uncollectability of financial assets

Background

In April 2009, *as mentioned in section 13.1*, the leaders of the G-20 called upon accounting standard setters to strengthen accounting recognition of loan-loss provisions by incorporating a broader range of credit information. During the financial crisis, the delayed recognition of credit losses associated with loans and other financial instruments was identified as a weakness in existing accounting standards. This is primarily because the impairment requirements under IAS 39 were based on an 'incurred loss model', i.e. credit losses were not recognised until a credit loss event occurs. The IASB has sought to address the concerns about the delayed recognition of credit losses by introducing in IFRS 9 a forward-looking expected credit loss model.

The expected credit loss model applies to:

- debt instruments measured at amortised cost or at FVOCI under IFRS 9 (which include debt instruments such as loans, debt securities and trade receivables)
- loan commitments and financial guarantee contracts that are not accounted for at FVPL under IFRS 9
- contracts assets under the revenue standard IFRS 15
- lease receivables under IFRS 16.

General approach

Under the general approach, entities must recognise expected credit losses in three stages. For credit exposures where there has not been a significant increase in credit risk since initial recognition (Stage 1), entities are required to provide for credit losses that result from default events 'that are possible' within the next 12 months. For those credit exposures where there has been a significant increase in credit risk since initial recognition (Stage 2), a loss allowance is required for credit losses expected over the remaining life of the exposure irrespective of the timing of the default.

An entity should determine whether the risk of a default occurring over the expected life of the financial instrument has increased significantly between the date of initial recognition and the reporting date. In making that assessment, an entity should not consider collateral as this only affects the expected credit loss but not the risk of a default occurring. An entity should make this assessment considering all reasonable and supportable information (including forward-looking information) that is available without undue cost or effort. IFRS 9 provides a non-exhaustive list of information — such as external market indicators, internal factors and borrower-specific information — that may be relevant in making the assessment (IFRS 9 paragraph B5.5.17). Some factors and indicators may not be identifiable at the level of individual financial instruments and should be assessed at a higher level of aggregation (e.g. portfolio level). If subsequently the credit risk improves significantly, the financial asset is transferred from Stage 2 to Stage 1 again.

If financial assets become credit-impaired (Stage 3), the loss allowance will still be based on the expected losses during the remaining term of the instrument, but from that moment onward interest revenue would be calculated by applying the effective interest rate to the amortised cost (net of loss allowance) rather than the gross carrying amount. This avoids an entity recognising interest revenue that needs to be considered impaired immediately. Financial assets are assessed as credit-impaired using the following criteria in Appendix A of IFRS 9:

(a) significant financial difficulty of the borrower
(b) a breach of contract or default in interest or principal payments
(c) a lender granting concessions related to the borrower's financial difficulty that the lender would not otherwise consider
(d) it becoming probable that a borrower will enter bankruptcy or other financial reorganisation (such as administration)
(e) the disappearance of an active market for the financial asset because of financial difficulties
(f) the purchase or origination of a financial asset at a deep discount that reflects the incurred credit losses.

IFRS 9 does not define 'default', but is clear that default is broader than failure to pay and entities would need to consider other qualitative indicators of default (e.g. covenant breaches). IFRS 9 requires an entity to apply a definition of 'default' that is consistent with the definition used for internal credit risk management purposes. However, there is a presumption that default does not occur later than when a financial asset is 90 days past due unless an entity can demonstrate that a more lagging default criterion is more appropriate.

Figure 13.7 provides an overview of the three stages of the model, the recognition of expected credit losses and the presentation of interest revenue.

FIGURE 13.7 Overview of the model

← Change in credit quality since initial recognition →		
Stage 1 Performing Initial recognition	Stage 2 Underperforming Assets with a significant increase in credit risk	Stage 3 Non-performing Credit-impaired assets
Recognition of expected credit losses		
12-month expected credit losses	Lifetime expected credit losses	Lifetime expected credit losses
Interest revenue		
Effective interest on gross carrying amount	Effective interest on gross carrying amount	Effective interest on amortised cost (net of loss allowance)

The standard provides detailed guidance in paragraphs B5.5.7 – B5.5.18 on how to determine whether a significant increase (or decrease) in credit risk has occurred. This may be a laborious process, in particular for entities with many financial assets at amortised cost or FVOCI. When applying the general approach, a number of operational simplifications and presumptions are available to help entities assess significant increases in credit risk since initial recognition, such as (IFRS 9 paragraph 5.5.10–5.5.11):

• If a financial instrument has low credit risk (equivalent to investment grade quality), then an entity may assume that no significant increases in credit risk have occurred.
• If forward-looking information (either on an individual or collective basis) is not available, there is a rebuttable presumption that credit risk has increased significantly when contractual payments are more than 30 days past due.

Simplified approach

IFRS 9 paragraph 5.5.15–16 also provides a simplified approach that does not require the tracking of changes in credit risk, but instead requires the recognition of lifetime expected credit losses at all times.

The simplified approach must be applied to trade receivables or contract assets that do not contain a significant financing component. However, for trade receivables or contract assets that contain a significant financing component, and for lease receivables, entities have an accounting policy choice to apply either the simplified approach or the general approach. This accounting policy choice should be applied consistently, but can be applied independently to trade receivables, contract assets and lease receivables.

Purchased or originated credit-impaired financial assets

The general approach does not apply to financial assets for which there is evidence of impairment upon purchase or origination. Instead of recognising a separate loss allowance, the expected credit loss would be reflected in a (higher) credit-adjusted effective interest rate. Subsequently, entities would recognise in profit or loss the amount of any change in lifetime expected credit loss as an impairment gain or loss (IFRS 9 paragraphs 5.5.13–14).

Measurement of expected credit losses

Lifetime expected credit losses should be estimated based on the present value of all cash shortfalls over the remaining life of the financial instrument. The 12-month expected credit losses are also based on the present value of cash shortfalls over the remaining life of the financial instruments, but only take into account the shortfalls resulting from possible default events that may occur within the 12 months after the reporting date.

In measuring expected credit losses, entities would, amongst others, need to take into account (IFRS 9 paragraphs 5.5.17–20 and B5.5.28–55):

- The period over which to estimate expected credit losses: entities would consider the maximum contractual period (including extension options). However, for revolving credit facilities (e.g. credit cards and overdrafts), this period extends beyond the contractual period over which the entities are exposed to credit risk and the expected credit losses would not be mitigated by credit risk management actions. This is to be calculated based on historical experience.
- Probability-weighted outcomes: although entities do not need to identify every possible scenario, they will need to take into account the possibility that a credit loss occurs, no matter how low that possibility is. This is not the same as the most likely outcome or a single best estimate.
- Time value of money: for financial assets, the expected credit losses are discounted to the reporting date using the effective interest rate that is determined at initial recognition and may be approximated. For loan commitments and financial guarantee contracts, the effective interest rate of the resulting asset will be applied and if this is not determinable, then the current rate representing the risk of the cash flows is used.
- Reasonable and supportable information: entities need to consider information that is reasonably available at the reporting date about past events, current conditions and forecasts of future economic conditions.

The expected credit loss calculation considers the amount and the timing of payments, which means that a credit loss arises even if an entity expects to be paid in full but later than when those payments are contractually due.

Impairment losses are recognised as follows for the different categories of financial assets:

(a) Debt instruments measured at amortised cost — an entity recognises the loss allowance as expense in profit and loss and reduces the carrying amount of these debt instruments in the statement of financial position.

(b) Debt instruments measured at FVOCI — an entity recognises the loss allowance as expense in profit and loss and reduces the carrying amount of these debt instruments in the statement of financial position. At the next reporting date, the debt instrument is recognised at its fair value in the statement of financial position. Any difference between its fair value and its carrying amount is recognised in OCI.

The impairment rules do not apply to equity instruments designated as measured at FVOCI and they do not apply to debt instruments, derivatives and equity instruments at FVPL.

Illustrative example 13.3 demonstrates the calculation of an impairment loss for a debt instrument measured at amortised cost.

Nurul Bank originates 2000 loans with a total gross carrying amount of €50,000,000. Nurul Bank segments its portfolio into two borrower groups (Groups Bagus and Roti) based on shared credit risk characteristics at initial recognition. Group Bagus comprises 1,000 loans with a gross carrying amount per client of €20,000, for a total gross carrying amount of €20,000,000. Group Roti comprises 1000 loans with a gross carrying amount per client of €30,000, for a total gross carrying amount of €30,000,000. There are no transaction costs and the loan contracts include no options (for example, prepayment or call options), premiums or discounts, points paid, or other fees.

Nurul Bank measures expected credit losses based on a loss rate approach for Groups Bagus and Roti. In order to develop its loss rates, Nurul Bank considers samples of its own historical default and loss experience for those types of loans. In addition, Nurul Bank considers forward-looking information, and updates its historical information for current economic conditions as well as reasonable and supportable forecasts of future economic conditions. Historically, for a population of 1,000 loans in each group, Group Bagus's 12-month expected loss rates are 0.3%, based on four defaults, and historical loss rates for Group Roti are 0.15%, based on two defaults. Nurul concludes the forward-looking information confirms data from historical experience, so used the latter.

Group	Number of clients in sample	Estimated per client gross carrying amount at default	Total estimated gross carrying amount at default	Historic per annum average defaults	Estimated total gross carrying amount at default	Present value of observed loss	Loss rate
	A	B	C = A × B	D	E = B × D	F	G = F ÷ C
Bagus	1,000	€20,000	€20,000,000	4	€80,000	€60,000	0.30%
Roti	1,000	€30,000	€30,000,000	2	€60,000	€45,000	0.15%
			€50,000,000			€105,000	

Nurul Bank would account for the following journal entry when it originates the loans that are measured at amortised cost as follows:

Investment in debt instrument	Dr	49,895,000	
Impairment loss (profit or loss)	Dr	105,000	
Cash	Cr		50,000,000

The expected credit losses should be discounted using the effective interest rate; however, for the purposes of this example, the present value of the observed loss is assumed.

At the reporting date, Nurul Bank expects an increase in defaults over the next 12 months compared to the historical rate. As a result, Nurul Bank estimates five defaults in the next 12 months for loans in Group Bagus and three for loans in Group Roti. It estimates that the present value of the observed credit loss per client will remain consistent with the historical loss per client.

Based on the expected life of the loans, Nurul Bank determines that the expected increase in defaults does not represent a significant increase in credit risk since initial recognition for the portfolios. Based on its forecasts, Nurul Bank measures the loss allowance at an amount equal to 12-month expected credit losses on the 1000 loans in each group amounting to €75,000 and €67,500 respectively. This equates to a loss rate in the first year of 0.375% for Group Bagus and 0.225% for Group Roti.

Group	Number of clients in sample	Estimated per client gross carrying amount at default	Total estimated gross carrying amount at default	Expected defaults	Estimated total gross carrying amount at default	Present value of observed loss	Loss rate
	A	B	C = A × B	D	E = B × D	F	G = F ÷ C

Bagus	1,000	€20,000	€20,000,000	5	€100,000	€75,000	0.375%
Roti	1,000	€30,000	€30,000,000	3	€90,000	€67,500	0.225%
			€50,000,000			€142,500	

Nurul Bank uses the loss rates of 0.375% and 0.225% respectively to estimate 12-month expected credit losses on new loans in Group Bagus and Group Roti originated during the year and for which credit risk has not increased significantly since initial recognition.

Nurul Bank would account for the increase in the 12-month expected credit losses on the debt instruments as follows:

Impairment loss (profit or loss)	Dr	37,500	
Investment in debt instrument	Cr		37,500

Illustrative example 13.4 shows the calculation of an impairment loss on a debt instrument measured at FVOCI.

ILLUSTRATIVE EXAMPLE 13.4 Impairment loss on a debt instrument measured at fair value through other comprehensive income

Branislava Ventures purchases a debt instrument with a fair value of £1,000,000 on 15 December 2026 and measures the debt instrument at FVOCI. The instrument has an interest rate of 5% over the contractual term of 10 years, and has a 5% effective interest rate. At initial recognition Branislava Ventures determines that the asset is not purchased or originated credit-impaired. Branislava Ventures determines that expected credit losses should be measured at an amount equal to 12-month expected credit losses, which amounts to £30,000.

Branislava Ventures would account for the following journal entry to recognise the investment in the debt instrument measured at fair value through other comprehensive income:

Investment in debt instrument	Dr	970,000	
Cash	Cr		1,000,000
Impairment loss (profit or loss)	Dr	30,000	

On 31 December 2026 (the reporting date), the fair value of the debt instrument has decreased to £950,000 because of changes in market interest rates. Branislava Ventures determines that there has not been a significant increase in credit risk since initial recognition and that expected credit losses should be measured at an amount equal to 12-month expected credit losses, which still amounts to £30,000. For simplicity, journal entries for the receipt of interest revenue are not provided.

Branislava Ventures would account for the difference between carrying amount (970,000) and fair value (950,000) of the debt instrument as follows:

Other comprehensive income	Dr	20,000	
Investment in debt instrument	Cr		20,000

Disclosure would be provided about the accumulated impairment amount of £30,000.

On 1 January 2027, Branislava Ventures decides to sell the debt instrument for £950,000, which is its fair value at that date. Branislava Ventures would derecognise the fair value through other comprehensive income asset and recycle amounts accumulated in other comprehensive income to profit or loss (i.e. £20,000) as follows:

Cash	Dr	950,000	
Investment in debt instrument	Cr		950,000
Loss (profit or loss)	Dr	20,000	
Other comprehensive income	Cr		20,000

The disclosure requirements are addressed *in section 13.15*. An illustration of how the Mercedes-Benz Group discloses movements between the various stages as well as the interaction with due date of its receivables from financial services is presented in figure 13.8.

FIGURE 13.8 Loss allowance and credit risk on receivables

Development of loss allowances for receivables from financial services due to expected credit losses

In millions of euros	12-month expected credit loss (Stage 1)		Not credit impaired (Stage 2)		Credit impaired (Stage 3)		Total	
	2023	2022	2023	2022	2023	2022	2023	2022
Balance at 1 January	**364**	339	**170**	142	**664**	556	**1198**	1,037
Additions	**141**	158	**48**	39	**123**	215	**312**	412
Remeasurement changes	**-23**	39	**115**	89	**216**	330	**308**	458
Utilization	**-4**	-2	**-19**	-14	**-107**	-104	**-130**	-120
Reversals	**-177**	-174	**-72**	-58	**-226**	-250	**-475**	-482
Transfer to stage 1	**56**	61	**-42**	-41	**-14**	-20	-	-
Transfer to stage 2	**-27**	-25	**88**	41	**-61**	-16	-	-
Transfer to stage 3	**-3**	-5	**-33**	-25	**36**	30	-	-
Exchange-rate effects and other changes	**2**	-27	**-15**	-3	**-145**	-77	**-158**	-107
Balance at 31 December	**329**	364	**240**	170	**486**	664	**1,055**	1,198

Credit risks included in receivables from financial services

In millions of euros	12-month expected credit loss (Stage 1)		Not credit impaired (Stage 2)		Credit impaired (Stage 3)		Total	
	2023	2022	2023	2022	2023	2022	2023	2022
Gross carrying amount at 31 December	**80,879**	80,852	**7,109**	4,277	**1,278**	1,618	**89,266**	86,747
thereof								
not past due	**80,071**	80,192	**5,442**	3,061	**254**	268	**85,767**	83,521
past due 30 days and less	**806**	631	**658**	537	**52**	239	**1,516**	1,407
past due 31 to 60 days	**2**	20	**704**	464	**50**	46	**756**	530
past due 61 to 90 days	**-**	9	**305**	215	**60**	42	**365**	266
past due 91 to 180 days	**-**	-	**-**	-	**335**	425	**335**	425
past due more than 180 days	**-**	-	**-**	-	**527**	598	**527**	598

Source: Mercedes-Benz Group, Annual Report (2023, Note 14, pp. 251–252).

Summary of the measurement rules of IFRS 9

Table 13.5 summarises the measurement rules of IFRS 9 *discussed earlier in this section.*

Table 13.5 Summary of the measurement rules in IFRS 9

Category of financial asset/liability	Initial measurement	Subsequent measurement	Reclassifications	Gains and losses	Impairment
Debt instruments measured at amortised cost	Fair value plus transaction costs	Amortised cost	Only when an entity changes its business model	Recognised in profit or loss	Changes in the expected credit loss allowance recognised in profit or loss
Debt instruments at fair value through other comprehensive income (FVOCI)	Fair value plus transaction costs	Fair value	Only when an entity changes its business model	Recognised in other comprehensive income, but recycled to profit or loss upon derecognition	Changes in the expected credit loss allowance recognised in profit or loss with offset in other comprehensive income
Equity instruments designated as measured at FVOCI	Fair value plus transaction costs	Fair value	Not permitted	Recognised in other comprehensive income without recycling to profit or loss	Not applicable
Debt instruments, derivatives and equity instruments at fair value through profit or loss (FVPL)	Fair value	Fair value	Debt instruments: only when an entity changes its business model Other instruments: not permitted	Recognised in profit or loss, unless a hedging instrument	Not applicable
Financial liabilities designated at FVPL	Fair value	Fair value	Not permitted	Recognised in profit or loss except for the effect of own credit which is recognised in other comprehensive income	Not applicable
Other financial liabilities at FVPL	Fair value	Fair value	Not permitted	Recognised in profit or loss, unless a hedging instrument	Not applicable
Financial liabilities at amortised cost	Fair value less transaction costs	Amortised cost	Not permitted	Recognised in profit or loss	Not applicable

13.12 FINANCIAL ASSETS AND FINANCIAL LIABILITIES: OFFSETTING

Often two entities may have both financial assets and financial liabilities in relation to each other. For example, a customer may have returned some goods to a supplier and expects repayment (financial asset) from the supplier while at the same time receiving invoices for new deliveries from the same supplier (financial liability). Or an entity may have multiple accounts with the same bank, some of which may have a debit balance (financial asset) while others may have a credit balance (financial liability). In those cases the question arises whether those financial assets and financial liabilities can be presented net (offset). This of course may be relevant for important key ratios such as solvency and liquidity ratios.

Paragraph 42 of IAS 32 states that a financial asset and a financial liability shall be offset and the net amount presented when, and only when, an entity:

(a) currently has a legally enforceable right to set off the recognised amounts; and
(b) intends either to settle on a net basis, or to realise the asset and settle the liability simultaneously.

The underlying rationale of this requirement is that when an entity has the right to receive or pay a single net amount and intends to do so, it has effectively only a single financial asset or financial liability.

Note that the right of set-off must be legally enforceable and therefore usually stems from a written contract between two parties. In rare cases, there may be an agreement between three parties allowing a debtor to apply an amount due from a third party against the amount due to a creditor. Assume, for example, that Company A owes Company B £1000, and Company Z owes Company A £1000. Company A has therefore recorded in its books the following:

| Amount Receivable from Company Z | Dr | 1,000 | |
| Amount Owing to Company B | Cr | | 1,000 |

Provided there is a legal right of set-off allowing Company A to offset the amount owing to Company B against the amount owed by Company Z, the amounts may be offset in Company A's accounts. Both Company B and Company Z must be parties to this legal right of set-off with Company A.

The conditions for offsetting are strict and essentially require written legal contracts resulting in net cash settlement. Many arrangements that create 'synthetic' (manufactured) offsetting do not result in offsetting under IAS 32, which also provides examples of common cases where offsetting is not permitted.

13.13 HEDGE ACCOUNTING

Entities enter into hedge arrangements for economic reasons; namely, to protect themselves from the types of risks *discussed in section 13.14* — currency risk, interest rate risk, other price risk and so on. Entities often enter into derivative and other contracts to manage these risk exposures. Hedging can be seen, therefore, as a risk management activity that changes an entity's risk profile. However, application of the normal IFRS® Standards accounting requirements to those risk management activities often results in accounting mismatches, when the gains or losses on a hedging instrument and hedged items are not recognised in the same period. The idea of hedge accounting is to reduce this mismatch in profit or loss by changing either the measurement or recognition of the hedged exposure, or the accounting for the hedging instrument.

Although the basic idea is simple, the development of hedge accounting standards raises difficult questions about when hedge accounting is more appropriate than the normal IFRS Standards accounting. In practice, this meant that some of the requirements in IAS 39 were arguably arbitrary and did not allow hedge accounting for certain risk management activities that are commonly applied by entities. Consequently, many entities would report 'accounting' hedges in their financial statements that did not correspond to the hedges that were entered into for risk management purposes, which was unhelpful for preparers and users alike.

The objective of the hedge accounting requirements in IFRS 9 is to present in the financial statements the effect of an entity's risk management activities. That is, hedge accounting under IFRS 9 is intended to align the accounting more closely to risk management. While the hedge accounting rules in IFRS 9 are less restrictive than those in IAS 39, the fact remains that hedge accounting is only permitted if all the qualifying criteria are met *(see section 13.13.3)*. Consequently, an entity would not apply hedge accounting to risk management activities that either do not meet the qualifying criteria or that are not designated by the entity as accounting hedges. In other words, even if the qualifying criteria are met, the entity is not required to apply hedge accounting. Hedge accounting is allowed if the qualifying criteria are met and the entity chooses to do so, by designating the specific hedge and only from the designation date. A number of important concepts need to be understood:

1. the hedging instrument
2. the hedged item
3. the conditions for hedge accounting and the three types of hedges
4. the hedge ratio, rebalancing and discontinuation.

13.13.1 The hedging instrument

A financial instrument must meet the following essential criteria for it to be classified as a hedging instrument:

1. It must be designated as such. This means that management must document the details of the hedging instrument and the item it is hedging, at the inception of the hedge.
2. It must be a derivative. Non-derivative financial assets or non-derivative financial liabilities can only be a hedging instrument if they are measured at FVPL, or are hedging foreign currency exchange risk to be designated as a hedging instrument. However, financial liabilities for which changes in the credit risk are presented in other comprehensive income cannot be a hedging instrument. Also, written options cannot be hedging instruments of the writer, unless they are designated as a hedge of a purchased option.
3. At the inception of the hedging relationship, there is formal designation and documentation of the hedging relationship and the entity's risk management objective and strategy for undertaking the hedge.
4. It must be with a party external to the reporting entity — external to the consolidated group or individual entity being reported on.
5. It cannot be split into component parts, except for separating the time value and intrinsic value in an option contract, and the interest element and spot price in a forward contract. However, the hedged item may be a combination of (portions of) derivatives or non-derivatives.
6. A proportion of the entire hedging instrument, such as 50% of the notional amount, may be designated as the hedging instrument. However, a hedging relationship may not be designated for only a portion of the period during which the hedging instrument remains outstanding.
7. A single hedging instrument in its entirety may be designated as a hedging instrument of more than one type of risk, if there is a specific designation of the hedging instrument and of the different risk positions as hedged items. Those hedged items can be in different hedging relationships.

IFRS 9 contains further detailed guidance, which is not discussed here in detail, that must be complied with and that further restricts which financial instruments can be treated as hedging instrument.

Examples of hedging instruments commonly used are forward foreign currency exchange contracts, interest rate swaps, futures contracts and loans in a foreign currency.

13.13.2 The hedged item

IFRS 9 defines the following terms:

- A *hedged item* can be a recognised asset or liability, an unrecognised firm commitment, a highly probable forecast transaction or a net investment in a foreign operation.
- A *forecast transaction* is an uncommitted but anticipated future transaction (e.g. expected future sales or purchases).
- A *firm commitment* is a binding agreement for the exchange of a specified quantity of resources at a specified price on a specified future date or dates (e.g. a purchase order to buy a machine for $50,000 in 3 months' time).

A hedged item:

1. can be a single item, a group of items or a component of such item(s)
2. can be a combination of a derivative with a hedged item as described above
3. must be reliably measurable
4. must arise from a transaction with a party external to the reporting entity (i.e. an entity that is not consolidated by the reporting entity), subject to certain exceptions regarding intragroup foreign currency balances
5. can be a risk component of financial item (e.g. only the interest or currency risk on a bond) or a risk component of a non-financial item (e.g. fuel price component in an electricity purchase contract), subject to certain conditions
6. can be a net nil position (i.e. on a group basis the hedged items themselves offset the risk being managed), subject to certain conditions
7. can be a 'layer' of an overall group of items (e.g. the bottom €60 million of a €100 million fixed rate loan), subject to certain conditions.

IFRS 9 contains further detailed requirements, which are not discussed here specifically, that restrict which exposures can be treated as hedged items.

13.13.3 The conditions for hedge accounting and the three types of hedges

Hedge accounting recognises the offsetting effects on profit or loss of changes in the fair values of the hedging instrument and the hedged item. Paragraph 6.4.1 of IFRS 9 sets out the following conditions that must be met in order for hedge accounting to be applied:

1. At the inception of the hedge, there must be formal designation and documentation of the hedging relationship and the entity's risk-management objective and strategy for undertaking the hedge. That documentation must include identification of:
   - the hedging instrument
   - the hedged item
   - the nature of the risk being hedged
   - how the entity will assess hedge effectiveness.
2. The hedging relationship consists only of eligible hedging instruments and eligible hedged items *as described in sections 13.13.1 and 13.13.2.*
3. The hedging relationship should meet the following hedge effectiveness requirements:
   (a) there is an economic relationship between the hedged item and the hedging instrument
   (b) credit risk does not dominate the value changes that result from that economic relationship
   (c) the hedge ratio of the hedging relationship is the same as that resulting from the quantity of the hedged item that the entity actually hedges and the quantity of the hedging instrument that the entity actually uses to hedge that quantity of hedged item.

   The three types of hedging relationships are:
- fair value hedge.
- cash flow hedge.
- hedge of a net investment in a foreign operation as defined in IAS 21. This is accounted for in a similar manner to cash flow hedges, but will not be discussed further in this chapter.

   Note the following points:
- A fair value hedge is a hedge of the exposure to changes in fair value of an asset, liability or unrecognised firm commitment.
- A cash flow hedge is a hedge of the exposure to variability in cash flows of a recognised asset or liability, or a highly probable forecast transaction.
- Paragraph 6.5.4 of IFRS 9 states that a hedge of the foreign currency risk of a firm commitment may be accounted for as either a fair value hedge or a cash flow hedge.
- A simple way of remembering the difference between the two types of hedge is that a cash flow hedge locks in future cash flows, whereas a fair value hedge does not.
- The most commonly occurring hedge transactions for average reporting entities are interest rate hedges and foreign currency hedges.

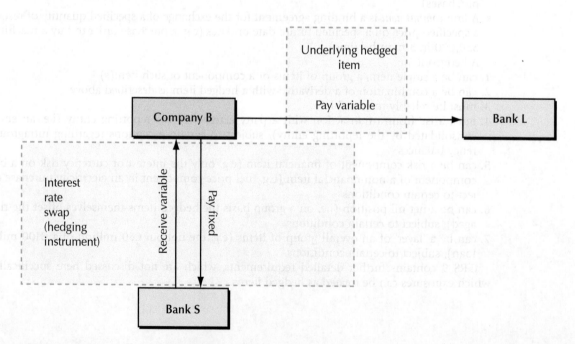

FIGURE 13.9 A simple cash flow hedge

As an example of a simple cash flow hedge, assume that Company B has a borrowing with lender Bank L that carries a variable rate of interest. Company B is worried about its exposure to future increases in the variable rate of interest and decides to enter into an interest rate swap with Bank S. The borrowing is the hedged item, and the risk being hedged is interest rate risk. Under the interest rate swap, Bank S pays Company B the variable interest rate, and Company B pays Bank S a specified fixed interest rate. The interest rate swap is the hedging instrument. The net cash flows for Company B are its payments of a fixed interest rate, so it has locked in its cash flows. This is therefore a cash flow hedge, assuming all the required criteria of IFRS 9 are met. Figure 13.9 illustrates this example of a simple cash flow hedge.

There is no exchange of principal in an interest rate swap — the cash flows are simply calculated using the principal as the basis for the calculation. For the example illustrated in figure 13.9, assume that the hedged item is a borrowing of $100,000 with a variable interest rate, currently 5%. The fixed rate under the interest rate swap is 6%. For the relevant period, Company B will pay Bank L $100,000 × 5% = $5,000. Under the swap, Company B will pay a net $1,000 (receive $100,000 × 5% and pay $100,000 × 6%) to bank S. Thus, Company B's net cash outflow is $5,000 + $1,000 = $6,000, which is the fixed rate. Note that Bank L is not a party to the swap — it continues to receive payments from Company B under its borrowing arrangement. Company B has locked in its cash flows at $6,000, and has certainty that this is what it will pay over the term of the swap. Currently the cash flows are higher than what it would pay under a variable rate, but Company B has entered into the swap in the expectation that the variable rate will rise.

Table 13.6 sets out the main requirements for fair value hedges and cash flow hedges.

Table 13.6 Summary of the main requirements of IFRS 9 for fair value hedges and cash flow hedges

	Fair value hedge	Cash flow hedge
Hedged item	Fair value exposures in a recognised asset or liability or unrecognised firm commitment	Cash flow variability exposures in a recognised asset or liability or highly probable forecast transaction
Gain or loss on hedging instrument	Recognised immediately in profit or loss. If hedging an equity instrument at fair value through other comprehensive income then recognise in other comprehensive income	Effective portion recognised directly in other comprehensive income. Ineffective portion recognised immediately in profit or loss
Gain or loss on hedged item	Generally, adjust hedged item for the effective portion of the value changes of the hedging instrument and recognise in profit or loss. This applies even if the hedged item is otherwise measured at cost However, if the hedged item is an equity instrument at fair value through other comprehensive income then recognise entire gain or loss on hedged risk in other comprehensive income	Not applicable because the exposure being hedged is future cash flows that are not recognised
Hedge ineffectiveness is recorded in profit or loss	Automatically, since the entire gain or loss on the hedging instrument is recorded in profit or loss	Must be calculated and separated from the amount recorded in other comprehensive income
Timing of recycling of hedge gains/losses in equity to profit or loss	Not applicable	Hedge of a forecast transaction that subsequently results in the recognition of a *financial* asset or financial liability: during the periods in which said asset/liability affects profit or loss, e.g. when the interest income or expense is recognised Hedge of a forecast transaction that subsequently results in the recognition of a *non-financial* asset or non-financial liability: include immediately in the initial cost of said asset/ liability Immediate recycling if hedge accounting is discontinued, unless future cashflows still expected to occur

A simple fair value hedge is demonstrated in illustrative example 13.5.

ILLUSTRATIVE EXAMPLE 13.5 A simple fair value hedge

Onur Holding has an investment in a debt instrument classified as at FVOCI. The cost of the investment on 1 September 2026 was $250,000. On 1 September 2026, Onur Holding enters into a derivative futures contract to hedge the fair value of the investment. All the conditions for hedge accounting are met, and the hedge qualifies as a fair value hedge because it is a hedge of an exposure to changes in the fair value of a recognised asset. At the next reporting date, 30 September 2026, the fair value of the investment (hedged item) was $230,000, based on quoted market bid prices. The fair value of the derivative (hedging instrument) at that date was $18,000. Onur Holding would record the journal entries shown below.

On initial recognition of the investment 1 September 2026:

Debt instrument at fair value through other comprehensive income	Dr	250,000	
Cash	Cr		250,000

On entering into the futures contract 1 September 2026:
No entries because the net fair value of the futures contract is zero.
On remeasurement at 30 September 2026:

Expense (profit or loss)	Dr	20,000	
Debt instrument at fair value through other comprehensive income	Cr		20,000
Futures Contract	Dr	18,000	
Income (profit or loss)	Cr		18,000

The hedge continues to meet the criteria in IFRS 9, so the hedge accounting may continue. The net effect of the hedge is that Onur Holding records a net loss in profit or loss of $2,000. The ineffective portion of the hedge ($2,000) is recorded automatically in profit or loss. Note that the decline in fair value of the debt instrument at fair value through other comprehensive income is recorded in profit or loss, even though the normal accounting for such investments is to recognise fair value changes directly in equity. This exception is made specifically for hedge accounting, to enable the matching effect of the hedging instrument with the hedged item in profit or loss to occur.

A cash flow hedge of a firm commitment is demonstrated in illustrative example 13.6.

ILLUSTRATIVE EXAMPLE 13.6 Cash flow hedge of a firm commitment

On 30 June 2026, King Kong enters into a forward exchange contract to receive foreign currency (FC) of 100,000 and deliver local currency (LC) of 109,600 on 30 June 2027. It designates the forward exchange contract as a hedging instrument in a cash flow hedge of a firm commitment to purchase a specified quantity of paper on 30 June 2027, and pay the same day. All hedge accounting conditions in IFRS 9 are met.

Note that a hedge of foreign currency risk in a firm commitment may be either a cash flow hedge or a fair value hedge. King Kong has elected to account for it as a cash flow hedge. Under IFRS 9, King Kong is required to adjust the cost of non-financial items acquired as a result of hedged forecast transactions.

The following table sets out the spot rate, forward rate and fair value of the forward contract at relevant dates.

Date	Spot rate	Forward rate to 30 June 2027	Fair value of forward contract
30 June 2026	1.072	1.096	—
31 December 2026	1.080	1.092	(388)[1]
30 June 2027	1.074	—	(2200)

1. This can be calculated if the applicable yield curve in the local currency is known. Assuming the rate is 6%, the fair value is calculated as follows: ([1.092 × 100,000] − 109,600)/1.06(6/12).

Journal entries are shown below:
At 30 June 2026:

Forward Contract	Dr	LC0		
Cash	Cr			LC0
(Initial recognition of forward contract)				

No entries because on initial recognition, the forward contract has a fair value of zero.
At 31 December 2026:

Other comprehensive income	Dr	LC388		
Forward Contract (liability)	Cr			LC388
(Recording the change in the fair value of the forward contract). The hedge is still considered to be 100% effective)				

At 30 June 2027:

Other comprehensive income	Dr	LC1,812		
Forward Contract (liability)	Cr			LC1,812
(Recording the change in the fair value of the forward contract)				
Paper (purchase price)	Dr	LC107,400		
Paper (hedging loss)	Dr	LC2,200		
Other comprehensive income	Cr			LC2,200
Payable	Cr			LC107,400

The last entry recognises the purchase of the paper at the spot rate (1.074 × FC100,000), and removes the cumulative loss that has been recognised in equity and includes it in the initial measurement of the purchased paper. The paper is thus recognised effectively at the forward rate (LC1,074,000 + 2,200 = LC 1,096,000 is the same as FC 100,000 × 1.096), and the hedge has been 100% effective.

If this transaction had been designated as a fair value hedge from the outset, then the entries recorded in equity for the cash flow hedge would instead be recorded as an asset or liability. IFRS 9 would then require the initial carrying amount of the asset acquired to be adjusted for the cumulative amount recognised in the statement of financial position. The adjusted journal entries would be as follows:

At 31 December 2026:

Asset	Dr	LC388		
Forward Contract (liability)	Cr			LC388
(Recording change in fair value of forward contract)				
At 30 June 2027				
Asset	Dr	LC1,812		
Forward Contract (liability)	Cr			LC1,812
(Recording change in fair value of forward contract)				
Paper (purchase price)	Dr	LC107,400		
Paper (hedging loss)	Dr	LC2,200		
Asset	Cr			LC2,200
Payable	Cr			LC107,400
(Recording purchase of paper and transferring cumulative amount recognised as an asset to the cost of the paper)				

Please note in illustrative example 13.6 that in a fully effective fair value hedge the hedged risk does not affect profit or loss, OCI or equity. However, in a fully effective cash flow hedge there is no impact on profit or loss, but since the effective portion of the hedge is recognised in OCI, there is still volatility in OCI and equity.

International Airline Group (IAG), parent company of airlines including British Airways and Iberia, hedges fuel price risk, foreign currency risk and interest rate risk. It applies fair value hedge accounting and cash flow hedge accounting. Figure 13.10 contains extracts from the notes containing the accounting policy for cash flow hedges in note 2 as well as the hedging of fuel price risk in note 29 sub a on financial risk management objectives and policies.

FIGURE 13.10 Cash flow hedge on fuel price risk

d   Cash flow hedges

Changes in the fair value of derivative financial instruments designated as in a cash flow hedge relationship of a highly probable expected future transaction are assessed for effectiveness and accordingly recorded in the Cash flow hedge reserve within equity.

Hedge effectiveness

Hedge effectiveness is determined at the inception of the hedge relationship, and through periodic prospective effectiveness assessments, to ensure that an economic relationship exists between the hedged item and hedging instrument. A hedging relationship qualifies for hedge accounting if it meets all of the following effectiveness requirements: (i) there is 'an economic relationship' between the hedged item and the hedging instrument; (ii) the effect of credit risk does not dominate the value changes that result from that economic relationship; and (iii) the hedge ratio is aligned with the requirements of the Group's risk management strategy and in all instances is maintained at a ratio of 1:1.

The Group assesses whether the derivative designated as the hedging instrument in a hedge relationship is expected to be on inception and at each reporting date effective in offsetting the changes in cash flows of the hedged item using the hypothetical derivative model.

Sources of ineffectiveness include the following:
- in hedges of fuel purchases, ineffectiveness may arise if the timing of the forecast transaction changes from what was originally estimated, or if there are changes in the credit risk of the Group or the derivative counterparty;
- in hedges of foreign currency purchases, ineffectiveness may arise if the timing of the forecast transaction changes from what was originally estimated, or if there are changes in the credit risk of the Group or the derivative counterparty;
- in hedges of interest rate payments, ineffectiveness may arise if there are differences in the critical terms between the interest rate derivative instrument and the underlying hedged item, or if there are changes in the credit risk of the Group or the derivative counterparty; and
- in all hedges, ineffectiveness may arise if there are differences between the critical terms of the hedging instrument and the hypothetical derivative, such as where on inception of the hedge relationship the fair value of the hedging instrument is not zero.

Ineffectiveness is recorded within the Income statement as Realised/unrealised (losses)/gains on derivatives not qualifying for hedge accounting and presented within Other non-operating credits.

Reclassification and transfer adjustments

Gains and losses accumulated in the Cash flow hedge reserve within equity are either reclassified from the Cash flow hedge reserve when the hedged item affects the Income statement, or transferred from the Cash flow hedge reserve when the hedged item gives rise to recognition in the Balance sheet as follows:
- where the forecast hedged item results in the recognition of expenses within the Income statement (such as the purchase of jet fuel for which both fuel and the associated foreign currency derivatives are designated as the hedging instrument), the accumulated gains and losses recorded in both the Cash flow hedge reserve and the Cost of hedging reserve are reclassified and included in the Income statement within the same caption as the hedged item is presented. Such reclassification occurs in the same period as the hedged item is recognised in the Income statement;
- where the forecast hedged item results in the recognition of a non-financial asset (such as the purchase of aircraft for which foreign currency derivatives are designated as the hedging instrument or where the purchase of jet fuel gives rise to the recognition of fuel inventory in storage facilities), or a non-financial liability (such as the sales in advance of carriage for which both foreign currency derivatives and non-financial derivative instruments are designated as the hedging instrument), the accumulated gains and losses recorded within both the Cash flow hedge reserve and the Cost of hedging reserve are transferred and included in the initial cost of the asset and liability, respectively. These gains or losses are recorded in the Income statement as the non-financial asset and the non-financial liability affects the Income statement (which for aircraft is through Depreciation, amortisation and impairment over the expected life of the aircraft, for fuel inventory through Fuel, oil costs and emission charges when it is consumed and for sales in advance of carriage through Passenger revenue when the flight is flown); and

- where the forecast hedged item results in the recognition of a financial asset or liability (such as variable rate debt for which interest rate swaps are designated as the hedging instrument), the accumulated gains and losses recorded within the Cash flow hedge reserve are reclassified to the Income statement to Interest expense within Finance costs at the same time as the interest income or expense arises on the hedged item.

a Fuel price risk

The Group is exposed to fuel price risk. In order to mitigate such risk, under the Group's fuel price risk management strategy a variety of over the counter derivative instruments are entered into. The Group strategy is to hedge a proportion of fuel consumption up to two years within the approved hedging profile.

The following table demonstrates the sensitivity of the Group's principal exposure to a reasonable possible change in the fuel price, based on current market volatility, with all other variables held constant on the profit before tax and equity[1]. The sensitivity analysis has been performed on fuel derivatives (both those designated in hedge relationships and those not designated in hedge relationships) at the reporting date only and is not reflective of the impact had the sensitised rates been applied through the duration of the years to 31 December 2023 and 2022.

2023			2022		
Increase/ (decrease) in fuel price per cent	Effect on profit before tax € million	Effect on equity € million	Increase/ (decrease) in fuel price per cent	Effect on profit before tax € million	Effect on equity € million
40	-	1,497	45	-	1,402
(40)	-	(1,526)	(45)	-	(1,200)

1 The sensitivity analysis on equity excludes the sensitivity amounts recognised in the profit before tax.

Source: International Airlines Group, Annual Report and Accounts (2023, notes 2 and 29 sub a, pp. 224 and 262).

13.13.4 Hedge ratio, rebalancing and discontinuation

IFRS 9 does not require a retrospective quantitative effectiveness assessment (i.e. was the hedge effective in the past?), but that does not mean that hedge accounting continues regardless of how effective a hedge is. A prospective effectiveness assessment is still required, in a similar manner as at the inception of the hedging relationship and on an ongoing basis, as a minimum at each reporting date. This process involves the steps shown in figure 13.11.

An entity first has to assess whether the risk management objective for the hedging relationship has changed. A change in risk management objective is a matter of fact that triggers discontinuation of the hedge relationship. Accordingly, a hedge relationship cannot be de-designated without an underlying change in risk management. An entity would also have to discontinue hedge accounting if the hedging instrument or hedged item was sold because in that case there would not be a hedge to account for. The same is true for the impact of credit risk; if credit risk is now dominating the hedging relationship, then the entity has to discontinue hedge accounting.

When an entity discontinues hedge accounting for a cash flow hedge the amount deferred in OCI:
- must be reclassified to profit or loss immediately, unless
- the hedged future cash flows are still expected to occur in which case the amounts stay in OCI (cash flow hedge reserve) until the cash flows occur.

The hedge ratio is the ratio between the amount of hedged item and the amount of hedging instrument. For many hedging relationships, the hedge ratio would be 1 : 1 as the underlying of the hedging instrument perfectly matches the designated hedged risk.

If the hedge ratio has been adjusted for risk management purposes or if it turns out that the hedged item and hedging instrument do not move in relation to each other as expected (i.e. there is an imbalance in the hedge ratio) then the hedge ratio may need to be adjusted to reflect this. In that case, the entity has to assess whether it expects this to continue to be the case going forward. If so, the entity is likely to rebalance the hedge ratio to reflect the change in the relationship between the underlying items.

Rebalancing can be achieved by increasing or decreasing the volume of the hedged item, or increasing or decreasing the volume of the hedging instrument. Rebalancing under IFRS 9 allows entities to refine their hedge ratio without having to account for a discontinuation of the entire hedge relationship, but it may result in a partial discontinuation if the hedged volume is reduced.

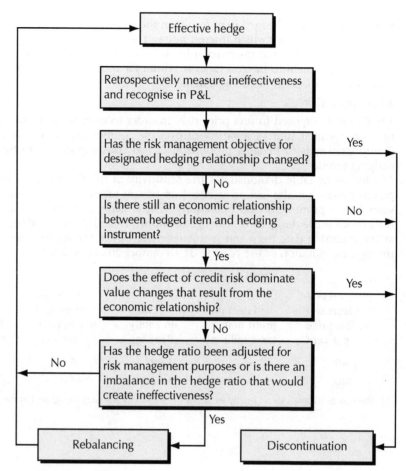

FIGURE 13.11 Effectiveness assessment and rebalancing

13.13.5 **Alternatives to hedge accounting**

IFRS 9 offers two important alternatives to hedge accounting. The first alternative is that IFRS 9 extends the FVPL option to contracts that meet the 'own use' scope exception (*see section 13.7.1*) if this eliminates or significantly reduces an accounting mismatch. In other words, by measuring 'own use' contracts at fair value, it would be possible to reduce the measurement mismatch with derivatives and other financial instruments that are also measured at fair value. This would alleviate the need for hedge accounting.

The second alternative applies to the many financial institutions that hedge the credit risk arising from loans or loan commitments using credit default swaps. This would often result in an accounting mismatch, as loans and loan commitments are typically not accounted for at FVPL, but the credit default swaps are. The simplest accounting would be to designate the credit risk as a risk component in a hedging relationship. However, the IASB noted that due to the difficulty in isolating the credit risk as a separate risk it does not meet the eligibility criteria for risk components. As a result, the accounting mismatch creates profit or loss volatility.

Under IFRS 9, an entity undertaking economic credit risk hedging may elect to account for a debt instrument (such as a loan or a bond), a loan commitment or a financial guarantee contract, at FVPL. This election can only be made if the asset referenced by the credit derivative has the same issuer and subordination as the hedged exposure (i.e. both the issuer's name and seniority of the exposure match). The accounting for the credit derivative would not change, i.e. it would continue to be accounted at FVPL. Consequently, even though it is not equivalent to fair value hedge accounting, this accounting does address several concerns of entities that use credit default swaps for hedging credit exposures.

13.14 **DISCLOSURES**

IFRS 7 contains many pages dealing with disclosures, but only relatively few 'black letter' requirements. This chapter does not address these requirements in detail, and readers are expected to have a general understanding of the requirements only.

The purpose of the disclosure requirements is to provide information to enhance understanding of the significance of financial instruments to an entity's financial position, performance and cash flows; and to assist in assessing the amounts, timing and certainty of future cash flows associated with those instruments.

Transactions in financial instruments may result in an entity assuming or transferring to another party one or more of the financial risks described in table 13.7. The purpose of the required disclosures is to assist users in assessing the extent of such risks related to financial instruments.

Table 13.7 Financial risks pertaining to financial instruments	
Type of risk	Description
Credit risk	The risk that one party to a financial instrument will fail to discharge an obligation and cause the other party to incur a financial loss.
Liquidity risk	The risk that an entity will encounter difficulty in meeting obligations associated with financial liabilities. This is also known as funding risk. For example, as a financial liability approaches its redemption date, the issuer may experience liquidity risk if its available financial assets are insufficient to meet its obligations.
Market risk	• *Currency risk* — the risk that the value of a financial instrument will fluctuate because of changes in foreign exchange rates. • *Interest rate risk* — the risk that the value of a financial instrument will fluctuate because of changes in market interest rates. For example, the issuer of a financial liability that carries a fixed rate of interest is exposed to decreases in market interest rates, such that the issuer of the liability is paying a higher rate of interest than the market rate. • *Other price risk* — the risk that the value of a financial instrument will fluctuate as a result of changes in market prices (other than those arising from interest rate risk or currency risk).

IFRS 7 applies to all entities for all types of financial instruments, other than those specifically excluded from its scope. Scope exclusions include:
• interest in subsidiaries, associates and joint ventures accounted for under IFRS 10, IAS 27, or IAS 28
• employers' rights and obligations arising from employee benefit plans, to which IAS 19 *Employee Benefits* applies
• insurance contracts as defined in IFRS 17 *Insurance Contracts*
• share-based payment transactions to which IFRS 2 *Share-based Payment* applies.

IFRS 7 applies to both recognised and unrecognised financial instruments. For example, loan commitments not within the scope of IFRS 9 are within the scope of IFRS 7.

IFRS 7 requires disclosure of financial instruments grouped by class. A class of financial instrument is a lower level of aggregation than a category, such as 'available-for-sale' or 'loans and receivables' *(see section 13.9)*. For example, government debt securities, equity securities, or asset-backed securities could all be considered classes of financial instruments.

IFRS 7 is divided into three main sections. The first section requires disclosure of the significance of financial instruments for financial position and performance. These disclosures are grouped into:
1. statement of financial position
2. statement of comprehensive income
3. other disclosures.

The second section requires disclosure about the nature and extent of risks arising from financial instruments. These include both quantitative and qualitative disclosures. The risks are grouped into the three categories noted above, that is, market risk, credit risk and liquidity risk. These risk disclosures shall be given either in the financial statements or incorporated by cross-reference from the financial statements to some other statement, such as a management commentary or risk report.

The third section requires disclosure about financial assets transferred to another entity.

Examples of the types of disclosures required in each of the sections are provided in tables 13.8 and 13.9.

Table 13.8 Significance of financial instruments for financial position and performance

Statement of financial position

Overall requirement	Summary of details required
Categories of financial assets and financial liabilities (paragraph 8)	• The carrying amount of specified categories, as defined in IFRS 9, for example, financial assets measured at fair value through profit or loss and financial assets measured at amortised cost.
Financial assets or financial liabilities at fair value through profit or loss (paragraphs 9, 10, 10A and 11)	• An entity that designates a *financial asset* as measured at fair value through profit or loss should disclose specified details including the maximum exposure to credit risk, the amount by which credit derivatives mitigate that exposure, the amount of fair value changes attributable to changes in credit risk and the change in the fair value of any credit derivative or similar instruments.
	• An entity that designates a *financial liability* at fair value through profit or loss should disclose specified details including the change in fair value that is attributable to changes in the credit risk, and the difference between the carrying amount of the liability and the amount the entity would be contractually required to pay at maturity.
Investments in equity instruments designated at fair value through other comprehensive income (paragraphs 11A and 11B)	• An entity that designates investments in equity instruments to be measured at fair value through other comprehensive income should disclose specified details including which investments have been designated and the reason for doing so, fair value of each investment, the related dividends received, and the cumulative gain or loss upon and reason for any disposal of such investments.
Reclassification (paragraph 12B, 12C and 12D)	• Disclosure is required of the circumstances around any change in business model that lead to a reclassification of financial assets and information about the financial performance of those reclassified assets after the reclassification.
Offsetting financial assets and financial liabilities (paragraphs 13A to 13F)	• Specified disclosures are required for all recognised financial instruments that are set off in accordance with IAS 32, such that users of the financial statements can assess the (potential) effect of netting arrangements on the entity's financial position.
Collateral (paragraphs 14 and 15)	• Collateral given: an entity must disclose the carrying amount of financial assets it has pledged as collateral (security) for liabilities or contingent liabilities. The terms and conditions of the pledge must also be disclosed.
	• Collateral received: specified details must be disclosed where an entity holds collateral (of financial and non-financial assets) and is permitted to sell or repledge that collateral.
Allowance for credit losses (paragraph 16A)	• The loss allowance related to financial assets measured at fair value through other comprehensive income should be disclosed.
Compound financial instruments with multiple embedded derivatives (paragraph 17)	• Disclosure is required of the existence of such features in compound financial instruments.
Defaults and breaches (paragraphs 18 and 19)	• For loans payable, disclosure is required of any defaults during the period, the carrying amount of loans payable in default at the end of the reporting period and whether the default was remedied before the financial statements were authorised for issue.

Table 13.8 *(continued)*

Statement of other comprehensive income

Items of income, expense, gains or losses (paragraphs 20 and 20A)	• Net gains or losses for each category of financial asset and financial liability. • Total interest income and total interest expense for financial assets or liabilities that are not at fair value through profit or loss. • Fee income and expense arising from financial assets or liabilities not at fair value through profit or loss, and from trust and other fiduciary activities. • Analysis of gains and of losses recognised in the statement of comprehensive income that resulted from the derecognition of financial assets measured at amortised cost.

Table 13.9 Significance of financial instruments for other disclosures

Other disclosures

Overall requirement	Summary of details required
Accounting policies (paragraph 21)	• Disclose relevant accounting policies. Where the accounting methods are prescribed in the relevant standards (e.g. in IFRS 9) then the entity should not repeat these but rather disclose where it has applied choices available.

Hedge accounting (paragraphs 21A to 21D, 23A to 23F and 24A to 24F)	• Disclose the risk management strategy, how it is applied to each risk category, a description of the hedging instruments used, the determination of the economic relationship between the hedged item and hedging instrument, and qualitative or quantitative information about how risk components were determined.
	• Disclose information about the terms and conditions of the hedging instruments and how hedging activities affect the amount, timing and uncertainty of future cash flows.
	• Tabular information about the effects of hedge accounting on the financial position and performance, which includes specified details separately by risk category and by type of hedge (i.e. fair value hedges, cash flow hedges and hedges of net investments in foreign operations) about:
	  • carrying amounts, presentation, change in fair value and nominal amounts of the items designated as hedging instruments;
	  • carrying amounts, presentation and accumulated fair value changes of the items designated as hedged items and information about hedge ineffectiveness.

Credit exposure measured at fair value through profit or loss (paragraph 24G)	• For financial instruments designated as measured at fair value through profit or loss because a credit derivative is used to manage the credit risk of that financial instrument, disclosure is required of specified information about the credit derivative, the amount recognised in profit or loss upon designation of the financial instrument and information about discontinuation of the treatment.
Fair value (paragraphs 25–29	• For each class of financial assets and liabilities, disclose the fair value of that class in a way that permits it to be compared with its carrying amount. • Other details are required in respect of gains or losses arising on initial recognition of certain financial instruments.

It should be noted that IFRS 7 does not prescribe how statement of profit or loss and OCI amounts are determined. For example, interest income on financial instruments carried at FVPL may be included in total interest income or it may be included in net gains or losses for that category.

Table 13.10 shows the disclosure requirements for the risks arising from financial instruments. These disclosures are intended to allow users of financial statements to assess the nature and extent of the risk that an entity is exposed to at the balance sheet date.

Table 13.10 Nature and extent of risks arising from financial instruments	
Overall requirement	Summary of details required
For each type of risk (credit risk, liquidity risk and market risk) disclose . . . (paragraph 33)	(a) the exposures to risk and how they arise (b) the entity's objectives, policies and processes for managing the risk and the methods used to measure the risk (c) any changes in (a) or (b) from the previous period. The policies and processes an entity uses would normally include the structure and organisation of its risk management function, the policies for hedging or otherwise mitigating risks, processes for monitoring hedge effectiveness, and policies and processes for avoiding large concentrations of risk.
For each type of risk (credit risk, liquidity risk and market risk) disclose . . . (paragraph 34)	(a) summary quantitative data about its exposure to that risk at the end of the reporting period. This disclosure must be based on the information provided internally to key management personnel of the entity (as defined in IAS 24 *Related Party Disclosures*) (b) the disclosures required by paragraphs 35A–42 (see below) to the extent not provided in (a) (c) concentrations of risk if not apparent from (a) and (b). Concentrations of risk arise from financial instruments that have similar characteristics and that are affected similarly by changes in economic or other conditions. For example, a risk concentration may be by geographic area, by industry or by currency.
Credit risk	
Scope and objectives (paragraphs 35A–35E)	The credit risk disclosures apply to the financial instruments to which the impairment requirements of IFRS 9 are applied. The objective of the credit risk disclosures is to enable users to understand the effect on the amount, timing and uncertainty of future cash flows by requiring: • information about credit risk management practices • quantitative and qualitative information • information about the entity's credit risk exposure.
Credit risk management practices (paragraphs 35F and 35G)	Disclose information about credit risk management practices and how they relate to the recognition and measurement of expected credit losses (including the methods, assumptions and information used to measure those losses). For example, an entity should disclose: • how it determined whether the credit risk of financial instruments has increased significantly since initial recognition • its definition of default • how it determined that financial assets are credit-impaired • the basis of inputs and assumptions and estimation techniques • how forward-looking information has been incorporated.
Quantitative and qualitative information about amounts arising from expected credit losses (paragraphs 35H–35L)	Disclose quantitative and qualitative information that allows users of financial statements to evaluate the amounts in the financial statements arising from expected credit losses, including changes in the amount of those losses and the reasons for those changes.

(continued)

Table 13.10 *(Continued)*

Overall requirement	Summary of details required
Credit risk exposure (paragraphs 35M, 35N and 36)	Disclose information about the entity's credit risk exposure; that is, the credit risk inherent in its financial assets and commitments to extend credit, including significant credit risk concentrations.
Collateral and other credit enhancements obtained (paragraph 38)	Specified details are required to be disclosed when an entity obtains financial or non-financial assets during the period by taking possession of collateral it holds as security.

Liquidity risk

Liquidity risk . . . (paragraph 39)	(a) a maturity analysis for financial liabilities that shows the remaining contractual maturities (b) a description of how the entity manages the liquidity risk inherent in (a). An entity must use judgement to determine the appropriate time bands for a maturity analysis, that is, for when amounts fall due. For example, an entity might determine that the following time bands are appropriate: • not later than 1 month • between 1 month and 3 months • between 3 months and 6 months • later than 6 months. The amounts disclosed in the maturity analysis must be the contractual undiscounted cash flows. This could be problematic for liabilities that mature later than 1 year because the amounts disclosed in the note would likely not reconcile to the statement of financial position where the discounted amount would be shown. Examples of how an entity might manage liquidity risk include: • having access to undrawn loan commitments • holding readily liquid financial assets that can be sold to meet liquidity needs • having diverse funding sources.

Market risk

Market risk — sensitivity analysis (paragraphs 40 and 41)	An entity must disclose: (a) for each type of market risk (i.e. currency risk, interest rate risk and other price risk) a sensitivity analysis showing how profit or loss or equity would have been affected by changes in the relevant risk variables that were reasonably possible at the end of the reporting period (b) the methods and assumptions used in preparing the sensitivity analysis (c) changes from the previous period in the methods and assumptions used. For example, if an entity has a floating interest rate (i.e. variable) liability at the end of the year, the entity would disclose the effect on interest expense for the current year if interest rates had varied by reasonably possible amounts. This effect could be disclosed as a range. For example, the entity could state that had the interest rate varied by between 0.25% and 0.5% then total interest expense would have increased by an amount of between $xx and $xy. If an entity prepares a sensitivity analysis that analyses the interdependencies between market risk variables (e.g. between interest rate risk and currency risk) then it need not make the disclosures in (a) but must rather disclose its own interdependent risk analysis.

Table 13.11 shows the disclosure requirements for financial assets transferred to another entity. The purpose of the required disclosures is to assist users in assessing the extent of such risks related to financial instruments.

Table 13.11 Transfers of financial assets	
Overall requirement	**Summary of details required**
Transfers of financial assets (paragraphs 42A–42C and 42H)	Disclose specified information for all transferred financial assets that are not derecognised and for any continuing involvement in a transferred asset existing at the reporting date.
	The objective of these requirements is to provide information that enables users of financial statements to understand the relationship between transferred financial assets that are not derecognised in their entirety and the associated liabilities. In addition, users should be able to evaluate the nature of, and risks associated with, an entity's continuing involvement in derecognised financial assets.
Transferred financial assets that are not derecognised in their entirety (paragraph 42D)	Disclose information such as, for example, the nature of the transferred assets, the nature of the risks and rewards of ownership to which the reporting entity is exposed, and a description of the nature of the relationship between the transferred assets and the associated liabilities.
Transferred financial assets that are derecognised in their entirety (paragraphs 42E–42G)	For transferred financial assets derecognised in their entirety but where the entity has continuing involvement in those assets, disclosure of certain specified qualitative and quantitative information is required for each type of continuing involvement.

13.15 SUMMARY

IAS 32 defines financial instruments, financial assets, financial liabilities and derivatives and distinguishes between financial liabilities and equity instruments. IFRS 7 prescribes disclosures. IAS 32 sets prescriptive rules for distinguishing financial liabilities from equity instruments, and for accounting for compound financial instruments that have elements of both. It requires that interest, dividends, gains and losses be accounted for consistent with the statement of financial position classification of the related financial assets and financial liabilities. It also sets prescriptive requirements for offsetting a financial asset and a financial liability.

IFRS 9 requires all financial instruments including derivatives to be initially recorded at fair value (with some adjusted for transaction costs). It defines an embedded derivative and establishes rules for separating an embedded derivative from the host contract. It creates four categories of financial instruments. Each category has its own rules for measurement, including initial and subsequent measurement, reclassifications, gains and losses and impairment.

IFRS 9 permits hedge accounting provided that strict criteria are met. These include meeting specified conditions before hedge accounting can be applied, meeting the definition of a hedging instrument and a hedged item, and identifying which of the three types of hedge the hedge transaction meets. IFRS 9 prescribes when hedge accounting must be rebalanced or discontinued and how this must be accounted for. It also contains rules for the derecognition of financial instruments, but these are not addressed in this chapter.

IFRS 9 is a new standard that was developed to address the criticisms raised during the financial crisis in 2008. Even though IFRS 9 offers many improvements over its predecessor standard, IAS 39, accounting for financial instruments remains challenging.

Discussion questions

1. Discuss the concept of 'equity risk' and how it is useful in determining whether a financial instrument is a financial liability or an equity instrument of the issuer.
2. Explain how IAS 32 distinguishes between financial liabilities and equity instruments.

3. Explain the conditions that must be met in order to apply hedge accounting.
4. Describe the main characteristics of a derivative. What is meant by an underlying?
5. Identify the main criticisms of accounting for financial instruments that emerged during the financial crisis. To what extent has the IASB addressed these?

Reference

Financial Crisis Advisory Group 2009, *Report of the Financial Crisis Advisory Group*, 28 July, www.ifrs.org.

Since several categories of financial instruments are measured at fair value, the Academic Perspective of *chapter 8* should be read in conjunction with this section. This review therefore concerns several other key areas, including loan losses, hedge accounting, debt–equity classification and securitisation of financial instruments.

The measurement and disclosure of accrued losses on loans and receivables has attracted significant interest in accounting research. This is an important issue especially for the banking sector. This is because banks carry large amounts of loans and receivables in their balance sheets owing to their lending activities. One would expect that greater loan losses are negatively related to stock prices and future cash flows. The empirical evidence, however, suggests otherwise. In particular, Beaver et al. (1989) examine the relation between the market-to-book ratio (a measure of the excess of market value of equity over book value of equity) and the allowance for doubtful debt (a contra-asset item). Surprisingly, they find that the two are positively related. A possible explanation of this is that in recognising larger loan impairments, banks signal to investors they acknowledge underlying problems and are ready to tackle them. Wahlen (1994) finds that larger than expected loan losses are associated with future earnings before loan losses. This suggests that managers recognise more losses in the current period when they anticipate better future performance. Wahlen (1994) also performs market-based tests and finds a positive relation between stock returns and unexpected loan losses. This supports the notion that investors also expect better future performance when recorded losses exceed expectations. Beaver and Engel (1996) decompose the allowance for loan losses into discretionary and non-discretionary components and examine their pricing implications. Specifically, they regress the allowance on a number of factors they argue should explain the amount recognised. The predicted amount, which is taken from the regression line, is regarded as the non-discretionary element and the residual the discretionary element. They predict that the 'nondiscretionary portion of the allowance is negatively priced because it reflects an impairment of the loan assets'. In contrast, the discretionary component should be unrelated to stock price, if it conveys no news. Alternatively, if it conveys some news, it should be positively related to prices. They report results that are consistent with these conjectures, implying that managers use the discretion that is available to them to convey useful information.

IFRS 9 changed the way loan impairments are measured by moving from the 'incurred loss model' to the 'expected credit loss model'. This means that whereas under IAS 39 losses were recognised upon observation of a clear loss event, IFRS 9 is based on forward-looking anticipation of losses over the lifetime of the financial instrument (e.g., a loan). Onali et al. (2021) find that market participants welcomed the new standard.

The lifetime expected loss model requires estimates of credit loss spanning potentially several years. Long-term forecasts are prone to estimation error, not to mention managerial discretion, and so researchers have attempted to develop good models. For example, Lu and Nikolaev (2022) develop a prediction model that performs more poorly as the forecasting period becomes longer. Nevertheless, they find that their estimates better explain future net charge-offs (loan write-offs) than reported allowances. Yet, there is not much research comparing the differences in decision-usefulness of the accounting outcomes between the two loss models adopted in IAS 39 and IFRS 9.

Hedging can be used by managers to reduce undesirable effects of volatility in earnings on their capacity to borrow by reducing bankruptcy risk. The incentive to hedge, however, may be affected by accounting rules. Specifically, hedge accounting may have two countervailing effects on hedging activity. On one hand, beyond the specific measurement rules, they require disclosure, which in turn improves the information environment and makes the statements clearer to investors (DeMarzo and Duffie, 1995). Better information can therefore enable investors to appreciate the reduction in risk and encourage hedging. On the other hand, too restrictive rules may discourage economically desirable hedging, if it does not qualify to be presented as such. Lins et al. (2011) provide survey-based evidence that introducing fair value measurement to derivative transactions both reduced speculative hedging, consistent with the theoretical prediction of Melumad et al. (1999), as well as economically desired hedging. Panaretou et al. (2013) show that the adoption of the more transparent and stricter IFRS Standards hedge rules in the UK resulted in lower information asymmetry.

The equity-or-debt classification of financial instruments would not be thought to have any real effects. Hopkins (1996) challenges this view. He conducts an experiment in which analysts are presented with different classifications of mandatorily redeemable preference shares (MRPS). Based on past empirical evidence that shows that issuing new shares reduces stock prices, but new debt does not, he conjectures and finds evidence that MRPS presented in equity cause subjects to assign lower stock price than the alternative classification as liability. Levi and Segal (2014) identify another real effect. They document that firms issued fewer MRPS following the change in US GAAP that required firms to classify MRPS as a liability rather than equity. De Jong et al. (2006) show that following the adoption of IFRS Standards in the Netherlands, Dutch companies repurchased MRPS or changed their terms.

During the financial crisis of 2008 the IASB amended IAS 39 to allow firms to retroactively reclassify financial assets that previously were measured at fair value to amortised cost, provided they can maintain a long position. The reclassification criteria were much stricter prior to the crisis. Many banks had taken the option up, as it allowed them to avoid reporting the adverse consequences of falling asset prices. Lim et al. (2013) find that this retroactive classification resulted in a loss of reliable information, as judged by decline in analyst forecast accuracy and an increase forecast dispersion.

Securitisation has been subjected to academic scrutiny because the accounting for derecognition of financial assets involves managerial discretion. Specifically, when an entity sells its receivables, but retains some cash flow streams, accounting rules require a gain or loss to be recorded based on the fair value of the retained cash flow streams. Dechow et al. (2010) examine whether such fair value gains tend to be higher in circumstances where managers face stronger incentives to inflate reported profit. They identify a sample of 305 firms that reported derecognition gains or losses. In this sample a higher pre-securitisation profit is inversely related to derecognition profit. In other words, firms whose pre-securitisation income is low tend to record higher gains from securitisation. The retained interest in securitised assets may also affect the selling entity's risk. Barth et al. (2012) examine the relation between bond rating (and yields) and retained interest in securitised assets and find that it is negative (positive). This suggests that securitisation increases default risk. This suggests that managers of securitising firms should employ high discount factors in calculating the gain or loss on derecognition. However this does not seem to be the case. Dechow et al. (2010) provide evidence that suggests managers of gain-reporting firms in fact employ *low* discount rates as it enables them to inflate earnings.

References

Barth, M. E., Ormazabal, G., and Taylor, D. J. 2012. Asset securitizations and credit risk. The Accounting Review, 87(2), 423–448.

Beaver, W., and Engel, E. 1996. Discretionary behavior with respect to allowances for loan losses and the behavior of security prices. Journal of Accounting and Economics, 22(1), 177–206.

Beaver, W., Eger, C., Ryan, S., and Wolfson, M. 1989. Financial reporting, supplemental disclosures, and bank share prices. Journal of Accounting Research, 27, 157–178.

De Jong, A., Rosellón, M., and Verwijmeren, P. 2006. The economic consequences of IFRS: The impact of IAS 32 on preference shares in the Netherlands. Accounting in Europe, 3(1), 169–185.

Dechow, P. M., Myers, L. A., and Shakespeare, C. 2010. Fair value accounting and gains from asset securitizations: A convenient earnings management tool with compensation side-benefits. Journal of Accounting and Economics, 49(1), 2–25.

DeMarzo, P. M., and Duffie, D. 1995. Corporate incentives for hedging and hedge accounting. Review of Financial Studies, 8(3), 743–771.

Hopkins, P. E. 1996. The effect of financial statement classification of hybrid financial instruments on financial analysts' stock price judgments. Journal of Accounting Research, 34, 33–50.

Levi, S., and Segal, B. 2014. The impact of debt–equity reporting classifications on the firm's decision to issue hybrid securities. The European Accounting Review, 24(4), 801–822.

Lim, C. Y., Lim, C. Y., and Lobo, G. J. 2013. IAS 39 reclassification choice and analyst earnings forecast properties. Journal of Accounting and Public Policy, 32(5), 342–356.

Lins, K. V., Servaes, H., and Tamayo, A. 2011. Does fair value reporting affect risk management? International survey evidence. Financial Management, 40(3), 525–551.

Lu, Y., and Nikolaev, V.V. 2022. Expected loan loss provisioning: An empirical model. The Accounting Review, 97(7), 319–346.

Melumad, N. D., Weyns, G., and Ziv, A. 1999. Comparing alternative hedge accounting standards: Shareholders' perspective. Review of Accounting Studies, 4(3–4), 265–292.

Onali, Enrico, Gianluca Ginesti, Giovanni Cardillo, and Giuseppe Torluccio. 2021. Market reaction to the expected loss model in banks. Journal of Financial Stability, 100884. 10.1016/j.jfs.2021.100884

Panaretou, A., Shackleton, M. B., and Taylor, P. A. 2013. Corporate risk management and hedge accounting. Contemporary Accounting Research, 30(1), 116–139.

Wahlen, J. M. 1994. The nature of information in commercial bank loan loss disclosures. The Accounting Review, 69(3), 455–478.

14

Share-based payment

ACCOUNTING STANDARDS IN FOCUS

IFRS 2 *Share-based Payment*

LEARNING OBJECTIVES

After studying this chapter, you should be able to:

 1   explain the objective and scope of IFRS 2

 2   distinguish between cash-settled and equity-settled share-based payment transactions

 3   demonstrate how equity-settled and cash-settled share-based payment transactions are recognised

 4   explain how equity-settled share-based payment transactions are measured

 5   explain the concept of vesting through differentiating between vesting and non-vesting conditions

 6   discuss several other considerations

 7   explain how modifications to granted equity instruments are treated

 8   demonstrate how cash-settled share-based payment transactions are measured

 9   describe and apply the disclosure requirements of IFRS 2.

INTRODUCTION

The purpose of this chapter is to examine share-based payments. The IFRS® Standard covering share-based payments is IFRS 2 *Share-based Payment*. Under IFRS 2, all transactions with employees or other parties — whether to be settled in cash (or settled in other assets) or settled in the equity instruments of an entity — must now be recognised in the entity's financial statements. The standard adopts the view that all share-based payment transactions ultimately lead to expense recognition, and entities must reflect the effects of such transactions in their profit or loss.

Organisations use various mechanisms to encourage their managers and employees to make decisions that improve the returns to shareholders, including offering remuneration that is linked to the share price of the organisation. This reflects a view that the behaviour of employees can be directed and controlled through the use of remuneration and other similar incentives. It is theorised that remuneration incentives linked to accounting and other performance measures will encourage managers and employees to take decisions and actions that positively impact the financial performance of the organisation and, in turn, the interests of shareholders of the organisation.

Share plans and share option plans are a common feature of remuneration for directors, senior managers and executives, and many other employees as a means of aligning employees' interests with those of the shareholders, and encouraging employee retention. Share plans reward employees by giving them shares or cash payments linked to the share price. Share option plans give the right to buy shares at a fixed price, which means that the option will expire worthless if the share price is below the exercise price at maturity. The value of the right to buy will increase as the share price increases once that price has been exceeded. Both types of plans reassure the shareholders that the directors and other employees have a direct financial interest in the share price increasing. The plans also provide an indirect incentive to remain with the company because rights to shares and share options rarely 'vest' until an agreed period, usually three years or more, have passed from the date on which the rights are 'granted' during which the person needs to remain employed. Thus, an employee who resigns is likely to sacrifice all or some of the value of rights under any share plan or share option plan that is in place.

Most countries require quoted companies to publish details of their executive remuneration schemes, including monetary value of the various components of executive pay. For example, the remuneration report of Woolworths Group Limited included in its 2023 annual report stretches over several pages of disclosure and comment on the company's remuneration policies. What Woolworths has awarded its executives in the financial year ending Change to 25 June 2023 (referred to as F23) in comparison to 2022 (referred to as F22) is summarised in figure 14.1.

As can be seen from figure 14.1, the company's executives receive cash payments, post-employment benefits (*see chapter 11*), as well as share-based payments. The latter amount to almost four million Australian dollars, or about 50% of total pay, indicating their importance.

Companies have been criticised over the size of executive remuneration, for failing to align executive incentives more closely with shareholder returns, and for using short terms (1–3 years) for share incentives to vest rather than longer-term incentives (5–10 years). A review of Woolworths Group Limited's approach shows a roughly balanced approach of short-term and long-term incentive components in its remuneration strategy. The amount of disclosure companies need to provide varies across countries, depending on the specific requirements of local regulations. Generally, the amount, quality and specificity of disclosures has improved over time following criticisms of failure to disclose details of executive performance hurdles, such as return on equity rates, which they usually justify on the basis of commercial sensitivity.

Some entities may also issue shares or share options to pay for the purchase of property or for professional advice or services. Before the issue of IFRS 2, there was no requirement to identify the expenses associated with this type of transaction or to measure and recognise such transactions in the financial statements of an entity. Accounting standard setters have decided that recognising the cost of share-based payments in the financial statements of entities should improve the relevance, reliability and comparability of financial information and help users of financial information to understand the economic transactions affecting entities.

Notwithstanding the above, the adoption of the idea of expensing share-based payments faced at the time significant opposition on theoretical grounds (see, for example, Guay et al. 2003). It also faced political pressure because of the anticipated effect on reported earnings (Rivlin, 2004). However, it seems that it is now well-accepted that instruments such as employee stock options should be expensed and explained in detail in the financial statements, as explained in this chapter.

FIGURE 14.1 Woolworth Group Limited's remuneration summary in 2023

| | | SHORT-TERM BENEFITS | | | | | SHARE-BASED PAYMENTS[6] | | |
		SALARY[1] $	CASH INCENTIVE[2] $	NON-MONETARY AND OTHER BENEFITS[3] $	POST EMPLOYMENT BENEFITS[4] $	OTHER LONG-TERM BENEFITS[5] $	EQUITY GRANTS AT RISK[7] $	OTHER EQUITY GRANTS[8] $	TOTAL $
Executive KMP									
B L Banducci	F23	2,561,222	1,193,010	3,905	27,500	36,160	2,650,623	1,239,075	7,711,495
	F22	2,633,419	766,627	4,734	27,500	36,490	3,227,557	861,130	7,557,457
A Bardwell	F23	969,722	471,813	3,905	97,841	47,767	1,041,036	460,180	3,092,269
	F22	932,202	300,967	4,734	85,273	60,158	1,047,193	312,095	2,742,622
N Davis	F23	1,037,622	471,818	3,905	27,500	26,583	970,204	428,321	2,965,953
	F22	947,280	294,850	4,734	27,500	13,785	931,687	233,488	2,503,324
S Harrison	F23	933,365	393,015	3,905	27,500	25,394	945,385	400,840	2,729,404
	F22	887,665	263,985	4,734	27,500	12,708	1,018,755	270,978	2,486,325

1 Salary includes the net change in accrued annual leave within the period and a car allowance.
2 Cash incentive represents the cash component of the F23 STI, which was 50% of the total F23 STI award. The remaining 50% is deferred as share rights for two years.
3 Non-monetary and other benefits include the deemed premium in respect of the Directors' and Officers' Indemnity insurance and, where applicable, relocation benefits and associated fringe benefits tax.
4 Post employment benefits represent superannuation paid directly to the executive KMP's nominated superannuation fund. If the Group is not required to pay superannuation, the payment may be made as cash and included in salary.
5 Other long-term benefits represents the net change in accrued long service leave within the period.
6 Share-based payments represent the portion of the fair value of share rights expected to vest and is recognised as an expense over the vesting period. Tha amount recognised is adjusted to reflect the expected number of instruments that will vest for non-market based performance conditions, including ROFE, sales per square metre and reputation. The reputation non-market based performance condition is applicable to the F22 and F23 LTI plans, and measures brand reputation across four key metrics. No adjustment for non-vesting is made for failure to achieve the relative TSR performance hurdle, as this is taken into account in the fair value at grant date.
7 For equity grants at risk, the fair value of share rights subject to the relative TSR performance measure is calculated using a Monte Carlo simulation model, whilst the fair value of other share rights is calculated using a Black-Scholes option pricing model.
8 Other equity grants are grants which are not subject to any further performance conditions except continuous employment, subject to the operation of the Group's malus policy.

Source: Woolworths Group Ltd (2023), p. 95).

14.1 APPLICATION AND SCOPE

IFRS 2 applies to share-based payment transactions. The standard was first issued with an effective date for financial statements covering periods beginning on or after 1 January 2005. IFRS 2 has since been amended several times, with most recent amendments in 2016.

The scope of IFRS 2 excludes equity instruments issued in a business combination in exchange for control of the acquiree; they are accounted for under IFRS 3 *Business Combinations* (*see chapter 19*). However, IFRS 2 applies to the cancellation, replacement or modification of existing share-based payment plans arising because of a business combination or restructuring.

Also excluded under paragraph 6 of IFRS 2 are share-based payments in which the entity receives or acquires goods or services under a contract within the scope of paragraphs 8–10 of IAS 32 *Financial Instruments: Presentation* or paragraphs 2.4–2.7 of IFRS 9 *Financial Instruments*.

14.2 CASH-SETTLED AND EQUITY-SETTLED SHARE-BASED PAYMENT TRANSACTIONS

IFRS 2 applies to share-based payments in which an entity acquires or receives goods or services. Goods can include inventory, consumables, property, plant or equipment, intangibles and other non-financial forms of assets; services, such as the provision of labour, are usually consumed immediately.

Measurement principles and specific requirements for three forms of share-based payments are dealt with in IFRS 2. These three forms are defined in paragraph 2 and Appendix A to IFRS 2 and are summarised as follows:

1. *equity-settled* share-based payment transactions, in which the entity receives goods or services as consideration for its own equity instruments (including shares or share options)
2. *cash-settled* share-based payment transactions, in which the entity acquires goods or services by incurring liabilities to transfer cash or other assets to the supplier (counterparty) for amounts that are based on the value (price) of the shares or other equity instruments of the entity
3. *other* transactions in which the entity receives or acquires goods or services, and the terms of the arrangement provide either the entity or the counterparty of the goods or services with a choice of settling the transaction in cash (or other assets) or equity instruments.

IFRS 2 also clarifies in paragraph 3A that paragraph 2 applies to cases where the entity receives goods or services, but another entity within the same group (or a shareholder of that other entity) has to settle the share-based payment. In addition, paragraph 2 applies when the entity has to settle a share-based payment when another entity within the group receives the goods or services.

The accounting treatment for these transactions differs depending on the form of settlement. The three forms and the essential features of share-based payment transactions are summarised in table 14.1.

TABLE 14.1 Form and features of share-based payment transactions	
Form	Features
Equity-settled share-based payment	Entity receives goods or services as consideration for its own equity instruments
Cash-settled share-based payment	Entity acquires goods or services by incurring liabilities for amounts based on the value of its own equities
Other	Entity receives or acquires goods or services and the entity, or the counterparty, has the choice of whether the transaction is settled in cash or equity

A transaction with an employee who holds equity instruments of the employing entity in his/her capacity as equity holder is not within the scope of IFRS 2 (paragraph 4). If, for example, the employee holds equity in the employer and the equity instrument entitles the holder to acquire additional equity at a price that is less than fair value (e.g. a rights issue), the granting or exercise of that right by the employee is not governed by IFRS 2.

14.3 RECOGNITION

LO3

Paragraph 7 of IFRS 2 requires goods or services received in a share-based payment transaction to be recognised when they are received. A corresponding increase in equity must be recognised if the goods or services were received in an equity-settled share-based payment transaction. An increase in a liability must be recognised if the goods or services were acquired in a cash-settled share-based payment.

Usually, an expense arises from the consumption of goods or services. For example, as services are normally consumed immediately, an expense is recognised as the service is rendered. If goods are consumed over a period of time or, as in the case of inventories, sold at a later date, an expense will not be recognised until the goods are consumed or sold. Sometimes it may be necessary to recognise an expense before the goods or services are consumed or sold because they do not qualify for recognition as assets. For example, this may occur if goods are acquired as part of the research phase of a project. Even though the goods may not have been consumed, they will not qualify for recognition as assets under other accounting standards. When the goods or services received in a share-based payment do not qualify for recognition as an asset, they must be expensed (IFRS 2 paragraph 8).

A share-based payment transaction would, depending on the principles for asset or liability recognition, be recognised in journal entries as shown below.

Asset or Expense	Dr	xxx	
Equity	Cr		xxx
(Recognition of an equity-settled share-based payment)			
Asset or Expense	Dr	xxx	
Liability	Cr		xxx
(Recognition of a cash-settled share-based payment)			

14.4 EQUITY-SETTLED SHARE-BASED PAYMENT TRANSACTIONS

LO4

The goods or services received in equity-settled share-based payments and the corresponding increase in equity must be measured at the fair value of the goods or services unless that fair value cannot be estimated reliably (IFRS 2 paragraph 10). For transactions with parties other than employees, there is a rebuttable presumption in IFRS 2 (paragraph 13) that the fair value of goods or services can be estimated reliably. In the unusual cases where the fair value cannot be reliably estimated, paragraph 10 requires that the goods or services and the corresponding increase in equity are to be measured indirectly by reference to the fair value of the equity instruments granted at the date the goods are obtained or the service is rendered.

It is normally considered that the fair value of services received in transactions with employees cannot be reliably measured. Thus, the fair value of the services received from employees is measured by reference to the equity instruments granted at grant date. In summary, under IFRS 2, equity-settled share-based payments are measured and recognised as follows:

Asset or Expense	Dr	Fair value of goods or
Equity	Cr	services received or acquired
(Recognition of a share-based payment in which fair value of goods or services can be reliably estimated)		
Asset or Expense	Dr	Fair value of the equity
Equity	Cr	instruments granted
(Recognition of a share-based payment where fair value of goods or services cannot be reliably estimated)		

14.4.1 Transactions in which services are received

Certain conditions may need to be satisfied before the counterparty in a share-based payment transaction becomes entitled to receive cash (or other assets) or equity instruments of the entity. When the conditions have been satisfied, the counterparty's entitlement is said to have 'vested'. Under a share-based payment arrangement, a counterparty's right to receive cash, other assets or equity instruments of the entity vests when the counterparty's entitlement is no longer conditional on the satisfaction of any vesting conditions (IFRS 2 Appendix A).

If the equity instruments vest immediately, the counterparty is not required to serve a specified period of service before becoming unconditionally entitled to the equity instruments (IFRS 2 paragraph 14). On grant date, the services received are recognised in full together with a corresponding increase in equity. However, if the equity instruments do not vest until a period of service has been completed, under paragraph 15 the services and the corresponding increase in equity are accounted for across the vesting period as the services are rendered.

The granting of equity instruments in the form of share options to employees conditional on completing a two-year period of service accounted for over the two-year vesting period is demonstrated in illustrative example 14.1.

ILLUSTRATIVE EXAMPLE 14.1 Recognition of share options as services are rendered across the vesting period

Wang Ltd grants 100 share options to each of its 50 employees. Each grant is conditional upon the employee working for Wang Ltd for the next two years. It is assumed that each employee will satisfy the vesting conditions. At grant date, the fair value of each share option is estimated as $25.

According to IFRS 2, paragraph 15(a), Wang Ltd will recognise the following amounts during the vesting period for the services received from the employees as consideration for the share options granted.

Year	Calculation	Remuneration expense for period and increase in equity $	Cumulative remuneration expense and increase in equity $
1	(100 × 50 options) × $25 × 1/2 years	62,500	62,500
2	(100 × 50 options) × $25 − $62,500	62,500	125,000

14.4.2 Transactions measured by reference to the fair value of the equity instruments granted

Paragraph 11 of IFRS 2 states that, if share-based payments are with employees and others providing similar services, it is not usually possible to measure the fair value of services received. If it is not possible to reliably estimate the value of goods or services received, then the transaction is measured by reference to the fair value of the equity instruments granted. If market prices are not available, or if the equity instruments are subject to terms and conditions that do not apply to traded equity instruments, then a valuation technique must be used to estimate what the price of the equity instruments would have been, in an arm's length transaction, on the measurement date.

While IFRS 2 (Appendix B11–41) discusses the inputs to option-pricing models such as the Black–Scholes–Merton formula, the choice of model is left to the entity. The valuation technique chosen must be consistent with generally accepted valuation methodologies for pricing financial instruments. It must also incorporate the terms and conditions of the equity instruments (e.g. whether or not an employee is entitled to receive dividends during the vesting period), and any other factors and assumptions that knowledgeable, willing market participants would consider in setting the price (IFRS 2 paragraph 17). For instance, many employee share options have long lives, and they are usually exercisable after the vesting period and before the end of the option's life. Option-pricing models calculate a theoretical price by using key determinants of the options.

Appendix B6 of IFRS 2 supplies the following list of factors that option-pricing models take into account as a minimum:
- exercise price of the option
- life of the option
- current price of the underlying shares
- expected volatility of the share price
- dividends expected on the shares
- risk-free interest rate for the life of the option.

Expected volatility is a measure of the amount by which a price is expected to fluctuate during a period. The value of the option is generally greater if the share price is more volatile. High volatility implies that future share price movements are likely to be large. A large increase in the share price will make the option far more valuable than a small increase and so the upside risk is valuable to the option's holder. If the share price falls below the striking price then it makes no difference to the option's holder whether it is slightly lower or significantly lower. Volatility is typically expressed in annualised terms, for example, daily, weekly or monthly price observations. Often there is likely to be a range of reasonable expectations about future volatility, dividends and exercise date behaviour. If so, an expected value would be calculated by weighting each amount within the range by its associated probability of occurrence.

Expectations about the future are generally based on experience and modified if the future is reasonably expected to differ from the past. For instance, if an entity with two distinctly different lines of business disposes of the one that was significantly less risky than the other, historical volatility may not be the best information on which to base reasonable expectations for the future. In other circumstances, historical information may not be available. For example, unlisted entities will have no historical share price data; likewise, newly listed entities will have little share price data available.

Whether expected dividends should be taken into account when measuring the fair value of shares or options granted depends on whether the counterparty is entitled to dividends. Generally, the assumption about expected dividends is based on publicly available information.

The risk-free interest rate is the implied yield currently available on zero-coupon government issues of the country in whose currency the exercise price is expressed, with a remaining term equal to the expected term of the option (IFRS 2 Appendix B37). It may be necessary to use an appropriate substitute if no such government issues exist or if circumstances indicate that the implied yield on zero-coupon government issues is not representative of the risk-free interest rate (e.g. in high inflation economies).

Woolworths Group Limited (introduced earlier in the chapter) discloses its use of an option pricing model in the determination of the fair value of options and performance rights. The company distinguishes vesting conditions that are non-market conditions—for example return on funds employed (ROFE) – from those that are market conditions, e.g. based on total shareholder return (TSR). The company uses the Black–Scholes option pricing model to deal with the valuation of rights with non-market vesting conditions and Monte Carlo simulation for the valuation of TSR-related rights. The detailed application of both Black–Scholes and Monte Carlo simulation are beyond the scope of this book. These are, however, well-established and supported models that enable Woolworths to base valuations on the assumptions that have to be made in the valuation process. Thus, shareholders are alerted to the fact that the valuations are matters of judgement, but that there is a clear structure in place for drawing a final conclusion.

Figure 14.2 captures the accounting policies of Woolworths Group Limited regarding share-based payment.

FIGURE 14.2 Woolworth Group Limited's accounting policies for remuneration policies of share-based payments in 2022

Significant Accounting Policies
Employee benefits expense includes remuneration and on-costs, superannuation expense and share-based payments expense.
Remuneration, on-costs and superannuation costs are mainly expensed as the related service is provided. A liability is recognised for the amount expected to be paid if the Group has a present legal or constructive obligation to pay this amount as a result of past service provided by the employee and the obligation can be estimated reliably. Refer to Note 3.11 for further details.

Share-based payments
Equity-settled share based payments to employees are measured at the fair value of the equity instruments at grant date. The fair value excludes the effect of non-market based vesting conditions. The fair value of instruments with market-based performance conditions (e.g. TSR) is calculated at the date of grant using a Monte Carlo simulation model. The probability of achieving market-based performance conditions is incorporated into the determination of the fair value per instrument. The fair value of instruments with non-market-based performance conditions (e.g. SQM, reputation, and ROFE), service conditions and retention rights is calculated using a Black–Scholes option pricing model.
The fair value determined at grant date is expensed on a straight-line basis over the vesting period based on the number of equity instruments that will eventually vest. At each reporting period, the Group revises its estimate of the number of equity instruments expected to vest as a result of non-market based vesting conditions. Any change in original estimates is recognised in profit or loss with a corresponding adjustment to reserves.

Source: Woolworths Group Ltd (2022, p. 162).

14.5 VESTING

14.5.1 Treatment of vesting conditions

If a grant of equity instruments is conditional on satisfying certain vesting conditions such as remaining in the entity's employment for a specified period of time, then the vesting conditions are not taken into account when estimating the fair value of the equity instruments. Instead, the vesting conditions are accounted for by adjusting the number of equity instruments included in the measurement of the transaction amount. Thus, the amount recognised for goods or services received as consideration for the equity instrument is based on the number of equity instruments that eventually vest. On a cumulative basis, this means that if a vesting condition is not satisfied then no amount is recognised for goods or services received.

In a situation where employees leave during the vesting period, the number of equity instruments expected to vest varies. This is demonstrated in illustrative example 14.2.

ILLUSTRATIVE EXAMPLE 14.2 Grant where the number of equity instruments expected to vest varies

Seers Company grants 100 share options to each of its 50 employees. The exercise price of each option is $10. Each grant is conditional on the employee working for the company for the next three years. The fair value of each share option is estimated as $25. On the basis of a weighted average probability, the company estimates that 10% of its employees will leave during the three-year period and therefore forfeit their rights to the share options.

During the year immediately following grant date (year 1) three employees leave, and at the end of year 1 the company revised its estimate of total employee departures over the full three-year period from 10% (five employees) to 16% (eight employees).

During year 2 a further two employees leave, and the company revised its estimate of total employee departures across the three-year period down to 12% (six employees). During year 3 a further employee leaves, making a total of six (3 + 2 + 1) employees who have departed. A total of 4,400 share options (44 employees × 100 options per employee) vested at the end of year 3.

The calculation of the periodic expense follows two steps. First, the cumulative remuneration expense is estimated at year end. This calculation takes into account all information available at the end of the period. Second, the difference between the cumulative amount calculated in the first step and the same amount calculated at the end of the previous period is the periodic expense.

Year	Calculation	Remuneration expense and increase in equity for period $	Cumulative remuneration expense and increase in equity $
1	(5,000 options × 84%) × $25 × 1/3 years	35,000	35,000
2	([5,000 options × 88%] × $25 × 2/3 years) − $35,000	38,333	73,333
3	(4,400 options × $25) − $73,333	36,667	110,000

Source: Adapted from IFRS 2, IG Example 1A.

When the options are exercised, the option holders (i.e. the employees) have to pay the exercise price. Assuming all 4,400 options were exercised, Seers Company passes this entry:

Cash	Dr	44,000	
Equity	Cr		44,000
(Recording of the exercise of 4,400 options with $10 exercise price)			

Paragraph 15(b) of IFRS 2 considers the case where the vesting period depends on meeting performance conditions, rather than a fixed vesting period (see illustrative example 14.1). Recall from figure 14.2 that performance conditions can relate to market conditions (e.g. vesting occurs when the entity's share price reaches certain value), or meeting certain operational targets (e.g. vesting occurs when sales growth target is met). This has implications for the recognition period, as follows:

Type of performance condition	Vesting period
Market condition	Should be consistent with the assumptions used in estimating the fair value of the options granted, and shall not be subsequently revised.
Non-market condition	Needs to be revised, if necessary, if subsequent information indicates that the length of the vesting period differs from previous estimates.

A grant of shares with a performance condition linked to the level of an entity's earnings may involve a variable vesting period which allows flexibility as to when the non-market performance condition is met. Such a case is demonstrated in illustrative example 14.3.

ILLUSTRATIVE EXAMPLE 14.3 Grant with a non-market performance condition linked to earnings

At the beginning of year 1, Benning Ltd grants 100 shares to each of its 50 employees, conditional on the employee remaining in the company's employ during the three-year vesting period. The shares have a fair value of $20 per share at grant date. No dividends are expected to be paid over the three-year period. Additionally, the vesting conditions allow the shares to vest at the end of:
- year 1 if the company's earnings have increased by more than 18%
- year 2 if earnings have increased annually by more than 13%, on average, across the two-year period
- year 3 if earnings have increased annually by more than 10%, on average, across the three-year period.

By the end of year 1, Benning Ltd's earnings have increased by only 14% and three employees have left. The company expects that earnings will continue to increase at a similar rate in year 2 and the shares will vest at the end of year 2 (implying the expected vesting period at the end of year 1 is two years). It also expects that a further three employees will leave during year 2, and therefore that 44 employees will vest in 100 shares each at the end of year 2.

Year	Calculation	Remuneration expense, and increase in equity, for period $	Cumulative remuneration expense and increase in equity $
1	(44 employees × 100 shares) × $20 × 1/2 years	44,000	44,000

By the end of year 2 the company's earnings have increased by only 10%, resulting in an annual average of only 12% ([14% + 10%]/2) and so the shares do not vest. Two employees left during the year. The company expects that another two employees will leave during year 3 and that its earnings will increase by at least 6%, thereby achieving the average of 10% per year over the three-year period.

The calculation of the periodic expense follows the two-step procedure, as in illustrative example 14.2.

Year	Calculation	Remuneration expense, and increase to equity, for period $	Cumulative remuneration expense and increase in equity $
2	([43 employees × 100 shares] × $20 × 2/3 years) − $44,000	13,333	57,333

Another three employees leave during year 3 and the company's earnings have increased by 8%, resulting in an average increase of 10.67% over the three-year period. Therefore, the performance condition has been satisfied. The 42 remaining employees (50 − [3 + 2 + 3]) are entitled to receive 100 shares each at the end of year 3.

Year	Calculation	Remuneration expense for period, and increase in equity $	Cumulative remuneration expense and increase in equity $
3	([42 employees × 100 shares] × $20) − $57,333	26,667	84,000

Source: Adapted from IFRS 2, IG Example 2.

Although the objective of equity compensation schemes like the ones presented in this chapter is to keep key personnel, it is possible that attractive employment opportunities lure many employees away during the vesting period. If a sufficiently large number of employees have left, there may be a reversal in expense. As an example, consider a share-based incentive scheme given to 10 key employees, as follows. Each employee is awarded 100 shares, and vesting takes place after four years of employment. The fair value at grant date of each share is $20. By the end of year 2 six key employees have left the entity. The remaining four are expected to stay in employment until the end of the vesting period. The calculation of the cumulative and periodic expenses is as follows:

Year	Calculation	Remuneration expense (income), and increase (decrease) in equity, for period $	Cumulative remuneration expense and increase in equity $
1	(10 employees × 100 shares) × $20 × 1/4 years	5,000	5,000
2	(4 employees × 100 shares) × $20 × 2/4 years − 5,000	(1,000)	4,000

The expense for the remaining four key employees in year 2 is equal to 40% of the year 1 expense, or $2,000. However, the year 1 expense relating to service (now withdrawn) of the six key employees who left is 60% of $5,000, or $3,000, which needs to be reversed. The net year 2 expense is therefore negative $1,000 (= $2,000 − $3,000). The entity then needs to debit equity and credit expenses by $1,000.

In some incentive plans the number of equity instruments awarded varies with the level of performance. Illustrative example 14.4 considers the accounting treatment in such a case.

ILLUSTRATIVE EXAMPLE 14.4 Grant with a non-market performance condition linked to earnings and with varying number of award shares

Assume the same facts as in illustrative example 14.3. However, instead of a fixed number of award shares, there will be an additional number of shares to be awarded. If earnings increase on average by 20% (rather than 18%, 13% or 10%), employees will be entitled to 150 shares, rather than 100. Suppose that at the end of year 1 Benning Ltd did not expect the 20% target to be met, but at end of year 2 Benning Ltd expects the year 3 earnings to grow enough to meet the 20% target. All other details are as in illustrative example 14.3. In year 2 Benning Ltd needs to record an expense of $42,000, calculated as follows:

Year	Calculation	Remuneration expense, and increase to equity, for period $	Cumulative remuneration expense and increase in equity $
2	([43 employees × 150 shares] × $20 × 2/3 years) − $44,000	42,000	86,000

Source: Adapted from IFRS 2, IG Example 3.

An entity may also grant equity instruments to its employees with a performance condition, and where the exercise price varies. This particular situation is demonstrated in illustrative example 14.5.

Because the exercise price varies depending on the outcome of a performance condition that is not a market condition, the effect of the performance condition (in illustrative example 14.5, the exercise price might be either $40 or $30) is not taken into account when estimating the fair value of the share options at grant date. Instead, the entity estimates the fair value of the share options at grant date and ultimately revises the transaction amount to reflect the outcome of the performance condition.

ILLUSTRATIVE EXAMPLE 14.5 Grant of equity instruments where the exercise price varies

At the beginning of year 1 Phillipe Ltd granted 5,000 share options with an exercise price of $40 to a senior executive, conditional upon the executive remaining with the company until the end of year 3. The exercise price drops to $30 if Phillipe Ltd's earnings increase by an average of 10% per year over the three-year period. On grant date the estimated fair value of the share options with an exercise price of $40 is $12 per option and, if the exercise price is $30, the estimated fair value of the options is $16 per option.

During year 1 the company's earnings increased by 12% and they are expected to continue to increase at this rate over the next two years. During year 2 the company's earnings increased by 13% and the company continued to expect that the earnings target would be achieved. During year 3 the company's earnings increased by only 3%. The earnings target was therefore not achieved and so the 5,000 vested share options will have an exercise price of $40. The executive completed three years' service and so satisfied the service condition.

The calculation of the periodic expense follows the two-step procedure, as in illustrative example 14.2. Note here that at the end of Year 1 and Year 2 earnings performance was on track to allow a decrease in the exercise price to $30, with a corresponding increase in option value to $16. If management expects earnings growth to meet the 10% average target, as is assumed below, the expense recognition must be based on option value of $16, as follows.

Year	Calculation	Remuneration expense for period, and increase in equity $	Cumulative remuneration expense and increase in equity $
1	5,000 options × $16 × 1/3 years	26,667	26,667
2	(5,000 options × $16 × 2/3 years) − $26,667	26,666	53,333
3	(5,000 options × $12) − $53,333	6,667	60,000

Source: Adapted from IFRS 2, IG Example 4.

Paragraph 21 of IFRS 2 requires that market conditions, such as a target share price, be taken into account when estimating the fair value of equity instruments. The goods or services received from a counterparty (e.g. an employee) that satisfies all other vesting conditions, such as remaining in service for a specified period of time, are recognised whether or not the market condition is satisfied.

A grant of equity instruments with a market condition is demonstrated in illustrative example 14.6.

ILLUSTRATIVE EXAMPLE 14.6 Grant with a market condition

At the beginning of year 1 Smallville Ltd grants 5,000 share options to a senior executive, conditional on that executive remaining in the company's employ until the end of year 3. The share options cannot be exercised unless the share price has increased from $15 at the beginning of year 1 to above $25 at the end of year 3. If the share price is above $25 at the end of year 3, the share options can be exercised at any time during the next seven years (that is, by the end of year 10). The company applies an option-pricing model that takes into account the probability that the share price will exceed $25 at the end of year 3. It estimates the fair value of the share options with this market condition to be $9 per option. The executive completes three years' service with Smallville Ltd when the share price is $27.

Year	Calculation	Remuneration expense for period, and increase in equity $	Cumulative remuneration expense and increase in equity $
1	5,000 options × $9 × 1/3 years	15,000	15,000
2	(5,000 options × $9 × 2/3 years) − $15,000	15,000	30,000
3	(5,000 options × $9) − $30,000	15,000	45,000

Source: Adapted from IFRS 2, IG Example 5.

As noted earlier, because the executive has satisfied the service condition, the company is required to recognise these amounts irrespective of the outcome of the market condition. In other words, even if the share price remains below $25 at the end of the three-year period, the entries depicted above are valid and should not be reversed.

14.5.2 Treatment of non-vesting conditions

Vesting conditions comprise service conditions (e.g. completion of a prespecified service period) and performance conditions (market-based or non-market-based) only, implying that other features of a share-based payment are not vesting conditions. A non-vesting condition may entail that, for example, the chief financial officer may be entitled to receive shares in three years' time, provided they did not enter employment with another entity in the industry.

All non-vesting conditions are taken into account when estimating the fair value of equity instruments granted (paragraph 21A). Under this provision, for grants of equity with non-vesting conditions, an entity must recognise the goods or services received from a counterparty that satisfy all vesting conditions that are not market conditions (such as services from an employee who remains in service for a specified period of time). This applies even if the non-vesting conditions remain unsatisfied.

14.6 OTHER CONSIDERATIONS

14.6.1 Events after vesting date

Having recognised the goods or services received and a corresponding increase in equity, paragraph 23 of IFRS 2 prevents an entity from making a subsequent adjustment to total equity after vesting date. For example, if an amount is recognised for services received from an employee, it may not be reversed if the vested equity instruments are later forfeited or, in the case of share options, if the options are not subsequently exercised. This restriction applies only to total equity; it does not preclude an entity from transferring amounts from one component of equity to another.

14.6.2 The fair value of the equity instruments cannot be estimated reliably

In the event that the fair value of equity instruments cannot be reliably estimated, they must instead be measured at their intrinsic value (IFRS 2 paragraph 24(a)). Intrinsic value is the difference between the share price and the exercise price (the amount the holder of the equity instrument needs to pay to be able to receive the share, or its worth in cash). The intrinsic value is measured at the date goods are obtained or services are rendered, at the end of each subsequent reporting period, and at the date of final settlement. Any change in intrinsic value must be recognised in profit or loss. For a grant of share options, the share-based payment arrangement is finally settled when the options are exercised, forfeited, or when they lapse. The amount to be recognised for goods or services is based on the number of equity instruments that ultimately vest or are exercised. The estimate must be revised if subsequent information indicates that the number of share options expected to vest differs from previous estimates. On vesting date, the estimate is then revised to equal the number of equity instruments that ultimately vest.

14.7 MODIFICATIONS TO TERMS AND CONDITIONS ON WHICH EQUITY INSTRUMENTS WERE GRANTED

An entity might choose to modify the terms and conditions on which it granted equity instruments. For example, it might change (reprice/retest) the exercise price of share options previously granted to employees at prices that were higher than the current price of the entity's shares. It might accelerate the vesting of share options to make the options more favourable to employees; or it might remove or alter a performance condition. If the exercise price of options is modified, the fair value of the options changes. A reduction in the exercise price would increase the fair value of share options. Irrespective of any modifications to the terms and conditions on which equity instruments are granted, paragraph 27 of IFRS 2 requires the services received, measured at the grant-date fair value of the equity instruments, to be recognised unless those equity instruments do not vest.

The incremental effects of modifications that increase the total fair value of the share-based payment arrangement, or that are otherwise beneficial to the employee, must also be recognised. The incremental fair value is the difference between the fair value of the modified equity instrument and that of the original equity instrument, both estimated at the date of modification (IFRS 2 Appendix B43(a)). Similarly, if the modification increases the number of equity instruments granted, the fair value of the additional equity instruments, measured at the date of modification, must be included in the amount recognised for services received.

If the modification occurs during the vesting period, the incremental fair value is included in the measurement of the amount recognised for services received from the modification date until the date when the modified equity instruments vest. This is in addition to the amount based on the grant-date fair value of the original equity instruments that is recognised over the remainder of the original vesting period. If the modification occurs after the vesting date, the incremental fair value is recognised immediately, or over the vesting period if the employee is required to complete an additional period of service before becoming unconditionally entitled to the modified equity instruments.

The terms or conditions of the equity instruments granted may be modified in a manner that reduces the total fair value of the share-based payment arrangement or that is not otherwise beneficial to the employee. If this occurs, then IFRS 2 (Appendix B44) requires the services received as consideration to be accounted for as if that modification had not occurred (i.e. the decrease in fair value is not to be taken into account).

Illustrative example 14.7 demonstrates the accounting treatment of a repricing modification to the terms and conditions of share options.

ILLUSTRATIVE EXAMPLE 14.7 Grant of equity instruments that are subsequently repriced

Merton Ltd grants 100 share options to each of its 50 employees, conditional upon the employee remaining in service over the next three years. The company estimates that the fair value of each option is $15. On the basis of a weighted average probability, the company also estimates that 10 employees will leave during the three-year vesting period and therefore forfeit their rights to the share options.

A Four employees leave during year 1, and the company estimates that a further seven employees will leave during years 2 and 3 (implying 39 employees are expected to vest). By the end of year 1 the company's share price has dropped, and it decides to reprice the share options. The repriced share options will vest at the end of year 3. At the date of repricing, Merton Ltd estimates that the fair value of each of the original share options is $5 and the fair value of each repriced share option is $8. The incremental value is $3 per share option, and this amount is recognised over the remaining two years of the vesting period along with the remuneration expense based on the original option value of $15.

Year	Calculation	Remuneration expense for period $	Cumulative remuneration expense $
1	39 employees × 100 options × $15 × 1/3 years	19,500	19,500

B During year 2, a further four employees leave, and the company estimates that another four employees will leave during year 3 to bring the total expected employee departures over the three-year vesting period to 12 employees.

Year	Calculation	Remuneration expense for period $	Cumulative remuneration expense $
2	38 employees × 100 options × [$15 × 2/3 years + $3 × 1/2 years] − $19,500	24,200	43,700

C A further three employees leave during year 3. For the remaining 39 employees (50 − [4 + 4 + 3]), the share options vested at the end of year 3.

Year	Calculation	Remuneration expense for period $	Cumulative remuneration expense $
3	39 employees × 100 options × ($15 + $3) − $43,700	26,500	70,200

Source: Adapted from IFRS 2, IG Example 7.

14.7.1 Repurchases

If vested equity instruments are repurchased, IFRS 2 (paragraph 29) specifies that the payment made to the employee is accounted for as a deduction from equity. This is similar to the treatment of treasury shares. If the payment exceeds the fair value of the equity instruments repurchased, the excess is recognised as an expense.

14.8 CASH-SETTLED SHARE-BASED PAYMENT TRANSACTIONS

Paragraphs 30–33 of IFRS 2 set out the requirements for share-based payments in which an entity incurs a liability for goods or services received, based on the price of its own equity instruments. These are known as cash-settled share-based payments. Because the ultimate payment is a function of the entity's share price, the amount to be paid is unknown at the grant date, but still there will be an ultimate cash outflow, and therefore there is a liability. Alternatively, an entity might grant to its employees a right to receive a future cash payment by granting to them a right to shares (including shares to be issued upon the exercise of share options) that are **redeemable**, either **mandatorily** (for example, upon cessation of employment) or at the **employee's option**. These latter features also imply there will be, ultimately, cash outflows, which the entity does not control and thus give rise to the recognition of a liability.

The fair value of the liability involved is remeasured at the end of each reporting period and the date of settlement, and any changes in the fair value are recognised in profit or loss for the period. In contrast, the fair value of equity-settled share-based payments is determined at grant date for employee services or at the date of receipt for other services and for goods. There is no remeasurement of the granted equity instruments subsequently.

Examples of cash-settled share-based payments included in paragraph 31 of IFRS 2 are share appreciation rights that might be granted to an employee as part of a remuneration package. Share appreciation rights entitle the holder to a future cash payment (rather than an equity instrument) based on increases in the share price. Another example is where an employee is granted rights to shares that are redeemable, providing the employee with a right to receive a future cash payment.

There is a presumption in IFRS 2 that the services rendered by employees in exchange for the share appreciation rights have been received. Where share appreciation rights vest immediately, the services and the associated liability must also be recognised immediately. Where the share appreciation rights do not vest until the employees have completed a specified period of service, the services received and the associated liability to pay for those services are recognised as the service is rendered. The liability is measured, initially and at the end of each reporting period until settled, at the fair value of the share appreciation rights by applying an option-pricing model that takes into account the terms and conditions on which share appreciation rights were granted, and the extent to which employees have rendered service (paragraph 33).

Illustrative example 14.8 shows the accounting treatment for cash-settled share appreciation rights.

Brierley Ltd grants 100 share appreciation rights (SARs) to each of its 50 employees, conditional upon the employee staying with the company for the next three years. The company estimates the fair value of the SARs at the end of each year as shown below. The intrinsic values of the SARs at the date of exercise (which equal the actual cash paid out) at the end of years 3, 4 and 5 are also shown. All SARs held by employees remaining at the end of year 3 will vest.

Year	Fair value	Intrinsic value (cash paid out)
1	$14.40	
2	$15.50	
3	$18.20	$15.00
4	$21.40	$20.00
5	$25.00	$25.00

The table below shows at the end of each year how many employees have left, the number of employees who exercised their SARs during the year and how many more are expected to leave.

Year	Have left	Expected to leave in subsequent years	Exercised their SARs
1	3	6	
2	4	3	
3	2	0	15
4			14
5			12

Year	Calculation	Expense $	Liability $
1	(50–9) employees × 100 SARs × $14.40 × 1/3 years	19,680	19,680
2	(50–10) employees × 100 SARs × $15.50 × 2/3 years – $19,680	21,653	41,333
3	(50–9) employees × 100 SARs × $18.20 – $41,333 Cash paid: 15 employees × 100 SARs × $15	33,287	74,620 (22,500) 52,120
4	(50–9–15) employees × 100 SARs × $21.40 – $52,150 Cash paid: 14 employees × 100 SARs × $20	3,520	55,640 (28,000) 27,640
5	12 employees × 100 SARs × $25 – $27,640 Cash paid: 12 employees × 100 SARs × $25	2,360	30,000 (30,000) 0
	Total	80,500	

Source: Adapted from IFRS 2, IG Example 12.

The table below summarises the annual journal entries based on the calculations above

Year 1				
	Expense	Dr	19,680	
	Liability	Cr		19,680

Recording of the SARs liability and corresponding expense

Year 2				
	Expense	Dr	21,653	
	Liability	Cr		21,653

Increasing the SARs liability and corresponding expense

Year 3				
	Expense	Dr	33,287	
	Liability	Cr		10,787
	Cash	Cr		22,500

Increasing the SARs liability for accrued expense and settlement of 1,500 SARs at $15 each

Year 4				
	Expense	Dr	3,520	
	Liability	Dr	24,480	
	Cash	Cr		28,000

Decreasing the SARs liability for reduction in accrued expense and settlement of 1,400 SARs at $20 each

Year 5				
	Expense	Dr	2,360	
	Liability	Dr	27,640	
	Cash	Cr		30,000

Decreasing the SARs liability for reduction in accrued expense and settlement of 1,200 SARs at $25 each

Source: Adapted from IFRS 2, IG Example 12A.

Illustrative example 14.9 shows the accounting treatment for cash-settled share appreciation rights when the vesting is linked to a (operation-based) performance condition.

ILLUSTRATIVE EXAMPLE 14.9 Cash-settled share appreciation rights subject to performance conditions

Grizzly Ltd grants 100 share appreciation rights (SARs) to each of its 50 employees, conditional on sales volume reaching $100 million by the end of year 3. By the end of year 1 managers estimate they will fail to meet the year 3 target. At the end of year 2, Grizzly's managers revise their assessment and expect to meet the target. The sales target is met in year 3. All 50 employees remain in employment throughout the example period.

The number of employees exercising their SARs exercised in years 3–5 are as follows:

Year 3 : 15; year 4 : 15; year 5 : 20.

The company estimates the fair value of the SARs at the end of each year as shown below. The intrinsic values of the SARs at the date of exercise (which equal the actual cash paid out) at the end of years 3, 4 and 5 are also shown.

Year	Fair value	Intrinsic value (cash paid out)
1	$14.40	
2	$15.50	
3	$18.20	$15.00
4	$21.40	$20.00
5	$25.00	$25.00

Year	Calculation	Expense $	Liability $
1	No liability, or expense, are recognised as management estimates sales target will not be met.		
2	50 employees × 100 SARs × $15.50 × 2/3 years	51,667	51,667
3	50 employees × 100 SARs × $18.20 – $51,667 Cash paid: 15 employees × 100 SARs × $15	39,333	91,000 (22,500) ──── 68,500
4	35 employees × 100 SARs × $21.40 – $68,500 Cash paid: 15 employees × 100 SARs × $20	6,400	74,900 (30,000) ──── 44,900
5	20 employees × 100 SARs × $25 – $44,900 Cash paid: 20 employees × 100 SARs × $25	5,100	50,000 (50,000) ──── 0
	Total	102,500	

14.8.1 Share-based payment transactions with cash alternatives

Some share-based payments may provide either the entity or the counterparty with the choice of having the transaction settled in cash (or other assets) or the issue of equity instruments. This section describes the required treatment in such cases.

Share-based payment transactions where the counterparty has settlement choice

If the counterparty to a share-based payment has the right to choose whether a transaction is settled in cash or equity instruments, a compound financial instrument has been created that includes a debt component and an equity component. The debt component represents the counterparty's right to demand a cash settlement, and the equity component represents the counterparty's right to demand settlement in equity instruments.

IFRS 2 (paragraphs 35, 36) requires that transactions with employees be measured at fair value on measurement date, by taking into account the terms and conditions on which rights to cash and equity were granted. For transactions with others in which the fair value of goods or services is measured directly, the equity component is measured as the difference between the fair value of the goods or services received and the fair value of the debt component at the date they are received. The fair value of the debt component is measured before the fair value of the equity component (paragraph 37), as the counterparty must forfeit the right to receive cash in order to receive equity instruments. The measurement of compound financial instruments with employees (and other counterparties) is summarised in table 14.2.

TABLE 14.2 Measurement of compound financial instruments	
Counterparty	Measurement approach
Employees	Measure fair value (FV) of the debt component then FV of the equity component, at measurement date, taking into account the terms and conditions on which rights to cash or equity were granted
Parties other than employees	Equity component is the difference between FV of goods or services received and FV of the debt component, at the date the goods or services are received

To illustrate assume an employee is given the choice between either a right to a cash payment equal to the value of 80 shares, or 100 shares. The grant is conditional upon the completion of two years' service. If the employee chooses the share alternative, the shares must be held for two years after vesting date. On grant date, the share price is $10. At the end of the first year, the share price increases to $11. The fair value of the grant with these features is $870. The fair value of the cash alternative is $800 = 80 × $10, which is a liability, and therefore the implied equity portion is 70 = 870 − 800. At the end of year 1 the liability's balance is $880 = 80 × $11. The entry below shows the recording of the expense, equity and liability in year 1:

Year 1	Expense	Dr	475	
	Liability	Cr		440
	Equity	Cr		35

Recording liability component at $880/2 and equity component $70/2 against expense of $475.

Note that at settlement date, the liability must be remeasured to fair value (IFRS 2 paragraph 39). Building on the previous example if the share price increases to $12 by the end of year 2, the liability's balance should stand at $960 = 80 × $12. The entry below shows the recording of the expense, equity and liability in year 2:

Year 2	Expense	Dr	555	
	Liability	Cr		520
	Equity	Cr		35

Recording liability component at $960–440, and equity component $70/2 against expense of $555.

If the employee selects the cash option, when cash is paid, the liability is eliminated. If shares are issued, instead, the liability is eliminated and equity is credited by $960.

The terms of equity-based compensation may turn unfavourable when the share price drops substantially. Many companies in such a case add a cash alternative to the package to provide additional incentive for the recipient of the grant to stay in employment. In some cases, the equity portion could be entirely replaced by the cash alternative. Paragraph 27 of IFRS 2 states that the recognition of the expense against the increase in equity continues over the vesting period, regardless of the drop in share price and the cash alternative, unless those equity instruments do not vest because of failure to satisfy a vesting condition (other than a market condition) that was specified at grant date. Therefore, the entity recognises the services received over the three-year period, based on the grant date fair value of the shares. Yet, the cash alternative needs to be recognised as a liability and balanced against a reduction in equity. A grant of shares with a cash alternative subsequently added that provides an employee with a settlement choice is demonstrated in illustrative example 14.10.

At the beginning of year 1, Scotland Ltd granted 10,000 shares with a fair value of $24 per share to a senior manager, conditional on the manager remaining in the company's employ for three years. By the end of year 2 the share price had dropped to $15 per share. At that date the company added a cash alternative to the grant, giving the manager the right to choose whether to receive the 10,000 shares or cash equal to the value of the shares on vesting date. On vesting date the share price had dropped to $12.

Year	Calculation	Expense $	Equity $	Liability $
1	10,000 shares × $24 × 1/3 years	80,000	80,000	

The addition of the cash alternative at the end of year 2 created an obligation to settle in cash. Scotland Ltd must recognise the liability to settle in cash based on the fair value of the shares at the modification date and the extent to which the specified services have been received. The liability must be remeasured at the end of each subsequent reporting period and at the date of settlement.

Year	Calculation	Expense $	Equity $	Liability $
2	10,000 shares × $24 × 2/3 years − $80,000	80,000	80,000	
	10,000 shares × $15 × 2/3 years		(100,000)	100,000*
3	10,000 shares × $24 − $160,000	80,000	80,000	
	10,000 shares × $15 − $100,000		(50,000)	50,000
	10,000 shares × $12 − $150,000	(30,000)		(30,000)
	Total	210,000	90,000	120,000*

* Total liability at date of settlement is $120,000 ($12 × 10,000 shares). The reduction of $30,000 brings the liability down to the settlement amount.

Source: Adapted from IFRS 2, IG Example 9.

Share-based payment transactions where the entity has settlement choice

Where an entity has a choice of settling in cash or equity instruments, it must determine whether it has a present obligation to settle in cash. Paragraph 41 of IFRS 2 states that an entity has a present obligation to settle in cash if the choice of settlement in equity instruments has no commercial substance (perhaps the entity is legally prohibited from issuing shares), it has a past practice or a stated policy of settling in cash, or if it generally settles in cash whenever the counterparty asks for cash settlement. If a present obligation exists, the transaction must be accounted for as a cash-settled share-based payment. If a present obligation to settle in cash does not exist, the transaction is accounted for as an equity-settled arrangement.

On settlement, if the entity elects to settle in cash, paragraph 43(a) of IFRS 2 requires the cash payment to be accounted for as the repurchase of an equity interest, resulting in a deduction from equity. Where there is an equity settlement, no further accounting adjustments are required. If, on settlement, the entity selects the settlement alternative with the higher fair value, an additional expense for the excess value given must be recognised. The excess value is either the difference between the cash paid and the fair value of the equity instruments that would have been issued, or the difference between the fair value of the equity instruments issued and the amount of cash that would have been paid, whichever is applicable.

14.9 DISCLOSURE

The global financial crisis which emerged in 2008 has resulted in much criticism about the inadequacy of disclosure in regard to performance hurdles and incentives used in share-based payment transactions. Corporate executives, on the other hand, complain about the onerous reporting and disclosure requirements necessary under the accounting rules. One difficulty faced by regulators is how to reduce the volume of required information yet still retain meaningful and useful disclosure.

Paragraphs 44–52 of IFRS 2 prescribe various disclosures relating to share-based payments. The objective of these disclosures is to provide significant additional information to assist financial statement users to understand the nature and extent of share-based payment arrangements that existed during the reporting period. The three principles that underpin the disclosures required by IFRS 2 are shown in table 14.3.

TABLE 14.3 Principles underpinning the disclosures in IFRS 2	
Disclosure principle	IFRS 2 paragraph
The nature and extent of the share-based payment arrangements.	44
How the fair value of goods or services received, or the fair value of equity instruments granted during the period, was determined.	46
The effect of share-based payment transactions on the entity's profit or loss for the period and on its financial position.	50

Paragraph 45 of IFRS 2 specifies the disclosures necessary to give effect to the principle in paragraph 44 as including at least the following:
- a description of each type of share-based payment arrangement that existed at any time during the period, including the general terms and conditions of each arrangement, such as vesting requirements, the maximum term of options granted, and the methods of settlement.

An entity with substantially similar types of share-based payments may aggregate this information unless separate disclosure of each arrangement is necessary to enable users to understand the nature and extent of the arrangements.

Other specific disclosures required by paragraph 45 are the number and weighted average exercise prices of share options for options that:
- are outstanding at the beginning of the period
- are granted during the period
- are forfeited during the period
- are exercised during the period
- have expired during the period
- are outstanding at the end of the period
- are exercisable at the end of the period.

In relation to share options exercised during the period, the weighted average share price at the date of exercise must be disclosed. If the options were exercised on a regular basis throughout the period, the weighted average share price during the period may be disclosed instead. For share options outstanding at the end of the period, the range of exercise prices and weighted average remaining contractual life must be disclosed. If the range of exercise prices is wide, the outstanding options must be divided into ranges that are meaningful for assessing the number and timing of additional shares that may be issued and the cash that may be received upon exercise of those options.

If the fair value of goods or services received as consideration for equity instruments of the entity has been measured indirectly by reference to the fair value of the equity instruments granted, the following information must be disclosed (paragraph 47):
- the weighted average fair value of share options granted during the period, at the measurement date, and information on how the fair value was measured including:
  - the option-pricing model used and the inputs to that model including the weighted average share price, exercise price, expected volatility, option life, expected dividends, the risk-free interest rate, and any other inputs to the model including the assumptions made to incorporate the effects of expected early exercise
  - how expected volatility was determined, including an explanation of the extent to which expected volatility was based on historical volatility
  - whether, and how many, other features of the option grant (such as a market condition) were incorporated into the measurement of fair value
- for equity instruments other than share options granted during the period, the number and weighted average fair value at the measurement date, and information on how that fair value was measured, including:
  - if not measured on the basis of an observable market price, how fair value was determined
  - whether and how expected dividends were incorporated
  - whether and how any other features of the equity instruments were incorporated

- for share-based payment arrangements that were modified during the period:
  - an explanation of the modifications
  - the incremental fair value granted as a result of the modifications and information on how the incremental fair value granted was measured.

If the entity has measured the fair value of goods or services received during the period directly, it is required to disclose how that fair value was determined (e.g. at market price).

If the entity has rebutted the assumption that the fair value of goods or services received can be estimated reliably, it is required to disclose that fact (paragraph 49) together with an explanation of why the presumption was rebutted.

Paragraph 51 gives effect to the principle that an entity must disclose information that enables financial statement users to understand the effect of share-based payments on the entity's profit or loss for the period and on its financial position. This paragraph requires disclosure of at least the following:
- the total expense recognised for the period arising from share-based payments in which the goods or services received did not qualify for recognition as assets, including separate disclosure of that portion of the total expense that arises from transactions accounted for as equity-settled share-based payments
- for liabilities arising from share-based payment transactions:
  - the total carrying amount at the end of the period
  - the total intrinsic value at the end of the period of liabilities for which the counterparty's right to cash or other assets had vested by the end of the period.

Finally, paragraph 52 requires the disclosure of such other additional information as may be needed to enable the users of the financial statements to understand the nature and extent of the share-based payment arrangements; how the fair value of goods or services received, or the fair value of equity instruments granted, was determined; and the effect of share-based payments on the entity's profit or loss and on its financial position.

A review of the corporate annual reports shows the large volume of space devoted to share-based payment disclosure. For example, it has already been stated that Woolworth Limited's 2014 remuneration report covers more than 20 pages, much of which relates to share-based payments. In addition, there is an extensive note to the consolidated financial statements that adds a further 8 pages of disclosure.

14.10 SUMMARY

IFRS 2 deals with the recognition and measurement of share-based payment transactions. Share-based payments are arrangements in which an entity receives or acquires goods or services as consideration for, or based on the price of (respectively) its own equity instruments. The main features of the standard are that it:
- requires financial statement recognition of the goods or services acquired or received under share-based payment arrangements, regardless of whether the settlement is cash or equity or whether the counterparty is an employee or another party.
- employs the general principle for cash-settled transactions that the goods or services received and the liability incurred are measured at the fair value of the liability; and, until it is settled, the fair value of the liability is remeasured at the end of each reporting period and at the date of settlement and any changes in fair value are recognised in profit or loss.
- employs the general principle for equity-settled transactions that the goods or services received and the corresponding increase in equity are measured at the grant date, and at the fair value of the goods or services received; and if the fair value cannot be measured reliably, the goods or services are measured indirectly by reference to the fair value of the equity instruments granted.
- allows an entity to choose appropriate option-valuation models to determine fair values and to tailor those models to suit the entity's specific circumstances.
- includes a lengthy set of disclosure requirements aimed at enabling financial statement users to understand the nature, extent and effect of share-based payments, and how the fair value of goods or services received or equity instruments granted was determined.

Discussion questions

1. Why do standard setters formulate rules on the measurement and recognition of share-based payment transactions?
2. What is the difference between equity-settled and cash-settled share-based payment transactions?
3. What is the different accounting treatment for instruments classified as debt and those classified as equity?
4. Outline the accounting treatment for the recognition of an equity-settled share-based payment transaction.
5. Explain when a counterparty's entitlement to receive equity instruments of an entity vests.
6. What are the minimum factors required under IFRS 2 to be taken into account in option-pricing models?

7. Distinguish between vesting and non-vesting conditions.
8. Explain what the 'retesting' of share options means.
9. Explain the measurement approach for cash-settled share-based payment transactions.
10. Are the following statements true or false?
    (a) Goods or services received in a share-based payment transaction must be recognised when they are received.
    (b) Historical volatility provides the best basis for forming reasonable expectations of the future price of share options.
    (c) Share appreciation rights entitle the holder to a future equity instrument based on the profitability of the issuer.

References

Guay, W., Kothari, S. P., & Sloan, R., 2003. Accounting for employee stock options. *American Economic Review*, 93(2), 405–409.

International Accounting Standards Board, *IFRS 2 Share-based Payments*, IFRS Foundation, London, www.ifrs.org.

Rivlin, G. 2004. Stock options debate comes to Silicon Valley. New York Times. https://www.nytimes.com/2004/06/25/business/stock-options-debate-comes-to-silicon-valley.htmlWoolworths Group Ltd 2023, *Annual Report 2023*, www.woolworthsgroup.com.au/content/dam/wwg/investors/reports/2023/f23-full-year/Woolworths%20Group%202023%20Annual%20Report.pdf

Share-based payments have received attention in academic research almost exclusively with respect to share-based compensation. One strand in this research challenges the accounting treatment of expensing this form of compensation and whether the use of fair value is relevant and reliable. A second strand has tried to understand the economic consequences of share-based compensation. A third strand reviewed here concerns how share-based compensation may affect earnings management.

In contrast to ordinary salary expense, share-based compensation has the important element of incentive that aligns employee interest with that of shareholders. That is, share-based payments carry both cost and value to issuing employers (Hall and Murphy 2002). It is therefore interesting to find out if investors agree with the treatment of expensing. An argument against expensing and in favour of recognition of an (intangible) asset is that share-based compensation may generate benefits (or, value) that exceed its cost. In addition, unlike cash payments, the related expense is measured by reference to fair values, which raises a concern whether the recorded amount is sufficiently reliable. Bell et al. (2002) examine how investors perceive share-based expense in a sample of 85 profitable firms. They find that market value of equity is positively related to the share-based compensation. Hanlon et al. (2003) argue that the positive effects documented by Bell et al. (2002) arise only in certain circumstances. They posit that share-based compensation is positively related to future performance only when firms issue employee stock options that are at a level that is appropriate for their underlying economic conditions and corporate governance mechanisms. Consistent with this prediction, Hanlon et al. (2003) find positive (negative) association with future performance for share-based compensation that is determined by (deviates from) these fundamentals. These two studies therefore suggest that the benefits of share-based compensation exceed the costs, at least in certain circumstances. Aboody (1996) examines the relation between the value of outstanding stock options and share prices. He finds a negative relation, suggesting options are net cost to employers. This evidence therefore justifies expensing. However, he also finds a positive relation when options are measured closer to the grant date. One interpretation of this is that benefits exceed costs at the outset, but are then incorporated into earnings and prices faster than the cost. In an attempt to separate between the incentive and cost effect, Aboody et al. (2004) proxy for the benefit effect by using analyst predictions of future growth. Once controlling for growth, they find that share-based expense is negatively related to stock prices and stock returns, as would be expected from an expense. Hence, from this strand of research we get mixed evidence as to whether share-based compensation is a net expense or net benefit. Nevertheless, establishing the above relations (whether positive or negative) suggests that share-based compensation is useful and reliable.

Dechow et al. (1996) turn attention to the economic consequences of share-based compensation. Many opponents to the treatment of expensing argue that this could limit their access to equity and debt markets, which in turn would

negatively affect their performance. In 1993 the FASB issued its Exposure Draft proposing the expense of employee stock options. Dechow et al. (1996) argue that if adverse consequences to the expensing are present, then one should find support in the behaviour of stock prices of firms that issue large amounts of employee stock options. They therefore examine stock returns around events that increased the probability of adopting the new expensing rule. However, their analysis fails to find a more pronounced effect on stock prices for firms that issue more employee stock options. They therefore conclude that markets did not anticipate any adverse real effect of the new accounting rule.

Another economic consequence of share-based payment is its scope to motivate risk-averse managers to engage in more risky projects for the benefit of well-diversified investors. Rajgopal and Shevlin (2002) test this theory in the Oil and Gas industry. They find a positive link between share-based compensation to managers and exploration activity, their proxy to managerial risk-taking. Cheng (2004) finds that share-based compensation encourages managers to engage in research and development (R&D) activity. Because R&D may be quite risky in nature (Kothari et al. 2002; Amir et al. 2007), this provides additional evidence as to the positive link between share-based compensation and risk-taking.

While share-based compensation works to align the incentives of managers with those of shareholders, managers may feel they are over-exposed to the specific risk of the company they run. To remedy this, they may want to diversify by selling vested options and shares (Ofek and Yermack, 2000).

Share-based compensation, especially in the form of options, can increase incentives to misreport. Burns and Kedia (2006) find a greater incidence of restatements where options are more sensitive to changes in share prices. Additionally, earnings management is expected prior to the sale of managers' shares to positively affect share price. To explore this possibility, Cheng and Warfield (2005) examine the propensity of earnings to meet certain targets, such as analyst forecasts. Consistent with the hypothesis of upward earning management, they find that firms that award high levels of share-based compensation to their managers are more likely to meet or beat analyst forecasts. Additionally, they find that managers that meet or beat analyst forecasts tend to sell more shares afterward than managers that do not meet analyst forecasts. Bergstresser and Philippon (2006) provide complementary evidence to both Cheng and Warfield (2005) and Burns and Kedia (2006). They find that managers whose overall compensation is more sensitive to changes in share prices, tend to manage accruals to a greater degree. This may explain the higher rate of restatements in these firms (Burns and Kedia 2006).

References

Aboody, D., 1996. Market valuation of employee stock options. *Journal of Accounting and Economics*, 22(1), 357–391.

Aboody, D., Barth, M.E., and Kasznik, R., 2004. SFAS no. 123 stock-based compensation expense and equity market values. *The Accounting Review*, 79(2), 251–275.

Amir, E., Guan, Y., and Livne, G. 2007. The association of R&D and capital expenditures with subsequent earnings variability. *Journal of Business Finance & Accounting*, 34(1–2), 222–246.

Bell, T.B., Landsman, W.R., Miller, B.L., and Yeh, S., 2002. The valuation implications of employee stock option accounting for profitable computer software firms. *The Accounting Review*, 77(4), 971–996.

Bergstresser, D., and Philippon, T., 2006. CEO incentives and earnings management. *Journal of Financial Economics*, 80(3), 511–529.

Burns, N. and Kedia, S., 2006. The impact of performance-based compensation on misreporting. *Journal of Financial Economics*, 79(1), 35–67.

Cheng, Q., and Warfield, T.D., 2005. Equity incentives and earnings management. *The Accounting Review*, 80(2), 441–476.

Cheng, S., 2004. R&D expenditures and CEO compensation. *The Accounting Review*, 79(2), 305–328.

Dechow, P.M., Hutton, A.P., and Sloan, R.G., 1996. Economic consequences of accounting for stock-based compensation. *Journal of Accounting Research*, 34, 1–20.

Hall, B.J., and Murphy, K.J., 2002. Stock options for undiversified executives. *Journal of Accounting and Economics*, 33, 3–42.

Hanlon, M., Rajgopal, S., and Shevlin, T., 2003. Are executive stock options associated with future earnings? *Journal of Accounting and Economics*, 36(1), 3–43.

Kothari, S.P., Laguerre, T.E., and Leone, A.J., 2002. Capitalization versus expensing: evidence on the uncertainty of future earnings from capital expenditures versus R&D outlays. *Review of Accounting Studies*, 7(4), 355–382.

Ofek, E., and Yermack, D., 2000. Taking stock: equity-based compensation and the evolution of managerial ownership. *The Journal of Finance*, 55(3), 1367–1384.

Rajgopal, S., and Shevlin, T., 2002. Empirical evidence on the relation between stock option compensation and risk taking. *Journal of Accounting and Economics*, 33(2), 145–171.

15 Income taxes

ACCOUNTING STANDARDS IN FOCUS

IAS 12 *Income Taxes*

LEARNING OBJECTIVES

After studying this chapter, you should be able to:

 1 understand the nature of income tax

 2 understand differences in accounting treatments and taxation treatments for a range of transactions

 3 explain the concept of tax-effect accounting

 4 calculate and account for current taxation expense

 5 discuss the recognition requirements for current tax

 6 account for the payment of tax

 7 explain the nature of and accounting for tax losses

 8 calculate and account for movements in deferred taxation accounts

 9 apply the recognition criteria for deferred tax items

 10 account for changes in tax rates

 11 account for amendments to prior year taxes and identify other issues

 12 explain the presentation requirements of IAS 12

 13 implement the disclosure requirements of IAS 12.

15.1 THE NATURE OF INCOME TAX

Income taxes are levied by governments on income earned by individuals and entities in order to raise money to fund the provision of government services and infrastructure. The percentage payable and the determination of taxable profit are governed by income tax legislation administered by a dedicated government body. Tax payable is normally determined annually with the lodgement of a taxation document, although some jurisdictions may require payment by instalment, with estimates of tax payable being made on a periodic basis.

This chapter analyses the accounting standard IAS 12 *Income Taxes*. According to paragraph 1 of IAS 12, the standard applies in accounting for income taxes, including all domestic and foreign taxes based on taxable profits. It also applies to withholding taxes that are payable by a subsidiary, associate or joint arrangement on distributions to a reporting entity. The standard does not deal with methods of accounting for government grants or investment tax credits, but it does deal with accounting for tax effects arising in respect of such transactions.

At first glance, accounting for income tax appears to be a simple matter of calculating the liability owing, recognising the liability and expense, and recording the eventual payment of the amount outstanding. Such a simplistic approach applies only if accounting profit is the same amount as taxable profit and the respective profits have been determined by the same rules. Because this is generally not the case, accounting for income taxes can be a complicated exercise; hence the need for an accounting standard.

In each country there are different legal requirements for calculating taxable profit. It is not the purpose of this chapter to deal with these requirements. Instead, the focus is on how to apply the principles in IAS 12 for accounting for income tax. The Standard adopts the balance sheet approach. As stated in the objective of IAS 12, the principal issue is to account for the current and future tax consequences of:

(a) the future recovery (settlement) of the carrying amount of assets (liabilities) that are recognised in an entity's statement of financial position; and

(b) transactions and other events of the current period that are recognised in an entity's financial statements.

The Standard distinguishes between current tax and deferred tax assets and liabilities. Current tax is defined in paragraph 5 of IAS 12 as the amount of tax that should be paid or will be received on the taxable profit or loss for the period. According to paragraph 5, deferred tax assets and deferred tax liabilities reflect the future tax consequences arising from the recovery of the entity's assets, such as prepaid insurance, and the settlement of liabilities, such as provisions. These future tax consequences of the entity's assets and liabilities arise because of differences between the principles and rules applied for accounting purposes and the rules applied for determining taxable profit. Some common differences between accounting profit and taxable profit will be assumed to illustrate the application of the requirements of IAS 12. It is also assumed in this chapter that the income tax rate is 30%.

15.2 DIFFERENCES BETWEEN ACCOUNTING PROFIT AND TAXABLE PROFIT

Accounting profit is defined in IAS 12, paragraph 5, as 'profit or loss for a period before deducting tax expense', profit or loss being the excess (or deficiency) of income less expenses for that period. Such income and expenses would be determined and recognised in accordance with accounting standards and the *Conceptual Framework*. Taxable profit is defined in the same paragraph as the profit for a period, determined in accordance with the rules established by the taxation authorities, upon which income taxes are payable. Taxable profit is thus the excess of taxable income over taxation deductions allowable against that income. Thus, accounting profit and taxable profit — because they are determined by different principles and rules — are unlikely to be the same figure in any one period. An important step in accounting for income taxes is identifying and accounting for the differences between accounting profit and taxable profit. These differences arise from a number of common transactions and may be either permanent or temporary in nature.

15.2.1 Differences between accounting profit and taxable profit that do not reverse over time ('permanent differences')

Differences between accounting profit and taxable profit arise when the treatment of a transaction by taxation legislation and accounting standards is such that amounts recognised as part of accounting profit are never recognised as part of taxable profit, or vice versa. For example, in some jurisdictions governments provide incentives for investment by allowing entities to claim a tax deduction for more than 100% of expenditure incurred on certain research and development activities undertaken during the taxation period. Assuming the entity recognises all the research and development expenditure as an expense and claims a tax deduction for it in the same period, there would still be a difference between accounting profit and taxable profit to the extent that the entity claims a tax deduction for more than 100% of the research and development expenditure. As a result of this extra deduction, taxable profit for the period is lower than accounting profit, and the extra amount for research and development is never recognised as an expense for accounting purposes. Other examples of permanent differences include income that is never subject to taxation such as dividend income, and expenditure, such as entertainment expenses, incurred by an entity that will never be an allowable tax deduction. Such differences will never reverse. While there are no direct accounting entries for permanent differences, we need to be aware of them when making adjustments to accounting profit to calculate taxable profit, and also in providing disclosures that explain the difference between tax expense and accounting profit (*see section 15.13*).

15.2.2 Differences between accounting profit and taxable profit that reverse over time

Some differences between accounting profit and taxable profit are temporary because they arise when the period in which revenues and expenses are recognised for accounting purposes is different from the period in which such revenues and expenses are treated as taxable income and allowable deductions for tax purposes. For example, interest revenue recognised on an accrual basis may not be included in taxable income until it is received as cash. Similarly, an insurance premium, which is often paid in advance, may be tax-deductible when the payment is made. However, the insurance premium is not immediately recognised as an expense in accounting profit; instead, the insurance premium is recognised as an expense over time. To the extent that the insurance premium has not expired, it is recognised as prepaid insurance, which is an asset. The key feature of these differences is that they are temporary, because sooner or later the amount of interest revenue will equal the amount of taxable interest income, and the amount deducted against taxable income for insurance will equal the insurance expense offset against accounting income. However, in any one individual accounting/taxation period, these amounts will differ when calculating accounting profit and taxable profit respectively.

IAS 12 takes a balance sheet approach, defining temporary differences in terms of the differences between the carrying amount of assets and liabilities and the amount attributed to that item for tax purposes, as explained in *section 15.8*. Differences that result in the entity paying more tax in the future (e.g. when interest is recognised for accounting purposes in a period before it is received and included in taxable income) are known as taxable temporary differences. Differences that result in the entity recovering tax via additional deductible expenses in the future (e.g. when accrued expenses are recognised for accounting purposes in a period before they are paid and included as a tax deduction) are known as deductible temporary differences. The existence of such temporary differences means that income tax payable that is calculated on taxable profit will vary in the current period from that based on accounting profit, but tax payments will eventually catch up. This is demonstrated in illustrative example 15.1.

ILLUSTRATIVE EXAMPLE 15.1 Reversal of temporary difference

Assume that the accounting profit of Aster Ltd for the year ended 30 June 2024 was £150,000, including £5,600 in interest revenue of which only £4,000 had been received in cash, resulting in an interest receivable of £1,600. The company income tax rate is 30%.

If tax is not payable on interest until it has been received in cash, the company's taxable profit will differ from its accounting profit, and a taxable temporary difference will exist in respect of the £1,600 interest receivable. If accounting profit for the next year is also £150,000 and the outstanding interest is received in August 2025, tax payable for the years ending 30 June 2024 and 2025 is calculated as follows:

	2024	2025
Accounting profit	£150,000	£150,000
Temporary difference:		
Interest revenue not taxable for year ended 2024	(1,600)	
Interest revenue taxable for year ended June 2025		1,600
Taxable profit	£148,400	£151,600
Tax payable (30%)	44,520	45,480

Note that tax of £90,000, which is equal to 30% of £300,000 (being 2 × £150,000), is paid over the 2 years. The temporary difference created in 2024 is reversed in 2025. The same process occurs with all temporary differences although it may take a number of periods for a complete reversal to occur.

Appendix A to IAS 12 gives examples of circumstances that give rise to temporary differences because of different treatments of transactions for accounting and taxation purposes. Some examples are listed below. However, in practice temporary differences may vary so it is necessary to consult the relevant taxation legislation for specific jurisdictions.

Circumstances that give rise to taxable temporary differences
Such circumstances include the following:
1. Interest revenue is received in arrears and is included in accounting profit on an accrual basis, resulting in interest receivable, but is included in taxable profit on a cash basis.
2. Revenue from the sale of goods is included in accounting profit when goods are delivered, resulting in accounts receivable, but is included in taxable profit only when cash is collected.
3. Depreciation of an asset is accelerated for tax purposes (the taxation depreciation rate is greater than the accounting rate), resulting in a difference between the carrying amount of the depreciable asset and the amount attributed to it for taxation purposes (often referred to as its written down value for tax).
4. Development costs are capitalised and amortised to the statement of profit or loss and other comprehensive income but are deducted in determining taxable profit in the period in which they are incurred.
5. Prepaid expenses are recognised as an asset but have already been deducted on a cash basis in determining the taxable profit of the current or previous periods.
6. Depreciation of an asset is not deductible for tax purposes and no deduction will be available for tax purposes when the asset is sold or scrapped *(see section 15.9)*. This results in a difference between the carrying amount of the depreciable asset and the amount attributed to it for taxation purposes, similar to item 3 above.
7. Financial assets or investment property are carried at fair value, which exceeds cost, but no equivalent adjustment is made for tax purposes.
8. An entity revalues property, plant and equipment, but no equivalent adjustment is made for tax purposes.

The tax treatment of temporary differences arising from revaluation to fair value (item 8) are discussed and illustrated in chapter 5 of the book *(see section 5.6.1 Applying the revaluation model: revaluation increases)*.

Circumstances that give rise to deductible temporary differences
Such circumstances include the following:
1. Post employment benefit costs are recognised on an accrual basis as provision for employee benefits. The associated employee benefits expenses are recognised in accounting profit in the period in which the service is provided by the employee, but are not deducted in determining taxable profit until the entity pays either retirement benefits or contributions to a fund. Similar temporary differences arise in relation to other accrued expenses — such as provision for product warranties, employee leave entitlements and interest — which are deductible on a cash basis in determining taxable profit.
2. Accumulated depreciation of an asset in the financial statements is greater than the cumulative depreciation allowed up to the end of the reporting period for tax purposes because the accounting depreciation rate is greater than the allowable taxation depreciation rate. Consequently, the carrying amount of the asset is less than the amount attributed to it for tax purposes (often referred to as its written down value for tax).
3. The cost of inventories sold before the end of the reporting period is deducted in determining accounting profit when goods or services are delivered, but is deducted in determining taxable profit only when cash is collected.
4. The net realisable value *(see chapter 4)* of an item of inventory, or the recoverable amount *(see chapter 5)* of an item of property, plant and equipment, is less than its costs less depreciation. The entity therefore reduces the carrying amount of the asset to its recoverable amount, but that reduction is ignored for tax purposes until the asset is sold.
5. Research costs (or organisation or other start-up costs) are recognised as an expense in determining accounting profit, but are not permitted as a deduction in determining taxable profit until a later period. This gives rise to a temporary difference because the carrying amount is nil (as the costs have been expensed) but the amount attributed to the research costs or start-up costs for tax purpose reflects the amount that can be claimed as a tax deduction in future periods.
6. Revenue received in advance is recognised as a liability in the statement of financial position but has already been included in taxable profit in current or prior periods (for example, subscriptions received in advance).

7. A government grant recognised as a liability in the statement of financial position will not be taxable in a future period as it has already been included in taxable profit in the current or prior period *(see section 15.9).*
8. Financial assets or investment property is carried at fair value, which is less than cost, but no equivalent adjustment is made for tax purposes. (Temporary differences arising in these circumstances are beyond the scope of this chapter.)

The illustrative examples, exercises and problems in this chapter assume that the revenue from selling goods and services is taxable irrespective of whether cash has been received for the sale, and that the cost of sales is an allowable deduction irrespective of whether cash has been paid to acquire those goods.

15.3 ACCOUNTING FOR INCOME TAXES

IAS 12 requires the tax consequences of transactions and other events to be accounted for in the same manner and the same period as the transactions themselves. Thus, if a transaction is recognised in profit or loss for the period, so too is the related tax payable or tax benefit. The same applies for transactions recognised in other comprehensive income. Similarly, if a transaction is adjusted directly to equity, so too is the related tax effect. Differing accounting and taxation rules *(as discussed in section 15.2)* mean that the actual payment (deduction) of tax relating to revenue (expense) items may take place in both current and/or future accounting periods but IAS 12, paragraph 58, requires that the total income tax expense relating to transactions is recorded in the current year irrespective of when it will be paid or deducted.

To illustrate: an entity recognises interest revenue of £21,000 for the year ended 30 June 2025. Of this amount, £15,000 has been received in cash and a receivable asset has been raised for the remaining £6,000. Tax legislation regards interest revenue as taxable only when it has been received. Therefore, the entity will pay tax of £4,500 (£15,000 × 30%) in the current year and tax of £1,800 (£6,000 × 30%) in the following year when the £6,000 interest receivable asset is settled (that is, when cash is received).

If the entity were to record only the current tax payable amount as income tax expense, the profit for the year would be overstated by £1,800 (£4,500 current tax as opposed to £6,300 tax expense on £21,000 of interest revenue). To ensure that the profit after-tax figure for the year is both relevant and reliable, IAS 12 requires the entity to record an income tax expense of £6,300 (£21,000 × 30%) for the current year in respect to the interest revenue. This comprises a current tax liability amount of £4,500 and a deferred tax liability of £1,800 for the taxable profit that will arise in the future when the interest receivable is settled.

The need to recognise both current and future tax consequences of current year transactions means that each transaction has two tax effects:
1. tax payable on profit earned for the year may be reduced or increased because the transaction is not taxable or deductible in the current year
2. future tax payable may be increased or decreased when that transaction becomes taxable or deductible.

If only current tax payable is recorded as an expense, then the profit for the current year will be understated or overstated by the amount of tax to be paid or tax benefit to be received in future years. Similarly, in the years that the tax or benefit on these transactions is paid or received, income tax expense will include amounts relating to prior periods and therefore be understated or overstated. As IAS 12 requires income tax expense to reflect all tax effects of transactions entered into during the year regardless of when the effects occur, two calculations are required at the end of the reporting period:
- the calculation of current tax asset/liability, which determines the amount of tax receivable/payable for the period
- the calculation of movements in deferred tax effects relating to the future tax consequences arising from assets and liabilities recognised in the statement of financial position.

Acknowledging the current and future tax consequences of all items recognised in the statement of financial position (subject to certain exceptions) should make the information about the tax implications of an entity's operations and financial position more relevant and reliable.

15.4 CALCULATION OF CURRENT TAX

Current tax is the amount of income taxes payable to the taxation authorities for the current period. Current tax is calculated by multiplying the taxable profit by the tax rate. The calculation of taxable profit involves identifying differences between accounting revenues and taxable income, and between accounting expenses and allowable deductions, for transactions during the year, as well as reversing temporary differences from prior years that occur in the current period.

According to paragraph 46 of IAS 12,

> current tax shall be measured using the tax rate that has been enacted, or substantively enacted, by the end of the reporting period.

Therefore, if a tax rate has changed — or, in some jurisdictions, if a change has been announced — the rate applicable to the taxable profit for the period must be applied.

Identifying differences between the current year's profit and taxable profit is a relatively simple exercise. All revenues and expenses are reviewed for amounts that are not taxable or deductible. Identifying reversals of prior year temporary differences may require referring back to prior year worksheets, transactions posted to asset and liability accounts during the current year, or reconstructions of ledger accounts. (The latter method is used in this chapter.) Such reversals include, where applicable, accrued expenses that have been paid and are now deductible, bad debts written off and now deductible, accrued revenue that has been received and is now taxable, and prepaid expenses deducted in a prior period but now expensed in accounting profit.

Once the differences have been isolated, there are two ways that the current tax could be determined: (i) the net differences could be adjusted against accounting profit to derive taxable profit, or (ii) the gross amounts of items with differences could be added back or deducted against accounting profit. (The latter method is adopted in this chapter.) A worksheet is used to perform this reconciliation between accounting profit and taxable profit using the following formula:

Accounting profit (loss)
　　+ (−) accounting expenses not deductible for tax
　　+ (−) accounting expenses where the amount differs from deductible amounts
　　+ (−) taxable income where the amount differs from accounting income
　　− (+) accounting income not subject to taxation
　　− (+) accounting income where the amount differs from taxable income
　　− (+) deductible amounts where the amount differs from accounting expense
= taxable profit (loss)

The current tax rate is then applied to taxable profit to derive the current tax payable (illustrative example 15.2).

ILLUSTRATIVE EXAMPLE 15.2 Determination of current tax worksheet

Iris Ltd's accounting profit for the year ended 30 June 2025 was £250,450. Included in this profit were the following items of income and expense:

Amortisation — development project	£30,000
Impairment of goodwill expense	7,000
Depreciation — equipment (15%)	40,000
Entertainment expense	12,450
Insurance expense	24,000
Doubtful debts expense	14,000
Loss on sale of equipment	6,667
Rent revenue	25,000
Annual leave expense	54,000

At 30 June 2025, the company's draft statement of financial position showed the following balances:

	30 June 2025	30 June 2024
Assets		
Cash	£ 55,000	£ 65,000
Accounts receivable	295,000	277,000
Allowance for doubtful debts	(16,000)	(18,000)
Inventories	162,000	185,000
Prepaid insurance	30,000	25,000

	30 June 2025	30 June 2024
Rent receivable	3,500	5,500
Development project	120,000	—
Accumulated amortisation	(30,000)	—
Equipment	200,000	266,667
Accumulated depreciation	(90,000)	(80,000)
Goodwill	35,000	35,000
Accumulated impairment	(14,000)	(7,000)
Deferred tax asset	?	24,900
Liabilities		
Accounts payable	310,500	294,000
Provision for annual leave	61,000	65,000
Mortgage loan	100,000	150,000
Deferred tax liability	?	17,150
Current tax liability	?	12,500

Additional information
1. Taxation legislation allows Iris Ltd to deduct 125% of the £120,000 spent on development during the year.
2. Iris Ltd has capitalised development expenditure relating to a filter project and amortises the balance over the period of expected benefit (4 years).
3. The taxation depreciation rate for equipment is 20%.
4. The equipment sold on 30 June 2025 cost £66,667 when it was purchased 3 years earlier.
5. Neither entertainment expenditure nor goodwill impairment expense is deductible for taxation purposes.
6. The insurance and annual leave expenses are deductible when paid.
7. The rent revenue is taxable when received.
8. The company income tax rate is 30%.

Calculation of current tax payable
Before completing the worksheet, all differences between accounting and taxation figures must be identified:

1. Development project
There are two differences here: a permanent difference arising from the extra 25% deduction allowed by tax legislation, and a temporary difference arising from the treatment of the development costs. For accounting purposes, the £120,000 has been capitalised and will be amortised over 4 years; for tax purposes, the entire expenditure is deductible in the current year. The tax deduction for development is therefore: £150,000 (being £120,000 + [25% × £120,000]).

2. Impairment of goodwill expense
No tax deduction is allowed for impairment expense, so the taxation deduction is nil. Paragraph 21 of IAS 12 does not permit the recognition of the deferred tax liability arising from the taxable temporary difference created by the recognition of goodwill *(see section 15.9)*.

3. Depreciation expense — equipment
Because equipment is being depreciated at a faster rate for taxation purposes, the tax deduction for depreciation is more than the depreciation expense included in the calculation of accounting profit. The amount of depreciation deductible is £53,333 (being £266,667 × 20%, rounded to the nearest £).

4. Entertainment expense
No deduction is allowed for entertainment expenditure, so the taxation deduction is nil and there is a permanent difference between accounting profit and taxable profit.

5. Insurance expense
Insurance expenditure is deductible when paid. The existence of a prepaid insurance asset account in the statement of financial position indicates that the insurance payment and insurance expense figures are different. It is therefore necessary to reconstruct the asset account to identify if any part of the expense has already been deducted for taxation purposes. This is done as follows:

Prepaid Insurance

Balance b/d	£25,000	Insurance expense	£24,000
Bank (Insurance paid)	29,000	Balance c/d	30,000
	54,000		54,000

The insurance paid figure of £29,000 represents the deduction allowable in determining taxable profit. The expense figure of £24,000 shows that the payment made includes £5,000 for insurance cover for the next accounting period. When this amount is expensed, no deduction will be available against taxable profit.

6. *Allowance for doubtful debts*
If, under taxation legislation, no deduction is allowed for bad debts until they have been written off, the taxation amount for doubtful debts will be nil. The draft statement of financial position shows that an allowance was raised in the previous year, so any debts written off against that allowance are deductible in the current year. To determine the amount (if any) of that write-off, the ledger account is reconstructed as follows:

Allowance for doubtful debts

Bad debts written off	£16,000	Balance b/d	£18,000
Balance c/d	16,000	Doubtful debts expense	14,000
	32,000		32,000

The allowable deduction for bad debts written off is therefore £16,000.

7. *Loss on sale of equipment*
The gain or loss on the sale of equipment is different for accounting and taxation purposes, and is calculated as shown in the following table.

	Accounting	Taxation
Cost	£66,667	£66,667
Accumulated depreciation	30,000	40,000
Carrying amount	36,667	26,667
Proceeds	30,000	30,000
Gain (loss)	£ (6,667)	£ 3,333

The difference in the loss or gain on sale is caused by the different depreciation rates for accounting and tax purposes, resulting in different carrying amounts. The carrying amount for accounting is £10,000 higher than the carrying amount for tax at the time of sale. This temporary difference has arisen because the depreciation expense for accounting is less than the amount of depreciation deducted for tax purposes over the 3 years that Iris Ltd has owned the equipment. Now that the equipment has been sold, the temporary difference is reversed. When preparing the current tax worksheet, the accounting loss of £6,667 is added back to profit and the taxation gain is also added. Thus, the effect of the higher depreciation deductions claimed for tax over the 3 years is reversed when the equipment is sold. Note that the proceeds are calculated by subtracting the loss on sale from the carrying amount (36,667 − 6,667).

8. *Rent revenue*
Rent revenue is taxable when received. The presence in the statement of financial position of a rent receivable asset indicates that part of the revenue has not yet been received as cash and is not taxable in the current year. A temporary difference therefore exists in respect of rent, as demonstrated by reconstructing the ledger account:

Rent receivable

Balance b/d	£ 5,500	Cash received	£27,000
Rent Revenue	25,000	Balance c/d	3,500
	30,500		30,500

In this instance, the cash received figure represents rent received for two different accounting periods: £5,500 outstanding at the end of the prior year, and £21,500 for the current year. Thus, the taxable amount combines the reversal of last year's temporary difference and the tax payable on the current year's income. A temporary difference still exists for the £3,500 rent for this year not yet received in cash.

9. *Annual leave expense*
The annual leave expense is deductible when paid in cash. The provision for annual leave indicates the existence of unpaid leave and therefore a taxation temporary difference. This is demonstrated by reconstructing the ledger account.

Provision for annual leave			
Leave paid	£ 58,000	Balance b/d	£ 65,000
Balance c/d	61,000	Leave Expense	54,000
	119,000		119,000

The reconstruction reveals a payment of £58,000, which is deductible in the current year and represents a partial reversal of the temporary difference related to the opening balance. As none of the current year expense has been paid, no deduction is available this year and further temporary difference is created.

This chapter assumes that sales revenue and cost of sales are taxable/deductible even when not received/paid in cash, so there are no differences with respect to the accounts receivable or accounts payable balances. If different assumptions applied, then the amounts of cash received for sales and cash paid for inventory would need to be determined in order to calculate the current tax payable.

Figure 15.1 contains the current worksheet used to calculate the current tax liability for Iris Ltd.

FIGURE 15.1 Completed current tax worksheet for Iris Ltd

IRIS LTD Current Tax Worksheet for the year ended 30 June 2025		
Accounting profit Add:		£ 250,450
Add:		
Amortisation of development expenditure	£ 30,000	
Impairment of goodwill expense	7,000	
Depreciation expense – equipment	40,000	
Entertainment expense	12,450	
Insurance expense	24,000	
Doubtful debts expense	14,000	
Accounting loss on sale of equipment	6,667	
Taxation gain on sale of equipment	3,333	
Annual leave expense	54,000	
Rent received	27,000	218,450
		468,900
Deduct:		
Rent revenue	25,000	
Bad debts written off	16,000	
Insurance paid	29,000	
Development costs paid	150,000	
Annual leave paid	58,000	
Depreciation of equipment for tax	53,333	(331,333)
Taxable profit		137,567
Current liability @ 30%		£ 41,270

15.5 RECOGNITION OF CURRENT TAX

Paragraph 12 of IAS 12 requires current tax and any tax receivable/payable for prior periods to be recognised as a current tax asset/liability, to the extent that it has not already been received/paid. If the amount of tax that has already been paid for current and prior periods exceeds the amount of tax payable for those periods, a current tax asset is recognised.

Additionally, paragraph 58 of the standard requires current tax to be recognised as income or an expense and included in the profit or loss for the period, except to the extent that the tax relates to a transaction recognised in other comprehensive income or directly in equity, or arises from a business combination. Therefore, the following journal entry is required to recognise the current tax payable for Iris Ltd at 30 June 2025:

30 June 2025			
Income tax expense (Current)	Dr	41,270	
Current tax liability	Cr		41,270
(Recognition of current tax liability)			

15.6 PAYMENT OF TAX

Taxation legislation may require taxation debts to be paid annually upon lodgement of a taxation return or at some specified time after lodgement (such as on receipt of an assessment notice, or at a set date or time). Alternatively, the taxation debt may be paid by instalment throughout the taxation year. In some jurisdictions, payments in advance relating to next year's estimated taxable profit may be required. Where one annual payment is required, the entry is:

Current tax liability	Dr	41,270	
Cash	Cr		41,270
(Payment of current liability)			

If payment by instalment is required, the process is a little more complicated. To pay by instalment, an estimate of taxable profit needs to be made; hence the reference in paragraph 12 of IAS 12 to amounts paid in excess of the amount due. To illustrate the process of payment by instalment, assume that Iris Ltd (from illustrative example 15.2) has to pay tax quarterly and has paid the following amounts for the first three quarters of the 2024–25 taxation year:

28 October 2024	£ 9,420
28 January 2025	10,380
28 April 2025	10,750

The journal entry to record the first payment is:

Current tax liability	Dr	9,420	
Cash	Cr		9,420
(Payment of first quarterly taxation instalment)			

Similar entries are passed at 28 January 2025 and 28 April 2025. At 30 June 2025, because the tax liability has been partially paid, an adjustment is required on the current tax worksheet to determine the balance of tax owing in relation to the 2024–25 year (see below).

IRIS LTD Current Tax Worksheet (extract) for the year ended 30 June 2025	
Taxable profit	£ 137,567
Tax payable @ 30%	41,270
Less: Tax already paid (£9,420 + £10,380 + £10,750)	(30,550)
Current tax liability	10,720

The effect of the adjusting journal entry is to change the debit balance of £30,550 in the current tax liability account (caused by the instalment payments) into a credit balance of £10,720, representing the amount owing to the tax authority:

30 June 2025			
Income tax expense (Current)	Dr	41,270	
Current tax liability	Cr		41,270
(Recognition of current tax liability)			

15.7 TAX LOSSES

Tax losses are created when allowable deductions exceed taxable income. IAS 12 envisages three possible treatments for tax losses: they may be carried forward, carried back, or simply lost. Where taxation legislation allows tax losses to be carried forward and deducted against future taxable profits, the carry-forward may be either indefinite or for a limited number of years. Other restrictions — such as requiring losses to be deducted against non-taxable income on recoupment — may also apply. Carry-forward tax losses create a deductible temporary difference and therefore a deferred tax asset in that the company will pay less tax on future taxable profits. *The recognition of a deferred tax asset for tax losses, which is subject to a recoverability test, is discussed in detail in section 15.9.2.*

Accounting for the creation and recoupment of carry-forward tax losses is demonstrated in illustrative example 15.3.

ILLUSTRATIVE EXAMPLE 15.3 Creation and recoupment of carry-forward tax losses

The following information relates to Poppy Ltd for the year ended 30 June 2026:

Accounting loss on income statement	£ 7,600
Depreciation expense	14,700
Depreciation deductible for tax	20,300
Entertainment expense (not tax-deductible)	10,000
Income tax rate	30%

The calculation of the tax loss appears below:

POPPY LTD Current Tax Worksheet (extract) for the year ended 30 June 2026	
Accounting loss	£ (7,600)
Add:	
Depreciation expense	14,700
Entertainment expense	10,000
	17,100
Deduct:	
Depreciation deduction for tax	(20,300)
Tax loss	(3,200)
Deferred tax asset @ 30%	£ 960

Assuming that recognition criteria are met, the adjusting journal entry is:

30 June 2026			
Deferred tax asset (Tax losses)	Dr	960	
Income tax expense	Cr		960
(Recognition of deferred tax asset from tax loss)			

If Poppy Ltd then makes a taxable profit of £23,600 for the year ending 30 June 2027, the loss is recouped as follows:

POPPY LTD Current Tax Worksheet (extract) for the year ended 30 June 2027	
Taxable profit before tax loss	£23,600
Tax loss recouped	(3,200)
Taxable profit	20,400
Current tax liability @ 30%	£ 6,120

The adjusting journal entry is:

30 June 2027			
Income tax expense (Current)	Dr	7,080	
Deferred tax asset (Tax Losses)	Cr		960
Current tax liability	Cr		6,120
(Recognition of current tax liability and reversal of deferred tax asset from tax loss)			

15.8 CALCULATION OF DEFERRED TAX

As already explained, IAS 12 adopts the philosophy that an entity should account for the current and future tax consequences of
- transactions and other events that occur during a period (*refer to sections 15.4 and 15.5*); and
- the future recovery (or settlement) of the assets and liabilities recognised in the statement of financial position.

As mentioned in section 15.2.2, temporary differences are defined in paragraph 6 of IAS 12 as the differences between the carrying amounts and the tax base of an entity's assets and liabilities. The tax base of an asset or liability refers to the amount attributed to it for taxation purposes, such as the amount that can be deducted in future periods for depreciation of plant and equipment (*discussed in section 15.8.2*). At the end of the reporting period, a comparison of an entity's carrying amounts of assets and liabilities and their tax bases will reveal the temporary differences that exist, and adjustments will then be made to deferred assets and liabilities. (The reference to 'deferred' tax adjustments comes from the fact that assets and liabilities reflect future inflows and outflows to an entity. The deferred tax balances are related to these future flows, and hence are deferred to the future rather than affecting current tax.) For assets and liabilities such as entertainment costs payable, differences between their tax bases and carrying amounts may be caused by permanent differences. Such differences will not give rise to deferred tax adjustments.

The following steps are required to calculate deferred tax:
1. Determine the carrying amounts of items recognised in the statement of financial position.
2. Calculate the tax bases of the items by determining the taxable economic benefits and deducible amounts arising from the recovery or settlement of each item (*discussed in section 15.8.2*).
3. Calculate and recognise the deferred tax assets and liabilities arising from these temporary differences after taking into account any relevant recognition exclusions (*see section 15.8.5*) and offset considerations (*see section 15.12.1*).
4. Recognise the net movement in deferred tax assets and liabilities during the period as deferred tax expense or income in profit or loss (unless an accounting standard requires recognition in other comprehensive income or directly in equity or as part of a business combination).

The first three steps are carried out on a worksheet. The final step requires an adjusting journal entry.

15.8.1 Determining carrying amounts

Carrying amounts are asset and liability balances net of valuation allowances, accumulated depreciation, amortisation and impairment losses (for example, accounts receivable less allowance for doubtful debts).

15.8.2 Determining tax bases

Tax bases need to be calculated for assets and liabilities.

Tax bases of assets

The economic benefits embodied in an asset are normally taxable when recovered by an entity through the use or sale of that asset. The entity may then be able to deduct all or part of the cost or carrying amount of the asset against those taxable amounts (that is, the taxable economic benefits) when determining taxable profits.

Paragraph 7 of IAS 12 describes the tax base of an asset as:

> the amount that will be deductible for tax purposes against any taxable economic benefits that will flow to an entity when it recovers the carrying amount of the asset. If those economic benefits will not be taxable, the tax base of the asset is equal to its carrying amount.

The following formula can be applied to derive the tax base from the carrying amount of the asset:

Carrying amount − Future taxable amounts + Future deductible amounts = Tax base

Figure 15.2 contains examples of the calculation of tax bases for assets.

	Carrying amount	Future taxable amounts*	Future deductible amounts	Tax base
Prepayments £3,000: fully deductible for tax when paid	£3,000	£(3,000)	£ 0	£ 0
Trade receivables of £52,000 less £2,000 allowance for doubtful debts: sales revenue is already Included in taxable profit	50,000	0	2,000	52,000
Plant and equipment costing £10,000 has a carrying value of £5,400: accumulated tax depreciation is £6,500	5,400	(5,400)	3,500**	3,500
Loan receivable £25,000: loan repayment will have no tax consequences	25,000	0	0	25,000
Interest receivable £1,000: recognised as revenue but not taxable until received	1,000	(1,000)	0	0

*Future taxable amounts are equal to carrying amounts unless economic benefits have already been included in taxable profit.
**The deductible amount represents the original cost of the asset less the accumulated depreciation based on taxation depreciation rates (being £10,000 − £6,500 = £3,500).

FIGURE 15.2 Calculation of the tax base of assets

Figure 15.2 illustrates the following situations:
- Where the future economic benefits are taxable, the carrying amount equals the taxable economic benefits. Hence, the tax base equals the future deductible amount. This can be seen in figure 15.2 for prepayments, plant and equipment, and interest receivable.
- Where there are no taxable economic benefits, generally the deductible amount is nil and the tax base equals the carrying amount. In figure 15.2, this applies to the loan receivable. An exception is trade receivables where, although there is no taxable economic benefit, there is a future deductible amount because of the existence of doubtful debts. In this case, the tax base equals the sum of the carrying amount and the future deductible amount.

Tax bases of liabilities

Liabilities, other than those relating to unearned revenue, do not generate taxable economic benefits. Instead, settlement may give rise to deductible items.

Paragraph 8 of IAS 12 describes the tax base of a liability as:

> its carrying amount, less any amount that will be deductible for tax purposes in respect of that liability in future periods. In the case of revenue which is received in advance, the tax base of the resulting liability is its carrying amount, less any amount of the revenue that will not be taxable in future periods.

The following formula can be applied to derive the tax base from the carrying amount of the liability:

Carrying amount + Future taxable amounts − Future deductible amounts = Tax base

Figure 15.3 contains examples of the calculation of the tax base for liabilities.

FIGURE 15.3 Calculation of the tax base of liabilities

	Carrying amount	Future taxable amounts	Future deductible amounts	Tax base
Provision for annual leave £3,900: not deductible for tax until paid	£ 3,900	£ 0	£(3,900)	£ 0
Trade payables £34,000: expense already deducted from taxable income	34,000	0	0	34,000
Loan payable £20,000: loan repayment will have no tax consequences	20,000	0	0	20,000
Accrued expenses £6,700: deductible when paid in cash	6,700	0	(6,700)	0
Accrued penalties £700: not tax-deductible	700	0	0	700

Figure 15.3 illustrates two situations:

- Where the carrying amount equals the future deductible amount, the tax base is nil. This applies to provisions for annual leave and accrued expenses.
- Where there is no future deductible amount, the carrying amount equals the tax base. This applies to trade payables and the loan payable.

Based on paragraph 8 of IAS 12, the following formula can be applied to derive the tax base from the carrying amount of a liability arising from revenue received in advance:

Carrying amount − Amount that will not be taxed in future periods = Tax base

For example, for an entity that has a liability of £500 for subscription revenue received in advance, which is taxed in the period in which it is received, the tax base can be calculated as £500 − £500 = £nil. The revenue of £500 will not be taxed in future periods because it has already been taxed in the period in which it was received.

Some items may have a tax base but are not recognised as assets and liabilities in the statement of financial position. Paragraph 9 of IAS 12 provides the example of research costs that are recognised as an expense in determining accounting profit in the period in which they are incurred but are not allowed as a deduction in determining taxable profit until a later period. Additionally, under paragraph 51A of IAS 12 the manner in which an asset/liability is recovered/settled may affect the tax base of that asset/liability in some jurisdictions.

15.8.3 Calculating temporary differences

When the carrying amount of an asset or liability is different from its tax base, a temporary difference exists. Temporary differences effectively represent the expected net future taxable amounts arising from the recovery of assets and the settlement of liabilities at their carrying amounts. Therefore, a temporary difference cannot exist where there are no future tax consequences from the realisation or settlement of an asset or liability at its carrying value.

Taxable temporary differences

A taxable temporary difference exists when the future taxable economic benefits of an asset or liability exceed any future deductible amounts. In the case of an asset, this means that the taxable economic benefits arising from the recovery of the asset exceed the deduction that can be claimed, giving rise to more tax being payable in the future. This is demonstrated in illustrative example 15.4.

ILLUSTRATIVE EXAMPLE 15.4 Calculation of a taxable temporary difference

An asset, which cost 150, has an accumulated depreciation of 50.
  Accumulated depreciation for tax purposes is 90 and the tax rate is 25%.

Carrying amount	= 100
Future taxable economic benefit	= 100
Future deductible amount	= 60
Tax base	= 100 − 100 + 60
	= 60 (= 150 cost less 90 tax depreciation)

Because the future taxable economic benefit is greater than the future deductible amount, a temporary taxable difference exists. In other words, the expectation is that the entity will pay income taxes in the future, when it recovers the carrying amount of the asset, because it expects to earn 100 but receive a tax deduction of 60. The entity has a liability to pay tax on that extra 40. As the payment occurs in the future, the liability is referred to as a 'deferred tax liability'.

Source: Adapted from IAS 12, paragraph 16.

Deductible temporary differences

A deductible temporary difference exists when the future taxable economic benefit of an asset or liability is less than any future deductible amounts. This is demonstrated in illustrative example 15.5.

ILLUSTRATIVE EXAMPLE 15.5 Calculation of a deductible temporary difference

Dalal Inc. recognises a liability of 100 for provision for warranty. For tax purposes, the product warranty costs will not be deductible until Dalal Inc. pays claims. The tax rate is 25%.

Carrying amount	= 100
Future taxable economic benefit	= 0
Future deductible amount	= 100
Tax base	= 100 + 0 − 100
	= 0

As the future deductible amount is greater than the tax base, a deductible temporary difference exists. In other words, in settling the liability for its carrying amount, Dalal Inc. will reduce its future tax profits and hence its future tax payments. Dalal Inc. then has an expected benefit relating to the future tax deduction. As the benefits are to be received in the future, the asset raised is referred to as a 'deferred tax asset'.

Source: Adapted from IAS 12, paragraph 25.

15.8.4 Calculating deferred tax liabilities and deferred tax assets

Paragraphs 15 and 24 of IAS 12 require (with some exceptions) that a deferred tax liability and a deferred tax asset be recognised for all taxable temporary differences and all deductible temporary differences, and that a total be determined for taxable temporary differences and for deductible temporary differences. An appropriate tax rate can then be applied to these totals to derive the balance of deferred tax liability and deferred tax asset at the end of the period. Paragraph 47 of the standard specifies that:

> Deferred tax assets and liabilities shall be measured at the tax rates that are expected to apply to the period when the asset is realised or the liability is settled, based on tax rates (and tax laws) that have been enacted or substantively enacted by the end of the reporting period.

Thus, if the tax rate is currently 30% but will rise to 32% in the next reporting period, deferred amounts should be measured at 32%. Should a change be enacted (or substantively enacted) between the end of the reporting period and the time of completion of the financial statements, no adjustment needs to be made to the tax balances recognised. However, disclosure of any material impacts should be made by note in compliance with IAS 10 *Events after the Reporting Period*.

Different tax rates may be required when temporary differences are expected to reverse in different periods, or when temporary differences relate to different taxation jurisdictions. Additionally, consideration should be given to the manner in which an asset/liability is recovered/settled in jurisdictions where the manner of recovery/settlement determines the applicable tax rate (IAS 12 paragraphs 51 and 51A).

Before determining the amounts of deferred tax liabilities and deferred tax assets, consideration must be given to the recognition criteria mandated by the accounting standard. *(See section 15.9.)*

15.8.5 Excluded differences

A deferred tax liability is usually recognised on taxable temporary differences. Likewise, a deferred tax asset is normally recognised on deductible temporary differences. However, IAS 12 specifies certain exceptions.

Paragraph 15 states that a *deferred tax liability* shall be recognised for all *taxable* temporary differences, *except* where the deferred tax liability arises from:

(a) goodwill; or
(b) the initial recognition of an asset or liability, which
   (i) did not arise through a business combination,
   (ii) at the time of the transaction, affects neither accounting profit nor taxable profit, and
   (iii) at the time of the transaction, does not give rise to equal taxable and deductible temporary differences.

Paragraph 24 states that a *deferred tax asset* shall be recognised for all *deductible* temporary differences, *except* where the deferred tax asset arises from the initial recognition of an asset or liability, which:

(a) did not arise through a business combination,
(b) at the time of the transaction, affects neither accounting profit nor taxable profit, and
(c) at the time of the transaction, does not give rise to equal taxable and deductible temporary differences.

Goodwill

Goodwill is the excess of the cost of the business combination over the acquirer's interest in the net fair value of the identifiable assets, liabilities and contingent liabilities *(see chapter 19)*. A taxable temporary difference is created because the tax base of goodwill is nil. IAS 12 does not permit the recognition of the deferred tax liability relating to goodwill, because goodwill is a residual amount and recognising the deferred tax amount would increase the carrying amount of goodwill (IAS 12 paragraph 21).

Initial recognition of an asset or liability

The tax base and carrying amount of an asset are usually the same on initial recognition but in some cases a temporary difference can arise on initial recognition. Consider the example of a non-deductible asset that is not acquired through a business combination. A non-deductible asset is an asset whose cost is not allowed as a deduction when calculating taxable profits and therefore the tax base on date of purchase is nil. A taxable temporary difference will arise on the initial recognition, being the difference between the carrying amount on date of purchase (the asset's cost) and its tax base (nil). Thus, although a deferred tax liability would normally be recognised on taxable temporary differences, the deferred tax liability is not recognised in this scenario because all the requirements of paragraph 15 of IAS 12 are met: the asset was not acquired in a business combination; the purchase did not affect accounting profit or loss, or tax profit or tax loss; and, at the time of recognition, it did not give rise to equal taxable and deductible temporary differences.

Following the introduction if IFRS 16 *Leases*, IAS 12 was amended by paragraph 22A to clarify that the exclusions from recognition of deferred tax liabilities and deferred tax assets (paragraph 15 and paragraph 24) does not apply to the temporary differences arising on the initial recognition of a lease.

15.8.6 Deferred tax worksheet

A deferred tax worksheet is shown in illustrative example 15.6. The purpose of the deferred tax worksheet is to calculate the movements in the deferred tax asset and the deferred tax liability accounts during the current period. Determining the temporary differences relating to assets and liabilities allows the closing balances of the deferred tax accounts to be calculated. A consideration of the beginning balances and movements during the year allows the calculation of the adjustments required to achieve those closing balances. All assets and liabilities may be included in the worksheet; alternatively, only those expected to have different accounting and tax bases could be shown.

ILLUSTRATIVE EXAMPLE 15.6 Deferred tax worksheet

Using the information provided in illustrative example 15.2, the deferred tax worksheet for Iris Ltd is shown in figure 15.4.

FIGURE 15.4 Deferred tax worksheet for Iris Ltd

IRIS LTD Deferred Tax Worksheet as at 30 June 2025						
	Carrying amount	Future taxable amount	Future deductible amount	Tax base	Taxable temporary differences	Deductible temporary differences
Relevant assets						
Receivables[1]	£ 279,000	£ 0	£16,000	£295,000		£16,000
Prepaid insurance[2]	30,000	(30,000)	0	0	£ 30,000	
Rent receivable[3]	3,500	(3,500)	0	0	3,500	
Development project[4]	90,000	(90,000)	0	0	90,000	
Equipment[5]	110,000	(110,000)	80,000	80,000	30,000	
Goodwill[6]	21,000	(21,000)	0	0	21,000	
Relevant liabilities						
Provision for annual leave[7]	61,000	0	(61,000)	0		61,000
Total temporary differences					174,500	77,000
Excluded differences[8]					(21,000)	—
Temporary differences					153,500	77,000
Deferred tax liability[9]					46,050	
Deferred tax asset[9]						23,100
Beginning balances[10]					(17,150)	(24,900)
Movement during year[11]					—	—
Adjustment[10]					28,900 Cr	(1,800) Cr

1. The carrying amount of receivables £279,000 (£295,000 – 16,000) represents the cash that the company expects to receive after allowing for any doubtful debts. Tax on this amount has already been paid via sales revenue recognised in the current year, so the future taxable benefit is nil. The allowance for doubtful debts raised as an expense in the current year is not deductible against taxable profit until the debts actually go 'bad' and are written out of the accounts receivable balance. Thus, there is a future deduction of £16,000 available. The tax base for receivables is £279,000, being the total of all debts outstanding at 30 June 2025 (doubtful or otherwise). Because the future deductible amount is greater than the future taxable benefit, a deductible temporary difference of £16,000 exists in respect of receivables.

2. The prepaid insurance asset represents the future benefit of insurance cover at 30 June 2025. The recovery of these benefits results in the flow of taxable economic benefits to Iris Ltd, giving a future taxable benefit of £30,000. The insurance premium was paid in the year ended 30 June 2025 and

was allowed as a deduction against the taxable profit for that year. This means that no deduction is available when the £30,000 is expensed in the year ended 30 June 2026, giving a tax base for the asset of £0. As the future taxable benefit exceeds the future deductible amount, a taxable temporary difference of £30,000 exists in respect of prepaid insurance.

3. The rent receivable asset represents monies to be received after 30 June 2025. The recovery of these benefits results in the flow of taxable economic benefits to Iris Ltd. Hence, a future taxable benefit of £3,500 exists. As this is a revenue item, no future deduction is available and the tax base is £0. As the future taxable benefit exceeds the future deductible amount, a taxable temporary difference of £3,500 exists in respect of the rent receivable.

4. The development project asset represents the future economic benefits expected to arise from development work undertaken in the current year. When those benefits are received, they are taxable. The total expenditure on development was deducted from taxable profit in the current year, so no future deduction is available. The tax base is £0 as the cash paid has already reduced taxable profit in the current year. As the future taxable benefit exceeds the future deductible amount, a taxable temporary difference of £90,000 exists in respect of the development project.

5. The carrying amount of equipment represents the future economic benefits expected to be received from that asset over the remainder of its useful life, £110,000 (£200,000 − £90,000). When those benefits are received, they are taxable. Iris Ltd will be able to claim a deduction against those taxable benefits, but only to the extent of the tax base of the asset. As the depreciation rate for tax purposes is greater than the accounting rate, the future deduction is only £80,000, being the original cost of £200,000 less £120,000 (i.e. 3 years' accumulated depreciation at 20% per annum). As the future taxable benefit exceeds the future deductible amount, a taxable temporary difference of £30,000 exists in respect of equipment.

6. The carrying amount of goodwill represents the future economic benefits expected to be received. Those benefits are taxable when received but, unlike equipment, no deduction against the benefits is available. The tax base of goodwill is £0 as taxation law does not allow a deduction for any amounts paid to acquire goodwill. As the future taxable benefit exceeds the future deductible amount, a taxable temporary difference of £21,000 exists in respect of goodwill (however, see exception to recognition in 8 below).

7. The provision for annual leave represents leave accrued by employees as at the end of the reporting period. As the leave represents future payments, there is no future taxable amount. When those payments are made, they are fully deductible against taxable profit. The tax base at 30 June 2025 is £0 because leave payments are only deductible in the year of payment. As the future deductible amount exceeds the future taxable amount, a deductible temporary difference of £61,000 exists in respect of the annual leave provision.

8. The adjustment for excluded differences recognises that IAS 12 (paragraphs 15 and 24) has prohibited the recognition of deferred tax amounts relating to certain temporary differences (see section 15.9.2). Paragraph 15 prohibits the recognition of the taxable temporary difference relating to goodwill, so it is removed from the total temporary differences existing at 30 June 2025.

9. The deferred tax liability figure of £46,050 is the future tax payable as a result of the existence of taxable temporary differences of £153,500. The deferred tax asset figure of £23,100 is the future deductions available as a result of the existence of deductible temporary differences of £77,000. These figures represent the closing balances of the deferred tax accounts.

10. Deferred tax amounts may accumulate over time; for example, the taxable temporary difference for equipment represents 3 years' differentials between accounting and taxation depreciation charges. This means that the deferred tax accounts have an opening balance representing prior year differences. If no adjustment is made for the opening balance, the deferred tax amounts are overstated. Accordingly, the opening balances are deducted from the total balances in order to determine the adjustment necessary to account for changes (additions and reversals) to deferred tax items during the current year. These adjustments are shown on the last line of the worksheet and form the basis of the adjusting journal entry for deferred tax. Positive figures are increases and negative figures are decreases in the account balances.

11. Normally, the deferred tax accounts are only adjusted at the end of each reporting period after the worksheet has been completed. Occasionally, however, adjustments are made to the deferred accounts during the year so the 'movements' line is used to adjust for such changes. Adjustments could be made for:
    - recoupment of prior year tax losses (see section 15.7)
    - a change in tax rates (see section 15.10)
    - an amendment to a prior year tax return (see section 15.11)
    - revaluation of property, plant and equipment items (see section 15.11.2)
    - business combinations (see section 15.11.3).

The flowcharts in figure 15.5 below summarise the measurement of deferred tax items according to IAS 12. While the flowcharts show the steps in the calculation of deferred tax items, they do not present the steps in determining whether the resultant deferred tax assets or deferred tax liabilities will be recognised. The criteria for the recognition of deferred tax assets and deferred tax liabilities are considered next, *in section 15.9.*

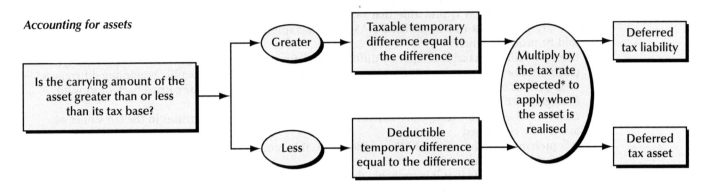

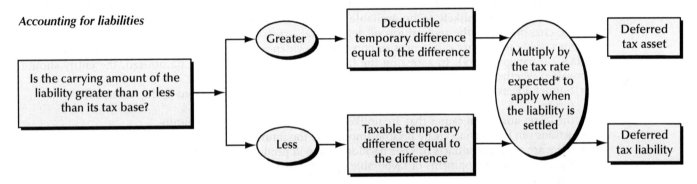

FIGURE 15.5 Accounting for deferred tax items
Note: *refers to the present tax rate or tax laws (tax rates) that have been enacted or substantively enacted by reporting date.
Source: CPA Australia (2010, p. 2)

15.9 RECOGNITION OF DEFERRED TAX LIABILITIES AND DEFERRED TAX ASSETS

The existence of temporary taxable and deductible differences may not result in the recognition of deferred tax assets and liabilities. Paragraphs 15 and 24 of IAS 12 specify recognition criteria that must be met before recognition occurs.

15.9.1 Deferred tax liabilities

Deferred tax liabilities must be recognised for all taxable temporary differences (except as outlined below). There is no need to explicitly consider the recognition criteria for a deferred tax liability because its recognition is derived from taxable temporary differences of recognised assets and liabilities. As the carrying amount of the asset or liability giving rise to the taxable temporary difference is recovered or settled, the temporary difference will reverse and give rise to taxable amounts that must be settled in future periods.

15.9.2 Deferred tax assets

Paragraph 24 of IAS 12 states that deferred tax assets must be recognised for all deductible temporary differences (subject to certain exceptions) and from the carry forward of tax losses, but only to the extent that it is probable that future taxable profits will be available against which the temporary differences can be utilised. The probability of future tax deductions is inherent in the recognition of the assets and liabilities that give rise to deductible temporary differences. For example, the recognition of a provision reflects the probability of an outflow to settle the obligation in future periods. The reversal of deductible temporary differences results in deductions against the taxable profits of future periods. However, the economic benefits in the form of reductions in tax payments will flow to the entity only if it earns sufficient taxable profits against which the deductions can be offset. Therefore, an entity recognises deferred tax assets only when it is probable that taxable profits will be available against which the deductible temporary differences can be utilised (IAS 12 paragraph 27). The realisation of a deferred tax asset would be probable where:

- there are sufficient taxable temporary differences relating to the same taxation authority and the same taxable entity that are expected to reverse in the same period as the deductible temporary differences, or in periods to which a tax loss arising from the deferred tax asset can be carried back or forward (paragraph 28)
- there would be taxable temporary differences arising if unrecognised increases in the fair values of assets were recognised
- it is probable that there will be other sufficient taxable profits arising in future periods against which to utilise the deductions
- other factors indicate that it is probable that the deductions can be realised.

If there are insufficient taxable temporary differences available against which to offset the deductible temporary differences, an entity can recognise a deferred tax asset only to the extent that sufficient taxable profits will be made in the future or that tax planning opportunities are available to create future taxable profits (IAS 12 paragraph 29).

A history of accounting losses, or the existence of unused tax losses, provides evidence that future taxable profits are unlikely to be available for the utilisation of deductible temporary differences. In these circumstances, the recognition of deferred tax assets would require either the existence of sufficient taxable temporary differences or convincing evidence that future taxable profits will be available (IAS 12, paragraph 35). In assessing the likelihood that tax losses will be utilised, the entity should consider whether:

- future budgets indicate that there will be sufficient taxable income derived in the foreseeable future
- the losses arise from causes that are unlikely to recur in the foreseeable future
- actions can be taken to create taxable amounts in the future
- there are existing contracts or sales backlogs that will produce taxable amounts
- there are new developments or favourable opportunities likely to give rise to taxable amounts
- there is a strong history of earnings other than those giving rise to the loss, and the loss was an aberration and not a continuing condition.

Where, on the balance of the evidence available, it is not probable that deductible temporary differences will be utilised in the future, no deferred tax asset is recognised. This probability assessment must also be applied to deferred tax assets that have previously been recognised and, if it is no longer probable that the benefits of such assets will flow to the entity, the carrying amount must be derecognised by passing the following entry:

30 June			
Income tax expense		Dr	xxx	
Deferred tax asset		Cr		xxx
(Derecognition of deferred tax assets where recovery is no longer probable)				

At the end of each reporting period, the entity should reassess the probability of recovery of all unrecognised deferred tax assets; it should recognise these assets to the extent that it is now probable that future taxable profit will allow the deduction of the temporary difference on its reversal. Changes in trading conditions, new taxation legislation, or a business combination may all contribute to improving the chance of recovering the deferred tax benefits. Paragraph 60 of IAS 12 requires that any adjustment to deferred tax be recognised in profit or loss, except to the extent that it relates to items previously recognised outside profit or loss (for example in other comprehensive income or charged or credited to equity).

The journal entries to record the movement in deferred tax for illustrative example 15.6 are provided in illustrative example 15.7.

Using the figures calculated in illustrative example 15.6 and assuming that the recognition criteria for deferred tax assets can be met, the adjusting journal for deferred tax movements is:

30 June 2025			
Income tax expense	Dr	30,700	
Deferred tax asset	Cr		1,800
Deferred tax liability	Cr		28,900
(Recognition of movements in deferred tax balances for the year)			

These movements can be checked back to the current worksheet as follows:
- Deferred tax assets arise in respect of doubtful debts and annual leave. In the current year, additional deductions of £2,000 (doubtful debts) and £4,000 (leave) are received. This indicates that more deductible temporary differences had been reversed than had been created, resulting in a decrease of £6,000 in future deductions and a £1,800 decrease in the deferred tax asset.
- Deferred tax liabilities arise in respect of development expenditure, equipment, insurance and rent. In the current year, additional deductions of £90,000 (development), £13,333 (depreciation) and £5,000 (insurance) are offset by additional taxable benefits of £10,000 (sale of equipment) and £2,000 (rent revenue), giving a net extra increase in taxable temporary differences and a £28,900 increase in the deferred tax liability.

The posting of this entry results in the deferred tax ledger accounts appearing as follows:

Deferred tax asset

1/724	Balance b/d	24,900	30/6/25	Income Tax Expense	1,800
			30/6/25	Balance c/d	23,100
		24,900			24,900
1/7/25	Balance b/d	23,100			

Deferred tax liability

30/6/25	Balance c/d	46,050	1/7/24	Balance b/d	17,150
			30/6/25	Income tax expense	28,900
		46,050			46,050
			1/7/25	Balance b/d	46,050

If the two taxation adjusting journals — current and deferred — are combined, then the total income tax expense recorded for the year ended 2025 by Iris Ltd is:

Income tax expense (Current) (see section 19.5)	£ 41,270
Income tax expense (Deferred) (see above)	30,700
Total	£ 71,970

This figure represents the total tax consequences of the transactions recorded in profit or loss for the year. It can be checked in this way: The accounting profit for the year is £250,450. All items of revenue and expense are taxable or deductible with the exception of goodwill impairment and entertainment expense. The development expenditure during the year gave rise to an 'extra' deduction of £30,000 against taxable profit. If the accounting profit adjusted for these permanent differences is multiplied by the tax rate, the result represents the total tax payable above (both now and in the future):

Accounting profit	£ 250,450
Add: Non-deductible amortisation	7,000
Add: Non-deductible entertainment expense	12,450
Less: Additional deduction for development	(30,000)
Taxable net profit	239,900
Tax @ 30%	£ 71,970

15.10 CHANGE OF TAX RATES

When a new tax rate is enacted (or substantively enacted), the new rate should be applied in calculating the current tax liability and adjustments to deferred tax accounts during the year. It should also be applied to the deferred amounts recognised in prior years. A journal adjustment must be passed to increase or reduce the carrying amounts of deferred tax assets and liabilities, in order to reflect the new value of future taxable or deductible amounts. Paragraph 60 of IAS 12 requires the net amount arising from the restatement of deferred tax balances to be recognised in profit or loss, except to the extent that the deferred tax amounts relate to items previously recognised in other comprehensive income or recognised directly in equity.

The accounting entries for the effects of a change in the tax rate are provided in illustrative example 15.8.

ILLUSTRATIVE EXAMPLE 15.8 Change of tax rate

As at 30 June 2026, the balances of deferred tax accounts for Carnation Ltd were:

Deferred Tax Asset	£29,600
Deferred Tax Liability	(72,800)

All deferred tax balances relate to items that were recorded in P&L. In September 2026, the government reduced the company tax rate from 40 pence to 30 pence in the pound, effective from 1 July 2027. The recorded deferred tax balances represent the tax effect of future taxable benefits and future deductible amounts at 40 pence in the pound, so they are now overstated and must be adjusted as follows:

	Deferred tax asset	Deferred tax liability
Opening balance	£29,600	£ 72,800
Adjustment for change in tax rate: ([40−30]/40)	(7,400)	(18,200)
Restated balance	£22,200	£ 54,600

The adjusting journal entry is:

Deferred Tax Liability	Dr	18,200	
Deferred Tax Asset	Cr		7,400
Income Tax Expense	Cr		10,800
(Recognition of the impact of a change of tax rate on deferred tax amounts)			

15.11 OTHER ISSUES

15.11.1 Amended prior year tax figures

It may take years before the tax filings have been assessed and approved by the tax authorities. So at the date the financial statements are approved for issuance, management will have to estimate the current tax asset and liability as well as any deferred tax balances. Subsequently, it is possible that the taxation authority will amend that assessment by changing the amount of taxable or deductible items. This amendment could result in the entity being liable to pay extra tax or becoming eligible for a taxation refund. Upon receipt of an amended assessment, the entity should analyse the reason for the adjustment and consider whether both current and deferred tax are affected. For example, if an entity has used an incorrect taxation depreciation rate, then the amendment to the correct rate will change both the prior year taxable profit and future taxable profits across the economic life of the depreciable asset. If only current tax for the previous year has changed, the following journal entry would be passed:

Income tax expense	Dr	xxx	
Current tax liability	Cr		xxx
(Amendment to prior year current tax on receipt of amended assessment)			

If the amendment also changes a deferred item, the new temporary difference will need to be calculated and the carry-forward balance adjusted accordingly. In the depreciation example used above, the adjustment (assuming the accounting depreciation rate is lower than the rate used to calculate taxable profit) is:

Income tax expense	Dr	xxx	
Deferred tax liability	Cr		xxx
Current tax liability	Cr		xxx
(Amendment to prior year current tax and deferred tax liability on receipt of amended assessment)			

Any amendment to the deferred tax liability or the deferred tax asset arising from amended assessments would appear on the deferred tax worksheet as a 'movement' adjustment.

15.11.2 Items recognised outside profit or loss

In general, the amount of current and deferred tax arising in a period must be recognised outside profit or loss if the tax relates to items that are recognised outside profit or loss (IAS 12 paragraph 61A). Examples of items that are recognised in other comprehensive income are:
- revaluation of items of property, plant and equipment to fair value *(see chapter 5)*. At the time of revaluation, an adjustment may be required to be made to the balance of the deferred tax liability account. For example, if an item of plant is revalued upwards from £100 to £200 and the tax rate is 30%, the entity would pass the following journal entry:

Plant	Dr	100	
(Revaluation of plant)			
Deferred tax liability	Cr		30
Asset revaluation surplus	Cr		70
(Revaluation of plant, recognition of deferred tax liability and accumulation of net revaluation gain in equity)			

- exchange differences arising on the translation of the financial statements of a foreign entity *(see chapter 24)*.

15.11.3 Deferred tax arising from a business combination

The amount of deferred tax arising in relation to the acquisition of an entity or business is recognised (subject to the recognition criteria) and included as part of identifiable assets acquired and liabilities assumed when determining the goodwill or gain on bargain purchase arising on acquisition. This may arise, for example, if the acquiree has a tax loss or other deferred tax asset that did not satisfy the recoverability criteria at the acquiree level but the criteria were satisfied at the level of the acquirer as a result of the business combination. *(Further discussion of the determination of goodwill and gain on bargain purchase can be found in chapter 19.)* When a deferred tax asset of the acquiree not recognised at the date of or during the measurement period of the business combination is subsequently recognised by the acquirer, the resulting deferred tax income is recognised in profit or loss (unless the standard requires it to be recognised outside profit and loss).

15.12 PRESENTATION IN THE FINANCIAL STATEMENTS

LO12

IAS 12 specifies the way in which tax items (income, expenses, assets and liabilities) are to be presented in the financial statements, including the circumstances in which items can be offset.

15.12.1 Tax assets and tax liabilities

Tax assets and tax liabilities must be classified as current and non-current as required by IAS 1 *Presentation of Financial Statements* (paragraph 60) and presented in the statement of financial position in accordance with IAS 1 paragraphs 54(n), 54(o) and 56. Paragraph 71 of IAS 12 allows current tax assets and current tax liabilities to be offset only when the entity has a legally enforceable right to offset the amount, and intends either to settle on a net basis or to realise the asset and settle the liability simultaneously. A legal right to set off the accounts would normally exist where the accounts relate to income taxes levied by the same taxing authority.

Deferred tax assets and deferred tax liabilities can be offset only if a legally enforceable right to offset current amounts exists; and the deferred items relate to income taxes levied by the same taxing authority on the same taxable entity, or on different taxable entities which intend either to settle on a net basis or to realise the asset and settle the liability simultaneously in each future period in which significant deferred amounts will reverse (IAS 12 paragraph 74).

Consequently, entities operating in a single country will normally offset both current and deferred tax assets and liabilities, and show only a net current tax liability or asset and a net deferred liability or asset.

15.12.2 Tax expense

The tax expense (or income) related to profit or loss for the period is required to be presented in the statement of profit or loss. The tax consequences of items in other comprehensive income must be recognised and presented separately in other comprehensive income (IAS 12 paragraph 77).

15.13 DISCLOSURES

LO13

Paragraphs 79–82A of IAS 12 contain the required disclosures relating to income taxes. These disclosures are very detailed, and provide significant additional information about the composition of income tax expense (or income), and both taxable and deductible temporary differences. Paragraph 79 requires separate disclosure of the major components of the tax expense (income) figure (examples of which are listed in paragraph 80), such as current tax expense and deferred tax arising from temporary differences. Paragraph 81 requires a wide range of disclosures including:

- tax relating to items recognised directly in equity
- tax expense relating to discontinued operations
- explanation of changes in tax rates, and
- the amount and expiry date, if applicable, of deductible temporary differences, unused tax losses and unused tax credits, for which a deferred tax asset has not been recognised in the statement of financial position.

Paragraph 81 also requires two detailed reconciliations to be prepared:

- Paragraph 81(c) requires entities to disclose 'an explanation of the relationship between tax expense (income) and accounting profit'. This essentially reconciles expected tax — accounting profit multiplied by tax rate — to the actual tax expense recognised. The reconciliation enables financial statement users to understand why the relationship between accounting profit and income tax expense is unusual, the factors causing the variance, and factors that could affect the relationship in the future. Entities are allowed to reconcile in either or both of the following ways:
  - a numerical reconciliation between tax expense and expected tax
  - a numerical reconciliation between the average effective tax rate (tax expense divided by the accounting profit) and the applicable tax rate.
  - Irrespective of the reconciliation method used, entities must disclose the basis on which the applicable tax rate is computed.
- Paragraph 81(g) requires disclosure of the following information for deferred tax items recognised in the statement of financial position:

  in respect of each type of temporary difference, and in respect of each type of unused tax loss and unused tax credit:

  i. the amount of the deferred tax assets and liabilities recognised in the statement of financial position for each period presented; and

  ii. the amount of the deferred tax income or expense recognised in profit or loss, if this is not apparent from the changes in the amounts recognised in the statement of financial position.

Normally, the second part of the paragraph 81(g) disclosure is required only if a change in tax rate or legislation has occurred during the year, or if some other event causes an adjustment to a deferred account during the period.

When an entity has suffered tax losses in either the current or previous period, and recognised a deferred tax asset related to those losses that is dependent on earning future taxable profits in excess of those arising on the reversal of taxable temporary differences, paragraph 82 requires disclosure of the amount of the deferred tax asset and the nature of the evidence supporting its recognition.

Paragraph 82A applies only in those jurisdictions where tax rates vary according to whether or not profit or retained earnings is distributed. In this situation, paragraph 82A requires the entity to disclose the nature and amounts (to the extent practicable) of the potential income tax consequences that would result from the payment of dividends to its shareholders.

Figure 15.6 provides an illustration of the disclosures required by IAS 12.

FIGURE 15.6 Example of selected disclosures required by IAS 12

Note 4: Income tax expense	Notes	2026 £	2025 £	IAS 12 paragraph
Major components of income tax expense				79
Current tax expense		126,600	117,600	80(a)
Deferred tax from origination and reversal of temporary differences		(20,250)	11,320	80(c)
Deferred tax relating to tax rate change		250	—	80(d)
Benefit from unrecognised tax loss used to reduce current tax expense		(1,500)	—	80(e)
Income tax expense		105,100	128,920	80(f)
Tax relating to items recognised in other comprehensive income				
Deferred tax relating to revaluation of land		12,500	—	81(ab)
Reconciliation of tax expense to prima facie tax on accounting profit				
The applicable tax rate is the company income tax rate of 30% (2025: 40%)				81(c)(i)
The prima facia on accounting profit differs from the tax expense provided in the accounts as follows:				
Accounting profit		402,000	397,000	
Prima facie tax at 30% (2025: 40%)		120,600	158,800	
Tax effect of non-deductible-expenses				
Goodwill impairment		3,900	5,200	
Non-taxable revenue		(1,500)	(2,000)	
Entertainment		3,600	2,300	
		126,600	164,300	
Increase in beginning deferred taxes resulting from reduction in tax rate		250	—	
Reduction in current tax from recoupment of tax losses		(1,500)	—	
Tax effect of net movements in items giving rise to:*				
Deferred tax assets		(8,250)	3,200	
Deferred tax liabilities		(12,000)	(38,580)	
Tax expense		105,100	128,920	81(d)
Change in tax rate				
As of 1 July 2025, the company tax rate changed from 40% to 30%				81(d)
Unrecognised deferred tax assets				
Tax losses in respect of which deferred tax has not been recognised as it is not probable that benefits will be received		20,000	40,000	81(e)
Unrecognised deferred tax liabilities				
Aggregate of temporary differences associated with investments in subsidiaries for which deferred tax liabilities have not been recognised		16,000	16,000	81(f)

*These figures represent the net effect of movements in assets and liabilities during the year which have increased or decreased current tax. The details can be found in disclosures required by paragraph 81(g)(ii).

(continued)

FIGURE 15.6 *(continued)*

Note 4: Income tax expense	Notes	2026 £	2025 £	IAS 12 paragraph
Deferred tax assets and liabilities				
The following items have given rise to deferred tax assets:				
Accounts receivable		12,000	15,000	
Employee entitlements		24,000	22,000	
Total deferred tax assets		36,000	37,000	
The following items have given rise to deferred tax liabilities:				
Land		12,500	—	
Plant and equipment		15,000	36,000	
Total: deferred tax liabilities		27,500	36,000	
Offset of deferred tax asset against liability		36,000	37,000	
Net deferred tax asset (liability)		8,500	(1,000)	*81(g)(i)*
Deferred tax expenses (income) recognised in the statement of comprehensive income for each type of temporary difference*				
Deferred tax expense in relation to:				
Plant and equipment		(12,000)	(38,580)	
Total deferred tax expense		(12,000)	(38,580)	
Deferred tax income in relation to:				
Accounts receivable		750	1,200	
Employee entitlements		7,500	2,000	
Total deferred tax income		8,250	3,200	*81(g) (ii)*

* This disclosure is required only if the movements in deferred items cannot readily be ascertained from other disclosures made with respect to deferred assets and liabilities. This is the case in this situation because the change in tax rate adjustments has obscured the movements in deferred items.

Figure 15.7 illustrates the disclosures about income taxes in Amazon Inc.'s consolidated financial statements for the year ended 31 December 2023.

NOTE 9 — INCOME TAXES

In 2021, 2022, and 2023, we recorded a net tax provision (benefit) of $4.8 billion, $(3.2) billion, and $7.1 billion. Our U.S. taxable income is reduced by accelerated depreciation deductions and increased by the impact of capitalized research and development expenses. Cash paid for income taxes, net of refunds, was $3.7 billion, $6.0 billion, and $11.2 billion for 2021, 2022, and 2023.

Certain foreign subsidiary earnings and losses are subject to current U.S. taxation and the subsequent repatriation of those earnings is not subject to tax in the U.S. The U.S. tax rules also provide for enhanced accelerated depreciation deductions by allowing us to expense a portion of qualified property, primarily equipment. These enhanced deductions are scheduled to phase out annually from 2023 through 2026. Our federal tax provision included a partial accelerated depreciation deduction election for 2021, and a full election for 2022 and 2023. Effective January 1, 2022, research and development expenses are required to be capitalized and amortized for U.S. tax purposes.

	December 31,	
	2022	2023
Deferred tax assets (1):		
Loss carryforwards U.S. – Federal/States	386	610
Loss carryforwards – Foreign	2,831	2,796
Accrued liabilities, reserves, and other expenses	3,280	3,751

	December 31,	
	2022	2023
Stock-based compensation	4,295	5,279
Depreciation and amortization	1,009	1,114
Operating lease liabilities	18,285	19,922
Capitalized research and development	6,824	14,800
Other items	1,023	745
Tax credits	950	1,582
Total gross deferred tax assets	38,883	50,599
Less valuation allowances (2)	(4,374)	(4,811)
Deferred tax assets, net of valuation allowances	34,509	45,788
Deferred tax liabilities:		
Depreciation and amortization	(9,039)	(12,454)
Operating lease assets	(17,140)	(18,648)
Other items	(817)	(1,489)
Net deferred tax assets (liabilities), net of valuation allowances	$ 7,513	$ 13,197

(1) Deferred tax assets are presented after tax effects and net of tax contingencies.
(2) Relates primarily to deferred tax assets that would only be realizable upon the generation of net income in certain foreign taxing jurisdictions or future capital gains, as well as tax credits.

Our valuation allowances primarily relate to foreign deferred tax assets, including substantially all of our foreign net operating loss carryforwards as of December 31, 2023. Our foreign net operating loss carryforwards for income tax purposes as of December 31, 2023 were approximately $10.2 billion before tax effects and certain of these amounts are subject to annual limitations under applicable tax Law. If not utilized, a portion of these losses will begin to expire in 2024.

INCOME Tax Contingencies

We are subject to income taxes in the U.S. (federal and state) and numerous foreign jurisdictions. Significant judgment is required in evaluating our tax positions and determining our provision for income taxes. During the ordinary course of business, there are many transactions and calculations for which the ultimate tax determination is uncertain. We establish reserves for tax-related uncertainties based on estimates of whether, and the extent to which, additional taxes will be due. These reserves are established when we believe that certain positions might be challenged despite our belief that our tax return positions are fully supportable. We adjust these reserves in light of changing facts and circumstances, such as the outcome of tax audits. The provision for income taxes includes the impact of reserve provisions and changes to reserves that are considered appropriate.

Source: Amazon Annual Report 2023

Note 9 provides information about major differences between accounting profit and taxable profit. The enhanced accelerated depreciation deducted in calculating taxable profit exceeds the depreciation expense recognised in accounting profit, reducing taxable profit compared with accounting profit. The requirement to capitalise research and development expenses and amortise them for purposes of calculating taxable profit increases taxable profit relative to accounting profit.

The disclosure of the components of deferred tax assets and deferred tax liabilities are consistent with the disclosures required by paragraph 81 (g) (i).

15.14 SUMMARY

This chapter analyses the content of IAS 12 *Income Taxes* and provides guidance on its implementation. The principal issue in accounting for taxes is how to account for the current and future tax consequences of transactions and other events of the current period. The accounting standard requires entities to recognise (with limited exceptions) deferred tax liabilities and deferred tax assets when the recovery or settlemer of an asset or liability will result in larger or smaller tax payments than would occur if such settlement or recovery had no tax consequence. The tax consequences of transactions are to be accounted for in the same way as the transaction to which they are related. Therefore, for transactions recognised in the statement of profit or loss and other comprehensive income, all related tax effects are also recognised in the statement of profit or loss and other comprehensive income. Where a transaction requires a direct adjustment to equity, so do any tax effects. Deferred tax assets, particularly those relating to tax losses, are recognised only if it is probable that the entity will have sufficient taxable profit in the future against which the tax benefit can be offset. All deferred tax liabilities must be recognised in full. IAS 12 requires extensive disclosures to be made in relation to both current and deferred tax items.

Discussion questions

1. What is the main principle of tax-effect accounting as outlined in IAS 12?
2. Explain the meaning of a temporary difference as it relates to deferred tax calculations and give three examples.
3. Explain how accounting profit and taxable profit differ, and how each is treated when accounting for income taxes.
4. In tax-effect accounting, the creation of temporary differences between the carrying amount and the tax base for assets and liabilities leads to the establishment of deferred tax assets and liabilities in the accounting records. List examples of temporary differences that create:
   (a) deferred tax assets
   (b) deferred tax liabilities.
5. In IAS 12, criteria are established for the recognition of a deferred tax asset and a deferred tax liability. Identify these criteria, and discuss any differences between the criteria for assets and those for liabilities.

References

Amazon 2023, *Annual Report*, https://amazon.com.
CPA Australia 2010, *International Financial Reporting Standards Fact Sheet — IAS 12 Income Taxes*, CPA Australia, February, www.cpaaustralia.com.au.
International Accounting Standards Board 2023, IAS 12 *Income Taxes*, www.ifrs.org.

Accounting researchers have been interested in whether differences between taxable profit and pre-tax profit (the accounting measure of profit before tax) provide information that is useful to investors. Additionally, accounting research has hypothesised that a greater book–tax difference may indicate poorer earnings quality and/or manipulation of recorded tax expense (Hanlon 2005).

Within research that looks at the usefulness of tax accounting, Amir et al. (1997) examine the pricing implications of six types of deferred tax assets and liabilities in 1992–1994. These include assets and liabilities created with respect to temporary differences in depreciation, losses carried forward, restructuring charges, environmental charges, employee benefits and valuation allowance (also see below). They find consistent evidence that deferred tax assets for employee benefit and restructuring charges are positively related to stock prices. This is consistent with these assets representing anticipated reduction in future cash payment for tax. They, however, find mixed evidence with respect to the other types of deferred tax assets and liabilities. Lev and Nissim (2004) explore if taxable income can help predict growth to assess the usefulness of tax accounting. They find that the ratio of taxable income to book income is positively associated with measures of future growth, suggesting that tax-based calculation of income can assist investors in predicting growth. They also find that this ratio and earnings-to-price are negatively related, consistent with the notion that earnings are more highly priced when taxable earnings are higher.

Laux (2013) extends Amir et al. (1997) by examining directly whether deferred tax assets (liabilities) predict reductions (increases) in future cash payments to tax authorities. He argues that this depends on the timing of the recognition of revenues and expenses in pre-tax income relative to taxable income. Specifically, he predicts lower future tax payments if expenses and revenues are first recognised in pre-tax income, and only later in taxable income (e.g. warranty expense). In contrast, he predicts no effect on future tax payments if the recognition of revenues and expenses in taxable income precedes recognition in pre-tax income (e.g. as in the case of unearned revenues and accelerated tax depreciation). His findings are consistent with these predictions. Laux (2013) also examines the valuation implications of the two categories of the timeliness of recognition of expenses and revenues. He finds that only expenses and revenues that are first recognised in pre-tax income (and recognised later in taxable income) are value relevant. Additionally, and similarly to Amir et al. (1997), he finds that deferred tax liabilities related to depreciation are not positively associated with stock prices. This is consistent with the possibility that these liabilities do not reverse and so do not trigger additional cash payments. This will be the case, for example, in growing firms that increase the depreciable asset base over time. As the asset base grows, origination of new deferred tax liabilities exceeds the reversal of old liabilities, implying no cash is returned to the tax authorities.

Laux (2013) uses a US sample, as many other studies reviewed here do. There is relatively little research using IFRS-reporting entities. One exception is Flagmeier (2022), who extends and refines Laux's (2013) classifications of deferred taxes using a sample of German firms. Flagmeier finds that deferred tax assets representing losses carryforward are not priced by the stock market. This is intriguing because she also finds that these deferred tax assets are associated with lower tax expense and payments in subsequent periods.

Deferred taxes may be indicative of managerial discretion in accruals, since this discretion typically does not affect current tax liability. Phillips et al. (2003) therefore conjecture that higher deferred tax expense is associated with more earnings management. Consistent with this, they find that companies are more likely to avoid earnings declines, and avoid losses when they show higher deferred tax expense. Ayers et al. (2010) examine the implications of book–tax differences for credit ratings. They find that larger changes in the difference between pre-tax income and taxable income are associated with lower credit ratings. They interpret this result as follows. As the amount by which book income exceeds tax income increases, credit analysts interpret this as poor earnings quality, which in turn suggests greater credit risk. This risk may stem from the lower earnings persistence that is documented by Hanlon (2005) for firms with large book–tax differences.

Deferred taxes themselves can be subject to manipulation. IAS 12 and US GAAP allow for partial recognition of deferred tax *assets*, to the extent that managers do not believe these assets will be recoverable. The accounting item that reduces the carrying amount of deferred tax asset under partial provisioning is called valuation allowance in the US (ASC 740-10-30-5). By changing their assessment of the valuation allowance managers can influence reported earnings. However, Bauman et al. (2001) do not find evidence consistent with this conjecture from contextual analysis of Fortune 500 firms. Miller and Skinner (1998) find that the valuation allowance is largely related to losses carried forward that may not be utilised. This is consistent with the view that the allowance is correctly stated, on average. Nevertheless, Schrand and Wong (2003) provide some evidence that banks in a strong financial position tend to have higher valuation allowance, suggesting they opportunistically create hidden reserves.

IAS 12 has removed much discretion that was previously available to companies under local standards. Specifically, in the UK, before 2005, both deferred tax assets and liabilities were recorded only to the extent that managers believed that a reversal would take place. That is, partial recognition was allowed for both deferred tax liabilities and deferred tax assets. Gordon and Joos (2004) examine how this discretion was used by UK managers and find that it was mostly deployed in highly leveraged firms that report larger unrecognised deferred tax liabilities. This enabled them to reduce the overall reported leverage of their firms, suggesting the allowance was measured opportunistically. The implication is that removing the level of discretion allowed by the new standard may have improved the quality of tax accounting.

References

Amir, E., Kirschenheiter, M., and Willard, K., 1997. The valuation of deferred taxes. *Contemporary Accounting Research*, 14(4), 597–622.

Ayers, B. C., Laplante, S. K., and McGuire, S. T., 2010. Credit ratings and taxes: The effect of book–tax differences on ratings changes. *Contemporary Accounting Research*, 27(2), 359–402.

Bauman, C. C., Bauman, M. P., and Halsey, R. F., 2001. Do firms use the deferred tax asset valuation allowance to manage earnings? *Journal of the American Taxation Association*, 23(s-1), 27–48.

Flagmeier, V. 2022. The information content of deferred taxes under IFRS. *European Accounting Review*, 31(2), 495–518.

Gordon, E. A., and Joos, P. R., 2004. Unrecognized deferred taxes: evidence from the UK. *The Accounting Review*, 79(1), 97–124.

Hanlon, M., 2005. The persistence and pricing of earnings, accruals and cash flows when firms have large book–tax differences. *The Accounting Review*, 80(1), 137–166.

Laux, R. C., 2013. The association between deferred tax assets and liabilities and future tax payments. *The Accounting Review*, 88(4), 1357–1383.

Lev, B., and Nissim. D., 2004. Taxable income, future earnings and equity values. *The Accounting Review*, 79(4), 1039–1074.

Miller, G. S., and Skinner, D. J., 1998. Determinants of the valuation allowance for deferred tax assets under SFAS No. 109. *The Accounting Review*, 73(2), 213–233.

Phillips, J., Pincus, M., and Rego, S. O., 2003. Earnings management: New evidence based on deferred tax expense. *The Accounting Review*, 78(2), 491–521.

Schrand, C. M., and Wong, M. H., 2003. Earnings management using the valuation allowance for deferred tax assets under SFAS No. 109. *Contemporary Accounting Research*, 20(3), 579–611.

Part 3

Presentation and Disclosures

16 Statement of cash flows *435*

17 Key notes disclosures *457*

18 Operating segments *479*

19 Business combinations *497*

16

Statement of cash flows

ACCOUNTING STANDARDS IN FOCUS

IAS 7 *Statement of Cash Flows*

LEARNING OBJECTIVES

After studying this chapter, you should be able to:

 1   explain the purpose of a statement of cash flows and its usefulness

 2   explain the definition of cash and cash equivalents

 3   explain the classification of cash flow activities and classify cash inflows and outflows into operating, investing and financing activities

 4   contrast the direct and indirect methods of presenting net cash flows from operating activities

 5   prepare a statement of cash flows and use a worksheet to prepare a statement of cash flows with more complex transactions

 6   prepare other disclosures required or encouraged by IAS 7

 7   be aware of future developments and changes in relation to IAS 7.

INTRODUCTION AND SCOPE

Ultimately, all existing and potential investors, lenders and other creditors would like to receive cash from their investment. Consequently, information about an entity's receipts and payments is important to such users of financial statements. The statement of cash flows provides this information by reporting cash inflows and outflows classified into operating, investing and financing activities, and the net movement in cash and cash equivalents during the period.

This chapter explains how to present a statement of cash flows in accordance with IAS 7 *Statement of Cash Flows*.

16.1 PURPOSE OF A STATEMENT OF CASH FLOWS

The overall purpose of a statement of cash flows is to present information about the historical changes in cash and cash equivalents of an entity during the period classified by operating, investing and financing activities. The statement of cash flows can help users of financial statements to:

- evaluate the entity's ability to generate cash and cash equivalents
- predict future cash flows
- evaluate the accuracy of past cash flow predictions and forecasts.

When used in combination with other financial statements, the statement of cash flows can help users to:

- evaluate an entity's financial structure (including liquidity and solvency) and its ability to meet its obligations and to pay dividends
- evaluate the entity's ability to affect the amount and timing of future cash flows, to enable it to adapt to changing business opportunities and circumstances
- understand the reasons for the difference between profit or loss for a period and the net cash flow from operating activities (the reasons for the differences are often helpful in evaluating the quality of earnings of an entity)
- compare the operating performance of different entities because cash flows are not directly affected by different accounting choices and judgements under accrual accounting.

16.2 DEFINING CASH AND CASH EQUIVALENTS

Paragraph 6 of IAS 7 defines cash and cash equivalents as follows:

Cash comprises cash on hand and demand deposits.

Cash equivalents are short-term, highly liquid investments that are readily convertible to known amounts of cash and which are subject to an insignificant risk of changes in value.

Paragraph 7 of IAS 7 explains that cash equivalents are held for the purpose of meeting short-term cash commitments, and not for investment or other purposes. Cash equivalents must be able to be converted into a known amount of cash. This means that the amount of cash that will be received must be known at the time of the initial investment in the cash equivalent. It must also have no more than an insignificant risk of changing in value. Therefore, an investment will qualify as a cash equivalent only if it has a short maturity (usually three months or less). Examples of cash and cash equivalents include cash on hand, cash at bank, short-term money market securities and 90-day term deposits. Equity investments typically do not qualify as cash equivalents, but it is necessary to consider their substance; equity instruments such as preferred shares acquired shortly before their specified maturity date may fall within the definition of cash equivalents.

Bank borrowings are ordinarily classified as a financing activity. A bank overdraft is a special case. It can arise where a customer has a facility with the bank that allows the customer's account to be overdrawn (i.e. to go below nil). The amount of the bank overdraft can vary on a daily basis up to an agreed limit. This would not usually be considered as part of cash and cash equivalents. However, if the bank overdraft is repayable on demand and forms an integral part of an entity's cash management, it is included in cash and cash equivalents. Such overdrafts may fluctuate from being overdrawn to being positive (i.e. cash at bank).

The statement of cash flows reports on changes in aggregate cash and cash equivalents. Therefore, movements between items classified as cash and cash equivalents, such as a transfer from cash at bank to a 90-day term deposit, are not reported in the statement of cash flows. The concept of cash and cash equivalents used in IAS 7 is summarised and illustrated in figure 16.1.

FIGURE 16.1 Concept of cash and cash equivalents used in IAS 7

	Form	Conditions	Examples
Cash	Cash on hand		Notes and coins
	Demand deposits		Call deposits held at financial institutions
Cash equivalents	Short-term, highly liquid investments	Readily convertible into known amounts of cash and subject to an insignificant risk of change in value	Bank bills Non-bank bills Deposits on short-term money market, such as 7-day deposits
	Bank overdraft	Repayable on demand and form an integral part of an entity's cash management	Cheque account that is in overdraft and which is repayable on demand

Source: Loftus et al. 2015.

16.3 CLASSIFYING CASH FLOW ACTIVITIES

As stated earlier, cash flow activities reported in the statement of cash flows are classified into operating, investing and financing activities. Paragraph 6 of IAS 7 defines these activities as follows:

Operating activities are the principal revenue-producing activities of the entity and other activities that are not investing or financing activities.

Investing activities are the acquisition and disposal of long-term assets and other investments not included in cash equivalents.

Financing activities are activities that result in changes in the size and composition of the contributed equity and borrowings of the entity.

Only expenditures that result in a recognised asset in the statement of financial position are eligible for classification as investing activities. For example, Green Company incurs expenditure of €50,000 on research for a carbon-neutral air conditioner. Expenditure incurred in the research phase must be recognised as an expense in accordance with IAS 38 *Intangible Assets*. Accordingly, the cash paid in relation to the research project is not classified as an investing cash flow because it has not resulted in the recognition of an asset in the statement of financial position of Green Company.

Note that the operating activities category is a default category; it includes all activities that are not classified as either investing activities or financing activities. Figure 16.2 summarises typical cash receipts and payments of an entity, classified by activity.

FIGURE 16.2 Typical cash receipts and payments classified by activity

Operating activities

Cash inflows from:
Sale of goods
Rendering of services
Royalties, fees, commissions
Interest received (or investing activity)
Dividends received (or investing activity)

Cash outflows for:
Payments to suppliers of goods and services
Payments to employees for services
Payments to the government for income tax and other taxes
Payments to lenders for interest or other borrowing cost (or finance activity)

Financing activities

Cash inflows from:
Issuing shares and other equity instruments
Issuing debentures, unsecured notes
Borrowings, such as loans

Investing activities

Cash inflows from:
Sale of property, plant and equipment
Sale of intangibles
Sale of shares and debt instruments of other entities
Repayment of loans by other parties

Cash outflows for:
Purchases of property, plant and equipment
Purchases of intangibles
Purchases of shares and debt instruments of other entities
Loans to other entities

Cash outflows for:
Buying back own shares (reduction in capital)
Repayment of debentures, unsecured notes
Repayment of borrowings, such as loans
Payment of dividends to shareholders (or operating)

16.3.1 Classifying interest and dividends received and paid

IAS 7 does not prescribe how interest and dividends received and paid should be classified. Rather, paragraph 31 of IAS 7 requires cash flows from interest and dividends received and paid to be disclosed separately and classified consistently from period to period as operating, investing or financing activities. Although most financial institutions classify interest paid and interest and dividends received as operating cash flows there is no consensus on how to classify these cash flows for other entities.

Some entities classify interest paid and interest and dividends received as operating cash flows because they may relate to items that determine profit or loss, while other entities classify interest paid as financing cash flows and interest and dividends received as investing cash flows, viewing them as the costs of financing or the returns on investments respectively. Paragraph 34 notes that dividends paid may be classified as financing cash flows because they are a cost of obtaining equity finance or as cash from operating activities, to assist users to determine the ability of the entity to pay dividends from operating cash flows.

Pick n Pay, a large South African supermarket reporting using IFRS, classifies interest received and paid as well as dividends received and paid as cash flows from operating activities as shown in figure 16.3.

FIGURE 16.3 Pick n Pay cash flows from operating activities for the year ended 28 February 2023

	Note	52 weeks to 26 February 2023 Rm	52 weeks to 27 February 2022 Rm
Cash flows from operating activities			
Trading profit	10	**3,048.0**	2,886.5
Adjusted for non-cash items	11	**3,626.3**	3,391.5
Depreciation of property, plant and equipment	9	**1,320.5**	1,216.0
Depreciation of right-of-use assets	3	**2,148.2**	1,979.9
Amortisation of intangible assets		**96.6**	123.4
Share-based payments expense		**59.4**	149.0
Lease adjustments		**(28.9)**	(42.4)
Movement in operating lease assets		**(1.0)**	3.1
Movement in retirement scheme assets		**51.8**	(4.0)
Fair value and foreign exchange adjustments		**(20.3)**	(33.5)
Cash generated before movements in working capital		**6,674.3**	6,278.0
Movements in working capital		**(968.2)**	(563.6)
Movements in trade and other payables, provisions and deferred revenue		**1,668.9**	898.2
Movements in inventory and right-of-return assets		**(2,338.2)**	(1,074.2)
Movements in trade and other receivables		**(298.9)**	(387.6)
Cash generated from trading activities		**5,706.1**	5,714.4
Other interest received	2	**251.7**	300.1
Other interest paid	3	**(431.4)**	(341.0)
Interest received on net investment in lease receivables	12	**191.9**	203.7
Interest paid on lease liabilities	25	**(1,446.0)**	(1,364.4)
Cash generated from operations		**4,272.3**	4,512.8
Dividends received		**16.0**	20.1
Dividends paid		**(1,112.8)**	(959.6)
Tax paid	6	**(458.4)**	(403.9)
Cash generated from operating activities		**2,717.1**	3,169.4

Source: Pick n Pay (2023, p. 29).

16.3.2 Classifying taxes on income

Paragraph 35 of IAS 7 requires income tax paid to be separately disclosed in the statement of cash flows and classified as cash flows from operating activities, unless it can be specifically identified with financing or investing activities. As noted in paragraph 36 of IAS 7, while the tax expense may often be readily identifiable with investing or financing activities, the associated cash flows may arise in different periods, making it very difficult to classify tax payments as cash paid for investing or financing activities. Accordingly, taxes paid are usually classified as cash flows from operating activities. Refer to figure 16.3 to identify the income tax paid reported by Pick n Pay in the operating activities section of the statement of cash flows.

16.4 FORMAT OF THE STATEMENT OF CASH FLOWS

The general format of a statement of cash flows follows the three cash flow activities. Cash flows from operating activities are presented first, followed by cash flows from investing activities and then those from financing activities. The resultant net increase or decrease in cash and cash equivalents during the period is then used to report the movement in cash and cash equivalents from the balance at the beginning of the period to the balance at the end of the period.

16.4.1 Reporting cash flows from operating activities

Cash flows from operating activities are primarily derived from the *principal revenue-producing activities* of the entity, therefore they generally result from transactions that are taken into account in the determination of profit or loss for a period.

The amount of cash flows arising from operating activities is an important indicator of the extent to which the operations of the entity have generated sufficient cash flows to repay loans, maintain the operating capability of the entity, pay dividends and make new investments without the need to obtain external sources of finance. Paragraph 14 of IAS 7 lists some examples of cash flows from operating activities:

• Cash receipts from the sale of goods, the rendering of services and other income;
• Cash payments to suppliers for goods and services;
• Cash payments to and on behalf of employees;
• Cash payments for, or refunds of, income tax.

Paragraph 18 of IAS 7 provides that cash flows from operating activities may be reported using one of two methods:

• the *direct method* – which presents major classes of gross cash receipts and gross cash payments in the statement of cash flows
• the *indirect method* – which adjusts the profit or loss for the effects of (a) changes during the period in inventories and operating receivables and payables; (b) non-cash items such as depreciation, provisions, deferred taxes, unrealised foreign currency gains and losses and undistributed profits of associates; and (c) all other items for which the cash effects are investing or financing cash flows (IAS 7 paragraph 20).

Although the standard permits both the direct and indirect method, IAS 7 encourages the use of the direct method. However, the indirect method is the predominant practice as that is most practical, as may become apparent from section 16.5 where the procedures are described to prepare the statement of cash flows under both methods. Figure 16.4 illustrates the typical format of a statement of cash flows that uses the direct method.

FIGURE 16.4 Typical format using the direct method of reporting cash flows from operating activities

Statement of Cash Flows for the year ended 31 December . . .	
Cash flows from operating activities	
Cash receipts from customers	$ xxx
Cash paid to suppliers and employees	(xxx)
Cash generated from operations	xxx
Interest received	xxx
Interest paid	(xxx)
Income taxes paid	(xxx)
Net cash from operating activities	xxx

(continued)

FIGURE 16.4 *(continued)*

Statement of Cash Flows for the year ended 31 December . . .		
Cash flows from investing activities		
Acquisition of subsidiary, net of cash acquired	(xxx)	
Purchase of property and plant	(xxx)	
Proceeds from sale of plant	xxx	
Net cash used in investing activities		(xxx)
Cash flows from financing activities		
Proceeds from share issue	xxx	
Proceeds from borrowings	xxx	
Payment of borrowings	(xxx)	
Dividends paid	(xxx)	
Net cash from financing activities		xxx
Net increase in cash and cash equivalents		xxx
Cash and cash equivalents at beginning of year		xxx
Cash and cash equivalents at end of year		xxx

Figure 16.5 illustrates the typical format of the indirect method of reporting cash flows from operating activities.

As can be seen in figure 16.5, depreciation expense is added back to profit in calculating cash flows from operating activities. This is because depreciation expense reduces profit but has no effect on cash flows. The loss on the sale of investment is added back to profit because it reduces profit but does not affect cash flows from operating activities. Conversely, a gain on the disposal of equipment would be deducted from profit in calculating cash flows from operations. The related cash flow (i.e. the cash proceeds on the sale of the equipment) is included in cash flows from investing activities.

Profit before tax is adjusted for the difference between an amount recognised in profit and the corresponding operating cash flows, such as the change in receivables, which reflects the difference between sales revenue and cash collected from customers. This process is explained in more detail later *(see section 16.5)*. In applying the indirect method, the total amount of interest income is deducted, rather than the difference between interest income measured on an accrual basis and the amount of interest received. This is because paragraph 31 of IAS 7 requires disclosure of interest received in the statement of cash flows, irrespective of whether cash flows from operating activities are presented using the direct method or the indirect method.

FIGURE 16.5 Typical format using the indirect method of reporting cash flows from operating activities

Statement of Cash Flows for the year ended 31 December . . .	
Profit before tax	$ xxx
Adjustments for:	
Depreciation	xxx
Foreign exchange loss	xxx
Loss on sale of equipment	xxx
Interest income	(xxx)
Interest expense	xxx
Increase in trade and other receivables	(xxx)
Decrease in inventories	xxx
Increase in accounts payable	xxx
Decrease in accrued liabilities	(xxx)
Cash generated from operations	xxx
Interest received	xxx
Interest paid	(xxx)
Income taxes paid	(xxx)
Net cash from operating activities	xxx

Can you tell the difference between the two methods of presenting the operating activities section of the statement of cash flows? Test yourself. Which method is used by Pick n Pay in figure 16.3?

16.4.2 Reporting cash flows from investing activities

Investing activities relate to the *acquisition and disposal of non-current assets*. Cash flows from investing activities represent the extent to which cash has been utilised for resources intended to generate future profits and cash flows. Paragraph 16 of IAS 7 lists some examples of cash flows from investing activities:

- Cash payments to acquire property, plant and equipment, intangibles and other long-term assets;
- Cash receipts from sales of property, plant and equipment, intangibles and other long-term assets;
- Cash payments to acquire shares or debentures of other entities;
- Cash receipts from sales of shares or debentures of other entities;
- Cash advances or loans made to other parties;
- Cash receipts from the repayment of cash advances or loans made to other parties.

Paragraph 21 of IAS 7 requires separate reporting of the major classes of gross cash receipts and gross cash payments arising from investing and financing activities, except for certain cash flows (outlined in the following section) that may be reported on a net basis.

16.4.3 Reporting cash flows from financing activities

Cash flows from financing activities are those that involve the entity's *equity and borrowings*. Information about cash flows from financing activities is useful in predicting claims on future cash flows by the providers of finance. Paragraph 17 of IAS 7 lists some examples of cash flows from financing activities:

- Cash proceeds from increases in equity;
- Cash paid to owners on repayment or redemption of the equity;
- Cash proceeds from long-term borrowings;
- Cash repayments of amounts borrowed.

16.4.3 Reporting cash flows on a net basis

Paragraph 22 of IAS 7 allows the following cash flows to be reported on a net basis:

(a) cash receipts and payments on behalf of customers when the cash flows reflect the activities of the customer rather than those of the entity, such as the acceptance and repayment of a bank's demand deposits, and rents collected from tenants by an agent and paid to the property owners; and

(b) cash receipts and payments for items in which the turnover is quick, the amounts are large, and the maturities are short. For example, assume an entity finances some of its operations with a 90-day bill acceptance facility with its bank. This means that the entity writes commercial bills, giving rise to a contractual obligation to pay the face value of the bill. The bank accepts the bill and pays the entity a discounted amount, with the difference being interest effectively paid by the entity. Thus, the entity is borrowing the discounted amount of the bill and repaying the face value, which is the sum of the amount borrowed and interest. The entity will have cash inflows from financing activities each time a commercial bill is accepted by the bank and cash outflows from financing activities each time one of its commercial bills matures. The entity may offset the cash received for the 90-day bills against the repayment on maturity, such that only the net movement in the level of borrowing is reported.

Paragraph 24 of IAS 7 permits the following cash flows to be reported on a net basis by financial institutions:

(a) cash receipts and payments for the acceptance and repayment of deposits with a fixed maturity date;
(b) the placement of deposits with and withdrawal of deposits from other financial institutions; and
(c) cash advances and loans made to customers and the repayment of those advances and loans.

16.5 PREPARING A STATEMENT OF CASH FLOWS

Unlike the statement of financial position and statement of profit or loss and other comprehensive income, the statement of cash flows is not prepared from an entity's general ledger trial balance. Preparation requires information to be compiled about the cash inflows and cash outflows of the entity for the reporting period. A statement of cash flows is usually prepared from comparative statements of financial position to determine the net amount of changes in assets, liabilities and equities over the period. This method can also be used to prepare the consolidated statement of cash flows for a group of entities. The comparative statements of financial position are supplemented by various items of information from the statement of profit or loss and other comprehensive income and additional information extracted from the accounting records of the entity to enable certain cash receipts and payments to be fully identified. The financial statements presented in figure 16.6 will be used to illustrate the preparation of a statement of cash flows.

FIGURE 16.6 Financial statements and additional accounting information of Violet Inc.

VIOLET INC.
Statement of Profit or Loss and Other Comprehensive Income
for the year ended 31 December 20X2

Income		
Sales revenue		$800,000
Interest income		5,000
Gain on sale of plant		4,000
		809,000
Expenses		
Cost of sales	$480,000	
Wages and salaries expense	120,000	
Depreciation — plant and equipment	25,000	
Interest expense	4,000	
Other expenses	76,000	705,000
Profit before tax		104,000
Income tax expense		30,000
Profit for the year		74,000
Other comprehensive income		
Gain on revaluation of land	2,000	
Income tax	(600)	
Other comprehensive income net of tax		1,400
Total comprehensive income for the year		$ 75 400

VIOLET INC.
Comparative Statements of Financial Position as at:

	31 December 20X1	31 December 20X2
Cash at bank	$ 60,000	$ 56,550
Accounts receivable	70,000	79,000
Inventory	65,000	70,000
Prepayments	8,000	9,500
Interest receivable	150	100
Plant and equipment[a]	150,000	165,000
Land	12,000	14,000
Intangible assets[b]	—	15,000
	$365,150	$409,150
Accounts payable	42,000	45,000
Wages and salaries payable	4,000	5,000
Accrued interest	—	200
Other expenses payable	3,000	1,800
Current tax payable	14,000	16,000
Deferred tax liability	5,000	8,600
Long-term borrowings[c]	60,000	70,000
Share capital	200,000	200,000
Retained earnings[d]	37,150	61,150
Revaluation surplus	—	1,400
	$365,150	$409,150

Additional information extracted from the company's records:
(a) Plant that had a carrying amount of $10,000 was sold for $14,000 cash. New equipment purchased for cash amounted to $50,000.
(b) All intangibles were acquired for cash.
(c) An additional borrowing of $10,000 in cash was made during the year.
(d) Dividends paid in cash were $50,000.

16.5.1 Cash flows from operating activities

The first step in preparing a statement of cash flows is to determine the cash flows from operating activities. The process used varies according to whether the direct or the indirect method of presentation is used.

Direct method

When using the direct method, the starting point is the cash receipts from customers. The cash payments made to suppliers and employees are deducted from the cash receipts from customers in order to arrive at the **cash generated from operations.** Payments to suppliers include suppliers of goods for resale as well as all suppliers relating to operating activities. Amounts paid for all distribution, administrative and other operating expenses are therefore included. Note that amounts paid to employees for salaries and wages are often included in distribution or administrative expenses, and are not shown separately.

The cash effects of non-operating items, dividends, interest and taxation are then taken into account in order to arrive at the **cash flow from operating activities.**

A. Determining cash receipts from customers

The starting point for determining how much cash was received from customers is the sales revenue reported in the statement of profit or loss and other comprehensive income. This figure reflects sales made by the entity during the period irrespective of whether the customers have paid for their purchases. Credit sales are recorded by a debit to accounts receivable and a credit to sales revenue. However, cash received from customers includes sales made in the previous period if cash is not collected until the current period, and excludes sales made in the current period if customers have not paid by the end of the current period. Hence, cash received from customers (assuming there have been no bad debts written off or settlement discounts given) equals:

Sales revenue + Beginning accounts receivable − Ending accounts receivable

Using the Violet Inc. information from figure 16.6, receipts from customers is determined as follows:

	Sales revenue	$ 800,000
+	Beginning accounts receivable	70,000
	Cash collectable from customers	870,000
−	Ending accounts receivable	(79,000)
	Receipts from customers	$ 791,000

The entity may offer settlement discounts to customers for prompt or early payment of their accounts. For example, if a customer who owes $100 takes advantage of an offer of a 5% discount for prompt payment, the customer would pay only $95 to settle the receivable, and the entity would record an expense of $5 for discount allowed for the non-cash reduction in receivables. Settlement discounts are accounted for as a non-cash expense (discount allowed) in profit or loss and a reduction in accounts receivable. Thus, settlement discounts allowed reduce the amount of cash that is collected from customers. Accordingly, discount allowed must be adjusted for in calculating cash receipts from customers. Similarly, adjustment would be necessary for bad debts written off if the entity used the direct write-off method of accounting for uncollectable debts. Calculation of cash receipts from customers under the allowance method of accounting for uncollectable debts is considered later in this chapter.

Assuming that there are no non-cash considerations for sales made, the following is the summarised Accounts Receivable account in the general ledger for the year:

Accounts Receivable			
Opening balance	70,000	Bad Debts Expense	—
Sales Revenue	800,000	Discount Allowed	—
		Cash receipts	791,000
		Closing balance	79,000
	870,000		870,000

The above summarised general ledger account can be reconstructed from the statement of financial position including comparative amounts (the opening and closing balances) and statement of profit or loss and other comprehensive income (bad debts expense, discount allowed and sales revenue). The cash receipts amount is then determined as the 'plug' figure (balancing item) in the Accounts Receivable account.

B. Determining cash paid to suppliers and employees

Payments to suppliers may comprise purchases of inventory and payments for services. However, not all inventory purchased during the year is reflected in profit or loss as cost of sales because cost of sales includes beginning inventory and excludes ending inventory. The cost of purchases of inventory made during the period equals:

$$\text{Cost of sales} - \text{Beginning inventory} + \text{Ending inventory}$$

Using a similar approach to that outlined for cash receipts from customers, it is then necessary to adjust for accounts payable at the beginning and end of the period to calculate cash paid to suppliers for purchases of inventory. Thus, cash paid to suppliers of inventories is calculated as:

$$\text{Purchases of inventories} + \text{Beginning accounts payable} - \text{Ending accounts payable}$$

Assuming no impairment of inventory, cash paid to suppliers for purchases is calculated as follows:

	Cost of sales	$480,000
−	Beginning inventory	(65,000)
+	Ending inventory	70,000
	Purchases for year	485,000
+	Beginning accounts payable	42,000
−	Ending accounts payable	(45,000)
	Payments to suppliers for purchases of inventory	$482,000

If the entity receives a discount from its suppliers for prompt or early payment of accounts payable the settlement discount received is accounted for as discount revenue and a reduction in accounts payable. Thus, settlement discounts reduce the amount of cash paid to suppliers and must be deducted in calculating cash paid to suppliers.

The logic of the previous calculations incorporating the adjustment for discount received is apparent from the following summarised inventory and accounts payable (for inventory) accounts in the general ledger for the year:

Inventory					Accounts Payable			
Opening balance	65,000	Cost of Sales	480,000	Discount Received	–	Opening balance	42,000
Purchases	485,000	Closing balance	70,000	Cash payments	482,000	Purchases	485,000
				Closing balance	45,000		
	550,000		550,000		527,000		527,000

The above summarised general ledger accounts can be reconstructed from the information contained in the comparative statements of financial position (the opening and closing balances) and the statement of profit or loss and other comprehensive income (cost of sales). The purchases amount is then determined in the Inventory account and inserted on the credit side of the Accounts Payable account. The amount of cash payments can then be determined as the 'plug' figure in reconciling the Accounts Payable account.

A similar approach is taken to determine the amount of payments made to suppliers for services and to employees. Adjustments must be made to the relevant expenses recognised in profit or loss for changes in the beginning and ending amounts of prepayments and relevant accounts payable and accrued liabilities. Thus, the amount of cash paid to suppliers for services is calculated as follows:

Expenses charged to profit or loss – Beginning prepayments
+ Ending prepayments
+ Beginning accounts payable / accruals
– Ending accounts payable / accruals

Thus cash paid to suppliers of services is calculated as follows:

Other expenses	$76,000
– Beginning prepayments	(8,000)
+ Ending prepayments	9,500
+ Beginning accruals (expenses payable)	3,000
– Ending accruals (expenses payable)	(1,800)
Payments to suppliers of services	$78,700

Similarly, cash paid to employees is calculated as follows:

Wages and salaries expense	$120,000
+ Beginning wages and salaries payable	4,000
– Ending wages and salaries payable	(5,000)
Payments to employees	$119,000

Using the previous calculations, total payments to suppliers and employees to be reported in the direct method statement of cash flows comprise:

Payments to suppliers for purchases	$ 482,000
Payments to suppliers for services	78,700
Payments to employees	119,000
Total payments to suppliers and employees	$679,700

The operating activities section of Violet Inc.'s statement of cash flows for the year is presented using the *direct method* in figure 16.7. For the moment, focus only on the two line items 'cash flows from operating activities' and 'cash paid to suppliers and employees' and the subtotal 'Cash generated from operations'. The difference in presentation of the statement of cash flows using the direct method and the indirect method lies only in the presentation of the cash generated from operations. The presentation of the remainder of the operating activities section (interest received/paid and income taxes paid) and the final subtotal 'net cash from operating activities' is identical for both the direct method and indirect method.

FIGURE 16.7 Cash flows from operating activities (direct method)

VIOLET INC. Statement of Cash Flows (extract) for the year ended 11 December 20X2	
Cash flows from operating activities	
Cash receipts from customers	$ 791,000
Cash paid to suppliers and employees	(679,700)
Cash generated from operations	111,300
Interest received*	5,050
Interest paid**	(3,800)
Income taxes paid	(25,000)
Net cash from operating activities	$ 87,550

* May be classified as investing   ** May be classified as financing

Indirect method

When using the indirect method, the starting point is the profit before tax on the statement of profit or loss. As this is an accrual basis figure, it is first adjusted for the *effect of non-cash items* included in the determination of profit — for example, depreciation expense or the gain on disposal of a non-current asset. It is then adjusted for the effect of *non-operating items* also included in the determination of profit — for example, investment income, interest expense and dividends. Although these items do involve the flow of cash, we reverse the effect of the accrual income or expense at this point and then take into account the cash inflow or outflow after *cash generated from operations*.

Then follow the effects of working capital movements — that is, movements in accounts receivable, accounts payable and inventory — to give the **cash generated from operations**.

Finally, and identical to the direct method, the cash effects of non-operating items (interest received and paid), dividends paid and taxation paid are taken into account to arrive at the **net cash flow from operating activities**.

The presentation of Violet Inc.'s cash flows from operating activities under the indirect method is shown in figure 16.8. The statement commences with profit before tax which is firstly adjusted for the non-cash items included in the determination of profit, in this case, the adding back of the deprecation of $25,000 and reversal of the gain on sale of plant of $4,000.

Secondly, it is necessary to reverse for the full amount of the interest income and interest expense as the amount of cash received or paid for these items is disclosed after the cash generated from operations subtotal.

Finally, the working capital movements are adjusted before arriving at the cash generated from operations. The increase in accounts receivable of $9,000 (which is the excess of accrual basis sales over cash receipts) must be subtracted from the profit on the statement of cash flows. The increase in accounts payable of $3,000 (which is the excess of accrual basis purchases over cash payments) is added to the profit on the statement of cash flows. The increase in inventory of $5,000 is then subtracted as it represents the amount by which purchases of inventory exceed the amount included in profit or loss as cost of sales.

In a similar way, movements in all other working capital items are taken into account (except for tax payable, which is disclosed separately). In this illustration, the increase in wages and salaries payable of $1,000 and the decrease in other expenses payable of $1,200 are combined as one line item and shown as a net reduction of $200.

FIGURE 16.8 Cash flows from operating activities (indirect method)

VIOLET INC. Statement of Cash Flows (extract) for the year ended 31 December 20X2	
Cash flows from operating activities	
Profit before tax	$104,000
Adjustment for:	
Depreciation	25,000
Gain on sale of plant	(4,000)
Interest income	(5,000)
Interest expense	4,000
Increase in accounts receivable	(9,000)
Increase in inventory	(5,000)
Increase in prepayments	(1,500)
Increase in accounts payable	3,000
Decrease in other payables	(200)
Cash generated from operations	111,300
Interest received*	5,050
Interest paid**	(3,800)
Income taxes paid	(25,000)
Net cash from operating activities	$ 87,550

* May be classified as investing   ** May be classified as financing

This example now turns to the line items in the operating activities section after the cash generated from operations. As mentioned previously, the presentation of these line items, leading to the final subtotal of cash generated from operating activities, is identical for both the direct and indirect methods.

C. Determining interest received

A similar approach is used to determine interest received, which equals:

Interest revenue + Beginning interest receivable – Ending interest receivable

Thus, Violet Inc.'s interest received is:

$$\$5,000 + \$150 - 100 = 5050$$

D. Determining interest paid

Using the same approach as for other expenses, Violet Inc.'s interest paid is determined as follows:

Interest expense + Beginning interest payable – Ending interest payable

Thus Violet Inc.'s interest paid is

$$\$4,000 + \$0 - \$200 = \$3,800$$

E. Determining income tax paid

The determination of income tax paid can be complicated because in addition to current tax payable, the application of tax effect accounting can give rise to deferred tax assets and deferred tax liabilities. Further, some of the movements in the current and deferred tax accounts might not be reflected in the income tax expense recognised in profit or loss. Certain gains and losses and associated tax effects are recognised in OCI and accumulated in equity accounts. For example, *as explained in chapter 15*, deferred tax may arise from a revaluation of property, plant and equipment that causes a difference between the book value and tax base of those assets, thereby resulting in a charge for income tax being made to the Revaluation Surplus account. As a result, it is often simpler to reconstruct the Deferred Tax Asset/Liability account to determine the allocation of income tax expense. We can use this reconstruction to determine the deferred component of income tax expense recognised in profit or loss, if this is not already identified in the statement of profit or loss and other comprehensive income.

Deferred Tax Liability			
		Opening balance	5,000
		Tax effect recognised in OCI	600
Closing balance	8,600	Income Tax Expense	3,000
	8,600		8,600

The above summarised general ledger account can be reconstructed from the comparative statements of financial position (opening and closing balances) and the statement of profit or loss and other comprehensive income. The income tax expense shown in the reconstruction of the Deferred Tax Liability account is the deferred component of income tax expense – that is, the amount of income tax expense pertaining to the movement in deferred tax balances.

• The movement in the Deferred Tax Liability account for Violet Inc. can be summarised as follows:

Opening balance	$5,000
+ Tax recognised directly in OCI	600
+ Income tax expense (deferred component)	3,000
Closing balance	$8,600

The current component of income tax expense can then be calculated by deducting the deferred component of income tax expense from the total income tax expense recognised in profit or loss. The current component of income tax expense for Violet Inc. can be calculated as follows:

Income tax expense	$30,000
– Deferred component of income tax expense	(3,000)
Current component of income tax expense	$27,000

The opening balance of Current Tax Payable of $14,000 is increased by the current component of income tax expense, $27,000. If no payments were made, the closing balance would be $41,000. However, as the closing balance is only $16,000, we can conclude that the amount of income tax paid must have been $25,000. To illustrate, the movement in Violet Inc's Current Tax Payable account may be summarised as follows:

Opening balance	$14,000
+ Income tax expense	27,000
− Income tax paid	(25,000)
Closing balance	$16,000

For Violet Inc., the amount of income tax paid consists of the final balance in respect of the previous year's current tax payable, and instalments paid in respect of the current year.

16.5.2 Cash flows from investing activities

Determining cash flows from investing activities requires identifying cash inflows and outflows relating to the acquisition and disposal of long-term assets and other investments not included in cash equivalents.

The comparative statements of financial position of Violet Inc. in figure 16.6 show that plant has increased by $15,000, land by $2000 and intangibles by $15,000. To determine the cash flows relating to these increases, it is necessary to analyse the underlying transactions.

The plant and equipment reported in the statement of financial position is net of accumulated depreciation. The net increase reflects the recording of purchases, disposals and depreciation of plant and equipment. Using the data provided, the analysis of the movement in plant and equipment (net of accumulated depreciation) is as follows:

Opening balance	$150,000
Purchases	50,000
Disposals	(10,000)
Depreciation for year	(25,000)
Closing balance	$165,000

The additional information provided in figure 16.6 states that the acquisitions were made for cash during the period, so no adjustment is necessary for year-end payables. The cash paid for equipment purchases for the year is $50,000 (note (a) in figure 16.6). Any payables for plant and equipment purchases outstanding at the beginning of the period would need to be added to purchases and any payables for plant and equipment outstanding at the end of the period would need to be deducted to calculate the amount of cash paid for plant and equipment during the period.

Plant with a carrying amount of $10,000 was sold, as stated in additional information (a) of figure 16.6. This amount is shown as a deduction from the net carrying amount plant and equipment.

The gain or loss on disposal of plant is the difference between the carrying amount and the proceeds on the sale of plant. Thus, the proceeds on sale of plant can be calculated as:

Carrying amount of plant sold + Gain *on* disposal of plant

or

−Loss *on* disposal of plant

For Violet Inc., the calculation is as follows:

$$\$10,000 + \$4,000 = \$14,000$$

Land increased by $2000 during the year, as shown in the comparative statements of financial position. This increase relates to the gain on revaluation of land reported in the statement of profit or loss and other comprehensive income. Thus the movement in land does not affect cash flows from investing activities.

The comparative statements of financial position for Violet Inc. show that the movement in intangibles equals the additional cash acquisitions made during the period, as detailed in the additional information presented in figure 16.6. Note, however, that the movement in intangibles equals the cash outflows for the year because there were no related accounts payable at the beginning or end of the year. If payables exist, the cash outflow is determined using the approach that was previously outlined for cash paid to suppliers and employees.

Using the above information, the cash flows from investing activities reported in Violet Inc.'s statement of cash flows for 20X2 are presented in figure 16.9.

FIGURE 16.9 Cash flows from investing activities

VIOLET INC. Statement of Cash Flows (extract) for the year ended 31 December 20X2	
Cash flows from investing activities	
Purchase of intangibles	$(15,000)
Purchase of equipment	(50,000)
Proceeds from sale of plant	14,000
Net cash used in investing activities	$(51,000)

16.5.3 Cash flows from financing activities

Determining cash flows from financing activities requires identification of cash flows that resulted in changes in the size and composition of contributed equity and borrowings.

Violet Inc.'s comparative statements of financial position report an increase in borrowings of $10,000. The additional information (c) in figure 16.6 confirms that the increase arose from an additional borrowing received in cash. It would normally be necessary to analyse the net movement in borrowings in order to identify whether the movement reflects repayments and additional borrowings, and whether any new borrowings arose from non-cash transactions, such as entering into a finance lease *(see chapter 9)*.

If the entity had issued shares during the period this would be reflected in a change in share capital. An alternative source of information about capital contributions is the statement of changes in equity. Any share issues for non-cash consideration, such as shares issued as part of a dividend reinvestment scheme, should be deducted from the movement in share capital to determine cash proceeds from share issues. Violet Inc.'s share capital is unchanged at $200,000, as shown in figure 16.6.

Dividends distributed by the entity can be identified by analysing the change in retained earnings. Profit increases retained earnings and losses decrease retained earnings. Dividends decrease retained earnings. Any non-cash dividends should be deducted from total dividends to determine cash dividends paid. Information about dividends is also reported in the statement of changes in equity. The movement in Violet Inc.'s retained earnings of $24,000 reflects:

Profit for the period	$ 74,000	
Dividends (paid in cash)	(50,000)	([d] in figure 16.6)
Net movement	$ 24,000	

Using the previous information, the financing cash flow section of Violet Inc.'s statement of cash flows for 20X2 is presented in figure 16.10.

FIGURE 16.10 Cash flows from financing activities

VIOLET INC. Statement of Cash Flows (extract) for the year ended 31 December 20X2	
Cash flows from financing activities	
Proceeds from borrowings	$ 10,000
Dividends paid*	(50,000)
Net cash used in financing activities	$(40,000)

*Dividends paid may be classified as an operating cash flow.

All that remains to complete the statement of cash flows for Violet Inc. is the determination of the net increase or decrease in cash held, and to use this net change to reconcile cash at the beginning and end of the year.

The complete statement of cash flows for Violet Inc. (using the **direct method** for reporting cash flows from operating activities) is shown in figure 16.11. The balance of cash at year-end of $56,550 shown in figure 16.11 agrees with the cash at bank balance shown in the statement of financial position at 31 December 20X2 in figure 16.6. There are no cash equivalents such as short-term deposits.

It is important to stress again that the only difference between this statement of cash flows prepared using the direct method and one prepared using the indirect method is in the presentation of cash generated from operations. Refer back to figure 16.8 to see the operating activities section of the statement of cash flows prepared using the indirect method.

FIGURE 16.11 Complete statement of cash flows of Violet Inc. applying the direct method

VIOLET INC. Statement of Cash Flows for the year ended 31 December 20X2		
Cash flows from operating activities		
Cash receipts from customers	$ 791,000	
Cash paid to suppliers and employees	(679,700)	
Cash generated from operations	111,300	
Interest received	5,050	
Interest paid	(3,800)	
Income taxes paid	(25,000)	
Net cash from operating activities		$ 87,550
Cash flows from investing activities		
Purchase of intangibles	$ (15,000)	
Purchase of plant	(50,000)	
Proceeds from sale of plant	14,000	
Net cash used in investing activities		(51,000)
Cash flows from financing activities		
Proceeds from borrowings	$ 10,000	
Dividends paid	(50,000)	
Net cash used in financing activities		(40,000)
Net decrease in cash and cash equivalents		(3,450)
Cash and cash equivalents at beginning of year		60,000
Cash and cash equivalents at end of year		$ 56,550

16.6 OTHER DISCLOSURES

IAS 7 prescribes additional disclosures in the notes to the financial statements, including information about the components of cash and cash equivalents, changes in ownership interests of subsidiaries and other businesses, and non-cash investing and financing transactions. Additional information is often necessary to obtain a complete understanding of the change in an entity's financial position because not all transactions are simple cash transactions. Significant changes can result from the acquisition or disposal of subsidiaries or other business units, or from financing and investing transactions that do not involve cash flows in the current period.

16.6.1 Components of cash and cash equivalents

The components of cash and cash equivalents must be disclosed and reconciled to amounts reported in the statement of financial position. The reconciliation provides better transparency of how items are reported in the financial statements. In some cases, cash and cash equivalents may include a bank overdraft. The end-of-period amount of cash and cash equivalents reported in the statement of cash flows may differ from that reported in the statement of financial position because the cash and short-term deposits are reported as current assets while the overdraft is a liability. Figure 16.12 illustrates the reconciliation between cash and cash equivalents in the statement of cash flows with the corresponding items reported in the statement of financial position for Pick n Pay.

Paragraph 48 requires disclosure of the amount of significant cash and cash-equivalent balances held that are not available for general use. This may include cash held by a foreign subsidiary that is subject to foreign exchange controls.

FIGURE 16.12 Disclosures about cash and cash equivalents for Pick n Pay at 26 February 2023

	52 weeks to 26 February 2023 Rm	52 weeks to 27 February 2022 Rm
Cash and cash equivalents		
Cash and cash equivalents	**1,997.8**	6,425.3
Bank overdraft and overnight borrowings	**(2,800.0)**	(2,800.0)
Cash and cash equivalents at end of period	**(802.2)**	3,625.3

Cash and cash equivalents
Cash and cash equivalents includes cash floats at stores as well as the Group's current account balances. The Group's primary banker, which at period-end, had a long-term credit rating of zaAA, facilitates the collection of cash at stores, provides general banking facilities and facilitates the payment of suppliers via an electronic banking platform. The interest rate on the current account varied between 2.5% and 6.7% per annum (2022: 2.8% and 3.3% per annum). Refer to note 30.3.2.

Cash investments
The Group invested its surplus cash in money market accounts during the period. The interest rate on these accounts varied between 4.6% and 8.3% per annum (2022: 4.0% to 5.4% per annum). Refer to note 30.3.2.

Bank overdraft
The Group utilised its bank overdraft during the period. The overdraft interest rate varied between 6.3% and 9.5% per annum (2022: 5.5% to 6.3% per annum). Refer to note 30.3.2.

Overnight borrowings
The Group utilised overnight borrowings during the period. Interest rates varied between 4.6% and 8.5% per annum (2022: 4.1% and 4.9% per annum). Refer to note 30.3.2.

Source: Pick n Pay (2023, p. 67).

16.6.2 Changes in ownership interests of subsidiaries and other businesses

Part 4 of this book deals with the financial reporting of consolidated groups of entities. When a parent entity obtains control of another entity, or loses control of an existing subsidiary, the comparative consolidated statement of financial position of the group before and after the acquisition or disposal will frequently reflect significant changes in the assets and liabilities arising from the acquisition or disposal. Financial statement users need to be aware of the effects of changes in ownership and control in order to understand the change in financial position of the consolidated group.

IAS 7 specifies additional reporting requirements relating to changes in control of subsidiaries and other businesses.

Paragraph 39 requires the aggregate cash flow effects of obtaining control of subsidiaries or other businesses to be reported as one item in the investing activities section of the statement of cash flows. When an entity obtains control of a subsidiary or other business, any cash and cash equivalents acquired are deducted from the cash consideration paid in determining the cash flow effects of obtaining control.

For example, Major plc obtained control over Minor plc by acquiring all of the ordinary shares of Minor plc. Major plc paid consideration of £1,500,000 in cash. Minor plc held cash and cash equivalents of £100,000 at the time of the acquisition. Thus, the net cash flow effect of Major plc obtaining control of Minor plc is a cash outflow of £1,400,000 (i.e. £1,500,000 − £100,000). This would be reported in the investing activities section of Major plc's consolidated statement of cash flows.

Similarly, paragraph 39 of IAS 7 requires the aggregate cash flow effects of losing control of subsidiaries or other businesses to be reported as one item in the investing activities section of the statement of cash flows. If an entity loses control of a subsidiary or other business, any cash and cash equivalents held by that subsidiary or other business at the time of the disposal are deducted from the cash consideration received in reporting the cash flow effects of losing control. For example, if Major plc sold its interest in several subsidiaries for a total cash consideration of £8,000,000, and those subsidiaries held cash and cash equivalents of £100,000, Major plc would report a net cash inflow of £7,900,000 for the proceeds from the sale of subsidiaries in the investing activities section of its statement of cash flows. Figure 16.13 illustrates the application of paragraph 39 of IAS 7 in the investing activities section of Major plc's statement of cash flows.

FIGURE 16.13 Investing activities section of statement of cash flows of Major plc for the year ended

	2024 £'000	2023 £'000
Cash flows from investing activities		
Payments for property, plant and equipment	(5,500)	(4,800)
Proceeds from sale of subsidiaries (net of cash held)	7,900	
Payment for purchase of subsidiary (net of cash acquired)	(1,400)	—
Proceeds from the sale of property, plant and equipment	1,100	1,300
Net cash from (used in) investing activities	2,100	(3,500)

Separate presentation of the cash flow effects of transactions to obtain or to surrender control of subsidiaries or other businesses is required. The cash flow effects of transactions resulting in the loss of control, such as the sale of a subsidiary, are not deducted from the cash flows of transactions that obtain control, such as the acquisitions of a subsidiary. Both the aggregate cash flow effects of obtaining control of subsidiaries and other businesses and the aggregate cash flow effects of losing control of subsidiaries and other businesses are reported separately in the investing activities section of the statement of cash flows as shown in figure 16.13.

Paragraph 40 of IAS 7 prescribes disclosure of the aggregate amounts of each of the following items:
(a) the total consideration;
(b) how much of the consideration comprises cash and cash equivalents;
(c) the amount of cash and cash equivalents held by the subsidiaries or other businesses; and
(d) the amount of other assets and liabilities held by the subsidiaries or other businesses, summarised by each major category.

Separate disclosures must be made for subsidiaries and other businesses over which control has been obtained, and those over which control has been lost. Disclosures provided by Major plc in accordance with paragraph 40(a)–(c) are shown in figure 16.14.

FIGURE 16.14 Selected disclosures about transactions resulting in the acquisition or loss of control over other entities by Major plc for the year ended 31 December 2024

During the year Major plc obtained control of Minor plc by acquiring all of the ordinary shares of Minor plc. All of the consideration was paid in cash. Details of the consideration and analysis of the cash flows are summarised below:

Total consideration (included in cash flows from investing activities)	£1,500,000
Cash acquired in subsidiary (included in cash flows from investing activities)	(100,000)
Net cash flows on acquisition	£1,400,000

During the year Major plc sold its retail business for total consideration of £9,000,000. Details of the consideration and analysis of the cash flows are summarised below:

Total consideration, comprising cash and equity investments	£9,000,000
Cash consideration (included in cash flows from investing activities)	£8,000,000
Cash acquired in subsidiary (included in cash flows from investing activities)	(100,000)
Net cash flows on disposal of the business	£7,900,000

16.6.3 Supplier finance arrangements

In May 2023, the IASB issued an amendment to IAS 7 disclosure requirements to assist users of financial statements in understanding the effects of supplier finance arrangements on an entity's liabilities, cash flows and exposure to liquidity risk.

In such arrangements, one or more finance providers pay amounts an entity owes to its suppliers. The entity agrees to settle those amounts with the finance providers according to the terms and conditions of the arrangements, either at the same date or at a later date than that on which the finance providers pay the entity's suppliers.

The amendments, set out in paragraph 44F of IAS 7, require an entity to provide information about the impact of supplier finance arrangements on liabilities and cash flows, including terms and conditions of those arrangements, quantitative information on liabilities related to those arrangements as at the beginning and end of the reporting period and the type and effect of non-cash changes in the carrying amounts of those arrangements. In terms of paragraph 44H, the information on those arrangements is required to be aggregated unless the individual arrangements have dissimilar or unique terms and conditions.

The amendments are effective for annual reporting periods beginning on or after 1 January 2024.

16.6.4 Non-cash transactions

Not all investing or financing transactions involve current cash flows. However, non-cash investing and financing activities need to be understood because they can significantly affect the financial position of an entity. Examples include:
- acquisition of assets by means of a finance lease or by assuming other liabilities
- acquisition of assets or an entity by means of an equity issue
- conversion of debt to equity
- conversion of preference shares to ordinary shares
- refinancing of long-term debt
- payment of dividends through a dividend reinvestment scheme.

Investing and financing transactions that do not involve the payment or receipt of cash and cash equivalents are not reported in the statement of cash flows. However, paragraph 43 of IAS 7 requires disclosure 'elsewhere in the financial statements in a way that provides all the relevant information about these investing and financing activities'.

16.6.5 Disclosures that are encouraged but not required

The following disclosures are specifically encouraged by paragraph 50 of IAS 7:
- the amount of undrawn borrowing facilities that may be available to pay for future operating activities or to settle commitments, and any restrictions on their use;
- the distinction between aggregate cash flows for increases in operating capacity and aggregate cash flows that are required to maintain operating capacity; and
- cash flows arising from the operating, investing and financing activities of each reportable segment.

16.7 FUTURE DEVELOPMENTS

IAS 1 will be superseded by IFRS 18 *Presentation and Disclosure in Financial Statements*, effective for periods beginning on or after 1 January 2027. In brief, IFRS 18 introduces new requirements on presentation within the statement of profit or loss, including specified totals and subtotals. Items of income and expense will be classified into operating, financing, investing, income tax or discontinued operations categories. This classification will depend on a combination of an assessment of the entity's main business activities and certain accounting policy choices. A subtotal for operating profit (a defined term in IFRS 18) will be required to be presented in financial statements.

The consequential amendments to IAS 7 will require all companies to use the operating profit subtotal as defined in IFRS 18 as the starting point for the indirect method of reporting cash flows from operating activities. Additionally, the presentation alternatives for cash flows related to interest and dividends paid and received will be removed. Companies (except financial entities) will have to present dividends and interest received as cash flow from investing activities, whereas dividends and interest paid will have to be presented as cash flows from financing activities.

The amendments need to be applied when IFRS 18 is applied, which is effective for annual periods beginning on or after 1 January 2027.

16.8 SUMMARY

IAS 7 *Statement of Cash Flows* is a disclosure standard requiring the presentation of a statement of cash flows as an integral part of an entity's financial statements. The statement of cash flows is particularly useful to investors, lenders and others when evaluating an entity's ability to generate cash and cash equivalents, and to meet its obligations and pay dividends. The statement is required to report cash flows classified into operating, investing and financing activities, as well as the net movement in cash and cash equivalents during the period. Net cash flows from operating activities may be presented using either the direct or the indirect method. IAS 7 requires additional information to be disclosed about investing and financing activities that do not involve cash flows and are therefore excluded from a statement of cash flows. The standard also requires additional disclosures relating to the cash flow effects of obtaining or losing control of subsidiaries and other businesses.

Discussion questions

1. What is the purpose of a statement of cash flows?
2. How might a statement of cash flows be used?
3. What is the meaning of 'cash equivalent'?
4. Explain the required classifications of cash flows under IAS 7.
5. What sources of information are usually required to prepare a statement of cash flows?
6. Explain the differences between the presentation of cash flows from operating activities under the direct method and their presentation under the indirect method. Do you consider one method to be more useful than the other? Why?
7. The statement of cash flows is said to be of assistance in evaluating the financial strength of an entity, yet the statement can exclude significant non-cash transactions that can materially affect the financial strength of an entity. How does IAS 7 seek to overcome this issue?
8. An entity may report profits over a number of successive years and still experience negative net cash flows from its operating activities. How can this happen?
9. An entity may report losses over a number of successive years and still report positive net cash flows from operating activities over the same period. How can this happen?
10. What supplementary disclosures are required when a consolidated statement of cash flows is being prepared for a group that has obtained or lost control of a subsidiary?

References

Pick n Pay 2023, *Annual Report 2023*, www.picknpayinvestor.co.za/downloads/annual-report/2023/2023-audited-annual-financial-statements-singles.pdf.

Loftus, J., Leo, K., Boys, N., Daniliuc, S., Luke, B., Hong, A., and Byrnes, K., 2015. *Financial Reporting*, John Wiley & Sons Australia.

Accounting researchers have been looking into the information content — that is, decision usefulness — of the statement of cash flows. In addition, accounting research has attempted to assess whether cash flows are as useful as earnings and accruals. For the purpose of understanding the various research findings described below, it will be constructive first to establish the link between earnings (E), accruals (ACCR) and operating cash flows (CFO). E = CFO + ACCR. Note that ACCR includes items such as changes in inventory, receivables and payables, as well as other items that appear under the indirect method.

In one of the earlier studies of cash flows, Wilson (1986) develops a model for the link between surprises in E, CFO and ACCR and abnormal stock returns. Specifically, abnormal stock returns are measured as the sum of returns in the two days around the earnings announcement and nine days around the filing day of the quarterly report. Employing a sample of 322 observations in 1981 and 1982, Wilson (1986) finds that abnormal stock returns are positively associated with surprises in earnings and CFO, but negatively related to the surprise in the current portion of ACCR. This is consistent with CFO and ACCR being useful to investors.

While the findings in Wilson (1986) suggest that this is the case, Bernard and Stober (1989) re-examine the evidence. In contrast to Wilson (1986), Bernard and Stober (1989) look at a longer period, 1977–1984, and assemble a much larger sample. Looking at the nine-days window centred at the filing date of the financials, they find no evidence of association between abnormal stock returns and cash flows. Because in their sample earnings announcements take place prior to the filing day, Bernard and Stober (1989) conclude that, conditional on knowing earnings, investors ignore cash flow information.

The above-mentioned studies were conducted before the introduction of the cash flow standard, SFAS, in the US. SFAS 95 (now ASC 230) (FASB, 1987) was the first to set formal requirements for a cash flow statement with its three parts (operating cash flows (CFO), investing cash flows (CFI) and financing cash flows (CFF)). Livnat and Zarowin (1990) were among the first to examine the value relevance of the three parts although they also employ pre-standard data. Their main findings are as follows. First, they show that cumulative abnormal annual stock returns (CAR) are positively associated with their estimates of CFO and ACCR. Second, when CFF and CFI are added as explanatory variables, they show that CAR is positively (negatively) related to CFF (CFI) although with a low magnitude. Third, they show that within CFO cash collections from customers are positively related to CAR, but cash payments to suppliers, employees and interest are negatively related to CAR. Overall, therefore, Livnat and Zarowin (1990) demonstrate the usefulness of the components of the cash flow statement.

Clinch et al. (2002) examine the usefulness of the direct and indirect methods for CFO. They take advantage of Australian rules from the time before the adoption of IFRS® Standards, which required the preparation of the statement of cash flows that is accompanied by disclosures of both methods. Their sample consists of 648 firm-year observa-

tions between 1992 and 1997. They provide evidence that some components of both direct CFO and indirect CFO are associated with annual stock returns. Clinch et al. (2002) interpret the association of various components of the direct and indirect method with annual returns as evidence of their usefulness in predicting future CFO. Consistent with this view they find that the usefulness of these components for investors is increasing with their predictive ability.

Barth et al. (2001) expand the analysis of the predictability of future cash flows using a large US sample during 1987–1996. They find that 1-year-ahead CFO is positively related to current and lagged earnings (up to six years). The magnitude of the relation, however, diminishes over time. They further show that components of current ACCR (e.g., changes in inventory and receivables) have predictive ability with respect to next year's CFO incrementally to that of current CFO. Interestingly, they find that depreciation and amortisation – non-cash expenses — also have predictive ability for future cash flows. Barth et al. (2001) then further explore the finding that current and prior earnings can predict future CFO. Specifically, they break current and two lags of earnings into their CFO and ACCR aggregate components. Here they find that while current and lagged CFO predict future CFO, past aggregate ACCR do not, only present ACCR. Nevertheless, when past aggregate ACCR are broken into the various components, Barth et al. (2001) show that these provide incremental predictive ability over current and past CFO. The overall conclusion is that the structure of the indirect method for CFO is quite useful for predicting future cash flows. Consistent with this, the various components of ACCR are found to be associated with market value of equity and stock returns.

In a more recent study, Clacher et al. (2013) investigate the value relevance of core direct cash flows, which they define as cash receipts from customers and cash paid to suppliers and employees. Using a sample of 459 Australian listed firms, they compare the value relevance of core cash flows before and after the adoption of IFRS Standards. They find that core cash flows are correlated with the value of the firm (i.e. value relevant) before the adoption of IFRS Standards. After adoption of IFRS Standards, core cash flows remain value relevant for firms in all industries and increase significantly in value relevance for industrial firms.

Although earnings and accruals are useful in that they are associated with stock returns, Cheng et al. (1996) argue that the relative information role of earnings is lower if earnings are more transitory. Using a large dataset from 1988 to 1992, the authors regress abnormal annual stock returns on earnings, change in earnings, CFO and change in CFO. They find that these variables are positively related to abnormal stock returns. This is consistent with both earnings and cash flows being useful to investors. However, the association between the earnings variables and abnormal stock returns is weaker when earnings take large extreme values (a proxy for transitory earnings). The explanation for this is that large earning changes are not seen as credible or sustainable and so investors rely more heavily on cash flows.

All the papers mentioned so far examine the usefulness of cash flows with respect to stock prices and returns. However, cash flow information may also be used by credit analysts and investors in debt markets. Using data reported under SFAS 95, Billings and Morton (2002) examine the link between cash-based interest coverage ratio and credit ratings while controlling for other common risk measures (e.g. CAPM's Beta). The authors find that the cash-based interest coverage ratio has incremental explanatory power for ratings. This suggests that rating agencies employ cash flow information in forming their rating assessments.

References

Barth, M.E., Cram, D.P., and Nelson, K.K., 2001. Accruals and the prediction of future cash flows. *The Accounting Review*, 76(1), 27–58.

Bernard, V.L. and Stober, T.L., 1989. The nature and amount of information in cash flows and accruals. *The Accounting Review*, 64(4), 624–652.

Billings, B.K. and Morton, R.M., 2002. The relation between SFAS no. 95 cash flows from operations and credit risk. *Journal of Business Finance & Accounting*, 29(5–6), 787–805.

Cheng, C.A., Liu, C.S. and Schaefer, T.F., 1996. Earnings permanence and the incremental information content of cash flows from operations. *Journal of Accounting Research*, 173–181.

Clacher, I., De Ricquebourg, A.D., and Hodgson, A., 2013. The value relevance of direct cash flows under International Financial Reporting Standards. *Abacus*, 49(3), 367–395.

Clinch, G., Sidhu, B., and Sin, S., 2002. The usefulness of direct and indirect cash flow disclosures. *Review of Accounting Studies*, 7(4), 383–404.

Financial Accounting Standards Board (FASB), 1987. Statement of Financial Accounting Standards No. 95. Norwalk, CT: FASB.

Livnat, J., and Zarowin, P., 1990. The incremental information content of cash-flow components. *Journal of Accounting and Economics*, 13(1), 25–46.

Wilson, G.P., 1986. The relative information content of accruals and cash flows: combined evidence at the earnings announcement and annual report release date. *Journal of Accounting Research*, 24(3), 165–200.

17

Key notes disclosures

ACCOUNTING STANDARDS IN FOCUS

IAS 24 *Related Party Disclosures*

IAS 33 *Earnings per Share*

LEARNING OBJECTIVES

After studying this chapter, you should be able to:

1. explain the potential effect of related party relationships
2. explain the objective and scope of IAS 24
3. identify an entity's related parties
4. identify relationships that do not give rise to a related party relationship as envisaged under IAS 24
5. describe and apply the disclosures required by IAS 24
6. explain why a government-related entity has a partial exemption from related party disclosures
7. explain the objective of IAS 33
8. discuss the application and scope of IAS 33
9. discuss the components of basic earnings per share and examine how it is measured
10. explain the concept of diluted earnings per share and how it is measured
11. explain the need for retrospective adjustment of earnings per share
12. describe and apply the disclosure requirements of IAS 33.

INTRODUCTION

Regardless of the industry or geographical location of an entity, there are two key aspects of disclosures that are commonly found in an entity's financial statements in accordance with IFRS® Standards — related party disclosures under IAS 24 *Related Party Disclosures* and earnings per share disclosures under IAS 33 *Earnings per Share*. Given the widespread application and importance to a user of an entity's financial statements, we will discuss the main requirements of both these standards in this chapter.

17.1 RELATED PARTY DISCLOSURES

It is not uncommon in business for entities to establish relationships with other entities and individuals, to interact with those parties, and to have outstanding balances and commitments with them. For example, groups of entities may conduct their business activities through subsidiary organisations, associated entities or joint venture operations. If an entity engages in transactions with other closely connected entities there is a danger that the economics of the transaction may not be the same had the transaction been negotiated by independent parties in an arm's length arrangement. For example, an entity might have an incentive to shift risks and returns in the form of profits or losses, income or expense flows, or assets or liabilities to a party that it is able to influence or control. Paragraph 6 of IAS 24 explains that related parties may enter into transactions on terms and conditions that would not apply to unrelated parties. For example, an entity might transact with an associate on more or less favourable terms than it would use with another, unrelated individual or entity. Thus, a related party association has the potential to have an impact on the profit or loss and financial position of an entity that might not otherwise occur.

Paragraph 9 of IAS 24 provides a definition of when one party is considered to be related to another party which includes close family members of a reporting entity, situations where control, joint control, or significant influence exists, and where a person or entity is a member of the key management personnel of a reporting entity.

The simple existence of a related party relationship has the potential to affect transactions with other parties. As an example, a subsidiary entity might operate on the instructions of its parent entity. Accordingly, knowledge of business relationships, related party transactions, outstanding balances and commitments with related parties may affect assessments of the business risks faced by entities. For these reasons, IAS 24 requires identification and disclosure of related parties, including related party transactions and any outstanding balances and commitments.

17.1.1 Objective and scope

As mentioned, IAS 24 applies to the identification of related party relationships and transactions and outstanding balances and commitments with related parties. It is used to identify the circumstances in which the disclosure of these items should occur, and the relevant disclosures to make.

The objective of IAS 24 as outlined in paragraph 1 is to ensure that an organisation's financial statements contain the disclosures necessary to an understanding of the potential effect of transactions and outstanding balances and commitments with related parties.

An alternative to the disclosure of related parties, transactions, balances and commitments could be to restate the events as though they had occurred between independent parties in arm's length transactions. However, in many instances valuation of the events and their impacts would be very difficult, if not impossible, to determine as comparable transactions simply may not exist. Thus, the objective of disclosing related party information is to ensure that the users of financial statements are provided with sufficient knowledge to enable them to undertake an independent assessment of the risks and opportunities facing entities which engage in related party transactions.

The major issues that must be considered, when determining the disclosures necessary to provide sufficient knowledge to financial statement users, include identifying related parties and related party arrangements, and deciding on the type and extent of the disclosure to be made. So, in summary, IAS 24 is applied in identifying related party relationships and transactions, identifying outstanding balances and commitments between related parties, and determining when and what related party disclosures must be made.

Paragraphs 3 and 4 of IAS 24 note that related party relationships, transactions, outstanding balances and commitments are disclosed in the consolidated and separate financial statements of a parent, venturer or investor presented in accordance with IFRS 10 *Consolidated Financial Statements* or IAS 27 *Separate Financial Statements*. However, intragroup transactions and balances are eliminated from consolidated financial statements.

17.1.2 Identifying related parties

IAS 24 considers close family who are able to control or significantly influence the activities of the other 'related' entity to be related parties. This relationship is detailed in paragraph 9 of IAS 24. If any of the conditions in paragraph 9 apply to an entity then it is regarded as a related party.

Definition of a related party

The conditions indicating whether one party is considered to be related to another are summarised in table 17.1.

Table 17.1 Definition of a related party — IAS 24 (paragraph 9a, b)	
Part a — A person or a close member of the person's family is related to a reporting entity if that person:	
(i)	has control or joint control of the reporting entity
(ii)	has significant influence over the reporting entity
(iii)	is a member of the key management personnel of the reporting entity or of a parent of the reporting entity
Part b — An entity is related to a reporting entity if any of the following conditions apply:	
(i)	The entity and the reporting entity are members of the same group
(ii)	The entity is an associate or joint venture of the entity (or an associate or joint venture of a member of a group of which the other entity is a member)
(iii)	Both entities are joint ventures of the same third party
(iv)	An entity is a joint venture of a third entity and the other entity is an associate of the third entity
(v)	The entity is a post-employment benefit plan for the benefit of employees of either the reporting entity or an entity related to the reporting entity. If the reporting entity is such a plan, the sponsoring employers are also related to the reporting entity
(vi)	The entity is controlled or jointly controlled by a person identified in part (a)
(vii)	A person identified in (a)(i) has significant influence over the entity or is a member of the key management personnel of the entity or of a parent of the entity

Source: IAS 24, paragraph 9.

A close member of the family of a person

Under paragraph 9, close family members are those who may be expected to influence or be influenced by that person in their dealings with the entity. Thus, in determining who to consider close family members, judgement is required. However, a person's children, spouse or domestic partner, children of the spouse or domestic partner, and dependants of the person or of their spouse or domestic partner, are always to be considered close family members of a person, regardless of whether they are expected to influence or be influenced by that person. Therefore, the close family members definition is an example of IFRS Standards combining an underlying principle with a rule-based approach in determining relevant disclosures.

Control, joint control, significant influence

Control is deemed to be when an investor is exposed, or has rights to variable returns from its involvement in the investee and has the ability to affect those returns through its power over the investee. Joint control is the contractually agreed sharing of control of an arrangement. Significant influence is the power to participate in the financial and operating policy decisions of an entity, and may be gained by share ownership, statute or agreement. A more detailed discussion of what constitutes control, joint control and significant influence can be found in *chapter 20 Consolidation: Controlled entities* and the online chapters *Associates and Joint Ventures* and *Joint Arrangements*.

Determining whether a close family relationship has related party disclosure consequences is demonstrated in illustrative example 17.1.

Xavier is married to Yvonne and he has a controlling investment in Alpha Ltd. Yvonne holds an investment in Bracken Ltd that gives her significant influence over that company. In this relationship:

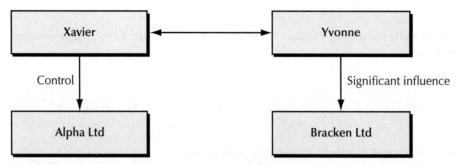

- Bracken Ltd is a related party of Alpha Ltd as Xavier controls Alpha Ltd and his close family member (his wife, Yvonne) has significant influence over Bracken Ltd.
- Alpha Ltd is a related party of Bracken Ltd as Yvonne has significant influence over Bracken Ltd and her close family member (her husband, Xavier) controls Alpha Ltd.
- If Xavier only has significant influence over Alpha Ltd, then Alpha Ltd and Bracken Ltd are not regarded as related entities under IAS 24.

Note: Several of the illustrative examples included in this chapter are derived from similar examples of the Illustrative Examples appendices of IAS 24 and IAS 33.

Key management personnel

Under paragraph 9, key management personnel of the entity or the entity's parent are related parties. Key management personnel are people who have authority and responsibility for planning, directing and controlling an entity's activities either directly or indirectly. This includes directors whether they are executive or otherwise.

Determining whether a party is related to a member of key management personnel is demonstrated in illustrative example 17.2.

Jack has a 100% interest in Henty Ltd and he is also a member of the key management personnel of Courier Ltd. Persimmon Ltd has a controlling interest in Courier Ltd.

In this set of circumstances:
- For Courier Ltd's financial statements, Henty Ltd is a related entity because Jack controls Henty Ltd and he is also a member of the key management personnel of Courier Ltd.
- For Henty Ltd's financial statements, Courier Ltd is a related entity because Jack controls Henty Ltd and he is also a member of Courier Ltd's key management personnel.
- Whether or not Henty Ltd and Persimmon Ltd are related entities would depend on whether Jack's membership of key management personnel of Courier Ltd also makes him key management personnel of the group of Persimmon Ltd, which depends on the facts and circumstances.

An associate of the entity

Under paragraph 9, any party that is determined to be an associate of the reporting entity is also considered to be a related party. An associated entity is one that is subject to the significant influence of another party as described in IAS 28 *Investments in Associates and Joint Ventures*. An associate includes subsidiaries of the associate (paragraph 12).

A joint venture

Any relationship that is determined to be a joint venture as defined in IAS 28 is regarded as a related party. A joint venture includes subsidiaries of the joint venture. For example, an investor that jointly controls a joint venture is related to the joint venture's subsidiary (paragraph 12).

Post-employment benefit plan

A post-employment benefit plan includes pensions and other retirement benefits and post-employment life insurance and medical care. IAS 24 does not provide an indication of why post-employment benefit plans are defined as related parties. However, it is likely that an entity sponsoring a post-employment benefit plan will have either control or significant influence over the plan. There may also be obligations or commitments outstanding at the end of a reporting period.

17.1.3 Relationships that are not related parties

Although the existence of related parties relationships are not uncommon in normal business life, there are many transactions and events between parties that do not necessarily give rise to a related party relationship as envisaged under IAS 24. For example, an employee of a large retailer such as Tesco Plc might purchase goods on normal trading terms in a Tesco store. It would be exceedingly difficult for all such transactions to be identified and recorded, and the benefit of reporting them to users is likely to be trivial. Further, in deciding whether a relationship exists that is subject to the disclosure requirements of IAS 24, paragraph 10 makes it clear that it is the substance, and not merely the legal form of a relationship or transaction, that is important. In this context, paragraph 11 identifies relationships that are not regarded as related parties. For instance, entities are not related parties simply because they have a director or a member of key management personnel in common, or because they share joint control in a joint venture. Similarly, parties an entity engages with for a significant volume of its business are not related parties to the entity simply as a result of the economic dependence that may arise.

17.1.4 Disclosures

In order for users of financial statements to form a view about the effects of the related party relationships of an entity, paragraphs 13 and 14 of IAS 24 require the disclosure of the relationship where control exists, irrespective of whether there have been transactions between the parties. If there have been transactions, then the nature of the relationship together with sufficient information to enable an understanding of the potential effect of the transactions on the financial statements must be disclosed.

An example of related parties identified by Ferrari N.V., and disclosed in its 2023 annual report, is shown in figure 17.1.

FIGURE 17.1 Disclosure of related party transactions.

> **28. RELATED PARTY TRANSACTIONS**
>
> Pursuant to IAS 24, the related parties of Ferrari include Exor N.V., and together with its subsidiaries the Exor Group, as well as all entities and individuals capable of exercising control, joint control or significant influence over the Group and its subsidiaries. Related parties also include companies over which the Exor Group is capable of exercising control, joint control or significant influence, including Stellantis N.V., and together with its subsidiaries the Stellantis Group, and CNH Industrial N.V. and its subsidiaries, as well as joint ventures and associates of Ferrari. In addition, members of the Ferrari Board of Directors and executives with strategic responsibilities and their families are also considered related parties.

Source: Ferrari N.V. 2023 Annual report and Form 20-F, note 28, p. 374.

Related party transactions and related party relationships

If the relationship is between parent and subsidiary entities, the identification of the parties is in addition to the disclosure requirements of IFRS 12 *Disclosure of Interests in Other Entities*, IAS 27 *Separate Financial Statements* and IAS 28. If the parent entity or the ultimate controlling entity does not make financial statements publicly available, then under paragraph 13 of IAS 24 the name of the next most senior parent that does so must be disclosed.

All entities

To assist users of financial statements to form their view about the effects of related party relationships on an entity, a range of information is required to be disclosed separately for each parent, entity with joint control or significant influence, subsidiary, associate, joint venture in which the entity is a venturer, key management personnel, and other related parties. The minimum disclosures are detailed under paragraph 18 and are summarised below.

(a) the amount of the transactions

(b) the amount of the outstanding balances and commitments including:
  (i) their terms and conditions and whether they are secured, and the nature of the settlement consideration to be provided
  (ii) details of any guarantees provided or received

(c) provisions for doubtful debts related to outstanding balances

(d) the expense recognised during the period in respect of bad or doubtful debts due from related parties.

A major focus of the disclosure requirements of IAS 24 is directed towards revealing the remuneration arrangements made for key management personnel. These requirements are intended to improve the transparency of related party relationships with directors and influential senior executives. These disclosures, contained in paragraph 17, are required in total and for each of a range of categories and are shown below:

(a) short-term employee benefits

(b) post-employment benefits

(c) other long-term benefits

(d) termination benefits

(e) share-based payment.

The key management personnel compensation disclosures provided by Ferrari N.V. in its 2023 annual report and Form 20-F are shown in figure 17.2.

FIGURE 17.2 Ferrari N.V. — key management personnel compensation.

Emoluments to Directors and Key Management

The fees of the Directors of Ferrari N.V. are as follows:

	For the years ended December 31,		
	2023	2022	2021
		(€thousand)	
Directors of Ferrari N.V.	9,791	7,660	6,668

The aggregate compensation to Directors of Ferrari N.V. for year ended December 31, 2023 was €9,791 thousand (€7,660 thousand in 2022 and €6,668 thousand in 2021), inclusive of the following:

- €6,688 thousand for salary and other short-term benefits, including short-term incentives (€5,650 thousand in 2022 and €5,445 thousand in 2021);
- €230 thousand for pension benefits (€230 thousand in 2022 and there were no pension benefits in 2021), and
- €2,873 thousand for share-based compensation awarded under the Company's equity incentive plans and other share-based payments, (€1,780 thousand in 2022 and €1,223 thousand in 2021). See Note 21 *"Share-based compensation"* for additional information related to the Company's equity incentive plans. There was no equity-settled compensation for Non-Executive Directors for the years ended December 31, 2023, 2022 and 2021.

The aggregate compensation for members of the FLT (excluding the CEO) in 2023 was €39,131 thousand (€33,935 thousand in 2022 and €18,728 thousand in 2021), inclusive of the following:

- €34,107 thousand for salary and other short-term benefits, including short-term incentives (€28,084 thousand in 2022 and €14,088 thousand in 2021);
- €4,479 thousand for share-based compensation awarded under the Company's equity incentive plans (€5,176 thousand in 2022 and €4,241 thousand in 2021); and
- €545 thousand for pension contributions (€675 thousand in 2022 and €399 thousand in 2021).

Source: Ferrari N.V. 2023 Annual report and Form 20-F, note 28, p. 376–377.

Examples of related party transactions that must be disclosed include the purchases or sales of goods or services whether incomplete or finished, and the acquisition or disposal of assets including property. Lease arrangements, transfers of research and development, transfers under licence agreements or finance arrangements including loans and equity contributions require disclosure. Provisions of guarantees, commitments including executory contracts, and the settlement of liabilities on behalf of the entity or by the entity on behalf of a related party must also be disclosed.

An example of transactions with related parties is shown in the notes accompanying Ferrari N.V.'s 2023 annual report and Form 20-F and is summarised in figure 17.3.

The Group carries out transactions with related parties on commercial terms that are normal in the respective markets, considering the characteristics of the goods or services involved. Transactions carried out by the Group with these related parties are primarily of a commercial nature and, in particular, these transactions relate to:

Transactions with Stellantis Group companies
- the sale of engines to Maserati S.p.A. ("Maserati");
- the purchase of engine components for the use in the production of Maserati engines from FCA US LLC;
- transactions with Stellantis Group companies, mainly relating to a technical cooperations agreement with the aim to enhance the quality and competitiveness of their respective products while reducing costs and investments, to services provided by Stellantis Group companies, including human resources, payroll, tax and the procurement of insurance coverage, as well as to sponsorship revenues received.

Transactions with Stellantis Group companies for the periods presented include transactions with FCA Bank until April 1, 2023. Following the sale by the Stellantis Group of its 50 percent ownership interest in FCA Bank to Crédit Agricole Consumer Finance S.A., FCA Bank (which was renamed CA Auto Bank) is now fully owned by Crédit Agricole Consumer Finance S.A. and is no longer a related party of Ferrari.

Transactions with Exor Group companies (excluding Stellantis Group companies)
- the Group incurs rental costs from Iveco S.p.A., a company belonging to Iveco Group, related to the rental of trucks used by the Formula 1 racing team;
- the Group earns sponsorship revenue from Iveco S.p.A.

Transactions with other related parties
- the purchase of components for Formula 1 racing cars from COXA S.p.A.;
- consultancy services provided by HPE S.r.l.;
- sponsorship agreement relating to Formula 1 activities with Ferrerti S.p.A.;
- sale of cars to certain members of the Board of Directors of Ferrari N.V. and Exor.

In accordance with IAS 24, transactions with related parties also include compensation to Directors and managers with strategic responsibilities.

The amounts of transactions with related parties recognized in the consolidated income statement are as follows:

| | For the years ended December 31, | | | | | | | | |
| | 2023 | | | 2022 | | | 2021 | | |
	Net revenues	Costs[1]	Financial expenses, net	Net revenues	Costs[1]	Financial expenses, net	Net revenues	Costs[1]	Financial expenses, net
					(€ thousand)				
Stellantis Group companies									
Maserati	50.391	2.091	—	78.946	2.989	—	119.083	2.428	—
FCA US LLC	—	6.803	—	14	14.861	—	—	18.465	—
Other Stellantis Group companies	11.489	6.280	1.032	10.953	5.950	2.696	11.799	6.238	2.103
Total Stellantis Group companies	**61,880**	**15,174**	**1,032**	**89,913**	**23,800**	**2,696**	**130,882**	**27,131**	**2,103**
Exor Group companies (excluding the Stellantis Group)	281	1.615	3	282	1.611	—	281	1.014	1
Other related parties	2.237	15.000	—	3.088	14.121	1	795	15.143	2
Total transactions with related parties	**64,398**	**31,789**	**1,035**	**93,283**	**39,532**	**2,697**	**131,958**	**43,288**	**2,106**
Total for the Group	**5,970,146**	**3,477,355**	**15,015**	**5,095,254**	**3,098,475**	**49,616**	**4,270,894**	**2,434,198**	**33,257**

(1) Costs include cost of sales, selling, general and administrative costs and other expenses, net.

FIGURE 17.3 Ferrari N.V. — transactions with related parties.

Non-financial assets and liabilities originating from related party transactions are as follows:

| | At December 31, | | | | | | | |
| | 2023 | | | | 2022 | | | |
	Trade receivables	Trade payables	Other current assets	Other liabilities	Trade receivables	Trade payables	Other current assets	Other liabilities
	(€ thousand)							
Stellantis Group companies								
Maserati	19.681	3.696	—	—	17.458	4.806	—	2.246
FCA US LLC	11	771	—	—	10	4.637	—	—
Other Stellantis Group companies	588	1.858	6	704	700	1.978	111	1.063
Total Stellantis Group companies	**20,280**	**6,325**	**6**	**704**	**18,168**	**11,421**	**111**	**3,309**
Exor Group companies (excluding the Stellantis Group)	—	392	214	218	343	418	68	73
Other related parties	118	2.726	—	51	673	3.341	499	504
Total transactions with related parties	**20,398**	**9,443**	**220**	**973**	**19,184**	**15,180**	**678**	**3,886**
Total for the Group	**261,380**	**930,560**	**130,228**	**1,022,967**	**232,414**	**902,968**	**153,183**	**952,025**

At December 31, 2023 there were no financial assets or financial liabilities with related parties (current financial receivables of €4,364 thousand and other financial payables of €429 thousand at December 31, 2022).

Source: Ferrari 2023 Annual report and Form 20-F (2023, Note 28, pp. 273–274).

17.1.5 Government-related entities

Numerous countries, for example, China, Germany, France, Russia and Eastern European nations, have a sizeable number of entities that are controlled by the government. Often the practical difficulties and costs for government-controlled entities of complying with the extensive disclosure requirements of IAS 24 are likely to outweigh the benefits to financial statement users. Accordingly, paragraph 25 provides an exemption from some of the disclosure requirements for transactions between entities that are controlled, jointly controlled or significantly influenced by a government and with other entities that are related because they are controlled by the same government.

If an entity chooses to apply the exemption, it is still required to identify the government to which it is related and to provide a range of other relevant disclosures. These include: the nature of the relationship; the nature and amount of each individually significant transaction; and either a qualitative or a quantitative indication of the extent of other transactions that are, in aggregate, significant.

17.2 EARNINGS PER SHARE

Earnings per share, commonly known as *EPS*, is a ratio that is calculated by comparing an entity's profit with the number of ordinary shares it has on issue. The earnings per share ratio is used to compare the after-tax profit available to ordinary shareholders of an entity on a per share basis, with that of other entities.

The purpose of this section is to examine and understand the earnings per share information that is presented in a reporting entity's financial statements. In an effort to improve the information provided by reporting entities, and with the objective of improving the consistency of comparisons between entities and across different time periods, IAS 33 prescribes the principles for the computation and the presentation of earnings per share.

Under paragraph 10 of IAS 33, the approach taken to the calculation of the earnings per share ratio is to divide profit or loss (earnings) attributable to ordinary shareholders of a parent entity, by the weighted average number of ordinary shares the entity has on issue (outstanding) during the reporting period.

FIGURE 17.4 L'Air Liquide S.A.'s remuneration report.

SUMMARY TABLE OF THE VARIABLE REMUNERATION FOR 2023

| Indicator | Approved elements by the General Meeting in 2023: | | | | Achievement | | | |
| | Target | | Maximum | | | | | |
	As a % of the fixed remuneration	As a % based on a 100	As a % of the fixed remuneration	As a % based on a 100	As a % of the target remuneration for this criterion	As a % of the fixed remuneration	As a % based on 100	In thousands of euros (rounded off)
Quantifiable financial criteria including:	**84**	**70**	**105**	**70**	**113**	**95**	**71**	**1,042**
Increase in recurring net earnings excluding the foreign exchange impact per share (recurring EPS)	60	50	75	50	125	75	56	825
Comparable growth in consolidated revenue	24	20	30	20	82	20	15	217

Source: L'Air Liquide S.A. (Universal Registration Document 2023, p. 178).

'Profit' is the numerator (top line) in the calculation and 'outstanding shares' is the denominator (bottom line). The resultant ratio is known as 'basic earnings per share', and the objective of providing this information is to show a measure of the interests of an ordinary shareholder in the performance (profit) of an entity across a reporting period.

The earnings per share ratio has other important uses including as an indicator of future performance and growth. Earnings changes which impact earnings per share, whether they indicate improvements or deteriorations, provide information to the market and are usually reflected in a changing share price. Earnings per share is also often used as a key performance indicator when determining the remuneration entitlements of directors and executives. For example, L'Air Liquide S.A. uses (recurring) earnings per share targets as one of the determining factors for the Chairman and CEO's variable remuneration. The relevant part of L'Air Liquide S.A.'s remuneration approach, targets and achievements, are presented in figure 17.4.

The utility of earnings per share has been criticised because of the flexibility that entities have in choosing accounting methods when determining their profit. While accounting policy *choice* enables entities to select the accounting methods that are the most appropriate to reflect their actual business operations, it results in inconsistencies between entities in the determination of their profit. For example, IFRS provides options between measurement methods such as the historical cost model and the revaluation model for property, plant and equipment (see IAS 16 *Property, Plant and Equipment*, paragraph 29). If one entity chooses the historical cost model, this generally leads to lower earnings per share in times of inflation, compared with the revaluation model. Therefore, it must be recognised that earnings per share data disclosed by reporting entities have limitations because of the different accounting methods that can be used in the determination of profit. Furthermore, it is not uncommon for entities to disclose so-called 'adjusted earnings' measures, accompanied by adjusted earnings per share. Comparing such non-GAAP measures across companies requires insight into the adjustments made. Entities disclosing adjusted earnings per share measures should therefore reconcile the adjusted earnings to the profit or loss measure applied under IAS 33 (paragraphs 73 and 73A). L'Air Liquide S.A. does so by including a reconciliation between net profit and recurring net profit, see figure 17.5.

Another limitation to the utility of the earnings per share ratio for comparison purposes is that it can be altered simply by changing the number of shares used in the denominator. The focus taken in IAS 33 is that a consistently determined denominator in the earnings per share calculation enhances financial reporting (paragraph 1). To enhance comparability, this means a number of adjustments may be required when calculating the earnings per share, as discussed in the remainder of this chapter.

Despite the limitations of earnings per share as an indicator of the performance of an entity, it is widely used in share analysis.

Recurring net profit Group share and recurring net profit Group share excluding currency impact
The recurring net profit Group share corresponds to the net profit Group share excluding exceptional and significant transactions that have no impact on the operating income recurring.

	FY 2022	FY 2023	2023/2022 variation
(A) Net Profit (Group Share) – As Published	**2,758.8**	**3,078.0**	**+11.6%**
(B) Exceptional and significant transactions after-tax with no impact on OIR			
■ Exceptional provisions on industrial assets in Russia and other related costs	(575.6)		
■ Exceptional income related to joint-venture take-over in Asia Pacific	205.5		
■ Provision for risks in Engineering & Construction activity	(32.8)		
■ Sales of Group stake in Hydrogenics		159.4	
■ Impairment of assets held for sale and of other assets identified in particular following a strategic review		(345.7)	
■ Restructuring costs of Home Healthcare activity in France		(55.7)	
(A) − (B) = Net profit recurring (Group share)	**3,161.7**	**3,320.0**	**+5.0%**
(C) Currency impact		(262.0)	
(A) - (B) - (C) = Net profit recurring (Group share) excluding currency impact		**3,582.0**	**+13.3%**

Source: L'Air Liquide S.A. (Universal Registration Document 2023, p. 64).

17.2.1 Scope

IAS 33 applies to the computation and presentation of earnings per share by reporting entities whose shares are publicly traded, or of entities that are in the process of issuing ordinary shares that will be traded in public markets (paragraph 1).

Under paragraph 4, if an entity presents both consolidated and separate financial statements, the IAS 33 disclosures need only be determined on the basis of consolidated information. As the parent entity earnings per share information may be helpful to some users, entities have the option of also disclosing earnings per share figures for the parent entity. However this information can only be presented in the parent's separate financial statements and not in the consolidated financial statements (IAS 33 BC paragraphs 5, 6). The earnings per share information presented by Nestlé Group in its 2023 consolidated income statement is presented in figure 17.6.

FIGURE 17.6 Earnings per share disclosed in income statement of Nestlé Group.

Earnings per share (in CHF)			
Basic earnings per share	15	4.24	3.42
Diluted earnings per share	15	4.23	3.42

Source: Nestlé Group (Financial Statements 2023, Note 15, p. 72) [only the EPS disclosures].

17.2.2 Basic earnings per share

As mentioned, earnings per share is measured by dividing profit (or loss) attributable to ordinary shareholders by the weighted average number of ordinary shares outstanding during the period. This measurement approach, which results in a ratio known as 'basic' earnings per share (paragraph 9), is demonstrated in figure 17.7.

FIGURE 17.7 Basic earnings per share ratio.

$$\frac{\text{Profit attributable to ordinary shareholders of the parent entity}}{\text{Weighted average number of ordinary shares outstanding during the reporting period}}$$

Earnings

The profit or loss (profit) that is used in the calculation of basic earnings per share must be from continuing operations. It must also include any income or expense attributable to ordinary shareholders that has been recognised in the reporting period. This will mean that any tax expense and any dividends on preference shares that have been classified as liabilities will already have been deducted as part of the determination of net profit. Tax expense is a normal component of the profit of an entity, and therefore it is a normal part of the calculation of profit. Any remuneration (such as preference dividend) of preference shares that are classified as equity and any other equity instruments not being ordinary shares do not belong to the ordinary shareholders. Therefore they must be deducted from net profit when determining the profit to be used in the calculation of earnings per share (paragraphs 12 and 13 of IAS 33, and demonstrated in figure 17.8.

FIGURE 17.8 Earnings calculation adjusting for tax expense and preference dividends.

Profit before tax expense	100,000
Less: Tax expense	(30,000)
Profit after tax	70,000
Less: Preference dividends	(10,000)
Profit attributable to ordinary equity holders (earnings)	60,000 (numerator)

The preference dividends are to be on an after-tax basis, and for non-cumulative preference dividends they are to include any amounts declared during the period. In respect of cumulative dividends, paragraph 14 requires the after-tax amount to be deducted whether or not a dividend is declared during the period. Any cumulative dividends paid during the period but which relate to prior periods are not part of the calculation.

The treatment of cumulative and non-cumulative dividends is demonstrated in illustrative example 17.3.

ILLUSTRATIVE EXAMPLE 17.3 Non-cumulative and cumulative preference dividends

Poulos Ltd has 100,000 Class A preference shares on issue, each carrying a non-cumulative dividend right of 3% of the $1 par value of the share. A non-cumulative dividend was declared during the reporting period. The company also has 200,000 Class B preference shares outstanding which carry a cumulative dividend right of 2% per share based on the par value of $1 per share. The company has a profit for the period from continuing operations amounting to $1.5 million, and tax is payable at the rate of 30%. Any dividend payment or redemption of Class A and Class B preference shares is at the full discretion of Poulos Ltd, so they are classified as equity instruments.

The earnings (profit attributable to ordinary shareholders) to be used in the calculation of basic earnings per share for Poulos Ltd is calculated as shown below.

Determination of earnings to include tax expense and preference dividends	
Calculation	**$**
Profit before tax	1,500,000
Tax expense	(450,000)
Profit after tax	1,050,000
Preference dividends	(7,000)[1]
Profit attributable to ordinary equity holders	1,043,000

[1]([100,000 × $1 × 3%] + [200,000 × $1 × 2%])

If an entity presents discontinued operations under IFRS 5 *Non-current Assets Held for Sale and Discontinued Operations*, the entity shall also disclose the earnings per share for the discontinued operations. An entity may choose to disclose earnings per share from discontinued operations in the notes, instead of on the face of the statement of comprehensive income. This is illustrated in the 2023 income statement of Enel SpA in figure 17.9.

FIGURE 17.9 Basic earnings from continuing and discontinued operations.

Earnings per share	18		
Basic earnings per share	18		
Basic earnings per share		*0.32*	*0.15*
Basic earnings/(loss) per share from continuing operations [a]		*0.36*	*0.34*
Basic earnings/(loss) per share from discontinued operations [a]		*(0.04)*	*(0.19)*

Source: Enel SpA (Integrated Annual Report 2023, p. 274) [only the basic EPS disclosures].

Repurchases and conversion of preference shares

If an entity chooses to repurchase preference shares it has on issue, then the excess of the fair value of the consideration paid over the carrying amount of the shares represents a return to preference share-holders and a charge against retained earnings. Paragraph 16 requires this amount to be included in the calculation of earnings per share, as a deduction when determining the profit attributable to ordinary shareholders.

Similarly, any excess of the fair value of the ordinary shares issued on conversion of preference shares over the fair value of the ordinary shares issuable under the original conversion terms must be deducted in calculating the profit attributable to ordinary shareholders (paragraph 17).

Shares

As the earnings per share calculation is focused on the ordinary equity of an entity, the denominator in the calculation contains only ordinary share capital. Because entities are able to issue new shares during a reporting period, the number of shares on issue can increase. They are also able to repurchase or cancel shares, which will decrease the number of shares on issue, and to split or to consolidate shares, which will vary the number of shares on issue. Other actions, including the conversion of convertible preference shares or other convertible securities into ordinary shares, can also vary the amount of shares outstanding. Accordingly, the number of ordinary shares that is used in the calculation of basic earnings per share is adjusted by a time-weighting factor, which is the number of days in the reporting period that the shares are outstanding as a proportion of the total number of days in the period (paragraph 20).

Shares are included in the calculation from the date that the consideration for shares is receivable (paragraph 21). For example, shares issued for cash is included when cash is receivable; ordinary shares issued on the reinvestment of dividends are included when the dividends are reinvested; shares issued when debt is converted or when the shares replace interest or principal on other financial instruments are included from the date interest ceases to accrue. If ordinary shares are issued in exchange for the settlement of a liability, then they are included from the settlement date or, if they are issued in exchange for services rendered, they are included from the date of rendering the services. Any ordinary shares issued as consideration for the acquisition of a non-cash asset are included in the calculation from the date on which the acquisition is recognised; and if shares are issued as part of the consideration in a business combination, they are included from the acquisition date as this reflects the date from which the acquiree's profits are included in the acquirer's income.

Share consolidation and share repurchase

While a consolidation of shares will decrease the number of shares on issue, there is no corresponding reduction in the entity's resources. However, when a repurchase occurs, the entity's resources (e.g. cash) will also be reduced. Shares that are repurchased and held by the issuing entity are termed 'Treasury' shares. If a purchase of Treasury shares (share repurchase) occurs, then the weighted average number of shares outstanding for the period in which the transaction takes place must be adjusted for the reduction in the number of shares from the date of the event (paragraph 29).

The calculation of the weighted average number of ordinary shares where a new share issue and a share repurchase have occurred during the period is demonstrated in illustrative example 17.4.

ILLUSTRATIVE EXAMPLE 17.4 Determining the weighted average number of shares

Singapore Ltd has 11,000 ordinary shares on issue at 1 January 20X1, which is the beginning of its reporting period, of which 500 have been repurchased in previous reporting periods. On 30 June 20X1, it issued a further 1,000 ordinary shares for cash. On 1 November 20X1, Singapore Ltd repurchased 300 shares at fair value in a market transaction.

		Issued shares	Treasury shares	Shares outstanding
1 January 20X1	Balance at the beginning of the year	11,000	500	10,500
30 June 20X1	Issue of new ordinary shares for cash	1,000		11,500
1 November 20X1	Repurchase of issued shares		300	11,200
31 December 20X1	Balance at the end of the year	12,000	800	11,200

The weighted average number of shares for use in the earnings per share calculation is determined as follows:

$$= (10,500 \times 6/12) + (11,500 \times 4/12) + (11,200 \times 2/12)$$
$$= 5,250 + 3,833 + 1,867$$
$$= 10,950 \text{ shares}$$

Contingently issuable shares

An entity may have contingently issuable shares outstanding. These are ordinary shares that the entity can issue for little or no cash or other consideration once a specified condition has been satisfied (paragraph 5). If an entity has contingently issuable shares, then these must be treated as outstanding and they are included in the calculation of basic earnings per share from the date when all necessary conditions have been satisfied (paragraph 24). The impact of contingently issuable shares on diluted earnings per share is discussed later (*see section 17.2.3*).

Bonus issues and share splits

If an entity announces a bonus issue of shares, or if it splits issued shares thereby increasing the number of shares outstanding, there is usually no consideration involved and therefore no corresponding increase in the entity's resources. The number of ordinary shares outstanding before the event must be adjusted for the proportionate change in the number of ordinary shares outstanding as if it had occurred at the beginning of the earliest period presented in the financial statements (paragraph 28). For example, under a two-for-one bonus issue, multiplying the number of ordinary shares outstanding before the bonus issue determines the number of additional ordinary shares. The effect of a bonus issue of shares on the basic earnings per share calculation is demonstrated in illustrative example 17.5.

ILLUSTRATIVE EXAMPLE 17.5 Bonus issue of shares

Jackson Ltd determined its profit attributable to ordinary shareholders for the reporting period ended 31 December 20X1 as $360,000 (20X4: $320,000). The number of ordinary shares on issue up to 30 April 20X1 was 50,000. Jackson Ltd announced a two-for-one bonus issue of shares effective for each ordinary share outstanding at 30 April 20X1 on 1 May 20X1.

Basic earnings per share is calculated as follows:

Bonus issue on 1 May 2015 $\qquad 50,000 \times 2 = 100,000$

Basic earnings per share 31 December 2015 $\dfrac{360,000}{50,000 + 100,000} = \$2.40$

Basic earnings per share 31 December 2014 $\dfrac{320,000}{50,000 + 100,000} = \$2.13$

Because the bonus shares were issued for no consideration, the event is treated as if it had occurred before the beginning of the 20X0 reporting period, the earliest period presented in the financial statements (paragraph 28).

Rights issues

In a bonus issue as the shares are usually issued for no consideration there is an increase in the number of shares outstanding, which is not accompanied by a corresponding increase in the resources of the issuing entity. However, in a rights issue the exercise price is usually lower than the fair value of the shares issued. This means that the rights issue includes a bonus element. In this case, the application guidance in IAS 33 (paragraph A2) requires that the number of ordinary shares used in the calculation of earnings per share, for all periods before the rights issue, is to be the number of ordinary shares outstanding before the rights issue multiplied by an adjustment factor. The components of the adjustment factor are shown in figure 17.10.

FIGURE 17.10 Adjustment factor for rights issues containing a bonus element

$$\frac{\text{Fair value per share immediately before the exercise of rights}}{\text{Theoretical ex-rights fair value per share}}$$

The 'theoretical ex-rights fair value per share' is calculated by adding the aggregate market value of the shares immediately before the exercise of the rights to the proceeds from the exercise of the rights, and then dividing by the number of shares outstanding after the exercise of the rights, as shown in figure 17.11.

FIGURE 17.11 Theoretical ex-rights value per share

$$\frac{\text{Fair value of all outstanding shares immediately before the exercise of rights +}}{\text{Number of shares outstanding after the exercise of the rights}}$$

Fair value is the share price at the close of the last day on which the shares were traded together with the rights. The calculation of basic earnings per share where there is a rights issue during the period is demonstrated in illustrative example 17.6.

ILLUSTRATIVE EXAMPLE 17.6 Rights issue

Georgiou Ltd determined its profit attributable to ordinary shareholders for the reporting period ended 31 December 20X1 as $5,000. At the beginning of the reporting period the company had 1000 ordinary shares on issue. It announced a rights issue with the following details:
- date of rights issue, 1 January 20X1
- last date to exercise rights, 1 March 20X1
- one new share for each four outstanding (250 total)
- exercise price, $10
- market price of one share immediately before exercise on 1 March 20X1, $12.

Determine the theoretical ex-rights value per share

$$\frac{\text{Fair value of all outstanding shares immediately before the exercise of rights} + \text{total proceeds from the exercise of the rights}}{\text{Number of shares outstanding after the exercise of the rights}}$$

$$\frac{(\$12 \times 1000\,\text{shares}) + (\$10 \times 250\,\text{shares})}{1000\,\text{shares} + 250\,\text{shares}} = \$11.60$$

Determine the adjustment factor

$$\frac{\text{Fair value per share immediately before the exercise of rights}}{\text{Theoretical ex} - \text{rights fair value per share}} \quad \frac{\$12}{\$11.60} = 1.03$$

Basic earnings per share for the year 20X1 is calculated as follows:

$$\text{Profit attributable to ordinary shareholders 30 June 2014} \frac{5,000}{(1,000 \times 1.03 \times 2/12) + (1,250 \times 10/12)} = \$4.12$$

17.2.3 Diluted earnings per share

In addition to calculating the basic earnings per share ratio, if an entity has options, warrants, contingently issuable shares or convertible securities, then it must also recognise the effect of potential dilution to its earnings per share ratio. The potential dilution effect stems from assumptions that the entity's convertible securities are converted, its warrants or options are exercised or that its contingently issuable shares are issued on the satisfaction of their specified conditions. Adjustments must be made to the profit (or loss) attributable to the ordinary shareholders. The adjustments are for the after-tax amount of dividends, interest or other income or expenses recognised in the reporting period in respect of the dilutive securities that would no longer arise if they were indeed converted into ordinary shares. Adjustments must also be made to increase the weighted average number of ordinary shares outstanding to reflect what the weighted average would have been, assuming that all potential ordinary shares (dilutive securities) had been converted.

FIGURE 17.12 Capgemini SE — potential (dilutive) ordinary shares.

Diluted earnings per share
Diluted earnings per share are calculated by assuming conversion into ordinary shares of all dilutive instruments outstanding during the year.

In 2023, instruments considered dilutive for the purpose of calculating diluted earnings per share include:
— shares delivered in October 2023 to non-French employees under the performance share plan approved by the Board of Directors on October 2, 2019 representing a weighted average of 670,155 shares;
— shares delivered in October 2023 to french employees and shares available for grant to non-French employees under the performance share plan approved by the Board of Directors on October 7, 2020, representing a weighted average of 1,512,694 shares;
— shares available for grant under the performance share plan approved by the Board of Directors on October 6, 2021, representing a weighted average of 1,643,331 shares and whose related performance conditions will be definitely assessed in October 2024;
— shares available for grant under the performance share plan approved by the Board of Directors on December 1, 2021, representing a weighted average of 9,681 shares and whose related presence conditions will be definitely assessed in December 2024;
— shares available for grant under the performance share plan approved by the Board of Directors on October 3, 2022, representing a weighted average of 1,913,097 shares and whose related performance conditions will be definitely assessed in October 2025;
— shares available for grant under the performance share plan approved by the Board of Directors on October 3, 2022, representing a weighted average of 11,865 shares and whose related presence conditions will be definitely assessed in October 2025;
— shares available for grand under the performance share plan approved by the Board of Directors on November 6, 2023, representing a weighted average of 285,385 shares and whose related performance conditions will be definitely assessed in November 2026.

Source: Capgemini SE (Universal Registration document 2023, Note 11, p. 293).

The information regarding potential (dilutive) ordinary shares appearing in the financial statements of Capgemini SE is presented in figure 17.12.

IAS 33 regards potential ordinary shares as dilutive only if their conversion to ordinary shares would decrease earnings per share (or increase loss per share) from the continuing operations of an entity (paragraph 41). Potential ordinary shares can be anti-dilutive. An anti-dilutive effect would occur if the conversion of potential ordinary shares would increase earnings per share (paragraph 5). Such anti-dilutive effects are ignored when calculating the diluted earnings per share.

If potential ordinary shares were to be converted, any dividends or interest payable in relation to those dilutive securities would no longer arise. Instead the new ordinary shares would be entitled to participate in profit. Therefore the profit must be increased to remove the impact of the dividends or interest that would otherwise have been payable. Similarly any other income or charges such as transaction costs, that are related to the potential ordinary shares and that have been included in profit, must be removed (paragraph 33).

Shares

The diluted earnings per share ratio must include an adjustment to increase the weighted average number of ordinary shares that would be outstanding if all of the dilutive securities were converted into ordinary shares.

Paragraph 36 deems that the potential ordinary shares are to be regarded as having been converted into ordinary shares at the beginning of the period or, if later, the date of the issue of the potential ordinary shares.

The potential ordinary shares shall be weighted for the period that they are outstanding. If any of the dilutive securities lapse or are cancelled, they are included in the calculation only for the portion of time during which they are outstanding. Any dilutive securities that are converted into ordinary shares during the period are included in the calculation of diluted earnings per share from the beginning of the period to the date of conversion (paragraph 38). If the terms of dilutive securities include more than one basis for conversion into ordinary shares, then under paragraph 39, the most favourable conversion rate or price from the perspective of the security holder is used.

Dilutive potential ordinary shares

As mentioned, potential ordinary shares are regarded by IAS 33 as dilutive only if their conversion to ordinary shares would decrease earnings per share or increase loss per share (paragraph 41). In deciding whether potential ordinary shares are dilutive (or anti-dilutive) each issue or series of potential dilutive securities is considered separately. The conversion, exercise or other issue of potential ordinary shares that would have an anti-dilutive effect on earnings per share is not assumed in the calculation of diluted earnings per share (paragraph 43).

When determining the dilutive effect of potential ordinary shares, each issue or series of dilutive securities is considered in sequence from most dilutive to least dilutive (paragraph 44). This means that the securities with the lowest earnings impact, per incremental share, are included in the calculation before those securities with the highest earnings impact per incremental share. This generally means that options and warrants are included first, because they do not usually affect the numerator (earnings) in the ratio.

Options and warrants

The proceeds from options and warrants are regarded as received from the issue of ordinary shares at the average market price during the period. Paragraphs 45–46 require that the difference between the number of ordinary shares issued and the number that would have been issued at the average market price be treated as an issue of ordinary shares for no consideration. The application guidance to IAS 33 indicates that a simple average of the weekly or monthly closing prices of ordinary shares is usually adequate for determining the average market price (paragraphs A4–A5). However, this approach will need to be adjusted when shares prices fluctuate widely.

Options and warrants are regarded as dilutive if they would result in the issue of ordinary shares for less than the average market price during the period (i.e. when they are 'in the money'). The amount of the dilution is determined as the average market price of ordinary shares during the period minus the issue price. Employee share options and non-vested ordinary shares are regarded as options in the calculation of diluted earnings per share (paragraph 48).

The effect of share options on basic and diluted earnings per share is demonstrated in illustrative example 17.7.

ILLUSTRATIVE EXAMPLE 17.7 Effect of share options on earnings per share

Harlem Ltd determined its profit attributable to ordinary shareholders for the reporting period ended 31 December 20X1 as $480,000. The average market price of the entity's shares during the period is $4.00 per share. The weighted average number of ordinary shares on issue during the period is 1,000,000. The weighted average number of shares under share options arrangements during the year is 200,000 and the exercise price of shares under option is $3.50.

	Earnings $	Shares	Per share $
Basic earnings per share is calculated as follows:			
Profit attributable to ordinary shareholders for the reporting period ended 31 December 20X1	480,000		
Weighted average shares on issue during the period		1,000,000	
Basic earnings per share			0.48
Diluted earnings per share is calculated as follows:			
Weighted average number of shares under option		200,000	
Weighted average number of shares that would have been issued at average market price is (200,000 × $3.50) / $4.00		(175,000)	
Diluted earnings per share	480,000	1,025,000	0.47

Convertible securities

If convertible preference shares are dilutive they are included in the diluted earnings per share calculation. They are regarded as anti-dilutive if the amount of the dividend declared or accumulated in the current period per ordinary share, obtainable on the conversion, exceeds basic earnings per share. Similarly, convertible debt is regarded as anti-dilutive whenever its interest (net of tax and other changes in income or expenses) per ordinary share obtainable on conversion, exceeds basic earnings per share.

Contingently issuable shares

Contingently issuable ordinary shares such as performance-based employee share options are regarded as outstanding, and if their conditions are satisfied they are included in the calculation of diluted earnings per share from the beginning of the period (or the date of the contingent share agreement, if later). If the conditions are not satisfied, the number of contingently issuable shares that is included in the diluted earnings per share calculation is based on the number of shares that would be issuable if the end of the reporting period were the end of the contingency period (paragraph 52).

If the number of contingently issuable ordinary shares is dependent on both future earnings and future prices of ordinary shares, then the number of ordinary shares included in the diluted earnings per share calculation is based on both conditions. That is, it is based on both earnings to date and on the current market price of the ordinary shares at the end of the reporting period (paragraph 55). Unless both conditions are met, contingently issuable ordinary shares are not included in the diluted earnings per share calculation.

Contracts that may be settled in ordinary shares or cash

If an entity has issued a contract that may be settled in cash or ordinary shares at the entity's option, then under paragraph 58 it is assumed that the settlement will be in ordinary shares. As a result the potential ordinary shares are included in the diluted earnings per share calculation if the effect is dilutive.

For contracts that can be settled in cash or in ordinary shares at the holder's option, then the more dilutive of either the cash settlement or the share settlement is used in the diluted earnings per share calculation (paragraph 60).

As mentioned, when determining the dilutive effect of potential ordinary shares, each issue or series of dilutive securities is considered in sequence from most dilutive to least dilutive (paragraph 44). Securities with the lowest earnings impact per additional share are included in the calculation first. Determining the order in which to include dilutive securities is demonstrated in illustrative example 17.8.

ILLUSTRATIVE EXAMPLE 17.8 Calculation of weighted average number when more than one issue of potentially dilutive securities exist

Brown Ltd extracted the following information from its financial records in order to determine its basic earnings per share and diluted earnings per share for its reporting period ended 31 December 20X1.

Profit from continuing operations	$12,400
Less: Dividends on preference shares	(6,400)
Profit from continuing operations attributable to ordinary shareholders	6,000
Ordinary shares on issue	2,000
Average market price of one ordinary share during the period	$7.50

Potential ordinary shares (potentially dilutive securities):

1. Options	10,000 with an exercise price of $6.00
2. Convertible preference shares	800 shares with an issue value of $100 entitled to a cumulative dividend of $8 per share. Each preference share is convertible to two ordinary shares.

Determine the increase in earnings attributable to ordinary shareholders on conversion of potential ordinary shares

Options	
Increase in earnings	$0
Additional shares issued for no consideration 10,000 × (7.50 − 6.00) / 7.50	2,000
Earnings per additional share	$0

Convertible preference shares	
Increase in earnings ($80,000 × 0.08)	$6,400
Additional shares (2 × 800)	1,600
Earnings per additional share	$4.00

The dilutive securities are included in the earnings per share calculation in the following order:
1. Options
2. Convertible preference shares

Determine dilutive effect of convertible securities

	$	Shares	$ per share	
Profit from continuing operations attributable to ordinary shareholders	10,000	2,000	5.00	
Increase in earnings from options	0	2,000		
	10,000	4,000	2.50	Dilutive
Increase in earnings from convertible preference shares[1]	6,400	1,600		
	16,400	5,600	2.93	Anti-dilutive

[1] *As the convertible preference shares increased diluted earnings per share they would be considered anti-dilutive and ignored in the calculation of diluted earnings per share.*

Conclusion: *Basic EPS is $5.00 and diluted EPS is $2.50*

17.2.4 Retrospective adjustments

Retrospective adjustments are made to restate the values of relevant items so that valid comparisons across time can be made. If, for example, the number of issued shares increases during a reporting period as a result of a bonus issue for no consideration, then the operating profit for the whole period in which the bonus issue occurred will be attributable to the increased number of shares and not to the lesser number of shares outstanding at the beginning of the reporting period.

IAS 33 paragraph 64 requires that if the number of ordinary shares or of potential ordinary shares outstanding increases as a result of a:
- capitalisation
- bonus issue
- share split;
   or if the number decreases as a result of a:
- consolidation (reverse share split); then,

the calculation of both basic earnings per share and diluted earnings per share must be adjusted retrospectively for all periods that are presented in the financial statements. The retrospective adjustment to the number of shares also applies to the period from the end of the reporting period but before the financial statements are authorised for issue. Further, basic and diluted earnings per share are both subject to retrospective adjustment for the effects of any errors or adjustments resulting from changes in accounting policies that are accounted for retrospectively. This is illustrated in illustrative example 17.9.

ILLUSTRATIVE EXAMPLE 17.9 Retrospective adjustment for share split

On 24 March 20X1 Green S.A. splits its ordinary shares outstanding in a 2:1 exchange, i.e. every 'old' ordinary share of Green Plc is exchanged for two 'new' shares. In doing so, the number of shares increases from 1,000,000 to 2,000,000. Profit from continuing operations during 20X0 and 20X1 amounts to €1,800,000 and €2,500,000 respectively.

Basic EPS for 20X1 as reported in the 20X1 financial statements amounts to €1.25 calculated as €2,500,000 / 2,000,000. Basic EPS for 20X0 is adjusted to €0.90 (€1,800,000 / 2,000,000) as comparative information about 20X0 in the 20X1 financial statements.

17.2.5 Disclosures

The basic earnings per share and diluted earnings per share ratios must be presented in an entity's statement of profit or loss and other comprehensive income (paragraph 66) even if the amounts are negative (paragraph 69). If the items of profit or loss are presented in a separate statement, then the basic and diluted earnings per share ratios are required to be presented in that separate statement. The two ratios must be displayed with equal prominence, and they must be calculated for each class of ordinary shares that have different rights to share in the profit of the period. If diluted earnings per share is presented for one period, then it must be shown for all periods that are presented in the financial statements, even if it is the same as the basic earnings per share. And, if the entity has a discontinued operation, then it must also calculate and disclose the basic and diluted earnings per share ratios for the discontinued operation in the statement of profit or loss and other comprehensive income.

Paragraphs 70–73 of IAS 33 prescribe various disclosures relating to earnings per share. The objective of these disclosures is to provide sufficient additional information to assist financial statement users to understand the composition of the earnings per share ratios.

For instance, Nestlé Group includes a reconciliation of the weighted average number of shares used in its basic and diluted earnings per share calculation in Note 15 in its 2023 financial statements. The reconciliations are presented in figure 17.11.

FIGURE 17.11 Reconciliation of weighted average number of shares – Nestlé Group

Reconciliation of weighted average number of shares outstanding (in millions of units)		
Weighted average number of shares outstanding used to calculate basic earnings per share	**2,646**	2,707
Adjustment for share-based payment schemes, where dilutive	**2**	2
Weighted average number of shares outstanding used to calculate diluted earnings per share	**2,648**	2,709

Source: Nestlé Group (2023, p. 145).

As discussed earlier *(see sections 17.2.2 and 17.2.3)*, if, in addition to calculating basic and diluted earnings per share, an entity uses a numerator other than the one required by IAS 33, then it must still use the denominator as prescribed under IAS 33 (paragraph 73). These additional ratios must be displayed with equal prominence as the prescribed basic EPS and diluted EPS ratios and presented in the notes to the financial statements. The basis on which the numerator is determined, including whether the amounts per share are before or after tax, must also be disclosed.

IAS 33 also encourages the voluntary disclosure of the terms and conditions of financial instruments and contracts that incorporate terms and conditions affecting the measurement of basic and diluted earnings per share.

17.3 SUMMARY

This chapter covers two common key disclosures in an entity's IFRS Standards financial statements — related party disclosures and earnings per share disclosures.

IAS 24 is a disclosure standard that defines related party relationships and prescribes the events, transactions, balances and commitments that must be revealed in the financial statements and reports of disclosing entities. As related party relationships can be expected to affect the profit or loss or the financial position of an entity, disclosures about them are particularly helpful to investors, lenders and other users when they evaluate and assess the risks and opportunities facing entities. The main features of IAS 24 are that it:
- considers key management personnel and their close family members to be related parties
- considers compensation benefits for key management personnel to be related party transactions.

Determining when related party relationships exist and identifying the circumstances in which disclosures about such relationships must be disclosed involves a certain amount of judgement. In making that judgement, entities must take into account the definitions of related parties provided in IAS 24. The definition of related parties includes:
- relationships affected by control or significant influence or joint venture arrangements
- key management personnel and close family members.

IAS 33 provides principles for the calculation and presentation of basic and diluted earnings per share. Earnings per share is a ratio which is used to compare the after-tax profit available to ordinary shareholders of an entity on a per share basis, with that of other entities. It is calculated by dividing profit or loss (earnings) attributable to ordinary shareholders, by the weighted average number of ordinary shares outstanding during a reporting period.

The objective of IAS 33 is to improve the information provided by reporting entities, and the consistency of comparisons between entities and across different time periods.

The main features of the standard are that it requires:

- the profit (or loss) used as a starting point in the calculation of basic earnings per share to be net profit from continuing operations, so net of any tax expense and dividends on preference shares that have been classified as liabilities
- The amount is adjusted for any dividends on other equity instruments than ordinary shares, such as preference shares classified as equity
- the denominator in the calculation to contain only ordinary shares
- the number of ordinary shares used in the calculation of basic earnings per share to be adjusted by a time-weighting factor which is the number of days in the reporting period that the shares are outstanding as a proportion of the total number of days in the period.

In addition to calculating the basic earnings per share ratio, if an entity has options, warrants, contingently issuable shares or securities that are convertible to ordinary shares, IAS 33 requires that the effect of dilution must be recognised in the entity's earnings per share. Adjustments to calculate diluted earnings per share must be made to:

- the profit (or loss) attributable to the ordinary shareholders for the after-tax amount of dividends, interest or other income or expenses that would no longer arise if the dilutive securities were converted into ordinary shares
- increase the weighted average number of ordinary shares outstanding to reflect what the weighted average would have been assuming that all potential ordinary shares (dilutive securities) had been converted.

Discussion questions

Related party disclosures

1. Why do standard setters formulate rules for the disclosure of related party relationships?
2. Explain why key management personnel are regarded as related parties.
3. Explain why a parent company and its subsidiary entities are regarded as related parties.
4. Distinguish between control, joint control and significant influence.
5. Explain how an entity determines whether a family member is a related party.

Earnings per share

1. What is the earnings per share ratio used for?
2. Why is a time-weighting factor used to determine the number of shares that is used in the calculation of basic earnings per share?
3. What is the treatment applied to treasury shares when calculating the weighted average number of shares used in the earnings per share calculation?
4. Distinguish between basic earnings per share and diluted earnings per share.
5. Explain the effect of potential ordinary shares on the calculation of diluted earnings per share.
6. Why are retrospective adjustments made to earnings per share ratios?

IFRS Standards prescribe, for each standard, a minimum set of additional information that should be disclosed in the notes. Disclosures about related parties are supplementary in nature and related figures do not get the same prominence as figures recognised directly in income or the statement of financial position. Since there is not much evidence on the disclosures of related parties transactions, we discuss here a more general question that academics have pondered in the context of disclosures: would managers provide disclosure even without regulation (or in the case of regulated disclosure such as related parties, to provide disclosure above the required level)? From a theoretical point of view, the answer seems to be yes. If investors maintain that lack of disclosure implies that managers withhold adverse information, then managers will furnish disclosure to avoid being seen as bad performers (Grossman 1981). However, in practice it seems that voluntary disclosure is not uniformly observed. One potential explanation of this phenomenon is that managers who do not disclose may be concerned that providing too much disclosure may benefit other parties, such as competitors, trade unions or litigants suing the corporation. Verrecchia (1983) argues that good news may be withheld owing to such disclosure costs. Hence, investors will not be certain if lack of disclosure is due to bad news or withholding of potentially costly good news. In equilibrium firms release good news only if the benefit from the good news exceeds the cost of its disclosure. Other firms will withhold information and will be assessed at the expected average value of non-disclosing firms.

One possible benefit of disclosures is a reduction in cost of equity capital. In the case of a single company, better disclosure reduces information asymmetry and hence cost of capital. This is less clear when investors can diversify and invest in a large number of firms and so individual risk becomes less of an issue. The theoretical model of Lambert et al. (2007) provides the necessary link between disclosure and cost of capital in a multi-security market. This is based on the argument that better disclosure helps investors to assess the covariance between a firm's future cash flows and that of the market as a whole. Because this covariance is a risk factor for investors, more disclosure therefore reduces this risk, increases current prices and reduces expected return. These disclosure effects are consistent with lower cost of capital.

Botosan (1997) empirically examines the link between voluntary disclosures in annual reports and cost of capital. She compiles a dataset of detailed disclosures made by 122 manufacturing firms in 1990. Based on a long list of 46 potential disclosure elements Botosan (1997) calculates a disclosure score for each company. Each firm is then ranked according to its disclosure score. Botosan (1997) then computes a measure of cost of equity capital by employing well-known valuation models. The main finding is that for firms with low level of analyst following, higher disclosure rank is negatively related to cost of equity capital. This suggests that the information environment is rich for firms that are followed by many analysts; hence the incremental effect of voluntary disclosure is small. In contrast, when the information environment is poor, voluntary disclosures work to reduce cost of capital.

Kothari et al. (2009) extend this line of research by looking at the link between three measures for the cost of equity capital and the content of corporate disclosures. Using special software that analyses the content of these disclosures for 889 firms between 1996 and 2001, Kothari et al. (2009) classify these disclosures as either favourable or unfavourable in nature. They find that favourable corporate disclosures reduce cost of capital while unfavourable disclosures increase cost of capital. However, the effect of favourable disclosures is quite small (and much smaller than the effect of unfavourable disclosures), suggesting that investors largely disregard positive corporate disclosures. The rather modest and mixed results may be due to the fact that theory suggests a link between the precision of disclosure and cost of capital, rather than a link between the favourableness of disclosures and cost of capital.

Another interesting question that has attracted academic scrutiny is whether recognition of a number in the main statements is assessed differently than if, instead, the same number is disclosed only in the accompanying notes. This has been termed as the 'recognition versus disclosure' concept. It should be nevertheless noted that disclosure in the notes can serve several purposes (Schipper 2007), not just as an alternative to recognition in the main statements.

One reason a disclosed amount could be assessed differently than a recognised amount is that the reliability of the two numbers differ. This can be the case if, for example, auditors scrutinise less carefully disclosed amounts than recognised ones. Barth et al. (2003) advance another reason for possible differences in valuation effects of disclosed versus recognised amounts. They argue that disclosed-only amounts may not be looked at by all investor types. Specifically, sophisticated investors would look at disclosed information while incurring some cost for exerting this effort. In contrast, unsophisticated investors prefer to look at recognised amounts only. In such a case the degree to which disclosed information is impounded in price is a function of the number of sophisticated investors in the market. Limited attention to disclosed amounts may also be relevant in this context (Hirshleifer and Teoh 2003).

One of the more persuasive studies of recognition vs. disclosure is conducted by Ahmed et al. (2006). The authors examine accounting regulation of derivatives in the US. Under old US standards information about fair value of derivatives was comprehensively provided. However, while a subset of derivatives was recognised on the balance sheet at fair value, other derivatives were either recognised at historical cost or zero cost. For these derivatives disclosure in the notes provided the relevant fair values. Under the new rules, all derivatives have to be recognised at fair value on the balance sheet. Crucially for this research, fair values were consistently estimated under both old and new rules. Ahmed et al. (2006) analyse the link between fair values of derivatives in 146 bank holding companies and the banks' market value of equity (MVE). They find that disclosed fair values (under old rules) are not associated with MVE, while recognised fair values (under old rules) exhibit positive relation with MVE. The authors then look at 82 banks that only disclosed fair values of derivatives under old rules but then had to recognise them under new rules. They find that recognised fair values (under new rules) are more closely related to MVE than disclosed amounts under old rules. This suggests that the value relevance of recognised fair values is greater than that of disclosed ones. Müller et al. (2015) provide corroborating results by taking advantage of the fact that under IFRS Standards fair values of investment properties may be either recognised or disclosed. Another interesting study on this issue is Aboody (1996). He examines a sample of 71 firms in the oil and gas industry, some of which had to recognise impairments of their wells in the income statement and some that only needed to disclose these impairments. He finds evidence suggesting that while recognised impairments affect stock prices, disclosed impairments do not.

Academic focus on earnings per share (EPS) mostly focuses on the role that EPS plays in managerial compensation, and hence, reporting incentives with Healy (1985) making notable early contribution. Healy (1985) identified the role of EPS targets embedded in compensation contracts through bonus payouts, arguing that upward earnings management is expected only up to a certain point; once the EPS target is achieved, managers have no incentive to manage earnings upward. Subsequent research also identified incentives to meet analyst forecasts of EPS. Thus, there may be a tension between meeting internal bonus targets and external bonus targets (Armstrong et al. 2024).

References

Aboody, D., 1996. Recognition versus disclosure in the oil and gas industry, Journal of Accounting Research, 34, 21–32.

Ahmed, A.S., Kilic, E. and Lobo, G.J., 2006. Does recognition versus disclosure matter? Evidence from value-relevance of banks recognized and disclosed derivative financial instruments, The Accounting Review, 81(3), 567–588.

Armstrong, C., Chau, J., Ittner, C.D. and Xiao, J.J., 2024. Earnings per share targets and CEO incentives. Review of Accounting Studies, 1-46. 10.1007/s11142-023-09815-3.

Barth, M.E., Clinch, G. and Shibano, T., 2003. Market effects of recognition and disclosure, Journal of Accounting Research, 41(4), 581–609.

Botosan, C.A., 1997. Disclosure level and the cost of equity capital, The Accounting Review, 72(3), 323–349.

Grossman, S.J. 1981. The informational role of warranties and private disclosure about product quality, The Journal of Law & Economics, 24(3), 461–483.

Healy, P.M., 1985. The effect of bonus schemes on accounting decisions. Journal of Accounting and Economics, 7(1–3), 85–107.

Hirshleifer, D. and Teoh, S.H., 2003. Limited attention, information disclosure, and financial reporting, Journal of Accounting and Economics, 36(1), 337–386.

Kothari, S.P., Li, X. and Short, J.E., 2009. The effect of disclosures by management, analysts, and business press on cost of capital, return volatility, and analyst forecasts: a study using content analysis, The Accounting Review, 84(5), 1639–1670.

Lambert, R., Leuz, C. and Verrecchia, R.E. 2007, Accounting information, disclosure, and the cost of capital, Journal of Accounting Research, 45, 385–420.

Müller, M., Riedl, E.J. and Sellhorn, T., 2015. Recognition versus disclosure of fair values, The Accounting Review, 90(6), 2411–2447.

Schipper, K., 2007. Required disclosures in financial reports, The Accounting Review, 82(2), 301–326.

Verrecchia, R., 1983. Discretionary disclosure, Journal of Accounting and Economics, 5, 365–380.

18 Operating segments

ACCOUNTING STANDARDS IN FOCUS

IFRS 8 *Operating Segments*

LEARNING OBJECTIVES

After studying this chapter, you should be able to:

 discuss the objectives of financial reporting by segments

 identify the types of entities that are within the scope of IFRS 8

 compare the management approach adopted by IFRS 8 with the risks and rewards approach

 identify operating segments in accordance with IFRS 8

 distinguish between operating segments and reportable segments

 apply the definition of reportable segments

 explain the disclosure requirements of IFRS 8

 analyse the disclosures made by companies applying IFRS 8 in practice.

18.1 OBJECTIVES OF FINANCIAL REPORTING BY SEGMENTS

IFRS 8 is primarily a disclosure standard and is particularly relevant for large organisations that operate in different geographic locations and/or in diverse businesses.

Paragraph 1 of IFRS 8 sets out the standard's core principle:

> An entity shall disclose information to enable users of its financial statements to evaluate the nature and financial effects of the business activities in which it engages and the economic environments in which it operates.

Many entities operate in different geographical areas or provide products or services that are subject to differing rates of profitability, opportunities for growth, future prospects and risks. Information about an entity's operating segments is relevant to assessing the risks and returns of a diversified or multinational entity where often that information cannot be determined from aggregated data. Therefore, segment information is regarded as necessary to help users of financial statements:

- better understand the entity's past performance
- better assess the entity's risks and returns
- make more informed judgements about the entity as a whole.

Many securities analysts rely on the segment disclosures to help them assess not only an entity's past performance but also to help them predict future performance. Analysts use these assessments to value an entity's shares price. Segment disclosures are widely regarded as some of the most useful disclosures in financial statements because of the extent to which they disaggregate financial information into meaningful and often revealing groupings. For example, an entity may appear profitable on a consolidated basis, but segment disclosures may reveal that one part of the business is performing poorly while another part is performing well. The part that is performing poorly may be significant to the entity as a whole and over time continued poor performance by that part (or segment) may cause the entire entity's performance to suffer. This is the kind of information that has an impact on an entity's share price because analysts frequently focus on predicting future cash flows in making their share valuations.

On the other hand, preparers of financial statements may not wish to reveal too much information on a disaggregated basis to their competitors. Some consider the disclosure requirements of IFRS 8 may provide information that is helpful to existing and potential competitors about favourable market opportunities. For example, a user may be able to determine an entity's profit margin by segment when reading the segment disclosures. This is a key reason why it is unlikely that entities would volunteer to disclose segment information (see section 18.2).

18.2 SCOPE

IFRS 8 applies to the financial statements of an entity 'whose debt or equity instruments are traded in a public market' or 'that files, or is in the process of filing, its financial statements with a securities commission or other regulatory organisation for the purpose of issuing any class of instruments in a public market' (IFRS 8 paragraph 2). Most commonly, 'traded in a public market' would mean a public stock exchange such as the London Stock Exchange or the Hong Kong Stock Exchange.

Where financial statements contain both consolidated financial statements and the parent's separate financial statements, segment information is required only for the consolidated financial statements (IFRS 8 paragraph 4). However, if consolidated financial statements are *not* prepared, and the entity is within the scope of the standard, it must apply the standard in its separate or individual financial statements (IFRS 8 paragraph 2(a)).

If an entity voluntarily chooses to disclose segment information then it must fully comply with IFRS 8; otherwise, it must not describe the disclosed information as segment information (IFRS 8 paragraph 3). Voluntary disclosure may occur, for example, where a large company that is not listed, but has a large number of dependent users such as a number of non-controlling shareholders, employees and creditors, elects to provide segment information.

18.3 MANAGEMENT APPROACH VS RISKS AND REWARDS APPROACH

In 2006, the International Accounting Standards Board (IASB®) issued IFRS 8 *Operating Segments*, which replaced IAS 14 *Segment Reporting*. The new Standard was part of the IASB's programme for achieving convergence with standards issued by the US Financial Accounting Standards Board (FASB) and essentially adopted the requirements of the FASB Statement of Financial Accounting Standards No. 131 (SFAS 131) *Disclosures about Segments of an Enterprise and Related Information*. The major change from IAS 14 was the adoption of the management approach to identifying segments as the only acceptable approach.

Under the management approach, the way that segment information is to be reported externally is based on how information is reported internally to the company's management *(see section 18.4)*. The identification of segments is based on how segment information is presented to the entity's chief operating decision maker (CODM) to make decisions about the allocation of resources between segments and to assess their performance. Further, IFRS 8 allows discretion in determining the content of segment profit or loss and segment assets and in making segment disclosures (e.g. disclosure of liabilities, statement of comprehensive income line items and geographical information). In contrast, under the former standard, IAS 14, the identification of segments was based on risks and rewards and the standard contained very prescriptive requirements as to what and how the entity should report on segments.

According to Véron (2007), the risks and rewards approach to identifying segments meets the needs of users while the management approach serves the needs of preparers. The discretion permitted by IFRS 8 in determining the content of segment profit or loss and segment assets and in making or not making certain disclosures contrasts with the prescribed measurement and disclosure requirements of IAS 14, favouring preparers over users (Véron, 2007).

An alternative perspective is that the information provided under the management approach is more useful to investors. The management approach enables investors to evaluate the entity on the same basis as that used by management in its decision making. Further, concerns about understandability are addressed by the reconciliation requirements of IFRS 8.

18.4 IDENTIFYING OPERATING SEGMENTS

An operating segment is defined in paragraph 5 of IFRS 8 as a component of an entity:

(a) that engages in business activities from which it may earn revenues and incur expenses (including revenues and expenses relating to transactions with other components of the same entity);
(b) whose operating results are regularly reviewed by the entity's chief operating decision maker to make decisions about resources to be allocated to the segment and assess its performance; and
(c) for which discrete financial information is available.

The CODM refers to the function of allocating resources and assessing performance of the operating segments, and not necessarily to a manager with a specific title (paragraph 7 of IFRS 8). That function may be carried out by a group of people, for example, an executive committee. In many large entities, an operating segment has a segment manager who is directly accountable to the CODM. As with the CODM, the term 'segment manager' refers to a function, rather than the job title of the person performing that function. Some entities adopt a matrix structure, which means there are several overlapping segments, with managers responsible for different components. For example, one manager may be responsible for different product and service lines and other managers responsible for specific geographic areas, with the operating results for both sets of components regularly reviewed by the CODM. An entity adopting a matrix structure must use the core principle *(see section 18.1 and Illustrative Example 18.2)* to determine its operating segments (IFRS 8 paragraph 10).

Figure 18.1 summarises the key decision points in identifying operating segments.

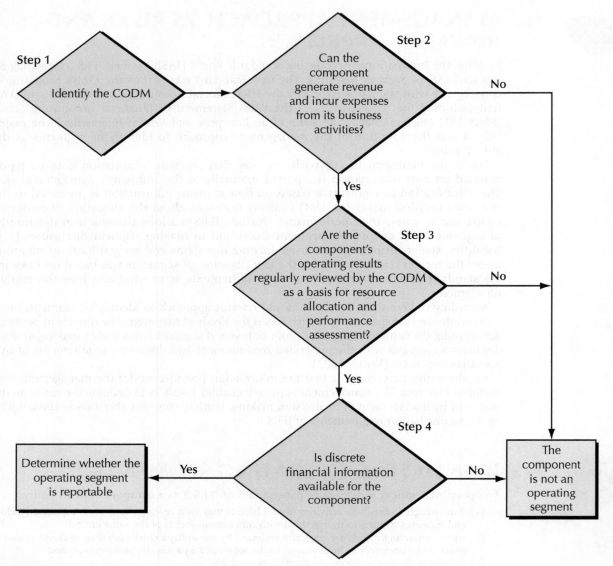

FIGURE 18.1 Identifying operating segments under IFRS 8
Source: Ernst & Young (2009, p. 9). © 2009 EYGM Limited. All rights reserved.

The following examples illustrate the steps in identifying operating segments.

ILLUSTRATIVE EXAMPLE 18.1 Identifying operating segments under IFRS 8 — the four steps

Sargsyan has a chief executive officer (CEO), a chief operating officer (COO) and an executive committee comprising the CEO, COO and the heads (general managers) of three business units — units X, Y and Z. Every month, financial information is presented to the executive committee for each of business units X, Y and Z and for Sargsyan as a whole in order to assess the performance of each business unit and of the company as a whole. Units X, Y and Z each generate revenue and incur expenses from their business activities. Unit Y derives the majority of its revenue from Unit Z. Corporate head office costs that are not allocated to units X, Y or Z are also reported separately each month to the executive committee in order to determine the results for Sargsyan as a whole.

Step 1: Identify the CODM
In this case, the CODM is likely to be the executive committee, since it is this group that regularly reviews the operating results of all business units and the company as a whole.

However, if we assume that the heads of the business units only join the committee meetings for the purpose of reporting on their specific business unit and then leave the meeting, we would form a different judgement. In that case, only the CEO and COO would review all the business units and the company as a whole The CEO and COO would make resource allocation decisions, such as whether to upgrade facilities in various business units. In that case, then the CODM would be the CEO and COO.

In practice, this would not likely make any difference to the identification of the operating segments since the operating results information regularly reviewed by the entire committee is likely to be identical to that reviewed by the CEO and COO (see step 2).

Step 2: Can the component generate revenue and incur expenses from its business activities?

For units X and Z, the answer is clearly yes. For Unit Y, the answer is also yes — even though a majority of its revenue is derived internally this does not prevent it from being identified as an operating segment (IFRS 8 paragraph 5(a)). For the corporate head office, the answer is no as it does not derive revenues; it only incurs costs. Therefore, the corporate head office would not be identified as an operating segment and would not require further assessment.

Step 3: Are the component's operating results regularly reviewed by the CODM as a basis for resource allocation and performance assessment?

Yes, the operating results for units X, Y and Z are regularly reviewed by the CODM.

Step 4: Is discrete financial information available for the component?

Yes, discrete financial information is available for units X, Y and Z.

Conclusion

Units X, Y and Z are identified as Sargsyan's operating segments.

ILLUSTRATIVE EXAMPLE 18.2 Identifying operating segments under IFRS 8 — matrix structure

Lothian has a chief executive officer (CEO), a COO and an executive committee comprising the CEO, COO and the heads (general managers) of three business units organised according to the company's main products — units A, B and C.

The company also operates in two distinct geographic regions — the United Kingdom and North America. The heads of these geographic regions attend executive committee meetings, have input into decisions about the distribution of the company's products into their geographic regions and give their views on the performance of the company's products in their regions. However, the CEO can override any decisions made by the committee.

Every month, financial information is presented to the executive committee for each of business units A, B and C, geographic regions UK and North America and for Lothian as a whole in order to assess the performance of each business unit, each geographic region and of the company as a whole. Corporate head office costs that are not allocated to units A, B or C or to the geographic regions are also reported separately each month to the executive committee in order to determine the results for Lothian as a whole. There is necessarily an overlap between the financial information presented for each of units A, B and C and UK and North American geographic regions because the product performance reported for each unit is reported again, with that of the other two product units, by geographic region.

Step 1: Identify the CODM

In this case, the CODM is likely to be the CEO, since he or she has overriding decision-making authority.

Step 2: Can the component generate revenue and incur expenses from its business activities?

For units A, B and C, the answer is clearly yes. For the geographic regions, the answer is also yes, even though the revenues are generated from deployment of the products from units A, B and C in the regions. For the corporate head office, the answer is no as it does not derive revenues; it only incurs costs. Therefore, the corporate head office would not be identified as an operating segment and would not require further assessment.

Step 3: Are the component's operating results regularly reviewed by the CODM as a basis for resource allocation and performance assessment?

For units A, B, C, the UK and North America, the answer is yes.

Step 4: Is discrete financial information available for the component?

For units A, B, C, the UK and North America, the answer is yes.

Conclusion

This leaves the entity potentially having two sets of operating segments — units A, B and C, and geographic regions, UK and North America. It is in this situation that paragraph 10 of IFRS 8 directs the entity to the core principle of the standard. This means management must exercise judgement consistent with the management approach founded on what is important to the CODM. For example, if the CEO uses the information and advice provided by the three business unit general managers in order to make decisions about the allocation of resources to those business units, such as whether to invest in new production technologies, but only looks to the geographical region heads for insight into regional product performance, then perhaps the CODM focuses more on the information provided by the three product line business units than the geographical information when allocating resources and assessing performance.

18.5 IDENTIFYING REPORTABLE SEGMENTS

18.5.1 The basic criteria

Paragraph 11 of IFRS 8 requires that an entity report separately information about each operating segment that:

(a) has been identified as an operating segment in accordance with the four steps discussed above, or results from aggregating two or more of those segments in accordance with specific aggregation criteria; and

(b) exceeds the specified quantitative thresholds.

The quantitative thresholds are specified in paragraph 13 of IFRS 8. An entity must report separately information about an operating segment that meets *any* of the following quantitative thresholds:

(a) its reported revenue is 10% or more of the combined revenue of all operating segments (revenue includes both external and internal revenue)

(b) its reported profit or loss is, in absolute terms, 10% or more of the greater of (1) the combined reported profit of all operating segments that reported a profit, and (2) the combined reported loss of all operating segments that reported a loss

(c) its assets are 10% or more of the combined assets of all operating segments.

If management believes that information about an operating segment would be useful to users, it may treat that segment as a reportable segment even if the quantitative thresholds are not met (IFRS 8 paragraph 13).

18.5.2 The aggregation criteria

The aggregation criteria in paragraph 12 provide that two or more operating segments may be aggregated into a single operating segment if aggregation is consistent with the core principle of the standard, the segments have similar economic characteristics and the segments are similar in *each* of the following respects:

(a) the nature of the products and services

(b) the nature of the production processes

(c) the type or class of customer for their products and services

(d) the methods used to distribute their products or provide their services

(e) if applicable, the nature of the regulatory environment, for example, banking, insurance or public utilities.

An entity may combine operating segments that do not meet the quantitative thresholds to produce a reportable segment only if the segments have similar economic characteristics and meet the above aggregation criteria (IFRS 8 paragraph 14).

Paragraph 15 of IFRS 8 requires that an entity must identify operating segments until at least 75% of the entity's consolidated *external* revenue is included in reportable segments.

Paragraph 16 of IFRS 8 states that business activities and operating segments that are not reportable must be combined and disclosed as 'all other segments' separately from the reconciling items required by paragraph 28 *(see section 18.7.5).*

Note that IFRS 8 does not distinguish between revenues and expenses from transactions with third parties and those from transactions *within the group* for the purposes of identifying operating segments (IFRS 8 paragraph 5). Therefore, in an entity with internal vertically integrated businesses, it is possible that such internal businesses might be identified as operating segments under IFRS 8.

IFRS 8 provides additional guidance to entities regarding the maximum number of reportable segments — indicating that 10 is a reasonable maximum (IFRS 8 paragraph 19).

Figure 18.2 summarises the key decision points in identifying reportable segments, and follows on from Figure 18.1

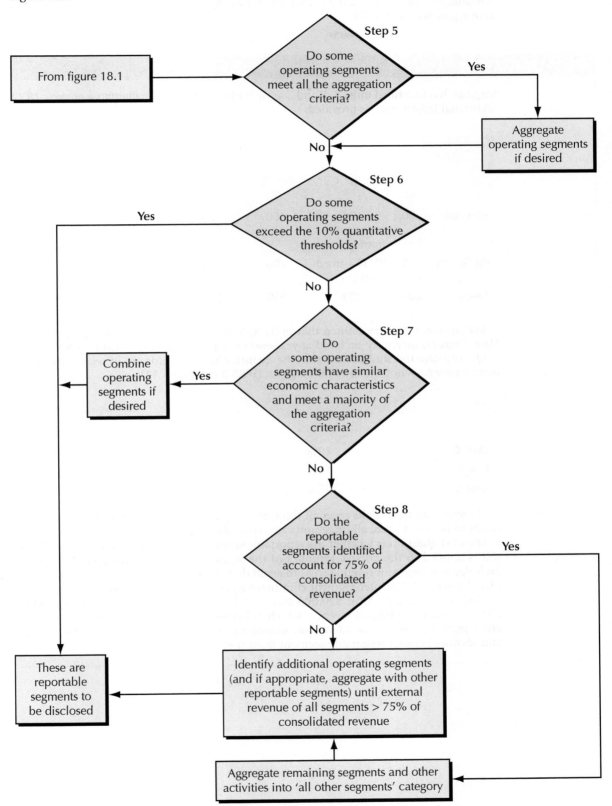

FIGURE 18.2 Identifying reportable segments under IFRS 8

Source: Adapted from IASB (2022) IFRS 8, Implementation Guidance, paragraph IG7.

18.6 APPLYING THE DEFINITION OF REPORTABLE SEGMENTS

Building on illustrative example 18.1, the following example illustrates how Sargsyan identifies its reportable segments under IFRS 8.

ILLUSTRATIVE EXAMPLE 18.3 Identifying reportable segments under IFRS 8

Sargsyan has identified units X, Y and Z as operating segments *(see illustrative example 18.1)*. The following additional information is provided:

	Unit X $'000	Unit Y $'000	Unit Z $'000	Total operating segments $'000	Corporate head office $'000	Other businesses $'000	Total Sargsyan (consolidated) $'000
Revenue	200	100 (80 earned from Unit Z)	400	700	—	230	850
Profit/(loss)	50	30 (10 earned from Unit Z)	100	180	(25)	20	165
Assets	800	300	950	2,050	250	200	2,500

Management has determined that units X, Y and Z do not meet the aggregation criteria of IFRS 8. Unit Z has no inventory on hand at year-end in respect of purchases from unit Y.

Quantitative thresholds: note that the quantitative thresholds are in respect of the *totals for the operating segments* — not the total for Sargsyan (IFRS 8 paragraph 13):

	Revenue % of total	Profit % of total	Assets % of total
Unit X	29%	28%	39%
Unit Y	14%	17%	15%
Unit Z	57%	55%	46%

Therefore, all three units meet all three of the quantitative thresholds. (Note that only one threshold needs to be met.) Thus, all three units are reportable segments.

The next question is whether the reportable segments account for 75% of consolidated revenue. This test is applied to the *external* revenues of the segments (IFRS 8 paragraph 15). Consolidated revenue excludes inter-segment revenue so as to avoid double-counting of revenue *(see chapter 22)*. Total consolidated revenue (after inter-segment eliminations) is $850,000. Total external operating segment revenue is: Unit X: $200,000; Unit Y: $20,000 and Unit Z: $400,000, giving a total of $620,000. This constitutes 73% of total consolidated revenue, which is below the 75% requirement. Therefore, additional operating segments need to be identified. Management will need to further analyse the 'other businesses' and identify another reportable segment from that component.

18.7 DISCLOSURE

18.7.1 Overall approach

IFRS 8 sets out a general approach to disclosure and largely allows management to determine what is disclosed and how the amounts disclosed are measured based on those measures used by the CODM for determining resource allocation and for assessing performance.

The general principle of disclosure is set out in paragraph 20 of IFRS 8, which is, in effect, a restatement of the core principle of the standard:

> An entity shall disclose information to enable users of its financial statements to evaluate the nature and financial effects of the business activities in which it engages and the economic environments in which it operates.

Paragraph 21 of IFRS 8 specifies three types of information that an entity must provide to comply with the disclosure principle: general information for each reportable segment; information about segment profit or loss, assets and liabilities; and reconciliation of totals for segment revenues, profit or loss, assets and liabilities to the corresponding amounts reported for the entity. Each type of information is discussed, in turn, in sections 18.7.2, 18.7.3 and 18.7.4.

18.7.2 General information

Paragraph 22 (a) requires an entity to disclose the factors it uses to identify the entity's reportable segments. This includes an explanation of how the organisation is structured. For example, the organisational structure may be based on its products and services, geographical areas, regulatory environments or a combination of factors.

The entity must also disclose details of the judgements made by management in applying the aggregation criteria *(see section 18.5.2)*. This must include a brief description of the operating segments that have been aggregated and the economic indicators that were used in determining that segments were sufficiently similar to be aggregated (IFRS 8, paragraph 22(a)).

Finally, paragraph 22(b) requires disclosure of the types of products or services from which revenue is derived for each reportable segment.

18.7.3 Information about profit or loss, assets and liabilities

Paragraph 23 of IFRS 8 requires an entity to report 'a measure' of profit or loss for each reportable segment. The entity is also required to report on segment assets and segment liabilities if they are reported to the CODM on a regular basis.

IFRS 8 does not specify how an entity should measure amounts reported as profit or loss, assets or liabilities for each segment. Instead, these amounts should be measured in the same way as they are presented to the CODM for making decisions about allocating resources to the segment and assessing its performance (IFRS 8 paragraph 25). This extends to allocations of amounts, such as head office costs, to segments. If the CODM uses information based on amounts that are allocated to segments, then those amounts should be allocated for the purposes of disclosing 'a measure'. If the CODM does not use that information, the amounts should not be allocated.

In respect of segment profit or loss, certain line items are also required to be disclosed *only* if these items are included in the measure of segment profit or loss reported to the CODM, or are otherwise regularly provided to the CODM:
(a) revenues from external customers
(b) inter-segment revenues
(c) interest revenue
(d) interest expense
(e) depreciation and amortisation
(f) material items of income and expense disclosed in accordance with paragraph 97 of IAS 1
(g) the entity's interest in the profit or loss of associates and joint ventures accounted for by the equity method
(h) income tax expense or income
(i) material non-cash items other than depreciation and amortisation (IFRS 8 paragraph 23).

Interest revenue and interest expense may be reported on a net basis only if a majority of the segment's revenues are from interest and the CODM relies primarily on net interest revenue to assess the performance of the segment. This may be the case, for example, in the banking industry.

In respect of segment assets, certain line items are also required to be disclosed if these items are included in the measure of segment assets reported to the CODM, or are otherwise regularly provided to the CODM:

(a) the amount of investment in associates and joint ventures accounted for by the equity method

(b) the amounts of additions to non-current assets (with certain exceptions, e.g., financial instruments, deferred tax assets) (IFRS 8 paragraph 24).

The notable feature of these disclosure requirements is the lack of prescription. If the items listed (with the exception of a measure of segment profit or loss, which must always be disclosed) are reported to the CODM, then they must be disclosed. This means that what is not reported internally is not disclosed externally. Furthermore, *how* the amount is measured internally is used for external measurement purposes, even if the measurement basis is not in accordance with IFRS.

Because management has discretion about measurement, IFRS 8 requires disclosure of *how* the entity has determined the measures of profit or loss, and, if applicable, assets and liabilities, for each reportable segment (IFRS 8 paragraph 27). This includes:

(a) the basis of accounting for any transactions between reportable segments;

(b) if not apparent from the required reconciliations *(see section 18.7.4)*, the nature of any differences between the measurements of total reported segment profit or loss and the entity's profit or loss before income taxes and discontinued operations (i.e. the profit or loss reported in the statement of profit or loss and other comprehensive income in accordance with IFRSs). For example, if the CODM uses concepts such as 'cash profit' for measuring the segment profit, the entity would need to disclose how 'cash profit' is determined and how it differs from the IFRS measure of profit before income taxes and discontinued operations. This could include, for example, the fact that the CODM determines 'cash profit' to be profit or loss before fair value movements, depreciation and amortisation, and impairment charges;

(c) if not apparent from the required reconciliations, the nature of any differences between the measurements of total reported segment assets and the entity's assets. For example, this could include accounting policies and policies for allocation of jointly used assets in determining segment assets;

(d) if not apparent from the required reconciliations, the nature of any differences between the measurements of total reported segment liabilities and the entity's liabilities. For example, this could include accounting policies and policies for allocation of jointly used liabilities in determining segment liabilities;

(e) the nature of any changes from prior periods in the measurement methods used to determine segment profit or loss, including the financial effect, if any, of those changes. For example, if the CODM decides to change the measure of segment profit or loss used from one that excludes fair value movements to one that includes fair value movements, this fact would need to be disclosed together with the impact on reported segment profit or loss to facilitate comparability; and

(f) the nature and effect of any asymmetrical allocations to reportable segments. For example, an entity might allocate depreciation expense to a segment without allocating the related depreciable assets to that segment.

18.7.4 Reconciliations

An entity is required to provide reconciliations of all of the following:

(a) the total of the reportable segments' revenues to the entity's revenue. In illustrative example 18.3, ignoring the identification of additional segments to meet the 75% threshold, this would be a reconciliation of total segment revenues of $700,000 to Sargsyan's revenue of $850,000;

(b) the total of the reportable segments' measures of profit or loss to the entity's profit or loss before income tax and discontinued operations (or, if items such as income tax are allocated to segments, to profit or loss after income tax). In illustrative example 18.3, ignoring the identification of additional segments to meet the 75% threshold, this would be a reconciliation of total segment profits of $180,000 to Sargsyan's profit of $165,000;

(c) the total of the reportable segments' assets (if reported) to the entity's assets. In illustrative example 18.3, ignoring the identification of additional segments to meet the 75% threshold, this would be a reconciliation of total segment assets of $2.05 million to Sargsyan's assets of $2.5 million;

(d) the total of segment liabilities (if reported) to the entity's liabilities; and

(e) the total of segment amounts for every other material item of information disclosed to the corresponding amount for the entity.

All material reconciling items must be separately identified and described. For example, in illustrative example 18.3, ignoring the identification of additional segments to meet the 75% threshold, the entity would need to disclose its reconciliation of total segment profits to Sargsyan's profit as follows:

	$'000
Total segment profits:	180
Less: Inter-segment profit	(10)
Less: Corporate head office costs not allocated to reportable segments	(25)
Add: Profit from other businesses not identified as reportable segments	20
Total Sargsyan profit	165

18.7.5 Entity-wide disclosures

The following disclosures apply to all entities subject to IFRS 8, including those that have only one reportable segment (unless the information is already provided as part of the reportable segment information).

- Information about products and services: revenues from external customers for *each product and service* or for each group of similar products and services. In this case, the amount of revenues must be based on the financial information used to produce the entity's financial statements, *not* based on amounts reported to the CODM. If the information is not available and the cost to develop it would be excessive, the entity need not disclose the information but it must state this fact (IFRS 8 paragraph 32). This requirement is potentially onerous in that it is possible that one reportable segment includes numerous products and/or services.
- Information about geographical areas: revenues from external customers and non-current assets (i) attributed to/located in the entity's country of domicile and (ii) attributed to/located in foreign countries. If revenues or non-current assets attributed to/located in an individual foreign country are material, those revenues/assets shall be disclosed separately. The entity must also disclose the basis for attributing revenues from external customers to individual countries. In this case, as in paragraph 32, the amount of revenues and assets must be based on the financial information used to produce the entity's financial statements. If the information is not available and the cost to develop it would be excessive then the entity need not disclose the information but it must state this fact (IFRS 8 paragraph 33).
- Information about major customers: if revenues from transactions with a single external customer account for 10% or more of an entity's total revenues, disclose that fact, the total amount of revenues from each such customer, and the reportable segment or segments reporting the revenues. The identity of the customer or customers does not have to be disclosed (IFRS 8, paragraph 34).

18.7.6 Comparative information

There are a few circumstances in which comparative information must be restated or otherwise taken into account.

(a) If an operating segment was a reportable segment for the immediately preceding prior period but is not for the current period, and management decides that the segment is of continuing significance, information about that segment must continue to be reported in the current period (IFRS 8 paragraph 17).

(b) If an operating segment becomes a reportable segment for the current period, comparative information must be restated to reflect the newly reportable segment, even if that segment did not meet the criteria for reportability in the prior period. This is required unless the information is not available and the cost to develop it would be excessive (IFRS 8 paragraph 18).

(c) If an entity changes any of its segment measures, including how segment profit or loss is determined, or changes the allocation of income, expenses, assets or liabilities to segments, without a change to the composition of its reportable segments, the general principles of IAS 1 for changes in presentation or classification apply *(see chapter 2)*. Therefore, comparative information would be restated, unless this is impracticable (IAS 1 paragraph 41).

(d) If an entity changes the structure of its internal organisation in a manner that causes the composition of its reportable segments to change, the corresponding information for prior periods, including interim periods, must be restated. This applies unless the information is not available and the cost to develop it would be excessive (IFRS 8 paragraph 29). Note that in this case the exemption from restatement applies to each individual item of disclosure, which could result in restatement of some items and not of others. If there has been a change in the composition of reportable segments, the entity must disclose whether comparative items of segment information have been restated.

(e) If an entity changes the structure of its internal organisation in a manner that causes the composition of its reportable segments to change and the corresponding information for prior periods is *not* restated, the entity must disclose the segment information for the current period on both the old and the new basis. This applies unless the information is not available and the cost to develop it would be excessive (IFRS 8 paragraph 30).

18.8 APPLYING THE DISCLOSURES IN PRACTICE

Figure 18.3 contains extracts from the 2023 annual report of Mercedes-Benz Group. Segment disclosures, in accordance with IFRS 8, are provided in Note 34 of the financial statements.

FIGURE 18.3 Extracts from Mercedes-Benz Group's annual report

Reported segments The Group comprises the segments Mercedes-Benz Cars, Mercedes-Benz Vans and Mercedes-Benz Mobility.

The breakdown of the segments corresponds to the internal organizational and reporting structure. The vehicle segments develop and manufacture premium and luxury cars as well as vans. In addition to the Mercedes-Benz brand, the brand portfolio of the Mercedes Benz Cars segment encompasses the brands Mercedes-AMG and Mercedes Maybach, as well as the G-Class product brand. Mercedes me provides access to the digital services of Mercedes-Benz Cars. At Mercedes-Benz Vans, the vans are sold under the Mercedes-Benz brand. Corresponding spare parts and accessories are also sold.

The Mercedes-Benz Mobility segment supports the sales of the Mercedes-Benz Group's automotive brands worldwide. The product range primarily includes customized mobility and financial services: from leasing and financing packages for end customers and dealers to insurance solutions, flexible subscription and rental models and fleet management services for business customers, with the latter primarily offered via the Athlon brand. Furthermore, Mercedes-Benz Mobility is active in the area of innovative and digital mobility services, seamless payment methods and the expansion of the charging infrastructure.

Reconciliation The reconciliation includes functions and services provided by the Group's headquarters as well as by equity investments not allocated to the segments (e.g. Daimler Truck Holding AG). In addition, the reconciliation includes items at the corporate level and the effects on earnings of eliminating intra-Group transactions between the segments.

Internal management and reporting structure The internal management and reporting structure at the Mercedes-Benz Group is principally based on the accounting policies according to IFRS that are described in Note 1.

The measure of the Group's net profit or loss used by the Mercedes-Benz Group's management and reporting structure is referred to as "EBIT". EBIT comprises gross profit, selling and general administrative expenses, research and non-capitalized development costs, other operating income/expense, and the gains/losses on equity-method investments, as well as other financial income/expense.

In justified individual cases, effects on the Group's Consolidated Statement of Income, Consolidated Statement of Financial Position, and Consolidated Statement of Cash Flows are not allocated to the corresponding segment based on a legal point of view, but the segment report rather follows an economic approach.

Intersegment revenue is principally recorded at prices that approximate market terms.

Transactions between the segments are generally eliminated in the reconciliation. The elimination of effects connected with intra-Group transfers of equity investments principally takes place in the segments involved. The effects on earnings at the Group are normally recognized in the corresponding segment upon completion of the external transaction. Some simplifications have been made in the segment reporting with regard to accounting for leasing agreements in connection with intra-Group transactions.

Segment assets principally comprise all assets. The assets of the Mercedes-Benz Cars and Mercedes Benz Vans segments exclude income tax assets, assets from defined benefit pension plans and other postemployment benefit plans, and certain financial instruments (including liquidity).

Segment liabilities principally comprise all liabilities. The Mercedes-Benz Cars and Mercedes-Benz Vans reporting segments' liabilities exclude income tax liabilities, liabilities from pensions and similar obligations and certain financial instruments (including financing liabilities).

The residual-value risks associated with the Group's operating leases and receivables from financial services are generally borne by the segments which manufactured the leased vehicles. Risk sharing is based on agreements between Mercedes-Benz Cars, MercedesBenz Vans and Mercedes-Benz Mobility; the terms vary by segment and geographic region. Non-current assets consist of intangible assets, property, plant and equipment, and equipment on operating leases.

Capital expenditures for intangible assets and property, plant and equipment reflect the cash-effective additions to these intangible assets and property, plant and equipment insofar as they do not relate to capitalized borrowing costs or goodwill.

Depreciation and amortization may also include impairments insofar as they do not relate to goodwill impairment according to IAS 36.

Amortization of capitalized borrowing costs is not included in the amortization of intangible assets or depreciation of property, plant and equipment.

The present segment information for the years 2023 and 2022 is as follows.

Segment Information

In millions of euros	Mercedes-Benz Cars 2023	2022	Mercedes-Benz Vans 2023	2022	Mercedes-Benz Mobility 2023	2022	Total Segments 2023	2022	Reconciliation 2023	2022	Mercedes-Benz Group 2023	2022
External revenue	107,805	107,067	19,661	16,719	25,752	26,231	153,218	150,017	—	—	153,218	150,017
Intersegment revenue	4,951	4,534	627	498	966	723	6,544	5,755	–6,544	–5,755	—	
Total revenue	112,756	111,601	20,288	17,217	26,718	26,954	159,762	155,772	–6,544	–5,755	153,218	150,017
Segment profit/ loss (EBIT)	14,224	16,340	3,138	1,897	1,302	2,428	18,664	20,665	996	–207	19,660	20,458
thereof gains/ losses on equity-method investments	1,355	1,586	126	122	–155	–209	1,326	1,499	803	233	2,129	1,732
thereof profit/ loss from compounding and effects from changes in discount rates of provisions for other risks	–338	457	–98	86	—	2	–436	545	–1	—	–437	545
Segment assets	93,435	91,908	10,486	10,036	145,057	142,524	248,978	244,468	–8,152	8,138	240,826	236,330
thereof carrying amounts of equity-method investments	3,922	4,479	325	328	208	271	4,455	5,078	8,649	8,452	13,104	13,530
Segment liabilities	51,668	51,964	9,232	9,025	132,043	128,948	192,943	189,937	–11,813	–12,290	181,130	177,647
Additions to non-current assets	14,939	12,687	1,570	1,295	13,541	11,277	30,050	25,259	–225	–173	29,825	25,086
thereof investments in intangible assets	4,055	3,197	372	179	50	43	4,477	3,419	–9	–1	4,468	3,418

(continued)

FIGURE 18.3 (continued)

thereof investments in property, plant and equipment	**3,345**	3,265	**351**	199	**49**	18	**3,745**	3,482	**—**	−1	**3,745**	3,481
Depreciation and amortization of non-current assets	**7,386**	7,213	**608**	620	**5,778**	6,130	**13,772**	13,963	**−75**	−72	**13,697**	13,891
thereof amortization of intangible assets	**2,232**	2,143	**159**	186	**64**	68	**2,455**	2,397	**4**	3	**2,459**	2,400
thereof depreciation of property, plant and equipment	**3,893**	3,800	**261**	266	**50**	56	**4,204**	4,122	**–**	−1	**4,204**	4,121

RECONCILIATION

The following table shows the reconciliation of EBIT according to segment reporting to the Consolidated Statement of Income.

Reconciliation of EBIT to Group figures

In millions of euros	2023	2022
Total of segments' profit/loss (EBIT)	**18,664**	20,665
Gains/losses on equity-method investments	**803**	233
Other reconciling Items	**55**	−458
Eliminations	**138**	18
EBIT as shown in the Consolidated Statement of Income/Loss	**19,660**	20,458

The **gains/losses on equity-method investments** includes the positive profit contribution of €797 million (2022: €226 million) from Daimler Truck Holding AG.

The line item **Other reconciling items** includes further items at the corporate level. In the prior year, the line item included expenses in connection with the sale of individual investments and business activities to Daimler Truck Holding AG or its subsidiaries.

The reconciliation of segment assets and liabilities to relevant amounts for the Group is shown in the next table.

Reconciliation of segment assets and liabilities to Group figures

In millions of euros	2023	2022
Total of segment assets	**248,978**	244,468
Equity method investment in DTHAG	**8,425**	8,199
Other equity-method investments[1]	**224**	253
Income tax assets[2]	**3,448**	3,107
Other reconciling items and eliminations	**−20,249**	−19,697
Segment assets Group	**240,826**	236,330
Unallocated financial instruments (including liquidity) and assets from pensions and similar obligations[2]	**22,196**	23,685
Total assets Group	**263,022**	260,015
Total of segment liabilities	**192,943**	189,937

		8,226	7,614
Income tax liabilities[2]		**8,226**	7,614
Other reconciling items and eliminations		**−20,039**	−19,904
Segment liabilities Group		**181,130**	177,647
Unallocated financial instruments and liabilities from pensions and similar obligations[2]		**−10,924**	−4,172
Total equity Group		**92,816**	86,540
Total equity and liabilities Group		**263,022**	260,015

[1] This mainly comprises the equity-method carrying amount of BAIC Motor.
[2] Unless these are attributable to Mercedes Peru Mobility.

Revenue and non-current assets by region With respect to information on geographical regions, revenue is allocated to countries based on the location of the customer; non-current assets are presented according to the physical location of these assets.

Revenue from external customers and non-current assets by region are shown in the following table.

Revenue and non-current assets by region

	Revenue		Non-current assets	
	2023	**2022**	**2023**	**2022**
In millions of euros				
Europe	**61,895**	56,487	**64,719**	61,983
thereof Germany	**25,799**	23,085	**46,511**	45,587
North America	**40,488**	40,091	**18,430**	19,722
thereof United States	**36,041**	35,829	**16,526**	17,883
Asia	**43,382**	45,558	**1,497**	1,626
thereof China	**25,284**	27,324	**507**	537
Other markets	**7,453**	7,861	**749**	1,341
	153,218	150,017	**85,395**	84,671

Source: Mercedes-Benz Group Annual Report (2023, pp. 310–333).

Points to note about figure 18.3:
1. The three segments, Mercedes-Benz Cars, Mercedes-Benz Vans and Mercedes-Benz Mobility, are identified in accordance with the internal management and reporting structure.
2. The 'measure' of segment profit or loss that is reported to Mercedes-Benz Group's management is referred to as 'EBIT' and comprises gross profit, selling and general administrative expenses, research and non-capitalised development costs, other income/expense and gains/losses arising from equity-method investments, as well as other financial income/expense. This means that EBIT is the measure considered relevant to and therefore reported to the CODM for the segments.
3. The segment result is reconciled to the IFRS profit before income taxes, consistent with the requirements of paragraph 28 of IFRS 8. The reconciliation shows that the difference between total segments' profit/loss (EBIT) and consolidated EBIT can be explained by the gains on equity-method investments not attributed to any segments, consolidation eliminations and other reconciling items, which include income/expense items at the corporate level.
4. There is disclosure of segment assets and liabilities. This means that these are reported internally to the CODM.
5. Mercedes-Benz Group discloses depreciation and amortisation expenses by segment, consistent with paragraph 23 (e) of IFRS 8.
6. At the end of Note 34 Mercedes-Benz Group reports on revenue and non-current assets by geographical region, consistent with the requirements of paragraph 33 of IFRS 8. However, there is no disclosure of the information about major customers as required by paragraph 34 of IFRS 8. Presumably this is because there is no single external customer whose revenues amount to 10% or more of the company's total revenues.

SUMMARY

IFRS 8 *Operating Segments* is primarily a disclosure standard and is particularly relevant for large organisations that operate in different geographical locations and/or in diverse businesses. Information about an entity's segments is relevant to assessing the risks and returns of a diversified or multinational entity where often that information cannot be determined from aggregated data.

Discussion questions

1. Segment disclosures are widely regarded as some of the most useful disclosures in financial statements because of the extent to which they disaggregate financial information into meaningful and often revealing groupings. Discuss this assertion by reference to the objectives of financial reporting by segments.
2. Explain what the 'management approach' used in IFRS 8 means.
3. Evaluate whether the reconciliations required by paragraph 28 of IFRS 8 address a concern about the lack of comparability between entities caused by management's ability to select any measurement basis it chooses in reporting segment information.
4. Describe how an entity determines its CODM for purposes of applying IFRS 8.

References

Ernst & Young 2009, *IFRS 8 Operating Segments: implementation guidance*, www.ey.com.

Véron, N. 2007, *EU adoption of the IFRS 8 standard on operating segments*, presented to the Economic Monetary Affairs Committee of the European Parliament, 19 September.

The academic literature on segment reporting has focused on how managers select reportable segments and which to aggregate with other segments (i.e., conceal). Another point of interest has been the effect of the changes in the rules governing segment reporting on reportable segments and resultant information environment. As discussed earlier in this chapter, the change from IAS 14 to IFRS 8 was hotly debated. The main concern was with respect to the management approach adopted by IFRS 8, which may be more prone to managerial discretion than IAS 14. The change in this standard followed a similar change in 1998 in the US from SFAS 14 (FASB, 1976) to SFAS 131 (now ASC 280) (FASB, 1997); hence many US studies are quite relevant to assessing the change in rules. (For a comparison between the various standards, see Nichols et al., 2013; this is also a good review paper on segment reporting.)

The analytical paper of Hayes and Lundholm (1996) provides some initial guidance on the issue of managers' discretion regarding which segments to report separately and which to conceal. In their model a disclosing manager is aware that segment information is used by a competitor. In the face of this competition, the disclosing manager prefers to aggregate segments so the competitor cannot infer which line of business is the more profitable one. However, if segment profitability is similar, there is little loss to the manager in disclosing the segments separately because (s)he is indifferent as to the competitor's action.

The proprietary cost argument identified by Hayes and Lundholm (1996) explains why profitable segments may be concealed. The reaction of a competitor to a disclosure of segment information is expected to be more harmful when a segment generates abnormal profit. The latter, in turn, is more likely in less competitive industries (e.g., in a duopoly). Harris (1998) examines this prediction employing several proxies for the degree of competition within an industry. Her sample consists of 929 multi-segment firms between 1987 and 1991. She shows that the number of reported segments (under old US rules) is lower than the actual number of industries a sample firm operates in. This suggests that many segments are not separately reported by sample firms. More importantly, the degree to which segments are unreported increases as competition weakens.

Managers may also have an incentive to conceal poorly performing lines of business, owing to agency costs. Berger and Hann (2007) posit that managers wishing to avoid scrutiny and criticism by boards and investors could do so by aggregating poor- with well-performing segments. Their results are based on a comparison of segment reporting in the US before and after SFAS 131 and are consistent with the presence of agency cost, but are mixed with respect to proprietary costs. Bens et al. (2011) employ a unique data review to further explore the aggregation issue and find that agency and proprietary costs drive aggregation when a firm discloses several segments, but not when it reports a single segment. Hope and Thomas (2008) also report results that are consistent with agency costs. Under SFAS 131 companies can reduce the number of foreign segments they report relative to SFAS 14. Hope and Thomas (2008) conjecture that

firms that stopped reporting geographical segments are poor-performing firms. They identify firms that under SFAS 14 disclosed foreign segments in the 5 years before the change in the rule and followed these firms over the first 5 years under SFAS 131. This results in a large sample of 4,773 firm-year observations. They find evidence that suggests that foreign operations in non-disclosing firms (firms that did not disclose at least two foreign segments in the first 2 years of SFAS 131) are less profitable and that the valuation of these firms is lower than that of firms that are identified as disclosers. While this is consistent with the presence of agency cost to disclosure, the evidence also suggests that SFAS 131 avails more latitude for managers to conceal poor performance.

Has the move to the management approach been successful? In the US several studies have documented an increase in the number of reported segments under SFAS 131 (e.g., Herrmann and Thomas, 2000; Berger and Hann, 2003; Botosan and Stanford, 2005). A similar trend is observed following the adoption of IFRS 8. Nichols et al. (2012) look at a sample of 326 large EU companies and find that in 62% there has been no change in the number of reported segments under IFRS 8 than under IAS 14. However, 27% (11%) of sample firms increased (decreased) the number of reported segments. The average increase is 0.35 segments. Leung and Verriest (2015) find that the effect of IFRS 8 on the number of reported segments, controlling for other confounding forces, is positive for both geographical and business segments.

Even if the number of reported segments has increased under new rules, it is not clear that the overall informativeness of financial statements has consequently improved. Both Nichols et al. (2012) and Leung and Verriest (2015) document a decline in overall items disclosed under IFRS 8, suggesting there may be less information available to users of segment reporting. Interestingly, Leung and Verriest (2015) find that the decline in the amount of information provided under IFRS 8 is more pronounced in firms that provided little disclosure under IAS 14. Aleksanyan and Danbolt (2015) also find that IFRS 8 disclosures differ in quantity and quality relative to previous standards.

Botosan and Stanford (2005) further examine this issue by looking at the effect of SFAS 131 on analysts. Specifically, they collect data on 615 firms in 1998 that reported a single segment under old US rules but multi-segment under new rules. They compare this sample to two other samples. The first is of 1945 firms that remained single-segment and the second including 592 firms that matched the main sample industry membership based on three-digit SIC code numbers. Botosan and Stanford (2005) present evidence that suggests that disclosure under new rules increased the amount of information common to all analysts. However, they do not find conclusive evidence on reduction in overall uncertainty and forecast error that financial analysts face following the new disclosure rules.

Ettredge et al. (2005) investigate a similar question using a different approach. They argue that if the new disclosure rules are more informative, this should be reflected in a stronger association between current stock returns and future earnings. That is predicated on the notion that stock returns are based on investors' expectation of future performance. Their sample is large, containing 6,827 firms and 21,698 firm-year observations between 1995 and 2001. They find that the association between stock returns and future earnings is larger following the adoption of SFAS 131. This suggests the management approach provides more useful information.

References

Aleksanyan, M. and Danbolt, J., 2015. Segment reporting: Is IFRS 8 really better? Accounting in Europe, 12(1), pp.37–60.

Bens, D.A., Berger, P.G., and Monahan, S.J., 2011. Discretionary disclosure in financial reporting: An examination comparing internal firm data to externally reported segment data. The Accounting Review, 86(2), 417–449.

Berger, P.G., and Hann, R., 2003. The impact of SFAS no. 131 on information and monitoring. Journal of Accounting Research, 41(2), 163–223.

Berger, P.G., and Hann, R., 2007. Segment profitability and the proprietary and agency costs of disclosure. The Accounting Review, 82(4), 869–906.

Botosan, C.A., and Stanford, M., 2005. Managers' motives to withhold segment disclosures and the effect of SFAS No. 131 on analysts' information environment. The Accounting Review, 80(3), 751–772.

Ettredge, M.L., Kwon, S.Y., Smith, D.B., and Zarowin, P.A., 2005. The impact of SFAS No. 131 business segment data on the market's ability to anticipate future earnings. The Accounting Review, 80(3), 773–804.

Financial Accounting Standards Board (FASB), 1976. Financial reporting for segments of a business enterprise. Statement of Financial Accounting Standards No. 14. Norwalk, CT: FASB.

Financial Accounting Standards Board (FASB), 1997. Disclosures about segments of an enterprise and related Information. Statement of Financial Accounting Standards No. 131. Norwalk, CT: FASB.

Harris, M., 1998. The association between competition and managers' business segment reporting decisions. Journal of Accounting Research, 36(1), 111–28.

Hayes, R.M., and Lundholm, R., 1996. Segment reporting to the capital market in the presence of a competitor. Journal of Accounting Research, 34(2), 261–79.

Herrmann, D., and Thomas W.B., 2000. An analysis of segment disclosures under SFAS No.131 and SFAS No. 14. Accounting Horizons, 14(3), 287–302.

Hope, O.K., and Thomas, W.B., 2008. Managerial empire building and firm disclosure. Journal of Accounting Research, 46(3), 591–626.

Leung, E., and Verriest, A., 2015. The impact of IFRS 8 on geographical segment information. Journal of Business Finance & Accounting, 42(3–4), 273–309.

Nichols, N., Street D., and Cereola, S., 2012. An analysis of the impact of applying IFRS 8 on the segment disclosures of European blue chip companies. Journal of International Accounting Auditing and Taxation, 21(2), 79–105.

Nichols, N.B., Street, D.L., and Tarca, A., 2013. The impact of segment reporting under the IFRS 8 and SFAS 131 management approach: A research review. Journal of International Financial Management & Accounting, 24(3), 261–312.

19

Business combinations

ACCOUNTING STANDARDS IN FOCUS

IFRS 3 *Business Combinations*

LEARNING OBJECTIVES

After studying this chapter, you should be able to:

1. understand the nature of a business combination and its various forms
2. explain the basic steps in the acquisition method of accounting for a business combination
3. recognise and measure the assets acquired and liabilities assumed in the business combination
4. understand the nature of and the accounting for goodwill and gain from bargain purchase
5. account for assets and liabilities subsequent to the business combination
6. provide the disclosures required under IFRS 3.

19.1 THE NATURE OF A BUSINESS COMBINATION

The accounting standard relevant for accounting for business combinations is IFRS 3 *Business Combinations* was originally issued in 2004 and revised by the International Accounting Standards Board (IASB®) in January 2008. There have been several subsequent amendments as a result of the IASB's annual improvement projects and revision of the *Conceptual Framework*.

A business combination is defined in Appendix A to IFRS 3 as arising when an acquirer obtains control of one or more businesses as a result of a transaction or other event.

> The definition explicitly includes transactions that are sometimes referred to as 'true mergers' or 'mergers of equals'.

The meaning of control is the same as in IFRS 10 *Consolidated Financial Statements*. Control exists when an investor is exposed, or has rights, to variable returns from its involvement with the investee and has the ability to affect those returns through its power over the investee.

The term business is defined in Appendix A as:

> An integrated set of activities and assets that is capable of being conducted and managed for the purpose of providing goods or services to customers, generating investment income (such as dividends or interest) or generating other income from ordinary activities.

The purpose of defining a business is to distinguish between the acquisition of a group of assets that does not constitute a business and the acquisition of a business. Appendix B of IFRS 3, which is an integral part of the Standard, provides application guidance on distinguishing between a group of assets and a business. An optional concentration test is described in paragraphs B7A and B7B. If the concentration test is satisfied, the set of activities is determined not to be a business. The concentration test is met if substantially all of the fair value of the gross assets acquired is concentrated in a single identifiable asset or group of similar identifiable assets, excluding cash and cash equivalents, deferred tax assets and goodwill. However, if the concentration test is not met, or if the entity elects not to apply it, the entity must perform the assessment in paragraphs B8 to B12D. To be considered a business, there must be an integrated set of activities and assets, that is, inputs and at least one substantive process applied to those inputs, which together significantly contribute to the ability to create output. Paragraphs B12A to B12D explain how to assess whether an acquired process is substantive.

While in all business combinations the acquirer obtains control of an integrated set of activities and assets, business combinations may take various forms. In this book we will consider two forms:

1. An acquisition in which the acquirer purchases assets, and possibly assumes liabilities, of the acquiree, as shown in figure 19.1. The acquirer subsequently recognises the assets and liabilities in its own financial statements

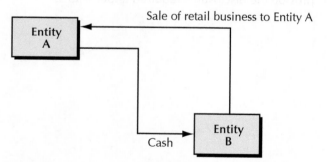

FIGURE 19.1 A business combination where the acquirer, A, purchases a business from another entity, B

2. In a more common form of acquisition, the acquirer purchases sufficient equity instruments (shares) in another entity to obtain control of that entity and, thus, its net assets. In this form of business combination, the transaction is between the acquirer and the former owners of the other entity, as shown in figure 19.2. The acquirer recognises the investment in equity instruments as an asset in its own financial statements, referred to as an investment in a subsidiary. The acquirer also prepares a single set of financial statements, referred to as the consolidated financial statements, to report on the financial position and financial performance of the parent and its subsidiaries as a combined entity or group. Accounting for this form of business combination in the consolidated financial statements requires the application of the principles for the recognition and measurement of assets and liabilities acquired in the business combination, including the recognition and measurement of goodwill. The preparation of consolidated financial statements is considered in chapters 20–23 of this book.

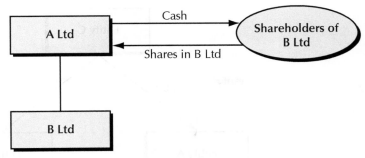

FIGURE 19.2 A business combination where the acquirer, A, obtains control of another entity, B

A business combination could also occur without any exchange of assets or equity between the entities involved in the exchange. For example, a business combination could occur where two entities merged under a contract. The shareholders of the two entities could agree to adjust the rights of each of their shareholdings so that they receive a specified share of the profits of both the combined entities. As a result of the contract, both entities would be under the control of a single management group.

IFRS 3 applies to all business combinations except those listed in paragraph 2 of the standard, namely:

- *Where the business combination results in the formation of a joint venture.* Such a business combination is accounted for under IFRS 11 *Joint Arrangements*. See online chapter D
- *Where the business combination involves entities or businesses under common control.* This occurs where all of the combining entities are controlled by the same party or parties both before and after the combination, and where control is not transitory. For example, P Ltd owns 100% of S Ltd's issued share capital. If P Ltd formed a new wholly owned entity, X Ltd, that acquired all of S Ltd's equity, then this would simply constitute an internal reconstruction. All of the combining entities would be controlled by P Ltd both before and after the reconstruction.
- Further, IFRS 3 does not apply to the acquisition of a group of assets that does not form a business combination. In those circumstances, the acquirer must apply the appropriate accounting standard, such as IAS 38 *Intangible Assets*, for each type of asset acquired or liability assumed.

19.2 ACCOUNTING FOR A BUSINESS COMBINATION — BASIC PRINCIPLES

The required method of accounting for a business combination under paragraph 4 of IFRS 3 is the *acquisition method*. The four key steps in this method are noted in paragraph 5 of the standard:

1. Identify the acquirer.
2. Determine the acquisition date.
3. Recognise and measure the identifiable assets acquired, the liabilities assumed, and any non-controlling interest in the acquiree.
4. Recognise and measure goodwill or a gain from a bargain purchase.

The acquisition date is the date that the acquirer obtains control of the acquiree. IFRS 3 deals with the acquisition itself and also with the subsequent measurement and accounting for assets and liabilities recognised initially at acquisition date.

19.2.1 Identifying the acquirer [step 1]

Identification of the acquirer is a critical step because, as explained below, it has implications for the measurement of assets and liabilities in the combined business. Paragraph 7 of IFRS 3 states that the acquirer is 'the entity that obtains *control* of another entity, i.e. the acquiree'.

The key criterion, then, in identifying an acquirer is that of control. This term is the same as that used in IFRS 10 *Consolidated Financial Statements* for identifying a parent–subsidiary relationship (see chapter 20). It is often straightforward to identify the acquirer. For example, entity A might acquire all shares in entity B.

In other situations, identification of an acquirer requires judgement. Consider the situation where entity A combines with entity B. To effect the combination, a new company (entity C) is formed, which issues shares to the existing shareholders of A and B as consideration for acquiring all the shares of both entities A and B. The subsequent organisational structure is as shown in figure 19.3.

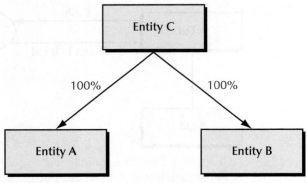

FIGURE 19.3 Example of entity combination and subsequent organisational structure

As entity C is created solely to formalise the organisation structure, it is not the acquirer, even though it is the legal parent of both of the other entities. Paragraph B18 of Appendix B to IFRS 3 states that one of the entities that existed before the combination must be identified as the acquirer. Entity C is not a party to the decisions associated with creating the business combination, it is just a vehicle used to facilitate the combination. If entity A is identified as the acquirer, then entity B's assets and liabilities are measured at fair value at acquisition date. If entity B is identified as the acquirer, then entity A's assets and liabilities are measured at fair value at acquisition date.

Paragraphs B14–B18 of Appendix B to IFRS 3 provide some indicators to assist in assessing which entity is the acquirer:

- *What are the relative voting rights in the combined entity after the business combination?* The acquirer is usually the entity whose owners have the largest portion of the voting rights in the combined entity. However, this is not always the case and the special case of a reverse acquisition is considered in paragraph B19 (refer to section 20.4.2 of chapter 20 of this book).
- *Is there a large minority voting interest in the combined entity?* The acquirer is usually the entity that has the largest minority voting interest in an entity that has a widely dispersed ownership.
- *What is the composition of the governing body of the combined entity?* The acquirer is usually the combining entity whose owners have the ability to elect or appoint or to remove a majority of the members of the governing body, such as the board of directors, of the combined entity.
- *What is the composition of the senior management that governs the combined entity subsequent to the combination?* This is an important indicator given that the criterion for identification of an acquirer is that of control. After X and Y combine, is the senior management group of the combined entity dominated by former senior managers of X or Y?
- *What are the terms of the exchange of equity interests?* Has one of the combining entities paid a premium over the pre-combination fair value of one of the combining entities, that is, an amount paid in order to gain control?
- *Which entity is the larger?* This could be measured by reference to the fair value of each of the combining entities, or relative revenues or profits. In a takeover, it is normally the larger company that takes over the smaller company (that is, the larger company is the acquirer).
- *Which entity initiated the exchange?* Normally the entity that is the acquirer is the one that undertakes action to take over the acquiree.

Determining the controlling entity is the key to identification of the acquirer. However, doing so may not be straightforward in many business combinations, and management might be required to make a reasoned judgement based on the circumstances.

Paragraph 6 requires an acquirer to be identified in every business combination, even though it may be argued that it is not always possible to do so. In the case of a 'true' merger, neither party would claim to be dominant.

It can also prove difficult to identify an acquirer under a combination achieved by contract alone. Such a combination may not involve the exchange of readily measurable consideration.

However, in all cases an acquirer must be identified. The need to identify the acquirer stems from the need to measure the acquiree's fair value and fair value of its assets and liabilities, but not those of the acquirer.

19.2.2 Determining the acquisition date [step 2]

The acquisition date is defined in Appendix A to IFRS 3 as:

[t]he date on which the **acquirer** obtains control of the **acquiree**.

Other dates, such as the date that the contract is signed or the date on which the assets are delivered may be important issues for management, but they do not necessarily reflect the acquisition date. As noted in paragraph 9 of IFRS 3, on the closing date of the combination, the acquirer legally transfers the consideration — cash or shares — and acquires the assets and assumes the liabilities of the acquiree. However, in some cases this may not be the acquisition date.

The definition of acquisition date then relates to the point in time when control passes, which determines as from which date the net assets of the acquiree become the net assets of the acquirer — in essence, the date on which the acquirer can recognise the net assets acquired in its own records.

Identifying the acquisition date is important because:

- The identifiable assets acquired and liabilities assumed by the acquirer are measured at their fair values on the acquisition date. If markets are volatile then the date could affect the fair value.
- The consideration paid by the acquirer is determined as the sum of the fair values of assets given, equity issued and/or liabilities undertaken in exchange for the net assets or shares of another entity. Share prices can fluctuate daily, so the choice of date can affect the measure of fair value.
- The acquirer may acquire only some of the shares of the acquiree. The owners of the balance of the shares of the acquiree are called the non-controlling interest. If non-controlling interest is measured at fair value, it is the fair value at acquisition date.
- The acquirer may have previously held an equity interest in the acquiree prior to obtaining control of the acquiree. For example, entity X may have previously acquired 20% of the shares of entity Y, and now acquires the remaining 80% giving it control of entity Y. The acquisition date is the date when entity X acquired the 80% interest. The 20% shareholding will be recorded as an asset in the records of entity X. At acquisition date, the fair value of this investment is measured. The effect of determining the acquisition date is that the financial position of the combined entity at acquisition date should report the assets and liabilities of the acquiree at that date, and any profits reported as a result of the acquiree's operations within the business combination should reflect profits generated after the acquisition date.

19.2.3 Recognition and measurement of assets acquired and liabilities assumed [step 3]

Where the acquirer purchases a business consisting of assets, liabilities and activities of another entity, it has to consider:

(a) the recognition and measurement of the identifiable assets acquired and the liabilities assumed (step 3 of the acquisition method)

(b) the recognition and measurement of goodwill or a gain from a bargain purchase (step 4 of the acquisition method).

Chapters 20–24 deal with the preparation of consolidated financial statements for business combinations where the acquirer purchases the shares of the acquiree. The only aspect of such business combinations that will be covered in this chapter is the recognition and measurement of the investment by the acquirer.

Recognition

Paragraph 10 of IFRS 3 requires the acquirer to recognise the identifiable assets acquired, the liabilities assumed and any non-controlling interest in the acquiree as of the acquisition date. (Non-controlling interests are discussed in chapter 23.)

Recognition of the identifiable assets acquired and liabilities assumed is subject to several conditions, which are specified in paragraphs 11 and 12:

Firstly, at the acquisition date, the assets and liabilities recognised by the acquirer must meet the definitions of assets and liabilities in the *Conceptual Framework*. For example, expected future costs cannot be included in the calculation of assets acquired and liabilities assumed.

Secondly, the item acquired or assumed must be part of the business acquired rather than the result of a separate transaction.

The first of these conditions can have implications for the treatment of contingent liabilities. If the contingent liability represents a possible obligation, for which the existence will be determined by a future event, such as the outcome of legal action against the acquiree, it is not recognised by the acquirer; the definition of a liability is not satisfied because there is no present obligation. However, if the contingent liability reflects a present obligation, but has been treated as contingent because the future outflows are not regarded as 'probable' or because the amounts cannot be measured with sufficient reliability, it must be recognised by the acquirer in the business combination (IFRS 3, paragraphs 21A and 21B).

The second condition applies substance over form. For example, suppose the acquiree had a claim outstanding against the acquirer before the acquisition date. If the acquirer agrees to settle the claim as part of the combination and part of the consideration includes a sum in settlement of the claim then it would be necessary to account for the acquisition as two transactions and the sum paid in settlement would have to be separated out from the consideration.

Paragraph 13 of IFRS 3 notes that a possible result of applying the principles of IFRS 3 may be the recognition of assets and liabilities as a result of the business combination that were not previously recognised by the acquiree. For example, internally generated intangibles that were not recognised by the acquiree because of the requirements of IAS 38 *Intangible Assets* may have to be recognised by the acquirer at fair value. Similarly, as explained earlier in this section, certain contingent liabilities are recognised by the acquirer in accordance with IFRS 3 even though IAS 37 *Provisions, Contingent Liabilities and Contingent Assets* prohibited their recognition by the acquiree in its financial statements before the business combination (see chapter 10).

Paragraph 15 of IFRS 3 requires that the acquirer classifies or designates assets and liabilities on the basis of the contractual terms, economic conditions, its operating or accounting policies and other pertinent conditions that exist at acquisition date. This could, for example, affect the classification of financial assets at fair value or at amortised cost.

As a part of the illustrative examples accompanying IFRS 3, the IASB provided examples of items acquired in a business combination that would meet the definition of an intangible asset (see figure 19.4).

FIGURE 19.4 Intangible assets, IFRS 3 Illustrative Examples, paragraphs IE18–44

CLASS	BASIS
Marketing-related intangible assets	
Trademarks, trade names, service marks, collective marks and certification marks	Contractual
Trade dress (unique colour, shape or package design)	Contractual
Newspaper mastheads	Contractual
Internet domain names	Contractual
Non-competition agreements	Contractual
Customer-related intangible assets	
Customer lists	Non-contractual
Order or production backlog	Contractual
Customer contracts and related customer relationships	Contractual
Non-contractual customer relationships	Non-contractual
Artistic-related intangible assets	
Plays, operas and ballets	Contractual
Books, magazines, newspapers and other literary works	Contractual
Musical works such as compositions, song lyrics and advertising jingles	Contractual
Pictures and photographs	Contractual
Video and audiovisual material, including motion pictures or films, music videos and television programs	Contractual
Contract-based intangible assets	
Licensing, royalty and standstill agreements	Contractual
Advertising, construction, management, service or supply contracts	Contractual
Lease agreements (whether the acquiree is the lessee or lessor)	Contractual
Construction permits	Contractual
Franchise agreements	Contractual
Operating and broadcasting rights	Contractual
Servicing contracts such as mortgage servicing contracts	Contractual
Employment contracts	Contractual
Use rights, such as drilling, water, air, timber cutting and route authorities	Contractual
Technology-based intangible assets	
Patented technology	Contractual
Computer software and mask works	Contractual
Unpatented technology	Non-contractual
Databases including title plants	Non-contractual
Trade secrets such as secret formulas, processes and recipes	Contractual

Measurement

Paragraph 18 requires an acquirer to measure the identifiable assets acquired and the liabilities assumed at their fair values on acquisition date, irrespective of their carrying amount in the accounts of the entity from which they were acquired. Thus, the assets and liabilities acquired are measured as if they were acquired separately at the acquisition date. Consistent with IFRS 13 *Fair Value Measurement* (see chapter 8), fair value is defined in Appendix A to IFRS 3 as:

> the price that would be received to sell an asset or paid to transfer a liability in an orderly transaction between market participants at the measurement date.

Paragraph BC198 of the Basis for Conclusions on IFRS 3 argues that fair values are relevant, comparable and understandable.

19.2.4 Goodwill and gain on bargain purchase [step 4]

Paragraph 32 of IFRS 3 states:

> The acquirer shall recognise goodwill as of the acquisition date measured as the excess of (a) over (b) below:
>
> (a) the aggregate of:
>   (i) the consideration transferred measured in accordance with this IFRS, which generally requires acquisition date fair value (see paragraph 37);
>   (ii) the amount of any non-controlling interest in the acquiree measured in accordance with this IFRS; and
>   (iii) in a business combination achieved in stages (see paragraphs 41 and 42), the acquisition-date fair value of the acquirer's previously held equity interest in the acquiree.
> (b) the net of the acquisition-date amounts of the identifiable assets acquired and the liabilities assumed measured in accordance with this IFRS.

Parts (a)(ii) and (iii) in paragraph 32 only arise in business combinations where the acquirer obtains control by acquiring shares in the acquiree. *This is discussed in chapters 20–23.* This means that for business combinations discussed in this chapter, goodwill is determined by comparing the consideration transferred by the acquirer with the net fair value of the identifiable assets and liabilities acquired.

The net fair value of the identifiable assets and liabilities acquired is determined as step 3. The first part of step 4 is then the measurement of consideration transferred.

Consideration transferred

Paragraph 37 specifies the following requirements for measuring the consideration transferred:
- the consideration is measured at fair value at acquisition date
- the fair value of the consideration is calculated as the sum of the acquisition-date fair values of the assets transferred by the acquirer, the liabilities incurred by the acquirer to the former owners of the acquiree, and the equity interest issued by the acquirer.

In a specific exchange, the consideration transferred to the acquiree could include just one form of consideration, such as cash, but could also include other assets, shares and contingent consideration. These are considered in the following pages.

Cash or other monetary assets

The fair value is the amount of cash or cash equivalent dispersed. The amount is usually readily determinable. However, it can become more complex if the settlement is deferred to a time after the acquisition date. For a deferred payment, the fair value to the acquirer is the amount the entity would have to borrow to settle the debt immediately. The discount rate used is the entity's incremental borrowing rate.

Use of cash, including a deferred payment, to acquire net assets results in the acquirer recording the following form of entry at the acquisition date (assume the consideration includes $100 payable 1 year later; the discount rate is 10%):

Net assets	Dr	xxx
Cash	Cr	xxx
Payable to Acquiree	Cr	91
(Acquisition of net assets with partially deferred payment)		

When the deferred payment is made to the acquiree, the interest component needs to be recognised:

Payable to Acquiree	Dr	91
Interest Expense	Dr	9
Cash	Cr	100
(Payment of deferred amount)		

Non-monetary assets

Non-monetary assets are assets such as property, plant and equipment, investments, licences and patents. *Chapter 8 discusses how fair values are determined.*

Where the consideration includes non-monetary assets, the acquirer is effectively selling the non-monetary asset. Hence, it is earning income equal to the fair value on the sale of the asset. Where the carrying amount of the asset in the records of the acquirer is different from fair value, a gain or loss on the asset is recognised at acquisition date. This principle is stated in paragraph 38 of IFRS 3: 'the acquirer shall remeasure the transferred assets or liabilities to their fair values as of the acquisition date and recognise the resulting gains or losses, if any, in profit or loss'.

Use of a non-monetary asset such as plant as part of the consideration to acquire net assets results in the acquirer recording the following entries (assume a cost of plant of $180, a carrying amount of $150 and fair value of $155):

Accumulated Depreciation	Dr	30	
Plant	Cr		25
Gain	Cr		5
(Remeasurement as part of consideration transferred in a business combination)			
Net Assets Acquired	Dr	xxx	
Plant	Cr		155
Other Consideration Payable	Cr		xxx
(Acquisition of net assets)			

The acquirer recognises a gain on the non-current asset and the asset is then included in the consideration transferred at fair value.

Equity instruments

If an acquirer issues its own shares as consideration, it needs to determine the fair value of those shares at the acquisition date. For listed entities, reference is made to the quoted prices of the shares.

Liabilities incurred

To be included in consideration, liabilities incurred by the acquirer must be obligations to the former owners of the acquiree. For example, the acquirer might incur a liability for deferred consideration payable to the former owners of the acquiree.

Costs of issuing debt and equity instruments

Paragraph 53 of IFRS 3 indicates costs to issue debt and equity instruments are accounted for in accordance with IAS 32 *Financial Instruments: Presentation* and IFRS 9 *Financial Instruments*. In issuing equity instruments such as shares as part of the consideration paid, transaction costs such as stamp duties, professional advisers' fees, underwriting costs and brokerage fees may be incurred. Paragraph 35 of IAS 32 states that these outlays should be treated as a reduction in the share capital of the entity as such costs reduce the proceeds from the equity issue, net of any related income tax benefit. However, this only applies to costs that are incremental and directly attributable to the equity issue that otherwise would have been avoided (IAS 32 paragraph 37). Hence, if costs of $1000 are incurred in issuing shares as part of the consideration paid, the journal entry in the records of the acquirer is:

Share Capital	Dr	1,000	
Cash	Cr		1,000
(Costs of issuing equity instruments)			

Similarly, the costs of arranging and issuing financial liabilities are an integral part of the liability issue transaction. These costs are included in the initial measurement of the liability. *Financial liabilities are discussed further in chapter 13.*

Contingent consideration

Appendix A to IFRS 3 provides the following definition of contingent consideration:

> Usually, an obligation of the acquirer to transfer additional assets or equity interests to the former owners of an acquiree as part of the exchange for control of the acquiree if specified future events occur or conditions are met. However, contingent consideration also may give the acquirer the right to the return of previously transferred consideration if specified conditions are met.

Consider two examples of contingencies. The first is where, because the future income of the acquirer is regarded as uncertain, the agreement contains a clause that requires the acquirer to provide additional consideration to the acquiree if the income of the acquirer exceeds a specified amount over some specified period. The second situation is where the acquirer issues shares to the acquiree and the acquiree is concerned that the issue of these shares may make the market price of the acquirer's shares decline over time. Therefore, the acquirer may offer additional cash or shares if the market price of its shares falls below a specified amount over a specified period of time.

However, where contingent consideration is linked to employment of the acquiree, or its shareholders, the contingent payment is considered to be remuneration expense, and not contingent consideration in a business combination, in accordance with International Financial Reporting Interpretations Committee (IFRIC) Agenda Decisions (January 2013 and April 2024). For example, entity A acquires a restaurant business and part of the acquisition agreement provides for the seller, Oliver, to continue as an employee of the acquired restaurant business. The seller's continued employment is to maintain the high-quality meals served by the restaurant. Entity A agrees to compensate Oliver for his services, that is, pay a salary, at an amount comparable to other leading chefs. Entity A also agrees to make additional payments to Oliver, contingent upon both the performance of the business and continued employment. Oliver forfeits the additional payments if his employment is terminated. In these circumstances, the additional payments are accounted for by entity A as post-business combination remuneration expenses.

According to paragraph 39 of IFRS 3, consistent with other measurements in transferred consideration, the acquirer shall recognise the acquisition-date fair values of contingent consideration as part of the consideration transferred.

Acquisition-related costs

Acquisition-related costs refer to the costs associated with bringing the business combination into effect. Acquisition-related costs include: 'finder's fees; advisory, legal, accounting, valuation and other professional or consulting fees; [and] general administrative costs, including the costs of maintaining an internal acquisitions department' (IFRS 3 paragraph 53).

For certain types of assets, accounting standards, such as IAS 16 *Property, Plant and Equipment* and IAS 38 *Intangible Assets*, require directly attributable costs to be capitalised as part of the cost of the asset acquired. In contrast, the acquisition-related costs associated with a business combination are accounted for as expenses in the periods in which they are incurred and the services are received. The key reasons given for this approach are provided in paragraph BC366 of the Basis for Conclusions on IFRS 3:

- Acquisition-related costs are not part of the fair value exchange between the buyer and seller.
- They are separate transactions for which the buyer pays the fair value for the services received.
- These amounts do not generally represent assets of the acquirer at acquisition date because the benefits obtained are consumed as the services are received.

The IFRS 3 accounting for these outlays is a result of the decision to record the identifiable assets acquired and liabilities assumed at fair value. In contrast, under IAS 16 and IAS 38, the assets acquired are initially recorded at cost.

ILLUSTRATIVE EXAMPLE 19.1 Consideration transferred in a business combination

The trial balance below represents the financial position of Whiting Ltd at 1 January 2026.

WHITING LTD Trial Balance as at 1 January 2026		
	Debit	Credit
Share capital		
Preference — 6,000 fully paid shares		$6,000
Ordinary — 30,000 fully paid shares		30,000
Retained earnings		21,500
Equipment	$42,000	
Accumulated depreciation — equipment		10,000
Inventory	18,000	
Accounts receivable	16,000	
Patents	3,500	
Debentures		4,000
Accounts payable		8,000
	$79,500	$79,500

At this date, the business of Whiting Ltd is acquired by Salmon Ltd The terms of acquisition are as follows:

1. Salmon Ltd is to take over all the assets of Whiting Ltd as well as the accounts payable of Whiting Ltd.
2. Salmon Ltd agreed to issue 2,000 preference shares to Whiting Ltd.
3. The fair value of Salmon Ltd's preference shares is $1.10 per share at the date of acquisition.
4. Whiting Ltd is to receive 50,000 fully paid ordinary shares in Salmon Ltd.
5. The fair value of Salmon Ltd's ordinary shares is $1.10 per share at the date of acquisition.
6. Salmon Ltd agreed to pay Whiting Ltd $19,930, of which $13,680 was payable at acquisition, and the balance, payable 1 year later.
7. The incremental borrowing rate for Salmon Ltd is 10% p.a.
8. Costs of issuing and registering the shares issued by Salmon Ltd amount to $40 for the preference shares and $100 for the ordinary shares.
9. Costs associated with the business combination and incurred by Salmon Ltd were $1,000.

The calculation of the consideration transferred in the business combination to Salmon Ltd is shown in figure 19.5.

FIGURE 19.5 Consideration transferred in the business combination

Consideration transferred:	Fair value $
Preference shares (2,000 × $1.10)	2,200
Ordinary shares (50,000 × $1.10)	55,000
Cash:	
Payable immediately	13,680
Deferred one year ($19,930 − $13,680)*	5,682
Fair value of consideration transferred	$76,562

*$5,682 is the cash payable in 1 year's time discounted at 10% p.a

In acquiring the net assets of Whiting Ltd, Salmon Ltd passes the journal entries shown in figure 19.6.

FIGURE 19.6 Journal entries in the acquirer's records

2026				
Jan. 1	Net Assets Acquired	Dr	76,562	
	Consideration Payable	Cr		19,362
	Share Capital – Preference	Cr		2,200
	Share Capital – Ordinary	Cr		55,000
	(Acquisition of the net assets of Whiting Ltd)			
	Consideration Payable	Dr	13,680	
	Cash	Cr		13,680
	(Payment of cash consideration to Whiting Ltd: $19,362 less $5,682 payable later)			
	Share Capital – Ordinary	Dr	100	
	Share Capital – Preference	Dr	40	
	Cash	Cr		140
	(Share issue costs)			
	Acquisition-Related Expenses	Dr	1,000	
	Cash	Cr		1,000
	(Acquisition-related expenses)			
Dec. 31	Consideration Payable	Dr	5,682	
	Interest Expense	Dr	568	
	Cash	Cr		6,250
	(Balance of consideration paid)			

Goodwill

As noted in section 19.2.4, goodwill is the excess of the consideration transferred over the net fair value of the identifiable assets acquired and liabilities assumed.

> Goodwill = Consideration transferred
>
> *less*
>
> Acquirer's interest in the net fair value of the acquiree's identifiable assets and liabilities

Goodwill is accounted for as an asset and is defined in Appendix A to IFRS 3 as:

> An asset representing the future economic benefits arising from other assets acquired in a **business combination** that are not individually identified and separately recognised.

The criterion of 'being individually identified' relates to the characteristic of 'identifiability' as used in IAS 38 *Intangible Assets* to distinguish intangible assets from goodwill. Note paragraph 11 of IAS 38 in this regard:

> The definition of an intangible asset requires an intangible asset to be identifiable to distinguish it from goodwill. Goodwill recognised in a business combination is an asset representing future economic benefits arising from other assets acquired in a business combination that are not individually identified and separately recognised. The future economic benefits may result from synergy between the identifiable assets acquired or from assets that, individually, do not qualify for recognition in the financial statements.

In order to be identifiable, an asset must be capable of being separated or divided from the entity, or arise from contractual or other legal rights. The notion of being 'separately recognised' is also then a part of the criterion of 'identifiability'. *This criterion is discussed further in chapter 6.*

Goodwill is then a residual, after the acquirer's interest in the identifiable tangible assets, intangible assets, and liabilities of the acquiree is recognised.

The components of goodwill

While the preceding discussion focuses on the calculation of goodwill, it is useful to consider what is represented by goodwill recognised in a business combination. This unidentifiable asset has two components as depicted in figure 19.7.

The *'going concern' component of the acquiree's existing business* represents the ability of the acquiree to earn a higher return on an assembled collection of net assets than would be expected from those net assets operating separately (Johnson and Petrone, 1998, p. 295). This reflects synergies of the assets, as well as factors relating to market imperfections such as an ability of an entity to earn a monopoly profit, or where there are barriers to competitors entering a particular market.

Further to the synergy of the acquired collection of assets comprising a business, additional synergy may arise through combination with the existing assets of the acquirer. The *combination component of goodwill* is the incremental fair value from combining the acquirer's and acquiree's businesses and net assets (Johnson and Petrone, 1998, p. 295).

While Johnson and Petrone (1998) identify other components of goodwill, they are not conceptually consistent with the approach to the recognition and measurement of goodwill adopted by IFRS 3.

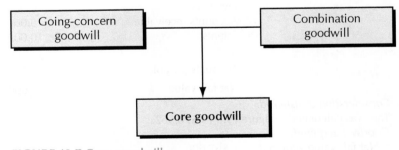

FIGURE 19.7 Core goodwill.
Source: Data derived from Johnson and Petrone (1998)

It is this 'core goodwill' that the IASB is concerned with in determining how to account for goodwill.

Is goodwill an asset?

IFRS 3 accounts for goodwill as an asset, although it is debatable whether it meets the definition of an asset as set out in the *Conceptual Framework*.

The problem with goodwill is that it is a unique asset. It arises as a residual. As Leo, Hoggett and Radford (1995, pp. 44–7) noted, the key difference between identifiable net assets and goodwill is measurement:

> The difference between the measurement method used for goodwill and that for measurement of all other assets of the business is whether the method involves determining the value of the business as a whole or part thereof.

The authors defined unidentifiable assets (p. 46) as those assets that meet the recognition criteria and cannot be measured without measuring the total net assets of a business entity. The existence of goodwill depends on the measurement of the entity as a whole. In recognising this, the IASB argued in paragraph BC323 of the Basis for Conclusions on IFRS 3:

> control of core goodwill is provided by means of the acquirer's power to direct the policies and management of the acquiree. Therefore, both the IASB and the FASB concluded that core goodwill meets the conceptual definition of an asset.

Accounting for goodwill

As noted earlier, goodwill is calculated as the excess of the consideration transferred in the business combination over the acquirer's interest in the net fair value of the identifiable assets acquired and liabilities assumed from the acquiree. Hence, to calculate goodwill as a part of the acquisition analysis it is necessary to calculate the consideration transferred and the net fair value of the identifiable assets acquired and liabilities assumed. A comparison of these two amounts determines the existence of goodwill. The acquirer then recognises goodwill as an asset in the same way as for all other identifiable assets acquired.

ILLUSTRATIVE EXAMPLE 19.2 Acquisition analysis

Using the figures from illustrative example 19.1, assume that Salmon Ltd assesses the fair values of the identifiable assets and liabilities of Whiting Ltd to be as follows:

Equipment	$36,000
Inventory	20,000
Accounts receivable	9,000
Patents	10,000
Accounts payable	8,000

To determine the entries to be passed by the acquirer, prepare an acquisition analysis that compares the consideration transferred with the net fair value of the identifiable assets, liabilities and contingent liabilities acquired. The analysis for this example is shown in figure 19.8.

FIGURE 19.8 Acquisition analysis by the acquirer

Acquisition analysis
Net fair value of identifiable assets acquired and liabilities assumed:

Equipment	$36,000
Inventory	20,000
Accounts receivable	9,000
Patents	10,000
	75,000
Accounts payable	8,000
Net fair value	$67,000

Consideration transferred:
This was calculated in figure 19.5 as $76,562.
Goodwill acquired:

Net fair value acquired	= $67,000
Consideration transferred	= $76,562
Goodwill	= $76,562 – $67,000
	= $9,562

The journal entries for Salmon Ltd at acquisition date are as shown in figure 19.9.

FIGURE 19.9 Journal entries of the acquirer, including recognition of goodwill, at acquisition date

Equipment	Dr	36,000	
Inventory	Dr	20,000	
Accounts Receivable	Dr	9,000	
Patents	Dr	10,000	
Goodwill	Dr	9,562	
Accounts Payable	Cr		8,000
Consideration Payable	Cr		19,362
Share Capital – Preference	Cr		2,200
Share Capital – Ordinary	Cr		55,000
(Acquisition of the assets and liabilities of Whiting Ltd)			
Consideration Payable	Dr	13,680	
Cash	Cr		13,680
(Payment of cash consideration)			
Acquisition-Related Expenses	Dr	1,000	
Cash	Cr		1,000
(Acquisition-related costs)			
Share Capital – Ordinary	Dr	100	
Share Capital – Preference	Dr	40	
Cash	Cr		140
(Share issue costs)			

Accounting for a gain on a bargain purchase

Where the acquirer's interest in the net fair value of the acquiree's identifiable assets and liabilities is greater than the consideration transferred, the difference is called a gain on a bargain purchase. In equation format, it can be represented as follows:

Gain on bargain purchase = Acquirer's interest in the net fair value of the acquiree's identifiable assets and liabilities

less

Consideration transferred

The existence of a bargain purchase is considered by the standard setters (paragraph BC371) as an anomalous transaction as parties to the business combination do not knowingly sell assets at amounts lower than their fair value. However, because the acquirer has excellent negotiation skills, or because the acquiree has made a sale for other than economic reasons or is forced to sell owing to specific circumstances such as cash flow problems, such situations do arise.

The standard setters adopt the view that most business combinations are an exchange of equal amounts, given markets in which the parties to the business combinations are informed and willing participants in the transaction. Therefore, the existence of a bargain purchase is expected to be an unusual or rare event.

Paragraph 36 of IFRS 3 requires that before a gain is recognised, the acquirer must reassess whether it has correctly:
• identified all the assets acquired and liabilities assumed
• measured at fair value all the assets acquired and liabilities assumed
• measured the consideration transferred.

The objective here is to ensure that all the measurements at acquisition date reflect all the information that is available at that date.

Note that one effect of recognising a bargain purchase is that there is no recognition of goodwill. A gain on bargain purchase and goodwill cannot be recognised in the same business combination.

Using the information regarding the consideration transferred in a business combination from illustrative example 19.1, assume the fair values of the identifiable assets and liabilities of Whiting Ltd are assessed to be:

Equipment	$45,000
Inventory	25,000
Accounts receivable	9,000
Patents	11,000
	90,000
Accounts payable	8,000
	$82,000

The acquisition analysis now shows:

Net fair value of assets and liabilities acquired = $82,000
Consideration transferred = $76,562
Gain on bargain purchase = $82,000 − $76,562
= $5,438

Assuming that the reassessment process did not result in any changes to the fair values calculated, the first journal entry in Salmon Ltd to record the acquisition of the net assets of Whiting Ltd is:

Equipment	Dr	45,000	
Inventory	Dr	25,000	
Accounts Receivable	Dr	9,000	
Patents	Dr	11,000	
Accounts Payable	Cr		8,000
Consideration Payable	Cr		19,362
Share Capital — Preference	Cr		2,200
Share Capital — Ordinary	Cr		55,000
Gain (Profit or Loss)	Cr		5,438
(Acquisition of assets and liabilities acquired from Whiting Ltd, and the gain on bargain purchase)			

19.3 SUBSEQUENT ACCOUNTING FOR A BUSINESS COMBINATION

Three areas where adjustments may need to be made subsequent to the initial accounting after acquisition date are:
• goodwill
• contingent liabilities
• contingent consideration.

19.3.1 Goodwill

Having recognised goodwill arising in the business combination, the subsequent accounting is directed from other accounting standards:
• goodwill is not subject to amortisation but is subject to an annual impairment test as detailed in IAS 36 *Impairment of Assets (see chapter 7)*.
• goodwill cannot be revalued because IAS 38 *Intangible Assets* does not allow the recognition of internally generated goodwill.

19.3.2 Contingent liabilities

Having recognised any contingent liabilities of the acquiree as liabilities, the acquirer must then determine a subsequent measurement for the liability. The liability is initially recognised at fair value. According to paragraph 56 of IFRS 3, subsequent to acquisition, and until it is cancelled or settled, the liability is measured as the higher of:

(a) the amount that would be recognised in accordance with IAS 37; and
(b) the amount initially recognised less, if appropriate, the cumulative amount of income recognised in accordance with IFRS 15 *Revenue from Contracts with Customers*.

Under IAS 37 paragraph 36, the liability would be measured at the best estimate of the expenditure required to settle the present obligation at the end of the reporting period. This would be used, for example, where a liability was recognised in relation to a court case. However, the requirements of paragraph 56 of IFRS 3 do not apply to contingent liabilities, such as guarantees or other financial liabilities, that are within the scope of IFRS 9 *Financial Instruments*.

19.3.3 Contingent consideration

Appendix A of IFRS 3 defines contingent consideration as an obligation of the acquirer to transfer additional assets or equity instruments to the former owners of the acquiree, which is contingent upon specified future events occurring or conditions, such as performance targets, being met. While usually an obligation of the acquirer, contingent consideration can also be a right of the acquirer to receive a return (refund) of some of the consideration paid, subject to specified conditions, such as a performance target not being achieved.

At acquisition date, the contingent consideration is measured at fair value, and is classified either as equity (e.g. the requirement for the acquirer to issue more shares subject to subsequent events) or as a liability or asset. Subsequent to the business combination, paragraph 54 of IFRS 3 requires the accounting for contingent consideration to be in accordance with the accounting standard that would normally apply to these accounts. However, IFRS 3 provides guidance on the measures to be used.

Where the contingent consideration is classified as equity, no remeasurement is required, and the subsequent settlement is accounted for within equity (IFRS 3 paragraph 58(a)). This means that if extra equity instruments are issued they are effectively issued for no consideration and there is no change to equity.

Other contingent consideration is accounted for at fair value with movements being recognised in profit and loss (IFRS 3 paragraph 58).

It should be noted that the subsequent accounting for contingent consideration is to treat it as a post-acquisition event; that is, not affecting the measurements made at acquisition date. Hence, any subsequent adjustments do not affect the goodwill calculated at acquisition date.

ILLUSTRATIVE EXAMPLE 19.4 Comprehensive example

Labrador Ltd's major business is in the pet food industry. It makes a number of canned pet foods, mainly for cats and dogs, as well as having a very promising line in dry dog food. It has been interested for some time in the operations of Pelican Ltd, an entity that deals with the processing of grain products for a number of other industries including flour-processing, health foods and, in more recent times, the production of grain products for feeding birds. Given its interest in the pet food industry and its desire to stay as one of the leaders in this area, Labrador Ltd began negotiations with Pelican Ltd to acquire its birdseed product division.

Negotiations began in July 2025. After months of discussion between the relevant parties of both companies, an agreement was reached on 15 February 2026 for Labrador Ltd to acquire the birdseed division. The agreement document was taken to the board of directors of Pelican Ltd who ratified the agreement on 1 March 2026. The net assets were exchanged on this date.

The net assets of the birdseed division at 1 March 2026, showing the carrying amounts at that date and the fair values as estimated by Labrador Ltd from documentation supplied by Pelican Ltd, were as shown below:

	Carrying amount	Fair value
Plant and equipment	$ 160,000	$ 167,000
Land	70,000	75,000
Motor vehicles	30,000	32,000
Inventory	24,000	28,000
Accounts receivable	18,000	16,000
Total assets	302,000	318,000

	Carrying amount	Fair value
Accounts payable	35,000	35,000
Bank overdraft	55,000	55,000
Total liabilities	90,000	90,000
Net assets	$212,000	$ 228,000

Details of the consideration Labrador Ltd agreed to provide in exchange for the net assets of the division are described below:

- 100,000 shares in Labrador Ltd — movements in the share price were as follows:

1 July 2025	$1.00
1 October 2025	1.10
1 January 2026	1.15
1 February 2026	1.30
15 February 2026	1.32
16 February 2026	1.45
1 March 2026	1.50

- Because of doubts as to whether it could sustain a share price of at least $1.50, Labrador Ltd agreed to supply cash to the value of any decrease in the share price below $1.50 for the 100,000 shares issued, this guarantee of the share price lasting until 31 July. Labrador Ltd believed that there was a 90% chance that the share price would remain at $1.50 or higher and a 10% chance that it would fall to $1.48.
- Cash of $40,000, half to be paid on the date of acquisition and half to be paid 1 year later.
- Supply of a patent relating to the manufacture of packing material. This has a fair value of $60,000 but has not been recognised in the records of Labrador Ltd because it resulted from an internally generated research project.
- Pelican Ltd was currently being sued for damages relating to a claim by a bird breeder who had bought some seed from the company, and claimed that this resulted in the death of some prime breeding pigeons. This uncertainty was delaying the negotiations so Labrador Ltd agreed to pay any resulting damages in relation to the court case. The expected damages were $40,000. Lawyers estimated that there was only a 20% chance of losing the case.

Labrador Ltd supplied the cash on the acquisition date as well as surrendering the patent. The shares were issued on 5 March, and the costs of issuing the shares amounted to $1,000. The incremental borrowing rate for Labrador Ltd is 10% p.a. Acquisition-related costs paid by Labrador Ltd in relation to the acquisition amounted to $5,000.

On 31 July the share price of Labrador Ltd's shares was $1.52.

On 31 August the lawsuit was settled out of court for $10,000, paid by Labrador Ltd.

Required

Prepare the journal entries in the records of the acquirer.

Solution

Acquisition analysis

Net fair value of assets acquired and liabilities assumed	
Plant and equipment	$ 167,000
Land	75,000
Motor vehicles	32,000
Inventory	28,000
Accounts receivable	16,000
	318,000
Accounts payable	35,000
Bank overdraft	55,000
Provision for damages (20% × $40,000)	8,000
	98,000
	$ 220,000

Consideration transferred

Purchase consideration:		
Shares: 100,000 × $1.50		$ 150,000
Guarantee: 10% ($1.50 − $1.48) × 100,000		200
Cash: Payable now		20,000
Deferred ($20,000 × 0.909,091)		18,182
Patent		60,000
		$ 248,382
Goodwill ($248,382 − $220,000)		$ 28,382

The journal entries of the acquirer, Labrador Ltd, are shown in figure 19.10.

FIGURE 19.10 Journal entries of the acquirer

2026				
March 1	Plant and Equipment	Dr	167,000	
	Land	Dr	75,000	
	Motor Vehicles	Dr	32,000	
	Inventory	Dr	28,000	
	Accounts Receivable	Dr	16,000	
	Goodwill	Dr	28,382	
	Accounts Payable	Cr		35,000
	Bank Overdraft	Cr		55,000
	Provision for Damages	Cr		8,000
	Share Capital	Cr		150,000
	Provision for Loss in Value of Shares	Cr		200
	Cash	Cr		20,000
	Consideration Payable	Cr		18,182
	Gain on Sale of Patent	Cr		60,000
	(Acquisition of birdseed division from Pelican Ltd)			
	Acquisition-Related Expenses	Dr	5,000	
	Cash	Cr		5,000
	(Acquisition-related costs)			
March 5	Share Capital	Dr	1,000	
	Cash	Cr		1,000
	(Costs of issuing shares)			
July 31	Provision for Loss in Value of Shares	Dr	200	
	Gain	Cr		200
	(Contingency not having to be paid)			
August 31	Provision for damages	Dr	8,000	
	Damages expenses	Dr	2,000	
	Cash	Cr		10,000

19.4 DISCLOSURE — BUSINESS COMBINATIONS

Paragraphs 59–63 of IFRS 3 contain information on disclosures required in relation to business combinations. To meet these disclosure requirements it is necessary to apply Appendix B of IFRS 3, which is an integral part of IFRS 3 containing application guidance.

Paragraph 59 requires entities to disclose information about the nature and financial effect of business combinations occurring during the current reporting period, or after the end of the reporting period but before the financial statements are authorised for issue. Paragraphs B64–B66 contain information to assist preparers to meet the disclosure objective in paragraph 59.

Note the qualitative information required to be disclosed under paragraph B64. In particular, note B64(d) which requires disclosure of the primary reasons for the business combination as well as a description of how the acquirer obtained control of the acquiree. This information should assist users to evaluate the success of the business combination and judge the ability of management to make investment decisions.

Also note that paragraph B64(e) requires disclosure of 'a qualitative description of the factors that make up goodwill recognised, such as expected synergies from combining operations of the acquiree and the acquirer, intangible assets that do not qualify for separate recognition or other factors'. Goodwill is not to be considered just a residual calculation. *As explained in section 19.2.4.3*, core goodwill can consist of elements such as combination goodwill and going-concern goodwill. An understanding of where the synergies exist will assist management in managing the earnings from goodwill as well as in any later impairment tests of goodwill *(see chapter 7 for more details concerning impairment testing)*. Unrecognised intangible assets may also be included in goodwill *(see chapter 6 for information on accounting for intangible assets in a business combination)*.

Quantitative disclosures are also required. In particular, paragraph B64(q) requires disclosure of (i) the amounts of revenue and profit or loss of the acquiree included in comprehensive income for the period and (ii) the amounts of revenue and profit or loss that would have been included if the business combination had occurred at the beginning of the annual reporting period.

Paragraph 61 of IFRS 3 requires the disclosure of information to assist in the evaluation of the financial effects of adjustments recognised in the current period that relate to business combinations occurring in previous periods. Paragraph B67 details disclosures required in meeting the information objective in paragraph 61.

Figure 19.11 illustrates the disclosures required by paragraph B64 and B67 for illustrative example 19.4.

FIGURE 19.11 IFRS 3 disclosures by Labrador Ltd for the year ended 30 June 2026

26. Business combinations		IFRS 3 paragraph
Acquisition of division from Pelican Ltd		
During the current reporting period, the company acquired the birdseed division of Pelican Ltd The acquisition date was 1 March 2026. The company has not had to dispose of any operations as a result of this combination. The primary reason for the business combination was to gain synergies in terms of the sales outlets for products sold by both entities.		B64(a) B64(b) B64(d)
The consideration transferred to Pelican Ltd was $248,382. The components of the cost were:		B64(f)
Shares in the company	$150,000	
Cash paid and payable	38,182	
Patent for packaging	60,000	
Guarantee relating to the maintenance of the company's share price	200	B64(g)(i)
The contingent consideration — the guarantee — was measured at acquisition date at $200 being based on an analysis of probable movements in share prices and budgeted information on future sales. The company issued 100,000 shares, determining a fair value of $1.50 based on the current market price of the company at 1 March 2026 as reported by the stock exchange.		B64(g)(ii) B64(f)(iv)
The assets acquired and liabilities assumed from Pelican Ltd were, as at 1 March 2026:		B64(i)

	Fair value
Plant and equipment	$167,000
Land	75,000
Motor vehicles	32,000
Inventory	28,000
Accounts receivable	16,000
	318,000
Accounts payable	35,000
Bank overdraft	55,000
	90,000
Contingent liability acquired	8,000
	98,000
Net assets acquired	$220,000

FIGURE 19.11 *(continued)*

		B64(h)
The contractual amount of receivables acquired is $18,000, with the uncollectable amount estimated at $2,000. Goodwill of $28,382 was recognised in the acquisition, the extra consideration being paid due to the excellent reputation and customer following relating to the quality of the birdseed products. None of the goodwill is tax deductible.		B64(e) B64(k)
The contingent liability acquired related to a court case involving a claim from a customer that certain bird food was of poor quality. If the court case were lost, which is not expected, the damages could be $40,000. A present obligation is regarded as existing at the end of the reporting period.		B64(j)
Subsequent to the end of the reporting period, the provision in relation to the company's guarantee in relation to maintenance of the share price expired. No extra payment was required, as the share price had been maintained.		B64(g)(iii)
Acquisition-related costs amounted to $5,000, all of which was recognised as an expense against the line item 'operating expenses'. Share issue costs of $1,000 were treated as a reduction in share capital.		B64(m)

27. Goodwill

	2026	2025	
Gross amount at beginning of period	$20,600	$19,600	B67(d)(i)
Accumulated impairment losses	500	300	
	20,100	19,300	
Goodwill acquired	28,382	3,000	B67(d)(ii)
	48,482	22,300	
Adjustments — tax assets recognised	—	2,000	B67(d)(iii)
		20,300	
Impairment losses for current period	—	200	B67(d)(v)
Carrying amount at end of period	$48,482	$20,100	
Consisting of:			
Gross amount at end of period	$48,982	$20,600	B67(d)(viii)
Accumulated impairment losses	500	500	
	$48,482	$20,100	

19.5 SUMMARY

IFRS 3 specifies accounting requirements for business combinations. While the standard applies to many different types of business combinations, this chapter focuses on business combinations in which one entity acquires a business from another entity, that is, where the assets and liabilities assumed constitute a business. The standard specifies how an acquirer accounts for the assets and liabilities acquired as well as the measurement of the consideration transferred. In making these calculations, the acquirer must determine the acquisition date as all fair value measurements are made at acquisition date. The identifiable assets and liabilities acquired are measured at fair value at the acquisition date. The standard interacts with other standards such as IAS 38 *Intangible Assets* and IAS 37 *Provisions, Contingent Liabilities and Contingent Assets* because the acquirer has to recognise intangible assets and liabilities acquired in a business combination. The nature and calculation of goodwill is also covered in this accounting standard, as is the treatment of a gain on a bargain purchase.

Goodwill or the gain on a bargain purchase is determined as a residual which, for the business combinations considered in this chapter, is generally determined by comparing the consideration transferred and the net fair value of the identifiable assets and liabilities acquired. Understanding the nature of goodwill is essential to understanding how to account for it. With the existence of the accounting standard on impairment of assets, goodwill is not required to be amortised. Where a bargain purchase arises, the gain is recognised in current period profit or loss.

On 1 January 2026, Trevally Ltd concluded agreements to take over the operations of Mackerel Ltd. The statements of financial position of the two companies as at that date were:

	Trevally Ltd	Mackerel Ltd
Cash	$ 20,000	$ 1,000
Accounts receivable	35,000	19,000
Inventory	52,000	26,500
Property, plant and equipment (net)	280,500	149,500
Debentures in Hangi Ltd	64,000	18,000
	$ 451,500	$ 214,000
Accounts payable	$ 78,000	$ 76,000
Loan payable	—	40,000
Share capital — issued at $1	300,000	80,000
Retained earnings	73,500	18,000
	$ 451,500	$ 214,000

Mackerel Ltd included in the notes to its accounts a contingent liability relating to a guarantee for a loan. Although a present obligation existed, a liability was not recognised by Mackerel Ltd because of the difficulty of measuring the ultimate amount to be paid.

The details of the acquisition agreements are as follows.

Mackerel Ltd
Trevally Ltd is to acquire all the assets (except cash) and assume all the liabilities of Mackerel Ltd. In consideration Trevally Ltd agreed to pay consideration to Mackerel Ltd comprising $25,000 in cash and 60,000 ordinary shares. Each share in Trevally Ltd has a fair value of $1.80. The assets of Mackerel Ltd are all recorded in Mackerel Ltd's records at cost (depreciated if applicable). The fair values of Mackerel Ltd's assets are:

Receivables	$ 17,500
Inventory	32,000
Property, plant and equipment	165,500
Debentures in Hangi Ltd	19,000

Mackerel Ltd had been undertaking research into new manufacturing machinery, and had expensed a total of $10,000 research costs. Trevally Ltd determined that the fair value of this in-process research was $2,000 at acquisition date. The contingent liability relating to the guarantee was considered to have a fair value of $1,500.

Trevally Ltd incurred costs amounting to $3,000 for external accounting advice and valuers' fees in relation to the acquisition.

Required

Prepare the acquisition analysis and journal entries necessary to record the business combination.

Solution

Prepare acquisition analyses and journal entries
The first step is to analyse the nature of the business combination, in particular what happens to each entity involved in the transactions. In this example, Trevally Ltd is the acquirer. It acquires assets and liabilities of Mackerel Ltd.

Considering the combination between Trevally Ltd and Mackerel Ltd, the first step is to prepare an acquisition analysis. This involves looking at the two sides of the transaction, determining the fair value of the identifiable assets acquired and liabilities assumed and calculating the consideration transferred. The difference between these two amounts will be goodwill or gain on bargain purchase.

Acquisition analysis
Trevally Ltd acquired all the assets except cash, and assumed all the liabilities of Mackerel Ltd. These assets and liabilities are now measured at fair value.

Accounts receivable	$ 17,500	
Inventory	32,000	
Property, plant and equipment	165,500	
Debentures in Hangi Ltd	19,000	
In-process research	2,000	
	236,000	
Provision for guarantee	1,500	
Loan payable	40,000	
Accounts payable	76,000	
	117,500	
Net fair value	$ 118,500	

Consideration transferred

The consideration transferred is the purchase consideration payable to Mackerel Ltd and is measured as the sum of the fair values of shares issued, liabilities undertaken and assets given up by the acquirer. In this example, Trevally Ltd issues shares and gives up cash. The share price is the fair value of the shares at the acquisition date.

Consideration transferred		
Shares issued by Trevally Ltd	60,000 × $ 1.80	$ 108,000
Cash		25,000
Consideration transferred		$ 133,000

The consideration transferred is then compared with the net fair value of the identifiable assets and liabilities acquired to determine whether goodwill or a gain arises. In this case the consideration transferred is greater; hence, goodwill has been acquired.

$$Goodwill = \$133,000 - \$118,500 = \underline{\underline{\$14,500}}$$

The general journal entries in Trevally Ltd can then be read from the acquisition analysis. Note that when shares are issued the relevant account is 'Share Capital'.

Accounts Receivable	Dr	17,500	
Inventory	Dr	32,000	
Property, Plant and Equipment	Dr	165,500	
Debentures in Hangi Ltd	Dr	19,000	
In-process Research	Dr	2,000	
Goodwill	Dr	14,500	
Accounts Payable	Cr		76,000
Loan Payable	Cr		40,000
Provision for Guarantee	Cr		1,500
Share Capital	Cr		108,000
Cash	Cr		25,000
(Acquisition of net assets of Mackerel Ltd)			
Acquisition-Related Expenses	Dr	3,000	
Cash	Cr		3,000
(Acquisition-related costs)			

On 1 July 2026, Smetana Ltd and Bay Ltd sign an agreement whereby the operations of Bay Ltd are to be taken over by Smetana Ltd. The statements of financial position of the two companies on that day were as shown below.

	Smetana Ltd	Bay Ltd
Cash	$ 50,000	$ 20,000
Accounts receivable	75,000	56,000
Inventory	46,000	29,000
Land	65,000	—
Plant and equipment	180,000	167,000
Accumulated depreciation — plant and equipment	(60,000)	(40,000)
Patents	10,000	
Shares in Cape Ltd	—	26,000
Debentures in Brett Ltd (nominal value)	10,000	—
	$ 376,000	$ 258,000
Accounts payable	$ 62,000	$ 31,000
Mortgage loan	75,000	21,500
10% debentures (face value)	100,000	30,000
Contributed equity:		
Ordinary shares of $1, fully paid	100,000	100,000
Retained earnings	39,000	75,500
	$ 376,000	$ 258,000

Smetana Ltd is to acquire all the assets of Bay Ltd (except for cash). The assets of Bay Ltd are recorded at their fair values except for:

	Carrying amount	Fair value
Inventory	$ 29,000	$ 39,200
Plant and equipment	127,000	155,000
Shares in Cape Ltd	26,000	22,500

The consideration is as follows:
   Smetana Ltd will issue 20,000 7% redeemable debentures to Bay Ltd. The fair value of each debenture is $3.50 at the date of the acquisition.
   Smetana Ltd will transfer one of its patents to Bay Ltd. The patent will give the holder a claim on future royalties. The patent is carried at $4,000 in the records of Smetana Ltd, but is considered to have a fair value of $5,000.
   Smetana Ltd will issue 40,000 ordinary shares to Bay Ltd. The fair value of each Smetana Ltd share is $2.70. Costs to issue these shares amount to $900.
   Smetana Ltd is to provide Bay Ltd with $86,700 in cash.
   Costs incurred in arranging the business combination amounted to $1,600.

Required

Prepare an acquisition analysis for the business combination.
   Prepare the journal entries in the records of Smetana Ltd to record the acquisition of the business conducted by Bay Ltd.

Solution

Prepare the journal entries of Smetana Ltd
   The nature of the transaction in this question is that the acquirer, Smetana Ltd, is acquiring the operations (assets and liabilities) of Bay Ltd.
   The first step is to prepare the acquisition analysis, which is a comparison of the fair value of the identifiable assets acquired and liabilities assumed with the consideration transferred.

Acquisition analysis
Note that all the assets acquired and the liabilities assumed by the acquirer are measured at fair value.

Accounts receivable	$ 56,000	
Inventory	39,200	
Plant and equipment	155,000	
Shares in Cape Ltd	22,500	
	$272,700	

Consideration transferred

The consideration transferred is measured by calculating the fair value of the assets given up, liabilities undertaken and shares issued by the acquirer. In this example, the acquirer issues shares and debentures in itself, gives up a patent and provides cash.

Purchase consideration
Shareholders

Debentures:	Debentures in Smetana	20,000 × $3.50		$ 70,000
Shares:	Shares in Smetana	40,000 × $2.70		108,000
Patent				5,000
Cash				86,700
Total consideration transferred				269,700

Because the total consideration transferred is less than the net fair value of the identifiable assets and liabilities acquired, the acquirer has to assess the measurements undertaken in the acquisition analysis. Having been assured that all relevant assets and liabilities have been included and that the fair values are reliable, the difference is then accounted for as a bargain purchase, and is included in current period profit or loss.

Gain on bargain purchase [$272,700 − $269,700] $3,000

The general journal entries can then be read from the acquisition analysis. Note that when shares are issued the relevant account is 'Share Capital'.

In relation to the patent, prior to accounting for the business combination, the acquirer remeasures the asset to fair value.

Patent	Dr	1,000	
Gain	Cr		1,000
(Remeasurement to fair value as part of consideration transferred on business combination)			
Accounts Receivable	Dr	56,000	
Inventory	Dr	39,200	
Property, Plant and Equipment	Dr	155,000	
Shares in Cape Ltd	Dr	22,500	
7% Debentures	Cr		70,000
Cash	Cr		86,700
Share Capital	Cr		108,000
Patent	Cr		5,000
Gain on Bargain Purchase	Cr		3,000
(Acquisition of net assets of Bay Ltd)			
Acquisition-Related Expenses	Dr	1,600	
Cash	Cr		1,600
(Acquisition-related costs)			
Share Capital	Dr	900	
Cash	Cr		900
(Payment of share issue costs)			

Note that the costs of share issue reduce the share capital issued with the Share Capital account then showing the net proceeds from share issues.

Discussion questions

1. What is meant by a 'business combination'?
2. Discuss the importance of identifying the acquisition date.
3. What is meant by 'contingent consideration' and how is it accounted for?
4. Explain the key components of 'core' goodwill.
5. What recognition criteria are applied to assets acquired and liabilities assumed in a business combination?
6. How is an acquirer identified?
7. Explain the key steps in the acquisition method.
8. How is the consideration transferred calculated?
9. How is a gain on bargain purchase accounted for?
10. What is the purpose of the disclosure requirements in IFRS 3?

References

Johnson, L. T., & Petrone, K. R. 1998, 'Is goodwill an asset?', *Accounting Horizons*, vol. 12, no. 3, pp. 293–303.

Leo, K. J., Hoggett, J. R., and Radford, J. 1995, *Accounting for identifiable intangibles and goodwill*, Australian Society of Certified Practising Accountants, Melbourne.

One of the interesting questions about business combinations is whether managerial discretion plays a role in the target's acquisition price. One context where this may be the case is when the acquisition is funded by stock-for-stock swap. Here managers of the acquiring firm may attempt to inflate earnings to increase the price of their stock. This, in turn, can produce a more favourable exchange ratio for the acquiring firm's shareholders. Erickson and Wang (1999) examine this question for 55 stock-for-stock mergers that took place between 1985 and 1990. Earnings management is captured by abnormal accruals and is shown to increase in the quarters preceding the merger announcement, but decrease following the announcement. To enhance the strength of the conclusion that earnings management is present mostly in stock-for stock acquisitions, the authors also analyse 64 cash deals, but do not find similar results. Louis (2004) extends this line of inquiry to mergers between 1992 and 2000 comprising 236 stock swaps and 137 cash deals. He finds that stock-swap acquirers experienced negative abnormal returns in the 2 years prior to the merger announcement. This poor performance may have exerted pressure on managers to manipulate earnings. Consistent with this, Louis (2004) finds strong evidence of greater earnings management in the quarter preceding the merger announcement in stock acquirers than cash acquirers. Additionally, he finds that abnormal stock returns in the 3 years following the merger are negatively related to the measure of abnormal accruals in the quarter preceding the announcement. This is consistent with successful earnings management by managers of stock swap-acquirers. Moreover, the evidence suggests that market participants do not fully understand the effect of pre-merger announcement earnings management.

As business combinations represent a major corporate event, investors would benefit from additional disclosures that could help them form expectations about future performance. Shalev (2009) assembles a sample of 297 acquiring firms involved in 1019 acquisitions between 1 July 2001 to 31 December 2004 to examine what determines the level of disclosure. He posits that acquirers that are more confident about the acquisition outcome would tend to be more forthcoming in their disclosures. He finds that disclosure levels are negatively related to the amount of goodwill recognised. This is consistent with goodwill capturing overpayment and hence bad news that acquirers would like to withhold. Acquirers that provide more disclosure also tend to report higher ROA in the year of acquisition and the following year. Consistent with Shalev's (2009) hypothesis, these acquirers also experience positive abnormal stock returns in the year following the filing of the annual report for the acquisition year.

Another question is whether earnings management plays a role in the allocation of the purchase consideration to net assets and goodwill. Under IFRS® Standards, the purchase consideration is allocated to goodwill after the fair value of net assets acquired is determined. This implies a one-to-one substitution effect between fair value adjustments and goodwill. For example, allocating purchase consideration to higher fair value of depreciable assets would reduce goodwill as well as future profits owing to higher depreciation. The opposite is also true since goodwill is not amortised. Shalev et al. (2013) explore how managerial compensation affects this price allocation. They examine 320 acquisitions between 2001 and 2008 and test for the association between a CEO's cash bonus (which is typically based on accounting numbers) and the percentage of the purchase price that is allocated to goodwill and intangibles with indefinite life. Shalev et al. (2013) provide evidence that suggests that greater bonus intensity is positively associated with the percentage of purchase price that is allocated to goodwill and intangibles with indefinite life. This is consistent with managers of acquiring firms using discretion to allocate a greater fraction of the purchase price to assets that are not subject to depreciation and amortisation which, in turn, boosts future profits.

Since goodwill is the difference between price paid and fair value of net assets acquired, it is not clear what its economic meaning is. Furthermore, insofar as goodwill is manipulated, it is interesting to see if it has any predictive value and whether its power to predict future performance is moderated by managerial discretion. These questions are addressed by Lee (2011). Lee (2011) first establishes that goodwill is positively related to 1 year ahead operating cash flows. This provides support to the view that goodwill is an asset. Importantly, this relation is not found to be sensitive to the degree of managerial discretion.

The above-mentioned studies are based on US samples; not much academic research has been conducted into IFRS 3. One of the few studies to do so is Glaum et al. (2013) who examine the degree of compliance with the disclosure requirements of IFRS 3 and IAS 36, the latter governing goodwill impairment rules. They examine compliance in a sample of 357 European firms involved in acquisitions in 2005 — the year when IFRS® Standards became mandatory in the EU. Glaum et al. (2013) develop a 100-item disclosure checklist that is based on the requirements of the two standards. Compliance is found to vary across countries, industries and auditor type. For example, Switzerland shows the highest level of compliance and Austria the lowest. Companies audited by big audit firms tend to comply more than companies audited by smaller auditors. Glaum et al. (2013) further find from a multivariate analysis that compliance increases with the size of recorded goodwill. A second study of IFRS 3 is Hamberg et al. (2011) who examine IFRS 3 adoption in a sample of Swedish firms. They find that goodwill-intensive firms experience higher stock returns than no-goodwill firms upon adoption of IFRS 3. It is not clear, however, if investors correctly interpret goodwill as a signal of better performance.

As noted in the chapter, IFRS 3 also mandates extensive qualitative disclosures. However, Amel-Zadeh et al. (2023) conclude that such disclosures are unsatisfactory. There may be several factors affecting the level of disclosures, one of which is the magnitude of goodwill relative to the overall purchase price. Florio et al. (2018) find that firms that allocate an unusually large proportion of the purchase price to goodwill, tend to disclose less.

References

Amel-Zadeh, A., Glaum, M. and Sellhorn, T., 2023. Empirical goodwill research: insights, issues, and implications for standard setting and future research. *European Accounting Review*, 32(2), pp.415–446.

Erickson, M., and Wang, S. W. 1999. Earnings management by acquiring firms in stock for stock mergers. Journal of Accounting and Economics, 27(2), 149–176.

Florio, C., Lionzo, A. and Corbella, S., 2018. Beyond firm-level determinants: The effect of M&A features on the extent of M&A disclosure. *Journal of International Accounting Research*, 17(3), pp.87–113.

Glaum, M., Schmidt, P., Street, D. L., and Vogel, S. 2013. Compliance with IFRS 3- and IAS 36-required disclosures across 17 European countries: Company- and country-level determinants. *Accounting and Business Research*, 43(3), 163–204.

Hamberg, M., Paananen, M., and Novak, J. 2011. The adoption of IFRS 3: The effects of managerial discretion and stock market reactions. *European Accounting Review*, 20(2), 263–288.

Lee, C. 2011. The effect of SFAS 142 on the ability of goodwill to predict future cash flows. *Journal of Accounting and Public Policy*, 30(3), 236–255.

Louis, H. 2004. Earnings management and the market performance of acquiring firms. *Journal of Financial Economics*, 74(1), 121–148.

Shalev, R. 2009. The information content of business combination disclosure level. *The Accounting Review*, 84(1), 239–270.

Shalev, R., Zhang, I. X., and Zhang, Y. 2013. CEO compensation and fair value accounting: Evidence from purchase price allocation. *Journal of Accounting Research*, 51(4), 819–854.

Part 4

Economic Entities

20 Consolidation: controlled entities 525

21 Consolidation: wholly owned subsidiaries 539

22 Consolidation: intragroup transactions 561

23 Consolidation: non-controlling interest 585

24 Translation of foreign currency transactions
and the financial statements of foreign entities 625

20 Consolidation: controlled entities

ACCOUNTING STANDARDS IN FOCUS	*IFRS 3 Business Combinations*
	IFRS 10 Consolidated Financial Statements;

LEARNING OBJECTIVES

After studying this chapter, you should be able to:

 explain the meaning of consolidated financial statements

 discuss the meaning and application of the criterion of control

 discuss which entities should prepare consolidated financial statements

 understand the relationship between a parent and an acquirer in a business combination

 explain the differences in disclosure requirements between single entities and consolidated entities.

20.1 INTRODUCTION

The purpose of this chapter is to discuss the preparation of a single set of financial statements, referred to as the consolidated financial statements. The preparation of consolidated financial statements views the group as the economic entity that is of interest to users of financial statements. It involves combining the financial statements of the individual entities so that they show the financial position and financial performance of the group of entities, presented as if they were a single economic entity.

The first issue covered in this chapter is the determination of which entities are required to prepare consolidated financial statements. This involves a discussion of the criterion for consolidation and its application to economic situations. The second issue in this chapter is the accounting procedures for preparing the consolidated financial statements. The application in this chapter is to a very simple group structure involving two entities, one of which owns all the issued shares in the other. Further issues associated with the preparation of consolidated financial statements are discussed in the chapters that follow (*see chapters 21–23*).

The accounting standards governing the preparation of consolidated financial statements are IFRS 3 *Business Combinations* issued in 2008 and IFRS 10 *Consolidated Financial Statements* issued in 2011. The objective of IFRS 3, as stated in paragraph 1, is to guide acquirers of other business in the recognition and measurement of assets acquired, liabilities assumed and how to measure non-controlling interests in the acquired company. In such acquisitions the price paid often differs from the fair value of net assets acquired giving rise to recognition of goodwill, and in some exceptional cases a gain on bargain purchase. IFRS 3 therefore sets the rules for measuring this goodwill or exceptional gain. Finally, IFRS 3 sets out the information that should be disclosed in relation to financial effects of business combinations.

The objective of IFRS 10 is stated in paragraph 1:

> to establish principles for the presentation and preparation of consolidated financial statements when an entity controls one or more other entities.

To achieve this, IFRS 10 then:

- requires a parent to present consolidated financial statements
- establishes control as the criterion for consolidation
- defines the criterion of control
- provides guidance on identifying when one entity controls another
- sets out the accounting requirements for the preparation of consolidated financial statements.

20.2 CONSOLIDATED FINANCIAL STATEMENTS

Consolidated financial statements are defined in Appendix A of IFRS 10 as follows:

> The financial statements of a **group** in which the assets, liabilities, equity, income, expenses and cash flows of the **parent** and its **subsidiaries** are presented as those of a single economic entity.

Consider figure 20.1. P Ltd has investments in several other companies. A shareholder's wealth in P Ltd is dependent not only on how well P Ltd performs, but also on the performance of the other entities in which P Ltd has an investment. Rather than require a shareholder in P Ltd to analyse each of the companies in the economic group, if P Ltd prepared a set of financial statements by adding together the financial statements of all entities in the group, this would assist investors in P Ltd to analyse their investment. Assuming that one share equals one voting right, it is clear that P Ltd can decide how to run S1, S2 and S3. Specifically, P Ltd owns 70% of S1. S1, in turn, controls S2, by the virtue of having 60% of the voting rights, thus enabling P Ltd to run S2 Ltd as it wishes even though the economic interest of P Ltd in S2 Ltd is only 42% (70% × 60%). P Ltd also owns and controls 100% of S3 Ltd.

Consolidated financial statements perform this function as they add together the financial statements of all entities within an economic entity. As stated in paragraph B86 of IFRS 10, consolidated financial statements 'combine like items of assets, liabilities, equity, income, expenses and cash flows' of the entities in the group.

This process of adding the financial statements together can be seen in its simplest form in figure 20.2. In this example there are two entities in the group, P Ltd and S Ltd. The consolidated financial statements are prepared by adding together the assets and liabilities of both entities. In chapter 21 a consolidation worksheet is used to perform this addition process.

This aggregation process is subject to several adjustments, and these are covered in detail in later chapters. However, in this chapter, the process of consolidation should be seen simply as a process of aggregation of the financial statements of all entities within the group. Note that the consolidation process does *not* involve making adjustments to the individual financial statements or the accounts of the entities in the group. This is because the individual companies within the group remain separate legal entities. The consolidated financial statements are an additional set of financial statements and are prepared using a worksheet to facilitate the addition and adjustment process.

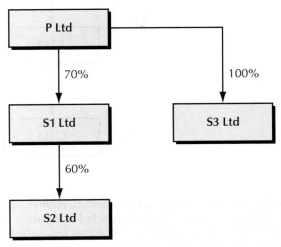

FIGURE 20.1 A group of entities

Note the focus of figure 20.2 is on the summation of assets and liabilities across the balance sheets of P and S after excluding P's investment in S. As a result, and as explained in chapter 21, the consolidated sum of net assets is therefore equal to P's equity.

The consolidated financial statements consist of a consolidated statement of financial position (i.e. the balance sheet), consolidated statement of profit or loss and other comprehensive income, a consolidated statement of changes in equity, and a consolidated statement of cash flows.

The following definitions are contained in Appendix A of IFRS 10:

Group	A **parent** and its **subsidiaries.**
Parent	An entity that **controls** one or more entities.
Subsidiary	An entity that is controlled by another entity.

The consolidated financial statements combine the financial statements of all the entities within a group. The entities in the group consist of two types; namely, parent and subsidiary. There is only one parent in a group, which is the controlling entity; that is, the entity that controls all other entities in the group. *Section 20.2* discusses the meaning of control. All other entities in the group — the controlled entities — are called subsidiaries. Hence, in figure 20.1, assuming that P Ltd controls all other companies in the figure, P Ltd is the parent entity, and all other entities in the group are subsidiaries.

FIGURE 20.2 The consolidation process

	P Ltd		S Ltd		Consolidation of P Ltd and S Ltd
Non-current assets*	150,000	+	120,000	=	270,000
Current assets	50,000	+	20,000	=	70,000
Total assets	200,000		140,000		340,000
Total liabilities	(80,000)	+	(30,000)	=	(110,000)
Net assets	$120,000		$110,000		$ 230,000

*Excluding P Ltd's investment in S Ltd (*explained in chapter 21*)

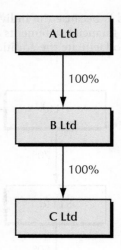

```
        ┌──────────┐
        │  A Ltd   │
        └──────────┘
              │
              │ 100%
              ▼
        ┌──────────┐
        │  B Ltd   │
        └──────────┘
              │
              │ 100%
              ▼
        ┌──────────┐
        │  C Ltd   │
        └──────────┘
```

FIGURE 20.3 Multiple groups

Note that for a number of entities that are interconnected there may be a number of groups. Consider figure 20.3. If B Ltd controls C Ltd, then B Ltd is a parent and C Ltd is its subsidiary, and together they form a group. If A Ltd controls both B Ltd and C Ltd, then A Ltd is a parent and both B Ltd and C Ltd are its subsidiaries, and all together they form a group.

20.2.1 Reasons for consolidation

There are several reasons why consolidated financial statements are prepared:

1. *Supply of relevant information.* The information obtained from the consolidated financial statements is relevant to investors in the parent entity. These investors have an interest in the group as a whole, not just in the parent entity. To require these investors to source their information from the financial statements of each of the entities comprising the group would place a large cost burden on the investors.
2. *Comparable information.* Some entities are organised into a group structure such that different activities are undertaken by separate members of the group. Other entities are organised differently, with some having all activities conducted within the one entity. For an investor to make useful comparisons between entities, access to consolidated financial statements makes the comparative analysis an easier task.
3. *Accountability.* A key purpose for all financial reporting is the discharge of accountability by management. Entities that are responsible or accountable for managing a pool of resources, being the recipients of economic benefits and responsible for payment of obligations, are generally required to report on their activities, and are held accountable for the management of those activities. The management of the parent entity is not just responsible for the management of the assets and liabilities of the parent itself. As the parent controls the assets of all subsidiaries, the assets under the control of the parent entity's management are the assets of the group. The consolidated financial statements report the assets under the control of the group management as well as the claims on those assets.
4. *Reporting of risks and benefits.* There are risks associated with managing an entity, and an entity rarely obtains control of another without obtaining significant opportunities to benefit from that control. The consolidated financial statements allow an assessment of these risks and benefits at a group level.

Notwithstanding these advantages, it should be noted that the aggregation process of the consolidation results in little information being available for the individual subsidiaries. Hence, users of consolidated financial statements would not normally be able to identify individual subsidiaries that exhibit better or worse financial position and performance.

20.3 CONTROL AS THE CRITERION FOR CONSOLIDATION

In Appendix A of IFRS 10, a parent is defined as an entity that *controls* one or more entities while a subsidiary is a controlled entity. The entity that is responsible for preparing the consolidated financial statements is the parent. An entity must then determine when it is a parent and which entities it controls. The determination of whether one entity controls another is crucial to the determination of which entities need to prepare consolidated financial statements. Paragraph 5 of IFRS 10 notes that 'an investor' must determine whether it is a parent by assessing whether it controls an 'investee'.

Under IFRS 10, the criterion for consolidation is control. It should first be noted that determination of whether control exists is a matter of judgement. In many situations it will not be clear cut that one entity controls another, and determination will have to be made by considering all available facts and circumstances (paragraph 8 of IFRS 10). As noted later in this section, IFRS 10 provides numerous factors to be considered in making the decision concerning the existence of control. Hence, it is important to understand the meaning of the term 'control' and what evidence may be accumulated to determine its existence or non-existence in specific circumstances. Further, if those circumstances change, there may be a need to assess whether control still exists.

Second, note that control is an exclusionary power. In a group there can be only one parent. If two or more investors join together to direct the activities of the investees, neither investor controls the investee — decision-making ability cannot be shared.

Control of an investee is defined in Appendix A of IFRS 10 as follows:

> An investor controls an investee when the investor is exposed, or has rights, to variable returns from its involvement with the investee and has the ability to affect those returns through its power over the investee.

Paragraph 7 of IFRS 10 identifies three elements, all of which must be held by an investor in order for it to have control, namely:
1. power over the investee
2. exposure, or rights, to variable returns from its involvement with the investee
3. the ability to use its power over the investee to affect the amount of the investor's returns. These three elements are discussed in detail in the following sections.

20.3.1 Power

Power is defined in Appendix A of IFRS 10 as follows:

> Existing rights that give the current ability to direct the *relevant activities*.

Note the key features of this definition.

Power arises from rights

These rights generally arise from some form of legal contract. For example, the rights that are held by the owner of an ordinary share in a company may include voting rights, rights to dividends or rights on liquidation of the company. Rights could also exist because of a contract between one entity and another entity. For example, an entity might engage another entity to manage its activities — the latter entity then has management rights but potentially no rights to dividends. The rights that are of importance in determining whether power exists are those relating to the ability to direct the relevant activities of an investee. Rights in relation to purely administration tasks are not rights that affect power. Examples of rights that affect who has power are listed in paragraph B15 of IFRS 10, namely:
- voting rights
- rights to appoint, reassign or remove members of an investee's key management personnel
- rights to appoint or remove another entity that participates in management decisions
- rights to direct the investee to enter into, or veto any changes to, transactions that affect the investee's returns.

Some questions that could be asked to assist in determining whether certain rights give rise to power are as follows (based on paragraph B18 of IFRS 10):
- Can the investor appoint or approve the investee's key management personnel who direct the relevant activities?
- Can the investor direct the investee to enter into or veto any changes to significant transactions that affect the investor's returns?
- Can the investor dominate either the nominations process of electing members of the investee's governing body or the obtaining of proxies from other holders of voting rights?

The rights must also be *substantive* rights. According to paragraph B22 of IFRS 10, for rights to be substantive the holders must have the practical ability to exercise the rights; that is, there are no barriers to the holders exercising the rights. The rights need to give the holder the current ability to direct the relevant activities when decisions about those activities need to be made.

As judgement is required in assessing whether rights are substantive, paragraph B23 of IFRS 10 provides some factors to consider in making that determination:
- whether the party or parties that hold the rights would benefit from the exercise of those rights, for example, potential voting rights.
- whether there are any barriers — economic or otherwise — that prevent a holder from the exercising of rights. Examples of such barriers are financial penalties, terms and conditions that make it unlikely that rights will be exercised, and the absence of specialised services necessary for exercising the rights. Paragraph B23(a) of IFRS 10 provides a detailed list of possible barriers.
- where more than one party is involved, whether there is a mechanism in place to enable those parties to practically exercise the rights.

If the rights are purely protective rights, the holder does not have power (paragraph 14). Protective rights are defined in Appendix A of IFRS 10 as follows:

Rights designed to protect the interest of the party holding those rights without giving that party power over the entity to which those rights relate.

Paragraph B28 of IFRS 10 provides examples of protective rights, which include:

(a) a lender's right to restrict a borrower from undertaking activities that could significantly change the credit risk of the borrower to the detriment of the lender.
(b) the right of a party holding a non-controlling interest in an investee to approve capital expenditure greater than that required in the ordinary course of business, or to approve the issue of equity or debt instruments.
(c) the right of a lender to seize the assets of a borrower if the borrower fails to meet specified loan repayment conditions.

A non-controlling interest is equity in a subsidiary not attributable to a parent. For example, if a parent owns 80% of the shares of a subsidiary, then the non-controlling interest in the subsidiary is 20%.

Power is the ability to direct

IFRS 10 stresses the point that control is the power to direct the activities of another entity. For example, Entity C may have two owners — Entity A that owns 55% of the shares in Entity C and Entity B that holds the remaining 45% of issued shares. Entity A may not be actively involved in the management of C while Entity B has been an active investor. Still, A has the power (ability) to control; hence it will be the parent company for consolidation purposes.

The ability to direct must be current

The investor must be able to exercise its rights to direct at the time decisions are made concerning the activities of an investee. However, there are circumstances where power is still held by an investor even though there may be a time period to pass, or an activity that needs to be undertaken, before the right to direct can be currently exercisable. Paragraph B24 of IFRS 10 provides examples of these circumstances. One example is:

An investor holds an option to acquire the majority of shares in an investee that is exercisable in 25 days and that would generate a profit for the investor upon exercising the option; that is, the value of the share exceeds the exercise price. A special meeting to change existing policies requires 30 days' notice. The existing shareholders cannot change existing policies before the exercise of the option. The investor has a substantive right that gives them the current ability to direct the relevant activities even before the option is exercised.

In contrast, assume the investor held a forward contract to acquire the majority of shares at a settlement date in 6 months' time. The existing shareholders would have the current ability to direct the activities of the investee as they can change the existing policies before the forward contract is settled.

It is relevant activities that are directed

Relevant activities are defined in Appendix A of IFRS 10 as:

activities of the investee that significantly affect the investee's returns.

The determination of relevant activities may change over time and differ between entities; hence it may be necessary to analyse the purpose and design of an investee. For many investees, the relevant decisions are those that govern the financial and operating policies of the investee. Paragraph B11 of IFRS 10 provides examples of some possible relevant activities, including:
• selling and purchasing goods and services
• managing financial assets
• selecting, acquiring and disposing of assets
• researching and developing new products
• determining a funding structure or obtaining funding.

To have power, an investor need not be able to make any decision it likes in relation to an investee, as the investor is constrained by corporate and contract laws under which the interests of non-controlling investors, creditors and others are protected.

Level of share ownership

Ownership of ordinary shares in a company normally provides voting rights that enable the holder of the majority of shares to dominate the appointment of directors or an entity's governing board. As paragraph B35 of IFRS 10 states, where an investor holds more than half of the voting rights of an investee, the investor has power providing:

(a) the relevant activities are directed by a vote of the holder of the majority of voting rights, or
(b) a majority of the members of the governing body that directs the relevant activities are appointed by a vote of the holder of the majority of the voting rights.

Hence, in the absence of other evidence, where an investor holds a majority of voting shares that investor would be considered to have power over the investee.

Where an investor holds less than 50% of the shares of an investee, the determination of whether the investor has power over the investee is more difficult. In determining the existence of power, it is necessary to examine the potential actions of the holders of the other shares in the investee. Some factors to assist in this process are:

- *Size of the voting interest.* The more voting shares an investor has, the more likely it is that it will have power. A further consideration is the number of shareholders who hold the remaining voting shares and the extent of their holdings. Where the remaining voting shares are held by a large number of shareholders, each holding a small number of shares, the probability of these other shareholders getting together to outvote the shareholder who holds a substantial proportion, but not a majority, of the shares must be considered. Note that, where the remaining shares are held by a small number of shareholders, the probability that they could get together and outvote the holder of the large parcel of shares is higher. Paragraphs B44–B45 of IFRS 10 provide examples of these circumstances.

  In the first example, investor A holds 45% of the voting rights of an investee. Two other investors each hold 26% of the voting rights of the investee. The remaining voting rights are held by investors who hold less than 1% each. There are no other arrangements that affect decision making. In this case, consideration of the size of investor A's voting interest and its relative size to the other shareholdings is sufficient to conclude that investor A does not have power. The two investors who hold 26% each would need to cooperate to be able to prevent investor A from controlling the investee.

  In the second example, an investor holds 40% of the voting rights of an investee, with the next two largest holdings of voting rights being 10% and 4%. The remaining voting rights are held by thousands of shareholders, none holding more than 1% of the voting rights. None of the shareholders has any arrangements to consult each other or make collective decisions. In this case, on the basis of the absolute size of its holding and the relative size of the other shareholdings, the investor has a sufficiently dominant voting interest to meet the power criterion without the need to consider any other evidence of power.

- *Attendance at annual general meetings.* Although all shareholders may attend general meetings and vote in matters relating to governance of the entity, it is rare for this to occur. If, therefore, only 60% of the eligible votes are cast at a general meeting and an entity has more than a 30% interest in that entity, it can cast the majority of votes at that meeting. It then has power over that entity.

- *The existence of contracts.* As noted in paragraph B39 of IFRS 10, the contractual arrangement between an investor and other holders of shares may give the investor sufficient voting rights to give the investor power. An example of such a contract is provided in application example 5 of paragraph B43 of IFRS 10:

  Investor A holds 40% of voting rights of an investee and twelve other investors each hold 5% of voting rights of the investee. A shareholder agreement grants investor A the right to appoint, remove and set the remuneration of management responsible for directing the relevant activities.

  In this case, consideration of the absolute size of the investor's holding and the relative size of the other shareholdings alone is not conclusive to determine the investor has rights sufficient to give it power. However, the fact that investor A has the contractual right to appoint, remove and set the compensation of key management is sufficient to conclude that investor A has power over the investee. The fact that investor A might not have exercised this right yet or the likelihood of investor A exercising their right to select, appoint or remove key management should not be considered when assessing whether investor A has power.

- *Level of disorganisation or apathy of the remaining shareholders.* This factor is affected by the dispersion of the shareholders, and reflected in their attendance at general meetings. Holders of small parcels of shares are often not organised into forming voting blocks. Shareholders with environmental or ethical concerns may be less apathetic about the actions of an entity and its management policies, and may form voting blocks.

The assessment of the existence of power where the investor holds less than a majority of voting shares is difficult and requires judgement. In many cases that assessment relies on an analysis of the non-action of other shareholders. Do the non-voting shareholders at an annual general meeting not vote because they are happy with the management ability of the investor, as opposed to being apathetic? Would they be willing to combine to outvote the investor if the latter's decisions were considered untenable? The success of the investee under the control of the investor is a further measure of the potential for generally passive shareholders to be sufficiently concerned to cast a vote at the next annual general meeting. When an investee is performing poorly, the interest of shareholders as well as their willingness to become involved generally increases. Poor performance with resultant lowering of share prices may also result in a current or new shareholder acquiring a large block of shares and changing the voting mix at general meetings.

Numerous problems arise in applying the concept of power under IFRS 10. First, there is the question of temporary control. Where the investor holds more than 50% of the voting shares of the investee, there is no danger of a change in the identity of the parent. However, if the identification of the parent is based on factors that may change over time, the process becomes more difficult. For example, the percentage of votes cast at general meetings may historically be 70%, but in a particular year it may be 50%. A shareholder with 30% of the voting shares has control in the latter circumstance but not in the former. Similarly, consider the situation where there are two substantial block holdings of voting shares, meaning that neither has power over the investee. One of the holders of a substantial block of shares may then sell its shares to a large number of buyers. The other holder of a substantial block may suddenly find that it has the power to control, regardless of whether this investor wants to exercise control or not.

Second, the ability of an entity to control another may be affected by relationships with other entities. For example, a holder of 40% of the voting shares may be 'friendly' with the holder of another 11% of shares. The 11% shareholder might be a financial institution that has invested in the holder of the 40% of votes and plans to vote with that entity to increase its potential for repayment of loans. However, business relationships and loyalties are not always permanent.

These two examples illustrate some of the practical issues in applying the concept of power in IFRS 10.

Potential voting rights

Paragraphs B47–B50 of IFRS 10 discuss the issue of whether potential voting rights should be considered in assessing the existence of power. Potential voting rights are rights to obtain voting rights of an investee, such as those within an option or convertible instrument (paragraph B47).

As noted earlier in this section:
- the rights must be substantive
- the investor must have a current ability to exercise those rights.

Where this occurs, potential voting rights must be taken into consideration when assessing the existence of power. Illustrative examples 20.1 and 20.2 provide some examples of potential voting rights adapted from paragraph B50 of IFRS 10.

ILLUSTRATIVE EXAMPLE 20.1 Potential voting rights — exercisable options

Arctic holds 70% of the voting rights of an investee. Baltic holds the other 30% but also holds an option to acquire half of Arctic's voting rights, with the option being exercisable at a fixed price over the next 2 years.

If the option is deeply 'out of the money' (that is, the fixed price is too high relative to the current share price of the investee) then Arctic would be considered to hold power as the current economic conditions are such that the rights associated with the option are not substantive, in that it is not practicable for Baltic to exercise the option.

If the option was 'in the money' (that is, where the underlying share price is well above the exercise price) then Baltic would be considered to have power as it could exercise the option and direct the activities of the investee.

Source: Adapted from IFRS 10, paragraph B50, Example 9.

ILLUSTRATIVE EXAMPLE 20.2 Potential voting rights — convertible debt instruments

An investee has three shareholders — Ant and two other investors. Each investor holds one-third of the voting rights. Ant also holds debt instruments that are convertible into voting shares of the investee at a fixed price that is 'out of the money', but not by a large amount. If the debt was converted, Ant would hold 60% of the shares of the investee. Because of the advantages of controlling the investee, it may be considered that Ant has power over the investee given Ant's ability to convert the debt instrument into shares. Additional information would need to be considered, including the current influence that Ant has on directing the activities of the investee.

Source: Adapted from IFRS 10, paragraph B50, Example 10.

20.3.2 Exposure or rights to variable returns

Besides having power to direct the activities of an investee, an investor must also have the rights to variable returns from that investee. Paragraph 6 of IFRS 10 ties control to exposure to risk. However, the International Accounting Standards Board (IASB®) then goes on to explain in the basis for conclusions BC32 that exposure to risk and rights to variable returns serve as an indicator of control, but on their own do not determine whether control is present. From an economic standpoint, the greater the risk exposure, the greater the incentives to control the activities of the investee.

Where an investor holds ordinary shares in an investee, it expects returns in relation to dividends, changes in the value of the investment, and residual interests on liquidation. These returns can be positive or negative; hence, the use of the term 'returns' rather than 'benefits'. The returns are not exclusive to the parent, but may also be received by other non-controlling shareholders. Other returns include (see paragraph B57 of IFRS 10 for examples of returns):

- returns from structuring activities with the investee; for example, obtaining a secure supply or raw material, access to a port facility, or a distribution network
- returns from denying or regulating access to a subsidiary's assets; for example, obtaining control of a patent for a competing product and stopping production
- returns from economies of scale
- remuneration from provision of services such as servicing of assets, and management.

The returns must have the potential to vary based on the performance of the investee. Examples of such variability are:

- dividends from ordinary shares that will change based on the profit performance of the investee
- fixed interest payments from a bond, as they expose the investor to the credit risk of the issuer of the bond, namely the investee
- fixed performance fees for management of the investee's assets, as they expose the investor to the performance risk of the investee.

20.3.3 Ability to use power to affect returns

Besides having power to direct the activities of the investee and rights to variable returns from the investee, a parent must have the ability to use its power over the investee to affect the returns received from the investee. This requires that the parent be able to use its power to increase its benefits and limit its losses from the subsidiary's activities. There is then a link between the holding of the power and the returns receivable. However, there is no specification of the level of returns to be received. IFRS 10 only requires that some variable returns be receivable and that the investor by its actions can affect the amount of those returns.

20.3.4 Agents

In determining whether control exists over an investee, an investor with decision-making rights needs to assess whether it is a principal or an agent.

Paragraph B58 of IFRS 10 explains that an agent is a party primarily engaged to act on behalf and for the benefit of another party or parties, being the principal and therefore does not control the investee when it exercises its decision-making authority. The agent has a fiduciary relationship to the principal.

Paragraph B60 of IFRS 10 provides a number of factors to consider in determining whether a decision maker is a principal or an agent:

- the scope of its decision-making authority over the investee — this relates to the range of activities that the decision maker is permitted to direct
- the rights held by other parties; for example, whether another entity has substantive removal rights over the decision maker
- the remuneration to which it is entitled in accordance with the remuneration agreement — the remuneration of an agent would be expected to be commensurate with the level of skills needed to provide the management service while the remuneration agreement would contain terms and conditions normally included in arrangements for similar services
- the decision maker's exposure to variability of returns from other interest that it holds in the investee — the greater the decision maker's exposure to variable returns from its involvement in the investee, the more likely it is that the decision maker is not an agent.

An agent cannot be a parent. Where a controlling decision maker is determined to be an agent, it is the principal that would be considered to be the parent. There may not be a parent if the agent is acting on behalf of a wide group of investors.

In relation to this, IFRS 10 paragraph 31 contains the so-called investment entity exception to consolidation. With investment entities as defined in IFRS 10 paragraph 27, that otherwise meet the criteria of controlling subsidiaries, the parent company should not prepare consolidated financial statements and instead measure its subsidiaries at fair value through profit or loss (IFRS 10 paragraph 31). The IASB was asked to make this exception to allow for venture capital and private equity companies to reflect in the financial statements that their business model is of holding the investments for a specific limited period with the purpose to benefit from fair value changes rather than exercise control.

20.4 PREPARATION OF CONSOLIDATED FINANCIAL STATEMENTS

Paragraph 4(a) of IFRS 10 requires *all* parents to prepare consolidated financial statements, except in those circumstances where it meets *all* the following conditions:

(i) it is a wholly owned subsidiary or is a partially owned subsidiary of another entity and all its other owners, including those not otherwise entitled to vote, have been informed about, and do not object to, the parent not presenting consolidated financial statements;

(ii) its debt or equity instruments are not traded in a public market (a domestic or foreign stock exchange or an over-the-counter market, including local and regional markets);

(iii) it did not file, nor is it in the process of filing, its financial statements with a securities commission or other regulatory organisation for the purpose of issuing any class of instruments in a public market; and

(iv) its ultimate or any intermediate parent produces consolidated financial statements that are available for public use and comply with IFRSs.

The essence of these conditions is to ensure that only companies with no public accountability are exempted from the requirement to prepare consolidated financial statements.

Consider the group structure in figure 20.4 (which is the same as in figure 20.3). A Ltd is a parent entity with two subsidiaries. According to paragraph 4 of IFRS 10, A Ltd is required to prepare consolidated financial statements, combining the financial statements of A Ltd, B Ltd and C Ltd. B Ltd is also a parent with C Ltd being its subsidiary. Is B Ltd also required to prepare consolidated financial statements?

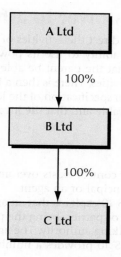

FIGURE 20.4 A parent and its subsidiaries

If B Ltd meets all the conditions in paragraph 4(a), it does not have to prepare consolidated financial statements. To determine this the following questions are asked:

- *Is B Ltd itself a wholly owned subsidiary?* In figure 20.4, B Ltd is itself a wholly owned subsidiary of A Ltd, hence this meets the first condition in paragraph 4(a)(i). Note also in paragraph 4(a)(i), that even if A Ltd owned only, say, 80% of B Ltd, making B Ltd a partially owned subsidiary, B Ltd may still be exempted from preparing consolidated financial statements if the 20% non-controlling interest in B Ltd has been informed about and do not object to the parent not presenting consolidated financial statements.

- *Has B Ltd filed its financial statements with a regulatory agency for the purpose of issuing any debt or equity instruments in a public market or are the debt and equity instruments of B Ltd traded in a public market?* If B Ltd intends to issue such instruments of if they are traded in a public market, then there are potential users for a set of consolidated financial statements from B Ltd. Where B Ltd is a wholly owned subsidiary, it is unlikely that its equity instruments would be traded in a public market.

- *Has A Ltd produced consolidated financial statements complying with IFRS® Standards?*

20.5 BUSINESS COMBINATIONS AND CONSOLIDATION

As noted in chapter 19, accounting for a business combination under the acquisition method requires the identification of an acquirer. The acquirer is the combining entity that obtains *control* of the other combining entities or businesses. Hence, as the criterion for identification of a parent–subsidiary relationship is control, it is expected that when a business combination is formed by the creation of a parent–subsidiary relationship, the parent will be identified as the acquirer. As noted in paragraph 3 of IFRS 10, the accounting requirements for business combinations and their effect on consolidation, including goodwill arising on a business combination, are set out in IFRS 3 *Business Combinations*.

However, there are situations where the parent entity is not the acquiring entity. In paragraph B19 of Appendix B to IFRS 3, a distinction is made between the legal acquirer/acquiree and the accounting acquirer/acquiree. The parent entity is usually the legal acquirer as it issues its equity interests as consideration in the combination transaction, with the subsidiary being the legal acquiree. This parent has control of the group subsequent to the business combination occurring. However, the accounting acquirer in a business combination is determined based on which entity participating in the business combination is the entity that obtains control of the other entities.

20.5.1 Formation of a new entity

Consider the situation in figure 20.5 in which A Ltd and B Ltd combine by the formation of a new entity, C Ltd, which acquires all the shares of both of these entities with the issue of shares in C Ltd to the existing shareholders of A Ltd and B Ltd. C Ltd controls both A Ltd and B Ltd.

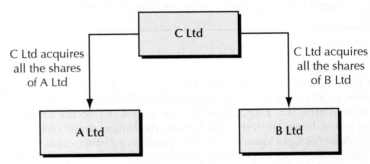

FIGURE 20.5 Identification of an acquirer where a new entity is formed

Even though C Ltd is acquiring the shares of both A Ltd and B Ltd, paragraph B18 of IFRS 3 disallows C Ltd to be considered the accounting acquirer; either A Ltd or B Ltd must be considered to be the accounting acquirer.

Deciding which entity is the acquirer involves a consideration of factors such as which of the combining entities initiated the combination, and whether the assets and revenues of one of the combining entities significantly exceed those of the others. The reasons for this decision by the IASB® are given in paragraphs BC98–BC101 of the Basis for Conclusions on IFRS 3 *Business Combinations*. The key reason for the standard setter's decision is in paragraph BC100. The argument is that the new entity, C Ltd, may have no economic substance, and the accounting result for the combination of the three entities should be the same if A Ltd simply combined with B Ltd without the formation of C Ltd. It is argued in paragraph BC100 that to account otherwise would 'impair both the comparability and the reliability of the information'.

However, the problem that then arises in the scenario in figure 20.5 is that a choice has to be made: is A Ltd or B Ltd the acquirer? In deciding on which entity is the acquirer, paragraphs B14–B18 of Appendix B to IFRS 3 provide some indicators to consider in situations where it may be difficult to identify an acquirer. The entity likely to be the acquirer is the one:
- that has a significantly greater fair value
- that gives up the cash or other assets, in the case where equity instruments are exchanged for cash or other assets
- whose management is able to dominate the business combination.

In this circumstance, although C Ltd is the legal parent of the subsidiaries A Ltd and B Ltd, it is not the acquirer in the business combination.

20.5.2 Reverse acquisitions

A further situation considered in paragraphs B19–B27 of IFRS 3 is the 'reverse acquisition' form of business combination. Consider the situation in figure 20.6.

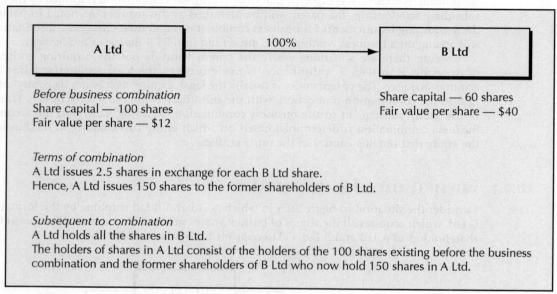

Before business combination
Share capital — 100 shares
Fair value per share — $12

Terms of combination
A Ltd issues 2.5 shares in exchange for each B Ltd share.
Hence, A Ltd issues 150 shares to the former shareholders of B Ltd.

Subsequent to combination
A Ltd holds all the shares in B Ltd.
The holders of shares in A Ltd consist of the holders of the 100 shares existing before the business combination and the former shareholders of B Ltd who now hold 150 shares in A Ltd.

Share capital — 60 shares
Fair value per share — $40

FIGURE 20.6 Reverse acquisition

A Ltd acquired all the shares in B Ltd, and A Ltd can therefore legally control the financial and operating policies of B Ltd. However, an analysis of the shareholding in A Ltd shows that the former shareholders of B Ltd hold 60% (i.e. 150/250) of the shares of A Ltd. So the substance of the business combination is that B Ltd has really taken over A Ltd because the former shareholders of B Ltd are in control. Paragraph BC96 of the Basis for Conclusions on IFRS 3 provides a further example of a reverse acquisition. In that example, a small public entity buys a large (and larger) private entity while the directors of the private entity replace the board of the public entity. The acquisition is funded by the public entity issuing shares to the owners of the private entity. After that, the owners of the private entity form the majority of shareholding in the public entity. The aim of the acquisition is to obtain a public listing status for the private entity. Thus, although from a legal point of view the private entity is the subsidiary, in substance it is the reverse; the private entity is the acquirer of the public entity.

The problem with the reverse acquisitions argument is that it relies on an analysis of which shareholders control the decision making — that is, the acquiring entity is the one whose owners control the combined entity and who have the power to govern the financial and operating policies of the entity so as to obtain benefits from its activities.

20.6 DISCLOSURE

There are no disclosures specified in IFRS 10. See chapter 19 regarding disclosures required by IFRS 12 and IAS 27.

Where entities form relationships with other entities, accounting standards often require additional disclosure so that users of financial statements can understand the economic substance of the entities involved. Where an entity is classified as a subsidiary of another, the parent, IFRS Standards establish principles for the preparation of consolidated financial statements. These statements are in addition to those prepared for either the parent or a subsidiary as separate legal entities. The consolidated financial statements are prepared by adding the financial statements of a parent and each of its subsidiaries, with adjustments being made during this process.

An important decision is the determination of whether the relationship between two entities is such as to be classified as a parent–subsidiary relationship. The existence of this relationship is determined by whether one entity has control over another. The existence of control requires the assessment of the power an entity has over another entity, whether the investor is exposed or has rights to variable returns from its involvement in the investee, and the ability of the investor to use its power over the investee to affect the amount of those returns. This analysis requires management to exercise judgement in analysing the specific relationships between entities, since the existence of control is not simply a matter of determining whether an entity owns a majority of shares in another.

In general, parent entities are responsible for the preparation of the consolidated financial statements. However, IFRS 10 exempts parent entities that meet specified criteria from the preparation of these statements. For those parents preparing consolidated financial statements, IFRS 3 will need to be applied as the formation of a parent–subsidiary relationship is normally also a business combination.

Discussion questions

1. What is a subsidiary?
2. What is meant by the term 'control'?
3. When are potential voting rights considered when deciding if one entity controls another?
4. Are only those entities in which another entity owns more than 50% of the issued shares classified as subsidiaries?
5. What benefits could be sought by an entity that obtains control over another entity?

21

Consolidation: wholly owned subsidiaries

ACCOUNTING STANDARDS IN FOCUS

IFRS 3 *Business Combinations*

IFRS 10 *Consolidated Financial Statements*

IFRS 12 *Disclosure of Interests in Other Entities*

LEARNING OBJECTIVES

After studying this chapter, you should be able to:

 1 understand the nature of the group covered in this chapter, and the initial adjustments required in the consolidation worksheet

 2 explain how a consolidation worksheet is used

 3 prepare an acquisition analysis for the parent's acquisition in a subsidiary

 4 prepare the worksheet entries at the acquisition date, being the business combination valuation entries and the pre-acquisition entries

 5 prepare the worksheet entries in periods subsequent to the acquisition date, adjusting for movements in assets and liabilities since acquisition date and dividends from pre-acquisition equity

 6 Prepare a consolidation worksheet when the parent company accounts for investment in subsidiary using the equity method rather than at cost

 7 Prepare the disclosures required by IFRS 3 and IFRS 12.

21.1 THE CONSOLIDATION PROCESS

This chapter discusses the preparation of consolidated financial statements. As discussed in chapter 20, under IFRS 10 *Consolidated Financial Statements* consolidated financial statements are the result of combining the financial statements of a parent and all its subsidiaries. *(The determination of whether an entity is a parent, or a subsidiary is discussed in chapter 20.)* The two accounting standards mainly used in this chapter are IFRS 10 and IFRS 3 *Business Combinations*. The accounting principles relevant for business combinations have been discussed earlier *(see chapter 19)* and an in-depth understanding of that chapter is essential to the preparation of consolidated financial statements because the parent's acquisition of shares in a subsidiary is simply one form of a business combination.

Although this chapter focuses on consolidation following an acquisition of an existing entity by paying shareholders of that subsidiary, it should be noted that the main steps of preparing a consolidated set of statements listed below apply when the parent company creates a new subsidiary (e.g. a newly-formed separate legal entity). Of course, in such a case there will be no fair-value adjustments of recognition of goodwill.

In IFRS 3 Appendix A, 'acquisition date' is defined as the date on which the acquirer obtains control of the acquiree. As discussed in chapter 19, both the fair values of the identifiable assets and liabilities of the subsidiary and the consideration transferred are measured at the acquisition date. In this chapter, the only combinations considered are those where the parent acquires its controlling interest in a subsidiary and, as a result, owns all the issued shares of the subsidiary — the subsidiary is then a wholly owned subsidiary.

This may occur by the parent buying all the shares in a subsidiary in one transaction, or by the parent acquiring the controlling interest after having previously acquired shares in the subsidiary. Note, however, as discussed in chapter 20, control of a subsidiary does not necessarily involve the parent acquiring shares in a subsidiary. The consolidated financial statements of a parent and its subsidiaries include information about a subsidiary from the date the parent obtains control of the subsidiary; that is, from the acquisition date. A subsidiary continues to be included in the parent's consolidated financial statements until the parent no longer controls that entity; that is, until the date of disposal of the subsidiary.

Before undertaking the consolidation process, it may be necessary to make adjustments in relation to the content of the financial statements of the subsidiary:

- If the end of a subsidiary's reporting period does not coincide with the end of the parent's reporting period, adjustments must be made for the effects of significant transactions and events that occur between those dates, with additional financial statements being prepared where it is practicable to do so (IFRS 10 paragraphs B92–B93). In most cases where there are different dates, the subsidiary will prepare adjusted financial statements as at the end of the parent's reporting period, so that adjustments are not necessary on consolidation. Where the preparation of adjusted financial statements is unduly costly, the financial statements of the subsidiary, prepared at a different date from the parent, may be used subject to adjustments for significant transactions. However, as paragraph B93 states, for this to be a viable option, the difference between the ends of the reporting periods can be no longer than 3 months. Further, the length of the reporting periods, as well as any difference between the ends of the reporting periods, must be the same from period to period.
- The consolidated financial statements are to be prepared using uniform accounting policies for like transactions and other events in similar circumstances (IFRS 10 paragraph 19). Where different policies are used, adjustments are made so that like transactions are accounted for under a uniform policy in the consolidated financial statements.

The preparation of the consolidated financial statements involves adding together the financial statements of the parent and its subsidiaries as well as processing a number of adjustments, these being expressed in the form of consolidating journal entries:

- As required by IFRS 3, at the acquisition date the acquirer must recognise the identifiable assets acquired and liabilities assumed of the subsidiary at fair value. Adjusting the carrying amounts of the subsidiary's assets and liabilities to fair value and recognising any identifiable assets acquired and liabilities assumed as a part of the business combination but not recorded by the subsidiary is a part of the consolidation process. The entries used to make these adjustments are referred to in this chapter as the *business combination valuation entries*. As noted later *(see section 21.2)* these adjusting entries are generally not made in the records of the parent or of the subsidiary, but in a consolidation worksheet.
- Where the parent has an ownership interest (i.e. owns shares) in a subsidiary, adjusting entries are made, referred to in this chapter as the *pre-acquisition entries*. As noted in paragraph B86(b) of IFRS 10, this involves eliminating the carrying amount of the parent's investment in each subsidiary (which we assume are carried at cost) and the parent's portion of pre-acquisition equity in each subsidiary. The name of these entries is derived from the fact that the equity of the subsidiary at the acquisition date is referred to as pre-acquisition equity, and it is this equity that is being eliminated. These entries are also made in the consolidation worksheet and not in the records of the parent or subsidiary.
- The third set of adjustments to be made is for transactions between the entities within the group subsequent to the acquisition date, including events such as sales of inventory or non-current assets.

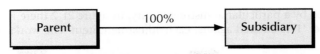

FIGURE 21.1 A wholly owned group

These *intragroup* transactions are referred to in IFRS 10 paragraph B86(c) *(adjustments for these transactions are discussed in detail in chapter 22)*.

In this chapter, the group under discussion is one where:

- there are only two entities within the group: one parent and one subsidiary (see figure 21.1)
- both entities have share capital
- the parent owns all the issued shares of the subsidiary; that is, the subsidiary is wholly owned (partially owned subsidiaries, where it is necessary to account for the non-controlling interest, are covered later *(see chapter 23)*)
- there are no intragroup transactions between the parent and its subsidiary after the acquisition date.

21.2 CONSOLIDATION WORKSHEETS

The consolidated financial statements are prepared by adding together the financial statements of the parent and the subsidiary. It is the *financial statements* of the parent and the subsidiary, rather than the underlying accounts, which are added together. There are no consolidated ledger accounts. The financial statements that are added together are the statements of financial position, statements of profit or loss and other comprehensive income and statements of changes in equity prepared by the management of the parent and the subsidiary. Consolidated statements of cash flows must also be prepared, but these are beyond the scope of this book.

To facilitate the addition process, particularly where there are several subsidiaries, as well as to make the necessary valuation and pre-acquisition entry adjustments, a worksheet or computer spreadsheet is often used. From the worksheet, the external statements are prepared — the consolidated statement of financial position, statement of profit or loss and other comprehensive income and statement of changes in equity.

The format for the worksheet is presented in figure 21.2, which contains the information used for the consolidation of the parent, P Ltd, and the subsidiary, S Ltd. Assume that P has paid £20,000 for all of the shares of S. At the time of acquisition S reported £15,000 in share capital and £5,000 in retained earnings. Note that this simple example does not deal with goodwill or fair value adjustments, which are discussed later.

FIGURE 21.2 Consolidation worksheet — basic format

Financial statements	Parent P Ltd	Subsidiary S Ltd	Adjustments				Consolidation
				Dr	Cr		
Investment in S Ltd	20,000	—			20,000	1	—
Other assets	35,000	27,000					62,000
	55,000	27,000			20,000		£62,000
Share capital	30,000	15,000	1	15,000			30,000
Retained earnings	25,000	12,000	1	5,000			32,000
	55,000	27,000		20,000			£62,000

Note the following points about the worksheet:

- The first column contains the names of the accounts, as the financial statements are combined on a line-by-line basis.
- The second and third columns contain the internal financial statements of the parent, P Ltd, and its subsidiary, S Ltd. These statements are obtained from the separate legal entities. The number of columns is expanded if there are more subsidiaries within the group.
- The next set of columns, headed 'Adjustments', are used to make the adjustments required in the consolidation process. These include adjustments for valuations at acquisition date, preacquisition equity, and intragroup transactions such as sales of inventory between the parent and subsidiary. The adjustments, written in the form of journal entries, are recorded on the worksheet. Where there are many adjustments, each journal entry should be numbered so that it is clear which items are being

affected by a particular adjustment entry. In figure 21.2 there is only one worksheet entry, hence the number '1' is entered against each adjustment item. The worksheet adjustment entry is:

(1) Share Capital of S	Dr	15,000	
(1) Retained Earnings of S (balance at acquisition)	Dr	5,000	
(1) Investment in S Ltd	Cr		20,000

- As noted earlier, the process of consolidation is one of adding together the financial statements of the members of the group and making various adjustments. Hence, figures for each line item in the right-hand column, headed 'Consolidation', arise through addition and subtraction as you proceed horizontally across the worksheet.
- The share capital and the retained earnings at acquisition date (on S Ltd's financial statements) are eliminated against the Investment in S Ltd (on P Ltd's financial statements).
- For example, for share capital, retained earnings and the shares in S Ltd, the effect of the adjustments are:

> Share capital : £30,000 + £15,000 − £15,000 = £30,000
> Retained earnings : £25,000 + £12,000 − £5,000 = £32,000
> Investment in S Ltd : £20,000 − £20,000 = £0

The figures in the right-hand column provide the information for the preparation of the consolidated financial statements of the group, P Ltd and S Ltd. Note that the retained earnings reported by the group include only £7,000 of the £15,000 reported by S. This is because S Ltd generated this amount in undistributed profit *since* acquisition. The subsidiary's retained earnings at acquisition amounted to £5,000 whereas at the date of consolidation this amount had increased to £12,000. Only the earnings of the subsidiary post acquisition are attributable to the group's performance and hence only £7,000 is absorbed into the consolidated retained earnings.

In preparing the consolidated financial statements, *no* adjustments are made in the accounting records of the individual entities that constitute the group. In addition, we assume the parent carries the investment in the subsidiary at cost and no further adjustment is made to the investment account (except for its elimination, as explained below). The adjusting entries recorded in the columns of the worksheet do not affect the accounts of the individual entities. They are recorded in a separate consolidation journal, not in the journals of any of the entities within the group and are then recorded on the consolidation worksheet. Hence, where consolidated financial statements are prepared over a number of years, a particular entry (such as a pre-acquisition entry) needs to be made *every time* a consolidation worksheet is prepared, because the entry never affects the actual financial statements of the individual entities.

21.3 THE ACQUISITION ANALYSIS: DETERMINING GOODWILL OR BARGAIN PURCHASE

On acquisition involving 100% of the shares in the acquired entity, there are three main measurement tasks that should be performed at acquisition date. First, the value of consideration paid to the previous shareholders of the acquired entity must be determined. In a simple case, this is the cash amount paid. Often, however, the acquirer uses other payment methods. Under one popular method, the acquirer issues its own shares in return for the shares in the target company (or a combination of cash and shares). In this case, the fair value of the shares issued should be determined. Occasionally, the fair value of the target's shares, rather than the acquirer's, may be measured more reliably and hence used instead (paragraph 33 of IFRS 10). The fair value of the consideration given should also take into account contingent payments (payments that are made in the future to the previous shareholders of the target company if certain conditions are met). These should also be fair-valued (paragraph 37). A slight complication arises when the acquisition is done in steps (step acquisition). For example, in the first step 30% of the target's shares are acquired and in the second step an additional 70% stake is purchased. In such a case the acquirer has to combine the value of consideration transferred in the last stage with the acquisition-date fair value of the initial 30% (paragraphs 41–42). The total of these two components is then regarded as the overall value of the 100% stake assumed *(see section 21.3.2)*.

The second measurement task requires the determination of the fair value of net assets (assets less liabilities) in the target's acquisition-date balance sheet. This typically involves fair-valuing of all on-balance-sheet assets and liabilities, as well as some off-balance-sheet items (e.g. intangible assets and contingent liabilities) *(see chapter 19)*.

The third measurement task is to assess the value of goodwill to show in the consolidated balance sheet. As discussed in chapter 19, this is done by comparing the value of considerations transferred (plus, possibly, the value of a previously held stake) to the fair value of net assets acquired. If the fair value of consideration transferred (plus, possibly, the value of a previously held stake) exceeds that of fair value of net assets acquired, then goodwill arises. If there is no excess whereby the fair value of net assets is higher, then negative goodwill arises. This is regarded as a bargain purchase. In such a case IFRS 10 (paragraph 36) requires the acquirer to conduct a review of its calculations. If the calculations hold, the negative goodwill is recorded in income (paragraph 35).

It should be noted that any acquisition-related costs, such as finders' fees; advisory, legal, accounting, valuation and other professional or consulting fees do not enter the above calculations and they need to be expensed (paragraph 53).

We discuss next several scenarios that may arise on acquisition date.

21.3.1 Parent has no previously held equity interest in the subsidiary

In this case, the parent acquires all the shares of the subsidiary at acquisition date in one transaction. In terms of paragraph 32 of IFRS 3 and as mentioned above, goodwill arises when the consideration transferred (32(a)(i)) is greater than the net fair value of the identifiable assets and liabilities acquired (32(b)). Where the reverse occurs, a gain on bargain purchase is recognised.

An acquisition analysis is conducted at acquisition date because it is necessary to recognise the identifiable assets and liabilities of the subsidiary at fair value, and to determine whether there has been an acquisition of goodwill or a bargain purchase gain.

The first step in the consolidation process is to undertake the above acquisition analysis in order to obtain the information necessary for making both the business combination valuation and pre-acquisition entry adjustments for the consolidation worksheet. Consider the example in figure 21.3.

FIGURE 21.3 Information at acquisition date

On 1 January 2024, Parent Ltd acquired all the issued share capital of Sub Ltd (300,000 shares), giving in exchange 100,000 shares in Parent Ltd, these having a fair value of £5 per share. At acquisition date, the statements of financial position of Parent Ltd and Sub Ltd, and the fair values of Sub Ltd's assets and liabilities, were as follows:

| | Parent Ltd | Sub Ltd | |
	Carrying amount	Carrying amount	Fair value
ASSETS			
Land	£120,000	£150,000	£170,000
Equipment	620,000	480,000	330,000
Accumulated depreciation	(380,000)	(170,000)	
Investment in Sub Ltd	500,000		
Inventory	92,000	75,000	80,000
Cash	15,000	5,000	5,000
Total assets	£967,000	£540,000	£585,000
LIABILITIES AND EQUITY			
Liabilities			
Provisions	30,000	60,000	60,000
Trade and other payables	27,000	34,000	34,000
Tax payable	10,000	6,000	6,000
Total liabilities	£ 67,000	£100,000	£100,000
Equity			
Share capital	550,000	300,000	
Retained earnings	350,000	140,000	
Total equity	900,000	440,000	
Total liabilities and equity	£967,000	£540,000	

At acquisition date, Sub Ltd has an unrecorded patent with a fair value of £20,000, and a contingent liability with a fair value of £15,000. This contingent liability relates to a loan guarantee made by Sub Ltd which did not recognise a liability in its records because it did not consider it could reliably measure the liability. The tax rate is 30%.

The analysis at acquisition date consists of comparing the fair value of the consideration transferred and the net fair value of the identifiable assets and liabilities of the subsidiary at acquisition date. The net fair value of the subsidiary could be calculated by revaluing the assets and liabilities of the subsidiary from the carrying amounts to fair values, remembering that under IAS 12 *Income Taxes* where there is a difference between the carrying amount and the tax base caused by the revaluation, the tax effect of such a difference has to be recognised. However, in calculating the net fair value of the subsidiary, because particular information is required to prepare the valuation and pre-acquisition entries, the calculation is done by adding the recorded equity of the subsidiary (which represents the recorded net assets of the subsidiary) and the differences between the carrying amounts of the assets and liabilities and their fair values, adjusted for tax. The adjustment for tax is done by comparing carrying values to the tax bases of assets and liabilities (*see chapter 15*). We assume here that the carrying values for tax purposes are equal to the reported carrying values in the statement of financial position of Sub Ltd. The book equity of the subsidiary in figure 21.3 consists of:

£300,000 capital + £140,000 retained earnings

These fair value adjustments are recorded initially against the *business combination valuation reserve* (BCVR). This reserve is not an account recognised in the subsidiary's records, but it is recognised in the consolidation process as part of the business combination. For example, using 30% tax rate, for land there is a difference of £20,000 on revaluation of the land to fair value, a business combination valuation reserve of £14,000 (i.e. £20,000 × (1–30%)) is raised. The total of pre-tax fair value adjustments is £50,000, giving rise to net deferred tax liability of £15,000. In this calculation we take into account the fair value of the contingent liability of £15,000 that is above its corresponding tax base (zero), giving rise to a deferred tax asset of £4,500. This deferred tax asset is offset against a deferred tax liability of £19,500 (= £65,000 × 30%) (*see chapter 15*).

The acquisition analysis, including the determination of the goodwill of the subsidiary, is as shown in figure 21.4.

FIGURE 21.4 Acquisition analysis — no previously held equity interests

	Sub Ltd		
	Carrying amount	Fair value adjustment	Fair value
ASSETS			
Land	£150,000	£20,000	£170,000
Equipment	310,000	20,000	330,000
Patent		20,000	20,000
Inventory	75,000	5,000	80,000
Cash	5,000		5,000
Total assets	£540,000	£ 65,000	£605,000
LIABILITIES			
Provisions	60,000		60,000
Trade and other payables	34,000		34,000
Contingent liability — loan guarantee		15,000	15,000
Deferred tax liability		15,000	15,000
Tax payable	6,000		6,000
Total liabilities	100,000	30,000	130,000
Net Assets	£440,000	£35,000	£475,000
Determination of goodwill:			
1 January 2024			
Consideration paid	500,000		
Less: Fair value of net assets acquired	475,000		
Goodwill	£ 25,000		

The information from the completed acquisition analysis is used to prepare the adjustment entries for the consolidation worksheet. These entries are illustrated below (*see section 21.4*).

In this book, it is assumed that the tax base of the subsidiary's assets and liabilities is unchanged as a result of the parent's acquisition of the subsidiary. In some jurisdictions, where the group becomes the taxable entity, there is a change in the tax base to the fair value amounts. In this case, no deferred tax effect would be recognised in relation to the assets and liabilities acquired.

21.3.2 Parent has previously held equity interest in the subsidiary

The situation used in figure 21.3 will be used here with the only difference being that on 1 January 2024 Parent Ltd acquires 80% of the shares in Sub Ltd, giving in exchange 80,000 shares in Parent Ltd, these having a fair value of £5 per share. Parent Ltd had previously acquired the other 20% stake in Sub Ltd for £75,000. On 31 December 2023, this investment in Sub Ltd was recorded at £92,000. The appreciation in value was recorded in income since the investment was classified as an equity instrument and measured at fair value through income. On 1 January 2024, these shares had been reassessed to have a fair value of £100,000.

In accordance with IFRS 3 paragraph 42, Parent Ltd revalues the previously held investment to fair value, recognising the £8,000 (= £100,000 − £92,000) increase in profit or loss. If previously changes in fair value are recognised in other comprehensive income, then the difference of £8,000 would be recognised in other comprehensive income. If previously the 20% interest would have been accounted for as an associate according to the equity method the difference would have been recognised in profit or loss. The journal entries in Parent Ltd at acquisition date, both for the previously held investment as well as the acquisition of the remaining shares in Sub Ltd, are as follows:

Investment in Sub Ltd	Dr	92,000	
Investment in Sub Ltd at fair value through Profit or Loss	Cr		92,000
Investment in Sub Ltd	Dr	8,000	
Profit or Loss	Cr		8,000
(Revaluation to fair value)			
Investment in Sub Ltd	Dr	400,000	
Share Capital	Cr		400,000
(Acquisition of shares in Sub Ltd: 80,000 at £5 per share)			

The first entry is to reclassify the investment account from fair value measurement through P&L to an investment carried at cost (in this case, the cost is the fair value prior to the acquisition of additional 80%). The second entry updates the fair value to £100,000, and the third records the value of the shares issued to fund the acquisition of 80%. If the acquisition of the 80% share is paid in cash instead, then a credit to the bank account of £400,000 would be recorded.

The determination of goodwill is shown in figure 21.5.

FIGURE 21.5 Determination of goodwill — previously held equity interests

Determination of goodwill:	
1 January 2024	
Value of previously acquired 20% stake	£100,000
Consideration paid	400,000
	500,000
Less: Fair value of net assets acquired	475,000
Goodwill	£ 25,000

As a result of the numbers used in this example, the goodwill number is the same as that shown in figure 21.4.

21.4 WORKSHEET ENTRIES AT THE ACQUISITION DATE

LO4

As noted earlier, the consolidation process does not result in any entries being made in the actual records of either the parent or the subsidiary. The adjustment entries are made in the consolidation worksheet. Hence, adjustment entries need to be passed each time a worksheet is prepared, and these entries change over time. In this section, the adjustment entries that would be passed in a consolidation worksheet prepared *immediately after the acquisition date* are analysed.

21.4.1 Business combination valuation entries

In figure 21.3, there are three identifiable assets recognised by the subsidiary whose fair values differ from their carrying amounts at acquisition date, as well as an intangible asset (the patent) and a contingent liability recognised as part of the business combination. The entries for the business combination valuations are done in the consolidation worksheet rather than in the records of the subsidiary *(see section 21.6 for a discussion on making these adjustments in the records of the subsidiary itself)*.

The identifiable assets and liabilities that require adjustment to fair value can be easily identified by reference to the acquisition analyses in figures 21.4 and 21.5, namely land, equipment, inventory, patent and the unrecorded guarantee. Goodwill also has to be recognised on consolidation. These differences are all recognised using business combination valuation entries. Consolidation worksheet adjustment entries for each of these assets and the unrecorded liability are given in figure 21.6.

The total balance of the business combination valuation reserve at this stage is £60,000. It will be cancelled to zero when the pre-acquisition entries are processed. The adjustments to assets and liabilities at acquisition date could also be achieved by one adjusting entry, giving a net balance to the business combination valuation reserve. However, in order to keep track of movements in that reserve as assets are depreciated or sold, liabilities paid or goodwill impaired, it is practical to prepare a valuation entry for each component of the valuation process. The valuation entries are passed in the adjustment columns of the worksheet, *which is illustrated in section 21.4.3.* Note that, in relation to entry (6) for goodwill, there is no deferred tax liability. This is because paragraph 21 of IAS 12 states that no such deferred tax liability is recognised, as goodwill is measured as a residual, and the recognition of a deferred tax liability would increase its carrying amount. Further, note that the goodwill is recognised on the consolidated balance sheet and not on the balance sheet of the acquiring company.

FIGURE 21.6 Business combination valuation entries at acquisition date

Business combination valuation entries			
(1) Land	Dr	20,000	
Deferred Tax Liability	Cr		6,000
Business Combination Valuation Reserve	Cr		14,000
(2) Accumulated Depreciation – Equipment	Dr	170,000	
Equipment	Cr		150,000
Deferred Tax Liability	Cr		6,000
Business Combination Valuation Reserve	Cr		14,000
(3) Inventory	Dr	5,000	
Deferred Tax Liability	Cr		1,500
Business Combination Valuation Reserve	Cr		3,500
(4) Patent	Dr	20,000	
Deferred Tax Liability	Cr		6,000
Business Combination Valuation Reserve	Cr		14,000
(5) Business Combination Valuation Reserve	Dr	10,500	
Deferred Tax Asset	Dr	4,500	
Provision for Loan Guarantee	Cr		15,000
(6) Goodwill	Dr	25,000	
Business Combination Valuation Reserve	Cr		25,000

21.4.2 Pre-acquisition entries

As noted in paragraph B86(b) of IFRS 10, an entry is required to eliminate the carrying amount of the parent's investment in the subsidiary against the parent's stake in the subsidiary's equity.

The investment in subsidiary on the parent's balance sheet represents the underlying assets and liabilities. As the consolidation process adds the net assets of the parent and subsidiary together to form the consolidated balance sheet, the investment in the subsidiary on the parent's balance sheet is eliminated to avoid double counting.

When the parent holds 100% of outstanding shares, this implies a full elimination of the subsidiary's equity as at the acquisition date. However, when the parent holds less than 100%, then the investment account is eliminated against the relevant portion of the subsidiary's equity on acquisition date (*see chapter 23*). The pre-acquisition entries, then, involve two areas:
- the Investment in Subsidiary, as shown in the financial statements of the parent
- the equity of the subsidiary at the acquisition date (i.e. the pre-acquisition equity). The pre-acquisition equity is not just the equity recorded by the subsidiary but includes the business combination valuation reserve recognised on consolidation via the valuation entries.

Using the example in figure 21.3, and reading the information from the acquisition analysis in figure 21.4 (including the business combination valuation reserve for the revalued assets including goodwill and the contingent liability), the pre-acquisition entry at acquisition date is as shown in figure 21.7. The pre-acquisition entry in this figure is numbered (7) because there were six previous valuation entries.

FIGURE 21.7 Pre-acquisition entry at acquisition date

Pre-acquisition entry			
(7) Retained Earnings (1 January 2024)	Dr	140,000	
Share Capital	Dr	300,000	
Business Combination Valuation Reserve	Dr	60,000	
Investment in Sub Ltd	Cr		500,000

The pre-acquisition entry is necessary to avoid overstating the equity and net assets of the group. To illustrate, consider the information in figure 21.3 relating to Parent Ltd's acquisition of the shares of Sub Ltd. Having acquired the shares in Sub Ltd, Parent Ltd records the asset 'Investment in Sub Ltd' at £500,000. This asset represents the actual net assets of Sub Ltd; that is, the ownership of the shares gives Parent Ltd the right to the net assets of Sub Ltd. To include both the asset 'Investment in Sub Ltd' and the net assets of Sub Ltd in the consolidated statement of financial position would double count the assets of the group, because the investment account is simply the right to the other assets. On consolidation, the investment account is therefore eliminated, and, in its place, the net assets of the subsidiary are included in the consolidated statement of financial position.

Similarly, to include both the equity of the parent and the equity of the subsidiary in the consolidated statement of financial position would double-count the equity of the group. In the example, Parent Ltd has equity of £900,000, which is represented by its net assets including the investment in the subsidiary. Because the investment in the subsidiary is the same as the net assets of the subsidiary, the equity of the parent effectively relates to the net assets of the subsidiary. To include in the consolidated statement of financial position the equity of the subsidiary at acquisition date as well as the equity of the parent would double-count equity in relation to the net assets of the subsidiary.

The credit balance on the business combination valuation reserve is also eliminated as it represents a valuation adjustment to the net assets of Sub Ltd and is also included in the £500,000 acquisition price.

21.4.3 Consolidation worksheet

Figure 21.8 contains the consolidation worksheet prepared at acquisition date, with adjustments being made for business combination valuation and pre-acquisition entries. The right-hand column reflects the consolidated statement of financial position, showing the position of the group. In relation to the figures in this column, note the following:
- In relation to the two equity accounts — share capital and retained earnings — only the parent's balances are carried into the consolidated statement of financial position. At acquisition date, all the equity of the subsidiary is pre-acquisition and eliminated as well as the business combination reserve. With the business combination valuation reserve, the valuation entry establishes the reserve, and the pre-acquisition entry eliminates it because it is by nature pre-acquisition equity.
- The assets of the subsidiary are carried forward into the consolidated statement of financial position at fair value.
- The adjusting journal entries have equal debits and credits (as shown in the line 'Total adjustments'), which is essential if the statement of financial position is to balance.

- The adjustments are applied following a simple process of aggregation, on a line-by-line basis, of the assets, liabilities, equity, and profit and loss of the parent and subsidiaries, as previously explained. For example, to get to the carrying value of land in the consolidated statement of financial position at £290,000 we first add £120,000 (at Parent Ltd) to £150,000 (at Sub Ltd) and then increase this sum by the debit adjustment of £20,000.

FIGURE 21.8 Consolidated worksheet at acquisition date

Financial statements	Parent Ltd	Sub Ltd	Adjustments Dr		Adjustments Cr		Consolidation
ASSETS							
Land	£ 120,000	£ 150,000	1	£ 20,000			£ 290,000
Equipment	620,000	480,000			150,000	2	950,000
Accumulated depreciation	(380,000)	(170,000)	2	170,000			(380,000)
Investment in Sub Ltd	500,000	—			500,000	7	—
Inventory	92,000	75,000	3	5,000			172,000
Cash	15,000	5,000					20,000
Patent	—	—	4	20,000			20,000
Goodwill	—	—	6	25,000			25,000
Total assets	£ 967,000	£ 540,000					£1,097,000
Provisions	£ 30,000	£ 60,000			£ 15,000	5	£ 105,000
Trade and other payables	27,000	34,000					61,000
Tax payables	10,000	6,000					16,000
Deferred tax liability			5	4,500	6,000	1	
					6,000	2	
					1,500	3	
	—	—			6,000	4	15,000
Total Liabilities	£ 67,000	£ 100,000					£ 197,000
EQUITY							
Share capital	550,000	300,000	7	300,000			550,000
Retained earnings (1 January 2024)	350,000	140,000	7	140,000			350,000
	900,000	440,000					900,000
Total liabilities and equity	£ 967,000	£ 540,000					£1,097,000
Business combination valuation reserve			5	10,500	14,000	1	
			7	60,000	14,000	2	
					3,500	3	
					14,000	4	
					25,000	6	
Total adjustment				£ 75,500	£ 75,500		

21.4.4 Subsidiary has recorded dividends at acquisition date

Using the information in figure 21.3, assume that one of the trade and other payables at acquisition date is a dividend payable of £10,000. The parent can acquire the shares in the subsidiary on a cum *div.* or an *ex div.* basis.

If the shares are acquired on a cum *div. basis*, then the parent acquires the right to the dividend declared at acquisition date. In this case, if Parent Ltd pays £500,000 for the shares in Sub Ltd, then the right to receive dividend effectively reduces the consideration given by £10,000 to £490,000. The entry it passes to record the business combination is:

Investment in Sub Ltd		Dr	490,000
Dividend Receivable		Dr	10,000
Share Capital		Cr		500,000

In other words, the parent acquires two assets — the investment in the subsidiary and the dividend receivable. In calculating the goodwill in the subsidiary therefore, the consideration given is £490,000. Deducting the fair value of net assets received of £475,000 then results in goodwill of £15,000. The pre-acquisition entry is:

(7) Retained Earnings (1 January 2024)	Dr	140,000	
Share Capital	Dr	300,000	
Business Combination Valuation Reserve	Dr	50,000	
Investment in Shares in Sub Ltd	Cr		490,000

A further consolidation worksheet entry is also required:

| Dividend Payable | Dr | 10,000 | |
| Dividend Receivable | Cr | | 10,000 |

This entry is necessary so that the consolidated statement of financial position shows only the assets and liabilities of the group; that is, only those benefits receivable from and obligations payable to entities external to the group. In relation to the dividend receivable recorded by Parent Ltd, this is not an asset of the group, because that entity does not expect to receive dividends from a party external to it. Similarly, the dividend payable recorded by the subsidiary is not a liability of the group. That dividend will be paid within the group, not to entities outside the group.

If the shares are acquired on an *ex div. basis*, then the parent only acquires the shares, as the dividend will be paid to previous shareholders and not the parent company. The dividend has no effect on the acquisition analysis. If Parent Ltd had paid £500,000 for the shares in Sub Ltd on an *ex div. basis*, then the acquisition analysis is:

Net fair value of identifiable assets and liabilities of Sub Ltd	= £475,000 (see the *cum. div.* basis)
Consideration transferred	= 100,000 shares × £5 = £500,000
Goodwill	= 500,000 − 475,000
	= 25,000

The pre-acquisition entry is:

Retained Earnings (1/1/2024)	Dr	140,000	
Share Capital	Dr	300,000	
Business Combination Valuation Reserve	Dr	60,000	
Investment in Sub Ltd	Cr		500,000

21.4.5 Gain on bargain purchase

In figure 21.3, Parent Ltd paid £500,000 for the shares in Sub Ltd. Consider the situation where Parent Ltd paid £470,000 for these shares. The gain on bargain purchase analysis is as shown in figure 21.9.

FIGURE 21.9 Gain on bargain purchase

Determination of gain on bargain purchase: 1 January 2024	
Consideration paid	£470,000
Less: Fair value of net assets acquired	475,000
Gain on bargain purchase	5,000

As the net fair value of the identifiable assets and liabilities of the subsidiary is greater than the consideration transferred, in accordance with paragraph 36 of IFRS 3 the acquirer must firstly reassess the identification and measurement of the subsidiary's identifiable assets and liabilities as well as the measurement of the consideration transferred. The expectation under IFRS 3 is that the excess of the net fair value over the consideration transferred is usually the result of measurement errors rather than being a real gain to the acquirer. However, having confirmed the identification and measurement of both amounts paid and net assets acquired, if an excess still exists, under paragraph 34 it is recognised immediately in the consolidated (rather than the acquirer's) profit as a gain on bargain purchase. This may happen, for example, when the subsidiary is in poor financial health and the subsidiary's shareholders are forced to offer a discount to a potential buyer.

Existence of a gain on bargain purchase implies that the entry (6) in figure 21.6 cannot be passed. However, if the subsidiary has previously recorded goodwill a business combination revaluation entry crediting goodwill and debiting business combination valuation reserve for the amount of goodwill recorded by the subsidiary would be required. The reason for this is that if the acquisition price paid by the parent is less than the subsidiary's identifiable net assets, this implies that no goodwill can exist in the subsidiary.

With a bargain purchase we replace entry (6) in figure 21.6, as follows:

| (6) Business Combination Valuation Reserve | Dr | 5,000 | |
| Gain on Bargain Purchase | Cr | | 5,000 |

The pre-acquisition entry for the situation in figure 21.9 is as shown in figure 21.10.

FIGURE 21.10 Pre-acquisition entry at acquisition date — gain on bargain purchase

Pre-acquisition entry			
(7) Retained Earnings (1 January 2024)	Dr	140,000	
Share Capital	Dr	300,000	
Business Combination Valuation Reserve	Dr	30,000	
Investment in Sub Ltd	Cr		470,000

21.5 WORKSHEET ENTRIES SUBSEQUENT TO THE ACQUISITION DATE

At acquisition date, the business combination valuation entries result in the economic entity recognising assets and liabilities not recorded by the subsidiary. Subsequently, changes in these assets and liabilities occur as assets are depreciated or sold, liabilities paid and goodwill impaired. Movements in the subsidiary's equity also occur as dividends are paid or declared and transfers are made within equity.

21.5.1 Business combination valuation entries

In the example used in figure 21.3, there were five items for which valuation entries were made — land, equipment, inventory, patent and the guarantee (a contingent liability). In this section, a 3-year time period subsequent to the acquisition date, 1 January 2024, is analysed (giving an end of reporting period of 31 December 2026) with the following events occurring:

- the land with original cost of £150,000 is sold in 2026 for net proceeds of £181,000 resulting in a gain of £31,000
- the equipment is depreciated on a straight-line basis over a 5-year period
- the inventory on hand at 1 January 2024 is all sold by 30 June 2024 (i.e. during the first year)
- the patent has an indefinite life, and is tested for impairment annually, with an impairment loss of £6,000 recognised in 2025
- the liability for the guarantee results in a payment of £10,000 in November 2024, with no further liability existing
- goodwill is written down by £5,000 in 2024, as a result of an impairment test (see chapter 7 for impairment of goodwill).

The statements of financial position of Parent Ltd and Sub Ltd, and the fair values of Sub Ltd's assets and liabilities, as of 31 December 2026 are shown in figure 21.11.

FIGURE 21.11 Statements of financial position at 31 December 2026

	Parent Ltd	Sub Ltd
	Carrying amount	Carrying amount
Assets		
Land	£170,000	£50,000
Equipment	750,000	680,000
Accumulated depreciation	(448,000)	(456,000)
Patent		
Investment in shares in Sub Ltd	500,000	
Inventory	52,000	75,000
Cash	65,000	95,000
Total assets	£1,089,000	£444,000
Equity and Liabilities		
Provisions	40,000	40,000
Trade and other payables	32,000	24,000
Tax payable	12,000	16,000
Total liabilities	£84,000	£80,000
Equity		
Share capital	550,000	300,000
Retained earnings	455,000	64,000
Total equity	£1,005,000	£364,000
Total liabilities and equity	£1,089,000	£444,000

The income statements for Parent Ltd and Sub Ltd for the year ended 31 December 2026 are shown in figure 21.12.

FIGURE 21.12 Income statements at 31 December 2026

Income statements	Parent Ltd	Sub Ltd
Revenue	120,000	95,000
Expenses	85,000	72,000
	35,000	23,000
Gain on sale of non-current assets	15,000	31,000
Profit before tax	50,000	54,000
Income tax expense	15,000	21,000
Profit for the period	35,000	33,000
Retained earnings (1 January 2026)	420,000	31,000
Retained earnings (31 December 2026)	455,000	64,000

We next analyse the effect of each of these items on the consolidation process.

21.5.1.1 Land

The land that was on Sub Ltd's balance sheet of 1 January 2024 was sold in 2026 for £181,000. Because Sub Ltd recorded a gain that is based on lower carrying value (£150,000) than what was recorded in the 31 December 2025 consolidated balance sheet, its 2026 after-tax profit is higher by £14,000 (= £20,000 × 70%). Sub Ltd's tax expense is also higher by £6,000 (= £20,000 × 30%). Therefore, the gain and tax expense should be reduced from Sub Ltd's income for the year.

Valuation entry for 2026:

(1) Gain on Sale of Land		Dr	20,000	
Tax Expense		Cr		6,000
Business Combination Valuation Reserve		Cr		14,000

21.5.1.2 Equipment

The equipment had a remaining useful life of 5 years on acquisition date. Hence, Sub Ltd recorded an annual depreciation expense of ((£480,000 − £170,000)/5 = £62,000) bringing total accumulated depreciation for acquisition date's equipment to £356,000 (= £170,000 + 3 × £62,000) and net book value of £124,000 (= £480,000 − £356,000).

However, from the group's perspective the initial fair value adjustment was £20,000. Hence on 1 January 2024 the equipment was restated to a revised cost of £330,000 with zero accumulated depreciation. This initial adjustment involved a reduction in the equipment cost account of £150,000 and a reduction in the accumulated depreciation account of £170,000 (see figure 21.6). For the purpose of consolidated statements, therefore, subsequent annual depreciation expense of £66,000 (= £330,000/5 years), is £4,000 higher than what was booked by Sub Ltd. After 3 years the net book value of this equipment is £132,000 (= £330,000 − £198,000). Note that the carrying value of the equipment at Sub Ltd's stand-alone balance sheet (£124,000) is lower than the carrying value in the consolidated balance sheet (£132,000). The difference of £8,000 reflects 40% of the fair value adjustment recorded on acquisition date, because the remaining useful life of this adjustment is 2 (out of 5) years.

Since the accumulated depreciation account in Sub Ltd's balance sheet is £356,000, but from the group's perspective it is £198,000, the adjustment entry needs to reverse £158,000 of Sub Ltd's accumulated depreciation account.

Note also the effect on the group's earning. The consolidation process effectively absorbs 100% of the profit reported by the subsidiary *since* acquisition. However, the calculation of this profit, which is reflected in Sub Ltd's equity, is **not** based on acquisition date's fair values. Hence, relative to the group, over the 3-year period, Sub Ltd's pre-tax profits are higher by £12,000 owing to lower annual depreciation expense (£32,000 vs. £36,000). After 30% tax, Sub Ltd's retained earnings are higher by £8,400. The £8,400 reduction in retained earnings is split between a reduction of £5,600 to opening retained earnings on 1 January 2026, and a reduction to the 2026 after-tax profit of £2,800 (£4,000 depreciation less £1,200 tax saving).

Figure 21.13 shows the valuation entry for 2026.

FIGURE 21.13 Business combination valuation entries at 31 December 2026

(2) Accumulated depreciation — Equipment	Dr	158,000	
Depreciation expense	Dr	4,000	
Retained earnings 1 January 2026	Dr	5,600	
Equipment — cost	Cr		150,000
Tax Expense	Cr		1,200
Deferred tax liability	Cr		2,400
Business Combination Valuation Reserve	Cr		14,000

Note that the total effect on consolidated retained earnings as at 31 December 2026 is a reduction of £8,400 (= £5,600 + £4,000 − £1,200). Also note that the credit adjustment of £150,000 to the equipment cost account remains the same since acquisition.

21.5.1.3 Inventory

The inventory was sold in 2024. Because Sub Ltd recorded gross profit that is based on lower carrying value than what was recorded in the 1 January 2024 consolidated balance sheet, its 2024 after-tax profit was higher by £3,500 (= £5,000 × 70%). This therefore works to reduce retained earnings on 1 January 2026 by this amount.

Valuation entry for 2026:

(3) Retained Earnings — 1 January 2026	Dr	3,500	
Business Combination Valuation Reserve	Cr		3,500

21.5.1.4 Patent

The patent was impaired in 2025 to £14,000. Since the patent is not recorded in Sub Ltd's stand-alone balance sheet, the impairment of £6,000 was recorded only in consolidated income in the previous year.

Hence, Sub Ltd's retained earnings as of 1 January 2026 should be reduced by £4,200 (= £6,000 × 70%). Deferred tax liability should also be reduced by £1,800 (= £6,000 × 30%) and stand at £4,200 (= £14,000 × 30%) in the 31 December 2026 consolidated statement of financial position.

Valuation entry for 2026:

(4) Patent	Dr	14,000	
Retained Earnings — 1 January 2026	Dr	4,200	
Deferred Tax Liability	Cr		4,200
Business Combination Valuation Reserve	Cr		14,000

21.5.1.5 Contingent liability

The guarantee liability was originally stated at £15,000 on the acquisition date consolidated balance sheet. Since in 2024 the settlement involved a payment of only £10,000, the group needs to record a pre-tax gain of £5,000. Sub Ltd's income statement in 2024 recorded a pre-tax loss of £10,000, because in its stand-alone balance sheet on 1 January 2024 no liability was recognised for the guarantee. Hence there is a difference of £15,000 between Sub Ltd's loss and the group's gain. Sub Ltd's retained earnings need to be increased by £10,500 (£15,000 × 70%) in the consolidation process.

Valuation entry for 2026:

(5) Business Combination Valuation Reserve	Dr	10,500	
Retained Earnings — 1 January 2026	Cr		10,500

21.5.1.6 Goodwill

Impairment tests for goodwill are undertaken annually. Goodwill is written down by £5,000 in 2024, as a result of an impairment test. In the consolidation worksheet prepared at 31 December 2024, the business combination valuation entry will recognise the loss and reduction in goodwill. Because goodwill impairment is not tax deductible (i.e. it is a permanent difference) there is no effect on deferred tax liability or tax expense.

Valuation entry for 2026:

(6) Retained Earnings — 1 January 2026	Dr	5,000	
Goodwill	Dr	20,000	
Business Combination Valuation Reserve	Cr		25,000

21.5.2 Pre-acquisition entry

With the above entries (1)–(6) recorded, the final entry is to eliminate the investment in Sub Ltd account against the equity of the subsidiary as it was on acquisition date:

(7) Retained Earnings	Dr	140,000	
Share Capital	Dr	300,000	
Business Combination Valuation Reserve	Dr	60,000	
Investment in Sub Ltd	Cr		500,000

We are now ready to prepare the consolidated statement of financial position and income statement — see figure 21.14.

FIGURE 21.14 Consolidation worksheet at 31 December 2026

	Parent Ltd	Sub Ltd	Adjustment number	Dr	Cr	Adjustment number	Consolidated
Statement of financial position							
Assets							
Land	£ 170,000	£50,000					£ 220,000
Equipment — cost	750,000	680,000			150,000	2	1,280,000
Equipment — accumulated depreciation	(448,000)	(456,000)	2	158,000			(746,000)
Patent			4	14,000			14,000
Investment in Sub Ltd	500,000				500,000	7	
Inventory	52,000	75,000					127,000
Cash	65,000	95,000					160,000
Goodwill			6	20,000			20,000
Total assets	£1,089,000	£444,000		£192,000	£650,000		£1,075,000
Liabilities							
Provisions	£40,000	£40,000					£80,000
Trade and other payables	32,000	24,000					56,000
Tax payable	12,000	16,000					28,000
Deferred tax liability					2,400	2	
					4,200	4	6,600
Total liabilities	£ 84,000	£ 80,000			£ 6,600		£ 170,600
Equity							
Share capital	£550,000	£300,000	7	£300,000			550,000
Retained earnings 1 January 2026	420,000	31,000	2	5,600			303,200
			3	3,500			
			4	4,200			
					10,500	5	
			6	5,000			
			7	140,000			
Total equity 1 January 2026	£ 970,000	£331,000		£458,300	£10,500		£853,200
Income statement							
Revenues	£120,000	£95,000					£215,000
Expenses	85,000	72,000	2	4,000			161,000
	35,000	23,000					54,000
Gain on sale of non-current assets	15,000	31,000	1	20,000			26,000
Profit before tax	50,000	54,000					80,000
Tax expense	15,000	21,000			6,000	1	28,800
					1,200	2	
Profit for 2026	£ 35,000	£ 33,000					£51,200
Total equity 31 December 2026	£1,005,000	£364,000		£482,300	£17,700		904,400
Total equity and liabilities 31 December 2026	£1,089,000	£444,000		£482,300	£24,300		£1,075,000
Business combination valuation reserve			5	10,500	14,000	1	
			7	60,000	14,000	2	
					3,500	3	
					14,000	4	
					25,000	6	
Total adjustments				£744,800	£744,800		

Total consolidated equity on 31 December 2026 is reported as follows:

Group's equity on 31 December 2026	
Share capital	£550,000
Retained earnings	354,400
	904,400

21.6 CONSOLIDATION WORKSHEET WHEN THE PARENT COMPANY ACCOUNTS FOR INVESTMENT IN SUBSIDIARY USING THE EQUITY METHOD

In section 21.5 above it was assumed that the parent company maintains its investment in Sub Ltd at cost. However, many parent companies use the equity method to account for the investment in subsidiaries. Online chapter 3 presents the equity method and explains how it works. For this section, we would assume you are familiar with this method, but essentially it is important to keep in mind that the investment account in the parent company's financial statements already incorporates many of the fair value adjustments and their consequences.

To illustrate, consider figure 21.15, which provides the stand-alone financial statements of Parent Ltd. and Sub Ltd on 31 December 2026:

FIGURE 21.15 Stand-alone financial statements of Parent Ltd and Sub Ltd on 31 December 2026

	Parent Ltd	Sub Ltd
Land	170,000	50,000
Equipment — cost	750,000	680,000
Equipment — accumulated depreciation	−448,000	−456,000
Investment in Sub Ltd	399,400	
Inventory	52,000	75,000
Cash	65,000	95,000
Total assets	988,400	444,000
Liabilities		
Provisions	40,000	40,000
Trade and other payables	32,000	24,000
Tax payable	12,000	16,000
Total liabilities	84,000	80,000
Equity		
Share capital	550,000	300,000
Retained earnings 1 January 2026	303,200	31,000
Profit and loss 2026		
Revenues	120,000	95,000
Expenses	85,000	72,000
	35,000	23,000
Gain on sale of non-current assets	15,000	31,000
Income from Sub	16,200	
Profit before tax	66,200	54,000
Tax expense	15,000	21,000
Profit for 2026	51,200	33,000
Total equity 31 December 2026	904,400	364,000
Total liabilities and equity	988,400	444,000

Sub Ltd was fully acquired on 1 January 2024. During 2026 Sub Ltd sold a piece of land whose carrying amount in the group's statement of financial position was higher by £20,000 than in Sub Ltd's statement of financial position. Sub Ltd also owns a patent that is off its balance sheet, but the group reports it at £14,000 and does not amortise it. For the group's reporting purposes, equipment is stated at £8,000 (31 December 2025: £12,000) more than in Sub Ltd's balance sheet. This amount is comprised from reduction in cost of £150,000 and reduction in accumulated depreciation of £158,000 (31 December 2025: £162,000). The group's annual depreciation expense is higher by £4,000, relative to the Sub Ltd's depreciation expense. Goodwill stands at £20,000, which has not changed since 31 December 2025. Tax rate is 30%.

Figure 21.16 below explains how the carrying amount of the investment account is calculated for both 2026 and 2025.

FIGURE 21.16 Analysis of the investment account under the equity method

On 31 December	2026	2025
Sub Ltd's book value of equity	£364,000	£331,000
Adjustment for land		20,000
Adjustment for PPE	8,000	12,000
Adjustment for patent	14,000	14,000
Deferred tax liability on the above adjustments	(6,600)	(13,800)
Adjusted equity	379,400	363,200
Goodwill	20,000	20,000
Investment in Sub Ltd	£399,400	£383,200

Parent Ltd reports in its stand-alone profit and loss in 2026 the item 'income from subsidiary' at £16,200. This is the profit reported by Sub Ltd adjusted for additional depreciation, lower gain on sale of land, partially offset by lower tax expense. Figure 21.17 summarises these adjustments.

FIGURE 21.17 Analysis of income form subsidiary under the equity method

Profit reported by Sub Ltd	33,000
Deduct adjustment for sale of land	−20,000
Adjustment for higher depreciation	−4,000
Lower tax expense related to the above adjustments	7,200
Income from subsidiary	16,200

With this information in mind, we can now proceed to the consolidation process, which is similar to the process followed when the investment is reported at cost. The consolidation process under the equity method is summarised in figure 21.18.

	Parent Ltd	Sub Ltd	Dr.	Cr.	Consolidated
Land	170,000	50,000			220,000
Equipment — cost	750,000	680,000		150,000	1,280,000
Equipment — accumulated depreciation	−448,000	−456,000	158,000		−746,000
Patent			14,000		14,000
Investment in Sub Ltd	399,400			399,400	0
Inventory	52,000	75,000			127,000
Cash	65,000	95,000			160,000
Goodwill			20,000		20,000
Total assets	988,400	444,000	192,000	549,400	1,075,000

FIGURE 21.18 Consolidation process under the equity method

	Parent Ltd	Sub Ltd	Dr.	Cr.	Consolidated
Liabilities					
Provisions	40,000	40,000			80,000
Trade and other payables	32,000	24,000			56,000
Tax payable	12,000	16,000			28,000
Deferred tax liability				6,600	6,600
Total liabilities	84,000	80,000	0	6,600	170,600
Equity					
Share capital	550,000	300,000	300,000		550,000
Retained earnings 1 January 2026	303,200	31,000	31,000		303,200
Profit and loss					
Revenues	120,000	95,000			215,000
Expenses	85,000	72,000	4,000		161,000
	35,000	23,000	4,000		54,000
Gain on sale of non-current assets	15,000	31,000	20,000		26,000
Income from Subsidiary	16,200		16,200		0
Profit before tax	66,200	54,000	40,200	0	80,000
Tax expense	15,000	21,000		7,200	28,800
Profit for 2026	51,200	33,000	40,200	7,200	51,200
Total equity 31 December 2026	904,400	364,000	371,200	7,200	904,400
Total liabilities and equity	988,400	444,000	371,200	13,800	1,075,000

The adjusting journal entry is passed after the two stand-alone statements are added together, see figure 21.19:

FIGURE 21.19 Adjusting entry under the equity method

Income from subsidiary	Dr	16,200
Depreciation expense	Dr	4,000
Gain on sale of noncurrent assets	Dr	20,000
Accumulated depreciation — equipment	Dr	158,000
Patent	Dr	14,000
Goodwill	Dr	20,000
Share capital	Dr	300,000
Retained earnings 1 January 2026	Dr	31,000
Tax expense	Cr	7,200
Deferred tax liability	Cr	6,600
Investment in Sub Ltd	Cr	399,400
Equipment — cost	Cr	150,000

21.7 DISCLOSURE

Paragraphs B64–B67 of Appendix B to IFRS 3 cover the disclosure of information about business combinations. These paragraphs require an acquirer to disclose information that enables users of its financial statements to evaluate the nature and financial effect of business combinations that occurred during the reporting period, as well as those that occur between the end of the reporting period and when the financial statements are authorised for issue. Examples of disclosures required by these paragraphs are given in figure 21.20.

FIGURE 21.20 Disclosure of business combinations

Note 4. Business combinations	IFRS 3 paragraph
On 20 October 2024, Libra Ltd acquired 100% of the voting shares of Pisces Ltd, a listed company specialising in the manufacture of electronic parts for sound equipment. The primary reason for the acquisition was to gain access to specialist knowledge relating to electronic systems. Control was obtained by acquisition of all the shares of Pisces Ltd.	B64(a), (b), (c) B64(d)

To acquire this ownership interest, Libra Ltd issued 600,000 ordinary shares, valued at £2.50 per share, which rank equally for dividends after the acquisition date. The fair value is based on the published market price at acquisition date. — *B64(f)(iv)*

The total consideration transferred was £1,800,000 and consisted of: — *B64(f)*

	£'000
Shares issued, at fair value	1,500
Cash paid	240
Cash payable in 2 years' time	60
Total consideration transferred	1,800

The fair values and the carrying amounts of the assets acquired and liabilities assumed in Pisces Ltd as at 20 October 2024 were — *B64(f)*

	Fair value £'000	Carrying amount £'000
Property, plant and equipment	1,240	1,020
Receivables	340	340
Inventory	160	130
Intangibles	302	22
Goodwill	54	0
	2,096	1,512
Payables	152	152
Provisions	103	103
Tax liabilities	41	41
	296	296
Fair value of net assets of Pisces Ltd	1,800	

Goodwill in Pisces Ltd can be attributed to the synergies existing within the company, and relate to the high level of training given to the staff as well as the professional expertise of the employees. Further, there exist in-process research activities in Pisces Ltd for which it was impossible to determine reliable fair values for the separate recognition of intangible assets. — *B64(e)*

Pisces Ltd earned a profit for the period from 20 October 2024 to 30 June 2025 of £520,000. This has been included in the consolidated statement of profit or loss and other comprehensive income for the year ended 30 June 2025. — *B64(q)(i)*

None of the above information has been prepared on a provisional basis. — *B67*

The consolidated profit is shown in the consolidated statement of profit or loss and other comprehensive income at £5,652,000, which includes the £520,000 contributed by Pisces Ltd from 20 October 2024 to the end of the period. If Pisces Ltd had been acquired at 1 July 2024, it is estimated that the consolidated entity would have reported: — *B64(q)(ii)*

	£'000
Consolidated revenue	36,654
Consolidated profit	6,341

In relation to the business combination in the 2023/24 period when Libra Ltd acquired all the shares in Orion Ltd, an adjustment was made in the current period relating to the provisional measurement of specialised equipment held by Orion Ltd. A loss of £250,000 was recognised in the current reporting period because of the write-down of this equipment. — *B67(a)(iii)*

FIGURE 21.20 *(continued)*

Included in the current period profit are gains on the sale of land acquired as a part of the business combination with Pisces Ltd. The gain amounted to £100,000 and arose due to an upsurge in demand for inner-city properties.	*B67(e)*

Goodwill		*B67(d)*
	£'000	
Gross amount at 1 July 2024	120	
Accumulated impairment losses	(15)	
Carrying amount at 1 July 2024	105	
Goodwill recognised in current period	54	
Carrying amount at 30 June 2025	159	
Gross amount at 30 June 2025	174	
Accumulated impairment losses	(15)	
Carrying amount at 30 June 2025	159	

IFRS 12 *Disclosure of Interests in Other Entities* also requires disclosures in relation to a parent's interest in its subsidiaries. Figure 21.21 illustrates some of these disclosures.

FIGURE 21.21 Disclosures concerning subsidiaries

Note 5. Subsidiaries	IFRS 12 paragraph
Aries Ltd has a 40% interest in Virgo Ltd. Although it has less than half the voting power, Aries Ltd believes it has control of the financial and operating policies of Virgo Ltd. Aries Ltd is able to exercise this control because the remaining ownership in Virgo Ltd is diverse and widely spread, with the next single largest ownership block being 11%.	*9(b)*
Aries Ltd has invested in a special purpose entity established by Pictor Ltd. Pictor Ltd established Cetus Ltd as a vehicle for distributing the sailing boats it makes. Aries Ltd currently owns 60% of the shares issued by Cetus Ltd. However, because of the limited decisions that the board of Cetus Ltd can make owing to the constitution of that entity, Aries Ltd believes that it does not have any real control over the operations of Cetus Ltd, so it sees its role in Cetus Ltd as that of an investor.	*9(a)*
Aries Ltd has a wholly owned subsidiary, Gemini Ltd, which operates within the electricity generating industry. The end of its reporting period is 31 May. Gemini Ltd continues to use this date because the government regulating authority requires all entities within the industry to provide financial information to it based on financial position at that date.	*11*
Aries Ltd has a wholly owned subsidiary, Hercules Ltd, in the country of Mambo. Because of constraints on assets leaving the country recently imposed by the new military government, there are major restrictions on the subsidiary being able to transfer funds to Aries Ltd.	*10(b)(i)*

Disclosures in relation to subsidiaries are set out in IFRS 12 *Disclosure of Interests in Other Entities*, issued in 2011. *These are discussed in chapter 20.* Note, however, the following extract from paragraph 10.

An entity shall disclose information that enables users of its consolidated financial statements
(a) to understand:
  (i) the composition of the group; and
  (ii) the interest that non-controlling interests have in the group's activities and cash flows (paragraph 12); and
(b) to evaluate:
  (i) the nature and extent of significant restrictions on its ability to access or use assets, and settle liabilities, of the group (paragraph 13);
  (ii) the nature of, and changes in, the risks associated with its interests in consolidated structured entities (paragraphs 14–17) . . .

21.8 SUMMARY

This chapter covers the preparation of the consolidated financial statements for a group consisting of a parent and a wholly owned subsidiary. Because of the requirements of IFRS 3 to recognise the identifiable assets acquired and liabilities assumed of an acquired entity at fair value, an initial adjustment to be made on consolidation concerns any assets or liabilities for which there are differences between fair value and carrying amount at the acquisition date. Further, although some intangible assets and liabilities of the subsidiary may not have been recognised in the subsidiary's records, they are recognised as part of the business combination.

The preparation of the consolidated financial statements is done using a consolidation worksheet, the left-hand columns of which contain the financial statements of the members of the group. The adjustment columns contain the consolidation worksheet entries that adjust the right-hand columns to form the consolidated financial statements. The adjustment entries have no effect on the actual financial records of the parent and its subsidiaries.

At acquisition date, an acquisition analysis is undertaken. The key purposes of this analysis are to determine the fair values of the identifiable assets and liabilities of the subsidiary, and to calculate any goodwill or gain on bargain purchase arising from the business combination. From this analysis, the main consolidation worksheet adjustment entries at acquisition date are the business combination valuation entries (to adjust carrying amounts of the subsidiaries' assets and liabilities to fair value) and the pre-acquisition entries.

In preparing consolidated financial statements in periods after acquisition date, the consolidation worksheet will contain valuation entries and pre-acquisition entries. However, these entries are not necessarily the same as those used at acquisition date. If there are changes to the assets and liabilities of the subsidiaries since acquisition date, or there have been movements in pre-acquisition equity, changes must be made to these entries.

Discussion questions

1. Explain the purpose of the pre-acquisition entries in the preparation of consolidated financial statements.
2. When there is a dividend payable by the subsidiary at acquisition date, under what conditions should the existence of this dividend be taken into consideration in preparing the pre-acquisition entries?
3. Is it necessary to distinguish pre-acquisition dividends from post-acquisition dividends? Why?
4. If the subsidiary has recorded goodwill in its records at acquisition date, how does this affect the preparation of the pre-acquisition entries?
5. Explain how the existence of a bargain purchase affects the pre-acquisition entries, both in the year of acquisition and in subsequent years.

22

Consolidation: intragroup transactions

ACCOUNTING STANDARDS IN FOCUS

IFRS 10 *Consolidated Financial Statements*

LEARNING OBJECTIVES

After studying this chapter, you should be able to:

 1 explain the need for making adjustments for intragroup transactions

 2 prepare worksheet entries for intragroup transactions involving profits and losses in beginning and ending inventory

 3 prepare worksheet entries for intragroup services such as management fees

 4 prepare worksheet entries for intragroup dividends

 5 prepare worksheet entries for intragroup borrowings.

INTRODUCTION

In this chapter, the group under discussion is restricted to one where:
- there are only two entities within the group (i.e. one parent and one subsidiary)
- the parent owns all the shares of the subsidiary.

Diagrammatically, then, the group is as shown in figure 22.1.

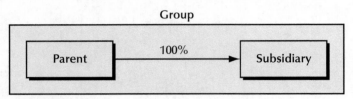

FIGURE 22.1 Group

In chapter 20, it is explained that the process of consolidation involves adding together the financial statements of a parent and its subsidiaries to reflect an overall view of the financial affairs of the group of entities as a single economic entity. It is also pointed out that two major adjustments are necessary to effect the process of consolidation:

(a) adjustments involving equity at the acquisition date, namely the business combination valuation entries (if any) and the elimination of investment in subsidiary, eliminating the investment account in the parent's financial statements against the pre-acquisition equity of the subsidiary *(see chapter 21)*

(b) elimination of intragroup balances and the effects of transactions whereby profits or losses are made by different members of the group through trading with each other.

This chapter focuses on (b), adjustments for intragroup balances and transactions. The chapter analyses transactions involving inventory, depreciable assets, services, dividends and borrowings.

22.1 RATIONALE FOR ADJUSTING FOR INTRAGROUP TRANSACTIONS

Whenever related entities trade with each other, or borrow and lend money to each other, the separate legal entities include the effects of these transactions in the assets and liabilities recorded and the profits and losses reported. For example, if a subsidiary sells inventory to its parent, the subsidiary records a sale of inventory, including the profit on sale and reduction in inventory assets, and the parent records the purchase of inventory at the amount paid to the subsidiary. If, then, in preparing the consolidated financial statements, the separate financial statements of the legal entities are simply added together without any adjustments for the effects of the intragroup transactions, the consolidated financial statements include not only the results of the group transacting with external entities (i.e. entities outside the group) but also the results of transactions within the group. This conflicts with the purpose of the consolidated financial statements to provide information about the financial performance and financial position of the group as a result of its dealings with external entities. Hence, the effects of transactions within the group must be eliminated in the preparation of the consolidated financial statements.

The requirement for the full adjustment for the effects of intragroup transactions is stated in paragraph B86(c) of IFRS 10 *Consolidated Financial Statements*:

> eliminate in full intragroup assets and liabilities, equity, income, expenses and cash flows relating to transactions between entities of the group (profits or losses resulting from intragroup transactions that are recognised in assets, such as inventory and fixed assets, are eliminated in full). Intragroup losses may indicate an impairment that requires recognition in the consolidated financial statements. IAS 12 *Income Taxes* applies to temporary differences that arise from the elimination of profits and losses resulting from intragroup transactions.

Besides adjusting for the effects of transactions occurring in the current period, it is also necessary to adjust the current period's consolidated financial statements for the ongoing effects of transactions in previous periods. Because the consolidation adjustment entries are applied in a worksheet only, and not in the accounts of either the parent or the subsidiary, any continuing effects of previous periods' transactions must be considered. For example, if the parent provided a loan to the subsidiary, it must be eliminated on consolidation each period for as long as it remains in the financial statements of the parent and subsidiary. Similarly, where assets such as inventory are transferred at the end of one period and then are still on hand at the beginning of the next period, consolidation adjustments are required to be made in both periods.

Some intragroup transactions do not affect the carrying amounts of assets and liabilities (e.g. where there is a management fee paid by one entity to another within the group). In that case, the items affected are fee revenue and fee expense. However, in other circumstances, there are assets and liabilities recognised by the group at amounts different from the amounts recognised by the individual legal entities. For example, consider the situation where a subsidiary sold an item of inventory to the parent for $1,000 and the inventory had cost the subsidiary $800. The parent recognises the inventory at cost of $1,000, whereas the cost of the inventory to the group is only $800. As is explained in more detail later in this chapter, consolidation adjustment entries are necessary to adjust for both the profit on the intragroup transaction and the carrying amount of the inventory.

Under IAS 12 *Income Taxes*, deferred tax accounts must be recognised where there are temporary differences between the carrying amount of an asset or liability and its tax base. Any difference between the carrying amount of an asset or a liability and its tax base in a legal entity within the group is accounted for by the legal entity. However, on consolidation, in relation to intragroup transactions, adjustments may be made to the carrying amounts of assets and liabilities. Hence, in adjusting for intragroup transactions wherever there are changes to the carrying amounts of assets and liabilities, any associated tax effect must be considered. Paragraph B86(c) of IFRS 10 recognises the need to apply tax-effect accounting for temporary differences arising from the elimination of profits and losses from intragroup transactions.

For example, assume an asset is transferred from the parent entity to the subsidiary at a transfer price of $1,000. The subsidiary recognises the asset at a carrying amount of $1,000. Assume also that the tax base is $800. In the records of the subsidiary, the application of tax-effect accounting will account for the temporary difference of $200, raising a deferred tax liability of $60, assuming a tax rate of 30%. On consolidation, any unrealised profit included in the carrying amount of assets arising from intragroup transactions must be eliminated. Assume the carrying amount of the asset held by the subsidiary includes $50 of unrealised profit arising from the transfer of the asset from the parent entity to the subsidiary. On consolidation, an adjustment is made to reduce the carrying amount of the asset by $50 to $950. The consolidation adjustment entries must include an adjustment for the tax effect of the change in the carrying amount of the asset, namely a reduction in the deferred tax liability of $15 (i.e. 30% × $50). The consolidated financial statements then show a deferred tax liability of $45 (i.e. $60 − $15). The combination of the tax-effect entries in the subsidiaries and the tax-effect adjustments on consolidation will account for the temporary difference caused by the group showing the asset at $950 and the tax base being $800, namely a deferred tax liability of $45 (i.e. 30% × ($950 − $800)). As can be seen in this example, in preparing the consolidation adjustments it is unnecessary to consider the tax-effect entries made in the individual entities in the group. If the appropriate tax-effect adjustments are made for changes in the carrying amounts of the assets, then the combination of those adjustments and the tax-effect entries made in the entities themselves will produce the correct answer.

In this book, it is assumed that each subsidiary is a tax-paying entity. Under the tax consolidation system in some countries, groups comprising a parent and its wholly owned subsidiaries can elect to consolidate and be treated as a single entity for tax purposes. Such entities prepare a consolidated tax return, and the effects of intragroup transactions are eliminated. Under such a scheme, the tax-effect adjustments demonstrated in this chapter would not apply.

Just as the elimination of investment in subsidiary is used in a consolidation worksheet to eliminate the investment and to adjust for pre-acquisition equity, adjustment journal entries are prepared for intragroup transactions and are recorded in the consolidation worksheet. The same two adjustment columns are used to effect these adjustments. For example, if it were necessary to adjust downwards by $10,000 the service revenue and the associated expense recorded by the legal entities, the consolidation worksheet would show the following line:

	Parent	Subsidiary	Adjustments Dr	Adjustments Cr	Group
Service revenue	100,000	80,000	10,000		170,000
Expense	30,000	30,000		10,000	50,000

In the following sections of this chapter, two types of intragroup transactions are discussed — transfers of inventory and intragroup services. In each of the specific sections covering these transactions, the process of determining when profits are realised for the different types of transactions is discussed.

22.2 TRANSFERS OF INVENTORY

In the following examples, assume that Jessica Ltd owns all the share capital of Amelie Ltd, and that the consolidation process is being carried out on 30 June 2026, for the year ending on that date. Assume also a tax rate of 30%. All entries shown as being for the individual entities assume the use of a perpetual inventory system, and adjustments will be made, where necessary, to cost of sales.

22.2.1 Sales of inventory

Example: Intragroup sales of inventory

On 1 January 2026, Jessica Ltd acquired $10,000 worth of inventory for cash from Amelie Ltd. The inventory had previously cost Amelie Ltd $8,000.

In the accounting records of Amelie Ltd, the following journal entries are made on 1 January 2026:

Cash	Dr	10,000	
Sales Revenue	Cr		10,000
Cost of Sales	Dr	8,000	
Inventory	Cr		8,000

In Jessica Ltd, the journal entry is:

Inventory	Dr	10,000	
Cash	Cr		10,000

From the viewpoint of the group in relation to this transaction, no sales of inventory were made to any party outside the group, nor has the group acquired any inventory from external entities. Hence, if the financial statements of Jessica Ltd and Amelie Ltd are simply added together for consolidation purposes, 'sales', 'cost of sales' and 'inventory' would be overstated in the consolidated financial statements of the group. Accordingly, we will need to adjust 'sales', 'cost of sales' and 'inventory' on consolidation so that the consolidated financial statements present the results of transactions with entities external to the group.

22.2.2 Realisation of profits or losses

Paragraph B86(c) of IFRS 10 states that the profits and losses resulting from intragroup transactions that require consolidation adjustments to be made are those 'recognised in assets'. These profits can be described as 'unrealised profits'. The test for realisation is the involvement of an external party in relation to the item involved in the intragroup transaction. If an item of inventory is transferred from a subsidiary to the parent entity (or vice versa), no external party is involved in that transaction. The profit made by the subsidiary is unrealised to the group. If the parent then sells that inventory item to a party external to the group, the intragroup profit becomes realised to the group. For example, assume a subsidiary, Amelie Ltd, sells inventory to its parent, Jessica Ltd, for $100, and that inventory cost Amelie Ltd $90. The profit on this transaction is unrealised. If Jessica Ltd sells the inventory to an external party for $100, the intragroup profit is realised. The group sold inventory that cost the group $90 to an external party for $100. The group has made $10 profit. Hence, the consolidation adjustments for profits on intragroup transfers of inventory depend on whether the acquiring entity has sold the inventory to entities outside the group. In other words, the adjustments depend on whether the acquiring entity still carries some or all of the transferred inventory as ending inventory at the end of the financial period.

22.2.3 Profits in ending inventory

The following example uses the information in the example in section 22.2.1 and provides information about whether the inventory transferred is still on hand at the end of the financial period.

Example: Transferred inventory still on hand

On 30 June 2026, all the inventory sold by Amelie Ltd to Jessica Ltd is still on hand. The adjustment entries in the consolidation worksheet at 30 June 2026 are:

Sales Revenue	Dr	10,000
Cost of Sales	Cr	8,000
Inventory	Cr	2,000

The sales adjustment is necessary to eliminate the effects of the original sale in the current period. Amelie Ltd recorded sales of $10,000. From the group's viewpoint, as no external party was involved in the transaction, no sales should be shown in the consolidated financial statements. To adjust sales revenue downwards, a debit adjustment is necessary. The effect of this adjustment on the consolidation process is seen in figure 22.2. Hence, an adjustment is necessary to eliminate the sales recorded by Amelie Ltd.

Using similar reasoning as with the adjustment for sales revenue, the subsidiary has recorded cost of sales of $8,000, but the group has made no sales to entities external to the group. Hence, the consolidation worksheet needs to have a reduction in cost of sales of $8,000 in order to show a zero amount in the consolidation column. Note also that adjusting sales by $10,000 and cost of sales by $8,000 effectively reduces consolidated profit by $2,000. In other words, the $2,000 profit recorded by Amelie Ltd on selling inventory to Jessica Ltd is eliminated and a zero profit is shown on consolidation. As no external party was involved in the transfer of inventory, the whole of the profit on the intragroup transaction is unrealised. This is illustrated in figure 22.2.

FIGURE 22.2 Extract from consolidation worksheet — profit in closing inventory

	Parent	Subsidiary	Adjustments Dr		Adjustments Cr		Group
Sales revenue	0	10,000	1	10,000			—
Cost of sales	0	8,000			8,000	1	—
		2,000					
Tax expense	0	600			600	2	—
Profit		1,400					—
Inventory	10,000	—			2,000	1	8,000
Deferred tax asset	—	—	2	600			600

The previous explanation dealing with the effect on profit covers only the statement of profit or loss and other comprehensive income part of the adjustment. Under the historical cost system, assets in the consolidated statement of financial position must be shown at cost to the group. Inventory is recorded in Jessica Ltd at $10,000, the cost to Jessica Ltd. The cost to the group is, however, $8,000, the amount that was paid for the inventory by Amelie Ltd to entities external to the group. Hence, if inventory is to be reported at $8,000 in the consolidated financial statements, and it is recorded in Jessica Ltd's records at $10,000, a credit adjustment of $2,000 is needed to reduce the inventory to $8,000, the cost to the group. This effect is seen in figure 22.2.

Jessica Ltd has recorded the inventory in its records at $10,000. This amount is probably also its tax base. However, *as explained in section 22.1*, any difference between the tax base and the carrying amount in Jessica Ltd is accounted for in the tax-effect entries in Jessica Ltd. On consolidation, a tax-effect entry is necessary where an adjustment entry causes a difference between the carrying amount of an asset or a liability in the records of the legal entity and the carrying amount shown in the consolidated financial statements. In the adjustment entry relating to profit in ending inventory in the above example, the carrying amount of inventory is reduced downwards by $2,000. The carrying amount and tax base of the inventory in Jessica Ltd is $10,000, but the carrying amount in the group is $8,000. This $2,000 difference is a deductible temporary difference giving rise to a deferred tax asset of $600 (i.e. 30% × $2,000), as well as a corresponding decrease in income tax expense. The appropriate consolidation worksheet adjustment entry is:

Deferred Tax Asset	Dr	600
Income Tax Expense	Cr	600

The effects of this entry are shown in figure 22.2.

The profit recorded by Amelie Ltd on the sale of inventory to Jessica Ltd increased Amelie Ltd's taxable profit by $2,000 and thus increased income tax expense and tax payable by $600. The consolidation worksheet adjustment entry reduces income tax expense by $600. Thus, from the perspective of the group there is no tax expense arising from the intragroup transaction.

The deferred tax asset recognises that the group is expected to earn profits in the future that will not require the payment of tax to the Taxation Office. When the inventory is sold by Jessica Ltd in a future period, this temporary difference is reversed. To illustrate this effect, assume that in the following period Jessica Ltd sells this inventory to an external entity for $11,000. Jessica Ltd will record a before-tax profit of $1,000 (i.e. $11,000 − $10,000) and an associated tax expense of $300. From the consolidated group position, the profit on sale is $3,000 (i.e. $11,000 − $8,000). The group will show current tax payable of $300, reverse the $600 deferred tax asset, and recognise an income tax expense of $900. These effects are further illustrated below.

Example: Transferred inventories partly sold

On 1 January 2026, Jessica Ltd acquired $10,000 worth of inventory for cash from Amelie Ltd. The inventory had previously cost Amelie Ltd $8,000. By the end of the year, 30 June 2026, Jessica Ltd had sold 75% of the transferred inventory for $14,000 to external entities. Thus, at 30 June 2026 Jessica Ltd has 25% of the transferred inventory on hand. Although Jessica Ltd records the inventory at $2,500, the cost to the group is only $2,000 ($8,000 × 25%).

The adjustment entry for the preparation of consolidated financial statements at 30 June 2026 is:

Sales	Dr	10,000	
Cost of Sales	Cr		9,500
Inventory	Cr		500

The total sales recorded by the *legal entities* are $24,000; that is, $10,000 by Amelie Ltd and $14,000 by Jessica Ltd. The sales by the *group*, being those sold to entities external to the group, are $14,000. The consolidation adjustment to sales revenue is then $10,000, being the amount necessary to eliminate the sales within the group.

The total cost of sales recorded by the *legal entities* is $15,500; that is, $8,000 by Amelie Ltd and $7,500 by Jessica Ltd (i.e. 75% × $10,000). The cost of sales to the *group*, being those to entities external to the group, is $6,000 (i.e. 75% × $8,000). Hence, the consolidation adjustment is $9,500; that is, $15,500 (sum of recorded sales) less $6,000 (group). The adjustment is that necessary to adjust the sum of the amounts recorded by the legal entities to that to be recognised by the group.

Note that the combined adjustments to sales and cost of sales result in a $500 reduction in before-tax profit. Of the $2,000 intragroup profit on the transfer of inventory from Amelie Ltd to Jessica Ltd, since three-quarters of the inventory has been sold by Jessica Ltd to an external party, $1,500 of the profit is realised to the group and only $500, the profit remaining in ending inventory, is unrealised. It is the unrealised profit that is adjusted for in the worksheet entry.

The group profit is then $500 less than that recorded by the legal entities. The sum of profits recorded by the legal entities is $8,500, consisting of $2,000 recorded by Amelie Ltd and $6,500 (being sales of $14,000 less cost of sales of $7,500) recorded by Jessica Ltd. From the group's viewpoint, profit on sale of inventory to external entities is only $8,000, consisting of sales of $14,000 less cost of sales of $6,000 (being 75% of original cost of $8,000). Hence, an adjustment of $500 is necessary to reduce recorded profit of $8,500 to group profit of $8,000.

The $500 adjustment to inventory reflects the proportion of the total profit on sale of the transferred inventory that remains in the inventory on hand at the end of the period. Since 25% of the transferred inventory is still on hand at the end of the period, then 25% of the total profit on transfer of inventory (i.e. 25% × $2,000) needs to be adjusted at the end of the period. The adjustment entry reduces the inventory on hand at 30 June 2026 from the recorded cost to Jessica Ltd of $2,500 to the group cost of $2,000 (being 25% of the original cost of $8,000).

The adjustments above have been determined by comparing the combined amounts recorded by the parent and the subsidiary with the amounts that the group should report in the consolidated financial statements. This process could be shown in the form of a table, as follows:

	Parent	Subsidiary	Total Recorded	Group	Adjustment
Sales	14,000	10,000	24,000	14,000	Dr 10,000
Cost of sales	(7,500)	(8,000)	(15,500)	(6,000)	Cr 9,500
Profit	6,500	2,000	8,500	8,000	
Inventory	2,500	0	2,500	2,000	Cr $500

Consider the *tax effect* of this adjustment. The carrying amount of the inventory is reduced by $500, reflecting the fact that the carrying amount to the group is $500 less than the carrying amount in the financial statements of Jessica Ltd. This gives rise to a deductible temporary difference of $500. Hence, a deferred tax asset of $150 (i.e. 30% × $500) must be raised on consolidation with a corresponding effect on income tax expense. Note that Amelie Ltd has recognised current tax expense and tax payable of $600 as a result of the taxable profit of $2,000 arising from the sales to Jessica Ltd. The recognition of the deferred tax asset and corresponding reduction in income tax expense of $150 partially offsets the current income tax expense. The tax expense of the group is thus $2,400 comprising $1,950 ($6,500 x 30%) recognised by Jessica Ltd, $600 recognised by Amelie Ltd, less $150 eliminated on consolidation.

The expectation of the group is that, in some future period, it will recognise the remaining $500 profit in transferred inventory when it sells the inventory to an external party, but will not have to pay tax on the $500 as Amelie Ltd has already paid the relevant tax. Note that the tax-deductible amount for Jessica Ltd is $2,500, being the cost to Jessica Ltd, not the cost to the group of $2,000. This expected tax saving to the group will be shown in the consolidated financial statements by a debit adjustment of $150 to the Deferred Tax Asset account.

The tax-effect adjustment entry is then:

Deferred Tax Asset	Dr	150
Income Tax Expense	Cr	150

Example: Transferred inventory completely sold

On 1 January 2026, Jessica Ltd acquired $10,000 worth of inventory for cash from Amelie Ltd. The inventory had previously cost Amelie Ltd $8,000. By the end of the year, 30 June 2026, Jessica Ltd had sold all the transferred inventory to an external party for $18,000.

> Amelie Ltd records a profit of $ 2,000 (i.e. $10,000 − $8,000)
> Jessica Ltd records a profit of $ 8,000 (i.e. $18,000 − $10,000)
> Total recorded profit is $10,000

> Profit to the group = Selling price to external entities less cost to the group
>   = $18,000 − $8,000
>   = $10,000

Since the recorded profit equals the profit to the group, there is no need for a profit adjustment on consolidation. Further, as there is no transferred inventory still on hand, there is no need for an adjustment to inventory. Because all the inventory has been sold to an external entity, the whole of the intragroup profit is realised to the group. Note, however, that an adjustment for the sales and cost of sales is still necessary. As noted previously, the sales within the group amount to $18,000 whereas the sales recorded by the legal entities total $28,000 (i.e. $10,000 + $18,000). Hence, sales must be reduced by $10,000. The total recorded cost of sales is $18,000, being $8,000 by Amelie Ltd and $10,000 by Jessica Ltd. The group's cost of sales is the original cost of the transferred inventory, $8,000. Hence, cost of sales is reduced by $10,000 on consolidation. The adjustment entry is then:

Sales	Dr	10,000
Cost of Sales	Cr	10,000

Since there is no adjustment to the carrying amounts of assets or liabilities, there is no need for any *tax-effect* adjustment.

Where inventory is transferred in the current period and some or all of that inventory is still on hand at the end of the period, the general form of the worksheet entries is:

Sales Revenue	Dr	xxx
Cost of Sales	Cr	xxx
Inventory	Cr	xxx
(The adjustment to inventory is based on the profit remaining in inventory on hand at the end of the period)		
Deferred Tax Asset	Dr	xxx
Income Tax Expense	Cr	xxx
(The tax rate times the adjustment to ending inventory)		

22.2.4 Profits in opening inventory

Any transferred inventory remaining unsold at the end of one period is still on hand at the beginning of the next period. Because the consolidation adjustments are made only in a worksheet and not in the records of any of the legal entities, any differences in balances between the legal entities and the consolidated group at the end of one period must still exist at the beginning of the next period.

Example: Transferred inventory on hand at the beginning of the period

On 1 July 2025, the first day of the current period, Amelie Ltd has on hand inventory worth $7,000, transferred from Jessica Ltd in June 2025. The inventory had previously cost Jessica Ltd $4,500. The tax rate is 30%.

In this example, in the preparation of the consolidated financial statements at *30 June 2025* the following adjustment entries for the $2,500 profit in ending inventory would have been made in the consolidation worksheet:

Sales	Dr	7,000	
Cost of Sales	Cr		4,500
Inventory	Cr		2,500
Deferred Tax Asset	Dr	750	
Income Tax Expense	Cr		750
(30% × $2,500)			

Since the ending inventory at 30 June 2025 becomes the beginning inventory for the next year, an adjustment is necessary in the consolidated financial statements prepared for the year ended 30 June 2026. The required adjustment is:

Retained Earnings (1/7/25)	Dr	2,500	
Cost of Sales	Cr		2,500

In making this consolidation worksheet adjustment, it is assumed that the inventory is sold to external entities in the current period. If this is not the case, then the adjustment to inventory that was made for the year ended 30 June 2025 will need to be made again in preparing the consolidated financial statements for the year ended 30 June 2026.

In making a *credit adjustment* of $2,500, cost of sales is reduced. The cost of sales recorded by Amelie Ltd for the year ended 30 June 2026 is $2,500 greater than that which the group should report, because the cost of sales recorded by Jessica Ltd is $7,000, whereas the cost of sales to the group is only $4,500. A reduction in cost of sales means an increase in profit. Hence, for the year ended 30 June 2026, the group's profit is greater than the sum of the legal entities' profit.

The *debit adjustment* to the opening balance of retained earnings reduces that balance; that is, the group made less profit in previous years than the sum of the retained earnings recorded by the legal entities. This is because, in June 2025, Jessica Ltd recorded a $2,500 profit on the sale of inventory to Amelie Ltd, this profit not being recognised by the group until the year ended 30 June 2026.

Consider the *tax effect* of these entries. If the previous period's tax-effect adjustment were carried forward into this year's worksheet it would be:

Deferred Tax Asset	Dr	750	
Retained Earnings (1/7/25)	Cr		750

On sale of the inventory during the year ended 30 June 2026, the deferred tax asset is reversed, with a resultant effect on income tax expense:

Income Tax Expense	Dr	750	
Deferred Tax Asset	Cr		750

On combining these two entries, the worksheet entry required is:

Income Tax Expense	Dr	750	
Retained Earnings (1/7/25)	Cr		750

In summary, the adjustment to cost of sales, retained earnings and income tax expense can be combined into one entry as follows:

Retained Earnings (1/7/25)	Dr	1,750
Income Tax Expense	Dr	750
Cost of Sales	Cr	2,500

Note that this entry has no effect on the closing balance of retained earnings at 30 June 2026. As the inventory has been sold outside the group, the whole of the profit on the intragroup transaction is realised to the group. There is no unrealised profit to be adjusted for at the end of the period.

Where inventory was transferred in a previous period and some or all of that inventory is still on hand at the beginning of the current period, the general form of the entries is:

Retained Earnings (opening balance)	Dr	xxx
Cost of Sales	Cr	xxx
Income Tax Expense	Dr	xxx
Retained Earnings (opening balance)	Cr	xxx

It can be seen that the consolidation worksheet entries for inventory transferred within the current period are different from those where the inventory was transferred in a previous period. *Before preparing the adjustment entries, it is essential to determine the timing of the transaction.*

Illustrative example 22.1 provides the consolidation worksheet entries for intragroup transfer of inventory.

ILLUSTRATIVE EXAMPLE 22.1 Intragroup transactions involving transfers of inventory

Leah Ltd acquired all the issued shares of Sophia Ltd on 1 January 2025. The following transactions occurred between the two entities:
1. On 1 June 2026, Leah Ltd sold inventory to Sophia Ltd for $12,000, this inventory previously costing Leah Ltd $10,000. By 30 June 2026, Sophia Ltd had sold 20% of this inventory to external entities for $3,000. The other 80% was all sold to external entities by 30 June 2027 for $13,000.
2. During the year ended 30 June 2027, Sophia Ltd sold inventory to Leah Ltd for $6,000, this being at cost plus 20% mark-up. Of this inventory, $1,200 remained on hand in Leah Ltd at 30 June 2027.

The tax rate is 30%.

Required

Prepare the consolidation worksheet entries for Leah Ltd at 30 June 2027 in relation to the intragroup transfers of inventory.

Solution

1. Sale of inventory in previous period

Retained Earnings (1/7/26)	Dr	1,120
Income Tax Expense	Dr	480
Cost of Sales	Cr	1,600

Working:
- this is a prior period transaction
- profit after tax remaining in inventory at 1/7/26 is $1,120 (= 80% × $2,000 (1 − 30%))
- cost of sales recorded by Sophia Ltd is $9,600 (= 80% × $12,000); cost of sales to the group is $8,000 (= 80% × $10,000). The adjustment is then $1,600.

2. Sale of inventory in current period

Sales	Dr	6,000
Cost of Sales	Cr	5,800
Inventory	Cr	200
Deferred Tax Asset	Dr	60
Income Tax Expense	Cr	60

Working:
- this is a current period transaction
- sales within the group are $6,000
- cost of sales recorded by the members of the group are $5,000 for Sophia Ltd and $4,800 (= 4/5 × $6,000) for Leah Ltd; a total of $9,800. Cost of sales for the group is $4,000 (= 4/5 × $5,000). The adjustment is then $5,800
- the inventory remaining at 30 June 2027 is recorded by Leah Ltd at $1,200. The cost to the group is $1,000 (= 1/5 × $5,000). The adjustment to inventory is then $200
- as the inventory is adjusted by $200, the tax effect is $60 (= 30% × $200).

22.3 INTRAGROUP SERVICES

Many different examples of services between related entities exist. For instance:

- Jessica Ltd may lend to Amelie Ltd some specialist personnel for a limited period of time for the performance of a particular task by Amelie Ltd. For this service, Jessica Ltd may charge Amelie Ltd a certain fee, or expect Amelie Ltd to perform other services in return.
- One entity may lease or rent an item of plant or a warehouse from the other.
- A subsidiary may exist solely for the purpose of carrying out some specific tasks, such as research activities for the parent, and a fee for such research is charged. In some circumstances, the cost of services may be capitalised. For example, certain services provided in the construction of an item of property, plant and equipment are included in the carrying amount of the asset in accordance with IAS 16 *Property, Plant and Equipment* (*see chapter 5*). However, throughout this section it is assumed that intragroup services result in service revenue in the separate financial statements of the entity providing the services and a corresponding expense in the separate financial statements of the entity receiving the services.
- The revenue and expense must be eliminated in the consolidation process because they do not result from transactions with a party outside the group.

Example: Intragroup services

During the year ended 30 June 2026, Jessica Ltd offered the services of a specialist employee to Amelie Ltd for 2 months; in return Amelie Ltd paid $30,000 to Jessica Ltd. The employee's annual salary is $155,000, paid for by Jessica Ltd.

The journal entries in the records of Jessica Ltd and Amelie Ltd in relation to this transaction are:

Jessica Ltd			
Cash	Dr	30,000	
Service Revenue	Cr		30,000
Amelie Ltd			
Service Expense	Dr	30,000	
Cash	Cr		30,000

From the group's perspective there has been no service revenue received or service expense made to entities external to the group. Hence, to adjust from what has been recorded by the legal entities to the group's perspective, the consolidation adjustment entry is:

Service Revenue	Dr	30,000	
Service Expense	Cr		30,000

No adjustment is made in relation to the employee's salary since, from the group's view, the salary paid to the employee is a payment to an external party.

Since there is no effect on the carrying amounts of assets or liabilities, there is no temporary difference and no need for any income tax adjustment.

Example: Intragroup rent

Jessica Ltd rents office space from Amelie Ltd for $150,000 for one year. Due to the short-term nature of the lease, it is accounted for as a short-term lease by Jessica Ltd, the lessee, and as an operating lease by Amelie Ltd, the lessor, in accordance with IFRS 16 *Leases* (*see chapter 9*).

In accounting for this transaction, Jessica Ltd records rent expense of $150,000 and Amelie Ltd records rent revenue of $150,000. From the group's view, the intragroup rental scheme is purely an internal arrangement, and no revenue or expense is incurred. The recorded revenue and expense therefore need to be eliminated. The appropriate consolidation adjustment entry is:

Rent Revenue	Dr	150,000	
Rent Expense	Cr		150,000

There is no tax-effect entry necessary as assets and liabilities are unaffected by the adjustment entry.

22.3.1 Realisation of profits or losses

With the transfer of services within the group, the consolidation adjustments do not affect the profit of the group. In a transaction involving a payment by a parent to a subsidiary for services rendered, the parent shows an expense and the subsidiary shows revenue. The net effect on the group's profit is zero. Any profit associated with the provision of services within the group is assumed to be realised in the period in which the service is provided. Hence, from the group's view, with intragroup services there is no unrealised profit.

22.4 INTRAGROUP DIVIDENDS

In this section, consideration is given to dividends declared and paid after Jessica Ltd's acquisition of Amelie Ltd. All dividends received by the parent from the subsidiary are accounted for as revenue by the parent, regardless of whether the dividends are paid from pre- or post-acquisition equity.

Two situations are considered in this section:
- dividends declared in the current period but not paid
- dividends declared and paid in the current period.

It is assumed that the company expecting to receive the dividend recognises revenue when the dividend is declared. In accordance with paragraph 12 of IAS 27 *Separate Financial Statements* an entity should recognise dividends from a subsidiary 'when the entity's right to receive the dividend is established'.

22.4.1 Dividends declared in the current period but not paid

Assume that, on 25 June 2026, Amelie Ltd declares a dividend of $4,000. At the end of the period, the dividend is unpaid. The entries passed by the legal entities are:

Amelie Ltd			
Dividend Declared (In retained earnings)	Dr	4,000	
Dividend Payable	Cr		4,000
Jessica Ltd			
Dividend Receivable	Dr	4,000	
Dividend Revenue	Cr		4,000

The entry made by Amelie Ltd both reduces retained earnings and raises a liability account. From the group's perspective, there is no reduction in equity and the group has no obligation to pay dividends outside the group. Similarly, the group expects no dividends to be received from entities outside the group. Hence, the appropriate consolidation adjustment entries are:

Dividend Payable	Dr	4,000	
Dividend Declared	Cr		4,000
(To adjust for the effects of the entry made by Amelie Ltd)			
Dividend Revenue	Dr	4,000	
Dividend Receivable	Cr		4,000
(To adjust for the effects of the entry made by Jessica Ltd)			

In the following period when the dividend is paid, no adjustments are required in the consolidation worksheet. As there are no dividend revenue, dividend declared, or receivable items left open at the end of the period, then the position of the group is the same as the sum of the legal entities' financial statements.

22.4.2 Dividends declared and paid in the current period

Assume Amelie Ltd declares and pays an interim dividend of $4,000 in the current period. Entries by the *legal entities* are:

Jessica Ltd				
Cash		Dr	4,000	
Dividend Revenue		Cr		4,000
Amelie Ltd				
Interim Dividend Paid (In retained earnings)		Dr	4,000	
Cash		Cr		4,000

From the outlook of the *group*, no dividends have been paid and no dividend revenue has been received. Hence, the adjustment necessary for the consolidated financial statements to show the affairs of the group is:

Dividend Revenue		Dr	4,000	
Interim Dividend Paid		Cr		4,000

Tax effect of dividends

Generally, dividends are tax-free. There are, therefore, no tax-effect adjustment entries required in relation to dividend-related consolidation adjustment entries, as shown in illustrative example 22.2.

ILLUSTRATIVE EXAMPLE 22.2 Intragroup dividends

Alice Ltd owns all the issued shares of Abigail Ltd, having acquired them for $250,000 on 1 January 2025. In preparing the consolidated financial statements at 30 June 2027, the accountant documented the following transactions:

2026	
Jan. 15	Abigail Ltd paid an interim dividend of $10,000.
June 25	Abigail Ltd declared a dividend of $15,000, this being recognised in the records of both entities.
Aug. 1	The $15,000 dividend declared on 25 June was paid by Abigail Ltd.

2027	
Jan. 18	Abigail Ltd paid an interim dividend of $12,000.
June 23	Abigail Ltd declared a dividend of $18,000, this being recognised in the records of both entities.

The tax rate is 30%.

Required

Prepare the consolidation worksheet adjustment entries for the preparation of consolidated financial statements at 30 June 2027.

Solution

The required entries are:

1. *Interim dividend paid*

Dividend Revenue		Dr	12,000	
Dividend Paid		Cr		12,000

2. *Final dividend declared*

Dividend Payable		Dr	18,000	
Dividend Declared		Cr		18,000
Dividend Revenue		Dr	18,000	
Dividend Receivable		Cr		18,000

22.5 INTRAGROUP BORROWINGS

Members of a group often borrow and lend money among themselves, and charge interest on the money borrowed. In some cases, an entity may be set up within the group solely for the purpose of handling group finances and for borrowing money on international money markets. Consolidation adjustments are necessary in relation to these intragroup borrowings because, from the stance of the group, loans receivable and loans payable are not assets or liabilities of the group. Similarly, the interest income and interest expenses should be eliminated because they do not arise from transactions with parties external to the group.

Example: Advances

Jessica Ltd lends $100,000 to Amelie Ltd, the latter paying $15,000 interest to Jessica Ltd. The relevant journal entries in each of the legal entities are:

Jessica Ltd				
Advance to Amelie Ltd		Dr	100,000	
Cash		Cr		100,000
Cash		Dr	15,000	
Interest Revenue		Cr		15,000
Amelie Ltd				
Cash		Dr	100,000	
Advance from Jessica Ltd		Cr		100,000
Interest Expense		Dr	15,000	
Cash		Cr		15,000

The consolidation adjustments involve eliminating the monetary asset created by Jessica Ltd, the monetary liability raised by Amelie Ltd, the interest revenue recorded by Jessica Ltd and the interest expense paid by Amelie Ltd:

Advance from Jessica Ltd		Dr	100,000	
Advance to Amelie Ltd		Cr		100,000
Interest Revenue		Dr	15,000	
Interest Expense		Cr		15,000

The adjustment to the asset and liability is necessary as long as the intragroup loan exists. In relation to any past period's payments and receipt of interest, no ongoing adjustment to accumulated profits (opening balance) is necessary as the net effect of the consolidation adjustment is zero on that item.

Because the effect on net assets of the consolidation adjustment is zero, no tax-effect entry is necessary.

22.6 SUMMARY

Intragroup transactions can take many forms and may involve transfers of inventory or property, plant and equipment, or they may relate to the provision of services by one member of the group to another member. To prepare the relevant worksheet entries for a transaction, it is necessary to consider the accounts affected in the entities involved in the transaction.

Intragroup transfers of inventory, services, dividends and debentures and their adjustment in the consolidation process are associated with a need to consider the implications of applying tax-effect accounting in the consolidation process.

The basic approach to determining the consolidation adjustment entries for intragroup transfers is:
(a) Analyse the events within the records of the legal entities involved in the intragroup transfer. Determine whether the transaction is a prior period or current period event.
(b) Analyse the position from the group's viewpoint.
(c) Create adjusting entries to change from the legal entities' position to that of the group.
(d) Consider the tax effect of the adjusting entries.

Note again that there are no actual adjusting entries made in the records of the individual legal entities which constitute the group. However, if required, a special journal could be set up by the parent entity to keep a record of the adjustments made in the process of preparing the consolidated financial statements. Alternatively, the consolidation process may be performed by the use of special consolidation worksheets.

Why a particular adjustment is the correct one involves an explanation of each line in the adjustment entry including why an account was adjusted, why it was increased or decreased, and why a particular adjustment amount is appropriate. This generally involves a comparison of what accounts were affected in the records of the legal entities with how the information should be presented in the consolidated financial statements.

DEMONSTRATION PROBLEM 22.1 Intragroup transfers of assets

The following example illustrates procedures for the preparation of a consolidated statement of profit or loss and other comprehensive income, a consolidated statement of changes in equity and a consolidated statement of financial position where the subsidiary is 100% owned. The consolidation worksheet adjustments for intragroup transactions including inventory are also demonstrated.

Details

On 1 July 2024, Eliza Ltd acquired all the share capital of Ebony Ltd for $472,000. At that date, Ebony Ltd's equity consisted of the following.

Share capital	$ 300,000
General reserve	96,000
Retained earnings	56,000

At 1 July 2024, all the identifiable assets and liabilities of Ebony Ltd were recorded at fair value. Financial information for Eliza Ltd and Ebony Ltd for the year ended 30 June 2026 is presented in the left-hand columns of the worksheet illustrated in figure 22.3. It is assumed that both companies use the perpetual inventory system.

Additional information

(a) On 1 January 2026, Ebony Ltd sold merchandise costing $30,000 to Eliza Ltd for $50,000. Half this merchandise was sold to external entities for $28,000 before 30 June 2026.
(b) At 1 July 2025, there was a profit in the inventory of Eliza Ltd of $6,000 on goods acquired from Ebony Ltd in the previous period.
(c) The tax rate is 30%.

Required

Prepare the consolidated financial statements for the year ended 30 June 2026.

Solution

The first step is to determine the pre-acquisition entries at 30 June 2026. These entries are prepared after undertaking an acquisition analysis.

At 1 July 2024:

Net fair value of the identifiable assets and liabilities of Ebony Ltd	= $300,000 + $96,000 + $56,000	
	= $452,000	
Consideration transferred	= $472,000	
Goodwill	= $20,000	

Consolidation worksheet entries

(1) *Business combination valuation entry*

As all the identifiable assets and liabilities of Ebony Ltd are recorded at amounts equal to their fair values, the only business combination valuation entry required is that for goodwill.

Goodwill	Dr	20,000	
Business Combination Valuation Reserve	Cr		20,000

(2) *Elimination of investment in subsidiary*

The entry at 30 June 2026 is the same as that at acquisition date as there have not been any events affecting that entry since acquisition date:

Retained Earnings (1/7/25)	Dr	56,000	
Share Capital	Dr	300,000	
General Reserve	Dr	96,000	
Business Combination Valuation Reserve	Dr	20,000	
Shares in Ebony Ltd	Cr		472,000

The next step is to prepare the adjustment entries arising because of the existence of intragroup transactions. It is important to classify the intragroup transactions into 'current period' and 'previous period' transactions. The resultant adjustment entries should reflect those decisions because previous period transactions would be expected to affect accounts such as retained earnings rather than accounts such as sales and cost of sales.

(3) *Profit in ending inventory*

The transaction occurred in the current period. The adjustment entries are:

Sales	Dr	50,000	
Cost of Sales	Cr		40,000
Inventory	Cr		10,000
($10,000 = ½ × [$50,000 − $30,000])			
Deferred Tax Asset	Dr	3,000	
Income Tax Expense	Cr		3,000
(30% × $10,000)			

Sales: The members of the group have recorded total sales of $78,000, being $50,000 by Ebony Ltd and $28,000 by Eliza Ltd. The group recognises only sales to entities outside the group, namely the sales by Eliza Ltd of $28,000. Hence, in preparing the consolidated financial statements, sales must be reduced by $50,000.

Cost of sales: Ebony Ltd recorded cost of sales of $30,000, and Eliza Ltd recorded cost of sales of $25,000 (being half of $50,000). Recorded cost of sales then totals $55,000. The cost of the sales to entities external to the group is $15,000 (being half of $30,000). Cost of sales must then be reduced by $40,000.

Inventory: At 30 June 2026, Eliza Ltd has inventory on hand from intragroup transactions, and records them at cost of $25,000 (being half of $50,000). The cost of this inventory to the group is $15,000 (being half of $30,000). Inventory is then reduced by $10,000.

Deferred tax asset/income tax expense: Under tax-effect accounting, temporary differences arise where the carrying amount of an asset differs from its tax base. In the first adjustment entry above, inventory is reduced by $10,000; that is, the carrying amount of inventory is reduced by $10,000. This then gives rise to a temporary difference, and because the carrying amount has been reduced, tax benefits are expected in the future when the asset is sold. Hence a deferred tax asset, equal to the tax rate times the change to the carrying amount of inventory (30% × $10,000), of $3,000 is raised. Given there is no Deferred Tax Asset in the worksheet in figure 22.3, the adjustment is made against the Deferred Tax Liability line item.

(4) *Profit in beginning inventory*

This is a previous period transaction. The required consolidation worksheet entry is:

Retained Earnings (1/7/25)	Dr	6,000
Cost of Sales	Cr	6,000
Income Tax Expense	Dr	1,800
Retained Earnings (1/7/25)	Cr	1,800
(30% × $6,000)		

Retained earnings: In the previous period, Ebony Ltd recorded a $6,000 before-tax profit, or a $4,200 after-tax profit on sale of inventory within the group. Because the sale did not involve external entities, the profit must be eliminated on consolidation.

Cost of sales: In the current period, the transferred inventory is sold to external entities. Eliza Ltd records cost of sales at $6,000 greater than to the group. Hence, cost of sales is reduced by $6,000. Note that this increases group profit by $6,000, reflecting the realisation of the profit to the group in the current period, when it was recognised by the legal entity in the previous period.

Income tax expense: At the end of the previous period, in the consolidated statement of financial position a deferred tax asset of $1,800 was raised because of the difference in cost of the inventory recorded by the legal entity and that recognised by the group. This deferred tax asset is reversed when the asset is sold. The adjustment to income tax expense reflects the reversal of the deferred tax asset raised at the end of the previous period.

Figure 22.3 shows the completed worksheet for preparation of the consolidated financial statements of Eliza Ltd and its subsidiary Ebony Ltd at 30 June 2026. Once the effects of all adjustments are added or subtracted horizontally in the worksheet to calculate figures in the right-hand 'consolidation' column, the consolidated financial statements can be prepared, as shown in figure 22.4(a), (b) and (c).

FIGURE 22.3 Consolidation worksheet — intragroup transfers of assets

Financial Statements	Eliza Ltd	Ebony Ltd		Adjustments Dr	Adjustments Cr		Consolidation
Sales revenue	1,196,000	928,000	3	50,000			2,074,000
Cost of sales	(888,000)	(670,000)			46,000	3,4	(1,512,000)
Wages and salaries	(57,500)	(32,000)					(89,500)
Depreciation	(5,200)	(4,800)					(10,000)
Other expenses	(4,000)	—					(4,000)
Total expenses	(954,700)	(706,800)					(1,615,500)
Profit before income tax	241,300	221,200					458,500
Income tax expense	(96,120)	(118,480)	4	1,800	3,000	3	(213,400)
Profit for the year	145,180	102,720					245,100
Retained earnings (1/7/25)	100,820	70,280	2	56,000	1,800	4	110,900
			4	6,000			
	246,000	173,000					356,000
Dividend paid	(80,000)	—					(80,000)
Retained earnings (30/6/26)	166,000	173,000					276,000
Share capital	500,000	300,000	2	300,000			500,000
Business combination valuation reserve			2	20,000	20,000	1	—
General reserve	135,000	96,000	2	96,000			135,000
	801,000	569,000					911,000

Financial Statements	Eliza Ltd	Ebony Ltd	Adjustments Dr		Cr		Consolidation
Other components of equity (1/7/25)	4,000	10,000					14,000
Gains on financial assets	1,000	3,000					4,000
Other components of equity (30/6/26)	5,000	13,000					18,000
Total equity	806,000	582,000					929,000
Deferred tax liability	52,000	30,000	3	3,000			79,000
Total equity and liabilities	858,000	612,000					1,008,000
Shares in Ebony Ltd	472,000	—			472,000	2	—
Cash	80,000	73,000					153,000
Inventory	169,000	36,000			10,000	3	195,000
Other current assets	10,000	300,000					310,000
Financial assets	15,000	68,000					83,000
Land	70,000	120,000					190,000
Plant and equipment	52,000	28,000					80,000
Accumulated depreciation	(10,000)	(13,000)					(23,000)
Goodwill	—	—	1	20,000			20,000
	858,000	612,000		552,800	552,800		1,008,000

FIGURE 22.4 (a) Consolidated statement of profit or loss and other comprehensive income

ELIZA LTD
Consolidated Statement of Profit or Loss and Other Comprehensive Income
for the year ended 30 June 2026

Revenues	$ 2,074,000
Expenses	1,615,500
Profit before income tax	458,500
Income tax expense	213,400
Profit for the year	$ 245,100
Other comprehensive income	
Gains on financial assets	4,000
TOTAL COMPREHENSIVE INCOME FOR THE YEAR	$ 249,100

FIGURE 22.4 (b) Consolidated statement of changes in equity

ELIZA LTD
Consolidated Statement of Changes in Equity
for the year ended 30 June 2026

TOTAL COMPREHENSIVE INCOME FOR THE YEAR	$ 249,100
Retained earnings at 1 July 2025	$ 110,900
Profit for the year	$ 245,100
Dividend paid	$ (80,000)
Retained earnings at 30 June 2026	$ 276,000
General reserve at 1 July 2025	$ 135,000
General reserve at 30 June 2026	$ 135,000
Other components of equity at 1 July 2025	$ 14,000
Gains on financial assets	$ 4,000
Other components of equity at 30 June 2026	$ 18,000
Share capital at 1 July 2025	$ 500,000
Share capital at 30 June 2026	$ 500,000

FIGURE 22.4 (c) Consolidated statement of financial position

ELIZA LTD
Consolidated Statement of Financial Position
as at 30 June 2026

Current assets			
Cash assets			$ 153,000
Inventories			195,000
Financial assets			83,000
Other			310,000
Total current assets			741,000
Non-current assets			
Property, plant and equipment;			
Plant and equipment	$ 80,000		
Accumulated depreciation	$(23,000)	$ 57,000	
Land		190,000	247,000
Goodwill			20,000
Total non-current assets			267,000
Total assets			1,008,000
Non-current liabilities			
Deferred tax liabilities			(79,000)
Net assets			$ 929,000
Equity			
Share capital			$ 500,000
General reserve			135,000
Retained earnings			276,000
Other components of equity			18,000
Total equity			$ 929,000

DEMONSTRATION PROBLEM 22.2 Dividends and borrowings

On 1 July 2025, Lilly Ltd acquired all the share capital of Tahlia Ltd and Eva Ltd for $187,500 and $150,000 respectively. At that date, equity of the three companies was:

	Lilly Ltd	Tahlia Ltd	Eva Ltd
Share capital	$150,000	$100,000	$100,000
General reserve	90,000	60,000	40,000
Retained earnings	20,000	17,500	10,000

At 1 July 2025, the identifiable net assets of all companies were recorded at fair values.

For the year ended 30 June 2026, the summarised financial information for the three companies shows the following details:

	Lilly Ltd	Tahlia Ltd	Eva Ltd
Sales revenue	$ 388,500	$ 200,000	$ 150,000
Dividend revenue	9,000	—	—
Other revenue	10,000	—	—
Total revenues	407,500	200,000	150,000
Total expenses	(360,000)	(176,000)	(138,000)
Profit before income tax	47,500	24,000	12,000

Income tax expense	(15,000)	(10,000)	(5,000)
Profit	32,500	14,000	7,000
Retained earnings (1/7/25)	20,000	17,500	10,000
Total available for appropriation	52,500	31,500	17,000
Interim dividend paid	(7,500)	(2,500)	—
Final dividend declared	(15,000)	(5,000)	(1,500)
Transfer to general reserve	(2,000)	(5,000)	—
	(24,500)	(12,500)	(1,500)
Retained earnings (30/6/26)	$ 28,000	$ 19,000	$ 15,500
Shares in Tahlia Ltd	$ 187,500	—	—
Shares in Eva Ltd	150,000	—	—
Dividend receivable	6,500	—	—
Loan receivable	5,000	—	—
Property, plant and equipment	18,500	$ 205,000	$ 167,000
Total assets	367,500	205,000	167,000
Final dividend payable	15,000	5,000	1,500
Loan payable	—	5,000	—
Other non-current liabilities	82,500	11,000	6,000
Total liabilities	97,500	21,000	7,500
Net assets	$ 270,000	$ 184,000	$ 159,500
Share capital	$ 150,000	$ 100,000	$ 104,000
General reserve	92,000	65,000	40,000
Retained earnings	28,000	19,000	15,500
Total equity	$ 270,000	$ 184,000	$ 159,500

Additional information
(a) Lilly Ltd has lent $5,000 to Tahlia Ltd, the loan having 10% interest rate attached.
(b) Lilly Ltd has recognised both the interim and final dividends from Tahlia Ltd and Eva Ltd as revenue.

Required

Prepare the consolidated financial statements as at 30 June 2026 for Lilly Ltd and its two subsidiaries, Tahlia Ltd and Eva Ltd. Assume all reserve transfers are from post-acquisition profits.

Solution

The relationship between the parent and subsidiaries may be expressed as shown in figure 22.5.

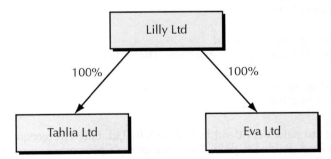

FIGURE 22.5 Relationship between parent and subsidiaries

Figure 22.6 overleaf illustrates the consolidation worksheet necessary to consolidate the financial statements of Lilly Ltd and its two subsidiaries. Detailed discussion of each adjustment is provided below. Note that:
- no adjustment entries are made for transfers to and from reserves if post-acquisition equity only is affected
- the dividends paid and declared by the parent to its shareholders are not adjusted for in the consolidated financial statements, because these dividends are paid by the group to external entities.

Acquisition analysis: Lilly Ltd and Tahlia Ltd
At 1 July 2025:

Net fair value of identifiable assets and liabilities of Tahlia Ltd	= $100,000 + $60,000 + $17,500
	= $177,500
Consideration transferred	= $187,500
Goodwill	= $10,000

Consolidation worksheet adjustment entries
(1) *Business combination valuation entry: Lilly Ltd and Tahlia Ltd*

| Goodwill | Dr | 10,000 | |
| Business Combination Valuation Reserve | Cr | | 10,000 |

(2) *Elimination of investment in subsidiary: Lilly Ltd and Tahlia Ltd*
The elimination of investment in subsidiary at 30 June 2026 is then:

Retained Earnings (1/7/25)	Dr	17,500	
Share Capital	Dr	100,000	
General Reserve	Dr	60,000	
Business Combination Valuation Reserve	Dr	10,000	
Shares in Tahlia Ltd	Cr		187,500

Acquisition analysis: Lilly Ltd and Eva Ltd
At 1 July 2025:

Net fair value of identifiable assets and liabilities of Eva Ltd	= $100,000 + $40,000 + $10,000
	= $150,000
Consideration transferred	= $150,000
Goodwill	= zero

No business combination valuation entry is required.

(3) *Elimination of investment in subsidiary: Lilly Ltd and Eva Ltd*
The elimination of investment in subsidiary at 30 June 2026 is then:

Retained Earnings (1/7/25)	Dr	10,000	
Share Capital	Dr	100,000	
General Reserve	Dr	40,000	
Shares in Eva Ltd	Cr		150,000

(4) *Interim dividend: Tahlia Ltd*
This is a current period transaction. The consolidation worksheet entry is:

| Dividend Revenue | Dr | 2,500 | |
| Dividend Paid | Cr | | 2,500 |

Tahlia Ltd paid a dividend in cash to Lilly Ltd. Lilly Ltd recognised dividend revenue and Tahlia Ltd recognised dividends paid. From the group's perspective, there were no dividends paid to entities external to the group. Hence, on consolidation it is necessary to eliminate both the Dividend Paid and Dividend Revenue accounts raised by the parent and the subsidiary.

(5) *Final dividend declared: Tahlia Ltd*
This is a current period transaction. The consolidation worksheet entry is:

Final Dividend Payable	Dr	5,000	
Final Dividend Declared	Cr		5,000
Dividend Revenue	Dr	5,000	
Dividend Receivable	Cr		5,000

The subsidiary declares a dividend, recognising a liability to pay the dividend and reducing retained earnings. The parent, which expects to receive the dividend, raises a receivable asset and recognises dividend revenue. From the group's point of view, because the dividend is not receivable or payable to entities external to the group, it does not want to recognise any of these accounts. Hence, on consolidation, all the accounts affected by this transaction in the records of the parent and the subsidiary are eliminated.

(6) *Final dividend declared: Eva Ltd*
This is a current period transaction. The consolidation worksheet entry is:

Final Dividend Payable	Dr	1,500	
Final Dividend Declared	Cr		1,500
Dividend Revenue	Dr	1,500	
Dividend Receivable	Cr		1,500

The explanation for this entry is the same as that for the dividend declared by Tahlia Ltd.

(7) *Loan: Lilly Ltd to Tahlia Ltd*
The loan may have been made in a previous period or the current period. The consolidation worksheet entry is the same:

Loan Payable	Dr	5,000	
Loan Receivable	Cr		5,000

This entry eliminates the receivable raised by the parent and the payable raised by the subsidiary. From the group's point of view, there are no loans payable or receivable to entities external to the group.

(8) *Interest on loan*
The interest paid/received is a current period transaction. In some situations where interest is accrued, interest may relate to previous or future periods. The consolidation worksheet entry is:

Interest Revenue	Dr	500	
Interest Expense	Cr		500
(10% × $5,000)			

The parent records interest revenue of $500 and the subsidiary records interest expense of $500. No interest was paid or received by the group from entities external to the group, so these accounts must be eliminated on consolidation.

Financial statements	Lilly Ltd	Tahlia Ltd	Eva Ltd		Dr	Cr		Group
				Adjustments				
Sales revenue	388,500	200,000	150,000					738,500
Dividend revenue	9,000	—	—	4	2,500			—
				5	5,000			
				6	1,500			
Other revenue	10,000	—	—	8	500			9,500
	407,500	200,000	150,000					748,000
Expenses	(360,000)	(176,000)	(138,000)			500	8	(673,500)
Profit before income tax	47,500	24,000	12,000					74,500
Income tax expense	(15,000)	(10,000)	(5,000)					(30,000)
Profit	32,500	14,000	7,000					44,500
Retained earnings (1/7/25)	20,000	17,500	10,000	2	17,500			20,000
				3	10,000			
	52,500	31,500	17,000					64,500

FIGURE 22.6 Consolidation worksheet — dividends

Financial statements	Lilly Ltd	Tahlia Ltd	Eva Ltd		Adjustments			Group
					Dr	Cr		
Interim dividend paid	(7,500)	(2,500)	—			2,500	4	(7,500)
Final dividend declared	(15,000)	(5,000)	(1,500)			5,000	5	(15,000)
						1,500	6	
Transfer to general reserve	(2,000)	(5,000)	0					(7,000)
	24,500	12,500	1,500					29,500
Retained earrings (30/6/26)	28,000	19,000	15,500					35,000
Share capital	150,000	100,000	100,000	2	100,000			150,000
				3	100,000			
General reserve	92,000	65,000	40,000	2	60,000			97,000
				3	40,000			
Business combination valuation reserve				2	10,000	10,000	1	—
Final dividend payable	15,000	5,000	1,500	5	5,000			15,000
				6	1,500			
Loan payable	—	5,000	—	7	5,000			—
Other non-current liabilities	82,500	11,000	10,000					103,500
Total equity and liabilities	367,500	205,000	167,000					400,500
Shares in Tahlia Ltd	187,500	—	—			187,500	2	—
Shares in Eva Ltd	150,000	—	—			150,000	3	—
Dividend receivable	6,500	—	—			5,000	5	—
						1,500	6	
Loan receivable	5,000	—	—			5,000	7	—
Property, plant and equipment	18,500	205,000	167,000					390,500
Goodwill	—	—	—	1	10,000			10,000
	367,500	205,000	167,000		368,500	368,500		400,500

From figure 22.6, after all adjustments have been entered in the worksheet and amounts totalled across to the consolidation column, the consolidated financial statements can be prepared in suitable format as shown in figure 22.7(a), (b) and (c).

FIGURE 22.7 (a) Consolidated statement of profit or loss and other comprehensive income

LILLY LTD Consolidated Statement of Profit or Loss and Other Comprehensive Income for the year ended 30 June 2026	
Revenues	$748,000
Expenses	673,500
Profit before income tax	74,500
Income tax expense	(30,000)
Profit for the year	$ 44,500
Other comprehensive income	—
TOTAL COMPREHENSIVE INCOME FOR THE YEAR	$ 44,500

FIGURE 22.7 (b) Consolidated statement of changes in equity

LILLY LTD Consolidated Statement of Changes in Equity for the year ended 30 June 2026	
TOTAL COMPREHENSIVE INCOME FOR THE YEAR	$ 44,500
Retained earnings at 1 July 2025	$ 20,000
Profit for the year	44,500
Interim dividend paid	(7,500)
Final dividend declared	(15,000)
Transfer to general reserve	(7,000)
Retained earnings at 30 June 2026	$ 35,000
General reserve at 1 July 2025	$ 90,000
Transfer from retained earnings	7,000
General reserve at 30 June 2026	$ 97,000
Share capital as at 1 July 2025	$ 150,000
Share capital at 30 June 2026	$ 150,000

FIGURE 22.7 (c) Consolidated statement of financial position

LILLY LTD Consolidated Statement of Financial Position as at 30 June 2026	
Non-current assets	
Property, plant and equipment	$390,500
Goodwill	10,000
Total non-current assets	400,500
Total assets	400,500
Current liabilities	
Final dividend payable	15,000
Non-current liabilities	103,500
Total liabilities	118,500
Net assets	$282,000
Equity	
Share capital	$150,000
Other reserves:	
General reserve	$ 97,000
Retained earnings	35,000
Total equity	$282,000

Discussion questions

1. Why is it necessary to make adjustments for intragroup transactions?
2. In making consolidation worksheet adjustments, sometimes tax-effect entries are made. Why?
3. Why is it important to identify transactions as current or previous period transactions?
4. Describe the adjustments required for loans between a parent and subsidiary when preparing consolidated financial statements. Why are the adjustments required?
5. What adjustments, if any, are required for service provided between entities within the group in the period in which the service is provided, and in subsequent periods?
6. What is meant by 'realisation of profits'?
7. When are profits realised in relation to inventory transfers within the group?

23 Consolidation: non-controlling interest

ACCOUNTING STANDARDS IN FOCUS

IFRS 10 *Consolidated Financial Statements*

IFRS 3 *Business Combinations*

IAS 1 *Presentation of Financial Statements*

IFRS 12 *Disclosure of Interests in Other Entities*

LEARNING OBJECTIVES

After studying this chapter, you should be able to:

 1 discuss the nature of the non-controlling interest (NCI)

 2 explain the effects of the NCI on the consolidation process

 3 explain how to calculate the NCI share of equity

 4 explain how the calculation of the NCI is affected by the existence of intragroup transactions

 5 explain how the NCI is affected by the existence of a gain on bargain purchase.

23.1 NON-CONTROLLING INTEREST EXPLAINED

In chapters 21 and 22, the group under consideration consisted of two entities where the parent owned *all* the share capital of the subsidiary. In this chapter, the group under discussion consists of a parent that has only a *partial* interest in the subsidiary; that is, the subsidiary is less than wholly owned by the parent.

23.1.1 Nature of the non-controlling interest (NCI)

Ownership interests in a subsidiary other than the parent are referred to as the non-controlling interest, or NCI. Appendix A of IFRS 10 *Consolidated Financial Statements* contains the following definition of NCI:

> Equity in a **subsidiary** not attributable, directly or indirectly, to a **parent**.

In figure 23.1, the group shown is illustrative of those discussed in this chapter. In this case, the parent entity owns 75% of the shares of a subsidiary. There are two owners in this group — the parent share-holders and the NCI. The NCI is a contributor of equity to the group.

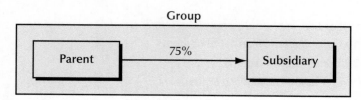

FIGURE 23.1 The group

According to paragraph 22 of IFRS 10, the NCI is to be identified and presented within equity, separately from the parent shareholders' equity; that is, it is regarded as an equity contributor to the group, rather than a liability of the group. This is because the NCI does not meet the definition of a liability as contained in the *Conceptual Framework*, because the group has no present obligation to provide economic outflows to the NCI. The NCI receives a share of consolidated equity, and is therefore a participant in the residual equity of the group.

Classification of the NCI as equity affects both the calculation of the NCI as well as how it is disclosed in the consolidated financial statements.

23.1.2 Calculation of the NCI share of equity

The NCI is entitled to a share of consolidated equity, because it is a contributor of equity to the consolidated group. Because consolidated equity is affected by profits and losses made in relation to transactions within the group, the calculation of the NCI is affected by the existence of intragroup transactions. In other words, the NCI is entitled to a share of the equity of the subsidiary adjusted for the effects of profits and losses made on intragroup transactions. *Intragroup transactions are discussed in more detail in section 22.4. The impact of intragroup transactions on NCI is discussed in section 23.2.4.*

23.1.3 Disclosure of the NCI

According to paragraph 22 of IFRS 10:

> A parent shall present non-controlling interests in the consolidated statement of financial position within equity, separately from the equity of the owners of the parent.

IAS 1 *Presentation of Financial Statements* confirms these disclosures. Paragraph 81B of IAS 1 requires the profit or loss and other comprehensive income for the period to be disclosed in the statement of profit or loss and other comprehensive income, showing separately the comprehensive income attributable to NCI, and that attributable to owners of the parent. Figure 23.2 shows how the statement of profit or loss and other comprehensive income may be shown. Note that in terms of the various line items in the statement, such as revenues and expenses, it is the total consolidated amount that is disclosed. It is only the consolidated profit and comprehensive income that is divided into parent share and NCI share.

According to paragraph 106(a) of IAS 1, the total comprehensive income for the period must be disclosed in the statement of changes in equity, showing separately the total amounts attributable to owners of the parent and to NCI. Figure 23.3 provides an example of disclosures in the statement of changes of equity. Note that the only line item for which the NCI must be shown is the total comprehensive income for the period. There is no requirement to show the NCI share of each equity account.

FIGURE 23.2 Disclosure of NCI in the statement of profit or loss and other comprehensive income

IRIS LTD Consolidated Statement of Profit or Loss and Other Comprehensive Income for the year ended 30 June 2026		
	2026 $ m	2025 $ m
Revenue	500	450
Expenses	280	260
Gross profit	220	190
Finance costs	40	35
	180	155
Share of after-tax profit of associates	30	25
Profit before tax	210	180
Income tax expense	(28)	(22)
PROFIT FOR THE YEAR	182	158
Other comprehensive income	31	24
TOTAL COMPREHENSIVE INCOME FOR THE YEAR	213	182
Profit attributable to:		
Owners of the parent	151	140
Non-controlling interests	31	18
	182	158
Total comprehensive income attributable to:		
Owners of the parent	179	160
Non-controlling interests	34	22
	213	182

FIGURE 23.3 Disclosure of NCI in the statement of changes in equity

IRIS LTD Consolidated Statement of Changes in Equity (extract) for the year ended 30 June 2026							
	Total equity					Non-controlling interest	Owners of the parent
	Share capital	Revaluation surplus	Translation reserve	Retained earnings	Total		
	$m	$m	$m	$m	$m	$m	$m
Balance at 1 July 2025	400	120	100	250	870	130	740
Changes in accounting policy	—	—	—	—	—	—	—
Total comprehensive income for the period	—	21	10	182	213	34	179
Dividends	—	—	—	(150)	(150)	(10)	(140)
Issue of share capital	—	—	—	—	—	—	—
Balance at 30 June 2026	400	141	110	282	933	154	779

Similarly, paragraph 54(q) of IAS 1 requires disclosure in the statement of financial position of the total NCI share of equity while paragraph 54(r) requires disclosure of the issued capital and reserves attributable to owners of the parent. The equity section of the statement of financial position could then appear as in figure 23.4. In the statement of financial position, only the total NCI share of equity is disclosed, rather than the NCI share of the different categories of equity. The NCI share of the various categories of equity and the changes in those balances can be seen in the statement of changes in equity. Note that the consolidated assets and liabilities are those for the whole of the group; it is only equity that is divided into parent and NCI shares.

FIGURE 23.4 Disclosure of NCI in the statement of financial position

IRIS LTD Statement of Financial Position (extract) as at 30 June 2026		
	2026 $m	2025 $m
EQUITY		
Share capital	400	400
Other reserves	251	220
Retained earnings	282	250
	933	870
Non-controlling interests	154	130
Equity attributable to owners of the parent	779	740

IFRS 12 *Disclosure of Interests in Other Entities* also contains disclosures required for subsidiaries in which there are NCIs. Paragraph 12 of IFRS 12 states:

> An entity shall disclose for each of its subsidiaries that have non-controlling interests that are material to the reporting entity:
>
> (a) the name of the subsidiary.
> (b) the principal place of business (and country of incorporation if different from the principal place of business) of the subsidiary.
> (c) the proportion of ownership interests held by non-controlling interests.
> (d) the proportion of voting rights held by non-controlling interests, if different from the proportion of ownership interests held.
> (e) the profit or loss allocated to non-controlling interests of the subsidiary during the reporting period.
> (f) accumulated non-controlling interests of the subsidiary at the end of the reporting period.
> (g) summarised financial information about the subsidiary.

23.2 EFFECTS OF NCI ON THE CONSOLIDATION PROCESS

Paragraph 32 of IFRS 3 states:

> The acquirer shall recognise goodwill as of the acquisition date measured as the excess of (a) over (b) below:
>
> (a) the aggregate of:
> (i) the consideration transferred measured in accordance with this IFRS, which generally requires acquisition date fair value;
> (ii) the amount of any non-controlling interest in the acquiree measured in accordance with this IFRS; and
> (iii) in a business combination achieved in stages, the acquisition date fair value of the acquirer's previously held equity interests in the acquiree.
> (b) the net of the acquisition-date amounts of the identifiable assets acquired and the liabilities assumed measured in accordance with this IFRS.

Consider a situation where A Ltd holds 20% of the shares in B Ltd and then acquires a further 50% of the shares of B Ltd. Holding 70% of the shares of B Ltd gives A Ltd control of that entity. At acquisition date, there is an NCI of 30%. Note:

- Where the parent acquires only a portion of the total equity or total net assets of the subsidiary, the consideration transferred is for only a portion of the net assets of the subsidiary; in this example, 50%.
- The 20% investment held prior to the parent obtaining control must be revalued at acquisition date to fair value.

The next step is to measure the amount of the 30% NCI in the subsidiary at the time of the acquisition. Paragraph 19 of IFRS 3 allows the entity to choose between two alternative approaches to the measurement of the NCI:

(a) fair value; or
(b) the present ownership instruments' proportionate share in the recognised amounts of the acquiree's identifiable net assets.

The choice of measurement approach for NCI is made for each business combination.

Which alternative is chosen affects the measurement of goodwill and the subsequent consolidation adjustments. This occurs because goodwill is measured as the residual in accounting for the business combination. Where the first alternative is used, the goodwill attributable to both the NCI and the parent is measured. Under the second alternative, only the goodwill attributable to the parent is measured. The methods are sometimes referred to as the 'full goodwill' and the 'partial goodwill' methods — see paragraph BC205 of the Basis for Conclusions on IFRS 3 for further elaboration. These terms are used in this chapter to distinguish between the two methods. *The methods are demonstrated in sections 23.2.1 and 23.2.2 and the reasons for the standard setters allowing optional measurements, as well as factors to consider in choosing between the methods, is discussed in section 23.2.3.*

23.2.1 Full goodwill method

Under this method, at acquisition date, the NCI in the subsidiary is measured at fair value. The fair value is determined on the basis of the market prices for shares not acquired by the parent, or, if these are not available, a valuation technique is used.

It is not sufficient to use the consideration paid by the acquirer to measure the fair value of the NCI. For example, if a parent paid $80,000 for 80% of the shares of a subsidiary, then the fair value of the NCI cannot be assumed to be $20,000 (i.e. 20/80 × $80,000). It may be that the acquirer paid a control premium in order to acquire a controlling interest in the subsidiary. Relating this to the nature of goodwill (refer section 19.5.3 of chapter 19), core goodwill includes the component of combination goodwill, relating to synergies arising because of the combination of the parent and the subsidiary. The parent would increase the consideration it was prepared to pay due to these synergies. However, these synergies may result in increased earnings in the parent and not the subsidiary. In this case, the NCI does not benefit from those synergies. Hence, the consideration paid by the parent could not be used to measure the fair value of the NCI in the subsidiary.

To illustrate the method, assume that P Ltd paid $169,600 for 80% of the shares of S Ltd on 1 July 2025. All identifiable assets and liabilities of the subsidiary were recorded at fair value, except for land for which the fair value was $10,000 greater than cost. The tax rate is 30%. The NCI in S Ltd was considered to have a fair value of $42,000. At acquisition date, the equity of S Ltd consisted of:

Share capital	$100,000
General reserve	60,000
Retained earnings	40,000

The acquisition analysis is as follows:

Net fair value of identifiable assets and liabilities of S Ltd	= $100,000 + $60,000 + $40,000 + $10,000(1 − 30%) (BCVR — land)
	= $207,000
(a) Consideration transferred	= $169,600
(b) Non-controlling interest in S Ltd	= $42,000
Aggregate of (a) and (b)	= $211,600
Goodwill	= $211,600 − $207,000
	= $4,600
Goodwill of S Ltd	
Fair value of S Ltd	= $42,000/20%
	= $210,000
Net fair value of identifiable assets and liabilities of S Ltd	= $207,000
Goodwill of S Ltd	= $210,000 − $207,000
	= $3,000
Goodwill of P Ltd	
Goodwill acquired	= $4,600
Goodwill of S Ltd	= $3,000
Goodwill of P Ltd — control premium	= $1,600

Note the following:
- The acquired goodwill of $4,600 calculated in the acquisition analysis consists of both the goodwill of the subsidiary and the premium paid by the parent to acquire control over the subsidiary.
- As the fair value of the NCI (20%) is determined to be $42,000, if P Ltd were to acquire 80% of S Ltd, it would expect to pay $168,000 (i.e. 80/20 × $42,000). As P Ltd paid $169,600, it paid a control

premium of $1,600. This is recognised as goodwill attributable to P Ltd. Effectively the goodwill of $4,600 is broken down into:

Control premium paid by P Ltd	$1,600
Parent's share of S Ltd's goodwill	$2,400 [$4,000 − $1,600 or 80% × $3,000]
NCI share of S Ltd's goodwill	$600 [20% × $3,000]

- The goodwill attributable to P Ltd — both share of S Ltd's goodwill and the control premium — could be calculated as follows:

Net fair value acquired by P Ltd	=	80% × $207,000
	=	$165,600
Consideration transferred	=	$169,600
Goodwill attributable to P Ltd	=	$169,600 − $165,600
	=	$4,000

- The control premium is recognised as part of goodwill on consolidation, but is not attributable to the NCI.

In accounting for the goodwill, a business combination valuation reserve is raised for the goodwill of the subsidiary, namely $3,000. This reserve is then attributed on a proportional basis to the parent and the NCI, being $2,400 to the parent and $600 to the NCI. The control premium goodwill is recognised in the adjustment to eliminate the investment in the subsidiary only as the earnings from this combination goodwill flow into the parent's earnings and not that of the subsidiary — otherwise it would be included in the valuation of the NCI in the subsidiary.

The consolidation worksheet entries are as follows:

1. Business combination valuation entries			
Land	Dr	10,000	
Deferred tax liability	Cr		3,000
Business combination valuation reserve	Cr		7,000
(Revaluation of land)			
Goodwill	Dr	3,000	
Business combination valuation reserve	Cr		3,000
(Recognition of subsidiary goodwill)			
2. Elimination of investment in subsidiary			
Retained earnings [80% × $40,000]	Dr	32,000	
Share Capital [80% × $100,000]	Dr	80,000	
General reserve [80% × $60,000]	Dr	48,000	
Business combination valuation reserve [80% ($7,000 + $3,000)]	Dr	8,000	
Goodwill	Dr	1,600	
Shares in S Ltd	Cr		169,000

Two *business combination valuation entries* are required: one for the revaluation of the land to fair value, and the second to recognise the goodwill of the subsidiary.

In relation to the equity on hand at acquisition date, 80% is attributable to the parent, and 20% is attributable to the NCI. The *elimination of investment in subsidiary* relates to the investment by the parent in the subsidiary, and thus relates to 80% of the amounts shown in the acquisition analysis. The adjustments to equity in the elimination of investment in subsidiary are then determined by taking 80% of the recorded equity of the subsidiary and 80% of the business combination valuation reserves recognised as a result of differences between fair values and carrying amounts of the subsidiary's identifiable assets and liabilities at acquisition date and the goodwill of the subsidiary. The goodwill relating to the control premium is recognised in the elimination of investment in subsidiary.

23.2.2 Partial goodwill method

Under the second option, at acquisition date, the NCI is measured as the NCI's proportionate share of the acquiree's identifiable net assets. Under this approach the measurement of the NCI does not reflect the goodwill because the NCI and the NCI's proportion of identifiable net assets are equal. The NCI therefore does not get a share of any equity relating to goodwill because goodwill is defined as the future economic benefits arising from assets that are not individually identified (Appendix A of IFRS 3). The only goodwill recognised is that acquired by the parent in the business combination — hence the term 'partial' goodwill. According to paragraph 32 of IFRS 3, using the measurement of the NCI share of equity based on the NCI's proportionate share of the acquiree's identifiable net assets:

Goodwill = consideration transferred *plus* previously acquired investment by parent *plus* NCI share of identifiable assets and liabilities of subsidiary *less* net fair value of identifiable assets and liabilities of subsidiary.

To illustrate, using the same example as in section 23.2.1, assume that P Ltd paid $169,600 for 80% of the shares of S Ltd on 1 July 2025. All identifiable assets and liabilities of the subsidiary were recorded at fair value, except for land for which the fair value was $10,000 greater than cost. The tax rate is 30%. At acquisition date, the equity of S Ltd consisted of:

Share capital	$100,000
General reserve	60,000
Retained earnings	40,000

The acquisition analysis is as follows:

Net fair value of identifiable assets and liabilities of S Ltd	= $100,000 + $60,000 + $40,000 + $10,000(1–30%) (BCVR — land)
	= $207,000
(a) Consideration transferred	= $169,600
(b) Non-controlling interest in S Ltd	= 20% × $207,000
	= $41,400
Aggregate of (a) and (b)	= $211,000
Goodwill	= $211,000 – $207,000
	= $4,000

Note that the $4,000 goodwill is the same as the parent's share calculated in section 23.2.1, consisting of the parent's share of the subsidiary's goodwill (80% × $3,000 = $2,400) and any control premium ($1,600).

The consolidation worksheet entries are:

Business combination valuation entry			
Land	Dr	10,000	
Deferred tax liability	Cr		3,000
Business combination valuation reserve	Cr		7,000
Elimination of investment in subsidiary			
Retained earnings [80% × $40,000]	Dr	32,000	
Share capital [80% × $100,000]	Dr	80,000	
General reserve [80% × $60,000]	Dr	48,000	
Business combination valuation reserve [80% × $7,000]	Dr	5,600	
Goodwill	Dr	4,000	
Shares in S Ltd	Cr		169,000

Note firstly that there is no business combination valuation entry for goodwill. This is because only the parent's share of the goodwill is recognised. A business combination valuation adjustment to recognise goodwill is only used under the full goodwill method where both the parent's and the NCI's share of goodwill is recognised.

In relation to the equity on hand at acquisition date, only 80% is attributable to the parent, and 20% is attributable to the NCI. The elimination of investment in subsidiary relates to the investment by the parent in the subsidiary, and thus relates to 80% of the amounts shown in the acquisition analysis. The adjustments to equity in the elimination of investment in subsidiary are then determined by taking 80% of the recorded equity of the subsidiary and 80% of the business combination valuation reserves recognised as a result of differences between fair value and carrying amounts of the subsidiary's identifiable assets and liabilities at acquisition date. Because only the parent's share of goodwill is recognised, this is accounted for in the elimination of investment in subsidiary which also relates to the investment by the parent in the subsidiary.

23.2.3 Reasons for, and choosing between, the options

The International Accounting Standards Board (IASB®) supports the principle of measuring all components of a business combination at fair value (paragraph BC212); however, paragraph BC213 notes some arguments against applying this to the NCI in the acquiree:

- It is more costly to measure the NCI at fair value than at the proportionate share of the net fair value of the identifiable net assets of the acquiree.
- There is not sufficient evidence to assess the marginal benefits of reporting the acquisition-date fair value of NCI.
- Respondents to the exposure draft saw little information of value in the reported NCI, regardless of how it is measured.

The IASB noted three main differences in outcome that occur where the partial goodwill method is used instead of the full goodwill method:

1. The amounts recognised for the NCI share of equity and goodwill would be lower.
2. Where IAS 36 *Impairment of Assets* is applied to a cash-generating unit containing goodwill, as the goodwill recognised by the CGU is lower, this affects the impairment loss relating to goodwill.
3. There is also an effect where an acquirer subsequently obtains further shares in the subsidiary at a later date. An explanation of this effect is beyond the scope of this book.

In choosing which method to use — full or partial goodwill — it is these three effects on the financial statements, both current and in the future, that must be taken into consideration. For example, if management has future intentions of acquiring more shares in the subsidiary (i.e. by acquiring some of the shares held by the NCI), then the potential impact on equity when that acquisition occurs will need to be considered.

23.2.4 Intragroup transactions

As noted in chapter 22, because the transactions occur within the economic entity, the full effects of transactions within the group are adjusted on consolidation. In essence, the worksheet adjustment entries used in chapter 22 are the same regardless of whether the subsidiary is wholly or partly owned by its parent. The only exception to the entries used in chapter 22 is for dividends.

Where an NCI exists, any dividends declared or paid by a subsidiary are paid proportionately (to the extent of the ownership interest in the subsidiary) to the parent and proportionately to the NCI. In adjusting for dividends paid by a subsidiary, only the dividend paid or payable to the parent is eliminated on consolidation. In other words, there is a proportional adjustment of the dividend paid or declared. As with other intragroup transactions, the adjustment relates to the flow within the group. A payment or a declaration of dividends by a subsidiary reduces the NCI share of subsidiary equity because the equity of the subsidiary is reduced by the payment or declaration of dividends. In calculating the NCI share of subsidiary equity, the existence of dividends must be taken into consideration *(see section 23.3.3)*. Where a dividend is declared, the NCI share of equity is reduced, and a liability to pay dividends to the NCI is shown in the consolidated statement of financial position.

To illustrate, assume a parent owns 80% of the share capital of a subsidiary. In the current period, the subsidiary pays a $1,000 dividend; that is, $800 is paid to the parent and $200 is paid to other shareholders of the subsidiary. The subsidiary also declares a further $1,500 dividend, of which 80% ($1,200) is payable to the parent. The parent recognises dividend revenue of $2,000 ($800 + $1,200) and a dividend receivable of $1,200 in its separate financial statements. The adjustment entries in the consolidation worksheet in the current period are:

Dividend revenue	Dr	800	
Dividend paid	Cr		800
(80% × $1,000)			
Dividend payable	Dr	1,200	
Dividend declared	Cr		1,200
(80% × $1,500)			
Dividend revenue	Dr	1,200	
Dividend receivable	Cr		1,200
(80% × $1,500)			

23.2.5 Consolidation worksheet

Because the disclosure requirements for the NCI require the extraction of the NCI share of various equity items, the consolidation worksheet is changed to enable this information to be produced. Figure 23.5 contains an example of the changed worksheet. In particular, note that two new columns are added, a *debit column* and a *credit column* for the calculation of the NCI share of equity. These two columns are not adjustment or elimination columns. Instead, they are used to divide consolidated equity into NCI share and parent entity share. The worksheet shown in figure 23.5 also contains a column showing the figures for the consolidated group. This column is shown between the adjustment columns and the NCI columns, and it is the summation of the financial statements of the group members and the consolidation adjustments. The parent figures are then determined by subtracting the NCI share of equity from the total consolidated equity of the group.

FIGURE 23.5 Consolidation worksheet containing NCI columns

Financial statements	P Ltd	S Ltd	Adjustments Dr	Cr	Group	Non-controlling interest Dr	Cr	Parent
Profit/(loss)	5,000	4,000			9,000	400		8,600
Retained earnings (opening balance)	10,000	8,000			18,000	800		17,200
Transfer from reserves	4,000	2,000			6,000	200		5,800
Total available for appropriation	19,000	14,000			33,000			31,600
Interim dividend paid	2,000	1,500			3,500		150	3,350
Final dividend declared	4,000	2,500			6,500		250	6,250
Transfer to reserves	3,000	1,000			4,000		100	3,900
	9,000	5,000			14,000			13,500
Retained earnings (closing balance)	10,000	9,000			19,000			18,100
Share capital	50,000	40,000			90,000	4,000		86,000
Other reserves	30,000	20,000			50,000	2,000		48,000
	90,000	69,000			159,000			152,100
Asset revaluation surplus (opening balance)	4,000	5,000			9,000	500		8,500
Revaluation increases	2,000	2,000			4,000	200		3,800
Asset revaluation surplus (closing balance)	6,000	7,000			13,000			12,300
Total equity: parent								164,400
Total equity: NCI							7,600	7,600
Total equity	96,000	76,000			172,000	8,100	8,100	172,000
Current liabilities	3,000	2,000			5,000			
Non-current liabilities	8,000	6,000			14,000			
Total liabilities	11,000	8,000			19,000			
Total equity and liabilities	107,000	84,000			191,000			

In figure 23.5, the amounts in the debit NCI column record the NCI share of the relevant equity item. This amount is subtracted in the consolidation process so that the consolidation column contains the parent's share of consolidated equity.

The first line in figure 23.5 is the consolidated profit/(loss) for the period. This amount is then attributed to the parent and the NCI. In all subsequent equity lines, the NCI share is recorded in the debit NCI column, and the parent's share of each equity account is calculated. The total NCI share of equity is then added to the parent column to give total consolidated equity.

The NCI share of retained earnings is increased by subsidiary profits and transfers from reserves, and decreased by transfers to reserves and payments and declarations of dividends. The total NCI share of equity is then the sum of the NCI share of capital, other reserves and retained earnings. The assets and liabilities of the group are shown in total and not allocated to the equity interests in the group — see, for example, the liabilities section in figure 23.5.

23.3 CALCULATING THE NCI SHARE OF EQUITY

NCI in the net assets consist of the amount of the NCI at the date of the original combination calculated in accordance with IFRS 3 and the NCI's share of changes in equity since the date of the combination.

Changes in equity since the acquisition date must be taken into account. Note that these changes are not limited to the recorded equity of the subsidiary, but also include other changes in consolidated equity. As noted earlier in this chapter, the NCI is entitled to a share of *consolidated* equity. This requires taking into account adjustments for profits or losses made as a result of intragroup transactions because these profits or losses are not recognised by the group.

The calculation of the NCI is done in two stages: (i) the NCI share of recorded equity is measured *(see section 23.3.1)*, and (ii) this share is adjusted for the effects of intragroup transactions *(see section 23.4)*.

23.3.1 NCI share of recorded equity of the subsidiary

The equity of the subsidiary consists of the equity contained in the actual records of the subsidiary as well as any business combination valuation reserves created on consolidation at the acquisition date, where the identifiable assets and liabilities of the subsidiary are recorded at amounts different from their fair values. The NCI is entitled to a share of subsidiary equity at the end of the reporting period, which consists of the equity on hand at acquisition date plus any changes in that equity between acquisition date and the end of the reporting period. The calculation of the NCI share of equity at a point in time is done in three steps:

1. Determine the NCI share of equity of the subsidiary at acquisition date.
2. Determine the NCI share of the change in subsidiary equity between the acquisition date and the beginning of the current period for which the consolidated financial statements are being prepared.
3. Determine the NCI share of the changes in subsidiary equity in the current period.

The calculation could be represented diagrammatically, as shown in figure 23.6.

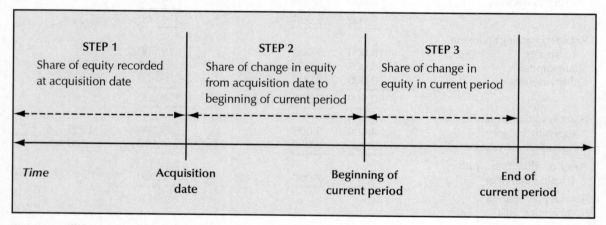

FIGURE 23.6 Calculating the NCI share of equity

Note that, in calculating the NCI share of equity at the end of the current period, the information relating to the NCI share of equity from steps 1 and 2 should be available from the previous period's consolidation worksheet.

To illustrate the above procedure, consider the calculation of the NCI share of retained earnings over a 5-year period. Assume the following information in relation to Cormorant Ltd:

Retained earnings as at 1 July 2021	$10,000
Retained earnings as at 30 June 2025	50,000
Profit for the year ended 30 June 2026	15,000
Retained earnings as at 30 June 2026	65,000

Assume that Pelican Ltd had acquired 80% of the share capital of Cormorant Ltd at 1 July 2021, and the consolidated financial statements were being prepared at 30 June 2026. The 20% NCI in Cormorant Ltd is therefore entitled to a share of the retained earnings balance of $65,000, a share equal to $13,000. This share is calculated in three steps:

Step 1. A share of the balance at 1 July 2021 (20% × $10,000)		= $ 2,000
Step 2. A share of the change in retained earnings from the acquisition date to the beginning of the current period (20% × [$50,000 − $10,000])	=	8,000
Step 3. A share of the current period increase in retained earnings (20% × $15,000)	=	3,000
		$13,000

The increase in retained earnings is broken into these three steps because accounting is based on time periods. The NCI is entitled to a share of the profits of past periods as well as a share of the profits of the current period. Note that, in calculating the NCI share of retained earnings for Cormorant Ltd at 30 June 2027 (1 year after the above calculation), the total of steps 1 and 2 for the 2027 calculation would be $13,000, as calculated above. The only additional calculation would be the share of changes in retained earnings for the year ended 30 June 2027.

The separate calculations are not based on a division of equity into pre-acquisition and post-acquisition equity. The division of equity is based on *time* — changes in equity are calculated on a period-by-period basis for accounting purposes.

The NCI columns in the consolidation worksheet contain the amounts relating to the three steps noted above. The journal entries used in the NCI columns of the consolidation worksheet to reflect the NCI share of equity are based on the three-step approach. The form of these entries is:

Step 1: NCI at acquisition date			
Share capital	Dr	xxx	
Business combination valuation reserve	Dr	xxx	
Retained earnings (opening balance)	Dr	xxx	
NCI	Cr		xxx
Step 2: NCI share of changes in equity between acquisition date and beginning of the current period			
Retained earnings (opening balance)	Dr	xxx	
NCI	Cr		xxx
Step 3: NCI share of changes in equity in the current period			
NCI share of profit/(Loss)	Dr	xxx	
NCI	Cr		xxx
Asset revaluation increases	Dr	xxx	
NCI	Cr		xxx
NCI	Dr	xxx	
Dividend paid	Cr		xxx
NCI	Dr	xxx	
Dividend declared	Cr		xxx

The effects of these journal entries can be seen in the consolidation worksheet in figure 23.5. The above entries are illustrative only, and there may be others where there are transfers to or from reserves that affect the balances of equity in the subsidiary. The effects of these transactions are illustrated in the next section.

23.3.2 Accounting at acquisition date

This section illustrates the effects that the existence of NCI has on the valuation entries, the acquisition analysis and the elimination of investment in subsidiary, as well as the step 1 calculation of the NCI share of equity at acquisition date. *As noted in section 23.2*, the acquisition analysis and subsequent consolidation worksheet entries are affected by whether the full goodwill or partial goodwill option is used in the measurement of the NCI's share of the subsidiary at acquisition date. The choice of method affects the accounting at acquisition date but has an effect on accounting subsequent to acquisition date only if there is an impairment of goodwill or the parent changes its equity interest in the subsidiary. Neither of these events is covered in this book.

Full goodwill method

Illustrative example 23.1 demonstrates the consolidation worksheet entries when the full goodwill method is applied.

ILLUSTRATIVE EXAMPLE 23.1 Consolidation worksheet entries at acquisition date

On 1 July 2025, Heron Ltd acquired 60% of the shares of Petrel Ltd for $45,000 when the equity of Petrel Ltd consisted of:

Share capital	$40,000
General reserve	2,000
Retained earnings	2,000

All the identifiable assets and liabilities of Petrel Ltd were recorded at fair value except for equipment and inventory:

	Carrying amount	Fair value
Equipment (cost $250,000)	$180,000	$200,000
Inventory	40,000	50,000

The tax rate is 30%. The fair value of the NCI in Petrel Ltd at 1 July 2025 was $28,000.

Acquisition analysis

Net fair value of identifiable assets and
  liabilities of Petrel Ltd
$$= \$40,000,\text{(capital)} + \$2,000,\text{(general reserve)}$$
$$+ \$2,000,\text{(retained earnings)}$$
$$+ \$20,000(1\text{–}30\%) \text{ (BCVR — equipment)}$$
$$+ \$10,000(1\text{–}30\%) \text{ (BCVR — inventory)}$$
$$= \$65,000$$

(a) Consideration transferred $= \$45,000$
(b) Non-controlling interest in Petrel Ltd $= \$28,000$
Aggregate of (a) and (b) $= \$73,000$
Goodwill $= \$73,000 - \$65,000$
  $= \$8,000$
Goodwill of Petrel Ltd
Fair value of Petrel Ltd $= \$28,000/40\%$
  $= \$70,000$

Net fair value of identifiable assets and
  liabilities of Petrel Ltd $= \$65,000$
Goodwill of Petrel Ltd $= \$70,000 - \$65,000$
  $= \$5,000$

Goodwill of Heron Ltd
Goodwill acquired $= \$8,000$
Goodwill of Petrel Ltd $= \$5,000$
Goodwill of Heron Ltd — control premium $= \$3,000$

Where NCI exist, because the parent acquires only a part of the ownership interest of the subsidiary, the parent acquires only a proportionate share of each of the equity amounts in the subsidiary.

(1) *Business combination valuation entries*

The valuation entries are unaffected by the existence of NCI. The purpose of these entries, in accordance with IFRS 3, is to show the assets and liabilities of the subsidiary at fair value at acquisition date. The entries for a consolidation worksheet (see figure 23.7) prepared at acquisition date are:

Accumulated depreciation — equipment	Dr	70,000	
Equipment	Cr		50,000
Deferred tax liability	Cr		6,000
Business combination valuation reserve	Cr		14,000
Inventory	Dr	10,000	
Deferred tax liability	Cr		3,000
Business combination valuation reserve	Cr		7,000
Goodwill	Dr	5,000	
Business combination valuation reserve	Cr		5,000

The business combination valuation reserve is pre-acquisition equity because it is recognised on consolidation at acquisition date. The NCI is entitled to a proportionate share of this reserve.

(2) *Elimination of investment and recognition of goodwill*

The first journal entry is read from the pre-acquisition analysis. The parent's proportional share of the various recorded equity accounts of the subsidiary, as well as the parent's share of the business combination valuation reserves, are eliminated against the investment account in the pre-acquisition entry. The goodwill relating to the control premium is also recognised. In this illustrative example, the elimination of investment in subsidiary is:

Retained earnings (1/7/25)	Dr	1,200	
[60% × $2,000]			
Share capital	Dr	24,000	
[60% × $40,000]			
Business combination valuation reserve	Dr	15,600	
[60% × ($14,000 + $7,000 + $5,000)]			
General reserve	Dr	1,200	
[60% × $2,000]			
Goodwill	Dr	3,000	
Shares in Petrel Ltd	Cr		45,000

(3) *NCI share of equity at acquisition date*

The NCI at acquisition date (the step 1 calculation) is determined as the proportional share of the equity recorded by the subsidiary at that date and the valuation reserves recorded on consolidation:

Share capital	40% × $40,000	=	$16,000
General reserve	40% × $2,000	=	800
Business combination valuation reserve	40% × ($14,000 + $7,000 + $5,000) =		10,400
Retained earnings	40% × $2,000	=	800
			$28,000

The following entry is then passed in the NCI columns of the consolidation worksheet:

Retained earnings (1/7/25)	Dr	800	
Share capital	Dr	16,000	
Business combination valuation reserve	Dr	10,400	
General reserve	Dr	800	
NCI	Cr		28,000

This entry is passed as the step 1 NCI entry in all subsequent consolidation worksheets. It is never changed. Any subsequent changes in pre-acquisition equity are dealt with in the step 2 NCI calculation.

Figure 23.7 shows an extract from a consolidation worksheet for Heron Ltd and its subsidiary, Petrel Ltd, at acquisition date. Only the equity section of the worksheet is shown. The worksheet entries are (i) the business combination valuation entries, (ii) the elimination of the investment and the recognition of goodwill, and (iii) the NCI step 1 entry.

FIGURE 23.7 Consolidation worksheet (extract) at acquisition date

Financial statements	Heron Ltd	Petrel Ltd	Adjustments				Group	Non-controlling interest					Parent
				Dr	Cr				Dr	Cr			
Retained earnings (1/7/25)	50,000	2,000	2	1,200			50,800	3	800				50,000
Share capital	100,000	40,000	2	24,000			116,000	3	16,000				100,000
General reserve	20,000	2,000	2	1,200			20,800	3	800				20,000
Business combination valuation reserve			2	15,600	14,000	1	10,400	3	10,400				0
					7,000	1							
					5,000	1							
Total equity: parent													170,000
Total equity: NCI										28,000	3		28,000
Total equity	170,000	44,000					198,000		28,000	28,000			198,000

Note that, in figure 23.7, the adjustment columns eliminate the parent's share of the pre-acquisition equity accounts and the NCI columns extract the NCI share of total equity. The parent column contains only the parent's equity and the parent's share of post-acquisition equity of the subsidiary, which in this case, being at acquisition date, is zero.

Partial goodwill method

Illustrative example 23.2 demonstrates the consolidation worksheet entries when the partial goodwill method is applied.

ILLUSTRATIVE EXAMPLE 23.2 Consolidation worksheet entries at acquisition date

On 1 July 2025, Heron Ltd acquired 60% of the shares of Petrel Ltd for $45,000 when the equity of Petrel Ltd consisted of:

Share capital	$40,000
General reserve	2,000
Retained earnings	2,000

All the identifiable assets and liabilities of Petrel Ltd were recorded at fair value except for equipment and inventory:

	Carrying amount	Fair value
Equipment (cost $250,000)	$180,000	$200,000
Inventory	40,000	50,000

The tax rate is 30%.

Acquisition analysis

Net fair value of identifiable assets
  and liabilities of Petrel Ltd
	= $40,000,(capital) + $2,000 (general reserve)
	  + $2,000 (retained earnings)
	  + $20,000(1–30%) (BCVR — equipment)
	  + $10,000(1–30%) (BCVR — inventory)
	  = $65,000

(a) Consideration transferred	= $45,000

(b) Non-controlling interest in
  Petrel Ltd
	= 40% × $65,000
	  = $26,000

Aggregate of (a) and (b)	= $71,000
Goodwill	= $71,000 – $65,000 = $6,000

Where there is NCI, because the parent acquires only a part of the ownership interest of the subsidiary, the parent acquires only a proportionate share of each of the equity amounts in the subsidiary.

(1) *Business combination valuation entries*

The valuation entries are unaffected by the existence of NCI. The purpose of these entries, in accordance with IFRS 3, is to show the assets and liabilities of the subsidiary at fair value at acquisition date. The entries for a consolidation worksheet (see figure 23.8) prepared at acquisition date are:

Accumulated depreciation — equipment	Dr	70,000	
Equipment	Cr		50,000
Deferred tax liability	Cr		6,000
Business combination valuation reserve	Cr		14,000
Inventory	Dr	10,000	
Deferred tax liability	Cr		3,000
Business combination valuation reserve	Cr		7,000

Note that there is no business combination valuation entry for goodwill as under the partial goodwill method only the parent's share of goodwill is recognised, and this is done in the preacquisition entry. The business combination valuation reserve is pre-acquisition equity because it is recognised on consolidation at acquisition date. The NCI is entitled to a proportionate share of this reserve. Because the reserve is recognised by the group, but not in the records of the subsidiary, this affects later calculations for the NCI share of equity.

(2) *Elimination of investment and recognition of goodwill*

The first elimination of investment in subsidiary is read from the pre-acquisition analysis. The parent's proportional share of the various recorded equity accounts of the subsidiary, as well as the parent's share of the business combination valuation reserves, are eliminated against the investment account in the pre-acquisition entry, and the parent's share of goodwill is recognised. In this illustrative example, the elimination of investment in subsidiary is:

Retained earnings (1/7/25) [60% × $2,000]	Dr	1,200	
Share capital [60% × $40,000]	Dr	24,000	
Business combination valuation reserve [60% × ($14,000 + $7,000)]	Dr	12,600	
General reserve [60% × $2,000]	Dr	1,200	
Goodwill	Dr	6,000	
Shares in Petrel Ltd	Cr		45,000

(3) *NCI share of equity at acquisition date*

The NCI at acquisition date (the step 1 calculation) is determined as the proportional share of the equity recorded by the subsidiary at that date and the valuation reserves recorded on consolidation:

Share capital	40% × $40,000	= $16,000
General reserve	40% × $2,000	= 800
Business combination valuation reserve	40% × ($14,000 + $7,000)	= 8,400
Retained earnings	40% × $2,000	= 800
		= $26,000

The following entry is then passed in the NCI columns of the consolidation worksheet:

Retained earnings (1/7/25)	Dr	800
Share capital	Dr	16,000
Business combination valuation reserve	Dr	8,400
General reserve	Dr	800
NCI	Cr	26,000

This entry is passed as the step 1 NCI entry in all subsequent consolidation worksheets. It is never changed. Any subsequent changes in pre-acquisition equity are dealt with in the step 2 NCI calculation.

Figure 23.8 shows an extract from a consolidation worksheet for Heron Ltd and its subsidiary, Petrel Ltd, at acquisition date. Only the equity section of the worksheet is shown. The worksheet entries are (i) the business combination valuation entries, (ii) the elimination of investment and recognition of goodwill, and (iii) the NCI step 1 entry.

Note that, in figure 23.8, the adjustment columns eliminate the parent's share of the pre-acquisition equity accounts and the NCI columns extract the NCI share of total equity. The parent column contains only the parent's equity and the parent's share of post-acquisition equity, which in this case, being at acquisition date, is zero.

FIGURE 23.8 Consolidation worksheet (extract) at acquisition date

Financial statements	Heron Ltd	Petrel Ltd	Adjustments				Non-controlling interest			Parent
				Dr	Cr	Group		Dr	Cr	
Retained earnings (1/7/25)	50,000	2,000	2	1,200		50,800	3	800		50,000
Share capital	100,000	40,000	2	24,000		116,000	3	16,000		100,000
General reserve	20,000	2,000	2	1,200		20,800	3	800		20,000
Business combination valuation reserve			2	12,600	14,000	1	8,400	3	8,400		0
					7,000	1					
Total equity: parent										170,000
Total equity: NCI									26,000	3	26,000
Total equity	170,000	44,000				196,000		26,000	26,000	196,000

23.3.3 Accounting subsequent to acquisition date

Using illustrative example 23.2, the consolidation worksheet entries at the end of the period 3 years after the acquisition date are now considered. These entries are based on the *partial goodwill* method. However, the effects of the events occurring subsequent to acquisition date on the elimination of investment and recognition of goodwill and business combination valuation entries are the same for the full goodwill method. Assume that:

- all inventory on hand at 1 July 2025 is sold by 30 June 2026
- the equipment has an expected useful life of 5 years
- goodwill has not been impaired
- in the 3 years after the acquisition date, Petrel Ltd recorded the changes in equity shown in figure 23.9.

In preparing the consolidated financial statements at 30 June 2028, the consolidation worksheet contains the valuation entries, the elimination of investment and recognition of goodwill entries, the NCI entries and the adjustments for the dividend transactions.

FIGURE 23.9 Changes in equity over a 3-year period

	2025–26	2026–27	2027–28
Profit for the period	$ 8,000	$12,000	$15,000
Retained earnings (opening balance)	2,000	7,800	16,000
	10,000	19,800	31,000
Transfer from general reserve	—	—	500
	10,000	19,800	31,500
Transfer to general reserve	—	1,000	—
Dividend paid	1,000	1,200	1,500
Dividend declared	1,200	1,600	2,000
	2,200	3,800	3,500
Retained earnings (closing balance)	7,800	16,000	28,000
Share capital	40,000	40,000	40,000
General reserve	2,000	3,000	2,500
Other components of equity*	2,000	2,500	2,400

* Resulted from movement in fair value of financial assets.

1. *Business combination valuation entries*

   The valuation entries for the 2027–28 period differ from those prepared at acquisition date because the equipment is depreciated, and the inventory has been sold. The entries at 30 June 2028 are:

Accumulated depreciation — equipment	Dr	70,000	
Equipment	Cr		50,000
Deferred tax liability	Cr		6,000
Business combination valuation reserve	Cr		14,000
Depreciation expense	Dr	4,000	
Retained earnings (1/7/27)	Dr	8,000	
Accumulated depreciation	Cr		12,000
(20% × $20,000 p.a.)			
Deferred tax liability	Dr	3,600	
Income tax expense	Cr		1,200
Retained earnings (1/7/27)	Cr		2,400
(30% × $4,000 p.a.)			

(If the full goodwill method had been used, the business combination entry relating to goodwill would be included at 30 June 2028 and would be the same as that used at acquisition date.)

2. *Elimination of investment and recognition of goodwill*

   The elimination of investment and recognition of goodwill entries have to take into consideration the following events occurring since acquisition date:
   - The inventory on hand at acquisition date has been sold.

The entry at 30 June 2028 is:

Retained earnings (1 July 2027)*	Dr	5,400
Share capital	Dr	24,000
Business combination valuation reserve**	Dr	8,400
General reserve	Dr	1,200
Goodwill	Dr	6,000
Shares in Petrel Ltd	Cr	45,000
* $1,200 + (60% × $7,000) (BCVR transfer — inventory)		
** 60% × $14,000		

3. *NCI share of equity at acquisition date (step 1)*

The NCI share of equity at acquisition date is as calculated previously. This entry is never changed from that calculated at that date — this applies whether the full goodwill or partial goodwill method is used.

Retained earnings (1/7/27)	Dr	800
Share capital	Dr	16,000
Business combination valuation reserve	Dr	8,400
General reserve	Dr	800
NCI	Cr	26,000

4. *NCI share of changes in equity between acquisition date and beginning of the current period* (i.e. from 1 July 2025 to 30 June 2027) (step 2)

To calculate this entry, it is necessary to note any changes in subsidiary equity between the two dates. The changes will generally relate to movements in retained earnings and reserves, but changes in share capital, such as when a bonus dividend is paid, could occur.

In this example, there are four changes in subsidiary equity, as shown in figure 23.9:

- Retained earnings increased from $2,000 to $16,000 — this will increase the NCI share of retained earnings.
- In the 2026–27 period, $1,000 was transferred to the general reserve. Because the transfer has reduced retained earnings, the NCI share of retained earnings as calculated above has been reduced by this transfer; an increase in the NCI share of general reserve needs to be recognised as well as an increase in NCI in total.
- The sale of inventory in the 2025–26 period resulted in a transfer of $7,000 from the business combination valuation reserve to retained earnings. Because the profits from the sale of inventory are recorded in the profits of the subsidiary, the NCI receives a share of the increased wealth relating to inventory. The NCI share of the business combination valuation reserve as recognised in step 1 must be reduced, with a reduction in NCI in total.
- Other components of equity increased by $2,500, increasing the NCI share of equity by $1,000.

Before noting the effects of these events in journal entry format, adjustments relating to the equipment on hand at acquisition date need to be considered. In the business combination valuation entry, the equipment on hand at acquisition date was revalued to fair value and the increase taken to the valuation reserve. By recognising the asset at fair value at acquisition date, the group recognises the extra benefits over and above the asset's carrying amount to be earned by the subsidiary. As expressed in the depreciation of the equipment (see the valuation entries above), the group expects the subsidiary to realise extra after-tax benefits of $2,800 (i.e. $4,000 depreciation expense less the credit of $1,200 to income tax expense) in each of the 5 years after acquisition. Whereas the group recognises these extra benefits at acquisition date via the valuation reserve, the subsidiary recognises these benefits as profit in its records only as the equipment is used. Hence, the profit after tax recorded by the subsidiary in each of the 5 years after acquisition date will contain $2,800 benefits from the equipment that the group recognised in the valuation reserve at acquisition date.

In calculating the NCI share of equity from acquisition date to the beginning of the current period, the NCI calculation will double-count the benefits from the equipment if there is no adjustment for the depreciation of the equipment. This occurs because the share of the NCI in equity calculated at acquisition date includes a share of the business combination valuation reserve created at that date in the consolidation worksheet. Therefore, giving the NCI a full share of the recorded profits of the subsidiary in the 5 years after acquisition date double-counts the benefits relating to the equipment. The NCI has already received a share of the valuation reserve in the step 1 calculation. Hence, in calculating the NCI share of changes in equity between acquisition date and the beginning of the current period (the step 2 calculation), there needs to be an adjustment for the extra depreciation of the equipment in relation to each of the years since acquisition date.

The adjustment for depreciation can be read directly from the valuation entry that records the depreciation on the equipment since acquisition date. In the valuation entry required for the 2027–28 consolidated financial statements (see (1) *Business combination valuation entries above*), there is a net debit adjustment to retained earnings (1/7/27) of $5,600 (i.e. the $8,000 adjustment for previous periods' depreciation less the $2,400 adjustment for previous periods' tax effect) in relation to the after-tax effects of depreciating the equipment. This reflects the extra benefits received by the subsidiary as a result of using the equipment and recorded by the subsidiary in its retained earnings account.

In this example, the only adjustment to retained earnings in the business combination valuation entry is that relating to the equipment. In other examples, there may be a number of adjustments to retained earnings depending on the number of assets being revalued. All such adjustments must be taken into account in order not to double-count the NCI share of equity. In other words, to determine the adjustments needed to avoid double-counting, all adjustments to retained earnings in the valuation entries must be taken into consideration.

In illustrative example 23.2, the NCI share of changes in *retained earnings* is determined by calculating the change in retained earnings over the period, less the adjustment against retained earnings in the valuation entry relating to depreciation of the equipment. The amount is calculated as follows:

$$40\% \times (\$16,000 - \$2,000 - [\$8,000 - \$2,400]) = \$3,360$$

The NCI is also entitled to a share of the change in *general reserve* between acquisition date and the beginning of the current period, the change being the transfer to general reserve in the 2026–27 period. As the general reserve is increased, the NCI share of that account is also increased. The calculation is:

$$40\% \times \$1,000 = \$400$$

The NCI is also entitled to a share of the movement in *other components of equity*. There was no balance in this account at acquisition date, and balance at 30 June 2027 is $2,500, so the NCI's share is:

$$40\% \times \$2,500 = \$1,000$$

The NCI is also affected by the transfer on consolidation from the *business combination valuation reserve* to retained earnings as a result of the sale of inventory. The NCI share of the valuation reserve is decreased, with a reduction in NCI in total. The calculation is:

$$40\% \times \$7,000 = \$2,800$$

The consolidation worksheet entries in the NCI columns for the step 2 NCI calculation are:

Retained earnings (1/7/27)	Dr	3,360	
NCI	Cr		3,360
(40% × [$16,000 − $2,000 − ($8,000 − $2,400)])			
General reserve	Dr	400	
NCI	Cr		400
(40% × $1,000)			
Other components of equity	Dr	1,000	
NCI	Cr		1,000
(40% × $2,500)			
NCI	Dr	2,800	
Business combination valuation reserve	Cr		2,800
(40% × $7,000)			

These entries may be combined as:

Retained earnings (1/7/27)	Dr	3,360	
General reserve	Dr	400	
Other components of equity	Dr	1,000	
Business combination valuation reserve	Cr		2,800
NCI	Cr		1,960

5. *NCI share of current period changes in equity (step 3)*

From figure 23.9 it can be seen that there are four changes in equity in the 2027–28 period:

- Petrel Ltd has reported a profit of $15,000.
- There has been a transfer from general reserve of $500.
- The subsidiary has paid a dividend of $1,500 and declared a dividend of $2,000.
- Other components of equity has decreased by $100.

In relation to both dividends and transfer to/from reserves, from an NCI perspective note that it is irrelevant whether the amounts are from pre- or post-acquisition equity. The NCI receives a share of all equity accounts regardless of whether it existed before acquisition date or was created after that date. In contrast, the parent shares in the post-acquisition equity but not the pre-acquisition equity of the subsidiary because the parent's share of pre-acquisition equity is eliminated in the consolidation.

The NCI share of *current period profit* is based on a 40% share of the recorded profit of $15,000. However, just as in step 2, there must be an adjustment made to avoid the double counting caused by the subsidiary recognising profits from the use of the equipment, these benefits having been recognised on consolidation in the business combination valuation reserve. Again, reference needs to be made to the valuation entries, and in particular to the amounts in these entries affecting current period profit. In the valuation entries, there is a debit adjustment to depreciation expense of $4,000 and a credit adjustment to income tax expense of $1,200. In other words, in the current period, Petrel Ltd recognised in its profit an amount of $2,800 from the use of the equipment that was recognised by the group in the business combination valuation reserve. Since the NCI has been given a share of the valuation reserve in step 1, to give the NCI a share of the recorded profit without adjusting for the current period's depreciation would double-count the NCI share of equity. The NCI share of current period profit is, therefore, 40% of the net of recorded profit of $15,000 less the after-tax depreciation adjustment of $2,800.

The consolidation worksheet entry in the NCI columns is:

NCI share of profit/(Loss)	Dr	4,880	
NCI	Cr		4,880
(40% × [$15,000 − ($4,000 − $1,200)])			

In the current period, a change in equity is caused by the $500 *transfer from general reserve* to retained earnings. This transaction does not change the amount of equity in total because it is a transfer between equity accounts, so there is no change to the NCI in total. However, the NCI share of general reserve has decreased and the NCI share of retained earnings has increased. For the latter account, the appropriate line item is 'Transfer from General Reserve'. The consolidation worksheet entry in the NCI columns is:

Transfer from general reserve	Dr	200	
General reserve	Cr		200
(40% × $500)			

The third change in equity in the current period relates to *dividends paid and declared*. Dividends are a reduction in retained earnings. The NCI share of equity is reduced as a result of the payment or declaration of dividends. Where dividends are paid, the NCI receives a cash distribution as compensation for the reduction in equity. Where dividends are declared, the group recognises a liability to make a future cash payment to the NCI as compensation for the reduction in equity. The consolidation worksheet entries in the NCI column are:

NCI	Dr	600	
Dividend paid	Cr		600
(40% × $1,500)			
NCI	Dr	800	
Dividend declared	Cr		800
(40% × $2,000)			

The fourth change in equity is the $100 reduction in *other components of equity*. This results in a reduction in the NCI share of this account that relates to financial assets as well as a reduction in NCI in total. The entry in the NCI columns is:

NCI	Dr	40	
Other components of equity	Cr		40
(40% × $100)			

6. *Adjustments for intragroup transactions: dividends*

The entries below and shown in the adjustment columns of the worksheet are necessary to adjust for the dividend transactions in the current period — note that the amounts are based on the proportion of dividends paid within the group.

Dividend revenue	Dr	900	
Dividend paid	Cr		900
(60% × $1,500)			
Dividend payable	Dr	1,200	
Dividend declared	Cr		1,200
(60% × $2,000)			
Dividend revenue	Dr	1,200	
Dividend receivable	Cr		1,200
(60% × $2,000)			

Using the figures for the subsidiary for the year ended 30 June 2028, as given in figure 23.9, and assuming information for the parent, a consolidation worksheet showing the effects of the entries developed in illustrative example 23.2 is given in figure 23.10.

FIGURE 23.10 Consolidation worksheet with NCI columns

Financial statements	Heron Ltd	Petrel Ltd		Adjustments Dr	Cr		Group		Non-controlling interest Dr	Cr		Parent
Profit/(loss) for the period	20,000	15,000	1 6 6	4,000 900 1,200	1,200	1	30,100	5	4,880			25,220
Retained earnings (1/7/27)	25,000	16,000	1 2	3,000 5,400	2,400	1	30,000	3	800			25,840
Transfer from general reserve	—	500					500	5	200			300
	45,000	31,500					60,600					51,360
Dividend paid	10,000	1,500			900 300	2 6	10,600			600	5	10,000
Dividend declared	5,000	2,000				6	5,800			800	5	5,000
	15,000	3,500					16,400					15,000
Retained earnings (30/6/28)	30,000	28,000					44,200					36,660
Share capital	100,000	40,000	2	24,000			116,000	3	16,000			
General reserve	20,000	2,500	2	1,200			21,300	3 4	800 400	200	5	20,300
Business combination valuation reserve	—	—	2	8,400	14,000	1	5,600	3	8,400	2,800	4	—
	150,000	70,500					187,100					156,660
Other components of equity (1/7/27)	10,000	2,500					12,500	4	1,000			11,500
Increases/(decreases)	2,000	(100)					1,900			40	5	1,940
Other components of equity (30/6/28)	12,000	2,400					14,400					13,440
Total equity: parent												170,100
Total equity: NCI								5 5 5	600 800 40	26,000 1,960 4,880	3 4 5	31,400
Total equity	162,000	72,900					201,500		37,280	37,280		201,500

23.3.4 Consolidation worksheet when the parent company applies equity accounting for the investment in the subsidiary

In the other examples in this chapter, it has been assumed that the parent company maintains its investment in Sub Ltd at cost in its separate financial statements. However, many parent companies use the equity method in their separate financial statements to account for the investment in subsidiaries, as discussed in section 21.6 of chapter 21. Online chapter 3 presents the equity method and explains how it works. For this section, we would assume you are familiar with this method, and the implications for the consolidation worksheet when the parent entity accounts for the investment in subsidiary using the equity method introduced in section 21.6. Accounting for NCI when the parent company has used the equity method to account for the subsidiary in its separate financial statements will be demonstrated by illustrative example, which is based upon the example from section 21.6 to incorporate NCI.

ILLUSTRATIVE EXAMPLE 23.3 Consolidation worksheet entries when the parent applies equity accounting for the investment in the susidiary

The financial statements of Parent Ltd and Sub Ltd on 31 December 2026 are as follows:

	Parent Ltd	Sub Ltd
Land	£170,000	£50,000
Equipment — cost	750,000	680,000
Equipment — accumulated depreciation	−448,000	−456,000
Investment in Sub Ltd	319,520	
Inventory	52,000	75,000
Cash	141,640	95,000
Total assets	985,160	444,000
Liabilities		
Provisions	40,000	40,000
Trade and other payables	32,000	24,000
Tax payable	12,000	16,000
Total liabilities	84,000	80,000
Equity		
Share capital	550,000	300,000
Retained earnings 1 January 2026	303,200	31,000
Profit or loss 2026		
Revenues	120,000	95,000
Expenses	85,000	72,000
	35,000	23,000
Gain on sale of non-current assets	15,000	31,000
Income from Sub	12,960	
Profit before tax	62,960	54,000
Tax expense	15,000	21,000
Profit for 2026	47,960	33,000
Total equity 31 December 2026	901,160	364,000
Total liabilities and equity	985,160	444,000

Parent Ltd acquired 80% of the shares of Sub Ltd on 1 January 2024. At that time, Sub Ltd held a parcel of land whose fair value was £20,000 higher than its carrying amount in Sub Ltd's statement of financial position. The land was subsequently sold during 2026. Sub Ltd owns a patent that is off its balance sheet, but its fair value at 1 January 2024 was £14,000. The group does not amortise the patent. The fair value of equipment held by Sub Ltd was £20,000 higher than its carrying amount at 1 January 2024 in the financial statements of Sub Ltd. This amount comprised a reduction in the gross (cost) of £150,000 and reduction in accumulated depreciation of £170,000. The group's annual depreciation expense is higher by £4,000, relative to Sub Ltd's financial statements. Thus, the fair value of the equipment was £8,000 higher than the carrying amount in Sub Ltd's financial statements at 31 December 2026 (31 December 2025: £12,000; 31 December 2024: £16,000). Goodwill stands at £16,000, which has not changed since 1 January 2024. Parent Ltd adopts the partial goodwill method. The tax rate is 30%.

Figure 23.11 shows how the carrying amount of the investment account is calculated for both 2026 and 2025. The book value of equity of Sub Ltd at the end of 2026 is the reported total equity at 31 December 2026. The book value of equity of Sub Ltd at the end of 2025 is the sum of Sub Ltd's share capital and retained earnings as it has no other equity items. Goodwill is calculated at acquisition as the excess of the consideration over the fair value of net assets acquired. In applying the equity method, goodwill is not recognised separately; it is included in the carrying amount of the investment.

FIGURE 23.11 Analysis of the investment account under the equity method

On 31 December	2026	2025
Sub Ltd's book value of equity	£ 364,000	£ 331,000
Adjustment for land		20,000
Adjustment for Equipment	8,000	12,000
Adjustment for patent	14,000	14,000
Deferred tax liability on the above adjustments	(6,600)	(13,800)
Adjusted equity of Sub Ltd	379,400	363,200
Parent's share of adjusted equity (80%)	303,520	290,560
Goodwill	16,000	16,000
Investment in Sub Ltd	£ 319,520	£ 306,560

Parent Ltd reports 'income from subsidiary' of £12,960 in its statement of profit or loss in 2026. This is the profit reported by Sub Ltd, adjusted for additional depreciation, lower gain on sale of land, and lower tax expense:

Profit reported by Sub Ltd	£33,000
Deduct adjustment for sale of land	−20,000
Adjustment for higher depreciation	−4,000
Lower tax expense related to the above adjustments	7,200
Income from subsidiary	16,200
Equity method share of profit (80% × 16,200)	12,960

With this information in mind, we can now proceed to the consolidation process, which is similar to the process followed when the investment is reported at cost. However, it is important to note that when equity accounting has been applied to the investment in subsidiary, the parent has already recognised its share of post-acquisition profits of the subsidiary in its own financial statements, which is also reflected in the carrying amount of the investment in the subsidiary. Thus, both pre-and post-acquisition equity must be considered in the business combination elimination entry to avoid double counting net assets of the subsidiary.

The following consolidation worksheet entry combines the business combination valuation entries, elimination of the investment and the parent's income from the subsidiary, and corresponding NCI entries.

Patent	Dr	14,000	
Accumulated depreciation — equipment	Dr	158,000	
Equipment — cost	Cr		150,000
Deferred tax liability	Cr		6,600
Business combination valuation reserve	Cr		3,080
Goodwill	Dr	16,000	
Share capital	Dr	240,000	
Retained earnings 1 January 2026	Dr	24,800	
Investment in Sub Ltd	Cr		319,520
Depreciation expense	Dr	4,000	
Gain on sale of noncurrent assets	Dr	20,000	
Tax expense	Cr		7,200
NCI share of profit	Cr		3,360
Income from subsidiary	Dr	12,960	

The business combination valuation entries correspond to the fair value adjustments shown in the calculation of the carrying amount of the Investment in Sub Ltd in figure 23.11. However, only Parent Ltd's share of the valuation adjustments is reflected in the Investment in Sub Ltd. Thus, the NCI portion of the valuation adjustments is recognised in the Business combination valuation reserve. The amount of £3,080 is calculated as [(14,000 + 158,000 − 150,000 − 6,600) × 20%].

Parent Ltd's share of Share capital (£300,000 × 80%) and Retained earnings at 1 January 2026 (£31,000 × 80%) are eliminated to avoid double counting of the subsidiary's net assets up to the beginning of the current period. As noted above, Parent Ltd's share of post-acquisition profit of Sub Ltd must also be eliminated to avoid double counting of post-acquisition profit recognised by Parent Ltd in the application of equity accounting for its Investment in Sub Ltd.

Adjustments are made for the effect of business combination valuations on the profit for the year ended 31 December 2026. The adjustments are for the gain on sale of land reported by Sub Ltd at an amount that is £20,000 more than would be reported by the group. The adjustment of £4,000 is for the additional depreciation arising from the fair value adjustment to equipment at acquisition. The combined tax effect of these two adjustments is £7,200 (24,000 × 30%). The net effect of the adjustments to Sub Ltd's profit is £16,800 (20,000 + 4,000 − 7,200). The NCI share of the adjustment to Sub Ltd's profit is £3,360. The carrying amount of the Investment in Sub Ltd, which has been determined by the application of equity accounting, is eliminated in full to avoid double-counting of net assets.

When the parent applies equity accounting to its investment in the subsidiary, the first two steps of calculating NCI are combined. Accordingly, the NCI entries for the first step, NCI at acquisition date, and the second step, NCI share of changes in equity up to the beginning of the current period, are combined, consistent with the elimination of the parent's share of equity up to the beginning of the current year. The third step is to determine the NCI share of the changes in the subsidiary's equity in the current period.

Steps 1 and 2: NCI share of equity of the subsidiary at 1 January 2026

Share capital	Dr	60,000	
Retained earnings 1 January 2026	Dr	6,200	
Business combination valuation reserve	Cr	3,080	
NCI	Cr		69,280

Share capital   £300,000 × 20% = £60,000
Retained earnings 1 January 2026 £31,000 × 20% = £6,200
Step 3

NCI share of profit	Dr	3,240	
NCI	Cr		3,240

The NCI share of Sub Ltd's profit is calculated, taking into consideration the adjustments for the gain on sale of land and the additional depreciation, net of related tax expense. The NCI share of profit is calculated as:

Profit reported by Sub Ltd	£33,000
Deduct adjustment for sale of land	−20,000
Adjustment for higher depreciation	−4,000
Lower tax expense related to the above adjustments	7,200
Income from subsidiary	16,200
Equity method share of profit (80% × 16,200)	12,960

In summary, the NCI share of Sub Ltd's equity is £72,520, comprising the NCI share of equity up to the beginning of 2026, £69,280 (steps 1 & 2) and the NCI share of the change in Sub Ltd's equity during 2026, £3,240 (step 3).

23.4 ADJUSTING FOR THE EFFECTS OF INTRAGROUP TRANSACTIONS

The justification for considering adjustments for intragroup transactions in the calculation of the NCI share of equity is that the NCI is classified as a contributor of capital to the group. Thus, the calculation of the NCI is based on a share of *consolidated equity* and not equity as recorded by the subsidiary.

Consolidated equity is determined as the sum of the equity of the parent and the subsidiaries after making adjustments for the effects of intragroup transactions. The NCI share of that equity must, therefore, be based on subsidiary equity after adjusting for intragroup transactions that affect the subsidiary's equity.

To illustrate, assume that during the current period a subsidiary in which there is an NCI of 20% has recorded a profit of $20,000 which includes a before-tax profit of $2,000 on sale of $18,000 inventory to the parent. The inventory is still on hand at the end of the current period. In the adjustment columns of the consolidation worksheet, the adjustment entries for the sale of inventory, assuming a tax rate of 30%, are:

Sales	Dr	18,000	
Cost of sales	Cr		16,000
Inventory	Cr		2,000
Deferred tax asset	Dr	600	
Income tax expense	Cr		600

The group does not regard the after-tax profit of $1,400 as being a part of consolidated profit. Hence, in calculating the NCI share of consolidated profit, the NCI is entitled to $3,720; that is, 20% × ($20,000 recorded profit — $1,400 intragroup profit).

The NCI share of equity is therefore adjusted for the effects of intragroup transactions. However, note that the NCI share of consolidated equity is essentially based on a share of *subsidiary* equity. Therefore, only intragroup transactions that affect the subsidiary's equity need to be taken into consideration. Profits made on inventory sold by the parent to the subsidiary do not affect the calculation of the NCI because the profit is recorded by the parent, not the subsidiary — the subsidiary equity is unaffected by the transaction.

In section 23.3, it is explained that the NCI share of the equity recorded by the subsidiary is calculated in three steps:

Step 1. share of equity at acquisition date

Step 2. share of changes in equity between acquisition date and the beginning of the current period

Step 3. share of changes in equity in the current period.

These calculations are based on the *recorded* subsidiary equity; that is, equity that will include the effects of the intragroup transactions. Having calculated the NCI as a result of the three-step process, the subsidiary needs to make further adjustments for the effects of intragroup transactions. Rather than adjust for these transactions in the NCI entries relating to the three-step process, the adjustments to the NCI are determined when the adjustments are made for the effects of the specific intragroup transactions.

For example, consider the case above where a subsidiary in which the NCI is 20% records a profit of $20,000, which includes a $2,000 before-tax profit on the sale of inventory to the parent (cost $4,000, selling price $6,000). In the step 3 NCI calculation, the worksheet entry passed in the NCI columns is:

NCI share of profit/(Loss)	Dr	4,000	
NCI	Cr		4,000
[20% × $20,000 recorded profit]			

In making the adjustment for the effects of intragroup transactions to be passed in the adjustment columns of the worksheet, the following entries are made:

Profit in closing inventory: subsidiary to parent			
Sales	Dr	6,000	
Cost of sales	Cr		4,000
Inventory	Cr		2,000
Deferred tax asset	Dr	600	
Income tax expense	Cr		600
[30% × $2,000]			

As this adjustment affects the profit of the subsidiary by an amount of $1,400 after tax (i.e. $2,000 − $600), this triggers the need to make an adjustment to the NCI, and the following entry is passed in the NCI columns of the worksheet:

NCI	Dr	280	
NCI share of profit/(Loss)	Cr		280
[20% × $1,400]			
[This entry is explained in more detail in illustrative example 23.4 later in this chapter.]			

The combined effect of the step 3 NCI entry and this last entry is that the NCI totals $3,720 — that is, $4,000 less $280. Thus, the NCI is given a share of recorded profit adjusted for the effects of intragroup transactions.

23.4.1 The concept of 'realisation' of profits or losses

Not all transactions require an adjustment entry for the NCI. For a transaction to require an adjustment to the calculation of the NCI share of equity, it must have the following characteristics:

- The transaction must result in the subsidiary recording a profit or a loss.
- After the transaction, the other party to the transaction (for two-company structures this is the parent) must have on hand an asset (e.g. inventory) on which the unrealised profit is accrued.
- The initial consolidation adjustment for the transaction should affect both the statement of financial position and the statement of profit or loss and other comprehensive income (including appropriations of retained earnings), such as affecting inventory and profit. In contrast, intragroup payments of interest affect only the statement of profit or loss and other comprehensive income.

In determining the transactions requiring an adjusting entry for the NCI, it is important to work out which transactions involve unrealised profit. *The concept of 'realisation' is discussed in chapter 22*. The test for realisation is the involvement of a party external to the group, based on the concept that the consolidated financial statements report the affairs of the group in terms of its dealings with entities external to the group. Consolidated profits are therefore realised profits as they result from dealing with entities external to the group. Profits made by transacting within the group are unrealised because no external entity is involved. Once the profits or losses on an intragroup transaction become realised, the NCI share of equity no longer needs to be adjusted for the effects of an intragroup transaction because the profits or losses recorded by the subsidiary are all realised profits.

In this section, the key point to note is when, for different types of transactions, unrealised profits on intragroup transactions become realised.

Inventory

With inventory, realisation occurs when the acquiring entity sells the inventory to an entity outside the group. Consolidation adjustments for inventory are based on the profit or loss remaining in inventory on hand at the end of a financial period. If inventory is sold in the current period by the subsidiary to the parent at a profit, giving the NCI a share of the recorded profit will overstate the NCI share of consolidated equity, because the group does not recognise the profit until the inventory is sold outside the group. Hence, whenever consolidated adjustments are made for profit remaining in inventory on hand at the end of the period, an NCI adjustment is necessary to reduce the NCI share of current period profit and the NCI total. Following the consolidation adjustment for the unrealised profit in inventory, an NCI adjustment entry is made in the NCI columns of the worksheet. The general form of the entry is:

| NCI | Dr | xxx | |
| NCI share of profit/(Loss) | Cr | | xxx |

If there is unrealised profit in inventory on hand at *the beginning of the current period*, the NCI share of the previous period's profit must be reduced as the subsidiary's previous year's recorded profit contains unrealised profit. As the group realises the profit in the current period when the inventory is sold to external parties, the NCI share of the current period profit must be increased. Following the worksheet adjustment for the profit remaining in beginning inventory, an NCI adjustment entry is made in the NCI columns of the worksheet. The general form of the NCI entry is:

| NCI share of profit/(Loss) | Dr | xxx | |
| Retained earnings (opening balance) | Cr | | xxx |

Intragroup transfers for services and interest

For transactions involving services and interest, the group's profit is unaffected because the general consolidation adjustment reduces both expense and revenue equally. For example, if the parent paid interest of $1,000 to the subsidiary, interest income of $1,000 and interest expense of $1,000 would be eliminated in the consolidation worksheet. The elimination of the interest income and the interest expense does not affect the group's consolidated profit. However, from the NCI's perspective, there has been a change in the equity of the subsidiary; for example, the subsidiary may have recorded interest revenue as a result of a payment from the parent entity relating to an intragroup loan. The revenue is unrealised in that no external entity has been involved in the transaction. Theoretically, the NCI should be adjusted for such transactions. However, as noted in paragraph B86(c) of IFRS 10, it is profits or losses 'recognised in assets' that are of concern. In other words, where there are transfers between entities that do not result in the retention within the group of assets on which the profit has been accrued, it is *assumed* that the profit is realised by the group immediately on payment within the group. For transactions such as payments for intragroup services and interest, there are no assets recorded with accrued profits attached. Hence, the profit is assumed to be immediately realised. The reason for the assumption of immediate realisation of profits on these types of transactions is a pragmatic one based on the cost benefit of determining a point of realisation.

An example of the process of calculating NCI when intragroup transactions exist is given in illustrative example 23.4.

ILLUSTRATIVE EXAMPLE 23.4 NCI and intragroup transactions

Bat Ltd owns 80% of the issued shares of Snake Ltd. In the year ending 30 June 2025, the following transactions occurred:
(a) In July 2024, Bat Ltd sold $2,000 worth of inventory that had been sold to it by Snake Ltd in May 2024 at a profit to Snake Ltd of $500.
(b) In February 2025, Bat Ltd sold $10,000 worth of inventory to Snake Ltd, recording a profit before tax of $2,000. At 30 June 2025, 20% of this inventory remained unsold by Snake Ltd.
(c) In March 2025, Snake Ltd sold $12,000 worth of inventory to Bat Ltd at a mark-up of 20%. At 30 June 2025, $1,200 of this inventory remained unsold by Bat Ltd.

Required
Given a tax rate of 30%, prepare the consolidation worksheet entries for these transactions as at 30 June 2025.

Solution
(a) *Sale of inventory in previous period: Snake Ltd to Bat Ltd*
   The entry in the adjustment columns of the worksheet is:

Retained earnings (1/7/24)	Dr	350	
Income tax expense	Dr	150	
Cost of sales	Cr		500

Since the inventory was originally sold by the subsidiary to the parent, the entry in the NCI columns of the worksheet is:

NCI share of profit/(Loss)	Dr	70	
Retained earnings (1/7/24)	Cr		70
(20% × $350)			

(b) *Sale of inventory in current period: Bat Ltd to Snake Ltd*

Sales	Dr	10,000	
Cost of sales	Cr		9,600
Inventory	Cr		400
Deferred tax asset	Dr	120	
Income tax expense	Cr		120

Because the sale was from parent to subsidiary, there is no NCI adjustment required.

(c) *Sale of inventory in current period: Snake Ltd to Bat Ltd*
The entries in the adjustment columns of the worksheet are:

Sales	Dr	12,000	
Cost of sales	Cr		11,800
Inventory	Cr		200
Deferred tax asset	Dr	60	
Income tax expense	Cr		60

Because the sale was from subsidiary to parent, the following entry is required in the NCI columns of the worksheet:

NCI	Dr	28	
NCI share of profit/(Loss)	Cr		28
(20% × $140)			

LO5

23.5 GAIN ON BARGAIN PURCHASE

This chapter has used examples of business combinations where goodwill has been acquired. In the rare case that a gain on bargain purchase may arise, such a gain has no effect on the calculation of the NCI share of equity. Further, whereas the goodwill of the subsidiary may be determined by calculating the goodwill acquired by the parent entity and then grossing this up to determine the goodwill for the subsidiary, this process is not applicable for the gain on bargain purchase. The gain is made by the parent paying less than the net fair value of the acquirer's share of the identifiable assets, liabilities and contingent liabilities of the subsidiary. The NCI receives a share of the fair value of the subsidiary, and has no involvement with the gain on bargain purchase.

To illustrate, assume a subsidiary has the following statement of financial position:

Equity	$ 80,000
Identifiable assets and liabilities	$ 80,000

Assume all identifiable assets and liabilities of the subsidiary are recorded at amounts equal to fair value. If a parent acquires 80% of the shares of the subsidiary for $63,000, then the acquisition analysis, assuming the use of the partial goodwill method, is:

Net fair value of subsidiary	= $80,000
(a) Consideration transferred	= $63,000
(b) Non-controlling interest in subsidiary	= 20% × $80,000
	= $16,000
Aggregate of (a) and (b)	= $79,000
Gain on bargain purchase	$80,000 − $79,000
	= $1,000

Assuming all fair values have been measured accurately, the consolidation worksheet entries at acquisition date are:
Business combination valuation entry
No entry required in this simple example.

Elimination of investment in subsidiary

Equity	Dr	64,000	
Gain on bargain purchase	Cr		1,000
Shares in subsidiary	Cr		63,000

Non-controlling interest (step 1)

Equity	Dr	16,000	
NCI	Cr		16,000
(20% × $80,000)			

Note that the NCI does not receive any share of the gain on bargain purchase.

23.6 SUMMARY

Where a subsidiary is not wholly owned, the equity of the subsidiary is divided into two parts, namely the parent's share and the NCI share. IAS 1 *Presentation of Financial Statements* requires that, with the disclosure of specific equity amounts, the parent's share and the NCI share should be separately disclosed. This affects the consolidation process. The NCI is classified as equity with the result that in statements of profit or loss and other comprehensive income and statements of financial position where equity amounts are disclosed the parent's share and the NCI share are separately disclosed.

The existence of an NCI will have different effects on the consolidation worksheet entries used, depending on whether the full goodwill or partial goodwill method is used. Under the full goodwill method, goodwill is recognised in the business combination valuation entries, and shared between the parent and the NCI. Where the partial goodwill method is used, the existence of an NCI has no effect on the business combination valuation entries. However, as a result of these entries, business combination valuation reserves are created of which the NCI has a share. With the elimination of investment in subsidiary, the existence of an NCI has an effect as this entry is based on the parent's share of pre-acquisition equity only. Hence, a proportionate adjustment is required. The adjustments for intragroup transactions also affect the calculation of the NCI share of equity. There is no effect on the adjustment for an intragroup transaction itself — this is the same regardless of the ownership interest of the parent in the subsidiary. However, the adjustment for an intragroup transaction affects the calculation of the NCI share of equity. Since the NCI is entitled to a share of consolidated equity rather than the recorded equity of the subsidiary, where an intragroup transaction affects the equity of the subsidiary, entries in the NCI columns of the worksheet are required, affecting the calculation of the NCI. It is then necessary to observe the flow of the transaction — upstream or downstream — to determine whether an NCI adjustment is necessary. One area where the NCI is unaffected is where a gain on bargain purchase arises, because the elimination of investment in subsidiary adjusts for the parent's share only. The gain calculated relates only to the parent and not the NCI.

DEMONSTRATION PROBLEM 23.1 Consolidated financial statements

Seal Ltd acquired 80% of the shares of Swan Ltd on 1 July 2022 for $540,000, when the equity of Swan Ltd consisted of:

Share capital	$500,000
General reserve	80,000
Retained earnings	50,000
Asset revaluation surplus	20,000

All identifiable assets and liabilities of Swan Ltd are recorded at fair value at this date except for inventory for which the fair value was $10,000 greater than carrying amount, and plant which had a carrying amount of $150,000 (net of $40,000 accumulated depreciation) and a fair value of $170,000. The inventory was all sold by 30 June 2023, and the plant had a further 5-year life with depreciation based on the straight-line method.

Financial information for both companies at 30 June 2026 is as follows:

	Seal Ltd	Swan Ltd
Sales revenue	$ 720,000	$ 530,000
Other revenue	240,000	120,000
	960,000	650,000
Cost of sales	(610,000)	(410,000)
Other expenses	(230,000)	(160,000)
	(840,000)	(570,000)
Profit before tax	120,000	80,000
Tax expense	(40,000)	(25,000)
Profit for the period	80,000	55,000
Retained earnings at 1/7/25	200,000	112,000
	280,000	167,000
Dividend paid	(20,000)	(10,000)
Dividend declared	(25,000)	(15,000)
	(45,000)	(25,000)
Retained earnings at 30/6/26	235,000	142,000
Share capital	600,000	500,000
Asset revaluation surplus*	20,000	60,000
General reserve	80,000	100,000
Total equity	935,000	802,000
Dividend payable	25,000	15,000
Other liabilities	25,000	25,000
Total liabilities	50,000	40,000
Total equity and liabilities	$ 985,000	$ 842,000
Receivables	$ 80,000	$ 30,000
Inventory	100,000	170,000
Plant and equipment	200,000	500,000
Accumulated depreciation	(115,000)	(88,000)
Land at fair value	100,000	80,000
Shares in Swan Ltd	540,000	—
Deferred tax assets	50,000	40,000
Other assets	30,000	110,000
Total assets	$ 985,000	$ 842,000

*The balances of the surplus at 1 July 2025 were $35,000 (Seal Ltd) and $50,000 (Swan Ltd).

The following transactions took place between Seal Ltd and Swan Ltd:
(a) During the year ended 30 June 2026, Swan Ltd sold inventory to Seal Ltd for $23,000, recording a profit before tax of $3,000. Seal Ltd has since resold half of these items.
(b) During the year ended 30 June 2026, Seal Ltd sold inventory to Swan Ltd for $18,000, recording a profit before tax of $2,000. Swan Ltd has not resold any of these items.
(c) On 1 June 2026, Swan Ltd paid $1,000 to Seal Ltd for services rendered.
(d) During the year ended 30 June 2025, Swan Ltd sold inventory to Seal Ltd. At 30 June 2025, Seal Ltd still had inventory on hand on which Swan Ltd had recorded a before-tax profit of $4,000.

Required

1. Given an income tax rate of 30%, prepare the consolidated financial statements for Seal Ltd for the year ended 30 June 2026 using the *partial goodwill method* to measure the non-controlling interest at acquisition date.
2. What differences would occur in the consolidation worksheet entries at 30 June 2026 if the *full goodwill method* was used to calculate the non-controlling interest at acquisition date? Assume the value of the non-controlling interest in the subsidiary at acquisition date is $134,500.

Solution

1. Consolidated financial statements using partial goodwill method

The first step is to prepare the acquisition analysis. Determining the net fair value is the same as for wholly owned subsidiaries. Where NCI exists, it is necessary to determine the net fair value acquired by the parent.

In this problem, the parent acquired 80% of the shares of the subsidiary. The net fair value of what was acquired is then compared with the consideration transferred, and a goodwill or gain on bargain purchase is determined. Note that the goodwill or gain is only that attributable to the parent, since the residual relates to what was paid by the parent and the proportion of net fair value of the subsidiary acquired by the parent.

Acquisition analysis

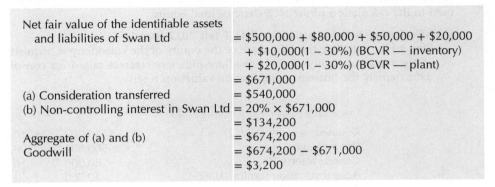

Net fair value of the identifiable assets
and liabilities of Swan Ltd
= $500,000 + $80,000 + $50,000 + $20,000
+ $10,000(1 − 30%) (BCVR — inventory)
+ $20,000(1 − 30%) (BCVR — plant)
= $671,000
(a) Consideration transferred = $540,000
(b) Non-controlling interest in Swan Ltd = 20% × $671,000
= $134,200
Aggregate of (a) and (b) = $674,200
Goodwill = $674,200 − $671,000
= $3,200

Consolidation worksheet entries at 30 June 2026

(1) *Business combination valuation reserve entries*

The business combination entries are unaffected by the existence of an NCI. Under IFRS 3, all identifiable assets and liabilities acquired in the acquiree/subsidiary must be measured at fair value. This principle is unaffected by the existence of NCI.

Accumulated depreciation	Dr	40,000	
Plant	Cr		20,000
Deferred tax liability	Cr		6,000
Business combination valuation reserve	Cr		14,000
Depreciation expense	Dr	4,000	
Retained earnings (1/7/25)	Dr	12,000	
Accumulated depreciation	Cr		16,000
Deferred tax liability	Dr	4,800	
Income tax expense	Cr		1,200
Retained earnings (1/7/25)	Cr		3,600

(2) *Elimination of investment in subsidiary*

Retained earnings (1/7/25)	Dr	45,600	
Share capital	Dr	400,000	
General reserve	Dr	64,000	
Asset revaluation surplus (1/7/25)	Dr	16,000	
Business combination valuation reserve	Dr	11,200	
Goodwill	Dr	3,200	
Shares in Swan Ltd	Cr		540,000

These elimination of investment and recognition of goodwill entries differ from the entries prepared for a wholly owned subsidiary in that the adjustment to equity accounts is measured as the parent's share of the equity accounts. This can be seen in the acquisition analysis where the parent's share of equity (80%) is applied to the net fair value before making a comparison with the cost of the combination. Hence the adjustment to share capital is $400,000; that is, 80% of the recorded $500,000. With retained earnings (1/7/25), the adjustment is calculated as:

$$(80\% \times \$50,000)(\text{opening balance}) + (80\% \times \$7,000)(\text{BCVR inventory})$$

The adjustment to the BCVR is:

$$80\% \times \$14,000 \, (\text{BCVR plant})$$

Non-controlling interest

The next three adjustment entries relate to the calculation of the NCI. These entries are passed in the NCI columns of the worksheet, not the adjustment columns. The three entries cover the three steps used in the calculation of the NCI share of total equity.

(3) *NCI share of equity at acquisition date, 1 July 2022 (step 1)*

Step 1 is to calculate the NCI share of the equity of the subsidiary at acquisition date. This consists of the recorded equity of the subsidiary plus any reserves raised on consolidation at acquisition date, namely the business combination valuation reserve.

Pre-acquisition equity of Swan Ltd		20%
Retained earnings (1/7/22)	$ 50,000	$ 10,000
Share capital	500,000	100,000
General reserve	80,000	16,000
Asset revaluation surplus (1/7/22)	20,000	4,000
Business combination valuation reserve	21,000	4,200
		$134,200

The worksheet entry in the NCI columns is:

Retained earnings (1/7/25)	Dr	10,000	
Share capital	Dr	100,000	
General reserve	Dr	16,000	
Asset revaluation surplus (1/7/25)	Dr	4,000	
Business combination valuation reserve	Dr	4,200	
NCI	Cr		134,200

Note that the adjustments to the equity accounts are debits, because these amounts will be subtracted from the balances in the group column in order to determine the parent's share of equity. On the other hand, the NCI account has a credit adjustment because the NCI is classified as equity, and the balance of pre-acquisition equity is a positive amount.

(4) *NCI share of equity from 1 July 2022 to 30 June 2025 (step 2)*

In step 2, the calculation is of the NCI share of equity between the acquisition date and the beginning of the current period; that is, between 1 July 2022 and 30 June 2025. This requires the calculation of movements in the subsidiary's equity accounts between these two dates.

General reserve: The balance at 30 June 2025, read from the financial information at 30 June 2026 and noting no transfers occurred in the current period, is $100,000. The difference between this and the balance at 1 July 2022 of $80,000 is $20,000. The NCI is entitled to 20% of this increase in equity. The combination of step 1 and step 2 effectively gives the NCI a 20% share of the total $100,000 balance.

Retained earnings: The balance at 30 June 2025 is the same as the opening balance in the current period, which is read from the financial information provided, namely $112,000. The difference between this amount and the balance recorded by the subsidiary at acquisition reflects movements in the amounts recorded by the subsidiary, such as reserve transfers and dividends. What is not reflected in the difference calculated are amounts affecting retained earnings not recorded by the subsidiary but recognised on consolidation. In this problem, the transaction that needs to be taken into account is the depreciation of the plant on hand at acquisition date, as shown in the business combination valuation reserve entries. As the plant is used, the recorded profit of the subsidiary recognises the extra benefits received. The NCI in relation to retained earnings (1/7/25) is therefore:

$$20\% \times [\$112,000 \, (\text{balance at 1/7/25}) - \$50,000 \, (\text{balance at acquisition}) - (\$12,000 - \$3,600)]$$

Asset revaluation surplus: The balance at acquisition date is $20,000 and the balance at 30 June 2025 is $50,000. The NCI is entitled to a 20% share of the difference between these two amounts.

Business combination valuation reserve: The balance at acquisition date was $21,000. As a result of the sale of the inventory, this has been reduced at 30 June 2025 to $14,000, a reduction of $7,000, because there has been a transfer from this reserve to retained earnings. Since the reserve has decreased in amount, this results in a decrease in the NCI share of this account. The total NCI in equity has not changed because the recorded retained earnings has increased by $7,000 as a result of the sale of inventory by the subsidiary.

A summary of these movements is then:

	Change in equity	20%
General reserve ($100,000 − $80,000)	$ 20,000	$ 4,000
Retained earnings ($112,000 − $50,000 − [$12,000 − $3,600])	53,600	10,720
Asset revaluation surplus ($50,000 − $20,000)	30,000	6,000
Business combination valuation reserve ($14,000 − $21,000)	(7,000)	(1,400)

The worksheet entry in the NCI columns is:

Retained earnings (1/7/25)	Dr	10,720	
General reserve	Dr	4,000	
Asset revaluation surplus	Dr	6,000	
Business combination valuation reserve	Cr		1,400
NCI	Cr		19,320

(5) *NCI in equity from 1 July 2025 to 30 June 2026 (step 3)*

Steps 1 and 2 determine the NCI share of equity recorded up to the beginning of the current year. Step 3 calculates the NCI share of changes in equity in the current year — 1 July 2025 to 30 June 2026.

The combination of all three steps determines the NCI share of equity at the end of the reporting period.

There are a number of changes in equity in the current period, with each change attracting its own adjustment entry in the NCI columns of the worksheet.

Profit for the period:
The NCI receives a share of recorded profit of the subsidiary. As with step 2, this is adjusted by the depreciation on the plant on hand at acquisition date. The recorded profit of the subsidiary includes benefits gained by use of the plant. The NCI share is then:

$$20\%\big[\$55,000 - (\$4,000 - \$1,200)\big]$$

The worksheet entry in the NCI columns is:

NCI Share of Profit/(Loss)	Dr	10,440	
NCI	Cr		10,440

The first line in the entry is a debit because in the consolidation worksheet this is deducted from group profit in order to calculate the parent share of profit. Note that, in later calculations, increases in the NCI share of profit require a debit adjustment to this account and decreases in the NCI share of profit require a credit adjustment.

Dividend paid:
The dividend paid by the subsidiary reduces the equity of the subsidiary. The adjustment to the NCI share of equity as a result of the dividend paid must take into consideration the full dividend paid with the effect of reducing the NCI share of total equity. The entry in the NCI columns of the worksheet is:

NCI	Dr	2,000	
Dividend paid	Cr		2,000
(20% × $10,000)			

Dividend declared:

As with the dividend paid, the NCI has been given a full share of equity before the declaration of dividends. Because the dividend declared reduces the equity of the subsidiary, the NCI share of equity is also reduced. The entry in the NCI columns of the worksheet is:

NCI	Dr	3,000	
Dividend declared	Cr		3,000
(20% × $15,000)			

Asset revaluation surplus:

The balance of the subsidiary's asset revaluation surplus at 1 July 2025 was $50,000. The balance at 30 June 2026 is $60,000. The NCI share of equity is increased by 20% of the change during the period. The debit adjustment is recognised in the worksheet against the Gains/Losses on Asset Revaluation account as this account reflects the increase in the reserve balance. The adjustment is a debit because it reduces the group gain so that the left-hand column of the worksheet shows the parent share of the gain. The entry in the NCI columns of the worksheet is:

Gains/losses on asset revaluation	Dr	2,000	
NCI	Cr		2,000
(20% × [$60,000 − $50,000])			

Intragroup transactions

(6) *Dividend paid*

The entry in the adjustment columns of the consolidation worksheet to adjust for the $10,000 dividend paid is:

Dividend revenue	Dr	8,000	
Dividend paid	Cr		8,000
(80% × $10,000)			

(7) *Dividend declared*

The subsidiary declared a dividend of $15,000 of which $12,000 is payable within the group. The entries in the adjustment columns of the worksheet are:

Dividend payable	Dr	12,000	
Dividend declared	Cr		12,000
Dividend revenue	Dr	12,000	
Dividend receivable	Cr		12,000

(8) *Sale of inventory: Swan Ltd to Seal Ltd*

The worksheet entries in the adjustment columns are:

Sales	Dr	23,000	
Cost of sales	Cr		21,500
Inventory	Cr		1,500
(Unrealised profit on sale of inventory 50% × $3,000)			
Deferred tax asset	Dr	450	
Income tax expense	Cr		450
(Tax effect, 30% × $1,500)			

(9) *Adjustment to NCI: unrealised profit in ending inventory*

The profit on sale was made by the subsidiary. The NCI is therefore affected. The total after-tax profit on the intragroup sale of inventory was $2,100 (i.e. $3,000 − $900 tax). However, since half the inventory is sold to an external entity, this portion is realised. The adjustment to the NCI relates only to the unrealised profits remaining in the inventory still on hand (half of $2,100, or $1,050). This is the same after-tax figure used to adjust profits in entry (8) above.

The transaction occurs in the current period. Therefore, it is the NCI share of current period profit that is affected. In adjustment entry (5), the NCI is given a share of the total recorded subsidiary profit for the current period. Because the realised profit is less than the recorded profit, the NCI share of equity must be reduced, specifically the NCI share of current period profit.

The worksheet entry in the NCI columns of the worksheet is:

NCI	Dr	210	
NCI share of profit/(Loss)	Cr		210
(20% × $1,050)			

The debit adjustment shows a reduction in total equity attributable to the NCI, and the credit adjustment shows a reduction in the NCI share of current period profits.

(10) *Sale of inventory: Seal Ltd to Swan Ltd*

The entries in the adjustment columns of the worksheet are:

Sales	Dr	18,000	
Cost of sales	Cr		16,000
Inventory	Cr		2,000
Deferred tax asset	Dr	600	
Income tax expense	Cr		600

Because the profit on the transaction is made by the parent entity and does not affect the equity of the subsidiary, there is no need to make any adjustment to the NCI.

(11) *Payment for services: Swan Ltd to Seal Ltd*

The entry in the adjustment columns of the worksheet is:

Other revenues	Dr	1,000	
Other expenses	Cr		1,000

The profit of the subsidiary is affected by the transaction even though the payment may, in effect, be from the parent to the subsidiary. However, if it is assumed that realisation occurs as the services are provided for this type of transaction, then no unrealised profit or loss exists in the subsidiary. Hence, there is no need to make any adjustment to the NCI share of equity.

(12) *Sale of inventory in previous period: Swan Ltd to Seal Ltd*

The entries in the adjustment columns of the worksheet are:

Retained Earnings (1/7/25)	Dr	2,800	
Income Tax Expense	Dr	1,200	
Cost of Sales	Cr		4,000

(13) *Adjustment to NCI: unrealised profit in beginning inventory*

The profit on this transaction was made by the subsidiary, so an adjustment to the NCI share of equity is required. There are two effects on the NCI because the transaction affects both last year's and the current period's figures.

First, the profit made by the subsidiary in the previous period was unrealised last year. Hence, the subsidiary's retained earnings (1/7/25) account contains $2,800 unrealised profit. An adjustment is necessary to reduce the NCI share of the previous period's profit:

NCI		Dr	560
Retained earnings (1/7/25)		Cr	560
(20% × $2,800)			

Second, in relation to the current period, because the inventory transferred last period is sold in the current period to an external entity, the profit previously recorded by the subsidiary becomes realised in the current period. Since the profit is realised to the NCI in the current period but was recorded by the subsidiary last period, the NCI share of current period profit needs to be increased. The adjustment is:

NCI share of profit/(Loss)		Dr	560
NCI		Cr	560
(20% × $2,800)			

These two entries can be combined and passed in the NCI columns of the worksheet:

NCI share of profit/(Loss)		Dr	560
Retained earnings (1/7/25)		Cr	560

This entry has no effect on the total NCI share of equity. It simply reduces the NCI share of equity recorded last period and increases the NCI share of current period profit. This reflects the fact that the subsidiary recorded the profit in the previous period whereas the group recognised the profit in the current period.

The consolidation worksheet for Seal Ltd at 30 June 2026 is shown in figure 23.12.

FIGURE 23.12 Consolidation worksheet showing NCI and the effects of intragroup transactions

Financial statements	Seal Ltd	Swan Ltd	Adjustments	Dr	Cr		Group	Non-controlling interest	Dr	Cr		Parent
Sales revenue	720,000	530,000	8	23,000			1,209,000					
			10	18,000								
Other revenues	240,000	120,000	6	8,000								
			7	12,000								
			11	1,000								
	960,000	650,000					1,548,000					
Cost of sales	(610,000)	(410,000)			21,500	8	(978,500)					
					16,000	10						
					4,000	12						
Other expenses	(230,000)	(160,000)	1	4,000	1,000	11	(393,000)					
	(840,000)	(570,000)					(1,371,500)					
Profit before tax	120,000	80,000					176,500					
Tax expense	(40,000)	(25,000)	12	1,200	1,200	1	(63,950)					
					600	10						
					450	8						
Profit	80,000	55,000					112,550	5	10,440	210	9	
								13	560			101,760

(continued)

Financial statements	Seal Ltd	Swan Ltd		Dr	Cr		Group		Dr	Cr		Parent
Retained earnings (1/7/25)	200,000	112,000	1	12,000	3,600	1		3	10,000	560	13	235,040
			2	45,600				4	10,720			
			12	2,800			242,600					
	280,000	167,000					355,150					336,800
Dividend paid	(20,000)	(10,000)			8,000	6	(22,000)			2,000	5	(20,000)
Dividend declared	(25,000)	(15,000)			12,000	7	(28,000)			3,000	5	(25,000)
	(45,000)	(25,000)					(50,000)					(45,000)
Retained earnings (30/6/26)	235,000	142,000					306,550					291,800
Share capital	600,000	500,000	2	400,000			700,000	3	100,000			600,000
General reserve	80,000	100,000	2	64,000			116,000	3	16,000			96,000
								4	4,000			
Business combination valuation reserve	0	0	2	11,200	14,000	1	2,800	3	4,200	1,400	4	0
	915,000	742,000					1,125,350					987,800
Asset revaluation surplus (1/7/25)	35,000	50,000	2	16,000			69,000	3	4,000			59,000
								4	6,000			
Gains/losses on asset revaluation	(15,000)	10,000					(5,000)	5	2,000			(7,000)
Asset revaluation surplus (30/6/26)	20,000	60,000					64,000					52,000
Total equity: parent												1,039,800
Total equity: NCI								5	2,000	134,200	3	160,750
								5	3,000	19,320	4	
								9	210	10,440	5	
										2,000	5	
Total equity	935,000	802,000					1,189,350		182,370	182,370		1,200,550
Dividend payable	25,000	15,000	7	12,000			28,000					
Other liabilities	25,000	25,000	1	4,800	6,000	1	51,200					
Total liabilities	50,000	40,000					79,200					
Total equity and liabilities	985,000	842,000					1,279,750					
Receivables	80,000	30,000			12,000	7	98,000					
Inventory	100,000	170,000			1,500	8	266,500					
					2,000	10						
Plant and equipment	200,000	500,000			20,000	1	680,000					
Accumulated depreciation	(115,000)	(88,000)	1	40,000	16,000	1	(179,000)					
Land	100,000	80,000					180,000					
Shares in Swan Ltd	540,000	0			540,000	2	0					
Deferred tax asset	50,000	40,000	8	450			91,050					
			10	600								
Goodwill	0	0	2	3,200			3,200					
Other assets	30,000	110,000					140,000					
Total assets	985,000	842,000		705,050	705,050		1,279,750					

The consolidated financial statements for Seal Ltd and its subsidiary, Swan Ltd, for the year ended 30 June 2026 are as shown in figures 23.13(a), (b) and (c).

FIGURE 23.13 (a) Consolidated statement of profit or loss and other comprehensive income

SEAL LTD Consolidated Statement of Profit or Loss and Other Comprehensive Income for the year ended 30 June 2026	
Revenue:	
Sales	$ 1,209,000
Other	339,000
Total revenue	1,548,000
Expenses:	
Cost of sales	(978,500)
Other	(391,000)
Total expenses	(1,371,500)
Profit before tax	176,500
Income tax expense	(63,950)
PROFIT FOR THE PERIOD	$ 112,550
Other comprehensive income	
Revaluation decreases	$ (5,000)
TOTAL COMPREHENSIVE INCOME	$ 107,550
Profit attributable to:	
Owners of the parent	$ 101,760
Non-controlling interest	10,790
	$ 112,550
Comprehensive income attributable to:	
Owners of the parent	$ 94,760
Non-controlling interest	12,790
	$ 107,550

FIGURE 23.13(b) Consolidated statement of changes in equity

SEAL LTD Consolidated Statement of Changes in Equity for the year ended 30 June 2026								
	Share capital	Retained earnings	General reserve	Asset revaluation surplus	Business combination valuation reserve	Total: Owners of the parent	Non-controlling interest	Total equity
Balance at 1 July 2025	$600,000	$235,040	596,000	$59,000	0	$ 990,040	$152,960	$1,143,000
Total comprehensive income		101,760		(7,000)		94,760	12,790	107,550
Dividends paid		(20,000)				(20,000)	(2,000)	(22,000)
Dividends declared		(25,000)				(25,000)	(3,000)	(28,000)
Balance at 30 June 2026	$600,000	$291,800	$96,000	$52,000		$1,039,800	$160,750	$1,200,550

FIGURE 23.13(c) Consolidated statement of financial position

SEAL LTD
Consolidated Statement of Financial Position
as at 30 June 2026

ASSETS	
Current assets	
Receivables	$ 98,000
Inventory	266,500
Total current assets	364,500
Non-current assets	
Plant and equipment	$ 680,000
Accumulated depreciation	(179,000)
Land	180,000
Deferred tax asset	91,050
Goodwill	3,200
Other	140,000
Total non-current assets	915,250
Total assets	$ 1,279,750
LIABILITIES	
Current liabilities: Dividend payable	$ 28,000
Non-current liabilities	51,200
Total liabilities	$ 79,200
Net assets	$ 1,200,550
EQUITY	
Share capital	$ 600,000
General reserve	96,000
Asset revaluation surplus	52,000
Retained earnings	291,800
Parent interest	$ 1,039,800
Non-controlling interest	$ 160,750
Total equity	$ 1,200,550

2. Consolidation worksheet changes under full goodwill method

Under the full goodwill method, the acquisition analysis would change as goodwill is calculated by taking into consideration the fair value of the NCI in the subsidiary.

Acquisition analysis

Net fair value of the identifiable assets and liabilities of Swan Ltd	= $500,000 + $80,000 + $50,000 + $20,000 + $10,000(1 − 30%) (BCVR — inventory) + $20,000(1 − 30%) (BCVR — plant)
	= $671,000
(a) Consideration transferred	= $540,000
(b) Non-controlling interest in subsidiary	= $134,500
Aggregate of (a) and (b)	= $674,500
Goodwill	= $674,500 − $671,000
	= $3,500
Goodwill of Swan Ltd	
Fair value of Swan Ltd	= $134,500/20%
	= $672,500
Net fair value of identifiable assets and liabilities of Swan Ltd	= $671,000
Goodwill of Swan Ltd	= $672,500 − $671,000
	= $1,500
Goodwill of Seal Ltd	
Goodwill acquired	= $3,500
Goodwill of Swan Ltd	= $1,500
Goodwill of Seal Ltd — control premium	= $2,000

Consolidation worksheet entries at 30 June 2026
(1) *Business combination valuation reserve entries*

Because the full goodwill method is used, there will need to an extra business combination valuation entry in relation to the goodwill of the subsidiary:

Goodwill	Dr	1,500	
Business combination valuation reserve	Cr		1,500

(2) *Elimination of investment and recognition of goodwill entries*

Retained earnings (1/7/25)	Dr	45,600	
Share capital	Dr	400,000	
General reserve	Dr	64,000	
Asset revaluation surplus (1/7/25)	Dr	16,000	
Business combination valuation reserve [80% × ($14,000 + $1500)]	Dr	12,400	
Goodwill	Dr	2,000	
Shares in Swan Ltd	Cr		540,000

(3) *NCI share of equity at acquisition date, 1 July 2022 (step 1)*

Under the full goodwill method this will change as the business combination valuation reserve in relation to goodwill has been recognised. The NCI share is calculated to be:

Pre-acquisition equity of Swan Ltd		
Retained earnings (1/7/22): 20% × $50,000	= $	10,000
Share capital: 20% × $500,000	=	100,000
General reserve: 20% × $80,000	=	16,000
Asset revaluation surplus (1/7/22): 20% × $20,000	=	4,000
Business combination valuation reserve: 20% × ($14,000 + $7,000 + $1,500)	= $	4,500
		$ 134,500

The worksheet entry in the NCI columns is:

Retained earnings (1/7/25)	Dr	10,000	
Share capital	Dr	100,000	
General reserve	Dr	16,000	
Asset revaluation surplus (1/7/25)	Dr	4,000	
Business combination valuation reserve	Dr	4,500	
NCI	Cr		134,500

No other changes are required.

Discussion questions

1. What is meant by the term 'non-controlling interest' (NCI)?
2. How does the existence of NCI affect the business combination valuation entries?
3. How does the existence of NCI affect the elimination of investment and recognition of goodwill entries?
4. Why is it necessary to change the format of the worksheet where NCI exists in the group?
5. Explain how the adjustment for intragroup transactions affects the calculation of the NCI share of equity.
6. Distinguish between the types of intragroup transactions for which NCI adjustment is needed and those for which no NCI adjustment is needed. Illustrate your answer with examples.
7. What is meant by 'realisation of profit'?

24

Translation of foreign currency transactions and the financial statements of foreign entities

ACCOUNTING STANDARDS IN FOCUS

IAS 21 *The Effects of Changes in Foreign Exchange Rates*

LEARNING OBJECTIVES

After studying this chapter, you should be able to:

 identify the reasons for translation of foreign currency transactions and financial statements and the applicable accounting standard

 explain exchange rates, monetary items and non-monetary items

 explain the difference between functional and presentation currencies

 apply the indicators in identifying the functional currency

 prepare journal entries to account for basic foreign currency transactions

 translate a set of financial statements from local currency into the functional currency

 translate financial statements into the presentation currency

 prepare consolidated financial statements including acquisition of foreign subsidiaries when the local currency is the functional currency

 prepare consolidated financial statements including foreign subsidiaries when the functional currency is that of the parent entity

 explain what constitutes the net investment in a foreign operation

 prepare the disclosures required by IAS 21.

24.1 TRANSLATION OF FOREIGN CURRENCY TRANSACTIONS AND FOREIGN SUBSIDIARY'S STATEMENTS

An entity operating in the UK may engage in transactions denominated in a currency other than the UK pound (£). Users of financial statements need transactions in foreign currencies to be consistently reported in one currency to obtain information that is comparable, relevant and faithfully represented. Therefore, it is necessary to translate all transactions, assets, liabilities and equity in foreign currencies into a single currency. If the financial statements of the entity are presented in pounds (£) then the financial effects of all elements must be recorded and reported in £, including transactions denominated in foreign currencies such as US dollars (US$) and euros (€).

Similarly, a parent entity may have subsidiaries that are domiciled in a foreign country. In most cases, the financial statements of the foreign subsidiary are prepared in the currency of the foreign country. In order for the financial statements of the foreign operation to be included in the consolidated financial statements of the parent, it is necessary to translate the foreign operation's financial statements to the currency used by the parent entity for reporting purposes.

The purposes of this chapter are:
- to explain how to apply the principles for accounting for foreign currency transactions, and
- to describe the process for translating and presenting the consolidated financial statements of a parent entity where at least one of its subsidiaries is a foreign subsidiary.

The accounting standard that deals with this process is IAS 21 *The Effects of Changes in Foreign Exchange Rates*.

24.2 KEY CONCEPTS IN FOREIGN CURRENCY TRANSLATION

In applying the principles in IAS 21 it is important to understand how exchange rates function and to be able to distinguish between monetary and non-monetary items.

24.2.1 Exchange rates

The local currency is the currency of a country or jurisdiction. For example, the local currency of the UK is pound sterling and the local currency of Hong Kong is the Hong Kong dollar. Foreign currencies can be bought and sold through banks, other financial institutions (that act as foreign exchange dealers) and other intermediaries. An exchange rate is defined in paragraph 8 of IAS 21 as the ratio of exchange between two currencies.

Exchange rates may be quoted using the indirect form or the direct form. The indirect form is often used in financial media. When the indirect form is used, the exchange rate is expressed as the equivalent amount of the foreign currency for one unit of the local currency. For the UK pound (£), an example of the indirect form is

> Indirect form: UK £1.00 = US$1.338 / 1.375

The exchange rate in the indirect form sets out the prices for buying and selling pound sterling as follows:
- US$1.338 is the buying rate for £1, being the price the foreign currency dealer will pay to buy £1 from a customer
- US$1.375 is the selling rate for £1, being the price the foreign currency dealer will ask to sell £1 to a customer

An alternative approach is to present exchange rates using the direct form that is expressed as the equivalent amount of the local currency for one unit of the foreign currency. For the UK£, an example of the direct form is

> Direct form : US$1.00 = £0.727 / 0.747

The exchange rate in the direct form sets out the prices for buying and selling pound sterling as follows:
- £0.727 is the buying rate for US$1, being the price the foreign currency dealer will pay to buy US$1 from a customer.
- £0.747 is the selling rate for US$1, being the price the foreign currency dealer will ask to sell US$1 to a customer.

Foreign currency transactions are initially recognised at the spot exchange rate, which is defined in paragraph 8 of IAS 21 as the exchange rate for immediate delivery. Thus, if a foreign currency transaction occurs on 26 September 2025, the spot exchange rate on 26 September is used to record that transaction. For example, Local plc purchases inventory from a supplier in Europe at a cost of €3,000 when the spot exchange rate is UK £1.00 = €1.20. Local plc translates the invoice amount of €3,000 at the spot exchange rate to £2,500 (€3,000/1.2 = £2,500). Local plc records the purchase of inventory as:

Inventory	Dr	£2,500
Accounts Payable	Cr	£2,500

24.2.2 Monetary and non-monetary items

As can be seen from the example, foreign currency transactions often result in the recognition of assets and liabilities, such as inventory and accounts payable. For purposes of applying principles in IAS 21, we need to distinguish between monetary and non-monetary items. Monetary items are defined in paragraph 8 of IAS 21 as:

Units of currency held and assets and liabilities to be received or paid in a fixed or determinable amount of units of currency.

By default, all other assets and liabilities are non-monetary items. Examples of monetary items include cash, accounts payable, accounts receivable and loans payable or receivable. Examples of non-monetary items include inventory, property, plant and equipment, patents and goodwill.

In accordance with paragraph 23 of IAS 21, at the end of each reporting period:

(a) foreign currency monetary items shall be translated using the closing rate, which is the spot exchange rate at the end of the reporting period;

(b) non-monetary items measured at historical cost in a foreign currency shall be translated at the exchange rate at the date of the transaction; and

(c) non-monetary items measured at fair value in a foreign currency shall be translated using the exchange rates at the date when fair value was measured.

The translation of foreign currency items is discussed in section 24.5.

24.3 FUNCTIONAL AND PRESENTATION CURRENCIES

As stated in paragraph 3 of IAS 21, the Standard applies to:
- accounting for transactions and balances in foreign currencies
- translating the results and financial position of foreign operations that are included in the financial statements of the entity by consolidation or the equity method
- translating an entity's results and financial position into a presentation currency.

In order to understand the different transaction processes, it is necessary to distinguish between three different concepts of currency: local currency, functional currency and presentation currency:

- *Local currency.* In this discussion the local currency refers to the currency of the country in which the foreign operation is based.
- *Functional currency.* This is defined in paragraph 8 of IAS 21 as 'the currency of the primary economic environment in which the entity operates'. As is explained in more detail later, this is the currency of the country in which the foreign operation is based. Economic environment is not defined in IAS 21.
- *Presentation currency.* Paragraph 8 defines this as 'the currency in which the financial statements are presented'.

To illustrate, Foreign Ltd is a subsidiary of Parent Ltd. Parent Ltd is an Australian company and Foreign Ltd is based in Singapore. The operations in Singapore are to sell goods manufactured in France. In this case, Foreign Ltd would most likely maintain its accounts in Singaporean dollars, the local currency, while the functional currency could be the euro, reflecting the major economic operations in France. Foreign Ltd would most likely present its financial statements in Singaporean dollars if reporting in Singapore, such as financial statements filed with the Singapore Securities and Exchange Commission. However, for presentation in the consolidated financial statements of Parent Ltd, the presentation currency could be the Australian dollar. As the accounts are maintained in Singaporean dollars, they may firstly have to be translated into the functional currency, the euro, and then translated again into the Australian dollar for presentation purposes. It is these two translation processes that are referred to in paragraph 3 of IAS 21.

What is the rationale for the choice of a functional currency and how is it related to foreign currency translation? This section relies heavily on the discussion in the seminal paper by Lawrence Revsine in which he emphasised the need to understand the rationale underlying the choice of currency as an entity's functional currency.

As noted by Revsine (1984, p. 514):

> A much more real danger is that firms, their auditors, and outside analysts may not understand the subtle philosophy that underlies the functional currency choice. As a consequence, innocent but incorrect choices and assessments may be made, and compatibility may not be achieved.

The Financial Accounting Standards Board (FASB) in the US outlined the following objectives of the translation process in paragraphs 4(a) and 4(b) of SFAS 52: Foreign Currency Translations:

1. to provide information that is generally compatible with the expected economic effects of an exchange rate change on an entity's cash flows and equity
2. to reflect in consolidated statements the financial results and relationships of the individual consolidated entities as measured in their functional currencies in conformity with US generally accepted accounting principles.

It is important that the financial effects on the parent entity of a change in the exchange rate are apparent from the translation process. The parent entity has an investment in a foreign operation and so has assets that are exposed to a change in the exchange rate. Capturing the extent of this exposure should be reflected in the choice of translation method. *(The relationship between the choice of functional currency and the method of translation of financial statements of a subsidiary in the application of principles in IAS 21 is discussed in section 24.6).* The difference between the economic environment of the parent and the subsidiary affects the extent to which a change in exchange rate affects the parent entity. This can be seen by noting the differences in the following three cases adapted from Revsine (1984).

24.3.1 Case 1

Protea Ltd is an Australian company that aims to sell its product in Hong Kong. On 1 January 2025 Protea Ltd acquires a building in Hong Kong to be used to distribute the Australian product. For purposes of this example, the exchange rate is assumed to be AUD$1 = HK$5 on 1 January 2025. The building cost HK$1 million, equal to AUD$200,000. Protea Ltd also deposited HK$275,000 (equal to AUD$55,000) in a Hong Kong bank. By 31 January 2025, Protea Ltd had made credit sales in Hong Kong of HK$550,000. Assume the exchange rate at this time was still AUD$1 = HK$5. The goods sold had cost AUD$90,000 to manufacture. The receivables were collected in February 2025 in the HK bank account of Protea. This cash receipt is transferred back to Australia immediately. Assume the exchange rate was AUD$1 = HK$5.5 at this time.

Note, in this case the company has no subsidiary but acquired an overseas asset, deposited money in an overseas bank and sold goods overseas. *As discussed in section 24.2,* the transactions are translated at the spot rate on the day of the transaction and monetary items are translated at the closing rate at the end of the period. Accordingly, Protea Ltd would record these transactions as follows, in Australian dollars:

Building	Dr	200,000	
Cash	Cr		200,000
Cash — HK Bank	Dr	55,000	
Cash	Cr		55,000
Receivables (550,000/5)	Dr	110,000	
Sales	Cr		110,000
Cost of Sales	Dr	90,000	
Inventory	Cr		90,000
Foreign Exchange Loss	Dr	10,000	
Receivables	Cr		10,000
(Loss on receivables when exchange rate changed from 1:5 to 1:5.5; 550,000/5–550,000/5.5)			
Cash	Dr	100,000	
Receivables	Cr		100,000
Foreign Exchange Loss	Dr	5,000	
Cash in HK Bank	Cr		5,000
(Loss on holding HK$275,000 when exchange rate changed from 1:5.0 to 1:5.5)			

Note two effects of this accounting procedure:

- Foreign currency transactions have an immediate or potentially immediate effect on the future cash flows of the parent. As a result, foreign currency gains/losses are recorded as they occur and immediately affect profit or loss.
- Non-monetary assets held in the foreign country are recorded at historical cost and are unaffected by exchange rate changes.

24.3.2 Case 2

Assume that, instead of transacting directly with customers in Hong Kong, Protea Ltd formed a subsidiary, Banksia Ltd, to handle the Hong Kong operation. As with case 1, all goods are transferred from the Australian parent to the Hong Kong subsidiary, which sells them in Hong Kong and remits profits back to the Australian parent.

Hence, Banksia Ltd is established with a capital structure of HK$1,275,000 (equal to AUD$255,000), an amount necessary to acquire the Hong Kong building and establish the bank account. On selling the inventory to Banksia Ltd, Protea Ltd passes the following entries:

Receivable — Banksia Ltd	Dr	110,000
Sales Revenue	Cr	110,000
Cost of Sales	Dr	90,000
Inventory	Cr	90,000

Assuming that Protea Ltd invoices the subsidiary in Hong Kong dollars, namely HK$550,000, the parent would pass the following entry to record in AUD the receipt of cash and the loss arising from the movement in the exchange rate:

Foreign Exchange Loss	Dr	10,000
Cash	Dr	100,000
Receivable	Cr	110,000

The subsidiary will show:

Sales	HK$	550,000
Cost of sales		550,000
Profit		—
Equity	HK$	1,275,000
Building	HK$	1,000,000
Cash		275,000
	HK$	1,275,000

Note that the underlying transactions are the same in case 1 and case 2. The organisational form does not change the underlying economic effects of the transactions. The translation of the HK subsidiary must therefore show the position as if the parent had undertaken the transactions itself. This is the purpose behind the choice of the functional currency approach.

Where the subsidiary is simply a conduit for transforming foreign currency transactions into cash flows in the functional currency of the parent (AUD in this example), the consolidation approach treats the foreign currency statements of the subsidiary as artefacts that must be translated into the currency of the parent.

In case 2, the translation of the subsidiary's statements must show:

- the assets of the subsidiary at cost to the parent; that is, what the parent would have paid in its currency at acquisition date
- the revenues and expenses of the subsidiary at what it would have cost the parent in its currency at the date those transactions occurred
- monetary gains and losses being recognised immediately in income as they affect the parent directly.

Note, in case 2, that the functional currency of the subsidiary is the Australian dollar. It is the currency of the primary economic environment in which the entity operates. The inventories are sourced in Australian dollars, the dollars financing the subsidiary are Australian dollars, and the cash flows that influence the actions of the parent in continuing to operate in Hong Kong are Australian dollars.

The key to determining the functional currency in case 2 is the recognition of the subsidiary as an *intermediary for the parent's activities*. The alternative is for the subsidiary to act as a *free-standing unit*. Consider case 3 in this regard.

24.3.3 Case 3

Assume that Protea Ltd establishes a subsidiary in Hong Kong for HK$1,250,000, the money again being used to acquire a building and set up a bank account. However, in this case the Hong Kong operation is established to manufacture products in Hong Kong for sale in Hong Kong.

Chinese labour is used in the manufacturing process and profits are used to reinvest in the business for expansion purposes. Remittances of cash to the parent are in the form of dividends.

The economics of case 3 are different from those in case 2. The subsidiary is not just acting as a conduit for the parent. Apart from the initial investment, the cash flows, both inflows and outflows, for the subsidiary are dependent on the economic environment of Hong Kong rather than Australia. The effect of a change in the exchange rate between Australia and Hong Kong has no immediate effect on the operations of the Hong Kong subsidiary. It certainly affects the worth of the parent's investment in the subsidiary, but it has no immediate cash flow effect on the parent. In this circumstance, the functional currency is the Hong Kong dollar rather than the Australian dollar.

In analysing the success of the overseas subsidiary, the interrelationships between variables such as sales, profits, assets and equity should be the same whether they are expressed in Hong Kong or Australian dollars. In other words, the translation process should adjust all items by the same exchange rate to retain these interrelationships.

The key point of Revsine's article is that the choice of translation method should be such as to reflect the underlying economics of the situation. In particular, it is necessary to select the appropriate functional currency to reflect these underlying economic events.

24.4 IDENTIFYING THE FUNCTIONAL CURRENCY

Paragraphs 9–14 of IAS 21 provide information on determining the functional currency. Paragraph 12 of IAS 21 requires management to give priority to the primary indicators in paragraph 9 over the additional indicators in paragraphs 10 and 11 when exercising judgement in determining the functional currency. The indicators are:

Paragraph 9: normally the one in which it primarily *generates and expends cash*
Consider the currency:
- in which *sales prices* are denominated or which influences sales prices
- of the country whose competitive forces and regulations influence *sales prices*
- in which *input costs* — labour, materials — are denominated and settled, or which influences such costs.

Paragraph 10: consider two factors:
- the currency in which funds from *financing activities* are generated
- the currency in which *receipts from operating activities* are retained.

Paragraph 11: consider:
- whether the activities of the foreign operation are carried out as an *extension* of the reporting entity
- whether *transactions with the reporting entity* are a high or low proportion of the foreign operation's activities
- whether *cash flows* from the activities of the foreign operation *directly affect* the cash flows of the reporting entity and are readily available for remittance to it
- whether *cash flows* from the foreign operation are sufficient to *service existing and expected debt* obligations without funds being made available by the reporting entity.

Paragraph 12: when the factors identified in paragraphs 10 and 11 provide mixed indicators of the functional currency, management should use judgement to determine which currency most faithfully reflects the economic effects of the underlying transactions and events. As noted above, in exercising judgement, management should give priority to the indicators referred to in paragraph 9.

Figure 24.1 illustrates the factors and how they serve as indicators of functional currency.

FIGURE 24.1 IAS 21 Indicators of functional currency

Indicator (IAS 21 paragraph)	Example	Functional currency is the currency of the parent	Functional currency is the local currency in which the foreign operation is based
Cash flows (para. 9)	Generates cash in local currency	Less likely	More likely
Sales prices (para. 9)	Sales prices in local currency	Less likely	More likely
Expenses (para. 9)	Purchases of supplier are priced in local currency	Less likely	More likely
Financing activities (para. 10)	Borrows funds in functional currency of the parent	More likely	Less likely
Retention of receipts from operations (para. 10)	Minimal retention of cash, most remitted to the parent	More likely	Less likely
Foreign operation is an extension of the parent (para. 11)	Foreign operation has a high level of autonomy	Less likely	More likely
Intragroup transactions (para. 11)	Transactions with the parent are a small proportion of total transactions of the foreign operation	Less likely	More likely
Cash flows from the activities of the foreign operation directly affect the cash flows of the parent (para. 11)	Cash generated by the foreign operation is readily available and frequently remitted to the parent and is a significant component of the parent's cash flows	More likely	Less likely
Sufficiency of the cash flows of the foreign operation to service its debt (para. 11)	The foreign operation faces difficulty servicing its debt and the parent is required to guarantee its loan from the bank	More likely	Less likely

In applying the criteria in paragraphs 9–14 of IAS 21, for a parent and a single subsidiary, such as an Australian parent and a subsidiary in Hong Kong, there are three scenarios.

1. the functional currency of the subsidiary is the Australian dollar
2. the functional currency is the Hong Kong dollar
3. the functional currency is another currency, say, the Malaysian ringgit.

The illustration of indicators of functional currency in figure 24.1 is generally applicable to the first two scenarios, in which the functional currency is the local currency of one of either the parent or the subsidiary. The third scenario, in which the functional currency is a different currency, is less common.

In relation to the choice between the first two alternatives, the extreme situations are those alluded to in the analysis of the Revsine cases in section 24.3. For the *Australian dollar* (AUD) to be the functional currency, the expectation is that the subsidiary is a conduit for the parent entity. In case 1, as the product is made in Australia, the AUD would most likely be the currency that influences labour and material costs. If the price for which goods are sold in Hong Kong is determined by the price for which the goods are sold in Australia, such as a fixed margin on AUD costs, this would suggest that the AUD influences sales prices as well. Further, because the entire product sold by the subsidiary emanates from the parent, there is significant traffic between the two entities, including cash being transferred from the subsidiary to the parent.

For the *Hong Kong dollar* to be the functional currency, it is expected that the Hong Kong operation is independent of the parent entity. The products are sourced in Hong Kong and the sales prices depend on the local currency. The only regular transactions between the two entities are the annual dividends.

However, between these two scenarios there are many others where the determination of the functional currency is blurred. For example, the product being sold may require some Australian raw materials but be assembled in Hong Kong using some local raw materials. There are then material transactions between the two entities, but the subsidiary may be self-sufficient in terms of finance. In these cases, cash is generated in Hong Kong but expended in both Australia and Hong Kong. In determining the functional currency, management will need to apply judgement.

In relation to the situation where another currency, such as the Malaysian ringgit, is the functional currency, this could occur where the Australian parent establishes a subsidiary in Hong Kong that imports raw materials from Malaysia and elsewhere, assembles them in Hong Kong and sells the finished product in Malaysia.

24.5 TRANSLATION OF TRANSACTIONS INTO THE FUNCTIONAL CURRENCY

Paragraph 21 of IAS 21 requires a foreign currency transaction to be recorded, on initial recognition in the functional currency, using the spot exchange rate at the date of the transaction. Subsequently, in accordance with paragraph 23 of IAS 21, at the end of the reporting period, monetary items are translated into the functional currency at the closing rate, which is the spot exchange rate at the end of the period. Non-monetary items are translated using the exchange rate at the date of the transaction if measured at cost, and using the exchange rate at the date that fair value was measured, for items measured at fair value.

Foreign currency gains and losses arising from the translation or settlement of monetary items are recognised in profit or loss.

The translation of foreign currency transactions, assets and liabilities is demonstrated in illustrative example 24.1.

ILLUSTRATIVE EXAMPLE 24.1 Translation of foreign currency transactions into the functional currency

On 12 December 2025 Glasgow plc purchased a machine from a supplier in France for €60,000, payable on 31 January 2026

Glasgow plc's functional currency is UK£.

Glasgow plc's reporting period ends on 31 December.

The following exchange rates applied:

12 December 2025 UK£ = €1.20
31 December 2025 UK£ = €1.25
31 January 2026 UK£ = €1.22

Required

Prepare journal entries to record the purchase of the machine and all payments made by Glasgow plc to the supplier.

The foreign currency payable is initially translated at the spot exchange rate of UK£ = €1.20 (£50,000 = €60,000/1.2). At the end of the reporting period, it is translated at the closing rate (£48,000 = €60,000/1.25), resulting in a foreign currency gain of £2,000 (£50,000 − £48,000) which is recognised in profit or loss. The amount payable on settlement is £49,180 (€60,000/1.22), resulting in a foreign currency loss of £1,180 (£48,000 − £49,180), which is recognised in profit or loss.

		£	£
12 December 2025			
Machine	Dr	50,000	
Payable to foreign supplier (€60,000/1.2)	Cr		50,000
31 December			
Payable to foreign supplier (€60,000/1.25)	Dr	2,000	
Foreign currency gain	Cr		2,000
31 January 2026			
Payable to foreign supplier	Dr	48,000	
Cash (€60,000/1.22)	Cr		49,180
Foreign currency loss	Dr	1,180	

24.6 TRANSLATION OF FINANCIAL STATEMENTS INTO THE FUNCTIONAL CURRENCY

This section deals with the translation of the financial statements of a subsidiary.

In the situation where it is determined that the functional currency for the foreign subsidiary is the parent's reporting currency, the financial statements of the subsidiary are automatically in the reporting currency of the parent. However, where the foreign subsidiary uses the currency where it is located as its functional currency, it is necessary to translate the subsidiary's financial statements to the reporting currency of the parent. For instance, in the example in *section 24.3*, if it is determined that the functional currency of Protea Ltd's Hong Kong subsidiary is the Hong Kong dollar, the financial statements of the subsidiary must be translated from Hong Kong dollars into Australian dollars before it can be consolidated into the group accounts of the parent.

The process of translating one currency into another is given in paragraphs 21 and 23 of IAS 21. As discussed in section 24.5, paragraph 21 deals with items reflected in the statement of profit or loss and other comprehensive income that concern transactions occurring in the current period.

Hence, in translating the revenues and expenses in the statement of profit or loss and other comprehensive income, theoretically each item of revenue and expense should be translated at the spot exchange rate between the functional currency and the foreign currency on the date that the transaction occurred. However, given the large number of transactions being reported on in the statement of profit or loss and other comprehensive income, paragraph 22 of IAS 21 allows the use of an approximation of the actual rate at the date of the transaction; for example, an average rate for a week or month might be used for all transactions within those periods. The extent to which averaging can be used depends on the extent to which there is a fluctuation in the exchange rate over a period and the evenness with which transactions occur throughout the period. For example, where the transactions are made evenly throughout a financial year — no seasonal effect, for example — and there is an even movement of the exchange rate over that year, a yearly average exchange rate could be used.

In relation to items presented in the statement of financial position, paragraph 23 of IAS 21 states:

At the end of each reporting period:
(a) foreign currency monetary items shall be translated using the closing rate;
(b) non-monetary items that are measured in terms of historical cost in a foreign currency shall be translated using the exchange rate at the date of the transaction; and
(c) non-monetary items that are measured at fair value in a foreign currency shall be translated using the exchange rates at the date when the value was measured.

Monetary items are defined in paragraph 8 as 'units of currency held and assets and liabilities to be received or paid in a fixed or determinable number of units of currency'. As noted in paragraph 16, examples of monetary liabilities include pensions and other employee benefits to be paid in cash and provisions to be settled in cash, including cash dividends that are recognised as a liability. Examples of monetary assets include cash and accounts receivable. All of these items are translated using the spot exchange rate at the end of the reporting period — the closing rate. As noted previously in case 1, this reflects the amounts available in the functional currency.

For non-monetary items such as plant and equipment, IAS 16 *Property, Plant and Equipment (see chapter 5)* allows the use of the cost basis or the revaluation model of measurement. Where the cost basis is used, the appropriate translation rate is the spot rate at the date the asset was initially recorded by the subsidiary. Where the revaluation model is used, the appropriate rate is the spot rate at the date of the valuation to fair value. Paragraph 25 of IAS 21 notes that certain non-monetary assets such as inventory are to be reported at the lower of cost and net realisable value in accordance with IAS 2 *Inventories*. In such a case, it is necessary to calculate the cost, translated using the spot rate at acquisition date, and the net realisable value translated at the spot rate at the date of valuation. The lower amount is then used — this may require a write-down in the functional currency statements that would not occur in the local currency statements.

The basic principles of the translation method follow.

24.6.1 Statement of financial position items

- *Assets.* Assets should first be classified as monetary or non-monetary. Monetary assets are translated at the current rate existing at the end of the reporting period. With a non-monetary asset, the exchange rate used is that current at the date at which the recorded amount for the asset has been entered into the accounts. Hence, for non-monetary assets recorded at historical cost, the rates used are those existing when the historical cost was recorded. For non-monetary assets that have been revalued, whether upwards or downwards, the exchange rates used will relate to the dates of revaluation.
- *Liabilities.* The principles enunciated for assets apply also for liabilities. The liabilities are classified as monetary and non-monetary and, for the latter, it is the date of valuation that is important.
- *Equity.* In selecting the appropriate exchange rate two factors are important. First, equity existing at the date of acquisition or investment is distinguished from post-acquisition equity. Second, movements

in other reserves and retained earnings constituting transfers within or internal to equity are treated differently from other reserves.

- *Share capital.* If on hand at acquisition or created by investment, the capital is translated at the rate existing at acquisition or investment. If the capital arises as the result of a transfer from another equity account, such as a bonus dividend, the rate is that current at the date the amounts transferred were originally recognised in equity.
- *Other reserves.* If on hand at acquisition, the reserves are translated at the rate existing at acquisition. If the reserves are post-acquisition and result from internal transfers, the rate used is that at the date the amounts transferred were originally recognised in equity. If the reserves are post-acquisition and not created from internal transfers, the rate used is that current at the date the reserves are first recognised in the accounts.
- *Retained earnings.* If on hand at acquisition, the retained earnings are translated at the rate of exchange current at the acquisition date. Any dividends paid from pre-acquisition profits are also translated at this rate. Post-acquisition profits are carried forward balances from translation of previous periods' statements of profit or loss and other comprehensive income.

24.6.2 Statement of profit or loss and other comprehensive income items

- *Income and expenses.* In general, these are translated at the rates current at the dates the applicable transactions occur. For items that relate to non-monetary items, such as depreciation and amortisation, the rates used are those used to translate the related non-monetary items.
- *Dividends paid.* These are translated at the rate current at the date of payment.
- *Dividends declared.* These are translated at the rate current at the date of declaration.
- *Transfers to/from reserves.* As noted earlier, if internal transfers are made, the rates applicable are those existing when the amounts transferred were originally recognised in equity.

The application of these rules will result in exchange differences. Exchange differences arise mainly from translating the foreign operation's monetary items at current rates in the same way as for the foreign currency monetary items of the entity. Because the non-monetary items are translated using a historical rate that is the same from year to year, no exchange differences arise in relation to the non-monetary items. Further, items in the statement of profit or loss and other comprehensive income such as sales, purchases and expenses give rise to monetary items such as cash, receivables and payables. Hence, the exchange difference over the period can be explained by examining the movements in the monetary items over the period. The accounting for the exchange difference is explained in paragraph 28 of IAS 21:

> Exchange differences arising on the settlement of monetary items or on translating monetary items at rates different from those at which they were translated on initial recognition during the period or in previous financial statements shall be recognised in profit or loss in the period in which they arise, except as described in paragraph 32.

The exchange differences are then taken to the current period's statement of profit or loss and other comprehensive income in the same way as movements in the exchange rates on an entity's own foreign currency monetary items. See section *24.10 for a discussion of the paragraph 32 exception.*

As stated in paragraph 34 of IAS 21, the application of the basic principles of the translation method means that when an entity keeps its records in a currency other than its functional currency all amounts are remeasured in the functional currency. This produces the same amounts in that currency as would have occurred had the items been recorded initially in the functional currency.

ILLUSTRATIVE EXAMPLE 24.2 Translation from local currency into functional currency

Patrick Ltd, a company operating in Ireland, is a wholly owned subsidiary of Harriet Ltd, a company listed in the UK. Harriet Ltd formed Patrick Ltd on 1 July 2025 with an investment of pound sterling £310,000 when the exchange rate was 1:1, thus providing capital of €310,000 for Patrick Ltd. Patrick Ltd's records and financial statements are prepared in euro (€). Patrick Ltd has prepared the financial information at 30 June 2026, as shown in figure 24.2.

PATRICK LTD
Statement of Financial Position
as at 30 June 2026

	2026 €
Current assets:	
Inventory	210,000
Monetary assets	190,000
Total current assets	400,000
Non-current assets:	
Land — acquired 1/7/25	100,000
Buildings — acquired 1/10/25	120,000
Plant and equipment — acquired 1/11/25	110,000
Accumulated depreciation	(10,000)
Deferred tax asset	10,000
Total non-current assets	330,000
Total assets	730,000
Current liabilities:	
Current tax liability	70,000
Borrowings	50,000
Payables	100,000
Total current liabilities	220,000
Non-current liabilities:	
Borrowings	150,000
Total liabilities	370,000
Net assets	360,000
Equity:	
Share capital	310,000
Retained earnings	50,000
Total equity	360,000

PATRICK LTD
Statement of Profit or Loss and Other Comprehensive Income
for the year ended 30 June 2026

	€	€
Sales revenue		1,200,000
Cost of sales:		
Purchases	1,020,000	
Ending inventory	210,000	810,000
Gross profit		390,000
Expenses:		
Selling	120,000	
Depreciation (plant and equipment)	10,000	
Interest	20,000	
Other	90,000	240,000
Profit before income tax		150,000
Income tax expense		60,000
Profit for the period		90,000

The only movement in equity, other than in profit, was a dividend paid during the period of €40,000.

Additional information
(a) Exchange rates over the period 1 July 2025 to 30 June 2026 were:

	EURO €$1.00 = POUND STERLING £
1 July 2025	1
1 October 2025	0.95
1 November 2025	0.90
1 January 2026	0.85
1 April 2026	0.75
30 June 2026	0.75
Average rate for year	0.85
Average rate for final quarter	0.77

(b) Proceeds of long-term borrowings were received on 1 July 2025 and are payable in four annual instalments commencing 1 July 2026. Interest expense relates to this loan.
(c) The inventory on hand at balance date represents approximately the final 3 months' purchases.
(d) Revenues and expenses are spread evenly throughout the year.
(e) Deferred tax asset relates to depreciation of the plant and equipment.
(f) The dividends were paid on 1 April 2026.

Required

The functional currency is determined to be the pound sterling. Translate the financial statements of Patrick Ltd into the functional currency.

Solution

The translation process is as shown in figure 24.2.

Exchange differences arise mainly from translating the foreign operation's monetary items at current rates in the same way as for the foreign currency monetary items of the entity. Because the non-monetary items are translated using a historical rate that is the same from year to year, exchange differences in relation to non-monetary items arise only in the periods in which they are acquired or sold. Items in the statement of profit or loss and other comprehensive income such as sales, purchases and expenses give rise to monetary items such as cash, receivables and payables. Hence, exchange differences are going to arise by examining the movements in the monetary items over the period.

FIGURE 24.2 Translation into functional currency

	€	Rate	£
Sales	1,200,000	0.85	1,020,000
Cost of sales:			
Purchases	1,020,000	0.85	867,000
Ending inventory	210,000	077	161,700
	810,000		705,300
Gross profit	390,000		314,700
Expenses:			
Selling	120,000	0.85	102,000
Depreciation (plant and equipment)	10,000	0.90	9,000
Interest	20,000	0.85	17,000
Other	90,000	0.85	76,500
	240,000		204,500
			110,200
Foreign exchange translation loss	0		1,000
Profit before tax	150,000		109,200
Income tax expense	60,000	0.85	51,000
Profit for the period	90,000		58,200
Retained earnings at 1/7/25	0		0
	90,000		58,200
Dividends paid	40,000	0.75	30,000
Retained earnings at 30/6/26	50,000		28,200

	€	Rate	£
Share capital	310,000	1.00	310,000
Non-current borrowings	150,000	0.75	112,500
Current tax liability	70,000	0.75	52,500
Current borrowings	50,000	0.75	37,500
Payables	100,000	0.75	75,000
	730,000		615,700
Inventory	210,000	0.77	161,700
Monetary assets	190,000	0.75	142,500
Land	100,000	1.00	100,000
Buildings	120,000	0.95	114,000
Plant and equipment	110,000	0.90	99,000
Accumulated depreciation	(10,000)	0.90	(9,000)
Deferred tax asset	10,000	0.75	7,500
	730,000		615,700

From figure 24.2, the net monetary assets of Patrick Ltd at 30 June 2026 consist of:

	€
Monetary assets	190,000
Deferred tax asset	10,000
Borrowings: non-current	(150,000)
Borrowings: current	(50,000)
Current tax liability	(70,000)
Payables	(100,000)
Net monetary assets at 30/6/26	(170,000)

The changes in the net monetary assets are determined from the statement of profit or loss and other comprehensive income. The exchange differences are calculated by comparing the difference between the exchange rate used in the translation process and the current rate at the closing rate:

	€	Current rate less rate applied	£ gain (loss)
Net monetary assets at 1 July 2025	310,000	(0.75–1.00)	(77,500)
Increases in monetary assets:			
Sales	1,200,000	(0.75–0.85)	(120,000)
	1,510,000		(197,500)
Decreases in monetary assets:			
Land	100,000	(0.75–1.00)	25,000
Buildings	120,000	(0.75–0.95)	24,000
Plant	110,000	(0.75–0.90)	16,500
Purchases	1,020,000	(0.75–0.85)	102,000
Selling expenses	120,000	(0.75–0.85)	12,000
Interest	20,000	(0.75–0.85)	2,000
Other expenses	90,000	(0.75–0.85)	9,000
Dividend paid	40,000	(0.75–0.75)	—
Income tax expense*	60,000	(0.75–0.85)	6,000
	1,680,000		196,500
Net monetary assets at 30 June 2026	(170,000)		(1,000)

*The entry for the period is:

		€	€
Income tax expense	Dr	60,000	
Deferred tax asset	Dr	10,000	
Current tax liability	Cr		70,000

In preparing the translated financial statements for the following period, it should be noted that the balance of retained earnings at 30 June 2026, as translated in figure 24.2, is carried forward into the next period. In other words, there is no direct translation of the retained earnings (opening balance) within the translation process.

24.7 TRANSLATION INTO THE PRESENTATION CURRENCY

Consider an entity operating in the UK that has two subsidiaries, one in Malaysia and one in Hong Kong, and the functional currency for each of these subsidiaries is the Hong Kong dollar. The UK parent will have to prepare a set of consolidated financial statements for the group. In which currency should the consolidated financial statements be prepared?

Theoretically, any currency could be the presentation currency. It may be pound sterling if management perceives it as the currency in which users prefer to read the financial statements. In that case, the two subsidiaries' financial statements would be prepared in Hong Kong dollars, which is the functional currency for them both. These would then be translated into pound sterling and consolidated with the parent entity's statements.

It is possible that the presentation currency could be the Hong Kong dollar, for example if the majority of shareholders in the parent entity were Hong Kong residents. In that case, the parent entity's statements would be translated from pound sterling into the Hong Kong dollar and consolidated with those of the subsidiaries as presented in their functional currency.

Hence, having prepared the parent's and the subsidiaries' financial statements in the relevant functional currencies, a presentation currency is chosen and all statements not already in that currency are translated into the presentation currency. Obviously, a number of presentation currencies could be chosen, and multiple translations undertaken.

Paragraph 39 of IAS 21 states the principles for translating from the functional currency into the presentation currency:

> The results and financial position of an entity whose functional currency is not the currency of a hyperinflationary economy shall be translated into a different presentation currency using the following procedures:
> (a) assets and liabilities for each statement of financial position presented (i.e. including comparatives) shall be translated at the closing rate at the date of that statement of financial position;
> (b) income and expenses for each statement presenting profit or loss and other comprehensive income (i.e. including comparatives) shall be translated at exchange rates at the dates of the transactions; and
> (c) all resulting exchange differences shall be recognised in other comprehensive income.

Paragraph 40 notes that average rates over a period for statement of profit or loss and other comprehensive income items may be used unless exchange rates fluctuate significantly over the period.

An elaboration of these procedures for a foreign subsidiary is as follows.

24.7.1 Statement of financial position items

- *Assets*. All assets, whether current or non-current, monetary or non-monetary, are translated at the exchange rate current at the reporting date. This includes all contra-asset accounts such as accumulated depreciation and allowance for doubtful debts.
- *Liabilities*. All liabilities are translated at the same rate as assets, namely the exchange rate current at the end of the reporting period.
- *Equity*. In selecting the appropriate rate, two factors need to be kept in mind. First, equity existing at the acquisition date or investment is distinguished from post-acquisition equity. Second, movements in other reserves and retained earnings constituting transfers within or internal to shareholders' equity are treated differently from other reserves.
  - *Share capital*. If on hand at acquisition date or created by investment, this is translated at the rate current at acquisition date or investment. If created by transfer from a reserve, such as general reserve via a bonus issue, this is translated at the rate current at the date the amounts transferred were originally recognised in equity.
  - *Other reserves*. If on hand at acquisition date, these are translated at the current exchange rate existing at acquisition date. If reserves are post-acquisition and created by an internal transfer within equity, they

are translated at the rate existing at the date the reserve from which the transfer was made was originally recognised in the accounts. If post-acquisition (e.g. an asset revaluation surplus) and not the result of an internal transfer, the rate used is that current at the date the reserve is recognised in the accounts.
- *Retained earnings*. If on hand at acquisition date, they are translated at the current exchange rate existing at acquisition. Any dividends from pre-acquisition profits are also translated at this rate. Post-acquisition profits are carried forward balances from translation of previous periods' statements of profit or loss and other comprehensive income.

24.7.2 Statement of profit or loss and other comprehensive income items

- *Income and expenses*. These are translated at the rates current at the applicable transaction dates. For items, such as purchases of inventory and sales, that occur regularly throughout the period, for practical reasons average or standard rates that approximate the relevant rates may be employed. This will involve considerations of materiality. In relation to items such as depreciation, which are allocations for a period, even though they may be recognised in the accounts only at year-end (because they reflect events occurring throughout the period) an average-for-the-period exchange rate may be used.
- *Dividends paid*. These are translated at the rates current when the dividends were paid.
- *Dividends declared*. These are translated at the rates current when the dividends are declared, generally at end-of-year rates.
- *Transfers to/from reserves*. As noted earlier, if these are transfers internal to equity, the rate used for the transfer and the reserve created is that existing when the amounts transferred were originally recognised in equity.

Using the example in figure 24.2 and, assuming that the functional currency of Patrick Ltd is the euro, the translation into pounds sterling as a presentation currency is shown in figure 24.3.

FIGURE 24.3 Translation into presentation currency

	€	Rate	£
Sales	1,200,000	0.85	1,020,000
Cost of sales:			
Purchases	1,020,000	0.85	867,000
Ending inventory	210,000	0.77	161,700
	810,000		705,300
Gross profit	390,000		314,700
Expenses:			
Selling	120,000	0.85	102,000
Depreciation	10,000	0.85	8,500
Interest	20,000	0.85	17,000
Other	90,000	0.85	76,500
	240,000		204,000
Profit before tax	150,000		110,700
Income tax expense	60,000	0.85	51,000
Profit for the period	90,000		59,700
Retained earnings at 1/7/25	0		0
	90,000		59,700
Dividends paid	40,000	0.75	30,000
Retained earnings at 30/6/26	50,000		29,700
Share capital	310,000	1.00	310,000
Non-current borrowings	150,000	0.75	112,500
Current tax liability	70,000	0.75	52,500
Current borrowings	50,000	0.75	37,500
Payables	100,000	0.75	75,000
Foreign currency translation reserve			(69,700)
	730,000		547,500

(continued)

FIGURE 24.3 (continued)

Inventory	210,000	0.75	157,500
Monetary assets	190,000	0.75	142,500
Land	100,000	0.75	75,000
Buildings	120,000	0.75	90,000
Plant and equipment	110,000	0.75	82,500
Accumulated depreciation	(10,000)	0.75	(7,500)
Deferred tax asset	10,000	0.75	7,500
	730,000		547,500

The exchange difference arising as a result of the translation is £(69,700) — there has been an exchange loss over the period. This loss arises for two reasons, as explained in paragraph 41 of IAS 21:

- *The income and expense items are translated at dates of the transactions and not the closing rate:* The profit represents the net movements in income and expenses:

Profit	= €90,000
Profit as translated	= £59,700
Profit × closing rate	= €90,000 × 0.75
	= £67,500
Translation gain	= £7,800

- *In the case of a net investment in a foreign operation, translating the opening net assets at an exchange rate different from the closing rate:*

Net investment at 1 July 2025	= €310,000
Net investment × opening rate	= €310,000 × 1.00
	= £310,000
Net investment × closing rate	= €310,000 × 0.75
	= £232,500
Translation loss	= £(77,500)

- The total translation loss is £(69,700) equal to (£7,800 + £(77,500)).

Note the following in relation to the translation into presentation currency:

- The exchange differences are not taken into current period income or expense. As explained in paragraph 41 of IAS 21, these exchange differences have little or no direct effect on the present and future cash flows from operations. The translation is for presentation only. It is the functional currency statements that recognise exchange differences in current period income and expense.
- In the Basis for Conclusions to IAS 21, in paragraphs BC10–BC14, the International Accounting Standards Board (IASB®) discusses whether the entity should (a) be permitted to present its financial statements in a currency other than the functional currency, (b) be allowed a limited choice of presentation currencies, or (c) be permitted to present their financial statements in any currency. The IASB concluded that entities should be permitted to present in any currency or currencies. The IASB noted that some jurisdictions require the use of a specific presentation which will put constraints on some entities anyway. Further, many large groups consist of many entities with different functional currencies and it is not clear which currency should be the presentation currency. In fact, in such circumstances management may prefer to use a number of presentation currencies.

24.8 CONSOLIDATING ACQUIRED FOREIGN SUBSIDIARIES — WHERE THE FUNCTIONAL CURRENCY IS NOT THE PRESENTATION CURRENCY

Paragraphs 44–47 of IAS 21 deal with matters relating to the consolidation of foreign subsidiaries. As noted in paragraph 45, normal consolidation procedures as set down in IFRS 10 apply to foreign subsidiaries. Where a parent establishes a subsidiary in a foreign country, the determination of what exists at acquisition date is relatively simple. This is because generally the investment recorded by the parent is equal to the initial share capital of the subsidiary. Where a parent entity obtains an overseas subsidiary by acquiring an already existing operation, the date of control determines the point of time at which historical rates for translation are determined.

For example, assume on 1 July 2025 York plc acquires all the shares of Palm Berhad, a Malaysian entity that has been in existence for many years. The group commences on the date of control, namely 1 July 2025. Palm Berhad may have some land that it acquired in 2016 for 1000 Malaysian ringgit (RM). The historical cost in the records of the company is 1000 RM. In other words, even though the overseas entity has held the land prior to the date that York plc obtained control over the foreign entity, the date for measurement of the historical rate is the date of control. This is because, under IFRS 3 *Business Combinations*, all assets and liabilities of the subsidiary are measured at fair value at acquisition date.

24.8.1 Acquisition analysis

Assume that York plc acquired all the shares of Palm Berhad at 1 July 2025 for £30,000, when the exchange rate between the pound sterling and the Malaysian ringgit was 1:5. At acquisition date, the equity of that company consisted of:

	RM	£
Share capital	100,000	20,000
Retained earnings	40,000	8,000

All the identifiable assets and liabilities of Palm Berhad were recorded at fair value except for plant, for which the fair value was RM5,000 (equal to £1,000) greater than the carrying amount. The plant has a further 5-year life. Assume the Malaysian tax rate is 20% and the British tax rate is 30%. At 30 June 2026, the exchange rate is £1 = RM6. The average rate for the year is A$1 = ¥5.5.

At acquisition date:		
Net fair value of identifiable assets and liabilities of Palm Berhad		= RM100,000 + 40,000 + 5,000 (1−20%) (BCVR — plant)
		= RM144,000
Consideration transferred	= £30,000 × 5	= RM150,000
Goodwill		= RM6,000

As noted in paragraph 47 of IAS 21, the goodwill is regarded as an asset of the subsidiary.

24.8.2 Business combination valuation entries

Goodwill

At acquisition date, the entry in Malaysian ringgit is:

		RM	RM
Goodwill	Dr	6,000	
Business Combination Valuation Reserve	Cr		6,000

The valuation reserve continues to be translated at the rate at acquisition date as it is pre-acquisition equity. Assuming the functional currency is the Malaysian ringgit, the financial statements of Palm Berhad would be translated into pound sterling for presentation purposes. The goodwill is translated at the closing rate of 1:6, giving rise to a foreign currency translation loss, recognised in equity. Hence, on consolidation at 30 June 2026, the worksheet would include an additional entry to recognise the foreign currency translation loss in the foreign currency translation reserve, as shown in the follow extract:

		£	£
Goodwill	Dr	1,200	
Business Combination Valuation Reserve			1,200
Foreign Currency Translation Reserve	Dr	200	
Goodwill	Cr		200

Plant

Similarly to goodwill, as noted in paragraph 47 of IAS 21, any fair value adjustments to the carrying amounts of assets and liabilities at acquisition date are treated as assets and liabilities of the foreign operation.

At acquisition date, the valuation entry is:

		£	£
Plant (RM5000/5)	Dr	1,000	
Deferred Tax Liability	Cr		200
Business Combination Valuation Reserve	Cr		800

At 30 June 2026, the valuation reserve is translated at the exchange rate at acquisition date and, as with goodwill, a foreign exchange loss is recognised — in this case on both the plant and the deferred tax liability:

		£	£
Plant (RM5000/6)	Dr	833	
Foreign Currency Translation Reserve (833 − 1000)	Dr	167	
Deferred Tax Liability (20% × 833)	Cr		167
Foreign Currency Translation Reserve (200 − 167)			33
Business Combination Valuation Reserve	Cr		800

The plant is depreciated at 20% per annum. This is based on the RM5,000 adjustment, giving a depreciation of RM1,000 per annum. The plant is translated at closing rates while the depreciation is translated at average rates.

		£	£
Depreciation Expense [RM1000/5.5]	Dr	182	
Accumulated Depreciation [RM1000/6.0]	Cr		167
Foreign Currency Translation Reserve	Cr		15
Deferred Tax Liability [RM200/6.0 or 20% × 167]	Dr	33	
Foreign Currency Translation Reserve	Dr	3	
Income Tax Expense [RM200/5.5]	Cr		36

24.8.3 Elimination of investment

The entry at acquisition date and at 30 June 2026 is:

		£	£
Retained Earnings (1/7/25)	Dr	8,000	
Share Capital	Dr	20,000	
Business Combination Valuation Reserve [800 + 1,200]	Dr	2,000	
Shares in Palm Berhad	Cr		30,000

24.8.4 Non-controlling interest (NCI)

The NCI receives a share of the recorded equity of the subsidiary as well as the valuation reserves raised on consolidation. The NCI also receives a share of the foreign currency translation reserve raised on the translation into the presentation currency. This share will need to be adjusted for any movements in that reserve as a result of movements raised via the revaluation process.

24.8.5 Intragroup transactions

As with any transactions within the group, the effects of transactions between a parent and its foreign subsidiaries, or between foreign subsidiaries, must be eliminated in full. Intragroup transactions can give rise to assets and liabilities that must be eliminated on consolidation (*refer to chapter 22*). If the functional currencies of the two entities differ, any foreign currency gain or loss remaining after elimination of the intragroup balances is recognised in profit or loss.

Foreign currency differences introduce additional complexity in the elimination of unrealised profit within a group. Neither IAS 21 nor IFRS 10 provide specific guidance in relation to transactions with foreign entities. A key matter of concern is whether the adjustment should be affected by changes in the exchange rate. In this regard, note paragraphs 136 and 137 of the Basis for Conclusions relating to the US Statement of Financial Accounting Standards (SFAS)

No. 52 *Foreign Currency Translation*:

> 136. An intercompany sale or transfer of inventory, machinery, etc., frequently produces an intercompany profit for the selling entity and, likewise, the acquiring entity's cost of the inventory, machinery, etc., includes a component of intercompany profit. The Board considered whether computation of the amount of intercompany profit to be eliminated should be based on exchange rates in effect on the date of the intercompany sale or transfer, or whether that computation should be based on exchange rates as of the date the asset (inventory, machinery, etc.) or the related expense (cost of sales, depreciation, etc.) is translated.
>
> 137. The Board decided that any intercompany profit occurs on the date of sale or transfer and that exchange rates in effect on that date or reasonable approximations thereof should be used to compute the amount of any intercompany profit to be eliminated. The effect of subsequent changes in exchange rates on the transferred asset or the related expense is viewed as being the result of changes in exchange rates rather than being attributable to intercompany profit.

It needs to be emphasised that the process of making the consolidation adjustments is to eliminate the *effects* of intragroup transactions. The exchange rate change is not an effect of the transaction but an economic effect on the group resulting from having assets in foreign entities.

Example 1 Parent sells inventory to foreign subsidiary

Assume Aust Ltd, an Australian company, owns 100% of the shares Windsor plc, a foreign operation based in the UK.

During the current period, when the exchange rate is £1 = AUD$2, Aust Ltd sells $10,000 worth of inventory to Windsor plc, at a before-tax profit of $2,000. At the end of the period, Windsor plc still has all inventory on hand. At the year-end reporting date, the exchange rate is £1 = $2.50. The Australian tax rate is 30%, while the tax rate in the foreign country is 25%.

Assuming the financial statements of Windsor plc have been translated from the functional currency (pound sterling) to the presentation currency (Australian dollars), the consolidation worksheet adjustment entries for the intragroup transaction are:

		AUD$	AUD$
Sales	Dr	10,000	
Cost of Sales	Cr		8,000
Inventory	Cr		2,000
Deferred Tax Asset	Dr	500	
Income Tax Expense	Cr		500
(25% × 2000)			

The above entries eliminate the sales and cost of sales as recorded by the parent. The inventory would have been recorded by Windsor plc at £5,000. The translation process at balance date would mean the £5,000 of inventory would be translated using the closing rate of £1 = AUD$2.50, giving a translated figure for inventory of AUD$12,500. After passing the consolidation adjustment entry, inventory in the consolidated statement of financial position would be reported at AUD$10,500 (i.e. AUD$12,500 − AUD$2,000). This figure is greater than the original cost of AUD$8,000 due to the exchange rate change between the transaction date and the balance date. The US FASB would argue that no further entry is necessary as the effect of changes in the exchange rates on the transferred asset is viewed as the result of changes in exchange rates rather than intragroup profit.

Note that the tax rate used is that of the country holding the asset — in this case, the foreign country. This is because the adjustment for the tax effect is required because of the adjustment to the carrying amount of the inventory in the first journal entry. As the inventory is held by the foreign entity, it is the foreign country's tax rate that is applicable.

Example 2 Foreign subsidiary sells inventory to parent

Assume Windsor plc, the foreign subsidiary, sells an item of inventory to Aust Ltd, the Australian parent, during the current period. The inventory had cost Windsor plc £5,000 and was sold to Aust Ltd for £7,500.

At the date of sale, the exchange rate was £1 = AUD$2. The tax rate in Australia is 30%. All inventory was still on hand at the end of the period when the closing exchange rate was £1 = $2.50.

The consolidation worksheet entry is:

		AUD$	AUD$
Sales	Dr	15,000	
Cost of Sales	Cr		10,000
Inventory	Cr		5,000
Deferred Tax Asset	Dr	1,500	
Income Tax Expense	Cr		1,500

Both sales and cost of sales as recorded by Windsor plc are translated at the exchange rate existing at the date of the transaction, namely £1 = AUD$2. The inventory sold to the parent is recorded by that entity at AUD$15,000. The profit on sale is adjusted against inventory at the exchange rate existing at date of sale, giving an adjustment of AUD$5,000. Hence, in the consolidated statement of financial position at the end of the period, the inventory is reported at AUD$10,000, equal to the original cost to Windsor plc.

ILLUSTRATIVE EXAMPLE 24.3 Consolidation — functional currency of the subsidiary is not the presentation currency

On 1 January 2026, Kent plc, a British company, acquired 80% of the shares of Continental Ltd, a European company, for £2,498,000. The 2026 trial balance of Continental Ltd prepared in euro, which is also its functional currency, showed the following information:

	1 January 2026 €'000	1 December 2026 €'000
Revenue		6,450
Cost of sales		4,400
Gross profit		2,050
Expenses:		
Depreciation		280
Other		960
		1,240
Profit before income tax		810
Income tax expense		120
Profit		690
Retained earnings at beginning of year		1,440
		2,130
Dividend paid		100
Dividend declared		100
		200
Retained earnings at end of year		1,930
Cash and receivables	1,000	1,760
Inventories	1,200	1,000
Land	800	800
Buildings	2,200	2,200
Accumulated depreciation	(900)	(990)
Equipment	1,130	1,330

| | 1 January 2026 | 1 December 2026 |
	€'000	€'000
Accumulated depreciation	(200)	(390)
Total assets	5,230	5,710
Current liabilities	590	420
Non-current liabilities	1,200	1,360
Total liabilities	1,790	1,780
Net assets	3,440	3,930
Share capital	2,000	2,000
Retained earnings	1,440	1,930
Total equity	3,440	3,930

Additional information

1. The exchange rates for pound sterling and the euro are as follows

	£	€
1 January 2026	1	1.20
1 July 2026	1	1.25
1 November 2026	1	1.35
31 December 2026	1	1.40
Average for the year	1	1.30

2. At 1 January 2026, all the assets and liabilities of Continental Ltd were recorded at fair value except for the land, for which the fair value was €1,000,000, and the equipment, for which the fair value was €1,010,000. The undervalued equipment had a further 4-year life. The tax rate in Continental Ltd's tax jurisdiction is 25%.
3. Additional equipment was acquired on 1 July 2026 for €200,000 by issuing a note for €160,000 and paying the balance in cash.
4. Sales and expenses were incurred evenly throughout the year.
5. Dividends of €100,000 were paid on 1 July 2026.
6. On 1 November 2026, Continental Ltd sold inventory to Kent plc for €25,000. The inventory had cost Continental Ltd €20,000. Half of the inventory is still on hand at 31 December 2026. Assume the tax rate in the UK is 30%.

Required

1. Translate the financial statements of Continental Ltd into pound sterling, which is the presentation currency.
2. Prepare the consolidation worksheet entries for consolidating the European subsidiary into the consolidated financial statements of Kent plc. The partial goodwill method is used.

Solution

1. Translation into presentation currency

	€	Rate	£
Revenue	6,450	1/1.30	4,962
Cost of sales	4,400	1/1.30	3,385
Gross profit	2,050		1,577
Depreciation	280	1/1.30	215
Other	960	1/1.30	739
	1,240		954
Profit before tax	810		623
Income tax expense	120	1/1.30	92
Profit	690		531
Retained earnings as at 1/1/26	1,440	1/1.20	1,200
	2,130		1,731
Dividend paid	100	1/1.25	80
Dividend declared	100	1/1.40	71
	200		151

	€	Rate	£
Retained earnings as at 31/12/26	1,930		1,580
Share capital	2,000	1/1.20	1,667
Non-current liabilities	1,360	1/1.40	971
Current liabilities	420	1/1.40	300
Foreign currency translation reserve			(439)
	5,710		4,079
Cash and receivables	1,760	1/1.40	1,257
Inventories	1,000	1/1.40	714
Land	800	1/1.40	572
Buildings	2,200	1/1.40	1,572
Accumulated depreciation	(990)	1/1.40	(707)
Equipment	1,330	1/1.40	950
Accumulated depreciation	(390)	1/1.40	(279)
	5,710		4,079

In relation to the foreign currency translation reserve:
- *The income and expense items are translated at dates of the transactions and not the closing rate:*
  The profit represents the net movements in income and expenses:

Profit	= €690,000
Profit as translated	= £530,800
Profit × closing rate	= €690,000 × 1/1.40
	= £492,857
Translation loss	= £(37,943)
Dividend paid as translated	= £80,000
Dividend paid at closing rate	= €100,000 × 1/1.40
	= £71,429
Translation gain	= £8,571

- *In the case of a net investment in a foreign operation, translating the opening net assets at an exchange rate different from the closing rate:*

Net investment at 1 January 2026	= €3,440,000
Net investment × opening rate	= €3,440,000 × 1/1.20
	= £2,866,667
Net investment × closing rate	= €3,440,000 × 1/1.40
	= £2,457,143
Translation loss	= £(409,524)

- Total translation loss is £(438,896) = (£(37,943) + £(409,524)) + £8,571
2. **Consolidation worksheet entries: (in $000)**

Net fair value of identifiable assets and liabilities of Continental Ltd	= €[2,000 + 1,440 + 200(1–25%) (land) + 80(1–25%) (equipment)] 1/1.20
	= £[1,667 + 1,200 + 125 + 50]
Net fair value acquired	= 80% × £[1,667 + 1,200 + 125 + 50]
	= £[1,334 + 960 + 100 + 40]
	= £2,434
Consideration transferred	= £2,498
Goodwill acquired	£64
	= €77 (i.e. 64 × 1.20)

(i) Business combination valuation entries

Land (200/1.40)	Dr	143	
Foreign Currency Translation Reserve	Dr	18	
Business Combination Valuation Reserve (150/1.20)	Cr		125
Deferred Tax Liability (50/1.40)	Cr		36
Accumulated Depreciation (200/1.40)	Dr	143	
Equipment (120/1.40)	Cr		86
Foreign Currency Translation Reserve	Dr	7	
Deferred Tax Liability (25% × [80/1.40])	Cr		14
Business Combination Valuation Reserve (60/1.20)	Cr		50
Depreciation Expense ([1/4 × 80]/1.30)	Dr	15	
Accumulated Depreciation ([1/4 × 80]/1.40)	Cr		14
Foreign Currency Translation Reserve	Cr		1
Deferred Tax Liability ([25% × 20]/1.30)	Dr	3.5	
Foreign Currency Translation Reserve	Dr	0.3	
Income Tax Expense ([25% × 20]/1.30)	Cr		3.8

(At acquisition the deferred tax liability was €20 = 25% × €80)

(ii) Elimination of investment

Retained Earnings (1/1/26)	Dr	960	
Share Capital	Dr	1,334	
Business Combination Valuation Reserve	Dr	140	
Goodwill	Dr	64	
Shares in Continental Ltd	Cr		2,498
Foreign Currency Translation Reserve	Dr	9	
Goodwill ([77/1.40] − 64)	Cr		9

(iii) Non-controlling interest
Share at acquisition date

Retained Earnings (1/1/26) (20% × 1200)	Dr	240	
Share Capital (20% × 1667)	Dr	333	
Business Combination Valuation Reserve (20% [125 + 50])	Dr	35	
NCI	Cr		608

Share from 1/1/26–31/12/26
(i) Current period profit — the share is based on the translated profit of the subsidiary

NCI Share of Profit	Dr	104	
NCI	Cr		104
(20% × £[531 − (15 − 3.8)])			

(ii) The share of the foreign currency translation reserve is based on the amount of the reserve calculated as a result of the translation process adjusted by any changes in that reserve recognised in the valuation entries

NCI	Dr	93	
Foreign Currency Translation Reserve	Cr		93
(20% [439 + 18 + 7 + 1 + 0.3])			

(iii) Dividend paid

NCI	Dr	16	
Dividend Paid	Cr		16
(20% × £80)			

(iv) Dividend declared

NCI	Dr	14	
Dividend Declared	Cr		14
(20% × £71)			

Intragroup transactions:
  (i) Dividends

Dividend Revenue	Dr	64	
Dividend Paid	Cr		64
(80% × [100/1.25])			
Dividend Revenue	Dr	57	
Dividend Receivable	Cr		37
(80% × [100/1.40])			
Dividend Payable	Dr	57	
Dividend Declared	Cr		57

(ii) Sale of inventory: subsidiary to parent on 1 November

Sales Revenue (25/1.35)	Dr	19	
Cost of Sales	Cr		17
Inventory (1/2 × 5 × 1/1.35)	Cr		2
Deferred Tax Asset (30% × 2)	Dr	0.6	
Income Tax Expense	Cr		0.6

(iii) Adjustment to NCI

NCI	Dr	0.28	
NCI Share of Profit	Cr		0.28
(20% × [2 − 0.6])			

24.9 CONSOLIDATING ACQUIRED FOREIGN SUBSIDIARIES — WHERE FUNCTIONAL CURRENCY IS THE PARENT'S REPORTING CURRENCY

While uncommon, IAS 21 deals with the situation in which an entity, such as a foreign subsidiary within a group, maintains its accounting records and prepares financial statements in a currency that is not its functional currency. We will consider the situation where the subsidiary has the same functional currency as the parent, and that currency is also the reporting currency of the group. Paragraph 34 of IAS 21 states that when an entity keeps its books and records in a currency other than its functional currency, the financial statements are translated into the functional currency in accordance with paragraphs 20–26 of IAS 21. The main difference from what is described in section 24.8 in preparing the consolidated financial statements in this case is the exchange rates used in translating items presented in the statement of financial position. This is because the translation of non-monetary assets differs when the translation is for presentation purposes rather than for functional currency purposes.

Under the method described in paragraph 23 of IAS 21, the non-monetary assets of the subsidiary are translated using exchange rates at the date of the transaction (i.e. historical rates). In contrast, in illustrative example 24.3, where the translation is based on paragraph 39 of IAS 21, the non-monetary assets are translated at the closing rate.

Using the information in illustrative example 24.3:
- at acquisition date, 1 January 2026, goodwill of the subsidiary was measured to be €96
- the land had a fair value-carrying amount difference of €200

- the equipment had a fair value-carrying amount difference of €80, with an expected remaining useful life of four years
- the tax rate in Continental Ltd's tax jurisdiction is 25%
- The exchange rates for pound sterling and the euro are as follows:

	£	€
1 January 2026	1	1.20
1 July 2026	1	1.25
1 November 2026	1	1.35
31 December 2026	1	1.40
Average for the year	1	1.30

The business combination valuation entries are then:

The goodwill balance is translated at the historical rate:

Goodwill (96/1.20)	Dr	80	
Business Combination Valuation Reserve (96/1.20)	Cr		80

The land is translated at the historical rate, but the deferred tax liability is translated at the closing rate. As the net monetary assets held at the beginning of the period are affected by changes in the exchange rate, an exchange gain is recognised:

Land (200/1.20)	Dr	167	
Foreign Exchange Gain	Cr		6
Business Combination Valuation Reserve (150/1.20)	Cr		125
Deferred Tax Liability (50/1.40)	Cr		36

The equipment and related accumulated depreciation are translated at the historical rate, while the deferred tax liability is translated at the closing rate, giving rise to a foreign exchange gain.

Subsequent depreciation is based on the historical rate:

Accumulated Depreciation (200/1.20)	Dr	167	
Equipment (120/1.20)	Cr		100
Foreign Exchange Gain	Cr		3
Deferred Tax Liability ([25% × 80]/1.40)	Cr		14
Business Combination Valuation Reserve (60/1.20)	Cr		50
Depreciation Expense ([1/4 × 80]/1.20)	Dr	17	
Accumulated Depreciation ([1/4 × 80]/1.20)	Cr		17
Deferred Tax Liability ([25% × 20]/1.40)	Dr	3.5	
Foreign Currency Exchange Loss	Dr	0.3	
Income Tax Expense ([25% × 20]/1.30)	Cr		3.8

(At acquisition the deferred tax liability was €20 = 25% × €80)

24.10 NET INVESTMENT IN A FOREIGN OPERATION

LO10

Paragraph 15 of IAS 21 notes that the investment in a foreign operation may consist of more than just the ownership of shares in that operation. An entity may have a monetary item that is receivable or payable to the foreign subsidiary. According to paragraph 15, where there is an item for which settlement is neither planned nor likely to occur in the foreseeable future, it is in substance a part of the entity's net investment in that foreign operation. These items include long-term receivables and payables but not trade receivables or payables.

Consider the situation where the parent entity, based in the UK, has made a long-term loan of CA$100,000 to a Canadian subsidiary when the exchange rate is £1 = CA$2. The parent entity records a receivable of £50,000, while the subsidiary records a payable of CA$100,000. If during the following financial period the exchange rate changes to £1 = CA$1.80, in accordance with paragraph 28 of IAS 21 the UK parent passes the following entry in its own records:

		Dr	5,556	
Loan Receivable		Dr	5,556	
Exchange Gain		Cr		5,556
CA$100000/1.8 – CA$100000/2.0				

This results in the receivable being recorded at £55,556. The subsidiary does not pass any entry because it still owes CA$100,000. On translation of the subsidiary into the presentation currency (pound sterling), the payable is translated into £55,556. On consolidation of the subsidiary, both the payable and the receivable are eliminated. However, because the receivable is regarded as part of the parent's net investment in the subsidiary, the accounting for the exchange gain is in accord with paragraph 32 of IAS 21:

> Exchange differences arising on a monetary item that forms part of a reporting entity's net investment in a foreign operation (see paragraph 15) shall be recognised in profit or loss in the separate financial statements of the reporting entity or the individual financial statements of the foreign operation, as appropriate. In the financial statements that include the foreign operation and the reporting entity (e.g. consolidated financial statements where the foreign operation is a subsidiary), such exchange differences shall be recognised initially in other comprehensive income and reclassified to profit or loss on disposal of the net investment in accordance with paragraph 48.

Hence, the exchange gain of £5,556 recognised as income by the parent must, on consolidation, be reclassified to other comprehensive income (OCI) and transferred to the foreign currency translation reserve raised as part of the translation process. Hence, in the consolidation worksheet the adjustment entry is:

		Dr	5,556	
Exchange Gain (P/L)		Dr	5,556	
OCI		Cr		5,556
OCI		Dr	5,556	
Foreign Currency Translation Reserve		Cr		5,556

On disposal of the net investment in the foreign operation, any foreign currency gain or loss for the current period is recognised in other comprehensive income, and the accumulated amount recognised in other comprehensive income is reclassified to profit or loss.

24.11 DISCLOSURE

LO11

Paragraphs 51–57 contain the disclosure requirements under IAS 21. In particular, an entity must disclose:
- the amount of exchange differences included in profit or loss for the period
- net exchange differences classified in a separate component of equity, and a reconciliation of the amount of such exchange differences at the beginning and end of the period
- when the presentation currency of the parent entity is different from the functional currency:
  - the fact that they are different
  - the functional currency
  - the reason for using a different presentation currency
- when there is a change in the functional currency, the fact that such a change has occurred.
  Illustrative disclosures relating to paragraph 52 of IAS 21 are given in figure 24.4.

FIGURE 24.4 Disclosures required by paragraph 52 of IAS 21

NOTE			IAS 21 paragraph
Movements in reserves			
Foreign Currency Translation Reserve	**2026**	**2025**	52(b)
Balance at beginning of period	(2,420)	(3,020)	
Exchange differences arising on translation of overseas operations	(540)	600	
Balance at end of period	(2,960)	(2,420)	
Profit from operations	**2026**	**2025**	
Profit from operations has been arrived at after charging:			
Amortisation	x	x	
Research and development costs	x	x	
Net foreign exchange gain/(loss)	765	(346)	52(a)

SUMMARY

A parent entity may have investments in subsidiaries that are incorporated in countries other than that of the parent. The foreign operation will record its transactions generally in the local currency. However, the local currency may not be that of the economy that determines the pricing of those transactions. To this end, IAS 21 requires the financial statements of a foreign operation to be translated into its functional currency, being the currency of the primary economic environment in which the entity operates. Determination of the functional currency is a matter of judgement, and the choice of the appropriate currency requires an analysis of the underlying economics of the foreign operation. A further problem addressed by IAS 21 is where the financial statements of the foreign operation need to be presented in a currency different from the functional currency. IAS 21 then provides principles relating to the translation of a set of financial statements into the presentation currency. Whenever a translation process is undertaken, foreign exchange translation adjustments arise. It is necessary to determine whether these adjustments are taken to profit or loss or to other comprehensive income.

Where the foreign operation is a subsidiary, having translated the financial statements of the foreign operation into the currency in which the consolidated financial statements are to be presented, consolidation worksheet adjustments are required as a part of the normal consolidation process. In assessing the assets and liabilities held by the subsidiary at acquisition date, as well as any goodwill or gain on bargain purchase arising as a result of the acquisition, the effects of movements in exchange rates on these assets and liabilities must be taken into consideration. The consolidation adjustments are affected by the process of translation used to translate the foreign entity's financial statements from the local currency into either the functional currency or the presentation currency.

Discussion questions

1. What is the purpose of translating financial statements from one currency to another?
2. What is meant by 'functional currency'?
3. What is the rationale behind the choice of an exchange rate as an entity's functional currency?
4. What guidelines are used to determine the functional currency of an entity?
5. How are statement of profit or loss and other comprehensive income items translated from the local currency into the functional currency?
6. How are statement of financial position items translated from the local currency into the functional currency?
7. How are foreign exchange gains and losses calculated when translating from local currency to functional currency?
8. What is meant by 'presentation currency'?
9. How are statement of profit or loss and other comprehensive income items translated from functional currency to presentation currency?
10. How are statement of financial position items translated from functional currency to presentation currency?
11. What causes a foreign currency translation reserve to arise?
12. Why are gains/losses on translation taken to a foreign currency translation reserve rather than to profit or loss for the period?

References

FASB 1981, *Foreign currency translation: Statement of Financial Accounting Standards No. 52*, Norwalk, CT: Financial Accounting Standards Board.
Revsine, L. 1984, The rationale underlying the functional currency choice, *The Accounting Review*, 59(3), 505–514.

GLOSSARY

Accounting estimates: Monetary amounts in financial statements that are subject to measurement uncertainty.

Accounting policies: The specific principles, bases, conventions, rules and practices applied by an entity in preparing and presenting financial statements.

Accounting profit: Profit or loss for a period before deducting tax expense.

Accrual basis: Recognising the effects of transactions and other events when they occur, rather than when cash or its equivalent is received or paid.

Acquiree: The business or businesses that the acquirer obtains control of in a business combination.

Acquirer: The entity that obtains control of the acquiree.

Acquisition date: The date on which the acquirer obtains control of the acquiree.

Active market: A market in which transactions for the asset or liability take place with sufficient frequency and volume to provide pricing information on an ongoing basis.

Adjusting event after the reporting period: An event that provides evidence of conditions that existed at the end of the reporting period.

Agreement date: The date that a substantive agreement between the combining parties is reached.

Agricultural produce: The harvested product of the entity's biological assets.

Allotment: The process whereby directors of the company allocate shares to applicants. Alternatively, an account recording an amount of money receivable from successful applicants once shares are allotted.

Amortisation: The systematic allocation of the depreciable amount of an intangible asset over its useful life. Generally used in the case of an intangible asset, instead of 'depreciation'. See also depreciation.

Amortised cost of a financial asset or financial liability: The amount at which the financial asset or financial liability is measured at initial recognition minus principal repayments, plus or minus the cumulative amortisation using the effective interest method of any difference between that initial amount and the maturity amount and, for financial assets adjusted for any loss allowance.

Asset: A present resource controlled by the entity as a result of past events.

Associate: An entity over which the investor has significant influence. See also Significant influence.

Balance sheet: See Statement of financial position.

Bargain purchase: A business combination in which the net of the acquisition-date amounts of the identifiable assets acquired and the liabilities assumed exceeds the aggregate of the consideration paid plus non-controlling interest.

Biological asset: A living animal or plant.

Bonus issue or bonus shares: An issue of shares to existing owners as a substitute for the payment of cash, particularly as a substitute for a cash dividend.

Business: An integrated set of activities and assets that is capable of being conducted and managed for the purpose of providing goods or services to customers, generating investment income (such as dividends or interest) or generating other income from ordinary activities.

Business combination: A transaction or other event in which an acquirer obtains control of one or more businesses. Transactions sometimes referred to as 'true mergers' or 'mergers of equals' are also business combinations as that term is used in IFRS 3.

Business segment: A distinguishable component of an entity that is engaged in providing an individual product or service or a group of related products or services and that is subject to risks and returns that are different from those of other business segments.

Call: An account used to record amounts of money receivable on shares that have been allotted by shareholders whose shares were forfeited.

Carrying amount: The amount at which an asset, a liability or equity is recognised in the statement of financial position.

Cash: Cash on hand and demand deposits.

Cash basis: Recognising the effects of transactions and other events when cash or its equivalent is received or paid, rather than when the transactions or other events occur.

Cash equivalents: Short-term, highly liquid investments that are readily convertible to known amounts of cash and which are subject to an insignificant risk of changes in value.

Cash flow statement: Provides information about the cash payments and cash receipts of an entity during a period.

Cash or settlement discount: An incentive for early payment of amounts owing on credit transactions, normally quoted as a percentage.

Cash-generating unit: The smallest identifiable group of assets that generates cash inflows that are largely independent of the cash inflows from other assets or groups of assets.

Cash-settled share-based payment transaction: A share-based payment transaction in which the entity acquires goods or services by incurring a liability to transfer cash or other assets to the supplier of those goods or services for amounts that are based on the price (or value) of equity instruments (including shares or share options) of the entity or another group entity.

Class of assets: A category of assets having a similar nature or function in the operations of an entity, and which, for the purposes of disclosure, is shown as a single item without supplementary disclosure.

Closing rate: The spot exchange rate at the end of the reporting period.

Comparability: The quality of accounting information that results from similar accounting recognition, measurement, disclosure, and presentation standards being used by all entities.

Component of an entity: Operations and cash flows that can be clearly distinguished, operationally and for financial reporting purposes, from the rest of the entity.

Conceptual Framework for Financial Reporting: The pronouncement of the International Accounting Standards Board that sets out the concepts underlying the preparation and presentation of financial statements for external users.

Consolidated financial statements: The financial statements of a group in which assets, liabilities, equity, income, expenses and cash flow of the parent and its subsidiaries are presented as those of a single economic entity.

Constructive obligation: An obligation that derives from an entity's actions where: (a) by an established pattern of past practice, published policies or a sufficiently specific current statement, the entity has indicated to other parties that it will accept certain responsibilities; and (b) as a result, the entity has created a valid expectation on the part of those other parties that it will discharge those responsibilities.

Contingency: A condition arising from past events that exists at reporting date and gives rise to either a possible asset or a possible liability, the outcome of which will be confirmed only on the occurrence of one or more uncertain future events that are outside the control of the entity.

Contingent asset: A possible asset that arises from past events and whose existence will be confirmed only by the occurrence or non-occurrence of one or more uncertain future events not wholly within the control of the entity.

Contingent consideration: Usually, an obligation of the acquirer to transfer additional assets or equity interests to the former owners of an acquiree as part of the exchange for control of the acquiree if specified future events occur or conditions are met. However, contingent consideration also may give the acquirer the right to the return of previously transferred consideration if specified conditions are met.

Contingent liability: Is: (a) A possible obligation that arises from past events and whose existence will be confirmed only by the occurrence or non-occurrence of one or more uncertain future events not wholly within the control of the entity, or (b) a present obligation that arises from past events but is not recognised because (i) it is not probable that an outflow of resources embodying economic events will be required to settle the obligation, or (ii) the amount of the obligation cannot be measured with sufficient reliability.

Contingent rent: The part of the lease payments that is not fixed in amount but is based on the future amount of a factor that changes other than with the passage of time.

Control of an economic resource: The present ability to direct the use of the economic resource and obtain the economic benefits that may flow from it.

Control of an investee: An investor controls an investee when the investor is exposed, or has rights, to variable returns from its involvement with the investee and has the ability to affect those returns through its power over the investee.

Corporate assets: Assets other than goodwill that contribute to the future cash flows of both the cash generating unit under review and other cash generating units.

Cost: The amount of cash or cash equivalents paid or the fair value of the other consideration given to acquire an asset at the time of its acquisition or construction or, when applicable, the amount attributed to that asset when initially recognised in accordance with the specific requirements of other IFRSs, e.g. IFRS 2 *Share-based Payment*.

Cost approach: A valuation technique that reflects the amount that would be required currently to replace the service capacity of an asset (often referred to as current replacement cost).

Costs of conversion: Costs directly related to the units of production plus a systematic allocation of fixed and variable overheads that are incurred in converting materials into finished goods.

Costs of disposal: Incremental costs directly attributable to the disposal of an asset or excluding finance costs and income tax expense.

Costs of purchase: Costs such as purchase price, import duties and other taxes (other than those subsequently recoverable by the entity from the taxing authorities), transport, handling and other costs directly attributable to the acquisition of finished goods, materials and services.

Costs to sell: The incremental costs directly attributable to the disposal of an asset (or disposal group), excluding finance costs and income tax expense.

Cumulative: In relation to preference shares, shares on which undeclared dividends in one year accumulate to the following year/s until paid.

Current liability: A liability that (a) is expected to be settled in the normal course of the entity's operating cycle, or (b) is at call or due or expected to be settled within 12 months of the reporting date.

Current tax: The amount of income taxes payable (recoverable) in respect of the taxable profit (tax loss) for a period.

Customer options: Customer options are opportunities provided to the customer to purchase additional goods or services. These additional goods and services may be priced at a discount or may even be free of charge. Options to acquire additional goods or services at a discount can come in many forms, including sales incentives, customer award credits (e.g. frequent flyer programmes), contract renewal options (e.g. waiver of certain fees, reduced future rates) or other discounts on future goods or services.

Date of exchange: The date when each individual investment is recognised in the financial report of the acquirer.

Deductible temporary differences: Temporary differences between the carrying amount of an asset or liability in the statement of financial position and its tax base that will result in amounts that are deductible in determining taxable profit (tax loss) of future periods when the carrying amount of the asset or liability is recovered or settled.

Deferred tax assets: The amounts of income taxes recoverable in future periods in respect of: (a) deductible temporary differences; (b) the carryforward of unused tax losses; and (c) the carryforward of unused tax credits.

Deferred tax liabilities: The amounts of income taxes payable in future periods in respect of taxable temporary differences.

Defined benefit plans: Post-employment benefit plans other than defined contribution plans.

Defined contribution plans: Post-employment benefit plans under which an entity pays fixed contributions into a separate entity (a fund) and will have no legal or constructive obligation to pay further contributions if the fund does not hold sufficient assets to pay all employee benefits relating to employee service in the current and prior periods.

Depreciable amount: The cost of an asset, or other amount substituted for cost (in the financial statements), less its residual value.

Depreciation (amortisation): The systematic allocation of the depreciable amount of an asset over its useful life. In the case of an intangible asset, the term 'amortisation' is generally used instead of 'depreciation'. The two terms have the same meaning.

Derivative: A financial instrument or other contract within the scope of IFRS 9 (see paragraph 2.1 of IFRS 9) with all three of the following characteristics (a) its value changes in response to the change in a specified interest rate, financial instrument price, commodity price, foreign exchange rate, index of prices or rates, credit rating or credit index, or other variable, provided in the case of a non-financial variable that the variable is not specific to a party to the contract (sometimes called the 'underlying'). (b) it requires no initial net investment or an initial net investment that is smaller than would be required for other types of contracts that would be expected to have a similar response to changes in market factors. (c) it is settled at a future date.

Development: The application of research findings or other knowledge to a plan or design for the production of new or substantially improved materials, devices, products, processes, systems or services before the start of commercial production or use.

Discontinued operation: A component of an entity that either has been disposed of or is classified as held for sale and (a) represents a separate major line of business or geographical area of operations; (b) is part of a single coordinated plan to dispose of a separate major line of business or geographical area of operations; or (c) is a subsidiary acquired exclusively with a view to resale.

Disposal group: A group of assets to be disposed of, by sale or otherwise, together as a group in a single transaction, and liabilities directly associated with those assets that will be transferred in the transaction. The group includes goodwill acquired in a business combination if the group is a cash-generating unit to which goodwill has been allocated in accordance with the requirements of paragraphs 80–87 of IAS 36 or if it is an operation within such a cash generating unit.

Dividends: Distributions of profits to holders of equity instruments in proportion to their holdings of a particular class of capital.

Economic life: Either the period over which an asset is expected to be economically usable by one or more users, or the number of production or similar units expected to be obtained from the asset by one or more users.

Effective interest method: The method that is used in the calculation of the amortised cost of a financial asset or a financial liability and in the allocation and recognition of the interest revenue or interest expense in profit or loss over the relevant period.

Effective interest rate: The rate that exactly discounts estimated future cash payments or receipts through the expected life of the financial asset or financial liability to the gross carrying amount of the financial asset or to the amortised cost of a financial liability. When calculating the effective interest rate, an entity shall estimate the expected cash flows by considering all the contractual terms of the financial instrument (for example, prepayment, extension, call and similar options) but shall not consider the expected credit losses. The calculation includes all fees and points paid or received between parties to the contract that are an integral part of the effective interest rate (see paragraphs B5.4.1–B5.4.3 of IFRS 9), transaction costs, and all other premiums or discounts. There is a presumption that the cash flows and the expected life of a group of similar financial instruments can be estimated reliably. However, in those rare cases when it is not possible to reliably estimate (see paragraphs AG8–AG8B or IAS 39) the cash flows or the expected life of a financial instrument (or group of financial instruments), the entity shall use the contractual cash flows over the full contractual term of the financial instrument (or group of financial instruments).

Embedded derivative: A component of a combined (or 'hybrid') instrument that also includes a non-derivative host contract, with the effect that some of the cash flows of the combined instrument vary in a way similar to a stand-alone instrument.

Employee benefits: All forms of consideration given by an entity in exchange for service rendered by employees or for the termination of employment.

Employee Compensation: Includes all employee benefits (as defined in IAS 19) including employee benefits to which IFRS 2 applies. Employee benefits are all forms of consideration paid, payable or provided by the entity, or on behalf of the entity, in exchange for services rendered to the entity. It also includes such consideration paid on behalf of a parent of the entity in respect of the entity. Compensation includes: (a) short-term employee benefits, such as wages, salaries and social security contributions, paid annual leave and paid sick leave, profit sharing and bonuses (if payable within twelve months of the end of the period) and non-monetary benefits (such as medical care, housing, cars and free or subsidised goods or services) for current employees; (b) post-employment benefits such as pensions, other retirement benefits, post-employment life insurance and post-employment medical care; (c) other long-term employee benefits, including long service leave or sabbatical leave, jubilee or other long service benefits, long-term disability benefits and, if they are not payable wholly within twelve months after the end of the period, profit sharing, bonuses and deferred compensation; (d) termination benefits; and (e) share-based payment.

Employees and others providing similar services: Individuals who render personal services to the entity and either (a) the individuals are regarded as employees for legal or tax purposes, (b) the individuals work for the entity under its direction in the same way as individuals who are regarded as employees for legal or tax purposes, or (c) the services rendered are similar to those rendered by employees. For example, the term encompasses all management personnel, ie, those persons having authority and responsibility for planning, directing and controlling the activities of the entity, including non-executive directors.

Entity-specific value: The present value of the cash flows an entity (1) expects to arise from the continuing use of an asset and from its disposal at the end of its useful life, or (2) expects to incur when settling a liability.

Entry price: The price paid to acquire an asset or received to assume a liability in an exchange transaction.

Equity: The residual interest in the assets of the entity after deducting all its liabilities.

Equity instrument: A contract that evidences a residual interest in the assets of an entity after deducting all of its liabilities.

Equity instrument granted: The right (conditional or unconditional) to an equity instrument of the entity conferred by the entity on another party, under a share-based payment arrangement.

Equity method: A method of accounting whereby the investment is initially recognised at cost and adjusted thereafter for the post-acquisition change in the investor's share of the investee's net assets. The investor's profit or loss includes its share of the investee's profit or loss and the investor's other comprehensive income includes its share of the investee's other comprehensive income.

Equity-settled share-based payment transaction: A share-based payment transaction in which the entity (a) receives goods or services as consideration for its own equity instruments (including shares or share options), or (b) receives goods or services but has no obligation to settle the transaction with the supplier.

Errors: Omissions from or misstatements in the financial statements.

Exchange difference: The difference resulting from translating a given number of units of one currency into another currency at different exchange rates.

Exchange rate: The ratio of exchange for two currencies.

Executory contract: A contract, or a portion of a contract, that is equally unperformed—neither party has fulfilled any of its obligations, or both parties have partially fulfilled their obligations to an equal extent.

Executory costs: Operating amounts (including insurance, maintenance, consumable supplies, replacement parts and rates) that are paid by the lessor on behalf of the lessee.

Exit price: The price that would be received to sell an asset or paid to transfer a liability.

Expenses: Decreases in assets, or increases in liabilities, that result in decreases in equity, other than those relating to distributions to holders of equity claims.

Fair value: The price that would be received to sell an asset or paid to transfer a liability in an orderly transaction between market participants at the measurement date.

Faithful representation: Information is faithfully represented if it is complete, neutral and free from error.

Finance lease: A lease that transfers substantially all the risks and rewards incidental to ownership of an underlying asset.

Financial asset: Any asset that is: (a) cash; (b) an equity instrument of another entity; (c) a contractual right: (i) to receive cash or another financial asset from another entity, or (ii) to exchange financial assets or financial liabilities with another entity under conditions that are potentially favourable to the entity; or (d) a contract that will or may be settled in the entity's own equity instruments that is: (i) a non-derivative for which the entity is or may be obliged to receive a variable number of the entity's own equity instruments, or (ii) a derivative that will or may be settled other than by the exchange of a fixed amount of cash or another financial asset for a fixed number of the entity's own equity instruments. For this purpose the entity's own equity instruments do not include puttable financial instruments classified as equity instruments in accordance with paragraphs 16A and 16B of IAS 32, instruments that impose on the entity an obligation to deliver to another party a pro rata share of the net assets of the entity only on liquidation and are classified as equity instruments in accordance with paragraphs 16C and 16D of IAS 32, or instruments that are contracts for the future receipt or delivery of the entity's own equity instruments.

Financial assets at fair value through profit or loss: Financial assets held for trading and measured at fair value with any gain or loss from a change in fair value recognised in profit or loss, or financial assets that upon initial recognition are designated by the entity as at fair value through profit or loss.

Financial instrument: Any contract that gives rise to a financial asset of one entity and a financial liability or equity instrument of another entity.

Financial liability: Any liability that is: (a) a contractual obligation: (i) to deliver cash or another financial asset to another entity, or (ii) to exchange financial assets or financial liabilities with another entity under conditions that are potentially unfavourable to the entity; or (b) a contract that will or may be settled in the entity's own equity instruments and is: (i) a non-derivative for which the entity is or may be obliged to deliver a variable number of the entity's own equity instruments, or (ii) a derivative that will or may be settled other than by the exchange of a fixed amount of cash or another financial asset for a fixed number of the entity's own equity instruments. For this purpose, rights, options or warrants to acquire a fixed number of the entity's own equity instruments for a fixed amount of any currency are equity instruments if the entity offers the rights, options or warrants pro rata to all of its existing owners of the same class of its own non-derivative equity instruments. Also, for these purposes the entity's own equity instruments do not include puttable financial instruments that are classified as equity instruments in accordance with paragraphs 16A and 16B of IAS 32, instruments that impose on the entity an obligation to deliver to another party a pro rata share of the net assets of the entity only on liquidation and are classified as equity instruments in accordance with paragraphs 16C and 16D of IAS 32, or instruments that are contracts for the future receipt or delivery of the entity's own equity instruments. As an exception, an instrument that meets the definition of a financial liability is classified as an equity instrument if it has all the features and meets the conditions in paragraphs 16A and 16B or paragraphs 16C and 16D of IAS 32.

Financial position: The assets, liabilities, and residual equity interest of an entity at a given point in time.

Financing activities: Activities that result in changes in the size and composition of the contributed equity and borrowings of the entity.

Firm commitment: A binding agreement for the exchange of a specified quantity of resources at a specified price on a specified future date or dates.

First-in, first-out (FIFO): A method of allocating cost to inventory items that assumes that the items first purchased will be the items first sold.

Forecast transaction: An uncommitted but anticipated future transaction.

Foreign currency: A currency other than the functional currency of the entity.

Foreign operation: An entity that is a subsidiary, associate, joint venture or branch of the reporting entity, the activities of which are based or conducted in a country or currency other than those of the reporting entity.

Forfeited shares account: An account initially recording the amount of funds supplied by shareholders whose shares were forfeited.

Framework for the Preparation and Presentation of Financial Statements: The pronouncement of the International Accounting Standards Board that sets out the concepts underlying the preparation and presentation of financial statements for external users. This has been superseded by the *Conceptual Framework for Financial Reporting*.

Functional currency: The currency of the primary economic environment in which the entity operates.

General purpose financial statements: A particular form of general purpose financial reports that provide information about the reporting entity's assets, liabilities, equity, income and expenses.

Going concern: An entity that is expected to continue in operation for the foreseeable future.

Goodwill: An asset representing the future economic benefits arising from other assets acquired in a business combination that are not individually identified and separately recognised.

Grant date: The date at which the entity and another party (including an employee) agree to a share-based payment arrangement, being when the entity and the counterparty have a shared understanding of the terms and conditions of the arrangement. At grant date the entity confers on the counterparty the right to cash, other assets, or equity instruments of the entity, provided the specified vesting conditions, if any, are met. If that agreement is subject to an approval process (for example, by shareholders), grant date is the date when that approval is obtained.

Gross investment in the lease: The sum of: (a) the lease payments receivable by a lessor under a finance lease; and (b) any unguaranteed residual value accruing to the lessor.

Group: A parent and its subsidiaries.

Guaranteed residual value: That part of the residual value of the leased asset guaranteed by the lessee or a third party related to the lessee.

Hedge effectiveness: The degree to which changes in the fair value or cash flows of the hedged item that are attributable to a hedged risk are offset by changes in the fair value or cash flows of the hedging instrument.

Hedged item: An asset, liability, firm commitment, highly probable forecast transaction or net investment in a foreign operation that (a) exposes the entity to risk of changes in fair value or future cash flows and (b) is designated as being hedged.

Hedging instrument: A designated derivative or (for a hedge of the risk of changes in foreign currency exchange rates only) a designated non-derivative financial asset or non-derivative financial liability whose fair value or cash flows are expected to offset changes in the fair value or cash flows of a designated hedged item.

Held-for-trading: A financial asset or financial liability that: (a) is acquired or incurred principally for the purpose of selling or repurchasing it in the near term; (b) on initial recognition is part of a portfolio of identified financial instruments that are managed together and for which there is evidence of a recent actual pattern of short-term profit-taking; or (c) is a derivative (except for a derivative that is a financial guarantee contract or a designated and effective hedging instrument).

Highest and best use: The use of a non-financial asset by market participants that would maximise the value of the asset or the group of assets and liabilities (e.g. a business) within which the asset would be used.

Highly probable: Significantly more likely than probable.

Impairment loss: The amount by which the carrying amount of an asset exceeds its recoverable amount.

Inception date of the lease (inception date): The earlier of the date of a lease agreement and the date of commitment by the parties to the principal terms and conditions of the lease.

Income: Increases in assets, or decreases in liabilities, that result in increases in equity, other than those relating to contributions from holders of equity claims.

Income approach: Valuation techniques that convert future amounts (e.g. cash flows or income and expenses) to a single current (e.g. discounted) amount; the fair value measurement is determined on the basis of the value indicated by current market expectations about those future amounts.

Incremental borrowing rate: The rate of interest the lessee would have to pay on a similar lease or, if that is not determinable, the rate that (at the inception of the lease) the lessee would incur to borrow over a similar term, and with a similar security, the funds necessary to purchase the asset.

Initial direct costs: Incremental costs of obtaining a lease that would not have been incurred if the lease had not been obtained, except for such costs incurred by a manufacturer or dealer lessor in connection with a finance lease.

Inputs (fair value): The assumptions that market participants would use when pricing the asset or liability, including assumptions about risk, such as the following: (a) the risk inherent in a particular valuation technique used to measure fair value (such as a pricing model); and (b) the risk inherent in the inputs to the valuation technique. Inputs may be observable or unobservable.

Intangible asset: An identifiable non-monetary asset without physical substance.

Interest rate implicit in the lease: The rate of interest that causes the present value of (a) the lease payments and (b) the unguaranteed residual value to equal the sum of (i) the fair value of the underlying asset and (ii) any initial direct costs of the lessor.

Intrinsic value: The difference between the fair value of the shares to which the counterparty has the (conditional or unconditional) right to subscribe or which it has the right to receive, and the price (if any) the counterparty is (or will be) required to pay for those shares. For example, a share option with an exercise price of CU15 (currency units) on a share with a fair value of CU20, has an intrinsic value of CU5.

Inventories: Assets (a) held for sale in the ordinary course of business; (b) in the process of production for such sale; or (c) in the form of materials or supplies to be consumed in the production process or in the rendering of services. Inventories encompass goods purchased and held for resale including, for example, merchandise purchased by a retailer and held for resale, or land and other property held for resale. Inventories also encompass finished goods produced, or work in progress being produced, by the entity and include materials and supplies awaiting use in the production process. Costs incurred to fulfil a contract with a customer that do not give rise to inventories (or assets within the scope of another Standard) are accounted for in accordance with IFRS 15 *Revenue from Contracts with Customers*.

Investee: An entity in which funds have been invested.

Investing activities: The acquisition and disposal of long-term assets and other investments not included in cash equivalents.

Investment property: Property (land or a building, or part of a building, or both) held (by the owner or by the lessee as a right-of-use asset) to earn rentals or for capital appreciation or both, rather than for (a) use in the production or supply of goods or services or for administrative purposes, or (b) sale in the ordinary course of business.

Investor: An entity which invests funds in an investee.

Joint arrangement: An arrangement of which two or more parties have joint control.

Joint control: The contractually agreed sharing of control of an arrangement, which exists only when decisions about the relevant activities require the unanimous consent of the parties sharing control.

Joint venture: A joint arrangement whereby the parties that have joint control of the arrangement have rights to the net assets of the arrangement.

Key management personnel: Those persons having authority and responsibility for planning, directing and controlling the activities of the entity, directly or indirectly, including any director (whether executive or otherwise) of that entity.

Lease: A contract, or part of a contract, that conveys the right to use an asset (the underlying asset) for a period of time in exchange for consideration.

Lease incentives: Payments made by a lessor to a lessee associated with a lease, or the reimbursement or assumption by a lessor of costs of a lessee.

Lease payments: Payments made by a lessee to a lessor relating to the right to use an underlying asset during the lease term, comprising the following: (a) fixed payments (including in-substance fixed payments), less any lease incentives; (b) variable lease payments that depend on an index or a rate; (c) the exercise price of a purchase option if the lessee is reasonably certain to exercise that option; and (d) payments of penalties for terminating the lease, if the lease term reflects the lessee exercising an option to terminate the lease. For the lessee, lease payments also include amounts expected to be payable by the lessee under residual value guarantees. Lease payments do not include payments allocated to non-lease components of a contract, unless the lessee elects to combine non-lease components with a lease component and to account for them as a single lease component. For the lessor, lease payments also include any residual value guarantees provided to the lessor by the lessee, a party related to the lessee or a third party unrelated to the lessor that is financially capable of discharging the obligations under the guarantee. Lease payments do not include payments allocated to non-lease components.

Lease term: The non-cancellable period for which a lessee has the right to use an underlying asset, together with both: (a) periods covered by an option to extend the lease if the lessee is reasonably certain to exercise that option; and (b) periods covered by an option to terminate the lease if the lessee is reasonably certain not to exercise that option.

Level 1 inputs: Quoted prices (unadjusted) in active markets for identical assets or liabilities that the entity can access at the measurement date.

Level 2 inputs: Inputs other than quoted prices included within Level 1 that are observable for the asset or liability, either directly or indirectly.

Level 3 inputs: Unobservable inputs for the asset or liability.

Liability: A present obligation of the entity to transfer an economic resource as a result of past events.

Loans and receivables: Non-derivative financial assets with fixed or determinable payments that are not quoted in an active market and which the entity has no intention of trading, e.g. loan to a subsidiary.

Market approach: A valuation technique that uses prices and other relevant information generated by market transactions involving identical or comparable (i.e. similar) assets, liabilities or a group of assets and liabilities, such as a business.

Market condition: A performance condition upon which the exercise price, vesting or exercisability of an equity instrument depends that is related to the market price (or value) of the entity's equity instruments (or the equity instruments of another entity in the same group), such as: (a) attaining a specified share price or a specified amount of intrinsic value of a share option; or (b) achieving a specified target that is based on the market price (or value) of the entity's equity instruments (or the equity instruments of another entity in the same group) relative to an index of market prices of equity instruments of other entities. A market condition requires the counterparty to complete a specified period of service (i.e. a service condition); the service requirement can be explicit or implicit.

Market participants: Buyers and sellers in the principal (or most advantageous) market for the asset or liability that have all of the following characteristics: (a) they are independent of each other, i.e. they are not related parties as defined in IAS 24, although the price in a related party transaction may be used as an input to a fair value measurement if the entity has evidence that the transaction was entered into at market terms; (b) they are knowledgeable, having a reasonable understanding about the asset or liability and the transaction using all available information, including information that might be obtained through due diligence efforts that are usual and customary; (c) they are able to enter into a transaction for the asset or liability; (d) they are willing to enter into a transaction for the asset or liability, i.e. they are motivated but not forced or otherwise compelled to do so.

Material: Information is material if omitting, misstating or obscuring it could reasonably be expected to influence decisions that the primary users of general purpose financial statements make on the basis of those financial statements, which provide financial information about a specific reporting entity.

Measurement: The process of determining the monetary amount at which an asset, liability, income or expense is reported in the financial statements.

Measurement date: The date at which the fair value of the equity instruments granted is measured for the purposes of IFRS 2. For transactions with employees and others providing similar services, the measurement date is the grant date. For transactions with parties other than employees (and those providing similar services), the measurement date is the date the entity obtains the goods or the counterparty renders service.

Minimum lease payments: The payments over the lease term that the lessee is or can be required to make, excluding contingent rent, costs for services and taxes to be paid by and reimbursed to the lessor, together with (a) for a lessee, any amounts guaranteed by the lessee or by a party related to the lessee, and (b) for a lessor, any residual value guaranteed to the lessor.

Monetary assets: Money held and assets to be received in fixed or determinable amounts of money.

Monetary items: Units of currency held and assets and liabilities to be received or paid in a fixed or determinable number of units of currency.

Most advantageous market: The market that maximises the amount that would be received to sell the asset or minimises the amount that would be paid to transfer the liability, after taking into account transaction costs and transport costs.

Net assets: Total assets minus total liabilities.

Net investment in a foreign operation: The amount of the reporting entity's interest in the net assets of that operation.

Net realisable value: The estimated selling price in the ordinary course of business less the estimated costs of completion and the estimated costs necessary to make the sale. Net realisable value refers to the net amount that an entity expects to realise from the sale of inventory in the ordinary course of business. Fair value reflects the amount for which the same inventory could be exchanged between knowledgeable and willing buyers and sellers in the marketplace. The former is an entity specific value; the latter is not. Net realisable value for inventories may not equal fair value less costs to sell.

Non-adjusting event after the end of the reporting period: An event that is indicative of conditions that arose after the end of the reporting period.

Non-cancellable lease: A lease that is cancellable only (a) upon the occurrence of some remote contingency, (b) with the permission of the lessor, (c) if the lessee enters into a new lease for the same or an equivalent asset with the same lessor, or (d) upon payment by the lessee of an additional amount such that, at inception of the lease, continuation of the lease is reasonably certain.

Non-controlling interest (NCI): Equity in a subsidiary not attributable, directly or indirectly, to a parent.

Non-performance risk: The risk that an entity will not fulfil an obligation. Non-performance risk includes, but may not be limited to, the entity's own credit risk.

Non-sequential acquisition: Where a parent acquires its shares in a subsidiary after that subsidiary has acquired shares in its subsidiary.

Notes: Notes contain information in addition to that presented in the statement of financial position, statement of comprehensive income, separate income statement (if presented), statement of changes in equity and statement of cash flows. Notes provide narrative descriptions or disaggregations of items presented in those statements and information about items that do not qualify for recognition in those statements.

Obligating event: An event that creates a legal or constructive obligation that results in an entity having no realistic alternative to settling that obligation.

Observable inputs: Inputs that are developed using market data, such as publicly available information about actual events or transactions, and that reflect the assumptions that market participants would use when pricing the asset or liability.

Offsetting: Grouping an asset and liability that are recognised and measured as separate units of account into a single net amount in the statement of financial position.

Onerous contract: A contract in which the unavoidable costs of meeting the obligations under the contract exceed the economic benefits expected to be received under it.

Operating activities: The principal revenue producing activities of an entity and other activities that are not investing or financing activities.

Operating lease: A lease that does not transfer substantially all the risks and rewards incidental to ownership of an underlying asset.

Operating segment: An operating segment is a component of an entity: (a) that engages in business activities from which it may earn revenues and incur expenses (including revenues and expenses relating to transactions with other components of the same entity); (b) whose operating results are regularly reviewed by the entity's chief operating decision maker to make decisions about resources to be allocated to the segment and assess its performance; and (c) for which discrete financial information is available.

Orderly transaction: A transaction that assumes exposure to the market for a period before the measurement date to allow for marketing activities that are usual and customary for transactions involving such assets or liabilities; it is not a forced transaction (e.g. a forced liquidation or distress sale).

Other comprehensive income: Items of income and expense (including reclassification adjustments) that are not recognised in profit or loss as required or permitted by other IFRSs.

Parent: An entity that controls one or more entities.

Participating: In relation to preference shares, shares that receive extra dividends above a fixed rate once a certain level of dividends has been paid on ordinary shares.

Performance: The ability of an entity to earn a profit on the resources that have been invested in it.

Periodic method: A system of recording inventory whereby the value of inventory is determined and recorded on a periodic basis (normally annually).

Perpetual method: A system of recording inventory whereby inventory records are updated each time a transaction involving inventory takes place.

Power: Existing rights that give the current ability to direct the relevant activities.

Pre-acquisition equity: The equity of the subsidiary at acquisition date. It is not just the equity recorded by the subsidiary, but is determined by reference to the cost of the business combination.

Presentation currency: The currency in which the financial statements are presented.

Principal market: The market with the greatest volume and level of activity for the asset or liability.

Private placement: An issue of shares usually to a large institutional investor such as a finance company, superannuation fund or life insurance company.

Probable: More likely than not.

Property, plant and equipment: Tangible items that (a) are held for use in the production or supply of goods or services, for rental to others, or for administrative purposes, and (b) are expected to be used during more than one period.

Prospective application: Prospective application of a change in accounting policy and of recognising the effect of a change in an accounting estimate, respectively, are (a) applying the new accounting policy to transactions, other events and conditions occurring after the date as at which the policy is changed; and (b) recognising the effect of the change in the accounting estimate in the current and future periods affected by the change.

Protective rights: Rights designed to protect the interest of the party holding those rights without giving that party power over the entity to which those rights relate.

Provision: A liability of uncertain timing or amount.

Public company: A company entitled to raise funds from the public by lodging a disclosure document with ASIC and have its shares or other ownership documents traded on the stock exchange. It may be a limited company, unlimited company or no-liability company.

Reciprocal shareholdings: Where two entities hold shares in each other.

Recognition: The process of capturing for inclusion in the statement of financial position or the statement(s) of financial performance an item that meets the definition of one of the elements of financial statements—an asset, a liability, equity, income or expenses. Recognition involves depicting the item in one of those statements—either alone or in aggregation with other items—in words and by a monetary amount, and including that amount in one or more totals in that statement.

Recoverable amount: The higher of an asset's (or cash generating unit's) fair value less costs of disposal and its value in use.

Related party: A person or entity that is related to the entity that is preparing its financial statements (in IAS 24 referred to as the 'reporting entity'). (a) A person or a close member of that person's family is related to a reporting entity if that person: (i) has control or joint control over the reporting entity; (ii) has significant influence over the reporting entity; or (iii) is a member of the key management personnel of the reporting entity or of a parent of the reporting entity. (b) An entity is related to a reporting entity if any of the following conditions applies: (i) The entity and the reporting entity are members of the same group (which means that each parent, subsidiary and fellow subsidiary is related to the others) (ii) One entity is an associate or joint venture of the other entity (or an associate or joint venture of a member of a group of which the other entity is a member). (iii) Both entities are joint ventures of the same third party. (iv) One entity is a joint venture of a third entity and the other entity is an associate of the third entity. (v) The entity is a post-employment benefit plan for the benefit of employees of either the reporting entity or an entity related to the reporting entity. If the reporting entity is itself such a plan, the sponsoring employers are also related to the reporting entity. (vi) The entity is controlled or jointly controlled by a person identified in (a). (vii) A person identified in (a)(i) has significant influence over the entity or is a member of the key management personnel of the entity (or of a parent of the entity). (viii) The entity, or any member of a group of which it is a part, provides key management personnel services to the reporting entity or to the parent of the reporting entity.

Related party transaction: A transfer of resources, services or obligations between a reporting entity and a related party, regardless of whether a price is charged.

Relevance: That quality of information that exists when the information influences economic decisions made by users.

Relevant activities: For the purpose of IFRS 10, relevant activities are activities of the investee that significantly affect the investee's returns.

Reload feature: A feature that provides for an automatic grant of additional share options whenever the option holder exercises previously granted options using the entity's shares, rather than cash, to satisfy the exercise price.

Reload option: A new share option granted when a share is used to satisfy the exercise price of a previous share option.

Remuneration: *See* compensation.

Reportable segment: An operating segment for which IFRS 8 requires information to be disclosed.

Reporting entity: An entity that is required, or chooses, to prepare general purpose financial statements.

Research: Original and planned investigation undertaken with the prospect of gaining new scientific or technical knowledge and understanding.

Reserve: A category of equity that is not contributed capital.

Residual value: The estimated amount that an entity would currently obtain from disposal of the asset, after deducting the estimated costs of disposal, if the asset were already of the age and in the condition expected at the end of its useful life.

Retrospective application: Applying a new accounting policy to transactions, other events and conditions as if that policy had always been applied.

Revaluation decrease (increase): The amount by which the revalued carrying amount of a non-current asset as at the revaluation date is less than (exceeds) its previous carrying amount.

Revenue: Income arising in the course of an entity's ordinary activities. See also Income.

Right-of-use asset: An asset that represents a lessee's right to use an underlying asset for the lease term.

Rights issue: An issue of new shares giving existing shareholders the right to an additional number of shares in proportion to their current shareholdings.

Segment accounting policies: Accounting policies adopted for preparing and presenting the financial statements of the consolidated group or entity as well as those accounting policies that relate specifically to a segment.

Segment assets: Operating assets that are employed by a segment in its operating activities and that either are directly attributable to the segment or can be allocated to the segment on a reasonable basis.

Segment expense: Expense resulting from the operating activities of a segment that is directly attributable to the segment and the relevant portion of an expense that can be allocated on a reasonable basis to the segment, including expenses relating to sales to external customers and expenses relating to transactions with other segments of the same entity.

Segment liabilities: Operating liabilities that result from the operating activities of a segment and that either are directly attributable to the segment or can be allocated to the segment on a reasonable basis.

Segment result: Segment revenue less segment expense. Segment result is determined before any adjustments for minority interest.

Segment revenue: Revenue reported in the entity's income statement that is directly attributable to a segment and the relevant portion of entity revenue that can be allocated on a reasonable basis to a segment, whether from sales to external customers or from transactions with other segments of the same entity.

Separate financial statements: Those presented by an entity in which the entity could elect, subject to the requirements in IAS 27, to account for its investments in subsidiaries, joint ventures and associates either at cost, in accordance with IFRS 9 Financial Instruments, or using the equity method as described in IAS 28 Investments in Associates and Joint Ventures.

Sequential acquisition: where a parent acquires its shares in a subsidiary before or on the same date that the subsidiary acquires shares in its subsidiary.

Share buy-back: The repurchase of a company's shares by the company from its shareholders.

Share issue costs: Costs incurred on the issue of equity instruments. These include underwriting costs, stamp duties and taxes, professional advisers' fees and brokerage.

Share option: A contract that gives the holder the right, but not the obligation, to subscribe to the entity's shares at a fixed or determinable price for a specified period of time.

Share-based payment arrangement: An agreement between the entity or another group entity or any shareholder of the group entity and another party (including an employee) that entitles the other party to receive (a) cash or other assets of the entity for amounts that are based on the price (or value)of equity instruments (including shares or share options) of the entity or another group entity, or (b) equity instruments (including shares or share options) of the entity or another group entity, provided the specified vesting conditions, if any, are met.

Share-based payment transaction: A transaction in which the entity (a) receives goods or services from the supplier of those goods or services (including an employee) in a share-based payment arrangement, or (b) incurs an obligation to settle the transaction with the supplier in a share-based payment arrangement when another group entity receives those goods or services.

Significant influence: The power to participate in the financial and operating policy decisions of the investee but is not control or joint control of those policies.

Specific identification: A method of allocating cost to inventory based on identifying and aggregating all costs directly related to each individual inventory item.

Spot exchange rate: The exchange rate for immediate delivery.

Statement of changes in equity: A financial statement prepared in accordance with IAS 1 for inclusion in general purpose financial reports. The statement reports on the changes in the entity's equity for the reporting period. Changes in equity disclosed may include movements in retained earnings for the period, items of income and expense recognised directly in equity, and movements in each class of share and each reserve.

Statement of financial position: A financial statement that presents assets, liabilities and equity of an entity at a given point in time, also known as the balance sheet.

Statement of profit or loss and other comprehensive income: A financial statement prepared in accordance with the requirements of IAS 1 for inclusion in general purpose financial statements. The statement reports the entity's income, expenses, profit or loss, other comprehensive income and total comprehensive income for the reporting period.

Subsidiary: An entity that is controlled by another entity.

Substance over form: The accounts will reflect the underlying economic reality of transactions and not their legal form.

Tax base of an asset or liability: The amount attributed to that asset or liability for tax purposes.

Tax expense (tax income): The aggregate amount included in the determination of profit or loss for the period in respect of current tax and deferred tax. Tax expense (tax income) comprises current tax expense (current tax income) and deferred tax expense (deferred tax income).

Taxable profit (tax loss): The profit (loss) for a period, determined in accordance with the rules established by the taxation authorities, upon which income taxes are payable (recoverable).

Taxable temporary differences: Temporary differences that will result in taxable amounts in determining taxable profit (tax loss) of future periods when the carrying amount of the asset or liability is recovered or settled.

Temporary differences: Differences between the carrying amount of an asset or liability in the statement of financial position and its tax base. Temporary differences may be either (a) taxable temporary differences; or (b) deductible temporary differences.

Trade discount: A reduction in selling prices granted to customers.

Transaction costs (financial instruments): Incremental costs that are directly attributable to the acquisition, issue or disposal of a financial asset or financial liability (see paragraph B5.4.8 of IFRS 9). An incremental cost is one that would not have been incurred if the entity had not acquired, issued or disposed of the financial instrument.

Transport costs: The costs that would be incurred to transport an asset from its current location to its principal (or most advantageous) market.

Understandability: The ability of financial information to be comprehended by financial statement users who have a reasonable knowledge of business and economic activities and accounting, and a willingness to study the information with reasonable diligence.

Underwriter: An entity which, for a fee, undertakes to subscribe for any shares not allotted to applicants as a result of an undersubscription.

Unguaranteed residual value: That portion of the residual value of the underlying asset, the realisation of which by a lessor is not assured or is guaranteed solely by a party related to the lessor.

Unit of account: The right or the group of rights, the obligation or the group of obligations, or the group of rights and obligations, to which recognition criteria and measurement concepts are applied.

Unobservable inputs: Inputs for which market data are not available and that are developed using the best information available about the assumptions that market participants would use when pricing the asset or liability.

Useful life: Either (a) the period over which an asset is expected to be available for use by an entity, or (b) the number of production or similar units expected to be obtained from the asset by an entity.

Value in use: The present value of future cash flows expected to be derived from an asset or cash-generating unit.

Venturer: A party to a joint venture that has joint control over that joint venture.

Vest: To become an entitlement. Under a share-based payment arrangement, a counterparty's right to receive cash, other assets or equity instruments of the entity vests when the counterparty's entitlement is no longer conditional on the satisfaction of any vesting conditions.

Vesting conditions: A condition that determines whether the entity receives the services that entitle the counterparty to receive cash, other assets or equity instruments of the entity, under a share-based payment arrangement. A vesting condition is either a service condition or a performance condition.

Vesting period: The period during which all the specified vesting conditions of a share-based payment arrangement are to be satisfied.

Weighted average: A method of allocating cost to inventory items based on the weighted average of the cost of similar items at the beginning of a period and the cost of similar items purchased or produced during the period.

A

accounting
accrual basis, 27
basis, 488
effects, asset-by-asset basis, 129–30
errors, changes, 45
information, 442f
losses, history, 422
policy/errors, changes, 321
accounting estimate, 45
change, accounting for, 48
changes, 45, 48
accounting policies, 45–9
application, judgements, 43
change, cumulative effect, 47
principles/conventions, 45
remuneration policies,
relationship, 385f
selecting/changing, 45–6
voluntary change, application, 46–7
accounting profit, 426
taxable profit, differences/permanent
differences, 404–7
temporary difference, reversal, 405–6
Accounting Standards Advisory
Forum (ASAF), 7
Accounting Standards Board, FRS 17
deliberation, 304
Accounting Standards Codification
(ASC) 842 *Leases*, 225
accounts receivable, 443
accruals (ACCR), 455
future stock returns, relationship, 108
managerial discretion, 431
reporting, 260
accrued benefit method prorated on
service method, 291
accrued losses, measurement/
disclosure, 376
accumulated benefit
determination, 298
present value, measurement, 298
accumulated depreciation account,
reduction, 552
acquired foreign subsidiaries,
consolidation
functional currency, parent's
reporting currency
(equivalence), 648–9
functional currency, presentation
currency (contrast), 640–8
acquirer
goodwill recognition, 503

identification, 499–500, 535f
records, journal entries, 506f
acquirer/vendor contracts, 341
acquisition date, 114–15, 540
accounting, 595–600
analysis, 544, 544f, 623, 641
balance sheet, 543
business combination valuation
entries, 546f
consolidated worksheet, 548f,
596–600, 598f, 600f
determination, 499, 500–1
information, 543f
measurement, 503
NCI share of equity, 600, 602
pre-acquisition entry, 547f
recorded dividends, subsidiary
holding, 548–9
share of equity, 609
subsequent accounting, 600–5
worksheet entries, 545–55
acquisition-related costs, 505
acquisitions
analysis, 508–9, 516–17, 542–5, 591
reverse acquisitions, 536, 536f
actuarial gains/losses, occurrence, 295
adjusted market assessment
approach, 66
adjusting events, 49
administrative overheads, 89
advertising/promotional activities,
expenditures, 160
agents, role/impact, 533
aggregate amounts, disclosure, 452
aggregate cash flow effects, 451
aggregation, 28, 484–5
process, 526, 548
allocation process, 118–19
amortised cost
calculation, IFRS 9 basis, 350–1
definition, 350
annual general meeting (AGM)
attendance, 531
dividends declaration/approval,
absence, 321
annual leave
accounting for. *see* employee benefits.
provision, 420
annual report, extract, 490f–3f
arm's length arrangement, 458
assessment, approach, 11
assets
accumulated depreciation, 406

alternative use, absence, 67, 68
asset for sale, holding (meaning), 84
carrying amount, 106, 118
intragroup transactions, impact
(absence), 563
temporary differences,
calculation, 416–17
cash flows, configuration, 114
ceiling, net-defined asset, limiting
(effect), 293
condition, 203
corporate assets, issues, 184–6
creation/enhancement, customer
control, 67
crypto assets, 87
depreciation, 238
derecognition, 110
disposal, 134–5
economic life, lease term, 244
economic performance, 176
expected disposal, 266
expense, contrast, 112
financial statement element, 11–12
group, 203
valuation premise, 211–12
identifiability, 154
identifiable assets, recognition/
measurement, 499, 501–3
identified assets, 226–7
impairment
accounting policies, 177f
test, 176–82
impairment loss
recognition/measurement, 180–2
reversal, 188–90
information, 487–8
initial measurement, 110
initial recognition, 418
intragroup transfers, 574–8
inventories, equivalence, 84
location, 203
market participants,
identification, 205
measurement, 203
multiple assets, acquisition, 115
non-monetary assets, 154
past event, 12
principal/advantageous markets,
defining, 204–5
projected cash flows, estimation, 189
purchase, lessee option, 244
qualifying asset, 89
recognition, 68, 76, 110

assets (*Continued*)
removal, 16
residual, equity (relationship), 14
revaluation
gains, 36
need, determination, 123
revaluation/reserve surplus,
322–3, 618
transfers, revaluation model
application, 130
right to payment, absence, 67, 68
risk, capture, 257
separate assets, 112
sharing, right, 310
tax bases, 415
transaction entry, ability/
willingness, 205
value, 175
associates, investments, 341
assumption, nature, 44
Australian GAAP, 171
available-for-sale (AFS) instruments, 52

B

balancing act, uncertainties
(impact), 15
bank borrowings, classification, 436
bank overdraft, 436
bargain purchase gain, 549–50, 612–13
determination, 542–5
recognition/measurement, 499, 501,
503–10, 510f
basic earnings per share, 465,
466–70, 466f
Basis for Conclusion, 9
beginning inventory, unrealised
profit, 619–20
Beller, Alan, 6
benchmark interest rate, 235
benefits/years of service method, 291
binding sale agreement, 270
Black-Scholes-Merton formula, 384
bonus issues, 317, 469
borrowings, problem, 578–83
broadcast rights, 85–6
business combinations, 498–9, 511–13
accounting for, principles, 499–510
acquirer purchase, 498f
acquisition, problem, 518–19
consideration transfer, 505–6, 506f
consolidation, relationship, 535–6
corporate event, 521
disclosure, 513–15, 557–9, 558f–9f
entity, acquirer control, 499f
occurrence, 499
results, joint venture formation
(impact), 499

subsequent accounting for, 510–13
valuation entries, 540, 546, 546f,
550–3, 552f, 599, 601, 608,
612, 641–2
voting rights, identification, 500
business combination valuation reserve
(BCVR), 544, 615
businesses
activities, expenses (incurring), 483
defining, purpose, 498
ownership interests, changes, 451–2
performing lines, problems
(concealment motivation), 495
risks, assessments, 458
businesses combinations
contingent consideration, 352
business models
assessment, delineation, 345
usage, 345–6

C

capital
concepts, 19
destruction, 332f
information, 44
structure, management
(equity reduction), 318
capital expenditure (CAPEX),
investment option, 257
Capital Markets Advisory Committee, 5
carry-forward tax loses, creation/
recoupment, 413–14
carrying amounts
determination, 414
recoverable amount, contrast, 187
sensitivity, 44
temporary differences,
calculation, 416–17
cash
alternatives, inclusion, 395–7, 437f
components, 450–1
contracts, settlement, 473
defining, 436
disclosures, 451f
profit, 488
receipts, determination, 443–4
receipts/payments, activity
classification, 437f
cash dividends, distribution, 321
cash equivalents
components, 450–1
concept, usage, 437f
defining, 436
disclosures, 451f
cash flows. *see* future cash flows
activities, classification, 437–9
characteristics, 347

configuration, 114
contractual cash flows, variability
(occurrence), 347
effects, presentation, 452
financing activities
impact, 449–50, 449f
income tax, relationship, 178
hedge, 362–3, 362f
fuel price risk, relationship, 366f–7f
reclassification/transfer
adjustments, 366–7
requirements, summary, 363t
interaction, 79f
interest paid, determination, 447
investing activities, impact, 448–9, 449f
net basis reporting, 441
operating activities
direct method, usage, 443–5, 445f
indirect method, usage,
446–8, 446f
relationship, 438f
usage, 443–8
projected cash flows, estimation, 178
reporting
financing activities/investing
activities, usage, 441
methods, 439
reporting, operating activities
usage, 439–41
direct method, usage,
439f–40f, 450
indirect method, usage, 440f
variation, 343–4
cash-generating units (CGUs), 176
goodwill
allocation, 187
exclusion, 182–4
relationship, 186–8
identification, 182–3
impairment, 184
impairment loss, 183–4
Level 2 input, 208
Level 3 input, 208
recoverable amount,
measurement, 190–1
cash-settled share appreciation rights
accounting treatment, 392, 393–4
performance conditions,
impact, 394–5
service conditions, impact, 393–4
cash-settled share-based payment
transactions, 382, 392–7
chief operating decision maker (CODM)
identification, 482–3
operating results review, 483
segment information presentation, 481
segment profit/loss report, 487–8

climate-related matters, effects, 205
commercial aircraft, sale/revenue, 69f
commodities, securities exchange
        trading, 208
company
    directors, voting right, 309–10
    executives, remuneration
        (criticism), 380
    gearing ratio, usage, 336
    solvency ratio, usage, 336
    winding-up/liquidation, 310
company-issued share option,
        impact, 316
comparability, 9–10
comparative information, 26
    minimum, IAS 1 requirements, 28–9
    usage, 489–90
compound financial instruments,
        339–40, 340f, 396t
compound securities, option
        type, 317
concentration test, meeting, 498
*Conceptual Framework for Financial
        Reporting* (*Conceptual Framework*)
        (CF), 4, 7
    equity definition, 308
    objective, 8
conceptual framework, overview/
        purpose, 7–8
conditional obligations, 12
confirmatory value, 8
consideration, transfer, 503
consignment inventory, 96
consolidated current/non-current
        assets, 30f
consolidated current/non-current
        liabilities, 31f
consolidated equity, 32f
consolidated financial statements,
        526–8, 613–24
    accountability, 528
    conditions, 534
    consolidation, reasons, 528
    definition, 526
    disclosure, 536–7
    financial statements,
        consolidation, 527, 527f
    information comparability, 528
    multiple groups, 528
    preparation, 534, 540, 542
    risks/benefits, reporting, 528
consolidated/non-current
        liabilities, 31f
consolidated statement of changes in
        equity, 40f, 577f, 583f, 622f
consolidated statement of financial
        position, 30, 578f, 583f, 623f

consolidated statement of profit or
        loss and other comprehensive
        income, 577f, 582f, 622f
consolidation
    business combinations,
        relationship, 535–6
    control, criterion, 528–33
    process, 540–2, 551
        equity method, usage, 557f
        NCI effects, 588–93
consolidation worksheets, 541–2, 541f,
        547–8, 554f, 555–7
    change, full goodwill method
        (impact), 623
    entries, 615
    extract, 565f
    journal entries, adjustment, 547
    non-controlling interest, 593, 593f
constructive obligations, 12, 261, 269
contingent assets, 273
contingent consideration, 504–5, 511
contingent liabilities, 262,
        263, 511, 553
contingently issuable shares, 469, 473
contingent settlement provisions, 339
continuing operations, earnings, 468f
continuity assumption, 10
contract(s)
    application issues, 72–6
    combination, 58
    context, 59
    continuation, 72
    creation, 72, 73
    disclosures, 77
    entry, 74
    existence, 57, 531
    financing component, 64
    identified asset presence,
        determination, 227–8, 230f
    judgements, 77
    lease, identification, 229
    negotiation, 58
    non-lease components, 233
    obtaining/fulfilment costs, asset
        recognition, 77
    performance obligations,
        identification, 56
    scope, increase, 72
    settlement, 473
    termination, 58, 72
contract assets
    interaction, 79f
    presentation, 76
contract costs, 70–2
    amortisation/impairment, 71–2
    capitalisation, 70–1
contract definitions, arrangements

absence, 57–8
presence, 57
contract fulfilment costs, 70-1
    entity responsibility, 76
contract liabilities
    interaction, 79f
    presentation, 76
contract modification, 72–4
    accounting for, decision tree, 73f
contractual cash flows, variability
        (occurrence), 347
contractual obligation, 338, 339
contributed equity
    share capital issuance, 312–14
    share capital movements, 314–18
control account/subsidiary ledger
        reconciliation, 96
control, importance, 12
conversion costs, 89
convertible debt instruments, potential
        voting rights, 532
convertible note, 340f
convertible securities, 473
convertible shares, non-convertible
        shares (contrast), 311
core goodwill, 507f
corporate assets
    accounting for, 185–6
    allocation, 191–5
    issues, 184
corporate structure
    features, 309–10
    limited liability, 310
    share capital, usage, 309–10
cost
    approach, 206, 209
    determination, 88–91, 113
    formulas, 100–3
    measurement techniques, 103
    model, 118–22, 143–6
        choosing, 133
        usage, 138, 161, 180–1
    other costs, 89
costing methods, application
        (consistency), 103
cost of capital, voluntary disclosures
        (link), 477
cost of sales (cost of goods sold),
        equation, 92
costs of disposal, subtraction, 177
counterparty
    cash settlement request, 397
    settlement choice, 397
covenants, company compliance, 30
COVID-19 pandemic, 89, 104f
credit adjustment, 568
credit-impaired financial assets, 355

credit risk
  increase, 354
  recognition, 348
  usage, 358f
crypto assets, 87
cumulative abnormal annual stock
    returns (CAR), 455
cumulative preference dividends, 467
cumulative preference shares, 311
  holder redemption, 337f
current assets
  description, 29
  inventories/receivables, inclusion, 31
current cost (entry price), 17
current exit price, 201
current period
  errors, 49
  NCI share of changes in equity,
    602, 604, 609
current service costs, profit/loss
    recognition, 291
current tax
  items, recognition, 425
  recognition, 412
  worksheet, determination, 408–11
current tax, calculation, 407–11
current value measurement, 17
current year profit, taxable profit
    (differences identification), 408
customers
  activities, affects exposure, 75
  benefits, receiving/consuming, 67
  cash receipts, determination, 443–4
  consideration paid/payable, 64
  contract(s), 56–8, 76, 77
  insolvency, 49
  options, determination, 61
cut-off procedures, 95

D

debt covenants, 336
  constraints, 133
debt instruments
  amortisation, 345
  amortised cost measurement, 355
  fair value through other
    comprehensive income (FVOCI),
    345, 349, 353
  FVOCI measurement, 355, 357
  FVPL, 345, 349
  measurement, 353, 359t
  portfolio, amortised cost
    measurement, 356–7
  securities exchange trading, 208
  term to maturity, extension, 344
debt, issuance (costs), 504
debtor, insolvency (information), 50

deductible temporary differences
  calculation, 417
  circumstances, 406–7
  usage, 422
deductions, payment (remitting), 281
deferred tax
  amounts, accumulation, 420
  business combination (impact), 425
  calculation, 414–21
  excluded differences, 418
  items, 421f, 425, 426
  liabilities/assets, calculation, 417–18
  managerial discretion,
    relationship, 431
  movement (recording), journal
    entries (usage), 423
  worksheet, 419–21
deferred tax assets
  calculation/recognition, 414
  recognition, 421–2
  types, 431
deferred tax liabilities
  account, reconstruction, 443, 447
  calculation/recognition, 414
  movement, 447
  recognition, 421
  types, 431
deficit/surplus
  asset/liability determination, 289–91
defined benefit (DB) obligation
    (present value determination),
    projected unit credit method
    (usage), 291–2
defined benefit (DB) pension
    plan 287–8
  accounting for, 290f, 295–7
  deficit/surplus, examination/
    determination, 289–90, 292
  modifications, 294
defined benefit (DB) post-employment
    benefit plans
  deficit/surplus, determination, 291–2
  employer accounting, 290–1
defined benefit (DB) post-employment
    benefits, accounting for, 289–97
defined contribution (DC) plan, 287
defined contribution (DC) post-
    employment benefits, accounting
    for, 288–9
depreciation, 118–22, 238, 649
  allocation process, 118–19
  charge, 242
  diminishing-balance method, 119–20
  expense, addition, 440
  inter-period allocation method, 148
  methods, 119–20
  movement, 139–42

residual value, 122
revalued assets, depreciation
    (revaluation model
    application), 131–2
significant parts depreciation, 122
straight-line method/basis, 119, 550
units-of-production method, 120
useful life, 121
derecognition, 16, 35
derivatives, 342–4
  definition/characteristics, 343
  financial instruments, bets, 343
  FVPL, 345
  measurement mismatch, 368
development costs, capitalisation/
    amortisation, 406
development outlays,
    capitalisation, 158
diluted earnings per share, 471–5
dilution effect, 471
dilutive potential ordinary shares, 472
dilutive securities, existence, 473–4
diminishing-balance method, 119–20
directly attributable costs, 116
direct method, 439, 445, 455
disclosure of accounting policy
    information, 42–3
disclosures, 18–19, 76–9, 514f–15f
  application, 490–3
  benefit, 477
  business combinations, 513–15,
    557–9, 558f–9f
  cash/cash equi9valents, 451f
  consolidated financial
    statements, 536–7
  earnings per share, 475
  encouragement, 453
  entity provision requirement, 77
  entity-wide disclosures, 489
  equity, 324
  fair value measurement, 215–18
  financial instruments, 368–74, 371t
  foreign currency, 650
  guidance, 18
  income taxes, 426–9
  intangible assets, 164–7
  inventories, 106–7
  investment properties, 138–9
  lessee, 241–3
  non-controlling interest
    (NCI), 586–8
  objective/requirements, 76
  operating segments, 487–90
  other disclosures, 44
  principles, 398t
  property, plant and equipment
    (IAS 16), 135–6

provisions, 273, 274f
related party disclosures, 458–64
requirements, 215–16, 216f–18f, 398, 650f
  focus, 462
  income taxes, 427f–8f
share-based payment, 397–9
statement of cash flows, 450–3
subsidiaries, 559f
voluntary disclosure, 477
discontinuation, 367
discontinued operations, 36, 37, 50, 468f
discount
  entity allocation, 65
  rate, determination, 178–9
  unwinding, 117
dissimilar items, 28
dividends
  consolidation worksheet, 582f
  current period payment, absence/presence, 571–2
  declaration, 321, 618, 634
  entity distribution, 449
  expectation, 384
  interim/final dividends, 321–2
  payment, 618
  preference dividends, earnings calculation adjustment, 467f
  problem, 578–83
  received/paid, classification, 438
dividends, intragroup transactions (adjustments), 605
due process, 6
Due Process Oversight Committee (DPOC), 7

E
earnings, 467
  calculation, adjustment, 467f
  changes, usage, 21
  continuing/discontinued operations, 468f
  management, importance, 521
earnings per share (EPS), 464–75
  academic focus, 478
  basic earnings per share, 465, 466–70, 466f
  diluted earnings per share, 471–4
  retrospective adjustments, 474
  scope, 466
  share options, effect, 472
  utility, limitation, 465
earnings-per-share (EPS) increase, 318
earnings response coefficient (ERC), 21
earnings to net profit, recurrence (reconciliation), 466f

economic benefits, rights, 228
economic conditions, management test estimate, 178
economic credit risk hedging, 368
economic resource, 11, 13
effective interest rate, definition, 350
embedded derivatives, 342, 343–4
Emerging Economies Group, 5
Emissions Trading System (EU ETS), launch, 86
empirical research, qualitative characteristics, 22
employee benefits
  accounting for, 280
  accumulated benefit, determination/present value measurement, 298
  annual leave, 280, 284–5
  bonus plans, 286–7
  CEO remuneration, 286f
  defined benefit post-employment benefits, accounting for, 289–97
  defined contribution post-employment benefits, accounting for, 288–9
  defining, 280
  IAS 19, scope/purpose, 280
  leave entitlements, 283
  long service leave (liability measurement), 298
  long-term employee benefits, 297–300
  non-monetary benefits, 280
  paid absences, accumulation, 283
  payments, remitting, 281
  payroll, accounting/usage, 281–2
  post-employment benefits, 287–8, 297
  profit-sharing arrangements, 286–7
  projected unit credit method, usage, 291–2, 298
  service leave payments, impact, 298
  short-term employee benefits, 280–7
  short-term paid absences, 283–6
  short-term profit-sharing arrangements/bonuses, liabilities, 287
  sick leave, 280, 285–6
  termination benefits, 301–2
  vesting/non-vesting paid absences, accumulation, 283
  wages/salaries, accrual, 282–3
employees
  bonuses, payment, 70
  cash payment, 396, 439, 444–5
  employer/pension plan, relationships, 287f
  expenses, 282f
  long service leave, 298–300

  long service leave eligibility estimation, 298
  sales commissions, 70
employee stock options (ESOP), usage, 328
employer, pension plan/employees (relationship), 287f
ending inventory, profits, 564–7, 619
end-of-period accounting, 95–6
end-of-period adjustments, 96–7
enforceable period, 231f, 232
entity (entities)
  activities, requirement, 75
  amount of consideration, collectability, 57
  changed use, 175
  combination, 500f
  control, 12
  debt covenants, constraints, 133
  economic benefits, production, 11
  economic credit risk hedging, 368
  environment/market, 175
  equity
    fair value measurement application, 215
    instruments, settlement, 338
  financial structure, evaluation, 436
  formation, 535, 535f
  governing body, composition, 500
  government-related entities, 464
  greenhouse gases, emission, 261
  group, 527f
  information disclosure, 559
  inventory risk, 76
  non-monetary exchanges, 56
  obligations
    meeting, restriction, 338
    performing, 58
  operations, entity-specific value, 114
  parent, equivalence (determination), 540
  policies/processes, 216
  present obligation, 261
  promise, nature (determination), 75
  relocation/reorganisation, expenditures, 160
  reported profit figure, scrutiny, 133
  risk-management, 362
  size, contrast, 500
  transactions, making, 540–1
entity-wide disclosures, 489
entry price, 201
environmental liabilities/environmental-related disclosures, 276
equipment
  remaining useful life, 552

equipment, depreciation, 550
equity, 308–9
  accounts, parent balance
      (carrying), 547
  charges, 601f
  compensation schemes,
      objective, 388
  components, 322–3, 340f
  contributed equity, share capital
      issuance/movement, 312–18
  corporate structure, features, 309–10
  disclosure, 324
  distributions, 340t
  financial statement element, 14
  for-profit companies, 309
  increase, profitable operations
      (impact), 14
  interests, 500–1
  investors, benefit, 21
  method, usage, 555–7, 556f, 557f
  NCI share, calculation, 586, 594–608
  ordinary shares, 310–11
  owner equity, 308f
  reduction, 318
  reserves, 320–23
  retained earnings, 321–2
  share capital, forms/decreases,
      310–11, 318–20
  statement of changes in equity, 26,
      39, 41, 324, 325f–6f
  statement of financial position
      components, 308
  treasury shares, holding/reissuance/
      cancellation, 319–20
equity-based compensation,
      problem, 396
equity-indexed interest,
      embedding, 344
equity instruments, 504
  acquirer purchase, 498
  considerations, 390
  designation, 345, 349
  exercise price, variation, 389
  fair value, 384–5, 390
  financial liabilities, distinctions, 336–9
  FVOCI, 349
  FVPL, 345
  granting terms/conditions,
      modification, 391–2
  grant, repricing, 391–2
  issuance, costs, 504
  number, vesting variation, 386
  number/weighted average fair
      value, 398
  repurchases, 392
  securities exchange trading, 208
  settlement, 338

equity/liability test,
      applications, 336–8
equity-or-debt classification, 276
equity-settled share-based payment
      transactions, 382, 383–5, 392
estimation uncertainty, nature, 44
exchange rates, 626–7
executives, remuneration
      (criticism), 380
exercisable options, potential voting
      rights, 532
exercise price, variation, 389
existence uncertainty, 15
expected cost plus margin
      approach, 66
expected credit losses, 354f, 355–7
expected credit loss model,
      application, 353
expected rate of return (ERR), 304
expected value, 61–3
expected volatility, measure, 384–5
expenditures, 160
expenses
  classification, 37f, 340f
  financial statement element, 13–14
  recognition, 160–1
expenses, translation, 634, 639
experience adjustments, 295

F
fair value
  accounting, 220, 332–3
  calculation, costs of disposal
      (subtraction), 177
  change, likelihood, 216
  current exit price, 201
  definition, 201–2, 349
  entity-specific characteristic,
      absence, 87
  fluctuation, gains/losses, 245
  framework, 202–8
  hedge, 362, 363t, 364
  hierarchy, 207, 215
  model, usage, 138
  orderly transactions, 201–2
  transaction/transportation costs, 202
fair value measurement, 113, 159, 244
  application, 212–15
  approaches, 213–14
  basis, 123
  categorisation, 216f–18f
  disclosure, 215–18, 216f–18f
  entity policies/processes,
      relationship, 216
  inputs, 207–9
  Level 1 inputs, 207–8
  Level 2 inputs, 208

Level 3 inputs, 208
  observable inputs, 207
  standard, need, 200
  unobservable inputs, 207
  valuation technique(s), 203, 206, 209
fair value through other comprehensive
      income (FVOCI), 345, 349
fair value through profit or loss
      (FVPL), 345, 348, 349
faithful representation, 9, 15
finance leases
  definition, 244
  lessor accounting, 246–9, 247f–9f
  manufacturer/dealer lessor
      accounting, 250–1
  manufacturer lessor
      recognition, 250–1
  measurement, 247
  operating leases, distinction, 225
  recognition, 246–7
Financial Accounting Standards
      Board (FASB)
  leasing project addition, 224
  revenue standard issuance, 56
  translation process objectives, 628
financial assets
  cash flow characteristics, 347
  categories, 345f, 346t
  credit impairment, 354
  definition, 335
  derecognition, 35, 353
  fair value carrying, 406, 407
  financial instrument category, 344–7
  gains/losses, recognition, 353
  general approach, 353–4
  impairment/collectability, 353–8
  initial measurement, 349
  management, business models
      (usage), 345–346
  measurement, 345, 348–59
  offsetting, 359–60
  originated credit-impaired financial
      assets, 355
  purchased credit-impaired financial
      assets, 355
  recognition criteria, 348
  scope, 341–2
  simplified approach, 355
  subsequent measurement, 349–51
  transfers, 374t
financial capital concept, 19
financial crisis (2008–2009), 315
financial guarantee contracts, 351, 353
financial information
  fundamental qualitative
      characteristics, 8–9, 15
  qualitative characteristics, 8–10

financial instruments, 337–8
  categories, 344–8
  compound financial instruments,
    339–40, 340f
  definition, 334
  derivatives, 342–4
  disclosures, 368–74
  embedded derivatives, 342–4
  equity-or-debt classification, 376
  fair value, 349
  financial assets, 335
    measurement, 348–59
    offsetting, 359–60
    recognition criteria, 348
    scope, 341–2
  financial liabilities
    measurement, 348–59
    offsetting, 359–60
    recognition criteria, 348
    scope, 341–2
  financial risks, relationship, 369t
  gains and losses, 37
  hedge accounting, 360–8
  identification, 334
  issuer, impact, 336
  items, exclusion, 334
  liabilities, 335
  model, 354f
  non-derivative financial instruments,
    addressing (absence), 339
  non-financial instruments, purchase/
    sale contracts, 334
  own use contracts, 342
  periodic payments, treatment, 336
  reclassifications, 348
  risks, nature/extent, 372t–3t
  rules, 336–8
  scope, 341
  settlement choice, 339
  significance, 370t–1t
  summary, 335t
  types, 334
financial item, risk component, 361
financial liabilities
  categories, 347t
  definition, 335
  derecognition, 353
  equity instruments, distinctions, 336–9
  financial instrument categories, 344,
    347–8, 347t
  gains/losses, recognition, 353
  initial measurement, 349
  measurement, 348–59
  offsetting, 359–60
  recognition criteria, 348
  scope, 341–2
  subsequent measurement, 349–51

financial performance, financial
    instruments (significance), 370f–1f
financial position
  comparative statements, 448
  financial instruments,
    significance, 370t–1t
  information, 8
financial reporting, 332f–3f
  cost constraint, 10
  objectives, segments (usage), 480
financial statements, 442f
  climate-related matters, effects, 205
  components, 26–7
  filing, 534
  lease-related items, presentation, 241f
  principles, 27–9
  reporting, frequency, 28
  scope, 480
  tax presentation, 425–426
financial statements, elements
  definition, 11–14
  measurement, 16–18
  recognition, 14–15
financing activities
  cash flows, relationship, 178
  definition, 437
  usage, 441
financing cash flows (CFF), 455
financing component, 63–4
finished goods/materials/services,
    transport/handling/costs, 88
finite useful lives, inclusion, 163–4
firm commitment
  binding agreement, 361
  cash flow hedge, 364–5
first-in, first-out (FIFO)
  cost formula, 99
  usage, 84
fixed payments, usage, 235, 244
fixed production overheads,
    allocation, 89
forecast transaction, 361
foreign currency
  disclosure, 650
  gains and losses on translation, 36
  transactions, 626
  transformation, subsidiary
    (conduit role), 629
  translation, 626–7
foreign operations, net investments,
    36, 640, 649–50
foreign subsidiaries, statements, 626
for-profit companies, listing (presence/
    absence), 309
forward contract, recognition, 348
forward-looking expected credit loss
    model, 332

Free Carrier (FCA), 95
free choice, basis, 62
Free On Board (FOB), 95–6
fuel price risk, cash flow
    hedges, 366f–7f
Fulfilment value (exit price), 17
full goodwill method, 589–90, 623
functional currency, 627–30
  financial statements,
    translation, 632–8
  foreign currency transactions,
    translation, 632
  IAS 21 indicators, 631f
  identification, 630–1
  local currency translation, 634–8
  presentation currency,
    contrast, 640–8
  transactions, translation, 632
  translation, 636f–7f
future cash flows
  determination, 178
  estimates, risk adjustment, 264–5
  prediction, 37
future costs, provision, 117
future events, 266
future lease payments, adjustment, 238
future operating losses, provision
    recognition (disallowance), 268

G
gains/losses, 340–1
gearing ratio, usage, 336
general ledger accounts,
    reconstruction, 444
general purpose financial reporting,
    objective, 8
general purpose financial
    statements, users, 28
Global Preparers Forum, 5
going concern, 10–11, 27
goods in transit, 95–6
goods/services
  activities, transferability (absence), 75
  consideration, expected amount, 72
  customer options, 60–1
  observable price, entity usage, 66
  payment terms, entity
    identification, 57
  prices establishment, entity
    discretion, 76
  promise, 58
  sales/purchases, 530
  transfer, arrangements (revenue
    recognition), 68–70
  transfer, promise, 58
  transferred goods/services,
    distinctiveness (absence), 73

goods/services, distinctiveness, 58
  capability, 58–9
  determination, 59
  payment, 64
  series, characteristic, 60
goodwill, 641
  absence, 193–5
  accounting for, 508
  asset, equivalence (question), 508
  balance, historical rate
    translation, 649
  calculation, 186
  components, 507
  core goodwill, 507f
  definition/calculation, 507
  determination, 542–5
  excluded difference, 418
  exclusion, 182–4
  full goodwill method, 589–90
  impairment tests, 553
  measurement, 499, 501, 503–10
  partial goodwill method, 590–1
  recognition, 499, 501, 503–10,
    599, 601–2
  recording, 550
  studies, 196
goodwill impairment, 196
  issues, relationship, 188
  test, 179f–80f, 187–8
governing body, composition, 500
government grant, recognition, 407
government-related entities, 464
gross-settled share options, 316
group earnings, impact, 552
growth rate, 178

H

hedge accounting, 360–8
  alternatives, 368
  conditions, 360, 362–6
  entity discontinuation, 367–8
  requirements, objective, 360
  standards, development
    (questions), 360
hedged item, 360, 361
hedges
  effectiveness, 362, 366, 368f
  ratio, 367
  ratio/rebalancing/
    discontinuation, 360
  types, 362–6
hedging instrument, 360, 361
hedging relationship, types, 362
high-quality corporate bonds, market
    yields (impact), 288
historical cost accounting
    (HCA), 220

hold to collect and sell business
    model, 345–6
hold to collect business model, 345–6

I

IASB and IFRS Interpretations Committee
    Due Process Handbook
    (DP Handbook), 6
identifiable assets
  acquirer recognition, 540
  acquisition, 501
  measurement, 499, 501, 503
  recognition, 499, 501–2, 546
identifiable, definition
    (absence), 154–5
identifiable liabilities, acquisition, 501
identified asset, 226–9, 230f
IFRS (see International Financial
    Reporting Standards)
IFRS Interpretations Committee
    (IFRIC), 5, 87, 88
  Agenda Decisions, 505
  1 Changes in existing decommissioning,
    restoration and similar
    liabilities, 117
  21 guidance/examples, 270,
    271timmaterial prior period
    errors, 49
impairment
  accounting policies, 177f
  cash-generating units, 182–4, 186–8
  disclosure, 190–1
  evidence, collection, 175–6
  goodwill, 179f–80f, 186–8
  indicators, 176
  issues, 188
  non-financial assets,
    application, 209–11
  test, 175–6, 177f, 188, 553
  value, calculation, 178–9
impairment loss
  accounting for, 183
  accumulation, 200
  calculation, 357
  corporate asset allocation, 191–5
  determination, 183
  goodwill, exclusion/absence,
    183, 193–5
  recognition/measurement, 180–2
  reversal, 188–90
import duties/taxes, 88
in-combination valuation
    premise, 210–11
income
  approach, 206, 209
  definition, 13
  financial statement element, 13

from subsidiary (analysis), equity
    method (usage by parent), 556f
  items of comprehensive
    income, 33–4
  statements, 551f
  tax, cash flows (relationship), 178
  translation, 634
income taxes, 404
  accounting for, 407
  classification, 438–9
  current tax, calculation, 407–11
  disclosures, 426–9
  effective tax rate, 426
  expense, component (calculation), 447
  issues, 424–5
  losses, 413–14
  net tax provision, 428–9
  paid, determination, 447–8
  payment, 412–13
incurred loss model, 376
indefinite useful lives, 163f, 164
indirect method, 439, 455
information
  comparability, 528
  error-free characteristic, 9
  external sources, 175
  internal sources, 175–6
  presentation requirement, 31–3
  uncertainty, sources, 43
initial public offering (IPO), 312, 328
input methods, 69–70
insurance contract
  defining, 369
  rights/obligations, 341
intangible assets, 110, 152f–3f,
    153–5, 502f
  accounting, 157, 162
  acquisition, 156, 157
  amortisation, 162–4
  balance sheet, extract, 159f
  brands/mastheads/publishing titles/
    customer lists, 159
  business combination, acquisition
    (relationship), 156–7
  cost model, usage, 161
  definition (IAS 38), 153–4
  development outlays, 158, 168–9
  development phase, 157–8
  disclosure, 164–7, 164f–7f
  expense, recognition, 160–1
  extract, 159f, 160f
  fair value measurement, 159
  finite useful lives, inclusion, 163–4
  identifiable, definition
    (absence), 154
  impairment, 181f–182f
  indefinite useful lives, 163f, 164

initial measurement, 155–61
initial recognition, 159, 161–4
internally generated assets,
    non-recognition
    (explanation), 158–60
internally generated goodwill, 161
internally generated intangible
    assets, 157–8
measurement, 157, 161–2
non-monetary, term (inclusion), 154
physical substance, absence, 155
recognition, 155–61
research phase, 157–8
retirements/disposals, 164
revaluation model, usage, 161–2
separability, criterion
    (inclusion), 155
separate acquisition, 156
subsequent expenditure, 162
unrecognised intangibles, 171
intangible R&D assets, amortised cost
    (estimation), 172
intellectual property, licenses, 74–5
interest, 340–1
    expenses, 242
    intragroup transfers, 610–1
    received/paid, classification, 438
    revenue, receiving, 406
interest-free loan, initial
    measurement, 349f
interest paid, determination, 447
interest rates, 175, 235
interim/final dividends, division, 321–2
internally generated assets,
    non-recognition
    (explanation), 158–60
internally generated goodwill, 161, 187
internally generated intangible
    assets, 157–8
internal organisation, structure (entity
    change), 489, 490
International Accounting Standards
    (IAS) (see International Financial
    Reporting Standards)
International Accounting Standards
    Board (IASB), 4. see also
    Conceptual Framework for
    Financial Reporting
formation, 4–5
IFRS 15 issuance, 56
independence, 5
US FASB, interaction, 333
International Accounting Standards
    Committee (IASC)
establishment, 4
operations, review, 5
shortcomings, 4

Standing Interpretations Committee,
    replacement, 5
International Chamber of Commerce
    (ICC), terminology (usage), 95
International Financial Reporting
    Standards (IFRSs)
IAS 1 Presentation of Financial
    Statements, 26–38, 43f,
    77, 134, 586
IAS 2 Inventories, 17, 70, 71, 87
IAS 7 Statement of Cash Flows, 85
IAS 8 Accounting Policies, Changes in
    Accounting Estimates and Errors,
    27–9, 42, 45–8, 68, 71, 117
IAS 10 Events after the Reporting
    Period, 27, 44, 49–50
IAS 12 Income Taxes, 32, 152, 407
IAS 16 Property Plant and Equipment, 17,
    114, 118, 122, 126, 134
IAS 19 Employee Benefits, 152, 280
IAS 20 Accounting for Government
    Grants and Disclosure of
    Government Assistance, 157
IAS 21 The Effects of Changes in Foreign
    Exchange Rates, 626
IAS 27 Separate Financial
    Statements, 56
IAS 28 Investments in Associates and
    Joint Ventures, 56
IAS 32 Financial Instruments:
    Presentation, 28, 333
IAS 33 Earnings per Share, 46
IAS 34 Interim Financial Reporting, 27
IAS 36 Impairment of Assets, 17, 174
IAS 37 Provisions, Contingent Liabilities
    and Contingent Assets, 260
IAS 38 Intangible Assets, 17, 71,
    86–7, 152, 155
IAS 40 Investment Property, 17
IAS 41 Agriculture, 225IFRS 2
    Share-based Payment, 369, 380
IFRS 3 Business Combinations,
    115, 152, 588
IFRS 4 Insurance Contracts, 274
IFRS 5 Non-current Assets Held for
    Sale and Discontinued Operations,
    32, 43, 152
IFRS 7 Financial Instruments:
    Disclosures, 200
IFRS 8 Operating Segments, 5, 480
IFRS 9 Financial instruments,
    17, 35, 38
IFRS 10 Consolidated Financial
    Statements, 56, 458, 562
IFRS 11 Joint Arrangements, 56
IFRS 12 Disclosure of Interests in Other
    Entities, 588

IFRS 13 Fair Value Measurement, 17,
    87, 104, 200
IFRS 15 Revenue from Contracts with
    Customers, 56–8, 60–1, 70,
    72, 76, 85
IFRS 16 Leases, 56, 110
IFRS 17 Insurance Contracts, 32, 35,
    56, 152, 341
IFRS 18 Presentation and Disclosure in
    Financial Statements, 50
compliance, 27, 41
management compliance, reporting
    requirements, 41f–42f
post-implementation reviews, 7
Practice Statement 1, Management
    Commentary, 26
Practice Statement 2 Making
    Materiality Judgments, 43
publication proposal,
    development, 7
publishing, 6–7
redeliberations/finalisations, 7
research programme, 6–7
International Financial Reporting
    Standards Advisory Council
    (IFRSAC), 5
International Financial Reporting
    Standards (IFRSs)
    Foundation, 4, 5–6
due process, 6
purpose/governance, 5–6
international standard setting,
    institutional structure, 6f
International Sustainability Standards
    Board (ISSB), 5
intragroup transactions, 541, 586,
    592, 642–4
adjustments, 562–3, 605
borrowings, 573
dividends, 571–3
effects, 562, 608–12, 620f–1f
inventory transfers,
    involvement, 569–70
non-controlling interest,
    relationship, 611–12
services, 570–1
inventory (inventories), 33f, 84–7
accounting policies, 100f, 103f
assets, equivalence, 84
broadcast rights, 85–6
classification, 85
cost, 84, 88
cost, determination, 88–9
costing methods, 10
crypto assets, 87
current programme rights, 86
definition, 84

inventory (inventories) (*Continued*)
emission rights, 86–7
IAS 2 definition, 84
impairment, disclosure, 104f
information role, 108
materials/supplies, write-down, 105
measurement principles, 84, 87
Note 1.11, extract, 86f
Note 11, extract, 85f
purchase costs, 88–9
realisation, 610
recording, periodic/perpetual
methods, 92
risk, 76
sale(s), 49, 550, 552, 564–6, 618, 619
scope, 85–7
sold, cost, 406
transactions, recording, 92
transfer, 564–70
write-downs, 36, 105
inventory on sale, costs
(assigning), 98–103
investee
activities, directing, 530
control, definition, 529
decision-making authority, 533
direct, ability, 530
management personnel, member
control, 529
investing activities, definition/
usage, 437, 441
investment properties, 136–9
ancillary services, 137
definition/classification, 136–7
disclosure, 138–9
fair value carrying, 406, 407
joint use properties, 137
measurement, 137–8
transfers, 137
investments
account (analysis), equity method
(usage), 555, 556f, 607f
amount, impact, 488
disposals, 236
elimination, 599, 601–2, 612,
615–6, 642
issued capital, amount, 324

J

joint control, 459
joint use properties, 137
joint ventures
determination, 460
formation, impact, 499
interest, 369
investments, 341
judgments, changes, 76

L

labelling, 326
labour, abnormal amounts, 89
leaseback arrangements, 253
leaseback transactions, 253–5, 253f
leases
agreement, lessor classification, 245–6
allocation, 233
arrangements, lessee option
(inclusion), 235
components, identification, 226
consideration, 232–3
current lease accounting, 224–5
expenses, 242
extract, 242f–3f
finance leases, operating leases
(distinction), 225
future lease payments,
adjustment, 238
identification, 225–33
interest rate, implicitness, 235f
lease-related items, presentation, 241f
lessee cancellation, 245
lessee measurement, 239–41
lessor classification, 243–6
liabilities, 234–5
accounting treatments, 238
interest expenses, 242
recognition, 236–7
maximum potential length,
determination, 231
minimum lease payments (MLPs),
disclosures (classification), 257
minimum/maximum length,
range, 231
non-cancellable period, 230–1
ownership transfer, 244
payments
discounting, 245
lessor perspective, 244–5
present value, 244
receivables, expected credit loss
model (application), 353
scope, 225
term, 230–2, 231f, 238
termination, payments/
penalties, 235, 244
legal obligation, 261, 272
lessee
accounting, 234–41
disclosure, 241–3
exemptions, 225
expense recognition, 238–9
initial measurement, 234–5
presentation, 241–3
purchase option, exercise price, 235
right-of-use asset measurement, 234

lessor
accounting, 246–53
classification, 243–6
perspective, 243f
levies, usage, 270
liabilities
asset holdings, 213–14
asset/transfer, sale/use
restrictions, 203
assumed, measurement/recognition,
499, 501–3
carrying amount, intragroup
transactions impact
(absence), 563
components, allocation, 340f
decommissioning, present value
technique, 214
definition, 12, 263
fair value measurement, application/
approaches, 212–14
financial statement element, 12–13
IAS 37 definition, 260–1
incurring, 504
information, 487–8
initial recognition, 418
market participants,
identification, 205
measurement, 203
removal, 16
residual, equity (relationship), 14
settlement, transfer (contrast), 212
tax bases, 415–16, 416f
timing/amount uncertainty, 260
transaction entry, ability/
willingness, 205
valuation, non-performance risk
(relationship), 213
licences, 74, 75
limited liability, protection ability, 310
line items, 36
liquidity, 29
litigation settlements, 37
loan commitments
accounting for, absence, 353
settling, impossibility, 341
local currency, 627
translation, 634–8
long service leave. *see* employee
benefits; employees
long-term benefits, 462
long-term employee benefits, 297–300
loss(es)
allowance, usage, 358f
information, 487–8
realisation, 564, 571, 610–12
lower of cost and net realisable
value, 87, 103–6

M

management
   approach, risks and rewards
      approach (contrast), 481
   commentary, integrated
      information, 26–7
   personnel compensation, 462f–3f
market
   approach, 206, 209
   capitalisation, 175
   condition, 389–90
   participants, identification, 205
   rent, 245
market-based tests, performing, 376
mark-to-market accounting, 332–3
material item, information, 28
materiality, 28
   concept, usage, 8–9
   definition, application, 42
   judgements (IAS 1),
      application, 43f
material prior period errors, 49
measurement, 16
   bases, 16–17
   basis, selection, 17–18
   rules, summary (IFRS 9), 359t
   uncertainty, 15, 17–18
military aircraft, sale/revenue, 69f
minimum lease payments (MLPs),
      disclosures (classification), 257
minority voting interest, presence, 500
monetary assets, 154, 503
monetary items, 627, 633

N

net assets
   fair value, determination, 543
   financial capital concept,
      comparison, 19
net basis reporting, 441
net cash inflows, generation, 162
net defined benefit liability
   adjustment, determination, 293
   net interest, definition, 293
   profit/loss amounts, recognition
      (determination), 293
   remeasurements, determination
      (OCI recognition), 294–5
remeasurement, 36
   determination, 291
net interest, definition, 293
net investment, hedge, 362
net nil position, 361
net realisable value (NRV), 103–6
   estimation, 104
   inventories write-downs, 36
   level, comparison, 406

measurement rule, lower of cost
      (application), 105–6
   rule, application, 87
   write-down, 105
net wages, payment (remitting), 281
neutrality (bias, absence), 9
new share capital, issuance, 50
non-accumulating short-term paid
      absences, 283, 284f
non-adjusting events, 49
non-cancellable period, 230–1, 231f
non-cash considerations, 64
non-cash transactions, 453
non-compliance, implications, 44
non-controlling interest (NCI), 35,
      501, 586, 642
   acquisition date,
      accounting, 595–600
   adjustment, 619
   amount, disclosure, 324
   consolidation worksheets, 593, 593f,
      603, 605f, 620f
   disclosure, 586–8
   effects, 588–93
   equity, equivalence, 530
   explanation, 586–8
   intragroup transactions,
      relationship, 611–12
   options, selection (reasons), 592
   recognition/measurement, 499
   share of changes in equity, 602
   share of current period changes in
      equity, 604
   share of equity, 586, 594–609,
      616–7, 624
non-cumulative, non-redeemable
      preference shares, issuance, 337
non-cumulative preference
      dividends, 467
non-current assets, 110
   additions, amount, 488
   disposal, 133
   expenditures (expensing), 9
non-derivative financial assets/
      liabilities, hedging instrument
      function, 361
non-derivative financial instruments
   addressing, absence, 339
   issuer examination, 339
non-financial asset
   application, 209–11
   highest/best use, 209–12
   valuation premise, 203
non-financial instruments, purchase/
      sale contracts, 334
non-lease components, 233
non-market performance condition

earnings, link, 388
   presence, 387–8
non-monetary assets,
      identification, 504
non-monetary items, 627
non-performance risk, 212–13
non-refundable upfront fee, charge, 60
non-vesting conditions, treatment, 390
no-par shares, issuance, 312
notes, 41–4
notes (accounting policies/explanatory
      information), 26

O

obligating events, 261, 272
obligation
   duty/responsibility, third-party
      involvement, 12
   existence, likelihood, 262
   legal/constructive/conditional
      characteristic, 12
   measurement, 264
   occurrence, 262
   present obligation, 12
obsolescence, 175
off-balance-sheet financing,
      achievement, 253
offsetting, 28, 359–60
onerous contracts, 268
opening inventory, profits, 568–9
operating activities
   definition, 437
   usage, 439–41
operating capability, 19
operating cash flows (CFO), 455
operating leases, lessor
      accounting, 251–3
operating segments
   definition, 481
   disclosure, 487–90
   identification, 481–4, 482f
   reportable segment, equivalence, 489
   scope, 480
option-pricing model, 384
options, 316, 472
   company-issued share option,
      impact, 316
   contract, function, 342–3
   employee stock options (ESOP),
      usage, 328
   equity instrument, 317
   exercise price, 384
   exercising, 386–7
   gross-settled share options, 316
   life, 384
   settlement options, 339
orderly transactions, 201–2

ordinary shares, 310–11
  contracts, settlement, 473
  equity/liability test, 336f–7f
organisational structure, 500f
originated credit-impaired financial
    assets, 355
other comprehensive income (OCI),
    34–6, 34f–5f, 52, 320
  credit risk, 348, 353
  recognition, 295–6
  revaluation increase, recognition, 124
  tax effects, recognition, 447
outcome uncertainty, 15
outlays, capitalisation decision, 118
output methods, 68
outstanding shares (denominator
    placement), 465
oversubscriptions, 313–14
own credit issue, 332
owner equity, 308f
ownership, transfer (absence), 244
own use contracts, 341

P
paid-in capital, addition, 313
parent
  company investment accounts,
      equity method (usage), 555–7
  financial statements, 541
  subsidiaries, 534f
    relationship, 579f
participating shares, non-participating
    shares (contrast), 311
partners, rights/responsibilities, 308–9
party rights, entity identification, 57
par value shares, issuance, 313
past event, impact, 12, 13
past performance, information, 8
patent, impairment, 552–3
payroll
  accounting for, 281–23
  usage, 281
pension plan
  assets, obligation, 289
  employer/employees,
      relationship, 287f
performance obligations
  criteria, application, 67
  customer options, determination, 61
  identification, 56, 58–61
  separate performance obligations,
      58–60
  time satisfaction, 70
  transaction price, allocations, 69f
  variable consideration, allocation, 65
performance obligation
  satisfaction, 56, 67–70

reporting period, revenue
    recognition, 77
  time duration, 67–9
periodic inventory method, 92–5
periodic payments, interest
    treatment, 336
perpetual inventory method, 92–5
personnel records, updating, 281
physical capital concept, 19
physical damage, 175
physical substance, absence, 155
post-employment benefit plan, 461
post-employment benefits,
    287–8, 297, 462
  accounting for, 290
comparability/transparency,
    enhancement, 290
Post-Implementation Review
    (PIR), 56
potential (dilutive) ordinary
    shares, 471f
  conversion, 471
power
  concept, application (problems), 532
  definition, 429
  directing ability, 530
  rights origin, 529–30
  usage, ability (impact), 533
pre-acquisition entries, 547–8,
    547f, 553–5
predictive value, 8
preference dividends
  earnings calculation
      adjustment, 467f
  non-cumulative/cumulative
      preference dividends, 467
preference shares, 311, 468
prepaid expenses, recognition, 406
presentation, 18–19, 76–9
  consistency, 29
  guidance, 18
presentation currency, 627–30
  translation, 638–40, 639f–40f
present obligation, 12
  economic benefits outflow,
      requirement (likelihood), 262
  future commitments, contrast, 12
  occurrence, 262
present value, 214, 264–5
price allocation, managerial
    compensation (impact), 521
principal considerations, agent
    considerations (contrast), 75
principal payments, embedding, 344
prior period error, 45
  correction, 349
  immateriality/materiality, 49

probability-weighted outcomes,
    usage, 355
production, costs/indirect costs, 89
profit
  information, 487–8
  numerator placement, 465
  realisation, 564, 571, 610–12
profitability ratios, usage, 33
progress, measure, 68–70
projected cash flows, estimation, 178
projected unit credit method, usage,
    291–2, 298
property, destruction, 50
property, plant and equipment (IAS
    16) (PPE), 110, 110f–11f
  accounting, effects (asset-by-asset
      basis), 129–30
  acquisition date, 114–15
  asset
    expense, contrast, 112
    movement, 139–42
  cost model, 118–22
  costs, inclusion/absence, 116
  depreciation, 118–22, 139–42
  derecognition, 133–4
  directly attributable costs, 116
  disclosure, 135–6
  dismantling/removal/restoration
      costs, 116–17
  funds, management outlay, 118
  future benefits, generation, 112–13
  initial measurement, 113–17
  initial recognition, 112–13, 117
  investment properties, 136–9
    ancillary services, 137
    cost model, usage, 138
    definition/classification, 136–7
    fair value model, usage, 138
    measurement, 137–8
    transfers, 137
  joint use properties, 137
  measurement, cost/revaluation
      models, 143–6
  multiple assets, acquisition, 115
  outlays, capitalisation decision, 118
  purchase price measurement, 113–15
  revaluation model, 123–32
  separate assets, 112
  separate classes, 123
proprietary cost argument, 495
protective rights, 530
provision
  accounting for, 266–7
  accrual, 276
  assets, expected disposal, 266
  best estimate, 263–4
  binding sale agreement, 270

changes, 266, 270
constructive obligation, usage, 269
contingent assets, 273
contingent liability, distinctions, 263
contingent settlement
    provisions, 339
decommissioning, 270
definition, 260–1, 268–73
disclosure, 273, 274f
estimation, decision tree, 264f
events/circumstances, risks/
    uncertainties, 264
future events, 266
future operating losses, provision
    recognition (disallowance), 268
identification, 260–2
levies, 270
measurement, 263–73
present value, 264–5
recognition, 268–73
    criteria, 262
    requirements, applications, 271–3
refurbishment costs, 273
reimbursements, 266
restructuring, 269–70
revaluation, 447
revaluation (UK firms), 148
risk-adjusted rate, calculation, 265
usage, 266
Public Interest Entity (PIE), 309
purchased credit-impaired financial
    assets, 355
purchase option
    exercise price, 235, 244
    reassessment, 238
purchase price, 88, 113–15
put option, embedding, 344

Q
qualifying asset, 89
qualitative characteristics,
    enhancement, 9–10
quantitative thresholds,
    specification, 484

R
rebalancing, 367
rebates, 88
receivables, loss allowance/credit
    risk, 358f
reclassification adjustments, 366–7
recognised assets, excess value over
    carrying amount, 187
recognition criteria, 14–15
recognition, expense, 106
reconciliations
    entity provision, 488–9

process, 92
recorded dividends, subsidiary
    holding, 548–9
recoverable amount
    carrying amount, contrast, 187
    definition, 176
redeemable preference shares, 311
refurbishment costs, 273
reimbursements, 266
related parties
    close family members, control/
        influence, 460
    control/joint control/significant
        influence, 459
    definition, 459, 459t
    disclosures, 461–4
    entities, 460–2
    family, close member, 459
    identification, 459–61
    joint venture, determination, 460
    key management personnel, 460
    post-employment benefit plan,
        relationship, 461
    relationships, 461
    transactions, disclosures,
        461f, 462, 464f
related party disclosures, 458–64
    objective/scope, 458
relevance
    existence uncertainty, impact, 15
    measurement uncertainty, impact, 15
    outcome uncertainty, impact, 15
    qualitative characteristic, 8
reliability, concept, 45
remuneration, 381f
    entitlement, 533
    policies, 385f
    report, 465f
reportable segments
    aggregation criteria, 484–5
    assets, total, 488
    asymmetrical allocations, 488
    basic criteria, 484
    definition, application, 486, 486f
    identification, 484–5, 485f
    information, 487
    transactions, 488
reported profit/loss, 484
reported segments, increase, 495
reporting, frequency, 28
reporting period
    adjusting event, accounting for, 50
    events, 49–50
    non-adjusting events, 50
    revenue recognition, 77
Report of the Financial Crisis Advisory
    Group, 332, 332f–3f

repurchases, 468
research costs, recognition, 406
reserves, 320–22, 324, 634
residual approach, 66
residual, fair value fluctuation, 245
residual value, 122, 238, 244
restructuring costs, qualifying, 269
retained earnings, 321–2, 547, 639
    revaluation surplus transfer, 130–1
    usage, 308
retrospective adjustments, 474
return on assets (ROA) ratio,
    usage, 257
return on plan assets (ROA)
    determination, 295
returns, power usage (impact), 533
revaluation
    asset/class of asset, distinction, 130f
    decrease, 126–9
    increase, 123–6
        depreciable assets,
            relationship, 125–6
        reversal, decrease (impact), 127–8
        tax effect, 125
    model, 123–32, 143–6
        application, 123–32
        choosing, 133
        usage, 161–2, 181
    regularity, 123
    surplus, transfer, 130–1
revalued assets, depreciation
    (revaluation model
    application), 131–2
revenue
    classification, 340t
    disaggregation, information, 77, 78f
    generation, 483
    interaction, 79f
    presentation, 76
    recognition, 406
revenue recognition, 56, 69
    cumulative amount, constraints, 62
    five-step model, IFRS 15
        (impact), 56f
    time duration, 69
reversals of provision, 237
reverse acquisitions, 500, 536, 536f
right of return, 65, 65f
right-of-use asset
    accounting treatments, 238
    carrying amount, 242
    depreciation charge, 242
    lessee measurement, 234
    recognition, 236–7
rights
    assets representation, 11
    issues (shares), 315, 470, 470f

risk-adjusted rate, calculation, 265
risk-free interest rate, implied yield (comparison), 385
risk management objective, entity assessment, 367
risks and rewards approach, management approach (contrast), 481

S

sale
  right of return, inclusion, 65
  transactions, 253f
    accounting, 253–5
    fixed payments/above-market terms, usage, 254–5
    qualification/nonqualification, 254, 255
sales
  adjustment, requirement, 565
  commissions, payment, 70
  royalties, 75
sales-based royalty, allocation, 75
scrip dividends, distribution, 321
seasoned equity offerings (SEOs), 328
segment information, presentation, 481
segment liabilities, total, 489
segment measures, entity changes, 489
segment profit/loss, determination, 488
selling costs, 89
senior management, composition, 500
sensitivity, 44, 216
separability, criterion (inclusion), 155
separate acquisition (intangible assets), 156
separate performance obligations, 58–60
service conditions, impact, 393–4
services
  fair value, 383
  intragroup transfers, 610–1
  payment, 619
set-off right, 360
settlement discount, availability, 88
settlement options, 339
share appreciation rights (SARs), granting, 392, 393–4
share-based payment, 462
  application/scope, 382
  arrangements, modification, 399
  disclosure, 397–9
  economic consequences, 401
  examination, 380
  expensing, 380
  Options, 379–399
  recognition, 383

remuneration policies, 385f
vesting, 386–90
share-based payment transactions, 369, 383
  cash alternatives, inclusion, 395–7
  counterparty, settlement choice, 395–6
  form/features, 382t
  liabilities, relationship, 399
  settlement, entity choice, 397
share bonus (stock dividend), 329
share capital, 311f, 547, 634, 638
  bonus issues, definition, 317
  buy-back
    management authorisation, 318
    programmes, management engagement, 328
  cancellation, 321
  cash representation, 308
  compound securities, option type, 317
  current price, 384
  decreases, 318–20, 318f
  forms, differences, 310–11
  granting
    cash alternative, addition, 397
    performance condition, 387
  increase, authorisation, 314f
  issuance, 310, 312–14
  movements, 314–18
  no-par shares, issuance, 312
  options, 316
  oversubscriptions, 313–14
  par value shares, issuance, 313
  placement, advantages, 314–15
  preference shares, 311
  price, expected volatility, 384
  repurchase, 320 (see also treasury shares)
  rights issues, 315
  share-based transactions, 318
  split, impact, 318
  stock dividends, issuance, 317
  usage, 309–10
  warrants, option type, 317
shareholders
  disorganisation/apathy level, 531
  money, returning, 328
  protection, limited liability feature, 310
  returns, 311
share issues
  costs, accounting for, 312
  issued at a discount, 313
  sharing right, 310
share options
  exercise, 392
  plans, 380

recognition, services function, 384
  weighted average fair value, 398
share plans, 380
share premium, 308, 313
shares, 468. see earnings per share
  bonus issue, 469
  consolidation/repurchase, 468
  contingently issuable shares, 269, 473
  dilutive potential ordinary shares, 472
  options, effect, 472
  ownership level, 530–2
  parent holding, 547
  potential (dilutive) ordinary shares, 471
  preferences shares, conversion, 468
  splits, 469, 474
  theoretical ex-rights value per share, 470f
  weighted average number, determination/reconciliation, 468–9, 475f
share warrants, option type, 317
short-term assets, leases (expenses), 242
short-term employee benefits, 280–7, 462
short-term paid absences, 283–6
  non-accumulating short-term paid absences, 283, 284f
short-term profit-sharing arrangements/bonuses, liabilities, 287
sick leave. see employee benefits
significant parts depreciation, 122
SME Interpretations Group, 5
solely payments of principal and interest (SPPI) test, 347
sole proprietor, multi-shareholder company (contrast), 308
solvency ratio, usage, 336
space systems/services, revenue/sale, 69f
Staff Accounting Bulletin (SAB) No.101, SEC issuance, 81
stand-alone asset, 203
stand-alone financial statements, 555f
stand-alone selling prices, 66
  allocation, 66
  method, application, 66
stand-alone valuation premise, 210
Standards Advisory Council (SAC), member appointment, 5
start-up activities, expenditures, 160
statement of cash flows, 26, 435-54
  direct method, usage, 450, 450f
  disclosures, 450–3

extract, 449f
financing activities section, 449-50
format, 439–41
investing activities section, 448-9, 452f
operating activities section, 443-8
preparation, 441–50
purpose, 436
statement of changes in equity, 26, 39, 41, 324, 325f–6f
information presentation, 41
information, reporting requirement, 39
NCI disclosure, 587f
presentation, 39
Statement of Financial Accounting Standards (SFAS)
52 *Foreign Currency Translation*, 643
130 *Reporting Comprehensive Income*, 52
131 *Disclosure about Segments of an Enterprise and Related Information*, 495
statement of financial position, 26, 29–33, 550f, 635, 638–9
carrying amounts, calculation, 414
classifications, 29–31
equity components, 308
information presentation requirement, 31–3
items, 633–4
NCI disclosure, 588f
statement of profit or loss and other comprehensive income, 26, 33–39, 124f, 634, 635, 639–40
expenses, classification, 34f–35f, 37f
IAS 32 requirement, 340
information presentation/ requirement, 36–8
NCI disclosure, 587f
reclassification adjustment, 38–9
stock dividends, issuance, 317
storage costs, 89
straight-line method (depreciation), 119
subsidiaries
assets, 547
disclosure, 559f
equity interest, parent holding (absence), 543–5
financial statements, 541
functional currency, presentation currency (contrast), 644–8
interest, 369
investments, 341, 555–7
elimination, 563, 615–6
equity accounting, parent company application (consolidation worksheet), 606–8

ownership interests, changes, 451–2
parent, relationship, 579f
recorded dividends, acquisition date (relationship), 584–5
recorded equity, NCI share, 594–5, 594f
reporting period, 540
substantive rights, 529
summary data, inclusion, 44
supplier finance arrangements, 452–3
suppliers, cash payments, 439, 444–5
surplus funds, return, 318

T
tangible assets, 110
taxable profit, accounting profit
differences, 404–7
permanent differences, 404–5
taxable temporary differences
calculation, 417
circumstances, 406
insufficiency, 422
taxation
debts, annual payment requirement, 412
legislation, requirements, 412
tax-effect adjustment, need (absence), 567
taxes. *see* current tax; income taxes
amended prior year tax figures, 424–5
assets, 415, 426
bases, 415–16, 416f
carry-forward tax loses, creation/ recoupment, 413–14
deferred tax, calculation, 414–21
effect, application (impact), 447
effective tax rate, 426
expense, 426, 467f
liabilities, 415–16, 426
losses, 413–14
payment, 412–13
rates, change, 408, 424
tax expenses, 36
termination benefits, 301–2, 462
theoretical ex-rights value per share, 470f
timeliness, meaning, 10
total comprehensive income, 34, 35
total expense, recognition, 399
total other comprehensive income, 34
trade discounts, 88
trademark, Level 3 input, 208
training activities, expenditures, 160
transaction price
allocation, 65–6

allocation, entity requirement, 65
determination, 56, 61–5
determination/allocation, 56
reduction, 64
transactions
cash flow effects, presentation, 452
costs, definition, 349
disclosures, 452f
entry, ability/willingness, 205
intragroup transactions, 541
measurement, equity instrument fair value reference, 384–5
non-cash transaction, 453
services, receiving, 383–4
transaction/transportation costs, 202
transfer adjustments, 366–7
transferred inventories
availability, 568–70
complete sale, 567
partial sale, 566–7
treasury shares, 318
cancellation, 320
company holding, 319
reissuance, 319
true and fair view (TFV), 52

U
uncertainties, 15
expected resolution, 44
source/s, 44
understandability, quality, 10
unit of account, 18, 203
units-of-production method, 120
unrealised profits, 564
unrecognised deferred tax assets, recovery (probability), 422
unrecognised identifiable net assets, 187
unused tax credits, 426
unused tax losses, 422, 426
usage-based royalties, 75
useful life, 121
US GAAP
finance/operating leases, distinction, 225
harmonisation, 133
reporting, 171

V
valuation
allowance, 431
methodologies, usage, 384
premise, identification, 210–11
techniques, usage, 206, 209
value in use, 183
calculation, 178–9
exit price, 17

variable consideration, 61–2
  entity allocation, 65
  estimation, 61–3
variable lease payments,
  usage, 234, 244
variable production overheads,
  identification, 89
variable returns, exposure/
  rights, 532–3
verifiability, quality, 10
vesting, 386–90
  conditions, treatment, 386–90
  date, events, 390
  non-vesting conditions,
    treatment, 390
vesting/non-vesting paid absences,
  accumulation, 283

voluntary disclosures, cost of capital
  (link), 477
voting interest, size, 531
voting rights, 529
  equivalence, 526
  identification, 500
  investor holding, 531
  potential voting rights, 532

W
wages/salaries
  accrual, 282–3
  recording, 281
warranty (warranties), 472
  provision, 271
  provision, amount (calculation), 45
wasted materials, abnormal amounts, 89

weighted average cost
  formula, 99–100
weighted average number of
  shares in basic earnings
  per share, calculation,
  473–4
wholly owned group, 541f
wholly owned subsidiary,
  consideration, 534
Working groups, establishment, 5
write-downs
  examination, 196
  reversal, 105

Z
zero-coupon government issues,
  implied yield, 385